LE NORD AND PICARDY
Pages 182–195

CHAMPAGNE
Pages 196–207

ALSACE AND LORRAINE
Pages 208–223

Reims

NORTHEAST FRANCE

Strasbourg

Troyes

Dijon

ENTRAL FRANCE AND THE ALPS

Lyon

Grenoble

BURGUNDY AND FRANCHE-COMTÉ
Pages 316–341

THE MASSIF CENTRAL
Pages 342–361

THE RHÔNE VALLEY AND FRENCH ALPS
Pages 362–381

THE SOUTH OF FRANCE

LANGUEDOC-ROUSSILLON
Pages 466–487

PROVENCE AND THE CÔTE D'AZUR
488–521

Ajaccio

CORSICA
Pages 522–533

EYEWITNESS *TRAVEL GUIDES*

FRANCE

EYEWITNESS *Travel Guides*

FRANCE

DK

DORLING KINDERSLEY
LONDON · NEW YORK · SYDNEY · MOSCOW
www.dk.com

A DORLING KINDERSLEY BOOK

www.dk.com

PROJECT EDITOR Rosemary Bailey
ART EDITOR Janis Utton
EDITORS Tanya Colbourne, Fiona Morgan,
Anna Streiffert, Celia Woolfrey
DESIGNERS Joy FitzSimmons, Erika Lang, Clare Sullivan
MAP CO-ORDINATORS Simon Farbrother, David Pugh
RESEARCHER Philippa Richmond

MANAGING EDITOR Douglas Amrine
MANAGING ART EDITOR Gaye Allen
SENIOR EDITOR Helen Partington
SENIOR DESIGNER Annette Jacobs
EDITORIAL DIRECTOR David Lamb
ART DIRECTOR Anne-Marie Bulat

PRODUCTION Hilary Stephens
PICTURE RESEARCH Naomi Peck
DTP DESIGNER Ingrid Vienings

MAIN CONTRIBUTORS
John Ardagh, Rosemary Bailey, Judith Fayard, Lisa Gerard-Sharp,
Colin Jones, Alister Kershaw, Alec Lobrano, Anthony Roberts,
Alan Tillier, Nigel Tisdall

MAPS
Jane Hugill, Jennifer Skelley (Lovell Johns Ltd, Oxford)

PHOTOGRAPHERS
Max Alexander, Neil Lukas, John Parker, Kim Sayer

ILLUSTRATORS
Stephen Conlin, John Lawrence, Maltings Partnership,
John Woodcock

Film outputting bureau Graphical Innovations (London)
Reproduced by Colourscan (Singapore)
Printed and bound by Dai Nippon Printing Co., (Hong Kong) Ltd

First published in Great Britain in 1994
by Dorling Kindersley Limited
9 Henrietta Street, London WC2E 8PS
Reprinted with revisions 1994, 1995, 1996, 1997, 1998, 1999

Copyright 1994, 1999 © Dorling Kindersley Limited, London

A CIP CATALOGUE RECORD IS AVAILABLE FROM THE BRITISH LIBRARY.

ISBN 0-75130-037-3

Every effort has been made to ensure that the information in this
book is as up-to-date as possible at the time of going to press.
However, details such as telephone numbers, opening hours,
prices, gallery hanging arrangements and travel information are
liable to change. The publishers cannot accept responsibility for
any consequences arising from the use of this book.
We would be delighted to receive any corrections and
suggestions for incorporation in the next edition. Please write to:
Managing Editor, Eyewitness Travel Guides,
Dorling Kindersley, 9 Henrietta Street, London WC2E 8PS.

CONTENTS

Bust of Charlemagne

INTRODUCING FRANCE

PARIS AND ILE DE FRANCE

The fishing village of St-Jean-de-Luz in the Pyrenees

Grape harvest in Alsace

Palais des Papes, Avignon

HOW TO USE THIS GUIDE

THIS GUIDE helps you to get the most from your visit to France. It provides both expert recommendations and detailed practical information. *Introducing France* maps the country and sets it in its historical and cultural context. The 15 regional chapters, plus *Paris and Ile de France,* describe important sights, with maps, pictures and illustrations. Throughout, features cover topics from food and wine to culture and beaches. Restaurant and hotel recommendations can be found in *Travellers' Needs.* The *Survival Guide* has tips on everything from the French telephone system to transport.

PARIS AND ILE DE FRANCE

The centre of Paris has been divided into five sightseeing areas. Each has its own chapter, which opens with a list of the sights described. A further section covers Ile de France. All sights are numbered and plotted on an area map. The detailed information for each sight follows the map's numerical order, making sights easy to locate within the chapter.

Sights at a Glance lists the chapter's sights by category: Churches, Museums and Galleries; Historic Buildings, Squares and Gardens.

All pages relating to Paris and Ile de France have green thumb tabs.

A locator map shows where you are in relation to other areas of the city centre.

1 Area Map
For easy reference, the sights are numbered and located on a map. Sights in the city centre are also shown on the Paris Street Finder *on pages 146–59.*

2 Street-by-Street Map
This gives a bird's eye view of the key areas in each chapter.

A suggested route for a walk is shown in red.

Stars indicate the sights that no visitor should miss.

3 Detailed information
The sights in Paris and Ile de France are described individually. Addresses, telephone numbers, opening hours and information on admission charges and wheelchair access are also provided for each entry.

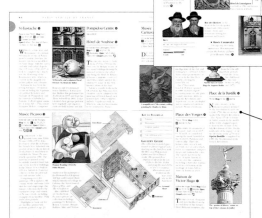

1 Introduction

The landscape, history and character of each region is described here, showing how the area has developed over the centuries and what it offers to the visitor today.

France Area by Area

Apart from Paris and Ile de France, France has been divided into 15 regions, each of which has a separate chapter. The most interesting towns and places to visit have been numbered on a *Pictorial Map*.

Each area of France can be quickly identified by its colour coding, shown on the inside front cover.

2 Pictorial Map

This shows the road network and gives an illustrated overview of the whole region. All interesting places to visit are numbered and there are also useful tips on getting around the region by car and train.

3 Detailed information

All the important towns and other places to visit are described individually. They are listed in order, following the numbering on the Pictorial Map. Within each town or city, there is detailed information on important buildings and other sights.

Story boxes highlight noteworthy features of the top sights.

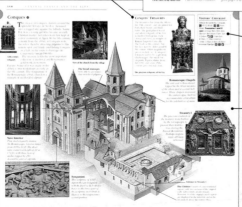

For all the top sights, a Visitor's Checklist provides the practical information you will need to plan your visit.

4 France's top sights

These are given two or more full pages. Historic buildings are dissected to reveal their interiors. The most interesting towns or city centres are shown in a bird's eye view, with sights picked out and described.

INTRODUCING
FRANCE

Putting France on the Map

France, one of the largest countries in Europe, has airline connections with most cities in the world. Paris is the major transport hub with two international airports; others include Bordeaux, Lille, Lyon, Nice and Toulouse. There are good, high-speed rail links with the rest of Europe, and a network of efficient motorways. A number of ferry routes cross the Mediterranean to Corsica and beyond. Cross-Channel ferries serve several ports, with the Channel Tunnel providing an alternative link by rail.

Europe

France, known as the "Hexagon" due to its six-sided shape, is bordered by six countries: Spain across the Pyrenees to the south; Italy and Switzerland beyond the Alps; Luxembourg and Belgium to the north; and Germany on the other side of the Rhine. The United Kingdom lies across the English Channel (La Manche).

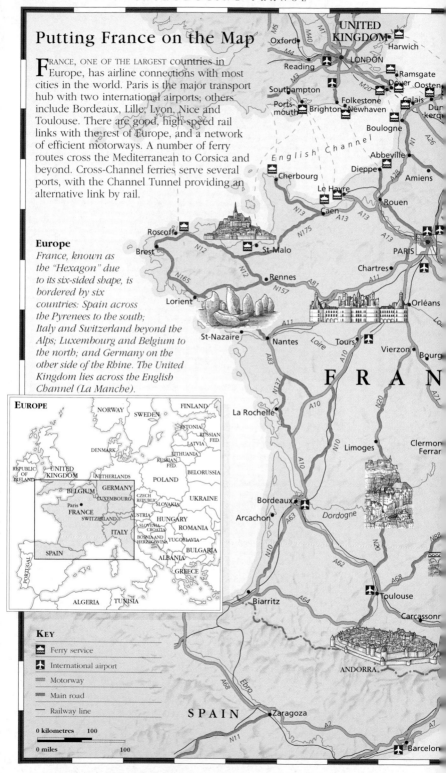

KEY

- 🚢 Ferry service
- ✈ International airport
- ▬▬ Motorway
- ▬▬ Main road
- — Railway line

0 kilometres   100

0 miles   100

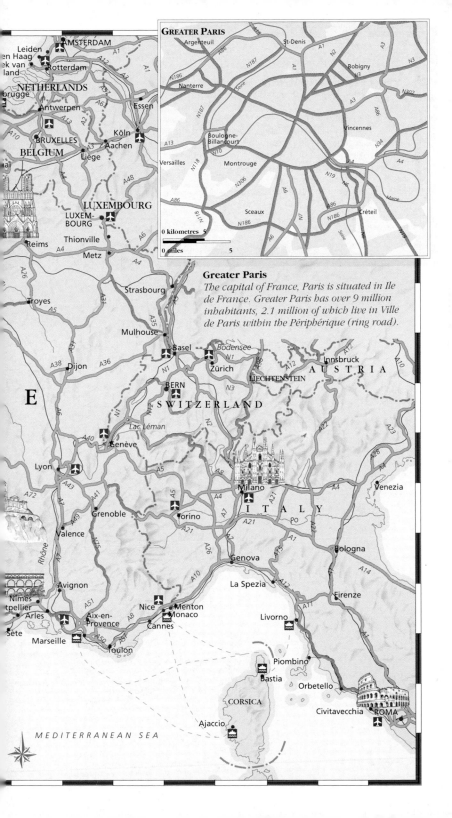

Greater Paris

The capital of France, Paris is situated in Ile de France. Greater Paris has over 9 million inhabitants, 2.1 million of which live in Ville de Paris within the Périphérique (ring road).

Regional France

FRANCE HAS A POPULATION of over 56 million, and
receives over 44 million visitors a year. It covers an
area of 543,965 sq km (210,025 sq miles). Paris is the
largest city, followed by Lyon, Marseille and the
conurbation of Lille-Lens-Valenciennes. The Loire,
Seine, Garonne and Rhône are the longest of France's
many rivers. This book divides the country into 15
regions, plus a separate
section for Paris and Ile de
France, although officially
France comprises 22 *régions*.

GETTING AROUND

In spite of its size, France is
relatively easy to travel around.
There is a well-organized rail
network, and travelling times
are considerably shortened
between towns with a high-
speed TGV link *(see p635)*.
Most motorways have expensive tolls but are fast and
efficient for longer distances.
Smaller roads are usually
a more interesting way to
discover the country's varied
landscape *(pp638–40)* and
they are almost invariably well-
maintained and signposted.

KEY

━━━ Motorway

━━━ Major road

═══ Minor road

0 kilometres   100

0 miles   100

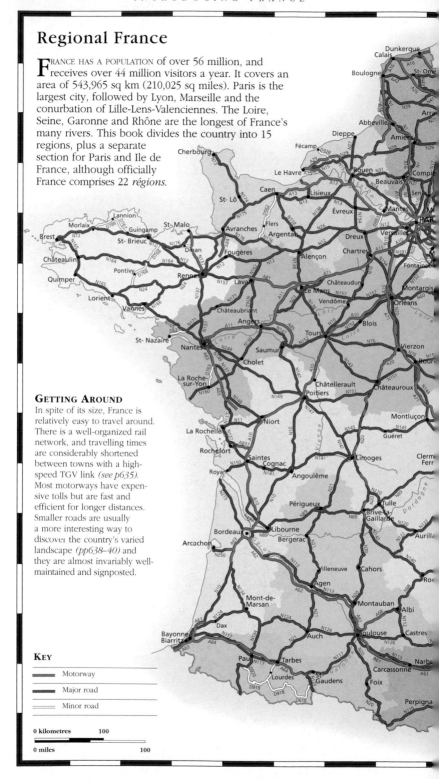

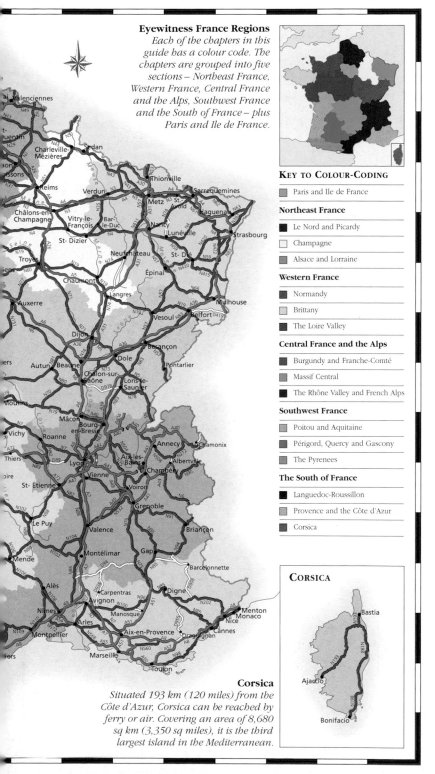

Eyewitness France Regions
Each of the chapters in this guide has a colour code. The chapters are grouped into five sections – Northeast France, Western France, Central France and the Alps, Southwest France and the South of France – plus Paris and Ile de France.

KEY TO COLOUR-CODING

- Paris and Ile de France

Northeast France

- Le Nord and Picardy
- Champagne
- Alsace and Lorraine

Western France

- Normandy
- Brittany
- The Loire Valley

Central France and the Alps

- Burgundy and Franche-Comté
- Massif Central
- The Rhône Valley and French Alps

Southwest France

- Poitou and Aquitaine
- Périgord, Quercy and Gascony
- The Pyrenees

The South of France

- Languedoc-Roussillon
- Provence and the Côte d'Azur
- Corsica

CORSICA

Corsica
Situated 193 km (120 miles) from the Côte d'Azur, Corsica can be reached by ferry or air. Covering an area of 8,680 sq km (3,350 sq miles), it is the third largest island in the Mediterranean.

A PORTRAIT OF FRANCE

THE FRENCH THEMSELVES *are the best advocates for visiting France, convinced that their way of life is best, and that their country is the most civilized on earth. The food and wine are justly celebrated. French culture, literature, art, cinema, and architecture can be both profound and provocative. Whether cerebral, sensual or sportif, France is a country where anyone might feel at home.*

France's landscape ranges from high mountain plateaux to lush farmland, traditional villages to chic boulevards. Its regional identities are equally diverse. The country belongs to both northern and southern Europe, and encompasses Brittany with its Celtic maritime heritage, the Mediterranean sunbelt, Germanic Alsace-Lorraine, and the hardy mountain regions of the Auvergne and the Pyrenees. Paris remains the linchpin, with its famously brusque citizens and intense tempo. Other cities range from the huge industrial conglomeration of Lille in the north, to Marseille, the biggest port on the Mediterranean. The differences between north and south, country and

Marianne, symbol of France

city are well-entrenched, indeed cherished, despite the determination of the forward-thinking French to link their country by TGV (high-speed train) and the home databank service, Minitel. High-tech advances like these have provoked an equal and opposite reaction: as life in France becomes more city-based and industrialized, so the desire grows to safeguard the old, traditional ways and to value rural life.

The idea of life in the country – *douceur de vivre* (the Good Life), long tables set in the sun for the wine and anecdotes to flow – is as seductive as ever for residents and visitors alike. Nevertheless, the rural way of life has been changing. Whereas in 1945 one

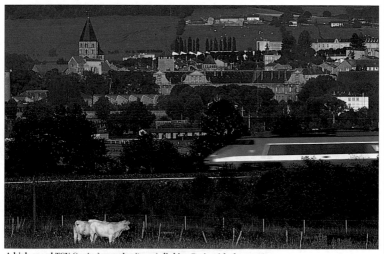

A high-speed TGV *(train à grande vitesse)*, linking Paris with the provinces

◁ Café life in St-Tropez, one of the country's many pleasures person in three worked in farming, today it is only one in 16. France's main exports used to be luxury goods like perfumes and Cognac; today, such exports have been overtaken by cars, telecommunications equipment, nuclear power stations and fighter aircraft.

People remain firmly committed to their roots, however, and often retain

The popular *moto* (scooter)

a place in the country where they go back for holidays or retirement. On average, there are more French people

who have second homes than any other nationality; and in many areas such as Provence, the dying villages have been finding a new life as chic summer residences for Parisians and foreigners.

Chanel chic

Many artists and artisans from the towns now go to live and work in the country; or entrepreneurs set up factory workshops there, more feasible in the age of the fax machine and the computer.

Social changes have come about since the steep decline in the influence of the Catholic Church. Today only 14 per cent of people attend mass regularly. Nearly half of all couples live together before marriage, and many never marry at all. Abortion is now legal.

Women, once treated as second-class citizens, have won legal equality in the last 30 years; in 1991 Edith Cresson was the first

woman to be appointed Prime Minister of France. Nevertheless, in France as in the rest of Europe, in politics, industry and big business there is still a reluctance to give senior posts to women. A flirtatious gallantry exists between the sexes, even in public and office life, and influential feminists take care to remain "feminine". Within the family, the old parental authoritarianism has waned; in schools, the harsh discipline has given way to a freer ambience – two trends resulting from the May 1968 political uprising that marked France so deeply *(see p63)*.

SOCIAL CUSTOMS AND POLITICS

French social life, except between close friends, has always been marked by formality – cheek kissing and handshakes, the use of titles *("Bonjour, Monsieur le President")*, the infrequent use of Christian names, the preference for the formal *vous* rather than the intimate *tu*. However, this has been changing among the younger generation, who

The May 1968 uprising, a catalyst for profound change in France

Farming in Alsace-Lorraine

will now call you by your Christian name, and use *tu* even in an office context. Standards of dress have become much more informal, too, though the French are still very concerned to dress well, and they judge others by their clothes: they prefer an elegantly casual Cardin pullover to an ill-fitting formal suit.

Formality lingers on, however, and France remains very legalistic – whether you are buying a house, exporting an antique or getting divorced. But the French also display a charming insouciance about their famous red tape. Rules and laws are there to be ingeniously evaded, twisted or made more human. This sport of avoiding cumbersome bureaucracy has a name of its own, *le système D*, to be accompanied with a shrug and a smile. For example, since 1992 a new law insists on non-smoking areas in public places, even in the most nicotine-stained of tiny bars – but no one really minds if it is not always applied too literally.

Today, the old sharp Left/Right ideological divide which used to dominate French politics is giving way to a more

Charles de Gaulle

gentle, centre-focused consensus. This has been fostered by François Mitterrand, who was re-elected president for another seven years in 1988 and has left more of a mark on French politics than any postwar politician since de Gaulle. However, the Republican spirit is still evident in recent confrontations, not least in the burning down of the Rennes Parliament building in 1993. The upper bourgeoisie still holds much of the real power in France, through both state and business appointments; the once powerful Communist Party is in steep decline. As in other European countries, there has recently been increased support for the far right. High unemployment – France's worst social problem today – has led to growing racism against black immigrants, many of whom are from former French colonies in North Africa.

CULTURE AND THE ARTS

Culture is taken seriously in France, and writers, intellectuals, artists and fashion designers are held in high social esteem. As a result, the state financed

Designer Thierry Mugler at the Paris collections

Défense – to the post-modern housing projects of Nîmes, Montpellier and Marseille in the south.

MODERN LIFE

The Government's eagerness to stimulate technology has brought innovations such as the Minitel, the videotext databank service, free to many homes. The Minitel can be used as a telephone directory, for booking plane or theatre tickets, and a huge range of communications services. In some ways, the French are already in the 21st century but remain ambivalent about modernism: they are conservative in many of their tastes and habits.

a large network of provincial arts centres in the 1960s, and has traditionally given subsidies which have allowed experimentation in art and design. The French remain justly proud of their own serious cinematic tradition, and are determined to defend it against pressures from Hollywood. Other activities – from the music industry to the French language itself – are subject to the same protectionist attitudes.

Decades after the introduction of the new franc (100 old francs) in 1960, for instance, many people still calculate in old francs, including those born long after the change. And the French still refuse to stagger their summer holidays, concentrating on the peak period of late July and August, when they take to the roads and coastal resorts.

Traditional Breton costumes, worn for festivals and *pardons*

Avant-garde art and literature and modern architecture all enjoy strong patronage in France. Some of the more exciting architectural projects range from the striking new buildings in Paris – the Louvre pyramid and La Grande Arche at La

Modernity has brought some major changes to daily life. For example,

A view through the base of La Grande Arche, part of the huge business complex on the edge of Paris

The traditional game of *boules* or *pétanque*, still extremely popular – especially in the south

France has Europe's largest hyper-markets, which have been steadily ousting the local grocery or corner shop. Though American in inspiration, these remain French in what they sell: a long delicatessen counter can have

a wonderful display of 100 or so French cheeses and *charcuterie* (prepared meats), while the huge range of fresh vegetables, fruit and herbs is a tribute to their role in French cuisine.

Southern produce: melons, peaches and apricots

However, under modern pressures, eating habits have been polarizing in a curious way. The French used to eat well every day as a matter of course. Today they are in a hurry, and for most meals of the week they will eat simply – either a quick fried steak or pasta dish at home, or a snack in town (hence the wave of fast-food places that have sprung up, in defiance of French tradition). But meals still remain an important part of French leisure activity – not just for the food and wines themselves, though these are perhaps the world's best, but also for the pleasure of lengthy, unhurried meals and good conversation around a table, among family or friends. They will reserve their gastronomy for the once-or-twice-a-week special occasion, maybe a dinner party, or a really good meal in a restaurant with a loved one, or the big family Sunday lunch which remains an important French ritual. It is at these times that the French zest for life really comes into its own.

Remote farm – a nostalgic reminder of rural life

The Classic French Menu

THE TRADITIONAL French meal consists of at least three courses. *Les entrées* or *hors d'oeuvre* (starters) include soups, egg dishes, salads or *charcuterie*, such as sliced sausage or ham. For *les plats* (main courses), fish or meat is served often with sauce, and accompanied by potatoes, rice or pasta and vegetables. Cheese comes before dessert, which can include sorbets, fruit tarts or *pâtisserie*. A fixed-price menu is the cheapest option. For more information on French restaurants, see pp576–9.

Soupe à l'oignon *is a favourite in bistros. Croutons, grated cheese and sometimes egg yolk are added to the onion soup.*

Oeufs en Cocotte *are prepared by baking eggs in a china rame-kin with cream and butter. They may be sprinkled with fresh herbs and garnished with mushrooms.*

Coquilles Saint-Jacques *are plump sea scallops. They are cooked simply in a little butter. Their orange tails, containing edible roe, are delicious.*

Fish soup

Endive salad with diced fried bacon

Goat's cheese melted on toast with salad

Omelette with herbs

Fried sole served with melted butter

Pike dumplings in a cream sauce

Minced beef with potato purée

Steak with pepper sauce

Veal stew enriched with egg and cream

Breast of duck

Pork chop

Veal sweetbreads

HORS D'OEUVRE
Soupe de poissons
Soupe à l'oignon
Salade frisée aux lardons
Crottin chaud en salade
Omelette aux fines herbes
Oeufs en cocotte

POISSONS
Sole Meunière
Quenelles de brochet
Coquilles St Jacques

VIANDES
Hachis parmentier
Noisettes d'agneau
Bifteck au poivre
Blanquette de veau
Magret de canard
Côte de porc
Ris de veau
Coq au vin

Noisettes d'Agneau *are small, tender lamb cutlets, sautéed in butter and served rare with mushrooms and herb and garlic butter.*

Coq au vin *is one of the best-known French dishes. A male chicken is braised in a sauce of red wine, herbs, garlic, small onions and button mushrooms.*

BREAKFAST

The French rarely eat cereal, eggs or meat for breakfast, so assorted breads, spread with butter and jams, are the morning choice. These include *croissants*, flaky, buttery crescent-shaped pastries; a piece of *baguette* (the classic long thin loaf) which is split in half and spread with butter and jam to create a *tartine*; *pain au chocolat*: a buttery square roll with a melted tablet of chocolate inside; and *brioche*, an airy muffin-shaped egg-enriched yeast bread. This is washed down with coffee or tea and, in some cafés, a glass of red wine, which is purported to maintain good digestion. The most common form of coffee at breakfast is *café au lait*, espresso coffee served with warm milk.

Croissants

Brioches

Pains au chocolat

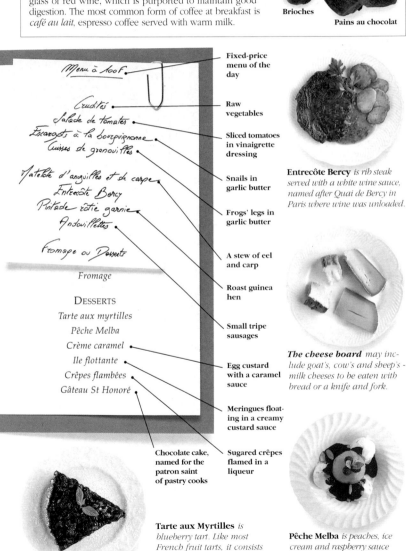

Menu à 100 F

Fixed-price menu of the day

Crudités

Raw vegetables

Salade de tomates

Sliced tomatoes in vinaigrette dressing

Escargots à la bourguignonne

Snails in garlic butter

Cuisses de grenouilles

Frogs' legs in garlic butter

Matelote d'anguilles et de carpe

A stew of eel and carp

Entrecôte Bercy

Entrecôte Bercy *is rib steak served with a white wine sauce, named after Quai de Bercy in Paris where wine was unloaded.*

Pintade rôtie garnie

Roast guinea hen

Andouillettes

Small tripe sausages

Fromage ou Desserts

Fromage

DESSERTS

Tarte aux myrtilles

Pêche Melba

Crème caramel

Egg custard with a caramel sauce

Ile flottante

Meringues floating in a creamy custard sauce

Crêpes flambées

Sugared crêpes flamed in a liqueur

Gâteau St Honoré

Chocolate cake, named for the patron saint of pastry cooks

The cheese board *may include goat's, cow's and sheep's - milk cheeses to be eaten with bread or a knife and fork.*

Tarte aux Myrtilles *is blueberry tart. Like most French fruit tarts, it consists of a shallow shortbread crust filled with fruit.*

Pêche Melba *is peaches, ice cream and raspberry sauce created by famed chef Escoffier for the singer Dame Nellie Melba.*

The Wine of France

Picker's hod

WINEMAKING IN FRANCE dates back to pre-Roman times, although it was the Romans who disseminated the culture of the vine and the practice of winemaking throughout the country. The range, quality and reputation of the fine wines of Bordeaux, Burgundy, the Rhône, and Champagne in particular have made them rôle models the world over. France's everyday wines can be highly enjoyable too, with plenty of good value wines now emerging from the southern regions.

Traditional vineyard cultivation

WINE REGIONS

Each of the 10 principal wine-producing regions has its own identity, based on grape varieties, climate and local culture. *Appellation contrôlée* laws guarantee a wine's origins and style.

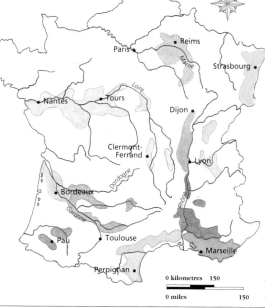

Paris • Reims
Strasbourg •
Nantes • Tours
Dijon •
Clermont-Ferrand •
Lyon •
Bordeaux
Toulouse
Pau • Marseille
Perpignan •

Marne
Loire
Dordogne
Garonne
Rhône

0 kilometres   150
0 miles   150

KEY

- Bordeaux
- Burgundy
- Champagne
- Alsace
- Loire
- Provence
- Jura and Savoie
- The Southwest
- Languedoc-Roussillon
- Rhône

HOW TO READ A WINE LABEL

Even the simplest label will provide a key to the wine's flavour and quality. It will bear the name of the wine and its producer, its vintage if there is one, and whether it comes from a strictly defined area (*appellation contrôlée* or VDQS) or is a more general *vin de pays* or *vin de table*. It may also have a regional grading, as with the *crus classés* in Bordeaux. The shape and colour of the bottle is also a guide. Most good-quality wine is bottled in green glass, which helps to protect it from light.

The property or producer

Château-bottled, rather than a blend from a merchant or grower's co-operative

MIS EN BOUTEILLE AU CHÂTEAU

CHÂTEAU MARGAUX
GRAND VIN

PREMIER GRAND CRU CLASSÉ
1985
MARGAUX
APPELLATION MARGAUX CONTRÔLÉE
S.C.A. CHÂTEAU MARGAUX PROPRIÉTAIRE A MARGAUX - FRANCE

Pictures may be accurate or fanciful

Capacity of the bottle

The vintage, from the French word *vendange*, or harvest

The wine's *appellation contrôlée*

HOW WINE IS MADE

Wine is the product of the juice of freshly picked grapes, after natural or cultured yeasts have converted the grape sugars into alcohol during the fermentation process. The yeasts, or lees, are normally filtered out before bottling.

Old wine press

WHITE WINE   RED WINE

Newly harvested grapes, whether red or white, are first lightly crushed to bring the sugar-rich juices into contact with the yeasts in the grape skins' "bloom".

Red wine gets its backbone from tannins present in red grape skins. The stems also contain tannins, but of a harsher kind; most winemakers de-stem most or all of their red grapes before they are pressed.

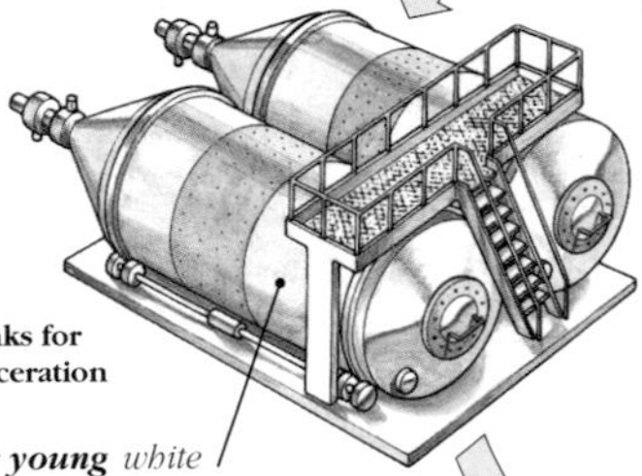

Tanks for maceration

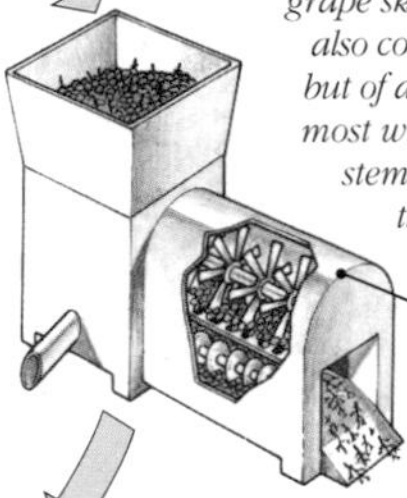

Crusher and de-stemmer

For young white wines and some reds (eg simple Beaujolais) that do not gain complexity from ageing, the crushed grape juice may be steeped, or macerated, with the grape skins for a few hours to add aroma and flavour.

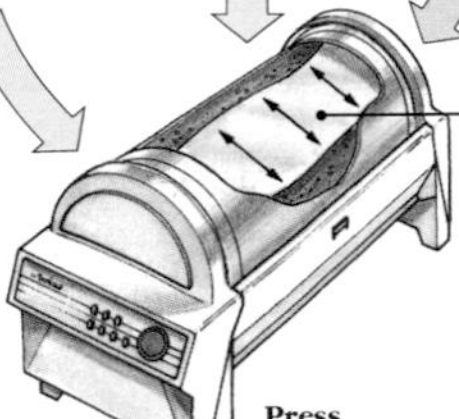

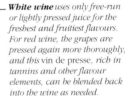

Press

White wine uses only free-run or lightly pressed juice for the freshest and fruitiest flavours. For red wine, the grapes are pressed again more thoroughly, and this vin de presse, rich in tannins and other flavour elements, can be blended back into the wine as needed.

Fermentation is a natural process, but can be unpredictable; nowadays, many growers use cultured yeasts and hygienic, temperature-controlled stainless-steel tanks to control fermentation and ensure consistent results.

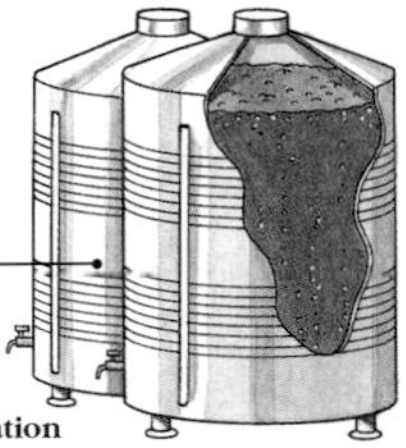

Early drinking wines may be filtered straight into their bottles, but barrels are used to age many finer wines. The flavours imparted by the oak are an integral part of many wines' identities – for example, the tobaccoey, "wood-shavings" character of red Bordeaux.

Fermentation vat

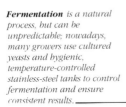

Oak casks

Different shades of glass identify the wine regions

Bottle shapes typical of red Bordeaux (left) and Burgundy

Artists in France

ARTISTS HAVE always been inspired by France, especially since landscape became a legitimate subject for art in the 19th century. Art and tourism have been closely linked for over a century, when the establishment of artists' colonies in the forest of Fontainebleau, Brittany and the south of France did much to make these areas attractive to visitors. Today, one of the pleasures of touring the countryside is the recognition of landscapes made famous in paintings.

Follower of *the French Classical tradition of landscape painting, Jean-Baptiste-Camille Corot recorded* The Belfry of Douai *(1871).*

Le Nord and Picardy

Gustave Courbet*, socialist and leader of the Realist School of painting, captured this famous coastal town in* The Cliffs at Etretat after a Storm *(1869).*

Normandy

Paris and Ile de France

Brittany

Loire Valley

Emile Bernard *was fascinated by the wild, almost primitive character of the Breton landscape and the individuality of its inhabitants. He was one of the community of artists based in Pont Aven. His* La Ronde Bretonne *(1892) portrays local Celtic customs.*

Poitou and Aquitaine

Neo-Impressionist *artist and exponent of Pointillism, Paul Signac indulged his love of maritime subjects on the coasts of France.* Entrance to the Port at La Rochelle *(1921) shows his use of myriad dots of colour to represent nature.*

Périgord, Quercy and Gascony

Pyrenees

Languedoc-Roussillon

Théodore Rousseau*, the leading light of the Barbizon School (see p171) of landscape painters, visited the Auvergne in 1830. It was here that he began to paint "en plein air" (in the open air). The results are seen in this sensitively observed scene,* Sunset, Auvergne *(c.1830).*

In his **Eiffel Tower** *(1926) Robert Delaunay investigated the abstract qualities of colour. His wife, artist Sonia Delaunay, said, "The Eiffel Tower and the Universe were one and the same to him."*

A few months before his tragic death in July 1890, Vincent Van Gogh painted the Church at Auvers. *He noted that the building "appears to have a violet-hued blue colour; pure cobalt".*

Alsace and Lorraine

Champagne

Scenes from everyday life were realistically rendered by Gustave Courbet, as here in Young Ladies of the Village Giving Alms to a Cow Girl in a Valley near Ornans *(1851–2).*

Burgundy and Franche-Comté

The Massif Central

The Rhône Valley and French Alps

Provence and the Côte d'Azur

Maurice Utrillo painted this village scene, The Church of Saint Bernard in Summer *(1924), while staying at his mother's home. The sombre tone and emptiness reflect his unhappy life.*

Landscape at Collioure *(1905) depicts the vivid colours of this little Catalan fishing village. It was here that Henri Matisse founded the art movement of the Fauves, or "Wild Beasts", who used exceptionally bright, expressive colours.*

The French Riviera attracted many artists (see pp462–3). Raoul Dufy particularly appreciated its pleasures, seen in this typical scene of blue skies and palm trees, La Jetée Promenade à Nice *(1928).*

| 0 kilometres | 100 |
| 0 miles | 100 |

Writers in France

Monument to
Baudelaire

WRITERS AND INTELLECTUALS traditionally enjoy high prestige in France. One of the most august of French institutions is the Academie Française, whose 40 members, most of them writers, have pronounced on national events and, on occasion, held public office.

The work of many French novelists is deeply rooted in their native area, ranging from the Normandy of Gustave Flaubert to Jean Giono's Provence. In addition to their literary merit, these novels provide a unique guide to France's regional identities.

Colette's house in Burgundy

THE NOVEL

The farmland of the Beauce, where Zola based his novel, *La Terre*

Marcel Proust, author of
Remembrance of Things Past

THE FIRST great French writer was Rabelais, in the 16th century, a boisterous, life-affirming satirist *(see p285)*. Many writers in the Age of Enlightenment which followed emphasized the classic tradition of reason,

clarity and objectivity in their work. The 19th century was the golden age of the French humanist novel, producing Balzac, with his vast fresco of contemporary society; Stendhal, a fierce critic of the frailties of ambition in *Scarlet and Black*; and Victor Hugo, known for epics such as *Les Misérables*. George Sand broke ground with her novels such as *The Devil's Pool* which depicted peasant life, albeit in an idealized way. In the same century, Flaubert produced his masterwork *Madame Bovary*, a study of provincialism and misplaced romanticism. In contrast, Zola wrote *Germinal, La Terre*, and other studies of lower-class life.

Marcel Proust combined a poetic evocation of his boyhood with a portrait of high society in his long novel,

Remembrance of Things Past. Others have also written poetically about their childhood, such as Alain-Fournier in *Le Grand Meaulnes* and Colette in *My Mother's House*.

A new kind of novel emerged after World War I. Jean Giono's *Joy of Man's Desiring*, and François Mauriac's masterly *Thérèse Desqueyroux*, explored the impact of landscape upon human character. Mauriac, and also George Bernanos in his *Diary of a Country Priest*, used lone spiritual struggle as a theme. The free-thinker André Gide was another leading writer of the interwar years with his *Strait is the Gate* and the autobiographical *If it Die*.

In the last 40 years, Alain Robbe-Grillet and others have promoted an experimental style known as the Nouveau Roman, subordinating character and plot to detailed physical description. Critics of the style feel that it has contributed to the recent decline of the novel.

Hugo's novel *Les Misérables*, made into a musical in the 1980s

THEATRE

THE THREE classic playwrights of French literature, Racine, Molière and Corneille, lived in the 17th century. Molière's comedies satirized the vanities and foibles of human nature. Corneille and Racine wrote noble verse tragedies. They were followed in the 18th century by Marivaux, writer of romantic comedies, and Beaumarchais whose *Barber of Seville* and *Marriage of Figaro* later became operas.

Molière, the 17th-century dramatist

Victor Hugo's dramas were the most vigorous product of the 19th century. The exceptional dramatists of the 20th century range from Jean Anouilh, author of urbane philosophical comedies, to Jean Genet, ex-convict critic of the establishment. In the 1960s, Eugene Ionesco from Romania and Samuel Beckett from Ireland were among the pioneers of a new genre, the "theatre of the absurd". Since then, no major playwrights have emerged but experimental work flourishes in state-subsidized theatre companies.

POETRY

THE GREATEST of early French poets was Ronsard, who wrote sonnets about nature and love in the 16th century. Lamartine, a major poet of the early 19th century, also took nature as one of his themes (his poem *Le Lac* laments a lost love). Later the same century, Baudelaire *(Les Fleurs du mal)* and Rimbaud *(Le Bateau Ivre)* were judged to be provocative in their day. Nobel prizewinner in 1904, Frédéric Mistral wrote in his native Provençal tongue. The greatest poet of the 20th century is considered to be Paul Valéry, whose work is profoundly philosophical.

PHILOSOPHY

FRANCE has produced a large number of leading philosophers in the European humanist tradition. One of

Novels by Albert Camus, who won the Nobel Prize in 1957

Sartre and de Beauvoir in La Coupole restaurant in Paris, 1969

the first was Montaigne, in the 16th century, an inspired moralist who established the essay as an art form. Then came Descartes, the master of logic, and the philosopher Pascal. The 18th century produced two great figures – Voltaire, the supreme liberal, and Rousseau, who preached the harmonizing influence of living close to nature.

In the 20th century, an element of philosophy entered the French novel, in the work of Sartre, de Beauvoir and Camus. Sartre led the existentialist movement in Paris in the early 1940s with his novel *Nausea* and his treatise *Being and Nothingness*. Camus' novel about alienation, *The Outsider,* was equally influential.

Barthes and Foucault were among the structuralists who followed. Their radical ideas dominated the Paris intellectual scene in the 1970s and 1980s.

FOREIGN WRITERS

Many foreign writers have visited and been inspired by France, from Petrarch in 14th-century Avignon to Goethe in Alsace in 1770–71. The Riviera attracted many English writers, including Somerset Maugham, Katharine Mansfield, and Graham Greene. In 1919 the American Sylvia Beach opened the first Shakespeare and Company bookshop in Paris, which became a cultural centre for expatriate writers. In 1922 she was the first to publish James Joyce's masterwork, *Ulysses*.

Hemingway with Sylvia Beach and friends, Paris 1923

Romanesque and Gothic Architecture in France

FRANCE IS RICH in medieval architecture, ranging from small Romanesque churches to great Gothic cathedrals. As the country emerged from the Dark Ages in the 11th century, there was a surge in Romanesque building, based on the Roman model of thick walls, round arches and heavy vaults. French architects improved this basic structure, leading to the flowering of Gothic in the 13th century. Pointed arches and flying buttresses were the key inventions that allowed for much taller buildings with larger windows.

LOCATOR MAP

① *Romanesque abbeys & churches*

⑬ *Gothic cathedrals*

ROMANESQUE FEATURES

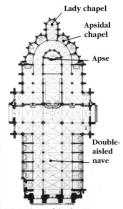

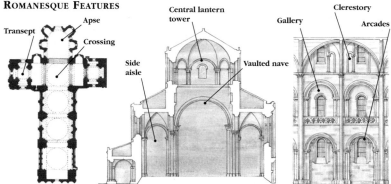

Transept · Apse · Crossing · Central lantern tower · Side aisle · Vaulted nave · Gallery · Clerestory · Arcades

The plan of Angoulême shows the cross-shape and the rounded eastern apse typical of Romanesque architecture.

A section of Le Puy reveals a high barrel-vaulted nave with round arches and low side aisles. Light could enter through windows in the side aisles and the central lantern tower.

The massive walls of the nave bays of St-Etienne support a three-storey structure of arcades, a gallery and clerestory.

GOTHIC FEATURES

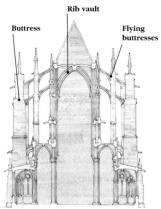

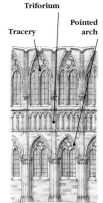

Lady chapel · Apsidal chapel · Apse · Double-aisled nave · Buttress · Rib vault · Flying buttresses · Triforium · Tracery · Pointed arch

The plan of Amiens shows the nave and apse flanked by a continuous row of chapels.

A section of Beauvais shows how the nave could be raised to staggering heights thanks to exterior support from flying buttresses.

Pointed arches withstood greater stress, permitting larger windou as in the nave at Re

WHERE TO FIND ROMANESQUE ARCHITECTURE

① St-Etienne, Caen *p244*
② Mont-St-Michel, Normandy *p248*
③ St-Pierre, Angoulême *p409*
④ Notre-Dame, Le Puy *p355*
⑤ St-Pierre, Moissac *pp432–3*
⑥ St-Sernin, Toulouse *pp436–7*
⑦ Ste-Foy, Conques *pp356–7*
⑧ Sacré-Coeur, Paray-le-Monial *p335*
⑨ St-Philibert, Tournus *p334*
⑩ St-Etienne, Nevers *p328*
⑪ Ste-Madeleine, Vézelay *pp326–7*
⑫ Marmoutier, Saverne *p223*

WHERE TO FIND GOTHIC ARCHITECTURE

⑬ Notre-Dame, Strasbourg *p221*
⑭ Notre-Dame, Reims *pp202–3*
⑮ Notre-Dame, Laon *p195*
⑯ Notre-Dame, Amiens *pp192–3*
⑰ St-Pierre, Beauvais *p190*
⑱ St-Denis, Ile-de-France *p162*
⑲ Sainte-Chapelle, Paris *pp80–81*
⑳ Notre-Dame, Paris *p82–3*
㉑ Notre-Dame, Chartres *pp298–301*
㉒ St-Etienne, Bourges *p303*

TERMS USED IN THIS GUIDE

Basilica: Early church with two aisles and nave lit from above by clerestory windows.

Clerestory: A row of windows illuminating the nave from above the aisle roof.

Rose: Circular window, often stained glass.

Buttress: Mass of masonry built to support a wall.

Flying buttress: An arched support transmitting thrust of the weight downwards.

Portal: Monumental entrance to a building, often decorated.

Tympanum: Decorated space, often carved, over a door or window lintel.

Vault: Arched stone ceiling.

Transept: Two wings of a cruciform church at right angles to the nave.

Crossing: Centre of cruciform where transept crosses nave.

Lantern: Turret with windows to illuminate interior, often with cupola (domed ceiling).

Triforium: Middle storey between arcades and clerestory.

Apse: Termination of the church, often rounded.

Ambulatory: Aisle running round east end, passing behind the sanctuary.

Arcade: Set of arches and supporting columns.

Rib vault: Vault supported by projecting ribs of stone.

Gargoyle: Carved grotesque figure, often a water spout.

Tracery: Ornamental carved stone pattern within Gothic window.

Flamboyant Gothic: Carved stone tracery resembling flames.

Capital: Top of a column, usually carved.

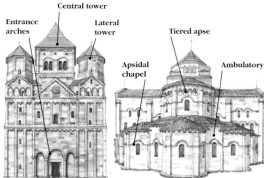

Central tower

Entrance arches

Lateral tower

Tiered apse

Apsidal chapel

Ambulatory

The west façade of Marmoutier Abbey with its towers, narrow windows and small portal give it a fortified appearance.

The east end of Nevers has a rounded apse surrounded by a semi-circular ambulatory and radiating chapels. The chapels were added to provide space for altars.

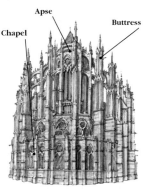

Stepped tower

Sculpted portal

Rose

Apse

Chapel

Buttress

The west façade of Laon has decorative, sculpted portals and a rose window characteristic of Gothic style.

The east end of Beauvais, with its delicate buttresses topped by pinnacles, is the culmination of High Gothic.

Rural Architecture

FRENCH FARMHOUSES ARE ENTIRELY products of the soil, built of stone, clay or wood, depending on what materials are found locally. As the topography changes so does the architecture, from the steeply-sloped roofs covered in flat tiles in the north to the broad canal-tiled roofs of the south.

Despite this rich regional diversity, French farmhouses fall into three basic categories: the *maison bloc,* where house and outbuildings share the same roof; the high house, with living quarters upstairs and livestock or wine cellar below; and courtyard farmsteads, their buildings set around a central court.

Shuttered window in Alsace

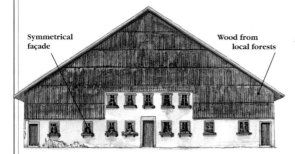

Symmetrical façade

Wood from local forests

The chalet is typical of the Jura, Alps and Vosges mountains. The maison bloc housed both family and livestock throughout the winter. Gaps between the gable planks allowed air to circulate around crops stored in the loft, and an earth ramp behind gave wagons access. Many lofts also had a threshing floor.

Half-timbered houses are typical of Normandy, Alsace, Champagne, Picardy, the Landes and Basque country. The filling between the timbers was wattle and daub or in some cases brick, but it is the arrangement of the smaller posts, different in each region, that best expresses the local style.

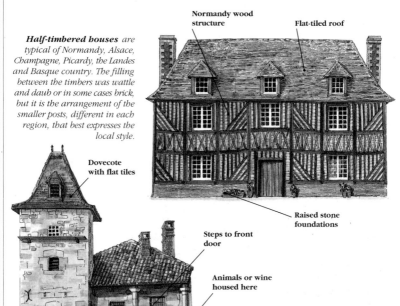

Normandy wood structure

Flat-tiled roof

Dovecote with flat tiles

Raised stone foundations

Steps to front door

Animals or wine housed here

The high house is most prominent in the southeast, and is normally built of stone with an exterior stone staircase and upstairs porch. Wine growers' barrels could be stored on the ground floor without hoisting, or livestock stabled there. High houses in the Lot Valley often boast a dovecote.

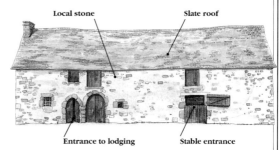

The long house is the oldest form of maison bloc, *with family and livestock at opposite ends of the building – originally one room. In this Breton version, separate doorways lead to house and stable. A dividing wall only became common in the 19th century.*

Local stone

Slate roof

Entrance to lodging

Stable entrance

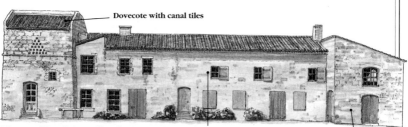

Dovecote with canal tiles

Ochre and beige colours of the south

Rendered façade

The word "mas" *generally refers to any Provençal farmhouse. In the Camargue and the Crau, it is a farmstead for large-scale sheep farming built in an "agglomerated" style: the outbuildings, although attached to one another, are of different heights. Often, a dovecote is included.*

Pebble and brick wall

Half-timber and brick

Compressed cob: *pisé*

Sun-dried adobe bricks

Pebbles in lime mortar

Brick, flint and chalk

WALLS

Limestone, granite, sandstone and pebbles were all used for building walls. But if no stone was available, clay was dug for infilling half-timbered houses, as wattle and daub. The alternative was to use a cob mixture *(pisé)*, pressed into blocks in a process called *banchange*. Adobe (sundried brick) was also used but fired brick was fairly rare as it was expensive to bake. However, brick was sometimes used as trim or combined with chalk or pebbles in a "composite" walling. Walls were generally rendered with mortar.

Flat terracotta tiles in colours of local sand

Pantiles, used in Flanders and Picardy

Canal clay tiles typical of the south

ROOFING

Two roof styles distinguish the north and south. Northern roofs are steeply pitched, so that any rainwater runs off easily. In the south, roofs are covered with canal clay tiles, and more gently sloped to prevent the tiles sliding off.

FRANCE THROUGH THE YEAR

THE FRENCH, with their farming roots, are deeply aware of the changing seasons, and the mild climate means they can celebrate outdoors most of the year. History and tradition are honoured with *fêtes*, such as Bastille Day (14 July). For culture lovers, thousands of arts festivals are held in venues ranging from the huge Avignon Theatre Festival down to small, village events. Large national sports events, such as the Tour de France cycle race, are a key feature in the calendar. Throughout the year, festivals take place celebrating every kind of food and wine. In high summer, the cities empty and French and foreign visitors flock to the beaches and countryside.

SPRING

FRANCE'S OUTDOOR life resumes in spring, terrace-cafés filling up in the sunshine. Easter is a time of Catholic processions, and concerts of sacred music. The Cannes Film Festival in May is the best known of the season's many conventions and trade fairs.

MARCH

Five Nations Rugby Tournament, Parc des Princes, Paris.
Tinta' Mars *(all month)*, Langres. Cabaret and musical evenings at various venues.
Montbéliard Chocolate Carnival *(usually second week)*.
International Dog-sled Championships *(second week)*, Chamrousse.
Grenoble Jazz Festival *(18–27 Mar)*. Jazz concerts.

Rugby ball

Formula One racing at the Monaco Grand Prix

Salon de Mars *(last week)*, Champ de Mars. Paris's most important art and antiques fair.
Wine Sales of the Hospices *(last weekend)*, Nuits-St-Georges.
Musical Flower Show *(end Mar–May)*, Epinal.

APRIL

Good Friday penitential processions Sartène (see p533), Perpignan (see p474) and Holy Week processions all over France.
Passion Plays *(Easter)*, re-enactments of the Crucifixion throughout France.
Bourges Spring Festival *(third week, see p303)*.
Europa Jazz Festival *(last*

two weeks), Le Mans. Young jazz musicians from all over the world come to play.
Horse-riding: International Competition *(last week)*, Saumur.
International Paris Fair *(end Apr–first week May)*, Parc des Expositions, Paris. Leisure and art exhibits.
Joan of Arc Festival *(end Apr–early May)*, Orléans (see p302).

Spring asparagus

MAY

Asparagus harvest, notably in the Loire Valley.
International Grand Prix de Monaco *(Ascension weekend, see p520)*.

La Bravade procession honouring Saint Torpes in St-Tropez

Oloron-Ste-Marie Agricultural Fair *(1 May, see p445)*.
Paris International Marathon *(mid-May)*, from place du Concorde to Château de Vincennes.
La Bravade *(16 18 May)*, St-Tropez *(see p506)*.
Cannes Film Festival *(second and third week)*.
International Sailing Week *(third week)*, La Rochelle.
Gypsy Pilgrimage *(24–26 May)*, Stes-Maries-de-la-Mer *(see p500)*.
Festival d'Amiens *(last week)*. Jazz and world music at various venues.

Traditional transhumance of animals to summer pastures

Fête de Transhumance *(end of May)*. Herds are taken up to summer pastures.
Nîmes Feria *(end May)*, bullfights and street music

festival *(see p486)*.
Grandes Eaux Musicales *(May–Oct, Sundays)*, Versailles. Classical music in the grounds of the château.

SUMMER

THE FRENCH holiday season begins in mid-July, with the return to work and school *(la rentrée)* in early September. Beaches, marinas and camp sites are all full to bursting. Every village has its *fête* and there are countless festivals and sporting events.

JUNE

French Tennis Open *(last week May – first week Jun)*, Stade Roland Garros, Paris.
Strasbourg International Music Festival *(until Jul)*.
Puy-du-Fou Pageant *(Jun–Sep)*, 18th-century village

brought to life in the park at Les Epesses, Vendée.
Le Mans 24-Hour Automobile Race *(third weekend, see p281)*.
Rose Show *(21 Jun)*, Bois de Boulogne, Paris.
Fête de St-Jean *(24 Jun)*, music, bonfires and fireworks all over France.
Tarasque Festival *(last week)*, Tarascon *(see p497)*.

JULY

Aix Festival *(all month)*, Aix-en-Provence *(see p501)*.
Avignon Theatre Festival *(all month, see p493)*.
Eté Girondin *(until Aug)*. Jazz concerts throughout Aquitaine *(see p411)*.

Bullfighting in Mont-de-Marsan

Tombées de la Nuit *(first week)*, Rennes. Arts festival.
Troménie *(11 Jul)*, Locronan. Procession of penitents *(see p263)*.
Comminges Festival *(mid-Jul–end Aug, see p452)*.
Foix Medieval Festival *(mid-Jul–mid Aug, see p453)*.
JVC Grand Parade du Jazz *(mid-Jul)*, Nice.
Mont-de-Marsan Feria *(third week)*. Bullfights and music *(see p415)*.
International Jazz Festival *(second half)*, Antibes and Juan-les-Pins *(see p511)*.
Jazz Vienne *(first two weeks)*, Vienne *(see p372)*.
Sète Festival *(second and third weeks, see p482)*.
Tour de France cycle race *(third week)*. The grand finale takes place on the Champs-Elysées, Paris.

The rose season in full bloom

Cyclists in the final stage of the Tour de France cycle race

Holiday-makers on a crowded beach in Cannes on the Côte d'Azur

AUGUST

Peak holiday season
(1–15 Aug).
Lourdes Pilgrimage
*(Palm Sun to 15
Aug, see p449).*
**International Organ
Festival** *(Jul–Sep),* organ
recitals in Chartres cathedral.
Pablo Casals Festival
(end Jul–mid-Aug),
Prades *(see p470).*

*Avignon Theatre
Festival performer*

Fête de la Véraison *(first
or second weekend),*
medieval celebration
of fruit harvest,
Châteauneuf-du-
Pape *(see p494).*
**Parade of Lavender
Floats** *(first or
second weekend),*
Digne *(see p507).*
**Interceltic Fes-
tival** *(second
week),* traditional

Celtic arts, crafts and music,
Lorient *(see p405).*
"Feria" – Bullfight *(mid-
Aug),* Dax *(see p415).*
**St-Jean-Pied-de-Port-Basque
Fête** *(mid-Aug, see p444).*
Son et Lumière (sound
and light) displays in historic
buildings everywhere and
15 August fireworks.
**International Sardana
Festival** *(third weekend),*
Céret *(see p472).*

AUTUMN

IN WINE REGIONS, the grape
harvest is the occasion for
much gregarious jollity, and
every wine village has its
wine festival. When the new
wine is ready in November
there are more festivities. The
hunting season begins –
everywhere there is game
shooting. In the southwest,
small migrating birds are
trapped in nets, often to the
fury of ecologists.

Ceremony for the Induction of new Chevaliers at the Hospice de Beaune

SEPTEMBER

Festival de l'Ile de France
(weekends, until mid-Oct),
Classical and jazz concerts.
Picardy Cathedral Festival
(mid-Sep), classical concerts
in the region's cathedrals.
"Musicades" *(first two
weeks),* Lyon. Classical
music concerts.
Le Puy "Roi de l'Oiseau",
(third week), Renaissance-
style festival *(see p355).*
Grape harvest, wine regions
throughout France.

OCTOBER

Paris Jazz Festival *(concerts
all month in various venues).*
Pottery-makers Festival
(first weekend), Lyon.
**Prix de l'Arc de
Triomphe** *(first Sun),*
Horse racing at
Longchamp, Paris.
**Espelette Red
Pepper Festival** *(last
weekend, see p443).*
Walnut season, through-
out Périgord region.

Classical cello

NOVEMBER

**Dijon International Food
and Wine Festival** *(first
two weeks).* Traditional
gastronomic fair.
Apple Festival *(mid-
Nov),* Le Havre.
**Wine Sales and Les
Trois Glorieuses**
(third weekend),
Beaune *(see p336).*
Truffle season *(until
Mar),* Périgord, Quercy
and Provence.

WINTER

AT CHRISTMAS, traditional nativity plays are held in churches and there are fairs and markets

Christmas wreath throughout France. In the Alps and the Pyrenees, and even the Vosges and Massif Central, the ski-slopes are crowded. In Flanders and Nice, carnivals take place before Lent.

DECEMBER

Men's International Skiing Competition *(mid-Dec)*, Val d'Isère. Most important skiing competition of the year.

JANUARY

Château de Thoiry Music Festival *(all year)*, concerts of every kind of music.
Abbaye de Fontevraud Season of Music *(until Jun, see p284)*.

Downhill skier on the slopes in the French Alps

The Taj Mahal re-created at the Lemon Festival in Menton

Monte-Carlo Rally *(usually mid-Jan, see p520)*.
Limoux Carnival *(until Mar)*. Street festival held since the Middle Ages.

FEBRUARY

Découvertes *(first week)*, Grand Palais. International art show for new artists.
Lemon Festival *(mid-Feb–Mar)*, Menton *(see p519)*.
Nice Carnival and the Battle of Flowers *(late Feb–early Mar, see p516)*.
International Jazz Festival *(mid–end Feb)*, Cannes.

Celebrating the Nice Carnival and the Battle of Flowers

Bastille Day parade past the Arc de Triomphe

PUBLIC HOLIDAYS

New Year's Day (1 Jan)
Easter Sunday and Monday
Ascension Day (sixth Thursday after Easter)
Whit Monday (second Monday after Ascension)
Labour Day (1 May)
VE Day (8 May)
Bastille Day (14 Jul)
Assumption Day (15 Aug)
All Saints' Day (1 Nov)
Remembrance Day (11 Nov)
Christmas Day (25 Dec)

The Climate of France

SET ON EUROPE'S western edge, France has a varied, temperate climate. An Atlantic influence prevails in the north-west, with westerly sea winds bringing humidity and warm winters. The east experiences Continental temperature extremes with frosty, clear winters and often stormy summers. The south enjoys a Mediterranean climate with hot, dry summers and mild winters, punctuated by violent winds.

PARIS AND ILE DE FRANCE

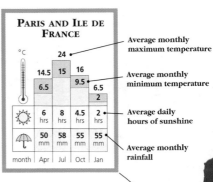

Average monthly maximum temperature
Average monthly minimum temperature
Average daily hours of sunshine
Average monthly rainfall

°C				
		24		
	14.5	15	16	
	6.5		9.5	6.5
				2
☀	6 hrs	8 hrs	4.5 hrs	2 hrs
☂	50 mm	58 mm	55 mm	55 mm
month	Apr	Jul	Oct	Jan

NORMANDY

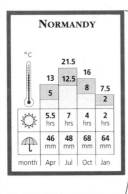

°C				
		21.5		
	13	12.5	16	
	5		8	7.5
				2
☀	5.5 hrs	7 hrs	4 hrs	2 hrs
☂	46 mm	48 mm	68 mm	64 mm
month	Apr	Jul	Oct	Jan

BRITTANY

°C				
		24		
	14.5	13	17	
	5.5		8.5	8
				2
☀	6 hrs	8 hrs	4.5 hrs	2 hrs
☂	44 mm	39 mm	62 mm	63 mm
month	Apr	Jul	Oct	Jan

LOIRE VALLEY

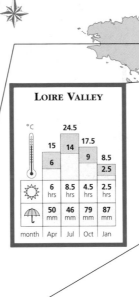

°C				
		24.5		
	15	14	17.5	
	6		9	8.5
				2.5
☀	6 hrs	8.5 hrs	4.5 hrs	2.5 hrs
☂	50 mm	46 mm	79 mm	87 mm
month	Apr	Jul	Oct	Jan

POITOU AND AQUITAINE

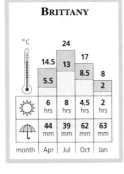

°C				
		26		
	16.5	14.5	19	
	6.5		9	9.5
				2.5
☀	6.5 hrs	9 hrs	5.5 hrs	2.5 hrs
☂	72 mm	47 mm	88 mm	100 mm
month	Apr	Jul	Oct	Jan

PYRENEES

°C				
		25		
	15	13.5	19	
	5		7.5	10
				0.5
☀	5 hrs	7.5 hrs	5.5 hrs	3.5 hrs
☂	98 mm	62 mm	78 mm	93 mm
month	Apr	Jul	Oct	Jan

PÉRIGORD, QUERCY AND GASCONY

°C				
		27		
	16.5	14.5	19	
	6		9	8.5
				2
☀	6 hrs	9 hrs	4.5 hrs	2.5 hrs
☂	60 mm	50 mm	57 mm	66 mm
month	Apr	Jul	Oct	Jan

Le Havre
PARIS
Rennes
Nantes
Tours
Bordeaux
Montauban
Biarritz

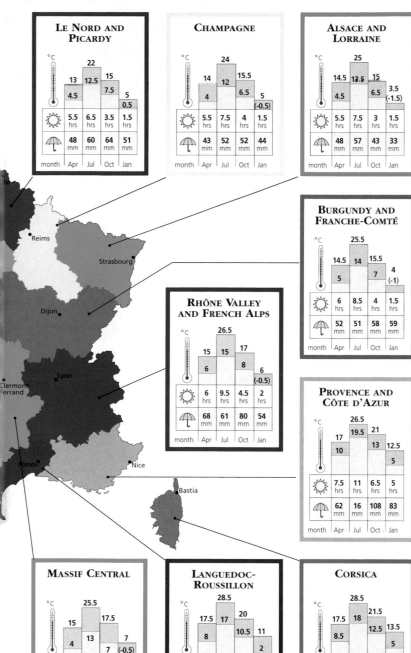

LE NORD AND PICARDY

°C

		22		
13	12.5		15	
4.5		7.5		5
				0.5

☀	5.5 hrs	6.5 hrs	3.5 hrs	1.5 hrs
☂	48 mm	60 mm	64 mm	51 mm
month	Apr	Jul	Oct	Jan

CHAMPAGNE

°C

		24		
	14	12	15.5	
	4		6.5	5
				(-0.5)

☀	5.5 hrs	7.5 hrs	4 hrs	1.5 hrs
☂	43 mm	52 mm	52 mm	44 mm
month	Apr	Jul	Oct	Jan

ALSACE AND LORRAINE

°C

		25		
	14.5	12.5	15	
	4.5		6.5	3.5
				(-1.5)

☀	5.5 hrs	7.5 hrs	3 hrs	1.5 hrs
☂	48 mm	57 mm	43 mm	33 mm
month	Apr	Jul	Oct	Jan

BURGUNDY AND FRANCHE-COMTÉ

°C

		25.5		
	14.5	14	15.5	
	5		7	4
				(-1)

☀	6 hrs	8.5 hrs	4 hrs	1.5 hrs
☂	52 mm	51 mm	58 mm	59 mm
month	Apr	Jul	Oct	Jan

RHÔNE VALLEY AND FRENCH ALPS

°C

		26.5		
	15	15	17	
	6		8	6
				(-0.5)

☀	6 hrs	9.5 hrs	4.5 hrs	2 hrs
☂	68 mm	61 mm	80 mm	54 mm
month	Apr	Jul	Oct	Jan

PROVENCE AND CÔTE D'AZUR

°C

		26.5		
	17	19.5	21	
	10		13	12.5
				5

☀	7.5 hrs	11 hrs	6.5 hrs	5 hrs
☂	62 mm	16 mm	108 mm	83 mm
month	Apr	Jul	Oct	Jan

MASSIF CENTRAL

°C

		25.5		
	15	13	17.5	
	4		7	7
				(-0.5)

☀	5.5 hrs	8.5 hrs	4.5 hrs	2.5 hrs
☂	45 mm	48 mm	51 mm	29 mm
month	Apr	Jul	Oct	Jan

LANGUEDOC-ROUSSILLON

°C

		28.5		
	17.5	17	20	
	8		10.5	11
				2

☀	7.5 hrs	11 hrs	6 hrs	4.5 hrs
☂	55 mm	20 mm	110 mm	72 mm
month	Apr	Jul	Oct	Jan

CORSICA

°C

		28.5		
	17.5	18	21.5	
	8.5		12.5	13.5
				5

☀	7 hrs	11 hrs	6.5 hrs	4.5 hrs
☂	66 mm	15 mm	107 mm	62 mm
month	Apr	Jul	Oct	Jan

Reims
Strasbourg
Dijon
Lyon
Clermont-Ferrand
Nîmes
Nice
Bastia

THE HISTORY OF FRANCE

THE ONLY European country facing both the North Sea and the Mediterranean, France has been subject to a particularly rich variety of cultural influences. Though famous for the rootedness of its peasant population, it has also been a European melting pot, even before the arrival of the Celtic Gauls in the centuries before Christ, through to the Mediterranean immigrations of the 20th century.

Fleur-de-lys, the royal emblem

Roman conquest by Julius Caesar had an enduring impact, but from the 4th and 5th centuries AD, waves of Barbarian invaders destroyed much of the Roman legacy. The Germanic Franks provided political leadership in the following centuries, but when their line died out in the late 10th century, France was socially and politically fragmented.

THE FORMATION OF FRANCE

The Capetian dynasty gradually pieced France together over the Middle Ages, a period of great economic prosperity and cultural vitality. The Black Death and the Hundred Years' War brought setbacks, and the dynasty's power was seriously threatened by the rival Burgundian dukes. France recovered, however, and flourished during the Renaissance, followed by the grandeur of Louis XIV's reign. During the Enlightenment, in the 18th century, French culture and institutions were the envy of Europe.

The Revolution of 1789 ended the absolute monarchy and introduced major social and institutional reforms, many of which were endorsed and consolidated by Napoleon. Yet the Revolution also inaugurated the instability which has remained a hallmark of French politics: since 1789, France has known five republics, two empires and three brands of royal power, plus the Vichy government during World War II.

Modernization in the 19th and 20th centuries proved a slow process. Railways, the military service and radical educational reforms were crucial in forming a sense of French identity among the citizens.

Rivalry with Germany dominated French politics for most of the late 19th and early 20th century. The population losses in World War I were traumatic for France, while during 1940–44 the country was occupied by Germany. Yet since 1945, the two countries have proved the backbone of the developing European Union.

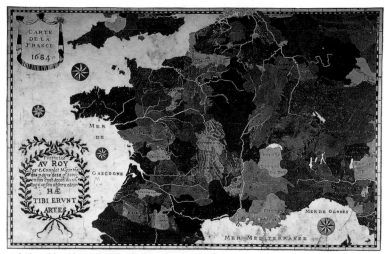

Inlaid marble table top showing the map of France in 1684

◁ *La République,* **painted by Charles Landelle in 1848**

Prehistoric France

THE EARLIEST TRACES of human life in France date back to around 2 million BC. From around 40,000 BC, *Homo sapiens* lived an itinerant existence as hunters and gatherers. Around 6000 BC, following the end of the Ice Age, a major shift in lifestyle occurred, as people settled down to herd animals and cultivate crops. The advent of metal-working allowed more effective tools and weapons to be developed. The Iron Age is associated particularly with the Celts, who arrived from the east during the first millennium BC. A more complex social hierarchy developed, consisting of warriors, farmers, artisans and druids (Celtic priests).

Bronze Age vase, Brittany

FRANCE IN 8000 BC

☐ *Former coastline*

☐ *Present-day land mass*

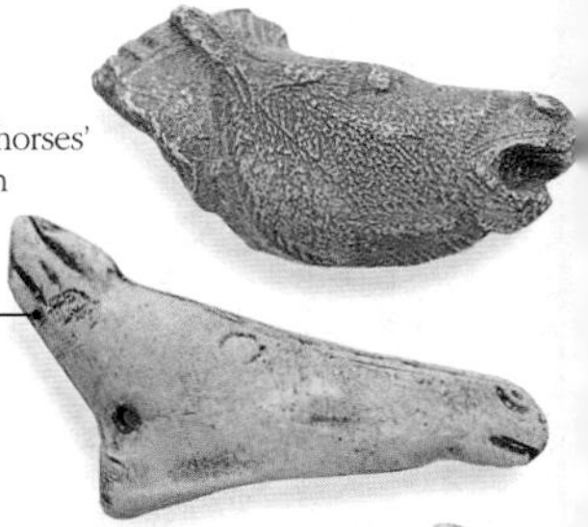

These carvings of horses' heads were found in the Pyrenees and date from around 9000 BC.

Carnac Stone Alignments *(4500–4000 BC)*
The purpose of the extensive networks of megaliths around Carnac (see p268) *remains obscure. They possibly served in pagan rituals or as an astronomical calendar.*

The mammoth, here carved from animal bone, was a thick-coated giant who died out after the end of the Ice Age.

Cro-Magnon Man
This skull, dating to c.25,000 BC, was discovered at Cro-Magnon in the Dordogne in 1868. In comparison with most of his predecessors, Cro-Magnon Man was tall, robust and had a large head. He differed only marginally from us.

PREHISTORIC ART

The rich deposits of cave art in France have only been recognized as authentic for just over a century. They include wall paintings and daubings but also various engraved objects. Venus figurines, carved with flint tools, probably had ritual and religious rather than erotic purposes.

TIMELINE

Painting of bulls in Lascaux

2,000,000 BC Early hominid societies

30,000 Cro-Magnon Man

2,000,000 BC	30,000	25,000	20,000

400,000 Discovery of fire by *Homo erectus*

28,000 The first Venus sculptures, possibly representing fertility goddesses

Primitive stone tool

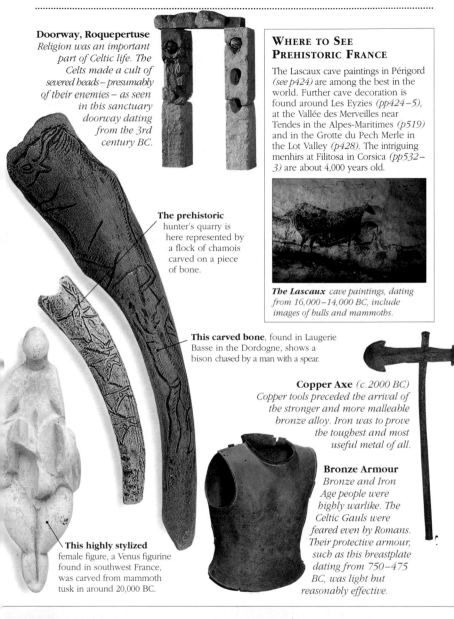

Doorway, Roquepertuse
Religion was an important part of Celtic life. The Celts made a cult of severed heads – presumably of their enemies – as seen in this sanctuary doorway dating from the 3rd century BC.

The prehistoric hunter's quarry is here represented by a flock of chamois carved on a piece of bone.

This carved bone, found in Laugerie Basse in the Dordogne, shows a bison chased by a man with a spear.

Copper Axe *(c. 2000 BC)*
Copper tools preceded the arrival of the stronger and more malleable bronze alloy. Iron was to prove the toughest and most useful metal of all.

Bronze Armour
Bronze and Iron Age people were highly warlike. The Celtic Gauls were feared even by Romans. Their protective armour, such as this breastplate dating from 750–475 BC, was light but reasonably effective.

This highly stylized female figure, a Venus figurine found in southwest France, was carved from mammoth tusk in around 20,000 BC.

WHERE TO SEE PREHISTORIC FRANCE

The Lascaux cave paintings in Périgord *(see p424)* are among the best in the world. Further cave decoration is found around Les Eyzies *(pp424–5)*, at the Vallée des Merveilles near Tendes in the Alpes-Maritimes *(p519)* and in the Grotte du Pech Merle in the Lot Valley *(p428)*. The intriguing menhirs at Filitosa in Corsica *(pp532–3)* are about 4,000 years old.

The Lascaux cave paintings, dating from 16,000–14,000 BC, include images of bulls and mammoths.

15,000 Hunters live on wandering herds of mammoth, rhinoceros and reindeer. Art includes the Lascaux caves and Val Camonica/Mont Bego engravings

7000–4500 Neolithic revolution: farming, megaliths and menhir stone sculptures

600 Greek colony at Marseille. Mediterranean luxury goods exchanged for tin, copper, iron and slaves. Early urban development

15,000	10,000	5,000

10,000 End of Ice Age. More regions become inhabitable

10,000–6000 Mammoth herds disappear and hunters must rely on animals of the forest, including wild boar and aurochs

1200–700 Arrival of the Celts during the Bronze and Iron Ages

500 Celtic nobles bury their dead with riches such as the Vix treasure *(see p324)*

Celtic helmet

Roman Gaul

THE ROMANS HAD ANNEXED the southern fringe of France by 125–121 BC. Julius Caesar brought the rest of Gaul under Roman control in the Gallic Wars (58–51 BC). The province of Gaul prospered: it developed good communications, a network of cities crammed with public buildings and leisure facilities such as baths and amphitheatres, while in the countryside large villas were established. By the 3rd century AD, however, barbarian raids from Germany were causing increasing havoc. From the 5th century barbarians began to settle throughout Gaul.

Roman mosaic from Vienne

FRANCE IN 58 BC

☐ *Roman Gaul*

Emperor Augustus, who was considered a living God, was worshipped at this altar.

Roman Dolce Vita
The Romans brought material comfort and luxury, and wine-growing became widespread. This 19th-century painting by Couture conveys a contemporary view of Roman decadence.

Vercingetorix
The Celtic chieftain Vercingetorix was Julius Caesar's greatest military opponent. This bronze statue is at Alise-Sainte-Reine (see p324), the Gauls' final stand in 51 BC.

LA TURBIE

This impressive monument near Monaco was erected in 6 BC by the Roman Senate. It celebrates Augustus's victory over the Alpine tribes in 14–13 BC. Badly pillaged for its stone, it was only partly restored in 1935.

TIMELINE

Augustus

125–121 BC Roman colonization of Southern Gaul

31 BC Frontiers of the Three Gauls (*Gallia Celtica, Gallia Aquitania* and *Gallia Belgica*) established by Augustus

200 BC	100	0	AD 100

58–51 BC Julius Caesar's Gallic Wars result in establishment of Roman Gaul

Julius Caesar

16 BC Maison Carrée built in Nîmes (*see pp486–7*)

52–51 BC Vercingetorix revolt

AD 43 Lugdunum (Lyon) established as capital of the Three Gauls

Dancing Girl
Celtic art continued uninfluenced by Roman naturalistic ideals. This bronze statuette of a young woman dates from the 1st–2nd century AD.

A statue of Augustus was placed at the top of the original monument.

Enamelled Brooch
This decorative Gallo-Roman brooch dates from the second half of the 1st century BC.

WHERE TO SEE GALLO-ROMAN FRANCE

Gallo-Roman remains are to be found all over France, many of them in Provence. In addition to La Turbie *(see p519)* there is the Roman amphitheatre in Arles *(p475)* and the theatre and triumphal arch in Orange *(p492)*. Elsewhere, there are ruins at Autun in Burgundy *(p329)*, the Temple d'Auguste et Livie in Vienne *(p372)*, Les Arènes at Nîmes *(pp486–7)* and fragments of Vesunna in Périgueux *(p424)*.

Les Arènes in Nîmes, *built at the end of the 1st century AD, is still in use today.*

The Claudian Tables
In AD 48, Emperor Claudius persuaded the Senate to allow Gauls full Roman citizenship. The grateful Gauls recorded the event on stone tables found at Lyon.

The 44 tribes subjugated by Augustus are listed on an inscription, with a dedication to the emperor.

Emperor Augustus
Augustus, the first Roman Emperor (27 BC–AD 14), upheld the Pax Romana, an enforced peace which allowed the Gauls to concentrate on culture rather than war.

AD 177 First execution of Christian martyrs, Lyon. Sainte Blandine is thrown to the lions, who refuse to harm her

Sainte Blandine

360 Julian, prefect of Gaul, proclaimed Roman Emperor. Lutetia changes name to Paris

200	300	400

275 First Barbarian raids

313 Christianity officially recognized as religion under the rule of Constantine, the first Christian emperor

406 Barbarian invasion from the east. Settlement of the Franks and Germanic tribes

476 Overthrow of the last Roman emperor leads to end of the western Roman Empire

The Monastic Realm

THE COLLAPSE of the Roman Empire led to a period of instability and invasions. Both the Frankish Merovingian dynasty (486–751) and the Carolingians (751–987) were unable to bring more than spasmodic periods of political calm. Throughout this turbulent period, the Church provided an element of continuity. As centres for Christian scholars and artists, the monasteries helped to restore the values of the ancient world. They also developed farming and viticulture and some became extremely powerful, dominating the country economically as well as spiritually.

9th-century gold chalice

FRANCE IN 751

☐ *Carolingian Empire*

Stable with lay brethren's quarters above

Charlemagne *(742–814)*
The greatest of Carolingian rulers, Charlemagne created an empire based on strictly autocratic rule. Powerful and charismatic, he could neither read nor write.

Bakery

The great infirmary hall could accommodate about 100 patients. It was flanked by the Lady Chapel.

CLUNY MONASTERY

The Benedictine abbey of Cluny *(see p335)* was founded in 910 with the aim of major monastic reforms. This major religious centre, here shown as a reconstruction (after Conant), had great influence over hundreds of monasteries throughout Europe.

Saint Benedict
Saint Benedict established the Benedictine rule: monks were to divide their time between work and prayer.

TIMELINE

481 Clovis the Frank becomes first Merovingian king

507 Paris made capital of the Frankish kingdom

c.590 Saint Colombanus introduces Irish monasticism to France

732 Battle of Poitiers: Charles Martel repulses Arab invasion

500	600	700

496 Conversion of Clovis, king of the Franks, to Christianity

628–37 Dagobert I, the last effective ruler of the Merovingian dynasty, brings temporary unity to the Frankish kingdom

Dagobert I

751 Pepin becomes first king of the Carolingian dynasty

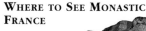

Baptism of Clovis
The Frankish chieftain Clovis was the first barbarian ruler to convert to Christianity. He was baptized in Reims in 496.

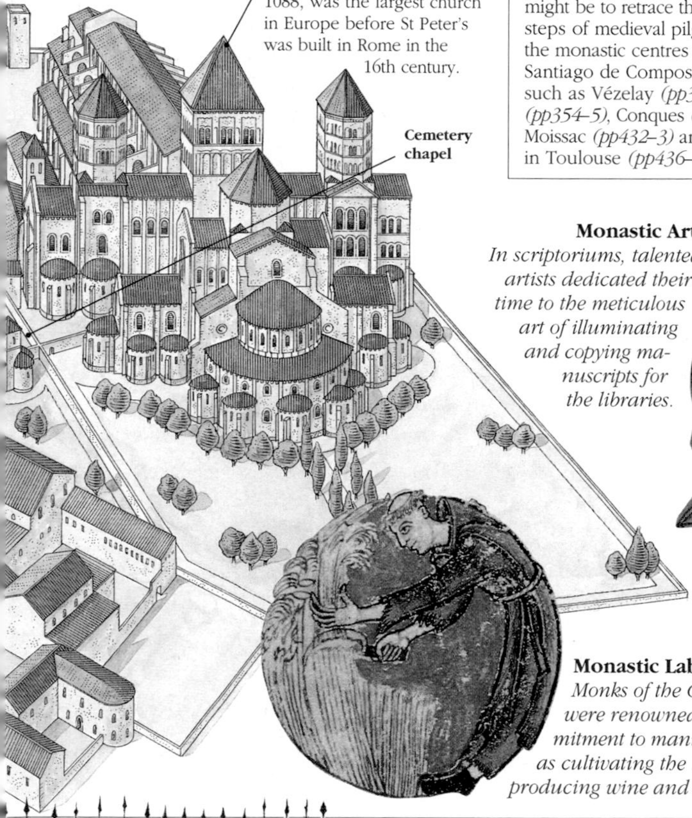

The abbey church, begun in 1088, was the largest church in Europe before St Peter's was built in Rome in the 16th century.

Cemetery chapel

WHERE TO SEE MONASTIC FRANCE

The monastic realm has survived in austere Cistercian abbeys in Burgundy, such as Fontenay *(see pp322–3)*. Little remains of Cluny, but some of the superb capitals can still be admired *(p335)*. The best way to experience monastic France might be to retrace the steps of medieval pilgrims and visit the monastic centres on the route to Santiago de Compostela *(pp390–91)*, such as Vézelay *(pp326–7)*, Le Puy *(pp354–5)*, Conques *(pp358–9)*, Moissac *(pp432–3)* and St-Sernin in Toulouse *(pp436–7)*.

Cluny capitals

Monastic Arts
In scriptoriums, talented artists dedicated their time to the meticulous art of illuminating and copying manuscripts for the libraries.

Monastic Labour
Monks of the Cistercian rule were renowned for their commitment to manual labour such as cultivating the land and producing wine and liqueurs.

1096 First Crusade

1066 Conquest of England by the Normans

Carolingian soldiers

987 Hugh Capet, first Capetian ruler

800	900	1000

843 Treaty of Verdun: division of the Carolingian Empire into three parts including West Francia

800 Coronation of Charlemagne as Holy Roman Emperor

910 Foundation of the Benedictine monastery of Cluny

1077 Bayeux tapestry

William the Conqueror steering his ship on the Bayeux tapestry

Gothic France

Tʜᴇ ɢᴏᴛʜɪᴄ ꜱᴛʏʟᴇ, epitomized by soaring cathedrals (*see pp28–9*), emerged in the 12th century at a time of growing prosperity and scholarship, crusades and an increasingly dominant monarchy. The rival French and Burgundian courts (*see p333*) became models of fashion and etiquette for all of Europe. *Chansons des gestes* (epic poems) performed by troubadours celebrated the code of chivalry.

Medieval knights in combat

FRANCE IN 1270

☐ *Royal territory*

▨ *Other fiefs*

Ciborium of Alpais
Alpais, a renowned 12th-century goldsmith in Limoges, made this superb ciborium used to hold wafers for the Holy Communion.

Winch to lift up stone sections

Courtly Love
According to the code of chivalry, knights dedicated their service to an ideal but unapproachable lady. Courtesy and romance were introduced in art and music.

The king supervised the building of the cathedral, accompanied by the architect.

Draper's Window
The textile trade benefited from the era of urban prosperity. This stained-glass window in a church in Semur-en-Auxois (see p325) shows wool washers at work.

TIMELINE

c.1100 First edition of the epic poem *Chanson de Roland*

1117 Secret marriage of the scholar Abelard and his student Héloise. Her uncle, canon Filibert, does not approve and forces him to become a monk while she retires as a nun

1154 Angevin Empire created by Anglo-Norman dynasty starting with Henry Plantagenet, count of Anjou and king of England (as Henry II)

1100	1125	1150	1175

1115 Saint Bernard founds the Cistercian abbey at Clairvaux

1120 Rebuilding of the abbey of St-Denis; birth of the Gothic style

King Philip Augustus, who adopted the fleur-de-lys emblem

1180–1223 Reign of Philip Augustus

The Crusades
In an attempt to win back the Holy Land from the Turks, Philip Augustus set out on the Third Crusade (1189) alongside England's Richard the Lion-Heart and Holy Roman Emperor Frederick Barbarossa.

Lacelike sculpture adorned the façades of the Gothic cathedrals.

Stone masons cut stones on site.

St Bernard *(1090–1153) Key figure of the Cistercian rule and counsellor to the pope, St Bernard preached rigorous simplicity of life.*

ELEANOR OF AQUITAINE

Strong-willed and vivacious Eleanor, duchess of independent Aquitaine, contributed to the conflict between France and England. In 1137 she married the pious Louis VII of France. Returning from a Crusade, Louis found that their marriage had broken down. After the annulment in 1152, Eleanor married Henry of Anjou, taking her duchy with her. Two years later Henry successfully claimed the throne of England. Aquitaine came under English rule and thus the Angevin Empire began.

Eleanor of Aquitaine and Henry II are buried in Fontevraud (p284).

Holy Relic
Throughout the Middle Ages most churches could boast at least one saint's relic. The cult of relics brought pilgrims and more riches.

THE BUILDING OF A CATHEDRAL
In affluent, mercantile towns, skilled masons constructed towering Gothic cathedrals of revolutionary design, such as Chartres *(see pp298–301)* and Amiens *(pp192–3)*. With their improbable height and lightness they were a testimony to both faith and prosperity.

Louis IX on his death bed

1226 Louis IX crowned king

1270 Death of Louis IX at Tunis in the Eighth Crusade

1305 Papacy established in Avignon

1200	1225	1250	1275	1300

1214 Battle of Bouvines. Philip Augustus begins to drive the English out of France

1259 Normandy, Maine, Anjou and Poitou acquired from England

1285 Philip the Fair crowned

1297 Louis IX is canonized, becoming Saint Louis

The Hundred Years' War

Public execution, in Froissart's 14th-century chronicle

THE HUNDRED YEARS' WAR (1337–1453), pitting England against France for control of French land, had devastating effects. The damage of warfare was amplified by frequent famines and the ravages of bubonic plague in the wake of the Black Death in 1348. France came close to being permanently partitioned by the king of England and the duke of Burgundy. In 1429–30 the young Joan of Arc helped rally France's fortunes and within a generation the English had been driven out of France.

FRANCE IN 1429

☐ France
▨ Anglo-Burgundy

Angels with trumpets announce the Last Judgment.

Men of War
One of the reasons men enlisted as soldiers was hope for plunder. Both the French and English armies lived off the land, at the expense of the peasantry.

The elect, springing resurrected from their graves, are ushered into heaven.

The Black Death
The plague of 1348–52 caused 4–5 million deaths, about 25 per cent of the French population. For want of medicines people had to put their faith in prayers and holy processions.

TIMELINE

14th-century flame-thrower

1346 Battle of Crécy: French defeated by English

1328 Philip VI, first Valois monarch

1356 French defeat at Battle of Poitiers

1325

1350

1375

1337 Start of the Hundred Years' War

Plague victims

1348–52 The Black Death

1358 Bourgeois uprising in Paris led by Etienne Marcel. The Jacquerie peasant uprising in Northern France

Medieval Medicine

The state of the heavens was widely held to influence earthly conditions, such as health, and a diagnosis based on the zodiac was considered reliable. The standby cure for all sorts of ailments was blood letting.

English Longbow

The king's troops fought against England, but the individual French duchies supported whichever side seemed more favourable. In the confused battles, English bowmen excelled. Their longbows caused chaos among the hordes of mounted French chivalry.

Christ as Supreme Judge is flanked by angels bearing the instruments of the Passion.

Archangel Michael, resplendent with peacock wings, holds the judgment scales. The weight of sinners outbalances the elect.

John the Baptist is accompanied by the 12 apostles and the Virgin Mary, dressed in blue.

The damned, with hideously twisted faces, fall into Hell.

THE LAST JUDGMENT

With war, plague and famine as constant visitors, many people feared that the end of the world was nigh. Religious paintings, such as the great 15th-century altarscreen by Rogier van der Weyden in the Hôtel-Dieu in Beaune *(see pp336–7)*, reflected the moral fervour of the time.

Attack on Heresy

The general anxiety spilled over into anti-Semitic pogroms and attacks on alleged heretics, who were burned at the stake.

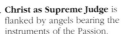

1415 Battle of Agincourt. French defeat by Henry V of England

1429 Intervention of Joan of Arc: Charles VII crowned king

1453 End of the Hundred Years' War. Only Calais remains in English hands

1400	1425	1450

1411 *Les Très Riches Heures du Duc du Berry* prayer book, by Paul and Jean de Limbourg *(see p194)*

1431 Joan of Arc burned at stake as witch by the English

1419 Charles VI of France makes Henry V of England his heir

Joan of Arc

Renaissance France

As a result of the French invasion of Italy in 1494, the ideals and aesthetic of the Italian Renaissance spread to France, reaching their height during the reign of François I. Known as a true Renaissance prince, he was skilled in letters and art as well as sports and war. He invited Italian artists, such as Leonardo and Cellini, to his court and enjoyed Rabelais' bawdy stories. Another highly influential Italian was Catherine de' Medici (1519–89). Widow of Henri II, she virtually ruled France through her sons, François II, Charles IX and Henri III. She was also one of the major players in the Wars of Religion (1562–93) between Catholics and Protestants, which divided the nobility and tore the country to pieces.

Masked lute-player

FRANCE IN 1527

☐ *Royal territory*
■ *Other fiefs*

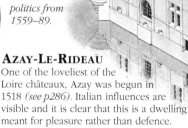

The corner towers are a Gothic feature transformed by Italian lightness of touch into pure decoration.

Galerie François I, Fontainebleau
The artists of the School of Fontaine-bleau blended late Italian Renaissance style with French elements.

Power Behind the Throne
Catherine de' Medici dominated French politics from 1559–89.

AZAY-LE-RIDEAU

One of the loveliest of the Loire châteaux, Azay was begun in 1518 (see p286). Italian influences are visible and it is clear that this is a dwelling meant for pleasure rather than defence.

TIMELINE

1470 First printing presses established in France

Prototype tank by Leonardo da Vinci

1519 Leonardo da Vinci dies in the arms of François I at the French court in Amboise

1536 Calvin's *Institutes of the Christian Religion* leads to a new form of Protestantism

1470	1480	1490	1500	1510	1520	1530

1477 Final defeat of the Dukes of Burgundy, who sought to establish a middle kingdom between France and Germany

1494–1559 France and Austria fight over Italian territories in the Italian Wars

1515 Reign of François I begins

Golden coin showing the fleur-de-lys and the salamander of François I

Gold Pomander
Pomanders containing sweet-smelling herbs such as amber and cinnamon were carried in time of plague to ward off the bad air held responsible for contagion.

Ballroom with Flemish tapestries

The staircase was in the new Italian fashion with double flights of steps rather than a spiral.

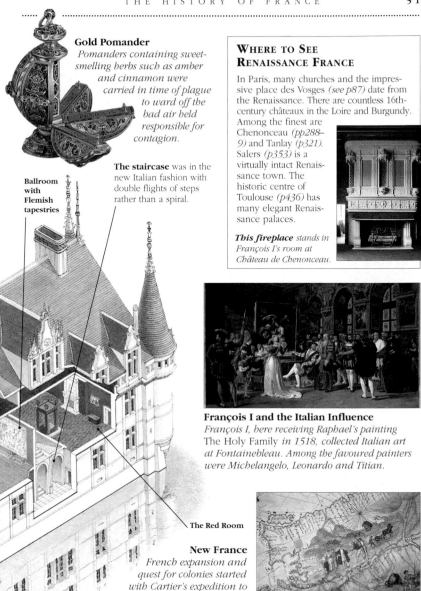

The Red Room

WHERE TO SEE RENAISSANCE FRANCE

In Paris, many churches and the impressive place des Vosges (see p87) date from the Renaissance. There are countless 16th-century châteaux in the Loire and Burgundy. Among the finest are Chenonceau (pp288–9) and Tanlay (p321). Salers (p353) is a virtually intact Renaissance town. The historic centre of Toulouse (p436) has many elegant Renaissance palaces.

This fireplace stands in François I's room at Château de Chenonceau.

François I and the Italian Influence
François I, here receiving Raphael's painting The Holy Family *in 1518, collected Italian art at Fontainebleau. Among the favoured painters were Michelangelo, Leonardo and Titian.*

New France
French expansion and quest for colonies started with Cartier's expedition to Canada in 1534 (see p272).

1540	1550	1560	1570	1580	1590	1600

1559 Treaty of Cateau–Cambrésis ends the Italian Wars

1572 Massacre of Protestants on St Bartholomew's Eve in Paris

1589 Henry III murdered. The Huguenot Henry IV becomes first Bourbon king of France

1598 Edict of Nantes: tolerance for Protestantism

1608 Foundation of Quebec

1539 Edict of Villers Cotterets makes French the official language of state

1562 Wars of Religion between Catholics and Protestants start

St Bartholomew's Eve Massacre

1593 Henry IV converts to Catholicism and ends the Wars of Religion

The Grand Siècle

Emblem of the Sun King

THE END OF THE RELIGIOUS WARS heralded a period of exceptional French influence and power. The cardinal ministers Richelieu and Mazarin paved the way for Louis XIV's absolute monarchy. Political development was matched by artistic styles of unprecedented brilliance: enormous Baroque edifices, the drama of Molière and Racine, and the music of Lully. Versailles *(see pp164–7)*, built under the supervision of Louis' capable finance minister Colbert, was the glory of Europe, but its cost and Louis XIV's endless wars proved expensive for the French state and led to widespread misery by the end of his reign.

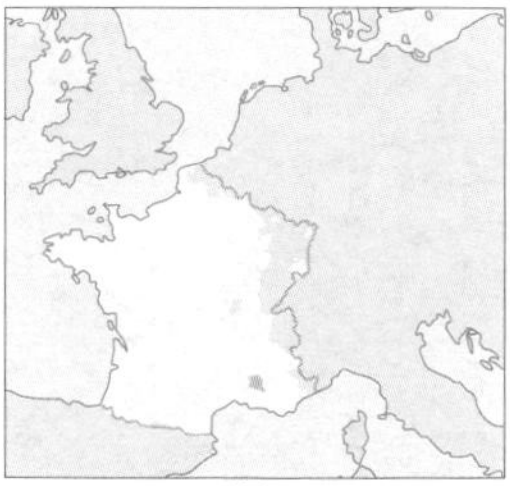

FRANCE IN 1661

☐ *Royal territory*

▨ *Avignon (papal enclave)*

OEUVRES DE MOLIERE.

Molière *(1622–73)*
Actor-playwright Molière performed many plays for Louis XIV and his court, though some of his satires were banned. After his death, his company became the basis of the French state theatre, the Comédie Française.

Madame (married to Monsieur) as Flora

Monsieur, the king's brother

Madame de Maintenon
In 1684, following the death of his first wife Marie-Thérèse, Louis secretly married his mistress Mme de Maintenon, then aged 49.

THE SUN KING AND HIS FAMILY

Claiming to be monarch by divine right, Louis XIV commanded court painter Jean Nocret to devise this allegorical scene in 1665. Surrounded by his family, the king appears as the sun god Apollo.

TIMELINE

1610–17
Marie de' Medici acts as Regent for Louis XIII

Cardinal Richelieu

1624 Cardinal Richelieu becomes principal minister

1634 Foundation of the literary society Académie Française

1642–3 Death of Louis XIII and Cardinal Richelieu. Accession of Louis XIV with Mazarin as principal minister

1610	1620	1630	1640	1650

1617 Louis XIII accedes at the age of 17

1631 Foundation of *La Gazette*, France's first newspaper

1637 Descartes' *Discourse on Method*

1635 Richelieu actively involves France in the Thirty Years' War

1648–52 The Fronde: French civil wars

Louis XIV's Book of Hours
After a lively and libertine youth, Louis became increasingly religious. His Book of Hours *(1688–93) is in Musée Condé (see p195).*

Royal Wedding
Louis XIII and Anne of Austria were married in 1615. After his death, Anne became regent for the young Louis XIV with Cardinal Mazarin as minister.

Louis XIV as Apollo

Anne of Austria as Cybele

Baroque Figurine
The royal glory was reflected in the arts. This objet d'art *features a Christ in jasper on a pedestal decorated with gilded cherubs and rich enamelling.*

The dauphin (the king's son)

Grande Mademoiselle, the king's cousin, as Diana

Queen Marie-Thérèse as Juno

WHERE TO SEE ARCHITECTURE OF THE GRAND SIÈCLE

Paris boasts many imposing Grand Siècle buildings, such as the Hôtel des Invalides *(see p110)*, the Dôme church *(p111)* and the Palais du Luxembourg *(pp122–3)*, but the Château de Versailles *(pp164–7)* is the ultimate example of the flamboyance of the period. Reminders of this glory include the sumptuous Palais Lascaris in Nice *(p518)* and the Corderie Royale in Rochefort *(p407)*. At the same time, military architect Vauban constructed mighty citadels, such as Neuf-Brisach *(see p216)*.

Versailles' *interior is a typical example of the gilded Baroque style.*

Playwright Jean Racine (1639–99)

1680 Creation of the theatre Comédie Française

1661 Death of Mazarin: Louis XIV becomes his own principal minister

1685 Revocation of the Edict of Nantes of 1598: Protestantism banned

1709 Last great famine in French history

1660	1670	1680	1690	1700

1662 Colbert, finance minister, reforms finances and the economy

1682 Royal court moves to Versailles

1689 Major wars of Louis XIV begin

1686 Opening of the Café Procope (first coffee house in Paris)

17th-century cannon

Enlightenment and Revolution

Plate of Louis
XVI's execution

IN THE 18TH CENTURY, Enlightenment philosophers such as Voltaire and Rousseau redefined man's place within a framework of natural principles, thus challenging the old aristocratic order. Their essays were read across Europe and even in the American colonies. But although France exported worldly items as well as ideas, the state's increasing debts brought social turmoil, triggering the 1789 Revolution. Under the motto "Freedom, Equality, Fraternity", the new Republic and its reforms had a far-reaching impact on the rest of Europe.

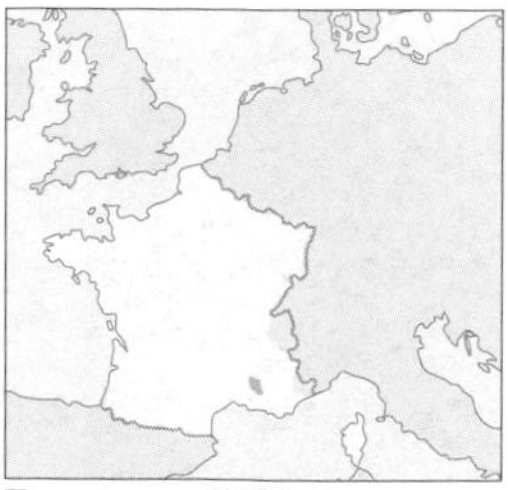

FRANCE IN 1789

☐ *Royal France*

▨ *Avignon (papal enclave)*

Voltaire *(1694–1778)*
Voltaire, master of satire, wrote numerous essays and the novel Candide.
His fierce critiques sometimes forced him into exile abroad.

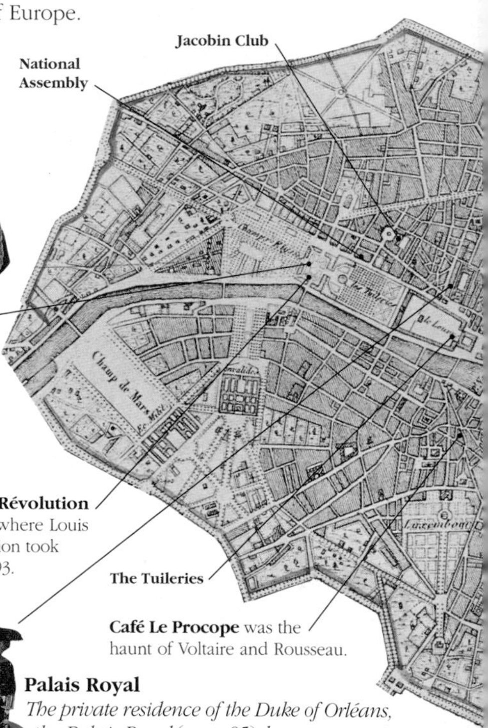

Jacobin Club

National Assembly

The Guillotine
This infamous invention was introduced in 1792 as a humane alternative to other forms of capital punishment, which had usually involved torture.

Place de la Révolution
(see p94) is where Louis XVI's execution took place in 1793.

The Tuileries

Café Le Procope was the haunt of Voltaire and Rousseau.

Palais Royal
The private residence of the Duke of Orléans, the Palais Royal (see p95) became a centre of revolutionary agitation from 1789. It was also the site of several printing presses.

TIMELINE

1715 Death of Louis XIV, accession of Louis XV

1743–64
Mme de Pompadour, Louis XV's favourite, uses her influence to support artists and philosophers during her time at court

1715	1725	1735	1745	1755

1720 Last outbreak of plague in France: population of Marseille decimated

Physician's protective costume worn during the plague

1751 Publication of the first volume of Diderot's *Encyclopaedia*

1756–63 Seven Years' War: France loses Canada and other colonial possessions

Revolutionary Symbols
The motifs of the Revolution such as the blue, white and red of the tricolor even appeared on wallpaper in the 1790s.

WHERE TO SEE 18TH-CENTURY FRANCE

The Palais de l'Elysée, built in 1718 (*see p104*), is an outstanding example of 18th-century Parisian architecture. Examples across France include the curious Saline Royale in Arc-et-Senans (*p340*), the Grand Théâtre in Bordeaux (*p412*), the elegant mansions in Condom (*p430*) and the merchants' houses in Ciboure (*p443*). The Château de Laàs in Sauveterre de Béarn is a feast of 18th-century art and furniture (*p448*).

The Grand Théâtre *in Bordeaux is an excellent example of elegant 18th-century architecture.*

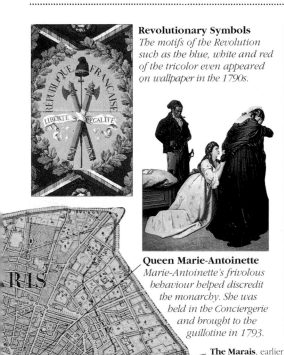

Queen Marie-Antoinette
Marie-Antoinette's frivolous behaviour helped discredit the monarchy. She was held in the Conciergerie and brought to the guillotine in 1793.

The Marais, earlier an aristocratic area, fell into decay as a result of the Revolution.

Bastille

REVOLUTIONARY PARIS
From 1789, Paris housed numerous political clubs, such as the left-wing Jacobins, and many revolutionary newspapers. The war tune *La Marseillaise*, introduced by volunteers from the south, was soon heard everywhere.

Revolutionary Calendar
A new calendar was introduced, the months named after seasonal events. This engraving shows Messidor, the month of harvest.

1768 Annexation of Corsica

1789 Storming of the Bastille, and establishment of constitutional monarchy: abolition of feudalism

1783 First balloon ascent, by the Montgolfier brothers

Model of the Bastille

1765	1775	1785	1795

1774 Accession of Louis XVI

Electors' card for the Convention of 1792

1794 Overthrow of Robespierre and end of the Terror

1762 Rousseau's *Emile* and the *Social Contract*

1778–83 France aids the 13 colonies in the War of American Independence

1792 Overthrow of Louis XVI: establishment of First Republic

Napoleonic France

TWO GENERATIONS of Napoleons dominated France from 1800 to 1870. Napoleon Bonaparte took the title of Emperor Napoleon I. He extended his empire throughout most of western Europe, placing his brothers and sisters on the thrones of conquered countries. Defeated in 1814 and replaced by the restored Bourbon dynasty, followed by the 1830 Revolution and the so-called July Monarchy, the Napoleonic clan made a comeback after 1848. Napoleon I's nephew, Louis Napoleon, became President of the Second Republic, then made himself emperor as Napoleon III. During his reign Paris was modernized and the industrial transformation of France began.

Légion d'Honneur

EUROPE IN 1812

☐ *Napoleonic rule*
☐ *Dependent states*

Musée du Louvre
The museum had opened in 1792, but it flourished during Napoleon's reign. He took a personal interest in both acquisitions and organization.

The Laurel, crown of the Roman emperors

Napoleon, as First Consul, is crowned by Chronos, the God of Time.

The revolutionary tricolor flag was kept throughout the empire.

Imperial Insignia
Napoleon I created a new titled aristocracy, who were allowed coats of arms. Only his, however, was permitted a crown. The eagle symbol was adopted in 1800, an evocation of Imperial Rome.

Légion d'Honneur medal

TIMELINE

1804 Napoleon crowned as Emperor. Napoleonic Civil Code established

Josephine's bed at Malmaison

1800 Establishment of the Bank of France

1809 Josephine and Napoleon divorce. She retains Château Malmaison *(see p163)*

1814 Defeat of Napoleon by the Allies (England, Russia, Austria and Prussia). Napoleon exiled to Elba

1800	1810	1820

1801–3 Treaty of Amiens brings temporary peace to Europe

1806 Arc de Triomphe commissioned

1803 Resumption of wars to create the Napoleonic Empire

1802 Establishment of the Légion d'Honneur

1815 The "Hundred Days": Napoleon returns from Elba, is defeated at Waterloo and exiled to St Helena

July Revolution
Three days of street-fighting in July 1830 ended unpopular Bourbon rule.

The Napoleons
This imaginary group portrait depicts Napoleon I (seated), his son "Napoleon II" – who never ruled (right) – Napoleon's nephew Louis Napoleon (Napoleon III) and the latter's infant son.

The Civil Code, created by Napoleon, is here shown as a tablet.

Napoleon on Campaign
A dashing general in the late 1790s, Napoleon remained a remarkable military commander throughout his reign.

EMPIRE FASHION

Greek and Roman ideals were evident in architecture, furniture, design and fashion. Women wore light, Classical tunics, the most daring with one shoulder or more bare. David and Gérard were the fashionable portraitists, while Delacroix and Géricault created many Romantic masterpieces.

Madame Récamier held a popular salon and was renowned for her beauty and wit. David painted her in 1800.

NAPOLEONIC GLORY

Though professing himself a true revolutionary, Napoleon developed a taste for imperial pomp. However, he also achieved some long-lasting reforms such as the Civil Code, the new school system and the Bank of France.

1832 Cholera epidemics begin

1838 Daguerre experiments with photography

1851 Coup d'état by Louis Napoleon

1848 Revolution of 1848: end of July Monarchy and establishment of the Second Republic

1852 Louis Napoleon crowned as Emperor Napoleon III

1830	1840	1850	1860

1830 Revolution of 1830: Bourbon Charles X replaced by the July Monarchy of King Louis-Philippe

1840 Large-scale railway building

Train on the Paris–St-Germain line

1853 Modernization of Paris by Haussmann

1857 Baudelaire (*Les Fleurs du Mal*) and Flaubert (*Mme Bovary*) prosecuted for public immorality

1859–60 Annexation of Nice and Savoy

The Belle Epoque

Art Nouveau vase by Lalique

THE DECADES before World War I became the *Belle Epoque* for the French, remembered as a golden era forever past. Nevertheless this was a politically turbulent time, with working-class militancy, organized socialist movements, and the Dreyfus Affair polarizing the country between Left and anti-semitic Right. New inventions such as electricity and vaccination against disease made life easier at all social levels. The cultural scene thrived and took new forms with Impressionism and Art Nouveau, the realist novels of Gustave Flaubert and Emile Zola, cabaret and cancan and, in 1895, the birth of the cinema.

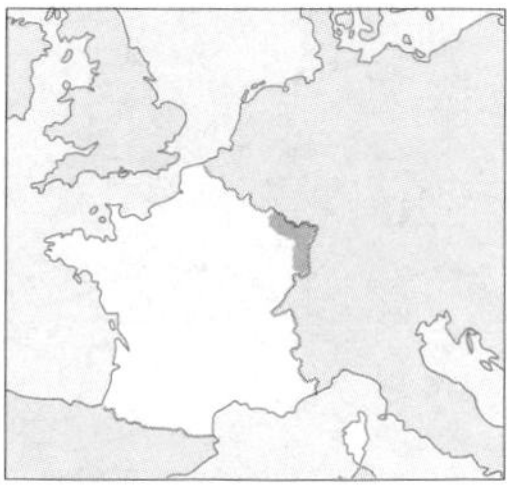

FRANCE IN 1871

☐ *Under Third Republic*

■ *Alsace and Lorraine*

Statue of Apollo by Aimé Millet

Universal Exhibition

The 1889 Paris exhibition was attended by 3.2 million people. Engineer Eiffel's breathtaking iron structure dominated the exhibition and caused great controversy at the time.

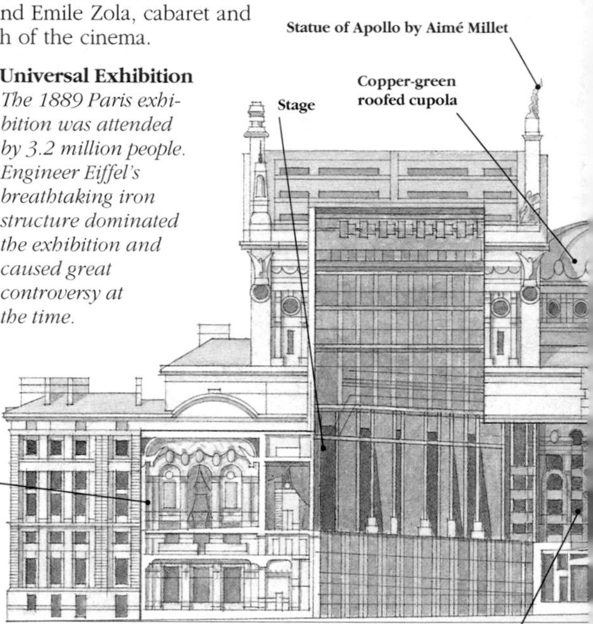

Stage

Copper-green roofed cupola

Backstage area

Peugeot Car *(1899)*
The car and bicycle brought new freedom, becoming a part of people's leisure time. Peugeot, Renault and Citroën were all founded before World War I.

The auditorium in gold and purple seated over 2,000 guests.

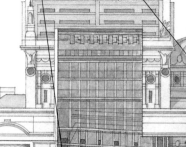

TIMELINE

1869 Opening of the Suez Canal, built by Ferdinand de Lesseps

1871 The Paris Commune leads to the Third Republic

Woman on the barricades in 1871

1880s Scramble for colonies in Africa and Asia begins

1889 Universal Exhibition in Paris; Eiffel Tower built

1865	1870	1875	1880	1885	1890

1870–71 Franco-Prussian War: defeat and overthrow of Napoleon III; France cedes Alsace and Lorraine to Germany

1874 Impressionist movement begins

1881–6 Reforms in education by Jules Ferry

1885 Pasteur produces vaccine for rabies, the first tested on a human

1890 Peugeot constructs one of the earliest automobiles

Poster Art
The poster was revolutionized by Art Nouveau, with designs by Alphonse Mucha particularly popular. This one from 1897 is for beer, the beverage of the lost Alsace and Lorraine, which became a "patriotic" drink.

Staircase at the Opera
The grand staircase had coloured marble columns and a frescoed ceiling. As this painting by Beroud from 1887 shows, it soon became a showcase for high society.

WHERE TO SEE THE BELLE EPOQUE

Belle Epoque buildings include the Negresco Hotel, Nice (see p516), the Grand Casino in Monte-Carlo (p520) and the Palais Hotel in Biarritz (p442). The Musée d'Orsay in Paris (pp116–17) exhibits Art Nouveau objects and furniture.

***Guimard's** Metro entrance is a typical example of the elegant, swirling lines of Art Nouveau.*

Emperor's pavilion

Grand Foyer with balconies and lavishly decorated ceiling

Grand staircase

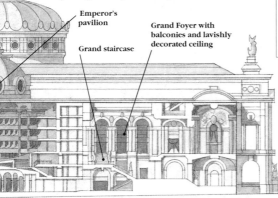

OPÉRA GARNIER
Founded by Napoleon III in 1862, the new opera was opened to great public acclaim in 1875 and became a focus of Belle Epoque social life. Designed by Charles Garnier, its extravagant exterior was matched by its sumptuous interior decor.

The Divine Sarah
Actress Sarah Bernhardt (1844–1923) worked in all theatrical genres, dominating the Paris stage.

1895 First public cinema by the Lumière brothers

Caricature of Zola

1894–1906 The alleged treason of Dreyfus sparks the Dreyfus Affair, involving the author Zola among others

1909 Blériot flies the Channel

1918 Armistice ends the war

1917 Mutinies in the army suppressed by Pétain

1916 Battle of Verdun

1895	1900	1905	1910	1915

1905 Official separation of church and state

1913 Publication of Proust's first volume of *Remembrance of Things Past*

1898 Marie and Pierre Curie discover radium

1914 World War I breaks out

French recruit, 1916

1919 Treaty of Versailles

Avant-Garde France

DESPITE THE DEVASTATION wrought by two world wars, France retained its international renown as a centre for the avant garde. Paris in particular was a magnet for experimental writers, artists and musicians. The cafés were full of American authors and jazz musicians, French surrealists and film makers. The French Riviera also attracted colonies of artists and writers, from Matisse and Picasso to Hemingway and Scott Fitzgerald, along with the wealthy industrialists and aristocrats arriving in automobiles or the famous Train Bleu. And from 1936 paid holidays meant that the working classes could also enjoy the new fashion for sunbathing.

FRANCE IN 1919

☐ *French territory*

African Gods of Creation

Art Deco 1925
The International Exhibition in Paris in 1925 launched the Art Deco style: geometrical shapes and utilitarian designs, adapted for mass-production.

Dancers in heavy cardboard costumes

The Jazz Age
Paris welcomed American jazz musicians, such as Sidney Bechet in 1925 and Dizzy Gillespie (left), co-founder of Bebop in the 1940s.

Citroën Goddess *(1956)*
This elegant model became an icon of the new French consumerism evident in the 1950s and '60s.

The costumes and scenery by the Cubist Léger were striking and made to look partly mechanical.

TIMELINE

1920 French Communist Party founded. Publication of Tristan Tzara's *Dadaist Manifesto*

1928 Premiere of *Un Chien Andalou* by Luis Buñuel and Salvador Dalí

Air France aircraft, 1937

1933 Air France begins operation

1937 Premiere of *La Grande Illusion* by Jean Renoir

1920

1930

1924 Olympic Games in Paris. André Breton publishes the *Surrealist Manifesto*

Detail of poster for the 1924 Olympics

1936–38 The "Popular Front": radical social programme introduced, including paid holidays

1929–39 The Depression

1938 Munich Conference: height of appeasement

Coco Chanel *(1883–1971)*
Chanel, here photographed by
Man Ray, revolutionized fashion
in the 1920s with her elegant
but comfortable clothes.

Par Avion
France pioneered the use of
airmail, starting in 1927.

WORLD WAR II

Following the collapse of the
Third Republic in 1940, Paris
and the north and west parts of
France were occupied by the
Germans until the Liberation in
1944. Southeast France formed
the collaborationist Vichy state,
led by Marshal Pétain and
Pierre Laval. Meanwhile, the
Free French movement was
led by Charles de Gaulle, with
Jean Moulin coordinating the
operations of the many
different Resistance factions.

German soldiers *liked to pose*
in front of the Eiffel Tower during
the occupation of Paris.

First Man and Woman

LA CRÉATION DU MONDE *(1923)*
Artistic experimentation thrived in the early
20th century. *La Création du Monde* by Les
Ballets Suédois had costumes by Léger and
music by Milhaud. Diaghilev's Ballets Russes
also competed for avant-garde artists like
Picabia, Cocteau, Satie and Sonia Delaunay.

The African theme
was based on text
by Blaise Cendrars.

Josephine Baker *(1906–75)*
The music hall flourished in the
1920s with Mistinguett and Josephine
Baker as its undisputed queens.

1940 German offensive:
the Fall of France. Vichy
government led by Pétain

1942 The whole of France
controlled by Germany

1949 Establishment of
NATO. Founding of the
Council of Europe

1958 5th Republic begins under
President de Gaulle

1956 Late in her career, Edith Piaf crowns
her success at Carnegie Hall, New York

1940   **1950**

1944 D-Day: Allied
landings in Normandy

1946 Sartre establishes
Les Temps Modernes.
First Cannes Film Festival

1954 France withdraws
from Indo-China after
Battle of Dien Bien Phu.
Start of Algerian
insurrection

1939 Declaration of
World War II

1945 End of the war.
Votes for women

Modern France

A FTER THE 1950s, the traditional foundations of French society changed: the number of peasant farmers plummeted, old industries decayed, jobs in the service sector and high-technology industries grew dramatically, and the French came to enjoy the benefits of mass culture and widespread consumerism. High prestige projects, such as Concorde, TGV, La Défense and the Pompidou Centre, brought international acclaim. Efforts for European integration and the inauguration of the Channel Tunnel aim towards closer relations with France's neighbours.

Lemon squeezer by Philippe Starck

FRANCE TODAY

☐ *France*
▨ *European Union*

Pompidou Centre *(1977)*
The Pompidou Centre's controversial building changed the aspect of the historic quarter of Beaubourg. A major arts centre, it has re-vitalized the formerly rundown area (see pp88–9).

New Wave Film
Directors like Godard and Truffaut launched a refresh-ing, personal style of films, such as Jules et Jim *(1961).*

La Grande Arche was opened in 1989 to commemorate the bicentenary of the Revolution.

Shopping centre

LA DÉFENSE
The huge modernist business centre at La Défense *(see p126)*, on the edge of Paris, was developed in the 1960s and has become a prime site for the headquarters of major multinational companies.

TIMELINE

1960 First French atomic bomb. Decolonization of black Africa	**1963** First French nuclear power station	**1968** May demonstrations	**1973** Extension of the Common Market (EU) from six to nine states
		1969 Pompidou replaces de Gaulle as president	
	1966 France leaves NATO		**1974** Giscard d'Estaing elected president
1960		**1970**	
	1965 First French satellite	**1970** Charles de Gaulle dies	**1976** First commercial flight for Concorde aeroplane
1962 Evian agreements lead to Algerian independence	**1967** Common Agricultural Policy, subsidizing Europe's farmers		

1977 Jacques Chirac first mayor of Paris since 1871. Opening of the Pompidou Centre

EU Flag
France has been one of the leading forces in the European Union ever since the move towards closer European collaboration began in the 1950s.

TGV
The TGV (Train à Grande Vitesse) is one of the world's fastest trains (see pp634–5). It typifies the French government's commitment to high technology and improved communications.

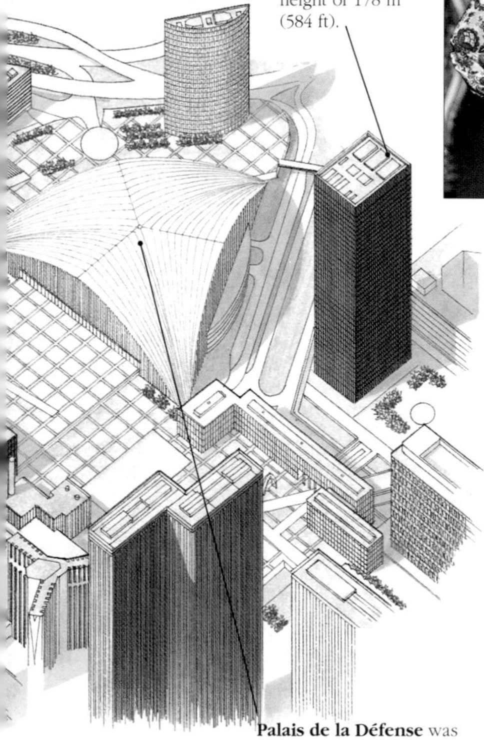

The Fiat Tower
is one of Europe's tallest towers, at a height of 178 m (584 ft).

Fashion by Lacroix
Despite less demand for haute couture, Paris is still a major fashion centre. The designs shown on the catwalk, here by Christian Lacroix, remain proof of the world-renowned skills of French designers.

May 1968

The events of May 1968 began as a political revolt by left-wing students against the Establishment and had a profound influence on French society. Around 9 million workers, and leading intellectuals like Jean-Paul Sartre, joined the rebellion, demanding better pay, better study conditions and the overhaul of traditional values and institutions.

***Student riots** starting in Nanterre, just outside Paris, sparked widespread rioting and industrial unrest in France.*

Palais de la Défense was built first and houses the centre for industry.

1980 Giverny, Monet's garden, opens to the public *(see p256)*

1989 Bicentennial celebration of the French Revolution

1991 Edith Cresson is first woman prime minister

1998 France hosts and wins the football World Cup

1980	1990	2000

1981 Mitterrand becomes president and heads Socialist governments 1981–6

François Mitterrand

1987 Mitterrand and Thatcher sign agreement for Channel Tunnel. Trial in Lyon of ex-SS Officer Klaus Barbie

1994 Channel Tunnel opens

1996 France mourns Mitterrand, who dies after a long illness

1995 Jacques Chirac is president

1997 Socialist Lionel Jospin becomes prime minister in landslide victory

Kings and Emperors of France

FOLLOWING THE BREAK-UP of the Roman Empire, the Frankish king Clovis consolidated the Merovingian dynasty. It was followed by the Carolingians, and from the 10th century by Capetian rulers. The Capetians established royal power, which passed to the Valois branch in the 14th century, and then to the Bourbons in the late 16th century, following the Wars of Religion. The Revolution of 1789 seemed to end the Bourbon dynasty, but it made a brief come-back in 1814–30. The 19th century was dominated by the Bonapartes, Napoleon I and Napoleon III. Since the overthrow of Napoleon III in 1870, France has been a republic.

768–814 Charlemagne

743–751 Childéric III
716–721 Chilpéric II
695–711 Childebert II
566–584 Chilpéric I
558–562 Clothaire I
447–458 Merovich
458–482 Childéric I

674–691 Thierri III
655–668 Clothaire III
628–637 Dagobert I

954–986 Lothaire
898–929 Charles III, the Simple
884–888 Charles II, the Fat
879–882 Louis III
840–877 Charles I, the Bald

1137–80 Louis VII
987–996 Hugh Capet
1031–60 Henri I
1060–1108 Philippe I

400	500	600	700	800	900	1000	110
MEROVINGIAN DYNASTY				**CAROLINGIAN DYNASTY**		**CAPETIAN DYNASTY**	
400	500	600	700	800	900	1000	110

751–768 Pépin the Short
721–737 Thierri IV
711–716 Dagobert III
691–695 Clovis III
668–674 Childéric II
637–655 Clovis II
584–628 Clothaire II
562–566 Caribert
511–558 Childebert I

996–1031 Robert II, the Pious
986–987 Louis V
936–954 Louis IV, the Foreigner
888–898 Odo, Count of Paris
882–884 Carloman
877–879 Louis II, the Stammerer
814–840 Louis I, the Pious

482–511 Clovis I

1108–37 Louis VI, the Fat

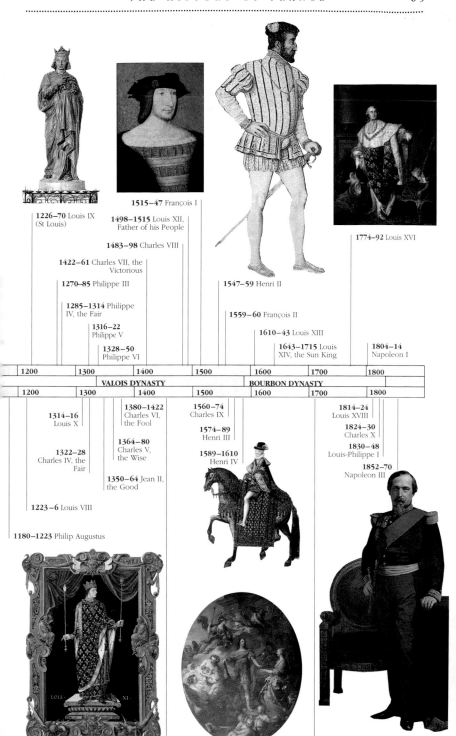

1226–70 Louis IX
(St Louis)

1498–1515 Louis XII,
Father of his People

1515–47 François I

1483–98 Charles VIII

1774–92 Louis XVI

1422–61 Charles VII, the
Victorious

1270–85 Philippe III

1547–59 Henri II

1285–1314 Philippe
IV, the Fair

1316–22
Philippe V

1559–60 François II

1328–50
Philippe VI

1610–43 Louis XIII

1643–1715 Louis
XIV, the Sun King

1804–14
Napoleon I

1200	1300	1400	1500	1600	1700	1800	

VALOIS DYNASTY   BOURBON DYNASTY

1200	1300	1400	1500	1600	1700	1800	

1314–16
Louis X

1380–1422
Charles VI,
the Fool

1560–74
Charles IX

1814–24
Louis XVIII

1574–89
Henri III

1824–30
Charles X

1364–80
Charles V,
the Wise

1830–48
Louis-Philippe I

1322–28
Charles IV, the
Fair

1589–1610
Henri IV

1852–70
Napoleon III

1350–64 Jean II,
the Good

1223–6 Louis VIII

1180–1223 Philip Augustus

1461–83 Louis XI, the Spider

1715–74
Louis XV

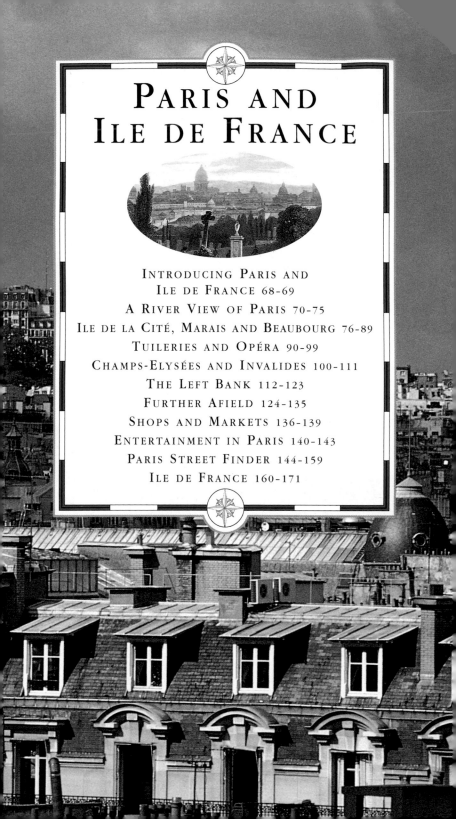

PARIS AND
ILE DE FRANCE

Introducing Paris and Ile de France

THE FRENCH CAPITAL is rich in museums, art galleries and monuments. The Louvre, Eiffel Tower and Pompidou Centre are among the most popular sights.

Surrounding Paris, the Ile de France takes in 12,000 sq km (4,600 sq miles) of busy suburbs and commuter towns punctuated by châteaux, the most celebrated being Versailles. Further out, suburbia gives way to farmland, forests and the magnificent palace of Fontainebleau.

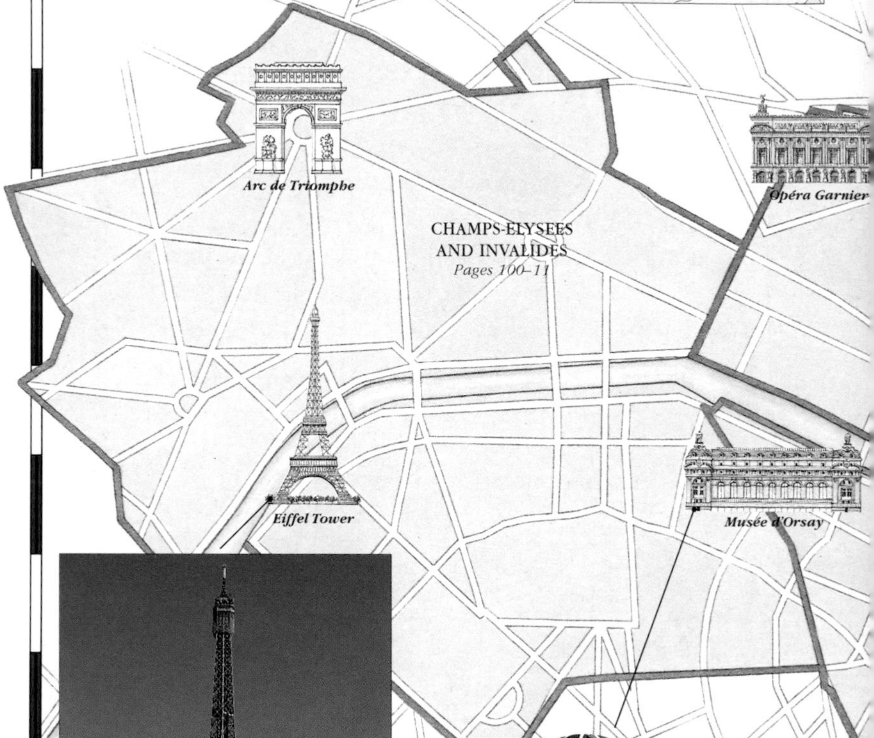

Arc de Triomphe

Opéra Garnier

CHAMPS-ELYSEES AND INVALIDES
Pages 100–11

Eiffel Tower

Musée d'Orsay

The Eiffel Tower, *designed for the Universal Exhibition of 1889, scandalized contemporary critics but is now the capital's most famous landmark* (see p109).

The Musée d'Orsay, *opened in 1986, was created from a late 19th-century railway terminus (see pp116–17). It houses a magnificent collection of 19th- and early 20th-century art, including Jean-Baptiste Carpeaux's* Four Quarters of the World *(1867–72).*

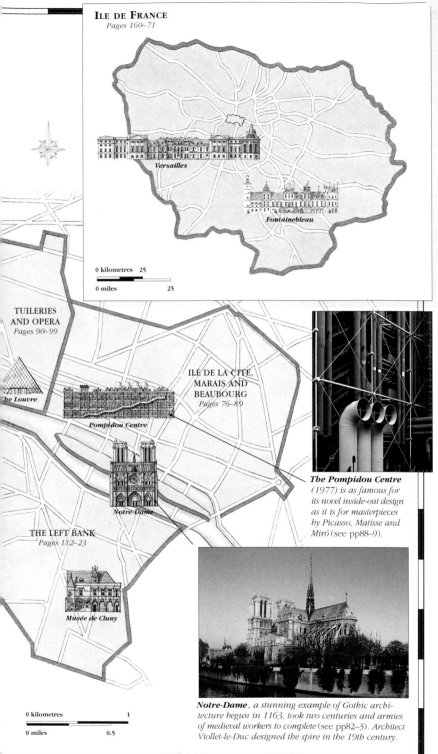

ILE DE FRANCE
Pages 160–71

Versailles

Fontainebleau

0 kilometres 25

0 miles 25

TUILERIES
AND OPERA
Pages 90–99

The Louvre

Pompidou Centre

ILE DE LA CITÉ,
MARAIS AND
BEAUBOURG
Pages 76–89

Notre-Dame

THE LEFT BANK
Pages 112–23

Musée de Cluny

0 kilometres 1

0 miles 0.5

The Pompidou Centre
*(1977) is as famous for
its novel inside-out design
as it is for masterpieces
by Picasso, Matisse and
Miró (see pp88–9).*

Notre-Dame, *a stunning example of Gothic architecture begun in 1163, took two centuries and armies
of medieval workers to complete (see pp82–3). Architect
Viollet-le-Duc designed the spire in the 19th century.*

A River View of Paris

Sculpture on the Pont Alexandre III

THE REMARK-ABLE French music-hall star Mistinguett described the Seine as a "pretty blonde with laughing eyes". The river most certainly has a beguiling quality, but the relationship that exists between it and the city of Paris is far more than one of flirtation.

No other European city defines itself by its river in the same way as Paris. The Seine is the essential point of reference to the city: distances are measured from it, street numbers determined by it, and it divides the capital into two distinct areas, the Right Bank on the north side of the river and the Left Bank on the south side. These are as well-defined as any of the official boundaries. The city is also divided historically: the east is linked to the city's ancient roots and the west to the 19th–20th centuries.

Practically every building of note in Paris is either along the river bank or within a stone's throw of it. The quays are lined by fine bourgeois apartments, magnificent town houses, world-renowned museums and striking monuments.

Above all, the river is very much alive. For centuries fleets of small boats used it, but motorized land traffic stifled this once-bustling scene. Today, the river is busy with commercial barges and massive *bateaux mouches* pleasure boats carrying sightseers up and down the river.

The Latin Quarter Quayside is on the left bank of the Seine. Associated with institutes of learning since the Middle Ages, it acquired its name from the early Latin-speaking students.

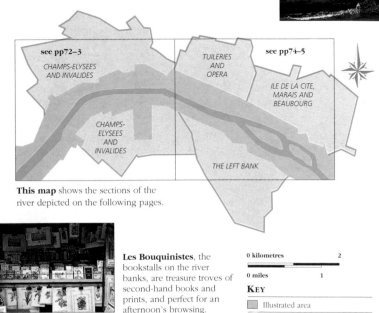

This map shows the sections of the river depicted on the following pages.

see pp72–3

CHAMPS-ELYSEES AND INVALIDES

TUILERIES AND OPERA

see pp74–5

ILE DE LA CITE, MARAIS AND BEAUBOURG

CHAMPS-ELYSEES AND INVALIDES

THE LEFT BANK

Les Bouquinistes, the bookstalls on the river banks, are treasure troves of second-hand books and prints, and perfect for an afternoon's browsing.

0 kilometres 2

0 miles 1

KEY

☐ Illustrated area

◁ **Pont Alexandre III, encrusted with exuberant statuary**

From Pont de Grenelle to Pont de la Concorde

THE GRAND monuments along this stretch of the river are remnants of the Napoleonic era and the Industrial Revolution. The elegance of the Eiffel Tower, the Petit Palais and the Grand Palais is matched by more recent buildings, such as the Palais de Chaillot and the skyscrapers on the Left Bank.

Palais de Chaillot
Built for the 1937 Exhibition, the spectacular colonnaded wings house four museums, a theatre and a cinema (p106).

The Palais de Tokyo forms part of the Film Library. Figures by Bourdelle adorn it.

The Pont Bir-Hakeim has a dynamic statue by Wederkinch rising at its north end.

Trocadéro M

Bateaux Parisiens Tour Eiffel

Vedettes de Paris Ile de France

Passerelle

Pont d'Iéna

Passy M

Maison de Radio France is an imposing circular building, designed in 1960, which houses studios as well as a radio museum.

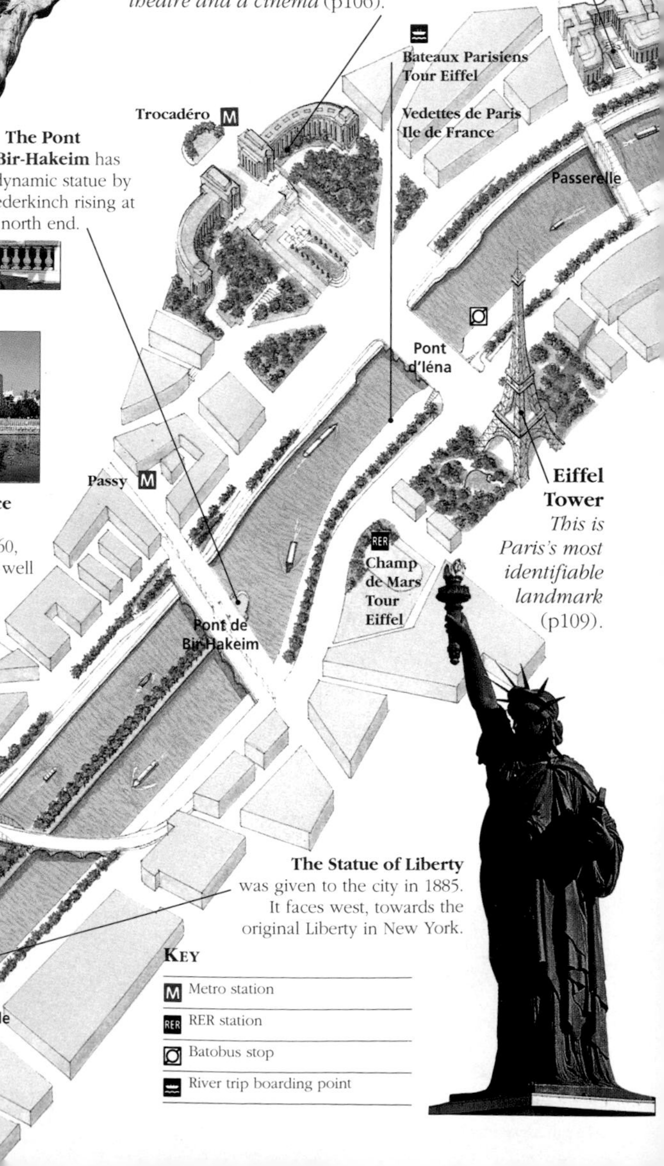

Champ de Mars Tour Eiffel RER

Eiffel Tower *This is Paris's most identifiable landmark (p109).*

Prés. Kennedy Radio France RER

Pont de Bir-Hakeim

The Statue of Liberty was given to the city in 1885. It faces west, towards the original Liberty in New York.

Pont de Grenelle

KEY

M	Metro station
RER	RER station
⬛	Batobus stop
▬	River trip boarding point

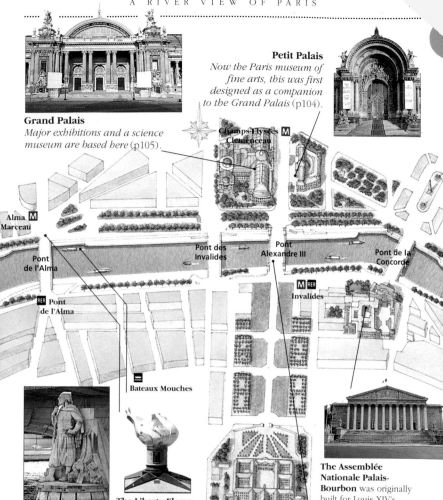

Grand Palais
Major exhibitions and a science museum are based here (p105).

Petit Palais
Now the Paris museum of fine arts, this was first designed as a companion to the Grand Palais (p104).

Champs-Élysées Clemenceau Ⓜ

Alma Ⓜ
Marceau

Pont
de l'Alma

RER Pont
de l'Alma

Pont des
Invalides

Pont
Alexandre III

Pont de la
Concorde

Ⓜ RER
Invalides

Bateaux Mouches

The Zouave, a statue on the central pier, is a useful gauge for checking flood levels.

The Liberty Flame is a memorial to the fighters of the French Resistance during World War II.

The Assemblée Nationale Palais-Bourbon was originally built for Louis XIV's daughter. It has accommodated the lower house of the French Parliament since 1830.

Dôme Church
The majestic gilded dome (p111) *is here seen from Pont Alexandre III. Napoleon's tomb is installed in the crypt.*

Pont Alexandre III
Flamboyant statuary decorates Paris's most ornate bridge (p105).

From Pont de la Concorde to Pont de Sully

THE HISTORIC heart of Paris lies on the banks and islands of the east river. At its centre is the Ile de la Cité, a natural stepping stone across the Seine and the cultural core of medieval Paris. Today it is still vital to Parisian life.

Jardin des Tuileries
These are laid out in the formal style (pp94–5).

Musée du Louvre
Before becoming the world's greatest museum and home to the Mona Lisa, *this was Europe's largest royal palace* (pp96–9).

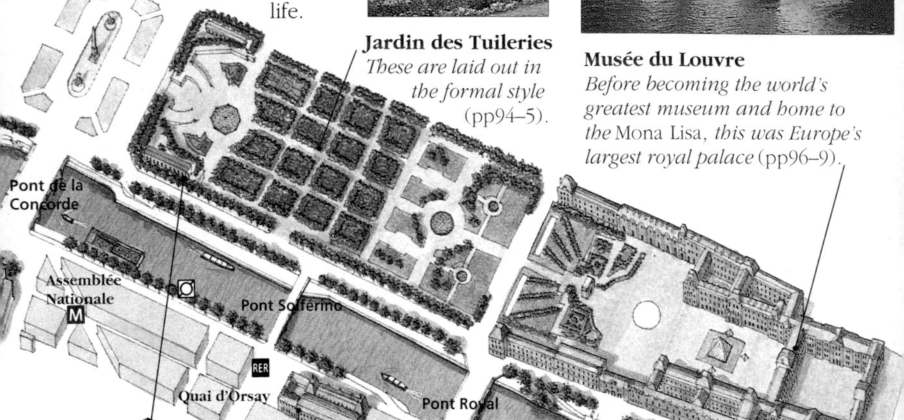

Pont de la Concorde

Assemblée Nationale M

Pont Solférino

Quai d'Orsay

Pont Royal

Pont du Carrousel

Pont des Arts

Musée de l'Orangerie
An important collection of 19th-century paintings is on display here (p94).

Musée d'Orsay
This converted railway station houses Paris's outstanding collection of Impressionist art (pp116–17).

Bateaux Vedettes du Pont Neuf

BATOBUS

The Batobus shuttle service departs May–Sep: 10am–7pm (9pm Jul & Aug) daily, every 25 min. Board at:
Eiffel Tower. Map 6 D3. M Bir Hakeim.
Musée d'Orsay. Map 8 D2. M Assemblée Nationale.
Louvre. Map 8 D2. M Palais Royal-Musée du Louvre.
Hôtel de Ville. Map 9 B4. M Hôtel de Ville.
Notre-Dame. Map 9 B4. M Saint-Michel.
Saint-Germain des Prés. Map 8 E3.
M Saint-Germain des Prés.

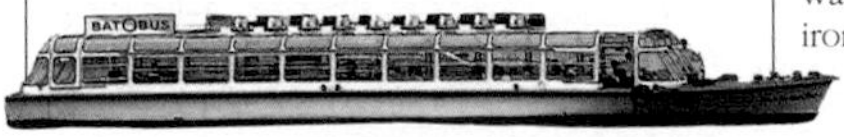

The Pont des Arts
was Paris's first cast-iron bridge. Completed in 1804, it took two years to build.

Hôtel des Monnaies, the Mint, was built in 1778, and has an extensive coin and medallion collection in its old milling halls.

HOW TO TAKE A SEINE CRUISE

Vedettes du Pont Neuf

Bateaux Vedettes Pont Neuf Seine Cruise
The boarding point is:
Square du Vert-Galant
(Pont Neuf). **Map** 8 F3.
C 01 53 00 98 98.
M *Pont Neuf.* **RER**
Châtelet. 🚌 *24, 27, 58,
67, 70, 72, 74, 75.*
Departures *Mar–Oct:
10:30am, 11:15am, noon,
(every 45 min), 1:30pm–
6:30pm, 9–10:30pm (every
30 min) daily; Nov–Mar:
10:30am, 11:15am, noon,
2–5:45pm, daily (every 45
min);* **Duration** *1 hr.*

BATEAUX-MOUCHES

Bateaux Mouches Seine Cruise
The boarding point is:
Pont de l'Alma. Map 6 F1.
C *01 42 25 96 10.* **M**
Alma-Marceau. **RER** *Pont de
l'Alma.* 🚌 *42, 63, 72, 80,
92.* **Departures** *Mar–Nov:
10am–10:30pm daily (every
30 min); Nov–Mar: 11am,
2:30pm, 4pm, 9pm (extra
departures Sat, Sun & public
hols).* **Duration** *1hr 15 min.*
Lunch cruise *Apr–Oct:
1pm Tue–Sun; Nov– Mar:
12:45pm Fri–Sun.* **Dinner
cruise** *8:30pm daily.*
*Bâteaux Mouches are the
largest cruise boats.*

ILE de FRANCE

Vedettes de Paris Ile de France Seine Cruise
The boarding point is:
Pont d'Iéna. Map 6 D2.
C *01 47 05 71 29 and 01
45 50 23 79.* **M** *Bir Hakeim.*
RER *Champ-de-Mars–Tour
Eiffel.* 🚌 *22, 30, 32, 44,
63, 69, 72, 82, 87.*
Departures *Apr–Oct: 10am–
11:30pm daily (every 30 min);
Nov–Mar: 11am–6pm Mon–Fri
(every hour); 11am–8pm Sat,
Sun (every 30 min).* **Duration**
*1hr. Vedettes are small
boats which allow passengers
to view the surroundings
through glass walls.*

BATEAUX PARISIENS

Bateaux Parisiens Tour Eiffel Seine Cruise
The boarding point is:
Pont d'Iéna. Map 6 D2.
C *01 44 11 33 44.* **M**
Trocadéro, Bir Hakeim.
RER *Champ-de-Mars–Tour
Eiffel.* 🚌 *42, 82, 72.*
Departures *Mar–Sep:
10am–10:30pm daily
(every 30 min); Oct–Feb:
10am–9pm daily (every
hour).* **Lunch cruise**
12:30pm daily. **Dinner
cruise** *8pm daily.* **Duration**
*2hr 30 min. Jacket and tie.
Bateaux Parisiens are a
more luxurious version of
Bateaux Mouches.*

Ile de la Cité
*This tiny island on
the Seine was first
inhabited around
200 BC by a Celtic
tribe known as the
Parisii (pp78–9).*

Conciergerie
*During the Revolution this
building, with its
distinctive
towers,
became
notorious as
a prison
(p79).*

The Ile St-Louis has been
a desirable address since
the 17th century,
when its elegant
houses
were built.

Pont Neuf **M**

Châtelet **M**

Hotel de Ville **M**

Pont au Change

Pont Notre Dame

Cité **M**

Pont d'Arcole

St-Michel **RER** **M**

Petit Pont

Pont au Double

Pont St-Louis

Pont Louis-Philippe

Pont Marie **M**

Pont Marie

Pont de l'Archevêché

Pont de la Tournelle

Pont de Sully

Sully Morland **M**

Notre-Dame
*This towering cathedral
surveys the river (pp82–3).*

🚏 **Bateaux Parisiens**

ILE DE LA CITÉ, MARAIS AND BEAUBOURG

THE RIGHT BANK is dominated by the modernistic Forum des Halles and Pompidou Centre in the Beaubourg. These are Paris's most thriving public areas, with millions of tourists, shoppers and students flowing between them. Young people flock to Les Halles, shopping for the latest street fashions beneath the concrete and glass bubbles of the underground arcades. All roads from Les Halles appear to lead to the Pompidou Centre, an avant-garde assembly of pipes, ducts and cables housing the Musée National d'Art Moderne. The smaller streets around the centre are full of art galleries housed in crooked, gabled buildings.

The motto of the city of Paris

The neighbouring Marais was abandoned by its royal residents during the 1789 Revolution, and it descended into architectural wasteland before being rescued in the 1960s. It has since become a very fashionable address, though small cafés, bakeries and artisans still survive in its streets.

Notre-Dame cathedral, the Palais de Justice and Sainte-Chapelle continue to draw tourists to the Ile de la Cité, despite extensive redevelopment of the island in the last century. At the eastern end a bridge connects with the Ile St-Louis, a former swampy pastureland transformed into a residential area with pretty, tree-lined quays.

SIGHTS AT A GLANCE

Museums and Galleries
Crypte Archéologique ❺
Hôtel de Sens ❽
Hôtel de Soubise ⓮
Maison de Victor Hugo ⓲
Musée Carnavalet ⓰
Musée Picasso ⓯
Pompidou Centre pp88–9 ⓭

Historic Buildings
Conciergerie ❷
Hôtel de Ville ❿
Palais de Justice ❸
Tour St-Jacques ⓫

Squares
Place de la Bastille ⓳
Place des Vosges ⓱

Churches
Notre-Dame pp82–3 ❻
Sainte-Chapelle ❹
St-Eustache ⓬
St-Gervais–St-Protais ❾
St-Louis-en-l'Ile ❼

Bridges
Pont Neuf ❶

GETTING THERE

Metro stations in the area include Châtelet, Hôtel-de-Ville and Cité. Bus routes 47 and 29 serve Beaubourg and the Marais respectively. Several bus routes cross Ile de la Cité and Ile St-Louis.

KEY

- ▨ Street-by-Street map *pp78–9*
- ▨ Street-by-Street map *pp84–5*
- Ⓜ Metro station
- ▣ Batobus boarding point
- Ⓟ Car park
- RER RER station

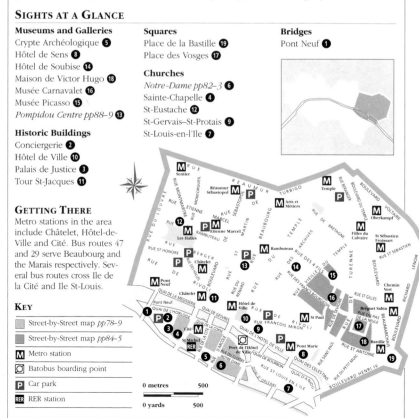

0 metres 500
0 yards 500

◁ **View of the Pont Neuf and Ile de la Cité from the Pont des Arts**

Street-by-Street: Ile de la Cité

T HE ORIGINS OF PARIS are on the Ile de la
Cité, the boat-shaped island on the
Seine first inhabited by Celtic tribes in the
3rd century BC. One tribe, the Parisii,
eventually gave its name to the city. The
island offered a convenient river crossing
on the route between northern and
southern Gaul and was easily defended.
In later centuries the settlement was
expanded by the Romans, the Franks
and the Capetian kings to form the
nucleus of today's city.

Remains of the first buildings can
still be seen today in the
archaeological crypt of the great
medieval cathedral of Notre-
Dame. At the other end of
the island is Sainte-
Chapelle, another Gothic
masterpiece.

★ Conciergerie
*This sinister-looking building was the country's
chief prison during the Revolution* ❷

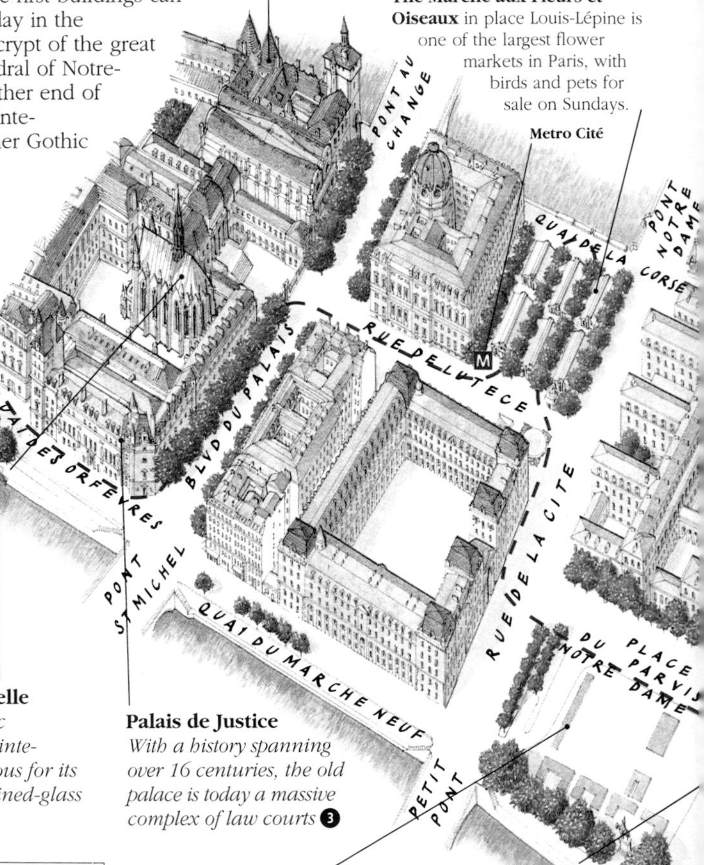

**The Marché aux Fleurs et
Oiseaux** in place Louis-Lépine is
one of the largest flower
markets in Paris, with
birds and pets for
sale on Sundays.

Metro Cité

To Pont Neuf

★ Sainte-Chapelle
*A jewel of Gothic
architecture, Sainte-
Chapelle is famous for its
magnificent stained-glass
windows* ❹

Palais de Justice
*With a history spanning
over 16 centuries, the old
palace is today a massive
complex of law courts* ❸

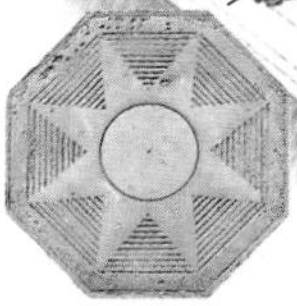

Point Zéro
marks the spot
from which all
road distances
are measured
in France.

To Latin Quarter

STAR SIGHTS

★ Notre-Dame

★ Sainte-Chapelle

★ Conciergerie

KEY

– – – Suggested route

Crypte Archéologique
*Deep under the square lie remnants
of houses dating back 2,000 years* ❺

Hôtel Dieu, a large hospital serving central Paris, was founded in AD 651 by St Landry, Bishop of Paris.

LOCATOR MAP
See Street Finder maps 8, 9

★ **Notre-Dame**
This cathedral is a superb example of French medieval architecture **6**

Musée Notre-Dame, founded in 1951, contains exhibits and documents commemorating the great events in Notre-Dame's history.

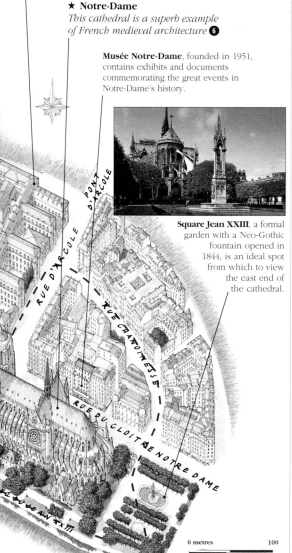

Square Jean XXIII, a formal garden with a Neo-Gothic fountain opened in 1844, is an ideal spot from which to view the east end of the cathedral.

0 metres   100
0 yards   100

Pont Neuf, the city's oldest bridge

Pont Neuf **1**

75001. **Map** 8 F3. **M** *Pont Neuf, Cité.*

DESPITE ITS NAME (New Bridge), this bridge is the oldest in Paris and has been immortalized by major literary and artistic figures. The first stone was laid by Henri III in 1578, but it was Henri IV (whose statue stands at the centre) who inaugurated it and gave it its name in 1607.

Conciergerie **2**

1 quai de l'Horloge 75001. **Map** 9 A3. **[** 01 53 73 78 50. **M** *Cité.* **Open** *Apr–Sep: 9:30–6pm daily; Oct–Mar: 10am–5pm daily (last adm: 30 mins before closing).* **Closed** *1 Jan, 1 May, 1 & 11 Nov, 25 Dec.* **[icons]** **[** *11am, 3pm daily.* **[**

FORMING PART of the huge Palais de Justice, the historic Conciergerie served as a prison from 1391–1914. Henry IV's assassin, François Ravaillac, was imprisoned and tortured here in 1610.
    During the Revolution the building was packed with over 4,000 prisoners. Its most celebrated inmate was Marie-Antoinette, who was held in a tiny cell until her execution in 1793. Others included Charlotte Corday, who stabbed Revolutionary leader Marat while he bathed.
    The Conciergerie has a superb four-aisled Gothic hall, where guards of the royal household once lived. Renovated during the 19th century, the building retains its 11th-century torture chamber and 14th-century clock tower.

A sculptured relief on the Palais de Justice

Palais de Justice ❸

4 boulevard du Palais (entrance by the Cour de Mai) 75001. **Map** 9 A3. ☎ *01 44 32 50 00*. Ⓜ *Cité*. **Open** *8:30am–6pm daily*.

THIS HUGE BLOCK of buildings making up the law courts of Paris stretches the entire width of the Ile de la Cité. It is a splendid sight with its Gothic towers lining the quays. The site has been occupied since Roman times when it was the governors' residence. It was the seat of royal power until Charles V moved the court to the Marais following a bloody revolt in 1358. In April 1793 the notorious Revolutionary Tribunal began dispensing justice from the Première Chambre Civile, or first civil chamber. Today the site embodies Napoleon's great legacy – the French judicial system. Trials are usually public and tourists are welcome.

Crypte Archéologique ❺

1 Place du Parvis Notre-Dame 75004. **Map** 9 A4. ☎ *01 43 29 83 51*. Ⓜ *Cité*. **Open** *Apr–Sep:10am–5:30pm daily; Oct–Mar:10am–5pm daily*. **Closed** *1 Jan, 1 May, 1 & 11 Nov, 25 Dec.*

SITUATED BENEATH the *parvis* (main square) of Notre-Dame and stretching 120 m (393 ft) underground, the crypt was opened in 1980 as Paris's museum of archaeology.

Exhibits include streets and houses from the Gallo-Roman period, sections of Lutetia's 3rd-century BC wall, and remains of the cathedral. Models explain the development of Paris from a settlement of the Parisii, the 3rd-century Celtic tribe who named the city.

Notre-Dame ❻

See pp82–3.

Sainte-Chapelle ❹

4 boulevard du Palais 75001. **Map** 9 A3. ☎ *01 53 73 78 51*. Ⓜ *Cité*. **Open** *Apr–Sep: 9:30am–6:30pm daily; Oct–Mar: 10am–5pm daily*. **Closed** *1 Jan, 1 May, 1 & 11 Nov, 25 Dec.*

ETHEREAL AND MAGICAL, Sainte-Chapelle has been hailed as one of the greatest architectural masterpieces of the Western world. In the Middle Ages the devout likened this church to "a gateway to heaven". Today no visitor can fail to be transported by the blaze of light created by the 15 magnificent stained-glass windows, separated by pencil-like columns soaring 15 m (50 ft) to the star-studded roof. The windows portray more than 1,000 biblical scenes in a kaleidoscope of red, gold, green and blue. Starting from the left near the entrance and proceeding clockwise, you can trace the scriptures from Genesis through to the Crucifixion and the Apocalypse.

The chapel was built in 1248 by Louis IX to house what was believed to be Christ's Crown of Thorns and fragments of the True Cross (now in the treasury at Notre-Dame). The king, who was canonized for his good works, purchased these relics from the Emperor of Constantinople, paying three times more for them than for the entire construction of Sainte-Chapelle.

The building actually consists of two separate chapels. The sombre lower chapel was used by servants and lower court officials, while the exquisite upper chapel, reached by means of a narrow spiral staircase, was reserved for the royal family and its courtiers. A discreetly placed window enabled the king to take part in the celebrations unobserved.

During the Revolution the building was badly damaged and became a warehouse for storing flour. It was renovated a century later by architect Viollet-le-Duc.

Today, evening concerts of classical music are held regularly in the chapel, taking advantage of its superb acoustics.

The magnificent interior of Sainte-Chapelle

St-Louis-en-l'Ile ❼

19 bis rue St-Louis-en-l'lle 75004.
Map 9 C4. 📞 *01 46 34 11 60.* Ⓜ *Pont Marie.* **Open** *9am–noon, 3–7pm Tue–Sun.* **Closed** *public hols.* 📷

Tʜᴇ ᴄᴏɴꜱᴛʀᴜᴄᴛɪᴏɴ of this church was begun in 1664 from plans by the royal architect Louis Le Vau, who lived on the island. It was completed and consecrated in 1726. Among its outstanding exterior features are the 1741 iron clock at the entrance and the pierced iron spire.

The interior, in the Baroque style, is richly decorated with gilding and marble. There is a statue of St Louis holding a crusader's sword. A plaque in the north aisle, given in 1926, bears the inscription "in grateful memory of St Louis in whose honour the City of St Louis, Missouri, USA is named". The church is also twinned with Carthage cathedral in Tunisia, where St Louis is buried.

The interior of St-Louis-en-l'Ile

Hôtel de Sens ❽

1 rue du Figuier 75004. **Map** 9 C4. 📞 *01 42 78 14 60.* Ⓜ *Pont-Marie.* **Open** *1:30–8:15pm Tue–Fri; 10am–8:15pm Sat.* **Closed** *public hols.* 📷

Oɴᴇ ᴏꜰ ᴏɴʟʏ a handful of medieval buildings still standing in Paris, the Hôtel de Sens is home to the Forney arts library. During the period of the Catholic League in the 16th

century, it was turned into a fortified mansion and occupied by the Bourbons, the Guises and Cardinal de Pellevé.

St-Gervais–St-Protais ❾

Place St-Gervais 75004. **Map** 9 B3. 📞 *01 48 87 32 02.* Ⓜ *Hôtel de Ville.* **Open** *6am–9pm Tue–Fri; 7am–8pm Sat & Sun.*

Nᴀᴍᴇᴅ ᴀꜰᴛᴇʀ Gervase and Protase, two Roman soldiers martyred by the Emperor Nero, the origins of this church go back to the 6th century. It boasts the earliest Classical façade in Paris, dating from 1621, with a triple-tiered arrangement of Doric, Ionic and Corinthian columns.

Behind the façade lies a late Gothic church renowned for its association with religious music. François Couperin (1668–1733) composed his two masses for this church's organ.

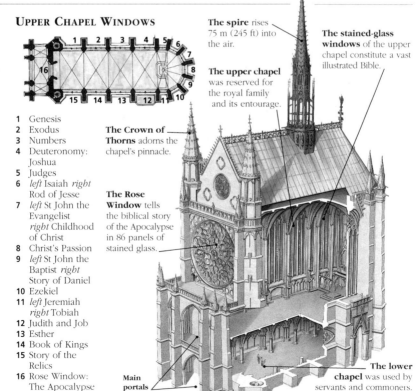

UPPER CHAPEL WINDOWS

1 Genesis
2 Exodus
3 Numbers
4 Deuteronomy: Joshua
5 Judges
6 *left* Isaiah *right* Rod of Jesse
7 *left* St John the Evangelist *right* Childhood of Christ
8 Christ's Passion
9 *left* St John the Baptist *right* Story of Daniel
10 Ezekiel
11 *left* Jeremiah *right* Tobiah
12 Judith and Job
13 Esther
14 Book of Kings
15 Story of the Relics
16 Rose Window: The Apocalypse

The spire rises 75 m (245 ft) into the air.

The stained-glass windows of the upper chapel constitute a vast illustrated Bible.

The upper chapel was reserved for the royal family and its entourage.

The Crown of Thorns adorns the chapel's pinnacle.

The Rose Window tells the biblical story of the Apocalypse in 86 panels of stained glass.

Main portals

The lower chapel was used by servants and commoners.

Notre-Dame ❻

NO OTHER BUILDING epitomizes the history of Paris more than Notre-Dame. Built on the site of a Roman temple, the cathedral was commissioned by Bishop de Sully in 1159. The first stone was laid in 1163, marking the start of two centuries of toil by armies of Gothic architects and medieval craftsmen. It has been witness to great events of French history ever since, including the coronations of Henry VI in 1422 and Napoleon Bonaparte in 1804. During the Revolution the building was desecrated and rechristened the Temple of Reason. Extensive renovations (including the addition of the spire and gargoyles) were carried out in the 19th century by architect Viollet-le-Duc.

★ West Façade
The beautifully proportioned west façade is a masterpiece of French Gothic architecture.

387 steps lead to the top of the south tower, where the famous Emmanuel bell is housed.

★ Galerie des Chimères
The cathedral's legendary gargoyles (chimères) gaze menacingly from the cathedral's ledge.

★ West Rose Window
This window depicts the Virgin in a medallion of rich reds and blues.

STAR FEATURES

- **★ West Façade and Portals**
- **★ Flying Buttresses**
- **★ Rose Windows**
- **★ Galerie des Chimères**

The Kings' Gallery features 28 stone images of the kings of Judah.

Portal of the Virgin
The Virgin surrounded by saints and kings is a fine composition of 13th-century statues.

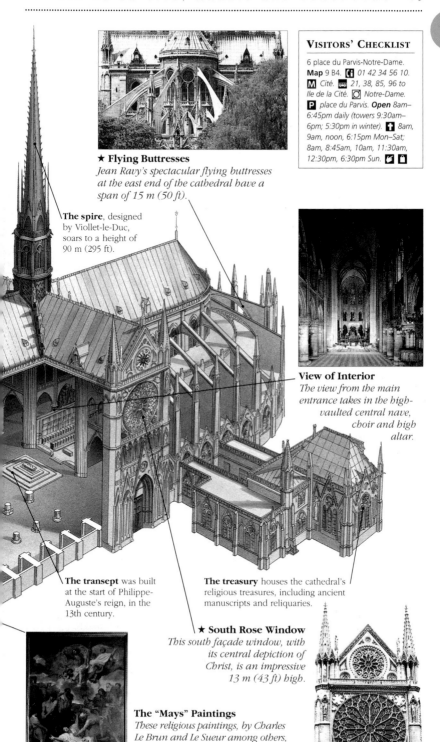

★ Flying Buttresses
Jean Ravy's spectacular flying buttresses at the east end of the cathedral have a span of 15 m (50 ft).

The spire, designed by Viollet-le-Duc, soars to a height of 90 m (295 ft).

VISITORS' CHECKLIST

6 place du Parvis-Notre-Dame.
Map 9 B4. 🚻 *01 42 34 56 10.*
Ⓜ *Cité.* 🚌 *21, 38, 85, 96 to Ile de la Cité.* Ⓞ *Notre-Dame.*
🅿 *place du Parvis.* **Open** *8am–6:45pm daily (towers 9:30am–6pm; 5:30pm in winter).* 🕆 *8am, 9am, noon, 6:15pm Mon–Sat; 8am, 8:45am, 10am, 11:30am, 12:30pm, 6:30pm Sun.* 📷 🖻

View of Interior
The view from the main entrance takes in the high-vaulted central nave, choir and high altar.

The transept was built at the start of Philippe-Auguste's reign, in the 13th century.

The treasury houses the cathedral's religious treasures, including ancient manuscripts and reliquaries.

★ South Rose Window
This south façade window, with its central depiction of Christ, is an impressive 13 m (43 ft) high.

The "Mays" Paintings
These religious paintings, by Charles Le Brun and Le Sueur among others, were presented by the Paris guilds every 1 May from 1630 to 1707.

Street-by-Street: The Marais

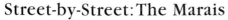

Once an area of marshland (*marais* means swamp), the Marais grew steadily in importance from the 14th century, by virtue of its proximity to the Louvre, the preferred residence of Charles V. Its heyday was in the 17th century, when it became a fashionable area for the moneyed classes. They built many grand and sumptuous mansions, the *hôtels* which still dot the Marais today. Many of these buildings have been restored and turned into museums.

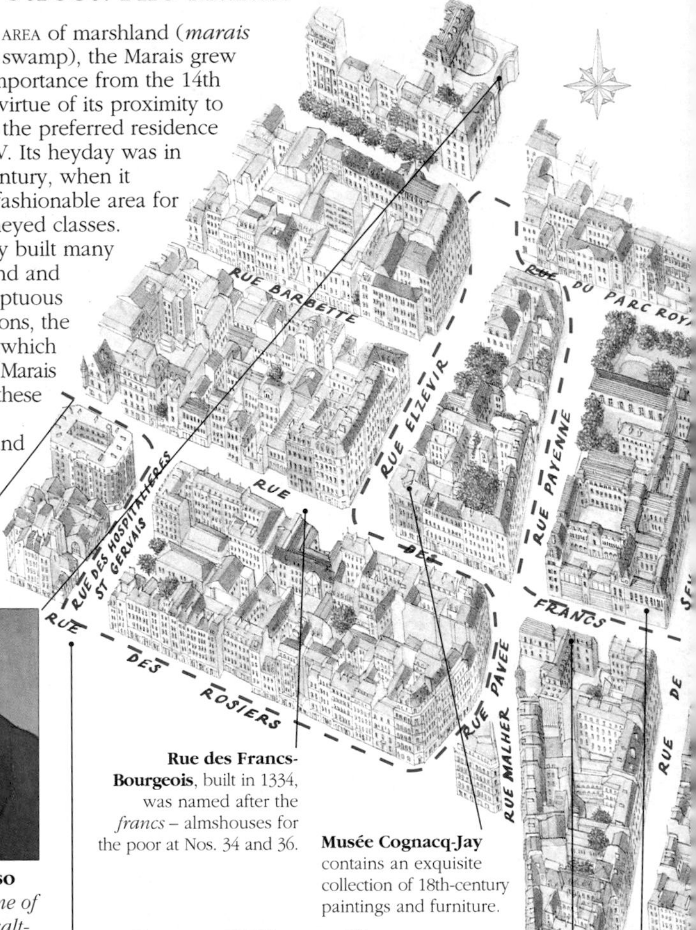

To the Pompidou Centre

Rue des Francs-Bourgeois, built in 1334, was named after the *francs* – almshouses for the poor at Nos. 34 and 36.

★ Musée Picasso
The palatial home of a 17th-century salt-tax collector is the setting for the most extensive collection of Picassos in the world ⑮

Musée Cognacq-Jay contains an exquisite collection of 18th-century paintings and furniture.

Hôtel de Lamoignon was built in 1584 and houses Paris's historical library.

Rue des Rosiers, in the heart of the Jewish quarter, is lined with 18th-century houses, shops and restaurants serving hot pastrami and borscht.

Key

 — Suggested route

0 metres	100
0 yards	100

★ Musée Carnavalet
Occupying two large mansions, this museum covers the history of Paris from Roman times ⑯

★ **Place des Vosges**
*This enchanting square is
an oasis of peace and
tranquillity* ⓱

LOCATOR MAP
See Street Finder maps 9, 10

Maison de Victor Hugo
Author of Les Misérables, *Victor Hugo
lived at No. 6 place des Vosges, now
a museum of his life and work* ⓲

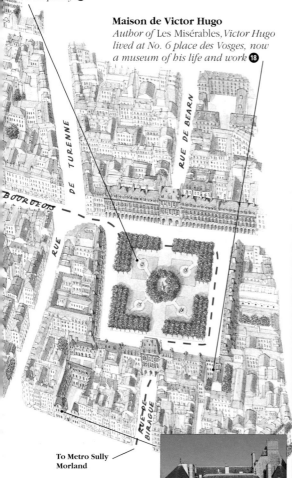

**To Metro Sully
Morland**

STAR SIGHTS

★ **Musée Picasso**

★ **Musée Carnavalet**

★ **Place des Vosges**

Hôtel de Sully, with its
orangerie and courtyard, is an
elegant Renaissance mansion.

Hôtel de Ville ⓾

4 place de l'Hôtel de Ville 75004.
Map 9 B3. **☎** *01 42 76 50 49.*
Ⓜ *Hôtel-de-Ville.* **Admission** by
guided tour only (phone to arrange).
Closed public hols, official functions
(phone to check). **&**

HOME OF THE city council,
the Hôtel de Ville is a
19th-century reconstruction of
the 17th-century town hall
burnt down by insurgents of
the Paris Commune in 1871.
It is a highly ornate example
of Third Republic architecture,
with elaborate stonework,
turrets and statues overlooking
a pedestrianized square.

The 16th-century Tour St-Jacques

Tour St-Jacques ⓫

Square de la Tour St-Jacques 75004.
Map 9 A3. **Ⓜ** *Châtelet.* **Not open**
to the public.

THIS IMPOSING late Gothic
tower, dating from 1522, is
all that remains of a medieval
church used as a rendezvous
by pilgrims setting out for
Compostela in Spain. The
building was destroyed by
revolutionaries in 1797.
Earlier, Blaise Pascal, the
17th-century philosopher,
mathematician, physicist and
writer, used the tower for
barometric experiments. His
statue stands at the base of
the tower, which is now used
as a meteorological station.

St-Eustache ⑫

Place du Jour 75001. **Map** 9 A1.
01 42 36 31 05. **M** Les Halles.
Châtelet-Les-Halles. **Open** 9am–7pm
Mon–Sat (9:15am–1, 3–7pm Sun).

Wᴵᵀᴴ ITS GOTHIC PLAN and Renaissance decoration, St-Eustache is one of Paris's most beautiful churches. Its massive interior is modelled on Notre-Dame, with five naves and side and radial chapels. The 105 years (1532–1637) it took to complete the church saw the flowering of the Renaissance style, which is evident in the magnificent arches, pillars and columns.

St-Eustache has been the setting for many ceremonial events including the baptisms of Cardinal Richelieu and Madame de Pompadour, and the funerals of fabulist La Fontaine, Colbert (prime minister of Louis XIV), 17th-century dramatist Molière, composer Rameau and the

**St-Eustache and sculptured head,
l'Ecoute, by Henri de Miller**

revolutionary orator Mirabeau. It was here that Berlioz first performed his *Te Deum* in 1855 and Liszt his *Messe Solenelle* in 1866. Today talented choir groups perform here regularly and organ recitals are held in June and July.

Pompidou Centre ⑬

See pp88–9.

Hôtel de Soubise ⑭

60 rue des Francs-Bourgeois 75003.
Map 9 C2. 01 40 27 61 78. **M**
Rambuteau. **Open** noon–6:45pm
Wed–Mon. **Closed** public hols.

Tʜɪs IMPOSING MANSION, built from 1705 to 1709 for the Princesse de Rohan, is one of two main buildings housing the national archives (the other one being the Hôtel de Rohan). It boasts a majestic courtyard and 18th-century interior decoration by some of the best-known artists of the time.

Natoire's *rocaille* work on the Oval Salon, the Princess's bedchamber, can be admired in the museum of French history now housed here. Other exhibits include Napoleon's will, in which he asks for his remains to be returned to France.

Musée Picasso ⑮

Hôtel Salé, 5 rue de Thorigny.
Map 10 D2. 01 42 71 25 21. **M**
St-Sébastien Froissart. **Open** Oct–Mar:
9:30am–5:30pm Wed–Mon; Apr–Sep:
9:30am–6pm Wed–Mon. **Closed**
1 Jan, 25 Dec. 🅐 🅞 ♿ 🅲 by appt.

Oɴ THE DEATH OF the Spanish-born artist Pablo Picasso (1881–1973), who lived most of his life in France, the French State inherited one quarter of his works in lieu of death duties. It used them to establish the Musée Picasso, which opened in 1986. The museum is housed in the beautifully restored Hôtel Salé, one of the loveliest buildings in the Marais. It was built in 1656 for Aubert de Fontenay, collector of the dreaded salt tax (*salé* means "salty").

Comprising over 200 paintings, 158 sculptures, 88 ceramic works and some 3,000 sketches and engravings, this unique collection shows the enormous range and variety of Picasso's work, including examples from his Blue, Pink and Cubist periods.

Highlights to look out for are his Blue period *Self-portrait*,

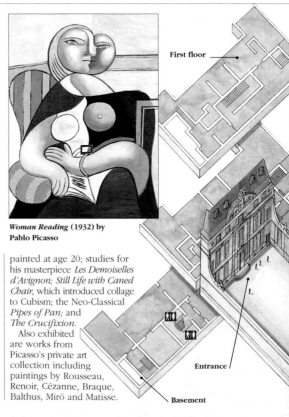

**Woman Reading (1932) by
Pablo Picasso**

painted at age 20; studies for his masterpiece *Les Demoiselles d'Avignon; Still Life with Caned Chair*, which introduced collage to Cubism; the Neo-Classical *Pipes of Pan;* and *The Crucifixion*.

Also exhibited are works from Picasso's private art collection including paintings by Rousseau, Renoir, Cézanne, Braque, Balthus, Miró and Matisse.

First floor

Entrance

Basement

Musée Carnavalet

23 rue de Sevigné 75003. **Map** 10 D3.
C 01 42 72 21 13. **M** St-Paul.
Open 10am–5:40pm Tue–Sun.
Closed public hols.
1:30pm Tue, 2:15pm Sun.

DEVOTED TO the history of Paris since Roman times, this vast museum occupies

A magnificent 17th-century ceiling painting by Charles Le Brun

KEY TO FLOORPLAN

- Paintings
- Illustrations
- Sculpture garden
- Ceramics
- Non-exhibition space

GALLERY GUIDE

The collection is mainly presented in chronological order, starting on the first floor with the Blue and Pink periods, Cubist and Neo-Classical works. The ground floor displays works from the late 1920s to the late 1930s, and from the mid-1950s to 1973. Ceramics, illustrations and work from the war years are in the basement.

Ground floor

Entrance and ticket office

two adjoining mansions. They include entire decorated rooms with gilded panelling, furniture and *objets d'art*; many works of art, such as paintings and sculptures of prominent personalities; and engravings showing Paris being built.

The main building is the Hôtel Carnavalet, built as a townhouse in 1548 by Nicolas Dupuis. The literary hostess Madame de Sévigné lived here between 1677 and 1696, entertaining the intelligentsia of the day and writing her celebrated *Lettres*. Many of her possessions are in the first-floor exhibit covering the Louis XIV era.

The 17th-century Hôtel le Peletier, opened in 1989, features superb reconstructions of early 20th-century interiors. Artifacts from the Revolution and Napoleonic era are on display, and reconstructed interiors include Proust's bedroom.

Place des Vosges

75003, 75004. **Map** 10 D3.
M Bastille, St-Paul.

THIS PERFECTLY symmetrical square, laid out in 1605 by Henri IV, is considered among the most beautiful in the world by Parisians and visitors alike. Thirty-six houses, nine on each side, are built over arcades which today accommodate antiques shops and fashionable cafés. The square has been the scene of many historical events over the centuries, including a three-day tournament in celebration of the marriage of Louis XIII to Anne of Austria in 1615.

Maison de Victor Hugo

6 place des Vosges 75004. **Map** 10 D4.
C 01 42 72 10 16. **M** Bastille.
Open 10am–5:40pm Tue–Sun.
Closed public hols. by appt.

THE FRENCH POET, dramatist and novelist lived on the second floor of the former Hôtel Rohan-Guéménée, the

largest house on the square, from 1832 to 1848. It was here that he wrote most of *Les Misérables* and completed other famous works. On display are reconstructions of some of the rooms in which he lived, complete with his desk, the furniture he made, his pen-and-ink drawings and mementos from the crucially important periods of his life, from his childhood to his exile between 1852 and 1870.

Marble bust of Victor Hugo by Auguste Rodin

Place de la Bastille

75004. **Map** 10 E4. **M** Bastille.

NOTHING REMAINS of the infamous prison stormed by the revolutionary mob on 14 July 1789, the event that sparked the French Revolution.

The 52-m (170-ft) Colonne de Juillet stands in the middle of the traffic-clogged square to honour the victims of the July Revolution of 1830. On the south side of the square (at 120 rue de Lyon) is the 2,700-seat **Opéra Bastille**, completed in 1989, the bicentennial of the French Revolution.

The "genius of liberty" statue on top of the Colonne de Juillet

Pompidou Centre ⓭

THE POMPIDOU IS LIKE a building turned inside out: escalators, lifts, air and water ducts and even the massive steel struts that make up the building's skeleton are all on the outside. This allowed the architects, Richard Rogers, Renzo Piano and Gianfranco Franchini, to create a flexible exhibition space. Among the artists featured in the museum are Matisse, Picasso, Miró and Pollock, representing such schools as Fauvism, Cubism and Surrealism. During the current renovation, most of the works will be lent to museums throughout the world. The Atelier Brancusi (Brancusi Workshop), in the piazza, is open indefinitely.

The top floor of the Centre affords superb views of other Parisian sights, such as the Eiffel Tower, Notre-Dame and the Sacré-Coeur.

This riotous jumble of glass and steel, known as Beaubourg, is Paris's top tourist attraction, built in 1977 and drawing over seven million visitors a year.

Mobile on Two Planes *(1955)*
20th-century American artist Alexander Calder introduced the mobile as an art form.

To the Atelier Brancusi ↙

GALLERY GUIDE
Much of the Pompidou Centre is closed to the public during the renovation work. The paintings shown on these pages are likely to be on display – on the fourth and fifth floors – when the centre reopens, but it is advisable to phone to check near the reopening time. There is also a permanent information kiosk located in the piazza.

Sorrow of the King *(1952)*
This collage was created by Matisse using gouache-painted paper cut-outs.

Portrait of the Journalist Sylvia von Harden *(1926) The surgical precision of Otto Dix's style makes this a harsh caricature.*

VISITORS' CHECKLIST

Centre d'Art et de Culture Georges Pompidou, Pl G Pompidou. **Map** 9 B2. [01 44 78 12 33. [M] *Rambuteau, Châtelet, Les Halles, Hôtel de Ville.* 21, 29, 38, 47, 58, 69, 70, 72, 74, 75, 76, 85. [RER] *Châtelet-Les-Halles.* [P] *Centre G Pompidou.* **Pompidou Centre Closed** *for refurbishment until Jan 2000.* **Atelier Brancusi open** *noon–10pm Mon–Fri; 10am–10pm Sat, Sun & public hols.* [&] [✔] [🎫] **Web site:** *www.cnac-gp.fr*

Man with a Guitar *(1914) Braque, along with Picasso, developed the Cubist technique of presenting many different views of the subject in one picture.*

With the Black Arc *(1912) The transition to Abstraction, one of the major art forms of the 20th century, can be seen in the works of Wassily Kandinsky.*

Picasso Fountain
This fountain, which was inaugurated in 1983, is in the Place Igor Stravinsky near the Pompidou Centre. It was designed by sculptors Jean Tinguely and Niki de Saint Phalle, both of whom are represented in the Pompidou Centre.

BRANCUSI WORKSHOP

The Atelier Brancusi, on the rue Rambuteau side of the piazza, is a reconstruction of the workshop of the Romanian-born artist Constantin Brancusi (1876–1957), who lived and worked in Paris. He bequeathed his entire collection of works to the French state on condition that his workshop be rebuilt as it was. The wide range of exhibits includes more than 200 sculptures and plinths, 1600 photographs, and tools Brancusi used to create his works. Also featured are some of his more personal items such as documents, pieces of furniture and his book collection.

Interior of the Brancusi workshop, designed by Renzo Piano

TUILERIES AND OPÉRA

THE 19TH-CENTURY grandeur of Baron Haussmann's *grands boulevards* offsets the bustle of bankers, theatre-goers, sightseers and shoppers who frequent the area around the Opéra. A profusion of shops and department stores, ranging from the exclusively expensive to the popular, draws the crowds. Much of the area's older character is found in the early 19th-century shopping arcades, with elaborate steel and glass roofs. They are known as *galeries* or *passages*, and were restored to their former glory in the 1970s. Galerie Vivienne, which is the smartest, has an elaborate, patterned mosaic floor. The passage des Panoramas, passage Verdeau and the tiny passage des Princes are more old-style Parisian. These streets abound with food shops of all kinds,

Lamppost of vestal virgin outside the Opéra

noted for their mouthwatering displays of expensive jams, spices, pâtés, mustards and sauces.

The Tuileries area lies between the Opéra and the river, bounded by the vast place de la Concorde in the west and the Louvre to the east. The Louvre palace combines one of the world's greatest art collections with IM Pei's avant-garde glass pyramid. Elegant squares and formal gardens give the area its special character. Monuments to monarchy and the arts coexist with modern luxury at its most ostentatious. Place Vendôme, home to exquisite jewellery shops and the luxurious Ritz Hotel, is a heady mix of the wealthy and the chic. Parallel to the Jardin des Tuileries are two of Paris's foremost shopping streets, the rue de Rivoli and rue St-Honoré, full of expensive boutiques, bookshops and five-star hotels.

SIGHTS AT A GLANCE

Museums and Galleries
Galerie National du Jeu de Paume ⑥
Musée des Arts Décoratifs ⑪
Musée Grévin ③
Musée du Louvre pp96–9 ⑭
Musée de l'Orangerie ⑧

Squares, Parks and Gardens
Jardin des Tuileries ⑨
Place de la Concorde ⑦
Place Vendôme ⑤

Monuments
Arc de Triomphe du Carrousel ⑫

Historic Buildings
Opéra de Paris Garnier ②
Palais Royal ⑬

Churches
La Madeleine ①
St-Roch ⑩

Shops
Les Galeries ④

GETTING THERE
This area is well served by the metro system, with stations at Tuileries, Pyramides, Palais Royal, Madeleine and Opéra, among others. Bus routes 24 and 72 pass along quai des Tuileries and quai du Louvre, while routes 21, 27 and 29 serve avenue de l'Opéra.

KEY

▨	Street-by-Street map *pp92–3*
Ⓜ	Metro station
Ⓟ	Car park

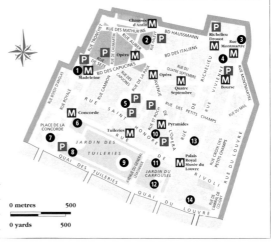

0 metres   500

0 yards   500

Street-by-Street: Opéra Quarter

IT HAS BEEN SAID that the whole world will pass you by if you sit for long enough at the Café de la Paix (opposite the Opéra Garnier). During the day, the area is a centre of commerce, tourism and shopping, with mammoth department stores lining the *grands boulevards*. In the evening, the clubs and theatres attract a totally different crowd, and the cafés along boulevard des Capucines throb with life.

Statue by Gurnery on the Opéra

★ Opéra Garnier
Dating from 1875, the grandiose opera house has come to symbolize the opulence of the Second Empire ❷

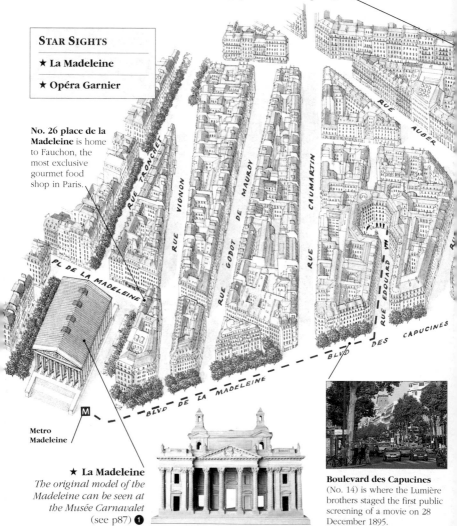

STAR SIGHTS

★ La Madeleine

★ Opéra Garnier

No. 26 place de la Madeleine is home to Fauchon, the most exclusive gourmet food shop in Paris.

Metro Madeleine

★ La Madeleine
The original model of the Madeleine can be seen at the Musée Carnavalet
(see p87) ❶

Boulevard des Capucines
(No. 14) is where the Lumière brothers staged the first public screening of a movie on 28 December 1895.

LOCATOR MAP
See Street Finder
maps 4, 7, 8

Musée de l'Opéra
contains the
scores of every
ballet and opera
performed at the
Opéra, and memor-
abilia ranging
from Nijinsky's
dancing shoes to
Pavlova's tiara.

PL DIAGHILEV

Metro
Opéra

**Place de
l'Opéra** was
designed by Baron
Haussmann and is one of
Paris's busiest intersections.

KEY

- - - Suggested route

| 0 metres | 100 |
| 0 yards | 100 |

Marochetti's *Mary Magdalene Ascending to Heaven* in La Madeleine

La Madeleine ❶

Pl de la Madeleine 75008.
Map 3 C5. **☎** *01 44 51 69 00.*
M *Madeleine.* **Open** *7:15am–5:15pm
Mon–Sat, 7:30am–1:30pm, 3:30–7pm
Sun.* 📷 🚻

MODELLED AFTER a Greek
temple, La Madeleine
was begun in 1764 but not
consecrated as a church until
1845. Before that, there
were proposals to turn
it into a stock exchange,
a bank, a theatre, a train
station or yet another
monument to Napoleon.
A colonnade of Corin-
thian columns encircles
the building and sup-
ports a sculptured frieze.
The inside is crowned
by three ceiling domes
and lavishly decorated
with fine sculptures, **Sign outside the**
rose marble and gilt. **Musée Grévin**

Opéra Garnier ❷

Place de l'Opéra 75009. **Map** 4 DF.
☎ *01 40 01 22 63.* **M** *Opéra.*
Open *11am–6:30pm daily.* **Closed**
14 Jul–15 Sep and public hols.

SOMETIMES COMPARED to a
giant wedding cake, this
extravagant building was
designed by Charles Garnier
for Napoleon III in 1862. The
Prussian War and the 1871
uprising delayed the opening
of the building till 1875.
The interior of the Opéra is
famous for its Grand Staircase
made of white Carrara marble,
towered over by a huge
chandelier. It is also renowned
for its five-tiered auditorium
bedecked in red velvet and
gold, with a false ceiling

painted by Chagall in 1964.
Though operas are now performed in the Opéra Bastille,
the Opéra Garnier is still Paris's
unrivalled centre for ballet.

Musée Grévin ❸

10 boulevard Montmartre 75009.
Map 4 F4. **☎** *01 47 70 85 05.* **M**
rue Montmartre. **Open** *1– 7pm
daily, 10am–7pm school
hols.* 📷 🚻

FOUNDED IN 1882, this
museum is a Paris
landmark, on a par
with Madame Tussauds
in London. The histori-
cal scenes include
Louis XIV at Versailles
and the arrest of Louis
XVI. Notable figures
from the worlds of art,
politics, film and sport
are also on display.
On the first floor is a
holography museum devoted
to optical tricks. The museum
also houses a 320-seat theatre.

Les Galeries ❹

75002. **Map** 4 F5. **M** *Bourse.*

THE EARLY 19th-century glass-
roofed shopping arcades
(known as *galeries* or *passages*)
are concentrated between
boulevard Montmartre and
rue St-Marc. They house an
eclectic mixture of small shops
selling anything from designer
jewellery to rare books and
art supplies. One of the most
charming is the Galerie
Vivienne (off the rue Vivienne
or the rue des Petits Champs)
with its mosaic floor and
excellent tearoom.

Place Vendôme ❺

75001. **Map** 8 D1. **M** *Tuileries.*

PERHAPS THE best example of 18th-century elegance in the city, the architect Jules Hardouin-Mansart's royal square was begun in 1698. The original plan was to house academies and embassies behind its arcaded façades, but instead bankers moved in and created sumptuous mansions for themselves. The square's most famous residents include Frédéric Chopin, who died here in 1849 at No. 12, and César Ritz, who established his famous hotel at No. 15 in 1898.

Galerie National du Jeu de Paume ❻

Jardin des Tuileries, place de la Concorde 75008. **Map** 7 C1.
C 01 47 03 12 50. **C** 01 42 60 69 69. **M** *Concorde.* **Open** *noon–9:30pm Tue, noon–7pm Wed–Fri, 10am–7pm Sat & Sun.* **Closed** *1 Jan, 1 May, 25 Dec.* 🎨 ♿ ✔

THE JEU DE PAUME – literally "game of the palm" – was built as two royal tennis courts by Napoleon III in 1851. When the game's popularity waned, the courts were converted into a gallery devoted to French Impressionist art. In 1986 the collection was moved to the Musée d'Orsay across the river *(see pp116–17)*. The Jeu de Paume now exhibits contemporary art.

Place de la Concorde ❼

75008. **Map** 7 C1. **M** *Concorde.*

ONE OF Europe's most magnificent and historic squares, covering over 8 ha (20 acres), the place de la Concorde was a swamp

The 3,200-year-old obelisk from Luxor

Monet's *Waterlilies (Nymphéas)* on display in the Musée de l'Orangerie

until the mid-18th century. It became the place Louis XV in 1775 when royal architect Jacques-Ange Gabriel was asked by the king to design a suitable setting for an equestrian statue of himself.

The monument, which lasted here less than 20 years, was replaced by the guillotine (the Black Widow, as it came to be known), and the square was renamed place de la Révolution. On 21 January 1793 Louis XVI was beheaded, followed by over 1,300 other victims including Marie Antoinette, Madame du Barry, Charlotte Corday (Marat's assassin) and revolutionary leaders Danton and Robespierre.

The blood-soaked square was optimistically renamed place de la Concorde after the Reign of Terror finally came to an end in 1794. A few decades later the 3,200-year-old Luxor obelisk was presented to King Louis-Philippe as a gift from the viceroy of Egypt (who also donated Cleopatra's Needle in London).

Flanking the rue Royale on the north side of the square are two of Gabriel's Neo-Classical mansions, the Hôtel de la Marine and the exclusive Hôtel Crillon.

Musée de l'Orangerie ❽

Jardin des Tuileries, place de la Concorde 75008. **Map** 7 C1.
C 01 42 97 48 16. **M** *Concorde.* **Closed** *for renovation from Jan 1999.* 🎨 📷 ♿ ✔

PAINTINGS from Claude Monet's crowning work, representing part of his water-lily series, fill the two oval ground floor rooms. Known as the *Nymphéas*, most of the canvases were painted between 1899 and 1921 in his garden at Giverny, near Paris.

This superb work is complemented by the Walter-Guillaume collection, including 24 canvases by Renoir, notably *Young Girls at the Piano*, dramatic works by Soutine and 14 Cézannes, including *The Red Rock*. Picasso is represented by early works including *The Female Bathers*, and Rousseau by 9 paintings, notably *The Wedding* and *Old Junier's Cart*. Other outstanding works are by Sisley, Derain, Modigliani and Utrillo.

Jardin des Tuileries ❾

75001. **Map** 8 D1. **M** *Tuileries, Concorde.*

THESE NEO-CLASSICAL gardens once belonged to the Palais des Tuileries, which the Communards razed to the ground in 1871. They were laid out in the 17th century by André Le Nôtre, who created the broad central avenue and topiary arranged in geometric designs. One of the most popular open spaces in the city, the Tuileries is a lovely spot for a picnic or leisurely stroll.

St-Roch ⑩

296 rue St-Honoré 75001. **Map** 8 E1. **C** 01 42 44 13 20. **M** Tuileries. **Open** 8:15am–7:30pm daily. **Closed** non-religious public hols. 📷

The Buren Columns in the main courtyard of the Palais Royal

THIS HUGE CHURCH was designed by Jacques Lemercier, architect of the Louvre, and its foundation stone was laid by Louis XIV in 1653. It is a treasure house of religious art, much of it from now-vanished churches and monasteries, and contains the tombs of the playwright Pierre Corneille, the royal gardener André Le Nôtre and the philosopher Denis Diderot.

Vien's *St Denis Preaching to the Gauls* (1767) in St-Roch

Musée des Arts Décoratifs ⑪

Palais du Louvre, 109 rue de Rivoli 75001. **Map** 8 E2. **C** 01 44 55 57 50. **M** Palais Royal, Tuileries. **Open** 11am –6pm Tue, Thu & Fri; 11am–9pm Wed; 10am–6pm Sat & Sun. **Library** 10am– 6pm Wed; 12:30pm– 6pm Thu–Tue.

OCCUPYING THE northwest wing of the Palais du Louvre, this museum offers a fascinating potpourri of decorative art and domestic design

from the Middle Ages to the present day. The Art Nouveau and Art Deco rooms include a reconstruction of the Left Bank home of couturier Jeanne Lanvin. Other floors show Louis XIV, XV and XVI styles of decoration and furniture. Contemporary designers such as Jean-Michel Wilmotte, Philippe Starck and Andrée Putman are also represented.

Arc de Triomphe du Carrousel ⑫

Place du Carrousel 75001. **Map** 8 E2. **M** Palais Royal.

THIS ROSE-MARBLE ARCH was built by Napoleon to celebrate various military triumphs including the Battle of Austerlitz in 1805. The crowning statues, added in 1828, are copies of the famous Horses of St Mark's which Napoleon stole from Venice, and which he was subsequently forced to return following his defeat at Waterloo in 1815.

Palais Royal ⑬

Place du Palais Royal 75001. **Map** 8 E1. **M** Palais Royal. **Buildings closed** to the public.

THIS FORMER royal palace has had a turbulent history. It was built by Cardinal Richelieu in the early 17th century, passing to the Crown on his death and becoming the childhood home of Louis XIV. Under the 18th-century royal dukes of Orléans, it became the epicentre of brilliant gatherings, interspersed with periods of gambling and debauchery. It was from here that the clarion call to revolution roused the mobs to storm the Bastille on 14 July 1789.

Today the southern section of the building houses the Councils of State and the Ministry of Culture. Just west of the palace at 2 rue de Richelieu is the Comédie Française, established by Louis XIV in 1680. Luxury shops occupy the rear section of the palace, where artists such as Colette and Cocteau once lived.

The Arc de Triomphe du Carrousel crowned by Victory riding a chariot

Musée du Louvre ⑭

The Louvre's east façade, facing St-Germain l'Auxerrois

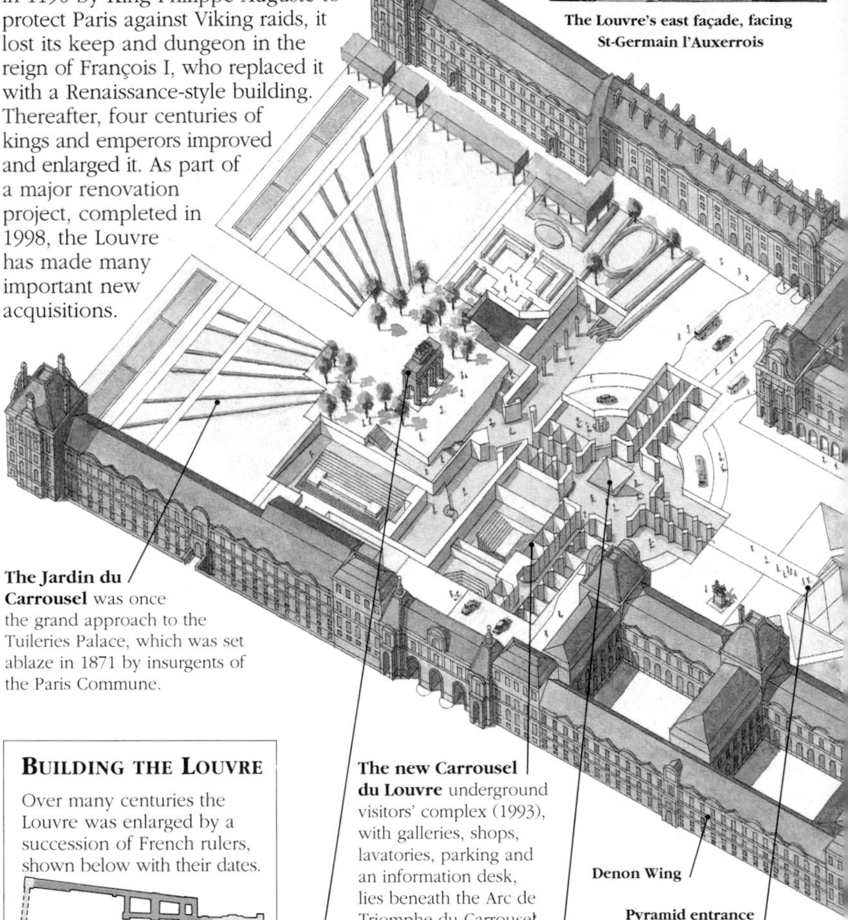

T HE MUSÉE DU LOUVRE, containing one of the most important art collections in the world, has a history dating back to medieval times. First built as a fortress in 1190 by King Philippe-Auguste to protect Paris against Viking raids, it lost its keep and dungeon in the reign of François I, who replaced it with a Renaissance-style building. Thereafter, four centuries of kings and emperors improved and enlarged it. As part of a major renovation project, completed in 1998, the Louvre has made many important new acquisitions.

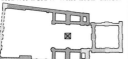

The Jardin du Carrousel was once the grand approach to the Tuileries Palace, which was set ablaze in 1871 by insurgents of the Paris Commune.

BUILDING THE LOUVRE

Over many centuries the Louvre was enlarged by a succession of French rulers, shown below with their dates.

MAJOR ALTERATIONS

- Reign of François I (1515–47)
- Catherine de' Medici (about 1560)
- Reign of Henri IV (1589–1610)
- Reign of Louis XIII (1610–43)
- Reign of Louis XIV (1643–1715)
- Reign of Napoleon I (1804–15)
- Reign of Napoleon III (1852–70)
- IM Pei (1989) (architect)

The new Carrousel du Louvre underground visitors' complex (1993), with galleries, shops, lavatories, parking and an information desk, lies beneath the Arc de Triomphe du Carrousel.

Denon Wing

Pyramid entrance

The inverted glass pyramid brings light to the subterranean complex, echoing the museum's new main entrance in the Cour Napoléon.

★ **Arc de Triomphe du Carrousel**
This triumphal arch was built to celebrate Napoleon's military victories in 1805.

STAR FEATURES

★ **Perrault Colonnade**

★ **Medieval Moats**

★ **Arc de Triomphe du Carrousel**

THE GLASS PYRAMID

Plans for the modernization and expansion of the Louvre were first conceived in 1981. They included the transfer of the Ministry of Finance from the Richelieu wing of the Louvre to new offices elsewhere, as well

as a new main entrance designed by architect IM Pei in 1989. Made of metal and glass, the pyramid enables the visitor to see the buildings around the palace, while allowing light down into the underground visitors' reception area.

VISITORS' CHECKLIST

Map 8 E2. 📞 *01 40 20 53 17.*
🖥 *01 40 20 51 51.* M *Palais Royal, Musée du Louvre.* 🚌 *21, 24, 27, 39, 48, 68, 69, 72, 81, 95.* RER *Châtelet-Les-Halles.* 🚇 *Louvre.* P *Carrousel du Louvre (entrance via avenue du General Lemmonier); place du Louvre, rue St-Honoré.* **Museum open** *9am–6pm Thu–Sun (last adm: 5:30pm); 9am–9:45pm Mon & Wed (last adm: 9:30pm).* **Hall Napoléon** *(including History of the Louvre, Medieval Louvre, auditorium, temporary exhibitions, restaurants, bookshop)* **open** *9am–10pm Wed–Mon.* 🎫 *(half price after 3pm and all day Sun. Free 1st Sun of month).* 🚹 *partial.* 🎥 *(every day except Sun) phone 01 40 20 52 09.* 🚻 **Web site** *http://www.louvre.fr*

Cour Marly is the glass-roofed courtyard that now houses the *Marly Horses (see p99).*

Richelieu Wing

Cour Puget

Hall Napoléon is situated under the pyramid.

Cour Khorsabad

Sully Wing

Cour Carrée

Cour Napoléon

★ **Perrault's Colonnade**
The east façade, with its majestic rows of columns, was built by Claude Perrault, who worked on the Louvre with Louis Le Vau in the mid-17th century.

The Salle des Caryatides is named after the four monumental statues created by Jean Goujon in 1550 to support the upper gallery. Built for Henri II, it is the oldest room in the palace.

The Louvre of Charles V
In about 1360, Charles V transformed Philippe-Auguste's old fortress, with its distinctive tower and keep, into a royal residence.

★ **Medieval Moats**
The base of the twin towers and the drawbridge support of Philippe-Auguste's fortress can be seen in the excavated area.

Exploring the Louvre's Collection

OWING TO THE VAST SIZE of the Louvre's collection, it is useful to set a few viewing priorities before starting. The collection of European paintings (1400–1848) is comprehensive, with over half the works by French artists. The exstensively renovated departments of Oriental, Egyptian, Greek, Etruscan and Roman antiquities feature numerous new acquisitions and rare treasures. The varied display of *objets d'art* includes furniture and jewellery.

The Raft of the Medusa (1819)
by Théodore Géricault

EUROPEAN PAINTING: 1400 TO 1848

PAINTING FROM northern Europe (Flemish, Dutch, German and English) is well covered. One of the earliest Flemish works is Jan van Eyck's *Madonna of the Chancellor Rolin* (about 1435), showing the Chancellor of Burgundy kneeling in prayer before the Virgin and Child. Hieronymus Bosch's *Ship of Fools* (1500) is a satirical account of the futility of human existence.

Mona Lisa (about 1504) by
Leonardo da Vinci

In the fine Dutch collection, Rembrandt's *Self-portrait*, his *Disciples at Emmaus* (1648) and *Bathsheba* (1654) are examples of the artist's genius.

The three major German painters of the 15th and 16th centuries are represented by important works. There is a youthful *Self-portrait* (1493) by Albrecht Dürer, a *Venus* (1529) by Lucas Cranach and a portrait of the great humanist scholar Erasmus by Hans Holbein.

The impressive collection of Italian paintings is arranged in chronological order from 1200 to 1800. The father figures of the early Renaissance, Cimabue and Giotto, are here, as is Fra Angelico, with his *Coronation of the Virgin* (1435), and Pisanello, with his delightful *Portrait of Ginevra d'Este* (about 1435). Several paintings by Leonardo da Vinci are on display, for instance the *Virgin with the Infant Jesus and St Anne* which is as enchanting as his *Mona Lisa*.

The Louvre's fine collection of French painting ranges from the 14th century to 1848.

Paintings after this date are housed in the Musée d'Orsay *(see pp116–17)*. Outstanding is Enguerrand Quarton's *Villeneuve-les-Avignon Pietà* (1455). The great 18th-century painter of melancholy, JA Watteau, is represented, as is JH Fragonard, master of the Rococo, whose delightfully frivolous subjects are evident in *The Bathers* from 1770.

EUROPEAN SCULPTURE: 1100 TO 1848

EARLY FLEMISH and German sculpture in the collection has many masterpieces such as Tilman Riemenschneider's *Virgin of the Annunciation* from the end of the 15th century and a life-size nude figure of the penitent Mary Magdalen by Gregor Erhart (early 16th century). An important work of Flemish sculpture is Adrian de Vries's long-limbed *Mercury and Psyche* from 1593, which was originally made for the court of Rudolph II in Prague.

The French section opens with early Romanesque works, such as the figure of Christ by a 12th-century Burgundian sculptor, and a head of St Peter. With its eight black-hooded mourners, the late 15th-century tomb of Philippe Pot (a high-ranking official in Burgundy) is one of the more unusual pieces. Diane de Poitiers, Henri II's mistress, had a large figure of her namesake Diana, goddess of the hunt, installed in the courtyard of her castle west of Paris. It is now in the Louvre.

The tomb of Philippe Pot (late 15th century) by
Antoine le Moiturier

The celebrated *Marly Horses* (1745) by Guillaume Coustou

The works of French sculptor Pierre Puget (1620–94) have been assembled in the Cour Puget. They include a figure of Milo of Crotona, the Greek athlete who got his hands caught in the cleft of a tree stump and was eaten by a lion. The wild horses of Marly now stand in the Cour Marly, surrounded by other masterpieces of French sculpture, including Jean-Antoine Houdon's early 19th-century busts of famous men such as Diderot and Voltaire.

The collection of Italian sculpture includes such splendid exhibits as Michelangelo's *Slaves* and Benvenuto Cellini's Fontainebleau *Nymph*.

ORIENTAL, EGYPTIAN, GREEK, ETRUSCAN AND ROMAN ANTIQUITIES

A SUBSTANTIAL OVERHAUL of the Louvre has boosted its collection of antiquities, which range from the Neolithic period to the fall of the Roman Empire. Among the new exhibits are Greek and Roman glassware dating from the 6th century BC. Important works of Mesopotamian art include one of the world's oldest legal documents, a basalt block bearing the code of the Babylonian King Hammurabi, dating from about 1700 BC.

The warlike Assyrians are represented by delicate carvings and a spectacular reconstruction of part of Sargon II's (722–705 BC) palace with its winged bulls. A fine example of Persian art is the enamelled brickwork depicting the king of Persia's personal guard of archers (5th century BC).

Most Egyptian art was made for the dead, who were provided with the things they needed for the after-life. Examples include the life-like funeral portraits such as the *Squatting Scribe*, and several sculptures of married couples.

The departments of Greek, Roman and Etruscan antiquities contain a vast array of fragments, among them some exceptional pieces. There is a geometric head from the Cyclades (2700 BC) and an elegant swan-necked bowl hammered out of a gold sheet (2500 BC). The two most famous Greek marble statues, the *Winged Victory of Samothrace* and the *Venus de Milo*, both belong to the Hellenistic period (late 3rd to 2nd century BC), when more natural-looking human forms were produced.

The undisputed star of the Etruscan collection is the terracotta sarcophagus of a married couple who look as though they are attending an eternal banquet, while the highlight of the Roman section is a 2nd-century bronze head of the Emperor Hadrian.

Venus de Milo
(Greece, late 3rd–early 2nd century BC)

OBJETS D'ART

T HE CATCH-ALL term *objets d'art* (art objects) covers a vast range of items: jewellery, furniture, clocks, watches, sundials, tapestries, miniatures, silver and glassware, cutlery, Byzantine and Parisian carved ivory, Limoges enamels, porcelain, French and Italian stoneware, rugs, snuffboxes, scientific instruments and armour. The Louvre has well over 8,000 pieces, from many ages and regions.

Many of these precious objects came from the Abbey of St-Denis, where the kings of France were crowned. The treasures include a serpentine stone plate from the 1st century AD with a 9th-century border of gold and precious stones, a porphyry vase which Suger, Abbot of St-Denis, had mounted in gold in the shape of an eagle, and the golden sceptre made for King Charles V in about 1380.

The French crown jewels include the coronation crowns of Louis XV and Napoleon, sceptres, swords and other accessories of the coronation ceremonies. On view also is the Regent, one of the purest diamonds in the world, which Louis XV wore at his coronation in 1722.

One whole room is taken up with a series of tapestries called the *Hunts of Maximilian,* originally executed for Emperor Charles V in 1530. The large collection of French furniture ranges from the 16th to the 19th centuries and is assembled by period, or in rooms devoted to donations by distinguished collectors. On display are pieces by exceptionally prominent furniture-makers such as André-Charles Boulle, cabinet-maker to Louis XIV, who worked at the Louvre in the late 17th to mid-18th centuries.

Squatting Scribe (about 2500 BC), a life-like Egyptian funeral sculpture

Gilded bronze statues by a number of sculptors, decorating the central square of the Palais de Chaillot

Champs-Elysées and Invalides

THE RIVER SEINE dissects this area, much of which is built on a monumental scale, from the imposing 18th-century buildings of Les Invalides to the Art Nouveau avenues surrounding the Eiffel Tower. Two of Paris's grandest thoroughfares dominate the neighbourhood to the north of the Seine: the Champs-Elysées has many smart hotels and shops but today is more down-

Ornate lamppost on Pont Alexandre III

market; and the rue du Faubourg St-Honoré boasts the heavily guarded Palais de l'Elysée. The village of Chaillot was absorbed into the city in the 19th century, and many of its opulent Second Empire mansions are now embassies or company headquarters. Streets around the place du Trocadéro and the Neo-Classical Palais de Chaillot are packed full of museums and elegant cafés.

SIGHTS AT A GLANCE

Historic Buildings and Streets
Avenue des Champs-Elysées ❷
Champ-de-Mars ⓰
Ecole Militaire ⓱
Hôtel des Invalides ⓳
Les Egouts ⓭
No. 29 Avenue Rapp ⓯
Palais de l'Elysée ❸

Museums and Galleries
Grand Palais ❺
Musée de l'Armée ⓴
Musée d'Art Moderne de la
    Ville de Paris ❼
Musée de la Mode et du
    Costume Palais Galliera ❽

Musée National des Arts
    Asiatiques Guimet ❾
Musée National d'Ennery ❿
Musée Rodin ㉓
Palais de Chaillot ⓬
Petit Palais ❹

Churches
Dôme Church ㉒
Sainte-Clothilde ㉔
St-Louis-des-Invalides ㉑

Monuments and Fountains
Arc de Triomphe ❶
Eiffel Tower p109 ⓮
Fontaine des Quatre Saisons ㉕

Modern Architecture
UNESCO ⓲

Gardens
Jardins du Trocadéro ⑪

Bridges
Pont Alexandre III ❻

GETTING THERE
Metro stations in this area include Etoile, Trocadéro and Champs-Elysées. Bus routes 42 and 73 serve the Champs-Elysées; routes 87 and 69 serve avenue de Suffren and rue St-Dominique respectively.

KEY

	Street-by-Street map *pp102–3*
M	Metro station
RER	RER station
▣	Batobus boarding point
P	Car park

0 metres   500

0 yards   500

Street-by-Street: Champs-Elysées

THE FORMAL GARDENS that line the Champs-Elysées from the place de la Concorde to the Rond-Point have changed little since they were laid out by the architect Jacques Hittorff in 1838. The gardens were used as the setting for the World Fair of 1855, which included the Palais de l'Industrie, Paris's response to London's Crystal Palace. The Palais was later replaced by the Grand Palais and the Petit Palais, which was created as a showpiece of the Third Republic for the Universal Exhibition of 1900. They sit on either side of an impressive vista that stretches from the place Clémenceau across the elegant curve of the Pont Alexandre III, with its four strong anchoring columns, to the Invalides.

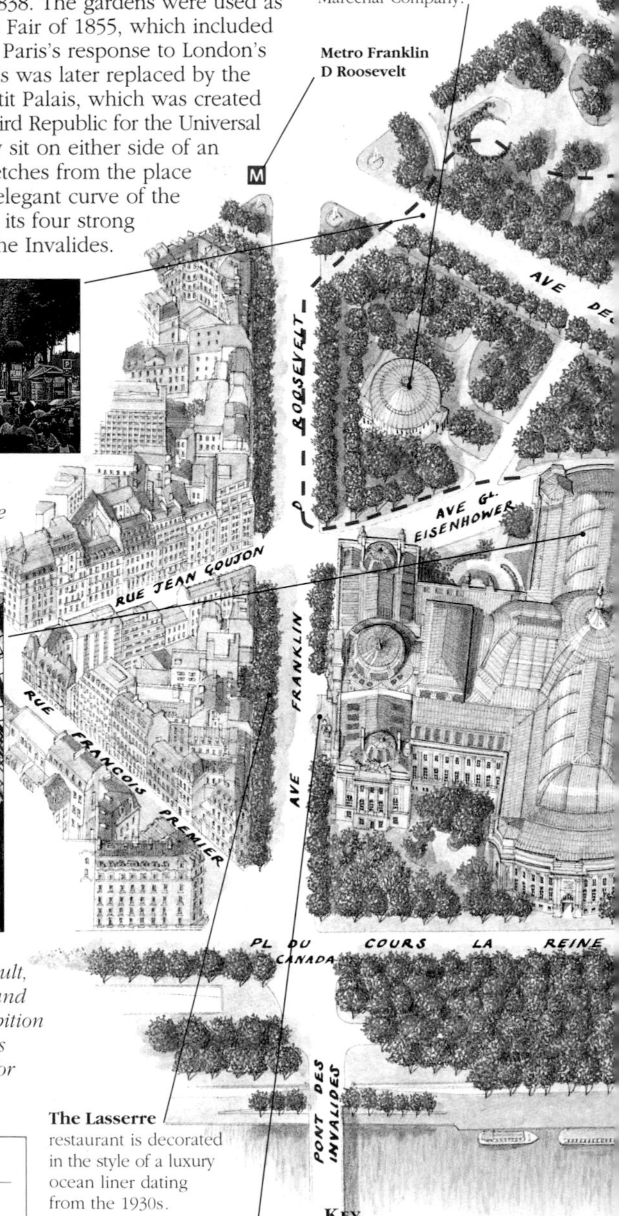

Théâtre du Rond Point, an original Champs-Elysées building, is home to the Marcel-Maréchal Company.

Metro Franklin D Roosevelt

★ Avenue des Champs-Elysées
This was the setting for the victory parades following the two World Wars ❷

★ Grand Palais
Designed by Charles Girault, and built between 1897 and 1900, this elaborate exhibition hall with its splendid glass dome is frequently used for major exhibitions ❺

The Lasserre restaurant is decorated in the style of a luxury ocean liner dating from the 1930s.

Palais de la Découverte, a museum of scientific discovery, was originally opened in the Grand Palais for the World Fair of 1937.

ROOSEVELT

AVE DE

AVE Gt. EISENHOWER

RUE JEAN GOUJON

RUE FRANÇOIS PREMIER

AVE FRANKLIN

PL DU CANADA

COURS   LA   REINE

PONT DES INVALIDES

STAR SIGHTS

★ Avenue des Champs-Elysées

★ Grand Palais

★ Petit Palais

KEY

- - - Suggested route

0 metres   100

0 yards   100

The Jardins des Champs-Elysées, with their fountains, flowerbeds and pleasure pavilions, have been a popular spot since the 19th century.

LOCATOR MAP
See Street Finder maps 2, 3, 6, 7

Metro Champs-Elysées-Clémenceau

To place de la Concorde

★ **Petit Palais**
The art collections of the city of Paris are housed here. They contain artifacts ranging from antique sculptures to landscape painters of the Barbizon school ➍

To the Invalides

Pont Alexandre III
This highly ornate, single-span structure symbolizes the optimism of the Belle Epoque at the turn of the century ➏

The east façade of the Arc de Triomphe

Arc de Triomphe ➊

Place Charles de Gaulle. **Map** 2 D4.
📞 *01 43 80 31 31.* **Open** *10am–10:30pm daily.* **Closed** *public hols.*

AFTER HIS greatest victory, the Battle of Austerlitz in 1805, Napoleon promised his men they would "go home beneath triumphal arches." The first stone of what was to become the world's most famous triumphal arch was laid the following year. But disruptions to architect Jean Chalgrin's plans, combined with the demise of Napoleonic power, delayed the completion of the bridge until 1836. Standing 50 m (164 ft) high, the Arc is encrusted with flamboyant reliefs, shields and sculptures. The viewing platform offers fascinating views of the city and the traffic circling far below.

On 11 November 1920 the body of the Unknown Soldier was placed beneath the arch to commemorate the dead of World War I. The tomb's eternal flame is lit every evening.

High relief by JP Corot, celebrating the Triumph of Napoleon

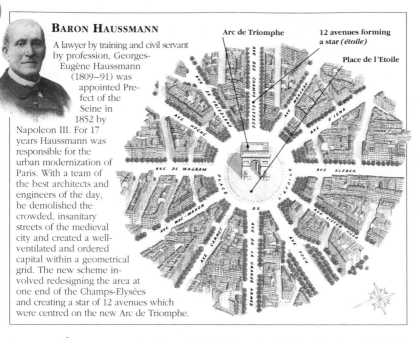

BARON HAUSSMANN

A lawyer by training and civil servant by profession, Georges-Eugène Haussmann (1809–91) was appointed Prefect of the Seine in 1852 by Napoleon III. For 17 years Haussmann was responsible for the urban modernization of Paris. With a team of the best architects and engineers of the day, he demolished the crowded, insanitary streets of the medieval city and created a well-ventilated and ordered capital within a geometrical grid. The new scheme involved redesigning the area at one end of the Champs-Elysées and creating a star of 12 avenues which were centred on the new Arc de Triomphe.

Arc de Triomphe

12 avenues forming a star *(étoile)*

Place de l'Etoile

Avenue des Champs-Elysées ❷

75008. **Map** 3 A5. **M** *Franklin D Roosevelt, George V.*

PARIS'S MOST well-known and popular thoroughfare was a desolate marshland until about 1667, when the master landscape-garden designer, André Le Nôtre *(see p169)*, created a tree-lined avenue which he named the Champs-Elysées. It has been the "triumphal way" ever since the home-coming of Napoleon's body from St Helena in 1840. Today, it is an ideal place to stop for a drink and observe the charm of Parisian life.

Palais de l'Elysée ❸

55 rue du Faubourg-St-Honoré 75008. **Map** 3 B5. **M** *St-Philippe-du-Roule.* **Not open** to the public.

SET AMID SPLENDID English-style gardens, the Elysée Palace was built in 1718 by Molet and has been the official residence of the President of the Republic since 1873. The palace has seen many changes over the centuries; Louis XV's mistress, Madame de Pompadour, had the site enlarged to suit her lavish lifestyle. It became a public entertainment park after the Revolution.

In the 19th century it was occupied by Napoleon's sister, Caroline, and her husband Murat. Two delightful rooms have been preserved from this period. General de Gaulle used to give press conferences in the Hall of Mirrors. Today, the President's apartments, with furniture by designer

Elysée guard

Philippe Starck, can be found on the first floor, in their English-style garden setting, opposite the rue de l'Elysée.

Petit Palais ❹

Av Winston Churchill 75008. **Map** 7 B1. **[** *01 42 65 12 73.* **M** *Champs-Elysées-Clémenceau.* **Open** 10am–5:40pm Tue–Sun. **Closed** public hols. ⚏ ⚼

BUILT FOR the Universal Exhibition in 1900, to stage a major display of French art, this jewel of a building now houses the Musée des Beaux-Arts de la Ville de Paris. The architect, Charles Girault, arranged the palace around a semi-circular

GRAND PALAIS

Exhibition space   Iron supports

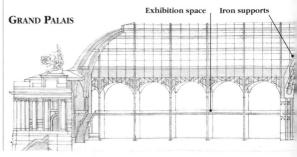

Pont Alexandre III, built between 1896–1900 for the Universal Exhibition

courtyard and garden, similar in style to the Grand Palais. The exhibits, which were donated by private collectors, are divided into sections. These include the Dutuit Collection of medieval and Renaissance *objets d'art*, paintings and drawings; the Tuck Collection of 18th-century furniture and *objets d'art*; and the City of Paris

Entrance to the Petit Palais

collection, with work by artists including Ingres, Delacroix and Courbet, and the landscape painters of the Barbizon School.

Grand Palais ❺

Porte A, avenue Eisenhower 75008. **Map** 7 A1. **⌂** *01 44 13 17 30.* **Ⓜ** *Champs-Elysées-Clémenceau.* **Open** *10am–8pm (10pm Wed) Wed–Mon.* **Closed** *public hols.* 🅰

Ｔｈｅ EXTERIOR of this huge palace combines an imposing Classical stone façade with a riot of Art Nouveau ironwork. It was built at the same time as the Petit Palais opposite, and has a splendid glass roof and bronze statues of flying horses and chariots at its four corners. The building looks most dramatic at night, when the glass roof glows with the lights from inside and the statues are silhouetted against the sky. The Great Hall and glass cupola can be seen from the interior during temporary exhibitions which are held in the Galeries Nationales du Grand Palais. The Salon des Antiquaires is temporarily closed for restoration.

Pont Alexandre III ❻

75008. **Map** 7 A1. **Ⓜ** *Champs-Elysées-Clémenceau.*

Ｔｈｉｓ ｉｓ PARIS'S prettiest bridge, with exuberant Art Nouveau decoration of gilt and bronze lamps, cupids and cherubs, nymphs and winged horses at either end. It was built between 1896 and 1900 to commemorate the 1892 French-Russian alliance, and in time for the Universal Exhibition in 1900. Pont Alexandre III was named after Tsar Alexander III (father of Nicholas II), who laid the foundation stone in October 1896.

The style of the bridge reflects that of the Grand Palais, to which it leads on the Right Bank. The construction of the bridge is a marvel of 19th-century engineering. It consists of a 6-m (18-ft) high single-span steel arch across the Seine. The design was subject to strict controls that prevented the bridge from obscuring the view of the Champs-Elysées or the Invalides, so today you can still enjoy the magnificent views from here.

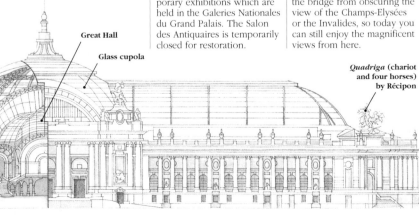

Great Hall

Glass cupola

Quadriga (chariot and four horses) by Récipon

Musée d'Art Moderne de la Ville de Paris ❼

11 avenue du Président-Wilson 75116. **Map** 6 E1. 🄲 *01 53 67 40 00.* 🄼 *Iéna.* **Open** *10am–7pm Sat, Sun, 10am–5:30pm Tue–Fri.* **Closed** *public hols.* 🈀 🈲 🈶

THIS MUSEUM covers trends in 20th-century art and is located in the east wing of the Palais de Tokyo. The Fauves and Cubists are well represented here. Highlights include Raoul Dufy's gigantic mural, *The Spirit of Electricity,* (created for the 1937 World Fair) and Matisse's *The Dance* (1932). Also exhibited here is a collection of Art Deco furniture from the period 1920–37.

Musée de la Mode et du Costume Palais Galliera ❽

10 av Pierre 1er de Serbie 75116. **Map** 6 D1. 🄲 *01 47 20 85 23.* 🄼 *Iéna, Alma–Marceau.* **Open** *10am–5:40pm Tue–Sun, but phone to check as only open for two exhibitions a year.* **Closed** *public hols.* 🈀

DEVOTED TO the evolution of fashion, this museum is housed in the Renaissance-style palace built for the Duchesse Maria de Ferrari Galliera in 1892. The collection includes more than 100,000 outfits and fashion accessories, from the 18th century to the present day. Donations have been made by such fashionable women as Baronne Hélène de Rothschild and Princess Grace of Monaco. Eminent couturiers such as Balmain and Balenciaga have donated their designs to the museum.

Because they are often extremely fragile, the fashion exhibits are displayed in rotation, usually in two major exhibitions each year. These shows can highlight a particular couturier's career or explore a single theme.

Trocadéro fountains in front of the Palais de Chaillot

Jardins du Trocadéro ⓫

75016. **Map** 6 D2. 🄼 *Trocadéro.*

THESE BEAUTIFUL gardens cover 10 ha (25 acres). Their centrepiece is a long rectangular ornamental pool, bordered by stone and bronze-gilt statues, which looks spectacular at night when the fountains are illuminated. The statues include *Woman* by Georges Braque and *Horse* by Georges Lucien Guyot. On either side of the pool, the slopes of the Chaillot hill lead gently down to the Seine and the Pont d'Iéna. There is a freshwater aquarium in the northeast corner of the gardens, which are richly laid out with trees, walkways, small streams and bridges.

Palais de Chaillot ⓬

17 place du Trocadéro 75016. **Map** 5 C2. 🄼 *Trocadéro.* **Open** *9:45am–6pm Wed–Mon.* **Closed** *public hols.* **Cinémathèque Française** *open for screenings:* 🄲 *01 56 26 01 01.*

THE PALAIS, with its huge, curved colonnaded wings each culminating in a vast pavilion, houses two museums, a theatre and a cinema. De- signed in Neo-Classical style for the 1937 Paris Exhibition by Azéma, Louis-Auguste Boileau and Jacques Carlu, it is adorned with sculptures and bas-reliefs. On the walls of the pavilions are gold inscriptions which were written by the poet and essayist, Paul Valéry.

The *parvis*, or square, situated between the two pavilions is highly decorated with bronze sculptures, ornamental pools and shooting fountains. On the terrace in front of the *parvis* stand two impressive bronzes, *Apollo* by Henri Bouchard and *Hercules* by Pommier. Steps lead down from the terrace to the Théâtre National de Chaillot which, after World War II, enjoyed fame for its avant-garde productions.

The basement of the palace houses Paris's main film institute, the Cinémathèque Française, founded by Henri Langlois in 1936. One of the areas devastated by a fire in 1997, the institute has been restored and screens a daily changing schedule of film classics. Still under renovation after the fire, the Musée du Cinéma Henri Langlois has a large collection of artifacts dating back to the origins of photography and cinema.

Musée National des Arts Asiatiques Guimet

6 place d'Iéna 75116. **Map** 6 D1. **C** 01 45 05 00 98. **M** Iéna. **Closed** for restoration until Dec 1999. New galleries opened at 19 avenue d'Iéna (phone to check opening hours).

ONE OF THE WORLD's leading museums of Asian art, the Guimet has the finest collection of Cambodian (Khmer) art in the West. It was originally set up in Lyon in 1879 by the industrialist and orientalist Emile Guimet, and moved to Paris in 1884. It includes an Asian research centre.

Buddha head from Musée Guimet

Musée National d'Ennery ⑩

59 avenue Foch 75016. **Map** 1 B5. **C** 01 45 53 57 96. **M** Porte Dauphine. **Open** 2–5:45pm Thu & Sun. **Closed** Aug.

THIS MANSION, which dates from the Second Empire period, contains two highly personal museums of precious *objets d'art*. Adolphe d'Ennery, the 19th-century dramatist and collector of Far Eastern art, assembled this array of Chinese and Japanese figures, ceramic boxes, ornaments and furniture, dating from the 17th to the 19th century.

PALAIS DE CHAILLOT

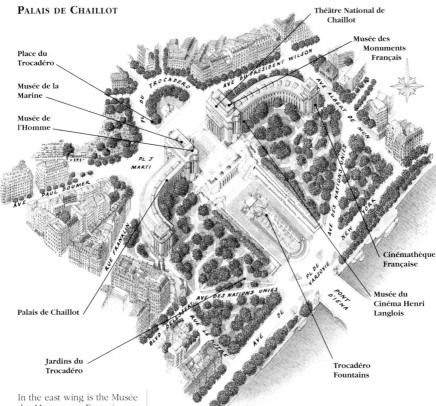

Place du Trocadéro

Musée de la Marine

Musée de l'Homme

Théâtre National de Chaillot

Musée des Monuments Français

Cinémathèque Française

Musée du Cinéma Henri Langlois

Palais de Chaillot

Jardins du Trocadéro

Trocadéro Fountains

In the east wing is the Musée des Monuments Français, designed in 1882 by Viollet-le-Duc. This museum plots the history of French monumental art from pre-Roman times to the 19th century. The Musée de l'Homme, in the west wing, portrays the history and development of humankind. Highlights include a mummy from the Incas and a rich African section. Also in the west wing is the Musée de la Marine, devoted to French naval history.

Some of these museums are due to move eventually to the nearby Palais de Tokyo, but the Palais de Chaillot will still be worth a visit, if only for the view of the Eiffel Tower.

Les Egouts

In front of 93 quai d'Orsay 75007.
Map 6 F2. 🄲 *01 47 05 10 29.*
Ⓜ *Pont-de-l'Alma.* **Open** *11am–4pm
(5pm in summer) Sat–Wed.* 🄰

O NE OF BARON HAUSSMANN'S
finest achievements, the
majority of Paris's sewers
(égouts) date from the Second
Empire. If laid end to end the
2,100 km (1,300 miles) of
sewers would stretch from
Paris to Istanbul. This century
the sewers became a popular
attraction with tourists. All
tours have been limited to a
small area around the quai
d'Orsay entrance and are now
on foot. A sewer museum has
been established here where
visitors can discover the
mysteries of underground
Paris. There are also displays
showing how the machinery
used in the sewers has
changed over the years.

Eiffel Tower ⑭

See p109.

No. 29 Avenue Rapp ⑮

75005. **Map** 6 E2. Ⓜ *Pont-de-l'Alma.*

A PRIME EXAMPLE of Art
Nouveau architecture, No.
29 avenue Rapp won its
designer, Jules Lavirotte, first
prize at the Concours des

**Original Art Nouveau doorway at
No. 29 avenue Rapp**

Façades de la Ville de Paris in
1901. Its ceramics and
brickwork are decorated with
animal and flower motifs
intermingling with female
figures. These are super-
imposed on a multi-coloured
sandstone base to produce a
façade that is deliberately
erotic, and was certainly
subversive in its day. Also
worth visiting nearby is
Lavirotte's building, complete
with watchtower, which can
be found in the square Rapp.

Champ-de-Mars ⑯

75007. **Map** 6 E3. Ⓜ *Ecole-Militaire.*
🆁🅴🆁 *Champ-de-Mars–Tour-Eiffel.*

T HE VAST GARDENS stretching
from the Eiffel Tower to
the Ecole Militaire (Military
School) were originally a
parade ground for
young officer cadets.
The area has
since been used
for horse-racing,
balloon ascents
and mass
ceremonies to
celebrate the
anniversary of the
Revolution on 14th
July. The first
ceremony was
held in 1790, in the
presence of a glum,
captive, Louis XVI.
Mammoth exhibitions were
held here in the late 19th
century, among them the
1889 World Fair for which the
Eiffel Tower was erected.

**A Paris balloon
ascent**

Ecole Militaire ⑰

1 place Joffre 75007. **Map** 6 F4.
Ⓜ *Ecole-Militaire.* **Visits** *by special
permission only – contact the
Commandant in writing.*

T HE ROYAL MILITARY academy
of Louis XV was founded
in 1751 to educate 500 sons of
impoverished officers. Louis XV
and Madame de Pompadour
commissioned architect
Jacques-Ange Gabriel to design
a building that would rival
Louis XVI's Hôtel des Invalides.
Financing the building became
a problem so a lottery was
authorized and a tax was
raised on playing cards.

**A 1751 engraving showing the
planning of the Ecole Militaire**

One of the main features
is the central pavilion – a
magnificent example of the
French Classical style, with
ten Corinthian columns
and a quadrangular
dome. Four figures
adorn the entab-
lature frieze,
symbolizing
France, Victory,
Force and Peace.
An early cadet at
the academy was
Napoleon, whose
passing-out report
stated that "he could
go far if the circum-
stances are right".

UNESCO ⑱

7 place de Fontenoy 75007.
Map 6 F5. 🄲 *01 45 68 10 00.*
Ⓜ *Ségur, Cambronne.* **Open** *9:30am–
12:30pm, 2:30–6pm Mon–Fri.*
Closed *public hols & during
conference sessions.* 🄰

T HIS IS the headquarters of
the United Nations
Educational, Scientific and
Cultural Organization
(UNESCO). The aim of the
organization is to contribute
to international peace and
security through education,
science and culture.
UNESCO is a treasure-trove
of modern art, including an
enormous mural by Picasso,
ceramics designed by Joan
Miró and sculptures by Henry
Moore. Another attractive
feature is the quiet Japanese
garden designed by Nogushi.

Eiffel Tower ⓮

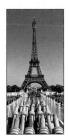

Eiffel Tower seen from the Trocadéro

BUILT FOR the Universal Exhibition of 1889, and to commemorate the centennial of the Revolution, the 320-m (1,051-ft) Eiffel Tower (Tour Eiffel) was meant to be a temporary addition to Paris's skyline. Designed by Gustave Eiffel, it was fiercely decried by 19th-century aesthetes. It stood as the world's tallest building until 1931, when New York's Empire State Building was completed.

Visitors' Checklist

Champ-de-Mars–Tour Eiffel. **Map** 6 D3. *01 44 11 23 11.* *Bir Hakeim.* *42, 69, 72, 82, 87, 91 to Champ-de-Mars.* *Champ-de-Mars.* *Tour Eiffel.* *on site.* ***Open*** *Sep–Jun: 9:30am–11pm; Jul & Aug: 9am–midnight.*

Daring Feats

The tower has always inspired crazy stunts. In 1912, Reichelt, a Parisian tailor, attempted to fly from the parapet with only a cape for wings. He plunged to his death in front of a large crowd.

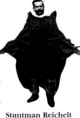

Stuntman Reichelt

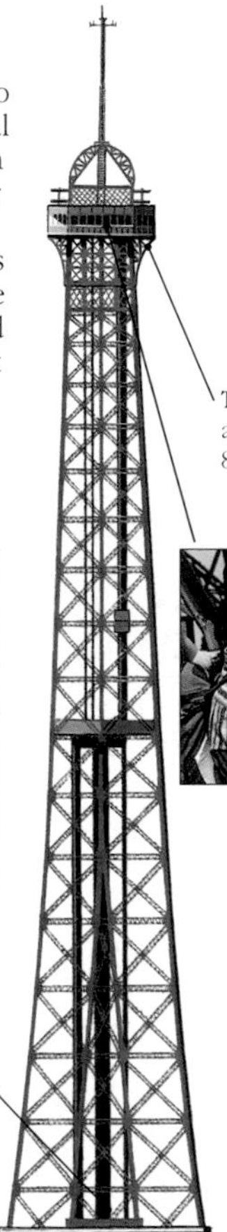

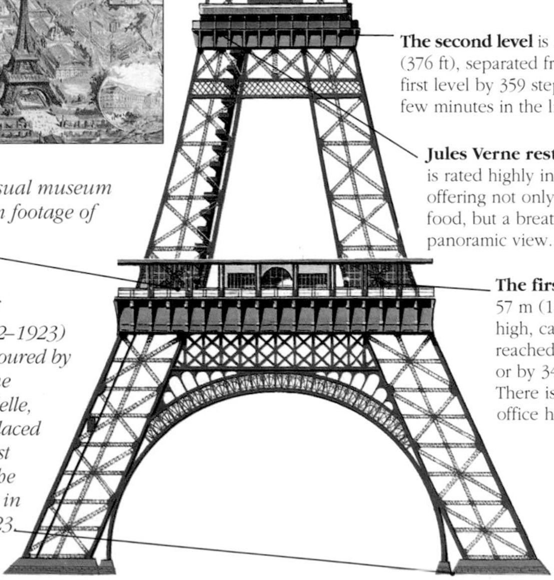

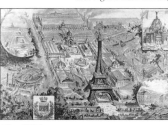

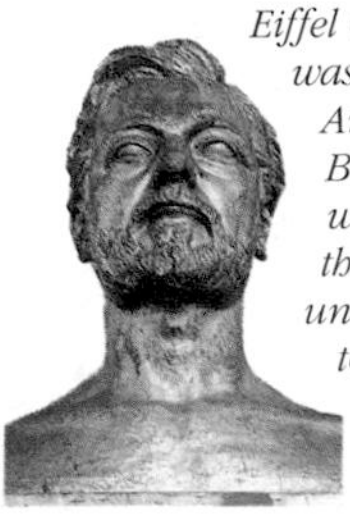

The third level, 276 m (899 ft) above the ground, can hold 800 people at a time.

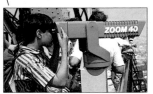

★ Viewing Gallery
On a clear day it is possible to see for 72 km (45 miles), including a distant view of Chartres Cathedral.

The double-decker lifts have a limited capacity, and during the tourist season there can be long waits. Queuing for the lifts requires patience and a good head for heights.

Star Features

- **★ Eiffel Bust**
- **★ Viewing Gallery**

Cineiffel
This small audio-visual museum shows historical film footage of the tower.

The second level is at 115 m (376 ft), separated from the first level by 359 steps or a few minutes in the lift.

Jules Verne restaurant is rated highly in Paris, offering not only superb food, but a breathtaking panoramic view.

★ Eiffel Bust
The achievement of Eiffel (1832–1923) was honoured by Antoine Bourdelle, who placed this bust under the tower in 1923.

The first level, 57 m (187 ft) high, can be reached by lift or by 345 steps. There is a post office here.

LES INVALIDES

Musée de l'Armée   Hôtel des Invalides   Cour d'Honneur

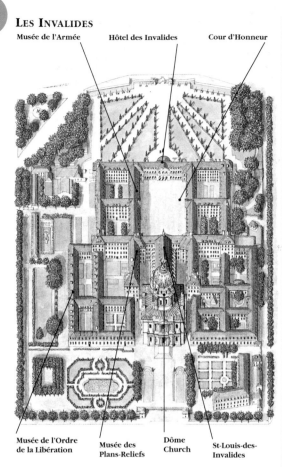

Musée de l'Ordre
de la Libération

Musée des
Plans-Reliefs

Dôme
Church

St-Louis-des-
Invalides

Hôtel des Invalides ⑲

75007. **Map** 7 A3. **☎** *01 44 42 37 70.*
M *Latour-Maubourg, Varenne.*
Open *10am–6pm daily.* **Closed** *1 Jan,
1 May, 1 Nov, 25 Dec.*

THIS IMPOSING building, from
which the area takes its
name, was commissioned by
Louis XIV in 1671 for his
wounded and homeless
veterans, many of whom had
become beggars. Designed
by Libéral Bruand, it was
completed in 1676 by Jules
Hardouin-Mansart. He later
incorporated the Dôme Church,
with its glittering golden roof,
which was built as Louis XIV's
private chapel. Nearly 6,000
soldiers once resided here.
Today there are less than 100.
The harmonious Classical
façade is one of the most
impressive sights in Paris, a
masterpiece of French 17th-
century architecture. The entire
ensemble is vast, brimming
with architectural and historical
splendour, with its tree-lined
esplanade stretching to the
Seine. The building houses
the Musée de l'Armée and
the Musée de l'Ordre de la
Libération. This was set up
to honour feats of heroism
during World War II under
the leadership of Charles de
Gaulle. The story is told using

documents, photographs and
mementos. The Musée des
Plans-Reliefs in the right wing
houses a large collection of
detailed military models of
French forts and fortified
towns considered top secret
until the 1950s. Bruand's Cour
d'Honneur is still used for
military parades.

Musée de l'Armée ⑳

Hôtel des Invalides 75007. **Map** 7 A3.
☎ *01 44 42 37 70.* **M** *Latour-
Maubourg, Varenne.* **Open** *10am–
6pm (5pm winter) daily.* **Closed** *1 Jan,
1 May, 1 Nov, 25 Dec.*

THIS IS ONE of the most
comprehensive museums
of military history in the world,
with exhibits ranging from
the Stone Age to World War II.
It is housed in two galleries,
situated on either side of the
magnificent courtyard of the
Hôtel des Invalides.
  Among the vast collection
is an exhibit recalling the
victories and defeats of France
through history, dedicated
mainly to the Napoleonic
era. Uniforms, weapons and
models are on display, as well
as the emperor's death mask
and stuffed horse, Vizier. Other
exhibits include François I's
ivory hunting horns, Oriental
arms from China, Japan and
Turkey, and a model of the
1944 Normandy landing.

St-Louis-des-Invalides ㉑

Hôtel des Invalides 75007. **Map** 7 A3.
M *Varenne, Latour-Maubourg.* **☎**
01 44 42 37 65. **Open** *9:30am–5pm
(4:30pm winter) daily.*

ALSO KNOWN AS the "soldiers'
church", this is the chapel
of the Hôtel des Invalides. It
was built from 1679 to 1708

The façade of the Musée de l'Armée

Altar of St-Louis-des-Invalides with banners seized in battle

by Jules Hardouin-Mansart, according to Bruand's design. The stark, Classical interior is well-proportioned, designed in the shape of a Greek cross.

There is a fine 17th-century organ, built by Alexandre Thierry, on which the first performance of Berlioz's *Requiem* was given on 5 December 1837, with more than 200 musicians and choristers participating.

Dôme Church ㉒

Hôtel des Invalides, avenue de Tourville.
Map 7 A3. 01 44 42 37 67.
Latour-Maubourg, Varenne. 32, 63, 93 to Les Invalides. Invalides. Tour Eiffel. **Open** Oct–Mar: 10am–5pm; Apr–Sep: 10am–6pm daily. **Closed** 1 Jan, 1 May, 17 Jun, 1 Nov, 25 Dec.

JULES HARDOUIN-MANSART was asked in 1676 by the Sun King, Louis XIV, to build the Dôme Church to complement the existing buildings of the Invalides military refuge, designed by Libéral Bruand, and to reflect the splendour of his reign. The Dôme was to be reserved for the exclusive use of the Sun King and as the location of royal tombs.

The resulting masterpiece complements the surrounding buildings and is one of the greatest examples of 17th-century French architecture, the period known as the *grand siècle*. After Louis XIV's death, plans to bury the royal

family in the church were abandoned; it became a monument to Bourbon glory.

The main attraction has to be the tomb of Napoleon; 20 years after his death on the island of St Helena, his body was returned to France on the authority of Louis-Philippe. His remains were installed in the crypt, encased in six coffins within an enormous red porphyry sarcophagus, resting on a pedestal of green granite. His son and brothers, Jerôme and Joseph, are also entombed in the crypt.

Marshal Foch, commander of the allied troops during World War I, is buried here. There is also a memorial to Sébastien le Prestre de Vauban, Louis XIV's military architect.

Dôme Church with cupola, first gilded in 1715

Musée Rodin ㉓

77 rue de Varenne 75007. **Map** 7 B3.
01 47 05 01 34. Varenne.
Open 9:30am–5:45pm (4:45pm winter) Tue–Sun. **Closed** 1 Jan, 1 May, 25 Dec. restricted.

AUGUSTE RODIN (1840–1917), widely regarded as one of the greatest French sculptors, lived and worked in the Hôtel Biron, an elegant 18th-century mansion, from 1908 until his death. In return for a state-owned flat and studio, Rodin left his work to the nation, and it is now exhibited here. Some of his most celebrated

sculptures are on display in the garden: *The Burghers of Calais, The Thinker, The Gates of Hell (see p116)* and *Balzac*.

The indoor exhibits are arranged in chronological order, spanning the whole of Rodin's career. Highlights of the collection include *The Kiss* and *Eve*.

Sainte-Clothilde ㉔

12 rue Martignac 75007.
Map 7 B3. 01 44 18 62 64.
Solférino, Varenne, Invalides.
Open 8am–7pm daily.

DESIGNED BY the German-born architect Franz Christian Gau and built in 1846–56, this Neo-Gothic church was inspired by the mid-19th-century enthusiasm for the Middle Ages, made fashionable by such writers as Victor Hugo. The church is noted for its imposing twin towers, clearly visible from across the Seine.

The interior decoration includes wall paintings by James Pradier and stained-glass windows with scenes relating to the patron saint of the church. The composer César Franck was organist here from 1858 to 1890.

Fontaine des Quatre Saisons ㉕

57–59 rue de Grenelle 75007.
Map 7 C4. rue du Bac.

THE EMINENT sculptor Edmé Bouchardon was commissioned in 1739 to design an attractive and practical fountain to supply water to the wealthy who lived around the boulevard Raspail. It is decorated with large allegorical figures of the city of Paris and bas-reliefs of the four seasons. In the house behind the fountain (No. 59) lived Alfred de Musset, the 19th-century novelist.

Rodin's *The Thinker* in museum garden

THE LEFT BANK

HE LEFT BANK has long been associated with poets, philosophers,
artists and radical thinkers of all
kinds. It still has its share of bohemian
street life and pavement cafés, but
the smart set has moved in,
patronizing Yves St-Laurent
and the exclusive interior
design shops in rue Jacob.
   The Latin Quarter is the
ancient area lying between
the Seine and Luxembourg
Gardens, and is today filled
with bookshops, art galleries
and cafés. The boulevard St-
Michel, bordering the Latin quarter
and St-Germain-des-Prés, has slowly
given way to commerce, and is full of

**Clock in the
Musée d'Orsay**

fast-food outlets and cheap shops.
The surrounding maze of narrow,
cobbled streets has retained its character, with ethnic shops and avant-
garde theatres dominated by the
façade of the Sorbonne, France's
first university, built in 1253.
   Many Parisians dream of
living near the Luxembourg
Gardens, a quiet area with
charming old streets, gateways and elaborate gardens
full of paths, lawns and tree-
lined avenues. Students come
here to chat, and on warm days,
old men still meet underneath the
chestnut trees to play chess or the
traditional French game of *boules*.

SIGHTS AT A GLANCE

Churches
Panthéon **13**
St-Etienne-du-Mont **12**
St-Germain-des-Prés **5**
St-Julien-le-Pauvre **10**
St-Séverin **9**

St-Sulpice **15**
Val-de-Grâce **17**

Museums and Galleries
Musée de Cluny **8**
Musée Eugène Delacroix **6**
Musée d'Orsay pp116–17 **1**

Fountains
Fontaine de l'Observatoire **16**

**Historic Buildings
and Streets**
Boulevard St-Germain **2**
Ecole Nationale Supérieure
   des Beaux Arts **4**
Palais du Luxembourg **14**
Quai Voltaire **3**
Rue de l'Odéon **7**
La Sorbonne **11**

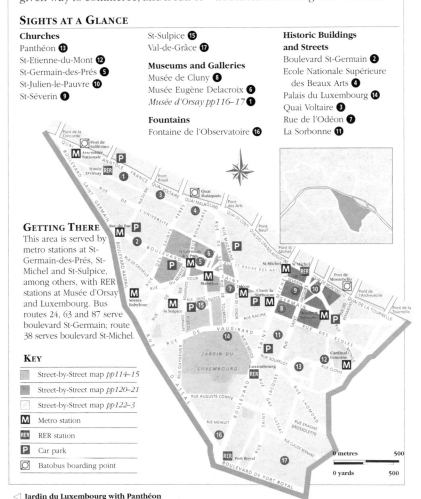

GETTING THERE
This area is served by
metro stations at St-
Germain-des-Prés, St-
Michel and St-Sulpice,
among others, with RER
stations at Musée d'Orsay
and Luxembourg. Bus
routes 24, 63 and 87 serve
boulevard St-Germain; route
38 serves boulevard St-Michel.

KEY

	Street-by-Street map *pp114–15*
	Street-by-Street map *pp120–21*
	Street-by-Street map *pp122–3*
M	Metro station
RER	RER station
P	Car park
	Batobus boarding point

◁ **Jardin du Luxembourg with Panthéon**

Street-by-Street: St-Germain-des-Prés

Aᶠᵗᵉʳ WORLD WAR II, St-Germain-des-Prés became synonymous with intellectual life centred on bars and cafés. Philosophers, writers, actors and musicians mingled in the cellar nightspots and brasseries, where existentialist philosophy co-existed with American jazz. The area is now smarter than in the heyday of Jean-Paul Sartre and Simone de Beauvoir, the enigmatic singer Juliette Greco and the New Wave film-makers. However, the writers are still around, enjoying the pleasures of sitting in Les Deux Magots, Café de Flore and other haunts. The 17th-century buildings have survived, but signs of change are evident in the affluent shops dealing in antiques, books and fashion.

Organ grinder in St-Germain

Les Deux Magots became a focus of bohemian and literary activity in the 1920s.

Café de Flore, the former favourite haunt of Jean-Paul Sartre, Simone de Beauvoir and other French intellectuals, still has a classic Art Deco interior.

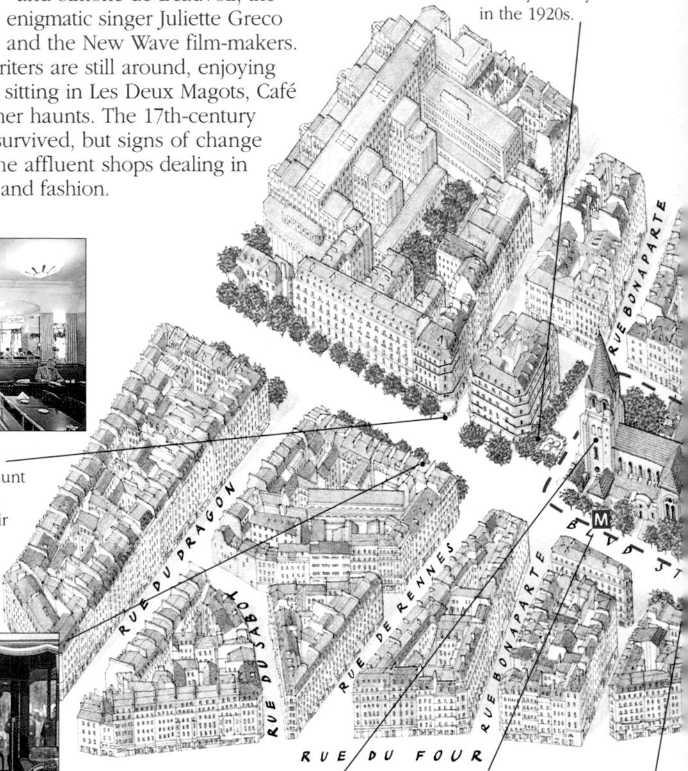

RUE DU DRAGON
RUE DU SABOT
RUE DE RENNES
RUE BONAPARTE
RUE BONAPARTE
RUE DU FOUR

Metro St-Germain-des-Prés

Brasserie Lipp, decorated with colourful ceramics, is a renowned brasserie frequented by politicians.

★ **St-Germain-des-Prés**
The philosopher René Descartes is among the notables buried here in Paris's oldest church ❺

★ **Boulevard St-Germain**
Café terraces, boutiques, cinemas, restaurants and bookshops characterize the central section of the Left Bank's main street ❷

See Street Finder maps 7, 8

STAR SIGHTS

★ St-Germain-des-Prés

★ Boulevard St-Germain

★ Musée Delacroix

KEY

− − − Suggested route

LOCATOR MAP
See Street Finder maps 7, 8

★ **Musée Delacroix**
The home of the Romantic painter Eugène Delacroix (1798–1863) is now a museum devoted to his art ⑥

Palais Abbatial was the residence of abbots from 1586 till the 1789 Revolution.

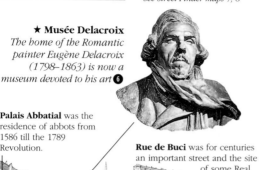

Rue de Buci was for centuries an important street and the site of some Real Tennis courts. It now holds a lively market.

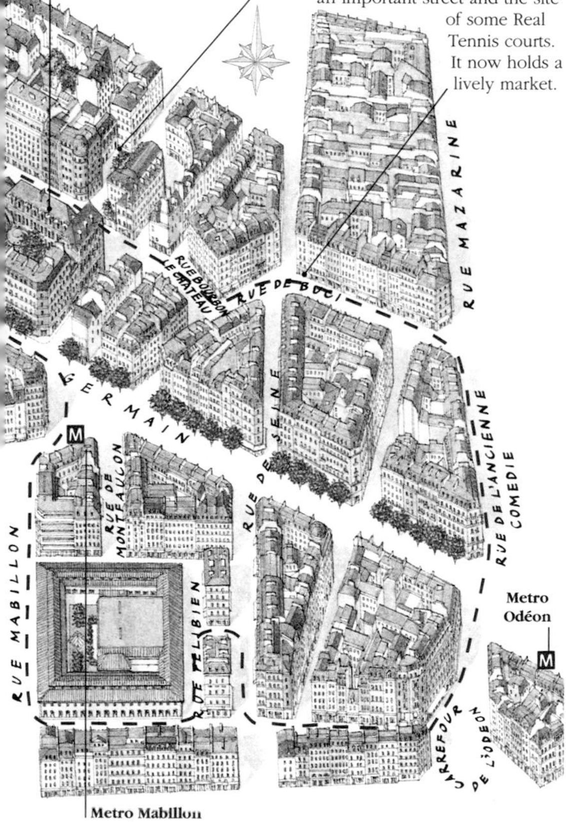

Metro Odéon

Metro Mabillon

| 0 metres | 100 |
| 0 yards | 100 |

Musée d'Orsay ①

See pp116–17.

Boulevard St-Germain ②

75006, 75007. **Map** 8 D4.
Ⓜ Solférino, Rue du Bac, St-Germain-des-Prés, Mabillon, Odéon.

THE LEFT BANK'S most celebrated thoroughfare curves across three districts from the Ile St-Louis to the Pont de la Concorde. The architecture is homogeneous because the boulevard was another of Baron Hauss-mann's bold strokes of 19th-century urban planning, but it encompasses a wide range of different lifestyles from bohemian to bourgeois.
    Starting from the east, it passes Musée de Cluny and the Sorbonne. It is most lively from boulevard St-Michel to St-Germain-des-Prés, with its café culture.

Quai Voltaire ③

75006, 75007. **Map** 8 D3.
Ⓜ Rue du Bac.

THE QUAI VOLTAIRE is now home to some of the most important antiques dealers in Paris. Many famous people have lived in the attractive 18th-century houses, among others Voltaire at No. 27 and Richard Wagner, Jean Sibelius and Oscar Wilde at No. 19.

Plaque marking the house in quai Voltaire where Voltaire died in 1778

Musée d'Orsay ●

IN 1986, 47 YEARS AFTER it had closed as a mainline railway station, Victor Laloux's superb turn-of-the-century building reopened as the Musée d'Orsay. Originally built as the Orléans railway terminus in the heart of Paris, it narrowly avoided demolition in the 1970s. During its conversion to a museum much of the original architecture was retained. The new museum presents the rich diversity of visual arts from 1848 to 1914 and explains the social, political and technological context in which they were created. Although the majority of the exhibits are paintings and sculptures, there are also displays of furniture, the decorative arts, cinema and the newspaper industry.

Young Dancer of Fourteen (1881) by Edgar Dégas

The Gates of Hell *(1880–1917)*
Rodin included figures that he had already created, such as The Thinker *and* The Kiss, *in this famous gateway.*

Dancing at the Moulin de la Galette *(1876)*
Renoir painted this picture outside to capture the light as it filtered through the trees.

The Dance *(1867–8)*
Carpeaux's dynamic sculpture caused a scandal when it was first unveiled in 1869.

KEY TO FLOORPLAN

Architecture & Decorative Arts	Naturalism and Symbolism
Sculpture	Art Nouveau
Painting before 1870	Temporary exhibitions
Impressionism	Non-exhibition space
Neo-Impressionism	

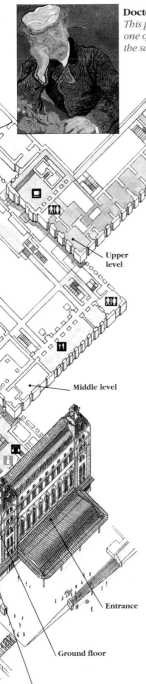

Doctor Paul Gachet *(1890)*
This portrait by Van Gogh is one of three and was painted the same year the artist died.

GALLERY GUIDE

The ground floor has works from the mid- to late 19th century. The middle level features Art Nouveau decorative art and late 19th- to early 20th-century paintings and sculptures. The upper level has Impressionist and Neo-Impressionist art.

Upper level

Middle level

Entrance

Ground floor

Shop entrance

VISITORS' CHECKLIST

1 rue de Bellechasse. **Map** 8 D2.
01 40 49 48 14. Solférino.
24, 68, 69, 84 to Quai A.
France; 73 to Rue Solférino; 63, 83, 84, 94 to Bd St-Germain.
Musée d'Orsay. Musée d'Orsay. Quai d'Anatole France. **Open** Jun–Sep: 9am–6pm Tue–Sun (9:45pm Thu); Oct–May: 10am–6pm Tue–Sat (9:45pm Thu), 9am–6pm Sun. **Closed** 1 Jan, 1 May, 25 Dec.

EXPLORING THE MUSÉE D'ORSAY

Many of the paintings in the Musée d'Orsay came from the Louvre and the Impressionist collection once in the Jeu de Paume. Paintings from before 1870 are on the ground floor, presided over by Thomas Couture's massive *Romans of Decadence*. Neo-Classical masterpieces, such as Ingres' *La Source*, hang near Romantic works like Delacroix's turbulent *Tiger Hunt*. These exotic visions contrast with Realist works by artists like Courbet and early canvases by Degas and Manet, including the latter's famous *Olympia*.

The museum's central aisle overflows with sculpture, from Daumier's satirical busts of members of parliament to Carpeaux's exuberant *The Dance* and Rodin's *The Gates of Hell*. Decorative arts and architecture are on the middle level, where there is also a display of Art Nouveau – sinuous lines

Blue Waterlilies (1919) **by Claude Monet**

characterize Lalique's jewellery and glassware and the designs of Hector Guimard, who produced the characteristic curvy entrances of the Paris metro.

Among the many highlights of the Impressionist rooms on the upper level are Monet's *Rouen Cathedral* series *(see p257)* and Renoir's joyful *Moulin de la Galette*. The Post-Impressionist collection includes the *Eglise d'Auvers* by Van Gogh and works by Cézanne, Seurat's pointillist compositions such as *Le Cirque*, Gauguin's highly coloured Symbolist works, Toulouse-Lautrec's depictions of Parisian women and nightlife, and Rousseau's charmingly naive dream world. Among the highlights of the post-1900 display is Matisse's *Luxe, Calme et Volupté*.

Le Déjeuner sur l'Herbe (1863) **by Edouard Manet**

The façade of the Ecole Nationale Supérieure des Beaux Arts

Ecole Nationale Supérieure des Beaux Arts ❹

14 rue Bonaparte 75006. **Map** 8 E3.
🇨 01 47 03 50 00. Ⓜ St-Germain-des-Prés. **Open** to the public 2–5pm 3rd Mon of each month. 🖼 by appt.

THE MAIN FRENCH school of fine arts has an enviable position at the corner of the rue Bonaparte and the riverside quai Malaquais. It is housed in several buildings, the most imposing being the 19th-century Palais des Etudes. A host of budding French and foreign painters and architects have crossed the large courtyard, which contains a 17th-century chapel, to study in the ateliers of the school. Young American architects, in particular, have come here to study over the past century.

St-Germain-des-Prés ❺

3 place St-Germain-des-Prés 75006.
Map 8 E4. 🇨 01 43 25 41 71.
Ⓜ St-Germain-des-Prés.
Open 8:30am–7:30pm daily.

THIS IS THE OLDEST CHURCH in Paris, originating in 542 as a basilica to house holy relics. It became an immensely powerful Benedictine abbey, rebuilt in the 11th century, but most of it was destroyed by fire in 1794. Major restoration took place in the 19th century. One of the three original towers survives, housing one of the oldest belfries in France. The interior of the church is an interesting mix of architectural styles, with 6th-century marble columns, Gothic vaulting and Romanesque arches. Famous tombs include that of 17th-century philosopher René Descartes.

Musée Eugène Delacroix ❻

6 rue de Fürstenberg 75006. **Map** 8 E4.
🇨 01 44 41 86 50. Ⓜ St-Germain-des-Prés. **Open** 9:30am–5pm Wed–Mon.
🖼 🖼 🖼

THE LEADING non-conformist Romantic painter Eugène Delacroix lived and worked here from 1857 till his death in 1863. Here he painted *The Entombment of Christ* and *The Way to Calvary* (which now hang in the museum). He also created superb murals for the Chapel of the Holy Angels in the nearby St-Sulpice church.

The apartment and garden studio has a portrait of George Sand, Delacroix self-portraits and sketches. There are also temporary exhibitions.

Jacob Wrestling with the Angel by Delacroix, in St-Sulpice *(see p123)*

Rue de l'Odéon ❼

75006. **Map** 8 F5. Ⓜ Odéon.

OPENED IN 1779 to improve access to the Odéon theatre, this was the first street in Paris to have pavements with gutters and it still has many 18th-century houses. Sylvia Beach's bookshop, the original Shakespeare & Company, stood at No. 12 from 1921 to 1940. It was a magnet for writers like James Joyce, Ezra Pound and Hemingway.

Musée de Cluny ❽

6 place Paul-Painlevé. **Map** 9 A5.
🇨 01 53 73 78 00. Ⓜ Cluny, St-Michel, Odéon. 🇷 St-Michel. **Open** 9:15am–5:45pm Wed–Mon. **Closed** 1 Jan, 1 Nov, 25 Dec. 🖼 🖼

THE MUSEUM, now officially known as the Musée National du Moyen Age – Thermes de Cluny, offers a unique combination of Gallo-

Stone heads of the Kings of Judah carved around 1220

St-Séverin ❾

1 rue-des-Prêtres-St-Séverin 75005.
Map 9 A4. 🇨 01 42 34 93 50. Ⓜ St-Michel. **Open** 11am–7:45pm Mon–Fri, 11am–8pm Sat, 9am–9pm Sun.

ST-SEVERIN, one of the most beautiful churches in Paris, is named after a 6th-century hermit. It is a perfect example of the Flamboyant Gothic style. Construction finished in the early 16th century and included a remarkable double aisle encircling the chancel. In the garden stands the church's medieval gable-roofed charnel house.

Gargoyles adorning the gables of the Flamboyant Gothic St-Séverin

The School **woodcarving (English, early 16th century)**

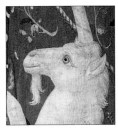
Roman ruins, incorporated into a medieval mansion, and one of the world's finest collections of medieval art and crafts. The museum's name came from the Abbot of Cluny in Burgundy, Pierre de Chalus, who bought the ruins in 1330. The present building was erected between 1485–98.

Among the star exhibits are the tapestries, remarkable for their quality, age and state of preservation. The highlight of the sculpture section is the Gallery of the Kings, while one of Cluny's most precious items, the Golden Rose of Basel from 1330, is found in the collection of jewellery and metalwork. Other parts of the collection include stained glass, woodcarvings, Books of Hours and enamelwork.

St-Julien-le-Pauvre ⑩

1 rue St-Julien-le-Pauvre 75005. **Map** 9 A4. **☎** 01 43 29 09 09. **M** St-Michel. **RER** St-Michel. **Open** 10am–noon, 3–6pm Sun–Fri.

THE CHURCH is one of the oldest in Paris, dating from between 1165 and 1220. The university held its official meetings in the church until 1524, when a student protest created so much damage that university meetings were barred from the church by parliament. It has belonged to the Melchite sect of the Greek Orthodox Church since 1889, and is now the setting for classical and religious concerts.

La Sorbonne ⑪

47 rue des Ecoles 75005. **Map** 9 A5. **☎** 01 40 46 22 11. **M** Cluny-La Sorbonne, Maubert-Mutualité. **Open** 9am–5pm Mon–Fri. **Closed** public hols.

THE SORBONNE, seat of the University of Paris until 1969, was established in 1253 by Robert de Sorbon, confessor to Louis IX, for 16 poor scholars to study theology. From these modest origins the college became the centre of scholastic theology. In 1469, three printing machines were brought from Mainz, and the first printing house in France was founded. The college's opposition to liberal 18th-century philosophical ideas led to its suppression during the Revolution. It was re-established by Napoleon in 1806, and the 17th-century buildings replaced. In 1969 the Sorbonne split into 13 separate universities, but the building still holds some lectures.

St-Etienne-du-Mont ⑫

Place Ste-Geneviève 75005. **Map** 13 A1. **☎** 01 43 54 11 79. **M** Cardinal Lemoine. **Open** 8am–noon, 2–7pm daily. **Closed** public hols, Mon during Jul–Aug. 📷

THIS REMARKABLE church houses the shrine of Saint Geneviève, patron saint of Paris, and the remains of the great literary figures Racine and Pascal. Some parts of the church are Gothic while others date from the Renaissance, including the magnificent rood screen.

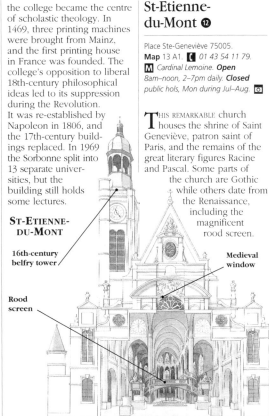

ST-ETIENNE-DU-MONT

16th-century belfry tower

Rood screen

Medieval window

Street-by-Street: Latin Quarter

Since the middle ages this riverside quarter has been dominated by the Sorbonne, and acquired its name from the early Latin-speaking students. It dates back to the Roman town across from the Ile de la Cité; at that time the rue St-Jacques was one of the main roads out of Paris. The area is generally associated with artists, intellectuals and a bohemian way of life; it also has a history of political unrest. In 1871, the place St-Michel became the centre of the Paris Commune, and in May 1968 it was a site of student uprisings. Today the eastern half has become sufficiently chic, however, to house members of the Establishment.

Latin jazz

★ **St-Séverin**
Begun in the 13th century, this church took three centuries to build and is a fine example of the Flamboyant Gothic style ⑨

Metro St-Michel Ⓜ

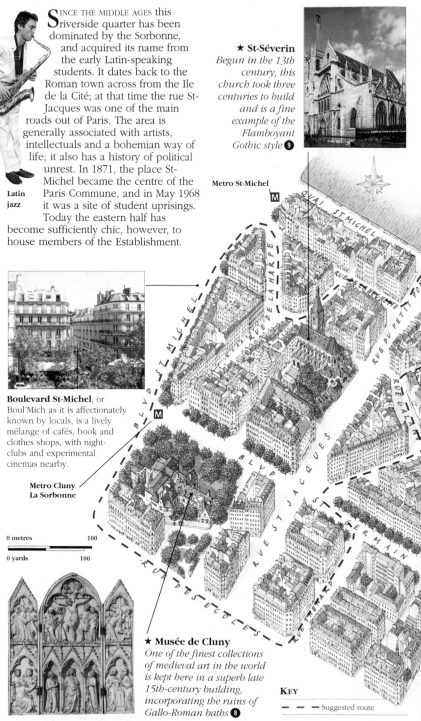

Boulevard St-Michel, or Boul'Mich as it is affectionately known by locals, is a lively mélange of cafés, book and clothes shops, with night-clubs and experimental cinemas nearby.

Metro Cluny La Sorbonne

0 metres   100
0 yards   100

QUAI ST MICHEL
BLVD ST MICHEL
RUE DE LA HARPE
RUE ST SÉVERIN
RUE DU PETIT PONT
RUE GALANDE
BLVD ST JACQUES
RUE ST JACQUES
BLVD ST GERMAIN
RUE DES ECOLES
RUE ST JACQUES

★ **Musée de Cluny**
One of the finest collections of medieval art in the world is kept here in a superb late 15th-century building, incorporating the ruins of Gallo-Roman baths ⑧

KEY

– – – Suggested route

LOCATOR MAP
See Street Finder maps 8, 9, 12, 13

★ **St-Julien-le-Pauvre**
Rebuilt in the 17th century, this church was used to store animal feed in the Revolution ⑩

Metro
Maubert
Mutualité

Ⓜ

STAR SIGHTS

★ Musée de Cluny

★ St-Séverin

★ St-Julien-le-Pauvre

Panthéon ⑬

Place du Panthéon 7500. **Map** 13 A1.
🄲 01 44 32 18 00. Ⓜ *Maubert-Mutualité, Cardinal-Lemoine.* **Open** *Oct–Mar: 10am–6:15pm; Apr–Sep: 9:30am–6:30pm daily.* **Closed** *1 Jan, 1 May, 11 Nov, 25 Dec.*

WHEN LOUIS XV recovered from a desperate illness in 1744, he was so grateful to be alive that he conceived a magnificent church to honour Saint Geneviève, the patron saint of Paris. The French architect Jacques-Germain Soufflot planned the church in Neo-Classical style. Work began in 1764 and was completed in 1790 under the control of Guillaume Rondelet,

The Panthéon Interior
The interior has four aisles arranged in the shape of a Greek cross, from the centre of which the great dome rises.

ten years after Soufflot's death. But with the Revolution underway the church was soon turned into a pantheon – a monument housing the tombs of France's great heroes. Napoleon returned it to the Church in 1806, but it was secularized and then desecularized once more before finally being made a civic building in 1885.

The façade, inspired by the Rome Pantheon, is decorated with a pediment relief by David d'Angers, depicting the mother country granting laurels to her great men. Among those resting here are Voltaire, Rousseau and Zola. Also here are the ashes of Pierre and Marie Curie and André Malraux.

Iron-Framed Dome
The fresco in the dome's stone cupola represents the Glorification of Sainte Geneviève, *commissioned by Napoleon in 1811.*

The dome lantern

The dome galleries

Entrance

Crypt
Under the building, the vast crypt divides into galleries flanked by Doric columns. Many French notables rest here, including Voltaire and Emile Zola.

Street-by-Street: Luxembourg Quarter

SITUATED ONLY A FEW STEPS from the bustle of St-Germain-des-Prés, this graceful and historic area offers a peaceful haven in the heart of a modern city. The Jardin du Luxembourg and Palais du Luxembourg dominate the surroundings. The gardens became fully open to the public in the 19th century under the ownership of the Comte de Provence (later to become Louis XVIII), when for a small fee visitors could come in and feast on fruit from the orchard. Today the gardens, palace and old houses on the streets to the north remain unspoilt and attract many visitors.

STAR SIGHTS

★ St-Sulpice

★ Palais du Luxembourg

To St-Germain-des-Prés

Place St-Sulpice, ringed by flowering chestnut trees, was begun in 1754.

★ St-Sulpice
This huge Classical church, by six different architects, took over a century to build ⓯

RUE HENRI DE JOUVENEL – RUE FÉROU

RUE SERVANDONI

RUE GARANCIÈRE

RUE DE TOURNON

RUE DE VAUGIRARD

Jardin du Luxembourg is a popular garden where people come to relax, sunbathe, sail boats in the pond or admire the many beautiful statues erected in the 19th century.

| 0 metres | 100 |
| 0 yards | 100 |

★ Palais du Luxembourg
First built as a royal residence, the palace has been used for various purposes from prison to Luftwaffe headquarters. This garden façade was added in 1841 ⓮

KEY

– – – Suggested route

LOCATOR MAP
See Street Finder maps 8, 12, 13

Fontaine de Médicis is a 17th-century fountain in the style of an Italian grotto. It is thought to have been designed by Salomon de Brosse.

Saint Geneviève, patron saint of Paris, whose prayers saved Paris from the Huns in AD 451, is honoured by this statue by Michel-Louis Victor in 1845.

Palais du Luxembourg 🄯

15 rue de Vaugirard 75006. **Map** 8 E5. ☎ 01 42 34 20 00. Ⓜ Odéon. Ⓡ *Luxembourg. **Visits** organized first Sun of each month through the Caisse Nationale de Monuments.* ☎ 01 44 61 20 89. *Apply by 1st of each month.* ♿

NOW THE HOME of the French Senate, this palace was built to remind Marie de' Médici, widow of Henri IV, of her native Florence. By the time it was finished (1631) she had been banished from Paris, but it remained a royal palace until the Revolution. Since then the palace has been used (briefly) as a prison, and in World War II it served as headquarters for the German Luftwaffe.

It was designed by Salomon de Brosse in the style of the Pitti Palace in Florence.

St-Sulpice 🄯

Place St-Sulpice 75006. **Map** 8 E5. ☎ 01 46 33 21 78. Ⓜ *St-Sulpice.* **Open** *7:30am–7:15pm daily.* 📷

THIS HUGE and imposing church was started in 1646 and took more than a century to finish. The result is a simple façade with two tiers of elegant columns and two mismatched towers at the ends. Large arched windows fill the vast interior with light.

In the side chapel to the right are murals by Eugène Delacroix, including *Jacob Wrestling with the Angel (see p118)* and *Heliodorus Driven from the Temple.*

Carpeaux's fountain sculpture

Fontaine de l'Observatoire 🄯

Place Ernest Denis, avenue de l'Observatoire 7500. **Map** 12 E2. Ⓡ *Port Royal.*

SITUATED AT THE southern tip of the Jardin du Luxembourg, this is one of the finest fountains in Paris. The central sculpture, by Jean-Baptiste Carpeaux, was erected in 1873. Made of bronze, it has four women holding aloft a globe representing four continents – the fifth, Oceania, was left out for reasons of symmetry. There are some subsidiary figures, including dolphins, horses and a turtle.

Val-de-Grâce 🄯

1 place Alphonse-Laveran 75005. **Map** 12 F2. ☎ 01 40 51 51 92. Ⓡ *Port Royal.* **Open** *1:30–5:30pm daily.*

THIS IS ONE of the most beautiful churches in France, built for Anne of Austria (wife of Louis XIII) in gratitude for the birth of her son. Young Louis XIV himself laid the first stone in 1645.

Designed by François Mansart, the church is noted for its lead-and-gilt dome. In the cupola is Pierre Mignard's enormous fresco, with over 200 triple-life-size figures. The six huge, twisted marble columns that frame the altar are similar to those made by Bernini for St Peter's in Rome.

The Classical two-storey west front of St-Sulpice with its two towers

FURTHER AFIELD

MANY OF PARIS'S famous sights are slightly out of the city centre. Montmartre, long a mecca for artists and writers, still retains much of its bohemian atmosphere, and Montparnasse is full of bustling cafés and theatre crowds. The famous Cimetière du Père Lachaise numbers Chopin, Oscar Wilde and Jim Morrison among its dead, and, along with the parks and gardens, provides a tranquil escape from sightseeing. Modern architecture can be seen at Fondation Le Corbusier and La Défense, and there is a huge selection of museums to visit. To the northeast, the science museum at La Villette provides an educational family day out.

SIGHTS AT A GLANCE

Museums and Galleries
Musée de Cristal de
   Baccarat ⑨
Musée Gustave Moreau ⑧
Musée Marmottan ⑤
Musée National d'Histoire
   Naturelle ㉓
Museum National des Arts
   Africains et Océaniens ⑲

Churches and Mosques
Mosquée de Paris/Institut
   musulman ㉖
Sacré-Coeur ⑪
St-Alexandre-Nevsky ⑥

Parks and Gardens
Bois de Boulogne ②
Jardin des Plantes ㉔
Parc André Citroën ㉗
Parc des Buttes-
   Chaumont ⑰

Parc Monceau ⑦
Parc Montsouris ㉒

Modern Architecture
La Défense ①
Fondation Le Corbusier ③
Institut du Monde Arabe ㉕

Historic Districts
Canal St-Martin ⑯
Montmartre pp128–9 ⑩
Montparnasse ㉘

Cemeteries
Cimetière de Montmartre ⑬
Cimetière du Montparnasse ㉙
Cimetière du Père Lachaise ⑱

KEY

■ Main sightseeing area
= Major roads

Markets
Marché aux Puces de
   St-Ouen ⑭

**Historic Buildings
and Streets**
Bibliothèque Nationale
   de France ㉑
Catacombes ㉚
Château de Vincennes ⑳
Moulin Rouge ⑫
Rue La Fontaine ④

Theme Parks
*Cité des Sciences et
   de l'Industrie pp132–3* ⑮

0 kilometres   4
0 miles   2

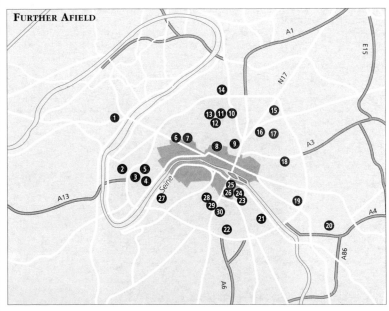

FURTHER AFIELD

◁ **The narrow rue St-Rustique winding up the hill to Sacré-Coeur**

West of the City

La Défense **①**

La Grande Arche. **⚟** *01 49 07 27 27.*
RER *La Défense.* **Open** *10am–6pm
daily.* 🎞 See **The History of France**
pp62–3.

THIS SKYSCRAPER business
city on the western edge
of Paris is the largest office
development in Europe. La
Grande Arche is an enormous
hollow cube large enough to
contain Notre-Dame cathedral.
Designed by Danish architect
Otto von Spreckelsen in the
late 1980s, the arch houses an
exhibition gallery and a
conference centre, and offers
a superb view over the city.

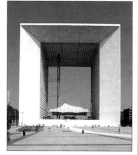

La Grande Arche in La Défense

Bois de Boulogne **②**

75016. **M** *Porte Maillot, Porte
Dauphine, Porte d'Auteuil, Sablons.*
Open *24 hrs daily.* 🎞 *to specialist
gardens and museum.* &

LOCATED BETWEEN the
western edges of
Paris and the river
Seine, this 865-ha
(2,137-acre) park offers
a vast belt of greenery
for strolling, cycling,
riding, boating, pic-
nicking or spending a
day at the races. The
Bois de Boulogne was
once part of the im-
mense Forêt du Rouvre.
In the mid-19th century
Napoleon III had the
Bois designed and
landscaped by Baron
Haussmann along the
lines of Hyde Park in
London. Several self-
contained parks within

the forest include the Pré
Catelan and the Bagatelle gardens, with architectural follies
and an 18th-century villa
famous for its rose garden.
The villa was built in just 64
days as the result of a bet
between the Comte d'Artois
and Marie-Antoinette.

By day the Bois is busy with
families, joggers and walkers,
but after dark it is notoriously
seedy – and best avoided.

Fondation Le Corbusier **③**

8–10 square du Docteur-Blanche
75016. **⚟** *01 42 88 41 53.*
M *Jasmin.* **Open** *10am–12:30pm,
1:30–6pm Mon–Fri (5pm Fri).* **Closed**
public hols, Aug, 24 Dec–2 Jan. 🎞

IN A QUIET CORNER of Auteuil
stand the villas La Roche
and Jeanneret, the first two
Parisian houses built by the
brilliant and influential 20th-
century architect Charles-
Edouard Jeanneret, better
known as Le Corbusier. Built
at the start of the 1920s, they
demonstrate his revolutionary
use of white concrete in Cubist
forms. Rooms flow into each
other allowing maximum light
and volume, and the houses
stand on stilts with windows
along their entire length.

Villa La Roche was owned
by the art patron Raoul La
Roche. Today, both villas
serve as a documentation
centre on Le Corbusier where
lectures on his work are given.

**An Art Nouveau window in the
rue la Fontaine**

Rue la Fontaine **④**

75016. **Map** 5 A4. **M** *Michel-Ange
Auteuil, Jasmin.* **RER** *Radio-France.*

THE RUE LA FONTAINE and
surrounding streets act
as a showcase for some of
the most exciting early 20th-
century, low-cost architecture,
featuring sinuous decorative
detail. At No. 14 stands the
Castel Béranger, which firmly
established the reputation of
architect Hector Guimard. He
went on to design the city's
Art Nouveau metro entrances.

Musée Marmottan **⑤**

2 rue Louis Boilly 75016.
⚟ *01 44 96 50 33.* **M** *Muette.*
Open *10am–5:30pm Tue–Sun.*
Closed *1 Jan, 1 May, 25 Dec.* 🎞 &

THE MUSEUM WAS
created in the 19th-
century mansion of the
famous art historian,
Paul Marmottan, in
1932. He bequeathed
his house, plus his
Renaissance, Consular
and First Empire paint-
ings and furniture, to
the Institut de France.

In 1971 the museum
acquired one of the
world's most important
collections of work by
Impressionist painter
Claude Monet, at the
bequest of his son,
Michel. Some of Monet's
most famous paintings
are here, including
Impression – Sunrise

A landscaped island in the Bois de Boulogne

(from which came the term "Impressionist"), a painting of Rouen Cathedral *(see p257)* and several from the *Water-lilies* series *(see p94)*. Also on show is the body of work painted at Giverny during the last years of Monet's life. This includes paintings such as *The Japanese Bridge* and *The Weeping Willow*. The wild, expressive brushstrokes and iridescent colours make these some of the museum's most powerful works.

Part of Monet's personal art collection was passed on to the museum, including work by fellow Impressionists Camille Pissarro, Pierre-Auguste Renoir and Alfred Sisley. The museum also displays medieval illuminated manuscripts and 16th-century Burgundian tapestries.

North of the City

St-Alexandre-Nevsky Cathedral

St-Alexandre-Nevsky **6**

12 rue Daru 75008. **Map** 2 F3.
[C] 01 42 27 37 34. [M] *Courcelles, Ternes.* **Open** *3–5pm Tue & Fri.*

THIS IMPOSING Russian Orthodox cathedral with its five golden-copper domes signals the presence of a large Russian community in Paris. Designed by members of the St Petersburg Fine Arts Academy and financed jointly by Tsar Alexander II and the local Russian community, the cathedral was completed in 1861. Inside, a wall of icons divides the church in two.

Colonnade beside the *naumachia* basin in Parc Monceau

The Greek-cross plan and the rich interior mosaics and frescoes are Neo-Byzantine in style, while the exterior and gilt domes are traditional Russian Orthodox in design.

Parc Monceau **7**

Bd de Courcelles 75017. **Map** 3 A3.
[C] 01 42 27 08 64. [M] *Monceau.*
Open *7am–9pm daily.*

THIS GREEN HAVEN dates back to 1778 when the Duc de Chartres commissioned the painter-writer and amateur landscape designer Louis Carmontelle to create a magnificent garden. The result was an exotic landscape full of architectural follies in the English and German style.

Over the years the land changed hands and in 1852 was acquired by the state and made into a chic public park. A few of the original features still remain. Among them is the *naumachia* basin – an ornamental version of a Roman pool used for simulating naval battles.

Musée Gustave Moreau **8**

14 rue de la Rochefoucauld 75009.
Map 4 E3. [C] 01 48 74 38 50.
[M] *Trinité.* **Open** *11am–5.15pm Mon & Wed, 10am–12.45pm, 2–5.15pm Thu–Sun.*

THE SYMBOLIST painter Gustave Moreau (1826– 98), known for his symbolic works depicting biblical and mythological fantasies, lived and worked in this handsome town house at the end of the 19th century. *Jupiter and Semele,* one of the artist's outstanding works is displayed here, along with other major paintings, and some of the 7,000 drawings and 1,000 oils and watercolours which Moreau bequeathed to the state.

Musée de Cristal de Baccarat **9**

30 bis rue de Paradis 75010.
[C] 01 47 70 64 30. [M] *Château d'Eau, Poissonnières.* **Open** *9:30am– 6pm Mon–Fri, 10am–5pm Sat.* **Closed** *public hols.* [icons] *by appt.*

THE RUE DE PARADIS has a number of glass and ceramics retailers, including the Baccarat company, founded in 1764 in Lorraine. The Musée de Cristal is beside the Baccarat showroom and displays over 1,200 articles made by the company. These include services created for the royal and imperial courts of Europe and many of the best pieces produced in the workshops.

Also on display are some of the techniques for shaping the crystal ware, which are as intricate as the finished work itself.

Le Vase d'Abyssinie, made of Baccarat crystal and bronze

Montmartre ⑩

THE STEEP *butte* (hill) of Montmartre has been associated with artists for 200 years. Théodore Géricault and Camille Corot came here at the start of the 19th century, and in the 20th century Maurice Utrillo immortalized the streets in his works. Today, street artists thrive predominantly on the tourist trade, but much of the area still preserves its rather louche, villagey pre-war atmosphere. The name of the area is ascribed to martyrs tortured and killed in the area around AD 250, hence *mons martyrium*.

Streetside painter

Montmartre Vineyard
This is the last Parisian vineyard. The harvest is celebrated on the first Saturday in October.

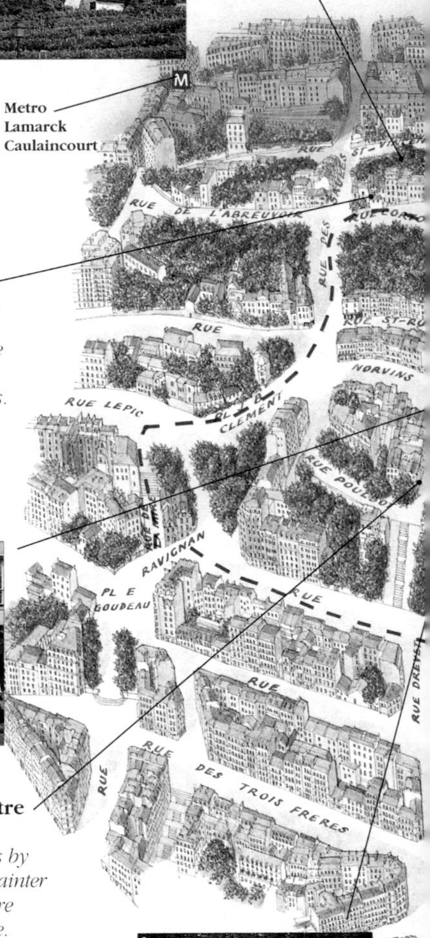

Metro Lamarck Caulaincourt

Au Lapin Agile
"The Agile Rabbit", once a literary haunt, is now one of the city's best-known nightclubs.

A la Mère Catherine
This was a favourite restaurant of Russian cossacks. They would shout "Bistro!" (meaning "quick") – which gave the bistro its name.

MAISON CATHERINE
A LA MERE CATHERINE

Espace Montmartre Salvador Dalí
Some 330 works by the Surrealist painter and sculptor are on display here.

Place du Tertre
The tourist centre of Montmartre is full of portraitists. Artists first exhibited in the square in the 19th century.

KEY

– – – Suggested route

| 0 metres | 100 |
| 0 yards | 100 |

Musée de Montmartre
Changing, Montmartre-related exhibitions usually include works by artists who lived here, such as this Portrait of a Woman *(1918) by Amedeo Modigliani.*

LOCATOR MAP
See Street Finder maps 3, 4

Sacré-Coeur
This Neo-Romanesque church, started in the 1870s and completed in 1914, contains many treasures, such as this figure of the Virgin Mary and Child *(1896) by P Brunet* ⓫

St-Pierre de Montmartre
This is an early Parisian church with origins dating back to the 6th century.

To metro Anvers

The funiculaire, or cable railway, at the end of the rue Foyatier takes you to the foot of the basilica of the Sacré-Coeur. Metro tickets are valid for it.

Square Willette lies below the forecourt of the Sacré-Coeur. It is laid out on the side of the hill in a series of descending terraces with lawns, shrubs, trees and flowerbeds.

Musée d'Art Naïf Max Fourny
Almost 600 examples of naive art are housed here, including The Wall *(1944) by F Tremblot.*

Sacré-Coeur

35 rue de Chevalier 75018. **Map** 4
F1. **[** 01 53 41 89 00. **M** *Abbesses
(then take the funiculaire to the steps
of the Sacré-Coeur), Anvers, Barbès-
Rochechouart, Château-Rouge,
Lamarck-Caulaincourt.* **:::** 30, 54,
80, 85. **Basilica open** 6:30am–11pm
daily. **Dome and crypt open** 9am–
7pm daily (6pm winter). **for
crypt and dome.** **restricted.**

THE SACRE-COEUR basilica,
dedicated to the Sacred
Heart of Christ, was built as a
result of a private religious
vow made at the outbreak of
the Franco-Prussian war.
Two businessmen, Alexandre
Legentil and Rohault de
Fleury promised to finance
the basilica should France be
spared from assault. Despite
the war and the Siege of
Paris, invasion was averted
and work began in 1875 to
Paul Abadie's designs. The
result has never been considered particularly graceful,
but the basilica is vast and
impressive, and is one of
France's most important
Roman Catholic buildings.

**The stained glass
gallery** affords a view
of the whole interior.

**The Great Mosaic
of Christ** (1912–22)
by Luc Olivier
Merson,
dominates the
chancel vault.

The ovoid dome is
the second-highest
point in Paris, after
the Eiffel Tower.

Bronze doors
in the portico
show the Last
Supper and
other biblical
scenes.

The crypt vaults house a
chapel containing Alexandre
Legentil's heart in a stone urn.

Moulin Rouge

82 bd de Clichy 75018. **Map** 4 E1.
[01 46 06 00 19. **M** *Blanche.* **Open**
9pm–1am daily. **See Entertain-
ment in Paris** p141.

BUILT IN 1885, the Moulin
Rouge was turned into
a dance hall in 1900; only
the red sails outside date
from the original nightclub.
Henri de Toulouse-Lautrec
immortalized the wild cancan
shows in his drawings, and
the high-kicking routines
continue today in glittering,
Las Vegas-style revues.

Cimetière de
Montmartre

20 avenue Rachel 75018. **Map** 4 D1.
[01 43 87 64 24. **M** *Place de
Clichy.* **Open** 8am–5:30pm Mon–Sat,
9am–5:30pm Sun.

THIS HAS been the resting
place for many luminaries
of the creative arts since the
beginning of the 19th century.

The composers Hector Berlioz
and Jacques Offenbach (who
wrote the famous cancan
tune), Russian dancer Waslaw
Nijinsky and film director
François Truffaut are just a
few of the famous people
who have been buried here
over the years.

There is also a Montmartre
cemetery near square Roland-
Dorgelès, known as the St-
Vincent cemetery. This is
where the French painter
Maurice Utrillo is buried.

**African stall in the Marché aux
Puces de St-Ouen**

Marché aux Puces
de St-Ouen

Rue des Rosiers, St-Ouen 75018.
M *Porte-de-Clignancourt.* **Open**
7am–6pm Sat–Mon. See **Shops
and Markets** p138.

THIS IS THE OLDEST and largest of the Paris flea markets, covering 6 ha (15 acres)
near the Porte de Clignancourt.
In the 19th century, rag merchants and tramps would
gather outside the fortifications that marked the city
limits and offer their wares
for sale. Today the area is
divided into separate markets,
and is well-known for its
heavy Second Empire furniture and ornaments. Although
there are few bargains to be
had, this does not deter the
huge weekend crowds.

Cité des Sciences et
de l'Industrie

See pp132–3.

Canal St-Martin ⑯

Ⓜ Jaurès, J Bonsergent, Goncourt.

A WALK ALONG THE QUAYS on either side of the Canal St-Martin gives a glimpse of how this thriving, industrial, working-class area of the city looked at the end of the 19th century. The 5-km (3-mile) canal, opened in 1825, provided a short-cut for river traffic between loops of the Seine. A smattering of brick-and-iron factories and warehouses survive from this time along the Quai de Jemmapes. Here, too, you will find the legendary Hôtel du Nord which featured in Marcel Carné's 1930s film of the same name. The canal itself is quietly busy with barges and anglers; around it the tree-lined quays, iron footbridges and public gardens are ideal for a leisurely stroll.

Boats moored at Port de l'Arsenal

Parc des Buttes-Chaumont ⑰

Rue Manin 75019 (access from Rue Armand Carrel). Ⓒ 01 53 35 89 35. Ⓜ Botzaris, Buttes-Chaumont. **Open** 7am–9pm (10pm summer) daily.

F OR MANY THIS is the most pleasant and unexpected park in Paris. Urban planner

Baron Haussmann converted the hilly site from a rubbish dump and quarry with gallows at the foot, to English-style gardens in the 1860s. His partner on the project was landscape architect Adolphe Alphand, who became chief organizer of a vast 1860s programme to provide the pavement-lined Parisian avenues with benches, streetlights, newspaper kiosks and urinals.

Others involved in the creation of this highly praised park were the engineer Darcel and the landscape gardener Barillet-Deschamps. They created a lake, made an island with real and artificial rocks, gave it a Roman-style temple and added a waterfall, streams, and footbridges leading to the island. Today, in summer, visitors will also find boating facilities, donkey rides and sunworshippers on the beautifully kept lawns.

East of the City

Cimetière du Père Lachaise ⑱

16 rue du Repos. Ⓒ 01 43 70 70 33. Ⓜ Père Lachaise, Alexandre Dumas. **Open** 8am–5:30pm daily.

P ARIS'S most prestigious cemetery is set on a wooded hill overlooking the city. The land was once owned by

Père de la Chaise, Louis XIV's confessor, but it was bought by order of Napoleon in 1803 to create a completely new cemetery. This became so popular with the Parisian bourgeoisie that the boundaries were extended six times during the 19th century. Here are buried celebrities such as

the writer Honoré de Balzac and the composer Frédéric Chopin, and more recently, the singer Jim Morrison and the actors Simone Signoret and Yves Montand.

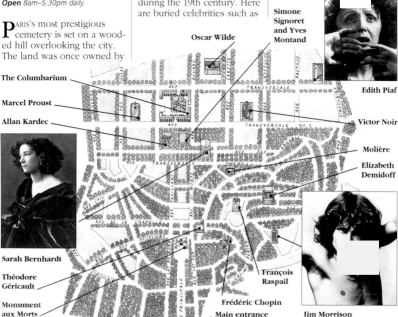

The Columbarium

Marcel Proust

Allan Kardec

Sarah Bernhardt

Théodore Géricault

Monument aux Morts

Oscar Wilde

François Raspail

Frédéric Chopin

Main entrance

Simone Signoret and Yves Montand

Edith Piaf

Victor Noir

Molière

Elizabeth Demidoff

Jim Morrison

Cité des Sciences et de l'Industrie ⑮

THIS HUGELY popular science and technology museum occupies the largest of the old Villette slaughterhouses, which now form part of a massive urban park. Architect Adrien Fainsilber has created an imaginative interplay of light, vegetation and water in the high-tech, five-storey building, which soars 40 m (133 ft) high, stretching over 3 ha (7 acres). At the museum's heart is the Explora exhibit, a fascinating guide to the worlds of science and technology. Visitors can take part in computerized games on space, the earth and ocean, computers and sound. On other levels there are cinemas, a science newsroom, a library and shops.

Modern folly in the Parc de la Villette

★ **Planetarium**
In this 260-seat auditorium, special effects projectors and the latest sound systems create exciting images of the stars and planets.

Starball
The Planetarium's 10,000 lenses reproduce images of the sky as it is viewed by astronauts beyond the earth's atmosphere.

★ **Ariane**
Rocket displays explain how astronauts are sent into space, and include an example of the European rocket Ariane.

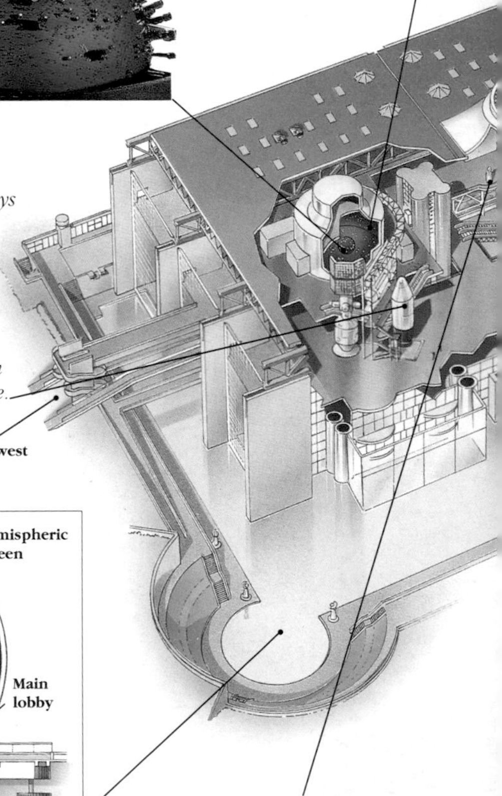

Entrance from the west

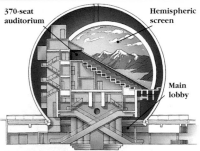

370-seat auditorium

Hemispheric screen

Main lobby

LA GÉODE

This giant entertainment sphere houses a huge hemispherical cinema screen, 1,000 sq m (11,000 sq ft), showing films on nature, travel and space.

The moat was designed by Fainsilber so that natural light could penetrate into the lower levels of the building.

The main hall is vast, with a soaring network of shafts, bridges, escalators and balconies, and has a cathedral-like atmosphere.

STAR EXHIBITS

★ **Planetarium**

★ **Ariane**

★ **La Géode**

Cupolas
*The two glazed domes,
17 m (56 ft) in diameter,
filter the flow of natural
light into the main hall.*

VISITORS' CHECKLIST

30 av Corentin-Cariou 75019.
☎ 01 40 03 75 00. Ⓜ *Porte de
la Villette.* 🚌 *150, 152, 250A to
Porte de la Villette.* 🅿 *on site.*
Open *9am–6pm (7pm Sun)
Tue–Sun (last adm: 5:30pm).* ♿
🅶 *Concerts. Films, videos.
Conference centre. Library.*

The greenhouses are
square hothouses, 32 m
(105 ft) high and wide,
linking the park to the
building.

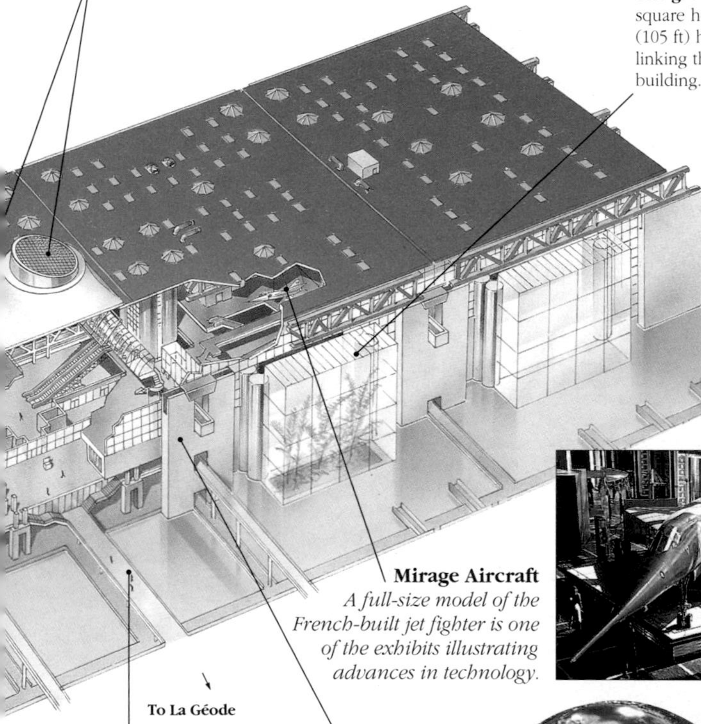

Mirage Aircraft
*A full-size model of the
French-built jet fighter is one
of the exhibits illustrating
advances in technology.*

To La Géode

Walkways
*The walkways cross the
encircling moat to link the
various floors of the museum
to the Géode and the park.*

Children's Science City
*In this lively, extensive area children can
experiment and play with machines that
show how scientific principles work.*

Bibliothèque Nationale de France

Museum National des Arts Africains et Océaniens ⓭

293 avenue Daumesnil 75012.
█ 01 44 74 84 80. Ⓜ Porte Dorée.
Open 10am–5:30pm Wed–Mon,
12:30–6pm Sat, Sun. **Closed** 1 May.

THIS MUSEUM IS housed in
an Art Deco building de-
signed by architects Albert La-
prade and Léon Jaussely, for
the city's grand colonial exhibition in 1931. Inside is a remarkable collection of African
and Australasian art, including
antelope masks from Mali,
Moroccan jewellery, Aborigine
bark paintings, and African
wood and copper figures on
the themes of life and death.

Château de Vincennes ⓮

Avenue de Paris 94300 Vincennes.
█ 01 43 28 15 48. Ⓜ Château de
Vincennes. Ⓡ Vincennes. **Open** 10am
–5pm daily (last adm 4:15pm); Apr–
Sep until 6pm. **Chapel** only.

THE CHATEAU de Vincennes
was the permanent royal
residence until the 17th century, before the court moved
to Versailles. The royal chambers and beautiful Gothic
chapel are all worth seeing;
so is the large, impressive
museum in the medieval keep.
Beyond the château moat
lies the Bois de Vincennes.
Once a royal hunting ground,
it is now a landscaped forest
with ornamental lakes and
cascades, and a zoo.

Bibliothèque Nationale de France ㉑

Quai François-Mauriac 75013.
█ 01 53 79 59 59. Ⓜ Quai de la
Gare. **Open** 10am–7pm Tue–Sat,
noon–6pm Sun. **Closed** public hols
& 2 weeks mid-Sep.

THESE FOUR great book-
shaped towers house ten
million volumes. The reference and research libraries, in
the central podium, offer over
400,000 titles. Other resources
include digitized illustrations,
sound archives and CD-ROMs.

South of the City

Parc Montsouris ㉒

Bd Jourdan 75014. █ 01 45 88 28 60.
Ⓜ Porte d'Orléans. Ⓡ Cité Univer-
sitaire. **Open** 7:30am–7pm daily.

THIS ENGLISH-STYLE park, the
second largest in Paris, was
laid out by the landscape architect Adolphe Alphand from
1865–1878. With its restaurant,
lawns and lake – home to a
variety of birds – it is popular
with students and children.

Skull of the reptile dimetrodon

Musée National d'Histoire Naturelle ㉓

2 rue Buffon 75005. **Map** 14 D1. █
01 40 79 30 00. Ⓜ Jussieu, Austerlitz.
Open 10am–5pm Wed–Mon. **Closed**
weekday public hols.

THE NATURAL HISTORY Museum
is organized into four
departments, with a new
evolution gallery in the offing.
The palaeontology section
features skeletons, casts of
various animals and an exhibition showing the evolution

of the vertebrate skeleton.
Palaeobotany is devoted to
plant fossils, and mineralogy
to rocks and gemstones. On
display in the entomology
department are some of the
world's oldest insect fossils.
The museum bookshop is
in the house where the
naturalist Buffon lived from
1772 until his death in 1788.

Jardin des Plantes ㉔

57 rue Cuvier 75005. **Map** 13 C1.
Ⓜ Jussieu, Austerlitz. **Open**
9am–6pm (5pm winter) daily.

THE BOTANICAL gardens were
established in 1626 when
Jean Hérouard and Guy de la
Brosse, Louis XIII's physicians,
obtained permission to found
a royal medicinal herb garden.
A school of botany, natural
history and pharmacy followed
and the garden opened to the
public in 1640. One of the
city's great parks, it contains
a natural history museum,
botanical school and zoo.
As well as beautiful vistas
and walkways flanked by
ancient statues, the park has
an alpine garden with plants
from Corsica, Morocco, the
Alps and the Himalayas, and
an unrivalled display of herbaceous and wild plants. The
Cedar of Lebanon here, originally from Britain's Kew
Gardens, was the first to be
planted in France.

**Rue Mouffetard, one of several
markets near Jardin des Plantes**

Institut du Monde Arabe

1 rue des Fossés St-Bernard 75005.
Map 9 C5. **[** *01 40 51 38 38.*
M *Jussieu, Cardinal-Lemoine.*
**Museum & temporary exhibitions
open** *10am–6pm Tue–Sun.* **Library
open** *1–8pm Tue–Sat.*

THIS MAGNIFICENT modern
building was designed by
French architect Jean Nouvel,
and cleverly combines high-
tech details with the spirit of
traditional Arab architecture.
   On the seventh floor there
is a comprehensive display
of Islamic works of art from
the 9th to the 19th centuries
including glassware, ceramics
and sculpture. The museum's
highlight is the fine collection
of *astrolabes*, the much-prized
tool used by the ancient
Arabic astronomers.

Mosquée de Paris/Institut musulman ㉖

Place du Puits de l'Ermite 75005.
[*01 45 35 97 33.* **M** *Place
Monge.* **Open** *9am–noon, 1–6pm
Sat–Thu.* **Closed** *Muslim hols.*

BUILT IN THE 1920s in the
Hispano-Moorish style,
these buildings are the spiritual centre for Paris's Muslim
community and the home of
the Grand Imam. Once used
solely by scholars, the mosque
has expanded over the years
and now houses the best Turkish baths in the city, a restaurant and beautiful *salon de thé.*

Parc André Citroën ㉗

Rue Balard 75015. **M** *Javel, Balard.*
Open *7:30am– dusk Mon–Fri,
9am–dusk Sat, Sun & public hols.*

DESIGNED BY both land-
scapers and architects, this
park is a fascinating blend of
styles, ranging from wildflower
meadow in the north to sophisticated monochrome mineral and sculpture gardens in
the southern section. Modern
water sculptures dot the park.

Institut du Monde Arabe, covered with photosensitive lightscreens

Tour Montparnasse

Montparnasse ㉘

75014 & 75015. **Map** 11 & 12.
M *Vavin, Raspail, Edgar Quinet.*

THE NAME Montparnasse
was first used ironically
in the 17th century, when
arts students performed their
work on a "mount" of rubble
left over from quarrying.
In ancient Greece, Mount
Parnassus was dedicated to
poetry, music and beauty.
By the 19th century, crowds
were drawn to the local
cabarets and bars by duty-
free prices. The mixture of
art and high living was particularly potent in the 1920s
and 1930s when Hemingway,
Picasso, Cocteau, Giacometti,
Matisse and Modigliani were
"Montparnos", as the residents
were called. This epoch ended
with World War II. The modern *quartier* is dominated
by the much-hated Tour
Montparnasse, visible from
all over Paris, and vast office
developments.

Cimetière du Montparnasse ㉙

3 bd Edgar Quinet. **Map** 12 D3. **[** *01
44 10 86 50.* **M** *Edgar Quinet.* **Open**
*8am–6pm Mon–Fri, 8:30am–6pm Sat,
9am–6pm Sun (5:30pm in winter).*

MONTPARNASSE cemetery
opened in 1824, and fast
became a chic burial place.
Among those buried here are
Serge Gainsbourg, Charles
Baudelaire, Left-Bank personalities Jean-Paul Sartre and
Simone de Beauvoir, and Guy
de Maupassant.

Catacombes ㉚

1 place Denfert-Rochereau 75014.
Map 12 E3. **[** *01 43 22 47 63.*
M *Denfert-Rochereau.* **Open** *2–
4pm Tue–Fri, 9–11am, 2–4pm Sat
& Sun.* **Closed** *public hols.*

A LONG SERIES of quarry
tunnels built in Roman
times, the catacombs are now
lined with ancient bones and
skulls. Thousands of rotting
corpses were transported
here in the 1780s to absorb
the excess from the insanitary
Les Halles cemetery.

**Skulls and bones stored in the
catacombs**

SHOPS AND MARKETS

FOR MANY PEOPLE, Paris epitomizes luxury and good living. Exquisitely dressed men and women sip wine by the banks of the Seine against the backdrop of splendid French architecture, or shop from small specialist shops. The least expensive way of joining the chic set is to create French style with accessories or costume jewellery. Alternatively, try shopping in the January or July sales. If your budget allows, take the opportunity to buy world-famous Paris fashions, or feast on the wonderful gourmet delicacies, displayed with consummate artistry. Parisian shopping streets and markets are the ideal place to indulge in the French custom of strolling for the express purpose of seeing and being seen. For up-to-the-minute high fashion, the rue du Faubourg-St-Honoré is hard to beat, with its exquisite couture window displays. Browsing around the bookstalls along the Seine is another favourite French pastime. A survey of some of the best and most famous places to shop follows.

Shopping in avenue de Montaigne

OPENING HOURS

SHOPS GENERALLY OPEN from 9:30am to 7pm, Monday to Saturday. Markets and local shops close on Mondays and some places also close for the summer holidays in August.

PAYMENT AND VAT

Traveller's cheques, Visa, American Express, Carte Bleue, Mastercard and, increasingly, Eurocheques are widely accepted. For further information, see pages 620–21. Prices will normally include the sales tax (TVA), which varies from 5% to 25%. Non-EU residents are entitled to a refund, provided you spend a minimum of F2,000 in one shop and are resident in France for under six months. Fill in a form (*bordereau de détaxe* or *bordereau de vente*) and present it at customs.

WOMEN'S FASHIONS

PARIS IS THE HOME of *haute couture*. Original *haute couture* garments, as opposed to imitations and adaptations, are one-off creations designed by the 23 couture houses listed with the Fédération Française de la Couture. The rules governing the classification *haute couture* are fairly strict, and many of the world's top designers, such as Claude Montana and Karl Lagerfeld, are not included on this prestigious list. Astronomical prices put *haute couture* beyond the reach of most pockets, yet it still remains the life-blood and focus of the French fashion industry.

The Chanel logo, recognized worldwide

Most couture houses are on or near rue du Faubourg-St-Honoré, including **Chanel**, **Christian Lacroix**, **Guy Laroche**, **Nina Ricci**, **Yves Saint Laurent** and **Christian Dior** to name just a few.

Hermès has classic country chic, and no one can resist **MaxMara**'s Italian elegance or a **Giorgio Armani** suit. **Karl Lagerfeld**, as well as designing for Chanel, has created his own sleek line. If your wardrobe lacks colour, try the exotic **Kenzo**. **Equipment** is well known for its classic silk shirts in a range of colours, and **Comme des Garçons** has avant-garde, quirky clothes for both sexes.

THE CENTRE OF PARIS COUTURE

The couture houses are concentrated on the Right Bank, around rue du Faubourg-St-Honoré and avenue Montaigne.

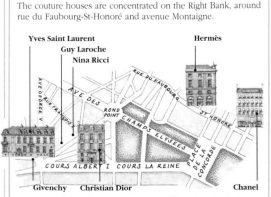

For accessories to complete the look, **Cartier** and **Christian Lacroix** are hard to beat.

Nearby rue Jean-Jacques Rousseau is now a prime shopping area. The eccentric but celebrated designer **Jean-Paul Gaultier** has a shop at Les Halles shop-ping centre, as does **Agnès B**, whose clothes combine the very latest chic with comfort. There are also inexpensive outlets selling copies of new designs in the centre. Rue des Rosiers in the Marais is full of new designers – try **Lolita Lempicka** or you may be tempted by the more daring **Azzedine Alaïa**.

Kenzo designerwear in the place des Victoires

MEN'S CLOTHES

MEN DON'T HAVE the luxury of *haute couture* dressing; their choice is limited to ready-to-wear, but most of the big name womenswear designers also produce a range for men, although they tend to be rather expensive. A good example is **Gianni Versace**, with his classic Italian clothes for men.

On the Right Bank, the household name designers include **Giorgio Armani**, the stylish **Pierre Cardin**, **Yves Saint Laurent** and **Lanvin**, who is particularly popular for his beautifully made leather accessories. Across the Seine, **Francesco Smalto**'s elegant creations are bought by the likes of Jean-Paul Belmondo, and for those who are not afraid to make a bold fashion statement, there is **Yohji Yamamoto**.

La Samaritaine department store in Beaubourg and Les Halles

DEPARTMENT STORES

IF TIME IS SHORT and you want to make all your purchases under one roof, try the *grands magasins* (department stores), all of which also have restaurants. Most still operate a ticket system for selling goods. The assistant writes a ticket for goods from their own boutique which you take to a cashier to be validated. You then return to the assistant to pick up your purchase. This can be time-consuming, so shop early in the day and avoid Saturdays. Be assertive, as the French don't pay attention to queues!

Au Printemps is huge, with separate buildings for menswear, household goods and women's and children's clothes. Fashion shows are held on Tuesdays at 10am (also Fridays in summer). The beauty department, with a vast perfume selection, is definitely worth a visit.

Cartier, one of the world's most exclusive stores

Au Bon Marché, on the Left Bank, was the first department store in Paris and is the most chic, with a good food hall. **Galeries Lafayette** has a wide range of clothes at all price levels. Fashion shows are held at 11am on Wednesdays and also Fridays in summer. **La Samaritaine** is one of the oldest shops in Paris, and full of bargains. It includes a sportswear shop and has good sales of household goods and furnishings. The store has a panoramic view of the Seine from the restaurant (closed in winter).

ART AND ANTIQUES

YOU CAN BUY art and antiques from shops and galleries of established reputations, or from flea markets and avant-garde galleries.

To avoid paying duty, you will need a certificate of authenticity when exporting *objets d'art* over 20 years old and any goods over a century old worth more than F1,000,000. Seek professional advice and declare the item at customs if in doubt.

Many of the prestigious antique shops and galleries are near the rue du Faubourg-St-Honoré, including **Le Louvre des Antiquaires** which comprises 250 different shops. On the Left Bank is the Carré Rive Gauche, an organization of 30 antiques dealers. **Didier Aaron** is an international expert on the 17th and 18th centuries. Two galleries worth a visit are **Artcurial**, for books and prints, and **Lavignes-Bastille**.

CHILDREN

THE CITY has many appeal-
ing toy shops, including
one of the world's most
famous, **Au Nain Bleu**,
situated in rue du Faubourg-
St-Honoré. Unfortunately, the
toys tend to be rather expensive so a visit to the store is
best kept as a special treat.

There is no shortage of
children's fashion in Paris, in
all styles and price ranges. A
good place to start is the rue
du Jour in Beaubourg and Les
Halles, which has a number
of children's boutiques. Many
designers of adult clothes also
have boutiques for children,
including **Kenzo**, **Baby Dior
and Agnès B**. Prices can be
extremely high, though. Ready-
to-wear chains such as **Bonpoint** sell chic, expensive but
well-made clothes and the
shops are serviceable and
wide-ranging. Perhaps not
surprisingly, the best-selling
children's garments at **Tartine
et Chocolat** on rue du
Faubourg-St-Honoré are
overalls.

For little feet, **Froment-
Leroyer** offers the best all-
round classics.

**Characters from the Tintin series,
Au Nain Bleu toy shop**

BOOKS, NEWSPAPERS AND MAGAZINES

ENGLISH AND AMERICAN pub-
lications are found at large
magazine stands and some
bookshops. If French is no
obstacle, weeklies *Pariscope*
and *L'Officiel des Spectacles*
have comprehensive listings.

Two English-language
newspapers are published in
France: the *International
Herald Tribune*, a daily, and
The European, a weekly. The
monthly *Boulevard* and the

Bookstall at Vanves market

bi-weekly *France–US Contacts*
are both published in English.

Some large department stores
have a books section, and
there are several English-
language bookshops, such as
WH Smith, **Brentano** and
Village Voice.
Gibert Joseph is
a good French-
language book-
shop selling
general and edu-
cational books
while **La Hune**
specializes in art,
design, cinema
fashion and photography. **Tea
and Tattered Pages** is a British
second-hand bookshop.

**Elegantly packaged
produce from Fauchon**

FOOD AND WINE

PARIS'S GASTRONOMIC treats
include *foie gras, char-
cuterie*, cheese and wine.
Some streets positively over-
flow with food shops – try rue
Montorgueil or rue Rambuteau, which has a marvellous
row of fishmongers, delica-
tessens and shops selling
prepared food. Charcuteries
such as **Fauchon**, in place
Madeleine, and the basement
of **Au Bon Marché** department
store sell cheese, snails, truffles,
caviar and regional produce.

L'établissement Poilâne
sells perhaps the only bread in
Paris known by the name of
its baker. Be prepared for big
queues at weekends and
around 4pm when a fresh
batch comes out of the oven.

Chocolate is another French
obsession. **Christian Constant**'s low-sugar creations,
well-known to connoisseurs,
are made from pure cocoa.
Barthélemy in the rue de
Grenelle has exceptional

Roquefort. **Caves Taillevent**,
an enormous wine cellar with
some of Paris's most expensive wine, is worth a tour.

MARKETS

THE FRENCH still shop daily,
hence food markets are
always packed. Most fruit and
vegetable markets are open
from around 8am to 1pm and
from 4pm to 7pm Tuesday to
Saturday, and 9am to 1pm
Sunday. Watch out for rotten
produce – buy products loose,
not in boxes. A little language
is useful for specifying *pas trop
mûr* (not too ripe), or *pour
manger ce soir* (to be eaten
tonight). The newly renovated
Marché St-Germain is a good
bet for Italian, Mexican, Greek,
Asian and organic
produce. The **Rue
Lepic** fruit and veg-
etable market, close
to Montmartre, is at
its most lively at
weekends. The
Rue Poncelet food
market is worth a
trip for its variety
of bakeries, pâtisseries and
charcuteries. **Rue de Seine** and
Rue de Buci have florists and
two excellent pâtisseries.

Paris's biggest and best-
known flea market is the
**Marché aux Puces de St-
Ouen**. Divided into separate
markets, it specializes in furniture, antiques, old jewellery
and second-hand clothes. The
smaller **Marché de la Porte
de Vanves** has good-quality
bric-a-brac – get there early
for the best choice.

**Lionel Poilâne's bread bearing his
trademark – a square**

DIRECTORY

WOMEN'S FASHION

Agnès B
6 rue de Jour 75001.
Map 9 A1.
📞 01 45 08 56 56.

Azzedine Alaïa
7 rue de Moussy 75004.
Map 9 C3.
📞 01 40 27 85 58.

Cartier
13 rue de la Paix 75002.
Map 4 D5.
📞 01 42 61 58 56.

Chanel
42 av Montaigne 75008.
Map 3 A5.
📞 01 47 20 84 45.

Christian Dior
30 av Montaigne 75008.
Map 6 F1.
📞 01 40 73 54 44.

Christian Lacroix
29 av Montaigne 75008.
Map 3 B5.
📞 01 42 68 69 50.

Comme des Garçons
40–42 rue Etienne-Marcel 75002.
Map 9 A1.
📞 01 42 33 05 21.

Equipment
46 rue Etienne-Marcel 75002.
Map 9 A1.
📞 01 40 26 17 84.

Giorgio Armani
6 pl Vendôme 75001.
Map 4 D5.
📞 01 42 61 55 09.

Guy Laroche
29 av Montaigne 75008.
Map 3 C5.
📞 01 40 69 69 50.

Jean-Paul Gaultier
6 rue Vivienne 75002.
Map 8 F1.
📞 01 42 86 05 05.

Hermès
24 rue du Faubourg-St-Honoré 75008. **Map** 3 C5.
📞 01 40 17 47 17.

Karl Lagerfeld
17 rue du Faubourg-St-Honoré 75008. **Map** 3 C5.
📞 01 42 66 64 64.

Kenzo
3 pl des Victoires 75001.
Map 8 F1.
📞 01 40 39 72 03.

Lolita Lempicka
3 bis rue des Rosiers 75004. **Map** 9 C3.
📞 01 42 74 50 48.

MaxMara
37 rue du Four 75006.
Map 8 D4.
📞 01 43 29 91 10.

Nina Ricci
39 av Montaigne 75008.
Map 6 F1.
📞 01 49 52 56 00.

Yves Saint Laurent
5 av Marceau 75016.
Map 6 E1.
📞 01 44 31 64 00.

MEN'S CLOTHES

Francesco Smalto
44 rue François 1er 75008. **Map** 2 F5.
📞 01 47 20 70 63.

Gianni Versace
62 rue du Faubourg-St-Honoré 75008. **Map** 3 C5.
📞 01 47 42 88 02.

Lanvin
15 rue du Faubourg-St-Honoré 75008. **Map** 3 C5.
📞 01 44 71 33 33.

Pierre Cardin
59 rue du Faubourg-St-Honoré 75008. **Map** 3 B5.
📞 01 42 66 92 25.

Yohji Yamamoto
3 rue de Grenelle 75006.
Map 8 D4.
📞 01 45 44 29 32.

DEPARTMENT STORES

Au Bon Marché
22 rue de Sèvres 75007.
Map 7 C5.
📞 01 44 39 80 00.

Au Printemps
64 bd Haussman 75009.
Map 4 D4.
📞 01 42 82 50 00.

Galeries Lafayette
40 bd Haussmann 75009.
Map 4 E4.
📞 01 42 82 34 56.

La Samaritaine
19 rue de la Monnaie 75001. **Map** 8 F2.
📞 01 40 41 20 20.

ART AND ANTIQUES

Artcurial
9 av Matignon 75008.
Map 3 A5.
📞 01 42 99 16 16.

Le Louvre des Antiquaires
2 pl du Palais-Royal 75001. **Map** 8 F2.
📞 01 42 94 27 00.

Didier Aaron
118 rue du Faubourg-St-Honoré 75008. **Map** 3 C5.
📞 01 47 42 47 34.

Lavignes-Bastille
27 rue de Charonne 75011. **Map** 10 F4.
📞 01 47 00 88 18.

CHILDREN

Au Nain Bleu
406–410 rue St-Honoré 75008. Map 3 C5.
📞 01 42 60 39 01.

Baby Dior
28 av Montaigne 75008.
Map 6 F1.
📞 01 40 73 55 44.

Bonpoint
15 rue Royale 75008.
Map 3 C5.
📞 01 47 42 52 63.

Froment-Leroyer
7 rue Vavin 75006.
Map 12 E1.
📞 01 43 54 33 15.

Tartine et Chocolat
105 rue du Faubourg-St-Honoré 75008. **Map** 3 B5.
📞 01 45 62 44 04.

BOOKS

Brentano
37 av de l'Opera 75002.
Map 4 E5.
📞 01 42 61 52 50.

Gibert Joseph
26 bd St-Michel 75006.
Map 8 F5.
📞 01 44 41 88 88.

La Hune
170 bd St-Germain 75006. **Map** 8 D4.
📞 01 45 48 35 85.

Tea and Tattered Pages
24 rue Mayet 75006.
Map 11 B1.
📞 01 40 65 94 35.

Village Voice
6 rue Princesse 75006.
Map 8 E1.
📞 01 46 33 36 47.

WH Smith
248 rue de Rivoli 75001.
Map 7 C1.
📞 01 44 77 88 99.

FOOD AND WINE

Barthélemy
51 rue de Grenelle 7007.
Map 8 D4.
📞 01 45 48 56 75.

Caves Taillevent
199 rue du Faubourg-St-Honoré 75008. **Map** 2 F3.
📞 01 45 61 14 09.

Christian Constant
37 rue d'Assas 75006.
Map 12 E1.
📞 01 45 48 45 51.

L'établissement Poilâne
8 rue du Cherche-Midi 75006. **Map** 8 D4.
📞 01 45 48 42 59.

Fauchon
26 pl de la Madeleine 75008. **Map** 3 C5.
📞 01 47 42 60 11.

MARKETS

Marché St-Germain
Rue Mabillon and rue Lobineau 75005.
Map 8 E4.

Rue Lepic
75018. **Map** 4 F1.

Rue Poncelet
75017. **Map** 2 E3.

Marché de la Porte de Vanves
Av Georges-Lafenestre & av Marc-Sangnier 75014.

Marché aux Puces de St-Ouen
Rue des Rosiers, St-Ouen 75018.

Rue de Seine and Rue de Buci
75006. **Map** 8 E4.

ENTERTAINMENT IN PARIS

W HETHER YOUR prefer-
ence is for classical
drama, avant-garde
theatre, ballet, opera or jazz, cinema or dancing the night away,
Paris has it all. There is plenty of
free entertainment too, from the
street performers outside the Pompidou Centre to musicians busking
all over town and in the metros.
Parisians themselves like nothing
better than strolling along the boulevards or sitting at a pavement café
nursing a drink as they watch
the world go by. If, however,
you're looking for the ultimate "Gay Paree" experience,
you can take in any of the
celebrated nightclubs.
For fans of spectator sports
there is tennis, the Tour de France or
horse racing. Recreation centres and
gyms cater to the more active. And
for those disposed to more leisurely
pursuits, there is always a quiet game
of boules to be played in the park.

The glass façade of the Bastille Opéra

BOOKING TICKETS

D EPENDING on the event,
tickets can often be bought
at the door, but for popular
events it is wiser to purchase
tickets in advance at the **FNAC**
chains or **Virgin Megastore**.
Theatre box offices open
daily from about 11am–7pm.
Most accept credit card bookings by telephone. The
Kiosque Théâtre sells left-
over tickets for up to half the
price the day of performance.

THEATRE

F ROM THE GRANDEUR of the
Comédie Française to
slapstick farce and avant-garde
drama, theatre is flourishing
in Paris. Founded in 1680 by
royal decree, the Comédie
Française is the bastion of
French theatre, aiming to keep
classical drama in the public
eye and to perform works by
the best modern playwrights.
Formerly the second theatre
of the Comédie Française, the
Odéon Théâtre de l'Europe
now specializes in plays from

other countries, performed in
their original language. In an
underground auditorium in the
Art Deco Palais de Chaillot, the
Théâtre National de Chaillot
stages lively productions of
European classics. The **Théâtre
National de la Colline** specializes in contemporary drama.
Among the most important
of the serious independents is
the **Comédie des Champs-
Elysées**, while for over 100
years the **Palais Royal** has
been the temple of risqué
farce. The café theatres such
as **Théâtre d'Edgar** and **Au
Bec Fin** provide a good
venue for seeing new talent.

In the summer, street theatre
thrives in tourist areas such as
the Pompidou Centre, Les
Halles and St-Germain-des-
Prés. Open-air performances
of Shakespeare and classic
French plays are given at the
Shakespeare Garden in the
Bois de Boulogne.

CLASSICAL MUSIC

T HE MUSIC SCENE in Paris has
never been so busy. There
are many first-class venues
with an excellent range of
opera, classical and contemporary music productions.
Opened in 1989, the ultra-
modern 2,700-seat **Opéra de
Paris Bastille** stages classic
and modern operas. The showcase for productions from
outside France is the **Opéra
Comique**, which also specializes in operettas.
The **Salle Pleyel** is Paris's
principal concert hall and home
of the Orchestre de Paris. Both
the **Théâtre des Champs-
Elysées** and the **Auditorium
du Châtelet** are recommended
for their varied, high-quality
programmes. The main venues
for chamber music and recitals

LISTINGS MAGAZINES

Pariscope and *L'Officiel des
Spectacles* are two of the best
listings magazines in Paris.
Published every Wednesday, you
can pick them up at any news-
stand. *Le Figaro* also has a good
listings section on Wednesdays.
Boulevard is published bi-monthly
in English, and is available at
newsstands or WH Smith (see p139).

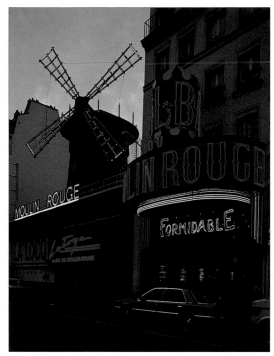

The famous silhouette of the Moulin Rouge nightclub

are the **Théâtre de la Ville** and the **Salle Gaveau**. Paris's newest venue is the **Cité de la Musique** in the Parc de la Villette. It is home to the renowned contemporary music group, the Ensemble InterContemporain, directed by Pierre Boulez.

DANCE

THE FRENCH are very vocal in their appreciation or dislike of dance, and those who fail to please are subjected to boos, hisses and mass walkouts in mid-performance.

The opulent **Opéra Garnier** has performance space for 450 artists and is home to the Ballet de l'Opéra de Paris, which has earned a reputation as one of the best classical ballet companies in the world. Government support has helped the **Théâtre de la Ville** to become Paris's most important venue for modern dance, with subsidies keeping ticket costs relatively low.

The **Maison des Arts de Créteil** stages famous overseas companies, as well as its own much praised productions.

CLUBS AND CABARET

MUSIC IN PARIS CLUBS tends to follow the trends set in the US and Britain. Only a few clubs such as **Balajo**, once frequented by Edith Piaf, and the ultra-hip **Folies Pigalle**, once a strip joint, are genuinely up-to-the-minute with their music.

La Locomotive attracts a mixed crowd to its three-level mainstream house nights. **Les Bains** is the old standby nightspot attracting fashion and show business people.

For a more Latin touch, try **La Java**. The dance floor of this club, where Edith Piaf once performed, now sways to Cuban and Brazilian sounds.

When it comes to picking a cabaret, the rule of thumb is simple: the better known places are best. The **Folies-Bergères** is the oldest music hall in Paris and probably the most famous in the world. It is closely rivalled by the **Lido** and the **Moulin Rouge**, birthplace of the cancan. **Paradis Latin** is the most "French" cabaret in the city. It shows variety acts whose sketches are enlivened by remarkable special effects and scenery.

ROCK, JAZZ AND WORLD MUSIC

THE TOP international acts are usually to be found at the enormous arenas such as **Palais Omnisports Paris-Bercy** or the **Zénith**. For a more intimate atmosphere, the legendary **Olympia** has assigned seating and good acoustics. To hear indigenous rock groups like Les Negresses Vertes and Mano Negra go to **La Cigale** or **Elysée-Montmartre** in the Pigalle area.

Jazz-crazy Paris has innumerable packed clubs where the best talent in the world can be heard on any evening. All the great jazz musicians have performed at **New Morning**, which also hosts African, Brazilian and other sounds. For Dixieland go to **Le Petit Journal St-Michael**.

World music and jazz lovers alike can see top acts and dance until dawn at the excellent **Chapelle des Lombards**.

La Locomotive, a huge disco on three levels

Cinema

Paris is the world's capital of film appreciation. It was the cradle of the cinematograph nearly 100 years ago. Then in the late 1950s and early 1960s the city nurtured that very Parisian vanguard movement, the New Wave, when film directors such as François Truffaut and Jean-Luc Godard revolutionized the way films were made and perceived.

There are now more than 300 screens within the city limits, distributed among 100 cinemas. Most are concentrated in cinema belts, which enjoy the added appeal of nearby restaurants and shops. The Champs-Elysées has the densest cinema strip in town, where you can see the latest Hollywood smash or French *auteur* triumph, as well as some classic re-issues.

In the vicinity of the Opéra de Paris Garnier, the cinemas in the Grands Boulevards include two notable landmarks: the 2,800-seat **Le Grand Rex**, with its Baroque decor, and the **Max Linder Panorama**, which was completely refurbished in the 1980s. The place de Clichy is the last Parisian stronghold of Pathé, while the newest nub of Right Bank cinema is in the Forum des Halles shopping mall. The largest screen in France, except for a specialist screen at **La Géode**, is the new **Gaumont** flagship in the place d'Italie district.

On the Left Bank, Odéon-St-Germain-des-Prés has taken over from the Latin Quarter as the city's heartland for art and repertory cinemas.

The dome of the 2,800-seat Le Grand Rex cinema

Sport

Paris is host to some of the foremost sporting events in the world. City-wide frenzy sweeps Paris when the Tour de France bicycle race finishes there in July. From late May to mid-June Parisians live and breathe tennis during the **Roland Garros** national tennis championship. The Prix de l'Arc de Triomphe, held at the **Hippodrome de Longchamp** on the first Sunday in October, provides the opportunity to see the rich in all their finery as well as first-class flat racing.

The **Palais Omnisports de Paris-Bercy** is the venue for a vast range of events, including the Paris tennis open, the six-day cycling race, show-jumping, martial arts as well as rock concerts. **Parc des Princes** is home to Paris's top football team, Paris St-Germain.

The Celebrated Cafés of Paris

One of the most enduring images of Paris is the Left Bank café scene where great artists, writers and eminent intellectuals consorted. Before World War I, hordes of Russian revolutionaries, including Lenin and Trotsky, whiled away their days in the Rotonde and the Dôme in Montparnasse. In the 1920s, Surrealists dominated café life. Later came the American writers led by Ernest Hemingway and Scott Fitzgerald, whose haunts included La Coupole. After World War II, Jean-Paul Sartre and other Existentialists shifted the cultural scene northwards to St-Germain.

Newspaper reading remains a typical café pastime

DIRECTORY

BOOKING TICKETS

FNAC
26–30 av des Ternes
75017. **Map** 2 D3.
[01 44 09 18 00.
Forum Les Halles, 1–7 rue
Pierre Lescot 75001.
Map 9 A2.
[01 40 41 40 00.

Virgin Megastore
52–60 av des Champs-
Elysées 75008.
Map 2 F5.
[01 49 53 50 00.

Kiosque Théâtre
15 pl de la Madeleine
75008.
Map 3 C5.

THEATRE

Au Bec Fin
6 rue Thérèse 75001.
Map 8 E1.
[01 42 96 29 35.

**Comédie des
Champs-Elysées**
15 av Montaigne 75008.
Map 6 F1.
[01 53 23 99 19.

Comédie Française
Place Colette 75001.
Map 8 E1.
[01 44 58 15 15.

**Odéon Théâtre de
l'Europe**
Pl de l'Odéon 75006.
Map 8 F5.
[01 44 41 36 36.

Palais Royal
38 rue Montpensier
75001.
Map 8 E1.
[01 42 97 59 81.

Théâtre d'Edgar
58 bd Edgar-Quinet
75014.
Map 12 D2.
[01 42 79 97 97.

**Théâtre National
de Chaillot**
1 pl du Trocadéro
75016.
Map 5 C2.
[01 53 65 30 00.

**Théâtre National
de la Colline**
15 rue Malte-Brun
75020.
[01 44 62 52 52.

CLASSICAL MUSIC

**Auditorium du
Châtelet**
(Auditorium des Halles)
Forum des Halles, Porte
St-Eustache.
Map 9 A2.
[01 42 28 28 40.

Cité de la Musique
221 av Jean-Jaurès 75019.
[01 44 84 44 84.

Opéra Comique
(Salle Favart) 5 rue Favart
75002. **Map** 4 F5.
[01 42 44 45 46.

**Opéra de Paris
Bastille**
120 rue de Lyon 75012.
Map 10 E4.
[01 44 73 13 99.

Salle Gaveau
45 rue la Boétie 75008.
Map 3 B4.
[01 49 53 05 07.

Salle Pleyel
252 rue du Faubourg St-
Honoré 75008. **Map** 2 E3.
[01 45 61 53 00.

**Théâtre des
Champs-Elysées**
15 av Montaigne 75008.
Map 6 F1.
[01 49 52 50 50.

Théâtre de la Ville
2 pl du Châtelet 75004.
Map 9 A3.
[01 42 74 22 77.

DANCE

**Maison des Arts de
Créteil**
Pl Salvador Allende 94000
Créteil.
[01 45 13 19 19.

Opéra Garnier
Pl de l'Opera 75009.
Map 4 E5.
[01 40 01 17 89.

Théâtre de la Ville
(See Classical Music.)

CLUBS AND
CABARET

Les Bains
7 rue du Bourg-L'Abbé
75003. **Map** 9 B1.
[01 48 87 01 80.

Balajo
9 rue de Lappe 75011.
Map 10 E4.
[01 47 00 07 87.

Folies-Bergères
32 rue Richer 75009.
[01 44 79 98 98.

Folies Pigalle
11 pl Pigalle 75009.
Map 4 E2.
[01 48 78 25 56.

La Java
105 rue du Faubourg-du-
Temple 75010.
[01 42 02 20 52.

La Locomotive
90 bd de Clichy 75018.
Map 4 D1.
[01 53 41 88 88.

Lido
116 bis av des Champs-
Elysées 75008. **Map** 2 E4.
[01 40 76 56 10.

Moulin Rouge
82 bd de Clichy 75018.
Map 4 E1.
[01 46 06 00 19.

Paradis Latin
28 rue du Cardinal-Lemoine
75005. **Map** 9 B5.
[01 43 25 28 28.

ROCK, JAZZ AND
WORLD MUSIC

**Chapelle des
Lombards**
19 rue de Lappe 75011.
Map 10 F4.
[01 43 57 24 24.

La Cigale
120 bd Rochechouart
75018. **Map** 4 F2.
[01 42 23 15 15.

Elysée-Montmartre
72 bd Rochechouart
75018. **Map** 4 F2.
[01 44 92 45 45.

New Morning
7–9 rue des Petites-Ecuries
75010.
[01 45 23 51 41.

Olympia
28 bd des Capucines
75009. **Map** 4 D5.
[01 47 42 25 49.

**Palais Omnisports
de Paris-Bercy**
8 bd de Bercy 75012.
Map 14 F2.
[fi 01 44 68 44 68.

**Le Petit Journal
St-Michel**
71 bd St-Michel 75005.
Map 12 F1.
[01 43 26 28 59.

Zénith
211 av de Jean-Jaurès
75019.
[01 42 08 60 00.

CINEMA

Gaumont Gobelins
58 & 73 av des Gobelins
75013. **Map** 13 B4.
[fi 01 47 07 55 88.

La Géode
26 av Corentin-Cariou
75019.
[fi 01 40 05 80 00.

Le Grand Rex
1 bd Poissonnière
75002.
[fi 01 42 36 83 93.

**Max Linder
Panorama**
24 bd Poissonnière
75009.
[fi 01 48 24 88 88.

SPORT

**Hippodrome de
Longchamp**
Bois de Boulogne 75016.
[01 44 30 75 00.

**Palais Omnisports
de Paris-Bercy**
(See Rock, Jazz and World
Music.)

Parc des Princes
24 rue du Commandant-
Guilbaud 75016.
[01 42 88 02 76.

**Stade Roland
Garros**
2 av Gordon-Bennett
75016.
[01 47 43 48 00.

PARIS STREET FINDER

THE MAP REFERENCES given with sights, shops and entertainment venues described in the Paris section of the guide refer to the maps on the following pages. Map references are also given for Paris hotels *(see pp540–44)* and restaurants *(pp580–84)*, and for useful addresses in the *Travellers' Needs* and *Survival Guide* sections at the back of the book. The maps include not only the main sightseeing areas but also the most important districts for hotels, restaurants, shopping and entertainment venues. The key map below shows the area of Paris covered by the *Street Finder*, with the arrondissement numbers for the various districts. The symbols used for sights and other features on the *Street Finder* maps are listed opposite.

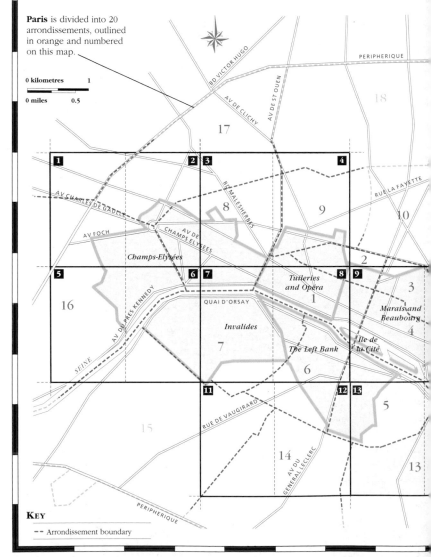

Paris is divided into 20 arrondissements, outlined in orange and numbered on this map.

0 kilometres   1

0 miles   0.5

BD VICTOR HUGO

PERIPHERIQUE

AV DE CLICHY

AV DE ST OUEN

18

17

1 **2** **3** **4**

AV CHARLES DE GAULLE

BD MALESHERBES

RUE LA FAYETTE

8   9   10

AV FOCH

AV DE CHAMPS ELYSEES

Champs-Elysées

2

5 **6** **7** **8** **9**

Tuileries and Opéra

3

16   QUAI D'ORSAY   1

Maraisand Beaubourg

AV DU PRES KENNEDY

Invalides

4

Île de la Cité

7   *The Left Bank*

SEINE

6

11 **12** **13**

5

RUE DE VAUGIRARD

15   14   13

AV DU GENERAL LECLERC

PERIPHERIQUE

KEY

-- Arrondissement boundary

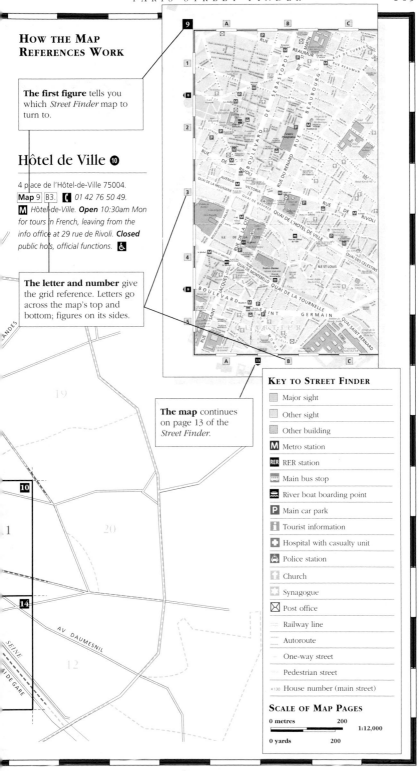

HOW THE MAP REFERENCES WORK

The first figure tells you which *Street Finder* map to turn to.

Hôtel de Ville ⑩

4 place de l'Hôtel-de-Ville 75004.
Map 9 B3. **[** 01 42 76 50 49.
M *Hôtel-de-Ville.* **Open** 10:30am Mon
for tours in French, leaving from the
info office at 29 rue de Rivoli. **Closed**
public hols, official functions. **&**

The letter and number give the grid reference. Letters go across the map's top and bottom; figures on its sides.

The map continues on page 13 of the *Street Finder.*

KEY TO STREET FINDER

	Major sight
	Other sight
	Other building
M	Metro station
RER	RER station
	Main bus stop
	River boat boarding point
P	Main car park
	Tourist information
	Hospital with casualty unit
	Police station
	Church
	Synagogue
⊠	Post office
	Railway line
	Autoroute
	One-way street
	Pedestrian street
«130	House number (main street)

SCALE OF MAP PAGES

0 metres   200
                              1:12,000
0 yards   200

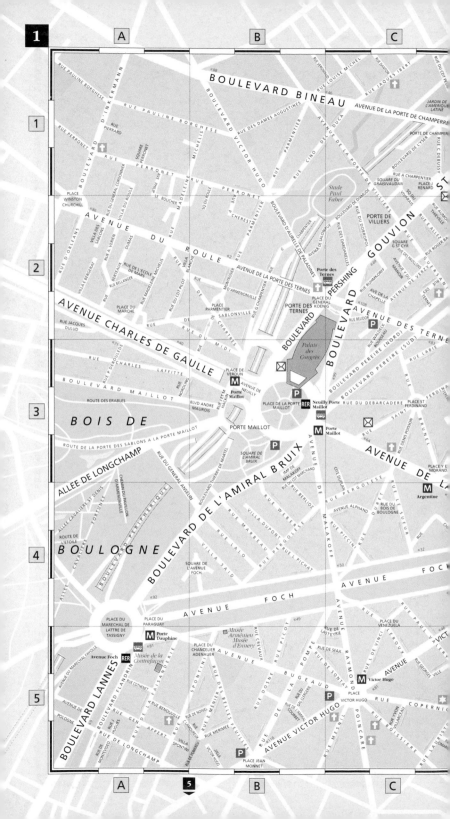

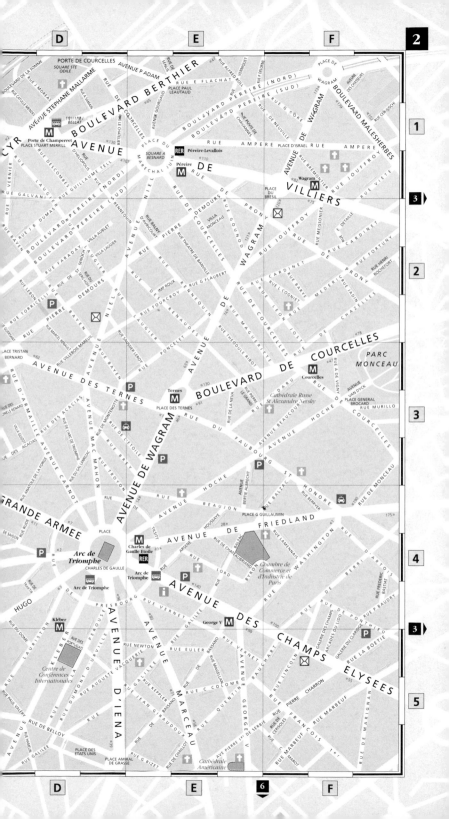

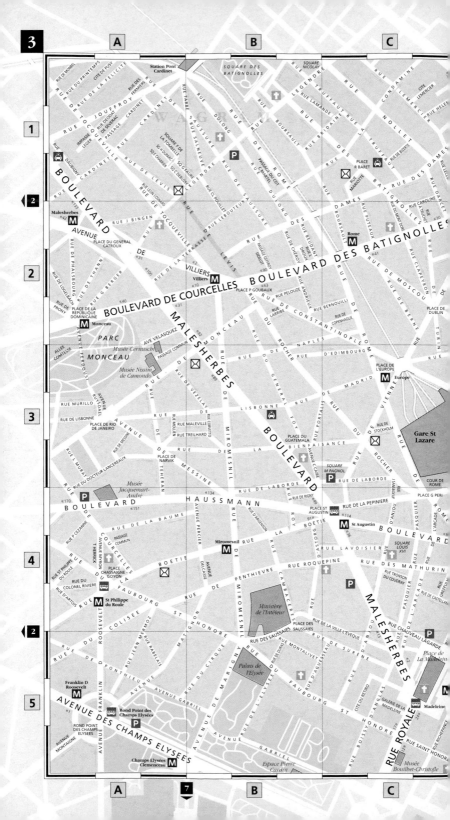

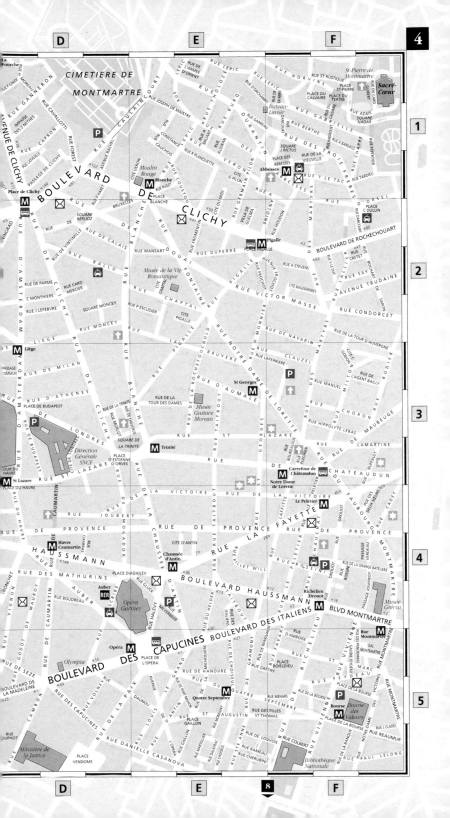

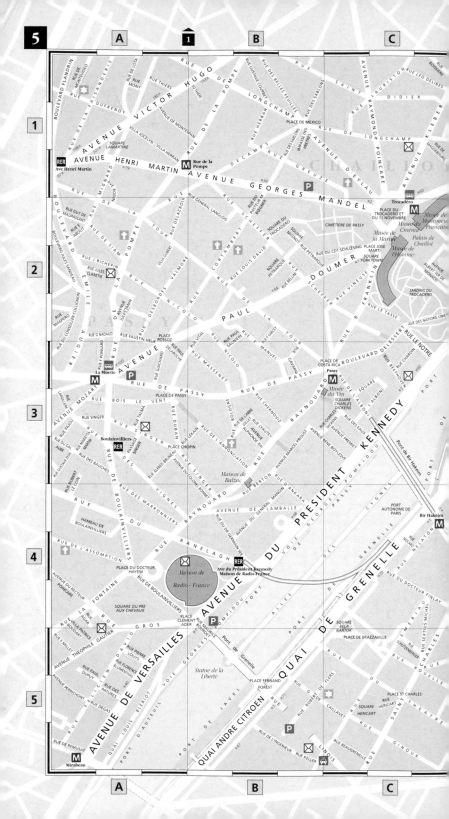

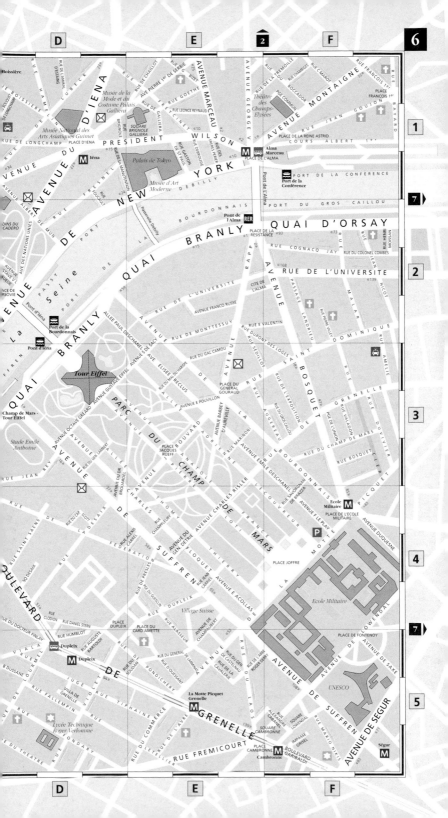

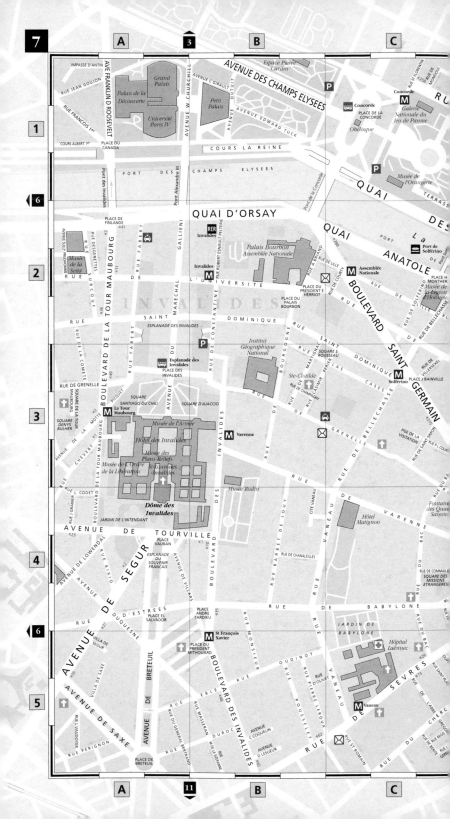

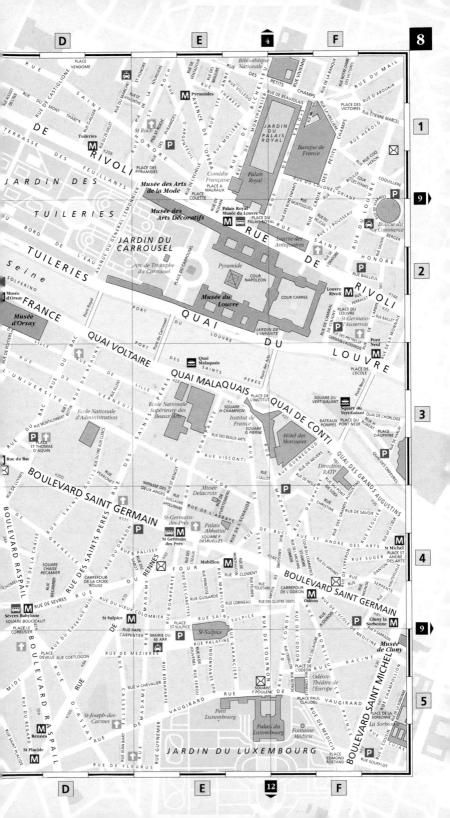

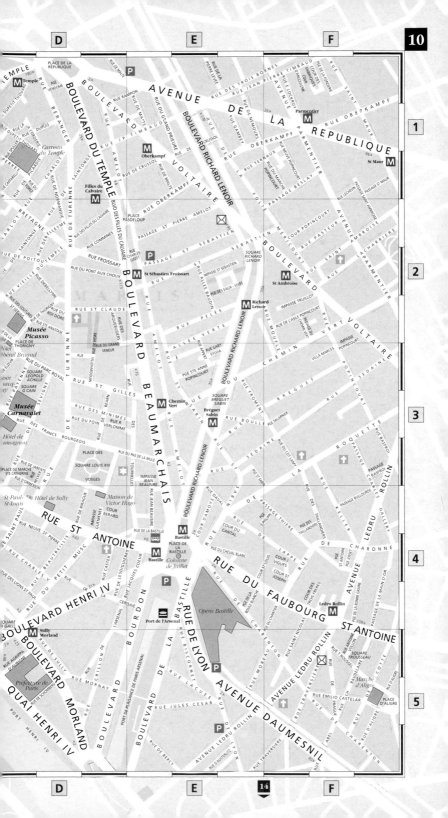

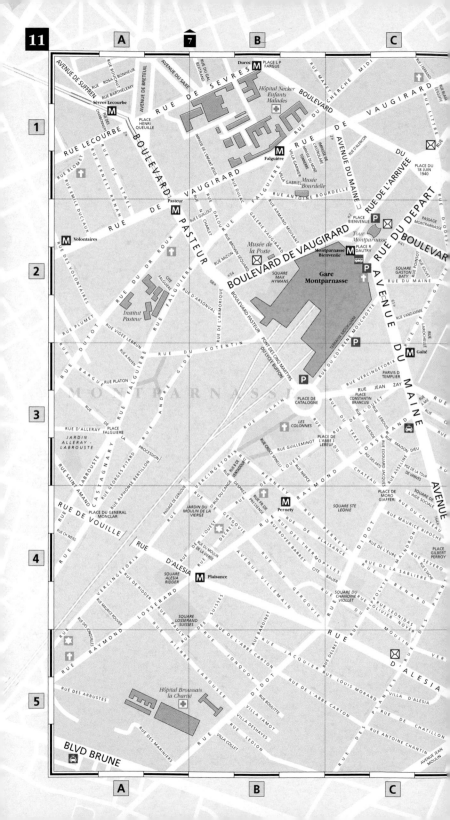

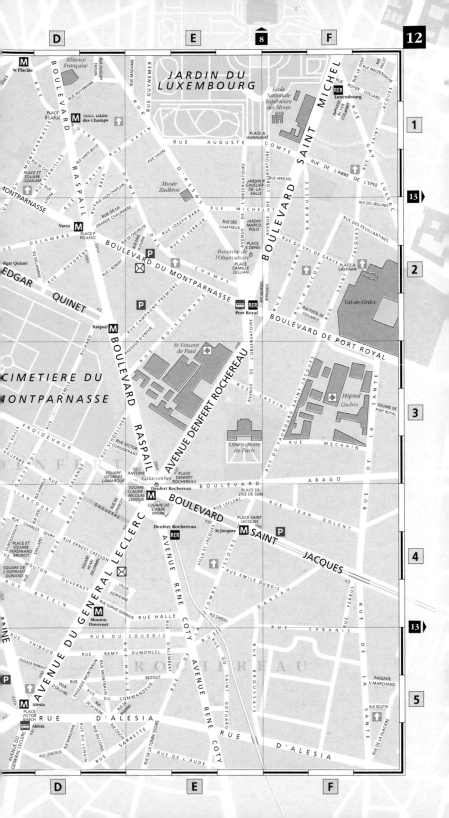

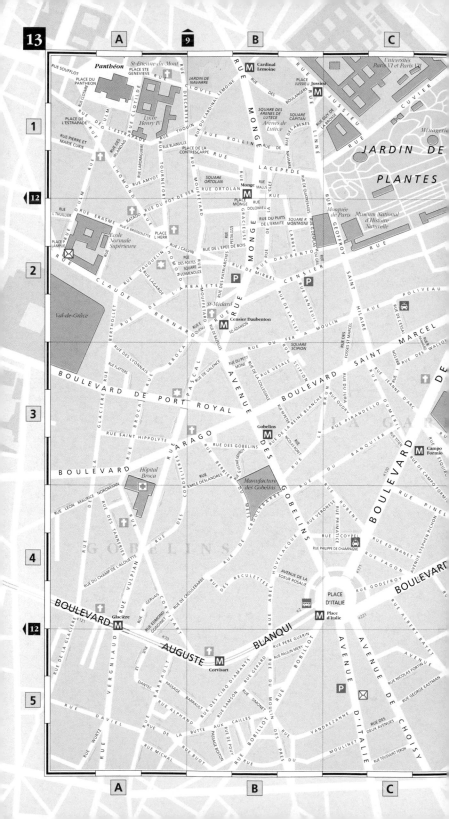

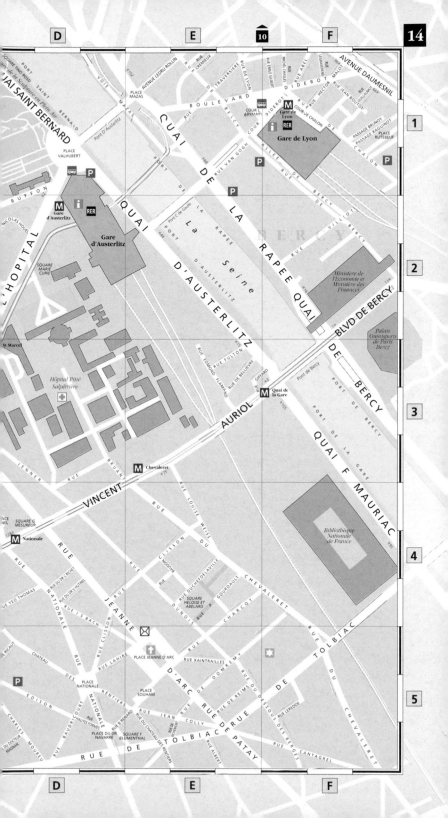

ILE DE FRANCE

SET AT THE HEART OF FRANCE, with Paris as its hub, Ile de France extends well beyond the densely populated suburbs of the city. Its rich countryside incorporates a historic royal region of monumental splendour central to *"la gloire de la France"*.

The region became a favourite with French royalty after François I transformed Fontainebleau into a Renaissance palace in 1528. Louis XIV kept the Ile de France as the political axis of the country when he started building Versailles in 1661. This Classical château created by the combined genius of Le Nôtre, Le Vau, Le Brun and Jules Hardouin-Mansart is France's most visited sight. It stands as a monument to the power of the Sun King and is still used for state occasions. Rambouillet, closely linked with Louis XVI, is now the summer residence of the French president, while Malmaison was the favourite home of Empress Josephine. To the north, the Château d'Ecouen offers a showcase of Renaissance life and to the south Vaux-le-Vicomte boasts some of the loveliest formal gardens in France.

Nourished by the Seine and Marne rivers, the Ile de France is a patchwork of chalky plains, wheatfields and forests. The serene, poplar-lined avenues and rustic charm of the region have been an inspiration to painters such as Corot, Rousseau, Pissarro and Cézanne.

SIGHTS AT A GLANCE

Châteaux and Museums
Château de Dampierre **8**
Château de Fontainebleau **13**
Château de Malmaison **5**
Château de Rambouillet **9**
Château de Sceaux **7**
Château de Vaux-le-Vicomte **11**
Château de Versailles **6**
Musée National de la
   Renaissance **2**

Towns
Provins **12**
St-Germain-en-Laye **4**

Abbeys and Churches
Abbaye de Royaumont **1**
Basilique St-Denis **3**

Theme Parks
Disneyland Paris **10**

KEY

☐   Greater Paris

▨   Central Paris

✈   International airport

▬   Motorway

▬   Major road

═   Minor road

0 kilometres   20

0 miles   10

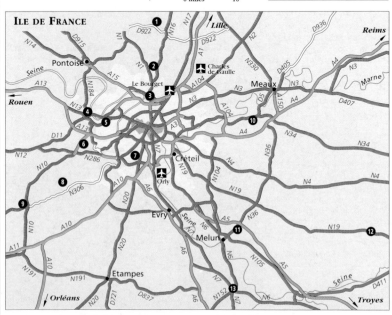

◁ **Magnificent formal gardens at the Château Vaux-le-Vicomte**

The vaulted Gothic refectory of Abbaye de Royaumont

Abbaye de Royaumont **①**

Fondation Royaumont, Asnières-sur-Oise, Val-d'Oise. **[** 01 30 35 59 00. **Open** daily. 📷 ♿ restricted. **☑** phone 01 30 35 59 91. **Concerts.**

SET AMONG WOODS "near water and far from mankind", 30 km (20 miles) north of Paris, Royaumont is the finest Cistercian abbey in the Ile de France. Chosen for its remoteness, the abbey's stark stonework and simplicity of line reflect the austere teachings of St Bernard. However, unlike his Burgundian abbeys, Royaumont was founded in 1228 by Louis IX and his mother, Blanche de Castille. "St Louis" showered the abbey with riches and chose it as a royal burial site.

The abbey retained its royal links until the Revolution, when much of it was destroyed. It was then a textiles mill and orphanage until its revival as a cultural centre. The original pillars still remain, along with a gravity-defying corner tower and the largest Cistercian cloisters in France, which enclose a charming Classical garden. The monastic quarters border one side of the cloisters.

The Château de Royaumont, erected as the abbot's palace on the eve of the Revolution, is set apart and resembles an Italianate villa. A stroll around the grounds will reveal the monks' workshops, woods, ponds and Cistercian canals.

The abbey is sometimes used for concerts: phone the Fondation Royaumont for details.

Musée National de la Renaissance **②**

Chateau d'Ecouen, Val-d'Oise. **[** 01 34 38 38 50. **Open** Wed–Mon. **Closed** 1 Jan, 1 May, 25 Dec. 📷 ♿

THIS IMPOSING moated château is curiously adrift, halfway between St-Denis and Royaumont. Now a Renaissance museum, Ecouen's magnificent quadrilateral exterior provides an authentic setting for an impressive collection of paintings, tapestries, coffers, carved doors and staircases salvaged from other 16th-century châteaux.

Ecouen was built in 1538 for Anne de Montmorency, adviser to François I and Commander-in-Chief of his armies. As the second most powerful person in the kingdom, he employed Ecole de Fontainebleau artists and craftsmen to adorn his palace. Their influence is apparent in the ravishing painted fireplaces, depicting biblical and Classical themes in mysterious landscapes. The most striking room is the chapel, containing a gallery and vaulted ceilings painted with the Montmorency coat of arms.

Upstairs, a long gallery contains one of the finest series of 16th-century tapestries in France. Equally compelling are the princely apartments, the Renaissance tiled floors, the library of illuminated manuscripts, a collection of vivid ceramics from Lyon, Nevers, Venice and Faenza and Iznik, and a display of early mathematical instruments and watches.

Since the ground floor is open in the morning and the second floor in the afternoon, lunching at Ecouen is advised.

Basilique St-Denis **③**

1 rue de la Légion d'Honneur, St-Denis. Seine-St-Denis. **Open** daily. **Closed** 1 Jan, 1 May, 1 & 11 Nov, 25 Dec. 📷 ♿

ACCORDING TO LEGEND, the decapitated St Denis struggled here clutching his head, and an abbey was erected to commemorate the martyred bishop. Following the burial of Dagobert I in the basilica in 638, a royal link with St-Denis began, which was to span 12 centuries. Most French kings were entombed in St-Denis, and all the queens of France were crowned here.

The elegant, early Gothic basilica rests on Carolingian and Romanesque crypts. Of the medieval effigies,

Statue of Louis XVI at St-Denis

the most impressive are of Charles V (1364) and a 12th-century likeness in enamelled copper of Blanche de France with her dog.

The mask-like serenity of these effigies is in sharp

The west wing of Musée National de la Renaissance

The Renaissance tomb of Louis XII and Anne de Bretagne in St-Denis

contrast with the graphically realistic Renaissance portrayal of agony present in the grotesque mausoleum of Louis XII and Anne de Bretagne. Both are represented as naked figures in the tabernacle, their faces eerily captured at the moment of death. Above the mausoleum, effigies of the finely dressed royal couple contemplate their own nakedness. As a reflection of humanity in the face of death, the basilica's tombs have few rivals.

St-Germain-en-Laye ❹

Yvelines. 41,000. *Maison Claude Debussy, 38 rue au Pain.* *01 34 51 05 12.* *Tue, Fri & Sun.*

DOMINATING the place Général de Gaulle in this chic suburb is the legendary Château de St-Germain, birthplace of Louis XIV. Louis VI built the original stronghold in 1124 but only the keep and St-Louis chapel remain. Under François I and Henri II, the medieval upper tiers were demolished, leaving a moated pentagon. Henri IV built the pavilion and terraces that run down to the Seine, and Louis XIV had Le Nôtre landscape the gardens before leaving for Versailles in 1682.

Today the château houses the **Musée des Antiquités Nationales**, which exhibits archaeological finds from prehistory to the Middle Ages. Created by Napoleon III, the collection includes a 22,000-year-old carved female, a megalithic tomb, a bronze helmet from the 3rd century BC and Celtic jewellery. The finest treasure is the Gallo-Roman mosaic pavement.

Musée des Antiquités Nationales
Château de St-Germain-en-Laye.
01 34 51 53 65. ***Open*** *Wed–Mon.*

Château de Malmaison ❺

Rueil-Malmaison, Hauts-de-Seine.
01 41 29 05 55. ***Open*** *9:30am–12:30pm, 1:30–5:45pm Wed–Fri, 10am–6:30pm Sat & Sun (6pm in winter).* *restricted.*

SITUATED 15 km (9 miles) west of Paris, this 17th-century estate is now best known for its Napoleonic associations. Bought by Josephine as a retreat from the formality of the Emperor's residences at the Tuileries and Fontainebleau, it has charming rural grounds. While Josephine loved this country manor, Napoleon scorned its entrance as fit only for servants. Instead, he had a curious drawbridge built at the back of the château.

The finest rooms are the frescoed and vaulted library, the canopied campaign room, and the sunny Salon de Musique, hung with paintings from Josephine's private collection. Napoleon's restrained yellow canopied bedroom contrasts the bedchamber Josephine died in, a magnificent indulgence bedecked in red. Many of the rooms overlook the romantic "English" gardens and the famous rose garden which was cultivated by Josephine after her divorce.

Memorabilia abound, from Imperial eagles to David's moody portrait of Napoleon, or Gérard's painting of the languid Josephine reclining on a chaise-longue.

Château Bois Préau, set in the wooded grounds, houses a museum dedicated to Napoleon's exile and death.

Empress Josephine's bed at Château de Malmaison

Château de Versailles ❻

Garden statue of a flautist

THE PRESENT PALACE, started by Louis XIV in 1668, grew around Louis XIII's original hunting lodge. Architect Louis Le Vau built the first section, which expanded into an enlarged courtyard. From 1678, Jules Hardouin-Mansart added north and south wings and the Hall of Mirrors. He also designed the chapel, completed in 1710. The Opera House (L'Opéra) was added by Louis XV in 1770. André Le Nôtre enlarged the gardens and broke the monotony of the symmetrical layout with expanses of water and creative use of uneven ground. Opposite the château is the Musée des Carrosses, housing a collection of royal carriages.

★ Formal Gardens
Geometric paths and shrubberies are features of the gardens.

The Orangery was built beneath the Parterre du Midi to house exotic plants in winter.

Fountain of Latona
Four marble basins rise to Balthazar Marsy's statue of the goddess Latona.

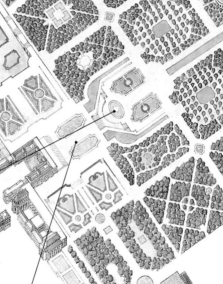

Water Parterre

★ Château
Under Louis XIV, Versailles became the centre of political power in France.

Dragon Fountain
The fountain's centrepiece is a winged monster.

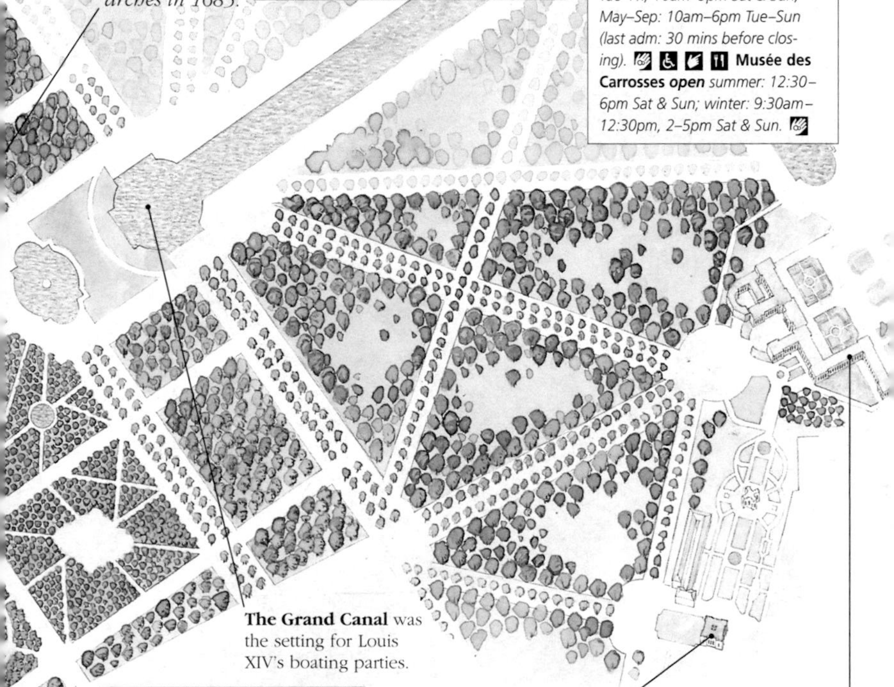

The King's garden features a mirror pool in the 19th-century garden created by Louis XVIII.

Colonnade
Mansart designed this circle of marble arches in 1685.

VISITORS' CHECKLIST

Versailles, Yvelines. 01 30 84 74 00. 171 from Paris. *Versailles Rive Gauche.* *Versailles Chantiers, Versailles Rive Droite.* **Château open** *Oct– Apr: 9am–5pm Tue–Sun; May– Sep: 9am–6pm Tue–Sun.* **Grand Trianon & Petit Trianon open** *Oct–Apr: 10am–noon, 2pm–5pm Tue–Fri, 10am–5pm Sat & Sun; May–Sep: 10am–6pm Tue–Sun (last adm: 30 mins before closing).* **Musée des Carrosses open** *summer: 12:30– 6pm Sat & Sun; winter: 9:30am– 12:30pm, 2–5pm Sat & Sun.*

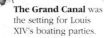

The Grand Canal was the setting for Louis XIV's boating parties.

Petit Trianon
Built in 1762 as a retreat for Louis XV, this small château became a favourite with Marie-Antoinette.

Fountain of Neptune
Groups of sculptures spray spectacular jets of water in Le Nôtre's 17th-century garden.

★ Grand Trianon
Louis XIV built this small palace of stone and pink marble in 1687 to escape the rigours of court life, and to enjoy the company of Madame de Maintenon.

STAR FEATURES

★ **Château**

★ **Formal Gardens**

★ **Grand Trianon**

Inside the Château de Versailles

THE SUMPTUOUS main apartments are on the first floor of this vast château complex. Around the Marble Courtyard are the private apartments of the king and queen. On the garden side are the state apartments where official court life took place. These were richly decorated by Charles Le Brun with coloured marble, stone and wood carvings, murals, velvet, silver and gilded furniture. Beginning with the Salon d'Hercule, each state room is dedicated to an Olympian deity. The climax is the Hall of Mirrors, where 17 great mirrors face tall arched windows.

KEY TO FLOORPLAN

- ☐ South wing
- ☐ Coronation room
- ☐ Madame de Maintenon's apartments
- ☐ Queen's apartments and private suite
- ☐ State apartments
- ☐ King's apartments and private suite
- ☐ North wing
- ☐ Non-exhibition space

★ **Queen's Bedroom**
In this room the queens of France gave birth to the royal children in public view.

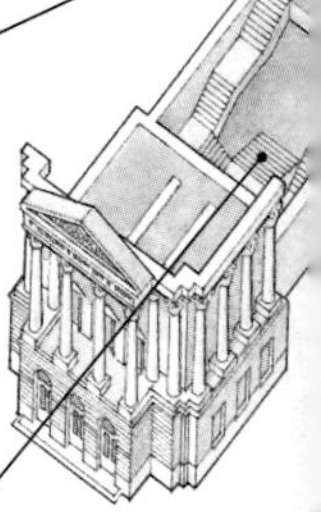

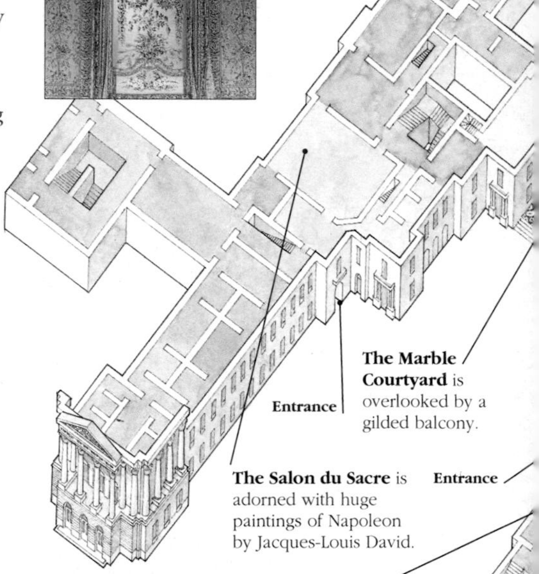

The Marble Courtyard is overlooked by a gilded balcony.

Entrance

The Salon du Sacre is adorned with huge paintings of Napoleon by Jacques-Louis David.

Entrance

★ **Salon de Vénus**
A statue of Louis XIV stands amid the rich marble decor of this room.

Stairs to ground floor reception area

★ **Chapelle Royale**
The chapel's first floor was reserved for the royal family and the ground floor for the court. The beautiful interior is decorated with Corinthian columns and white marble, gilding and Baroque murals.

STAR FEATURES

★ Chapelle Royale

★ Salon de Vénus

★ Hall of Mirrors

★ Queen's Bedroom

★ Hall of Mirrors
Great state occasions were held in this room stretching 70 m (233 ft) along the west façade. Here in 1919 the Treaty of Versailles was ratified, ending World War I.

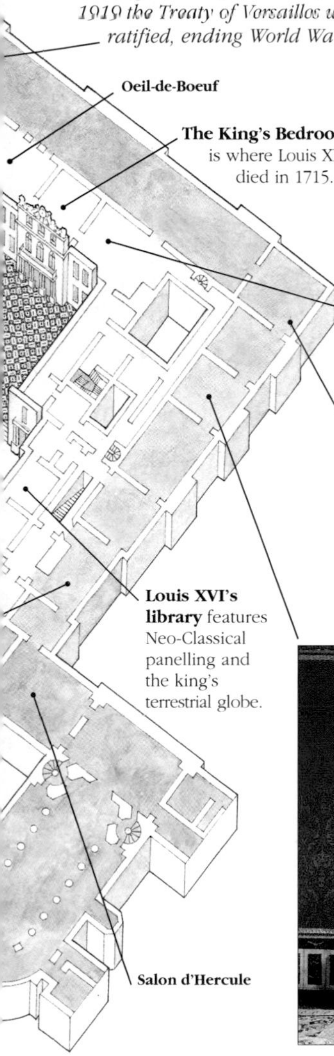

Oeil-de-Boeuf

The King's Bedroom is where Louis XIV died in 1715.

The Cabinet du Conseil was used by the king to receive his ministers and family.

Salon de la Guerre
The room's theme of war is reinforced by Antoine Coysevox's stuccoed relief of Louis XIV riding to victory.

Louis XVI's library features Neo-Classical panelling and the king's terrestrial globe.

Salon d'Apollon
Designed by Le Brun and dedicated to the god Apollo, this was Louis XIV's throne room. A copy of Hyacinthe Rigaud's famous portrait of the king (1701) hangs here.

Salon d'Hercule

TIMELINE

Louis XV

1667 Grand Canal begun

1668 Construction of new château by Le Vau

1722 12-year-old Louis XV occupies Versailles

1793 Louis XVI and Marie-Antoinette executed

1833 Louis-Philippe turns the château into a museum

1650	1700	1750	1800	1850

1671 Interior decoration by Le Brun begun

1661 Louis XIV enlarges château

1682 Louis XIV and Marie-Thérèse move to Versailles

1715 Death of Louis XIV. Versailles abandoned by court

1774 Louis XVI and Marie-Antoinette live at Versailles

1789 King and Queen forced to leave Versailles for Paris

1919 Treaty of Versailles signed on 28 June

Château de Sceaux ❼

Sceaux, Hauts-de-Seine. **☎** *01 46 61 06 71.* **Open** *Wed–Mon.* **Closed** *public hols.* 🖼 ♿

T HE PARC DE SCEAUX, bounded by elegant villas, is an appealing mixture of formal gardens, woods and water containing Classical gardens designed by Le Nôtre. The gardens use water to great effect, with tiered waterfalls and fountains presenting a moving staircase that cascades into an octagonal basin. This feeds into the Grand Canal and offers a poplar-lined view to the Pavillon de Hanovre. This elegant pavilion is one of several that adorn the park, which also contains Mansart's Classical Orangerie. Today this is the setting for exhibitions and, in summer, classical music concerts.

Built for Colbert in 1670, the original château was demolished and rebuilt in Louis XIII style in 1856. The stylish fake contains the Musée de l'Ile de France, which celebrates the landscapes, châteaux and history of the region through paintings, furniture, sculpture and ceramics.

Château de Dampierre ❽

Dampierre-en-Yvelines, Yvelines. **☎** *01 30 52 53 24.* **Open** *Apr–mid-Oct: daily pm.* 🖼 ♿ *restricted.*

A FTER VERSAILLES and Rambouillet, Dampierre is the most celebrated château southwest of Paris. Built in

---

1675 for the Duc de Chevreuse, the exterior of the château is a harmonious composition of rose-coloured brick and cool stone, designed by Hardouin-Mansart.

By contrast, the interior sumptuously evokes Versailles, particularly in the royal apartments and the Louis XIV dining room. The grandest room is the frescoed Salle des Fêtes, remodelled in the 19th century in triumphal Roman style. The rooms overlook gardens landscaped round a canal by Le Nôtre.

Château de Rambouillet

Château de Rambouillet ❾

Rambouillet, Yvelines. **☎** *01 34 83 00 25.* **Open** *Wed–Mon.* **Closed** *1 Jan, 1 May, 1 & 11 Nov, 25 Dec, and when president in residence.* 🖼

T HE CHATEAU borders the deep Forêt de Rambouillet, once the favourite royal hunting ground. This ivy-covered red-brick château, flanked by five stone towers, is curious rather than beautiful. Adopted

---

as a feudal castle, country estate, royal palace and Imperial residence, it reflects a composite of French royal history. Since 1897, it has been the president's official summer residence.

Inside, oak-panelled rooms are adorned with Empire-style furnishings and Aubusson tapestries. The main façade overlooks Classical parterres. Nearby is the Queen's Dairy, given by Louis XVI to Marie-Antoinette so that she could play milkmaid.

Environs
About 28 km (17 miles) north on the D11 is the **Château de Thoiry,** which has a large zoo of around 800 animals in its grounds and an innovative play area for children.

Disneyland Paris ❿

Marne-la-Vallée, Seine-et-Marne. **☎** *01 60 30 60 30.* **Open** *daily.* 🚇 *Marne-la-Valée-Chessy.* 🚆 *TGV from Lille or Lyon.* 🚌 *from Charles de Gaulle and Orly airports.* ♿

T HE RESORT covers 600 ha (1,500 acres) of which the theme park covers 40 ha (99 acres). The park is divided into five themes: Frontierland, Adventureland, Main Street USA, Fantasyland and Discoveryland. Although themes rely heavily on Hollywood nostalgia, Disneyland Paris has tried to give this park a European touch. The **Minnie Mouse**
resort's rides include Space Mountain which tests even the sturdiest of dispositions.

Château de Vaux-le-Vicomte ⓫

Maincy, Seine-et-Marne. **☎** *01 64 14 41 90.* **Open** *Mar–11 Nov: daily.* 🖼

S ET NORTH OF MELUN, not far from Fontainebleau, the château enjoys a peaceful rural location. Nicolas Fouquet, a

---

SÈVRES PORCELAIN

In 1756 Madame de Pompadour and Louis XV opened a porcelain factory near Versailles at Sèvres to supply the royal residences with tableware and *objets d'art*. Thus began the production of exquisite dinner services, statuettes, Etruscan-style vases, romantic cameos and porcelain paintings, depicting grand châteaux or mythological scenes. Sèvres porcelain is typified by its translucence, durability and narrow palette of colours.

***Le Pugilat* (1832), one of a pair of vases from Sèvres**

ANDRÉ LE NÔTRE

As the greatest French landscape gardener, Le Nôtre (1613–1700) created masterpieces in château gardens all over France. His Classical vision shaped many in the Ile de France, such as those at Dampierre, Sceaux and Vaux-le-Vicomte. At Vaux he perfected the concept of the *jardin à la française*: avenues framed by statues and box hedges; water gardens with fountains and ornate pools; graceful terraces and geometrical parterres "embroidered" with motifs. His genius lay in architectural orchestration and a sense of symmetry, typified by the sweeping vistas of Versailles, his greatest triumph.

powerful court financier to Louis XIV, challenged the architect Le Vau and the decorator Le Brun to create the most sumptuous palace of the day. The result, one of the greatest 17th-century French châteaux, surpassed Fouquet's dreams. However, it also led to his downfall. Louis and his ministers were so enraged – because its luxury cast the royal palaces into the shade – that they arrested Fouquet and confiscated all his estates.

As befits Fouquet's grand tastes, the interior is a gilded banquet of frescoes, stucco, caryatids and giant busts. The Salon des Muses boasts Le Brun's magnificent frescoed ceiling of dancing nymphs and poetic sphinxes. La Grande Chambre Carrée is decorated in Louis XIII style with panelled walls and an impressive triumphal frieze, evoking Rome. Unlike Versailles or even Fontainebleau, its many rooms feel touchingly intimate and the scale is not overwhelming.

Yet Vaux-le-Vicomte's continuing fame is due to André Le Nôtre's stunning gardens, the finest in the Ile de France. The landscape designer's early training as a painter is evident in the magnificent succession of terraces, ornamental lakes and fountains, which descend to a formal canal.

Provins ⑫

Seine-et-Marne. 🚶 *12,000.* 🚉 🚌
🛈 *Chemin de Villecran (01 64 60 26 26).* 🚍 *Sat.*

AS A ROMAN OUTPOST, Provins commanded the border of Ile de France and Champagne. Today, it offers a coherent vision of the medieval world. Ville Haute, the upper town, is clustered within high 12th-century ramparts, complete with crenellations and defensive ditches. The ramparts to the west are the best preserved. Here, between the fortified gateways of Porte de Jouy and Porte St-Jean, the fortifications are dotted with square, round and rectangular towers.

The town is dominated by Tour César, a keep with four corner turrets and a pyramid shaped roof. The moat and fortifications were added by the English during the Hundred Years' War. A guard-room leads to a gallery and views over the place du Chatel, a busy square of medieval gabled houses, and the Grange aux Dîmes to the endless wheatfields beyond.

Provins is proud of its crimson roses. Every June, a floral celebration is held in the riverside rose garden, marked by a medieval festival.

Château de Vaux-le-Vicomte seen across the gardens designed by Le Nôtre

Château de Fontainebleau ⑬

Ceiling detail from the Salle de Bal

F ONTAINEBLEAU is not the product of a single vision but is a bewildering cluster of styles from different periods. Louis VII built an abbey here which was consecrated by Thomas à Beckett in 1169. A medieval tower survives but the present château harks back to François I. Originally drawn by the local hunting, the Renaissance king created a decorative château modelled on Florentine and Roman styles.

Fontainebleau's abiding charm comes from its relative informality and spectacular forest setting. While impossible to cover in a day, the *grands appartements* provide a sumptuous introduction to this royal palace.

Ground floor

Jardin de Diane
Now more romantic than Classical, the garden features a bronze fountain of Diana as huntress.

★ Escalier du Fer-à-Cheval
This imposing horseshoe-shaped staircase by Jean Androuet du Cerceau, built in 1634, lies at the end of Cour du Cheval Blanc. Its ingenious design allowed carriages to pass beneath the two arches.

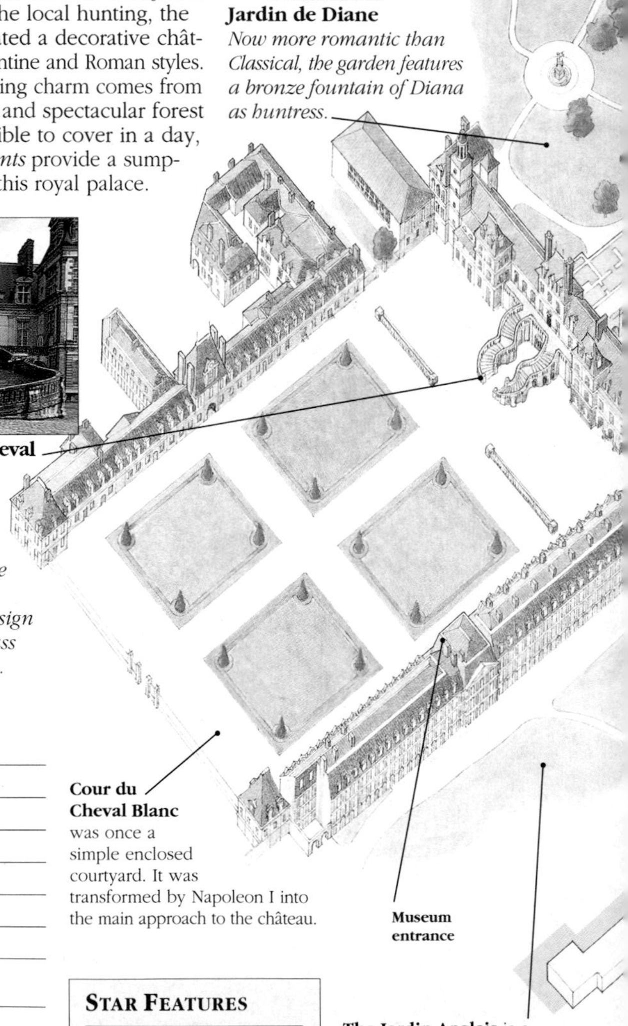

KEY TO FLOORPLAN

- ☐ Petits Appartements
- ☐ Galerie des Cerfs
- ▨ Musée Chinois
- ☐ Musée Napoléon
- ☐ Grands Appartements
- ▨ Salle Renaissance
- ☐ Appartements de Madame de Maintenon
- ☐ Grands Appartements des Souverains
- ▨ Escalier de la Reine/ Appartements des Chasses
- ☐ Chapelle de la Trinité
- ▨ Appartement Intérieur de l'Empereur

Cour du Cheval Blanc was once a simple enclosed courtyard. It was transformed by Napoleon I into the main approach to the château.

Museum entrance

The Jardin Anglais is a romantic "English" garden, planted with cypress and plantain trees. It was redesigned in the 19th century.

STAR FEATURES

- ★ Escalier du Fer-à-Cheval
- ★ Salle de Bal
- ★ Galerie François I

Porte Dorée
Originally a feudal gate-house, this was transformed into the entrance pavilion to the forest by Gilles Le Breton for François I.

VISITORS' CHECKLIST

Seine-et-Marne. ☎ 01 60 71 50 70. **Open** 9:30am–12:30pm, 2–5pm Wed–Mon. **Closed** 1 Jan, 1 May, 25 Dec.

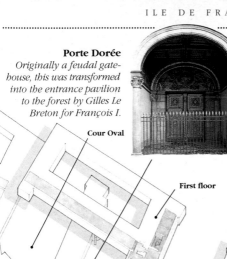

Cour Oval

First floor

★ **Salle de Bal**
The Renaissance ballroom, de-signed by Primaticcio (1552), was finished under Henri II. His emblems adorn the walnut cof-fered ceiling, forming a pattern reflected in the parquet floor.

The Appartements de Napol-éon I house his grandiose throne in the Emperor's Salle du Trône, formerly the Chambre du Roi.

Cour de la Fontaine

Chapelle de la Sainte Trinité was designed by Henri II in 1550. The chapel acquired its vaulted and frescoed ceiling under Henri IV and was completed by Louis XIII.

★ **Galerie François I**
This gilded gallery is a tribute to the Italian artists in the Ecole de Fontainebleau. Rosso Fiorentino's allegorical frescoes pay homage to the king's wish to create "a second Rome".

THE BARBIZON SCHOOL

Artists have been drawn to the glades of Fontainebleau since the 1840s, when a group of landscape painters, determined to paint only from nature, formed around Théodore Rousseau and Millet. They settled in the nearby hamlet of Barbizon where the Auberge Ganne, a museum dedicated to the Ecole de Barbizon, is located.

Spring at Barbizon, painted by Jean-François Millet (1814–75)

NORTHEAST
FRANCE

Introducing Northeast France

T HE FLAT, OPEN PLAINS of the Northeast are bordered
by the Vosges mountains and the forests of the
Ardennes. Apart from the sombre battle memorials,
the area is best known for the fine wines of
Champagne and Alsace, and some of France's finest
Gothic cathedrals. Its traditional coal, steel and
textile industries have declined but wheat and
wine production prosper, and the
Channel Tunnel promises
economic revival. This
map indicates some of
the many interesting
sights to see.

LE NORD AND PICARDY
(See pp182–95)

Amiens Cathedral

Amiens cathedral *is renowned
for its fine wood carvings and
its nave, the highest in France
(see pp192–3).*

*Beauvais
Cathedral*

Château de Compiègne

*Reim.
Cathed*

The pride of Beauvais *is its Gothic
cathedral and astronomical clock
(see p190) which escaped heavy
bombing during World War II.*

Half-timbered houses *and
Renaissance mansions line the
streets and alleys of Troyes' Old
Town (see p206) rebuilt after the
great fire in 1524. Its cathedral has
remarkable stained-glass windows.*

*Troyes
Cathedral*

The legacy of World War I *is strong in this area of former battlefields. The Douaumont Memorial outside Verdun* (see pp180–81), *with its 15,000 graves, is only one of many memorials and cemeteries here.*

Haut-Koenigsbourg, *a castle rebuilt in Neo-Gothic style by Kaiser Wilhelm II when Alsace-Lorraine was under German rule, is one of Alsace's most popular attractions* (see p218).

Strasbourg*, seat of the European Council, has a fine Gothic cathedral* (see pp220–21) *surrounded by delightful historic buildings.*

Douaumont Memorial

Porte Chaussée, Verdun

Place Stanislas, Nancy

Strasbourg Cathedral

CHAMPAGNE
(See pp196–207)

ALSACE AND LORRAINE
(See pp208–23)

Haut-Koenigsbourg

0 kilometres   50

0 miles   50

Regional Food: Northeast France

Visitors to Boulogne, Le Touquet and Calais know the northeast best for its sea catch. Besides the heaped platters of *fruits de mer*, a plate of steamed mussels and chipped potatoes is one of the greatest pleasures of this coast. A giant waffle dusted with sugar completes the meal.

Hops, used to make the local beer, grow inland, along with fields of chicory. Both hops and chicory are served as vegetables. Alsace and Lorraine share in the ancient tradition of beer-making. Beer is commonly used in the cuisine of Lorraine, while Riesling wine is more popular in the Alsace region. Alsatian cooking centres on *charcuterie* (cooked meats), culminating in the classic *choucroute garnie* (sauerkraut with pork and sausages).

Rich cakes and tarts are also popular, especially the *kougelhopf*, a ring-shaped cake studded with raisins, currants and almonds, and sometimes soaked in Kirsch.

Potato salad with sausage *reveals the German influence in robust Alsatian fare. This dish is usually served warm.*

Herrings, *found along the northeast coast of France, are popular grilled or cured, and served with potatoes.*

Brioche *is a buttery, egg-enriched bread. In Alsace, various brioches are associated with festivals –* neujohweka *are eaten on New Year's Day, and on St Nicholas Day (6 Dec) bakers make small brioche figures called* bonshommes.

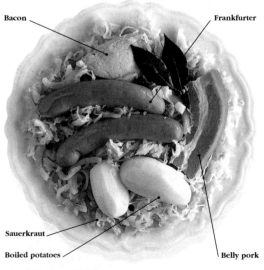

Bacon

Frankfurter

Sauerkraut

Boiled potatoes

Belly pork

Pâté en croûte *is cooked in a pastry case. The pastry keeps the pâté moist and faintly pink while it is baked in the oven.*

Choucroute garnie *is an earthy dish of sauerkraut with bacon, cured pork loin or knuckle, and fresh and smoked sausages – among them* boudin noir *(black pudding),* saucisse de Strasbourg *(a plump frankfurter) and* boudin blanc *(white pork sausage). It should be accompanied by boiled potatoes and strong* moutarde de Meaux, *along with a glass of chilled Alsatian Riesling wine.*

Pea soup, *also known as* Potage St-Germain, *is made with fresh peas which abound in the market gardens of Amiens.*

Truite Ardennaise, *pan-fried trout with smoked ham and cream, is an old-time classic from the Ardennes region.*

Zewelwai or onion quiche *is a tart made with a filling of onions, eggs and cream, typical of Lorraine.*

Porc aux deux pommes *is the quintessential Alsatian dish, consisting of pork served with potatoes and apples.*

Ardennes ham, *cured in the traditional local method, takes its name from the area. It is then salted and cold-smoked.*

Carbonnade *is a beef stew braised in beer; the name derives from "carbon", when the meat was grilled over coals.*

Tarte Alsacienne *is a fruit- and custard-filled tart, often made with yeast dough instead of shortcrust pastry.*

Madeleines *are tea cakes made famous by Marcel Proust in* Remembrance of Things Past.

Rum babas *are rum and sugar syrup-soaked yeast pastries baked in individual moulds.*

Macaroons *are almond meringue biscuits, a speciality of Nancy, capital of Lorraine.*

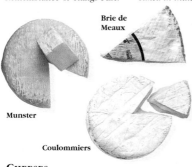

Brie de Meaux

Munster

Coulommiers

CHEESES

In addition to the familiar Brie de Meaux and tangy Munster of Alsace, the northeast has many lesser known but equally flavoursome cheeses such as the pungent Maroilles, Vieux Lille, Boulette d'Avesnes, Dauphin, Rollot and Coulommiers.

DRINKS

Beer is often drunk with meals in the northeast. Traditional methods of beer-making are still followed by big breweries such as Kronenbourg as well as many smaller breweries.

Savenne   **Kronenbourg**   **Bière de Garde**

France's Wine Regions: Champagne

Giant carved barrel, Épernay

SINCE ITS FABLED "INVENTION" by the monk Dom Pérignon in the 17th century, no other wine has rivalled champagne as the symbol of luxury and celebration. Most champagne is non-vintage: the skill of the blenders *(see p200)*, using reserves of older wines, creates consistency and excellence year on year. The "big names" *(grandes marques)*, command the prestige and the prices here; however, many small growers and cooperatives also produce excellent-value wines. Along with vintage champagnes, made only in the best years, they are well worth seeking out.

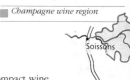

LOCATOR MAP

 *Champagne wine region*

Grapes going for pressing, Montagne de Reims

WINE REGIONS

Champagne is a compact wine region, largely in the French *département* of the Marne. Certain areas within it are particularly identified with certain styles of wine. The Aube is famous not only for champagne but also for an eccentric and pricy still wine, Rosé des Riceys.

Soissons

D1

A4

Château Thierry

N3

La Ferté-sous-Jouarre

RD33

Petit Morin

Grand Morin

KEY FACTS ABOUT CHAMPAGNE

 Location and Climate
The cool, marginal climate creates the finesse that other sparkling wines strive for, but seldom achieve. Chalky soils and east- and north-facing aspects help produce the relatively high acidity champagne needs.

Grape Varieties
Three varieties are grown, red **Pinot Noir** and **Pinot Meunier**, and white **Chardonnay**. Most champagne is a blend of all three, though Blanc de Blancs is 100 per cent Chardonnay and Blanc de Noirs, although white, is made only from red grapes.

Good Producers
Grandes Marques: Bollinger, Krug, Louis Roederer, Pol Roger, Deutz, Billecart-Salmon, Veuve Clicquot, Charles Heidsieck, Taittinger, Ruinart, Laurent Perrier.
Négociants, cooperatives and growers: A Bonnet, Boizel, Bricout, Drappier, Ployez-Jacquemart, Union Champagne, Cattier, Gimmonet, Andre Jacquart, Jacques Selosses, Chartogne-Taillet, Alfred Gratien, Emile Hamm, Albert Beerens, Vilmart.

 Good Vintages
1996, 1990, 1989, 1988, 1985, 1983.

BOLLINGER
Spécial Cuvée
BRUT
Champagne   *Ay-France*

***From a name** famous even to non-wine lovers, this is in the classic brut (dry) style; only brut non dosage or brut sauvage is drier.*

Nogent-sur-Seine

KEY

☐	Champagne *appellation* area
☐	Vallée de la Marne district
■	Montagne de Reims district
☐	Côte de Sézanne district
☐	Côte des Blancs district
☐	Aube district

0 kilometres   15

0 miles   15

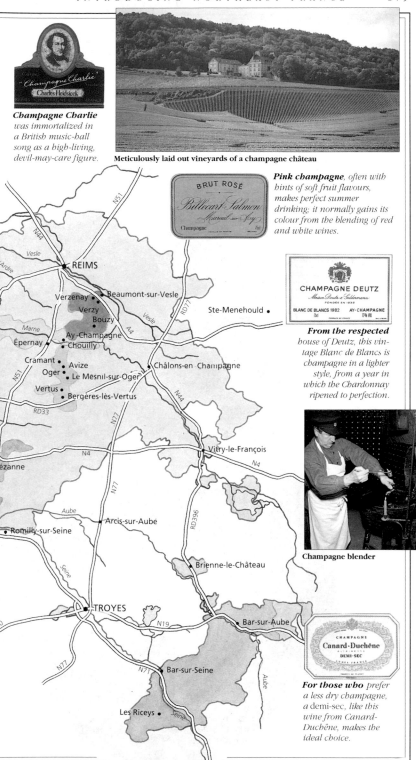

Champagne Charlie *was immortalized in a British music-hall song as a high-living, devil-may-care figure.*

Meticulously laid out vineyards of a champagne château

Pink champagne, *often with hints of soft fruit flavours, makes perfect summer drinking; it normally gains its colour from the blending of red and white wines.*

From the respected house of Deutz, this vintage Blanc de Blancs is champagne in a lighter style, from a year in which the Chardonnay ripened to perfection.

Champagne blender

For those who prefer a less dry champagne, a demi-sec, like this wine from Canard-Duchêne, makes the ideal choice.

The Battle of the Somme

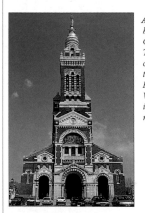

British World War I soldier

THE MANY CEMETERIES that cover the Somme region serve as a poignant reminder of the mass slaughter that took place on the Western Front in World War I (which ended with the Armistice on 11 November 1918). Between 1 July and 21 November 1916, the Allied forces lost more than 600,000 men and the Germans at least 465,000. The Battle of the Somme, a series of campaigns conducted by British and French armies against fortified positions held by the Germans, relieved the hard-pressed French at Verdun; but hopes of a breakthrough never materialized, and the Allies only managed to advance 16 km (10 miles).

LOCATOR MAP

▨ Somme battlefield

Beaumont Hamel Memorial Park, a tribute to the Royal Newfoundland Regiment, has a huge bronze caribou.

Thiepval Memorial was designed by Sir Edwin Lutyens. It dominates the landscape of Thiepval, one of the most hard-fought areas of the battle, appropriately chosen as a memorial to the 73,412 British soldiers with no known grave.

Albert was the site of heavy bombardment by German artillery in 1916. Today, the town is a convenient centre for visiting the battlefields. The Albert Basilique, with its leaning Virgin statue, was damaged but is now restored. It was a landmark for thousands of troops.

Lochnager Mine Crater, formed by the largest of the British mines exploded on 1 July 1916, lies on the ridge by La Boiselle.

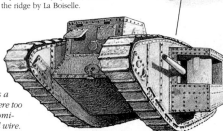

The British Tank Memorial, on the main road from Albert to Bapaume, commemorates the first use of tanks in warfare on 15 September 1916. The attack was a limited success; the tanks of World War I were too slow and unreliable to transform warfare dominated by artillery, machine guns and barbed wire.

Propaganda in World War I was employed by both sides to maintain support at home. This French postcard has a popular image for civilian consumption. It shows a dying soldier kissing the flag, under the tender gaze of a ministering nurse, affirming his faith in the cause with his last breath.

Delville Wood South African Memorial and Museum show the importance of Commonwealth forces in the Somme.

VISITORS' CHECKLIST

D929, D938 from Albert. **i** *9 rue Gambetta, Albert.* **C** *03 22 75 16 42.* **Albert Basilique, Beaumont Hamel Memorial Park, Thiepval, La Boiselle, Delville Wood and Pozières memorials open** *daily.* **Ulster Tower open** *May–Sep: Tue–Sun; Oct–Apr: Sun.* **South African Memorial Museum,** *Delville Wood, Longueval.* **C** *03 22 85 02 17.* **Open** *Feb–mid-Dec: Tue–Sun.* **Closed** *public hols.* **Historial de Péronne** **C** *03 22 83 14 18.* **Open** *Apr–Sep: daily; Oct– May: Tue–Sun.* **Closed** *mid-Dec–mid-Jan.*

Bapaume

D929

N17

A1

A2

• Flers

Morval •

Ginchy •

Canal du Nord

D917

Maricourt

• Maurepas

N17

Canal de la Somme

A1

D1

Péronne

Poppies were one of the few plants to grow on the battlefield. Ghengis Khan brought the first white poppy from China and, according to legend, it turned red after battle. Today poppies are a symbol of remembrance.

KEY

▨	Allied forces
▨	German forces
☐	Front Line before 1 July 1916
▨	Front Line progress July–September 1916
▨	Front Line progress September–November 1916

0 kilometres   5

0 miles   5

The Front Line trenches stretched from the North Sea to the Swiss frontier; only by keeping underground could men survive the terrible conditions. Trenches remain in a few areas, including the Beaumont Hamel Park.

LE NORD AND PICARDY

···

PAS DE CALAIS · NORD · SOMME · OISE · AISNE

BENEATH THE MODERN SKIN *of France's northernmost region, the sights and monuments bear witness to the triumphs and turbulence of its past: soaring Gothic cathedrals, stately châteaux along the river Oise, and the battlefields and memorials of World War I.*

The Channel ports of Dunkerque, Calais and Boulogne, and the refined resort of Le Touquet, are the focal points along a busy coastline that stretches from the Somme estuary to the Belgian frontier. Boulogne has a genuine maritime flavour, and the white cliffs running from here to Calais provide the most dramatic scenery along the Côte d'Opale.

Flemish culture holds sway along the border with Belgium: an unfamiliar France of windmills and canals where the local taste is for beer, hot-pots and festivals with gallivanting giants. Lille is the dominant city here, a sprawling modern metropolis with a lively historic heart and an excellent art museum. To the southwest, the grace of Flemish architecture is handsomely displayed in the central squares of Arras, the capital of Artois.

From here to the Somme valley the legacy of World War I, with its memorial cemeteries and poppy-strewn battlefields, makes compelling viewing.

Cathedrals are the main appeal of Picardy. In Amiens, its capital, Cathédrale Notre-Dame is a pinnacle of the Gothic style – its magnificence echoed by the dizzying achievements at Beauvais further south. Splendid cathedrals at Noyon, Senlis and the delightful hilltop town of Laon chart the evolution of the Gothic. Closer to Paris, two châteaux command attention. Chantilly, the epicentre of French equestrianism, boasts gardens by Le Nôtre and a 19th-century château housing copious art treasures. Compiègne, bordered by a large and inviting forest, plays host to a lavish royal palace favoured by French rulers from Louis XV to Napoleon III.

Memorial cemetery in Vallée de la Somme, an area still haunted by the memory of World War I

◁ Catamarans on the busy beach of Le Touquet Paris-Plage

Exploring Le Nord and Picardy

As the gateway to England and Belgium, this northern corner of France is buzzing with business and industries, with the large, Euro-oriented city of Lille offering great culture as well as a new hi-tech district. Yet peace and quiet is never far away. The coast between the historic port of Boulogne-sur-Mer and the Vallée de la Somme has a rich birdlife and is perfect for a relaxing seaside visit. Inland, the many Gothic cathedrals such as Amiens and Beauvais make an impressive tour, and the World War I battlefields and memorials provide an important insight into 20th-century history. Further south, the grand châteaux at Compiègne and Chantilly – which has the fascinating Musée Condé – are easily visited en route to or from Paris.

Key

- Motorway
- Major road
- Minor road
- Scenic route
- River
- ⁂ Viewpoint

0 kilometres   25

0 miles   25

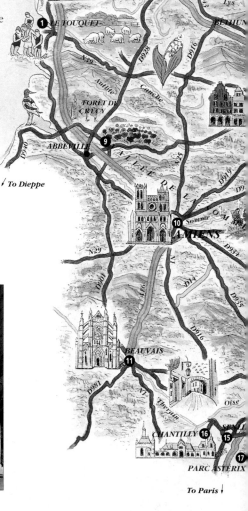

Lively outdoor café in the historic Grand' Place in the heart of Arras

SIGHTS AT A GLANCE

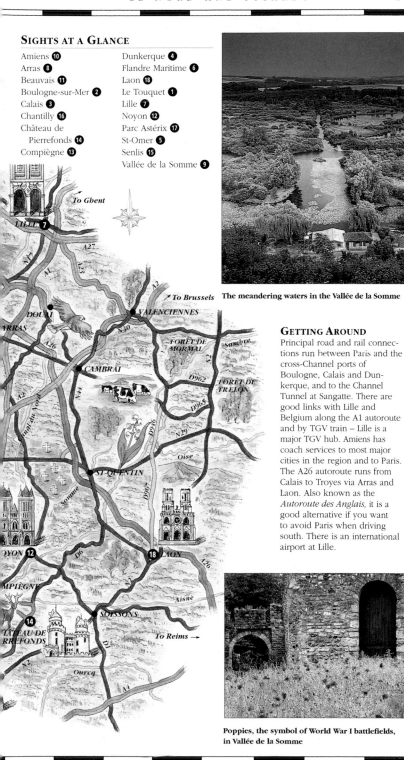

The meandering waters in the Vallée de la Somme

GETTING AROUND

Principal road and rail connections run between Paris and the cross-Channel ports of Boulogne, Calais and Dunkerque, and to the Channel Tunnel at Sangatte. There are good links with Lille and Belgium along the A1 autoroute and by TGV train – Lille is a major TGV hub. Amiens has coach services to most major cities in the region and to Paris. The A26 autoroute runs from Calais to Troyes via Arras and Laon. Also known as the *Autoroute des Anglais,* it is a good alternative if you want to avoid Paris when driving south. There is an international airport at Lille.

Poppies, the symbol of World War I battlefields, in Vallée de la Somme

Le Touquet beach at low tide

Le Touquet ❶

Pas de Calais. 🏛 6,000. 🚉 🚌 🚊
🛈 Palais de l'Europe (03 21 06 72 00).
🐟 Thu & Sat (Jun–mid-Sep: also Mon).

PROPERLY KNOWN as Le Touquet Paris-Plage, this resort was created in the 19th century and became fashionable with the rich and famous between the two World Wars.

A vast pine forest, planted in 1855, spreads around the town sheltering stately villas. To the west, a grid of smart hotels, holiday residences and sophisticated shops and restaurants borders a long, sandy beach. A racecourse and a casino help retain Le Touquet's affluent atmosphere, complemented by seaside amusements and sports facilities, including golf, horse-riding and land yachting.

Further inland, the hilltop town of **Montreuil** has lime-washed 17th-century houses, abundant restaurants and a tree-shaded rampart walk.

Boulogne-sur-Mer ❷

Pas de Calais. 🏛 44,000. 🚌 🚊 🛳
🛈 Forum Jean Woël, quai de la Poste
(03 21 31 68 38). 🐟 Wed & Sat.

AN IMPORTANT fishing port and popular cross-Channel terminus, Boulogne rewards its visitors well. Its historical attractions come neatly boxed in a walled Haute Ville, with the Porte des Dunes opening on to a 17th–19th-century ensemble of Palais de Justice,

Bibliothèque and Hôtel de Ville in **place de la Résistance**.

The 19th-century **Basilique Notre-Dame** is capped by a huge dome visible for miles around. Inside, a bejewelled wooden statue represents Boulogne's patroness, Notre-Dame de Boulogne. She is wearing a *soleil*, a radiant head-dress also worn by the women of the town during the *Grande Procession* held annually in her honour. Nearby, the powerful moated 13th-century **Château**, built for the Counts of Boulogne, is now a well-organized historical museum.

In the centre of town, shops, hotels and fish restaurants line the quai Gambetta on the east bank of the river Liane. To the north lie Boulogne's beach and **Nausicaa**, a spectacular and innovative aquarium and Sea Centre.

North of the town, the **Colonne de la Grande Armée** was erected in 1841 as a monument to Napoleon I's planned invasion of England in 1803–5. From the top there is a panoramic view along the coast towards Calais. This is the most scenic stretch of the Côte d'Opale (Opal Coast),

with the windblown headlands of **Cap Gris-Nez** and **Cap Blanc-Nez** offering extensive views across the Channel.

⚓ **Château**
Rue de Bernet. 📞 03 21 10 02 20.
Open Wed–Mon. **Closed** 1 Jan, 1 May, 25 Dec. 🎫
🐠 **Nausicaa**
Bd Sainte-Beuve. 📞 03 21 30 98 98.
Open daily. **Closed** 2 weeks in Jan, 1 Jan, 25 Dec. 🎫 ♿

Calais ❸

Pas de Calais. 🏛 80,000. 🚉 🚌 🛳
🛈 12 bd Clémenceau (03 21 96 62 40). 🐟 Wed, Thu & Sat.

CALAIS IS A BUSY cross-Channel port with a sandy beach to the west. Clumsily rebuilt after World War II, it seems to have little to offer at first sight.

The **Musée des Beaux Arts et de la Dentelle**, however, has works by the Dutch and Flemish Schools, and recalls the town's lace-making industry. Also on show are studies for Auguste Rodin's famous statue *The Burghers of Calais* (1895). This monument stands outside the

The windswept Cap Blanc-Nez on the Côte d'Opale

The Burghers of Calais by Auguste Rodin (1895)

⋔ Musée Portuaire
9 quai de la Citadelle. **[** 03 28 63 33 39. **Open** Wed–Mon. **Closed** 1 Jan, 1 May, 25 Dec. 🈲 &

⋔ Musée des Beaux Arts
Place du Général de Gaulle. **[** 03 28 59 21 65. **Open** Wed–Mon. **Closed** some public hols. 🈲 &

⋔ Musée d'Art Contemporain
Avenue des Bains. **[** 03 28 59 21 65. **Open** Wed–Mon. **Closed** some public hols. 🈲 &

St-Omer ❺

Pas de Calais. 🏠 15,000. 🚉 🚌 **ℹ** bd Pierre Guillain (03 21 98 08 51). 🛒 Sat.

REFINED and old-fashioned St-Omer seems untouched by the war. The elegant 17th- and 18th-century houses lining the cobbled streets. Among them is **Hôtel Sandelin**, built in 1777, now a museum of fine and decorative arts. The **Cathédrale Notre-Dame** features original 13th-century tiles and a huge Classical organ. Nearby, the **Bibliothèque Municipale** contains rare manuscripts and early books from the Abbaye St-Bertin, a ruined 15th-century abbey east of St-Omer.

⋔ Hôtel Sandelin
14 rue Carnot. **[** 03 21 38 00 94. **Open** Wed–Sun. **Closed** public hols. 🈲 & ground floor only.

⋔ Bibliothèque Municipale
40 rue Gambetta. **[** 03 21 38 35 08. **Open** Tue–Sat. **Closed** public hols.

rebuilt Flemish Renaissance-style Hôtel de Ville in the southern part of town. It celebrates an event during Edward III's siege of Calais in 1347, when six burghers offered their lives to save the rest of the town. They were later spared.
Musée de la Guerre, housed in a battle-scarred German blockhouse, offers a detailed account of local events during World War II.

⋔ Musée des Beaux Arts et de la Dentelle
25 rue Richelieu. **[** 03 21 46 48 40. **Open** Wed–Mon (Sun pm). **Closed** public hols. 🈲 &

⋔ Musée de la Guerre
Parc Saint Pierre. **[** 03 21 34 21 57. **Open** Feb–Nov: Wed–Mon. 🈲 &

Dunkerque ❹

Nord. 🏠 70,000. 🚉 🚌 ⛴ **ℹ** 4 place Général de Gaulle (03 28 66 79 21). 🛒 Wed & Sat.

DUNKERQUE is a major port and industrial centre with a cross-Channel ferry terminal to the west. Place du Minck, with fresh fish stalls, is a good starting point for exploring the port, by foot or boat. A stroll along the Bassin du Commerce leads to **Musée Portuaire**, celebrating the port's maritime past and present.
In the town centre, a statue commemorates the local hero, 17th-century corsair Jean Bart, who lies buried in **Eglise St-Eloi**. The belfry (1440) offers views and a Jean Bart tune.

Musée des Beaux Arts has an exhibition of the dramatic evacuation of 350,000 British and French troops in 1940. Also on display are works by artists Vasarely and César.
To the northeast, near Malo-les-Bains, the **Musée d'Art Contemporain** features ceramics and glassware.

The port at Dunkerque

CHANNEL CROSSINGS

Calais is only 36 km (22 miles) southeast of the English coast, and crossing the waters of the Channel – which the French know as La Manche (the Sleeve) – has inspired many intrepid exploits. The first crossing by balloon was in 1785 by Jean Pierre Blanchard; Captain M Webb made the first swim in 1875; and Louis Blériot's pioneering flight followed in 1909. Plans for an undersea tunnel, first laid as early as 1751, were finally achieved in 1994 with the opening of a railway link between Sangatte and Folkestone.

Children watching Louis Blériot taking off, 1909

Flandre Maritime **6**

Nord. ✈ *Lille.* ▤ *Bergues.*
🚢 *Dunkerque.* ℹ *Bergues, La Mairie
(03 28 68 60 44).*

SOUTH OF DUNKERQUE lies a
flat, agricultural plain with
narrow waterways and expansive skies – an archetypal
Flemish landscape with canals,
cyclists and ancient windmills.
The **Noordmeulen**, built just
north of Hondschoote in 1127,
is thought to be the oldest
windmill in Europe.

From Hondschoote the D3
follows the Canal de la Basse
Colme west to Bergues, a
fortified wool town with fine
16th–17th-century Flemish
works in its **Musée Municipal**.
Further south, the hilltop
town of **Cassel** has a cobbled
Grande Place with 16th–18th-
century buildings, and views
across Flanders and Belgium
from its Jardin Public.

🏛 Musée Municipal

1 rue du Mont de Piété, Bergues.
📞 *03 28 68 13 30.* **Open** *Feb–Dec:
Wed–Mon.* ♿

Lille **7**

Nord. 🗺 *175,000.* ✈ ▤ ▣ ℹ
Palais Rihour (03 20 21 94 21). 🛒 *daily.*

LILLE IS THE CAPITAL of Le Nord
and the most important city
in northern France. Close to
the Belgian border, it is
the heart of a conurbation of

**Flower stalls in the arcades of the
Vieille Bourse in Lille**

industrial estates, suburbs and
new towns with over a million
inhabitants. Lille is set to play
a pivotal role in the new
barrier-free Europe – a hi-
tech business district is under
construction, known as
EuraLille and served by its
own rail station, Lille-Europe.

The city's charm lies in its
historic centre, Vieux Lille – a
vibrant concentration of
cobbled squares and narrow
streets packed with stylish
shops, cafés and restaurants.
Place du Général de Gaulle
forms its hub, bordered by
the impressive façades of the
Art Deco **Voix du Nord**
newspaper offices and the
17th-century **Vieille Bourse**
(Old Exchange). To the east
lie the imposing **Nouvelle
Bourse** (New Exchange) and
the **Opéra**, both built at the
start of the 20th century.

For an overview of the Lille
region, ascend the belfry of
the city's 1920s town hall.

Musicians in place du Général de Gaulle, in the heart of Vieux Lille

⛪ Hospice Comtesse

32 rue de la Monnaie. 📞 *03 20 49 50
90.* **Open** *Wed–Mon.* **Closed** *1 Jan,
1 May, 14 Jul, 1 Nov, 25 Dec.* ♿
♿ *restricted.*

A hospital was first founded
here in 1237. Today its 15th-
and 17th-century buildings are
used for exhibitions. The Sick
Room (1470) has a splendid
barrel-vaulted ceiling and in
the Community Wing is a
beautiful Delft-tiled kitchen. The
hospice also has a collection
of ancient musical instruments.

🏛 Musée des Beaux Arts

Pl de la République. 📞 *03 20 06 78 00.*
Open *Wed–Mon.* ♿ ♿
One of the best art collections
outside Paris, the museum is
strong on Flemish works, including Rubens and Van Dyck.
Other highlights are *Paradise
and Hell* by Dirk Bouts, Van
Goyen's *The Skaters*, Goya's
The Letter, Delacroix's *Médée*
as well as works by Courbet
and Impressionist paintings.

Arras

Pas de Calais. 🖼 *42,000.* 🚉 🚏
🛈 *Hôtel de Ville, place des Héros
(03 21 51 26 95).* 🚌 *Wed & Sat.*

THE CENTRE of Arras, capital
of the Artois region, is
graced by two picturesque
cobbled squares enclosed by
155 houses with 17th-century
Flemish-style façades. A
triumph of postwar recon-
struction, each residence in the
Grand' Place and the smaller
Place des Héros has a slightly
varying design, with some
original shop signs still visible.

A monumental **Hôtel de
Ville** rebuilt in the Flamboyant
Gothic style stands at the
west end of place des Héros
– in the foyer are two giants,
Colas and Jacqueline, who
swagger round the town
during local festivals. From
the basement you can
take a lift up to the belfry,
which offers superb
views, or take a guided
tour into the labyrinth of
underground passages
below Arras. These were
cut in the limestone as
early as the 10th century.
They have often
served as shelter,
and during
World War I as
a subterranean
army camp.

The huge Abbaye
St-Vaast includes an
18th–19th-century
Neo-Classical cathedral
and the **Musée des
Beaux-Arts**. In the museum
fine medieval sculpture
includes a pair of beautifully
carved 13th-century angels.

Among other exhibits are a
local *arras* (hanging tapestry),
souvenirs of the town's best-
known son Maximilien de
Robespierre, and 19th-century
works by the School of Arras,
influenced by Corot.

🏛 **Hôtel de Ville**
Pl des Héros. 📞 *03 21 51 26 95.*
Open *daily.* **Closed** *1 Jan, 25 Dec.* 📷
🏛 **Musée des Beaux Arts**
22 rue Paul Doumer. 📞 *03 21 71 26
43.* **Open** *Wed–Mon.* **Closed** *public
hols.* 📷

Vallée de la Somme ❾

Somme. 🚉 🚏 🚌 *Amiens.*
🛈 *Péronne (03 22 84 42 38).*

MEANDERING west from St-
Quentin to St-Valéry-sur-
Somme, the river Somme
acts as a natural guide
through northern Picardy.
Its name is well known
from the battles fought here
during World War I (*see
pp180–81*). For a thought-
provoking introduction, visit
the **Historial de la Grande
Guerre**, which makes
imaginative use of
archive film, posters,
weapons, toys and
the savage art
of Otto Dix.
From
Péronne
west to
Amiens (*see
p190*), small lakes
and wooded
islands make the Somme
Valley an attractive area for
camping, walking and fishing.
In summer a small steam train

**Roadside shrine,
Somme Valley**

Boating on the river Somme

offers scenic rides between
Froissy and Dompierre.

West of Amiens lies **Samara**,
the largest archaeological park
in France. Adopting Amiens'
Gallo-Roman name, the park
has realistic reconstructions
of prehistoric dwellings. Exhibitions explain primitive crafts
like flint-cutting, dyeing and
corn-grinding. There are also
botanical gardens.

Further downstream, **Abbeville** is worth a stop for the
time-battered Eglise St-Vulfran.
Begun in 1488, it has a Flamboyant Gothic west front with
beautiful door panels carved
in the 16th century.

From here the Canal de la
Somme guides the river to
St-Valery-sur-Somme. This
fishing port-cum-resort has a
Haute Ville with partly preserved ramparts and a tree-
shaded seaside promenade.

A pleasant way to enjoy the
sea, sand and marsh landscape
of the bay is to take the little
train that loops between
Cayeux-sur-Mer and Le Crotoy
during the summer. Bird-
watchers can visit the **Maison
de l'Oiseau** on the D3 towards Cayeux-sur-Mer and
the **Parc Ornithologique de
Marquenterre** at St-Quentin-
en-Tourmont north of the bay.

🏛 **Historial de la Grande
Guerre**
Château de Péronne. 📞 *03 22 83 14
18.* **Open** *Oct–Apr: Tue–Sun; May–
Sep: daily.* **Closed** *1 Nov.*
📷 ♿ 📷
🏛 **Samara**
La Chaussée-Tirancourt. 📞 *03 22 51 82
83.* **Open** *Jan–mid-Dec: daily.* 📷 ♿

16th-century carvings on Eglise St-Vulfran in Abbeville, Somme Valley

Amiens ⑩

Somme. 🚶 *130,000.* 🚊 🚌
ℹ️ *6 bis rue Duseval (03 22 71 60
58).* 🚌 *Wed & Sat.*

T HERE IS MORE to Amiens, the
capital of Picardy, than its
Cathédrale Notre-Dame *(see
pp192–3).* The picturesque
quarter of St-Leu is a pedestrianized area of low houses and
flower-lined canals with waterside restaurants, bars and
artisans' shops. Further east are
Les Hortillonages, a colourful patchwork of marshland
market gardens, once tended
by farmers using punts and
now a protected natural site.
   Musée de Picardie displays
medieval religious sculpture
and 19th-century marble and
bronze statues. Among its fine
range of 16th–20th-century
paintings are a remarkable set
of 16th-century group portraits,
commissioned annually as an
offering to the cathedral. To
the south lies the circus created
by author Jules Verne (1828–
1905). His home, **Maison à la
Tour**, is now a documentation
centre. **Musée d'Art Local et
d'Histoire Régionale** has
exhibits of furniture and
objets d'art from the region.

🏛️ **Musée de Picardie**
48 rue de la République. 📞 *03 22 91
36 44.* **Open** *daily.* **Closed** *1 Jan, 1
May, 1 Nov, 11 Nov, 25 Dec.* 📷 ♿
🏛️ **Musée d'Art Local et
d'Histoire Régionale**
36 rue V Hugo. 📞 *03 22 91 81 12.*
Open *Easter–Sep: Thu–Sun; Oct–
Easter: Sun.* **Closed** *1 Jan, 1 May,
1 Nov, 11 Nov, 25 Dec.* 📷 ♿

The clock depicts
Christ surrounded by
the 12 apostles.

Solstice
indicator

Mechanical figures
perform scenes from
the Last Judgment.

Clock
showing
age of the
world

Astronomical clock in Beauvais cathedral

Beauvais ⑪

Oise. 🚶 *56,000.* 🚊 🚉 🚌
ℹ️ *1 rue Beauregard (03 44 45 08
18).* 🚌 *Wed & Sat.*

H EAVILY BOMBED in World
War II, Beauvais is now a
modern town with one out-
standing jewel. Though never
completed, **Cathédrale St-
Pierre** is a poignant, neck-
cricking finale to the vaulting
ambition that created the great
Gothic cathedrals. In 1227
work began on a building
designed to soar above all predecessors, but the roof of the
chancel caved in twice from
lack of support before its
completion in the early 14th
century. Delayed by wars and
inadequate funds, the transept
was not completed until 1550.
In 1573 its crossing collapsed
after a tower and spire were
added. What remains today is
nevertheless a masterpiece,
rising 48 m (157 ft) high.
In the transept much of the
original 16th-century stained
glass survives, while near the
north door is a 90,000-part
astronomical clock assembled
in the 1860s. What would
have been the nave is still
occupied by the remnants of
a 10th-century church known
as the Basse-Oeuvre.
   The former Bishop's Palace
is now home to the **Musée
Départemental de l'Oise**.
The collection includes
archaeological finds, medieval
sculpture, tapestries and local
ceramics. Beauvais has a long
tradition of tapestry manufacture, and examples from

VIOLLET-LE-DUC

The renowned architectural theorist Viollet-le-Duc (1814–79)
was the first to fully appreciate Gothic architecture. His
1854 dictionary of architecture celebrated medieval building
techniques, showing that the
arches and tracery of Gothic
cathedrals were solutions
to architectural problems,
not mere decoration. His
restoration work included
Château de Pierrefonds,
Notre-Dame in Paris
(see pp82–3) and Car-
cassonne *(see pp478–9).*

**Medieval architects, as
drawn by Viollet-le-Duc**

the French national collection are shown in the **Galerie Nationale de la Tapisserie**.

🏛 **Musée Départemental de l'Oise**
Ancien Palais Episcopal, 1 rue du Musée. 📞 *03 44 48 48 88.* **Open** *Wed–Mon.* **Closed** *1 Jan, Easter Mon, Whit Mon, 1 May, 25 Dec.* 📷 ⛺
🏛 **Galerie Nationale de la Tapisserie**
22 Rue St-Pierre. 📞 *03 44 05 14 28.* **Open** *Tue–Sun (phone to check).* 📷

Noyon ⓬

Oise. 🏘 *15,000.* 🚉 🛈 *place de l'Hôtel de Ville (03 44 44 21 88).* 🛒 *Wed & Sat, first Tue of each month.*

Noyon has long been a religious centre. The **Cathédrale de Notre-Dame**, dating from 1150, is the fifth to be built on this site and was completed by 1290. It provides a harmonious example of the transition from Romanesque to Gothic style. A local history museum, the **Musée du Noyonnais**, occupies part of the former Bishop's Palace, and at the cathedral's east end is a rare half-timbered chapter library built in 1506.

Jean Calvin, the Protestant theologian and one of the leaders of the Reformation, was born here in 1509 and is commemorated in the small **Musée Jean Calvin**.

🏛 **Musée du Noyonnais**
Ancien Palais Episcopal, 7 rue de l'Evêché. 📞 *03 44 09 43 41.* **Open** *Wed–Mon.* **Closed** *1 Jan, 11 Nov, 25 Dec.* 📷

The rib-vaulted nave of Cathédrale de Notre-Dame, Noyon

Path through Forêt de Compiègne

Compiègne ⓭

Oise. 🏘 *50,000.* 🚉 🚌 🛈 *Hôtel de Ville (03 44 40 01 00).* 🛒 *Wed & Sat.*

Compiègne is where Joan of Arc was captured by the Burgundians in 1430. A 16th-century Hôtel de Ville with a towering belfry rules over the centre, but the town is most famous for its royal **Château**. Designed as a summer residence for Louis XV by Jacques Anges Gabriel, the château was completed by Louis XVI, restored by Napoleon and later became a favourite residence of Napoleon III and Empress Eugénie. Guided tours of the Imperial Apartments progress through stately and private chambers, such as the sumptuous bedrooms of Napoleon I and Marie-Louise.

Within the château, the Musée du Second Empire and Musée de l'Impératrice display furniture, memorabilia and portraits, while the Musée de la Voiture is an entertaining assembly of historic carriages, bicycles and early motor cars.

South and east of the town the old hunting grounds of **Forêt de Compiègne** spread as far as Pierrefonds, with ample space for walks and picnics beneath its oaks and beeches. East of the D130 Les Beaux Monts provide majestic views back to the château.

The Clairière de l'Armistice, north of the N31, marks the spot where the armistice of World War I was signed on 11 November 1918. The small **Musée Wagon de l'Armistice**

has a replica of the railway carriage where the ceremony took place, which was used again in World War II by Hitler as a humiliating venue for the signing of the French surrender on 22 June 1940.

⚜ **Château de Compiègne**
Place du Général de Gaulle. 📞 *03 44 38 47 00.* **Open** *Wed–Mon.* **Closed** *1 Jan, 1 May, 1 Nov, 25 Dec.* 📷 ⛺
🏛 **Musée Wagon de l'Armistice**
Clairière de l'Armistice (in direction of Soissons). 📞 *03 44 85 14 18.* **Open** *Wed–Mon.* **Closed** *1 Jan, 25 Dec.* 📷

Château de Pierrefonds

Château de Pierrefonds ⓮

Oise. 📞 *03 44 42 72 72.* **Open** *daily.* **Closed** *1 Jan, 1 May, 1 Nov, 25 Dec.* 📷

The immense Château de Pierrefonds dominates the small village below. A mighty castle was constructed here by Louis d'Orléans in the 14th century, but by 1813 it had become a picturesque ruin which Napoleon I purchased for less than 3,000 francs.

In 1857, Napoleon III commissioned the architect Viollet-le-Duc to restore it, and in 1884 Pierrefonds was reborn as an imperial residence. The exterior, with its moat, drawbridge, towers and double sentry walks, is a diligent reconstruction of medieval military architecture. The interior, by contrast, is enlivened by the romantic fancies of Viollet-le-Duc and his patron. There are guided tours and a historical exhibition.

Amiens Cathedral

Work on the largest cathedral in France started in 1220, financed by profits from the cultivation of woad, a plant valued for its blue dye. It was built to house the head of St John the Baptist, brought back from the Crusades in 1206 and a magnet for pilgrims. It is still displayed in the Treasury. Within 50 years Notre-Dame was complete, a masterpiece of engineering – Gothic architecture carried to a bold extreme. Restored in the 1850s by Viollet-le-Duc *(see p190)*, and having miraculously survived two World Wars, the cathedral is famous for its rich array of statues and reliefs, which inspired John Ruskin's *The Bible of Amiens* in 1884.

★ West Front
The King's Gallery, a row of 22 colossal statues repre-senting the kings of France, spans the west front. The statues are also thought to symbolize the Kings of Judah.

St Firmin Portal is decorated with figures and scenes from the life of St Firmin, the martyr who brought Christianity to Picardy and became the first bishop of Amiens.

The Calendar shows signs from the Zodiac, with the corresponding monthly labours below. It depicts everyday life in the 13th century.

Weeping Angel
Sculpted by Nicolas Blasset in 1628, this sentimental statue in the ambulatory became a popular image during World War I.

Central Portal
Scenes from the Last Judg-ment decorate the tympanum, with the Beau Dieu, *a statue of Christ, between the doors.*

STAR FEATURES

- **★ West Front**
- **★ Nave**
- **★ Choir Stalls**
- **★ Choir Screens**

Towers
Two towers of unequal height frame the west front. The south tower was completed in 1366; the north in 1402. The spire was replaced twice, in 1627 and 1887.

VISITORS' CHECKLIST

Cathédrale Notre-Dame, place Notre-Dame. 03 22 71 60 50. **Open** Apr–Oct: 8:30am–7pm; Nov–Mar: 9am–noon, 2–5pm (6pm Sat). **Closed** last Sun of Sep, 23 Dec. 9am, 10:15am, 11:30am, 6pm Sun.

The Flamboyant tracery of the rose window was created in the 16th century.

A double row comprising 22 elegant flying buttresses supports the construction.

★ **Nave**
Soaring 42 m (138 ft) high, with support from 126 slender pillars, the brightly illuminated interior of Notre-Dame is a hymn to the vertical.

★ **Choir Stalls**
The 110 oak choir stalls (1508–19) are delicately carved with 4,000 biblical, mythical and contemporary figures.

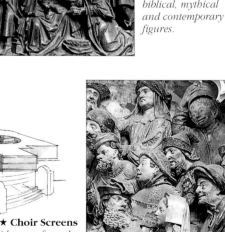

The flooring was laid down in 1288 and reassembled in the late 19th century. The faithful followed its labyrinthine shape on their knees.

★ **Choir Screens**
Vivid scenes from the lives of St Firmin and St John, carved in the 15th–16th centuries, adorn the ambulatory.

Senlis ⑮

Oise. 🏠 *16,000.* 🚊 ℹ️ *place du Parvis Notre-Dame (03 44 53 06 40).* 🛒 *Tue & Fri.*

Senlis, 10 km (6 miles) east of Chantilly, is worth visiting for its Gothic cathedral and the well-preserved historic streets in the old town that surround it. **Cathédrale Notre-Dame** was constructed during the second half of the 12th century and the sculpted central doorway of its west front, depicting the Assumption of the Virgin, influenced later cathedrals such as Amiens *(see pp192–3).* The spire of the south tower dates from the 13th century, while the Flamboyant south transept, built in the mid-16th century, makes an ornate contrast with the austerity of earlier years. Opposite the west front, a gateway leads to the ruins of the Château Royal and its gardens. Here the **Musée de la Vénerie**, housed in a former priory, celebrates hunting through paintings, old weapons and trophies.

The **Musée d'Art** recalls the town's Gallo-Roman past, and also has an excellent collection of early Gothic sculpture.

🏛 **Musée de la Vénerie**
Château Royal, place du Parvis Notre-Dame. 📞 *03 44 53 00 80 ext. 1315.* **Open** *Thu–Mon, Tue pm.* **Closed** *1 May.* 📷 🎫 *obligatory.*

🏛 **Musée d'Art**
Ancien Evêché, 2 place Notre-Dame. 📞 *03 44 53 00 80 ext. 1247.* **Open** *Wed pm–Mon.* **Closed** *1 May.* 📷

Les Très Riches Heures du Duc de Berry, on show in Chantilly

Chantilly ⑯

Oise. 🏠 *11,000.* 🚊 🚌 ℹ️ *23 avenue du Maréchal Joffre (03 44 57 08 58).* 🛒 *Wed, & Sat.*

The horse-racing capital of France, Chantilly offers a classy combination of château, park and forest that has long made it a popular excursion.

With origins from Gallo-Roman times, the château of today started to take shape in 1528, when the famous Anne de Montmorency, constable of France, had the old fortress replaced and added the Petit Château. During the time of the Great Prince of Condé (1621–86), renovation work continued and Le Nôtre created a park and fountains which made even Louis XIV jealous.

Destroyed in the Revolution, the Grand Château was again

CHANTILLY HORSE RACING

Chantilly is the capital of thoroughbred racing in France, a shrine to the long-standing love affair between the French upper classes and the world of horses. It was the firm belief of Prince Louis-Henri de Bourbon, creator of Chantilly's monumental Grandes Ecuries, that he would one day be reincarnated as a horse. Horse racing was introduced from England around 1830 and soon became very popular. The first official race meeting was held here in 1834 and today around 3,000 horses are trained in the surrounding forests and countryside. Every June, Chantilly becomes the focus of the social and flat racing season when top riders and their thoroughbreds compete for its two historic trophies, the Prix du Jockey-Club and Prix de Diane-Hermès.

Prix Equipage de Hermès, one of many prestigious races at Chantilly

rebuilt and its receptions and hunting parties became crowded by the fashionable high society of the 1820s–30s. It was finally replaced by a Renaissance-style château in the late 19th century.

Today the Grand Château and the Petit Château form the **Musée Condé**, displaying art treasures collected by its last private owner, the Duke of Aumale. These include work by Raphael, Botticelli, Poussin and Ingres, and an entertaining gallery of 16th-century portraits by the Clouet brothers. Among the most precious items is the famous 15th-century illuminated manuscript *Les Très Riches Heures du Duc de Berry*, reproductions of which are on view. You can also tour the stately apartments, with decorative conceits ranging from frolicking monkeys to triumphant battles.

Both châteaux are somewhat upstaged by the magnificent stables (Grandes Ecuries), an equestrian palace designed by Jean Aubert in 1719 which could accommodate 240 horses and 500 dogs. Adjacent to the hippodrome, it is occupied by the **Musée Vivant du Cheval**, presenting various breeds of horses and ponies as well as riding displays.

Asterix with friends, Parc Astérix

🏛 **Musée Condé**
Château de Chantilly. 🕻 *03 44 62 62 62.* **Open** *Wed–Mon.* 🈺
🐎 **Musée Vivant du Cheval**
Grandes Ecuries du Prince de Condé, Chantilly. 🕻 *03 44 57 40 40.* **Open** *Wed–Mon.* 🈺 ♿

Parc Astérix ⑰

Plailly. 🕻 *03 36 68 30 10.* **Open** *Apr–Aug: daily; Sep–Oct: Wed, Sat, Sun.* **Closed** *some Mon & Fri in May & Jun (phone to check).* 🈺 ♿

A SHORT DRIVE north of Charles de Gaulle Airport on the A1 Autoroute stands a fortified Gallo-Roman encampment with its own customs controls, currency, Menhir FM radio station and security staff wearing plastic-winged helmets. This atmospheric theme parc, very popular with families, gives visitors a real feeling for the comic-strip heroes created by Goscinny and Uderzo.

A stroll along Via Antiqua reveals architecture and souvenirs from Asterix's journeys, while the Asterix Village and the Roman camp are reconstructions from the cartoons. Fairground thrills range from high-speed water rides – strictly for the adventurous – to more sedate old-fashioned merry-go-rounds.

Rue de Paris represents Paris through the centuries, including the construction of Notre-Dame in Paris and the heroic exploits of the Three Musketeers. Souvenir shops are never very far away.

Laon ⑱

Aisne. 🏘 *36,000.* 🚉 🅸 *place du Parvis de la Cathédrale (03 23 20 28 62).* 🚌 *Thu & Sat.*

T HE CAPITAL of the Aisne *département*, Laon occupies a dramatic site on top of a long, narrow ridge surrounded by wide plains.

The pedestrianized rue Châtelaine, a major shopping street in Laon

Rose window in the 13th-century Cathédrale de Notre-Dame, Laon

The old town, on top of the mount, is best approached by Poma, an automated cable car that swings up from the railway station to the place du Général Leclerc.

The pedestrianized rue Châtelaine leads to Laon's splendid **Cathédrale de Notre-Dame**. Completed in 1235, the cathedral lost two of its original seven towers in the Revolution but remains an impressive monument to the early Gothic style.

Notable details include the deep porches of the west façade, the four-storey nave, and the carved Renaissance screens enclosing its side chapels. The immense 13th-century rose window in the apse beautifully represents the Glorification of the Church. Protruding from the cathedral's western towers are statues paying tribute to the oxen used to haul up stone for its construction.

The rest of medieval Laon rewards casual strolling: a promenade rings the 16th-century **Citadelle** further east, while to the south you can follow the ramparts past the Porte d'Ardon and Porte des Chenizelles to **Eglise St-Martin**, with good views back over the rooftops to the cathedral from rue Thibesard.

South of Laon is Chemin des Dames, named after Louis XV's daughters who used to take this route, but more often remembered as a World War I battlefield and lined with cemeteries and memorials.

CHAMPAGNE

···

MARNE · ARDENNES · AUBE · HAUTE-MARNE

C HAMPAGNE IS A NAME *of great resonance, conjuring up images of celebration and the world-famous cathedral at Reims. Yet beyond the glamour lies an unspoilt rural idyll of two strikingly contrasting landscapes: the rolling plains of Champagne, giving way to lakes and water meadows to the south, and the dense forests and hills of the Ardennes in the north.*

The so-called "sacred triangle of Champagne", linking Épernay, Reims and Châlons-en-Champagne, is like a magnet for wine lovers. Here, the experience of drinking fine champagne is enhanced by gourmet meals of stuffed trout, Ardennes ham and the famous sausages called *andouillettes*.

The sign-posted *route touristique du champagne* wends its way through vineyards towards endless cereal plains stretching southwards to the "lake district", an area of oak forests, water meadows and streams.

On the border between France and Belgium lies the Ardennes, named after the Celtic word for deep forest. This wild border land of dramatic valleys, deciduous forests and hills is cut by the meanderings of the river Meuse. Border fortifications include the vast citadel of Sedan and the star-shaped bastion of Rocroi, as well as the Maginot Line outposts built before World War II. The Ardennes may offer appealing countryside but Champagne is culturally superior, with impressive towns that have painstakingly restored historic centres. It has some striking churches, from the Gothic majesty of Reims cathedral to the rustic charm of its typical wooden *champenois* churches. These feature vivid stained-glass windows by the famous School of Troyes, whose subtle craftsmanship seems to typify the appeal of this quiet region.

Timber-framed *champenois* church at Lac du Der-Chantecoq

Cathédrale St-Etienne at Châlons-en-Champagne

Exploring Champagne

Champagne's fizz draws wine lovers to the sacred triangle between Reims, Épernay and Châlons-en-Champagne, but the region also attracts culture lovers to its great churches, notably Reims Cathedral. Reims abounds in gastronomic restaurants but Troyes, the former capital of Champagne, makes the most delightful base. Although much of Champagne is flat, the wild and wooded Ardennes to the north attracts walkers and nature-lovers. North of Reims, the Ardennes canal can be explored by barge or pleasure boat from Rethel; to the south, water sports are popular on the lakes to the east of Troyes.

Fishing by a canal in Montier-en-Der near Lac du Der-Chantecoq

GETTING AROUND

International flights to Reims-Champagne airport usually involve a change in Paris. By road, Reims, which is the main focus for visitors, is easily reached along the A4 motorway from Alsace or Paris. The train from Paris takes 90 minutes. Rail transport within the region is reasonably good, and so are the roads.

The subtleties of the wine-growing landscape can be explored from Reims along the many signposted roads marked "Route de Champagne".

To Brus
RO
N43

To St-Quentin
Amiens

RETHEL

Aisne

REIMS 1

PARC NATUREL
RÉGIONAL DE LA
MONTAGNE DE REIMS

ÉPERNAY 2

CHÂLONS-
EN-CHAMPAGNE

RD33

N4

To Provins

Aube

D441

Saine

TROYES 10

N77

Windmill at Verzenay, Parc Naturel de la Montagne de Reims

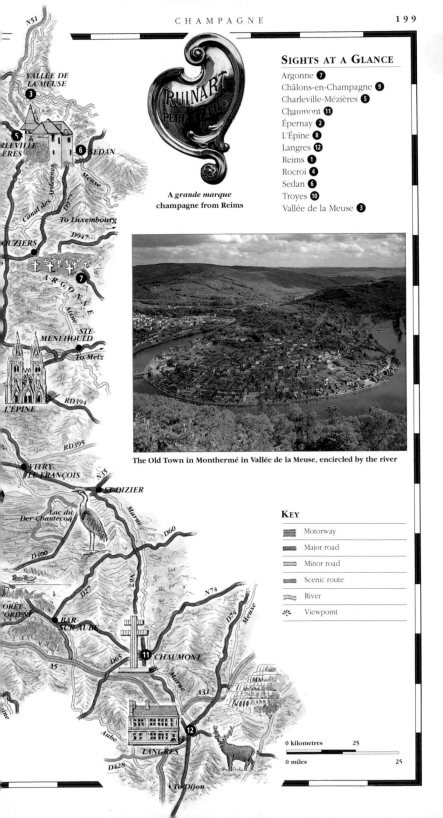

A grande marque
champagne from Reims

The Old Town in Monthermé in Vallée de la Meuse, encircled by the river

KEY

▬	Motorway
▬	Major road
▬	Minor road
▬	Scenic route
∿	River
☀	Viewpoint

0 kilometres   25

0 miles   25

(map labels)
N51
VALLÉE DE LA MEUSE **3**
CHARLEVILLE-MÉZIÈRES **5**
SEDAN **6**
Meuse
Canal des Ardennes
Dyle
To Luxembourg
D947
OUZIERS
ARGONNE **7**
Aisne
STE-MENEHOULD
To Metz
L'ÉPINE
RD394
RD395
VITRY-LE-FRANÇOIS
N35
ST-DIZIER
Lac du Der-Chantecoq
Marne
D60
D700
D27
FORÊT D'ORIENT
BAR-SUR-AUBE
N74
Meuse
A5
D65
CHAUMONT **11**
Marne
A31
Aube
LANGRES **12**
D428
To Dijon

Gilded reliquary (1896), with body of St Remi, in Basilique St-Remi, Reims

Reims ❶

Marne. 🏠 185,000. ✕ 🚉 🚌
🛈 2 rue Guillaume de Machault
(03 26 77 45 25). 🚉 daily.

RENOWNED the world over
from countless champagne
labels, Reims is home to some
of the best known *grandes
marques*. But the city has
another, much earlier, claim
to fame: since the 11th century, all the kings of France
have come to this "city of
coronations" to be crowned
in its remarkable Gothic
Cathédrale Notre-Dame
(see pp202–3).

Although World War II
bombing destroyed much of
Reims' architectural coherence,
there are some remarkable
monuments here. The **Crypto-
portique**, part of the forum,
and Porte Mars, a triumphal
Augustan arch, recall the
city's Roman past. In 1945,
the German surrender was
taken in the **Musée de la
Reddition** in Eisenhower's
French headquarters during
World War II. **Musée des
Beaux Arts** houses a fine
collection of 15th- and 16th-
century canvases depicting
biblical scenes, portraits
by the Cranachs, *The
Death of Marat* by
David, and more than 20
landscapes by Corot.
Also featured are the
Barbizon School, Impres-
sionists and modern masters.

In 1996 Reims was the
venue for celebrations
marking the 1,500-year
anniversary of the baptism,
in the cathedral, of Clovis,
the first King of the Franks.

🏛 Ancien Collège des Jésuites & Planetarium

1 place Museux. 🇨 03 26 85 51 50.
College open daily. **Closed** public hols.
Planetarium open Sat & Sun. 🎫
Founded in 1606, this college
was a hospice until 1976.
Nowadays its 300-year-old

vines, Romanesque wine cellars and Baroque interior play
their part as atmospheric film
sets, notably for the film of
Zola's *Germinal* (1992) and
Queen Margot (1993), starring
Isabelle Adjani. Highlights include the refectory's marquetry
ceiling and the kitchen, the
only room where fireplaces
were permitted in an austere
Jesuit establishment. A double
spiral staircase leads to a
Baroque library topped by a
ceiling like an upturned boat.
Housed in the same building
since 1979 is the **Planetarium**,
with views of the sky from
everywhere in the world.

🏠 Basilique St-Remi

Place de Lenoncourt. **Open** daily. 🚹
Now marooned in a modern
quarter, this Benedictine abbey
church, the oldest church in
Reims, began as a Carolingian

Porte Mars, a reminder of Reims in Roman times

MÉTHODE CHAMPENOISE

To produce its characteristic bubbles, champagne has
to undergo a process of double fermentation.
• **First fermentation:** The base wine, made from rather
acidic grapes, is fermented at 20°–22°C in either stainless steel
tanks or, occasionally, in oak barrels. It is then siphoned off
from the sediment and kept at colder temperatures to clear completely, before being drawn off and blended with
wines from other areas and years (except in
the case of vintage champagne). The wine
is bottled and the *liqueur de tirage*
(sugar, wine and yeast) is added.
• **Second fermentation:** The bottles
are stored for a year or more in cool,
chalky cellars. The yeast converts the
sugar to alcohol and carbon dioxide,
which produces the sparkle, and the
yeast cells die leaving a deposit. To
remove this, the inverted bottles are turned
and tapped daily to shift
the deposits into the neck of the bottle
(remuage). Finally, the deposits are expelled by
the process known as *dégorgement*, and a bit of
sugar *(liqueur d'expédition)* is added to adjust
the sweetness before the final cork is inserted.

Champagne
Mumm of
Reims

basilica dedicated to Saint Remi (440–533). Inside, an Early Gothic choir and radiating chapels can be seen, as well as sculpted Romanesque capitals in the north transept.

🏛 Musée St-Remi
53 rue Simon. **[** 03 26 85 23 36. **Open** daily pm only. **Closed** 1 Jan, 1 May, 14 Jul, 1 & 11 Nov, 25 Dec. **🖼**

Set in the former abbey, the adjoining museum encloses the original Gothic chapter-house within its cloistered 17th-century shell. On display in the museum are archeological artifacts, 15th-century tapestries depicting the life of Saint Remi, and a varied collection of weapons dating from the 16th–19th centuries.

Épernay ❷

Marne. 🏘 28,000. 🚌 🚗 **i** 7 av de Champagne (03 26 53 33 00). 🗓 Wed, Sat & Sun.

T HE SOLE REASON for visiting Épernay is to burrow into the chalky *caves* and taste the champagne. This rather undistinguished town lives off the fruits of its profitable champagne industry. As proof, the avenue de Champagne quarter abounds in mock-Renaissance mansions. **Moët et Chandon**,

Statue of Dom Perignon at Moët

dating back to 1743, is the largest and slickest *maison*, the star of the Moët-Hennessy stable. Its cellars stretch some 28 km (18 miles) underground.

The group also owns other brands, such as Ruinart, Dom Perignon, Pommery, Mercier and even Parfums Dior. When the recession took the fizz out of Champagne in 1993, Moët took the step of making a number of people redundant, and provoked the first ever

strike in the industry. There is little to choose between a visit to the cellars of Moët or **Mercier** – they are both based in avenue de Champagne. Mercier has the distinction of displaying a giant tun created for the 1889 Paris Exhibition, and takes visitors trundling through the *caves* in an electric train.

De Castellane, in avenue de Verdun, offers a more personalized tour, accompanied by a heady *dégustation*.

🍷 Moët et Chandon
20 avenue de Champagne. **[** 03 26 51 20 00. **Open** Apr–mid-Nov: daily; mid-Nov–Mar: Mon–Fri. **🖼**

🍷 Mercier
70 avenue de Champagne. **[** 03 26 51 22 22. **Open** Mar–Nov: daily; Dec–Feb: Thu–Mon. **Closed** 25 Dec–1 Jan. **🖼 ♿**

🍷 De Castellane
57 rue de Verdun. **[** 03 26 51 19 11. **Open** Apr–Nov: daily. **🖼**

Dégorgement *is the final removal of the yeast deposits from the bottle. The neck of the bottle is plunged in freezing brine and the frozen block of sediment is then removed.*

Seductive marketing of champagne since the last century has ensured its continuing success.

The bubbles in champagne *are produced during the second fermentation. Ageing for several years or more improves the quality of champagne.*

Reims Cathedral

THE MAGNIFICENT GOTHIC Cathédrale Notre-Dame at Reims is noted for its harmony and monumentality. A cathedral has stood on this site since 401 but the present building was begun in 1211. Reims has been the backdrop for coronations from medieval times till 1825, when Charles X was crowned. The coronation of Charles VII here in 1429 was attended by Joan of Arc.

During the Revolution, the rood screen and windows were destroyed but the stonework survived. World War I damage was finally fully restored in 1996, to coincide with the 1,500th anniversary of the baptism of Clovis, King of the Franks, at Reims, which was considered the first coronation of a French king.

★ Great Rose Window
Best seen at sunset, the 13th-century window shows the Virgin surrounded by the apostles and angel musicians. It is set within a larger window, a feature common in 13th-century architecture.

The Nave
Compared with the nave at Chartres (see pp298–301), Reims is taller. Its elegant capitals are decorated with naturalistic floral motifs such as ivy and berries.

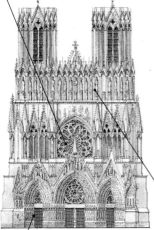

WEST FAÇADE

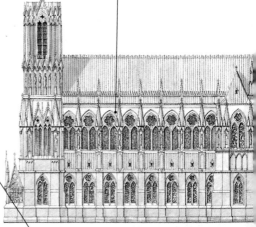

SOUTH FAÇADE

★ Smiling Angel
Rich in statuary, Reims is often called "the cathedral of angels". Situated above the left (north) portal, this enigmatic angel with unfurled wings is the most celebrated of the many that grace the building.

★ Gallery of the Kings
The harmonious west façade, decorated with over 2,300 statues, is the most notable feature at Reims. Fifty-six stone effigies of French kings form the Gallery of the Kings.

Palais du Tau

The archbishop's palace adjoining the cathedral is named after its T-shaped design, based on early episcopal crosses. (Tau is Greek for T.) The palace, built in 1690 by Mansart and Robert de Cotte, encloses a Gothic Chapel and the 15th-century Salle du Tau, rooms associated with French coronations. On the eve of a coronation, the future king spent the night in the palace. After being crowned in the cathedral, he held a magnificent banquet in the palace. The Salle du Tau, or banqueting hall, is the finest room in the palace, with a magnificent barrel-vaulted ceiling and walls hung with 15th-century Arras tapestries. The palace now houses a museum of statuary and tapestries from the cathedral, including a 15th-century tapestry of the baptism of Clovis, the first Christian king.

Salle du Tau – the banqueting hall

Visitors' Checklist

Cathédrale Notre-Dame, place du Cardinal Luçon. *03 26 47 55 34.* ***Open*** *7:30am–7:30pm daily.* *8am & 7pm Mon–Fri; 9am, 10:15am & noon Sun.*

Palais du Tau *03 26 47 81 79.* ***Open*** *daily.* ***Closed*** *1 Jan, 1 May, 1 & 11 Nov, 25 Dec.*

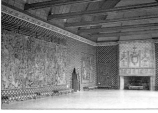

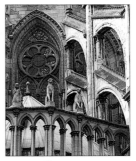

Apse Gallery
The restored claire-voie *(open work) gallery on the apse is crowned by statues of mythological beasts.*

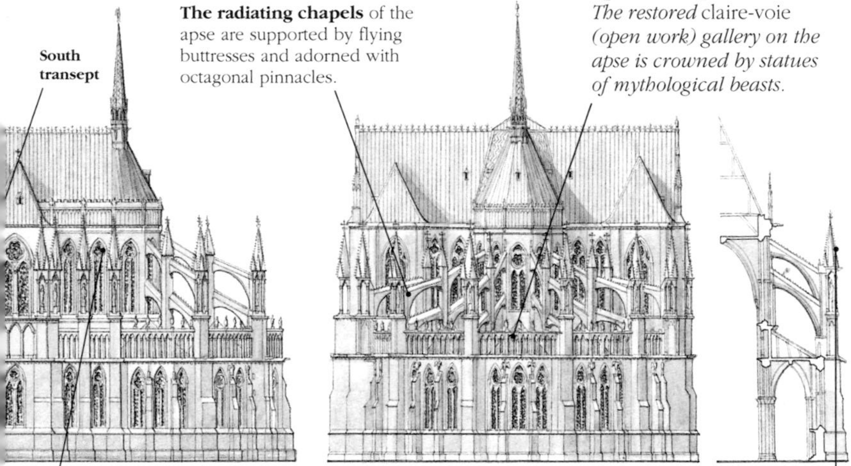

South transept

The radiating chapels of the apse are supported by flying buttresses and adorned with octagonal pinnacles.

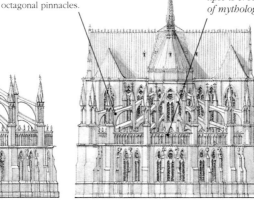

Apse

Side Section

The clerestory windows pioneered Gothic tracery by dividing the lights with slender bars of stone, creating a decorative, intersecting pattern.

Pinnacles on the flying buttresses shelter guardian angels, symbolic protectors of the cathedral.

Star Features

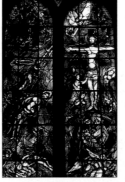

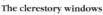

- ★ **Gallery of the Kings**
- ★ **Smiling Angel**
- ★ **Great Rose Window**

Chagall Window
The windows in the axial chapel were designed by the 20th-century artist Marc Chagall and made by local craftsmen. This one depicts the Crucifixion and the Sacrifice of Isaac.

The *sentier touristique*, a walk along the ramparts of Rocroi

Vallée de la Meuse ❸

Ardennes. 🚊 *Revin*. 🛈 *Revin (03 24 40 19 59).*

THE MEUSE meanders through the Ardennes among spectacular scenery of wild gorges, woods and warped rock formations of granite or schist.

Dramatically situated on a double meander of the Meuse, **Revin** is an unremarkable town in an exceptional site, with the Vieille Ville enfolded in the north bend. From the quay, you can see wooded **Mont Malgré Tout** and a route dotted with observation points and steep trails. Just south is **Dames de la Meuse**, a rocky outcrop over the river gorge.

Monthermé lies on two banks, with the Vieille Ville clustered on the charming left bank. The rocky gorges around **Roche à Sept Heures** on the far bank entice climbers and ramblers. Further on is **Rocher des Quatre Fils d'Aymon**, a ridge whose jagged crest suggests the silhouette of four legendary local horsemen.

Rocroi ❹

Ardennes. 🚶 *2,600.* 🚊 🛈 *place d'Armes (03 24 54 20 06).* 🚌 *Tue.*

SET ON the Ardennes plateau, the star-shaped citadel of Rocroi was originally built under Henri II in 1555, and later made impregnable by Vauban in 1675 *(see p216).*

The main attraction is the *sentier touristique*, a walk along the ramparts beginning in the Porte de France, the southern gateway. The nature reserve at Rièzes is home to orchids and carnivorous plants.

Charleville-Mézières ❺

Ardennes. 🚶 *57,000.* 🚊 🚊 🛈 *4 place Ducal (03 24 32 44 80).* 🚌 *Tue, Thu & Sat.*

KNOWN AS the gateway to the Ardennes, this riverside ford was originally two towns. The sombre medieval citadel of Mézières only merged with the neat Classical town of Charleville in 1966. Mézières has irregular slate-covered houses curving around a bend in the Meuse. Battered fortifications and gateways are visible from avenue de St-Julien. Tucked into the ramparts is the much remodelled Gothic **Notre-Dame de l'Espérance**.

The centrepiece of Charleville is **place Ducale**, a model of Louis XIII urban planning,

echoing place des Vosges in Paris *(see p87).* The poet Arthur Rimbaud was born nearby in 1854. His modest birthplace at No. 12 rue Thiers is still there, along with his childhood home on the Meuse at 7 quai Arthur Rimbaud.

Just along the quayside is the Vieux Moulin, the town house whose view inspired *Le Bateau ivre*, Rimbaud's greatest poem. Inside is the small **Musée Rimbaud**, with manuscripts and photographs by the poet.

🏛 Musée Rimbaud
Quai Arthur Rimbaud. 📞 *03 24 32 44 65.* **Open** *Tue–Sun.* **Closed** *1 Jan, 1 May, 25 Dec.* 🎫

Sedan ❻

Ardennes. 🚶 *22,000.* 🚊 🚊 🛈 *Château Fort, place du Château (03 24 27 73 73).* 🚌 *Wed & Sat.*

JUST TO THE EAST of Charleville is the **Château de Sedan**, the largest fortified castle in the whole of Europe. There has been a bastion on these slopes since the 11th century, but each Ardennes conflict has spelt a new tier of defences for Sedan.

In 1870, during the Franco-Prussian War, with 700 Prussian cannons turned on Sedan, Napoleon III surrendered and 83,000 French prisoners were deported to Prussia. In May 1940 after capturing Sedan, German forces reached the French coast a week later.

The seven-storeyed bastion contains sections dating from medieval times to the 16th

The 19th-century poet Rimbaud, whose birthplace was Charleville

century. Highlights of any visit are the ramparts, the 16th-century fortifications and the magnificent 15th-century eaves in one tower. A jumbled **Musée du Château**, which is located in the south wing, has a section devoted to military campaigns.

The bastion is surrounded by 17th-century slate-roofed houses which hug the banks of the Meuse. These reflect the city's earlier prosperity as a Huguenot stronghold.

🏛 Musée du Château
1 place du Château. **☎** *03 24 27 73 75.* **Open** *Mar–Oct: Tue–Sun.* 📷

Environs
Further south is **Fort de Vitry-la-Ferté**, one of the few forts on the Maginot line to have come into direct and devastating combat with the enemy in 1940.

Courtyard inside the heavily fortified Château de Sedan

Gargoyle on Basilique de Notre-Dame de l'Épine

Argonne ❼

Ardennes & Meuse. 🚌 *Vouziers.*
ℹ *Vouziers (03 24 71 97 57).*

EAST OF REIMS, the Argonne is a compact region of picturesque valleys and forests, a countryside dotted with priories, trenches and war cemeteries.

As a wooded border between the rival bishoprics of Champagne and Lorraine, the Argonne was home to abbeys and priories. Now ruined, the Benedictine abbey of **Beaulieu-en-Argonne** boasts a fine wine press and has forest views. Just north is **Les Islettes**,

known for its faïence pottery and tiles. The hilly terrain here was a battleground during the Franco-Prussian War and lay on the Western front in World War I. The disputed territory of **Butte de Vauquois**, north of Les Islettes, bears a war memorial.

L'Épine ❽

Marne. 🏠 *650.* 🚌

L'ÉPINE IS WORTH visiting if only for a glimpse of the **Basilique de Notre-Dame de l'Épine** surrounded by wheatfields. Designed on the scale of a cathedral, this 15th-century Flamboyant Gothic church has been a pilgrimage site, especially in summer, since medieval times. Even French kings have come here to venerate a "miraculous" statue of the Virgin.

On the façade, three gabled portals are offset by floating tracery, a gauzy effect reminiscent of Reims cathedral. All around are gruesome gargoyles, symbolizing evil spirits and deadly sins, chased out by the holy presence within. Unfortunately, the most risqué sculptures were destroyed, judged obscene by 19th-century puritans. The subdued Gothic interior contains a 15th-century rood-screen and the venerated statue of the Virgin.

CHAMPAGNE TIMBER CHURCHES

Skirting Lac du Der-Chantecoq lies a region of woodland, water meadows and characteristic Romanesque and Renaissance timber-framed churches with curious pointed gables and *caquetoirs*, rickety wooden porches. Many have intimate and often beautifully carved interiors with stained-glass windows designed in the vivid colours of the School of Troyes. Rural roads link churches at Bailly-le-Franc, Chatillon-sur-Broué, Lentilles, Vignory, Outines, Chavanges and Montier-en-Der.

16th-century timber church in Lentilles

Châlons-en-Champagne ❾

Marne. 48,000. 3 quai des Arts (03 26 65 17 89). Wed & Sat.

ENCIRCLED BY the river Marne and minor canals, Châlons' sleepy bourgeois charm is made up of half-timbered houses and gardens mirrored in canals. Nearby are vineyards producing Blanc de Blancs.

From quai de Notre-Dame there are views of old bridges and the Romanesque towers of **Notre-Dame-en-Vaux**, a masterpiece of Romanesque-Gothic. Behind the church is a well-restored medieval quarter and the **Musée du Cloître de Notre-Dame-en-Vaux**, containing the original Romanesque cloisters.

Cathédrale St-Etienne, by the canal, is a cool Gothic affair with a Baroque portal, Romanesque crypt and vivid medieval windows. Beyond is **Le Petit Jard**, riverside gardens overlooking the Château du Marché, a turreted toll gate built by Henri IV. The neighbouring place de la République has lively bars and restaurants.

Musée du Cloître de Notre-Dame-en-Vaux

Rue Nicolas Durand. 03 26 64 03 87. ***Open*** *Wed–Mon.* ***Closed*** *1 Jan, 1 May, 1 & 11 Nov, 25 Dec.*

Troyes ❿

Aube. 60,000. 16 bd Carnot (03 25 82 62 50). Sat.

TROYES IS A DELIGHT, a city of magnificent Gothic churches and charming 16th-century courtyards, in a historical centre shaped like a champagne cork. The city is famous for its heritage of stained glass and sausages *(andouillettes)*, its knitwear industry and factory shops.

The battered Flamboyant Gothic west front of the **Cathédrale St-Pierre-et-St-Paul** opens on to a splendid vaulted interior. The nave is bathed in mauvish-red rays from the 16th-century rose window, complemented by the discreet turquoise of the Tree of Jesse window and the intense blue of the medieval windows of the apse.

Statuary in Troyes' Cathédrale St-Pierre-et-St-Paul

Nearby, **Eglise St-Nizier** glitters in the faded quarter behind the cathedral with its shimmering tiled Burgundian roof. Inside, it is lit by windows in a range of warm mauves and soothing blues.

The harmonious Gothic **Basilique St-Urbain** boasts grand flying buttresses (and fine windows, although these are currently undergoing restoration). **Eglise Ste-Madeleine** is noted for its elaborate 16th-century rood screen resembling lacey foliage, grapes and figs. Beyond is a wall of windows in browns, reds and blues. The ruelle des Chats, which is a quaint covered passageway, connects rue Charbonnet and rue Champeaux.

Rue Larivey, a typical street with half-timbered houses, in Troyes

Set in one of the best-preserved quarters, **Eglise St-Pantaléon** faces a Renaissance mansion. A Gothic and Renaissance interior houses an imposing collection of 16th-century statuary and severe *grisaille* windows.

Musée d'Art Moderne

Palais Episcopal, place St-Pierre. 03 25 76 26 80. ***Open*** *Wed–Mon.* ***Closed*** *public hols.*

Beside the cathedral, the former episcopal palace is now a museum of modern art, with a sculpture by Rodin, and an especially fine collection of Fauvist paintings, as well as other modern art.

Hotel du Petit Louvre

Rue de la Montée St-Pierre.

Courtyard only *open* *daily.*

Set off quai Dampierre, this newly restored *hôtel particulier* boasts a fish-scale roof, medieval tower, Renaissance courtyard, staircase and well. The highlight is a façade adorned with quizzical multi-coloured faces.

Environs

The city's green playground, **Lac et Forêt d'Orient**, is 25 km (15 miles) east of Troyes. The forest is dotted with marshes, nature reserves and smaller lakes. Lac d'Orient, a large artificial lake, is popular for sailing, with water-skiing on Lac Amance, and fishing at Lac du Temple.

Chaumont ⓫

Haute-Marne. 🏘 29,000. 🚊 🚌
🛈 place du Général de Gaulle (03 25 03 80 80). 🛒 Wed & Sat.

AS THE FORMER residence of the Counts of Champagne, this feudal town enjoyed great prestige in the 13th century. On the far side of a ravine, the old town is on a rocky spur, with the Palais de Justice and the medieval castle keep dominating.

The keep is a reminder that this quiet administrative centre had a formidable past. This impression is confirmed by the Renaissance town houses which are bulging with *tourelles d'escaliers*, turreted staircases.

Basilique St-Jean-Baptiste, a grey-stone Champenois church, is the most remarkable monument in Chaumont. The interior is enlivened by a spider's web of vaulting, a striking turreted staircase and Renaissance galleries. Near the entrance is a tiny chapel containing an unsettling *Mise au Tombeau* (1471), an intense multi-coloured stone group of 11 mourners gathered around Christ laid out on a shroud in his tomb. In the left transept is a bizarre but beguiling *Tree of Jesse*. On this ill-lit Renaissance stone relief, a family tree sprouts from the sleeping Jesus, who slumbers unawares – much like Chaumont itself.

Environs

Twenty-three kilometres (14 miles) to the northwest of Chaumont, **Colombey-les-Deux-Eglises** will forever be associated with General Charles de Gaulle. The de Gaulles bought their home, **La Boisserie**, in 1933, but

Cathédrale St-Mammès in Langres

had to abandon it during the war, when it was badly damaged. After its restoration, de Gaulle would return to La Boisserie from Paris at weekends to write his memoirs and plan come-backs. He eventually died here on 9 November 1970. The house is now a museum, with memorabilia from his life.

In the village churchyard, the General and President of France lies in a simple tomb. However, a giant granite cross of Lorraine, erected in 1972, dominates the skyline – a grandiose memorial more in keeping with de Gaulle's notion of *la gloire*.

🏛 La Boisserie

Colombey-les-Deux-Eglises. 【 03 25 01 52 52. **Open** Mar–Dec: Wed–Mon. **Closed** 25 Dec. 🎦 ♿

Langres ⓬

Haute-Marne. 🏘 10,000. 🚊
🛈 square O Lahalle (03 25 87
🛒 Fri.

SET ON A ROCKY SPUR, Langres lies beyond Chaumont, in the backwaters of southern Champagne. This ancient bishopric was one of the gateways to Burgundy and the birthplace of the encyclopedist, Denis Diderot (1713–84). Langres promotes itself as a land of springs, claiming that its proximity to the sources of the Seine and Marne grant it mystical powers.

Virtually the whole town is enclosed by medieval ramparts, Langres' undoubted attraction. A succession of towers and parapets provide glimpses of romantic town gates, sculpted Renaissance mansions and dim alleys. From the ramparts stretch panoramic views of the Marne valley, the Langres plateau, the Vosges, and, on a clear day, even Mont Blanc.

Near Porte Henri IV is the much-remodelled **Cathédrale St-Mammès**. The gloomy vaulted interior, in Burgundian Romanesque style, is redeemed by the sculpted capitals in the apse, reputedly taken from a temple of Jupiter.

Langres runs a lively summer season, featuring re-creations of a Renaissance tavern and the Nightwatchmen's Round, a folkloric evening stroll.

Memorial to General de Gaulle at Colombey-les-Deux-Eglises

ALSACE AND LORRAINE

MEURTHE-ET-MOSELLE · MEUSE · MOSELLE · BAS-RHIN
HAUT-RHIN · VOSGES

A S BORDER REGIONS, *Alsace and Lorraine have been fought over for centuries by France and Germany, their beleaguered past recalled by many a military stronghold and cemetery. Today, the region presents only a peaceful aspect with pastel-painted villages, fortified towns and sleepy vineyards.*

At the northeast frontier of France, bordered by the Rhine, Alsace forms a fertile watershed between the mountains of the Vosges and the Black Forest in Germany. Lorraine, with its gentle rolling landscape on the other side of the mountains, is the poorer cousin but appears more overtly French in character.

EMBATTLED TERRITORY

Caught in the wars between France and Germany, Alsace and Lorraine have changed nationality four times since 1871. Centuries of strife have made border citadels of Metz, Toul and Verdun in Lorraine, while Alsace abounds with castles, from the pastiche folly of Haut-Koenigsbourg to Saverne's ruined fortress, built to guard a strategic pass in the Vosges. However, the area has a strong identity of its own, taking pride in local costumes, traditions and dialects. In Alsace, Route du Vin vineyards nudge pretty villages in the Vosges foothills. Strasbourg, the capital, is a cosmopolitan city with a 16th-century centre, while Nancy, Lorraine's historical capital, represents elegant 18th-century architecture and town planning.

Much of the attraction of this region lies in its cuisine. Lorraine offers beer and quiche lorraine. In Alsace, cosy *winstubs*, or wine cellars, serve sauerkraut and flowery white wines, such as Riesling and Gewürztraminer.

Villagers enjoying the view from their window in Hunspach, north of Strasbourg in the northern Vosges

◁ Half-timbered houses with flower-clad balconies along the Route du Vin in Alsace

Exploring Alsace and Lorraine

VISITORS SEEKING ART and architecture will be amply rewarded by the charming medieval towns and excellent city museums of the region. Undiscovered Lorraine is the place to clamber over military citadels, walk in unspoiled countryside and unwind at relaxing spas. By contrast, Alsace offers magnificent forests and rugged mountain drives in the Vosges, quaint villages and rich wines. The Route du Vin *(see pp222–3)* is one of the region's many scenic routes. It is particularly popular during the wine harvest festivities but is worth visiting in any season.

SIGHTS AT A GLANCE

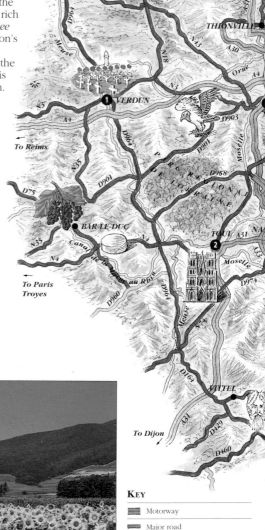

Field of sunflowers just outside the village of Turckheim

KEY

▬	Motorway
▬	Major road
▬	Minor road
▬	Scenic route
〰	River
☆	Viewpoint

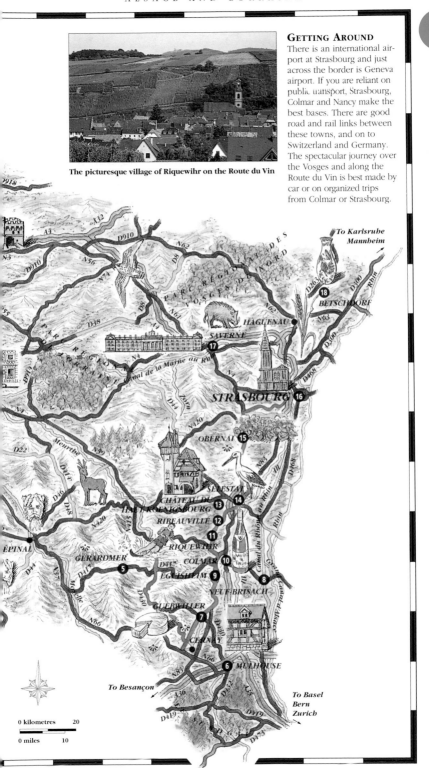

The picturesque village of Riquewihr on the Route du Vin

GETTING AROUND
There is an international airport at Strasbourg and just across the border is Geneva airport. If you are reliant on public transport, Strasbourg, Colmar and Nancy make the best bases. There are good road and rail links between these towns, and on to Switzerland and Germany. The spectacular journey over the Vosges and along the Route du Vin is best made by car or on organized trips from Colmar or Strasbourg.

To Karlsruhe
Mannheim

BETSCHDORF

HAGUENAU

SAVERNE

STRASBOURG

OBERNAI

SELESTAT

CHÂTEAU DU HAUT-KŒNIGSBOURG

RIBEAUVILLÉ

RIQUEWIHR

COLMAR

EGUISHEIM

NEUF-BRISACH

ÉPINAL

GÉRARDMER

GUEBWILLER

CERNAY

MULHOUSE

To Besançon

To Basel
Bern
Zurich

0 kilometres   20

0 miles   10

The Ossuaire de Douaumont, a sentinel for the regiments of crosses on the battlefields of Verdun

Verdun ❶

Meuse. 🏘 23,000. 🚊 🚌 ℹ️ *place de la Nation (03 29 86 14 18).* 🛒 *Tue & Fri.*

THICK WALLS, drawbridges and gateways bear witness to Verdun's militaristic past. Based strategically at the mouth of the Meuse and near the border, it has been caught up in countless wars over the centuries. In 1916, Verdun became the symbol of French resistance when over 400,000 Frenchmen died defending the citadel.

The crenellated **Porte Chausée**, a medieval river gateway, still guards the eastern entrance to the town and is the most impressive of the remaining fortifications.

Although battered by war damage, the **Citadelle de Verdun** retains its 12th-century tower, the only relic from the original abbey that Louis XIV's architect, Vauban, incorporated into his new military design. Now a war museum, the **Musée de la Citadelle Militaire**, it recreates through an audio-visual display Verdun's role in World War I. The citadel casemates come to life as grim trenches, and the presentation ends by showing how the "Unknown Soldier" was chosen for the symbolic tomb under the Arc de Triomphe in Paris (*see p103*).

The **Cathédrale de Notre-Dame**, perched on high, looks dramatic, but the impression is marred by the clumsiness of its remodelling. The Rhenish cathedral retains Romanesque elements, from a tympanum showing Christ in Majesty to sculptures of Adam and Eve which are visible from the medieval cloisters. In the 18th-century, the Roman-esque sections were bricked up in deference to prevailing Baroque taste, but they were revealed once again by the bombardments of 1916.

Environs

It is Verdun's fate to be forever associated with the horrors of 1916–17. The harrowing battlefields of Verdun lie north of the city, on both banks of the Meuse. As most of the villages in the area were razed, little has remained but the trenches and a few forts. The landscape is now littered with sombre memorials, most notably the **Ossuaire de Douaumont**, a repository for the unidentified remains of 130,000 French and German soldiers of World War I.

🏛 Musée de la Citadelle Militaire

La Citadelle. 📞 *03 29 86 14 18.* **Open** *daily.* **Closed** *1 Jan, 25 Dec.* 📷 ♿

The 16th-century cloisters of Eglise St-Gengoult in Toul

Toul ❷

Meurthe-et-Moselle. 🏘 18,000. 🚊 🚌 ℹ️ *parvis de la Cathédrale (03 83 64 11 69).* 🛒 *Wed & Fri.*

LYING WITHIN dark forests west of Nancy, the octag-onal fortress city of Toul is encircled by the Moselle and the Canal de la Marne. Along with Verdun and Metz, Toul was one of the 4th-century bishoprics. In the early 18th century, Vauban built the cita-del, from which the ring of defensive waterways, the octagonal city ramparts and the **Porte de Metz** remain.

The **Cathédrale St-Etienne**, begun in the 13th century, took over 300 years to build and so reflects a composite of styles, with Flamboyant Gothic predominating. It suffered damage in World War II but the purity of the Champenois style has survived, notably in the arched, high-galleried interior. The imposing Flam-boyant Gothic façade is flanked by octagonal towers. Other highlights are the two Renaissance chapels close to the transepts and the vast Champenois cloisters, decorated with sculpted foliage and stone gargoyles.

The Gothic façade of **Eglise St-Gengoult** is flanked by towers and adorned by Gothic stained-glass windows depic-ting the life of St Gengoult.

Rue du Général-Gengoult, behind the church, contains a clutch of sculpted Renais-sance houses, and just north of the city are vineyards which produce the local "grey" Côtes de Toul wines.

Environs

Accessible from either Metz or Toul, the vast **Parc Régional de Lorraine** takes in red-tiled cottages, vineyards, forests, cropland, *chaumes* (high pastureland), marshes and lakes. Inns in the area are especially noted for their quiche lorraine and *potée lorraine*, a bacon casserole.

Jupiter Slaying a Monster **on the Column of Merten in La Cour d'Or**

Metz ❸

Moselle. 🚹 *124,000.* ✈ 🚆 🚌
🛈 *place d'Armes (03 87 55 53 76).*
📅 *Wed, Thu & Sat.*

AN AUSTERE yet appealing city, Metz sits at the confluence of the Moselle and the Seille. Twenty bridges criss-cross the rivers and canals, and there are pleasant walks along the banks. This Gallo-Roman city, now the capital of Lorraine, has always been a pawn in the game of border chess – annexed by Germany in 1870, regained by France in 1918.

Set on a hill above the Moselle, the **Cathédrale St-Etienne** overlooks the historic centre. The Gothic exterior flaunts impressive flying buttresses and long-necked gargoyles. Inside, stained-glass windows, from Gothic to modern, including some by Chagall, present walls of shimmering light.

To the northwest of the cathedral, a narrow wooden bridge leads across to the island of Petit Saulcy, site of the oldest French theatre still in use. Located on the other side of the cathedral, the **Porte des Allemands**, spanning a river, more resembles a medieval castle because of its bridge, defensive towers and 13th-century gate with pepper-pot towers.

In the Vieille Ville, place St-Louis is a delightful square bordered by lofty, arcaded 14th-century mansions. **Eglise St-Pierre-aux-Nonnains** claims to be one of the oldest churches in France. The external walls and the ruined façade date from Roman times, while much of the rest belongs to the 7th-century convent that occupied the site. Nearby is the frescoed 13th-century **Chapelle des Templiers**, built by the Knights Templar.

🏛 Musée de la Cour d'Or
2 rue du Haut-Poirier. 📞 *03 87 75 10 18.* **Open** *daily.* **Closed** *some public hols.* 📷
Also known as the Musée d'Art et d'Histoire, this fascinating collection is set in the Petits-Carmes, a deconsecrated 17th-century monastery incorporating Gallo-Roman thermal baths and a medieval tithe barn. On display are Merovingian stone carvings, Gothic painted ceilings and German, Flemish and French paintings.

WHITE STORKS

Until recently, the white stork, traditionally a symbol of good fortune, was a frequent sight in northeast France. White storks spend the winter in Africa, but migrate north to breed. However, the gradual draining of marshy ground, pesticides and electric cables have threatened their survival here. A programme to reintroduce them to the area has set up breeding centres, as at Molsheim and Turckheim, which means these striking birds can once again be seen in Alsace-Lorraine.

The 13th-century Chapelle des Templiers, with restored frescoes, in Metz

Place Stanislas in Nancy, with statue of Stanislas Leczinski, Duke of Lorraine and father-in-law of Louis XV

Nancy ❹

Meurthe-et-Moselle. 🏛 100,000.
🚆 🚌 🏛 ℹ 14 place Stanislas
(03 83 35 22 41). 🛒 Tue–Sat.

Lorraine's HISTORIC capital
backs on to the Canal du
Marne and the river Meurthe.
In the 18th century, Stanislas
Leczinski, Duke of Lorraine
(see p292), embellished Nancy
beyond recognition, making it
a model of the golden age of
18th-century town planning.

The second golden age was
at the turn of this century,
when glassmaker Emile Gallé
founded the Ecole de Nancy,
a forerunner of the Art
Nouveau movement in France.

Nancy's principal and most
renowned landmark is **place
Stanislas**. Laid out in the
1750s, this elegantly proportioned square is enclosed by
highly ornate gilded wrought-
iron gates and railings, a
hallmark of the city. Lining
the square are pavilions, including the Hôtel de Ville (town
hall) and stylish restaurants.

An Arc de Triomphe leads
to place de la Carrière, a
gracious, tree-lined square. At
the far end, flanked by semi-
circular arcades, is the Gothic
Palais du Gouvernement.
Next door in the Parc de la

Pépinière is Rodin's statue of
Claude Lorrain, the landscape
painter, born near Nancy.

The Grande Rue provides a
glimpse of medieval Nancy.
Of the original fortifications
only the Porte de la Craffe,
which was used as a prison
after the Revolution, remains.

🔒 Eglise et Couvent des
Cordeliers et Musée
Régional des Arts et
Traditions Populaires
64 & 66 Grande Rue. [03 83 32 18
74. **Open** Wed–Mon. **Closed** 1 Jan,
1 May, 14 Jul, 1 Nov, 25 Dec. 🖼
The Dukes of Lorraine are
buried in the crypt and the
adjoining converted monastery
contains the Musée Régional
des Arts et Traditions Populaires, covering folklore,
furniture, costumes and crafts.

🏛 Musée des Beaux Arts
3 place Stanislas. [03 83 85 30 72.
Open Wed–Mon. **Closed** for
renovation until 1999. 🖼
The fine arts museum is noted
for Delacroix's dramatic *Death
of Charles the Bold at Nancy*
(1833), as well as for pastoral
scenes by Poussin and Claude
Lorrain. On the ground floor
are 19th- and 20th-century
paintings by artists such as
Manet, Monet, Berthe Morisot,
Utrillo, Dufy and Modigliani.

🏛 Musée Historique
Lorraine
Palais Ducal, 64 Grande Rue. [03 83
32 18 74. **Open** Wed–Mon. **Closed** 1
Jan, 1 May, 14 Jul, 1 Nov, 25 Dec. 🖼
The museum of the history of
Lorraine has a rich collection
of archaeological finds, sculp-
tures and paintings, including
two by Georges de la Tour.

🏛 Musée de l'Ecole de
Nancy
36–38 rue de Sergent Blandan.
[03 83 40 14 86. **Open**
Wed–Sun, Mon pm. **Closed** 1 Jan, 1
May, 14 July, 1 Nov, 25 Dec. 🖼
Exhibits in reconstructed Art
Nouveau settings include
furniture, fabrics and jewellery,
as well as the fanciful glassware of Emile Gallé, founder
of the Ecole de Nancy.

Arc de Triomphe in place Stanislas,
leading to place de la Carrière

Vosges landscape seen from the Route des Crêtes

THE ROUTE DES CRÊTES

This strategic mountain road (83 km, 50
miles long) connects the Vosges valleys from
Col du Bonhomme to Cernay, east of Thann,
often through woodland. Hugging the
western side of the Vosges, the Route des
Crêtes was created during World War I to
prevent the Germans from observing French
troop movements. When not shrouded in
mist, there are breathtaking views over
Lorraine from its many "crests" (crêtes).

Gérardmer ❺

Vosges. 🏠 10,000. 🚊 🚟 🅸 place des Déportés (03 29 27 27 27). 🚢 Thu & Sat.

Nestling on the Lorraine side of the Vosges, on the shore of a magnificent lake stretching out before it, Gérardmer is a setting rather than a city. In November 1944, just before its liberation, Gérardmer was razed by the Nazi scorched-earth policy, but has since been reconstructed. Saw mills and wood-carving remain local trades, though tourism is fast replacing the textile industry.

Gérardmer is now a popular holiday resort. In winter, the steep slopes of the Vosges Cristallines around the town turn it into a ski resort, while the lake is used for watersports in summer. The town's attractions also include lakeside walks and boat trips, as well as Géromée cheese, similar to the more famous Munster, from just over the Alsatian border. Gérardmer also boasts the oldest tourist information office in the country, dating from 1875.

Yet, ultimately, it is the scenic drives and mountain hikes in the Vosges that attract adventurous visitors. Most leave the lakeside bowl to head for the Alsatian border via the magnificent **Route des Crêtes**, which can be joined at the mountain pass of Col de la Schlucht.

Recreating village crafts in Ecomusée d'Alsace in Ungersheim

Mulhouse ❻

Haut Rhin. 🏠 109,000. 🛫 🚊 🚟 🅸 9 av du Maréchal Foch (03 89 35 48 48). 🚢 Tue, Thu & Sat.

Close to the Swiss border, Mulhouse is an unprepossessing industrial city, badly damaged in World War II. However, there are numerous technical museums and shopping galleries, as well as Alsatian taverns and Swiss wine bars. Most visitors use the city as a base for exploring the rolling hills of the Sundgau on the Swiss border.

Of the museums, **Musée de l'Impression sur Etoffes**, at 14 rue Jean-Jaques Henner, is devoted to textiles and fabric painting, while **Musée Français du Chemin de Fer**, at 2 rue Alfred Glehn, has a collection of steam and electric locomotives. **Musée de l'Automobile**, at 192 avenue de Colmar, boasts over 100 Bugattis, a clutch of Mercedes and Ferraris and Charlie Chaplin's Rolls Royce. In place de la République, the liveliest part of town, is the **Musée Historique**, in the Renaissance former town hall.

Alsatian black pig in Ecomusée d'Alsace in Ungersheim

Environs

At Ungersheim, north of Mulhouse, the **Ecomusée d'Alsace** consists of rural settings transplanted here to preserve and display the region's heritage. The 12th-century fortified house from Mulhouse is a dramatic building, complete with Gothic garden. Farms are run along traditional lines, with livestock such as the Alsatian black pig. Rural crafts can be seen in their original settings.

🏛 **Ecomusée d'Alsace**
Chemin du Grosswald.
🕻 03 89 74 44 74. **Open** daily. 📷 ♿

The lake at Gérardmer, offering sporting and leisure activities

Guebwiller ⓲

Haut Rhin. 🏃 *11,000.* 🚌 ℹ️ *73 rue de la République (03 89 76 10 63).* 🛒 *Tue & Fri.*

SURROUNDED BY vineyards and flower-filled valleys, Guebwiller is known as "the gateway to the valley of flowers". However, as an industrial town producing textiles and machine tools, it feels cut off from this rural setting. The houses are digni-fied, but the *caves* and churches make it worth a visit.

Set on a pretty square, **Eglise Notre-Dame** combines Baroque theatricality with Neo-Classical elegance, while **Eglise des Dominicains** boasts Gothic frescoes and a fine rood screen. **Eglise St-Léger**, the richly ornamented Romanesque church, is the most rewarding, especially the façade, triple porch and portal.

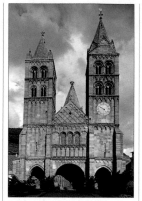

Eglise St-Léger in Guebwiller

Environs
The scenic Lauch valley, north-west of Guebwiller, is known as "Le Florival" because of its floral aspect. **Lautenbach** is used as a starting point for hikes through this recognized *zone de tranquillité*. The

village has a pink Roman-esque church, whose portal depicts human passion and the battle between Good and Evil. The square leads to the river, a small weir, *lavoir* (public washing place) and houses overhanging the water.

Neuf-Brisach ⓳

Haut Rhin. 🏃 *2,100.* 🚌 ℹ️ *Palais du Gouverneur, 6 place d'Armes (03 89 72 56 66).* 🛒 *1st & 3rd Mon of each month.*

SITUATED NEAR the German border, this octagonal citadel is the military strategist Vauban's masterpiece. Built between 1698 and 1707, the citadel forms a typical star-shaped pattern, with symmetrical towers enclosing 48 equal squares. In the centre, from where straight streets radiate for ease of defence, is

THE CITADEL OF NEUF-BRISACH

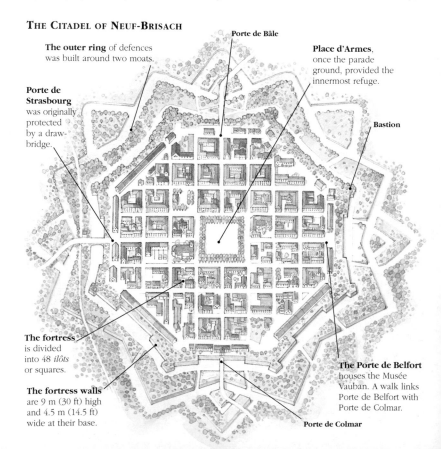

The outer ring of defences was built around two moats.

Porte de Bâle

Place d'Armes, once the parade ground, provided the innermost refuge.

Porte de Strasbourg was originally protected by a draw-bridge.

Bastion

The fortress is divided into 48 *ilôts* or squares.

The fortress walls are 9 m (30 ft) high and 4.5 m (14.5 ft) wide at their base.

The Porte de Belfort houses the Musée Vauban. A walk links Porte de Belfort with Porte de Colmar.

Porte de Colmar

The celebrated Isenheim altarpiece by Matthias Grünewald in Colmar

the place d'Armes and the Eglise St-Louis, which was added in 1731–6. It was Vauban's usual homage to his patron, Louis XIV, implying that the church was dedicated to the Sun King, rather than the saint.

The Porte de Belfort houses the **Musée Vauban**, which includes a model of the town, showing the outlying defences, now concealed by woodland. They represent Vauban's barrier to the fortress and it is to his credit that the citadel was never taken.

🏛 Musée Vauban

Place Porte de Belfort. **📞** 03 89 72 56 66. **Open** Apr–Oct: Wed–Mon. **Open** Nov–Mar: groups only, by appt. 📷 ♿

Eguisheim ❾

Haut Rhin. 🏠 1,500. 🚌 📕 22a Grand'Rue (03 89 23 40 33).

Eguisheim is a most exquisite small town, laid out within three concentric rings of ramparts. Curled up within these 13th-century walls, the ensemble of austere fortifications and domestic elegance makes for a surprisingly harmonious whole.

In the centre of town is the octagonal feudal **castle** of the Counts of Eguisheim. A Renaissance fountain in front has the statue of Bruno Eguisheim, born here in 1002. He became Pope Léon IX and was later canonized.

The Grand'Rue is lined with half-timbered houses, many showing their construction

date. Close to the castle is the **Marbacherhof**, a monastic tithe barn and cornhall. On a neighbouring square, the modern parish church retains the original Romanesque sculpted tympanum.

The rest of the town has its share of Hansel-and-Gretel atmosphere, while inviting courtyards offer tastings of *grands crus*. From rue de Hautvilliers, outside the ramparts, a marked path leads through scenic vineyards.

Colmar ❿

Haut Rhin. 🏠 65,000. 🚌 🚋 📕 4 rue d'Unterlinden (03 89 20 68 92). 🖉 Wed, Thu & Sat.

Colmar is the best preserved city in Alsace. As a trading post and river port, Colmar had its heyday in the 16th century, when wine merchants shipped their wine along the waterways running through the picturesque canal quarter,

now known as **Petite Venise**. "Little Venice" is best seen on a leisurely boat trip that takes you from the tanners' quarter to the rue des Tanneurs. The adjoining place de l'Alsacienne Douane is dominated by the **Koifhüs**, a galleried customs house with a Burgundian tiled roof, overlooking half-timbered pastel houses which sport sculpted pillars.

Nearby, the place de la Cathédrale quarter is full of 16th-century houses with picturesque hanging signs. **Eglise St-Martin**, essentially Gothic, has a noted south portal. Just to the west, the place des Dominicains, with cafés, is dwarfed by the Gothic **Eglise Dominicains**. Inside is *La Vierge au Buisson de Roses* (1473), the glittering red and gold "Virgin of the Rose-bush" by Martin Schongauer, a renowned Alsatian painter and native of Colmar.

Place d'Unterlinden, the adjoining square, has the **Musée d'Unterlinden**. Set in a Dominican monastery, it displays early Rhenish paintings. The highlight is the Isenheim altarpiece. A master-piece of emotional intensity, it is part of an early 16th-century Alsatian panel painting by Matthias Grünewald.

In the historic centre, the quaint rue des Têtes has the former wine exchange, a Renaissance town house known as the Maison des Têtes because of the grimacing heads on the gabled façade. And in rue Mercière, **Maison Pfister**, with its slender stair turret and galleried flower-decked façade, has come to typify the city.

Along the quai de la Poissonerie in the Petite Venise area of Colmar

Riquewihr ⓫

Haut Rhin. 🏛 *1,100.* 🚉
🛈 *2 rue de 1ère Armée (03 89 49 08 40).* 🚗 *Fri.*

VINEYARDS RUN right up to the ramparts of Riquewihr, the prettiest village on the Route du Vin *(see pp222–3).* Deeply pragmatic, Riquewihr wine makers plant roses at the end of each row of vines – both for their pretty effect and as early detectors of parasites. The village belonged to the Counts of Wurtemberg until the Revolution and has grown rich on wine, from Tokay and Pinot Gris to Gewürztraminer and Riesling. Virtually an open-air museum, Riquewihr abounds in cobbled alleys, geranium-clad balconies, galleried courtyards, romantic double ramparts and watchtowers.

From the Hôtel de Ville, the **rue de Gaulle** climbs gently past medieval and Renaissance houses, half-timbered, stone-clad or corbelled. Oriel windows vie with sculpted portals and medieval sign boards. On the right lies the idyllic **place des Trois Eglises**.

A passageway leads through the ramparts to the vineyards, stacked up on the hill. Further up lies the **Dolder**, a 13th-century belfry, followed by the **Tour Haute**, marking the second tier of ramparts. Beyond the gateway are **Cours des Bergers**, gardens laid out around the 16th-century ramparts. The picture-postcard image is only challenged by the crowds in summer or during the wine harvest, when visitors out-number the local population several times over.

The pretty – and popular – village of Riquewihr, set among vineyards

Ribeauvillé ⓬

Haut Rhin. 🏛 *4,800.* 🚉 🚌
🛈 *1 Grand'Rue (03 89 73 62 22).* 🚗 *Sat.*

OVERLOOKED by three ruined castles, Ribeauvillé is stiflingly prettified, as may be expected from a favoured town on the Route du Vin. This status is partly due to healthy sales of the cele-brated *grands crus* of Alsace, especially Riesling. There are ample opportunities for tastings, particularly near the park, in the lower part of town *(see pp222–3).*

On the Grand'Rue (No. 14) is the **Pfifferhüs**, the minstrels' house, now a regional restau-rant. As local cooks declare, Ribeauvillé is the capital of the *kougelhopf*, the light, almond-flavoured Alsatian cake.

Tortuous alleys wind past steep-roofed artisans' and *vignerons'* houses in the upper part of the town. Beyond are Renaissance fountains, painted façades and **St Grégoire-le-Grand**, the Gothic parish church. A marked path, which begins in this part of town, leads into the vineyards.

Château du Haut-Koenigsbourg ⓭

Orschwiller. 📞 *03 88 92 11 46.* **Open** *2nd week Feb–2nd week Jan: daily.* **Closed** *1 Jan, 1 & 11 Nov, 25 Dec.* 📷

LOOMING ABOVE the pretty village of St-Hippolyte, Haut-Koenigsbourg castle, the most popular attraction in Alsace, dominates the horizon. In 1114, the Swabian Emperor, Frederick of Hohenstaufen, built the first Teutonic castle here, which was destroyed in 1462. Rebuilt and added to under the Habsburgs, it burned down in 1633. At the end of the 19th century, Kaiser Wilhelm II commissioned Berlin architect Bodo Ebhardt to restore the castle. The result of his painstaking work was a precise reconstruction of the original building.

Despite a drawbridge, fierce keep and rings of fortifications, this warm sandstone hybrid is too sophisticated for a feudal château. The Cour d'Honneur is a breathtaking re-creation, with a pointed corner turret and creaky arcaded galleries. Within the castle are suitably gloomy "Gothic" chambers and airy "Renaissance" rooms. La Grande Salle is the most far-fetched, with a Neo-Gothic gallery and ornate panelling. From the battlements stretches a glorious Rhineland panorama, bordered by the Black Forest and the Alps. On the other side are sweeping views, from the high Vosges to wine villages and vineyards below.

Upper garden

West bastion

West wing

Outer walls

Chapelle St-Sébastien outside Dambach-la-Ville, along the Route du Vin

Sélestat ⓴

Bas Rhin. 🏛 16,000. 🚊 🚌
🛈 Commanderie Saint Jean, boulevard du Général Leclerc (03 88 58 87 20). 🚌 Tue.

D URING THE RENAISSANCE, Sélestat was the intellectual centre of Alsace, with a tradition of humanism fostered by Beatus Rhenanus, a friend of Erasmus. The famous **Biblio- thèque Humaniste** has a magnificent collection of leather-bound editions of some of the earliest printed books and unique illuminated manuscripts. Nearby are the Cour des Prélats, a turreted ivy-covered mansion, and the Tour de l'Horloge, a medieval clocktower. **Eglise Ste-Foy** is 12th-century, with an octagonal belltower. Opposite is **Eglise St- Georges**, glittering with green and red "Burgundian tiles".

🏛 Bibliothèque Humaniste
1 rue de la Bibliothèque.
☎ 03 88 92 03 24.
Open Jul–Aug: daily; Sep–Jun: Mon–Sat am.
Closed public hols. 🚫

Obernai ⓯

Bas Rhin. 🏛 10,000. 🚊 🚌
🛈 place du Beffroi (03 88 95 64 13).
🚌 Tue & Thu.

Young **Alsaciens** in traditional costume

A T THE NORTH END of the Route du Vin, Obernai retains a flavour of authentic Alsace: residents speak Alsatian, at festivities women wear traditional costume, and church services are well-attended in the cavernous Neo-Gothic **Eglise St-Pierre- et-St-Paul**. The place du Marché is well-preserved, and features the gabled **Halle aux Blés**, a 16th-century corn hall above a former butcher's shop, with a façade adorned with cows' and dragons' heads. Place de la Chapelle, the adjoining square, has a Renaissance fountain. The square is home to the 16th-century **Hôtel de Ville** and the **Kapellturm**, the galleried Gothic belfry. Side streets have Renaissance and medieval timber-framed houses. A stroll past the cafés on rue du Marché ends in a pleasant park by the ramparts.

Environs
Odile, Alsace's seventh-century patron saint, was born in Obernai but she is venerated on **Mont Sainte-Odile** to the west, where she is buried in the Chapelle Ste-Odile.
Molsheim, a former bishopric and fortified market town 10 km (6 miles) north, is noted for its attractive marketplace with fountain. The star attraction is the Metzig, a Renaissance-style butchers' guildhall, now the town hall.

Environs
Medieval **Dambach-la-Ville**, another pretty town, is linked to Andlau and red-tiled Itterswiller by a delightful rural road through vineyards.
Ebersmunster, a picturesque hamlet, has an onion-domed abbey church, whose Baroque interior is a sumptuous display of gilded stucco.

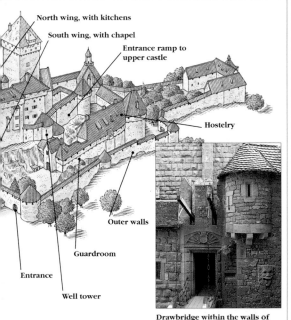

North wing, with kitchens

South wing, with chapel

Entrance ramp to upper castle

Hostelry

Outer walls

Guardroom

Entrance

Well tower

Drawbridge within the walls of Château du Haut-Koenigsbourg

Strasbourg ⑯

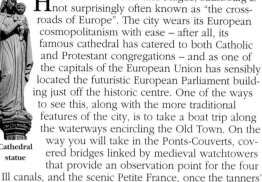
Cathedral statue

HALFWAY BETWEEN PARIS and Prague, Strasbourg is not surprisingly often known as "the cross-roads of Europe". The city wears its European cosmopolitanism with ease – after all, its famous cathedral has catered to both Catholic and Protestant congregations – and as one of the capitals of the European Union has sensibly located the futuristic European Parliament building just off the historic centre. One of the ways to see this, along with the more traditional features of the city, is to take a boat trip along the waterways encircling the Old Town. On the way you will take in the Ponts-Couverts, covered bridges linked by medieval watchtowers that provide an observation point for the four Ill canals, and the scenic Petite France, once the tanners' district, dotted with mills and criss-crossed by bridges.

Barge on the canal

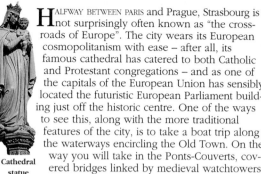
The central portal of the west façade of the cathedral

⛪ Cathédrale Notre-Dame
A masterpiece of stone lace-work, the sandstone cathedral "rises like a most sublime, wide-arching tree of God", as Goethe marvelled. Though construction began in the 11th century (the choir is Romanesque, the nave is Gothic), it ended only in 1439, with the completion of the west façade, begun in 1277. The three portals are ornamented with statues. But the crowning glory is the kaleidoscope of the rose window. The south portal leads

to the Gothic Pilier des Anges, or Pillar of Angels (built around 1230), set beside the Astrono-mical Clock: mechanical figures appear accompanied by chimes at 12:31pm. There are wonderful views over the city from the viewing platform, and on some summer evenings there are organ concerts.
In place de la Cathédrale, Maison Kammerzell, now a popular restaurant, was once a rich merchant's mansion, and is the most elaborately carved in Alsace. The ground floor

dates from 1467, the rest from 1589. From place du Château, behind the cathedral, a tourist "mini-train" plies the main sights in the historic centre and Petite France.

🏛 Musée de l'Oeuvre de Notre-Dame
3 place du Château. **📞** 03 88 52 50 00.
Open Tue–Sun. **Closed** 1 Jan, Good Fri, 1 May, 1 Nov, 25 Dec. 🈺
♿ ground floor only.
The cathedral's impressive museum contains much of its original sculpture, as well as magnificent stained glass from the 11th century. A collection

IPE, the European Parliament building on the outskirts of the city centre

VISITORS' CHECKLIST

Bas Rhin. 250,000. 12 km
(7.5 miles) SW Strasbourg.
place de la Gare (08 36 35
35 35). place des Halles (03
88 77 70 70). 17 place de la
Cathédrale (03 88 52 28 28).
Mon–Sat. Classical Music
Festival (Jun); Jazz Festival (Jun);
Musica, contemporary music
festival (mid-Sep–early-Oct).

Bishops of Strasbourg. It
houses three museums; the
Musée des Beaux Arts: the
Musée Archéologique;
and the Musée des Arts
Décoratifs, which contains
the sumptuous State
Apartments and one of
the finest collections
of ceramics in France.
Nearby, in the old Customs
House, the Musée d'Art
Moderne has temp-
orary exhibitions
featuring works by
modern artists.

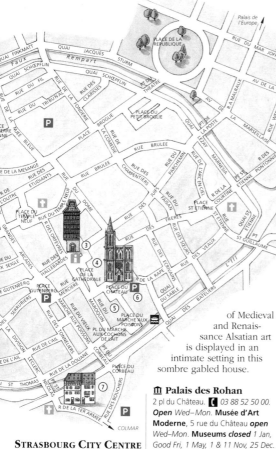

STRASBOURG CITY CENTRE

Cathédrale Notre-Dame ④
Maison Kammerzell ③
Musée Alsacien ⑦
Musée de l'Oeuvre
  de Notre-Dame ⑤
Palais des Rohan ⑥
Petite France ②
Ponts-Couverts ①

| 0 metres | 250 |
| 0 yards | 250 |

KEY

	River boat service
P	Parking
	Tourist information
	Church

of Medieval
and Renais-
sance Alsatian art
is displayed in an
intimate setting in this
sombre gabled house.

🏛 Palais des Rohan

2 pl du Château. 03 88 52 50 00.
Open Wed–Mon. **Musée d'Art
Moderne**, 5 rue du Château **open**
Wed–Mon. **Museums closed** 1 Jan,
Good Fri, 1 May, 1 & 11 Nov, 25 Dec.

Designed by the king's architect, Robert de Cotte, in 1730,
this grand Classical palace
was intended for the Prince-

🏛 Musée
Historique

3 place de la Grande Boucherie.
03 88 52 50 00. **Closed** for
renovation until 1999.
The museum occupies the
cavernous 16th-century city
abattoir and focuses on Strasbourg's political, economic
and military history.

🏛 Musée Alsacien

23 quai St-Nicolas. 03 88 35 55 36.
Open Wed–Mon. **Closed** 1 Jan, Good
Fri, 1 May, 1 Nov, 25 Dec.
Housed in a series of interconnecting Renaissance
buildings, the museum has
exhibits on local traditions
and popular arts and crafts.

Ponts-Couverts with medieval
watchtowers over the canals

The Alsace Route du Vin

MEANDERING over 180 km (110 miles) from Marlenheim to Thann, the picturesque wine route takes in historic towns with cobbled streets, medieval timber-framed houses and Renaissance fountains. Romantically appointed *winstubs,* or cellars, offer traditional *choucroute garnie* and flowery white Alsatian wines. Dedicated wine lovers could spend two or three days covering the route at leisure, or may want to make shorter trips in either direction to or from Colmar. For a refreshing contrast from the unremitting charm of the towns and villages, escape occasionally into *sentiers viticoles* – lovely paths through the vineyards themselves.

Alsatian wine master

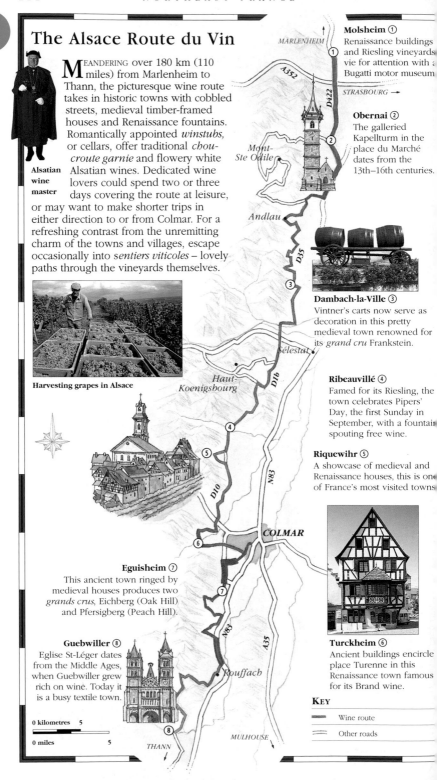

Harvesting grapes in Alsace

Molsheim ①
Renaissance buildings and Riesling vineyards vie for attention with a Bugatti motor museum.

STRASBOURG →

Obernai ②
The galleried Kapellturm in the place du Marché dates from the 13th–16th centuries.

Dambach-la-Ville ③
Vintner's carts now serve as decoration in this pretty medieval town renowned for its *grand cru* Frankstein.

Ribeauvillé ④
Famed for its Riesling, the town celebrates Pipers' Day, the first Sunday in September, with a fountain spouting free wine.

Riquewihr ⑤
A showcase of medieval and Renaissance houses, this is one of France's most visited towns.

Turckheim ⑥
Ancient buildings encircle place Turenne in this Renaissance town famous for its Brand wine.

Eguisheim ⑦
This ancient town ringed by medieval houses produces two *grands crus*, Eichberg (Oak Hill) and Pfersigberg (Peach Hill).

Guebwiller ⑧
Eglise St-Léger dates from the Middle Ages, when Guebwiller grew rich on wine. Today it is a busy textile town.

MARLENHEIM

Mont-Ste-Odile

Andlau

Sélestat

Haut-Koenigsbourg

COLMAR

Rouffach

MULHOUSE

THANN

0 kilometres   5

0 miles   5

KEY

▬▬ Wine route

═══ Other roads

ALSACE WINE

Alsace wines are usually aromatic, dry and full-bodied. All are white except Pinot Noir, used for light reds.

late-harvested Alsatian classic

KEY FACTS

Location and climate
Protected by the Vosges, Alsace has a semi-continental, fairly dry, warm climate.

Grape varieties
Alsace wines are known simply by their grape variety. **Gewürztraminer**, with its exotic rose-petal character, is most typically Alsatian, although the **Riesling** is arguably the finest. **Muscat** is another aromatic variety. Spicy but less assertive than Gewürztraminer, **Pinot Gris** and the crisper, dry **Pinot Blanc** go well with food. **Pinot Noir** is the only red variety.
Lusciously rich, sweet, late-harvested wines are an Alsace speciality.

Best producers
Albert Boxler, Marcel Deiss, Marc Kreyden-weiss, Bernard & Robert Schoffit, Kuentz-Bas, Domaine Weinbach, Josmeyer, Olivier Zind-Humbrecht, Charles Schléret, Domaines Schlumberger, Domaine Ostertag, Domaine Trimbach, Hugel & Fils, Cave de Turckheim.

Good vintages
1996, 1995, 1994, 1990, 1989, 1988.

The 12th-century chapel of the Château du Haut-Barr, near Saverne

Saverne ⑰

Bas Rhin. 🚹 10,600. 🚉 🚌
🚹 Château des Rohan (03 88 91 80 47). 🛒 Tue, Thu & Sat.

FRAMED BY HILLS, and situated on the river Zorn and the Marne-Rhine canal, Saverne is a pretty sight. The town was a fief of the prince-bishops of Strasbourg and its sandstone Château des Rohan was a favourite summer residence. Today, it houses the **Musée de la Ville de Saverne**, whose collection traces Saverne's past. On the far side of the château, the Grand'Rue is studded with restaurants and timber-framed Renaissance houses.

🏛 **Musée de la Ville de Saverne**
Château des Rohan. 📞 03 88 91 06 28. **Open** Mar–Nov: Wed–Mon; Dec–Feb: Sun. 📷 ♿

Environs
To the southwest, perched on a rocky spur, the ruined **Château du Haut-Barr** – the "Eye of Alsace" – once commanded the vital pass of Col de Saverne.
In **Marmoutier**, 6 km (3.5 miles) south of Haut-Barr, is a renowned abbey church with a Romanesque-Lombard façade and octagonal towers.

Betschdorf ⑱

Bas Rhin. 🚹 3,600. 🚹 La Mairie (03 88 54 48 00).

THE VIBRANT village of Betschdorf borders the Forêt de Haguenau, 45 km (27 miles) north of Strasbourg. Many residents occupy timber-framed houses dating from the 18th century, when pottery made the village prosperous. Generations of potters have passed down the knowledge of the characteristic blue-grey glaze to their sons, while the women have been entrusted with decorating it in cobalt blue. A pottery museum, with a workshop attached, displays rural ceramics. Also worth visiting are the frescoed Gothic Niederbetschdorf church and the Lutheran Kuhlendorf church, the only timber-framed church in Alsace. Nearby is the Wacht, the former nightwatchmen's quarters. Betschdorf is a good place to try *tartes flambées* – hot, crispy bases topped with cheese or fruit.

Betschdorf pottery

Environs
Another pottery village, **Soufflenheim**, lies 10 km (6 miles) southeast. Its earth-coloured pottery is usually painted with bold flowers.

WESTERN FRANCE

Introducing Western France

THE WESTERN REGIONS of France have played very
different historical roles, from the royal heartland
of the Loire Valley to separatist Celtic Brittany. These
are mainly rich farming regions, with fishing important
along the coasts. Heavy industry and oil refineries are
concentrated around Rouen and Le Havre. Visitors
come for the wonderful beaches, quiet rural byways
and the sumptuous Loire châteaux. This map shows
the region's most celebrated sights.

*The evocative silhouette of Mont-St-Michel has welcomed
pilgrims since the 11th century. Today nearly one million visitors
a year walk across the sands to the island abbey (see pp246–51).*

Guimiliau Parish Close

Mont-St-Michel

BRITTANY
(See pp258–75)

Carnac Megaliths

*The megaliths of Carnac are evidence of early settlers
in Brittany. These ancient granite blocks, arranged in
intriguing patterns, date back to 4000 BC and are thought
to have had a religious or astronomical purpose (see p269).*

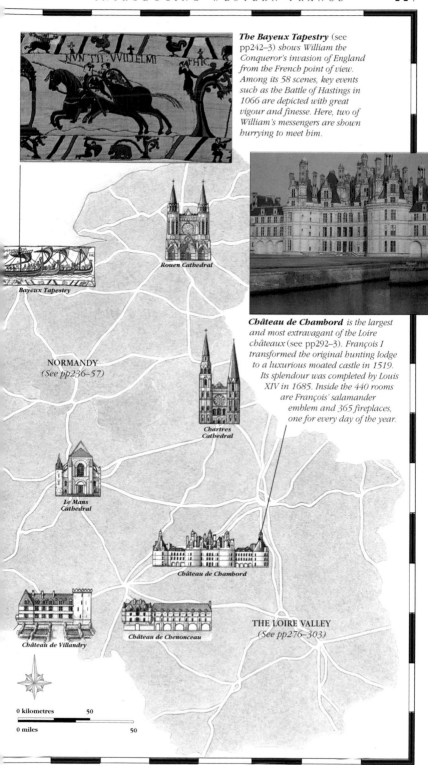

The Bayeux Tapestry (see pp242–3) *shows William the Conqueror's invasion of England from the French point of view. Among its 58 scenes, key events such as the Battle of Hastings in 1066 are depicted with great vigour and finesse. Here, two of William's messengers are shown hurrying to meet him.*

Bayeux Tapestry

Rouen Cathedral

Château de Chambord *is the largest and most extravagant of the Loire châteaux* (see pp292–3). *François I transformed the original hunting lodge to a luxurious moated castle in 1519. Its splendour was completed by Louis XIV in 1685. Inside the 440 rooms are François' salamander emblem and 365 fireplaces, one for every day of the year.*

NORMANDY
(See pp236–57)

Chartres Cathedral

Le Mans Cathedral

Château de Chambord

Château de Villandry

Château de Chenonceau

THE LOIRE VALLEY
(See pp276–303)

0 kilometres   50

0 miles   50

Regional Food: Western France

Moules marinières *are mussels cooked in white wine, with onions, shallots, parsley and butter.*

WITH 480 KM (300 MILES) of coastline, Normandy cooking naturally draws on an abundance of fish and shellfish. Lambs graze on the salt-marshes, giving the meat its slightly salty, distinctive flavour. Inland, dairy cattle produce rich milk for cream, cheese and butter. Calvados, the famous apple brandy, is derived from the apples that thrive here. Seafood, salt-marsh lamb, cider, and cider *eau-de-vie* all cross the border into Breton cuisine, but particular to Brittany is fresh curd cheese or buttermilk with buckwheat *crêpes* – foods once regarded as humble but which have now become much sought-after ingredients of chic regional cuisine.

In the Loire Valley, the river is a source of tasty fresh-water fish, and plump mushrooms are cultivated in caves along the riverbanks. The rich alluvial soils produce luscious vegetables, fruit, cheese and wine.

Camembert cheese

Pure sea salt crystals, seen glistening on the Guérande peninsula of southeast Brittany, are raked in pans by farmers in the traditional way. This fine natural salt retains all its minerals and the unmistakable scent of the sea.

Oysters *can be eaten raw straight from the shell or grilled quickly and served with a sauce.*

Rillettes *are chunks of pork or goose meat seasoned with herbs, cooked in lard and pounded to a paste.*

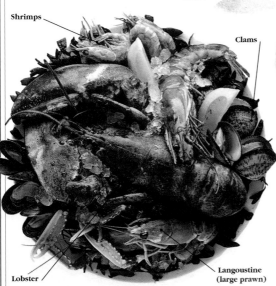

Shrimps / Clams / Lobster / Langoustine (large prawn)

Fruits de mer *is a selection of local seafood which includes oysters, clams, mussels, crabs, langoustines, whelks, shrimps and periwinkles, often served on a great bed of ice and seaweed. Necessary accompaniments include lemons, shallot-and-vinegar sauce, chilled Muscadet, fresh rye bread and butter.*

Artichokes *can be cooked in water or wine with herbs, stuffed, or served with herb or lemon-flavoured butter.*

Gigot d'agneau à la Bretonne *is roast lamb served with haricot beans simmered with tomatoes, garlic and onions.*

Salmon with beurre blanc, *a sauce of butter, wine and shallots, is a popular dish in both Brittany and the Loire.*

Tripe à la mode de Caen *is a Normandy dish of steamed tripe and vegetables cooked together very slowly in cider.*

Tarte tatin *is a caramelized upside-down apple tart, originally created at the Hôtel Tatin in the Loire Valley.*

Crêpes Suzettes, *one of Brittany's most famous dishes, is flavoured with oranges and Grand Marnier liqueur.*

Galette biscuits *from Brittany are quite noticeably flavoured with the slightly salty butter used in the regional cuisine.*

CHEESES
Some of France's finest cheeses come from Normandy – Camembert, pungent Livarot and creamy Pont-l'Evêque. Crottin de Chavignol from the Loire is one of the most popular *chèvres* (goat's cheeses).

Pont l'Eveque

Crottins de Chavignol

Livarot

Camembert

Benedictine   **Calvados**   **Cider**

DRINKS
In Normandy and most of Brittany, sparkling alcoholic and non-alcoholic cider is the local drink, an excellent accompaniment to savoury *crêpes*. Much stronger is the apple brandy known as Calvados (*lambig* in Brittany). The herbal liqueur Benedictine was first concocted by a monk at Fécamp in 1510.

France's Wine Regions: the Loire

WITH A FEW EXCEPTIONS, the Loire is a region of good rather than great wines. The fertile agricultural soils of the meandering flatlands of the "Garden of France" are fine for fruit and vegetables, less so for the production of great wines. The cool, northern, Atlantic-influenced climate nonetheless produces refreshing reds and summer rosés, aromatic white wines and attractively bracing sparkling wines. The white wines are very much in the majority here, and are usually intended for early consumption, so vintages in the Loire tend to matter less than in the classic red wine regions.

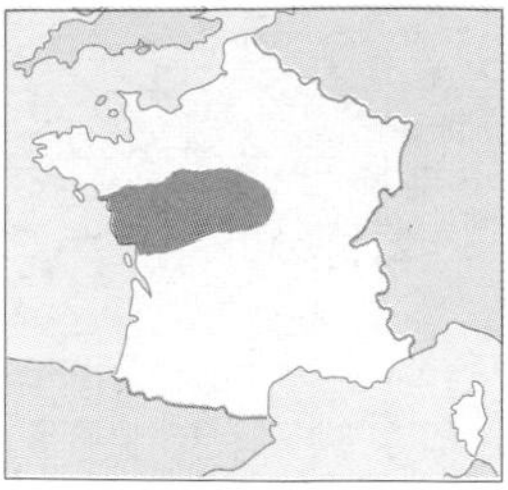

Cabernet Franc, red grape of the Loire

LOCATOR MAP

▨ Loire wine region

The great sweet wine of the Coteaux du Layon, Quarts de Chaume, is little-known outside France.

Muscadet with the words sur lie on the label has been aged on its "lees" (see page 23), giving the wine more flavour and interest.

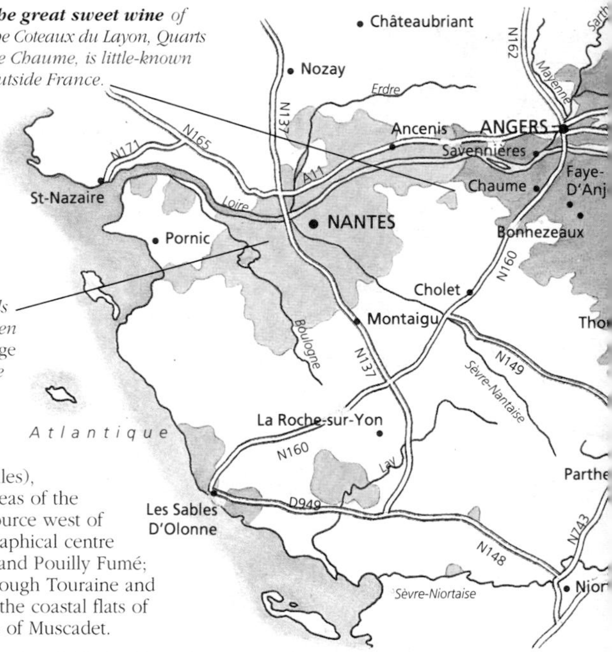

WINE REGIONS

The Loire, flowing for some 1,000 km (620 miles), links the major wine areas of the Loire Valley. Near its source west of Burgundy, in the geographical centre of France, lie Sancerre and Pouilly Fumé; the river flows west through Touraine and Anjou, finally reaching the coastal flats of the Pays Nantais, home of Muscadet.

Châteaubriant • Nozay • Ancenis ANGERS Savennières • St-Nazaire Chaume • Faye-D'Anj • NANTES Bonnezeaux • Pornic Cholet • Tho Montaigu

Atlantique La Roche-sur-Yon Parthe

Les Sables D'Olonne Njor Sèvre-Niortaise

KEY

▨ Pays Nantais
▨ Anjou-Saumur
▨ Haut-Poitou
☐ Touraine
▨ Central Vineyards

0 kilometres   15

0 miles   15

Clos de l'Echo, Chinon, producer of fine, herbaceous red wine

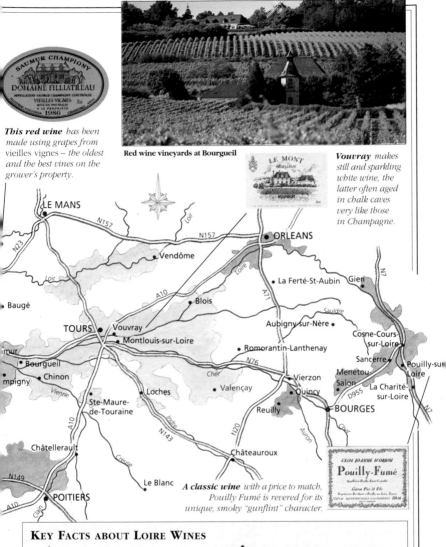

This red wine has been made using grapes from vieilles vignes – *the oldest and the best vines on the grower's property.*

Red wine vineyards at Bourgueil

Vouvray makes still and sparkling white wine, the latter often aged in chalk caves very like those in Champagne.

LE MANS

N157

N23

Loir

Loir

Vendôme

Baugé

A10

Loire

Blois

TOURS • Vouvray

Montlouis-sur-Loire

mur

• Bourgueil

Chinon

mpigny

Vienne

Ste-Maure-de-Touraine

Loches

Cher

Châtellerault

Creuse

N143

Indre

N149

A10

Clain

POITIERS

Le Blanc

N120

Châteauroux

ORLEANS

N157

Loir

La Ferté-St-Aubin   Gien

N7

Aubigny-sur-Nère •

Romorantin-Lanthenay

Sauldre

Cosne-Cours-sur-Loire

Vierzon

Sancerre •   • Pouilly-sur-Loire

Menetou-Salon

D955

La Charité-sur-Loire

Valençay

Quincy

Reuilly

BOURGES

Auron

Cher

N7

A classic wine with a price to match, Pouilly Fumé is revered for its unique, smoky "gunflint" character.

Pouilly-Fumé

KEY FACTS ABOUT LOIRE WINES

Location and Climate
Fertile agricultural soils support fruit, vegetables and cereals as well as grapes. The climate is cool, influenced by the nearby Atlantic, giving the wines a refreshing acidity.

Grape Varieties
The *Muscadet* makes simple, dry white wines. The *Sauvignon* makes gooseberryish, flinty dry whites; it is at its finest in Sancerre and Pouilly Fumé, but is also good in Touraine. The *Chenin Blanc* makes dry and medium Anjou, Savennières, Vouvray, Montlouis and Saumur, sparkling Vouvray and Saumur, and the famous sweet whites, Bonnezeaux,

Vouvray and Quarts de Chaume. Summery reds are made from the *Gamay* and the grassy, herbaceous *Cabernet Franc*.

Good Producers
Muscadet: Sauvion, Guy Bossard, Luneau. *Anjou, Savennières, Vouvray*: Richou, Domaine de la Bizolière, Coulée de Serrant, Huet, Domaine des Aubuissières, Bourillon-Dorléans. *Touraine* (white): Domaine des Acacias. *Saumur* (red): Filliatreau, Domaine des Roches Neuves. *Chinon/Bourgueil* (red): Joguet, Taluau, Druet. *Sancerre, Pouilly Fumé, Ménétou-Salon*: Dagueneau, Reverdy, Vacheron, Mellot, Henry Natter, Henry Pelle.

From Defence to Decoration

THE GREAT CHATEAUX of the Loire Valley gradually evolved from purely defensive structures to decorative palaces. With the introduction of firearms, castles lost their defensive function and comfort and taste predominated. Defensive elements like towers, battlements, moats and gatehouses were retained largely as symbols of rank and ancestry. Renaissance additions, like galleries and dormer windows, added elegance.

Salamander emblem of François 1

Slate and stone walls

Angers (see p281), *a fortress built from 1230–40 by Louis IX, stands on a rocky hill in the town centre. In 1585, Henri III removed the pepper-pot shaped towers from 17 fortifications which were formerly 30 m (98 ft) high.*

Fortifications with pepper-pot towers removed

Circular tower, formerly defensive

Corbelled walkways, once useful in battle

Chaumont (see p296) *was rebuilt in 1498–1510 in Renaissance style by the Amboise family. Although it has a defensive appearance, with circular towers, corbelled walkways and a gatehouse, these features are mainly decorative. It was restored after 1875.*

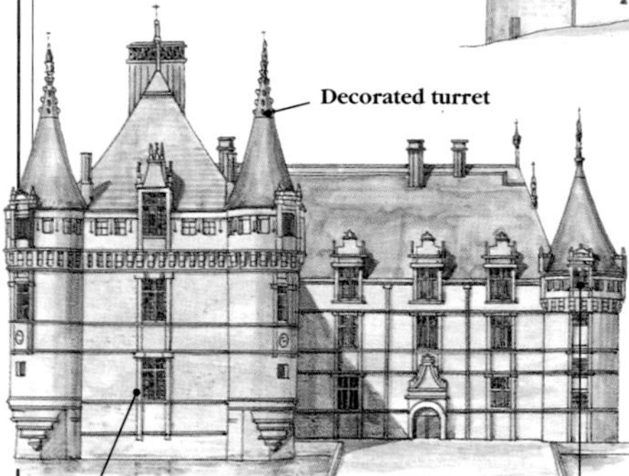

Decorated turret

Azay-le-Rideau (see p286), *regarded as one of the most elegant and well-designed Renaissance châteaux , was built by finance minister Gilles Berthelot (1518–1527) and his wife Philippa Lesbahy. It is a mixture of traditional turrets with Renaissance pilasters and pinnacles. Most dramatic is the interior staircase with its three storeys of twin bays and an intricately decorated pediment.*

Renaissance carved windows

Pilasters (columns)

Cylindrical tower

Dormer windows

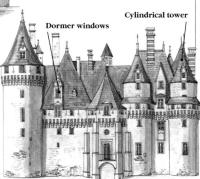

Ussé (see p285) *was built in 1462 by Jean de Bueil as a fortress with parapets containing openings for missiles, battlements and gunloops. The Espinay family, chamberlains to both Louis XI and Charles VIII, bought the château and changed the walls overlooking the main court-yard to Renaissance style with dormer windows and pilasters. In the 17th century the north wing was demolished to create palatial terraces.*

Breton Traditions

BRITTANY WAS CHRISTENED Breiz Izel (Little Britain) by the Welsh and Cornish migrants who fled here from Cornwall and Wales in the 5th and 6th centuries AD and imposed their customs, language and religion on the local Gauls. Brittany resisted Charlemagne, the Vikings, the Normans, English alliances and even French rule until 1532. Today, Breton is still taught in schools, and a busy calendar keeps Brittany in touch with its past and with other Celtic regions.

Bigouden lace headdresses

Breton music has strong Celtic links. Instruments like the biniou, similar to the bagpipes, and the oboe-like bombarde are often heard at local festivals.

***A pardon** is an annual religious festival honouring a local saint. The name derives from the granting of indulgences to pardon the sins of the past year. Some* pardons, *like those at Ste-Anne d'Auray and Ste-Anne-la-Palud, still attract thousands of pilgrims who carry banners and holy relics through the streets. Most* pardons *take place between April and September.*

Lace *coiffe*   Felt hat   Linen *coiffe*   Small headdress

Wooden clogs

***Breton costumes**, still seen at* pardons *and weddings, varied as each area had distinctive headdresses or* coiffes. *Artists like Gauguin often painted the costumes. There are good museum collections in Quimper* (see p264) *and Pont-l'Abbé in Pays Bigouden* (see p263).

Embroidered apron

Baggy Breton trousers

Brittany's Coastal Wildlife

Starfish

WITH ITS GRANITE CLIFFS, sweeping bays and deep estuaries, the Brittany coastline contains a wealth of different wildlife habitats. Parts of the coast have a tidal range of more than 50 m (150 ft), the highest in France, and this great variation in sea level divides marine life into several distinct zones. Most of the region's famous shellfish, including mussels, clams and oysters, live on the lower shore, either on rocks or in muddy sand where they are submerged for most of the day. Higher zones are the preserve of limpets and barnacles and several kinds of seaweed which can survive out of the water for long periods. Above the sea, towering cliffs offer a nursery for seabirds and a foothold for many kinds of wild flowers.

Cliffs at the Pointe du Raz, Brittany

The Ile de Bréhat at low tide

FEATURES OF THE COAST
This scene shows some of the wildlife habitats found on the Brittany coastline. When exploring the shore, make a note of the tide times, particularly if you plan to walk along the foot of the cliffs.

Saltmarsh flowers are at their best in late summer

Dunes, where marram grass grows, stabilize the sand.

Mud and sand is inhabited by clams and cockles which filter food from the water.

Rock stacks provide secure nurseries for nesting seabirds.

OYSTER BEDS

Like most marine molluscs, oysters begin their lives as tiny floating larvae. The first step in *ostréculture*, or oyster cultivation, consists of providing the larvae with somewhere to settle, which is usually a stack of submerged tiles. The developing oysters are later transferred to beds and left to mature before being collected for the market.

Oyster beds at Cancale

Clifftop turf often contains a narrow band of wild flowers sandwiched between fields and the sea.

Rockpools are flooded twice daily by the tide. They are inhabited by fish, molluscs, sea anemones and sponges.

COASTAL WILDLIFE

The structure of this shore determines the wildlife that lives on it. In a world beset by wind and waves, rocks provide solid anchorage for plants and a secure habitat for many small animals. Muddy sand is rich in nutrients, and has a greater abundance of life – although most of this is concealed beneath the surface.

Cliffs

The rock dove *is a cliff-dwelling ancestor of the well-known city pigeon.*

Thrift *is a common spring flower, found on exposed ledges near the sea.*

Rocks and Rockpools

Seaweed *of many different varieties is exposed each day by the falling tide.*

The limpet*, a slow-moving creature, scrapes tiny plants from the rock surface.*

The goby*, with its sharp eyesight, dashes for cover at the first sign of movement above.*

Crabs *live at many different water depths. Some species are extremely good swimmers.*

Mud and Sand

Cockles *live in large numbers just beneath the surface of muddy sand.*

The curlew *has a forceps-like curved beak for extracting shell-fish from mud and sand.*

NORMANDY

EURE · SEINE-MARITIME · MANCHE · CALVADOS · ORNE

THE QUINTESSENTIAL IMAGE *of Normandy is of a lush, pastoral region of apple orchards and contented cows, cider and pungent cheeses – but the region also spans the windswept beaches of the Cotentin and the wooded banks of the Seine valley. Highlights include the great abbey churches of Caen, the mighty island of Mont-St-Michel and Monet's garden at Giverny.*

Normandy gets its name from the Viking Norsemen who sailed up the river Seine in the 9th century. Pillagers turned settlers, they made their capital at Rouen – today a cultured cathedral city that commands the east of the region. Here the Seine meanders seaward past the ancient abbeys at Jumièges and St-Wandrille to a coast that became an open-air studio for Impressionist painters during the mid- and late 19th century.

North of Rouen are the chalky cliffs of the Côte d'Albâtre. The mood softens at the port of Honfleur and the elegant resorts of the Côte Fleurie to the west. Inland lies the Pays d'Auge, with its half-timbered manor houses and patch-eyed cows. The western half of Normandy is predominantly rural, a *bocage* countryside of small, high-hedged fields with windbreaks composed of beech trees.

The modern city of Caen is worth visiting for its two great 11th-century abbey churches built by William the Conqueror and his queen, Matilda. Close by in Bayeux, the story of William's invasion of England is told in detail by the town's famous tapestry. Memories of another invasion, the D-Day Landings of 1944, still linger along the Côte de Nacre and the Cotentin peninsula. Thousands of Allied troops poured ashore on to these magnificent beaches in the closing stages of World War II. The Cotentin peninsula is capped by the port of Cherbourg, still a strategic naval base. At its western foot stands one of France's greatest attractions: the monastery island of Mont-St-Michel.

Half-timbered manor house in the village of Beuvron-en-Auge, near Lisieux

◁ Rich pastures and brown and white Norman cattle, the traditional wealth of the province

Exploring Normandy

NORMANDY'S RICH HISTORICAL SIGHTS and diverse landscape make it ideal for touring by car or bicycle.
Rewarding coastal drives and good beaches can be
found along the windswept Côte d'Albâtre and the
Cotentin Peninsula. Further south is one of France's
most celebrated sights, Mont-St-Michel. Inland,
follow the meanders of the Seine valley, passing cider
orchards and half-timbered houses along the way, to
visit historic Rouen and Monet's garden at Giverny.

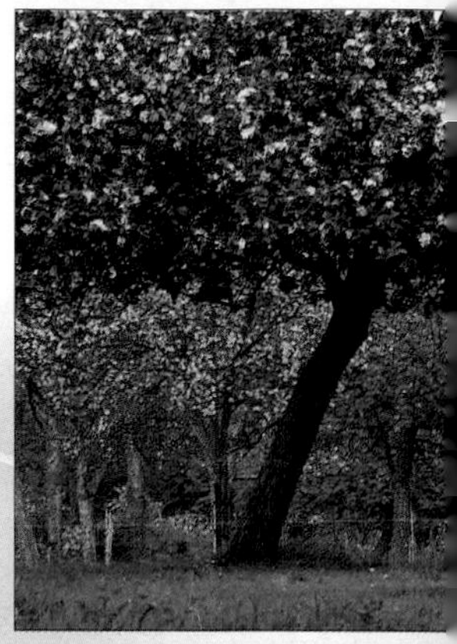

Apple trees in blossom in the
Pays d'Auge

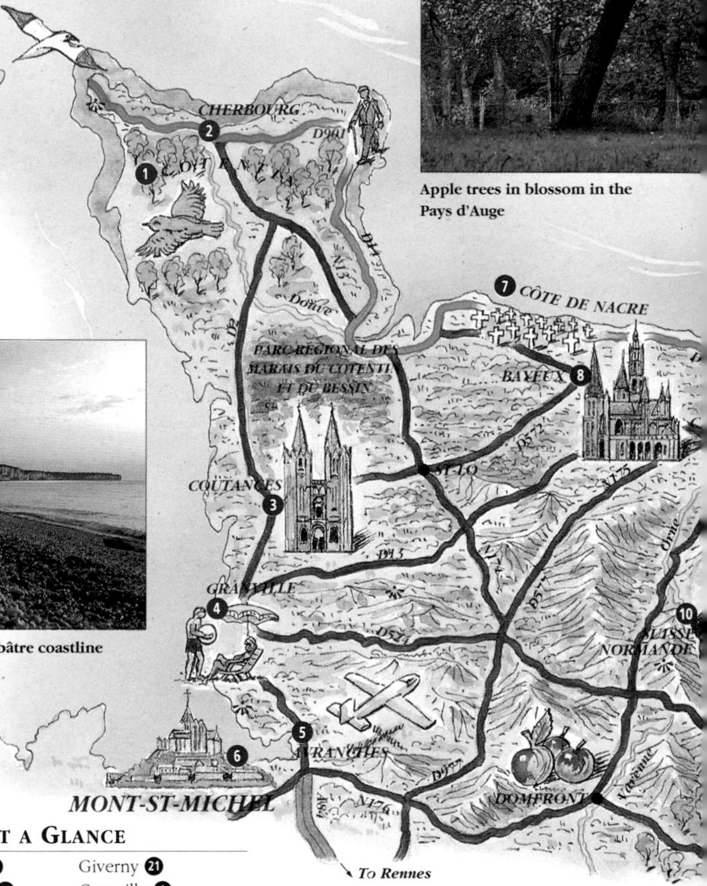

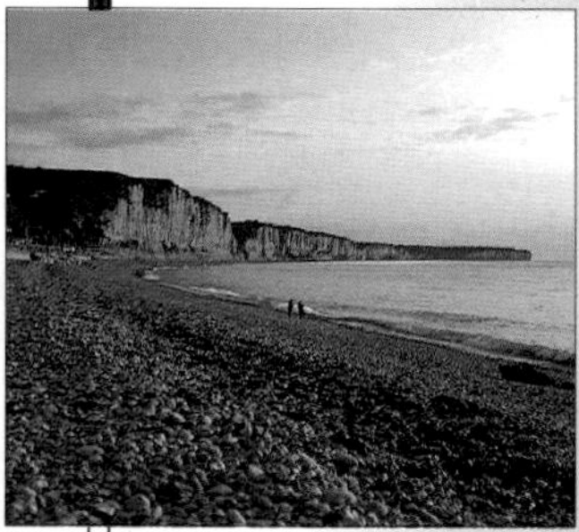

The Côte d'Albâtre coastline

SIGHTS AT A GLANCE

To Rennes

KEY

▬▬	Motorway
▬▬	Major road
▬▬	Minor road
▬▬	Scenic route
～	River
⚹	Viewpoint

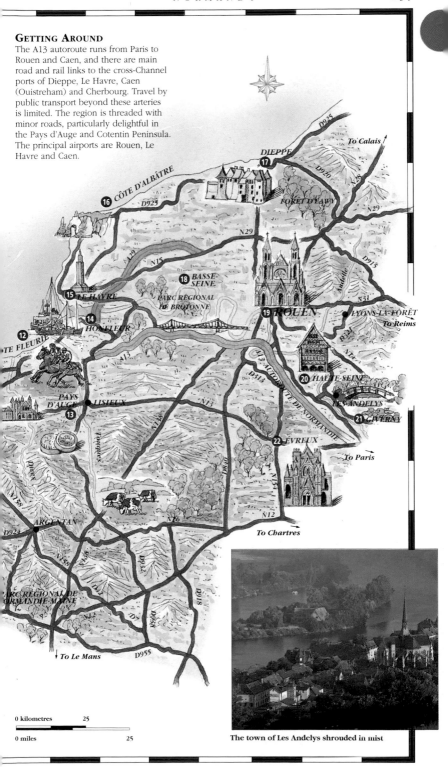

GETTING AROUND

The A13 autoroute runs from Paris to Rouen and Caen, and there are main road and rail links to the cross-Channel ports of Dieppe, Le Havre, Caen (Ouistreham) and Cherbourg. Travel by public transport beyond these arteries is limited. The region is threaded with minor roads, particularly delightful in the Pays d'Auge and Cotentin Peninsula. The principal airports are Rouen, Le Havre and Caen.

To Calais

DIEPPE 17

CÔTE D'ALBÂTRE 16

D925

FORÊT D'EAWY

N29

N15

BASSE-SEINE 18

15 LE HAVRE

PARC RÉGIONAL DE BROTONNE

19 ROUEN

LYONS-LA-FORÊT
To Reims

14 HONFLEUR

12
TE FLEURIE

A13

HAUTE-SEINE 20

PAYS D'AUGE
13

LISIEUX

LES ANDELYS

21 GIVERNY

A13 AUTOROUTE DE NORMANDIE

22 EVREUX

To Paris

ARGENTAN

D924

To Chartres

PARC RÉGIONAL DE NORMANDIE-MAINE

To Le Mans   D955

0 kilometres   25

0 miles   25

The town of Les Andelys shrouded in mist

Rugged cliffs on the Cotentin Peninsula

Cotentin ❶

Manche. 🏕 🚌 🚗 ⛴ *Cherbourg.*
ℹ️ *Cherbourg (02 33 93 52 02).*

Thrusting into the English Channel, the Cotentin Peninsula has a landscape similar to Brittany's. Its long sandy beaches are relatively undeveloped, with wild and windblown headlands around Cap de la Hague and Nez de Jobourg. The latter is a worthwhile goal for bird-watchers – gannets and shearwaters fly by in large numbers. Along the east coast stretch the expansive sands of Utah Beach, where American troops landed as part of the Allied invasion on 6 June 1944. Inland, Ste-Mère-Eglise commemorates these events with its poignant **Musée des Troupes Aéroportées** (Airborne Troops Museum). Just outside Ste-Mère-Eglise, the **Musée de la Ferme du Cotentin** offers an insight into rural life in the early 1900s, while further north in the market town of Valognes the **Musée Régional du Cidre et du Calvados** celebrates the thriving local talent for making cider and Calvados.

Two fishing ports command the Peninsula's northeast corner: Barfleur and St-Vaast-la-Hougue, the latter famous for oysters and a base for boat trips to the Ile de Tatihou. The Val de Saire is ideal for a scenic drive, with a view point at La Pernelle the best place to survey the coast. On the west side of the peninsula, the resort of Barneville-Carteret offers sandy beaches and summer boat trips to the Channel Islands. The low-lying, marshy landscape east of Carentan forms the heart of the Parc Régional des Marais du Cotentin et du Bessin.

🏛 **Musée des Troupes Aéroportées**
Place du 6 Juin, Ste-Mère-Eglise.
📞 *02 33 41 41 35.* **Open** *Feb–mid-Nov: daily; mid-Nov–mid-Dec: Sat & Sun.* 🈳 ♿

🏛 **Musée de la Ferme du Cotentin**
Route de Beauvais, Ste-Mère-Eglise.
📞 *02 33 41 30 25.* **Open** *Easter–Oct: Wed–Mon (Jul & Aug: daily).* 🈳

🏛 **Musée Régional du Cidre et du Calvados**
Rue du Petit-Versailles, Valognes.
📞 *02 33 40 22 73.* **Open** *Apr–Sep: Wed–Mon (Jul & Aug: daily).* **Closed** *Sun am.* 🈳

Cherbourg ❷

Manche. 🏙 *28,000.* 🏕 🚌 🚗 ⛴ ℹ️ *2 quai Alexandre III (02 33 93 52 02).* ⛴ *Tue, Thu & Sat.*

Cherbourg has been a strategic port and naval base since the mid-19th century. The French Navy still uses its harbours, along with transatlantic ships and cross-Channel ferries from England and Ireland. For a commanding view over the port, drive to the hill-top **Fort du Roule**, which houses the **Musée de la Libération**, recalling the D-Day invasion and the subsequent liberation of

Cherbourg. Most activity is centred on the flower-filled market square, place Général de Gaulle, and along shopping streets such as rue Tour-Carrée and rue de la Paix. The town's collection of fine art is displayed in the spacious **Musée Thomas-Henry**, and includes some enjoyable 17th-century Flemish works, and portraits by Jean François Millet, who was born in the nearby village of Gréville-Hague.

Parc Emmanuel Liais has some small botanical gardens and a densely packed **Musée d'Histoire Naturelle**.

🏛 **Musée de la Libération**
Fort du Roule. 📞 *02 33 20 14 12.* **Open** *Apr–Sep: daily; Oct–Mar: Tue–Sun.* **Closed** *1 Jan, 1 Nov, 25 Dec.* 🈳 ♿

🏛 **Musée Thomas-Henry**
Rue Vastel. 📞 *02 33 23 02 23.* **Open** *Tue–Sun.* **Closed** *public hols.* 🈳 ♿

🏛 **Musée d'Histoire Naturelle**
Parc Emmanuel Liais, 9 rue de l'Abbaye.
📞 *02 33 53 51 61.* **Open** *Tue–Sun.* **Closed** *Sun am, public hols.* 🈳 ♿

Cherbourg town centre

Coutances ❸

Manche. 🏙 *12,000.* 🚌 🚗 ℹ️ *place Georges Leclerc (02 33 45 17 79).* ⛴ *Thu.*

From roman times until the Revolution, the hill-top town of Coutances was the capital of the Cotentin. The slender **Cathédrale Notre-Dame**, a fine example of Norman Gothic architecture, was begun in the 1040s by the local De Hauteville family, with a soaring 41-m (135-ft) lantern tower, and double flying buttresses added in the 13th century. Also of interest are the Gothic stained-glass windows. Much of the town was severely damaged during World War II but the cathedral, the churches of St Nicholas and St Peter, and the beautiful public gardens with their rare plants, all survived.

The back of Coutances cathedral with its squat lantern tower

Granville ❹

Manche. 🚶 *13,000.* 🚌 🚉 ⛴
ℹ️ *4 cours Jonville (02 33 91 30 03).*
🛒 *Wed & Sat.*

RAMPARTS enclose the upper town of Granville, which sits on a rocky spur overlooking the Baie du Mont-St-Michel. The walled town developed from fortifications built by the English in 1439 as part of their assault on Mont-St-Michel. Granville's long-established seafaring tradition is borne out by the **Musée de Vieux Granville**, found in the town gatehouse. The chapel walls of the **Eglise de Notre-Dame** are lined with tributes from local fishermen to their patroness Notre-Dame du Cap Lihou.

The lower town is an old-fashioned seaside resort with a casino, promenades, public gardens and amusements such as an aquarium, a wax-works and a *Féerie du Coquillage* (Shell Wonderland). From the port there are boat trips to the Iles Chausey, a scattering of low-lying granite islands that supplied the stone for the abbey of Mont-St-Michel.

🏛 Musée de Vieux Granville
2 rue Lecarpentier. 📞 *02 33 50 44 10.* **Open** *Apr–Jun: Wed–Sun; Jul–Sep: Wed–Mon; Oct–Mar: Wed, Sat & Sun.* **Closed** *1 Jan, 1 May, 1 & 11 Nov, 25 Dec.* 🎫

D-DAY LANDINGS

In the early hours of 6 June 1944, Allied forces began landing on the shores of Normandy, the first step in a long-planned invasion of German-occupied France, known as Operation Overlord. Parachutists were dropped near Ste-Mère-Eglise and Pegasus Bridge, and sea-borne assaults were made along a string of code-named beaches. US troops landed on Utah and Omaha in the west, while British and Canadian troops, which included a contingent of Free French commandos, landed at Gold, Juno and Sword. Fifty years on, the beaches are still referred to by their code names.

American troops coming ashore during the Allied invasion of France

Pegasus Bridge, where the first French house was liberated, is a natural starting point for a tour around the sights and memorials. Further west, evocative ruins of the artificial harbour towed across from England survive at Arromanches-les-Bains.

There are British, German and American war cemeteries at La Cambe, Ranville and St-Laurent-sur-Mer. War museums at Bayeux, Caen, St-Mère-Eglise and Cherbourg provide background on D-Day and the ensuing Battle for Normandy.

ALLIED LANDINGS ON 6 JUNE 1944

Cherbourg

Douve

Le Havre

Seine

Ste-Mère-Eglise

UTAH

St-Laurent-sur-Mer

OMAHA

GOLD JUNO SWORD

KEY

Carentan

La Cambe

Arromanches-les-Bains

Bayeux

Pegasus Bridge

Vire

Ranville

━━━ American troops

━━━ British troops

━━━ Canadian troops

✝ War cemetery

Parachute drop

St-Lô

Orne

Caen

0 kilometres   25

0 miles   25

By the end of D-Day, over 135,000 men had been brought ashore, with losses totalling around 10,000.

Avranches ❺

Manche. 🏘 8,500. 🚊 🚌 🛈 2 rue Général de Gaulle (02 33 58 00 22). 🛍 Sat.

AVRANCHES has been a religious centre since the 6th century and is the final staging-post for visitors to the abbey on Mont-St-Michel. The origins of the famous abbey lie in a vision experienced by Aubert, the Bishop of Avranches. One night in 708 the Archangel Michael instructed him to build a church on the nearby island. Aubert's skull, with the finger-hole made in it by the angel, can be seen in the treasury of **St-Gervais** church in Avranches.

The best views of Mont-St-Michel are from the **Jardin des Plantes**. After the Revolution, 203 illuminated manuscripts were rescued from Mont-St-Michel's abbey and some are exhibited at the **Musée Hôtel de Ville**. Nearby, the **Musée Municipal** introduces exhibits showing life in the Cotentin over the past centuries, with a model of Avranches cathedral, which was pulled down in 1794.

🏛 **Musée Hôtel de Ville**
Place Littré. 【 02 33 89 29 40. **Open** Jun & Sep: Mon–Sat; Jul & Aug: daily. 🌐 &

🏛 **Musée Municipal**
Palais Episcopal, place Jean de Saint-Avit. 【 02 33 58 25 15. **Open** Easter–Jun & Sep: Wed–Mon; Jul & Aug: daily. **Closed** 1 May. 🌐

Remains of Mulberry Harbour from World War II off the Côte de Nacre

Mont-St-Michel ❻

See pp246–9.

Côte de Nacre ❼

Calvados. ✈ Caen. 🚊 🚌 Caen, Bayeux. 🚢 Caen-Ouistreham. 🛈 Caen (02 31 27 14 14).

THE STRETCH of coast between the mouths of the rivers Orne and Vire was dubbed the Côte de Nacre (Mother of Pearl Coast) in the 19th century. More recently it has become known as the site of the D-Day Landings when Allied troops poured ashore at the start of Operation Overlord (see p241). The associated cemeteries, memorials and museums, and the remnants of the Mulberry Harbour at Arromanches-les-Bains, provide focal points for a visit. However, the coastline is equally popular as a summer holiday destination, offering long, sandy beaches backed by seaside resorts such as Courseulles-sur-Mer and Luc-sur-Mer. Both are less expensive and more relaxed than the resorts of the Côte Fleurie further east.

Bayeux ❽

Calvados. 🏘 15,000. 🚊 🚌 🛈 Pont-St-Jean (02 31 51 28 28). 🛍 Sat.

BAYEUX was the first town to be liberated by the Allies in 1944 and fortunate to escape war damage. Today, an attractive nucleus of 17th–19th-century buildings around its central high streets, rue St-Martin and rue St-Jean.

BAYEUX TAPESTRY

A lively comic strip justifying William the Conqueror's invasion of England, this 70-m (230-ft) long embroidered hanging was probably commissioned by Bishop Odo of Bayeux. Offering insights into 11th-century life, and an action-packed account of Harold, King of England's defeat at the Battle of Hastings, the tapestry is valued as a work of art, an historical document and an entertaining read.

Harold's retinue sets off for France to inform William that he will succeed to the English throne.

Trees with interlacing branches are sometimes used to divide the tapestry's 58 scenes.

The latter, now pedestrianized, is lined with shops and cafés. Above the town rise the spires and domed lantern tower of the Gothic **Cathédrale Notre-Dame**. Beneath its harmoniously proportioned interior is an 11th-century crypt decorated with restored 15th-century frescoes of angels playing musical instruments. The original Romanesque church that stood here was consecrated in 1077, and it is likely that Bayeux's famous tapestry was commissioned for this occasion by one of its key characters, Bishop Odo.

The tapestry is displayed in a renovated seminary, **Centre Guillaume-le-Conquérant**, which gives a detailed audiovisual explanation of events leading up to the Norman conquest. On the southwest side of the town's ring road, the **Musée Mémorial de la Bataille de Normandie** traces the events of the Battle of Normandy in World War II, including an excellent film compilation made from contemporary newsreels.

🏛 Centre Guillaume-le-Conquérant
Rue de Nesmond. 📞 02 31 51 25 50. *Open* daily. *Closed* 1 Jan, 25 Dec. 📷 ♿

🏛 Musée Mémorial de la Bataille de Normandie
Boulevard Fabian-Ware. 📞 02 31 92 93 41. *Open* daily. *Closed* 1 Jan, last 2 weeks of Jan, 25 Dec. 📷 ♿

The Abbaye aux Hommes in Caen

Caen ❾

Calvados. 🏙 116,000. 🚉 🚌 🚗
🚢 🛈 place St-Pierre (02 31 27 14 14). 🗓 Fri & Sun.

IN THE MID-11TH century Caen became the favoured residence of William the Conqueror and Queen Matilda, and despite the destruction of three-quarters of the city during World War II, much remains of their creation. The monarchs built two great abbeys and a castle on the north bank of the river Orne, bequeathing Caen a core of historic interest that justifies penetrating its industrial estates and postwar housing.

Much-loved by the citizens of Caen, the **Eglise St-Pierre** was built on the south side of the castle in the 13th–14th centuries, with an impressively ornate Renaissance east end added in the early 16th century. The frequently copied 14th-century belltower was destroyed in 1944 but has now been restored. To the east, rue du Vaugeux is the central street in Caen's small Vieux Quartier (Old Quarter). Now pedestrianized, the street still has some lovely half-timbered buildings. A walk west, along rue St-Pierre or boulevard du Maréchal Leclerc, leads to the city's main shopping district.

The English have a last meal on land before boarding with hunting dogs and falcons.

Wide moustaches distinguish the English characters from the clean-shaven French.

The coloured wool used to embroider the linen has faded little since the 11th century.

Latin inscriptions caption each main scene in the work and embody the heroic ideals shared by all the participants.

Borders provide wry comment through fables and asides.

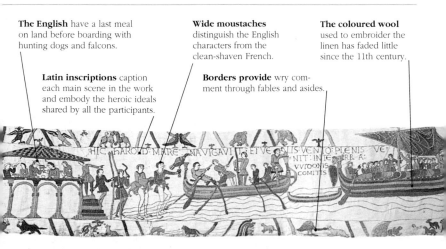

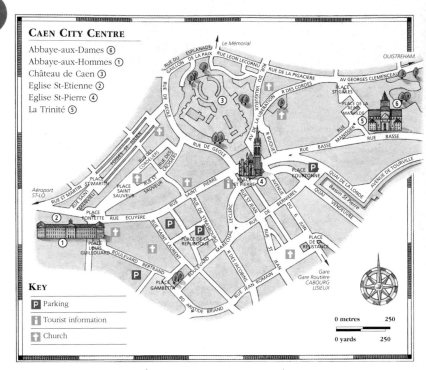

CAEN CITY CENTRE

Abbaye-aux-Dames ⑥
Abbaye-aux-Hommes ①
Château de Caen ③
Eglise St-Etienne ②
Eglise St-Pierre ④
La Trinité ⑤

KEY

P Parking

i Tourist information

✝ Church

| 0 metres | 250 |
| 0 yards | 250 |

⛪ Abbaye aux Hommes

Esplanade Jean-Marie Louvel. **Open** daily. **Closed** 1 Jan, 25 Dec. 🎦 ♿ 🎥 obligatory.
Work began on William's Abbey for Men in 1066 and was almost complete by his death 20 years later. The abbey church, **Eglise St-Etienne**, is a masterpiece of Norman Romanesque, with a severe, unadorned west front crowned with 13th-century spires. The sparingly decorated nave was roofed in the early 12th-century with stone vaulting that anticipates the Gothic style.

⛪ Abbaye aux Dames

Place de la Reine Mathilde. **Open** daily. **Closed** 1 Jan, 1 May, 25 Dec. 🎥 obligatory. ♿
Like William's Abbaye aux Hommes, Matilda's Abbey for Women also has a Norman Romanesque church, **La Trinité**, flanked by 18th-century buildings. Begun in 1060, it was consecrated six years later. Queen Matilda lies buried in the choir, and her beautifully restored abbey, with its creamy Caen stone, makes a serene and dignified mausoleum.

🏛 Château de Caen

Esplanade du Château. **Musée des Beaux Arts** 【 02 31 85 28 63. **Musée de Normandie** 【 02 31 86 06 24. **Museums open** Wed–Mon. **Closed** 1 Jan, Easter, 1 May, Ascension, 1 Nov, 25 Dec. 🎦 ♿
The ruins of Caen's castle offer spacious lawns, museums and rampart views over the city. A wide-ranging fine art collection, strong on 17th-century French and Italian painting, is exhibited in the **Musée des Beaux Arts**. The **Musée de Normandie** recalls traditional life in the region with displays and utensils – some dating from prehistoric times – on farming and lace.

🏛 Mémorial

Esplanade Dwight-Eisenhower. 【 02 31 06 06 44. **Open** mid-Jan–Dec: daily. **Closed** 25 Dec. 🎦 ♿
In the northwest of Caen, close to the N13 ring-road, Mémorial is a museum dedicated to peace, placing the events of D-Day into the context of World War II and other conflicts of the 20th century. Opened in 1988, the museum uses a host of interactive and audio-visual techniques, including stunning compilations of archive and fictional film to explain the war's origins, document its horrors and consider the failed peace that has followed.

Lush Orne valley in the Suisse Normande

Suisse Normande

Calvados & Orne. Caen.
Caen, Argentan. Putanges-
Pont-Ecrepin (02 33 35 86 57).

THOUGH HARDLY LIKE the
mountains of Switzerland,
the cliffs and valleys carved
out by the river Orne as it
winds north to Caen have
become a popular site for
walking, climbing, camping
and river sports. The area is
also ideal for a lazy, rural
drive. Its highest and most
impressive point is the Oëtre
Rock, off the D329, where
you can look down over the
dramatic gorges created by
the river Rouvre.

Parc Régional de Normandie-Maine

Orne & Manche. Alençon.
 Argentan. Carrouges (02 33
27 40 62).

THE SOUTHERN FRINGES of
central Normandy have
been incorporated into
France's largest regional park.
Among the farmland and
forests of oak and beech are
several small towns. **Dom-
front** rests on a spur overlooking the river Varenne.
The lake-side spa town
Bagnoles-de-l'Orne offers a
casino and sports facilities,
while further east **Sées** has an
attractive Gothic cathedral.
The **Maison du Parc** at Carrouges provides information

Poster of Deauville, about 1930

on walks, horseriding and
cycling in the park.

🎿 Maison du Parc
Carrouges. 📞 02 33 81 75 75.
Open Mon–Fri. **Closed** public hols.

Environs
Just north of the park, outside
Mortrée, is the **Chateau d'O**,
a moated Renaissance château
with fine 17th-century frescoes.
The **Haras du Pin** nearby is
France's national stud, called
"a horses' Versailles" for its
grandeur and 17th-century
architecture. Horse shows,
dressage events and tours take
place throughout the year.

Côte Fleurie

Calvados.   Deauville.
 Deauville (02 31 88 78 88).

THE COTE FLEURIE (Flowery
Coast) between Villerville
and Cabourg has been planted
with chic resorts which burst
into bloom every summer.
Trouville was once a humble
fishing village, but in the mid-
19th century caught the
attention of writers Gustave
Flaubert and Alexandre
Dumas. By the 1870s Trouville
had acquired grand hotels, a
railway station and pseudo-
Swiss villas along the beach-
front. It has, however, long
been outclassed by its neighbour, **Deauville**, created by
the Duc de Morny in the
1860s. This resort boasts a
casino, racecourses, marinas
and the famous beachside
catwalk, Les Planches.

For something quieter, head
west to smaller resorts such
as Villers-sur-Mer or
Houlgate. **Cabourg** further
west is dominated by the
turn-of-the-century Grand
Hôtel *(see p551)* where
novelist Marcel Proust spent
many summers. Proust used
the resort as a model for the
fictional Balbec in his novel
Remembrance of Things Past.

Pays d'Auge

Calvados. Deauville. Lisieux.
 Lisieux (02 31 62 08 41).

INLAND from the Côte Fleurie,
the Pays d'Auge is classic
Normandy countryside, lushly
woven with fields, wooded
valleys, cider orchards, dairy
farms and manor houses. Its
capital is **Lisieux**, a cathedral
town devoted to Ste Thérèse
of Lisieux, canonized in 1925,
who attracts many thousands
of pilgrims each year. Lisieux
is an obvious base for exploring the region, though nearby
market towns, such as St-
Pierre-sur-Dives and Orbec, are
smaller and more attractive.

The best way to enjoy the
Pays d'Auge is to potter
around its minor roads. Two
signposted tourist routes are
devoted to cider and cheese,
while splendid farmhouses,
manors and châteaux testify
to the wealth gained from this
fertile land. Two typical
manor houses that admit
visitors are at **Crèvecoeur-
en-Auge** and **St-Germain-de-
Livet**, while the half-timbered
village of **Beuvron-en-Auge**
is equally photogenic.

APPLES AND CIDER

Apple orchards are a familiar feature of the Normandy
countryside, and their fruit a fundamental ingredient in the
region's gastronomic repertoire. No self-respecting
pâtisserie would be without its *tarte normande* (apple
tart), and every country lane seems to sport an *Ici Vente
Cidre* (cider sold here) sign. Much of the harvest forms the
raw material for cider and Calvados, an apple brandy aged
in oak barrels for at least two years. A local brew is also
made from pears, and known as *poiré* (perry).

A crop ranging from sour cider apples to sweet eating varieties

Mont-St-Michel ❻

The 10th-century abbey

The 11th-century abbey

St Michael

SHROUDED BY MIST, engulfed by sea, soaring proud above glistening sands – the silhouette of Mont-St-Michel is one of the most enchanting sights in France. Now linked to the mainland by a causeway, the island of Mont-Tombe (Tomb on the Hill) stands at the mouth of the river Couesnon, crowned by a fortified abbey that almost doubles its height. Lying strategically on the frontier between Normandy and Brittany, Mont-St-Michel grew from a humble 8th-century oratory to become a Benedictine monastery that had its greatest influence in the 12th and 13th centuries. Pilgrims known as *miquelots* journeyed from afar to honour the cult of St Michael, and the monastery was a renowned centre of medieval learning. After the Revolution the abbey became a prison. It is now a national monument that draws some 850,000 visitors a year.

The mid-18th-century abbey

St Aubert's Chapel
A small 15th-century chapel built on an outcrop of rock is dedicated to Aubert, the founder of Mont-St-Michel.

Gabriel Tower

★ **Ramparts**
English attacks during the Hundred Years' War led to the construction of fortified walls with imposing towers.

Entrance

TIMELINE

700	1000	1300	1600	1900
966 Benedictine abbey founded by Duke Richard I	**1211–28** Construction of La Merveille	**1434** Last assault by English forces. Ramparts surround the town	**1789** French Revolution: abbey becomes a political prison	**1874** Abbey declared a national monument
				1922 Services again held in abbey church
1017 Work on abbey church starts		**1516** Abbey falls into decline	**1877–9** Causeway built	**1895–7** Belfry, spire and statue of St Michael added
708 St Aubert builds an oratory on Mont-Tombe		**1067–70** Mont-St-Michel depicted in Bayeux Tapestry *Bayeux Tapestry detail*		**1969** Benedictine monks return

VISITORS' CHECKLIST

to Pontorson, then bus.
boulevard de l'Avancée
(02 33 60 14 30). St-Michel
de Printemps (May).
Abbey 02 33 60 14 14.
02 33 60 14 14. **Open**
May–Sep: 9am–5:30pm; Oct–Apr:
9am–4:30pm (during school hols:
9:30am–5pm). **Closed** 1 Jan, 1
May, 1 Nov, 11 Nov, 25 Dec.
12:15pm daily.

Tides of Mont-St-Michel
Extremely strong tides in the Baie du Mont-St-Michel act as a natural defence. They rise and fall with the lunar calendar and can reach speeds of 10 km/h (6 mph) in spring.

★ Abbey
Protected by high walls, the abbey and its church occupy an impregnable position on the island.

Gautier's Leap
At the top of the Inner Staircase, this terrace is named after a prisoner who leaped to his death.

Eglise St-Pierre

Liberty Tower

The Arcade Tower provided lodgings for the abbot's soldiers.

King's Tower

STAR FEATURES

★ Abbey

★ Ramparts

★ Grande Rue

★ Grande Rue
Now crowded with tourists and souvenir shops, the pilgrims' route, followed since the 12th century, climbs up past Eglise St-Pierre to the abbey gates.

The Abbey of Mont-St-Michel

THE PRESENT BUILDINGS bear witness to the time when the abbey served both as a Benedictine monastery and, for 73 years after the Revolution, as a political prison. In 1017 work began on a Romanesque church at the island's highest point, building over its 10th-century predecessor, now the Chapel of Our Lady Underground. A monastery built on three levels, La Merveille (The Miracle) was added to the church's north side in the early 13th century.

Cross in the choir

★ Church
Four bays of the Romanesque nave survive. Three were pulled down in 1776, creating the West Terrace.

★ La Merveille
The Miracle is a Gothic masterpiece – a three-storey monastic complex built in only 16 years.

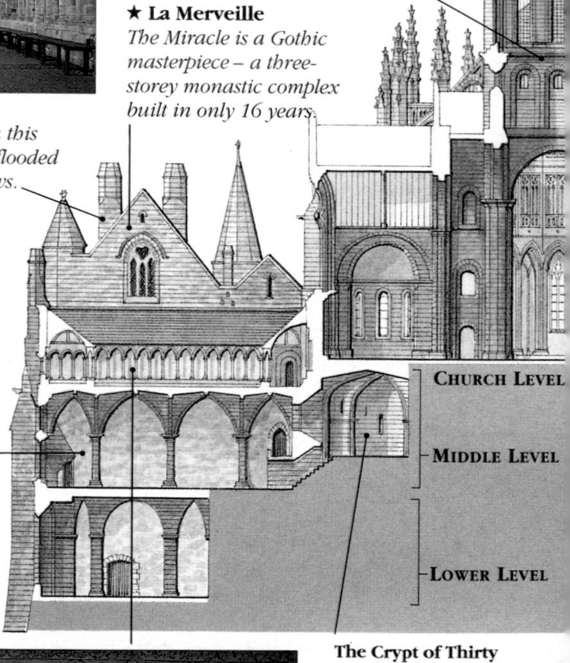

Refectory
The monks took their meals in this long, narrow room, which is flooded with light through tall windows.

Knights' Room
The rib vaults and finely decorated capitals are typically Gothic.

CHURCH LEVEL

MIDDLE LEVEL

LOWER LEVEL

The Crypt of Thirty Candles is one of two 11th-century crypts built to support the transepts of the main church.

★ Cloisters
The cloisters with their elegant columns in staggered rows are a beautiful example of early 13th-century Anglo-Norman style.

VISITING THE ABBEY

The three levels of the abbey reflect the monastic hierarchy. The monks lived at the highest level, in an enclosed world of church, cloister and refectory. The abbot entertained his noble guests on the middle level. Soldiers and pilgrims further down on the social scale were received at the lowest level. Guided tours begin at the West Terrace at the church level and end in the almonry, where alms were dispensed to the poor. The almonry is now a bookshop and souvenir hall.

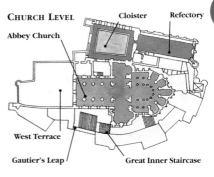

CHURCH LEVEL

Cloister · Refectory · Abbey Church · West Terrace · Gautier's Leap · Great Inner Staircase

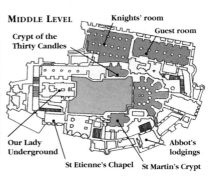

MIDDLE LEVEL

Knights' room · Guest room · Crypt of the Thirty Candles · Our Lady Underground · St Etienne's Chapel · St Martin's Crypt · Abbot's lodgings

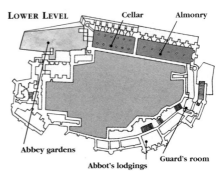

LOWER LEVEL

Cellar · Almonry · Abbey gardens · Abbot's lodgings · Guard's room

Church Interior

A Flamboyant Gothic choir was built in 1446–1521, held up by crypts with massive supporting pillars.

St Martin's Crypt is an 11th-century barrel-vaulted chapel that preserves the austere forms of the original Romanesque abbey.

The abbot's lodgings were close to the abbey entrance, and he received prestigious visitors in the guest room. Poorer pilgrims were received in the almonry.

Benedictine Monks

Today a small monastic community lives in the abbey, continuing the religious traditions introduced by the Benedictines in 966.

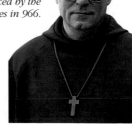

STAR FEATURES

★ Church

★ La Merveille

★ Cloisters

Mont-St-Michel by night ▷

Honfleur ⑭

Calvados. 🏙 8,400. 🚉 Deauville.
🚗 🛈 place Arthur Boudin (02 31
89 23 30). 🚌 Sat.

A MAJOR DEFENSIVE PORT in the 15th century, Honfleur has blossomed into one of Normandy's most appealing harbours. At its heart is the Vieux Bassin (Old Dock). Constructed in the late 17th century, it is bordered on the western quayside by houses six or seven storeys tall.

Honfleur became a centre of artistic activity in the 19th century. Eugène Boudin, the seascape painter, was born here in 1824. Courbet, Sisley, Pissarro, Renoir and Cézanne all visited Honfleur, often meeting at the Ferme St-Siméon, which is now a luxury hotel. Painters still work from Honfleur's quayside and exhibit in the **Greniers à Sel**, two warehouses built in 1670 for storing salt. These lie to the east of the Vieux Bassin in an area known as l'Enclos, which made up the fortified heart of the town in the 13th-century.

The **Musée de la Marine** displays mementos of Honfleur's nautical past, with a warren of Norman interiors next door in the former prison. To the west of the Vieux Bassin is a wooden church in the place Ste-Catherine, built by ship's carpenters in the 15th century. The **Musée Eugène Boudin** documents the artistic appeal of Honfleur and the Seine estuary, with works ranging from Eugène Boudin

Woman with Parasol (1880) by Boudin in the Musée Eugène Boudin

---

to Raoul Dufy. From here a steep walk, which is particularly enjoyable at sunset, leads to the hill-top chapel of **Notre-Dame de Grace**.

🏛 Greniers à Sel
Rue de la Ville/quai de la Tour.
📞 02 31 89 02 30. **Open** for guided tours, and during exhibitions (phone for details). 🎫 obligatory, except during summer exhibitions. 📷 ♿

🏛 Musée de la Marine
Quai St Etienne. 📞 02 31 89 14 12.
Open mid-Feb–mid-Nov: Tue–Sun; Jul & Aug: daily. **Closed** 1 May. 📷 ♿

🏛 Musée Eugène Boudin
Place Erik Satie, rue de l'Homme de Bois. 📞 02 31 89 54 00. **Open** mid-Mar–Oct: Wed–Mon; Nov, Dec, mid-Feb–mid-Mar: Wed–Fri & Mon pm, Sat, Sun. 📷 ♿

The quayside at Honfleur

Le Havre ⑮

Seine-Maritime. 🏙 195,000. ✈ 🚉
🚌 🚢 🛈 Forum de l'Hôtel de Ville
(02 32 74 04 04). 🚌 Mon, Wed & Fri.

S TRATEGICALLY positioned at the head of the Seine estuary, Le Havre (The Harbour) was created in 1517 by François I after the nearby port of Harfleur silted up.

During World War II it was virtually obliterated by Allied bombing, but despite the vast oil refineries and industrial zone which stands beside the port, it still has some appeal. Much of the city centre was rebuilt in the 1950s and 1960s from designs by August Perret, whose towering **Eglise St-Joseph**, on boulevard François I, pierces the skyline in an emphatic manner.

The **Musée des Beaux Arts**, which has a stunning structure built entirely of glass and metal, has an exhilarating collection of works by the Le Havre-born artist Raoul Dufy.

🏛 Musée des Beaux Arts
Place Guynemer. 📞 02 35 42 33 97.
Closed for renovation until 1999.

Côte d'Albâtre ⑯

Seine-Maritime. ✈ 🚉 🚌 🚢
🛈 Dieppe (02 35 84 11 77).

T HE ALABASTER COAST gets its name from the chalky cliffs and milky waters that characterize the Normandy coastline between Le Havre and Le Tréport. It is best known for the **Falaise d'Aval** west of Etretat, eroded into an arch. The author Guy de Maupassant, born near Dieppe in 1850, compared these cliffs to an elephant dipping its trunk into the sea. From Etretat, a chain of coastal roads runs east across a switchback of breezy headlands and wooded valleys to Dieppe.

Fécamp is the only major town along this route. Its Benedictine abbey, now in ruins, was once an important pilgrimage centre after a tree trunk containing drops of Christ's Blood was washed ashore here during the 7th century. This is enshrined in a reliquary at the entrance to the Lady Chapel of the abbey church, La Trinité.

The vast **Palais Bénédictine** is a mock Gothic-and-Renaissance homage to the ego of Alexander Le Grand, a local wine merchant who rediscovered the monks' recipe for Bénédictine, the famous herbal liqueur. Building of the palace began in 1880 and

The cliffs at Falaise d'Aval, famously likened to an elephant dipping its trunk into the sea

today incorporates a distillery and an eccentric museum packed with art treasures and curios. The adjacent halls provide an aromatic account of the 27 herbs and spices which make up the elixir.

🏛 Palais Bénédictine
110 rue Alexandre Le Grand, Fécamp. ☎ 02 35 10 26 00. **Open** daily. **Closed** 1 Jan, 25 Dec. 🎫 🅿

View of Dieppe from the château and museum above the town

Dieppe ⓱

Seine-Maritime. 🏘 40,000. ✕ 🚂 🚌 ⛴ 🛈 pont Jean Ango (02 35 84 11 77). 🖙 Tue, Thu & Sat.

Dieppe exploits a break in the chalky cliffs bordering the Pays de Caux, and has won historical prestige as a Channel fort, port and resort. Prosperity came during the 16th and 17th centuries, when local privateer Jean Ango raided the Portuguese and English fleets, and a trading post called Petit Dieppe was founded on the West African coast. At that time, Dieppe's population was almost double what it is today, and included a 300-strong community of

craftsmen carving imported ivory. This maritime past is celebrated in the **Musée du Château**, housed in a 15th-century castle crowning the headland to the west of the seafront. Here you can see historical maps and model ships, a collection of Dieppe ivories, and paintings that evoke the town's development as a fashionable seaside resort during the 19th century. Dieppe had the nearest beach to Paris and it quickly responded to the developing passion for promenading, seawater cures and bathing.

Today Dieppe's broad seafront is given over to lawns, seaside amusements and car parks, and its liveliest streets surround the battle-scarred **Eglise St-Jacques** to the south. If the weather is poor, head for the **Cité de la Mer**, an exhibition centre with models on maritime themes, and fun for children.

🏛 Musée du Château
☎ 02 35 84 19 76. **Open** Jun–Sep: daily; Oct–May: Wed–Mon. **Closed** 1 Jan, 1 May, 1 Nov, 25 Dec. 🎫
🏛 Cité de la Mer
37 Rue de l'Asile Thomas. ☎ 02 35 06 93 20. **Open** daily. 🎫 ♿

Basse-Seine ⓲

Seine-Maritime & Eure. ✈ Le Havre, Rouen. 🚂 🚌 Yvetot. ⛴ Le Havre. 🛈 Yvetot (02 35 95 08 40).

Meandering seaward from Rouen to Le Havre, the river Seine is crossed by three spectacular road bridges, the Pont de Brotonne and, further west, the Pont de Tancarville.

The third bridge, the Pont de Normandie, was completed in 1995 and links Le Havre and Honfleur. The grace and daring of these modern bridges echoes the soaring aspirations of the abbeys founded on the river's banks in the 7th and 8th centuries. The abbeys now provide good stepping stones for a tour of the Lower Seine valley.

West of Rouen is the harmonious Eglise de St-Georges at **St-Martin-de-Boscherville** which until the Revolution was the church of a small walled abbey. Its 12th-century chapter house has remarkable biblical statues and carved capitals. From here the D62 runs south to the riverside village of La Bouille.

As you head northwest, an hourly car ferry at Mesnil-sous-Jumièges takes you over to the colossal ruins of the **Abbaye de Jumièges**. The abbey was founded in 654 and once housed 900 monks and 1,500 servants. The main abbey church dates from the 11th century; its consecration in 1067 was a major event, with William the Conqueror in attendance.

The D913 strikes through oak and beech woods in the Parc Régional de Brotonne to the 7th-century **Abbaye de St-Wandrille**. The Musée de la Marine de Seine at **Caudebec-en-Caux** gives an engrossing account of life on this great river over the past 120 years.

Monk from Abbaye de St-Wandrille

Rouen ⓲

FOUNDED AT THE LOWEST POINT where
the Seine could be bridged, Rouen
has prospered through maritime trade
and industrialization to become a rich
and cultured city. Despite the severe
damage of World War II, the city boasts
a wealth of historic sights on its right
bank, all within walking distance of
the central Cathédrale Notre-Dame,
frequently painted by Monet. In turn a
Celtic trading post, Roman garrison and
Viking colony, Rouen became the capital of the Norman
Duchy in 911. It was captured by Henry V in 1419
after a siege during the Hundred Years' War. In
1431 Joan of Arc was burned at the stake
here in place du Vieux-Marché.

Rouen, a thriving port on the river Seine

Exploring Rouen

From the cathedral, the rue
du Gros Horloge runs west
under the city's Great Clock,
to the place du Vieux
Marché and its post-
war Eglise Ste-Jeanne-
d'Arc. Rue aux Juifs
leads past the 15th-
century Gothic
Palais de Justice,
once Normandy's
parliament, to
the smart shops
and cafés
around rue des
Carmes. Further
east, between
the St-Maclou and
St-Ouen churches,
are half-timbered houses in
the rue Damiette and rue Eau
de Robec. North, in place
Général de Gaulle, is the
18th-century **Hôtel de Ville**.

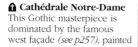

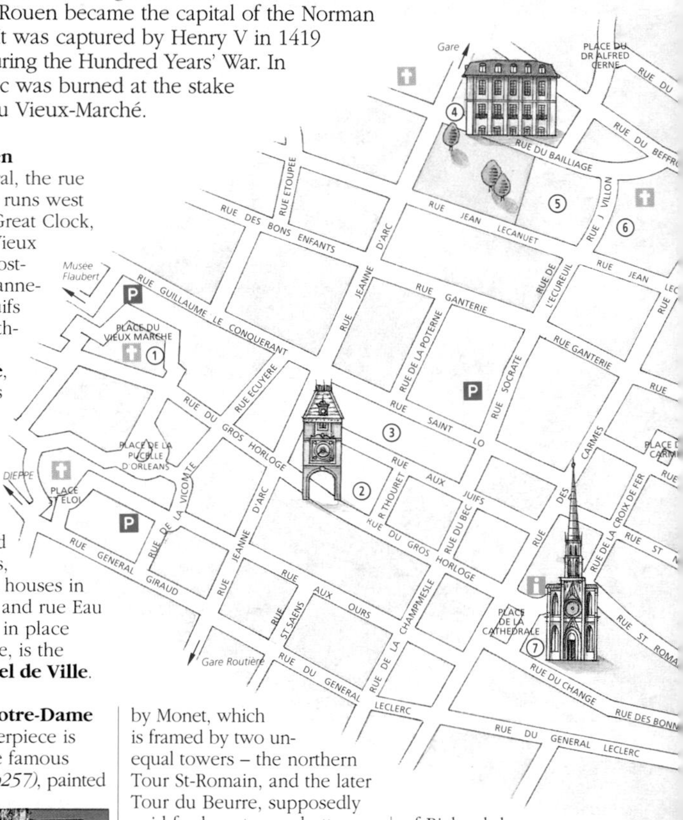

⛪ Cathédrale Notre-Dame

This Gothic masterpiece is
dominated by the famous
west façade *(see p257)*, painted

Cathédrale Notre-Dame, Rouen

by Monet, which
is framed by two un-
equal towers – the northern
Tour St-Romain, and the later
Tour du Beurre, supposedly
paid for by a tax on butter
consumption in Lent. Above
the central lantern tower rises
a Neo-Gothic spire, made
from cast iron and erected in
1876. If the cathedral's
programme of restoration
allows, both the 13th-century
northern Portail des Libraires
and the 14th-century southern
Portail de la Calende are
worth seeing for their precise
sculpting and delicate tracery.
Many of the cathedral's riches
are accessible by guided tour
only. Highlights are the tomb

of Richard the
Lion-Heart, whose heart
was buried here, and
the unusual 11th-century
semi-circular hall crypt,
rediscovered in 1934.

KEY

P	Parking
i	Tourist information
⛪	Church

0 metres   250

0 yards   250

🔒 Eglise St-Maclou

This Flamboyant Gothic church has an intensively decorated west façade with a five-bay porch and carved wooden doors depicting biblical scenes. Behind the church, its *aître*, or ossuary, is a rare surviving example of a medieval cemetery for the burial of plague victims. The timbers of its buildings, set around the quadrangle, are carved with a macabre array of grinning skulls, crossed bones, coffins, hourglasses, buckets, beds and grave-diggers' implements.

Jug from Musée de la Céramique

🔒 Eglise St-Ouen

Once part of a formidable Benedictine abbey, St-Ouen is a solid Gothic church with a lofty, unadorned interior made all the more beautiful by its restored 14th-century stained glass. Behind the church there is a pleasant park which is an ideal spot for picnics.

🏛 Musée des Beaux Arts

Square Verdrel. **(** 02 35 71 28 40.
Open Wed–Mon. **Closed** public hols.
The city's collection includes major art works: masterpieces by Caravaggio and Velázquez, and paintings by Normandy-born artists Théodore Géricault, Eugène Boudin and Raoul Dufy. Also on display is Monet's *Rouen Cathedral, The Portal, Grey Weather.*

VISITORS' CHECKLIST

Seine Maritime. 🚼 103,000.
✈ 11 km (7 miles) SE Rouen.
🚉 gare rive droite, place Bernard Tissot (08 36 35 35 35). 🚌 25 rue des Charrettes (02 35 52 92 00).
🛈 25 place de la Cathédrale (02 32 08 32 40). 🖭 Tue–Sun. 🎪 Feast of Joan of Arc (late May).

🏛 Musée de la Céramique

Hôtel d'Hocqueville, 1 rue Faucon.
(** 02 35 71 28 40. **Open Wed–Mon.
Closed public hols.
Exhibits of 6,000 pieces of Rouen faïence – colourful glazed earthenware – together with other pieces of French and foreign china are displayed in a 17th-century town house. The works trace the history of Rouen faïence to its zenith in the 18th century.

🏛 Musée Le Secq des Tournelles

Rue Jacques-Villon. **(** 02 35 71 28 40. **Open** Wed–Mon. **Closed** public hols.
Located in a 15th-century church, this wrought ironwork museum exhibits antique iron-mongery ranging from keys to corkscrews, Gallo-Roman spoons to mighty tavern signs.

🏛 Musée Flaubert

51 rue de Lecat. **(** 02 35 15 59 95.
Open Tue–Sat. **Closed** public hols.
Flaubert's father was a surgeon at Rouen Hospital, and the house where the family lived combines mem-orabilia with an awesome – and occasionally gruesome – display of 17th–19th-century medical equipment.

SIGHTS AT A GLANCE

GUSTAVE FLAUBERT

The novelist Gustave Flaubert (1821–80) was born and raised in Rouen, and the city provides the backdrop for some memorable scenes in his masterpiece, *Madame Bovary*.
Published in 1857, this realistic study of a country doctor's wife driven to despair by her love affairs provoked a scandal that made Flaubert's name. His famous stuffed green parrot, which can be seen in the Musée Flaubert, was always perched on his writing desk.

Flaubert's stuffed parrot

Château Gaillard and the village of Les Andelys, in a loop of the river Seine

Haute-Seine 🔟

Eure. ✈ Rouen. 🚊 Gaillon,
Pont St-Pierre. 🚌 Pont de l'Arche,
Louviers, Les Andelys. ℹ️ Les Andelys
(02 32 54 41 93).

SOUTHEAST OF ROUEN, the
river Seine follows a
convoluted course, with most
points of interest on its north
bank. At the centre of the
Forêt de Lyons, once the
hunting ground for the Dukes
of Normandy, is the country
town of **Lyons-la-Forêt**, with
half-timbered houses and an
18th-century covered market.

To the south the D313
follows the gracefully curving
Seine to the village of **Les
Andelys**. Above it tower the
ruins of Château Gaillard
which Richard the Lion-Heart
built in 1197 to defend Rouen
from the French. They
eventually took the castle in
1204 by forcing a way in
through the latrines.

Giverny 🔟

Eure. 👥 600. ℹ️ 36 rue Carnot,
Vernon (02 32 51 39 60).

IN 1883 the Impressionist
painter Claude Monet
rented a house in the small
village of Giverny, and

worked here until his death at
the age of 86. The house,
known as the **Fondation
Claude Monet**, and its magnificent garden are open to the
public. The house is decorated
in the original colour schemes
that Monet admired; the gardens are famous as the subject
of some of the artist's best-
loved studies. Only copies are
on show in the small gallery,
but there are outstanding original 19th- and 20th-century
art works in the **Musée d'Art
Américain Giverny** nearby.

🏛 **Fondation Claude Monet**
Giverny, Gasny. 📞 02 32 51 28 21.
Open Apr–Oct: Tue–Sun. 🖼
🏛 **Musée d'Art Américain
Giverny**
99 rue Claude Monet, Giverny.
📞 02 32 51 94 65. **Open** Apr–Oct:
Tue–Sun. 🖼 ♿

Évreux 🔟

Eure. 👥 55,000. 🚊 🚌 ℹ️ 3 place de
du Général de Gaulle (02 32 24 04 43).
🕓 Wed & Sat.

THOUGH CONSIDERABLY dam-
aged in the war, Évreux is
a pleasant cathedral town set
in wide, agricultural plains. At
its heart, the **Cathédrale
Notre-Dame** is renowned for
its 14th–15th century stained
glass. The building is
predominantly Gothic, though
Romanesque arches survive
in the nave and Renaissance
screens adorn its chapels.
Next door, the former Bishop's
Palace houses the **Musée
Municipal**, with exhibits
ranging from two Roman
bronze statues of Jupiter and
Apollo to fine 18th-century
furniture and decorative art.

Monet's garden at Giverny, restored to its original profuse glory

Monet's Cathedral Series

IN THE 1890s Claude Monet made almost 30 paintings of Rouen's cathedral, several of which are now in the Musée d'Orsay in Paris *(see pp116–17)*. He studied the effects of changing light on its façades, and described both the surface detail and huge bulk, putting colour before contour. The archetypal Impressionist, Monet said he conceived this series when he watched the effects of light on a country church, "as the sun's rays slowly dissolved the mists . . . that wrapped the golden stone in an ideally vaporous envelope".

HARMONY IN BLUE AND GOLD *(1894)*
Monet selected a close vantage point for the series and was keen on this southwest view. The sun would cast afternoon shadows across the carved west front, accentuating the cavernous portals and the large rose window.

Monet's sketch, *one of many of Rouen, parallels the shimmering effect of the paintings.*

Harmony in Brown *(1894) is the only finished version of a frontal view of the west façade. Analysis has shown that it was begun as a southwest view like the others.*

Harmony in Blue *(1894), compared with Harmony in Blue and Gold, shows the stone of the west façade further softened by the diffuse light of a misty morning.*

The Portal, Grey Weather *(1894) was one of several canvases in the grey colour group which showed the cathedral façade in the soft light of an overcast day.*

BRITTANY

FINISTÈRE · CÔTES D'ARMOR · MORBIHAN · ILLE-ET-VILAINE

JUTTING DEFIANTLY INTO THE ATLANTIC, *France's northwest corner has long been culturally and geographically distinct from the main bulk of the country. Known to the Celts as Armorica, the land of the sea, Brittany's past swirls with the legends of drowned cities and Arthurian forests. Prehistoric megaliths arise mysteriously from land and sea, and the medieval is never far from the modern.*

A long, jagged coastline is the region's great attraction. Magnificent beaches line its northern shore, swept clean by huge tides and interspersed with well-established seaside resorts, seasoned fishing ports and abundant oysterbeds. The south coast is gentler, with wooded river valleys and a milder climate, while the west, being exposed to the Atlantic winds, has a drama that justifies the name Finistère – the End of the Earth.

Inland lies the Argoat – once the Land of the Forest, now a patchwork of undulating fields, woods and rolling moorland. Parc Régional d'Armorique occupies much of central Finistère, and it is in western Brittany that Breton culture remains most evident. In Quimper, and in the Pays Bigouden, crêpes and cider, traditional costumes and Celtic music are still a genuine part of the Breton lifestyle. Eastern Brittany has a more conventional appeal. Vannes, Dinan and Rennes, the Breton capital, have well-preserved medieval quarters where half-timbered buildings shelter inviting markets, shops, crêperies and restaurants. The walled port of St-Malo on the Côte d'Emeraude recalls the region's maritime prowess, while the remarkably intact castles at Fougères and Vitré are a reminder of the mighty border-fortresses that protected Brittany's eastern frontier before its final union with France in 1532.

Women dressed in traditional costume and *coiffe,* the typical Breton lace head-dress

◁ Characteristic pink granite cliffs on the Côte de Granit Rose, northern Brittany

Exploring Brittany

IDEAL FOR A SEASIDE HOLIDAY, Brittany offers enjoyable drives
along the headlands and beaches of the northern Côte
d'Emeraude and Côte de Granit Rose, while the south coast
boasts wooded valleys and the prehistoric sites of Carnac and
the Golfe du Morbihan. The parish closes (see pp266–7) provide
an intriguing insight into Breton culture, as does the cathedral
town of Quimper. Be sure to visit the regional
capital, Rennes, and the great castle at Fougères,
and in summer take a boat trip to one
of Brittany's islands.

SIGHTS AT A GLANCE

0 kilometres   25

0 miles   25

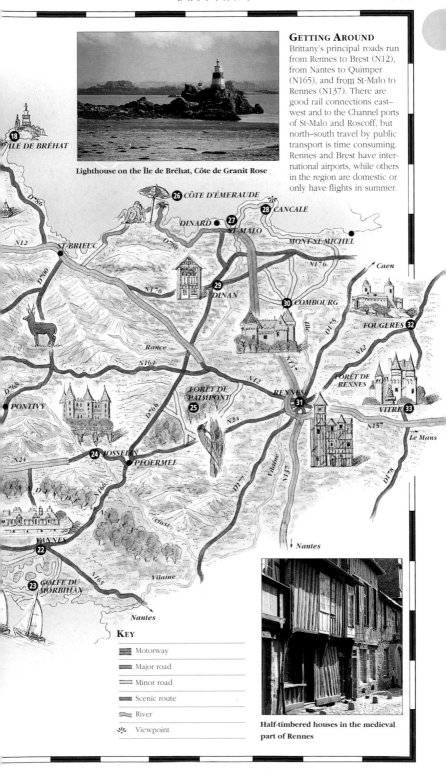

GETTING AROUND

Brittany's principal roads run from Rennes to Brest (N12), from Nantes to Quimper (N165), and from St-Malo to Rennes (N137). There are good rail connections east–west and to the Channel ports of St-Malo and Roscoff, but north–south travel by public transport is time consuming. Rennes and Brest have international airports, while others in the region are domestic or only have flights in summer.

Lighthouse on the Île de Bréhat, Côte de Granit Rose

KEY

- Motorway
- Major road
- Minor road
- Scenic route
- River
- Viewpoint

Half-timbered houses in the medieval part of Rennes

Île d'Ouessant ❶

Finistère. ✈ *Ouessant (via Brest).*
🚉 *Brest, then boat.* 🚌 *Le Conquet,
then boat.* ℹ *place de l'Eglise,
Lampaul (02 98 48 85 83).*

A WELL-KNOWN Breton proverb
declares "He who sees
Ouessant sees blood". Also
known as Ushant, the island
is notorious among sailors for
its fierce storms and strong
currents. However, this most
westerly point of France has a
pleasant climate in summer
and, though often bleak and
stormy, can be surprisingly
mild in winter. Part of the Parc
Régional d'Armorique, the
windswept island is a popular
stopover for migrating birds.
These, along with a small seal
population, may be observed
from the Pern and Pen-ar-
Roc'h headlands.

Two museums shed light on
the island's defiant history,
dogged by shipwreck and
tragedy. At Niou Uhella, the
Eco-Musée d'Ouessant has
furniture made from driftwood
and wrecks, often painted blue
and white in honour of the
Virgin Mary. Nearby at Phare
du Créac'h, the **Musée des
Phares et Balises** explains
the history of Brittany's many
lighthouses and the daily life
of a lighthouse keeper.

🏛 Eco-Musée d'Ouessant
Niou Uhella. 🕿 *02 98 48 86 37.*
Open *Apr–Sep: daily; Oct–Mar:
Tue–Sun (pm only).* ▨ 🚫 *restricted.*
🏛 Musée des Phares et
Balises
Phare du Créac'h. 🕿 *02 98 48 80 70.*
Open *May–Sep: daily; Oct–Apr:
Tue–Sun (pm only).* ▨ 🚫

Brest ❷

Finistère. 🚗 *153,000.* ✈ 🚉 🚌 ⚓
ℹ *av Clémenceau (02 98 44 24 96).*
🚌 *daily.*

A NATURAL HARBOUR protected
by the Presqu'île de
Crozon, Brest is France's
premier naval port with a rich
maritime history. Heavily
bombed during World War II,
it is now a modern commercial
city where cargo vessels and
fishing boats ply the waters.
There are extensive views of

Windswept moorlands near Ménez-Meur, Parc Régional d'Armorique

the Rade de Brest from the
Cours Dajot promenade. The
12th–17th-century **Château**
houses a naval museum with
a collection ranging from
historic maps and maritime
paintings to model ships,
carved wooden figureheads
and nautical instruments.

Across the Penfeld river –
reached by Europe's largest
lifting bridge, the Pont de
Recouvrance – is the 16th-
century **Tour Tanguy**, which
has dioramas evoking old
Brest. Down by the Port de
Plaisance, **Océanopolis** is an
entertaining and educational
"sea centre" with hands-on
exhibits, seals and aquariums.

⚓ Château de Brest
🕿 *02 98 22 12 39.* **Open** *Wed–
Mon.* ▨
🏰 Tour Tanguy
Square Pierre Peron. 🕿 *02 98 00 88
60.* **Open** *Jun–Sep: daily; Oct–
May: Wed, Thur, Sat & Sun pm only.*
🐟 Océanopolis
Port de Plaisance du Moulin Blanc.
🕿 *02 98 34 40 40.* **Open** *daily.*
Closed *Sep–May: Mon pm.* ▨ 🚫

**Traditional boatbuilding at Le
Port-Musée, Douarnenez**

Parc Régional
d'Armorique ❸

Finistère. ✈ *Brest.* 🚉 *Chateaulin,
Landernau.* 🚌 *Le Faou, Huelgoat.*
ℹ *Ménez-Meur (02 98 21 90 69).*

T HE ARMORICAN Regional
Nature Park stretches west
from the moorlands of the
Monts d'Arrée to the Presqu'île
de Crozon and Ile d'Ouessant.
Within this protected area lies
a mixture of farmland, heaths,
remains of ancient oak forest
and wild, open spaces. The
park and its scenic coastline
is ideal for walking, riding
and touring by bicycle or car.

Huelgoat is a good starting
point for inland walks, and
there are splendid views from
Ménez-Hom (300 m, 1,082 ft).

The main information centre
for the park is at **Ménez-Meur**,
where there is a wooded estate
with wild and farm animals,
and a Breton horse museum.
Scattered around the park are
another nine small, specialist
museums, some paying
tribute to country traditions
like hunting, fishing and
tanning. Works by contemporary artists and craftsworkers
are exhibited at the **Maison
des Artisans** in Brasparts.

The **Musée de l'Ecole
Rurale** at Trégarven recreates
a rural school from the beginning of the 20th century,
while other museums are
devoted to subjects as diverse
as medieval monastic life, rag-
and-bone men and the lifestyle of a Breton country priest.

Douarnenez ❹

Finistère. 🏘 16, 700. 🚉
🛈 2 rue Docteur Mével (02 98 92
13 35). 🚏 Mon–Sat.

A T THE START of this century
Douarnenez used to be
France's leading sardine port,
with a fleet of almost 1,000
boats. Today it is still devoted
to fishing, but is also a tourist
resort with beaches on both
sides of the Pouldavid estuary.

Nearby lies the tiny **Île
Tristan**, linked with the tragic
love story of Tristan and Iseult.
In the 16th century it was the
stronghold of a notorious
brigand, La Fontenelle.

The picturesque **Port du
Rosmeur** offers cafés, fish
restaurants and boat trips
around the bay, with a lively
early morning *criée* (fish
auction) held in the nearby
Nouveau Port. The Port-Rhu
has been turned into a floating
museum, **Le Port-Rhu
Musée**, with over 100 boats
and several shipyards. Some
of the larger vessels can be
visited in high season.

🏛 Le Port-Rhu Musée

Place de l'Enfer. 📞 02 98 92 65 20.
Open daily (winter: Tue–Sun). 🅿 ♿

**Locronan's 15th-century Eglise St-
Ronan, seen from the churchyard**

Locronan ❺

Finistère. 🏘 800. 🛈 place de la
Mairie (02 98 91 70 14).

D URING THE 15th–17th
centuries Locronan grew
wealthy from the manufacture
of sail-cloth. After Louis XIV
ended the Breton monopoly
on this trade, the town
declined – leaving an elegant
ensemble of Renaissance

The awe-inspiring cliffs of Pointe du Raz

buildings that today attract
huge numbers of visitors. In
the town's central cobbled
square stands a late 15th-
century church dedicated to
the Irish missionary St Ronan.
Down Rue Moal is the delightful **Chapelle Notre-Dame-
de-Bonne-Nouvelle** with
a calvary and a fountain.

Every July Locronan is the
scene of a *Troménie*, a
hilltop pilgrimage held in
honour of St Ronan. The more
elaborate *Grande Troménie*
takes place every six years.

Pointe du Raz ❻

Finistère. 🚉 Quimper. 🚌 Quimper,
then bus. 🛈 Audierne (02 98 70
12 20).

T HE DRAMATIC Pointe du
Raz, almost 80 m (262 ft)
high, is a narrow headland
jutting into the Atlantic at the
tip of Cap Sizun. The views
of jagged rocks and pounding
seas are breathtaking. Further
west lies the flat, treeless Ile
de Sein and beyond that the
lighthouse of Ar Men. Despite
being only an average 1.5 m
(5 ft) above sea level, Ile de

Sein is nevertheless home to
some 500 resolute inhabitants,
and can be reached by boat
from Audierne in an hour.

Pays Bigouden ❼

Finistère. 🚌 Pont l'Abbé. 🛈 Pont
l'Abbé (02 98 82 30 30).

B RITTANY'S SOUTHWEST tip
is known as the Pays
Bigouden, a windy peninsula
with proud and ancient traditions. The region is famous
for the tall *coiffes* that are still
worn by women at festivals
and *pardons (see p233)* and
there are many examples at
the **Musée Bigouden**.

Along the Baie d'Audierne
is a brooding landscape of
weather-beaten hamlets and
isolated chapels – the 15th-
century calvary at **Notre-
Dame-de-Tronoën** is the
oldest in Brittany. There are
invigorating sea views from
Pointe de la Torche and from
the **Eckmühl lighthouse**.

🏛 Musée Bigouden

Le Château, Pont l'Abbé. 📞 02 98
66 09 09. **Open** Easter–Sep: Mon–Sat.
Closed 1 May. 🅿

Quimper 8

Finistère. 63,000. ✈ 🚊 🚌 🚢
i place de la Résistance (02 98 53
04 05). 🕭 daily.

THE ANCIENT capital of
Cornouaille, Quimper has
a distinctly Breton character.
Here you can find Breton
language books and music
on sale, buy a traditional
costume and tuck into some
of the best crêpes and cider
in Brittany. Quimper gets its
name from *kemper*, a Breton
word meaning the confluence
of two rivers, and the Steir
and Odet still flow through
this relaxed cathedral city.

West of the cathedral lies a
pedestrianized area known
as **Vieux Quimper**, full of
shops, crêperies and half-
timbered houses. Rue Kéréon
is the main thoroughfare, with
the place au Beurre and the
picturesque *hôtel particuliers*
(mansions) of rue des
Gentilshommes to the north.

Quimper has been pro-
ducing faïence, elegant hand-
painted pottery, since 1690.
The design often features
decorative flowers and
animals framed by blue and
yellow borders. Originally
created as wedding presents
and heirlooms, faïence
is today exported to
collectors all over
the world. In the
southwest of the
city lies the
oldest factory,
**Faïenceries
HB-Henriot**,
which is open
to visitors from
March to October.

**A Cathédrale
St-Corentin**

*Typical faïence plate
from Quimper*

Quimper's cathedral
is dedicated to the city's
founder-bishop St Corentin.
Begun in 1240, it is the
earliest Gothic building in
Lower Brittany, and was
bizarrely constructed with the
choir standing at a slight angle
to the nave, perhaps to fit in
with some since-disappeared
buildings behind. The two
spires of the west façade were
only added in 1856. Between
them rides a statue of King
Gradlon, the mythical founder

The Martyrdom of St Triphine (1910) by Sérusier, Pont-Aven School

of the drowned city of Ys. After
this deluge he chose Quimper
as his new capital and St
Corentin as his spiritual guide.

🏛 Musée des Beaux-Arts
40 place St-Corentin. **[** 02 98 95 45
20. **Open** Jul–Aug: daily; Sep–Jun:
Wed–Mon. **Closed** most public hols;
Nov–Mar: Sun am. 🎫 🕭
Quimper's art museum, one of
the best in the region, was extensively restored in 1993. The
collection is strong on late
19th- and early 20th-century
artists, and their work – such
as Jean-Eugène Buland's *Visite
à Ste-Marie de Bénodet* –
offers a valuable in-
sight into the way
visiting painters
perpetuated a
romantic view
of Brittany.
Also on show
are works by
members of
the Pont-Aven
School and local
artists like J-J
Lemordant and
Max Jacob.

**🏛 Musée Departemental
Breton**
1 rue de Roi-Gradlon. **[** 02 98 95 21
60. **Open** Jun–Sep: daily; Oct–May:
Tue–Sun. **Closed** public hols. 🎫 🕭
The 16th-century Bishop's
Palace houses a well-presented
collection of Breton costumes,
furniture and faïence. Exhibits
include elaborate *coiffes* from
around Cornouaille, ornately
carved box-beds and ward-
robes, and turn-of-the-century
tourist posters for Brittany.

Concarneau 9

Finistère. 19,000. 🚊 🚢
i quai d'Aiguillon (02 98 97 01 44).
🕭 Mon & Fri.

AN IMPORTANT fishing port,
Concarneau's principal
attraction is its 14th-century
Ville Close (walled town),
built on an island in the
harbour and completely
encircled by massive lichen-
covered granite ramparts.
Access is by bridge from the
place Jean Jaurès. Parts of the
ramparts can be toured, and
the narrow streets are full of
shops and restaurants. The
Musée de la Pêche, housed
in the port's ancient barracks,
explains the local techniques
and history of sea-fishing.

🏛 Musée de la Pêche
Rue Vauban. **[** 02 98 97 10 20.
Open daily. **Closed** Jan. 🎫 🕭

**Fishing boats in Concarneau's
busy harbour**

Pont-Aven ⑩

Finistère. 🚶 3,000. 🚌 🚉 *place de l'Hôtel de Ville (02 98 06 04 70).* 🗓 *Tue.*

ONCE A MARKET town of "14 mills and 15 houses", Pont-Aven's picturesque location in the wooded Aven estuary made it attractive to many late 19th-century artists.

In 1888 Paul Gauguin, along with like-minded painters Emile Bernard and Paul Sérusier, developed a crude, colourful style of painting known as Synthetism. Drawing inspiration from the Breton landscape and its people, the Ecole de Pont-Aven (Pont-Aven School) worked here and in nearby Le Pouldu until 1896.

Today the town remains devoted to art and has some 50 private galleries, along with the informative **Musée de Pont-Aven** which documents the achievements of the Pont-Aven School. The surrounding woods proved inspirational to many visiting artists, and offer pleasant walks in their footsteps – one leads through the Bois d'Amour to the **Chapelle de Trémalo**, where the wooden Christ in Gauguin's *Le Christ Jaune* still hangs.

🏛 **Musée de Pont-Aven**
Pl de l'Hôtel de Ville. 📞 *02 98 06 14 43.*
Open *daily.* **Closed** *between exhibitions.* 📷 ♿

Notre-Dame-de-Kroaz-Baz, Roscoff

Le Pouldu ⑪

Finistère. 🚶 4,000. 🚌 🚉 *boulevard Charles Filiger (02 98 39 93 42).*

A QUIET PORT at the mouth of the river Laïta, Le Pouldu has a small beach and good walks. Its main attraction is **Maison de Marie Henry**, a reconstruction of the inn where Paul Gauguin and other artists stayed between 1889 and 1893. They covered every inch of the dining room, including the window-panes, with self-portraits, caricatures and still-lifes. These were discovered in 1924 beneath layers of wallpaper.

🏛 **Maison de Marie Henry**
Rue des Grandes Sables. 📞 *02 98 39 98 51.* **Open** *mid-Jun–mid-Sep: daily; mid-Sep–mid-Jun: by appt. only, phone to arrange.* 📷

Roscoff ⑫

Finistère. 🚶 3,700. 🚉 🚌 🚢
🛈 *46 rue Gambetta (02 98 61 12 13).* 🗓 *Wed.*

ONCE A CORSAIRS' haunt, Roscoff is now a thriving Channel port and seaside resort. Signs of its wealthy seafaring past can be found in the old port, particularly along rue Amiral Réveillère and in place Lacaze-Duthiers. Here the granite façades of the 16th- and 17th-century ship-owners' mansions, and the weather-beaten caravels and cannon decorating **Eglise Notre-Dame-de-Kroaz-Baz**, testify to the days when the privateers of Roscoff were as notorious as those of St-Malo *(see p272)*. Notre-Dame, built in the early 16th century, has an elaborate lantern belfry.

Charles Perez Aquarium nearby is devoted to the weird and wonderful creatures that swim in the Channel. From the harbour you can take a short boat trip to the peaceful **Ile de Batz**. Salt-water cures are available at Roscoff's two thalassotherapy institutes and there is also a seaweed research centre, Thalado. Near the Pointe de Bloscon are colourful tropical gardens.

🐟 **Charles Perez Aquarium**
Place Georges Teissier. 📞 *02 98 29 23 23.* **Open** *Easter– Sep: daily.* 📷 ♿ *restricted.*

PAUL GAUGUIN IN BRITTANY

Carving, Chapelle de Trémalo

Paul Gauguin's (1848–1903) story reads like a romantic novel. At the age of 35 he left his career as a stockbroker to become a full-time painter. From 1886 to 1894 he lived and worked in Brittany, at Pont-Aven and Le Pouldu, where he painted the landscape and its people. He chose to concentrate on the intense, almost "primitive" quality of the Breton Catholic faith, attempting to convey it in his work. This is evident in *Le Christ Jaune* (Yellow Christ), inspired by a woodcarving in the Trémalo chapel. In Gauguin's painting, the Crucifixion is a reality in the midst of the contemporary Breton landscape, rather than a remote or symbolic event. This theme recurs in many of his paintings from the period, including *Jacob Wrestling with the Angel* (1888).

Le Christ Jaune (1889) by Paul Gauguin

St-Thégonnec ⑬

Finistère. 🚉 *Open* daily. ♿

This is one of the most complete parish closes in Brittany. Passing through its triumphal archway, the ossuary is to the left. The calvary, directly ahead, was built in 1610 and perfectly illustrates the extraordinary skills Breton sculptors developed as they worked with the local granite. Among the many animated figures surrounding the central cross, a small niche contains a statue of St Thégonnec with a cart pulled by wolves.

Guimiliau ⑭

Finistère. *Open* daily. ♿

Almost 200 figures adorn Guimiliau's intensely decorated calvary (1581–88), many wearing 16th-century dress. Among them you can contemplate the legendary torment of Katell Gollet, a servant girl tortured by demons for stealing a consecrated wafer to please her lover. The church is dedicated to St Miliau and has a richly decorated south porch. The baptistry's elaborate carved oak canopy dates from 1675.

Font canopy from 1675, Guimiliau

Lampaul-Guimiliau ⑮

Finistère. *Open* daily. ♿

Entering through the monumental gate, the chapel and ossuary lie to the left, while the calvary is to the right. Here, however, it is the church that demands most attention. The interior is zealously painted and carved, including some naive scenes from the Passion depicted along the 16th-century rood-beam dividing the nave and choir.

Parish Closes

Reflecting the religious fervour of the Bretons, the Enclos Paroissiaux (parish closes) were built during the 16th–18th centuries. At that time Brittany had few urban centres but many wealthy rural settlements that profited from maritime trading and the manufacture of cloth. Grand religious monuments, some taking over 200 years to complete, were built by small villages inspired by spiritual zeal and the more earthly desire to rival their neighbours. Some of the finest parish closes lie in the Elorn valley, linked by a well-signposted Circuit des Enclos Paroissiaux.

***The enclosure**, surrounded by a stone wall, is the hallowed area. By following the wall, visitors are drawn towards the triumphal arch, shown here in Pleyben.*

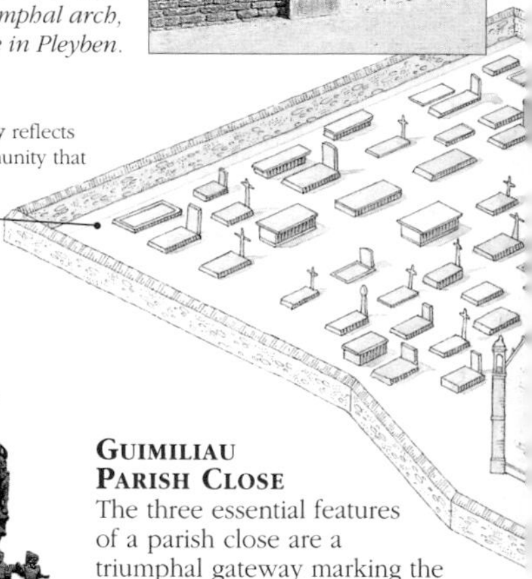

The small cemetery reflects the size of the community that built these great churches.

GUIMILIAU PARISH CLOSE
The three essential features of a parish close are a triumphal gateway marking the entry into the hallowed enclosure, a calvary depicting scenes from the Passion and Crucifixion, and an ossuary beside the church porch.

***The calvary** is unique to Brittany, and may have been inspired by the crosses set on top of menhirs (see p269) by the early Christians. They provide a walk-around Bible lesson, often with the characters in 17th-century costumes as in this example from St-Thégonnec.*

Brittany's parish closes are mainly concentrated in the Elorn Valley. As well as St-Thégonnec, Guimiliau and Lampaul-Guimiliau, other parish closes to visit include Bodilis, La Martyre, La Roche-Maurice, Ploudiry, Sizun and Commana. Further afield lie Plougastel-Doulas and Pleyben, while Guéhenno is in the Morbihan region.

Church interiors are usually adorned with depictions of local saints and scenes from their lives, along with ornately carved beams and furniture. This is the altarpiece in Guimiliau.

In the ossuary bones exhumed from the cemetery would be stored. Built close to the church entrance, the ossuary was considered a bridge between the living and the dead.

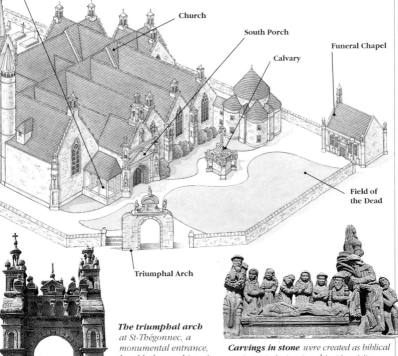

Church

South Porch

Calvary

Funeral Chapel

Field of the Dead

Triumphal Arch

The triumphal arch at St-Thégonnec, a monumental entrance, heralds the worshipper's arrival on sacred ground, like the righteous entering heaven.

Carvings in stone were created as biblical cartoons to instruct and inspire visitors. Their clear message is now often obscured by weather and lichen, but this one in St-Thégonnec is well preserved.

The chapel of Notre-Dame, perched on the cliffs above the beach of Port-Blanc, Côte de Granit Rose

Côte de Granit Rose ⑯

Côtes d'Armor. ⊠ 🚊 🚌 *Lannion.* ℹ *Lannion (02 96 46 41 00).*

THE COAST between Paimpol and Trébeurden is known as the Côte de Granit Rose due to its reddish-pink cliffs. These are best seen between Trégastel and Trébeurden, but the pink granite also features as building material in the neighbouring towns. The stretch of coast between Trébeurden and Perros-Guirec is one of Brittany's most popular family holiday areas.

Further east there are quieter beaches and coves, as at **Trévou-Tréguignec** and **Port-Blanc**. Beyond the cathedral town of Tréguier, **Paimpol** is a working fishing port that once sent huge cod and whaling fleets to fish off Iceland and Newfoundland.

Tréguier ⑰

Côtes d'Armor. 🏘 *2,900.* ℹ *Hôtel de Ville (02 96 92 30 19).* 🛒 *Wed.*

SET ON A HILL overlooking the estuary of the Jaundy and Guindy rivers, Tréguier stands apart from the seaside resorts of the Côte de Granit Rose. It is a typically Breton market town, content with its one major attraction, **Cathédrale St-Tugdual**, and makes few concessions to tourism. The cathedral, built in the 14th–15th centuries, is dedicated to the monk St

Tugdual. It has three towers – one Romanesque, one Gothic and an 18th-century spire pierced with holes in order to withstand strong winds.

Île de Bréhat ⑱

Côtes d'Armor. 🚊 🚌 *Paimpol, then bus to Pointe de l'Arcouest (Mon–Sat in winter; daily in summer), then boat.* ℹ *Paimpol (02 96 20 83 16).*

A 15-MINUTE CROSSING from the Pointe de l'Arcouest, the Île de Bréhat is actually two islands, joined by a small bridge, which together are only 3.5 km (2.2 miles) long. With motorized traffic banned, and a climate mild enough for oleander, mimosa and a variety of fruit trees to flourish, it has a relaxing, pastoral atmosphere. Bicycle hire and boat tours are available in the main town, **Port-Clos**, and you can walk to the island's highest point, the **Chapelle St-Michel**.

Chapelle St-Michel, a landmark on Ile de Bréhat

Carnac ⑲

Morbihan. 🏘 *4,400.* 🚌 ℹ *74 avenue des Druides (02 97 52 13 52).*

CARNAC IS ONE of the world's great prehistoric sites, with almost 3,000 menhirs in parallel rows north of the town centre and an exceptional **Musée de Préhistoire**.

In the town the 17th-century **Eglise St-Cornély** is dedicated to St Cornelius, patron saint of horned animals. Scenes from the saint's life are painted on its wooden ceiling. To the south, the long, sandy beach makes the town a popular seaside resort.

🏛 **Musée de Préhistoire**
10 place de la Chapelle.
📞 *02 97 52 22 04.* **Open** *Wed–Mon.* **Closed** *1 Jan, 1 May, 25 Dec.*
🎦 ♿

Presqu'île de Quiberon ⑳

Morbihan. ⊠ *Quiberon (via Lorient).* 🚊 *Jul & Aug.* 🚌 ⛴ *Quiberon.* ℹ *Quiberon (02 97 50 07 84).*

ONCE AN ISLAND, the slender Quiberon peninsula has a bleak and windy west coast with sea-punished cliffs, known as the Côte Sauvage. The east is more benign with sheltered beaches. At the southern tip of the peninsula is the fishing port and resort of **Quiberon**, from where the car ferry departs for Belle-Ile.

In 1795 10,000 Royalist troops were massacred here in an ill-fated attempt to reverse the French Revolution.

Brittany's Prehistoric Monuments

AT CARNAC, thousands of ancient granite rocks were arranged in mysterious lines and patterns by Megalithic tribes as early as 4000 BC. Their original purpose remains obscure: the significance was probably religious, but the precise patterns also suggest an early astronomical calendar. Celts, Romans and Christians have since adapted them to their own beliefs.

The Gavrinis Tumulus, Golfe du Morbihan

MEGALITHS

There are many different formations of megaliths, all with a particular purpose. Words from the Breton language, such as *men* (stone), *dole* (table) and *hir* (long), are still used to describe them.

Menhirs, *the most common megaliths, are upright stones, standing alone or arranged in lines. Those in circles are known as cromlechs.*

Dolmen, *two upright stones roofed by a third, were used as a burial chamber, such as the Merchant's Table at Locmariaquer.*

Allée couverte, *upright stones placed in a row and roofed to form a covered alley, can be seen at Carnac.*

A tumulus *is a dolmen covered with stones and soil to form a burial mound.*

BAIE DE QUIBERON

Carnac
Gavrinis
Quiberon

KEY

Megalithic sites
Alignments

0 kilometres 10
0 miles 5

Brittany's major megalithic sites

Alignment at Carnac

Menhirs of all shapes in a field near Carnac

Belle-Île ㉑

Morbihan. ☒ *Quiberon (via Lorient).*
🚢 *from Quiberon.* ⓘ *Le Palais
(02 97 31 81 93).*

BRITTANY'S largest island lies
14 km (9 miles) south of
Quiberon and can be reached
in 45 minutes by car ferry
from Quiberon. Its coast
offers both rugged cliffs and
good beaches, while inland
lie exposed highlands inter-
sected by sheltered valleys.
In the main town, Le Palais,
stands the **Citadelle Vauban**,
a 16th-century star-shaped
fortress, and there are fine
walks and views along the
southern Côte Sauvage.

Cloisters of St-Pierre in Vannes

Vannes ㉒

Morbihan. 🏠 48,500. 🚉 🚌 ⓘ *1 rue
Thiers (02 97 47 24 34).* 🛒 *Wed & Sat.*

STANDING AT THE HEAD of the
Golfe du Morbihan, Vannes
was the capital of the Veneti,
a seafaring Armorican tribe
defeated by Caesar in 56 BC.
In the 9th century Nominoë,
the first Duke of Brittany,
made it his power base. The
city remained influential up
until the signing of the union
with France in 1532, when
Rennes became the Breton
capital. Today it is a busy
commercial city with a well-
preserved medieval quarter,
and a good base for exploring
the Golfe du Morbihan.

The impressive eastern
walls of old Vannes can be
viewed from the promenade
de la Garenne. Two of the
city's old gates survive at
either end: Porte-Prison in the
north, and the southern Porte-

Breton seafarer, off Belle-Île's coast

Poterne with a row of 17th-
century wash houses close by.

Walking up from Porte St-
Vincent, you find the city's
old market squares, still in
use today. The **place des
Lices** was once the scene of
medieval tournaments and the
streets around the rue de la
Monnaie are full of well-
preserved 16th-century houses.

Begun in the 13th century,
Cathédrale St-Pierre has since
been drastically remodelled
and restored. The Chapel of
the Holy Sacrament houses
the revered tomb of Vincent
Ferrier, a Spanish saint who
died in Vannes in 1419.

Opposite the west front of
the cathedral, the old covered
market **La Cohue** (meaning
throng or hubbub) was once
the city's central meeting place.
Parts of the building date from
the 13th century, and a small
museum inside displays art
and artifacts relevant to the
history of Vannes and the
Golfe du Morbihan.

Housed in the 15th-century
Château Gaillard, the **Musée
d'Archéologie du Morbihan**

is a rich assembly of finds
from Morbihan's many
prehistoric sites, including
jewellery, pottery and
weapons. There is also a
gallery of medieval and
Renaissance *objets d'art*.

🏛 **Musée d'Archéologie du
Morbihan**
Château Gaillard, 2 rue Noé.
📞 *02 97 42 59 80.* **Open** *Apr–Oct:
Mon–Sat; Nov–Mar: Mon–Sat pm.*
Closed *public hols.* 📷

Environs
To the south of the city the
Parc du Golfe is a leisure
park with many amusements,
a butterfly conservatory and
an aquarium with over 400
species of fish. Northeast of
Vannes, off the N166, lie the
romantic ruins of the 15th-
century **Tours d'Elven**.

Golfe du Morbihan ㉓

Morbihan. ☒ *Lorient.* 🚉 🚌 🚢
Vannes. ⓘ *Vannes (02 97 47 24 34).*

MORBIHAN MEANS "little sea"
in Breton, an apt de-
scription for this landlocked
expanse of tidal water. Only
connected to the Atlantic by a
small channel between the
Locmariaquer and Rhuys
peninsulas, the gulf is dotted
with islands. Around 40 are
inhabited, with the **Ile d'Arz**
and the **Ile aux Moines** the
largest. These are served by
regular ferries from Conleau
and Port-Blanc respectively.

Around the gulf several small
harbours earn a living from
fishing, oyster cultivation and
tourism. There is a wealth of

The picturesque fishing port of Le Bono in Golfe du Morbihan

Young holidaymakers on the beach at Dinard, a classic seaside resort on the Emerald Coast

megalithic sites, notably the island of **Gavrinis** where a tumulus has been excavated to reveal extraordinary stone carvings *(see p269)*. There are boat trips to Gavrinis from Larmor-Baden and around the gulf from Locmariaquer, Auray, Vannes and Port-Navalo.

The medieval Château de Josselin on the banks of the river Oust

Josselin ㉔

Morbihan. ⚑ 2,600. ⊟ ⓘ place de la Congrégation (02 97 22 36 43). ⊜ Sat.

OVERLOOKING the river Oust, Josselin is dominated by a medieval **Château** owned by the Rohan family since the end of the 13th century. Only four of its nine towers survive. The elaborate inner granite façade incorporates the letter "A" – a tribute to the much-loved Duchess Anne of Brittany (1477–1514), who presided over Brittany's "Golden Age". Tours are given of the 19th-century interior, and in the former stables there is a Musée des Poupées with 600 dolls. In the town, **Basilique Notre-Dame-du-Roncier** contains

the mausoleum of the castle's most famous owner and constable of France, Olivier de Clisson (1336–1407). West of Josselin at Kerguéhennec, the grounds of an 18th-century château have become a modern sculpture park.

♟ Château de Josselin

📞 02 97 22 36 45. **Open** Apr–May & Oct: Wed, Sat, Sun & public hols, pm only; Jun & Sep: daily pm; Jul & Aug: daily. 🎫 ♿

Forêt de Paimpont ㉕

Ille-et-Vilaine. 🚶 Rennes. 🚌 Rennes, then bus. 🚌 Ploêrmel. ⓘ Paimpont, summer (02 99 07 84 23).

ALSO KNOWN AS the Forêt de Brocéliande, this forest is a last remnant of the dense primeval woods that once covered much of Armorica. It has long been associated with the legends of King Arthur, and visitors still come to search for the magical

Legendary sorcerer Merlin and Viviane, the Lady of the Lake

spring where the sorcerer Merlin first met Viviane, the Lady of the Lake. The small village of **Paimpont** provides a good base for exploring both the forest and its myths.

Côte d'Emeraude ㉖

Ille et Vilaine & Côtes d'Armor. ✈ Dinard–St-Malo. 🚌 ⊟ 🚢 ⓘ St-Malo (02 99 56 64 48).

BETWEEN Le Val-André and the Pointe du Grouin, near Cancale, sandy beaches, rocky headlands and classic seaside resorts stretch along Brittany's northern shore. Known as the Emerald Coast, its self-proclaimed Queen is the aristocratic resort of **Dinard**, "discovered" in the 1850s and still playing host to the international rich.

To its west the summer holiday mood is sustained by resorts like St-Jacut-de-la-Mer, St-Cast-le-Guildo, Sables d'Or-les-Pins and Erquy, all with tempting beaches. In the Baie de la Frênaye, the medieval **Fort La Latte** provides good views from its ancient watch-tower, while the lighthouse that dominates **Cap Fréhel** nearby offers even more extensive panoramas.

East of Dinard, the D186 runs across the **Barrage de la Rance** to St-Malo. Built in 1966 it was the world's first dam to generate electricity by using tidal power. Beyond St-Malo, coves and beaches surround La Guimorais, while around the Pointe du Grouin the seas are often truly emerald.

SEAFARERS OF ST-MALO

St-Malo owes its wealth and reputation to the exploits of its mariners. In 1534 Jacques Cartier, born in nearby Rothéneuf, discovered the mouth of the St Lawrence river in Canada and claimed the territory for France. It was Breton sailors who voyaged to South America in 1698 to colonize the Iles Malouines, known today as Las Malvinas or the Falklands. By the 17th century St-Malo was the largest port in France and famous for its corsairs – privateers licensed by the king to prey on foreign ships. The most illustrious were the swashbuckling René Duguay-Trouin (1673–1736), who captured Rio de Janeiro from the Portuguese in 1711, and the intrepid Robert Surcouf (1773–1827), whose ships hounded vessels of the British East India Company. The riches won by trade and piracy enabled St-Malo's ship-owners to build great mansions known as *malouinières*.

Explorer Jacques Cartier (1491–1557)

St-Malo ㉗

Ille-et-Vilaine. 🏙 49,000. 🚢 🚉
🚌 🛥 🛈 *esplanade St-Vincent
(02 99 56 64 48).* 🍴 Mon–Sat.

ONCE A FORTIFIED island, St-Malo stands in a commanding position at the mouth of the river Rance.

The city is named after Maclou, a Welsh monk who came here in the 6th century to spread the Christian message. During the 16th–19th centuries the port won prosperity and power through the exploits of its seafarers. St-Malo was heavily bombed in 1944 but has since been scrupulously restored and is now a major port and ferry terminal as well as a resort.

Intra-muros, the old walled city, is encircled by ramparts that provide fine views of St-Malo and its offshore islands. Take the steps up by the **Porte St-Vincent** and walk clockwise, passing the mighty 15th-century **Grande Porte**.

Within the city is a web of narrow, cobbled streets with tall 18th-century buildings housing souvenir shops, fish restaurants and crêperies. Rue Porcon-de-la-Barbinais leads to **Cathédrale St-Vincent**, with its sombre 12th-century nave contrasting with the brilliant modern stained glass of the chancel. On cour La Houssaye, the 15th-century Maison de la Duchesse Anne has been carefully restored.

St-Malo seen at low tide through the gate of Fort National

♠ Château de St-Malo
🅲 *02 99 40 71 57.* **Open**
Easter–Sep: daily; Oct–Easter: Tue–Sun.
Closed *1 Jan, 1 & 11 Nov, 25 Dec.* 🎟
St-Malo's castle dates from the 14th–15th centuries. The great keep, built in 1424, contains a museum of the city's history, including the adventures of its state-sponsored corsairs. From its watch towers there is an impressive view of sea and coast. The adjacent tower, the Quic-en-Groigne, contains a museum of historical wax-works. Nearby, in the place Vauban, an aquarium has been built into the ramparts.

🏰 Fort National
Open *Easter–end Sep: daily at low tide.* 🎟
Constructed in 1689 by Louis XIV's famous military architect, Vauban, this fort can be reached on foot at low tide and offers good views of St-Malo and its ramparts. At low tide you can walk out to the island of **Grand Bé**. From the top there are great views along the whole of Côte d'Emeraude *(see p271).* The St-Malo-born writer François-René de Chateaubriand lies buried here.

🏰 Tour Solidor
St-Servan. 🅲 *02 99 40 71 58.*
Open *Easter–Sep: daily; Oct–Easter:
Tue–Sun.* **Closed** *1 Jan, 1 May,
1 & 11 Nov, 25 Dec.* 🎟
To the west of St-Malo in St-Servan, the three-towered Tour Solidor was built in 1382. Formerly a prison, it now houses an intriguing museum devoted to the ships and sailors that rounded Cape Horn, displaying ship models, logs and various instruments of a nautical flavour.

Environs
When the tide is out, good beaches are revealed around St-Malo and in the nearby suburbs of St-Servan and Paramé. A regular passenger ferry runs across to Dinard *(see p271)* and the Channel Islands and there are boat trips up the Rance to Dinan, and out to the Iles Chausey, Ile de Cézembre and Cap Fréhel.

At Rothéneuf you can visit the **Manoir Limoëlou**, home of the navigator Jacques Cartier. Nearby, on the coast, Les Rochers Sculptés is a beguiling array of granite

Cancale oysters, prized for their taste since Roman times

faces and figures carved into the cliffs by a local priest, Abbé Fouré, at the end of the 19th century.

♦ Manoir Limoëlou
Rue D Macdonald-Stuart, Limoëlou-Rothéneuf. **⚏** 02 99 40 97 73.
Open Jun–Aug: daily; Sep–May: Mon–Fri. 🖼 🕭

Cancale ㉘

Ille-et-Vilaine. **🚶** 5,000. **🚌**
ℹ 44 rue du Port (02 99 89 63 72).
🚍 Sun.

A SMALL PORT with views across the Baie du Mont-St-Michel, Cancale is entirely devoted to the cultivation and consumption of oysters. Prized by the Romans, the acclaimed flavour of Cancale's oysters is said to derive from the strong tides that wash over them daily. You can survey the beds from a *sentier des douaniers* (coastguards' footpath, the GR34) running along the cliffs.

There are plenty of opportunities for sampling the local speciality provided by a multitude of bars and restaurants along the busy quays of the Port de la Houle, where the fishing boats arrive at high tide. Devotees should pay a visit to the **Musée de l'Huître et du Coquillage**.

🏛 Musée de l'Huître et du Coquillage
Aurore. **📞** 02 99 89 69 99.
Open Mid-Feb–mid-Nov: daily. 🖼

Dinan ㉙

Côtes d'Armor. **🚶** 12,800. **🚌 🚍**
ℹ 6 rue de l'Horloge (02 96 39 75 40).
🚍 Thu.

S ET ON A HILL overlooking the wooded Rance valley, Dinan is a modern market town with a medieval heart. Surrounded by ramparts, the well-kept, half-timbered houses and cobbled streets of its Vieille Ville have an impressive, unforced unity best appreciated by climbing to the top of its 15th-century **Tour d'Horloge**, in rue de l'Horloge. Nearby, **Basilique St-Sauveur** contains the heart of Dinan's most famous son, the 14th-century warrior Bertrand du Guesclin.

Behind the church, Les Jardins Anglais offer good views of the river Rance and the viaduct spanning it. A couple of streets further north, the steep, geranium-decorated rue du Jerzual winds down through the 14th-century town gate to the port. Once a busy harbour from which cloth was shipped, it is now a quiet backwater where you can take a pleasure cruise, or follow a towpath walk around to the restored 17th-century **Abbaye St-Magloire** at Léhon.

For an introduction to Dinan's history, the **Musée-Château** houses a small museum. Next to it is the 15th-century **Tour de Coëtquen**. From here there are pleasant walks beside the ramparts along the promenade des Petits Fossés and the promenade des Grands Fossés.

♦ Musée-Château
Château de la Duchesse Anne, rue du Château. **📞** 02 96 39 45 20.
Open second wk Feb–May & mid-Oct–Dec: Wed–Mon; Jun–mid-Oct: daily. **Closed** 25 Dec. 🖼 🕭

Author and diplomat François-René de Chateaubriand (1768–1848)

Combourg ㉚

Ille-et-Vilaine. **🚶** 4,800. **🚌 🚍**
ℹ place Albert Parent (02 99 73 13 93). **🚍** Mon.

A SMALL, SLEEPY town beside a lake, Combourg is completely overshadowed by the great, haunting **Château de Combourg** first built in the 11th century. The buildings seen today date from the 14th and 15th centuries. In 1761 the château was bought by the Comte de Chateaubriand, and the melancholic childhood spent there by his son, the author and diplomat François-René de Chateaubriand (1768–1848), is candidly described in his entertaining chronicle, *Mémoires d'Outre-Tombe*.

Empty after the Revolution, the château was restored in the late 19th century and is now open for guided tours. In one room are papers and furniture relating to the life of François-René de Chateaubriand.

♦ Château de Combourg
23 rue des Princes. **📞** 02 99 73 22 95.
Open Apr–Oct: Wed–Mon. 🖼

View over Dinan and the Gothic bridge crossing the river Rance

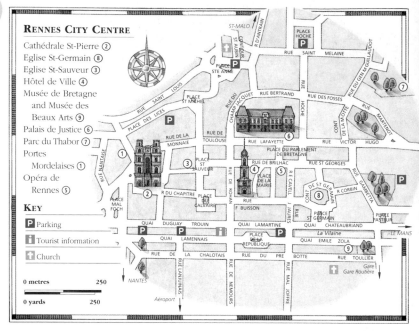

RENNES CITY CENTRE

Cathédrale St-Pierre ②
Eglise St-Germain ⑧
Eglise St-Sauveur ③
Hôtel de Ville ④
Musée de Bretagne
  and Musée des
  Beaux Arts ⑨
Palais de Justice ⑥
Parc du Thabor ⑦
Portes
  Mordelaises ①
Opéra de
  Rennes ⑤

KEY

P Parking

i Tourist information

✝ Church

0 metres   250

0 yards   250

Rennes ⓷¹

Ille-et-Vilaine. 🏛 204,000. ✈ 🚉
🚌 ℹ *pont de Nemours*
(02 99 79 01 98). 🛒 *Tue–Sat.*

F OUNDED BY the Gauls and
colonized by the Romans,
Rennes is strategically located
where the Vilaine and Ille
rivers meet. After Brittany's
union with France in 1532, the
town became regional capital.
In 1720 a fire lasting for six
days devastated the city. Today
a small part of the medieval
city survives, together with
the neat grid of 18th-century

**The lively market at place des
Lices in the heart of Rennes**

buildings that arose from the
ashes. Around this historic
core are the tower blocks and
hi-tech factories of modern
Rennes – a confident provincial
capital with two universities
and a thriving cultural life.
  Wandering through the
streets that radiate from the
place des Lices and the place
Ste-Anne, it is easy to imagine
what Rennes was like before
the Great Fire. Now mostly
pedestrianized, this area has
become the city's youthful
heart with plenty of bars,
crêperies and designer shops.
At the western end of rue de
la Monnaie stands the 15th-
century **Portes Mordelaises**,
once part of the city's ramparts.
  Close by, **Cathédrale St-
Pierre** was completed in 1844,
the third on this site. Note the
carved 16th-century Flemish
altarpiece. Nearby is the 18th-
century **Eglise St-Sauveur**.
Just south of the attractive rue
St-George, **Eglise St-Germain**
has a typically Breton belfry
and wooden vaulting. In the
place de la Mairie stands the
early 18th-century **Hôtel de
Ville** and the Neo-Classical
Opéra de Rennes. The **Parc
du Thabor**, once part of a
Benedictine monastery,
is ideal for walks and picnics.

**Half-timbered houses lining the
narrow streets of old Rennes**

🏛 Palais de Justice
Place du Parlement. *Closed for
restoration until at least 2000.*
Rennes' Law Courts, built in
1618–55 and designed by
Salomon de Brosse, were the
seat of the region's governing
body until the Revolution.
  Parts of the building were
still used as criminal courts
until it was severely damaged
by fire during the riots over
fish prices in February 1994.
A restoration project will
return its interior as well as
exterior to their original state,
including the unique coffered
ceiling and gilded woodwork
of the Grande Chambre.

🏛 Musée de Bretagne, Musée des Beaux Arts

20 quai Emile Zola. 📞 *02 99 28 55 84 (Musée de Bretagne)*. 📞 *02 99 28 55 85 (Musée des Beaux Arts)*. **Open** *Wed–Mon*. **Closed** *public hols*. 📷 ♿

The Musée de Bretagne, on the south bank of the Vilaine river, provides a stimulating introduction to Brittany's history. There are examples of traditional Breton furniture and costume, and displays on Brittany's prehistoric megaliths, the growth of Rennes, rural crafts and the fishing industry.

In the same building, the **Musée des Beaux Arts** has a wide-ranging collection of art from the 14th century to the present, including a room devoted to art on Breton themes. There are paintings by Gaugin, Bernard and other members of the Pont-Aven School *(see p265)*, and three works by Picasso, including the lively *Baigneuse* painted at Dinard in 1928.

Environs

Just south of Rennes, the **Eco-musée du Pays de Rennes** traces the history of a local farm since the 17th century.

Some 16 km (10 miles) to the southeast of Rennes is **Châteaugiron**, a charming medieval village, with an imposing castle and houses preserving their wooden eaves.

🏛 Ecomusée du Pays de Rennes

Ferme de la Bintinais, route de Châtillon-sur-Seiche. 📞 *02 99 51 38 15*. **Open** *mid-Jan–Feb: Wed–Mon*. **Closed** *Sat & Sun am, public hols*. 📷 ♿

♟ Château de Châteaugiron

📞 *02 99 37 89 02*. **Open** *Jul–Aug: daily; May–Jun & Sep: Sun pm*. 📷

Fougères ㉜

Ille-et-Vilaine. 🚶 *23,000*. 🚉 ℹ️ *1 place Aristide Briand (02 99 94 12 20)*. 🚌 *Sat*.

A FORTRESS TOWN close to the Breton border, Fougères rests on a hill overlooking the Nançon river. In the valley below, and still linked to the Haute Ville by a curtain of ancient ramparts, stands the mighty 11th–15th century

The mighty fortifications of Château de Fougères

Château de Fougères. To get a good overview of the château, go to the gardens of place aux Arbres behind the 16th-century **Eglise St-Léonard**. From here you can descend to the river and the medieval houses around place du Marchix. The Flamboyant Gothic **Eglise St-Sulpice**, with its 18th-century wood-panelled interior and granite retables, is well worth visiting.

A walk around the castle's massive outer fortifications reveals the ambitious scale of its construction, with 13 towers and walls over 3 m (10 ft) thick. You can still climb the castle's ramparts and towers to get a feel of what it was like to live and fight within its staggered defences. Much of the action in Balzac's novel *Les Chouans* (1829) takes place in and around Fougères and its castle.

♟ Château de Fougères

Place Pierre-Simon. 📞 *02 99 99 79 59*. **Open** *Feb–Dec: daily*. 📷

Overhanging timber-frame houses on rue Beaudrairie, Vitré

Vitré ㉝

Ill-et-Vilaine. 🚶 *14,000*. 🚉 🚉 ℹ️ *place St-Yves (02 99 75 04 46)*. 🚌 *Mon*.

T HE FORTIFIED TOWN of Vitré is set high on a hill overlooking the Vilaine valley. Its medieval **Château** is complete with pencil-point turrets and picturesque 15th–16th century buildings in attendance. The castle was rebuilt in the 14th–15th centuries and follows a triangular plan, with some of its ramparts walkable. There is a museum of local treasures in the Tour St-Laurent.

To the east, rue Beaudrairie and rue d'Embas have overhanging timber-frame houses with remarkable patterning.

The 15th–16th century **Cathédrale Notre-Dame**, built in Flamboyant Gothic style, has an elaborate south façade with an exterior stone pulpit. Further along rue Notre-Dame, the promenade du Val skirts around the town's ramparts.

To the southeast of Vitré on the D88, the **Château des Rochers-Sévigné** was once the home of Mme de Sévigné (1626–96), famous letter-writer and chronicler of life at the court of Louis XIV. The park, chapel and some of her rooms are open to the public.

♟ Château de Vitré

📞 *02 99 75 04 54*. **Open** *Apr–Sep: daily*. **Closed** *Sat am, Sun am, Mon am, 1 Jan, Easter, 1 Nov, 25 Dec*. 📷

♟ Château des Rochers-Sévigné

📞 *02 99 96 76 51*. **Open** *Apr–Sep: daily*. **Closed** *1 Jan, Easter, 1 Nov, 25 Dec*. 📷 ♿ *restricted*.

THE LOIRE VALLEY

INDRE · INDRE-ET-LOIRE · LOIR-ET-CHER · LOIRET · EURE-ET-LOIR
CHER · VENDÉE · MAINE-ET-LOIRE · LOIRE-ATLANTIQUE · SARTHE

R ENOWNED FOR ITS SUMPTUOUS CHATEAUX, *the relics of royal days gone by, the glorious valley of the Loire is rich in both history and architecture. Like the river Loire, this vast region runs through the heart of French life. Its sophisticated cities, luxuriant landscape and magnificent food and wine add up to a bourgeois paradise.*

The lush Loire Valley is supremely regal. Orléans was France's intellectual capital in the 13th century, attracting artists, poets and troubadours to the royal court. But the medieval court never stayed in one place for long, which led to the building of magnificent châteaux all along the Loire. Chambord and Chenonceau, the two greatest Renaissance châteaux, remain prestigious symbols of royal rule, resplendent within their ornamental gardens.

Due to its central location, culture and fine cuisine, Tours is the natural visitors' capital. Angers is a close second but more authentic are the historic towns of Amboise, Blois, Saumur and Beaugency, strung out like jewels along the river. This is the classic Loire Valley, a château trail which embraces the Renaissance gardens of Villandry and the fairytale turrets of Azay-le-Rideau. Venture northwards and the cathedral cities of Le Mans and Chartres reign supreme, their medieval centres bordered by Gallo-Roman walls. Nantes in the west is a breezy, forward-looking port and gateway to the Atlantic.

Southwards, the windswept Vendée is edged by a wild, sandy coastline that is perfect for windsurfers and nature lovers alike. Inland, the Loire's more peaceful tributaries and the watery Sologne beg to be explored. Also ripe for discovery are troglodyte caves, sleepy hamlets, and small Romanesque churches decorated with frescoes. Inviting inns offer game, fish and abundant fresh vegetables to be lingered over with a light white Vouvray wine or full-bodied Bourgeuil. Overindulgence is no sin in this rich region.

The river Loire at Montsoreau, southeast of Saumur

◁ The fairytale Château de Saumur towering above the town and the river Loire

Exploring the Loire Valley

THE LUSH VALLEY LANDSCAPE, studded with France's greatest châteaux, is the main attraction. River cruises are available from Angers and Nantes, while the sandy Atlantic coast offers beach holidays. Peaceful country holidays can be had in the Vendée, and in the Loir and Indre valleys. Wine tours focus on Bourgueil, Chinon, Muscadet and Vouvray. The most charming bases are Amboise, Blois, Beaugency and Saumur, but culture-lovers are well-provided for throughout the region.

Countryside around Vouvray

To Caen

To Rennes Brest

LAVAL

To Rennes St-Malo

CHÂTEAUBRIANT

Erdre

NANTES

CLISSON

ÎLE DE NOIRMOUTIER

ÎLE D'YEU

ANGERS

SAUMUR

LANGEAIS

USSÉ

ABBAYE DE FONTEVRAUD

CHOLET

MONTREUIL-BELLAY

To Poitiers

LA ROCHE-SUR-YON

VENDÉE

LES SABLES D'OLONNE

KEY

▬	Motorway
▬	Major road
▬	Minor road
▬	Scenic route
～	River
✿	Viewpoint

0 kilometres   25

0 miles   25

The 16th-century Château de Villandry, set amid gardens

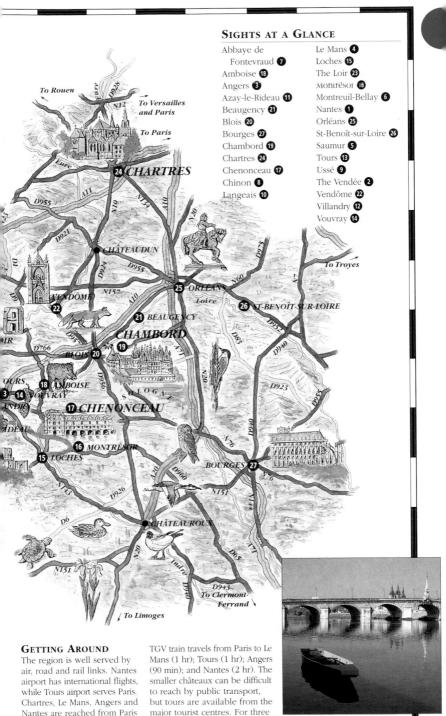

SIGHTS AT A GLANCE

GETTING AROUND

The region is well served by air, road and rail links. Nantes airport has international flights, while Tours airport serves Paris. Chartres, Le Mans, Angers and Nantes are reached from Paris by the A11, and the A10 links Orléans, Blois and Tours. The TGV train travels from Paris to Le Mans (1 hr); Tours (1 hr); Angers (90 min); and Nantes (2 hr). The smaller châteaux can be difficult to reach by public transport, but tours are available from the major tourist centres. For three or four people, car rental may be cheaper than public transport.

A bridge over the river Loire pictured at dawn

Tomb of François II and his wife, Marguerite de Foix, in Cathédrale St-Pierre

Nantes ❶

Loire-Atlantique. 🏙 250,000.
🛬 🚊 🚌 🛈 place du Commerce
(02 40 20 60 00). 🚢 daily.

For centuries, Nantes disputed with Rennes the title of capital of Brittany. Yet links with the Plantagenets and Henri IV also bound it to the "royal" river Loire. Since the 1790s it has officially ceased to be part of Brittany, and, though still Breton at heart, it is today capital of the Pays de la Loire.

Visually, Nantes is a city of variety, with high-tech towers overlooking the port, canals and Art Nouveau squares. Chic bars and restaurants cram the medieval nucleus, bounded by place St-Croix and the château.

The stark **Cathédrale St-Pierre**, started in 1434 but not completed until 1893, is notable for its sculpted Gothic portals and Renaissance tomb of François II, the last duke of Brittany. More impressive is the **Château des Ducs de Bretagne**, where Anne of Brittany was born in 1477 and where the Edict of Nantes was signed by Henri IV in 1598, granting Protestants religious freedom. Inside one wing of the castle is the **Musée des Salorges**, a naval museum that charts Nantes' colonial links and slave-trading activities in the 18th and 19th centuries. On display are Indian prints, a slave trader's study and a re-creation of the horrific conditions endured by the galley slaves.

⚓ Château des Ducs de Bretagne/Musée des Salorges
Pl Marc Elder. 🕻 02 40 41 56 56.
Open Jul–Aug: daily; Sep–Jun:
Wed–Mon. **Closed** public hols. 🈺

Environs
From Nantes, boats cruise the rivers Erdre and Sèvre, passing a succession of minor châteaux, Muscadet vineyards and gentle countryside.

Some 16 km (10 miles) southeast of Nantes is **Clisson**, a town razed to the ground during the Vendée Uprising of 1793, and later rebuilt along Italian lines, acquiring Neo-Classical villas, brick belltowers and red-tiled roofs. On a rocky spur overlooking the river Sèvre is the ruined 13th-century **Château de Clisson**, parts of which are under restoration.

⚓ Château de Clisson
🕻 02 40 54 02 22. **Open** Wed–Mon.
Closed Christmas school hols. 🈺

The Vendée ❷

Vendée and Maine-et-Loire.
🛬 Nantes. 🚊 🚌 La Roche-sur-Yon.
🛈 La Roche-sur-Yon (02 51 36 00 85).

The counter-revolutionary movement which swept western France between 1793 and 1799 began as a series of uprisings in the Vendée, still an evocative name to the French. As a bastion of the *Ancien Régime*, the region rebelled against urban Republican values. But a violent massacre in 1793 left 80,000 royalists dead in one day as they tried to cross the Loire at St-Florent-le-Vieil. The Vendée farmers were staunch royalists, and, although they ultimately lost, the region remains coloured by conservatism and religious fervour to this day.

1993 marked the bicentennial of the Vendée Uprising, which was commemorated by the opening of two new museums in Cholet and Challans. Other memorials include the war cemetery at the twice-besieged village of La Gaubretière and stained-glass windows in the parish church of Luc-sur-Boulogne.

Today, the tranquil Vendée welcomes green tourism. East and north of La Roche-sur-Yon lies the *bocage vendéen*, a wooded backwater with bridle paths and nature trails. The Atlantic coast between the Loire and Poitou is one of the cleanest and least explored in France, the only significant resort being **Les Sables d'Olonne**, which boasts a marina, a fort and the Vendée war museum. To the north, the

The harbour at Ile de Noirmoutier in the Vendée

marshy **Ile de Noirmoutier** is connected to the mainland at low tide via the Gois causeway.

Inland lies the remote **Marais Poitevin** *(see p398)*, its marshes home to bird sanctuaries and hamlets bordered by canals. Maillezais offers a Romanesque abbey as well as punting along the canals, while neighbouring Chaillé-les-Marais has fine 17th-century churches. With the largest complex of man-made waterways in France, this lush area is graced with the name Venise Verte (Green Venice).

The Apocalypse Tapestry in Angers

Angers ❸

Maine-et-Loire. 🏢 *140,000.* 🚉 🚏
🛈 *pl Kennedy (02 41 23 51 11).*
🏪 *Wed & Sat.*

A NGERS SEES ITSELF as the quintessential Loire city. It is the historic capital of Anjou, home of the Plantagenets and gateway to the Loire Valley.

Angers has a formidable 13th-century **Château** *(see p232)*. Inside is one of France's finest medieval tapestries, woven between 1375 and 1378. It tells the story of the Apocalypse, depicting battles between hydras and angels.

A short walk from the castle is the **Cathédrale St-Maurice**, noted for its Romanesque façade and 12th-century stained-glass windows. Close by, in place St-Croix, is the timber-framed **Maison d'Adam** with carvings representing the tree of life. The nearby **Musée David d'Angers**, housed in the glass-covered ruins of a 13th-century church, is a tribute to the eponymous 19th-century sculptor born in Angers. Across the river Maine, the Hôpital St-Jean, a hospital for the poor from 1174 to 1854, is today the home of the **Musée Jean Lurçat**. Its prize exhibit is the dramatic *Chant du Monde* tapestry created by Lurçat in 1957.

⚓ **Château d'Angers**
🄲 *02 41 87 43 47.* **Open** *daily.* **Closed**
1 Jan, 1 May, 1 & 11 Nov, 25 Dec. 🎫
🏛 **Musée David d'Angers**
33 bis rue Toussaint. 🄲 *02 41 87 21 03.* **Open** *mid-June–mid-Sep: daily; mid-Sep–mid-Jun: Tue–Sun.* 🎫 🦽
🏛 **Musée Jean Lurçat**
4 boulevard Arago. 🄲 *02 41 24 18 45.*
Open *mid-Jun–mid-Sep: daily; mid-Sep–mid-Jun: Tue–Sun.* **Closed** *public hols.* 🎫 🦽

Environs
Within a 16-km (10-mile) radius of Angers lie the Classical **Château de Serrant** and the moated **Château du Plessis-Bourré**, a decorative pleasure dome encased in a feudal shell. For a quiet taste of the countryside, follow the Loire east along the sandbanks and dykes, enjoying the rustic fish restaurants and a vigorous game of *boule de fort* en route.

⚓ **Château de Serrant**
St-Georges-sur-Loire. 🄲 *02 41 39 13 01.* **Open** *Jul–Aug: daily; Mar–Jun & Sep–Oct: Wed–Mon.* 🎫
⚓ **Château du Plessis-Bourré**
Ecuillé. 🄲 *02 41 32 06 01.*
Open *Mar–Nov: Thu pm–Tue; Dec–Feb: groups by appt.* 🎫

Le Mans ❹

Sarthe. 🏢 *150,000.* ✈ 🚉 🚏
🛈 *Hôtel des Ursulines, rue de l'Etoile (02 43 28 17 22).* 🏪 *Wed, Fri & Sun.*

E VER SINCE Monsieur Bollée became the first designer to place an engine under a car bonnet, Le Mans has been synonymous with the motor trade. Bollée's son created an embryonic Grand Prix, since when the event *(see p33)* and associated **Musée de l'Automobile** have remained star attractions.

Stained-glass Ascension window in the Cathédrale St-Julien, Le Mans

Vieux Mans, the ancient fortified centre, is surrounded by the greatest Gallo-Roman walls in France, best seen from the quai Louis Blanc. Once insalubrious and abandoned, the area has been extensively restored, and is now used as a recherché film set where epics such as *Cyrano de Bergerac* are filmed. Its pleasures lie in the Renaissance mansions, half-timbered houses, arcaded alleys and tiny courtyards. The crowning point is the Gothic **Cathédrale St-Julien**, borne aloft on flying buttresses, with its Romanesque portal rivalling that of Chartres. Inside, the Angevin nave opens into a Gothic choir, complemented by sculpted capitals and a 12th-century Ascension window.

🏛 **Musée de l'Automobile**
Circuit des 24 Heures du Mans.
🄲 *02 43 72 72 24.* **Open** *Jun–Sep: daily.* 🎫 🦽

Le Mans racetrack: a 1933 print from the French magazine *Illustration*

Saumur ❺

Maine-et-Loire. 🏘 *32,000.* 🚉 🚌 🛈
pl de la Bilange (02 41 40 20 60). 🚢 *Sat.*

Saumur is celebrated for its
fairytale château, cavalry
school, mushrooms and
sparkling wines. Its stone
mansions recall the city's
17th-century heyday, when it
was a bastion of Protestantism
and vied with Angers as the
intellectual capital of Anjou.

Towering high above both
town and river is the turreted
Château de Saumur. The
present structure was started
in the 14th-century
by Louis I of Anjou
and remodelled a
century later by his
grandson, King
René. A 90-minute
guided tour covers
porcelain and
equestrian exhibits.

Saumur is predomi-
nantly a city of stone,
but **place St-Pierre**
boasts a number of
well-restored, half-
timbered houses and a
medieval church containing
16th-century tapestries. Steps
lead up to the galleried
Maison des Compagnons,

The Château de Saumur and spire of St-Pierre seen from the Loire

King René's
coat of arms

the setting for Balzac's novel
Eugénie Grandet.

On the south bank of the
Loire in the western suburb
of St-Hilaire-St-Florent is the
Ecole Nationale d'Equitation
(National Riding
School) where the
prestigious Cadre
Noir puts on exciting
equestrian shows.

The nearby **Musée
du Champignon**
organizes tours of
the region's tufa
caves, where 75 per
cent of the country's
mushrooms are
cultivated. Before
returning to the
town centre, be sure to
sample the local *méthode
champenoise* sparkling wine –
the best in France outside
Champagne.

♣ **Château de Saumur**
🔃 *02 41 40 24 40.* **Open** *Apr–Sep:
daily; Oct–Mar: Wed–Mon.* **Closed**
1 Jan, 25 Dec. 📷

⚕ **Ecole Nationale
d'Equitation**
St-Hilaire-St-Florent. 🔃 *02 41 53 50
50.* **Open** *Apr–Sep: Mon–Sat; Oct–Mar:
by appt.* **Closed** *public hols.* 📷 ♿ ✔

🏛 **Musée du Champignon**
St-Hilaire-St-Florent. 🔃 *02 41 50 31 55.*
Open *mid-Feb–mid-Nov: daily.* 📷 ♿

Environs
Downriver from Saumur is the
lovely **Eglise de Cunault**, an
11th-century Romanesque
abbey church with a fine west
door and carved capitals.

Montreuil-Bellay ❻

Maine-et-Loire. 🏘 *4,000.* 🚉 *Saumur.*
🚌 🛈 *place du Concorde (02 41 52
32 39).* 🚢 *Tue (Jun–Sep: Sun also).*

Set on the river Thouet 17 km
(11 miles) south of Saumur,
Montreuil-Bellay is one of the
region's most gracious small
towns. It makes an ideal base
for touring Anjou. Walled mansions overlook Gothic churches
and the **Chapelle St-Jean**, an
ancient hospice and pilgrimage centre. A stroll along the
river bank leads past a priory,
a miller's house and city gate.

The imposing **Château de
Montreuil-Bellay**, established
in 1025, is a veritable fortress
with its 13 interlocking towers,
barbican and ramparts. A
gracious 15th-century house lies
beyond the fortified gateway,
complete with vaulted medieval
kitchen, ancient wine cellars
(wine-tasting recommended),
and an oratory decorated with
15th-century frescoes.

♣ **Château de
Montreuil-Bellay**
🔃 *02 41 52 33 06.* **Open**
Easter–Nov: Wed–Mon. 📷

TROGLODYTE DWELLINGS

Some of the best troglodyte settlements in France have been
carved out of the soft limestone (tufa) of the Loire Valley, especially around Saumur, Vouvray and along the river Loir. The
caves, cut out of cliff-faces or dug underground, have been a
source of cheap, secure accommodation for centuries. Today
they are popular as *résidences secondaires*, or used for wine
storage and mushroom growing. Some are now restaurants or
hotels, and old quarries at Doué-la-Fontaine accommodate a
zoo and a 15th-century amphitheatre. At Rochemenier, near
Saumur, is a well-preserved troglodyte village museum. A
central pit is surrounded by a warren of caves, barns, wine
cellars, dwellings and even a simple underground chapel.

Heralded by chimney pots, the underground hamlet of
nearby La Fosse is inhabited by one family who have made
their eccentric home into a living museum open to visitors.

A typical troglodyte dwelling

Court Life in the Renaissance

FRANÇOIS I'S REIGN, from 1515 to 1547, witnessed the apogee of the French Renaissance, characterized by an intense period of château-building and an interest in humanism and the arts. The itinerant court travelled between the pleasure palaces of Amboise, Blois and Chambord in the Loire. Days were devoted to hunting, falconry, *fêtes champêtres* (country festivals) or *jeu de paume*, a forerunner of tennis. Nights were given over to feasting, balls, poetry and romantic assignations.

Lute and mandolin *music were much in vogue, as were Italian recitals and masquerades. Musicians played at the twice-weekly balls, where the pavane and galliard were danced.*

The antics *of François I's fools, Triboulet and Caillette, amused the court. Yet they were often mistreated: courtiers regularly nailed Caillette's ears to a post for fun, daring him to remain silent.*

RENAISSANCE FEASTS

Dinner usually took place before 7pm to the accompaniment of Italian music. Humanist texts were read aloud and the king's fools amused the courtiers.

Courtiers used their own knives at dinner. Forks were still rare, although their use was spreading from Italy.

A typical royal dinner comprised smoked eel, salted ham, veal pâté, egg and saffron soups, roast game and boiled meats, as well as fish dishes in lemon or gooseberry sauce.

The cost of lavish damask, satin and silk costumes often sent courtiers into debt.

Diane de Poitiers *(1499–1566) became the mistress of the future Henri II when he was 12 years old. Two years later he married Catherine de' Medici, but Diane remained his favourite until his death.*

Artists symbolized love *in different ways during the Renaissance. Winged hearts charmingly perform the function here.*

The Grand Moûtier cloisters

Abbaye de Fontevraud **⓿**

Maine-et-Loire. 🚉 from Saumur.
📞 02 41 51 71 41. **Open** daily. **Closed**
1 Jan, 1 & 11 Nov, 25 Dec. 🅿 ⚟

The Plantagenets

The legendary counts of Anjou were named after the
genêt, the sprig of broom Geoffrey Plantagenet wore in his
cap. He married Matilda, daughter of England's Henry I.
In 1154, when their son Henry – who had married
Eleanor of Aquitaine *(see p47)* – acceded to the
English throne, the Plantagenet dynasty of English kings was
founded, fusing French and English destinies for 200 years.

**Effigies of Henry II, Plantagenet king
of England, and Eleanor of Aquitaine**

THE ABBAYE DE FONTEVRAUD is the largest and most remarkably intact medieval abbey in France. It was founded in the early 12th century by Robert d'Arbrissel, a visionary itinerant preacher who set up a Benedictine community of monks, nuns, nobles, lepers, vagabonds and repentant prostitutes.

The radical founder entrusted the running of the abbey to an abbess, usually from a noble family, and the abbey became a favourite sanctuary for the female aristocracy, including Eleanor of Aquitaine.

From 1804 to 1963 the abbey was used as a prison, since when the buildings have been painstakingly restored by the French government.

Wandering around the abbey buildings, orangery and gardens gives a fascinating insight into monastic life. The focal point was the Romanesque abbey church, consecrated in 1119. It boasts beautifully carved capitals and an immense single nave with four domes, the finest example of a cupola nave in France. Inside are the painted effigies of the Plantagenets dating from the early 13th century: Henry II of England, his redoubtable wife Queen Eleanor of Aquitaine, their Crusading son Richard the Lion-Heart and the sly Isabelle d'Angoulême, who poisoned her husband, King John.

The abbey's nuns lived around the Renaissance **Grand Moûtier cloisters**, forming one of the largest nunneries in France, and the leper colony's nurses were housed in the **St-Lazare priory**, now the atmospheric abbey hotel *(see p555)*. Little remains of the monastic quarters, but the **St-Benoît hospital** survives. Most impressive is the octagonal kitchen with its fireplaces and chimneys in the **Tour Evraud**. Restored by Viollet-le-Duc in the 19th century, it is a rare example of secular Romanesque architecture.

The abbey, now an important arts centre, regularly hosts concerts and exhibitions.

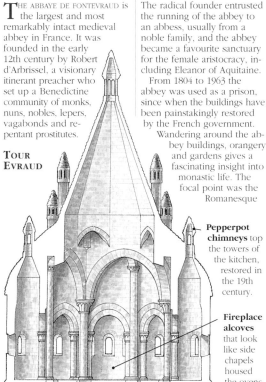

Tour Evraud

Pepperpot chimneys top the towers of the kitchen, restored in the 19th century.

Fireplace alcoves that look like side chapels housed the ovens.

Chinon **⓿**

Indre-et-Loire. 👥 9,000. 🚉 🚌 ℹ 12
rue Voltaire (02 47 93 17 85). 🚌 Thu.

THE CHATEAU DE CHINON is an important shrine in Joan of Arc country and, as such, wheedles francs from all passing pilgrims. It was here in 1429 that the saint first recognized the disguised dauphin (later Charles VII), and persuaded him to give her an army in order to drive the English out of France. Before that, Chinon was the Plantagenet kings' favourite castle, and witnessed the death of Henry II. Although the **château** is now mostly in ruins, the ramparts are an impressive sight from the opposite bank of the Vienne river.

The town's bijou centre is like a medieval film set. **Rue Voltaire**, lined with 15th- and 16th-century houses and once enclosed by the castle walls, represents a cross-section of Chinonais history. At No. 12 is the **Musée Animé du Vin**, where animated figures tell the story of wine-making. **No. 44** is a stone mansion where, in 1199, Richard the

**Chinon's medieval
summer pageant**

Vineyard in the Chinon wine region

Lion-Heart is said to have died. The grandest mansion is the **Hôtel du Gouvernement**, with its double staircase and loggia. More charming is the **Maison Rouge** in the Grand Carroi, studded with a red-brick herringbone pattern.

The 15th-century **Hostellerie Gargantua**, where Rabelais' lawyer father once practised, is now an agreeable inn (see p555). The great Renaissance writer lived nearby in the rue Jean-Jacques Rousseau.

The August medieval market is Chinon's most colourful pageant, when the town is given over to minstrels, strolling players, fire-eaters and jugglers.

🏛 Musée Animé du Vin
12 rue Voltaire. 📞 02 47 93 25 63.
Open Apr–Sep: daily. 🖼

Environs
Some 5 km (3 miles) southwest of Chinon is the rustic manor house of La Devinière, now the **Maison Rabelais**, where the 16th-century writer, priest and humanist scholar was born.

🏛 Maison Rabelais
Seuilly. 📞 02 47 95 91 18. **Open** daily. **Closed** 1 Jan, 25 Dec. 🖼

Château d'Ussé 🄋

Indre-et-Loire. 🚉 Langeais, then taxi. 📞 02 47 95 54 05.
Open mid-Feb–mid-Nov: daily. 🖼

THE FAIRYTALE Château d'Ussé enjoys a bucolic setting overlooking watery meadows and the river Indre. Its romantic white turrets, pointed towers and chimneys inspired Charles Perrault's *Sleeping Beauty*.

Constructed in the 15th century, the castle was gradually transformed into an aristocratic château, which is still privately owned (see p232). However, the sunless and musty interior is rather disappointing and the *Sleeping Beauty* tableaux are clumsily presented.

The château's delightful Renaissance chapel, framed by the oak forest of Chinon, has lost its Aubusson tapestries, but retains a lovely della Robbia terracotta *Virgin*.

Château de Langeais 🄌

Indre-et-Loire. 🚉 Langeais.
📞 02 47 96 72 60. **Open** daily.
Closed 25 Dec. 🖼

COMPARED with neighbouring towns, Langeais is distinctly untouristy and has a welcoming, unpretentious feel. Its château is fiercely feudal, built strictly for defence with a drawbridge, portcullis and no concessions to the Renaissance. It was constructed by Louis XI in just six years, from 1465–9, with hardly an alteration since then. The ruins of an impressive keep, built by Foulques Nerra in AD 994, stand in the small château courtyard.

Unconvincing waxworks represent the marriage of Charles VIII and his child-bride Anne of Brittany in 1491, a ceremony held in the Salle du Mariage. The room is decorated with intricate tiled floors, carved chests and a fine collection of 15th- and 16th-century Flemish and Aubusson tapestries.

FRANÇOIS RABELAIS

Rabelais, born in 1494, was a priest, doctor, diplomat and humanist scholar noted for his wisdom and tolerance. He is best remembered for his many ribald satires: *Pantagruel* and *Gargantua*, stories about a giant father and his son, were set around Chinon where Rabelais grew up.

Infant Pantagruel, depicted by Doré in 1854, was fed on the milk of 4,200 cows.

Château d'Azay-le-Rideau ⓫

Indre-et-Loire. 🚉 Azay-le-Rideau.
📞 02 47 45 42 04. **Open** daily. **Closed**
1 Jan, 1 May, 1 & 11 Nov, 25 Dec. 🖼

BALZAC CALLED Azay-le-Rideau
"a multi-faceted diamond
set in the Indre". It is the most
beguiling and feminine of Loire
châteaux, created in the early
16th century by Philippa Lesbahy, wife of François I's cor-
rupt finance minister. Although
Azay is superficially Gothic
(see pp50–51, 232), the turrets
are purely decorative and the
moats are picturesque pools.
Azay was a pleasure palace,
lived in during fine weather
and deserted in winter. The
illusion is sustained by a complex system of moats and
weirs with Renaissance-style
boats gliding across the lilies.
   The interior is equally delightful, an airy, creaking
mansion smelling faintly of
cedarwood and full of lovingly
re-created domestic detail. The
period furniture, family portraits and exquisite tapestries
confirm the impression of Azay
as a Renaissance museum.
Features include the portable
Spanish cabinets and embroidered bed canopies. The four-
storey grand staircase is
unusual for its time, being
straight as opposed to spiral.
   Wine-tasting opportunities
in the village are a welcome
reminder that vineyards are
all around. Unlike most Loire
villages, Azay is lively at night,
thanks to the popularity of its
poetic son et lumière.

The Château de Villandry's *jardin d'ornament*

Château de Villandry ⓬

Indre-et-Loire. 🚉 Savonnières or
Tours, then taxi. 📞 02 47 50 02 09.
Château open mid-Feb–mid-Nov:
daily; mid-Nov–mid-Feb: guided tours
only. **Gardens open** daily. 🖼

VILLANDRY was the last great
Renaissance château built
in the Loire Valley, a perfect
example of 16th-century
architecture. Its spectacular
gardens were restored to their
Renaissance splendour earlier
this century by Dr Joachim
Carvallo, whose grandson continues his work unstintingly.
   The result is a patchwork of
sculpted shrubs and flowers on
three levels: the kitchen garden
(jardin potager), the ornamental garden (jardin d'ornament)
and, on the highest level, the
water garden (jardin d'eau).
There are signs to explain the
history and meaning behind
each plant: the marrow, for instance, symbolized fertility; the
cabbage, sexual and spiritual
corruption. Plants were also
prized for their medicinal prop-

erties: cabbage helped to cure
hangovers, while pimento
aided digestion. In the *jardin
d'amour*, flowers depict the
many faces of love: passionate,
romantic, tragic and fickle.
While tragic love is represented
by crossed swords, fickleness is
symbolized by yellow blooms.

A chocolatier in Tours

Tours ⓭

Indre-et-Loire. 👥 140,000. 🚄 🚉 🚌
🛈 78 rue Bernard Palissy
(02 47 70 37 37). 🛒 daily.

TOURS IS THE MOST appealing
of the major Loire cities,
thanks to bourgeois prosperity,
an intelligent restoration programme and a lively university population. It is built on
the site of a Roman town, and
became an important centre of
Christianity in the 4th century
under St Martin, bishop of
Tours. In 1461 Louis XI made
Tours the French capital and
the city prospered on arms and
fabrics. However, during Henri
IV's reign the city lost favour
with the monarchy and the
capital left Tours for Paris.
   Bombarded by the Prussians
in 1870, and bombed in
World War II, Tours suffered
extensive damage. By 1960,
the middle classes had abandoned the historic centre and

Château d'Azay-le-Rideau reflected in the river Indre

it became a slum, full of crumbling medieval masonry. Regeneration of the city has succeeded due to the popular policies of Jean Royer, mayor of Tours from 1958 to 1996.

The pedestrianized **place Plumereau** is Tours' most atmospheric quarter, set in the medieval heart of the city and full of cafés, boutiques and galleries. Streets such as rue Briçonnet reveal half-timbered façades, hidden courtyards and crooked towers. A gateway leads to place St-Pierre-le-Puellier, a square with sunken Gallo-Roman remains and a Romanesque church converted into a café. A few streets away in place de Châteauneuf lies the Romanesque **Tour Charlemagne**, all that remains of St Martin's first church. West of here is the highly yuppified artisans' quarter, centred on the rue du Petit St-Martin.

The **Cathédrale St-Gatien**, in the eastern sector of the city, was begun in the early 13th century and completed in the 16th. Its Flamboyant Gothic façade is blackened and crumbling but still truly impressive, as are the medieval stained-glass windows.

Tours has several unusual museums. Considered the

Cathédrale St-Gatien in Tours

finest Renaissance building in Touraine, the **Hôtel Gouin** was a silk merchant's house and is now the archaeological museum, filled with medieval statuary. The **Musée des Beaux Arts**, set in the former episcopal palace, overlooks Classical gardens and a giant cedar of Lebanon. Its star exhibits are *The Resurrection* and *Christ in the Garden of Olives* by Mantegna, but more typical are the Loire landscapes and portraits. The **Historial de Touraine** in the nearby Château Royal is a perfect

introduction to the Loire, with 165 wax figures animating 15 centuries of local history.

Just west of here off rue Colbert is the **Eglise St-Julien**, whose Gothic monastic cells and chapterhouse contain a small wine museum and a crafts museum displaying the traditional work of the guilds.

⋔ Hôtel Gouin
25 rue du Commerce. **[** *02 47 66 22 32.* **Open** *mid-Mar–Sep: daily; Feb–mid-Mar & Oct–Nov: Sat–Thu.*
⋔ Musée des Beaux Arts
18 place François Sicard.
[*02 47 05 68 73.* **Open** *Wed–Mon.* **Closed** *1 Jan, 1 May, 14 Jul, 1 & 11 Nov, 25 Dec.*
⋔ Historial de Touraine
Château Royal, 25 av André Malraux.
[*02 47 61 02 95.* **Open** *daily.*

Backgammon players in Tours' place Plumereau

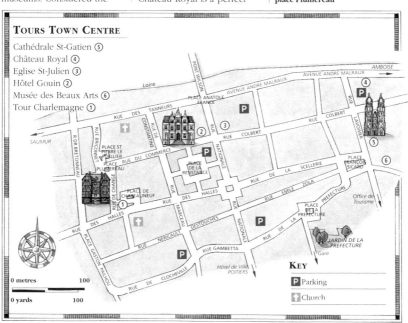

TOURS TOWN CENTRE
Cathédrale St-Gatien ⑤
Château Royal ④
Eglise St-Julien ③
Hôtel Gouin ②
Musée des Beaux Arts ⑥
Tour Charlemagne ①

KEY
P Parking
Church

Château de Chenonceau ⓱

A ROMANTIC PLEASURE PALACE, Chenonceau was created from the Renaissance onwards by a series of aristocratic women. A magnificent avenue bordered by plane trees leads to symmetrical gardens and the serene vision that Flaubert praised as "floating on air and water". The château stretches across the river Cher with a 60-m (197-ft) gallery built over a series of arches, its elegant beauty reflected in the languid waters. The grandeur continues inside with splendidly furnished rooms, airy bedchambers and fine paintings and tapestries.

Turreted Pavilion
This was built between 1513 and 1521 by Catherine Briçonnet and her husband, Thomas Bohier, over the foundations of an old water mill.

Chapelle
The chapel has a vaulted ceiling and pilasters sculpted with acanthus leaves and cockle-shells. The stained glass, destroyed by a bomb in 1944, was replaced in 1953.

Catherine de' Medici's Gardens
Lavish court receptions and transvestite balls were held under Catherine's auspices.

TIMELINE

Catherine de' Medici

1533 Marriage of Catherine de' Medici (1519–89) to Henri II (1519–59). Chenonceau becomes a Loire royal palace

1559 On Henri's death, Catherine forces the disgraced Diane to accept the Château de Chaumont in exchange for Chenonceau

1789 Chenonceau is spared in the French Revolution, thanks to Madame Dupin

1575 Louise de Lorraine (1554–1601) marries Henri III, Catherine's third and favourite son

1547 Henri II offers Chenonceau to Diane de Poitiers, his lifelong mistress

1512 Thomas Bohier acquires medieval Chenonceau. His wife, Catherine Briçonnet, rebuilds it in Renaissance style

1863 Madame Pelouz restores the château t its original stat

1730–99 Madame Dupin, a farmer-general's wife, makes Chenonceau a salon for writers and philosophers

1500	1600	1700	1800

VISITORS' CHECKLIST

Chenonceau. from Tours.
02 47 23 90 07. **Open** 16 Mar–
15 Sep: 9am–7pm daily; 16 Sep–
15 Mar: closing times vary –
phone for details.

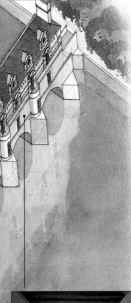

The Creation of Chenonceau

THE WOMEN RESPONSIBLE for Chenonceau each left their mark. Catherine Briçonnet, wife of the first owner, built the turreted pavilion and one of the first straight staircases in France here; Henri II's mistress, Diane de Poitiers, added the formal gardens and arched bridge over the river Cher; Catherine de' Medici transformed the bridge into an Italian-style gallery (having evicted Diane following her husband's death in 1559); Louise de Lorraine, bereaved wife of Henri III, inherited the château in 1590 and painted the ceilings black and white, the colours of royal mourning; Madame Dupin, a cultured 18th-century châtelaine, saved the château from destruction during the Revolution; and Madame Pelouze undertook a complete restoration in 1863.

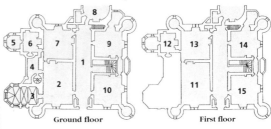

Ground floor   **First floor**

CHÂTEAU GUIDE

The main living area was in the square-shaped turreted pavilion in the middle of the river Cher. Four principal rooms open off the Grande Galerie on the ground floor: the Salle des Gardes and the Chambre de Diane de Poitiers, both hung with 16th-century Flemish tapestries; the Chambre de François I, with a Van Loo painting; and the Salon Louis XIV. On the first floor, reached via the vestibule, are other sumptuous apartments including the Chambre de Catherine de' Medici and the Chambre de Vendôme.

1 Vestibule
2 Salle des Gardes
3 Chapelle
4 Terrasse
5 Librairie de Catherine de' Medici
6 Cabinet Vert
7 Chambre de Diane de Poitiers
8 Grande Galerie
9 Chambre de François I
10 Salon Louis XIV
11 Chambre des Cinq Reines
12 Cabinet des Estampes
13 Chambre de Catherine de' Medici
14 Chambre de Vendôme
15 Chambre de Gabrielle d'Estrée

Grande Galerie
The elegant gallery crowning the bridge is Florentine in style, created by Catherine de' Medici from 1570–76.

1913 The château is bought by the Menier family, the *chocolatiers* who still own it today

1940 Chenonceau chapel is damaged in a bombing raid

Diane de Poitiers

Chambre de Catherine de' Medici

Vouvray ⓮

Indre-et-Loire. 👥 *3,000.*
ℹ️ *Le Moirie (02 47 52 70 48).*
🚌 *Tue & Fri.*

JUST EAST OF TOURS is the village of Vouvray, home of the delicious white wine that Renaissance author Rabelais likened to taffeta. A visit to the **Ecomusée du Pays de Vouvray** wine museum rewards the visitor with a presentation and a film, followed by a wine-tasting. If in Vouvray on a market day, buy a picnic lunch and head for the vineyards.

The star vineyard is **Huet**. In 1829 Sir Walter Scott sang the praises of the estate, toasting the dry white wines, the growers' quaint troglodyte homes hewn out of the rock, and the Gothic church in the vineyards. Little has changed in Vouvray. Huet's methods are still traditional, with wine fermented in oak barrels. Supported by local wine growers, Gaston Huet hit the headlines in 1990 with his protests against the building of tracks for the TGV train over Vouvray vineyards. A French compromise was eventually reached and tunnels were built under the hilly vineyards.

The medieval town of Loches

🏛 **Ecomusée du Pays de Vouvray**
30 rue Victor Herault. 📞 *02 47 52 66 04.* **Open** daily. 🅿️ ♿
🍷 **Huet**
Le Manoir du Haut-Lieu, 11–13 rue de la Croix-Buisée. 📞 *02 47 52 78 87.* **Open** Jul & Aug: Mon–Sat; Sep–Jun: by appt only. **Closed** public hols. 🅿️

Loches ⓯

Indre-et-Loire. 👥 *7,000.* 🚉 🚌
ℹ️ *pl de la Marne (02 47 59 07 98).*
🚌 *Wed & Sat.*

THIS UNSPOILT medieval town is slightly removed from the château trail in the Indre valley. It is a backwater of late Gothic gateways and sculpted façades. Its **Château** dominates the scene and boasts the deepest dungeons in the Loire. The building is associated with Charles VII and his beautiful mistress Agnès Sorel. It is also where Joan of Arc, after her historic victory in Orléans, pleaded with Charles to go to Reims and be crowned. Anne of Brittany's chapel is decorated with ermines (her emblem), and contains a poignant alabaster effigy of Agnès Sorel.

♟ **Château de Loches**
📞 *02 47 59 01 32.* **Open** daily. 🅿️

THE HEROINE OF FRANCE

Joan of Arc is the quintessential French national heroine, a virginal warrior, a woman martyr, a French figurehead. Her divinely led campaign to "drive the English out of France" during the Hundred Years' War has inspired plays, poetry and films from Voltaire to Cecil B de Mille. Responding to heavenly voices, she appeared on the scene as champion of the dauphin, the uncrowned Charles VII. He faced an Anglo-Burgundian alliance which held most of northern France, and had escaped to the royal châteaux on the Loire.

Earliest known drawing of Joan of Arc (1429)

Joan convinced him of her mission, mustered the French troops and in May 1429 led them to victory over the English at Orléans. She then urged the dithering Charles to go to Reims to be crowned. However, in 1430 she was captured and handed over to the English. Accused of witchcraft, she was burnt at the stake in Rouen in 1431 at the age of 19. Her legendary bravery and tragic martyrdom led to her canonization in 1920.

Portrait of Joan of Arc *in the Maison Jeanne d'Arc in Orléans (see p302). She saved the city from the English on 8 May 1429, a date the Orléannais still celebrate annually.*

Montrésor ⑯

Indre-et-Loire. 🕮 *400*. 🛈 *Grande Rue (02 47 92 71 04).*

CLASSED "the most beautiful village in France", Montrésor does not disappoint. It is set on the river Indrois, in the loveliest valley in Touraine. Once a fief of the Cathédrale de Tours, the village became a Polish enclave in the 1840s. In 1849 a Polish nobleman, Count Branicki, bought the 15th-century **Château**, built on the site of one of Foulques Nerra's

Farm building and poppy fields near the village of Montrésor

11th-century fortifications. It has remained in the family ever since, its interior virtually unchanged since Branicki's time.

⛪ **Château de Montrésor**
📞 *02 47 92 60 04.* **Open** *Apr–Oct: daily.* 📷 🅿 🚻

Château de Chenonceau ⑰

See pp288–9.

Amboise ⑱

Indre-et-Loire. 🕮 *12,000.* 🚊 🚌
🛈 *Quai du Général de Gaulle (02 47 57 09 28).* 🅐 *Fri & Sun.*

FEW BUILDINGS are more historically important than the **Château d'Amboise**. Louis XI lived here; Charles VIII was born and died here; François I and later Catherine de' Medici were regular visitors. The château was also the setting for the Amboise Conspiracy of 1560, an ill-fated Huguenot plot against François II. Visitors are shown where the corpses of 1,200 conspirators were hung from iron hooks on the façade of the château.

The **Tour des Minimes**, the château's original entrance, is

Amboise seen from the Loire

famous for its huge spiral ramp up which horsemen could ride to deliver provisions.

Perched on the ramparts is the Gothic **Chapelle St-Hubert**, believed to be Leonardo da Vinci's burial place. Under the patronage of François I, the artist spent the last years of his life in the nearby manor house of **Clos-Lucé**, whose cellars exhibit models of Leonardo's inventions constructed from his mechanical sketches.

⛪ **Château d'Amboise**
📞 *02 47 57 00 98.* **Open** *daily.*
Closed *1 Jan, 25 Dec.* 📷
🏛 **Clos-Lucé**
2 rue de Clos-Lucé. 📞 *02 47 57 62 88.*
Open *daily.* **Closed** *1 Jan, 25 Dec.* 📷

A romantic heroine, Joan of Arc was a popular subject for artists. This painting of her is by François Léon Benouville (1821–59).

Burnt at the stake *– a scene from* St Joan, *Otto Preminger's 1957 epic film, which starred Jean Seberg.*

Château de Chambord ⑲

HENRY JAMES ONCE SAID, "Chambord is truly royal – royal in its great scale, its grand air, and its indifference to common considerations." The Loire's largest residence, brainchild of the extravagant François I, began as a hunting lodge in the Forêt de Boulogne. In 1519 the original building was razed and the creation of Chambord began, to a design probably initiated by Leonardo da Vinci. By 1537 the towers, keep and terraces had been completed by 1,800 men and two master masons. At one point, François suggested diverting the Loire to flow in front of his château, but he settled for redirecting the nearer Closson instead. His son Henry II continued his work, and Louis XIV completed the 440-roomed edifice in 1685.

The Château de Chambord with the river Closson, a tributary of the Loire, in the foreground

The Salamander
François I chose the salamander as his enigmatic emblem. It appears over 700 times throughout the château.

The chapel was begun by François I shortly before his death in 1547. Henri II added the second storey and Louis XIV the roof.

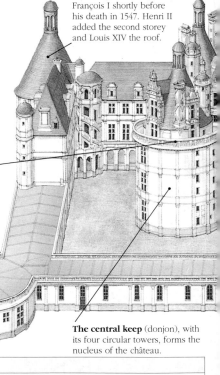

★ **Roof Terraces**
This skyline of delicate cupolas has been likened to a miniature Oriental town. The roof terraces include a forest of elongated chimney pots, miniature spires, shell-shaped domes and richly sculpted gables.

The central keep (donjon), with its four circular towers, forms the nucleus of the château.

STAR FEATURES

★ **Roof Terraces**

★ **Vaulted Guardrooms**

★ **Grand Staircase**

TIMELINE

1519–47 The Count of Blois' hunting lodge demolished by François I and the château created		**1725–33** Inhabited by Stanislas Leczinski, exiled king of Poland who was made duke of Lorraine		
	1547–59 Henri II adds the west wing and second storey of the chapel	**1748** The Maréchal de Saxe acquires Chambord. On his death two years later, the château falls into decline		

1500	1600	1700	1800	1900
	1547 On François' death, the court leaves Chambord for Chenonceau and Blois	**1669–85** Louis XIV completes the building	**1840** Chambord declared a *Monument Historique*	
		1670 Molière's *Le Bourgeois Gentilhomme* staged at Chambord	**1970s** Giscard d'Estaing restores and refurnishes Chambord, and re-digs the moats	

Molière

★ Vaulted Guardrooms
Arranged in the form of a Greek cross around the Grand Staircase, the vaulted guard-rooms were once the setting for royal balls and plays. Their ceilings are decorated with François I's initials and salamander motif.

VISITORS' CHECKLIST
from Blois. 02 54 50 40 00. **Open** 9:30am–6:15pm daily (Jul Aug until 7:15pm; Oct–Mar: 9:30am–5:15pm). Last adm: 30 min before closing. **Closed** 1 Jan, 1 May, 25 Dec.

The lantern tower is 32 m (105 ft) high. Surmounting the terrace, it is supported by arched buttresses and crowned by a fleurs-de-lys.

François I's Bedchamber is where the king, hurt by a failed romance, scratched a message on a pane of glass: "*Souvent femme varie, bien fol est qui s'y fie.*" (Every woman is fickle, he who trusts one is a fool.)

Cabinet de François I
The king's barrel-vaulted study (cabinet) in the outer north tower was turned into an oratory in the 18th century by Queen Catherine Opalinska, wife of Stanislas Leczinski (Louis XV's father-in-law).

★ Grand Staircase
This innovative double-helix staircase was supposedly designed by Leonardo da Vinci. It ensures that the person going up and the person going down cannot meet.

Louis XIV's Bedchamber
Louis XIV's bedchamber lies within the Sun King's state apartments, the grandest quarters in the château.

Blois' Cathédrale St-Louis and Hôtel de Ville seen from across the Loire

Blois ⑳

Loir-et-Cher. 👥 *50,000.* 🚉 🚌
ℹ️ *Pavillon Anne de Bretagne, 3 av
Jean Laigret (02 54 74 06 49).*
🛒 *Tue, Thu, Sat & Sun.*

ONCE A FIEF of the counts of
Blois, the town rose to
prominence as a royal domain
in the 15th century, retaining
its historic façades and refined
atmosphere to this day. Architectural interest abounds in
Vieux Blois, the hilly, partially
pedestrianized quarter enclosed
by the château, cathedral and
river. A well-signposted walking tour, the *route royale*, is
a gentle introduction to the
noble mansions and romantic
courtyards that grace the
Loire's most beguiling town.

Set back from the north
bank of the river, the **Château
de Blois** was the principal
royal residence until Henri IV
moved the court to Paris in
1598 – Louis XIV's creation
of Versailles (*see pp164–7*)
was to mark the final eclipse
of Blois. The château's four
contrasting wings make a har-

monious whole. The Salle des
Etats, the only part of the
building surviving from the
13th century, housed the
council and court, and is the
best-preserved Gothic hall in
the Loire. The adjoining late
15th-century Louis XII wing
infuses Gothic design with
Renaissance spirit, sealed with
the king's porcupine symbol
and motto: "From near and
afar, I can defend myself."

The 16th-century François I
wing is a masterpiece of the
French Renaissance containing
a monumental spiral staircase
in an octagonal tower. By
contrast, the 17th-century
Gaston d'Orléans wing is a
model of Classical sobriety.

Blois is authentically furnished and hung with
paintings portraying its
troubled past. These
include a graphic
portrayal of the
murder of the Duc
de Guise in 1588.
Suspected of head-
ing a Catholic plot
against Henri III,
he was stabbed to

King Louis XII's porcupine symbol

death by guards in the king's
chamber. The most intriguing
room is Catherine de' Medici's
study, its walls containing 237
secret cabinets, full of jewels,
state papers and potions.

François I Staircase

*Built between 1515 and
1524, this octagonal
staircase is a master-
piece of the
early French
Renaissance.*

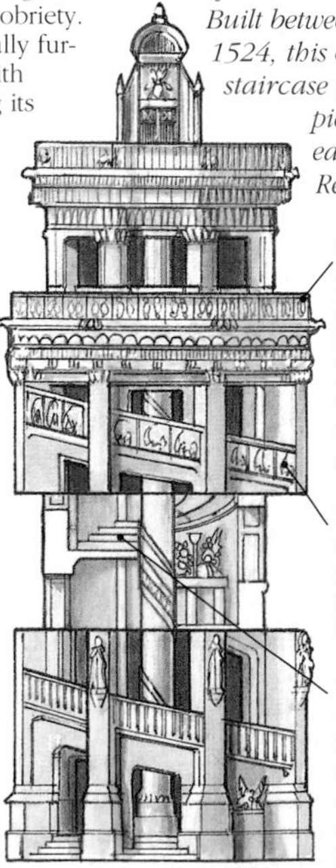

The gallery
provided an
ideal setting
for viewing
jousts and re-
ceptions held
in the inner
courtyard.

**François I's
salamander
motif** adorns
the openwork
balustrades.

The staircase
within the
tower slopes
appreciably
more steeply
than the
balustrades.

Louis XII wing of the Château de Blois

Dominating the eastern sector of the city, the **Cathédrale St-Louis** is a 17th-century reconstruction of a Gothic church that was almost completely destroyed by a hurricane in 1678. Behind the cathedral the former bishop's palace, built in 1725, has been used as the **Hôtel de Ville** (town hall) since 1940. The surrounding terraced gardens have lovely views over the city and river.

Place Louis-XII, the marketplace until the 18th century, is overlooked by splendid 17th-century façades, balconies and half-timbered houses. The finest of them is the **Maison des Acrobates**, carved with characters from medieval farces including acrobats and jugglers.

Rue Pierre de Blois, a quaint alley straddled by a Gothic passageway, winds downhill to the medieval Jewish ghetto. The dilapidated rue des Juifs boasts several distinguished *hôtels particuliers* (mansions), including the galleried **Hôtel de Condé**, with its Renaissance archway and courtyard. The most striking courtyard belongs to **Hôtel Belot**, a 16th-century mansion adorned with barrel-vaulted loggias and an external spiral staircase. The alley leads down to rue du Puits-Châtel, rich in Renaissance mansions.

Place Vauvert is the most charming square in Vieux Blois, bordered by restaurants and the galleried **Hôtel Sardini**, once owned by Renaissance bankers.

♣ Château de Blois
📞 02 54 78 06 62. **Open** daily. **Closed** 1 Jan, 25 Dec. 🖼

Covered Gothic passageway in rue Pierre de Blois

The nave of the abbey church of Notre-Dame in Beaugency

Beaugency 🅴

Loiret. 🏛 7,000. 🚊 🚌 🛈 3 pl de Docteur-Hyvernaud (02 38 44 54 42). 🚌 Sat.

BEAUGENCY has long been the eastern gateway to the Loire. This compact medieval town makes a peaceful base for exploring the Orléanais region. Exceptionally for the Loire, it is possible to walk along the river banks and stone *levées*. At quai de l'Abbaye there is a good view of the 14th-century bridge which, until modern times, was the only crossing point between Blois and Orléans. An obvious target for enemy attack, it was captured four times by the English during the Hundred Years' War before being re-taken by Joan of Arc in 1429.

The centre of town is dominated by a ruined 11th-century castle keep. It stands on **place St-Firmin**, along with a 16th-century belltower (the church was destroyed in the Revolution) and an equestrian statue of Joan of Arc. The stone square is bordered by period houses, including the **Château Dunois**, a Renaissance manor house built on the site of the feudal castle. It houses an appealing regional museum featuring an array of costumes, furniture and antique toys.

Facing the Château Dunois is **Notre-Dame**, a Romanesque abbey church that witnessed the annulment of the marriage between Eleanor of Aquitaine and Louis VII in 1152, leaving Eleanor free to marry the future Henry II of England.

Nearby is the medieval clocktower in rue des Trois Marchands and the Gothic **Hôtel de Ville**, with its Renaissance façade adorned with the town arms. Equally charming are the streams in the nearby mill district, linking rue du Pont with rue du Rü.

♣ Château Dunois (Musée Régional de l'Orléanais)
Place Dunois. 📞 02 38 44 55 23. **Open** Wed–Mon. **Closed** 1 Jan, 1 May, 25 Dec. 🖼

Châteaux Tour of the Sologne

THE MYSTERIOUS SOLOGNE is a secretive landscape of woods and marshes edged by vineyards. Wine-lovers can indulge in tastings of Cheverny wine, accompanied by a dinner of succulent wild game from the region's forests, popular hunting grounds for centuries. The Sologne is a hunter's paradise and devotees of the sport can see the hounds used today, as well as hunting trophies of the past.

This ambling rural route takes in some of the Loire's most varied châteaux. The five on this tour – for which a couple of days is required – represent a delightful encapsulation of regional architecture. All styles are here, from feudal might to Renaissance grace and Classical elegance. Several are inhabited but can still be visited.

Château de Beauregard ②
Beauregard was built around 1520 as a hunting lodge for François I. It contains a gallery with 363 portraits of royalty.

Château de Chaumont ①
Chaumont is a feudal castle with Renaissance embellishments and lofty views over the river Loire (see p232).

```
0 kilometres    5
0 miles         5
```

KEY

▬ Tour route

═══ Other roads

Pontlevoy

Vendôme ㉒

Loir-et-Cher. 🚶 18,000. 🚉 🚌
🛈 47 rue Poterie (02 54 77 05 07).
🛒 Fri & Sun.

ONCE AN IMPORTANT STOP for pilgrims en route to Compostela in Spain, Vendôme is now popular with modern pilgrims, thanks to the TGV rail service. Though a desirable address with Parisian commuters, the town still manages to retain its provincial charm. Vendôme's old stone buildings are encircled by the river Loir, its lush gardens and chic restaurants reflected in the water.

The town's greatest monument is the abbey church of **La Trinité**, founded in 1034. Its Romanesque belltower (all that remains of the original structure) is overshadowed by the church portal, a masterpiece of Flamboyant Gothic tracery. The interior is embellished with Romanesque capitals and 14th-century choir stalls.

Commanding a rocky spur high above the Loir is the ruined **château**, built by the counts of Vendôme in the 13th and 14th centuries. Below is the watery **Parc Ronsard** with a medieval *lavoir*, a two-storey washing- and drying-room. Leading downriver are delightful walks past willows, ruined towers, weirs and mills.

Vendôme's native son Rochambeau, hero of the American Revolution

The Loir ㉓

Loir-et-Cher. ✈ Tours. 🚉 🚌
Vendôme. 🛈 Montoire-sur-Loir (02 54 85 00 29).

COMPARED WITH the royal river Loire, the tranquil Loir to the north has undeniable charm. The stretch between Vendôme and Trôo is the most rewarding, offering troglodyte caves (see p282), walking trails, wine-tasting, fishing and boat trips.

Les Roches-l'Evêque is a fortified village with cave dwellings carved into the cliffs. Just downstream is **Lavardin**, with its Romanesque church, half-timbered houses, Gothic bridge and a château ringed by ramparts. In **Montoire-sur-Loir**, the Chapelle St-Gilles boasts Romanesque frescoes in a former leper colony. **Trôo**, the next major village, is known for its Romanesque Eglise de St-Martin and a labyrinth of troglodyte dwellings.

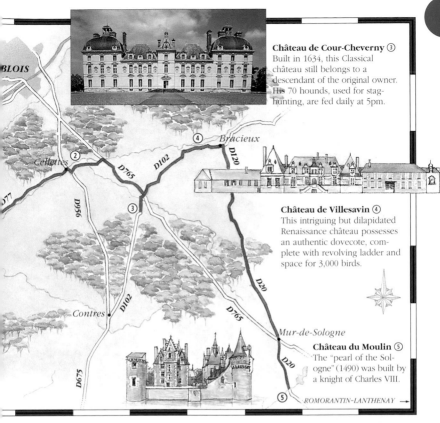

Château de Cour-Cheverny ③
Built in 1634, this Classical
château still belongs to a
descendant of the original owner.
His 70 hounds, used for stag-
hunting, are fed daily at 5pm.

BLOIS

Cellettes ②

Bracieux ④

Château de Villesavin ④
This intriguing but dilapidated
Renaissance château possesses
an authentic dovecote, complete with revolving ladder and
space for 3,000 birds.

Contres

Mur-de-Sologne

Château du Moulin ⑤
The "pearl of the Sol-
ogne" (1490) was built by
a knight of Charles VIII.

⑤ *ROMORANTIN-LANTHENAY →*

St-Jacques-des-Guérets, facing
the village of Trôo, has a frescoed Romanesque chapel, as
does **Poncé-sur-le-Loir**, further
downstream. On the slopes are
vineyards producing Jasnières
and Côteaux du Vendômois.
Wine-tastings enliven sleepy
Poncé and **La Chartre-sur-le-
Loir**. The cliffs on the opposite
bank are studded with caves,
commonly used as wine cellars.

Northwards, the **Forêt de
Bercé** abounds with paths and
streams, while to the west the
small town of **Le Lude** sits on
the south bank of the Loir, its
romantic château combining
fountains and fireworks in a
magnificent *son et lumière*.

Some 20 km (12 miles)
west of Le Lude lies the town
of **La Flèche**, whose main
attraction is the Prytanée
National Militaire, originally a
Jesuit college founded by
Henri IV in 1604. Philosopher
René Descartes was one of
the college's earliest and most
illustrious pupils.

Chartres ㉔

Eure-et-Loir. 🚶 *42,000.* 🚉 🚌
🛈 *pl de la Cathédrale (02 37 21 50
00).* 🛍 *Sat.*

CHARTRES MAY have the greatest Gothic cathedral in
Europe *(see pp298–301)*, but
the town's churches should not
be ignored. The Benedictine
abbey church of **St-Pierre** has
lovely medieval stained-glass
windows, while **St-Aignan**
abuts 9th-century ramparts. By
the river is the Romanesque
Eglise de St-André, a deconsecrated church used for art
exhibitions and jazz concerts.
The **Musée des Beaux Arts**,
beside the cathedral in the
former episcopal palace,
offers a fine collection of
tapestries, Fragonard paintings
and temporary exhibitions.

As one of the first urban
conservation sites in France,
Chartres is a success story.
Quirky half-timbered houses
abound along such cobbled

**One of the many washhouses
along the river Eure**

streets as the rue des Ecuyers.
Steep staircases known as
tertres lead down to the river
Eure providing views of mills,
medieval tanneries, humpback
stone bridges, washhouses
and the cathedral.

A major new on-site archaeological museum is being built
by architect Richard Rogers to
house ruins from the Gallo-
Roman city, excavated in the
shadow of the cathedral.

🏛 **Musée des Beaux Arts**
29 cloître Notre-Dame. 📞 *02 37 36 41
39.* **Open** *Wed–Mon.* **Closed** *1 Jan, 1
& 8 May, 1 & 11 Nov, 25 Dec.* 📷

Chartres Cathedral

Aᶜᶜᴼᴿᴰᴵᴺᴳ ᵀᴼ ᴬᴿᵀ ᴴᴵˢᵀᴼᴿᴵᴬᴺ Emile Male, "Chartres is the mind of the Middle Ages manifest." Begun in 1020, the Romanesque cathedral was destroyed by fire in 1194. Only the north and south towers, south steeple, west portal and crypt remained; the sacred *Veil of the Virgin* relic was the sole treasure to survive. Peasant and lord alike helped to rebuild the church in just 25 years. Few alterations were made after 1250 and, fortunately, Chartres was unscathed by the Wars of Religion and the French Revolution. The result is a Gothic cathedral with a true "Bible in stone" reputation.

Part of the Vendôme Window

Elongated Statues

These statues on the Royal Portal represent Old Testament figures.

The taller of the two spires dates from the start of the 16th century. Flamboyant Gothic in style, it contrasts sharply with the solemnity of its Romanesque counterpart.

STAR FEATURES

★ **Stained-Glass Windows**

★ **South Porch**

★ **Royal Portal**

Gothic Nave
As wide as the Romanesque crypt below it, the nave reaches a lofty height of 37 m (121 ft).

★ Royal Portal
The central tympanum of the Royal Portal (1145–55) shows Christ in Majesty.

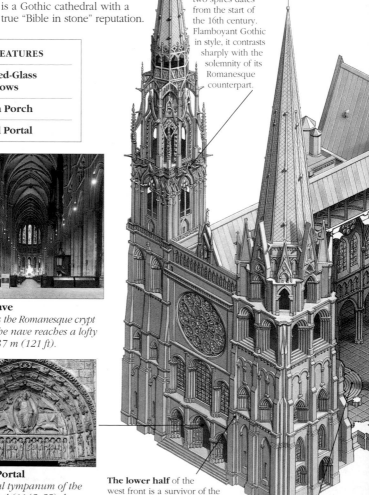

The lower half of the west front is a survivor of the original Romanesque church, the portal dating from the mid-12th century.

Labyrinth

THE LABYRINTH

The 13th-century labyrinth, inlaid in the nave floor, was a feature of most medieval cathedrals. As a penance, pilgrims used to follow the tortuous route on their knees, echoing the Way of the Cross. The journey of 262 m (851 ft), around 11 bands of broken concentric circles, took at least one hour to complete.

VISITORS' CHECKLIST

Pl de la Cathédrale. 02 37 21 75 02. **Open** 7:30am–7:15pm Mon–Sat; 8:30am Sun & public hols. 11:45am & 6pm Mon–Sat; 9:30am, 11am, 6pm Sun. in English: noon & 2:45pm; French: 10:30am & 3pm.

Apsidal Chapel
This chapel houses the oldest cathedral treasure, the Veil of the Virgin relic, which miraculously survived the fire of 1194. More artifacts can be found in the St Piat Chapel.

Vaulted Ceiling
A network of ribs supports the vaulted ceiling.

★ **Stained-Glass Windows**
The windows cover a surface area of over 3,000 sq m (32,300 sq ft).

★ **South Porch**
Sculpture on the South Porch (1197–1209) reflects New Testament teaching.

The Crypt
This is the largest crypt in France, most of it dating from the early 11th century. It comprises two parallel galleries, a series of chapels and the 9th-century St Lubin's vault.

The Stained Glass of Chartres

DONATED BY royalty, aristocracy and the merchant brotherhoods between 1210 and 1240, this glorious collection of stained glass is world-renowned. Over 150 windows illustrate biblical stories and daily life in the 13th century. During both World Wars the windows were dismantled piece by piece and removed for safety. There is an on-going programme, begun in the 1970s, to restore the windows in the cathedral.

Stained glass above the apse

Redemption Window

Six scenes illustrate Christ's Passion *and death on the* Cross (c.1210).

★ Tree of Jesse

This 12th-century stained glass shows Christ's genealogy. The tree rises up from Jesse, father of David, at the bottom, to Christ enthroned at the top.

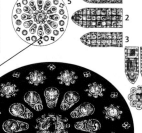

★ West Rose Window

This window (1215), with Christ seated in the centre, shows the Last Judgment.

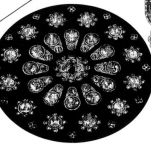

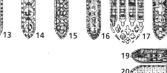

KEY

1 Tree of Jesse	**12** Noah
2 Incarnation	**13** St John the Evangelist
3 Passion and Resurrection	**14** Mary Magdalene
4 North Rose Window	**15** Good Samaritan and Adam and Eve
5 West Rose Window	**16** Assumption
6 South Rose Window	**17** Vendôme Chapel Windows
7 Redemption Window	**18** Miracles of Mary
8 St Nicholas	**19** St Apollinaris
9 Joseph	**20** Modern Window
10 St Eustache	**21** St Fulbert
11 St Lubin	

22 St Anthony and St Paul	**33** St Theodore and St Vincent
23 Blue Virgin	**34** St Stephen
24 Life of the Virgin	**35** St Cheron
25 Zodiac Window	**36** St Thomas
26 St Martin	**37** Peace Window
27 St Thomas à Becket	**38** Modern Window
28 St Margaret and St Catherine	**39** Prodigal Son
29 St Nicholas	**40** Ezekiel and David
30 St Remy	**41** Aaron
31 St James the Greater	**42** Virgin and Child
32 Charlemagne	**43** Isaiah and Moses
	44 Daniel and Jeremiah

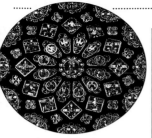

North Rose Window
This depicts the Glorification of the Virgin, *surrounded by the kings of Judah and the prophets (c.1230).*

GUIDE TO READING THE WINDOWS

Each window is divided into panels, usually read from left to right, bottom to top (earth to heaven). The number of figures or abstract shapes used is thought to be symbolic: three stands for the Church, while the number four symbolizes the material world or the four elements.

Mary and Child in the sacred mandorla (c.1150)

Two angels doing homage before the celestial throne

Christ's triumphal entry into Jerusalem on Palm Sunday

Upper panels of the Incarnation Window

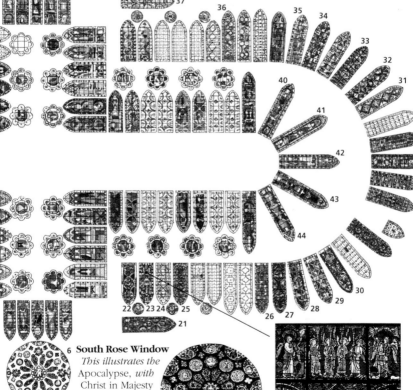

South Rose Window
This illustrates the Apocalypse, *with* Christ in Majesty *(c.1225).*

STAR WINDOWS

★ West Rose Window

★ Tree of Jesse

★ Blue Virgin Window

★ **Blue Virgin Window**
The window's bottom panel depicts the conversion of water into wine by Christ at The Marriage at Cana.

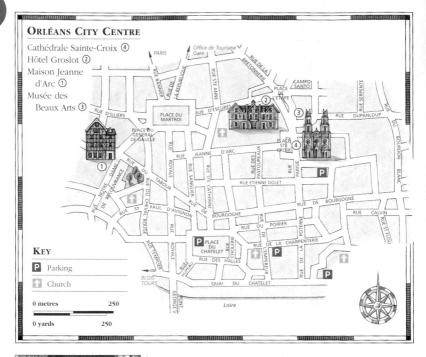

ORLÉANS CITY CENTRE

Cathédrale Sainte-Croix ④
Hôtel Groslot ②
Maison Jeanne
    d'Arc ①
Musée des
    Beaux Arts ③

KEY

P Parking

✝ Church

0 metres   250

0 yards   250

Orléans' Cathédrale Sainte-Croix

Orléans ㉕

Loiret. 🏛 *150,000.* ✈ 🚉 🚌
ℹ *place Albert 1er (02 38 24 05 05).*
🚌 *Tue–Sun.*

ORLÉANS has a royal and
republican tradition yet
feels curiously blank, despite its
Renaissance façades. However,
the city is not as soulless as it
seems, especially in its attach-
ment to Joan of Arc. It was
here that the Maid of Orléans
saved France from the English
in 1429 *(see p290)*. Since her

martyrdom at Rouen in 1431,
Joan remains a presence in
Orléans. Every 29 April and 7
and 8 May her liberation of the
city is re-enacted in a pageant
and a blessing in the cathedral.

Orléans' historic centre was
badly damaged in World War
II, but much has been reconstructed, and a faded grandeur
lingers in Vieil Orléans, the
quarter bounded by the cathedral, the river Loire and the
place du Martroi. The latter,
a Classical but windswept
square, boasts lively bars and
an equestrian statue of the
city's heroine. Nearby, the
half-timbered **Maison Jeanne
d'Arc** was rebuilt from period
dwellings in 1965 on the site
where Joan lodged in 1429.
Inside are audiovisual re-
creations of her life.

From place du Martroi, the
rue d'Escures leads past
Renaissance mansions to the
cathedral. **Hôtel Groslot** is the
grandest, a 16th-century red-
brick mansion where kings
Charles IX, Henri III and Henri
IV all stayed. The 17-year-old
François II died here in 1560
after attending a meeting of
the Estates General with his
child-bride, Mary, later Queen

of Scots. The building served
as Orléans' town hall from
1790 to 1982. Its sumptuously
decorated interior contains
Joan memorabilia and some
fine Renaissance paintings.

Virtually opposite the Hôtel
Groslot and alongside the new
town hall is the **Musée des
Beaux Arts**, displaying French
works from the 15th to the
20th century. Foreign painters
including Tintoretto, Correggio,
Van Ruysdael and Velázquez
are also represented.

The **Cathédrale Sainte-
Croix**, just to the south of the
museum, is an imposing
edifice that was begun in the
late 13th century, destroyed by
the Huguenots (Protestants) in
1568, and then rebuilt in supposedly Gothic style between
the 17th and 19th centuries.

🏨 **Hôtel Groslot**
Pl de l'Etape. 【 *02 38 79 22 30.* **Open**
daily. **Closed** sporadically & 8 May.
🏛 **Musée des Beaux Arts**
place Sainte-Croix. 【 *02 38 53 39
22.* **Open** Wed–Mon. **Closed** 1 Jan,
May, 8 May, 1 Nov, 25 Dec. 🈲 ♿
🏛 **Maison Jeanne d'Arc**
3 place du Général de Gaulle. 【 *02 38
52 99 89.* **Open** Tue–Sun. **Closed** 1 Jan,
1 May, 25 Dec; Nov–May: Sun am. 🈲

Joan of Arc stained-glass window in Orléans' Cathédrale Sainte-Croix

St-Benoît-sur-Loire 26

Loiret. 🏠 2,000. 🚉 ℹ️ *La Mairie (02 38 35 79 00).*

SITUATED ALONG the river Loire between Orléans and Gien, St-Benoît-sur-Loire boasts one of the finest Romanesque abbey churches in France, constructed between 1067 and 1108. It is all that survives of an important monastery founded in AD 650 and named after St Benedict, patron saint of Europe. His relics were transported from Italy at the end of the 7th century.

The church's belfry porch is graced with carved capitals depicting biblical scenes. The nave is tall and light, and the choir floor is an amazing patchwork of marble. Daily services with Gregorian chant are open to the public.

Bourges 27

Cher. 🏠 76,000. ✈ 🚉 🚌
ℹ️ *21 rue Victor Hugo (02 48 24 75 33).* 🚌 *Thu–Sun.*

THIS GALLO-ROMAN city retains its original walls but is best known as the city of Jacques Coeur, financier and foreign minister to Charles VII. The greatest merchant of the Middle Ages and a self-made man *par excellence*, it was in his capacity as an arms dealer that he established a tradition the city maintains to this day as the centre of France's armaments industry.

Built over part of the walls, the **Palais Jacques Coeur** is a Gothic gem and a lasting memorial to its first master. It was finished in 1453, and incorporates Coeur's two emblems, scallop shells and hearts, as well as his punning family motto: *"A vaillan coeur, rien impossible"* – to the valiant heart, nothing is impossible. The obligatory tour reveals a barrel-vaulted gallery, a painted chapel and a chamber that housed Turkish baths.

Bourges also flourishes as a university town and cultural mecca, renowned for its spring festival of music and dance.

Rue Bourbonnoux leads to **St-Etienne**, the widest Gothic cathedral in France and the one most similar to Paris's Notre-Dame. The west façade has five sculpted portals, the central one depicting an

Statue of Jacques Coeur

enthralling *Last Judgment*. In the choir are vivid 13th-century stained-glass windows presented by the guilds. The crypt holds the marble tomb of the 14th-century Duc de Berry, best known for commissioning the illuminated manuscript the *Très Riches Heures (see pp194–5)*. From the top of the north tower stretch views of the beautifully restored medieval quarter and the marshes beyond. Beside the cathedral is a magnificent tithe barn and the remains of the Gallo-Roman ramparts.

Stained-glass window in the Cathédrale St-Etienne

The **Jardin des Prés Fichaux**, set along the river Yèvre, contains pools, parterres and an open-air theatre. On the northern edge of town lie the **Marais de Bourges**, some of the loveliest water meadows in France, best explored by flat-bottomed boat.

⌂ Palais Jacques Coeur
Rue Jacques Coeur. ☎ 02 48 24 06 87. **Open** *daily.* **Closed** *1 Jan, 1 May, 1 & 11 Nov, 25 Dec.* 🎟️ 📷

Environs
About 35 km (22 miles) south of Bourges in the Berry region is the **Abbaye de Noirlac**. Founded in 1136, it is one of the best-preserved Cistercian abbeys in France.

Statue in the Jardin des Prés Fichaux

CENTRAL FRANCE
AND THE ALPS

Introducing Central France and the Alps

THE GEOLOGICAL CONTRASTS of this region reflect its enormous variety, from the industrial and gastronomic metropolis of Lyon to the largely agricultural landscape of Burgundy. The mountains of the Massif Central and the Alps attract visitors for winter sports, superb walking and other outdoor activities. The major sights of this richly rewarding area, both natural and architectural, are shown here.

Basilique Ste-Madeleine, *the famous pilgrimage church crowning the hill-top village of Vézelay, is a masterpiece of Burgundian Romanesque. It is renowned for its vividly decorated tympanum and capitals* (see pp326–7).

The Abbaye de Ste-Foy *in the village of Conques* (see pp356–7) *is one of the great pilgrimage churches of France, with a fabulous treasury of medieval and Renaissance gold reliquaries.*

THE MASSIF CENTRAL
(See pp342–61)

Abbaye de Ste-Foy, Conques

The Gorges du Tarn *have some of France's most spectacular natural scenery. The road which follows the plunging course of the river Tarn gives dramatic viewpoints along the canyon and across the limestone Causses* (see pp360–61).

The Abbaye de Fontenay, founded by Saint Bernard in the early 12th century, is the oldest Cistercian monastery in France (see pp322–3). This well-preserved Romanesque abbey is a perfect testimony to the severe ideal of the Cistercian life.

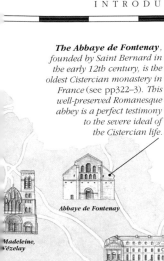

Abbaye de Fontenay

Madeleine, Vézelay

Palais des Ducs, Dijon

Théâtre Romain, Autun

BURGUNDY AND FRANCHE-COMTE
(See pp316–41)

Brou Abbey Church, Bourg-en-Bresse

Mont Blanc

Temple d'Auguste et Livie, Vienne

THE RHONE VALLEY AND FRENCH ALPS
(See pp362–81)

Palais Idéal du Facteur Cheval, Hauterives

Le Puy

Gorges du Tarn

| 0 kilometres | 50 |
| 0 miles | 50 |

Regional Food: Central France

R ENOWNED FOR ITS gastronomic tradition, Lyon is the place to savour Lyonnais and Burgundian food at its best – from sophisticated three-star cuisine to the more robust, homely fare of the *"mères"*, the women cooks of Lyon. This eminent culinary flair is complemented by the wealth of fine local produce: the famed chicken from Bresse; prime lean beef from Charolais; ham from the Morvan hills; wild fowl and frogs from the marshes of the Dombes; fish from the Saône and the Rhône; and snails known as the "oysters of Burgundy". Franche-Comté and the Jura contribute to the regional repertoire with smoked sausages, farmhouse cheeses, walnut oil and fish from glacier-fed lakes. In the Auvergne, regional fare features salted hams, pork, cheeses, potatoes, cabbage and lentils.

Oeufs en meurette *is a famous Burgundian dish of eggs poached in a red wine sauce with onions, mushrooms and bacon.*

Pain d'epices

Dijon mustard owes *its distinctive flavour to the combination of high-quality mustard seeds, local wine, and* verjus *(the fermented juice of unripe grapes). A staple condiment in French households, the smooth and coarse-grained varieties are also used in cooking.*

Coarse-grained Dijon mustard

Smooth Dijon mustard

Rosette de Lyon *is the most famous of Lyon sausages. It is made of meat from leg of pork and served in chunky slices.*

Bacon

Mushrooms

Beef

Wine sauce

Boeuf bourguignon, *the famous classic stew, is more refined than many other French stews. Burgundians use cuts of beef from Charolais cattle for preference. The marinated meat is cooked slowly in Burgundy or Beaujolais wine until tender. Cubes of bacon, baby onions and mushrooms are then added.*

Escargots à la Bourguignonne *are snails served with parsley and garlic butter. Small tongs are used to pluck the snails out of the shells.*

Falette *(stuffed breast of veal) is a speciality from the Auvergne. It can be served hot with braised cabbage, or cold with a salad.*

Minute steak Dijonnaise *is steak served in a cream and mustard sauce. Veal, rabbit and pork are also served in this way.*

Bresse chicken, *the appellation contrôlée chicken, is delicious served with a creamy sauce and wild morels.*

Andouillettes à la Lyonnaise *are tripe sausages stuffed with veal. Served with fried onions, they are typically Lyonnaise.*

Salt pork with lentils, *a speciality of the Auvergne, is salt-cured pork poached in wine with tiny green Puy lentils.*

Walnut and pear pie *is a double-crusted pie made with ground walnut pastry and filled with sliced pears.*

***Cherry flan* or** *clafoutis is made with dark cherries covered in a batter-like dough and laced with kirsch, a cherry liqueur.*

CHEESES

Central France produces the richest selection of cheeses in France. These range from soft, tangy, brandy-soaked Epoisses from Burgundy and the Swiss-type cheeses of the Alps, used in *fondue*, to cheddar-like Cantal and blue-veined cheeses such as Roquefort.

Burgundy cheeses

Epoisses   Pipo Crem'   Bleu de Bresse

Alpine cheeses

Tomme au raisin   Raclette   Emmenthal Français   Vacherin

Massif Central cheeses

St-Nectaire   Roquefort   Fourme d'Ambert   Cantal

France's Wine Regions: Burgundy

Grape-picker's basket

BURGUNDY and its fine wines have inspired awe for centuries. The fame of the region's wines spread throughout Europe in the 14th century, under the Valois Dukes of Burgundy. After the French Revolution, Napoleonic laws of equal inheritance split vineyards into tiny fractions, resulting in a bewildering number of *appellations*. Even today, the classification system remains dauntingly complex. But despite its impenetrable image, this is unmissable territory for the "serious" wine lover, with its rich vinous history and tradition and dazzling *grands crus*.

LOCATOR MAP

▨ *Burgundy wine region*

Clos de Vougeot on the Côte de Nuits

PRINCIPAL WINE AREAS

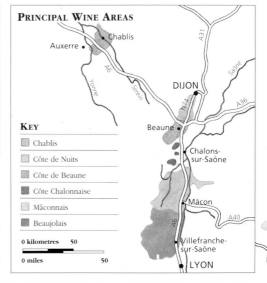

Chablis
Auxerre •

DIJON

Beaune •

Chalons-sur-Saône

Mâcon

Villefranche-sur-Saône

LYON

KEY

▨ Chablis
▨ Côte de Nuits
▨ Côte de Beaune
▨ Côte Chalonnaise
▨ Mâconnais
▨ Beaujolais

0 kilometres   50
0 miles   50

WINE REGIONS

Between Chablis in the north and the Côte Chalonnaise and Mâconnais in the south is the Côte d'Or, incorporating Côte de Nuits and Côte de Beaune. The Beaujolais region *(see pp366–7)* lies below Mâcon.

KEY FACTS ABOUT BURGUNDY

Location and Climate
The continental climate (bleak winters and hot summers) can be very variable, making vintages a crucial quality factor. The best vineyards have chalky soil and face south or east.

Grape Varieties
Burgundy is at least relatively simple in its grape varieties. Red Burgundy is made from **Pinot Noir**, with its sweet flavours of raspberries, cherries and strawberries, while the **Gamay** makes red Mâcon and Beaujolais. **Chardonnay** is the principal white variety for Chablis and white Burgundy, though small amounts of **Aligoté** and **Pinot Blanc** are grown and the **Sauvignon** is a speciality of St Bris.

Good Producers
White Burgundy: Jean-Marie Raveneau, René Dauvissat, La Chablisienne, Comtes Lafon, Guy Roulot, Etienne Sauzet, Pierre Morey, Louis Carillon, Jean-Marc Boillot, André Ramonet, Hubert Lamy, Jean-Marie Guffens-Heynen, Olivier Merlin, Louis Latour, Louis Jadot, Olivier Leflaive.
Red Burgundy: Denis Bachelet, Daniel Rion, Domaine Dujac, Armand Rousseau, Joseph Roty, De Montille, Domaine de la Pousse d'Or, Domaine de l'Arlot, Jean-Jacques Confuron, Robert Chevillon, Georges Roumier, Leroy, Drouhin.

Good Vintages
(Reds) 1996, 1993, 1990, 1988.
(Whites) 1996, 1995, 1993, 1992.

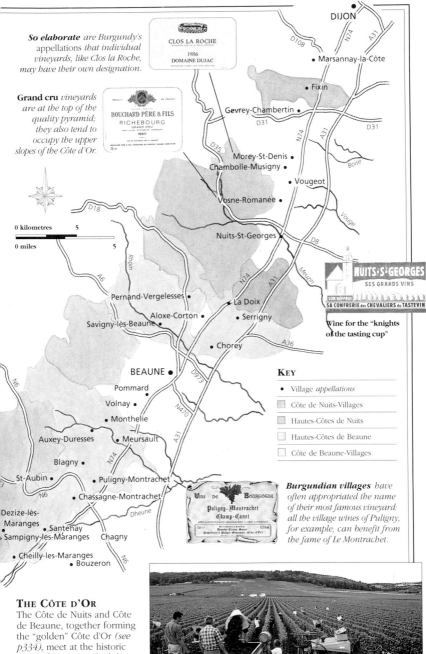

So elaborate are Burgundy's appellations *that individual vineyards, like Clos la Roche, may have their own designation.*

Grand cru *vineyards are at the top of the quality pyramid; they also tend to occupy the upper slopes of the Côte d'Or.*

CLOS LA ROCHE
1986
DOMAINE DUJAC

BOUCHARD PÈRE & FILS
RICHEBOURG
GRAND CRU
1985

DIJON

D108 · N74 · A31

Marsannay-la-Côte

Fixin

Gevrey-Chambertin
D31 · N74 · A31 · D31

Morey-St-Denis
Chambolle-Musigny

Vougeot

Vosne-Romanée

Nuits-St-Georges

0 kilometres 5
0 miles 5

Pernand-Vergelesses
La Doix
Aloxe-Corton
Serrigny
Savigny-lès-Beaune

Chorey

BEAUNE

Pommard

Volnay

Monthelie

Auxey-Duresses · Meursault

Blagny

St-Aubin

Puligny-Montrachet

Chassagne-Montrachet

Dezize-lès-Maranges
Santenay
Sampigny-les-Maranges · Chagny

Cheilly-les-Maranges
Bouzeron

NUITS·S⸱GEORGES
SES GRANDS VINS
SON BEFFROI
SA CONFRERIE des CHEVALIERS du TASTEVIN

Wine for the "knights of the tasting cup"

KEY

•	Village *appellations*
▢	Côte de Nuits-Villages
▢	Hautes-Côtes de Nuits
▢	Hautes-Côtes de Beaune
▢	Côte de Beaune-Villages

Vins de Bourgogne
Puligny-Montrachet
Champ-Canet

Burgundian villages have often appropriated the name of their most famous vineyard: all the village wines of Puligny, for example, can benefit from the fame of Le Montrachet.

THE CÔTE D'OR
The Côte de Nuits and Côte de Beaune, together forming the "golden" Côte d'Or *(see p334)*, meet at the historic town of Beaune, which hosts the most famous annual wine auction in the world *(see p336)*. "Hautes-Côtes" and "Villages" wines are made by those not fortunate enough to possess land in the starry individual *appellations*.

Teams of grape-pickers at the vineyards of Nuits-St-Georges

The French Alps

IN ANY SEASON, the Alps are one of the most spectacular regions of France – a majestic mountain range stretching south from Lake Geneva almost to the Mediterranean, and climaxing in Europe's loftiest peak, the 4,800-m (15,770-ft) Mont Blanc. The area encompasses the old regions of Dauphiné and Savoie, once remote and independent (Savoie only became part of France in 1860). They have prospered since alpine holidays and skiing became popular over the last century, but are still very conscious of their distinct identity.

Children in traditional Savoie costumes

The Alpine landscape in winter: chalets and skiers on the slopes at Courchevel

WINTER

THE SKI SEASON usually starts just before Christmas, and finishes at the end of April. Most resorts offer both cross-country and downhill skiing,

A cable car at Courchevel, part of Les Trois Vallées complex

with many pistes linking two or more ski stations. The less energetic can still enjoy the landscape from some of the highest cable cars (*téléphériques*) in the world.

Of the 100 or more French Alpine resorts, the most popular include **Chamonix-Mont Blanc**, the historic capital of Alpine skiing and site of the first Winter Olympics in 1924; **Megève**, which boasts one of the best ski schools in Europe; **Morzine**, a year-round resort on the Swiss border, overlooked by the modern, car-free resort of **Avoriaz**; modern **Albertville**, site of the 1992 Winter Olympics; **Les Trois Vallées**, which include glamorous

A downhill skier at Val d'Isère

Courchevel and **Méribel**, and the lesser-known **Val Thorens/Les Ménuires**; **Tignes**, a year-round resort; **Les Arcs** and **La Plagne**, both purpose-built; and **Val d'Isère**, a favourite among the rich and famous.

ALPINE FLOWERS

In spring and early summer the pastures of the French Alps are ablaze with flowers. These include blue and yellow gentians, bellflowers, lilies, saxifrages and a variety of orchids. Steep mountain meadows cannot be farmed intensively, and the absence of fertilizers and weed killers enables wild flowers to flourish.

Spring gentian *(Gentiana verna)*

Martagon lily *(Lilium martagon)*

The French Alps in spring: flower-filled meadows overlooked by brilliant white peaks

SPRING AND SUMMER

T HE ALPINE summer season starts in late June, extending to early September – most resorts close in October and November

Bell-ringing dairy cows in an Alpine pasture

between the hiking and skiing seasons. After the spring thaw, flower-filled pastures, snow-fed mountain lakes and a huge number of marked trails make this area a hiker's paradise. In the Chamonix area alone there are over 310 km (195 miles) of hiking trails. The best known long-distance route is the **Tour du Mont Blanc**, a 10-day hike via France, Italy and Switzerland. The **GR5** traverses the entire Alps, passing through the **Parc National de la Vanoise** and **Parc Régional du Queyras** (*see p377*) to the south. *Téléphériques* give access to the higher trails, where the views are even more awesome. Be sure to bring plenty of warm,

waterproof clothing: the weather can change very quickly.

Many resorts are now concentrating on broadening their summer appeal – golf, tennis, mountain biking, horse-riding, paragliding, canoeing, white water rafting, glacier skiing and mountain climbing are all widely available.

Mountain climbers scaling the heights around Mont Blanc

Geology of the Massif Central

THE MASSIF CENTRAL covers almost one-fifth of France and is over 250 million years old. Most of its peaks have been eroded to form a vast plateau split into deep valleys. The heart of the Massif consists of hard, igneous rocks like granite, with softer rocks such as limestone at its margins. Different rock types are reflected in the landscape and buildings; in the eroded Gorges du Tarn, the houses are built of russet-coloured limestone. Massive granite farmhouses are a feature of Limousin and Le Puy-en-Velay is distinguished by its giant basalt pillars.

LOCATOR MAP

■ *Extent of the Massif Central*

This granite portal *is found in the Romanesque church at Moutier d'Ahun (see p346). Granite underlies much of the Massif Central.*

Basalt *is a dark, fine-grained rock formed by volcanic lava. A common building stone in the Auvergne, it is often cut into blocks and bonded with lighter-coloured mortar. In the medieval town of Salers (see p353), basalt was used for most of the buildings, including this one in the Grande Place.*

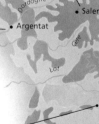

Montluçon •

Moutier d'Ahun •

Limoges •

Clermont-Ferrand •

Dordogne

• Salers

• Argentat

Cère

Lot

Schist tiling *is featured on these roofs at Argentat. Schist is a crystalline rock which splits readily into layers. It is particularly common on the edge of the Massif, and provides an effective roofing material.*

Limestone walls *can be seen on houses in Espalion (see p356). Of all the rocks in the Massif Central, it is among the most easily worked. It splits readily and is soft enough to be cut into blocks with a hand saw. As with granite, its colour and consistency vary from area to area.*

Millau •

Tarn

0 kilometres   50

0 miles   50

Crystallized lava, *like this dramatic curtain of columns at Prades, formed when liquid basalt seeped through the surrounding rock and solidified to form giant crystals.*

KEY

- Sedimentary rock
- Surface volcanic rock
- Granite
- Metamorphic rock

Nevers

Loire

Saône

Lyon •

St-Etienne •

• Le-Puy-en-Velay

Rhône

Limestone plateaux (causses) *are typical of this region. Gorges, where rivers have cut through layers of this slightly soluble rock, run deep into the Massif Central.*

This mature landscape at Mont Aigoual is the highest point in the Cévennes (see p357), dividing rivers flowing into the Atlantic and the Mediterranean. Its granite and schist rocks show erosion.

RECOGNIZING ROCKS

Geologists divide rocks into three groups. Igneous rocks, like granite, are formed by volcanic activity and either extruded on to the surface or intrude into other rocks below ground. Sedimentary rocks are produced by sediment build-up. Metamorphic rocks have been transformed by heat or pressure.

SEDIMENTARY ROCK

Oolitic limestone often contains fossils and small amounts of quartz.

SURFACE VOLCANIC ROCK

Basalt, *which can form very thick sheets, is the most common lava rock.*

GRANITE

Pink granite, *a coarse-grained rock, is formed deep in the earth's crust.*

METAMORPHIC ROCK

Muscovite schist is a medium-grained mud or clay-based rock.

BURGUNDY
AND FRANCHE-COMTÉ

YONNE · NIÈVRE · CÔTE D'OR · SAÔNE-ET-LOIRE
HAUTE-SAÔNE · DOUBS · JURA

BURGUNDY CONSIDERS *itself the heart of France, a prosperous region with world-renowned wine, earthy but excellent cuisine and magnificent architecture. Franche-Comté to the east combines gentle farmland with lofty Alpine forests.*

Under the dukes of Valois, Burgundy was France's most powerful rival, with territory extending well beyond its present boundaries. By the 16th century, however, the duchy was ruled by governors appointed by the French king, but it still managed to keep its privileges and traditions. Once a part of Burgundy, Franche-Comté – the Free County – struggled to remain independent of the French crown, and was a province of the Holy Roman Empire until annexed by Louis XIV in 1674.

Burgundy, now as in the past, is a wealthy region, a centre of medieval religious faith which produced Romanesque masterpieces at Vézelay, Fontenay, and Cluny. Dijon is a splendid city, filled with the great palaces of the old Burgundian nobility and a collection of great paintings and sculptures in the Musée des Beaux Arts. The vineyards of the Côte d'Or, the Côte de Beaune and Chablis yield some of the world's most venerated wines.

Other richly varied landscapes – from the wild forests of the Morvan to the lush farmland of the Brionnais – produce snails, Bresse chickens and Charolais beef.

Franche-Comté has none of this opulence, though its capital, Besançon, is an elegant 17th-century city with a tradition of clockmaking. Topographically the Franche-Comté is divided into two, with gently-rolling farmland in the Saône valley and high Alpine scenery to the east. This forest country of Alpine torrents filled with trout is also the home of great cheeses, notably Vacherin and Comté, and of the characteristic yellow wine of Arbois.

The prehistoric site of the Roche de Solutré near Mâcon

◁ **Vineyards at Santenay in the world-renowned Côte de Beaune district**

Exploring Burgundy and Franche-Comté

BURGUNDY IS FRANCE'S RICHEST province –
historically, culturally, gastronomically and
economically. This lush kernel of a once
great power possesses a concentration of
unique Romanesque architecture in Fontenay
and Vézelay, along with
some of the world's
most venerated wines.
Dijon is a must for
lovers of art, archi-
tecture and food.
Franche-Comté is
better suited for
outdoor holidays,
such as trekking
and canoeing in
wild scenery and
crystal-clear rivers.

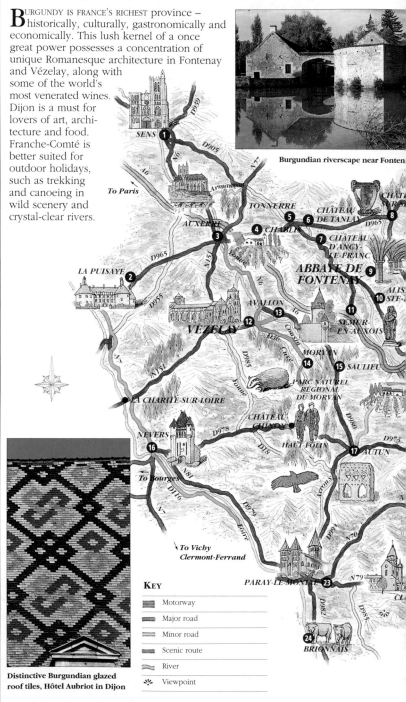

Burgundian riverscape near Fonten

To Paris

SENS ❶

TONNERRE
❺ ❻ CHÂTEAU
DE TANLAY

CHÂTEAU
SUR-S
❽ D965

CHABLIS ❹

AUXERRE
❸

❼ CHÂTEAU
D'ANCY-
LE-FRANC

LA PUISAYE ❷

ABBAYE DE
FONTENAY
❾

ALIS
STE-
❿

AVALLON
❸
VÉZELAY ❷

❶
SEMUR-
EN-AUXOIS

MORVAN
❹   ❺ SAULIEU

LA CHARITÉ-SUR-LOIRE

PARC NATUREL
RÉGIONAL
DU MORVAN

CHÂTEAU
CHINON

NEVERS
⓯

HAUT-FOLIN

⓱ AUTUN

To Bourges

*To Vichy
Clermont-Ferrand*

PARAY-LE-MONIAL ㉓

CL

㉔
BRIONNAIS

KEY

▬▬	Motorway
▬▬	Major road
▬▬	Minor road
▬▬	Scenic route
〰	River
⚹	Viewpoint

**Distinctive Burgundian glazed
roof tiles, Hôtel Aubriot in Dijon**

Sights at a Glance

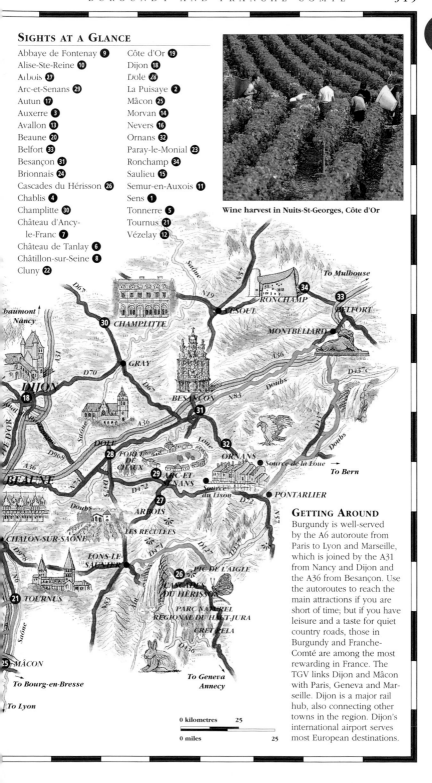

Wine harvest in Nuits-St-Georges, Côte d'Or

Getting Around

Burgundy is well-served by the A6 autoroute from Paris to Lyon and Marseille, which is joined by the A31 from Nancy and Dijon and the A36 from Besançon. Use the autoroutes to reach the main attractions if you are short of time; but if you have leisure and a taste for quiet country roads, those in Burgundy and Franche-Comté are among the most rewarding in France. The TGV links Dijon and Mâcon with Paris, Geneva and Marseille. Dijon is a major rail hub, also connecting other towns in the region. Dijon's international airport serves most European destinations.

0 kilometres   25

0 miles   25

Reliquary in the cathedral treasury at Sens

Sens ❶

Yonne. 🏛 27,000. 🚊 🚌
ℹ place Jean-Jaurès (03 86 65 19 49). 🖴 Mon & Fri.

THE LITTLE TOWN of Sens was important well before Caesar came to Gaul. Indeed, the Senones were the tribe whose stealthy attempt to sack the Roman Capitol in 390 BC was so famously thwarted by a flock of geese.

The **Cathédrale St-Etienne** is Sens' outstanding glory. Begun before 1140 it is the oldest of the great Gothic cathedrals and its noble simplicity influenced many other churches. Louis IX (see p47) did the town the honour of getting married here in 1234.

The exquisite stained-glass windows from the 12th–16th centuries show biblical scenes, including the Tree of Jesse, and a tribute to Thomas à Becket who was exiled here. His liturgical robes can be seen in the rich treasury, now housed in the **Musée de la Cathédrale St-Etienne**. Among the other exhibits is a beautiful 11th-century Byzantine coffer.

The market held around the cathedral is excellent and the town is renowned for its robust Burgundian fare.

🏛 **Musée de la Cathédrale St-Etienne**
Place de la Cathédrale. 📞 03 86 64 15 27. **Open** Jun–Sep: daily; Oct–May: Mon pm, Wed, Thu pm, Fri pm Sat, Sun. 🖼 ♿

La Puisaye ❷

Yonne, Nièvre. 🚊 Auxerre, Clamecy, Bonny-sur-Loire, Cosne-Cours-sur-Loire. 🚌 St-Fargeau, St-Sauveur-en-Puisaye. ℹ Maison de la Puisaye, St-Fargeau (03 86 74 15 72).

THE STRANGE, secret forest country of the Puisaye was immortalized by Colette (1873–1954), who was born at **St-Sauveur** in "a house that smiled only on its garden side . . .". The **Musée Colette**, housed in the town's 17th-century château, displays the writer's photographs, books, furniture and other objects.

The best way to explore the region is on foot or by bike around its watery woodlands, orchards and meadows, so unlike the rest of Burgundy. There are many interesting destinations, notably the 13th-century **Château de Ratilly** near St-Sauveur, with a pottery workshop and art exhibitions. More of this can be seen in **St-Amand**, the centre of Puisaye stoneware production. The pink brick **Château de St-Fargeau** housed the exiled Grande Mademoiselle (see p53). The church in **La Ferté-Loupière** contains a 15th-

Colette in the 1880s at St-Sauveur

century Danse Macabre fresco, while the frescoes in Eglise St-Pierre in **Moutiers** show John the Baptist and the Creation.

🏛 **Musée Colette**
Château St-Sauveur-en-Puisay.
📞 03 86 45 61 95. **Open** Apr–Sep: Wed–Mon; Oct–Mar: Sat, Sun and public hols. 🖼

Auxerre ❸

Yonne. 🏛 39,000. 🚊 🚌
ℹ 1–2 quai de la République (03 86 52 06 19). 🖴 Tue & Fri.

BEAUTIFULLY SITED overlooking the Yonne river, Auxerre justly prides itself on a fine collection of churches along with a charming pedestrianized main square, the place Charles-Surugue.

The Gothic **Cathédrale St-Etienne** took over three centuries to build and was completed in about 1560. It is famous for its intricate 13th-century stained glass. The choir with its slender columns and colonettes is the epitome of Gothic weightlessness and elegance, while the western portals are decorated with beautiful flamboyant sculpture which has been sadly mutilated by war and weather. The Romanesque crypt is adorned by unique 11th–13th-century frescoes, including one depicting Christ on a white horse. The badly pillaged treasury is less impressive, but still has an interesting collection of illuminated manuscripts.

St Germanus, mentor of St Patrick and bishop of Auxerre

Château de St-Fargeau in the Puisaye region

in the 5th century, was buried at the former abbey church of **St-Germain**. The abbey was founded by Queen Clothilde, wife of Clovis *(see pp44–5)*, the first Christian king of France, and hence is a great shrine. The crypt is partly Carolingian, with tombs and 11th–13th century frescoes. The former abbey houses the **Musée St-Germain** with an exhibition of Gallo-Roman finds from the region, witness to Auxerre's long history.

🏛 Musée St-Germain
2 pl St-Germain. **[** 03 86 51 09 74. **Open** *Wed–Mon.* **Closed** *public hols.*

The intriguing spring of Fosse Dionne in Tonnerre

Medieval fresco in Cathédrale St-Etienne at Auxerre

Chablis ❹

Yonne. 🏘 2,300. 🚊 🚌 quai du Biez (03 86 42 80 80). 🛒 Sun.

THERE CAN BE no question that Chablis tastes best in Chablis. Although this is one of the most famous wine villages on earth, its narrow stone streets still have an air of sleepy prosperity. Saint Vincent, the patron saint of wine-growers, is celebrated by processions in February, attended by the wine brother-hood of Piliers Chablisiens.

Tonnerre ❺

Yonne. 🏘 6,000. 🚊 🚌 🛈 12 rue du Collège (03 86 55 14 48). 🛒 Sat.

THE MYSTICAL cloudy-green spring of **Fosse Dionne** is a good reason to visit the small town of Tonnerre. An astonishing volume of water bursts up from the ground into an 18th-century washing-place. Due to its depth and strong currents it has never been thoroughly explored and local legend has it that a serpent lives on undisturbed at the bottom.

The **Hôtel-Dieu** is 150 years older than the Hôtel-Dieu in Beaune *(see p336–7)*. It was founded by Margaret of Burgundy in 1293 to care for the poor. In the Revolution it lost its tiling but the barrel-vaulted oak ceiling survived.

🏥 Hôtel-Dieu
Rue du Prieuré. **[** 03 86 55 33 00. **Open** *Easter–May & Oct: Sat, Sun & hols; Jun–Sep: Wed–Mon.* 🎫 ♿

Château de Tanlay ❻

Tanlay. **[** 03 86 75 70 61. **Open** *Apr–mid-Nov: Wed–Mon.* 🎫

THE MOATED Château de Tanlay is a beautiful ex-ample of French Renaissance, built in the mid-16th century. There is a *trompe l'oeil* in the Grande Galerie and, in the corner tower, an intriguing School of Fontainebleau painted ceiling. Its antique divinities represent famous Protestants and Catholics in the 16th century, such as Diane de Poitiers as Venus.

The Renaissance façade and *cour d'honneur* of Château de Tanlay

Abbaye de Fontenay ❾

Tʜᴇ ᴛʀᴀɴQᴜɪʟ ᴀʙʙᴇʏ of Fontenay is the oldest surviving Cistercian foundation in France and offers a rare insight into the Cistercian way of life. It represents the spirit of the order in the sublime gravity of its Romanesque church and its plain but elegant chapterhouse, in early Gothic style. The abbey was founded in 1118 by St Bernard. Situated deep in the forest, it offered the peace and seclusion the Cistercians sought. Supported by the local aristocracy, the abbey began to thrive and remained in use until the Revolution when it was sold and converted into a paper mill. In 1906 the abbey came under new ownership and was restored to its original appearance.

Dovecote
A magnificent circular dovecote, built in the 17th century, is situated next to the kennel where the precious hunting dogs of the dukes of Burgundy were guarded by servants.

The 17th-century abbot's lodgings were built when the abbots were appointed by royal favour.

The bakehouse is no longer intact but the 13th-century oven and chimney have survived.

The visitors' hostel is where weary wanderers and pilgrims were offered board and lodging by the monks.

★ Cloisters
For a 12th-century monk a walk through the cloisters was an opportunity for meditation and provided shelter from the weather.

Warming Room

In the forge monks produced their own tools and hardware.

Fontenay "Prison"
It may be that this 15th-century building was actually used to lock up not local miscreants but important abbey archives, in order to protect them against damage by rats.

Scriptorium
Manuscripts were copied here. The adjacent Warming Room was used to warm chilled hands.

★ Abbey Church
Rich decoration has no place in this church from the 1140s. But the severe architectural forms, the warm colour of the stone and the diffused light convey a grandeur of their own.

VISITORS' CHECKLIST

Marmagne. **[** 03 80 92 15 00
◻ Montbard. **Open** 9am–noon,
2– 6pm (5pm Oct–Mar). **▨ 良 ✔**

Dormitory
Monks slept in long rows on straw mattresses in this large, unheated room. The timberwork roof is from the late 15th century.

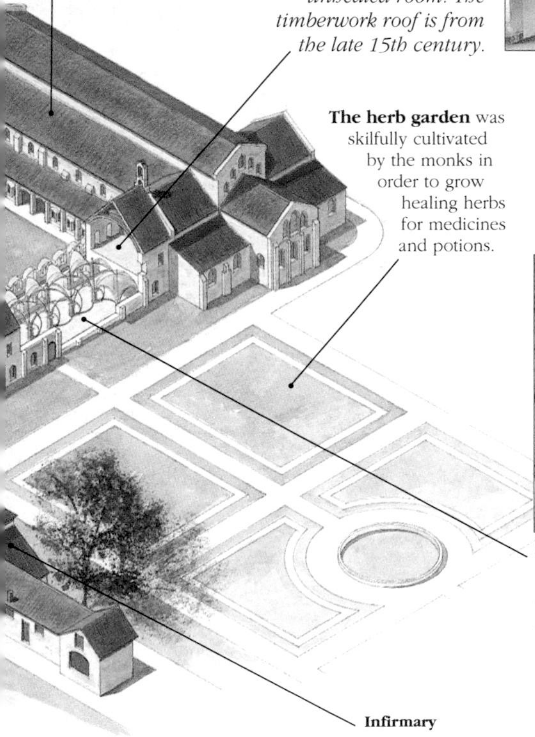

The herb garden was skilfully cultivated by the monks in order to grow healing herbs for medicines and potions.

STAR FEATURES

★ **Abbey Church**

★ **Cloisters**

Chapterhouse
Once a day, monks and abbot assembled in this room to discuss matters concerning the community. It derives much of its charm from the elegant 12th-century piers and the rib-vaults.

Infirmary

ST BERNARD AND THE CISTERCIANS

In 1112 Bernard, a young Burgundian nobleman, joined the Cistercians. At the time the order was still obscure, founded 14 years earlier by a group of monks who wanted to turn their back on the elaborate lifestyle of Cluny *(see pp44–5)*, renounce the world and espouse poverty and simplicity of life. During Bernard's lifetime the Cistercians became one of the largest and most famous orders of its time. Part of this success was clearly due to Bernard's powerful personality and his skills as a writer, theologian and statesman. He reinforced the poverty rule, rejecting all forms of embellishment. In 1174, only 21 years after his death, he was canonized.

The Virgin Protecting the Cistercian Order, by Jean Bellegambe

Château d'Ancy-le-Franc **⑦**

Ancy-le-Franc. **[** 03 86 75 14 63.
Open Apr–mid-Nov: daily. **[**
obligatory.

THE CLASSICAL Renaissance
façade of Château d'Ancy-
le-Franc gives an austere impression. Its inner courtyard,
however, has rich ornamen-
tation. The château was built
in the 1540s by the Italian
Sebastiano Serlio, for the
Duke of Clermont-Tonnerre.
Most of the interior decorations were carried out by
Primaticcio and other members
of the Fontainebleau School
(see pp170–71). Diane de
Poitiers, the duke's sister-in-
law and mistress of Henry II,
is portrayed in the *Chambre
de Judith e Holophernes.*
   In the outbuildings a vintage
car and carriage museum
displays over 80 vehicles.

The vase of Vix in the Musée du
Châtillonnais, Châtillon-sur-Seine

Châtillon-sur-Seine **⑧**

Côte d'Or. 7,500. **place**
Marmont (03 80 91 13 19). Sat.

WORLD WAR II left Châtillon
a smoking ruin, hence
the town's resolutely modern
aspect. But the past is still
present in the **Musée du
Châtillonnais**, where the
magnificent Vix treasure is
displayed. In 1953, the tomb
of a Gaulish princess, dating
from the 6th century BC, was
discovered near Vix at Mont
Lassois. The trove of jewellery
and artifacts of Greek origin
includes a stunning bronze
vase, 164 cm (66 in) high and
weighing 208 kg (459 lb).

The staid façade of Château d'Ancy-le-Franc

Another point of interest is the
Romanesque **Eglise St-Vorles**
containing an *Entombment*
with Christ and mourners
splendidly sculpted (1527).
   At the nearby source of the
river Douix, which runs into
the Seine, is a beautiful grotto.

🏛 Musée du Châtillonnais
7 rue du Bourg. **[** 03 80 91 24 67.
Open Wed– Mon. **Closed** 1 Jan, 1
May, 25 Dec.

Abbaye de Fontenay **⑨**

See pp322–3.

Alise-Ste-Reine **⑩**

Côte d'Or. 670. **[]** Venarey-les-
Laumes, 3 km (2 miles) (03 80 96 89 13).

MONT AUXOIS, above the
little village of Alise-Ste-
Reine, was the site of Caesar's
final victory over the heroic
Gaulish chieftain Vercingetorix

in 52 BC after a six-week siege
(see p42). The first excavations
here were undertaken in the
mid-19th century, and they
uncovered the vestiges of a
thriving Gallo-Roman town,
with theatre, forum and well-
laid-out street plan. The
Musée Alésia has a collection
of artifacts, jewellery and
bronze figures from the site.
   Alise is dominated by Aimé
Millet's gigantic moustachioed
statue of Vercingetorix, which
was placed here in 1865 to
commemorate the first excavations. Cynics feel that it
bears a more than passing
resemblance to Napoleon III,
who sponsored the dig.

🏛 Musée Alésia
Rue de l'Hôpital. **[** 03 80 96 10 95.
Open Apr–11 Nov: daily.

Environs
In the vicinity lies **Château de
Bussy-Rabutin**. The spiteful
17th-century soldier and wit
Roger de Bussy-Rabutin
created its highly individualistic

Excavations at the Roman site near Alise-Ste-Reine

decor, while exiled from Louis XIV's court. One room is dedicated to portraits of his many mistresses, as well as a couple of imaginary ones.

♣ **Château de Bussy-Rabutin**
Bussy-le-Grand. **[** 03 80 96 00 03.
Open daily; Nov–Mar: Thu–Mon.
Closed 1 Jan, 1 May, 1 & 11 Nov,
25 Dec. 🖼 🚻

Semur-en-Auxois ⓫

Côte d'Or. 🏘 4,500. 🚌
🛈 2 place Gaveau (03 80 97 05 96).
🛒 Thu & Sat.

APPROACHED from the west, Semur-en-Auxois comes as a surprise on an otherwise uneventful road. Its massive round bastions built in the 14th century (one of them with an unnerving gash in it) suddenly appear, towering over the Pont Joly and the peaceful river Armançon.

The **Eglise Notre-Dame** dates from the 13th and 14th centuries, and was modelled on the cathedral of Auxerre. The fragile high walls had to be restored in the 15th and 19th centuries. The church houses significant art-works, from the tympanum showing the legend of Doubting Thomas on the north doorway, to the 15th-century *Entombment* by Antoine le Moiturier. The stained glass presents the legend of Saint Barbara, and the work of different guilds such as butchers and drapers.

Environs
The village of Epoisses is the site of the moated **Château d'Epoisses**, its 11th–18th-century construction blending medieval towers with fine Renaissance details, and a huge 15th-century dovecote. Epoisses is also the home of

Stained-glass window in Eglise Notre-Dame at Semur-en-Auxois

Semur-en-Auxois by the river Armançon

one of Burgundy's most re-vered cheeses, to be sampled at the local café or *fromagerie*.

♣ **Château d'Epoisses**
Epoisses. **[** 03 80 96 40 56. **Open** Jul–Aug: Wed–Mon (grounds: all year). 🖼 🚻 ground floor only.

Vézelay ⓬

See pp326–7.

Avallon ⓭

Yonne. 🏘 8,600. 🚌 🚂 🛈 4 rue Bocquillot (03 86 34 14 19). 🛒 Sat.

A FINE OLD fortified town, Avallon is situated on a granite spur between two ravines by the river Cousin.

Avallon suffered much in the wars of Saracens, Normans, English and French, which accounts for its coldly defen-sive aspect. Today the town is quiet and rather beautiful, all passion spent, full of charming details. The main monument is the 12th-century Roman-esque **Eglise St-Lazare**, with two carved doorways. The larger illustrates the signs of the zodiac, the labours of the month, and the musicians of

the Apocalypse. The nave is decorated with sophisticated acanthus capitals and poly-chrome statuary.

The **Musée de l'Avallonnais** has a wide-ranging collection, featuring an intricate Venus mosaic from the 2nd century AD, and Georges Rouault's (1871–1958) series of Expres-sionist etchings, the *Miserere*.

🏛 **Musée de l'Avallonnais**
Place de la Collégiale. **[** 03 86 34 03 19. **Open** May–Oct: Wed–Mon. 🖼

Environs
To the southwest of Avallon is the 12th-century Château de Bazoches, which was trans-formed into a military garrison by Vauban in the 17th century.

Miserere by Georges Rouault in the Musée d'Avallonnais, Avallon

Vézelay ⑫

Decorated capital

THE GOLDEN GLOW of the Basilique Ste-Madeleine crowning Vézelay's hill is visible from afar. Tourists follow in the footsteps of medieval pilgrims, ascending the narrow street up to the former abbey church. In the 12th century, at the height of its glory, the abbey claimed to house relics of Mary Magdalene and was also an important meeting point for pilgrims en route to Santiago de Compostela in Spain *(see pp390–91)*. Today its attraction lies in the Romanesque church with its magnificent sculpture and Gothic choir.

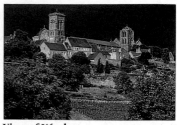

View of Vézelay
The abbey dominates Vézelay's surroundings as it once dominated the religious and worldly affairs of the area.

Nave of Ste-Madeleine
The nave was rebuilt between 1120–35, using alternate dark and light stone in the transverse arches.

Tour St-Michel was built in 1230–40. It derives its name from the statue of the archangel in the tower's southwest corner.

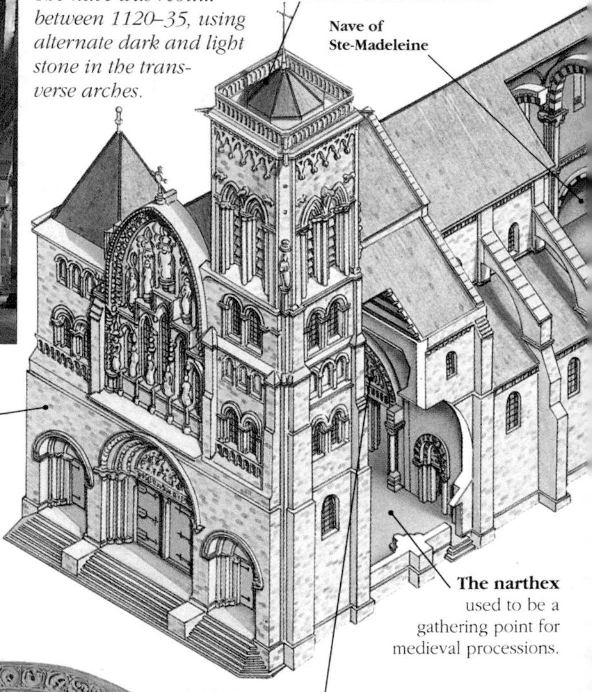

Nave of Ste-Madeleine

The façade dates from 1150 and has a large 13th-century window. It was about to collapse when Viollet-le-Duc was commissioned to restore it according to old plans in 1840.

The narthex used to be a gathering point for medieval processions.

★ **Tympanum**
This masterpiece of sculpture (1120–35) shows Christ on His throne, stretching out His hands from which rays of light descend on to the apostles.

STAR FEATURES

★ **Tympanum**

★ **Capitals**

Tour St-Antoine was built at the same time as the choir, in the late 12th century. Its counterpart on the north side was never finished.

VISITORS' CHECKLIST

Basilique Ste-Madeleine, Vézelay.
📞 03 86 33 26 73. 🚉 Sermizelles.
Open Apr–Oct: 6am–8pm daily;
Nov–Mar: 7am–6pm. ♿ ✝ 7am,
12:30pm, 6pm, 6:30pm Tue–Fri;
8am, 12:30pm, 6pm, 6:30pm
Sat; 8am, 11am Sun. 📷 🚫

The chapterhouse and cloister are the only parts remaining from the 12th-century monastic buildings. Viollet-le-Duc rebuilt the cloister and restored the rib-vaulted chapterhouse, once a graceful background for the monks' daily assemblies.

Crypt of Ste-Madeleine
The Carolingian crypt houses relics once thought to be Mary Magdalene's. The vault was rebuilt in 1165.

★ Capitals
The capitals in the nave and narthex are exquisitely carved, and give a vivid rendering of the stories of Classical antiquity and the Bible. The master who created them remains unknown.

Choir of Ste-Madeleine
The choir was rebuilt in the last quarter of the 12th century in the then modern Gothic style of the Ile de France.

Morvan, a region of rivers and forests, well-suited to fishing and other outdoor pursuits

Morvan ⑭

Yonne, Côte d'Or, Nièvre, Saône et Loire. 🚉 Dijon. 🚌 Autun, Corbigny. 🚌 Château-Chinon, Saulieu, Avallon. 🅸 Château-Chinon (03 86 85 06 58); Maison du Parc, St-Brisson (03 86 78 79 00).

MORVAN is a Celtic word meaning Black Mountain, which is a good description of this area seen from afar. The immense, sparsely inhabited plateau of granite and woodland appears suddenly in the centre of the rich Burgundy hills and farmland. Stretching roughly north to south, it gains altitude as it proceeds southwards, reaching a culminating point of 901 m (2,928 ft) at **Haut-Folin**.

The Morvan's two sources of natural wealth are abundant water and dense forests of oak, beech and conifer. In the old days lumber used to be floated out of the area to Paris via the river Yonne. Today it travels by truck, and the Yonne, Cousin and Cure rivers are instead used for the production of electricity.

The population continues to shrink, for the Morvan has always been a poor, remote area. Each of its largest towns, Château-Chinon in the centre and Saulieu on the outskirts, has barely 3,000 inhabitants.

During World War II, the Morvan was a bastion of the French Resistance. Today a Regional Nature Park, its attraction is its wildness. Information on a wide variety of outdoor activities, including cycling, canoeing, skiing, and horse trekking, is available at the Maison du Parc at St-Brisson where there is also a **Musée de la Resistance**. There are plenty of short walking trails, in addition to two well-signed long-distance paths: the GR13 (Vézelay to Autun) and the Tour du Morvan par les Grands Lacs.

🏛 **Musée de la Résistance**
Maison du Parc, St-Brisson. 📞 03 86 78 79 00. **Open** Apr–Jun: Sat, Sun; Jul–Oct: daily; Nov–Mar: by appt. 🅰 🅱

Saulieu ⑮

Côte d'Or. 🏘 2,900. 🚉 🚌 🅸 24 rue d'Argentine (03 80 64 00 21 or 03 80 64 09 22). 🛒 Thu & Sat.

ON THE EDGE of the Morvan, Saulieu has been a shrine of Burgundian cooking ever since the 17th century. The town was then a staging post on the Paris to Lyon coach road. Today the tradition is maintained by the famous chef Bernard Loiseau at the **Côte d'Or** restaurant (see p599). Yet there is more to Saulieu than *ris de veau de lait braisé* or *poularde truffée à la vapeur.* The Romanesque **Basilique St-Andoche**, built in the early 12th century, has decorated capitals with representations of the Flight into Egypt and a comical version of the story of Balaam and his donkey waylaid by the Angel.

Nevers ⑯

Nièvre. 🏘 44,000. 🚉 🚌 🅸 Palais Ducal, rue Sabatier. (03 86 68 46 00). 🛒 Sat.

LIKE ALL Burgundian towns fronting the Loire, Nevers should be approached from the west side of the river for a full appreciation of its noble site. Though lacking historical importance, the town has much to show. The Romanesque 11th-century **Eglise St-Etienne** has graceful monolithic columns and a wreath of radiating chapels. In the crypt of the Gothic **Cathédrale St-Cyr** is a 15th-century sculpted *Entombment.* The contemporary stained-glass windows are also worth a look.

The overlordship of Nevers passed to the Italian Gonzaga family in the 16th century. The Gonzagas brought a school of artists skilled in the fine arts of faïence making and glassblowing. The industry has remained in the town and the modern pottery, still decorated in the traditional white, blue, yellow and green colours, is charming, with its curious trademark, the little green arabesque knot, or *noeud*

Nevers faïence vase

vert. The best place to view it is at the **Musée Municipal**, and the best place to buy is the 17th-century **Faïencerie Montagnon** close by. The 12th-century **Porte du Croux** houses the **Musée Archéologique** with some remarkable Romanesque sculpture.

🏛 **Musée Municipal Frédéric Blandin**
Promenade des Ramparts. 📞 03 86 23 92 89. **Open** Wed–Mon. 🎫
🏛 **Musée Archéologique**
Rue de la Porte-du-Croux. 📞 03 86 59 17 85. **Open** Wed–Mon. 🎫

Environs
Just south of Nevers, the 19th-century **Pont du Guetin** carries the Loire Canal majestically across the Allier river. The church at **St-Parize-le-Châtel** has a jolly Burgundian menagerie sculpted on the capitals of the crypt.

The *Temptation of Eve* in Autun

Autun ⑰

Saône-et-Loire. 🚉 17,900. 🚌 🚆 🅘 2 av Charles de Gaulle (03 85 86 80 38). 🅐 Wed, Fri & Sun.

AGUSTODUNUM, the town of Augustus, was founded in the late 1st century BC. It was a great centre of learning,

The imposing Porte St-André in Autun, once part of the Roman wall

with a population four times what it is today. Its theatre, built in the 1st century AD, could seat 20,000 people.

Today Autun is still a delight, deserving gastronomic as well as cultural investigation.

The magical **Cathédrale St-Lazare** was built in the 12th century. It is special because of the genius of its sculptures, most of them by the mysterious 12th-century artist Gislebertus. He sculpted both the capitals inside and the glorious Last Judgment tympanum over the main portal. This masterpiece, called a "Romanesque Cézanne" by writer André Malraux, was saved from destruction during the Revolution by an extraordinary stroke of luck. It had been plastered over in the 18th century and escaped any further damage. Inside, some of the capitals can be seen close-up in a room in the tower. Look also

for the sculpture of Pierre Jeannin and his wife. Jeannin was the president of the Dijon parliament who prevented the Massacre of St Bartholomew *(see pp50–51)* spreading to Burgundy with the immortal remark, "the commands of very angry monarchs should be obeyed very slowly".

The brilliant collection of medieval art at **Musée Rolin** includes the lovely bas relief *Temptation of Eve*, by Gislebertus. There is also the painted stone Virgin of Autun (15th century), and the *Nativity of Cardinal Rolin* by the Master of Moulins, from about 1480.

The monumental **Porte St-André**, the **Porte d'Arroux** and the ruins of the **Théâtre Romain** and the **Temple de Janus** are reminders of Autun's glorious Roman past.

🏛 **Musée Rolin**
5 rue des Bancs. 📞 03 85 52 09 76. **Open** Wed–Mon. **Closed** 1 Jan, 1 May, 14 Jul, 1 & 11 Nov, 25 Dec. 🎫

Remains of the Roman theatre at Autun, dating from the 1st century AD

Street by Street: Dijon ⑱

THE CENTRE of Dijon is noted for its architectural splendour – a legacy from the Dukes of Burgundy *(see p333)*. Wealthy parliament members also had elegant *hôtels particuliers* built in the 17th–18th centuries. The capital of Burgundy, Dijon today has a rich cultural life and a renowned university. The city's great art treasures are housed in the Palais des Ducs. Dijon is also famous for its mustard *(see p308)* and *pain d'épice* (gingerbread), a reminder of the town's position on the spice route. It became a major rail hub during the 19th century and now has a TGV link to Paris.

Hôtel de Vogüé
This elegant 17th-century mansion is decorated with Burgundian cabbages and fruit garlands by Hugues Sambin.

★ Notre-Dame
This magnificent 13th-century Gothic church has a façade with gargoyles, columns and the popular Jacquemart clock. The chouette *(owl) is reputed to bring good luck when touched.*

Musée des Beaux Arts
The collection of Flemish masters here includes this 14th-century triptych by Jacques de Baerze and Melchior Broederlam.

Place de la Libération was created by Mansart in the 17th century.

★ Palais des Ducs
The dukes of Burgundy held court here, but the building seen today was mainly built in the 17th century for the parliament. It now houses the Musée des Beaux Arts.

Rue Verrerie
This cobbled street in the old merchants' quarter is lined with medieval half-timbered houses. Some have fine wood-carvings, such as Nos. 8, 10 and 12.

VISITORS' CHECKLIST

Côte d'Or. 🏠 151,000. ✈ 5 km (3 miles) SSE Dijon. 🚊 🚌 Cours de la Gare. 🚹 place Darcy (03 80 44 11 44). 🛒 Tue, Fri & Sat. 🎪 Florissimo (every 3 years: 1999, 2002, etc); Festival de Musique (Jun); Fêtes de la Vigne (Sep). *Hôtel de Vogüé* only inner courtyard open to the public. *Musée Magnin* (03 80 67 11 10) *open* Tue–Sun. *Closed some public hols.* 🖼

★ St-Michel
Begun in the 15th century and completed in the 17th century, St-Michel's façade combines Flamboyant Gothic with Renaissance details. On the richly carved porch, angels and biblical motifs mingle with mythological themes.

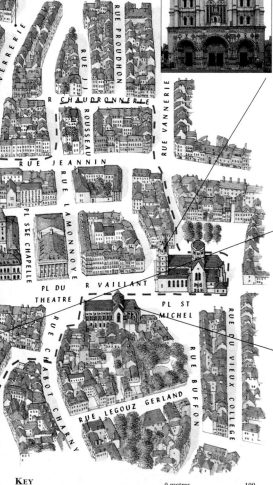

Musée Magnin
A collection of French and foreign 16th–19th-century paintings are displayed among period furniture in this 17th-century mansion.

Eglise St-Etienne dates back to the 11th century but has been rebuilt many times. Its characteristic lantern was added in 1686.

STAR SIGHTS

★ Palais des Ducs

★ Notre-Dame

★ St-Michel

KEY

– – – Suggested route

0 metres 100

0 yards 100

Well of Moses by Claus Sluter, in
the Chartreuse de Champmol

Exploring Dijon

The centre of Dijon is a warren
of little streets that reward
exploration. The rue des
Forges, behind the Palais de
Ducs, was the main street
until the 18th century and is
named after the jewellers and
goldsmiths who had work-
shops there. The tourist office,
housed in Hôtel Chambellan at
No. 34, is Flamboyant Gothic
with a stone spiral staircase
and wooden galleries. At No.
38 the Maison Milsand, built
in 1561, has a stone façade
decorated by Hugues Sambin.

Rue Chaudronnerie has a
number of houses of note,
especially the Maison des
Cariatides at No. 28, with ten
fine stone carved caryatids
framing the windows. Place

Darcy is lined with hotels and
restaurants; the Jardin Darcy is
delightful.

🏛 Musée des Beaux Arts

Place de la Ste-Chapelle. **☎** *03 80 74
52 70.* **Open** *Wed–Mon.* **Closed** *1 Jan,
1 May, 8 May, 14 Jul, 1 & 11 Nov, 25
Dec.* 🎥 🚻

Dijon's prestigious art collection is housed in the former
Palais des Ducs *(see p330)*.
The Salle des Gardes on the
first floor is dominated by the
giant mausoleums of the
dukes, with tombs sculpted
by Claus Sluter (c.1345–1405).
Other exhibits include two
gilded Flemish retables and a
portrait of Philip the Good by
Rogier van der Weyden.

The art collection has many
Dutch and Flemish masters
and sculpture by Sluter and
François Rude. There is also a
large collection of Swiss and
German primitives, 16th–18th
century French paintings, and
the Donation Granville of 19th-
and 20th-century French art.
Also note the vast ducal
kitchens with six giant fireplaces, and the Tour Philippe
le Bon, 46 m (150 ft) tall with
a fine view of Burgundian
tiled roof tops.

⛪ Cathédrale St-Benigne

Little remains of the 11th-
century Benedictine abbey
first founded in honour of St
Benigne, but beneath the
Gothic church is a magni-
ficent Romanesque crypt with
a fine rotunda ringed by
three circles of columns.

🏛 Musée Archéologique

5 rue du Docteur Maret. **☎** *03 80
30 88 54.* **Open** *Wed–Mon.* **Closed**
most public hols. 🎥

The museum is housed in the
old dormitory of the Benedictine abbey of St-Bénigne. The
11th-century chapterhouse, its
stocky columns supporting a
barrel-vaulted roof, houses a
fine collection of Gallo-Roman
sculpture. The ground floor,
with its lovely fan vaulting,
houses the famous head of
Christ by Claus Sluter, originally from the *Well of Moses.*

⛪ Chartreuse de Champmol

1 bd Chanoine Kir. **Open** *daily.*

This was originally the site
of a family necropolis built
by Philip the Bold, destroyed
during the Revolution. All
that remains is a chapel doorway and the famous *Well of
Moses* by Claus Sluter. It is now
in the grounds of a psychiatric
hospital east of Dijon railway
station, not very easy to find
but definitely worth the effort.
Despite its name, it is not a
well, but a monument, its
lower part probably originally
surrounded by water. Sluter is
renowned for his deeply cut
carving and here his work,
depicting six prophets, is
exquisitely lifelike.

The tomb of Philip the Bold by Claus Sluter, now in the Salle des Gardes of the Musée des Beaux Arts

The Golden Age of Burgundy

WHILE THE FRENCH Capetian dynasty fought in the Hundred Years' War *(see pp48–9)*, the dukes of Burgundy built up one of the most powerful states in Europe, which included Flanders and parts of Holland. From the time of Philip the Bold (1342–1404), the ducal court became a cultural force, supporting many of Europe's finest artists, such as painters Rogier Van der Weyden and the Van Eyck brothers and sculptor Claus Sluter. The duchy's dominions were, however, broken up after the death of Duke Charles the Bold in 1477.

The tomb of Philip the Bold in Dijon was made by the Flemish sculptor Claus Sluter, who was among the most brilliant artists of the Burgundian golden age. The dramatic realism of the mourners is one of the most striking features of this spectacular tomb, begun while the duke was still alive.

BURGUNDY IN 1477

■ *Extent of the duchy at its peak*

THE MARRIAGE OF PHILIP THE GOOD

Philip the Good, duke from 1419–67, married Isabella of Portugal in 1430. This 17th-century copy of a painting by Van Eyck shows the sumptuous wedding feast, when Philip also inaugurated the chivalric Order of the Golden Fleece.

The dukes surrounded themselves with luxury, including fine gold and silverware.

Isabella of Portugal

The Duchess of Bedford, Philip's sister

Greyhounds were popular hunting animals at the Burgundian court.

Philip the Good is dressed in white ceremonial finery.

Burgundian art, such as this Franco-Flemish Book of Hours, reflected the Flemish origins of many of the dukes' favourite artists.

Dijon's Palais des Ducs was rebuilt in 1450 by Philip the Good to reflect the glory of the Burgundian court, a centre of art, chivalry and glorious feasts. Empty after Charles the Bold's death, it was reconstructed in the 17th century.

Wine harvest in the vineyards of Nuits-St-Georges, part of the Côte d'Or district

Côte d'Or ⑲

Côte d'Or. ✈ Dijon. 🚉 🚌 Dijon,
Nuits-St-Georges, Beaune, Santenay.
ℹ Santenay (03 80 20 63 15:
summer only); Beaune (03 80 26 21 30).

IN WINEMAKING TERMS, the Côte
d'Or includes the Côte de
Beaune and the Côte de Nuits
in a nearly unbroken line of
vines from Dijon to Santenay.
Squeezed in between the flat
plain of the Saône to the
southeast and a plateau of
rough woodland to the northwest, this narrow escarpment
is about 50 km (30 miles)
long. The grapes of the great
Burgundy vineyards grow in
the golden reddish soil of the
slope (hence the name).
    The classification of the
characteristics of the land is
fabulously technical and elaborate, but for the layman a
rough rule of thumb might be
that 95 per cent of the best

Narrow street in Beaune's historic
centre

vines are on the uphill side of
the N74 thoroughfare (see
pp310–11). The names on the
signposts haunt the dreams of
wine lovers the world over:
Gevrey-Chambertin, Vougeot,
Chambolle-Musigny, Vosne-
Romanée, Nuits-St-Georges,
Aloxe-Corton, Meursault and
Chassagne Montrachet.

Typical grape basket in the Musée
du Vin de Bourgogne at Beaune

Beaune ⑳

Côte d'Or. 🚶 22,000. 🚉 🚌 ℹ
rue de l'Hôtel Dieu (03 80 26 21 30).
🛒 Sat & Wed.

THE OLD CENTRE of Beaune,
snug within its ramparts
and encircling boulevards, is
easy to explore on foot. Its
indisputable treasure is the
Hôtel-Dieu (see pp336–7).
The Hôtel des Ducs de
Bourgogne, built in the 14th–
16th centuries, houses the
Musée du Vin de Bourgogne.
The building, with its flamboyant façade, is as interesting
as its display of traditional
winemaking equipment.
    Further to the north lies
the **Collégiale Notre-Dame**,
begun in the early 12th
century. Inside this mainly
Romanesque church hang five
very fine 15th-century woollen
and silk tapestries. With hints

of early Renaissance style they
delicately illustrate the life of
the Virgin Mary in 19 scenes.

🏛 **Musée du Vin de
Bourgogne**
Rue d'Enfer. 📞 03 80 22 08 19.
Open Apr–Nov: daily; Dec–Mar:
Wed–Mon. 📷 ♿ ground floor only.

Tournus ㉑

Saône-et-Loire. 🚶 7,400. 🚉 🚌 ℹ
place Carnot (03 85 51 13 10). 🛒 Sat.

ONE OF BURGUNDY's oldest
and greatest Romanesque
buildings is found in Tournus.
The **Abbaye de St-Philibert**
was founded by a group of
monks from Noirmoutier who
had been driven from their
island by invading Normans in
the 9th century, taking with
them relics of their patron
saint, Philibert. Rebuilt in the
10th–12th centuries, the well-
fortified abbey church is made
from lovely pale pink stone.

Dovecote in Cormatin château
gardens, Mâconnais

Nave of St-Philibert in Tournus

A narthex leads into the nave with its soaring pillars and black and white vaulting. The bones of St Philibert can be seen in the choir, while in the niche on the south side is a 12th-century wood carving of Notre-Dame-la-Brune.

Environs
Southwest of Tournus lies the Mâconnais landscape of hills, vineyards, orchards, red-tiled farmhouses and Romanesque churches. **Brancion** is a pretty hill village, **Chapaize** has an 11th-century church and there is a sumptuous Renaissance château at **Cormatin**. The village of **Taizé** is the centre of a world-famous ecumenical community. To the north, **Chalon-sur-Saône** features old quarters and the Musée Niepce, dedicated to the inventor of photography.

Cluny ❷

Saône-et-Loire. 4,400. 6 rue Mercière (03 85 59 05 34). Sat.

THE LITTLE TOWN of Cluny is overshadowed by the ruins of its great abbey. The **Ancienne Abbaye de Cluny** was once the most powerful monastic foundation in Europe *(see pp44–5)*.

The abbey was founded by William the Pious, Duke of Aquitaine in 910. Within 200 years, Cluny had become the head of a major reforming order with monasteries all over Europe. Its abbots were considered as powerful as monarchs or popes, and four

of them are venerated as saints. By the 14th century, however, the system was in decline. The abbey was closed in 1790 and the church was later dismantled for building materials.

The guided tour presents the abbey remains, notably the Clocher de l'Eau Bénite (Holy Water Belltower), **Musée d'Art**, housed in the former abbot's palace, and its figured capitals displayed in the 13th-century flour-store. In the town, don't miss the 12th-century **Eglise St-Marcel**.

Southwest of the town, the chapel in **Berzé-la-Ville** is decorated with superb 12th-century frescoes, similar to those once seen at Cluny.

⚑ Ancienne Abbaye de Cluny
03 85 59 12 79. **Open** daily. **Closed** public hols.
🏛 Musée d'Art
Palais Jean de Bourbon. 03 85 59 23 97. **Open** daily. **Closed** 1 Jan, 1 May, 1 & 11 Nov, 25 Dec.

Paray-le-Monial ❷

Saône-et-Loire. 10,500. 25 av Jean-Paul II (03 85 81 10 92). Fri.

DEDICATED to the cult of the Sacred Heart of Jesus, the **Basilique du Sacré-Coeur** has made Paray-le-Monial one of the most important sites of pilgrimage in modern-day France. The cult was founded by Marguerite-Marie Alacoque who was born here in 1647, but it didn't develop until the 19th century. The church is a small version of the now lost abbey church of Cluny and features extraordinary harmony and purity in its Romanesque architecture.

The **Musée de la Faïence** in the priory contains some remarkable examples of 19th-century Charolles porcelain with pastoral decorations.

Situated on place Guignaud is the ornate **Maison Jayet**, dating from the 16th century, which houses the town hall.

Basilique du Sacré-Coeur at Paray-le-Monial

Hôtel-Dieu

Christ-de-Pitié

AFTER THE HUNDRED Years' War, many of Beaune's inhabitants suffered the effects of poverty and famine. To remedy this, the chancellor, Nicolas Rolin, and his wife founded a hospice here in 1443, which was inspired by the architecture of Northern French hospitals. The Rolins provided an annual grant, and vines and salt-works for income. Today the hospice is considered a medieval jewel, with its superb geometric multi-coloured Burgundian roof tiles. It houses two religious masterpieces: the *Christ-de-Pitié* statue, carved from wood, and Rogier van der Weyden's polyptych.

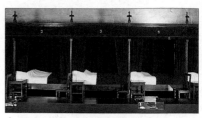

★ Great Hall of the Poor
The hall, with its carved, painted roof, has 28 four-poster beds, each one often used by several patients at a time. Meals were served from central tables.

Tribute to Rolin's Wife
A recurring motif features the entwined letters N and G, birds and stars, and the word "Seulle" referring to Rolin's wife Guigone, his "one and only".

Saint Hugues' Room contains a painting of the saint curing two children. Frescoes by Isaac Moillon show the miracles of Christ.

Entrance

Saint Anne's Room has a tableau of nuns working in what was once the linen room, and a colourful feast-day tapestry.

ANNUAL CHARITY WINE AUCTION

On the third Sunday in November, an annual charity auction in Beaune is the centrepiece of three days of festivities known as *Les Trois Glorieuses*. Saturday sees the banquet of the Confrérie des Chevaliers du Tastevin at the Château Clos de Vougeot. On Sunday the auction of wine from the 61 ha (151 acres) of vineyards, owned by nearby hospitals, takes place. Its prices are the benchmark for the entire vintage. On Monday at La Paulée de Meursault there is a party where growers bring along bottles of their best vintages to enjoy.

Wine sold at the famous auction

STAR FEATURES

★ Great Hall

★ Last Judgment Polyptych by Rogier van der Weyden

Kitchen

The centrepiece of the kitchen is a Gothic fireplace with a dual hearth and a mechanical spit, made in 1698, which is turned by a wooden "robot".

VISITORS' CHECKLIST

Rue de L'Hôtel-Dieu, Beaune.
📞 03 80 24 45 00. **Open**
Apr–mid-Nov: 9–6:30pm daily;
Dec–Mar: 9–11:30am, 2–5pm
daily. 🅿 📷 ✔
Wine Auction Les Halles
de Beaune (03 80 24 45 00).
Date 3rd Sunday in Nov.

Cour d'Honneur

The buildings of Hôtel-Dieu are arranged around a splendid central courtyard. This is flanked by a wooden gallery, above which rise high dormer windows topped by weather vanes. The courtyard well is a fine example of Gothic wrought-iron work.

Glazed roof tiles, in a colourful geometric pattern, are the most dramatic feature of the Hôtel-Dieu.

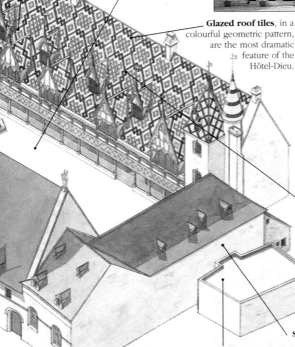

Pharmacy

Such unusual potions as woodlouse powder, shrimps' eyes and vomit nut powder are stored in these earthenware pots. Nearby is a bronze mortar used to prepare the remedies.

St Louis' Room

★ Last Judgment Polyptych

The naked figures shown in Rogier van der Weyden's 15th-century polyptych were briefly given clothing in the 19th century. At the same time, the altarpiece was cut in half so that the outer and inner panels could be seen together.

Château de Pierreclos in the Mâconnais region

Brionnais ㉔

Saône-et-Loire. ✈ Mâcon.
🚌 Paray-le-Monial, La Clayette.
🚌 Paray-le-Monial, Anzy-le-Duc.
ℹ Marcigny (03 85 25 39 06).

THE BRIONNAIS is a small and peace-ful rural district, squeezed between the river Loire and the Beaujolais foot-hills in the far south of Burgundy.

Its agricultural staple is the white Charolais cow, which can be seen grazing everywhere. For a closer look at this regional symbol, visit the lively cattle-market in **St-Christophe** early on Thursday mornings.

The area has an abundance of Romanesque churches, most of which are built of the local ochre-coloured stone. The 11th-century church of **Anzy-le-Duc** has a majestic

Capital in St-Julien-de-Jonzy

three-tiered polygonal tower and exquisitely carved capitals. **Semur-en-Brionnais** was the birthplace of Cluny's famous abbot St Hugues. Its church is inspired by his great monastery. The church at **St-Julien-de-Jonzy** has a very finely carved tympanum.

A small town by the river Genette, **La Clayette** is graced by a château set in a lake. It is not open to the public, but has a vintage car museum and in summer is the setting for a *son et lumière* show.

Southeast of La Clayette the lonely **Montagne de Dun** rises just over 700 m (2,300 ft) and offers a pano-rama over the gentle, green Brionnais hills. This is some of the best picnic country in Burgundy, full of sleepy corners and quiet byways.

Mâcon ㉕

Saône-et-Loire. 🏠 38,000. ✈ 🚊
🚌 ℹ 187 rue Carnot (03 85 39 71 37). 🛒 Sat.

AT THE FRONTIER between Burgundy and the south, Mâcon is an industrial town and wine centre on the Saône.

The lack of churches is due to fervent anti-clericalism during the Revolution, when 14 were destroyed. A 17th-century convent has been turned into the **Musée des Ursulines**. Its collections include French and Flemish painting and an exhibition on the prehistoric site of Solutré. On the charming place aux Herbes, where the market is held, the **Maison de Bois** is a 15th-century wooden house covered with bizarre carvings.

🏛 **Musée des Ursulines**
Allée de Matisco. 📞 03 85 39 90 38. **Open** Mon, Wed–Sat, Sun pm only. **Closed** most public hols. 🚫

Environs
The great **Roche de Solutré** rises dramatically above the Pouilly-Fuissé vineyards in the Mâconnais district *(see p.335)*. Below the rock, bones and flints from the Stone Ages have established it as an important archaeological site.

Mâconnais is also the land of the Romantic poet Lamartine (1790–1869). Born in Mâcon, he spent his childhood at Milly Lamartine and later lived at Château de St-Point. **Château de Pierreclos** is associated with his epic poem *Jocelyn*.

Charolais cattle grazing on the gentle hills of the Brionnais

Franche-Comté

A REGION OF WOODS and water, the Franche-Comté offers exceptional natural beauty combined with opportunities for canoeing, trekking and skiing. Apart from towns well worth visiting, this is a region to explore in the wild. Glorious scenery with grottoes and cascading waterfalls can be found all along the Vallée du Doubs. Further south are the spectacular sources of the rivers Lison and Loue. The Reculées is an area of extraordinary formations of ridges and waterfalls such as Baume-les-Messieurs. In Région des Lacs, the silent, peaceful lakes are surrounded by mountain peaks and virgin forests.

Cascades du Hérisson ㉖

Pays-des-Lacs. **⌂** *Clairvaux-les-Lacs (03 84 25 27 47).*

Nature at its purest at Source du Lison in the Franche-Comté

THE VILLAGE of Doucier, at the foot of the Pic de l'Aigle, is the starting point for the valley of the river Hérisson, one of the finest natural settings in the Jura. Leave the car at the park by the Moulin Jacquand and walk up the trail through the woods to a spectacular waterfall, the 65-m (213-ft) Cascade de L'Eventail, and beyond to the equally impressive Cascade du Grand Saut. The walk, which takes about two hours there and back, is steep at times and can be slippery, so proper shoes are essential.

Arbois ㉗

Jura. **⌂** *4,000.* 🚉 🚌 **⌂** *10 rue de l'Hôtel de Ville (03 84 37 47 37).* 🛒 *Fri.*

THE JOLLY wine town of Arbois lies on the vine-covered banks of the river Cuisance. It is famous for its wines, especially the sherry-like *vin jaune* (yellow wine) of the district. On the north side

of the town is **Maison de Pasteur**, the preserved house and laboratory of the great practical scientist Louis Pasteur (1822–95), the first to test vaccines on humans.

Environs
Southeast of Dole is the 18th-century **Château d'Arlay**, with immaculately kept gardens.

Dole ㉘

Jura. **⌂** *27,000.* 🚉 🚌 **⌂** *6 pl Grevy (03 84 72 11 22).* 🛒 *Tue, Thu & Sat.*

THE BUSY TOWN of Dole lies where the Doubs meets the Rhine-Rhône canal. The former capital of the Comté was always a symbol of the region's resistance to the French. The region had become used to relative independence, first under the Counts of Burgundy and then as part of the Holy Roman Empire. Though always French-speaking, its people did not appreciate the idea of the French absolute

monarchy and in 1636 endured a very long siege. The town finally submitted to Louis XIV, first in 1668, and again in 1674.

There is a charming historic quarter in the centre of town, full of winding alleys, houses dating back to the 15th century, and quiet inner court-yards. Place aux Fleurs offers an excellent view of this part of town and the mossy-roofed, 16th-century **Eglise Notre-Dame** with its high belltower.

Virgin and Child on the north portal of Eglise Notre-Dame, Dole

The Saline Royale at Arc-et-Senans

Arc-et-Senans ㉙

Doubs. 🏘 *1,300.* 🚋
ℹ️ *03 81 57 46 44.*

Designated a world heritage
site since 1982, the Saline
Royale (royal salt works) at
Arc-et-Senans were designed
by the great French architect
Claude-Nicolas Ledoux (1736–
1806). He envisaged a development built in concentric
circles around the main buildings. However, the only ones
to be completed (in 1775)
were the buildings meant for
salt production. Nevertheless,
these show the staggering
scale of Ledoux's idea: salt
water was to be piped from
Salins-les-Bains nearby, and
fuel to reduce it was to come
from the Chaux forest. The
enterprise, which was never a
financial success, was closed
down in 1895, but the terrific
buildings remain.

The **Musée Ledoux** displays
intriguing models of this and
other grand projects imagined
by the visionary architect.

🏛 **Musée Ledoux**
Ancienne Saline Royale.
📞 *03 81 54 45 45.* **Open** *daily.*
Closed *1 Jan, 25 Dec.* 🎫

Champlitte ㉚

Haute Saône. 🏘 *1,900.* 🚋 ℹ️ *La
Mairie (03 84 67 68 78).*

At a time when the small-
farm life of the French
countryside is fast disappearing, the **Musée des Arts et
Traditions Populaires** at the
small town of Champlitte has
a special relevance. This
museum of folk arts and

traditions (in a Renaissance
château) was created by a local
shepherd who collected objects
and artifacts connected with
disappearing local customs.
One of the most poignant displays recalls the emigration of
400 inhabitants to Mexico in
the mid-19th century.

🏛 **Musée des Arts et
Traditions Populaires**
Place de l'Eglise. 📞 *03 84 67 82 00.*
Open *Apr–Sep: daily; Oct–Mar:
Wed–Mon.* **Closed** *1 Jan, 1 Nov, 25
Dec.* 🎫

Besançon ㉛

Doubs. 🏘 *120,000.* 🚋 🚌
ℹ️ *2 place de la 1re Armée Française
(03 81 80 92 55).* 🅰️ *Tue, Fri & Sun.*

Besançon supplanted Dole
as the capital of the
Franche-Comté in the 17th
century. It began as an ecclesiastical centre and is now
an industrial one, specializing
in precision engineering. The
stately architecture of the old
town, often enriched with
elegant wrought-iron work,
is a 17th-century legacy.

A walk along the Grande
Rue reveals varying aspects of
the town's past. The **Palais
Granvelle**, built for the Chancellor of the Holy Roman
Emperor in 1534–42, has a
beautiful Renaissance façade.
Further on are the birthplaces
of the titanic novelist Victor
Hugo (1802–85) at No. 140
and the Lumière brothers *(see
p59)* at place Victor Hugo.
Behind **Porte Noire**, a Roman
arch, is the 12th-century
Cathédrale St-Jean. In its belltower is the extraordinary
Horloge Astronomique,

a true symbol of Besançon's
watchmaking past. Try to be
there on the hour, when the
automats pop out of the clock
as if by magic.

The stunning **Musée des
Beaux Arts et d'Archéologie**
occupies the old corn market.
Its collection includes works
by Bellini, Cranach, Rubens,
Fragonard, Boucher, Greuse,
Ingres, Courbet, David, Goya,
Matisse and Picasso.

Vauban's citadel, built on a
strategic site overlooking the
river Doubs, offers magnificent
views and houses the intriguing **Musée Comtoise** with a
collection of local artifacts.

⌚ **Horloge Astronomique**
Rue de la Convention. 📞 *03 81 81
12 76.* **Open** *Apr–Sep: Wed–Mon;
Oct–Dec, Feb–Mar: Thu–Mon.*
Closed *1 Jan, 1 May, 1 & 11 Nov, 25
Dec.* 🎫

🏛 **Musée des Beaux Arts et
d'Archéologie**
1 pl de la Révolution. 📞 *03 81 81 44
47.* **Open** *Wed–Mon.* **Closed** *1 Jan, 1
May, 1 Nov, 25 Dec.* 🎫 *except Sun.* ♿

🏛 **Musée Comtois**
La Citadelle, rue des Fusillés de la
Résistance. 📞 *03 81 65 07 44.*
Open *daily.* **Closed** *1 Jan, 25 Dec.* 🎫

**The fantastic astronomical clock
in Besançon, made in 1857–60**

Ornans ㉜

Doubs. 🏘 *4,300.* 🚋 ℹ️ *7 rue
Pierre Vernier (03 81 62 21 50).*

The great Realist painter
Gustave Courbet was born
at Ornans in 1819. He painted
the town in every possible
light. His *Enterrement à
Ornans* proved to be one of
the most influential paintings

The striking Chapelle Notre-Dame-du-Haut by Le Corbusier at Ronchamp

of the 19th century. A stream of Courbet enthusiasts makes the pilgrimage to this delightful riverside town to see his grave and the paintings in his childhood home, now turned into the **Musée Courbet**.

⑪ Musée Courbet
Place Robert Fernier. **【** 03 81 62 23 30. **Open** Apr–Oct: daily; Nov–Mar: Wed–Mon. **Closed** 1 Jan, 1 May, 1 Nov, 25 Dec. 🖼

Environs
A canoeist's paradise, the **Vallée de la Loue** is the loveliest in the Jura. The D67 follows the river from Ornans eastwards to Ouhans, from where it is only a 15-minute walk to its magnificent source. Various belvederes offer splendid views over the area.

Southwest of Ornans, the spectacular **Source du Lison** (see p339) is a 20-minute walk from Nans-sous-Ste-Anne.

Belfort ㉝

Territoire de Belfort. 🏛 52,000. 🚊 🚌 🚏 2 bis rue Clemenceau (03 84 55 90 90). 🚌 daily.

THE SYMBOL of Belfort is an enormous pink sandstone lion. It was built (rather than carved) by Frédéric Bartholdi (1834–1904), whose other major undertaking was the Statue of Liberty.

Belfort's immensely strong **citadel**, designed by Vauban under Louis XIV, withstood three sieges, in 1814, 1815 and 1870. Today this remarkable array of fortifications provides an interesting walk and extensive views of the surroundings. The **Musée d'Art et d'Histoire**, housed in some of the billets, displays models of the original fortifications as well as regional art and artifacts and contemporary exhibitions.

Ronchamp ㉞

Haute Saône. 🏛 3,100. 🚊 🚏 place du 14 juillet (Apr–Nov: 03 84 63 50 82). 🚌 Sat.

LE CORBUSIER'S remarkable **Chapelle Notre-Dame-du-Haut** dominates this former miners' town. A sculpture rather than a building, its swelling concrete form was finalized in 1955. Light, shape and space form a successful unity in the interior.

There is also a **Musée de la Mine** evoking the industry and the life of local miners.

Le Miroir d'Ornans in the Musée Courbet, Ornans

THE MASSIF CENTRAL

ALLIER · AVEYRON · CANTAL · CORRÈZE · CREUSE · HAUTE-LOIRE
HAUTE-VIENNE · LOZÈRE · PUY DE DÔME

*T*HE MASSIF CENTRAL *is the keystone of France, holding the country together by the sheer force of its grandeur. It is surprisingly little known beyond its sprinkling of spas and the major cities of Clermont-Ferrand, Vichy and Limoges. This remarkable, remote and rugged region is one of France's best-kept secrets.*

The huge central plateau of ancient granite and crystalline rock that makes up the Massif Central embraces the dramatic landscapes of the Auvergne, Limousin, Aveyron and Lozère. Once a testing crossroads for pilgrims, and strung with giant volcanoes, it is a region of unsuspected richness, from the spectacular town of Le Puy-en-Velay, to the unique treasures at Conques.

With its crater lakes and hot springs, the Auvergne is the Massif Central's lush volcanic core, an outdoor paradise offering activities from hiking in summer to skiing in winter. It also has some of France's most beautiful Romanesque churches, medieval castles and Renaissance palaces. To the east are the mountain ranges of Forez, Livardois and Velay; to the west are the giant chains of extinct volcanoes, the Monts Dômes, Monts Dore and the Monts du Cantal. The Limousin, on the northwestern edge of the Massif Central, is gentler country with green pastures and blissfully empty roads.

The Aveyron spreads into the southwest from the Aubrac mountains, carrying with it the rivers Lot, Aveyron and Tarn through gorges and valleys with their cliff-hanging villages. To the east in the Lozère are the Grands Causses, the vast, isolated uplands of the Cévennes. These barren plateaux give farmers a poor living, but have been a favourite route with adventurous travellers across the centuries.

La Bourboule, a spa town in the Monts Dore

◁ **The summit of Puy Mary, 1,787 m (5,863 ft), offering a superb view to walkers who attempt the ascent**

Exploring the Massif Central

NATURE IS AT ITS MOST MAGNIFICENT in the volcanic mountain ranges and wild river gorges of the Massif Central. This is a vast and unspoiled territory which offers spectacular sightseeing and every imaginable outdoor activity, with rafting, paragliding, canoeing and hiking among the many choices. There are hundreds of churches, châteaux and museums to nourish lovers of history, architecture and art; and good, hearty regional cooking and wonderful local wines for lovers of good living.

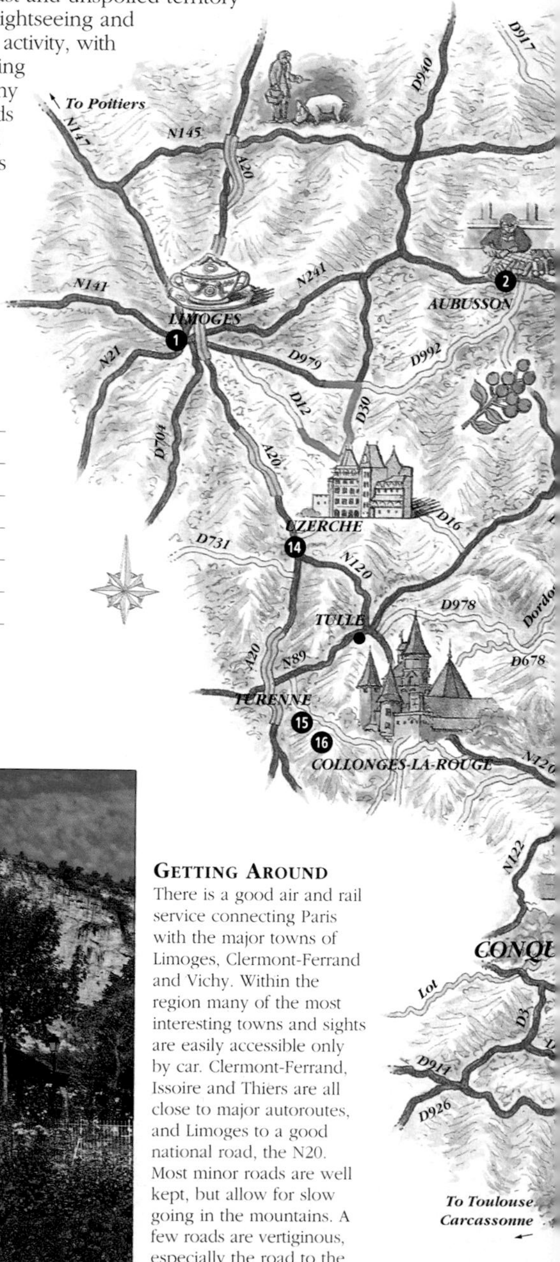

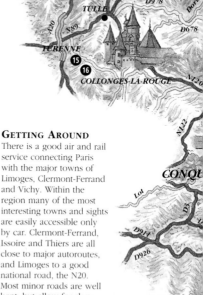

KEY

▬ Motorway

▬ Major road

▬ Minor road

▬ Scenic route

〰 River

☆ Viewpoint

0 kilometres   25

0 miles   25

Limestone cliffs of the Gorges du Tarn

GETTING AROUND

There is a good air and rail service connecting Paris with the major towns of Limoges, Clermont-Ferrand and Vichy. Within the region many of the most interesting towns and sights are easily accessible only by car. Clermont-Ferrand, Issoire and Thiers are all close to major autoroutes, and Limoges to a good national road, the N20. Most minor roads are well kept, but allow for slow going in the mountains. A few roads are vertiginous, especially the road to the summit of Puy Mary, which is breathtaking.

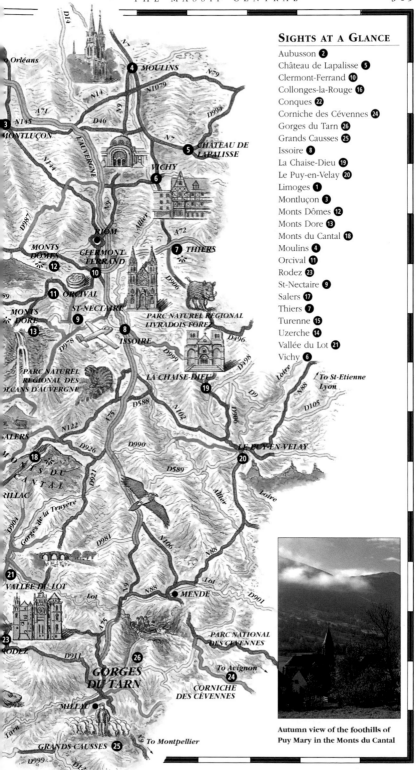

Autumn view of the foothills of
Puy Mary in the Monts du Cantal

A Limoges enamel plaque, **The Bad Shepherd**

Limoges ❶

Haute-Vienne. 👥 150,000. ✈ 🚊
🚌 🛈 *bd de Fleurus (05 55 34 46 87).*
🚢 *daily.*

THE CAPITAL of the Limousin
has two hearts: the old
Cité, which grew up around
the cathedral on a plateau
overlooking the river Vienne,
and the rival château on an
adjacent rise, now the commercial centre of the modern
city. The Cité was ravaged by
the Black Prince in 1370
during the Hundred Years'
War and never recovered;
today it is a quiet place to
wander among half-timbered
houses and narrow streets.

The area was famous for
enamelwork in the Middle Ages
and Renaissance period, but it
was not until the 1770s, when
kaolin deposits were discovered
nearby, that Limoges became
synonymous with porcelain.
The legendary local ware is on
display at the superb **Musée
National Adrien-Dubouché**.
More than 10,000 exhibits, including early Greek and
Chinese pieces, trace the history of ceramics to the present

day. The **Musée Municipal
de l'Evêché** houses some 500
Limousin enamels.

🏛 Musée National Adrien-
Dubouché

Place Winston Churchill.
📞 *05 55 33 08 50.* **Open** *Wed–Mon.*
Closed *1 Jan, 1 May, 25 Dec.* 📷
🏛 Musée Municipal de
l'Evêché

Place de la Cathédrale. 📞 *05 55 45
61 75.* **Open** *Jul, Aug: daily; Oct–Jun:
Wed–Mon.* **Closed** *1 Jan, 1 May,
1 & 11 Nov, 25 Dec.*

Environs

Intense Resistance activity in
the Limousin during World
War II led to severe reprisals
by the occupying army. On
10 June 1944 at the village
of Oradour-sur-Glane, SS
troops burned alive the entire
population of 650. The ruins
have been kept as a shrine,
and a new village built next
to them. The lively town of
St-Junien, a glove-making
centre since the Middle Ages,
has an intriguing 11th-century
church (the Collégiale St-
Junien) containing a statue of
Sainte Madeleine clothed entirely in her own blonde hair.

Aubusson ❷

Creuse. 👥 6,000. 🚊 🚌 🛈 *rue
Vieille (05 55 66 32 12).* 🚢 *Sat.*

AUBUSSON OWES its renown
to the exceptionally pure
waters of the Creuse, perfect
for making the delicately
coloured dyes used for
tapestries and rugs. Tapestry
production was at its zenith in
the 16th and 17th centuries,
but by the end of the 18th
century the Revolution and
patterned wallpaper had
swept away the clientele.

In the 1940s, Aubusson was
revived, largely due to the
artist Jean Lurçat, who persuaded other modern artists
to design for tapestry. The
**Musée Departemental de la
Tapisserie**, across the river
from the Old Town, displays
a permanent collection of
these modern works. Visitors are
welcome at the **Manufacture
St Jean**, where they may watch
tapestries and custom-made
carpets being expertly restored
and made by hand.

🏛 Musée Departemental de
la Tapisserie

Avenue des Lissiers. 📞 *05 55 66 33
06.* **Open** *Wed–Mon.* 📷 ♿
🏛 Manufacture St Jean

3 rue St Jean. 📞 *05 55 66 10 08.*
Open *Mar–Oct: daily; Nov–Feb:
Mon–Fri.* **Closed** *23 Dec–1 Jan.* 📷

Environs

A single street of 15th-century
houses and a Roman bridge
comprise **Moûtier-d'Ahun**,

**Tapestry restoration at the
Manufacture St Jean in Aubusson**

Romanesque church at Moûtier-d'Ahun near Aubusson

tucked into the lush Creuse valley. Vestiges of a Benedictine abbey can still be detected in the half-Romanesque, half-Gothic church with its elaborate stone portal. The choir has wooden stalls, for which it is worth paying a visit to the church. They are masterpieces of late 17th-century carving with fantastical and intricately worked motifs of flora and fauna representing the many different facets of Good and Evil in figurative form. Today there is a garden where the nave once was.

Montluçon 3

Allier. ⚑ 45,000. ✕ 🚆 🚌 🛈 5 Place Piquand (04 70 05 11 44). 🛒 Sat.

MONTLUÇON is the economic centre of the region, a small town with a medieval core. At its heart there is a Bourbon château, now the **Musée des Instruments et des Musiques**, housing a collection of *vielles* (hurdy-gurdies). Upstairs are 19th- and 20th-century prints by local artists and displays of regional faïence. The 12th-century **Eglise de St-Pierre** is a surprise, with giant stone columns and a huge barrel-vaulted ceiling.

🏛 Musée des Instruments et des Musiques Populaires
Château des Ducs de Bourbon. **Closed** until Jun 1997.

Moulins 4

Allier. ⚑ 23,000. 🚆 🚌 🛈 place de l'Hôtel de Ville (04 70 44 14 14). 🛒 Tue & Fri.

CAPITAL of the Bourbonnais and seat of the Bourbon Dukes since the 10th century, Moulins flourished during the early Renaissance, and is now an appealing backwater.

Moulins' most celebrated sight is the Flamboyant Gothic **Cathédrale Notre-Dame**, where members of the Bourbon court appear amid the saints in the 15th- and 16th-century stained-glass windows.

The treasury contains a luminous 15th-century Virgin and Child triptych by the "Master of Moulins". Benefactors Pierre II, Duke of Bourbon, and his wife Anne de Beaujeu, bedecked in embroidery and jewels, are shown being introduced to a less richly dressed Madonna in the central panel.

The tower keep and the single remaining wing of the Bourbon **Vieux Château** house a superb collection of sculpture, painting and decorative art from the 12th to the 16th centuries.

🔒 Cathédrale Notre-Dame
Rue Louis Mantin. **Treasury open** Apr–Sep: daily; Oct–Mar: Wed–Mon. 🎟 **Closed** Sun am.

Stained-glass windows at the Cathédrale Notre-Dame in Moulins

Château de Lapalisse ❺

Allier. 📞 04 70 99 08 51, 04 70 55 01 12. **Open** Easter– Oct: Wed–Mon. 🖼️

IN THE EARLY 16th century, the Marshal of France, Jacques II de Chabannes, hired Florentine architects to reconstruct the feudal château-fort at Lapalisse, creating a refined Renaissance castle, inhabited ever since by his descendants. The *salon doré* (gilded room) has a beamed ceiling panelled in gold, and two huge 15th-century Flemish tapestries showing the Crusader Knight Godefroy de Bouillon and Greek hero Hector, two of the nine classic braves of chivalric legend.

Environs
From Lapalisse, the D480 leads up through the beautiful Besbre valley past a handful of other small, well-preserved châteaux. Only **Château de Thoury**, with ancient hunting memorabilia and *objets d'art* on show, is open to the public.

♣ **Château de Thoury**
Dompierre. 📞 04 70 42 00 41. **Open** Apr–Oct: daily. 🖼️ 🅿️ restricted.

Gilded ceiling, Château de Lapalisse

Vichy ❻

Allier. 🏠 26,000. 🚊 🚌 🛈 19 rue du Parc (04 70 98 71 94). 🍴 Wed.

THIS SMALL CITY on the river Allier has been known since the Roman era for its hot and cold springs, and reputed cures for rheumatism, arthritis and digestive complaints. The celebrated letter-writer Madame de Sévigné and the daughters of Louis XV came here in the late 17th and 18th centuries – the former compared the showers to "a rehearsal for Purgatory". The

Interior of the original Thermal Establishment building in Vichy

visits of Napoleon III in the 1860s put Vichy on the map and made taking the waters fashionable. The small town was spruced up and became a favourite among the French nobility and the world's wealthy middle classes. These days, the grand old Thermal Establishment, built in 1900, has been turned into shopping galleries. The modern baths are state-of-the-art and strictly

Vichy poster (about 1930–50) by Badia-Vilato

for medical purposes. A doctor's prescription and a reservation 30 days in advance are required for all treatments.

Vichy's fortunes changed for the better once again in the 1960s with the damming of the Allier, creating a huge lake in the middle of town, which rapidly became a thriving centre for watersports and international events. For a small fee, you can have a taste of sports from aikido to waterskiing or learn canoeing on the 3-km (2-mile) long artificial river.

The focal point of life in Vichy is the **Parc des Sources** in the centre of town, with its turn-of-the-century bandstand (afternoon concerts in season), Belle Epoque glass-roofed shopping galleries, and the Grand Casino and Opera House. Here there is gambling every afternoon and musical performances in the evenings, and an atmosphere of gaiety pervades. Also open to the public are the beautiful bronze taps of the **Source**

Celestin, in a riverside park containing vestiges of a convent bearing the same name. Only by making an effort to imagine the city in grainy black-and-white newsreel style is there the slightest reminder of the wartime Vichy government which was based in the town from 1940–44 *(see p61)*.

🌺 **Source Celestin**
Boulevard Kennedy.
Open daily. ♿

Thiers ⓞ

Puy de Dôme. 🚶 *15,000.* 🚌 🚉
🛈 *Maison de Pirou (04 73 80 10 74).*
🍽 *Thu & Sat.*

ACCORDING TO the writer La Bruyère, Thiers "seems painted on the slope of the hill", hanging dramatically as it does on a ravine over a sharp bend in the river Durolle. The city has been renowned for cutlery since the Middle Ages, when legend has it that Crusaders brought back techniques of metalwork from the Middle East. With grindstones powered by dozens of waterfalls on the opposite bank of the river, Thiers produced everything from table knives to guillotine blades, and cutlery remains its major industry today, much of it on display in the Cutlery Museum, the **Musée de la Coutellerie**.

The Old Town is filled with mysterious quarters like "the Corner of Chance" and "Hell's Hollow", honeycombed with tortuous streets and well-restored 15th–17th-century houses. Many have elaborately carved wooden façades, like the Maison du Pirou in place

Pirou. The view to the west from the rampart terrace, towards the Monts Dômes and the Monts Dore, is often splendid at sunset.

🏛 **Musée de la Coutellerie**
Maison des Coutelliers, 21–23 & 58 rue de la Coutellerie. 📞 *04 73 80 58 86.* **Open** *Jun–Sep: daily; Oct–May: Tue–Sun.* **Closed** *1 Jan, 1 May, 14 Sep, 1 Nov, 25 Dec.* 📷

Issoire ⓞ

Puy de Dôme. 🚶 *14,000.* 🚌
🛈 *place du Général de Gaulle (04 73 89 15 90).* 🍽 *Sat.*

MOST OF OLD ISSOIRE was destroyed in the 17th-century Wars of Religion. The present-day town has been an important industrial centre

since the end of World War II. Not only does Issoire have a thriving aeronautical tradition, it is also a mecca for glider pilots who come from miles around to take advantage of the strong local air currents.

One of the few relics of old Issoire, the colourful 12th-century abbey church of **St-Austremoine** is one of the great Romanesque churches of the region. The capitals depict scenes from the *Life of Christ* (one of the Apostles at the Last Supper has fallen asleep at the table), or imaginary demons and beasts. The 15th-century fresco of the *Last Judgment* shows Bosch-like figures of sinners being cast into the mouth of a dragon, with one damsel being carted off to hell in a hand basket.

Thiers from the south, spreading over the slopes above the river Durolle

St-Nectaire ❾

Puys de Dôme. 🏠 650. 🔲 🚹 *Les Grandes Thermes (04 73 88 50 86).*

THE AUVERGNE is noted for Romanesque churches. The **Eglise St-Nectaire** in the upper village of St-Nectaire-le-Haut, with its soaring, elegant proportions, is one of the most beautiful. The 103 stone capitals, 22 of them poly-chrome, are vividly carved, and the treasury includes a gold bust of St Baudime and a wooden Notre-Dame-de-Mont-Cornadore, both marvels of 12th-century work-manship. The lower village, St-Nectaire-le-Bas, is a spa with more than 40 hot and cold springs, used in the treatment of kidney and meta-bolic problems.

Environs

The 12th-century citadel of **Château de Murol**, partially in ruins, offers costumed guides demonstrating medieval life and knightly pursuits. It is wonderful for children.

🏛 **Château de Murol**
Murol. 📞 *04 73 88 67 11.* **Open** *Apr–Sep: daily; Oct–Mar: Sun & school hols.* 🈺

Fontaine d'Amboise (1515) in Clermont-Ferrand

Clermont-Ferrand ❿

Puy de Dôme. 🏠 140,000. ✈ 🚊 🔲 🚹 *place de la Victoire (04 73 98 65 00).* 🈺 *Mon–Sat.*

CLERMONT-FERRAND began as two distinct – and rival – cities, united only in 1630. Clermont is a lively and bust-ling commercial centre and student town, with thriving cafés and restaurants. It was a Celtic settlement before the Roman era, had a cathedral as early as the 5th century, and by 1095 was significant enough for the pope to announce the First Crusade there. The Counts of Auvergne, challenging the episcopal power of Clermont, established their base in what is now old Montferrand, a short drive from Clermont city centre. Built on a bastide pattern, this is a time warp of quiet streets and Renaissance houses.

Place St-Pierre is Clermont's principal marketplace, with a daily food market which is especially good on Saturdays. Nearby, the **Fontaine d'Amboise** (1515), a tiered fantasy in black lava, looks out to the Puy de Dôme peak. The pedestrianized rue du Port, lined with small shops, leads steeply downhill from the fountain to the **Basilique Notre-Dame-du-Port**. This is one of the most important Romanesque churches in the region. The stone interior is beautifully proportioned, with a magni-ficent raised choir and vivid carved capitals – look for Charity battling Avarice, in the form of two knights with chain mail and pikes.

The contrast with the black lava **Cathédrale de Notre-Dame-de-l'Assomption** is startling, from austere 12th-century Romanesque to high-flying 13th-century Gothic. The graceful lines of the

Raised choir in the Basilique Notre-Dame-du-Port

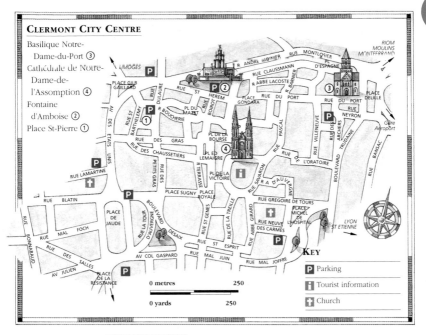

CLERMONT CITY CENTRE

Basilique Notre-
  Dame-du-Port ③
Cathédrale de Notre-
  Dame-de-
  l'Assomption ④
Fontaine
  d'Amboise ②
Place St-Pierre ①

KEY

P Parking

ℹ Tourist information

✝ Church

0 metres 250

0 yards 250

---

interior are due to the strong local stone used for construction, allowing pillars to be thinner and the whole structure lighter. The dark volcanic rock provides a foil for the jewel-like 12th–15th-century stained-glass windows, which are believed to be from the same workshop as Sainte-Chapelle's in Paris *(see pp80–81)*.

The old section of Montferrand thrived from the 13th to the 17th centuries, and many fine houses – known as *hôtels particuliers* – built by prosperous merchants have survived. Some of the best of

Michelin man, c.1910

these, with Italianate loggias, mullioned windows and intriguing courtyards, line ancient **rue Kléber**. Between Clermont and old Montferrand lies a third mini-city, the headquarters and factories of the Michelin rubber-and-tyre company, founded here in 1830, which dominates the town.

Environs

Once the rival of Clermont-Ferrand for supremacy in Auvergne, **Riom** is a sombre provincial town of black stone houses and lava fountains. The 14th-century château of Duke Jean de Berry was razed in the 19th century to build the Palais de Justice; all that remains is the delicate Sainte-Chapelle with its lovely 15th-century stained-glass windows.

Riom's greatest treasure is a graceful Madonna holding an infant with a small bird in his hand. The statue is housed in the Eglise de Notre-Dame-du-Marthuret, originally built in the 14th century, but much rearranged since then.

Choir inside the Cathédrale de Notre-Dame-de-l'Assomption

Orcival ⑪

Puy de Dôme. 🚶 *300.*
ℹ *04 73 65 82 55.*

CRAMMED WITH HOTELS and crowded in summer, Orcival is nevertheless well worth visiting for its Romanesque church, the **Basilique d'Orcival**, which many would say is the best in the region. Completed at the beginning of the 12th century, and typically Auvergne Romanesque in style, the apse is multi-tiered and the side walls are supported by powerful buttresses and strong arches. Inside, the ornate silver and vermilion *Virgin and Child* (in the formal, forward-facing position known as "in majesty") is enigmatic in its rigid, square chair. With an interior lit by 14 windows and a spacious crypt, the proportions of the building itself are the most graceful aspect.

Virgin and Child in the Basilique d'Orcival

Aerial view of Puy de Dôme in the Monts Dômes range

Monts Dômes ⑫

Puy de Dôme. 🎿 🚋 🚻 *Clermont-Ferrand.* 🛈 *Puy de Dôme summit (04 73 62 21 45: Apr–Oct). Montlosier (04 73 65 64 00).*

THE YOUNGEST RANGE of the Auvergne volcanoes at 4,000 years old, the Monts Dômes, or Chaîne des Puys, encompasses 112 extinct volcanoes aligned over a 30-km (19-mile) stretch just west of Clermont-Ferrand. At the centre, the **Puy de Dôme** towers above a high plateau. A concentric road off the N922 spirals up the peak at a steady 12 per cent gradient, while the steeper, original switchback Roman path is still used by hikers.

At the summit – a further half-hour walk – are the vestiges of the Roman temple of Mercury and a telecommunications tower. But on a rare clear day, the view across the volcano will take away whatever breath the walker has left.

The volcanic Roche Tuilière below Col de Guéry in the Monts Dore

In the southwest corner of the Monts Dômes region is the **Château de Cordès**, a small, privately owned 15th-century manor house. The formal gardens were laid out by Le Nôtre *(see p169)*, who also designed the gardens at Versailles.

♣ **Château de Cordès**
Orcival. 🕻 *04 73 65 81 34.* **Open** *Easter–Oct: daily (phone for visits out of season).* 🅿

Monts Dore ⑬

Puy de Dôme. 🚋 *Clermont-Ferrand.* 🚋 🚻 *Le Mont-Dore.* 🛈 *Montlosier (04 73 65 64 00).*

THREE GIANT VOLCANOES – the Puy de Sancy, the Banne d'Ordanche and the Puy de l'Aiguiller – and their secondary cones make up the Monts Dore: dark green, heavily wooded mountains laced with rivers and lakes and dotted with summer and winter resorts for skiing, hiking, paragliding, canoeing and sailing.

The 1,885-m (6,185-ft) **Puy de Sancy** is the highest point in Central France. Its peak can be reached by taking the cable car from the town of Le Mont-Dore, followed by a long hike across open terrain. From Le Mont-Dore, there is an exhilarating scenic drive on the D36 which leads to the **Couze de Chambon valley**, a beautiful stretch of high moorland threaded with waterfalls.

The area has two very popular spa towns: **La Bourboule** is a sunny resort mainly devoted to children's ailments, and it even has a Children's

Casino attached to the **Grand Casino**. At Le Mont-Dore, the **Etablissement Therma**, for asthma and respiratory ailments, has a grandiose turn-of-the-century interior.

Below the Col de Guéry on the D983, the eroded volcanic **Roche Sanadoire** and **Roche Tuilière** stand up like two gigantic gateposts; from their peaks there are far-reaching views over the wooded Cirque de Chausse and the valley beyond.

🚻 **Etablissement Thermal**
1 place du Panthéon, Le Mont-Dore. 🕻 *04 73 65 05 10.* **Open** *mid-May– 9 Oct: Mon–Sat.* 🅿 🅱

Church at La Bourboule in the Monts Dore

Uzerche ⑭

Corrèze. 🏘 *3,500.* 🚋 🚻 🛈 *place de la Lunade (05 55 73 15 71).*

UZERCHE is an impressive sight: grey slate roofs, turrets and belltowers rising from a hill above the Vézère river. This prosperous town never capitulated during the conflicts of the Middle Ages, and earlier withstood a seven-year siege by Moorish forces in 732. On the point of surrender, the townspeople sent a feast out to their enemy – in fact, the last of their supplies. The Moors, thinking such lavish offerings meant the city had stores to spare, gave up.

The Romanesque **Église St-Pierre** crests the hill above the town. Beyond Uzerche, the Vézère cuts through the green gorges of the Saillant.

CANTAL CHEESE

Transhumance is still practised in the Auvergne, with the local Salers cattle kept in barns in the valleys during winter and led up to mountain pastures for the summer. The robust grasses and flowers – gentian, myrtle, anemone – on which the cows graze produce a flavoursome milk that is the basis for the region's great cheese, Cantal. Curds were once turned and pressed through cheesecloth by hand, but now modern methods prevail. Cantal is the key ingredient in *aligot* – the potato-and-cheese purée flavoured with garlic that is one of the region's most famous dishes.

Salers cattle enjoying rich pastures

Turenne ⓯

Corrèze. 750.
Ancienne Mairie (summer: 05 55 85 94 38; winter: 05 55 85 91 15).

TURENNE is one of the most appealing medieval towns in the Corrèze. Crescent-shaped and clustered on the cliffside, the town was the last independent feudal fiefdom in France, under the absolute rule of the La Tour d'Auvergne family until 1738. Henri de la Tour d'Auvergne, their most illustrious member, was a marshal of France under Louis XIV, and one of the greatest soldiers of modern times.

Now the sole remains of the **Château du Turenne** are the 13th-century Clock Tower and 11th-century Tower of Caesar, from which there is an amazing 360-degree view of the Cantal mountains across to the Dordogne valley. Not far away is the 16th-century collegiate church and the **Chapelle des Capucins** dating from the 18th century.

⚓ **Château du Turenne**
05 55 85 91 87. **Open**
Easter–Oct: daily; Nov–Feb: Sun.

Collonges-la-Rouge ⓰

Corrèze. 400.

THERE'S SOMETHING a little unsettling about Collonges' unique carmine sandstone architecture, quite beautiful in individual houses but somewhat sinister *en masse*, especially in those buildings with bands of white mortar outlining the red stone blocks. Founded in the 8th century, Collonges came under the rule of Turenne, whose burghers built the sturdy turreted houses in the surrounding vineyards. Look out for the communal bread oven in the marketplace, and the 11th-century church, which was later fortified with a tower keep. The unusual carved white limestone tympanum shows a man driving a bear, among several other lively figures.

Salers ⓱

Cantal. 450. place Tyssandier d'Escous (04 71 40 70 68). Wed.

A SOLID, HANDSOME TOWN of grey lava houses and 15th-century ramparts, Salers sits atop a steep escarpment at the edge of the Cantal mountains. It is one of few virtually intact Renaissance villages in the region. The church has an admirable polychrome *mise en tombeau* (entombment), dated 1495, and five elaborate 17th-century Aubusson tapestries.

From the fountain, streets lead up to the cliff edge, and allow views of the surrounding valleys, with the ever-present sound of cowbells in the distance. The town is very crowded in summer, but it makes a good starting point for excursions to the Puy Mary (*see p354*), the huge barrage at Bort-les-Orgues, the nearby Château de Val and the Cère valley to the south.

Medieval Château de Val at Bort-les-Orgues near Salers

Puy Mary peak in the volcanic Monts du Cantal

Monts du Cantal ⓲

Cantal. ✈ Aurillac. 🚉 🚌 Lioran.
🛈 Super-Lioran (04 71 49 50 08).

THE CANTAL MOUNTAINS were originally one enormous volcano – the oldest and the largest in Europe, dating from the Tertiary period. The highest peaks, the **Plomb du Cantal** at 1,855 m (6,086 ft) and the **Puy Mary** at 1,787 m (5,863 ft), are surrounded by ranges of smaller crests and deep river valleys. Driving the narrow, precipitous roads is a giddy experience, compounded by the grand vistas at every hairpin turn. Between peaks and gorges, rich mountain pastures provide summer grazing for red-gold Salers cows *(see p353)*. From the **Pas de Peyrol**, the highest road pass in the country at 1,582 m (5,191 ft), it's about a 45-minute journey on foot to the summit of the Puy Mary.

Environs
One of the finest of the Auvergne châteaux, **Château d'Anjony** was built by Louis II d'Anjony, a supporter of Joan of Arc *(see pp290–91).* Highlights are the 16th-century frescoes: in the chapel, scenes from the Life and Passion of Christ, and upstairs in the *Salle des Preux* (Room of the Knights), a dazzling series of the nine heroes of chivalry. To the southwest lies the small market town of **Aurillac**, a good base from which to explore the Cantal region.

⛪ **Château d'Anjony**
Tournemire. 📞 04 71 47 61 67.
Open mid-Jan–mid-Nov: daily. 🎦

La Chaise-Dieu ⓳

Haute-Loire. 🏠 950. 🚌 🛈 place de la Mairie (04 71 00 01 16). 🕒 Thu.

SOMBRE AND MASSIVE, midway between Romanesque and Gothic, the abbey church of **St-Robert** is the prime reason to visit the small village of La Chaise-Dieu. The building dates from the 14th century and is an amalgam of styles and tastes. The choir, however, is sensational: 144 oak stalls carved with figures of Vice and Virtue. Above them, entirely covering the walls, are some of the loveliest tapestries in France. Made in Brussels and Arras in the early 16th century and depicting scenes from the Old and New Testaments, they are rich in colour and detail.

On the outer walls of the choir the 15th-century wall painting of the *Danse Macabre* shows Death in the form of skeletons leading rich and poor alike to their inevitable end. Beyond the cloister is the Echo room, in which two people whispering in opposite corners can hear one another perfectly – this was a clever medieval solution for hearing the confessions of lepers.

Le Puy-en-Velay ⓴

Haute-Loire. 🏠 23,000. ✈ 🚉 🚌
🛈 place du Breuil (04 71 09 38 41).
🕒 Sat. 🎪 Sep.

Statue of Notre-Dame-de-France at Le Puy

LOCATED IN THE BOWL of a volcanic cone, the extraordinary town of Le Puy teeters on a stunning series of rock outcrops and giant basalt pillars. The town appears to have three peaks, each topped with a landmark church or statue. Seen from afar, the ensemble is one of the most dramatic sights in France.

Now a commercial and tourist-oriented town, Le Puy's star attraction is its medieval **Holy City**. This became a pilgrimage centre after the Bishop of Le Puy, Gotescalk, made one of the first pilgrimages to Santiago de Compostela in 962, and built the **Chapelle St-Michel d'Aiguilhe** on his return.

Detail of *Danse Macabre* at St-Robert, in La Chaise-Dieu

THE AUVERGNE'S BLACK MADONNAS

The cult of the Virgin Mary has always been strong in the Auvergne and this is reflected in the concentration of her statues in the region. Carved in dark walnut or cedar, now blackened with age, the Madonnas are believed to originate from the Byzantine influence of the Crusaders. Perhaps the most famous Madonna is the one in Le-Puy-en-Velay, a 17th-century copy of one which belonged to Louis IX in the Middle Ages.

Louis IX's Black Virgin

Pilgrims from eastern France and Germany assembled at the **Cathédrale de Notre-Dame** with its famous Black Madonna and "fever stone" – a Druid ceremonial stone with healing powers embedded in one of its walls – before setting off for Compostela.

Built on an early pagan site, the Cathédrale de Notre-Dame is a huge Romanesque structure. Multiform arches, carved palm and leaf designs and a chequerboard façade show the influences of Moorish Spain, and indicate the considerable cultural exchange that took place with southern France in the 11th and 12th centuries. In the transept are Romanesque frescoes, notably an 11th–12th-century St Michael; in the sacristy, the treasury includes the Bible of Theodolphus, a hand-written document from the era of Charlemagne. The cathedral is the centre of the Holy City complex that dominates the upper town, encompassing a baptistry, cloister, Prior's house and Penitents' chapel.

The colossal red statue of **Notre-Dame-de-France**, on the pinnacle of the Rocher Corneille, was erected in 1860, cast from 213 cannons captured at Sebastopol during the Crimean War. The statue is reached by a steep pathway, and can be climbed by an iron ladder on the inside.

The Chapelle St-Michel, like the cathedral, shows Moorish influences in the trefoil decoration and coloured mosaics on the rounded arch over the main entrance. It seems to grow out of a giant finger of lava rock and is reached by a steep climb. The church is thought to be located on the site of a Roman temple to Mercury, and its centre dates from the 10th century, although most of the building was constructed a century later. The floor has been constructed to follow the contours of the rock in places,

and the interior is ornamented with faded 10th-century murals and 20th-century stained glass.

In the lower city, narrow streets of 15th- and 16th-century houses lead to the Vinay Garden and the **Musée Crozatier**, which has a collection of hand-made lace from the 16th century to the present – a craft which is now enjoying a revival. The museum also has a surprisingly good collection of medieval *objets d'art* and 15th-century paintings, with works attributed to Rubens, de Heem and Salomon Ruysdael.

In mid-September, Le Puy transforms itself into a masked and costumed Renaissance carnival for the Bird King Festival, an ancient tradition celebrating the skill of the city's best archers *(see p34)*.

⛪ Chapelle St-Michel d'Aiguilhe

Aiguilhe. 📞 *04 71 09 50 03.* **Open** *mid-Feb–mid-Nov & 21 Dec–5 Jan: daily.* **Closed** *1 Jan, 25 Dec.* 🈳

⛪ Notre-Dame-de-France

Rocher Corneille. 📞 *04 71 04 11 33.* **Open** *Feb–Nov: daily; Dec, Jan & school hols: pm only.* **Closed** *1 Jan, 25 Dec.* 🈳

🏛 Musée Crozatier

Jardin Henri Vinay. 📞 *04 71 09 38 90.* **Open** *Wed–Mon.* **Closed** *1 Jan, 1 Nov, 25 Dec.* 🈳

Chapelle St-Michel d'Aiguilhe, standing on a finger of lava rock

Ruins of the Castle of
Calmont d'Olt at Espalion
in the Lot Valley

Vallée du Lot ㉑

Aveyron. ✈ *Aurillac, Rodez.*
🚊 *Rodez, Séverac-le-Château.*
🚌 *St-Geniez, Conques.* 🛈 *Espalion
(05 65 44 10 63).*

From Mende and the old
river port of La Canourgue
all the way to Conques, the
river Lot (or Olt in old usage)
courses through its fertile
valley past orchards, vineyards
and pine forests. **St Côme
d'Olt**, near the Aubrac mountains, is an unspoiled, fortified
village whose 15th-century
church is surrounded by
Medieval and Renaiss-
ance houses. At **Espalion**,
the pastel stone houses
and a turreted 16th-
century castle are
reflected in the river,
which runs beneath a
13th-century arched
stone bridge. The
town has one of the
best markets in the
region on Friday
mornings. Just outside
town is the 11th-century
Perse Church, whose carved
capitals portray battling
knights and imaginary birds
sipping from a chalice.

Estaing was once the fiefdom of one of the greatest
families of the Rouergue, dating back to the 13th century.
The village nestles beneath its
massive château (now a convent) on the river bank. The
road passes through the Lot
Gorge on the way to **Entraygues** ("between waters")
where the old quarter and
13th-century Gothic bridge
are worth a visit. Beyond
Entraygues the river widens
to join the Garonne.

Conques ㉒

See pp358–9.

Rodez ㉓

Aveyron. 🏙 *25,000.* ✈ 🚊 🚌
🛈 *place Foch (05 65 68 02 27).*
🛒 *Wed & Sat.*

Like many medieval French
cities, Rodez was politi-
cally divided: the shop-lined
place du Bourg on one side
of town and **place de la Cité**,
near the cathedral, on the

Entombment in Rodez Cathedral

other, reflect conflicting secular and ecclesiastical interests.
Rodez's commercial centre,
the largest in the region, is
probably the main attraction
now, though if you find
yourself here for a morning,
the **Cathédrale Notre-Dame**
makes a worthwhile diversion.
This huge, pink stone building was constructed in 1277
and has a fortress-like west
façade which once played a
part defending the town. The
narrow streets around only
permit a view skywards to its
magnificent, ornate belltower.

The Gothic interior is
dominated by a series of
giant pillars and a soar-
ing silver-piped organ
topped by carved
wooden angels. The
15th-century choir
stalls show a mag-
nificent panoply of
creatures, including a
winged lion, some fair
demoiselles and one
naughty fellow who is
exposing his derrière.

ROBERT LOUIS STEVENSON

Robert Louis Stevenson (1850–94),
best known for his novels *Treasure
Island, Kidnapped* and *Dr Jekyll
and Mr Hyde*, was also an accom-
plished travel writer. In 1878, he
set off across the remote Cévennes
mountain range with only a
small donkey, Modestine,
for company. His classic
account of this eventful
journey, *Travels with a
Donkey in the Cévennes*,
was published in the
following year.

Robert Louis Stevenson

Dramatic scenery in Corniche des Cévennes national park

Corniche des Cévennes ⓸

Lozère, Gard. ✈ Rodez-Marcillac.
🚉 Alès. 🚌 St-Jean-du-Gard.
ℹ St-Jean-du-Gard (04 66 85 32 11).

THE DRAMATIC corniche road from Florac on the Tarn to St-Jean-du-Gard was cut in the early 18th century by the army of Louis XIV in pursuit of the Camisards, Protestant rebels who had no uniforms but fought in their ordinary shirts (*camiso* in the *langue d'oc*). The route of the D983 makes a spectacular drive. Fascination with the history of the Camisards was one of the reasons that the famous Scots writer Robert Louis Stevenson undertook his fabled trek in the Cévennes with Modestine, recounted in his *Travels with a Donkey*.

At St-Laurent-de-Treves, where fossil remains suggest dinosaurs once roamed the lagoon, there is a sweeping view of the Grands Causses and the peaks of Lozère and Aigoual. The Corniche finishes in St-Jean-du-Gard, where the **Musée des Vallées Cévenoles**, depicting typical peasant life, is located in a former 17th-century inn.

🏛 Musée des Vallées Cévenoles

95 Grand' rue, St-Jean-du-Gard.
📞 04 66 85 10 48. **Open** Jul–Aug: daily; May–Jun & Sep: Tue–Sun; Oct–Apr: Tue, Thu & Sun pm by appt. **Closed** 1 Jan, 25 Dec. 🎫 ♿

Grands Causses ⓶⓹

Aveyron. ✈ Rodez-Marcillac. 🚉
🚌 Millau. ℹ Millau (05 65 60 02 42).

THE CAUSSES are vast, arid limestone plateaux, alternating with surprisingly green, fertile canyon valleys. The only sign of life at times is a bird of prey wheeling in the sky, or an isolated stone farm or shepherd's hut. The whole area makes for some desolate hiking for those who like solitude.

The four Grands Causses – Sauveterre, Méjean, Noir and Larzac – stretch out east of the city of Millau, from Mende in the north to the valley of the Vis river in the south.

Among the sights in the Causses are the *chaos* – bizarre rock formations reputed to resemble ruined cities, and named accordingly: there's the *chaos* of **Montpellier-le-Vieux**, **Nîmes-le-Vieux** and **Roquesaltes**. **Aven Armand** and the **Dargilan Grotto** are vast and deep natural underground grottoes with equally astonishing formations.

A good place to head for in the windy reaches of the Larzac Causse is the strange, rough-hewn stone village of **La Couvertoirade**, a fully-enclosed citadel of the Knights Templar in the 12th century. The unpaved streets and medieval houses are an austere reminder of the dark side of the Middle Ages. The only drawback is the entrance fee to the village, payable at a toll.

The Causse du Larzac's best-known village is probably **Roquefort-sur-Soulzon**, a small grey town terraced on the side of a crumbled limestone outcrop. It has one main street and one major product, Roquefort cheese. This is made from unpasteurized sheep's milk, seeded with a distinctive blue mould grown on loaves of bread, and aged in the warren of damp caves above the town.

View over Méjean, one of the four plateaux of the Grands Causses

Conques ㉒

THE VILLAGE of Conques clusters around the splendid Abbaye de Ste-Foy, hemmed into a rugged site against the hillside. Sainte Foy was a young girl who became an early Christian martyr; her relics were first kept at a rival monastery in Agen. In the 9th century a monk from Conques stole the relics, thereby attracting pilgrims to this remote spot and firmly establishing Conques as a halt on the route to Santiago de Compostela *(see pp390–91)*.

12th-century reliquary

The treasury holds the most important collection of medieval and Renaissance gold work in western Europe. Some of it was made in the abbey's own workshops as early as the 9th century. The Romanesque abbey church has beautiful stained-glass windows and its tympanum is a triumph of medieval sculpture.

View of the church from the village

The broad transepts were able to accommodate crowds of pilgrims.

Nave Interior
Pure and elegantly austere, the Romanesque interior dates from 1050–1135. The short nave soars to a height of 22 m (72 ft), with three tiers of arches topped by 250 decorative carved capitals.

Tympanum
This sculpture of 1135 depicts the Last Judgment, *with the Devil in Hell (shown here) in the lower part of the sculpture and Christ in Heaven in the tympanum's central position.*

CONQUES' TREASURES

The treasures date from the 9th to the 16th century, and are prized for both their beauty and their rarity. The gold-plated wood and silver reliquary of Ste Foy is studded with gems, rock crystal and even an *intaglio* of Roman Emperor Caracalla. The body is 9th century, but the face may be older, possibly 5th century. Other magnificent pieces include an "A"-shaped reliquary said to be a gift from Charlemagne; the small but exquisite Pepin's shrine from AD 1000; and a late 15th-century processional cross.

The precious reliquary of Ste-Foy

VISITORS' CHECKLIST

Abbaye de Ste-Foy, Conques.
☎ 05 65 69 85 12.
🚌 🚉 from Rodez.
Treasuries I and II open Jul–Aug: 9am–7pm daily; Sep–Jun: 9am–noon (11am: Sun) & 2–6pm.
🎨 ✝ 8:15am & 11:30am Mon–Sat, 7:45am & 11am Sun.
📷 ♿ restricted. 🎫

Romanesque Chapels
The east end is three-tiered, topped by the blind arcades of the choir and a central bell-tower. Three chapels surround the eastern apse, built to accommodate extra altars for the celebration of mass.

Treasury I
The precious contents of the treasury were hidden by the townspeople to prevent their destruction during the French Revolution. Perhaps surprisingly, all were returned.

Entrance to Treasury I

The Cloister consists of a reconstructed square: only two sections of the original early 12th-century arcades remain. However, 30 of the original carved capitals are displayed in the refectory and in the Treasury II above the tourist office.

Gorges du Tarn ㉖

NEAR THE BEGINNING of its journey to meet the river Garonne, the Tarn flows through some of Europe's most spectacular gorges. For millions of years, the Tarn and its tributary the Jonte have eaten their way down through the limestone plateaux of the Cévennes, creating a sinuous forked canyon some 25 km (15 miles) long and nearly 600 m (2,000 ft) deep. The gorges are flanked by rocky bluffs and scaled by roads with dizzying bends and panoramic views, which are incredibly popular in the high season. The surrounding plateaux, or *causses*, are eerily different, forming an open, austere landscape, dry in summer and snow-clad in winter, where wandering sheep and isolated farms are sometimes the only signs of life.

Point Sublime
From 800 m (2,600 ft) up, there are stunning views of a major bend in the Tarn gorge, with the Causse Méjean visible in the distance.

Outdoor Activities
The Tarn and Jonte gorges are popular for canoeing and river-rafting. Although relatively placid in summer, melting snow can make the rivers hazardous in spring.

Pas de Souci
Just upriver from Les Vignes, Pas de Souci flanks a narrow point in the gorge as the Tarn makes its way northwards.

0 kilometres   5
0 miles   3

D46

D995

GORGES DU TARN

D907

le Rozier

D996

GORGES DE LA JONTE

Tarn

D110

CAUSSE NOIR

N9

Millau

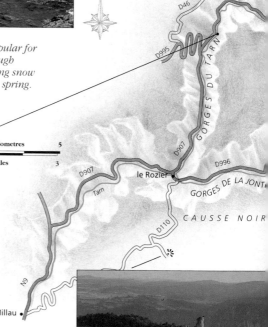

Chaos de Montpellier-le-Vieux
Situated on the flank of the Causse Noir off the D110 is a remarkable geological site – bizarre rock formations created by limestone erosion.

La Malène
An old crossing-point between the Causse de Sauveterre and the Causse Méjean, this village, with its 14th-century fortified manor, is a good starting point for boat trips.

VISITORS' CHECKLIST

Lozère. ✈ Rodez-Marcillac.
🚌 Mende, Banassac, Séverac-le-Château. 🚏 Florac, Le Rozier.
ℹ Le Rozier (summer: 05 65 62
60 89). St-Enimie (04 66 48 53 44).

Aven Armand Caves
On the Causse Méjean, many stalactites in the caves are tinted by minerals that are deposited by the slowly trickling water.

Causse Méjean
The high plateaux or causses *are a botanist's paradise in spring and summer, with over 900 species of wild flowers, including orchids.*

THE WILD CÉVENNES

One of the least populated parts of France, this area is well known for its wild flowers and birds of prey, and griffon vultures were once common here. These giant but harmless scavengers nearly died out earlier this century through being hunted, but now a reintroduction programme has led to growing numbers breeding in the Gorges de la Jonte.

Yellow wort

Kidney vetch

Green-winged orchid

Wild flowers *found in this thinly populated area include unusual alpine plants.*

The griffon vulture, *which now breeds in the region, has a wingspan of over 2.5 m (8 ft).*

THE RHÔNE VALLEY AND FRENCH ALPS

LOIRE · RHÔNE · AIN · ISÈRE · DRÔME
ARDÈCHE · HAUTE-SAVOIE · SAVOIE · HAUTES-ALPES

I TS TWO MOST IMPORTANT *geographical features, the Alps and the river Rhône, give this region both its name and its dramatic character. The east is dominated by majestic snowcapped peaks, while the Rhône provides a vital conduit between north and south.*

The Romans recognized this strategic route when they founded Lyon over 2,000 years ago. Today Lyon, with its great museums and fine Renaissance buildings, is the second city of France. It is one of the country's most vital commercial and cultural centres as well as the undisputed capital of French gastronomy. To the north lie the flat marshlands of the Dombes and the rich agricultural Bresse plain. Here, too, are the famous Beaujolais vineyards which, along with the Côtes du Rhône, make the region such an important wine producer.

The French Alps are among the most popular year-round resort areas in the world, with internationally renowned ski stations such as Chamonix, Mégève and Courchevel, and historic cities like Chambéry, capital of Savoy before it joined France. Elegant spa towns line the shores of Lac Léman (Lake Geneva).

Grenoble, a bustling university city and high-tech centre, is flanked by two of the most spectacular nature reserves in France, the Chartreuse and the Vercors.

To the south, orchards and fields of sunflowers give way to brilliant rows of lavender interspersed with vineyards and olive groves. Châteaux and ancient towns dot the landscape. Mountains and pretty, old-fashioned spa towns characterize the rugged Ardèche, and the deeply scoured gorges along the river Ardèche offer some of the wildest scenery in France.

The restored Ferme de la Forêt at St-Trivier-de-Courtes, north of Bourg-en-Bresse

◁ **Annecy's medieval quarter**

Exploring the Rhône Valley and French Alps

LYON is the region's largest city, famed for its historic buildings and gastronomic tradition. Wine lovers can choose between the vineyards of the Beaujolais, Rhône Valley and Drôme region to the south. To the west, the Ardèche offers rugged wilderness, canoeing and climbing. Spa devotees from around the world flock to Évian-les-Bains and Aix-les-Bains, while the Alps are a favourite destination for sports enthusiasts *(see pp312–13).*

SIGHTS AT A GLANCE

The Pont des Amours in Annecy

0 kilometres   25

0 miles   25

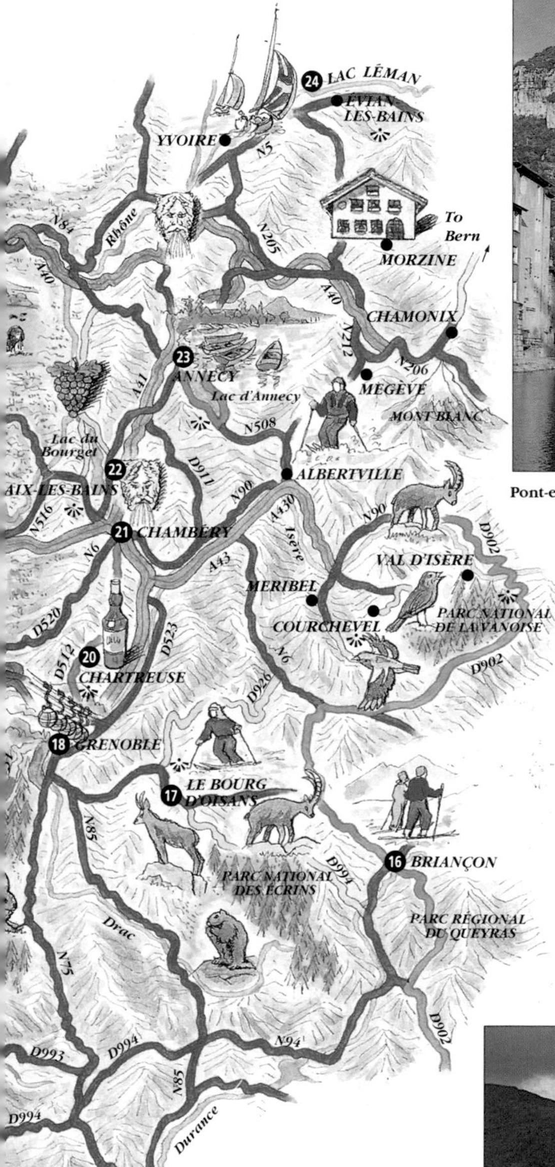

KEY

- Motorway
- Major road
- Minor road
- Scenic route
- River
- Viewpoint

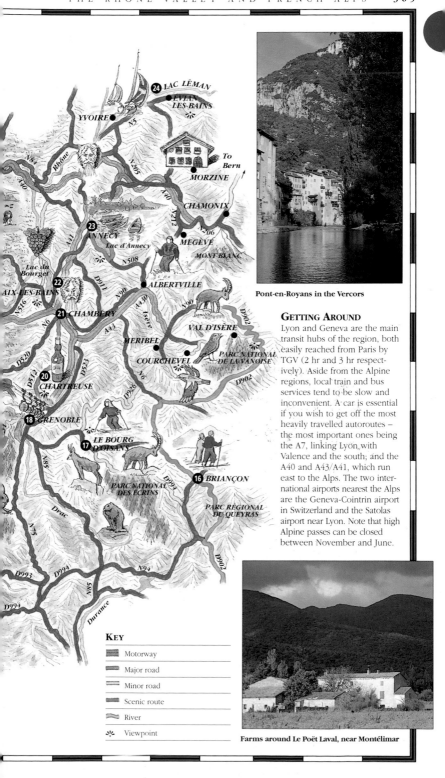

Pont-en-Royans in the Vercors

GETTING AROUND

Lyon and Geneva are the main transit hubs of the region, both easily reached from Paris by TGV (2 hr and 3 hr respectively). Aside from the Alpine regions, local train and bus services tend to be slow and inconvenient. A car is essential if you wish to get off the most heavily travelled autoroutes – the most important ones being the A7, linking Lyon with Valence and the south; and the A40 and A43/A41, which run east to the Alps. The two international airports nearest the Alps are the Geneva-Cointrin airport in Switzerland and the Satolas airport near Lyon. Note that high Alpine passes can be closed between November and June.

Farms around Le Poët Laval, near Montélimar

Bourg-en-Bresse **①**

Ain. 🚶 *43,000.* 🚉 🚌 🚹 *Centre
Culturel Albert Camus, 6 av Alsace-
Lorraine (04 74 22 49 40).*
🛒 *Wed & Sat.*

BOURG-EN-BRESSE is a busy
market town, with some
beautifully restored half-
timbered buildings. It is best
known for its tasty *poulet de
Bresse* (chickens raised in the
flat agricultural region of Bresse
and designated *appellation
contrôlée, see p309*); and its
abbey church of **Brou** on the
southeast edge of town.

The latter, no longer a place
of worship, has become one
of the most visited sites in
France. Flamboyant Gothic in
style, it was built between
1505 and 1536 by Margaret of
Austria after the death of her
husband Philibert, Duke of
Savoy, in 1504.

The couple's finely sculpted
Carrara marble tombs can be
seen in the choir, along with
the tomb of Margaret of
Bourbon, Philibert's mother,
who died in 1483. Notice also
the beautifully carved choir
stalls, stained-glass windows,
and rood screen with its elegant basket-handle arching.

The adjacent cloisters house
a small museum with a good
collection of 16th- and 17th-
century Dutch and Flemish
masters, as well as contemporary works by local artists.

Tomb of Margaret of Austria in the abbey church of Brou at Bourg-en-Bresse

Environs
About 24 km (15 miles)
north of Bourg-en-Bresse at
St-Trivier-de-Courtes, the
restored **Ferme-Musée de la
Forêt** offers a look at farm
life in the region during the
17th century. The ancient
house has what is known
locally as a Saracen chimney,
with a brick hood
in the centre of the
room, similar to
constructions
in Sicily and
Portugal, and a
collection of
antique farm
implements.

Bresse chickens

🏛 **Ferme-Musée de la Forêt**
📞 *04 74 30 71 89.* **Open** *Easter–Jun
& Oct–Nov: Sat, Sun & public hols;
Jul–Sep: daily.* ♿

The Dombes **②**

Ain. ✈ *Lyon.* 🚉 *Lyon, Villars les
Dombes, Bourg-en-Bresse.* 🚌 *Villars-
les-Dombes (from Bourg-en-Bresse).*
🚹 *3 pl de Hôtel de Ville, Villars-les-
Dombes (04 74 98 06 29).*

THIS FLAT, glacier-gouged
plateau south of Bourg-
en-Bresse is dotted with small
hills, ponds and marshes,
making it popular with anglers
and bird-watchers.

In the middle of the area at
Villars-les-Dombes
is an ornithological
park, the **Parc des
Oiseaux**. Over 400
species of native
and exotic birds live
here, including tufted
herons, vultures,
pink flamingoes,
emus and ostriches.

🦅 **Parc des Oiseaux**
Route Nationale 83, Villars-les-
Dombes. 📞 *04 74 98 05 54.*
Open *daily.* ♿

Pérouges **③**

Ain. 🚶 *900.* 🚉 *Meximieux-
Pérouges.* 🚌 🚹 *04 74 60 01 14.*

ORIGINALLY the home of a
colony of immigrants from
Perugia, Pérouges is a fortified
hilltop village of medieval
houses and cobblestone
streets. In its heyday in the
13th century it was a thriving
centre of linen-weaving, but
with the mechanization of the
industry in the 19th century,
the local population dwindled
from 1,500 to 90.

Restoration of its historic
buildings and a new influx of
craftsmen have breathed new
life into Pérouges. Not surprisingly, the village has often
been used as the setting for
historical dramas such as *The
Three Musketeers* and *Monsieur
Vincent.* The village's main
square, place de la Halle, is
shaded by a huge lime tree
planted in 1792 to honour
the Revolution.

A Tour of Beaujolais

BEAUJOLAIS is an ideal area for wine tasting, offering delicious, affordable wine and glorious countryside. The south of the region produces most of the Beaujolais Nouveau, released fresh from the cellars on the third Thursday of November each year. In the north are the ten superior quality *cru* wines – St-Amour, Juliénas, Moulin-à-Vent, Chénas, Fleurie, Chiroubles,

Morgon, Brouilly, Côte de Brouilly and Regnié – most of which can be visited in a day's drive. The distinctive *maisons du pays* have living quarters built over the wine cellar. Almost every village has its *cave* (wine cellar), offering tastings and a glimpse of the wine culture that dominates local life.

Côte de Brouilly

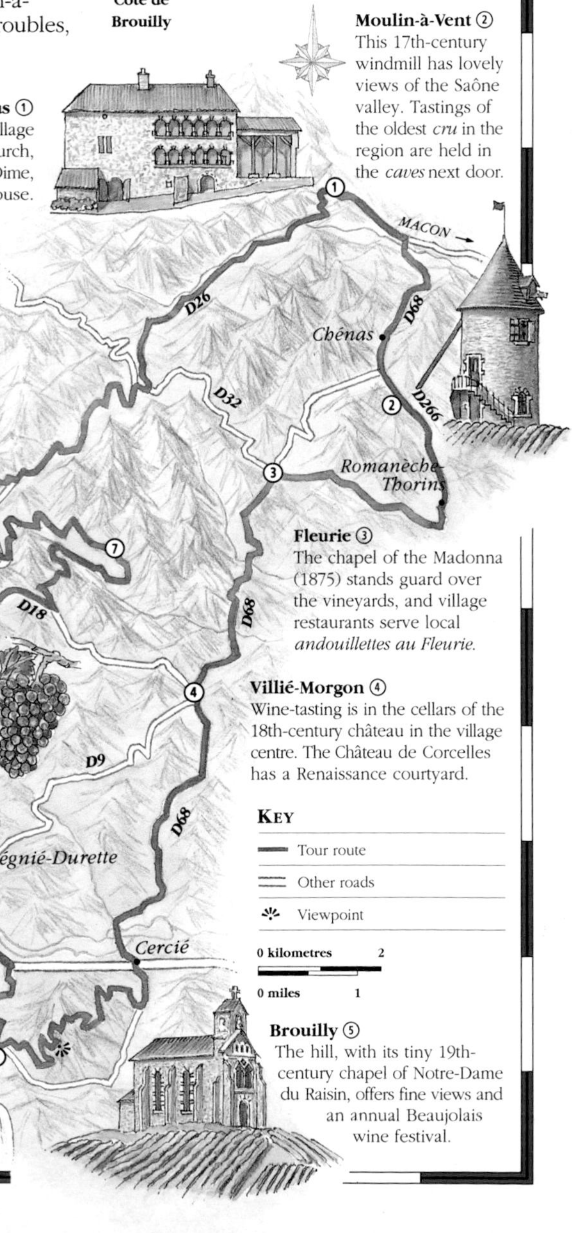

Juliénas ①
Famous for *coq au vin*, this village stores and sells wine in its church, château, and the Maison de la Dime, a 16th-century tithe house.

Moulin-à-Vent ②
This 17th-century windmill has lovely views of the Saône valley. Tastings of the oldest *cru* in the region are held in the *caves* next door.

MACON →

Chénas

Vineyard of Gamay grapes

Romanèche-Thorins

Chiroubles ⑦
A bust in the village square honours Victor Pulliat, who saved the vines from the phylloxera blight in the 1880s by using American vine stocks.

Fleurie ③
The chapel of the Madonna (1875) stands guard over the vineyards, and village restaurants serve local *andouillettes au Fleurie*.

Villié-Morgon ④
Wine-tasting is in the cellars of the 18th-century château in the village centre. The Château de Corcelles has a Renaissance courtyard.

Régnié-Durette

Cercié

KEY

━━━ Tour route

═══ Other roads

☼ Viewpoint

0 kilometres   2

0 miles   1

Beaujeu ⑥
Once the ancient capital of the region, Beaujeu offers tastings in this Renaissance wooden house, and in the 17th-century Hospices de Beaujeu.

VILLEFRANCHE-SUR-SAONE ↓

Brouilly ⑤
The hill, with its tiny 19th-century chapel of Notre-Dame du Raisin, offers fine views and an annual Beaujolais wine festival.

Street-by-Street: Lyon ❹

O N THE WEST BANK of the river Saône, the restored old quarter of Vieux Lyon is an atmospheric warren of cobbled streets, *traboules* (covered passageways), Renaissance palaces, first-class restaurants, lively *bouchons* (bistros) and chic designer shops. It is also the site of the Roman city of Lugdunum, the commercial and military capital of Gaul founded by Julius Caesar in 44 BC. Vestiges of this prosperous city can be seen in the superb Gallo-Roman museum at the top of Fourvière hill. Two excavated Roman theatres still stage performances from opera to rock concerts. At the foot of the hill is the finest collection of Renaissance mansions in France – a testimony to the enormous wealth brought to the city by banking, printing and the silk trade.

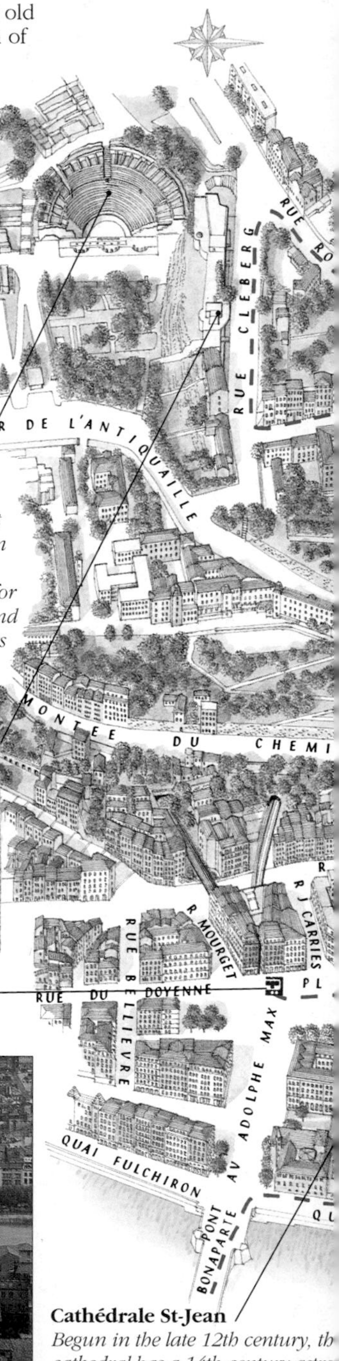

★ Théâtres Romains
There are two Roman amphitheatres here: the Grand Théâtre, the oldest theatre in France, built in 15 BC to seat 10,000 spectators and still used for modern performances; and the smaller Odéon, with its geometric tiled flooring.

★ Musée de la Civilisation Gallo-Romaine
This underground museum contains a rich collection of statues, mosaics, coins and inscriptions evoking Lyon's Roman past.

Entrance to funicular

STAR SIGHTS

- ★ Théâtres Romains

- ★ Musée de la Civilisation Gallo-Romaine

- ★ Basilique Notre-Dame de Fourvière

Cathédrale St-Jean
Begun in the late 12th century, the cathedral has a 14th-century astronomical clock that shows religious feast days till the year 2019.

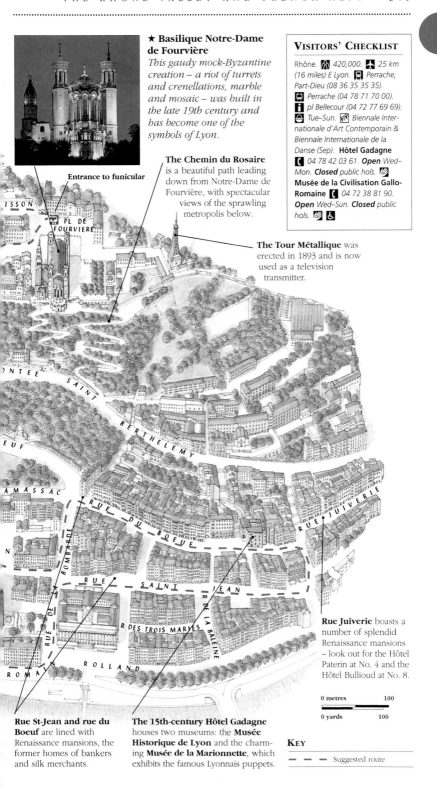

★ Basilique Notre-Dame de Fourvière
This gaudy mock-Byzantine creation – a riot of turrets and crenellations, marble and mosaic – was built in the late 19th century and has become one of the symbols of Lyon.

Entrance to funicular

The Chemin du Rosaire is a beautiful path leading down from Notre-Dame de Fourvière, with spectacular views of the sprawling metropolis below.

The Tour Métallique was erected in 1893 and is now used as a television transmitter.

Rue Juiverie boasts a number of splendid Renaissance mansions – look out for the Hôtel Paterin at No. 4 and the Hôtel Bullioud at No. 8.

Rue St-Jean and rue du Boeuf are lined with Renaissance mansions, the former homes of bankers and silk merchants.

The 15th-century Hôtel Gadagne houses two museums: the **Musée Historique de Lyon** and the charming **Musée de la Marionnette**, which exhibits the famous Lyonnais puppets.

VISITORS' CHECKLIST

Rhône. 420,000. 25 km (16 miles) E Lyon. Perrache, Part-Dieu (08 36 35 35 35). Perrache (04 78 71 70 00). pl Bellecour (04 72 77 69 69). Tue–Sun. Biennale Internationale d'Art Contemporain & Biennale Internationale de la Danse (Sep). **Hôtel Gadagne** 04 78 42 03 61. *Open* Wed–Mon. *Closed* public hols. **Musée de la Civilisation Gallo-Romaine** 04 72 38 81 90. *Open* Wed–Sun. *Closed* public hols.

0 metres   100
0 yards   100

KEY

– – – Suggested route

Exploring Lyon

FRANCE'S SECOND CITY, dramatically sited on the banks of the Rhône and Saône rivers, has been a vital gateway between the north and south since ancient times. On arriving you immediately feel a *brin du sud*, or touch of the south. The crowds are not as quick-stepping as they are in Paris, and the sun is often shining here when it's rainy and cold in the north. Despite its importance as a banking, textile and pharmaceutical centre, most of the French immediately associate Lyon with their palates. The city is packed with restaurants, ranging from simple *bouchons* (bistros) to some of the most opulent tables in France.

The rue St-Jean in Vieux Lyon

The Presqu'île

The heart of Lyon is the Presqu'île, the narrow peninsula of land between the Saône and Rhône rivers, just north of their confluence. A pedestrianized shopping street, the rue de la République, links the twin poles of civic life: the vast **place Bellecour**, with its equestrian statue of Louis XIV in the middle, and the **place des Terreaux**. The latter is overlooked by Lyon's ornate 17th-century Hôtel de Ville (town hall) and the Palais St-Pierre, a former Benedictine convent and now the home of the **Musée des Beaux Arts**. In the middle of the square is a monumental 19th-century fountain by Bartholdi, sculptor of the Statue of Liberty.

Behind the town hall, architect Jean Nouvel's futuristic **Opéra de Lyon** – a black barrel vault of steel and glass encased in a Neo-Classical shell – was remodelled to a controversial design in 1993.

A few blocks to the south, the **Musée de l'Imprimerie** illustrates Lyon's contribution to the early days of printing in the late 15th century.

Two other museums worth visiting in the Presqu'île are the **Musée Historique des Tissus**, which houses an extraordinary collection of silks and tapestries dating from early Christian times to the present day, and the **Musée des Arts Décoratifs**, which displays a range of tapestries, furniture, porcelain and *objets d'art*.

Nearby, the **Abbaye St-Martin d'Ainay** is an impressively restored Carolingian church dating from 1107.

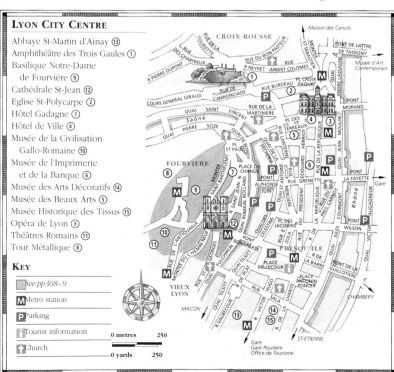

LYON CITY CENTRE

Abbaye St-Martin d'Ainay ⑬
Amphithéâtre des Trois Gaules ①
Basilique Notre-Dame
  de Fourvière ⑨
Cathédrale St-Jean ⑫
Eglise St-Polycarpe ②
Hôtel Gadagne ⑦
Hôtel de Ville ④
Musée de la Civilisation
  Gallo-Romaine ⑩
Musée de l'Imprimerie
  et de la Banque ⑥
Musée des Arts Décoratifs ⑭
Musée des Beaux Arts ⑤
Musée Historique des Tissus ⑮
Opéra de Lyon ③
Théâtres Romains ⑪
Tour Métallique ⑧

KEY

☐ See pp368–9
Ⓜ Metro station
Ⓟ Parking
🅸 Tourist information
✝ Church

0 metres   250

0 yards   250

Food market on quai St-Antoine

La Croix-Rousse
This working-class area north
of the Presqu'île became the
centre of the city's silk-weaving
industry in the 15th century. It
is traced with covered passages
known as *traboules*, used by
the weavers to transport their
finished fabrics. To get a sense
of them, enter at No. 6 place
des Terreaux and continue
along till you reach the **Eglise
St-Polycarpe**. From here, it
is a short walk to the ruins of
the **Amphithéâtre des Trois
Gaules**, built in AD 19, and
the **Maison des Canuts**,
where you can see a traditional
silk loom in operation.

La Part-Dieu
This modern business area on
the east bank of the Rhône is
the site of the TGV railway
station, a huge shopping complex and a public library. The
**Auditorium Maurice-
Ravel**, a venue for im-
portant cultural events,
is also found nearby.

🏛 **Musée de
l'Imprimerie**
13 rue de la Poulaillerie.
📞 04 78 37 65 98.
Open Wed–Sun. **Closed**
public hols. 🖼

🏛 **Musée Historique
des Tissus**
34 rue de la Charité. 📞 04 78 37 15
05. **Open** Tue–Sun. **Closed** public
hols. 🖼

🏛 **Musée des Arts Décoratifs**
30 rue de la Charité. 📞 04 78 37 15
05. **Open** Tue–Sun. **Closed** public
hols. 🖼

🏛 **Maison des Canuts**
10–12 rue d'Ivry. 📞 04 78 28 62 04.
Open Mon–Sat. **Closed** public hols.
🖼 ♿

Musée des Beaux Arts

LYON'S RECENTLY RENOVATED Musée des Beaux Arts
showcases the country's largest and most important
collection of art after the Louvre. The museum is housed
in the 17th-century Palais St-Pierre, a former Benedictine
convent for the daughters of the nobility. The Musée d'Art
Contemporain, formerly located in the Palais St-Pierre, is
now at 81 Cité Internationale, north of the Jardin Tête
d'Or. Housed in a building designed by Renzo Piano,
it specializes in works dating from after the mid-1900s.

ANTIQUITIES

INCLUDED in this wide-ranging
collection on the first floor
are Egyptian archaeological
finds, Etruscan statuettes and
4,000-year-old Cypriot ceramics. Temporary exhibits, with
a separate entrance on 16 rue
Edouard Herriott, are also on
the ground and first floors.

SCULPTURE
AND OBJETS D'ART

OCCUPYING the old chapel
on the ground floor, the
sculpture department includes
works from the French Romanesque period and Italian
Renaissance, as well as late
19th- and early 20th-century
pieces. Represented are Rodin
and Bourdelle (whose statues
also appear in the courtyard),
Maillol, Despiau and
Pompon among
others. The huge
objets d'art collection,
on the first floor,
comprises medieval
ivories, bronzes
and ceramics,
coins, medals,
weapons, jew-
ellery, furniture
and tapestries.

Odalisque (1841)
by James Pradier

PAINTINGS
AND DRAWINGS

THE MUSEUM'S superb col-
lection of paintings occupies the first and second floors.
It covers all periods and includes works by Spanish and
Dutch masters, the French
schools of the 17th, 18th and
19th centuries, Impressionist

Fleurs des Champs (1845) by
Louis Janmot of the Lyon School

and modern paintings, as well
as works by the Lyon School,
whose exquisite flower paintings were used as sources of
inspiration by the designers of
silk fabrics through the ages.
On the first floor, the Cabinet
d'Arts Graphiques has over
4,000 drawings and etchings
by such artists as Delacroix,
Poussin, Géricault, Degas and
Rodin (by appointment only).

🏛 **Musée des Beaux Arts**
Palais St-Pierre, 20 place des Terreaux.
📞 04 72 10 17 40. **Open**
Wed–Sun. **Closed** public hols. 🖼

La Méduse (1923) by Alexeï von
Jawlensky

Châtiment de Lycurgue in the Musée Archéologique, St-Romain-en-Gal

Vienne ❺

Isère. 🏛 *29,000.* 🚉 🚌 🛈 *cours Brillier (04 74 85 12 62).* 🚢 *Sat.*

No OTHER CITY in the Rhône Valley offers such a concentration of architectural history as Vienne. Located in a natural basin of land between the river and the hills, this site was recognized for both its strategic and aesthetic advantages by the Romans, who vastly expanded an existing village when they invaded the area in the 1st century BC.

The centre of the Roman town was the **Temple d'Auguste et Livie** (25 BC) on place du Palais, a handsome structure supported by Corinthian columns. Not far away off place de Miremont

Vienne's Temple d'Auguste et Livie (1st century BC)

are the remains of the **Théâtre de Cybèle**, a temple dedicated to the goddess Cybele, whose worship involved orgiastic rites.

The **Théâtre Romain**, at the foot of Mont Pipet off rue du Cirque, was one of the largest amphitheatres in Roman France, capable of seating over 13,000 spectators. It was restored in 1938, and is now used for a variety of events, including an international jazz festival in the first two weeks of July each year. From the very top seats the view of the town and river is spectacular.

Other interesting Roman vestiges include a fragment of Roman road in the public gardens and, on the southern edge of town, the **Pyramide du Cirque**, a curious structure about 20 m (65 feet) high that was once the centrepiece of the chariot racetrack. The **Musée des Beaux Arts et d'Archéologie** also has a good collection of Gallo-Roman artifacts, as well as 18th-century French faïence and 17th-century paintings by lesser-known artists from the region.

The **Cathédrale de St-Maurice** is the city's most important medieval monument. It was built between the 12th and 16th century and represents an unusual hybrid of Romanesque and Gothic styles. The interior has three aisles but no transept, and contains many fine Romanesque sculptures.

Two of Vienne's earliest Christian churches are the 12th-century **Eglise St-André-le-Bas**, with richly carved capitals in its nave and cloister, and the **Eglise St-Pierre**, parts of which date from the 5th and 6th centuries. The latter houses the **Musée Lapidaire**, a museum of stone-carving with a collection of bas-reliefs and statues from Gallo-Roman buildings.

🏛 **Musée des Beaux Arts et d'Archéologie**
Place de Miremont 📞 *04 74 85 50 42.* **Open** *Apr–mid-Oct: Wed–Mon; mid-Oct–Mar: Wed–Sat, Sun pm.* **Closed** *1 Jan, 1 May, 1 & 11 Nov, 25 Dec.* 🖋
🏛 **Musée Lapidaire**
Place St-Pierre. 📞 *04 74 85 20 35.* **Open** *Apr–mid-Oct: Wed–Mon; mid-Oct–Mar: Wed–Sat, Sun pm.* **Closed** *1 Jan, 1 May, 1 & 11 Nov, 25 Dec.* 🖋 ♿

Vienne's Cathédrale de St-Maurice

St-Romain-en-Gal ❻

Rhône. 🏛 *1,300.* 🚉 *Vienne.*

IN 1967, BUILDING WORK in this commercial town directly across the Rhône from Vienne revealed extensive remains of a significant Roman community dating from 100 BC to AD 300. It comprises the remnants of villas, public baths, shops and warehouses. Of particular interest is the House of the Ocean Gods, with a magnificent mosaic floor depicting the bearded Neptune and other ocean images.

Much of what has been unearthed during the ongoing excavations is housed in the **Musée Archéologique** adjoining the ruins. The impressive collection includes household objects, murals and mosaics. The star exhibit is the *Châtiment de Lycurgue (Chastisement of Lycurgus)*, a mosaic discovered in 1907.

🏛 Musée Archéologique
📞 04 74 53 74 01. **Open** *Tue–Sun.*
Closed *public hols.* 🈺 ♿

St-Étienne ➐

Loire. 🏘 *200,000.* ✈ 🚉 🚌
ℹ *3 place Roannelle (04 77 25 12 14).* 🅿 *daily.*

THE DOUR industrial renown brought to this city by coal-mining and armaments is no longer really deserved. The downtown area around place des Peuple is lively and animated, and, nearby, the **Musée d'Art et d'Industrie** will fascinate anyone with a mechanical bent. It covers St-Étienne's industrial background, including the development of the revolutionary Jacquard loom.

The city's main attraction, however, is its **Musée d'Art Moderne**, a sprawling contemporary building on the northern edge of the city just off the N82. The museum houses changing exhibitions and also a growing collection of 20th-century art, including works by Andy Warhol and Frank Stella.

Detail of the bizarre Palais Idéal du Facteur Cheval at Hauterives

🏛 Musée d'Art et d'Industrie
Place Louis Comte. **📞** 04 77 33 04 85. **Closed** *for renovation until early 1999.* 🈺 ♿
🏛 Musée d'Art Moderne
La Terrasse. **📞** 04 77 79 52 52.
Open *daily.* **Closed** *1 Jan, 1 May, 14 Jul, 15 Aug, 1 Nov, 25 Dec.* 🈺 ♿

THE RHÔNE'S BRIDGES

The Rhône has played a crucial role in French history, transporting armies and commercial traffic between the north and south. It has always been dangerous, a challenge to boatmen and builders for centuries. In 1825 the brilliant engineer, Marc Seguin, built the first suspension bridge using steel wire cables. This was followed by another 20 along the length of the Rhône, forever transforming communications between east and west.

Suspension bridge over the Rhône at Tournon-sur-Rhône

Palais Idéal du Facteur Cheval ➑

Hauterives, Drôme. 🚉 *Romans-sur-Isère* **📞** 04 75 68 81 19. **Open** *daily.*
Closed *1 Jan, 25 Dec.* 🈺 ♿

AT HAUTERIVES, 25 km (15 miles) north of Roman-sur-Isère on the D538, is one of the greatest follies of France, an eccentric "palace" constructed entirely of stones and evoking Egyptian, Roman, Aztec and Siamese styles of architecture. It was built single-handedly by a local postman, Ferdinand Cheval, who collected the stones during his daily rounds on horseback. His neighbours thought him mad, but the project attracted the admiring attention of surrealist André Breton and other artists.

The interior of the palace is inscribed with numerous mottos and exhortations by Cheval, the most poignant of which refers to his assiduous efforts to realize his lifelong fantasy: "1879–1912: 10,000 days, 93,000 hours, 33 years of toil".

The town of Tournon-sur-Rhône

Tournon-sur-Rhône **9**

Ardèche. 🏠 10,000. 🚌 🚂 Hôtel de la Tourette (04 75 08 10 23). 🛒 Wed & Sat.

SITUATED AT THE FOOT of impressive granite hills, Tournon is a lovely town with gracious tree-lined promenades and an imposing 11th–16th-century **château**. The latter houses a museum of local history, and has fine views of the town and river from its terraces.

The adjacent **Collégiale St-Julien**, with its square bell-tower and elaborate façade, is an interesting example of the Italian influence on architecture in the region during the 14th century. Inside is a powerful *Resurrection*, painted in 1576 by Capassin, a pupil of Raphael.

On quai Charles de Gaulle, the **Lycée Gabriel-Fauré** is the oldest secondary school in France, dating from 1536.

Directly across the Rhône from Tournon, the village of **Tain l'Hermitage** is famous for its steep-climbing vineyards which produce both red and white Hermitage, the finest (and most expensive) of all Côtes du Rhône wines.

Environs
From Tournon's main square, the place Jean Jaurès, a narrow, twisting road signposted the **Route Panoramique** leads via the villages of Plats and St-Romain-de-Lerps to St-Péray. This route offers breathtaking views at every turn, and, at St-Romain, you are rewarded with a superb panorama extending over 13 *départements*.

Valence **10**

Drôme. 🏠 65,000. 🚌 🚂 🛈 parvis de la Gare (04 75 44 90 40). 🛒 Wed & Sat.

VALENCE is a large, thriving market town set on the east bank of the Rhône and looking across to the cliffs of the Ardèche. Its principal sight is the Romanesque **Cathédrale St-Apollinaire** on place des Clercs, founded in 1095 and rebuilt in the 17th century.

Alongside the cathedral in the former bishop's palace, the small **Musée des Beaux Arts** contains a collection of late 18th-century chalk drawings of Rome by Hubert Robert.

A short walk from here are two Renaissance mansions. The **Maison des Têtes** at No. 57 Grande Rue was built in 1532 and is embellished

with the sculpted heads of various ancient Greeks including Aristotle, Homer and Hippocrates. On rue Pérollerie, the **Maison Dupré-Latour** has a finely sculptured porch and staircase.

The **Parc Jouvet**, south of avenue Gambetta, offers 6 hectares (14 acres) of pools and gardens, with fine views across the river to the ruined **Château de Crussol**.

🏛 **Musée des Beaux Arts**
4 place des Ormeaux. 📞 04 75 79 20 80. **Open** daily. **Closed** Mon, Tue, Thu & Fri am, public hols. 📷 except Sun.

The limestone Pont d'Arc

The Ardèche **11**

Ardèche. ✈ Avignon. 🚂 Montélimar, Pont St-Esprit. 🚌 Montélimar, Vallon Pont d'Arc. 🛈 Vallon Pont d'Arc (04 75 88 04 01).

OVER THE COURSE OF thousands of years, wind and water have endowed this south-central region of France

---

Harvest in a Côtes du Rhône vineyard

CÔTES DU RHÔNE

Rising in the Swiss Alps and travelling south to the Mediterranean, the mighty Rhône is the common thread that links the many vineyards of the Rhône Valley. A hierarchy of *appellations* divides into three levels of quality: at the base, the regional Côtes du Rhône provides the bulk of the Rhône's wines; next, Côtes du Rhône-Villages comprises a plethora of picturesque villages; and, at the top, there are 13 individual *appellations*. The most famous are the steep slopes of Hermitage and Côte Rôtie in the northern Rhône, and historic Châteauneuf-du-Pape (*see p493*) in the south. The lion's share of production is of red wine, which, based on the syrah grape, is often spicy, full-bodied and robust.

with such a wild and rugged landscape that it is often more reminiscent of the American southwest than the verdure commonly associated with the French countryside. This visible drama is repeated underground as well, since the Ardèche is honeycombed with enormous stalagmite- and stalactite-ornamented caves. The most impressive are the **Aven d'Orgnac** (*aven* meaning pothole) to the south of Vallon-Pont-d'Arc, and the **Grotte de la Madeleine**, reached via a signposted path from the D290.

For those who prefer to stay above ground, the most arresting natural scenery in the region is the **Gorges de l'Ardèche**, best seen from the D290, a two-lane road with frequent viewpoints that parallels the recessed river for 32 km (20 miles). Nearly at the head of the gorge, heading west, is the **Pont d'Arc**, a natural limestone "bridge" spanning the river, created by erosion and the elements.

Canoeing and white-water rafting are the two most popular sports here. All the equipment necessary can be rented locally; operators at Vallon-Pont-d'Arc (among many other places) rent out two-person canoes and organize return transport from St-Martin d'Ardèche, 32 km (20 miles) downstream. Note that the river Ardèche is one of France's fastest flowing rivers – it is safest in May and June; by autumn its waters can be

The Gorges de l'Ardèche, between Vallon-Pont-d'Arc and Pont St-Esprit

The village of Vogüé on the banks of the river Ardèche

unpredictable and dangerous, especially for beginners.

The softer side of the region is found in its ancient and picturesque villages, gracious spa towns, vineyards and plantations of Spanish chestnuts (from which the delectable *marron glacé* is produced).

Some 13 km (8 miles) south of Aubenas, the 12th-century village of **Balazuc** is typical of the region, its stone houses built on a clifftop overlooking a secluded gorge of the river Ardèche. There are fine views as you approach and leave the village on the D294.

Neighbouring **Vogüé** is nestled between the river Ardèche and a limestone cliff. A tiny but atmospheric village, its most commanding sight is the 12th-century **Château de Vogüé**, once the seat of the barons of Languedoc. Rebuilt in the 17th century, the building houses a museum featuring exhibitions about the region.

♠ **Château de Vogüé**
📞 04 75 37 76 50. **Open** Easter–15 Jun: Sun & public hols; 16 Jun–15 Sep: Sun–Fri.

Vals-les-Bains ⑫

Ardèche. 🏠 3,700. 🚌 🛈 Gare Routière (04 75 37 49 27). 🛒 Thu & Sun.

THIS SMALL SPA TOWN retains a hint of its past elegance. It is situated in the valley of the Volane, where there are at least 150 springs, of which all but two are cold. The water, which contains bicarbonate of soda and other minerals, is said to help with digestive problems, rheumatism and diabetes.

Discovered around 1600, Vals-les-Bains is one of the few spas in southern France to have been overlooked by the Romans. The town reached the height of its popularity in the late 19th century, and most of its parks and architecture recall a little of the *Belle Epoque*. With its casino, landscaped parks, and a selection of hotels and restaurants, Vals is a convenient first stop for an exploration of the Ardèche.

Environs
About 15 km (9 miles) east of Vals is the superb Romanesque church of **St-Julien du Serre**.

A farm near Le Poët Laval, east of Montélimar

Montélimar ⓭

Drôme. 🏛 31,000. 🚌 🚉
🛈 Allées Provençales (04 75 01 00
20). 🚌 Wed & Sat.

WHETHER you choose to
make a detour to
Montélimar will largely depend
on how sweet a tooth you
might have. The main curiosity
of this market town is its medieval centre, chock-full of shops
selling almond-studded nougat.
This splendid confection has
been made here since the start
of the 17th century, when the
almond tree was first introduced into France from Asia.
The **Château des Adhémar**,
a mélange of 12th-, 14th- and
16th-century architecture,
surveys the town from a tall
hill to the east.

♟ Château des Adhémar
🇮 04 75 01 07 85. **Open** Apr–Oct:
daily; Nov–Mar: Wed–Mon. **Closed**
1 Jan, 25 Dec. 🈸 🅱

Environs
The countryside east of
Montélimar is full of picturesque medieval villages and
scenic routes. **La Bégude-de-
Mazenc** is a thriving little holiday centre, with its fortified
Old Town perched on a hilltop.
Further east is **Le Poët Laval**, a
tiny medieval village of honey-
coloured stone buildings set in
the Alpine foothills. **Dieulefit**,
the capital of this beautiful
region, has several small hotels
and restaurants, as well as
facilities for tennis, swimming
and fishing. To the south, the
fortified village of **Taulignan**
is known for its cuisine based
on truffles, the local delicacy.

Grignan ⓮

Drôme. 🏛 1,300. 🚌 🛈 Grande
Rue (04 75 46 56 75). 🚌 Tue.

ATTRACTIVELY SITUATED on a
rocky hill surrounded by
fields of lavender, this charming
little village owes its fame to
Madame de Sévigné, who
wrote many of her celebrated
letters when she was staying
at the **Château de Grignan**.
Built during the 15th and
16th centuries, the château is
one of the finest Renaissance
structures in this part of France.
Its interior contains a good
collection of Louis XII furniture and Aubusson tapestries.
From the château's terrace,
a panoramic view extends as
far as the Vivarais mountains
in the Ardèche. Directly below
the terrace, the **Eglise de St-
Saveur** was built in the 1530s,
and contains the tomb of
Madame de Sévigné, who
died in the château in 1696 at
the age of 69.

♟ Château de Grignan
🇮 04 75 46 51 56. **Open** Apr–Oct:
daily; Nov–Mar: Wed–Mon. **Closed**
1 Jan, 25 Dec. 🈸

Nyons ⓯

Drôme. 🏛 7,000. 🚌 🛈 place de
la Libération (04 75 26 10 35). 🚌 Thu.

NYONS is synonymous with
olives in France, since
the region is a major centre of
olive production. All manner of
olive products can be bought
here at the colourful Thursday
morning market, from soap to
tapenade, the olive paste so
popular in the south.
The **quartier des Forts** is
Nyons' oldest quarter, a warren
of narrow streets and stepped
alleyways, the most rewarding
of which is the covered rue
des Grands Forts. Spanning the
river Aygues is a graceful 13th-
century bridge; on its town side
are several old mills turned
into shops where you can see
the enormous presses once
used to extract olive oil. The
Musée de l'Olivier further
explains the cultivation of the
olive tree and the myriad
local uses found for its fruit.
There is a fine view of the
area from the belvedere overlooking the town. Sheltered
as it is by mountains, Nyons
enjoys an almost exotic climate,
with all the trees and plants of
the Riviera to be found here.

🏛 Musée de l'Olivier
Ave des Tilleuls. 🇮 04 75 26 12 12.
Open Mar–Oct: daily; Nov–Feb:
Mon–Sat. 🈸 🅱

Environs
From Nyons, the D94 leads
west to **Suze-la-Rousse**, a
pleasant wine-producing village which, during the Middle
Ages, was the most important
town in the area. Today, it is
best known for its "university
of wine", one of the most respected centres of oenology in

The hilltop town of Grignan and its Renaissance château

Olive groves just outside Nyons

the world. It is housed in the 14th-century **Château de Suze-la-Rousse**, the hunting lodge of the princes of Orange. The interior courtyard is a masterpiece of Renaissance architecture and some rooms preserve original paint and stuccowork.

♣ Château de Suze-la-Rousse
🎬 *04 75 04 81 44.* **Open** *Easter–Oct: daily; Nov–Easter: Wed–Mon.* **Closed** *1 Jan, 25 Dec.* 🖼

Playing *boules* in Nyons

Briançon ⓰

Hautes Alpes. 🏔 *12,000.* 🚉 🚏 🛈 *place du Temple. (04 92 21 08 50).* 🗓 *Wed.*

BRIANÇON – the highest town in Europe at 1,320 m (4,330 feet) – has been an important stronghold since pre-Roman times, guarding as it does the road to the Col de Montgenèvre, one of the

oldest and most important passes into Italy. At the beginning of the 18th century, the town was fortified with ramparts and gates – still splendidly intact – by Louis XIV's military architect, Vauban. If driving, park at the Champs de Mars, and enter the pedestrianized Old Town via the **Porte de Pignerol**.

This leads to the **Grande Rue**, a steep, narrow street with a stream running down the middle, bordered by lovely period houses. The nearby **Eglise de Notre-Dame** dates from 1718, and was also built by Vauban with an eye to defence. To visit Vauban's **citadel**, stop by the tourist office, which organizes guided tours.

Today, Briançon is a major sports centre, offering skiing in winter; rafting, cycling and *parapente* in summer.

LIFE ON HIGH

The Alpine ibex is one of the rarest inhabitants of the French Alps, living high above the treeline in all but the coldest part of the year. Until the creation of the Parc National de la Vanoise, this sure-footed climber had become almost extinct in France, but as a result of rigorous conservation there are now over 500. Both males and females have horns; in the oldest males they can be almost 1 m (3 ft) long.

An ibex in the Parc National de la Vanoise

Environs
Just west of Briançon, the **Parc National des Ecrins** is the largest of the French national parks, offering lofty peaks and glaciers, and a magnificent variety of Alpine flowers.

The **Parc Régional du Queyras** is reached from Briançon over the rugged Col de l'Izoard. A wall of 3,000-m (9,850-ft) peaks separates this wild and beautiful national park from neighbouring Italy.

Le Bourg d'Oisans ⓱

Isère. 🏔 *2,900.* 🚉 🛈 *quai Girard (04 76 80 03 25).* 🗓 *Sat.*

LE BOURG D'OISANS is an ideal base from which to explore the Romanche valley and other adjoining valleys. The area provides numerous opportunities for outdoor sports such as cycling, rock-climbing and skiing, in the nearby resort of **L'Alpe d'Huez**.

Silver and other minerals have been mined here since the Middle Ages, and today the town has a scientific reputation as a centre for geology and mineralogy. Its **Musée des Mineraux et de la Faune des Alpes** is renowned for its collection of crystals and precious stones.

🏛 Musée des Minéraux et de la Faune des Alpes
🎬 *04 76 80 27 54.* **Open** *daily (Oct–mid-Nov: pm only).* **Closed** *1 Jan, 25 Dec.* 🖼 ♿

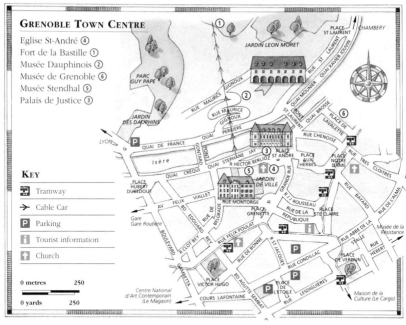

GRENOBLE TOWN CENTRE

Eglise St-André ④
Fort de la Bastille ①
Musée Dauphinois ②
Musée de Grenoble ⑥
Musée Stendhal ⑤
Palais de Justice ③

KEY

🚊	Tramway
✈	Cable Car
🅿	Parking
ℹ	Tourist information
✝	Church

0 metres   250
0 yards   250

Grenoble's former town hall, now the Musée Stendhal

Grenoble ⑱

Isère. 🏔 200,000. ✈ 🚉 🚌
ℹ 14 rue de la République
(04 76 42 41 41). 🛒 Tue–Sun.

ANCIENT CAPITAL of the Dauphiné region and site of the 1968 Winter Olympics, Grenoble is a thriving city, home to the science-oriented University of Grenoble, and a centre of chemical and electronics industries and nuclear research. It is attractively situated at the confluence of the Drac and Isère rivers, with the Vercors and Chartreuse massifs to the west and north.

A cable car starting at quai Stéphane-Jay whisks you up to the 16th-century **Fort de la Bastille**, where you are rewarded with superb views of the city and surrounding mountains. From here, paths lead down through the Parc Guy Pape and Jardin des Dauphins to the **Musée Dauphinois**, a regional museum in a 17th-century convent devoted to local history, arts and crafts.

On the left bank of the Isère, the focus of life is the pedestrian area around place Grenette, a lively square lined with sidewalk cafés. Nearby, the place St-André is the heart of the medieval city, overlooked by Grenoble's oldest buildings including the 13th-century **Eglise St-André** and 15th-century **Palais de Justice**.

In the former town hall, the **Musée Stendhal** houses an exhibition on the life of the 19th-century novelist from Grenoble. The **Musée de Grenoble**, on the place de Lavalette, exhibits art from every period, including a superb modern collection with works by Chagall, Picasso and Matisse among others. On rue Hébert, the **Musée de la Résistance** has a collection of documents relating to the French Resistance.

Temporary displays of modern art can be seen at the **Centre National d'Art Contemporain** (better known as "Le Magasin"), a renovated warehouse on the Cours Berriat. In the quartier Malherbe, the **Maison de la Culture** ("Le Cargo") hosts everything from film festivals to orchestral concerts. It is due to undergo extensive renovation from mid-1998, and events will be moved to other venues.

🏛 **Musée Dauphinois**
30 rue Maurice Gignoux. 【 04 76
85 19 01. **Open** Wed–Mon. **Closed**
1 Jan, 1 May, 25 Dec. 🌐 ⛾
🏛 **Musée Stendhal**
1 rue Hector Berlioz. 【 04 76 54 44
14. Phone for opening times. ⛾

Grenoble's gondola cable car

🏛 **Musée de Grenoble**
5 place de Lavalette. **☎** 04 76 63 44
44. **Open** Wed–Mon. **Closed** 1 Jan,
1 May, 25 Dec. 🅿 ♿
🏛 **Musée de la Résistance**
14 rue Hébert. **☎** 04 76 42 38 53.
Open Wed–Mon. **Closed** 1 Jan,
1 May, 25 Dec. 🅿 ♿
🏛 **CNAC (Le Magasin)**
155 Cours Berriat. **☎** 04 76 21 95 84.
Open Tue–Sun (during exhibitions).
Closed mid-Sep–Oct. 🅿 ♿
🏛 **Maison de la Culture**
4 rue Paul Claudel. **☎** 04 76 25 92
00. **Open** Sep–Jun: Tue–Sat pm. 🅿
obligatory. **Closed** 24 Dec–4 Jan, some
school hols & all public hols. 🅿 ♿

The Vercors ⑲

Isère & Drôme. ✈ Grenoble. 🚉
Romans-sur-Isère, St-Marcellien,
Grenoble. 🚌 Pont-en-Royans,
Romans-sur-Isère. 🛈 Pont-en-Royans
(04 76 36 09 10).

T O THE SOUTH and west of
Grenoble, the Vercors is
one of the most magnificent
regional parks in France – a
wilderness of pine forests,
mountains, waterfalls, caves
and deep, narrow gorges.
The D531 out of Grenoble
passes through **Villard-de-
Lans** – a good base for
excursions in the area – and
continues west to the dark
Gorges de la Bournes. About
8 km (5 miles) further west,
the hamlet of **Pont-en-Royans**
is sited on a very narrow
limestone gorge, its stone
houses built into the rocks
overlooking the river Bourne.
South of Pont-en-Royans
along the D76, the **Route de
Combe-Laval** snakes along a
sheer cliff above the roaring
river below. The **Grands
Goulets**, 6.5 km (4 miles) to
the east, is a spectacularly
deep, narrow gorge overlooked
by sheer cliffs that virtually
shut out the sky above. The
best-known mountain in the
park is the **Mont Aiguille**, a
soaring outcrop of rock rising
2,086 m (6,844 ft).
The Vercors was a key base
for the French Resistance
during World War II. In July
1944 the Germans launched
an aerial attack on the region,
flattening several of its villages.
There are Resistance museums
at Vassieux and Grenoble.

Cows grazing in the Chartreuse

The Chartreuse ⑳

Isère & Savoie. ✈ Grenoble,
Chambéry. 🚉 Grenoble, Voiron.
🚌 St-Pierre-de-Chartreuse. 🛈 St-
Pierre-de-Chartreuse (04 76 88 62 08).

F ROM GRENOBLE, the D512
leads north towards
Chambéry into the Chartreuse,
a majestic region of mountains
and forests where hydroelec-
tricity was invented in the late
19th century. The **Monastère
de la Grande Chartreuse** is
the main local landmark, situated just west of St-Pierre-de-
Chartreuse off the D520-B.
Founded by St Bruno in
1084, the monastery owes its
fame to the sticky green and
yellow Chartreuse liqueurs first
produced by the monks in
1605. The recipe, based on
a secret herbal elixir of 130
ingredients, is now produced
in the nearby town of Voiron.
The monastery itself is
inhabited by about 40 monks
who live in silence and seclusion. It is not open to visitors,
but there is a museum at the
entrance, the **Musée de la
Correrie**, which faithfully
depicts the daily routine of
the Carthusian monks.

🏛 **Musée de la Correrie**
St-Pierre-de-Chartreuse. **☎** 04 76 88
60 45. **Open** Easter–Oct: daily. 🅿

A farm in the pine-clad mountains of the Chartreuse

Chambéry ㉑

Savoie. 🏔 *55,000.* ✈ 🚆 🚌
ℹ️ *24 boulevard de la Colonne
(04 79 33 42 47).* 🛒 *Sat.*

ONCE THE CAPITAL of Savoy, this dignified city has aristocratic airs and a distinctly Italianate feel. Its best-loved monument is the splendidly extravagant **Fontaine des Eléphants** on rue de Boigne. It was erected in 1838 to honour the Comte de Boigne, a native son who left to his home town some of the fortune he amassed in India.

The **Château des Ducs de Savoie**, at the opposite end of rue de Boigne, was built in the 14th century and is now mostly occupied by the Préfecture (police). Only parts of the building can be visited, such as the late Gothic Ste-Chapelle.

On the southeast edge of town is the 17th-century country house, **Les Charmettes**, where the Romantic philosopher Rousseau lived with his mistress Madame de Warens from 1732–42. It is worth a visit for its vine-covered gardens and small museum of Rousseau memorabilia.

♣ **Les Charmettes**
892 chemin des Charmettes.
📞 *04 79 33 39 44.*
Open *Wed–Mon.* **Closed**
public hols. 📷

The Lac du Bourget at Aix-les-Bains

Aix-les-Bains ㉒

Savoie. 🏔 *25,000.* ✈ 🚆 🚌
ℹ️ *pl Jean Mollard (04 79 35 05 92).*
🛒 *Wed & Sat.*

THE GREAT Romantic poet Lamartine rhapsodized over the beauty of Lac du Bourget, site of the gracious spa town of Aix-les-Bains. The heart of the town is the 19th-century **Thermes Nationaux**, thermal baths which were first enjoyed by the Romans over 2,000 years ago – in the basement the remains of the original Roman baths can still be seen. Today, this huge establishment receives more *curistes* than any other spa in France. Opposite

Roman statue in the Temple of Diana

the baths, the 2nd-century AD **Temple of Diana** contains a collection of Gallo-Roman artifacts. The nearby **Musée Faure** is an art-lover's paradise, with its collection of Impressionist paintings, including Degas and Sisley, Rodin sculptures and Lamartine memorabilia.

🏛 **Thermes Nationaux**
Pl Maurice Mollard. 📞 *04 79 35 38 50.*
Open *Wed pm.* 🎫 *obligatory.*
Closed *mid-Dec– mid-Jan, 1 May, 14 Jul, 15 Aug.* 📷
🏛 **Musée Faure**
Villa des Chimères, 10 bd des Côtes.
📞 *04 79 61 06 57.* **Open** *Wed–Mon.*
Closed *18 Dec–2 Jan, public hols.*
📷 ♿

Environs
Boats leave from Aix's Grand Port and sail across Lac du Bourget to the **Abbaye d'Hautecombe**, a Benedictine abbey containing the mausoleum of the Savoyard dynasty.

The small town of **Le Revard**, just east of Aix on the D913, has spectacular views of the lake on one side and Mont Blanc on the other.

Annecy ㉓

Haute Savoie. 🏔 *51,000.* ✈ 🚆
🚌 ℹ️ *1 rue Jean Jaurès (04 50 45 00 33).* 🛒 *Tue, Fri & Sun.*

ANNECY IS ONE of the most charming and attractive towns in the Alps, set at the

Annecy's 12th-century Palais de l'Isle, with the Thiou canal in the foreground

Cycling along the shores of Lac Léman (Lake Geneva)

northern tip of Lac d'Annecy and surrounded by snow-capped mountains. Its small medieval quarter is laced with canals, flower-covered bridges and arcaded streets. Strolling around is the main attraction, particularly on market day, though there are a couple of specific sights worth having a look at: the formidable **Palais de l'Isle**, a 12th-century prison in the middle of the Thiou canal; and the turreted **Château d'Annecy**, set high on a hill above the town with fine views of Vieil Annecy and the crystal-clear lake beyond.

The best spot for swimming and watersports is at the eastern end of the avenue d'Albigny near the Imperial Palace hotel, while boat trips leave from the quai Thiou.

Environs
One of the best ways to enjoy the area's spectacular scenery is to take a boat from Annecy to **Talloires**, a tiny lakeside village celebrated for its hotels and restaurants. Facing Talloires across the lake is the 15th-century **Château de Duingt** (not open to visitors).

On the west bank of the lake, the Semnoz mountain and its summit, the **Crêt de Châtillon**, offer superb views of Mont Blanc and the Alps (see pp312–13).

Lac Léman ⚑

Haute Savoie & Switzerland. ✈ Geneva. 🚊 🚌 Geneva, Thonon-les-Bains, Évian-les-Bains. 🛈 Thonon-les-Bains (04 50 71 55 55).

THE STIRRING SCENERY and gentle climate of the French shore of Lake Geneva (Lac Léman to the French) has made it a popular and fashionable resort area since the first spa buildings were erected at Évian-les-Bains in 1839.

Yvoire is a fine place to begin a visit to the area. This medieval walled fishing port is guarded by a massive 14th-century castle, and its tightly-packed houses are bedecked with colourful flower boxes.

Further east along Lac Léman is **Thonon-les-Bains**, a prosperous, well-manicured little spa town perched on a cliff overlooking the lake. A funicular takes you down to Rives, the small harbour at the foot of the cliffs, where sailboats can be rented and excursion boats to the Swiss cities of Geneva and Lausanne call in. Just outside the town is the 15th-century **Château de Ripaille**, made famous by its one-time resident, Duke Amadeus VIII, who later became antipope (Felix V).

Though it has been modernized and acquired an international reputation for its eponymous spring water, **Évian-les-Bains** still exudes a polite *vie en rose* charm. The tree-lined lakefront promenade teems with leisurely strollers, while more energetic types can avail themselves of all kinds of sporting facilities including tennis, golf, riding, sailing and skiing in the winter. State-of-the-art spa treatments are available, and the exotic domed casino is busy at night, offering blackjack, roulette and baccarat among other games.

From Évian there are daily ferries across Lake Geneva to Lausanne in Switzerland, as well as coach excursions into the surrounding mountains.

Évian-les-Bains' Hôtel Royal (see p563)

SOUTHWEST FRANCE

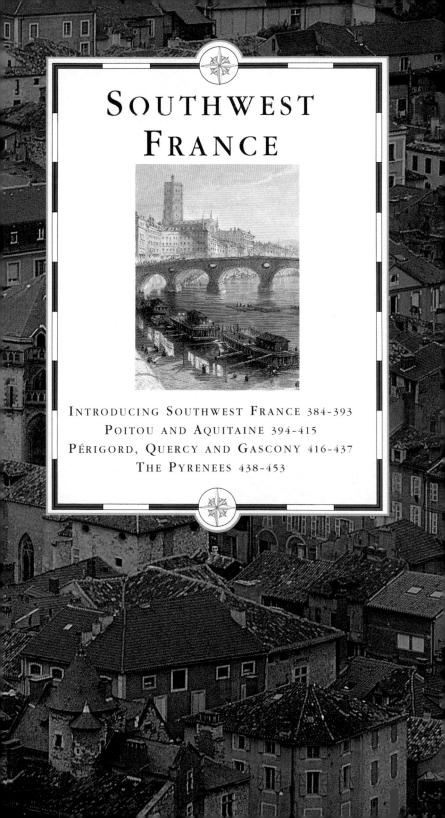

Introducing Southwest France

T HE SOUTHWEST IS FARMING FRANCE, a green and peaceful land
nurturing crops from sunflowers to *foie gras*. Other key country
products include Landes forest timber, Bordeaux wines and Cognac.
Major modern industries, including aerospace, are focused on the
two chief cities, Bordeaux and Toulouse. Visitors are mainly drawn to
the wide Atlantic beaches, the ski slopes of the Pyrenees and
the rural calm of the Dordogne. The major sights of this
favoured region are shown here and include some of
France's most celebrated Romanesque buildings.

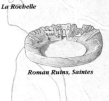

La Rochelle

Grand Théâtre, Borde

La Rochelle's harbour *is today a haven for pleasure
yachts as well as an important commercial port (see p406).
Tour de la Chaîne and Tour St-Nicolas protect the
entrance of the old port. The town's historic centre is filled
with cobbled streets lined by merchants' houses.*

Roman Ruins, Saintes

POITOU AND AQUITAINE
(See pp394–415)

THE PYRENEES
(See pp438–53)

Bordeaux *is a town of grand buildings
and monuments, including its theatre.
The Monument aux Girondins, with its
magnificent bronze statues and fountains, stands at the 18th-century Esplanade des Quinconces (see pp410–12).*

| 0 kilometres | 50 |
| 0 miles | 50 |

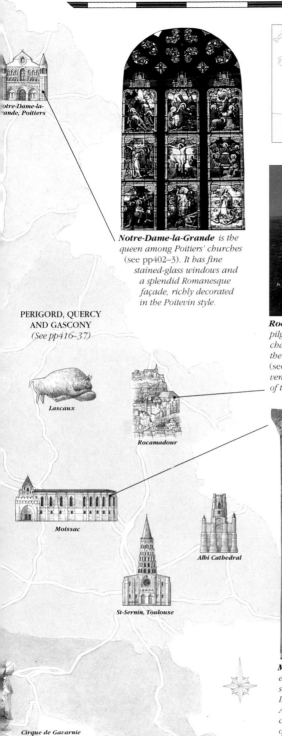

Notre-Dame-la-Grande is the queen among Poitiers' churches (see pp402–3). It has fine stained-glass windows and a splendid Romanesque façade, richly decorated in the Poitevin style.

PERIGORD, QUERCY AND GASCONY
(See pp416–37)

Lascaux

Rocamadour

Moissac

Albi Cathedral

St-Sernin, Toulouse

Cirque de Gavarnie

Rocamadour is both a place of pilgrimage and a tourist sight, its chapels and shrines clinging to the edge of the rocky hillside (see pp426–7). Among its many venerated features is the statue of the Black Virgin and Child.

Moissac Abbey is the pre-eminent medieval monastery in southwest France (see pp432–3). Its tympanum, representing the Apocalypse, and the cloister capitals are outstanding examples of Romanesque sculpture.

Regional Food: Southwest France

The RENAISSANCE KING HENRI IV'S declaration, "Great cooking and great wines make a paradise on earth," sums up the wonderful and varied cuisine of southwest France. Oysters and mussels proliferate along the Arcachon and Marennes coastline, and in the countryside around Bordeaux, the vine dominates to such an extent that wines are used in the cooking of practically every regional dish – *à la bordelaise* generally translates as "with a wine sauce".

Garlic

In Périgord, Quercy and Gascony, geese, ducks and goats are raised for *foie gras, confit* and cheese. Truffles found in the forests are highly prized and costly, and are used sparingly in soups, sauces, *pâté* and stuffings. Goose fat is used for cooking dishes such as *cassoulet* and *daube de boeuf*.

In Basque country, the local chilli pepper, the *piment d'Espelette*, spices everything from Bayonne's famous ham and *piperade*, to fish and stews.

Piperade *is a popular Basque country dish of fluffy omelette or scrambled eggs mixed with garlic, peppers and ham.*

Foie gras *is the enlarged liver of a goose or duck which has been force-fed on maize. It may be cooked in port or brandy.*

Pain de campagne, *the traditional round, rustic country loaf, is quite hard to find today, but a few dedicated bakers still make it. The sour dough is baked in a traditional wood-fired oven, with the smoke from the fire helping to flavour the bread.*

Toulouse sausage

Duck

Haricot beans

Garlic sausage

Cassoulet *is a dish that arouses fierce competition among the dedicated cooks of the southwest. It is a thick stew of white haricot beans, cooked with a variety of sausages and cuts of meat. There are several versions of* cassoulet, *which can include duck, fresh or salt pork, or mutton.*

Homard persillé *is a lobster terrine cooked in a flavoured stock with parsley and herbs.*

Chèvre tiede sur un lit de salade *is grilled goat's cheese, served on a bed of green salad, usually with croutons.*

Duck with cèpes *is made from confit of duck (meat cooked and preserved in its own fat) with wild mushrooms and garlic.*

Fresh truffles *are often cooked in an omelette to bring out their earthy flavour. Périgord truffles are considered the best.*

Rabbit *with prunes is a classic casserole combination, using the celebrated local Agen prunes for a sweet-sour flavour.*

Saucisson sec

Saucisson au poivre

Saucissons *are fresh or dried (sec) sausages available all over France. They can include a variety of meat, herbs and spices.*

Goat's cheese *is often preserved in olive oil, with bay leaves, black peppercorns and thyme added for flavour.*

Marzipan loaf, *a Basque speciality known as* touron, *is made of almond paste with pistachios, hazelnuts and fruit.*

WILD MUSHROOMS

Mushroom hunting is a favourite pastime for the French. Varieties include the big and fleshy *cèpes (Boletus edulis)*, the egg-yolk coloured *chanterelles (Cantharellus cibarius)*, and the brown *morilles* (morels). Fresh wild mushrooms make a less expensive but equally delicious substitute for truffles.

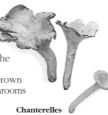

Chanterelles

Morille

Cèpe

Walnut oil *is a popular dressing for salads in the southwest. Walnut trees grow in the valleys here, thriving even in the thin soil of the uplands. The Dordogne produces more walnuts than any other French region.*

Armagnac

Cognac

Quercy Noix

DRINKS

Besides fine wines, the region's most famous drink is brandy, a spirit made from white grapes. Brandies are distilled in both Cognac and Armagnac, and are best drunk following a meal. In Quercy, there is an aperitif called Quercy Noix, which is made from walnuts.

France's Wine Regions: Bordeaux

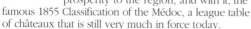

B ORDEAUX IS THE WORLD'S largest fine wine region, and, for red wines, certainly the most familiar outside France. Following Henry II's marriage to Eleanor of Aquitaine, three centuries of courtly commerce with Great Britain ensured that claret was served at the finest foreign tables. In the 19th century, canny merchants capitalized on this **Barrel-making** fame and brought fantastic financial prosperity to the region, and with it, the famous 1855 Classification of the Médoc, a league table of châteaux that is still very much in force today.

LOCATOR MAP
■ *Bordeaux wine region*

Picking red Merlot grapes at Château Palmer

Cos d'Estournel, like all the châteaux included in the 1855 league of crus classés ("classed growths"), proudly proclaims the fact on its label.

WINE REGIONS
The great wine-producing areas of Bordeaux straddle two great rivers; the land between the rivers ("Entre-Deux-Mers") produces lesser, mainly white wines. The rivers, and the river port of Bordeaux itself, have been crucial to the trade in Bordeaux wines; some of the prettiest châteaux line the river banks, enabling easy transportation.

Lac d'H

KEY FACTS ABOUT BORDEAUX WINES

Location and Climate
Climatic conditions may vary not only from one year to another, but also within the region itself. The soils tend to be gravelly in the Médoc and Graves, and clayey on the right bank.

Grape Varieties
The five main red grape varieties are the *Cabernet Sauvignon, Cabernet Franc, Merlot, Petit Verdot* and *Malbec,* with Cabernet the dominant grape on the west side of the Gironde, Merlot to the east. Most Bordeaux reds are, however, a blend of grapes. *Sauvignon Blanc* and *Sémillon* are grown and often blended for both dry and sweet whites.

Good Producers
(reds) Latour, Margaux, Haut-Brion, Cos d'Estournel, Montrose, Léoville Lascases, Léoville Barton, Lascombes, Pichon Longueville, Pichon Lalande, Lynch-Bages, Palmer, Rausan-Ségla, Duhart Milon, Clerc Milon, Grand Puy Lacoste, Sociando-Mallet, d'Angludet, Monbrison, Les Ormes de Pez, de Pez, Phélan-Segur, Chasse-Spleen, Poujeaux, Domaine de Chevalier, Pape Clément, Cheval Blanc, Canon, Pavie, l'Angelus, Le Tertre Rôteboeuf, Larmande, Troplong Mondot, La Conseillante.

Good Vintages
(reds) 1990, 1989, 1988, 1986, 1985.

Haut-Brion, in the top division of Bordeaux's Classification, was and still is the single Graves château in this league of Médoc properties.

Arcachon

Cap Ferret

Lac de Ca et de Sang

The famous legend that guarantees château-bottling originated in Bordeaux, as a check to unscrupulous merchants.

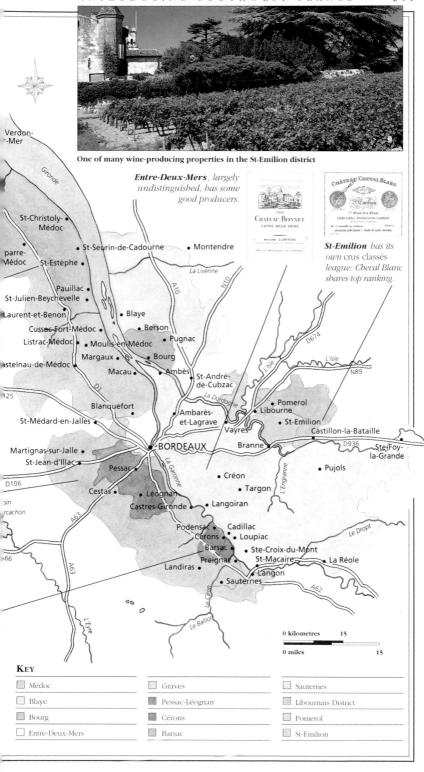

One of many wine-producing properties in the St-Emilion district

Entre-Deux-Mers, largely undistinguished, has some good producers.

St-Emilion has its own crus classés league: Cheval Blanc shares top ranking.

Verdon-
-Mer

Gironde

St-Christoly-
Médoc

parre-
Médoc   St-Estèphe

St-Seurin-de-Cadourne   Montendre

Pauillac

St-Julien-Beychevelle

Laurent-et-Benon   Blaye

Cussac-Fort-Médoc   Berson

Listrac-Médoc   Moulis-en-Médoc   Pugnac

Margaux   Bourg

astelnau-de-Médoc   Macau   Ambès

125   St-André-
de-Cubzac

Blanquefort   Pomerol
Libourne

St-Médard-en-Jalles   Ambarès-
et-Lagrave   St-Emilion

Vayres   Castillon-la-Bataille

Martignas-sur-Jalle   BORDEAUX   Branne   Ste-Foy-
la-Grande

St-Jean-d'Illac

D106   Pessac   Créon   Pujols

Cestas   Targon

sin
rcachon   Castres-Gironde   Langoiran

66   Podensac   Cadillac

Léognan

Cérons   Loupiac

Barsac   Ste-Croix-du-Mont

Preignac   St-Macaire   La Réole

Landiras   Langon

Sauternes

La Livenne

A10   N110

D674

L'Isle   L'Isle   N89

La Dordogne

D936

L'Engranne

Le Dropt

La Garonne

Le Ciron

L'Eyre   Le Balliot

A63

A62

0 kilometres   15

0 miles   15

KEY

☐ Médoc	☐ Graves	☐ Sauternes
☐ Blaye	☐ Pessac-Léognan	☐ Libournais District
☐ Bourg	☐ Cérons	☐ Pomerol
☐ Entre-Deux-Mers	☐ Barsac	☐ St-Emilion

The Road to Compostela

Scallop symbol

Throughout the Middle Ages millions of Christians visited Santiago de Compostela in Spain to pay homage at the shrine of St James (Santiago). They travelled across France staying in monasteries or simple shelters and would return with a scallop shell, the symbol of St James, as a souvenir. Most pilgrims went in hope of redemption and were often on the road for years. In 1140, a monk called Picaud wrote one of the world's first travel guides about the pilgrimage. Today, travellers can follow the same routes, passing through ancient towns and villages with their magnificent shrines and churches.

Foreign pilgrims joined at ports such as St Malo.

The original cathedral of Santiago de Compostela was built in 813 by Alfonso II over the tomb of St James. In 1075 construction started on the grandiose Romanesque church seen today which has, among other later additions, a resplendent 17th–18th-century Baroque façade.

The routes converged on Santiago de Compostela.

Most pilgrims crossed the Pyrenees at Roncesvalles.

James the Greater, an apostle, came to Spain to spread the Gospel, according to legend. On his return to Judaea, he was martyred by Herod. His remains were taken to Spain by boat and lay hidden for 800 years.

The powerful Cluny monastery in Burgundy (see pp44–5), and its affiliated monasteries, played an important role in promoting the pilgrimage. They built shelters and set up churches and shrines housing precious relics, to encourage the pilgrims on their way.

THE PILGRIMS' WAY

Paris, Vézelay *(see pp326–7)*, Le Puy *(see p354)* and Arles are the rallying points for the four "official" routes across France. They cross the Pyrenees at Roncesvalles and Somport, and merge at Puente la Reina to form one route, culminating at the shrine on the Galician coast.

Conques purloined relics to boost its prestige.

Le Puy was a main rallying point for pilgrims.

The reliquary of Ste-Foy, at Conques, is in one of many elaborate shrines on the way which drew crowds of pilgrims. A saint's relics were thought to have miraculous powers.

The name Santiago de Compostela is believed to originate from the Latin Campus stellae *(field of stars). Legend has it that strange stars were seen hovering over a field in 814 and on 25 July, now the feast of Santiago, the saint's remains were found.*

WHAT TO SEE TODAY

Huge Romanesque churches, including Ste-Madeleine at Vézelay *(see p326)*, Ste-Foy at Conques *(pp358–9)* and St-Sernin at Toulouse *(p437)*, along with many small chapels, were built to accommodate large numbers of pilgrims.

Basilique Ste-Madeleine, Vézelay

The first recorded pilgrim was the bishop of Le Puy in 951. But pilgrims have probably been coming to Santiago since 814, soon after the saint's tomb was found.

Caves of the Southwest

SOUTHWEST FRANCE is well-known for its spectacular rock formations, created by the slow accumulation of dissolved mineral deposits. Caves and rock shelters exist throughout limestone country in France. But in the foothills of the Pyrenees and the Dordogne they also have something else to offer the visitor: a collection of extraordinary rock paintings, some dating back to the last Ice Age. These art forms were created when prehistoric peoples evolved and began engraving, painting and carving. This unique artistic tradition lasted for more than 25,000 years, reaching its zenith around 17,000 years ago. Some very fine examples of cave painting are still visible today.

Ancient cave paintings at Lascaux

CAVES OF THE DORDOGNE

There are many different cave systems to visit in or near the Dordogne valley. The entire Périgord region contains one of the densest concentrations of prehistoric sites anywhere in the world. In an uncertain climate, its rivers flanked by caves and rock shelters proved very attractive to prehistoric man.

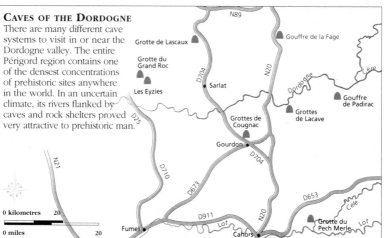

CAVE FORMATION

Limestone is laid down in layers containing fissures that allow water to penetrate beneath the surface. Over thousands of years, the water slowly dissolves the rock, first forming potholes and then larger caverns. Stalactites develop where water drips from the cave roof; stalagmites grow upwards from the floor.

Grotte du Grand Roc in the Vézère valley, Limousin

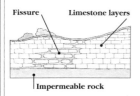

1 *Water percolates through fissures, slowly dissolving the surrounding rock.*

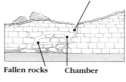

2 *The water produces potholes and loosens surrounding rocks, which gradually fall away.*

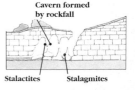

3 *Dripping water containing dissolved limestone forms stalactites and stalagmites.*

GOUFFRE DE PADIRAC

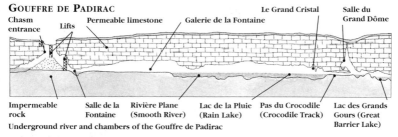

Chasm entrance | Lifts | Permeable limestone | Galerie de la Fontaine | Le Grand Cristal | Salle du Grand Dôme

Impermeable rock | Salle de la Fontaine | Rivière Plane (Smooth River) | Lac de la Pluie (Rain Lake) | Pas du Crocodile (Crocodile Track) | Lac des Grands Gours (Great Barrier Lake)

Underground river and chambers of the Gouffre de Padirac

Prehistoric caves at Les Eyzies

VISITING THE CAVES

Cougnac contains chasms ("gouffres") and galleries and its prehistoric paintings include human figures. Around **Les Eyzies** *(see pp424–5)* are the major caves of **Font de Gaume**, **Les Combarelles** and **La Mouthe**, which have some beautiful prehistoric paintings and drawings, as does **Rouffignac** in its extensive network of caves. **Grand Roc** has chambers containing a profusion of stalactites and stalagmites. For more unusual rock formations, the chasm at **La Fage**, northeast of Les Eyzies, leads to chambers and galleries with some magnificent examples.

On the south bank of the Dordogne, an underground river and lake with extraordinary rock formations can be seen at **Lacave**. The gigantic chasm and caverns at **Padirac** *(p428)* are even more spectacular. The caves at **Lascaux** with the finest prehistoric paintings have been closed but the exceptional replica at **Lascaux II** *(p424)* is well worth seeing. Further south, **Pech-Merle's** caverns *(p428)* have impressive rock formations.

THE STORY OF CAVE ART

The first prehistoric cave paintings in Europe were discovered in northwest Spain in 1879. Since then, over 200 decorated caves and rock shelters have been found in Spain and France, mainly in the Dordogne region. A wide range of clues, from stone lamps to miraculously preserved footprints, has helped prehistorians to work out the techniques the cave artists used. But their motives are still not clear. Nearly all the paintings are of animals, with few humans, and many of them are in inaccessible underground chambers. The paintings undoubtedly had a symbolic or magical significance; a new theory suggests they were the work of shamens.

The techniques used by Ice Age artists, who worked by lamplight, included cutting outlines into soft rock, using natural contours as part of the design. Black lines and shading were produced by charcoal, while colour washes were applied with mineral pigments such as kaolin and haematite. Hand silhouettes were made by sucking up diluted pigment and blowing it through a plant stem to form a fine spray. When the hand was removed from the rock, its eerie shape was left behind.

Decorated stone lamp discovered in Lascaux cave

Kaolin

Charcoal

Haematite

The Great Bull from the Hall of Bulls frieze at Lascaux

POITOU AND AQUITAINE

DEUX-SÈVRES · VIENNE · CHARENTE-MARITIME
CHARENTE · GIRONDE · LANDES

THIS VAST AREA *of southwest France spans a quarter of the country's windswept Atlantic coastline, a great expanse of fine sandy beaches. The region stretches from the marshes of the Marais Poitevin to the great pine forests of the Landes. Central to it is the celebrated wine region of Bordeaux and its great châteaux.*

The turbulent history of Poitou and Aquitaine, fought over for centuries, has left a rich architectural and cultural heritage. The great arch and amphitheatre at Saintes bear witness to Roman influence in the area. In the Middle Ages, the pilgrimage route to Santiago de Compostela *(see pp390– 91)* created an impressive legacy of Romanesque churches, such as those at Poitiers and Parthenay, as well as tiny chapels and glowing frescoes. The Hundred Years' War *(see pp48–9)* caused great upheaval but also resulted in the construction of mighty defence keeps by the English Plantagenet kings. As a result of the Wars of Religion *(see pp50–51)*, many towns, churches and châteaux were destroyed and had to be rebuilt.

Present-day Poitiers is a big, thriving commercial centre. To the west are the historic ports of La Rochelle and Rochefort. Further south, the wine-producing district of Bordeaux combines with Cognac, famous for its brandy, to supply an important part of the region's income. The city of Bordeaux is as prosperous today as in Roman times, combining a lively cultural scene with elegant 18th-century architecture. Its wines complement the region's cuisine: eels, mussels and oysters from the coast; and salty lamb and goat's cheeses from the inland pastures.

Shuttered houses in St Martin de Ré, on Ile de Ré, off the coast of La Rochelle

◁ **The seaside resort of Arcachon by the sandy dunes of the Bassin d'Arcachon**

Exploring Poitou and Aquitaine

Blessed with a seemingly endless Atlantic coastline, abundant navigable waterways, excellent ports and the finest wine and brandy in the world, the region is ideal for a relaxing holiday. Today most summer visitors head straight for the beaches with their thundering waves, but there is also a lush countryside inland with a lot to offer. Fine medieval architecture can be seen along the pilgrim's route to Santiago de Compostela *(see pp390–91)*, and châteaux of all shapes and sizes characterize the wine districts around Bordeaux. The only modern city of major importance in the region, Bordeaux is worth a visit for its elegant 18th-century architecture as well as for its rich cultural life. The vast man-made forest of Les Landes also adds to this greatly undervalued corner of France.

Beachlife in Bassin d'Arcachon on the Côte d'Argent

GETTING AROUND

The region's main highway is the A10 autoroute connecting Paris and Poitiers with Bordeaux and points east, such as Toulouse, west to Rochefort and south to Bayonne and Spain. This road carries most of the heavy traffic in the area, relieving the excellent smaller roads, which are largely a joy to drive along. The Paris-Poitiers-Angoulême-Bordeaux TGV line has halved rail travel times (Paris–Bordeaux 3 3/4 hr). Bordeaux operates an international airport, and has coach services serving most European capitals. From Poitiers there are buses to nearby towns, including Parthenay, Chauvigny and St-Savin.

To Tours

ANGLES-SUR-ANGLIN 9

POITIERS 6

7

8

10 *ST-SAVIN*

ABBAYE DE NOUAILLÉ-MAUPERTUIS

CHAUVIGNY

11 *MONTMORILLON*

ELLE

13

CONFOLENS

CHARROUX 12

23 *ANGOULÊME*

To Limoges

CHÂTERRE-R-DRONNE 24

MILION

To Toulouse

The harbour at Île de Ré

SIGHTS AT A GLANCE

KEY

▬ Motorway

▬ Major road

▬ Minor road

▬ Scenic route

〰 River

☼ Viewpoint

0 kilometres   25

0 miles   25

Boats moored at Coulon in the Marais Poitevin

Rose window of St-Médard, Thouars

Thouars **①**

Deux-Sèvres. 🚹 12,600. 🚊 🚌 🛈
3 bis bd Pierre Curie (05 49 66 17 65).
🍴 Tue & Fri.

THOUARS, on a rocky outcrop
surrounded by the river
Thouet, is on the border between Anjou and Poitou. There
are as many roofs of northern
slate as of southern red tiles.

In the centre lies **Eglise St-
Médard**. Its Romanesque
façade is a perfect example of
the Poitevin style that is typical
of the region *(see p402)*, although a splendid Gothic rose
window has been added. Lined
with half-timbered medieval
houses, the rue du Château
leads up to the 17th-century
château which dominates the
town. It now houses a lycée
and is open to the public
during the summer.

East of Thouars lies the
moated **Château d'Oiron**,
which now hosts contemporary
art exhibitions. A masterpiece
of Renaissance architecture, it
was built in 1518–49.

♣ Château d'Oiron
79100 Oiron. **⚊** 05 49 96 51 25.
Open daily. **Closed** public hols. ⌾

Parthenay **②**

Deux-Sèvres. 🚹 11,000. 🚊 🚌
🛈 8 rue de la Vaux-St-Jacques (05 49
64 24 24). 🍴 Wed.

PARTHENAY is a classic, sleepy
provincial town, typical of
western France, except on
Wednesday mornings, when
France's second biggest livestock market is held here. In
the Middle Ages, the town was
an important halt on the route
to Santiago de Compostela
(see pp390–91) and it is easy
to imagine the processions of
pilgrims in the medieval
quarter. Steep and cobbled,
rue de la Vaux-St-Jacques
winds up to the 13th-century
ramparts, leading on from the
fortified Porte St-Jacques
which guards a 13th-century
bridge over the river Thouet.

West of Parthenay, the 12th-
century church of **St-Pierre
de Parthenay-le-Vieux** has a
splendid Poitevin façade,
featuring Samson and the Lion
and a cavalier with a falcon.

Marais Poitevin **③**

Charente-Maritime, Deux-Sèvres,
Vendée. ✈ La Rochelle. 🚊 Niort,
Coulon, Marans. 🚌 Coulon, Arcais.
🛈 Coulon (05 49 35 99 29).

THE POITEVIN MARSHES, which
have been slowly drained
with canals, dykes and sluices
for a thousand years, cover
about 90,000 hectares (222,000
acres) between Niort and the
sea. The area is now a national
park, divided into two parts.
To the north and south of the
Sèvre estuary is the fertile
Marais Désséché (dry marsh),
where cereal crops are grown.
The huge swathe of the Marais
Mouillé (wet marsh) is upstream towards Niort.

The wet marshes, known
as the Venise Verte (Green
Venice), are the most interesting. They are crisscrossed by
a labyrinth of weed-choked
canals, adorned by orchids and
waterlilies, shaded by poplars
and beeches, and supporting a
rich variety of birds and other
wildlife. The *maraîchins* who
live here stoutly maintain that
much of the huge, water-
logged forest is unexplored.
The picturesque whitewashed
villages hereabouts are all
built on high ground, and the
customary means of trans-
port is a flat-bottomed boat,
known as a *platte*.

Coulon, St-Hilaire-la-Palud,
La Garette and Arçais, as well
as Damvix and Maillezais in
the Vendée, are all convenient
starting points for boat trips
around the marshes (allow at
least three hours). Boats can

Medieval houses lining the cobbled rue de la Vaux-St-Jacques in Parthenay

Flat-bottomed boats moored at Coulon in the Marais Poitevin

be rented with or without a guide. Make sure you bring plenty of insect repellent.

Coulon is the largest and best equipped village, and the district's capital. In the aquarium here lurks the largest and ugliest freshwater fish in captivity in France, a 20-kilo (45-lb) *silure*, or sheat-fish. From here there are also river cruises departing along the main channel of the Sèvre.

The Plantagenet donjon in Niort, now housing a local museum

Niort ➍

Deux-Sèvres. 58,000. 🚊 🚌
🛈 *rue Ernest Perochon (05 49 24 18 79).* 🖙 *Thu & Sat.*

ONCE A MEDIEVAL PORT by the green waters of the Sèvre, Niort is now a prosperous industrial town specializing in machine tools, electronics, chemicals and insurance.

Its closeness to the marshes is evident in local specialities – eels, snails and angelica. This herb has been cultivated in the wetlands for centuries and is used for anything from liqueur to ice cream.

The town's immediate attraction is the huge 12th-century donjon overlooking the Vieux Ponts. Built by Henry II and Richard the Lion-Heart, it played an important role during the Hundred Years' War and was later used as a prison. One prisoner was the father of Madame de Maintenon *(see p52),* who was born in Niort and spent

her childhood there. The donjon is now a museum concentrating on local arts and crafts, and archaeology.

Environs

Half way to Poitiers is the small town of **St-Maixent-L'Ecole**. A marvel of light and space, its abbey church is a Flamboyant Gothic recon-struction by François Le Duc (1670) of a building destroyed during the Wars of Religion. Further west, the **Tumulus de Bougon** consists of five tumuli (burial mounds), the oldest dating from 4500 BC.

Melle ➎

Deux-Sèvres. 4,000. 🚌 🛈 *place de la Poste (05 49 29 15 10).* 🖙 *Fri.*

A ROMAN SILVER MINE was the origin of Melle, which in the 9th century had the only mint in Aquitaine. Later its fame derived from the *baudet de Poitou,* an especially sturdy mule bred in the area. Now Melle is better known for its churches, of which the finest is **St-Hilaire**. Built in a delight-ful riverside setting it has a 12th-century Poitevin façade with an equestrian statue, thought to be of the Emperor Constantine, above the north door. The capitals in the nave have elaborate motifs ranging from angels to bizarre beasts.

Environs

To the northwest, the abbey in **Celles-sur-Belle** has a great Moorish doorway which con-trasts strongly with the rest of the church, a 17th-century restoration in Gothic style.

Equestrian statue of Constantine on the façade of St-Hilaire, Melle

Canal in the Venise Verte region of the Marais Poitevin ▷

Poitiers ⑥

THREE OF THE GREATEST BATTLES in French history were fought around Poitiers, the most famous in 732 when Charles Martel halted the Arab invasion. After two periods of English rule *(see p47)* the town thrived during the reign of Jean de Berry (1369–1416), the great sponsor of the arts. Its university, founded in 1431, made Poitiers a major intellectual centre and saw Rabelais among its students. The Wars of Religion left Poitiers in chaos and not until the late 19th century did any major development take place. Today, however, the town is a modern and dynamic regional capital with a rich architectural heritage in its historic centre.

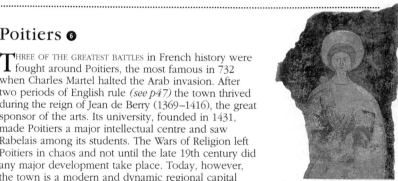

Fresco in Eglise St-Hilaire-le-Grand

🛆 Notre-Dame-la-Grande
Despite its name, Notre-Dame-la-Grande is not a large church. One of Poitiers' great pilgrim churches, it is most celebrated for its 12th-century masterpiece of lively Poitevin sculpture. In the choir is a Romanesque fresco of Christ and the Virgin. Most of the chapels were added during the Renaissance.

♟ Palais de Justice
Pl Alphonse-le-Petit. **☎** *05 49 50 22 00.* **Open** *Mon – Fri; Jul & Aug:daily.*
Behind the bland Renaissance façade is the 12th-century great hall of the palace of the Angevin kings, Henry II and Richard the Lion-Heart. This is thought to be the scene of Joan of Arc's examination by a council of theologians in 1429.

🛆 Cathédrale St-Pierre
The 13th-century carved choir stalls in St-Pierre are by far the oldest in France. Note the huge 12th-century east window showing the Crucifixion. The tiny figures of the cathedral's

Pillars with colourful geometrical patterns in Notre-Dame-la-Grande

NOTRE-DAME-LA-GRANDE

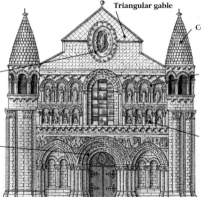

Triangular gable

Cone-shaped pinnacles

Christ in Majesty is shown in the centre of the gable, surrounded by symbols of the evangelists.

Blind arcading is a distinctive feature of the Poitevin façade.

The portals on the Poitevin façade are deep and richly sculpted, often showing a pronounced Moorish influence.

The 12 apostles are represented by statues in the arcatures, together with the first bishop St Hilaire and his disciple St Martin.

FUTUROSCOPE

Futuroscope is a fantastic theme park exploring state-of-the-art visual technology in a futuristic architectural environment. Attractions include the "magic carpet" cinema, with one of its two screens placed on the floor, creating the sensation of "flying" over land. The crystal-like Kinemax has the biggest screen in Europe.

Futuroscope's Kinemax

patrons (Henry II and Eleanor of Aquitaine) are crouched at the foot of the window.

Eglise Ste-Radegonde

Housed in this church is the 6th-century tomb of Radegonde, who founded the Abbaye de Ste-Croix – the first nunnery in France – on this site. In the choir are 13th-century windows recounting the life of the saint.

Baptistère St-Jean

Rue Jean Jaurès. **Open** Jul–Aug: daily; Sep–Jun: Wed–Mon. The polygonal 4th-century Baptistère St-Jean is one of the oldest Christian buildings in France. Many of the earliest converts were baptized here. Now a museum, it contains Romanesque frescoes of Christ and Emperor Constantine, and some Merovingian sarcophagi.

Musée Sainte-Croix

3 bis rue Jean Jaurès. 05 49 41 07 53. **Open** Tue–Sun. **Closed** public hols. Musée Sainte-Croix exhibits an eclectic mixture of Classical and medieval archaeology, and a wide range of paintings and sculpture. Three bronzes by Camille Claudel are on show, including La Valse. There is also a gallery of local artifacts and paintings.

Eglise St-Hilaire-le-Grand

Fires and reconstructions have made St-Hilaire a mosaic of different styles. With its origins in the 6th century, the church still displays an 11th-century belltower and a 12th-century nave.

Médiathèque François Mitterrand

4 rue de l'Université. 05 49 52 31 51. **Open** Tue–Sat. This modern building, in the historic quarter, is renowned for its communications technology. Inside, the **Musée du Moyen Age** displays medieval manuscripts and engravings.

Environs

The **Futuroscope**, 7 km (4.5 miles) north of Poitiers, is a museum of developments in visual communications.

Futuroscope

Jaunay-Clan. 05 49 49 30 00. **Open** daily.

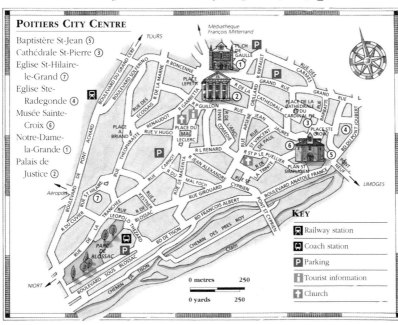

POITIERS CITY CENTRE

Baptistère St-Jean ⑤
Cathédrale St-Pierre ③
Eglise St-Hilaire-le-Grand ⑦
Eglise Ste-Radegonde ④
Musée Sainte-Croix ⑥
Notre-Dame-la-Grande ①
Palais de Justice ②

KEY

- 🚉 Railway station
- 🚌 Coach station
- 🅿 Parking
- ℹ Tourist information
- ✝ Church

0 metres 250
0 yards 250

The castle ruins of Angles-sur-Anglin with the old watermill in the foreground

Abbaye de Nouaillé-Maupertuis ❼

Nouaillé-Maupertuis. 📞 05 49 55 90 25. **Church open** daily (pm only). ♿ restricted.

O N THE BANKS of the river Miosson lies the Abbaye de Nouaillé-Maupertuis. First mentioned in 780, the abbey became independent in 808 and followed the Benedictine rule. Apart from the beauty of the site, it is also worth a visit for its church, built in the 11th–12th century and reconstructed several times. Behind the altar is the 10th-century sarcophagus of St-Junien, with three great heraldic eagles carved on the side.

More interesting is the nearby battlefield, scene of the great English victory at Poitiers by the Black Prince in 1356. The view has altered little in 600 years. Drive down the small road to La Cardinerie (to the right off the D142), which leads to the river crossing at Gue de L'Omme, the epicentre of the battle. There is a monument halfway up the hill where the heaviest fighting took place and where the French king Jean le Bon was isolated and captured. He had put up a heroic single-handed resistance with nothing but his battle-axe and his small son Philippe to tell him from where the next English knight was coming.

Chauvigny ❽

Vienne. 🏠 8,000. 🚉 🛈 5 rue St-Pierre (05 49 46 39 01). 🚌 Sat.

C HAUVIGNY, on its steep promontory overlooking the broad river Vienne, has the distinction of being able to display the ruins of no fewer than four fortified medieval castles. Stone from the local quarry was so plentiful that nobody ever bothered to demolish earlier castles for building material.

Nevertheless, the best thing in this town is the 11th–12th-century **Eglise St-Pierre**, whose decorated capitals are a real treasure – particularly those in the choir. The carvings represent biblical scenes along with monsters,

Monster capitals in Eglise St-Pierre in Chauvigny

sphinxes and sirens. Look for the one which says *Gofridus me fecit* (Gofridus made me), with wonderfully natural scenes of the Epiphany.

Environs
Nearby is the lovely **Château de Touffou**, a Renaissance dream on the banks of the Vienne, with terraces and hanging gardens. Just to the north of it is the sleepy village of **Bonneuil-Matours**. Its Romanesque church has richly ornate choir stalls.

⚓ **Château de Touffou**
Bonnes. 📞 05 49 56 40 08. **Open** mid-Jun–mid-Sep: Tue–Sun; Oct–May: Sat & Sun. 🈲

Angles-sur-Anglin ❾

Vienne. 🏠 420. 🛈 La Mairie (05 49 48 86 87 or 05 49 48 61 20). 🚌 Sun.

T HE VILLAGE OF ANGLES lies in an extremely beautiful riverside setting, dominated by its castle ruins. Adding to the charm is an old watermill by the slow-running river Anglin, graced by waterlilies and swaying reeds.

Angles is also famous for its tradition of fine needlework, the *jours d'Angles*, which is determinedly maintained by the local women today.

The village is delightful to visit off season, but in summer the narrow streets become too crowded for comfort.

St-Savin ⑩

Vienne. 🚶 *1,100.* 🚉
🛈 *15 rue St-Louis (05 49 48 11 00).*
🗓 *Fri.*

THE GLORY of St-Savin is its 11th-century abbey church with its slender Gothic spire and huge nave.

The abbey had enormous influence until the Hundred Years' War, when it was burnt down. It was later pillaged several times during the Wars of Religion. Despite restoration work by monks in the 17th century and again in the 19th century, the church seems quite untouched.

Its interior contains the most magnificent series of 12th-century Romanesque frescoes in Europe. These wallpaintings were among the very first in France to be classified *Monument Historique* in 1836, by Prosper Merimée, author of *Carmen*, and Inspector of Historical Monuments. Some of the frescoes were restored between 1967–74 and the collection is now protected by UNESCO. A full-scale replica of the St-Savin murals can be seen at the Palais de Chaillot in Paris *(see pp106–7).*

Belltower of St-Savin

Montmorillon ⑪

Vienne. 🚶 *7,200.* 🚉 🛈 *2 pl du Marechal Leclerc (05 49 91 11 96).*
🗓 *Wed & Sat.*

MONTMORILLON, built on both banks of the calm river Gartempe, has its origins in the 11th century. Like most towns in the region it had a difficult time during the Hundred Years' War and the Wars of Religion. Some buildings survived, such as **Eglise Notre-Dame**, which has beautiful frescoes in its 12th-century crypt. They include scenes from the life of St Catherine of Alexandria.

Environs

Half an hour's walk from the Pont de Chez Ragon, south of Montmorrillon, is the **Portes d'Enfer**, a dramatically shaped rock above the sudden rapids of the Gartempe.

Confolens ⑫

Charente. 🚶 *3,150.* 🚉 🛈 *place des Marronniers (05 45 84 22 22).*
🗓 *Wed & Sat.*

ON THE BORDER with Limousin, Confolens was once an important frontier town with eight churches, but now suffers from rural exodus. Efforts to prevent the town's isolation include the annual international folklore festival. Every August the town is transformed into a tumultuous mix of music, costumes and crafts from all over the world.

Of historical interest is the medieval bridge across the Vienne, heavily restored in the early 19th century.

Charroux ⑬

Vienne. 🚶 *1,400.* 🛈 *2 route de Chatain (05 49 87 60 12).* 🗓 *Thu.*

THE 8TH-CENTURY **Abbaye du St-Sauveur** in Charroux was once one of the richest abbeys in the region. Today it has become no more than a ruin open to the sky.

Its chief contribution to history was made in the 10th century, when the Council of Charroux declared the "Truce of God", the earliest-known attempt to regulate war in the manner of the Geneva convention. Rules included: "Christian soldiers may not plunder churches, strike priests or steal peasants' livestock while campaigning."

The huge tower marking the centre of the church, and some superb sculpture from the original abbey portal in the small museum here, give an idea of what Charroux must have been like in its heyday.

ST-SAVIN WALL PAINTINGS

The frescoes of St-Savin represent Old Testament history from the Creation to the Ten Commandments. The sequence starts to the left of the entrance with the Creation of the stars and of Eve. It continues with scenes from Noah's Ark to the Tower of Babel, the story of Joseph and the parting of the Red Sea. It is believed that all the frescoes were created by the same group of artists, due to the similarity in style. Their harmonious colours – red and yellow ochre, green, black and white – have been softened by time.

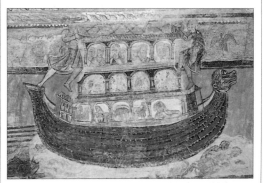

Noah's Ark, from a 12th-century wall painting in St-Savin

Aulnay ⑭

Charente-Maritime. 🏛 *1,400.*
ℹ️ *290 avenue de l'Eglise (05 46 33 14 44).* 🚌 *Sun.*

PERHAPS the most unusual fact about the lovely 12th-century **Eglise St-Pierre** at Aulnay is that it was all built at once; there is no ill-fitting apse or transept added to an original nave. Surrounded by nothing but cypresses, it has remained the same since the time of the great pilgrimages.

The church is covered in glorious sculpture, particularly the outside of the south transept. It is a rare example of a complete Romanesque façade, with rank on rank of raucous monsters and graceful human figures. Look for the donkey with a harp. Inside the church there is a pillar decorated with elephants, inscribed "Here be Elephants".

Façade of Eglise St-Pierre at Aulnay

La Rochelle ⑮

Charente-Maritime. 🏛 *71,000.* ✈
🚉 🚌 ℹ️ *pl de la Petite Sirène, Le Gabut (05 46 41 14 68).* 🚌 *daily.*

LA ROCHELLE, a commercial centre and busy port since the 11th century, has suffered much from a distressing tendency to back the wrong side – the English and the Calvinists, for example. This led to the ruthless siege of the city by Cardinal Richelieu in 1628, during which 23,000 people starved to death. The walls were destroyed and the city's

Tour St-Nicolas in La Rochelle

privileges withdrawn. The glory of La Rochelle is the old harbour surrounded by stately buildings. The harbour is now the biggest yachting centre on France's Atlantic coast. On either side of its entrance are **Tour de la Chaîne** and **Tour St-Nicolas**. A huge chain used to be strung between them to ward off attack from the sea.

La Rochelle is easy to explore on foot, though its cobbled streets and many arcades can be impossibly congested in high summer. To get an overview, climb the 15th-century **Tour de la Lanterne**. Its inner walls were covered in graffiti by prisoners, mostly foreign mariners, in the 17th–19th centuries. Ships are the most common motif.

The study of the 18th-century scientist Clément Lafaille is preserved in the **Muséum d'Histoire Naturelle**, complete with shell collection and display cabinets. There are also stuffed animals and African masks. The town's relation to the New World is treated in the **Musée du Nouveau Monde**. Emigration as well as commerce and the slave trade are explained through old maps, paintings and artifacts.

The richly decorated 16th-century courtyard façade of the **Hôtel de Ville** is worth a visit, as is the delightful collection of perfume bottles in the **Musée du Flacon à Parfum** in the parfumerie at No. 33 rue du Temple.

Outside the old centre is the huge **Aquarium**. Glassed tunnels lead through tanks with different marine biotopes, including sharks and turtles.

🏰 **Tour de la Lanterne**
Le Port. 📞 *05 46 41 56 04.* **Open** *Apr–15 Sep: daily; 15 Sep–Mar: Tue–Sun.* **Closed** *1 Jan, 1 May, 1 & 11 Nov, 25 Dec.* 🎫
🏛 **Muséum d'Histoire Naturelle**
28 rue Albert Premier. 📞 *05 46 41 18 25.* **Open** *Tue–Sat & Sun pm.* **Closed** *public hols.* 🎫
🏛 **Musée du Nouveau Monde**
10 rue Fleuriau. 📞 *05 46 41 46 50.* **Open** *Wed–Mon.* **Closed** *1 Jan, 1 May, 14 Jul, 1 & 11 Nov, 25 Dec.* 🎫
🐟 **Aquarium**
Port des Minimes. 📞 *05 46 34 00 00.* **Open** *daily.* 🎫 ♿

Environs
Ile de Ré, also known as the white island, is a long stretch of chalky cliffs and dunes, with a rich birdlife. Since 1988 it has been connected to the mainland by a 3-km (2-mile) long bridge.

Head for **St-Martin-de-Ré**, the island's main village. Apart from its 17th-century ramparts there are plenty of seafood restaurants serving oysters from the island's oyster beds.

Arcade in rue du Palais, La Rochelle

Rochefort ⑯

Charente-Maritime. 🏛 *28,000.* 🚉
🚌 ℹ️ *av Sadi-Carnot (05 46 99 08 60).* 🚌 *Tue, Thu & Sat.*

THE HISTORIC RIVAL of La Rochelle, Rochefort was purpose-built by Colbert *(see pp52–3)* in the 17th century

Phare des Baleines on the eastern point of Ile de Ré, just outside La Rochelle

to be the greatest shipyard in France, producing over 300 sailing vessels per year.

Today this maritime heritage can be traced in the **Corderie Royale** (royal ropeworks) from 1670. Beautifully restored, the building now houses an exhibition on ropemaking. The **Musée de la Marine** displays splendid models of all ships built in the arsenal.

The noble and somewhat austere town is now more famous as the birthplace of the flamboyant writer Pierre Loti (1850–1923). The author's extravagant **Maison de Pierre Loti** is filled with lush souvenirs in an oriental decor.

The **Musée d'Art et d'Histoire** has an interesting ethnographic collection and a relief map of the old shipyard.

♛ La Corderie Royale
Centre International de la Mer, rue Audebert. 【 05 46 87 01 90. **Open** daily. **Closed** 1 Jan, 25 Dec. 🖼 ⛦
🏛 Musée de la Marine
Place de la Galissonnière. 【 05 46 99 86 57. **Open** Wed–Mon. **Closed** public hols (except Easter & Pentecost). 🖼
🏛 Maison de Pierre Loti
141 rue Pierre Loti. 【 05 46 99 16 88. **Open** Wed–Mon; Jul–mid-Sep: daily. **Closed** 20 Dec–20 Jan, public hols. 🖼
🏛 Musée d'Art et d'Histoire
63 avenue Charles de Gaulle. 【 05 46 99 83 99. **Open** Tue–Sat: pm only. **Closed** public hols. 🖼

Environs
Ile d'Aix is served by a ferry from Fouras on the mainland. Napoleon was briefly kept here before being exiled to St Helena. There are Napoleonic mementos in the **Musée Napoléonien**. The camel he rode in the Egyptian campaign is in the **Musée Africain**.

🏛 Musée Napoléonien
30 Rue Napoléon. 【 05 46 84 66 40. **Open** Wed–Mon. **Closed** 1 May. 🖼
🏛 Musée Africain
Rue Napoléon. 【 05 46 84 66 40. **Open** Thu–Tue. **Closed** 1 May. 🖼 ⛦

Napoleon, who was detained at Ile d'Aix in 1814

Île d'Oléron ⑰

Charente-Maritime. ✈ La Rochelle. 🚉 Rochefort, Marennes (summer), then bus. 🚤 from La Rochelle. 🛈 Château d'Oléron (05 46 47 60 51).

OLERON is the second largest French island after Corsica, and a very popular holiday resort. Its south coast, the **Côte Sauvage**, is all dunes and pine forest, with excellent beaches at Vert Bois and Grande Plage, near the fishing port of La Cotinière. The north is more prosaic, largely given over to farming and fishing.

The miniature train from **St-Trojan** makes an interesting excursion through dunes and woodlands to the Pointe de Maumusson (summer only).

Brouage ⑱

Charente-Maritime. 🏘 180.
🛈 2 rue de Québec, Hiers-Brouage (05 46 85 19 16).

CARDINAL Richelieu's fortress at Brouage, his base during the Siege of La Rochelle (1627–8), once overlooked a thriving harbour, but its wealth and population declined in the 18th century as the ocean receded. In 1659, Marie Mancini was sent into exile here by her uncle, Cardinal Mazarin, who did not approve of her liaison with Louis XIV. The king never forgot the beautiful Marie. Even on his way back from his wedding, he stayed alone at Brouage in the room once occupied by his first great love. Today the **ramparts** form a peaceful backdrop for the villagers working in the oyster beds below.

Environs
There are two reasons to go to **Marennes**, southwest of Brouage: the famous green-tinged oysters and the view from the steeple of Eglise St-Pierre-de-Sales. Nearby is the 18th-century **Château de la Gatandière** with an exhibition of horsedrawn vehicles.

One of Royan's five popular beaches

Royan **⑲**

Charente-Maritime. 🏛 *17,500.* 🚉
🚌 🛳 *to Verdon only.* ℹ *Rond-Point de la Poste (05 46 05 04 71).*
🗓 *daily.*

BADLY DAMAGED by Allied carpet-bombing at the end of World War II, Royan is now thoroughly modern and completely different in tone from the rest of the towns on this weather-beaten coast. With five beaches of fine sand, here called *conches*, it becomes a heavily populated resort in the summer months.

Built between 1955 and 1958, **Eglise Notre-Dame** is a remarkable early example of reinforced concrete architecture. Its interior is flooded with colour and light by the stained-glass windows.

A change from all the modern architecture is offered by the outstanding Renaissance **Phare de Cordouan**. Various lighthouses have been erected on the site since the 11th century. The present one was finished in 1611, with a chapel

inside. The construction was later reinforced and 40 m (130 ft) added to its height. Since 1789 the only thing that has changed is the lighting method. Boat trips which include Phare de Cordouan leave from Royan harbour.

Talmont **⑳**

Charente-Maritime. 🏛 *83.*

THE TINY Romanesque **Eglise Ste-Radegonde** in Talmont occupies an extraordinary position on a spit of land overlooking the Gironde. Built in 1094, the church has a unique apse, designed to resemble the prow of a ship – which is appropriate, since the nave has already fallen into the sea. A 15th-century façade closes off what's left. Inside are richly decorated capitals, including a representation of St George and the Dragon.

Talmont is a jewel of a village, packed full of little white houses covered with climbing roses in summer.

Saintes **㉑**

Charente-Maritime. 🏛 *27,000.* 🚉
🚌 ℹ *Villa Musso, 62 cours National (05 46 74 23 82).* 🗓 *Tue–Sun.*

CAPITAL OF the Saintonge region, Saintes has an extraordinarily rich architectural heritage. For centuries it boasted the only bridge over the lower Charente, well used by pilgrims on their way to Santiago de Compostela. The Roman bridge no longer exists but you can still admire the magnificent **Arch of Germanicus** (AD 19) which used to mark its entrance.

On the same side of the river is the simple and beautiful **Abbaye aux Dames**. Consecrated in 1047, the church was modernized in the 12th century. During the 17th–18th centuries many young noble ladies were educated here. Look for the decorated portal and the vigorous 12th-century head of Christ in the apse.

On the left bank is the 1st-century Roman **amphitheatre**. Further away lies the rather unknown gem, **Eglise St-Eutrope**. In the 15th century, this church had the misfortune to effect a miraculous cure of the dropsy on Louis XI. In a paroxysm of gratitude, he did his best to wreck it with ill-considered Gothic additions. Luckily, its rare Romanesque capitals have survived.

Arch of Germanicus in Saintes

Cognac **㉒**

Charente. 🏛 *20,000.* 🚉 🚌
ℹ *16 rue du 14 Juillet (05 45 82 10 71).* 🗓 *daily.*

WHEREVER YOU SPOT the telltale black lichen stains from alcohol evaporation on the exterior of the

Necropolis in the monolithic Eglise St-Jean in Aubeterre-sur-Dronne

buildings in this old river port, you may be sure that you are looking at yet another storehouse of cognac.

Head for the best distillery, **Cognac Otard**, situated in the 15th–16th-century château where François I was born. The distillery was established in 1795 by a Scot named Otard, who ruthlessly demolished an old chapel in the process. However, a great part of the Renaissance architecture has been saved and can be enjoyed during the tour, which includes a cognac-tasting.

Cognac in traditional snifter

The basic material for cognac is local white wine low in alcohol, which is then distilled. The resultant pale spirit is aged in oak barrels for 5–40 years before being bottled. The skill lies in the blending – therefore the only guide to quality is the name and the duration of ageing.

🍷 **Cognac Otard**
Château de Cognac, bd Denfert-Rochereau. 📞 05 45 36 88 86. **Open** Apr–Sep: daily; Oct–Mar: Mon–Fri. **Closed** public hols.

Angoulême ㉓

Charente. 🏠 46,000. 🚉 🚌
ℹ️ 7 bis rue du Chat (05 45 95 16 84). 🛒 daily.

THE CELEBRATED 12th-century Cathédrale St-Pierre, which dominates this thriving industrial centre, is the fourth to be built on the site. One of its most interesting features is the Romanesque frieze on the façade, wonderfully rich in detail. Some exaggerated restoration work was carried out by the 19th-century architect Abadie. In his eagerness to wipe out all details added after the 12th century, he even managed to destroy a 6th-century crypt.

Unfortunately he was also let loose on the old château, transforming it into a Neo-Gothic **Hôtel de Ville** (town hall). However, the 15th-century tower where Marguerite d'Angoulême was born in 1492 still stands. A statue of her can be seen in the garden. Sister of François I, she spoke six languages, had an important role in foreign politics and wrote the very popular novel *Heptameon*.

The ramparts offer a long bracing walk with views over the Charente Valley.

The **Centre National de la Bande Dessinée et de l'Image** has a reference collection of French print and film cartoons since 1946. Its museum presents cartoon personalities such as Tintin, Asterix and Snoopy.

🏛️ **Centre National de la Bande Dessinée et de l'Image**
121 rue de Bordeaux. 📞 05 45 38 65 65. **Open** Tue–Sun (daily during school hols). **Closed** 1 Jan, 1 May, 25 Dec. 📷 ♿

Environs
Angoulême used to be famous for its papermills. The **Moulin de Fleurac** at Nersac has a museum and still produces rag paper in the traditional 18th-century manner.

🍷 **Moulin de Fleurac**
Nersac. 📞 05 45 91 50 69. **Open** Wed–Mon. 📷

Aubeterre-sur-Dronne ㉔

Charente. 🏠 390. 🚌 ℹ️ rue St Jean (05 45 98 57 18). 🛒 Thu & Sun.

THE CHIEF ORNAMENT of this pretty white village is the weird monolithic **Eglise St-Jean**. Dug out of the white chalky cliff that gave the village its name (Alba Terra – White Earth), some parts of it date back to the 6th century. Between the Revolution and 1860, it served as the village's cemetery. It contains an early Christian baptismal font and an octagonal reliquary.

Detail from the Romanesque façade of Cathédrale St-Pierre in Angoulême

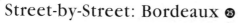

Street-by-Street: Bordeaux ㉕

B<small>UILT ON A CURVE</small> of the river Garonne, Bordeaux has been a major port since pre-Roman times and for centuries a focus and crossroads of European trade. Today Bordeaux shows little visible evidence of the Romans, Franks, English or the Wars of Religion that have marked its past. This forward-looking town, the fifth largest in France, is an industrial and maritime sprawl surrounding a noble 18th-century centre.

Along the waterfront of this wealthy wine metropolis is a long sweep of elegant Classical façades, first built to mask the medieval slums behind. Adding to the magnificence is the Esplanade des Quinconces, the Grand Théâtre and the Place de la Bourse.

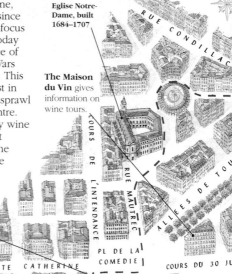

Eglise Notre-Dame, built 1684–1707

The Maison du Vin gives information on wine tours.

★ Grand Théâtre
Built in 1773–80, the theatre is a masterpiece of the Classical style, crowned by 12 statues of the muses.

STAR SIGHTS

- ★ Grand Théâtre

- ★ Esplanade des Quinconces

- ★ Place de la Bourse

KEY

– – – Suggested route

0 metres   100

0 yards   100

The quais, lined with graceful façades, make a beautiful walk along the Garonne.

★ Place de la Bourse
This elegant and harmonious square is flanked by two majestic 18th-century buildings, Palais de la Bourse and Hôtel des Douanes.

★ Esplanade des Quinconces
Replacing the 15th-century Château de Trompette, this vast space of tree-lined esplanades with statues and fountains was created in 1827–58.

VISITORS' CHECKLIST

Gironde. 214,000. 10 km (6 miles) W Bordeaux. Gare St-Jean, rue Charles Domerq. place des Quinconces. 12 cours du 30 Juillet (05 56 00 66 00). Mon–Sat. L'Eté Girondin (jazz; Jul–Aug); Fête du Vin Nouveau (end Oct).

Quartier des Chartrons, the old merchants' quarter, has fine 18th-century buildings.

The Monument aux Girondins is a richly adorned monument (1804–1902). It commemorates the Girondists sent to the guillotine by Robespierre during the Terror (1793–5).

COURS DE TOURNON
RUE BOUDET
COURS DE GOURGUE
DES QUINCONCES
COURS DU MARECHAL FOCH
ESPLANADE DES QUINCONCES
ALLEE DE CHARTRES
ALLEE DE BRISTOL
RUE VAUBAN
RUE FERRERE
RUE FOY
DE MUNICH
QUAI LOUIS XVIII

Le CAPC
This museum of contemporary art and cultural centre opened in 1990 in an early 19th-century warehouse.

Terraces provide good views over the river.

Loading wine barrels in 19th-century Bordeaux

THE BORDEAUX WINE TRADE

After Marseille, Bordeaux is the oldest trading port in France. From Roman times the export of wine was the basis for a modest prosperity, but under English rule (1154–1453, see pp46–9), the merchants began making immense fortunes from their monopoly of wine sales to England. After the discovery of the New World, Bordeaux took advantage of its Atlantic position to diversify and extend its wine market. Today the Bordeaux region produces over 44 million cases of wine per year.

GRAND THÉÂTRE DE BORDEAUX

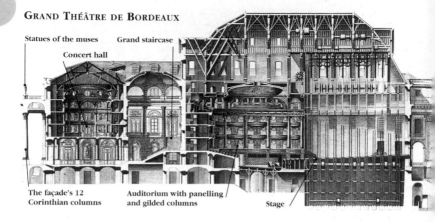

Statues of the muses   Grand staircase

Concert hall

The façade's 12
Corinthian columns

Auditorium with panelling
and gilded columns

Stage

Exploring Bordeaux

The liveliest part of Bordeaux is the triangle formed by Cours de l'Intendance, Cours Clemenceau and Allées de Tourny, where the fashionable boutiques and famous cafés are. Department stores line the pedestrianized rue Ste-Catherine and Porte-Dijeaux.

⛲ Grand Théâtre

Place de la Comédie. **[** 05 56 48 58 54.
Built by the architect Victor Louis, the 18th-century Grand Théâtre is one of the finest Classical constructions of its type in France. The auditorium is renowned for its extraordinary acoustics. The spectacular main staircase was later imitated by Garnier for the Paris Opéra (see p93).

⛪ Eglise St-Seurin

This church is somewhat chaotic with a patchwork of styles ranging from the 11th to the 18th century. Most interesting are the 6th-century Gallo-Roman sarcophagi in the crypt, and a fine bishop's throne of sculpted stone, dating from the 14th century.

⛪ Basilique St-Michel

It took 200 years to build the massive Basilique St-Michel, begun in 1350. Cleaned and restored in the 1990s, this triple-naved edifice prides itself on the remarkable statue of St Ursula with her flock of penitents, in one of the side-chapels. Its freestanding belfry, built in 1472–92, is the tallest in southern France at 114 m (375 ft).

🏛 Musée des Beaux Arts

20 cours d'Albret. **[** 05 56 10 16 93. **Open** Wed–Mon. **Closed** public hols. 📷 ♿
Housed in the northern and southern wings of the Hôtel de Ville, this museum possesses an excellent collection of paintings, ranging from the Renaissance to our time. Special masterpieces include works by Titian, Veronese, Rubens, Delacroix, Corot, Renoir, Matisse and Boudin.

🏛 Musée d'Aquitaine

20 cours Pasteur. **[** 05 56 01 51 00. **Open** Tue–Sun. **Closed** public hols. 📷 ♿
This important museum traces life in the region from prehistoric times to the present, through artifacts, furniture and viticulture tools. Among its more spectacular exhibits are the Tayac treasure from the 2nd century BC, including a magnificent gold torque, and the Garonne treasure, a hoard of over 4,000 Roman coins.

**Calm street in Bordeaux by the
Porte de la Grosse Cloche**

⛪ Cathédrale St-André

The nave of this gigantic church was begun in the 11th century and modified 200 years later. The Gothic choir and transepts were added in the 14th and 15th centuries. The excellent medieval sculptures on the Porte Royale include scenes from the Last Judgment.

🏛 Le CAPC

Entrepôt Lainé, 7 rue Ferrère. **[** 05 56 00 81 50. **Open** Tue–Sun pm only. **Closed** 1 Jan, 1 May, 25 Dec. 📷 ♿
The CAPC (Centre d'Arts Plastiques Contemporains) is housed in a superbly converted 19th-century warehouse and opened as a museum in 1990. There are regular themed exhibitions from the permanent collection of contemporary art. The museum also functions as a cultural centre, with special film projections, lectures and debates.

St-Émilion ㉖

Gironde. 👥 2,800. 🚉 🚌 place de Créneaux (05 57 24 72 03). 🚌 Sun.

To MOST PEOPLE, St-Émilion is the *appellation* of a fine red wine (see pp388–9). It is, however, also the name of a charming village in the middle of the wine growing district. Its origins go back to the 8th century when the hermit Émilion dug out a cave for himself in the rock. A monastery followed, and by the Middle Ages St-Émilion had become a small town. Today medieval houses still line the narrow streets, and parts of the 13th-century ramparts remain. There is also an interesting monolithic church, dug out of the chalky cliff by followers of Saint Émilion after his death.

Famous châteaux in the district include the elegant **Figeac**, **Cheval Blanc** and **Ausone**, all of them St-Émilion Premier Crus Classés.

Vineyard close to Margaux in the Médoc region west of Bordeaux

Pauillac ㉗

Gironde. 🏛 5,700. 🚊 🚌
🛈 quai de Pauillac, la Verrerie (05 56 59 03 08). 🛥 Tue & Sat.

O NE OF THE MOST famous areas in the Médoc wine region *(see pp388–9)* is the commune of Pauillac. Three of its châteaux are Médoc Premier Crus Classés. The

Château Mouton-Rothschild uses leading artists to create its wine labels and houses a small museum of paintings on wine themes from all over the world. The **Château Lafite-Rothschild** is of medieval origin and the **Château Latour** is recognizable by its distinctive stone turret. They can be visited by appointment

(contact the tourist office). The town of Pauillac is situated on the west bank of the Gironde. In the 19th century it was the bustling arrival point for transatlantic steamships, but now the sleepy port is mostly used by pleasure boats. There are picturesque river views from the quais and plenty of cafés serving the local wine.

BORDEAUX WINE CHÂTEAUX

The château is at the heart of the quality system in Bordeaux, the world's largest fine wine region. A château includes a vineyard and a building which can range from the most basic to the grandest, historic as well as modern. But the château is also the symbol of a tradition and the philosophy that a wine's quality and character spring from the soil. Some châteaux welcome visitors for wine tasting as well as buying. The Maison du Vin and the tourist office in Bordeaux *(see p411)* offer information and tours.

Latour in Pauillac *is famous for its powerful wines and the medieval stone turret that appears on its label.*

Cheval Blanc, *a great château in the St-Émilion area, boasts a rich, spicy Premier Grand Cru.*

Margaux, *built in 1802, produces a classic Margaux Premier Cru of the same elegant proportions as its Palladian façade.*

Palmer, *dating from 1856, is Neo-Renaissance in style and produces a very fine Margaux Troisième Cru.*

Gruaud-Larose *is a cream-coloured château with a Classical façade, distinguished by its full-bodied St-Julien Deuxième Cru Classé.*

Vieux Château Certan *is Belgian-owned and one of the great historic properties of Pomerol. Its wines are consistently in the first rank in the district, challenged only by Pétrus.*

The immense Dune du Pilat, stretching almost 3 km (2 miles) south of the inlet to Bassin d'Arcachon

La Côte d'Argent ㉘

Gironde, Landes. ✈ Bordeaux, Biarritz. 🚌 Soulac-sur-Mer, Arcachon, Labenne, Dax. 🚌 Lacanau, Arcachon, Mimizan. 🅸 Lacanau (05 56 03 21 01), Mimizan-Plage (05 58 09 11 20), Capbreton (05 58 72 12 11).

THE LONG STRETCH of coast between Pointe de Grave on the Gironde estuary and Bayonne *(see p442)* is called La Côte d'Argent – the Silver Coast. It is virtually one vast beach of shifting sand dunes. Treeplanting has now slowed down their progress.

The coast is dotted with seaside resorts like **Soulac-sur-Mer** in the north, followed by the big **Lacanau-Océan** and **Mimizan-Plage**. Down in the south is **Hossegor** with its salty lake, and **Capbreton**. Modern holiday resorts have been integrated with the old.

Inland is a string of lakes popular for fishing and boating. They are connected to each other and the ocean by *courants*, lively water currents, such as the **Courant d'Huchet** from Etang de Léon. Boat trips are available.

Bassin d'Arcachon ㉙

Gironde. 👥 12,000. 🚌 🚌 🅸 esplanade Georges Pompidou (05 56 83 01 69). 🖭 daily.

IN THE MIDDLE of the Côte d'Argent the straight coastline suddenly forms a lagoon. Famous for its natural beauty,

fine beaches and oysters, the Bassin d'Arcachon is a protected area, perfect for holidaymakers, sailing enthusiasts and oyster-eaters.

The basin is dotted with smaller amorphous resorts, beaches and fishing/oyster villages, all worth exploring.

Cap Ferret, the northern headland that protects the basin from stiff Atlantic winds, is a preserve of the wealthy, whose luxurious villas stand among the pines. Look for the small road under the trees from Lège, which leads to the wild, magnificent beach of Grand-Crohot.

Between Cap Ferret and Arcachon, near Gujan-Mestras, the **Parc Ornitho-logique du Teich** provides care and shelter for damaged birds and endangered species. For the bird watcher, there are two fascinating walks, each carefully marked: an introductory one, and another of greater length. Both

provide concealed observation points from which people can watch the wild fowl without disturbing them.

Arcachon was created as a seaside resort in 1845. Its popularity grew and in the late 19th and early 20th centuries the elegant villas in the calm Ville d'Hiver were built. The livelier Ville d'Eté, facing the lagoon, has a casino and sports facilities.

The immense **Dune du Pilat** is the largest sand dune in Europe. It is nearly 3 km (2 miles) long, 115 m (375 ft) high and 500 m (1,625 ft) wide. Aside from its panoramic view, the dune is a magnificent vantage point in autumn for viewing flocks of migratory birds as they pass overhead on their way to the sanctuary at Le Teich.

🦋 **Parc Ornithologique du Teich**
Le Teich. 📞 05 56 22 80 93. **Open** daily. 🖭 🅰

Parc Ornithologique du Teich, a bird sanctuary in Bassin d'Arcachon

LANDES FOREST

The vast, totally artificial 19th-century forest of Les Landes was an ambitious project to make use of an area of sand and marshes. Pines and grasses were planted to anchor the coastal dunes, and inland dunes were stabilized with a mixture of pines, reeds and broom. In 1855 the land was drained, and is now covered with pine groves and undergrowth, preserving a delicate ecological balance.

Pine trees in the Landes forest

Les Landes ⑳

Gironde, Landes. 🚋 *Bordeaux.*
🚌 *Morcenx, Dax, Mont de Marsan.*
🚌 *Mont de Marsan.* ⓘ *Mont de Marsan (05 58 05 87 37).*

A LMOST ENTIRELY covered by an immense pine forest, the Landes area extends over the two *départements* of Gironde and Landes. The soil here is uniformly sandy. Until a century ago the whole region became a swamp in winter, because of a layer of tufa (porous rock) just under the surface which retained water from the brackish lakes. Any settlement or agriculture close to the sea was impossible due to the constantly shifting dunes. Furthermore, the mouth of the Adour river kept moving from Capbreton to Vieux-Boucau and back, a distance of 32 km (20 miles).

The Adour was fixed near Bayonne by a canal in the 16th century. This was the start of the slow conquest of the Landes. The planting of pine trees ultimately wiped out the migrant shepherds and their flocks. Today the inner Landes is still very under-populated,

but wealthy from its pinewood and pine derivatives. The coastal strip has a large influx of holidaymakers.

In 1970, part of the forest was made into a nature park. Here, a small steam train takes visitors to **Marqueze**, where a typical 19th-century *airial* (clearing) has been restored. It commemorates the vanished world of Les Landes before the draining of the marshes, when shepherds still used stilts to get about. There are traditional *auberges landaises*, wooden houses with sloping roofs, as well as henhouses built on stilts because of the foxes. In **Luxey** a museum recalls old techniques of tapping and distillation of resin.

Lévignacq, near the coast, is a perfect Landais village with a remarkable 14th-century fortified church full of charming naive frescoes.

Mont-de-Marsan ㉛

Landes. 🚋 *32,000.* 🚌 🚌
ⓘ *6 place du Général Leclerc (05 58 05 87 37).* 🖥 *Tue–Sat.*

A BULLFIGHTING MECCA, Mont-de-Marsan attracts all the great bullfighters of France and Spain during the summer season. A less bloodthirsty local variant of the sport, very popular here, is the *course landaise*, in which the object is to vault over the horns and back of a charging cow.

The administrative capital of the Landes is also known for its hippodrome and the production of poultry and *foie gras*.

Sculpture from the first half of the 20th century can be seen at **Musée Despiau-Wlérick**.

Dax ㉜

Landes. 🚋 *20,000.* 🚌 🚌 ⓘ *place Thiers (05 58 56 86 86).* 🖥 *Sat.*

T HE THERMAL SPA of Dax is second only to Aix-les-Bains *(see p.380)* in importance. Its hot springs, with a constant temperature of 64° C (147° F) and tonic mud from the Adour, have been soothing aches and pains and promoting tranquillity since the time of Emperor Augustus.

Apart from the 13th-century doorway of the otherwise 17th-century **Cathédrale Notre-Dame**, there isn't much of architectural interest in this warm, peaceful town. But the promenade along the river Adour is charming and the bullring is world-renowned.

La Force **(1937) by Raoul Lamourdieu, in the bullfighting capital of Mont-de-Marsan**

PÉRIGORD, QUERCY AND GASCONY

DORDOGNE · LOT · TARN · HAUTE GARONNE · LOT-ET-GARONNE
TARN-ET-GARONNE · GERS · CORRÈZE

*I*F ARCHAEOLOGY IS ANY GUIDE, *the southwest of France has been continuously inhabited by mankind for tens of thousands of years, longer than any other area in Europe. The landscape of these historic regions seems to have an ancient familiarity, derived from centuries of people living in harmony with the land.*

The great cave sites around Les Eyzies and Lascaux harbour the earliest evidence we possess of primitive art. The castles, bastides *(see p435)* and churches that grace the countryside from Périgueux to the Pyrenees, from the Bay of Biscay to Toulouse and beyond to the Mediterranean, belong to a far more recent past. From the coming of Christianity until the late 18th century, this lovely region was the battlefield for a string of conflicts. The English fought and lost the Hundred Years' War for Aquitaine (1345–1453); this was followed by intermittent Wars of Religion, in which Catholics fought Huguenots (French Protestants) in a series of massacres and guerilla wars *(see pp48–49).*

Today nothing is left of these old struggles but crumbling ramparts, keeps and bastides, which are part of the region's cultural and artistic heritage, attracting thousands of visitors every year. Yet it is as well to remember that all the great sights here, from the abbey church at Moissac, whose 12th-century portal is a masterpiece of Romanesque art, to the awesome clifftop site of Rocamadour, have suffered at one time or another from the attacks of marauding soldiers.

This region may seem incomparably rich in all the ingredients for a good holiday – uncluttered landscapes, empty roads, clean rivers and good regional cuisine – but the economy is fragile. Over the last century, the southwest has suffered a decline in the old peasant way of life, resulting in a population migration from the countryside to the towns.

Périgord geese, reared for the area's celebrated *foie gras*

◁ La Roque-Gageac in the Dordogne Valley

Exploring Périgord, Quercy and Gascony

THE MARKET TOWNS of Périgueux, Cahors and Albi make good bases for exploring the region, and are quieter alternatives to Toulouse – the only major urban centre. Elsewhere, the green hills and sleepy villages of Gascony and Périgord are mainly for those who appreciate the slow pace of life in the countryside. But if you want more than peace and good food, this region offers some of the finest medieval architecture in France, along with Europe's most important prehistoric caves, notably Lascaux.

The medieval hilltop town of Cordes

GETTING AROUND

The west–east Autoroute des Deux Mers (A62) is the main road route through the region, linking Bordeaux, the Atlantic coast and the Mediterranean. The N20 from Limoges provides alternative access to the Dordogne and Quercy. Buses and mainline railways, including a Bordeaux–Marseille TGV, pass along the same two axes. They meet at Toulouse, where an international airport has daily flights to and from most European destinations.

KEY

▬	Motorway
▬	Major road
▭	Minor road
▬	Scenic route
⌇	River
⭒	Viewpoint

0 kilometres   25

0 miles   25

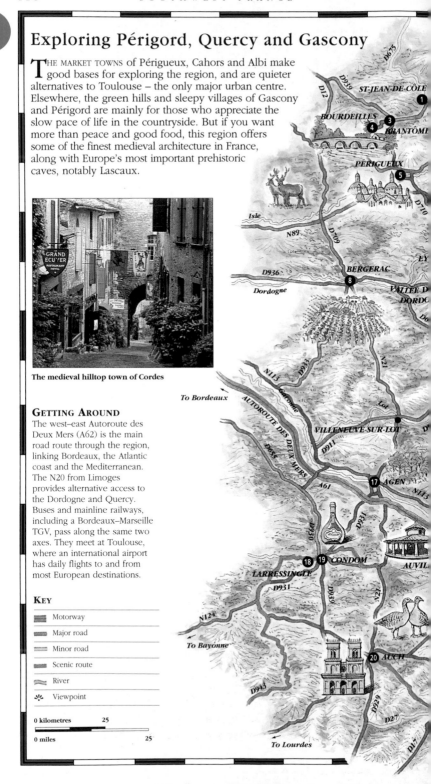

SIGHTS AT A GLANCE

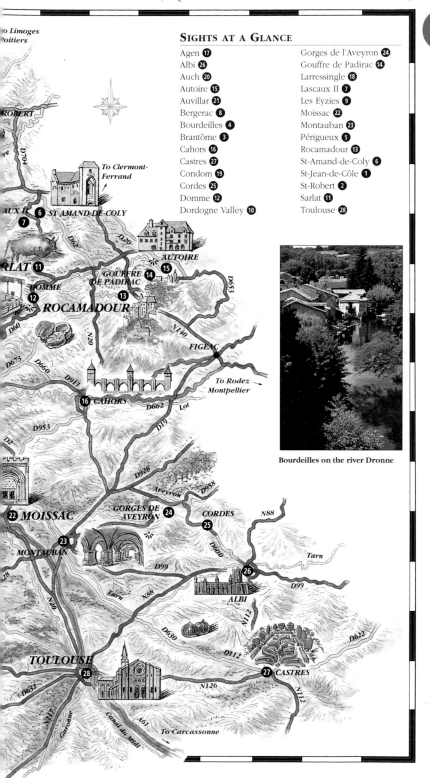

Bourdeilles on the river Dronne

St-Jean-de-Côle **●**

Dordogne. **⚑** *350.*
ℹ *05 53 62 14 15*

ST-JEAN-DE-COLE'S medieval, humpbacked bridge gives the best view of this lovely Dordogne village set in hilly countryside. Stone and half-timbered houses, roofed with the distinctive red-brown tiles of the region, cram the narrow streets around the main square. Here stand a covered market place, château and 12th-century church.

The cupola of the church used to be the largest in the region, bigger even than those of the cathedrals. Too large, it seems, for it fell down twice in the 18th and 19th centuries. The second time it happened the builders gave up, and there has been a plank ceiling ever since.

Main square in the lovely village of St-Jean-de-Côle

St-Robert **●**

Corrèze. **⚑** *350.* **ℹ** *Le Mairie (05 55 25 11 12).*

ST-ROBERT IS a substantial hilltop village with wide views over the meadows, poplars and walnut trees of the Dordogne countryside. There is also an early 12th-century priory filled with appealing details, many in a tongue-in-cheek Romanesque style. Look for the capital attached to the ambulatory wall with the carving of two old men pulling each others' beards; and the 13th-century wooden Christ figure from the Spanish School. Classical concerts take place in the central square in summer, during the last week of July and the first week of August.

Brantôme Abbey, with belfry

Brantôme **●**

Dordogne. **⚑** *2,100.* **🚌** **ℹ** *Pavillon Renaissance (05 53 05 80 52).* **🛒** *Fri.*

SURROUNDED on all sides by the brisk river Dronne, and bisected by heavy traffic, Brantôme boasts a solid reputation for good restaurants, some ancient riverside gardens, and a medieval abbey now occupied by the town hall.

The massive abbey, topped by an ornate 11th-century belfry, overshadows the village. Its most unlikely abbot, appointed at the age of 15, was the poet Pierre de Bourdeille (1540–1614), whose lovers allegedly included Mary, Queen of Scots. After a crippling fall, Bourdeille retired here in 1569 to write his racy memoirs. It is possible to wander the stone staircases and cloisters, passing through the main courtyard to a series of caves which have been hollowed out of the cliffs behind. In one is a huge crucifixion scene cut into the

stone during the 16th century. Across the river is the **Musée Rêve et Miniatures**, a private collection of doll houses in a variety of period styles. Each one is authentically furnished down to the smallest detail, such as textiles and crockery.

Outside Brantôme stands the fine Renaissance **Château de Puyguilhem**.

🏛 Musée Rêve et Miniatures
8 rue Puyjoli. **📞** *05 53 35 29 00.*
Open *Apr–Nov: Tue–Sun (Jul–Sep: daily).* 🖼

♣ Château de Puyguilhem
Villars. **📞** *05 53 54 82 18.* **Open** *Feb –Dec: Tue–Sun (Jul–Aug: daily).* 🖼 ♿

Bourdeilles **●**

Dordogne. **⚑** *800.* **ℹ** *Le Mairie (05 53 03 42 96; winter: 05 53 03 73 13).*

THIS SMALL TOWN has everything – a narrow Gothic bridge with cutwater piers spanning the Dronne, a mill upstream and a medieval **château**. The 16th-century additions to the castle were designed in a hurry by the châtelaine Jacquette de Montbron, who was expecting a visit from Queen Catherine de' Medici. When the royal visit was called off, so were the building works. The highlight of the château is the gilded salon on the first floor, decorated in the 1560s by Ambroise le Noble, an artist of the Fontainebleau School.

♣ Château de Bourdeilles
📞 *05 53 03 73 36.* **Open** *Feb–Dec: Wed–Mon (Jul–Aug: daily).* 🖼

The impressive Château de Bourdeilles towering above the town

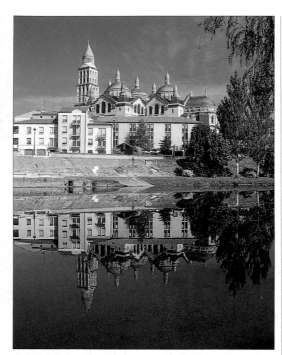

Cathédrale St-Front in Périgueux, restored in the 19th century

Périgueux ❺

Dordogne. 👥 32,000. ✈ 🚊 🚌
ℹ 26 place Francheville (05 53 53 10 63). 🛒 Wed & Sat.

THE ANCIENT and truly gastro-nomic city of Périgueux, like its neighbours Bergerac and Riberac, should be visited on market day, when stalls in the lively medieval core offer the pick of local specialities, including truffles, *charcuterie* (prepared meats) and the succulent pies called *pâtés de Périgord.*

Périgueux, now the busy regional capital, has long been the crossroads of Péri-gord. The earliest part remaining today is the quarter known as **La Cité**, once the important Gallo-Roman settlement of Vesunna. Those interested in archaeology should begin here. From Roman times to the Middle Ages, this was the focus of Périgueux. Most of the fabric of Vesunna

was pulled down in the 3rd century, but some vestiges of a temple, a huge arena and a sumptuous villa remain. In this area is also the **Eglise St-Etienne**, with origins dating to the 12th century.

Walking up the hill from La Cité to the city's dazzling white cathedral you pass through bustling streets and squares, each with its market activity. This is the medieval quarter of **Le Puy St-Front**, which began to flourish as pilgrims on their way to Santiago de Com-postela *(see pp390–91)* visited the cathedral. As they brought prestige and wealth to the quarter, it gradually eclipsed La Cité in political importance.

At the top stands the imposing **Cathédrale St-Front**, the largest in southwestern France. The Romanesque con-struction was heavily restored (some say to

19th-century stained glass in Cathédrale St-Front

death) in the 19th century, when architect Paul Abadie added the fanciful domes and cones. He later used St-Front as inspiration for the Sacré-Coeur in Paris *(see p130).*

Other gems of medieval and Renaissance architecture in this newly cleaned-up area include **Maison Estignard**, at No. 3 rue Limogeanne with its un-usual corkscrew staircase, and houses along rue Aubergerie and rue de la Constitution.

Also in the cathedral quarter is the **Musée du Périgord**, one of the most comprehensive prehistory museums in France. High-lights are remnants of burials dating back 70,000 years, and beautiful Roman mosaics, glass, earthenware and other artifacts from Vesunna.

🏛 **Musée du Périgord**
22 cours Tourny. 📞 05 53 06 40 70.
Open Wed–Mon. **Closed** public hols. 🚫

St-Amand-de-Coly ❻

Dordogne. 📞 05 53 51 67 50.
Open daily (by appt in winter). 🚫

THIS abbey church is an outstanding example of fortress architecture, built in the 12th–13th century by Augustinian monks to protect their monastery. There are two lines of defence: a high stone rampart and, behind it, the arched tower of the church itself. The tower looks more like a castle keep, and was once pierced by a score of arrow slits.

Inside, the church is beauti-fully simple, with pure lines, a flat ribbed vault, 12th-cen-tury cupola, a soaring nave, and a stone floor sloping upwards to the altar. Yet even this interior was arranged for defence, with a gallery from which enemies within the building could be attacked.

St-Amand was heavily dam-aged during the Hundred Years' War. Later, in 1575, it survived a siege by 2,000 Huguenot cavalry and a six-day bombardment by cannon. Religious life here finally came to an end after the Revolution.

Sarlat ⑪

Sculptures of geese in Sarlat

S ARLAT-LA-CANEDA possesses the highest concentration of medieval, Renaissance and 17th-century façades of any town in France. Its prosperity was a reflection of the privileged status it was granted in return for loyalty to the French crown during the Hundred Years' War. Behind the nondescript rue de la République are narrow lanes and archways, and ancient, ochre-coloured stone town houses rich in ornamental detail. Protected by law since 1962, Sarlat's buildings now form an open-air museum. The town is also famous for one of the best markets in France.

Place de la Liberté
The Renaissance heart of Sarlat is now lined with luxury shops and cafés.

Rue des Consuls contains 16th- and 17th-century mansions, built for the town's middle-class merchants, magistrates and church officials.

Rue Jean-Jacques Rousseau was the main street until rue de la République (known as "La Traverse") was built in the 19th century.

Walnuts, a key Périgord crop

SARLAT MARKET

Every Saturday, the great Sarlat market is held in place de la Liberté, and once a month there is a full-scale fair which attracts locals from all around. Sarlat lies at the heart of the nation's *foie gras* and walnut trades. These typical Périgord products absorb much of the town's attention and supply a good proportion of its revenue, as they did during Sarlat's heyday in the 13th and 14th centuries. Other local specialities are black truffles dug up in the woods in January, and wild mushrooms. Seek out, too, the cheeses of every shape, age and hue, and the huge range of pork delicacies available, which may be potted, fresh, smoked, dried, salted, fried, baked or boiled.

Bulbs of pink garlic

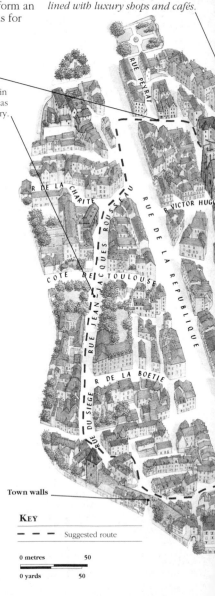

Town walls

KEY

- - - Suggested route

| 0 metres | 50 |
| 0 yards | 50 |

Rue de la Salamandre
This lane was named after the salamander emblem of King François I, seen on many of the town's 16th-century houses.

VISITORS' CHECKLIST

Dordogne. 🏠 10,000. 🚋 av de la Gare (05 53 59 00 21). 🚌 31 rue de Cahors (05 53 59 01 48). 🛈 pl de la Liberté (05 53 59 27 67). 🛒 Wed & Sat. 🎭 Theatre (3 weeks Jul–Aug); Film (Nov).

Lanterne des Morts (Lantern of the Dead)
The conical tower in the cemetery was built to commemorate St Bernard's sermons in Sarlat in August 1147.

Cathédrale St-Sacerdos
Built largely in the 16th and 17th centuries, the cathedral is remarkable for its magnificent 18th-century organ.

The Chapelle des Pénitents Bleus, built in pure Romanesque style, is the last vestige of the 12th-century abbey.

The former Bishop's Palace, with remains of a 16th-century loggia and a Renaissance interior, is now the municipal theatre.

Cour des Fontaines
A pure spring here attracted the monks who founded Sarlat's first abbey in the 9th century.

Painting of a bull from the original cave at Lascaux

Lascaux II ❼

Montignac. ▐ 05 53 51 95 03.
Open Feb–Jun & Sep–Dec: Tue–Sun;
Jul–Aug: daily. **Closed** 1 Jan, 25 Dec. ▨

L ASCAUX is the most famous
of the prehistoric sites
clustered around the junction
of the rivers Vézère and Beune
(see pp392–3). Two young
boys and their dog, Robot,
came across the caves and
their astonishing palaeolithic
paintings in 1940, and the
importance of their discovery
was swiftly recognized.

Lascaux has been closed to
the public since 1963 because
of deterioration, but an exact
copy, known as Lascaux II,
has been created a few
minutes' walk down the hillside, using the same materials.
The replica is beautiful and
should not be spurned: high-
antlered elk, bison and plump
horses cover the walls,
moving in herds or files,
surrounded by arrows and
geometric symbols thought to
have had ritual significance.

Bergerac ❽

Dordogne. 🐾 28,000. ✕ ▤ ▥
🅷 rue Neuve d'Argenson (05 53 57
03 11). ▤ Wed & Sat.

T HIS SMALL PORT, a tobacco
farming and commercial
centre, spreads itself over
both sides of the Dordogne.
Chief attractions are its extraordinary **Musée du Tabac**
(tobacco museum), and its
food and wine which are
invariably excellent. Bergerac's

most celebrated wine is Mon-
bazillac, a sweet white wine,
often drunk on ceremonial
occasions. On show in the
small, lively museum are
some Native American pipes
and ivory tobacco graters.

🏛 Musée du Tabac
Maison Peyrarède, place du Feu.
▐ 05 53 63 04 13. **Open** Tue–Sun.
Closed public hols. ▨ ⚹

Les Eyzies ❾

Dordogne. 🐾 900. ▤ 🅷 place de
la Mairie (05 53 06 97 05). ▤ Mon.

F OUR MAJOR prehistoric sites
and a group of smaller
caves cluster around the
unassuming village of Les
Eyzies. Head first for the
**Musée National de Préhis-
toire**, in a 16th-century castle
overlooking the village. The
timelines and other exhibits
are useful for putting the vast
warren of prehistoric painting
and sculpture into context.

The **Grotte de Font de
Gaume**, a good 20-minute
walk from the road, is the
logical first stop after the museum at Les Eyzies. This cave,
discovered in 1901, contains
the finest ensemble of prehistoric paintings still open to
the public in France. Close by
is the **Grotte des Combarelles**, with paintings of
bison, reindeer, magic
symbols and human figures,
and a major series of

Les Eyzies, a centre for the area's concentration of prehistoric caves carvings. Further on, you reach the rock shelter of **Abri du Cap Blanc**, discovered in 1911, with a rare, life-size frieze of horses and bison sculpted in the rock.

On the other side of Les Eyzies is the cave system at **Rouffignac**, a favourite place for excursions since the 15th century. There are 8 km (5 miles) of caves here, 2.5 km (1.5 miles) of which are served by electric train. The paintings include drawings of mammoths, and a frieze of two bison challenging each other to combat.

Tickets for all the caves sell out fast, especially in the summer months, so arrive early to be sure of a place.

Musée National de Préhistoire

🏛 Musée National de Préhistoire
📞 *05 53 06 45 45.* **Open** *Wed–Mon.* **Closed** *25 Dec, 1 Jan.* 🎫
Grotte de Font de Gaume
📞 *05 53 06 90 80.* **Open** *Thu–Tue by appt.* **Closed** *1 Jan, 1 May, 1 Nov, 11 Nov, 25 Dec.* 🎫
Grotte des Combarelles
📞 *05 53 06 90 80.* **Open** *Thu–Tue.* **Closed** *1 Jan, 1 May, 1 Nov, 11 Nov, 25 Dec.* 🎫
Abri du Cap Blanc
Marquay, Les Eyzies. **📞** *05 53 59 21 74.* **Open** *Apr–Nov: daily.* 🎫 ♿
Grotte de Rouffignac
📞 *05 53 05 41 71.* **Open** *Apr–Oct: daily.* 🎫 ♿

Dordogne Valley ⓾

Dordogne. ✈ *Bergerac.* 🚌 *Beynac, Bergerac, Le Buisson de Cadouin.* 🛈 *Le Buisson de Cadouin (05 53 22 06 09).*

PROBABLY no river in France crosses so varied a landscape and such different geological formations as the

View of Domme from the medieval gateway of Porte de la Combe

Dordogne. Starting in deep granite gorges in the Massif Central, it continues through fertile lowlands, then enters the limestone Causse country around Souillac. By the time the Dordogne has wound down to the Garonne, it is almost 3 km (2 miles) wide.

Don't be put off by the touristy image of this famous valley. Despite being a popular holiday location, it is a beautiful area for wandering. Several villages make good stopping-off points, such as Limeuil, Beynac and La Roque-Gageac from where flat-bottomed *gabarres* (river boats) ferry visitors in summer.

Perched high above the river, southwest of Sarlat, is the 17th-century **Château de Marqueyssac**. Its topiary park offers panoramic views from Domme to Beynac, and of the Château de Castelnaud on the opposite river bank.

Sarlat ⓫

See pp422–3.

Domme ⓬

Dordogne. 🏠 *1,000.* 🛈 *place de la Halle (05 53 28 37 09).* 🚍 *Thu.*

HENRY MILLER wrote: "Just to glimpse the black, mysterious river at Domme from the beautiful bluff . . . is something to be grateful for all one's life." Domme itself is a neat bastide *(see p435)* of golden stone, with medieval gateways still standing. People come here to admire the view, which takes in the Dordogne valley from Beynac in the west to Montfort in the east, and wander the maze of old streets inside the walls. There is also a large cavern under the 19th-century covered market (access by lift from April to December) where the inhabitants hid at tense moments during the Hundred Years' War and the 16th-century Wars of Religion. Despite a seemingly impregnable position, 30 intrepid Huguenots managed to capture Domme by scaling the cliffs at night and opening the gates.

A *cingle* (loop) of the river Dordogne, seen from the town of Domme

Rocamadour ⑬

The Château stands on the site of a fort which protected the sanctuary from the west.

ROCAMADOUR BECAME one of the most famous centres of pilgrimage following the discovery in 1166 of an ancient grave and sepulchre containing an undecayed body, said to be that of the early Christian hermit St Amadour. The discovery unleashed a spate of miracles heralded, it is claimed, by the bell above the Black Virgin and Child in the Chapel of Notre-Dame. Although the town suffered with the decline of pilgrimages in the 17th and 18th centuries, it was heavily restored in the 19th century. Still a holy shrine, as well as a popular tourist destination, Rocamadour's site on a rocky peak above the Alzou valley is phenomenal. The best views are to be had from the village of L'Hospitalet.

Black Virgin and Child

St Michael's Chapel contains well-preserved 12th-century frescoes.

General View
Rocamadour is at its most breathtaking in the sunlight of early morning: the cluster of medieval houses, towers and battlements seems to sprout from the base of the cliff.

The Tomb of St Amadour once held the body of the hermit called *roc amator* (lover of rock), from whom the town took its name.

Museum of Sacred Art

Grand Stairway
Pilgrims would climb this broad flight of steps on their knees as they said their rosaries. The stairway leads to a square on the next level, around which the main pilgrim chapels are grouped.

The Chapel of St John the Baptist faces the fine Gothic portal of the Basilica of St-Sauveur.

The Basilica of St-Sauveur, a late 12th-century sanctuary, backs on to the bare rock face.

St Anne's Chapel dates from the 19th century, and contains a 17th-century gilded altar screen.

Ramparts

Cross of Jerusalem

VISITORS' CHECKLIST

Lot. 🚹 630. 🚉 5 km (3 miles) SW Rocamadour. 🅹 Hôtel de Ville (05 65 33 62 59).
Chapel of Notre-Dame open Apr–Oct: 8am–8.30pm; Nov–Mar: 8:30am–6:30pm daily. 📷

Stations of the Cross
Pilgrims encounter the Cross of Jerusalem and 12 stations marking Jesus's journey to the Cross on their way up the hillside to the château.

Chapel of St Blaise (19th-century)

Rocamadour Town
Now a pedestrian precinct, its main street is lined with souvenir shops to tempt the throngs of pilgrims.

Chapel of Notre-Dame (Miracles)
St Amadour's body was found underneath the courtyard of this hallowed shrine. A statue of the Black Virgin, the supreme object of veneration, stands on the altar.

Gouffre de Padirac ⑭

Lot. 📞 05 65 33 64 56. **Open** Apr–mid-Oct: daily. 📷

FORMED BY THE COLLAPSE of a cave, this huge crater measures 35 m (115 ft) wide and 75 m (245 ft) deep. The stunning succession of galleries at the bottom *(see p393)* has been a great tourist attraction since their discovery in the late 19th century, and deservedly so, as the immense chamber known as the Salle du Grand Dôme dwarfs the tallest of cathedrals.

Autoire ⑮

Lot. 🏘 250.

THIS IS ONE of the loveliest places in Quercy, the fertile area east of Périgord. There are no grand monuments or dramatic history, just a beautifully unspoiled site at the mouth of the Autoire gorge. The **Château de Limarque** on the main square, and the **Château de Busqueille** overlooking it, are both built in characteristic Quercy style, with turrets and small towers. Elsewhere, elaborate, raised dovecotes typical of the region stand in the middle of fields or are attached to houses.

Outside Autoire, past a 30-m (100-ft) waterfall, a path climbs to a rock amphitheatre giving panoramic views of the region.

The picturesque village of Autoire, seen from across the gorge

Cahors ⑯

Lot. 🏘 20,000. 🚉 🚌 ℹ️ place François Mitterrand (05 65 53 20 65). 📅 Wed & Sat.

THE CHIEF TOWN of rural Quercy, 2,000-year-old Cahors is encircled by the natural defences of the river Lot. This small commercial centre is famous for truffles, a Saturday morning market, and the dark, heady Cahors wine which was produced as far back as Roman times. Cahors' main street is boulevard Gambetta, a typical southern thoroughfare lined with plane trees, cafés and shops. This street, like many others in France, was named after the dashing radical Léon Gambetta (1838–82), who was born in Cahors and led France to recovery after the war with Prussia in 1870.

Cathédrale de St-Etienne, entrenched behind the narrow streets of Cahors' Old Town,

A Tour of Two Rivers

FLANKED BY SPECTACULAR LIMESTONE CLIFFS, the beautiful Lot and Célé valleys feature ancient medieval villages and castles, narrow gorges and rushing waterfalls along lazy stretches of river. An unhurried tour of both valleys, around 160 km (100 miles), is best spread over two days, so that some gastronomic delights can be enjoyed as well as the superb views. The slow, winding road from Cahors, well-known for the 14th-century Pont Valentré, meanders beside the wide river Lot. This is the home of truffles, *confit* (conserve) of duck and goose, delicious goat's cheese and the almost black Cahors wine. The town of Figeac, with its old quarter and choice of hotels and restaurants, offers an ideal overnight stop.

Grotte du Pech-Merle ①
This 25,000-year-old prehistoric site outside Cabrerets has huge chambers painted with mammoths, horses, bison and human figures.

CAHORS

St-Cirq-Lapopie ⑥
Perched high above the Lot, one of France's prettiest villages has a 15th-century church and timber-framed houses built into the cliffs.

Cabrerets

Vers

Bouziès

dates back to 1119. It has some fine medieval details: don't miss the lively figures of the Romanesque north door and tympanum, which depict the Ascension, or the huge cupola above the nave (said to be the largest in France). They are covered in 14th-century frescoes depicting the stoning of St Stephen (St Étienne). The Renaissance cloisters are decorated with some intricate, though damaged, carvings.

Also worth seeking out in the cathedral quarter is the ornate 16th-century **Maison de Roaldès**, its north façade decorated with tree, sun and rose of Quercy motifs. It was here that Henri of Navarre (who later became King Henri IV) stayed for one night in 1580 after besieging and capturing Cahors.

The town's landmark monument is the **Pont Valentré**, a fortified bridge with seven pointed arches and

The fortified Pont Valentré spanning the river Lot at Cahors

three towers that spans the river. It was built between 1308 and 1360, and has withstood many attacks since then. A breathtaking sight, it is claimed that the bridge is one of the most photographed monuments in the whole of France. Inside the middle tower, the Tour du Diable (Devil's Tower), is a small museum with displays relating to the history of the bridge and the town.

Environs
Situated about 60 km (37 miles) to the west of Cahors is the **Château de Bonaguil**, a superb example of military architecture dating from the Middle Ages.

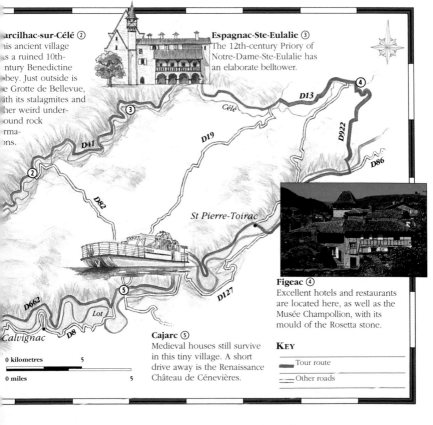

arcilhac-sur-Célé ②
his ancient village is a ruined 10th-century Benedictine bey. Just outside is e Grotte de Bellevue, ith its stalagmites and her weird under-ound rock rma-ns.

Espagnac-Ste-Eulalie ③
The 12th-century Priory of Notre-Dame-Ste-Eulalie has an elaborate belltower.

Célé

D13

D22

D86

D41

D19

②

③

④

D82

St Pierre-Toirac

D662

D8

Lot

⑤

D127

Calvignac

0 kilometres   5

0 miles   5

Figeac ④
Excellent hotels and restaurants are located here, as well as the Musée Champollion, with its mould of the Rosetta stone.

Cajarc ⑤
Medieval houses still survive in this tiny village. A short drive away is the Renaissance Château de Cénevières.

KEY

━━━ Tour route

═══ Other roads

Orchards and vineyards outside Agen

Agen ⑰

Lot-et-Garonne. 🚶 32,000. ✕ 🚉 🚌 ℹ 107 boulevard Carnot (05 53 47 36 09). 🛒 Wed, Sat, Sun.

I N A RECENT, nationwide poll, the inhabitants of Agen – an attractive, unhurried provincial capital on the Garonne – were shown to be easily the most contented people in the country. The town is the mecca of French rugby (its team has won three championship titles in recent years), and the prune production centre of France.

But the town has other treasures in addition to happy citizens and succulent plums. The **Musée Municipal des Beaux Arts** contains fine paintings by Goya, including his *Ascent in a Hot-Air Balloon;* Sisley's *September Morning;* and one of Corot's best landscapes, *L'étang de Ville Avray.* Undisputed jewel of the collection is the Greek

marble *Vénus du Mas*, a beautifully proportioned statue dating from the 1st century BC, discovered nearby in 1876.

Around the town, vast orchards of regimented plum trees are a prominent feature of the landscape. Crusaders returning from the Middle East brought the fruit to France in the 11th century, and monks in the Lot valley nearby were the first to dry plums for prunes in commercial quantities. Agen's factories now produce approximately 35,500 tonnes of prunes each year.

🏛 Musée Municipal des Beaux Arts

Place du Docteur Esquirol. ☎ 05 53 69 47 23. **Open** Wed–Mon. **Closed** 1 Jan, 1 May, 1 Nov, 25 Dec. 📷

Environs

The fortified village of Moirax has a 12th-century Romanesque church of great beauty and symmetry, formerly part

of a Cluniac priory. Two of the appealingly sculpted capitals depict biblical accounts of Daniel in the lions' den, and Original Sin.

Larressingle ⑱

Gers. 🚶 150. 🚌 to Condom. ℹ Larressingle (05 62 28 00 80).

W ITH ITS RAMPARTS, ruined donjon (defence tower) and fortress gate, Larressingle is a tiny fortified village in the middle of the Gascon countryside. It dates from the 13th century, and is one of the last remaining Gascon villages with its walls still intact. The state of preservation is unique, and gives an idea of what life must have been like for the small, embattled local communities, which had to live for decades under conditions of perpetual warfare.

Condom ⑲

Gers. 🚶 8,000. 🚌 ℹ place Bossuet (05 62 28 00 80). 🛒 Wed.

L ONG A CENTRE for the Armagnac trade, Condom is a market town built around the late-Gothic **Cathédrale St-Pierre**. In 1569 during the Wars of Religion, the Huguenot (French Protestant) army threatened to demolish the cathedral, but Condom's citizens averted this by paying a ransom of F30,000.

The river Baïse skirts the town centre. Notable among Condom's fine 17th–18th-century mansions is the **Hôtel de Cugnac** on avenue Général de Gaulle, with its ancient *chai* (wine and spirit storehouse) and distillery. On the other side of the town centre, the **Musée de l'Armagnac** is the place to find out, finally, what the difference between the brandy of Armagnac and Cognac really is.

🏛 Musée de l'Armagnac

2 rue Jules Ferry. ☎ 05 62 28 31 41. **Open** Wed–Mon. **Closed** public hols. 📷 ♿

ARMAGNAC

Armagnac is one of the world's most expensive brandies. It is also one of the most jealously guarded: about 40 per cent of it never leaves Gascony, and 4/5 of the remainder never leaves France. The vineyards of Armagnac roughly straddle the border between the Gers and the Lot-et-Garonne regions and the Landes. Similar in style to Cognac, its more famous neighbour, Armagnac's single distillation leaves more individual flavours in the spirit. The majority of small, independent producers offer direct sale to the public: look out for the battered, often half-hidden farm signs advertising *Vente Directe.*

A Tenarèze Armagnac

D'ARTAGNAN

Gascons call their domain the "Pays d'Artagnan" after Alexandre Dumas' rollicking hero from *The Three Musketeers* (1844). The character of d'Artagnan was based on Charles de Batz, a typical Gascon whose chivalry, passion and impetuousness made him ideal as a musketeer, or royal body-guard. De Batz's life was as fast and furious as that of the fictional hero, and he performed a feat of courtliness by arresting Louis XIV's most formid-able minister without causing the slightest offence. The French have other opinions on the Gascon nature too: a *promesse de Gascon,* for example, means an empty promise.

Statue of Dumas' musketeer d'Artagnan in Auch

windows show a mix of prophets, patriarchs and apostles, with 360 individually characterized figures and exceptional colours. Three depict the key biblical events of Creation, the Crucifixion and the Resurrection.

Auch went through an urbanization programme in the 18th century, when the Allées d'Etigny, flanked by the grand Hôtel de Ville and Palais de Justice, were built. Some fine houses from this period line the pedestrianized rue Dessoles. Auch's restaurants are known for their hearty dishes, including *foie gras de canard* (fattened duck liver).

Auch ⓴

Gers. 🏘 *25,000.* ▤ ▤ 🅸 *1 rue Dessoles (05 62 05 22 89).* 🄴 *Thu & Sat.*

THE ANCIENT capital of the Gers department, Auch (pronounced "Ohsh") has long been a sleepy place which comes alive on market days. The new town by the station is not a place which encourages you to linger. Head instead for the Old Town on

Medallion from Cathédrale de Ste-Marie

the outcrop overlooking the river Gers. If you climb the 232 stone steps from the river, you arrive directly in front of the late-Gothic **Cathédrale de Ste-Marie**, begun in 1489. The furnish-ings of the cathedral are remarkable: highlights are the carved wooden choir stalls depicting more than 1,500 biblical, historical and mythological characters, and the equally mag-nificent 15th-century stained glass, attri-buted to Arnaud de Moles. The

Auvillar ㉑

Tarn-et-Garonne. 🏘 *1,000.* 🅸 *La Mairie (05 63 39 57 33).*

A PERFECT complement to the high emotion of Moissac *(see pp432–3),* Auvillar is one of the loveliest hilltop villages in France. It has a triangular marketplace lined with half-timbered arcades at its centre, and extensive views from the promenade overlooking the river Garonne. There are picnic spots along this panor-amic path plus an orientation map. This includes all but the chimneys visible in the distance, belonging to the nuclear plant at Golfech.

Sunflowers, a popular crop in southwest France grown for their seeds and oil

Moissac ㉒

Abbot Durand

THE VILLAGE OF MOISSAC nestles among vineyards of sweet Chasselas grapes, with the abbey of St-Pierre its undisputed highlight. Founded in the 7th century by a Benedictine monk, the abbey was subsequently ransacked by Arabs, Normans and Hungarians. In 1047, Moissac abbey was united with the rich foundation at Cluny and prospered under the direction of Abbot Durand de Bredon. By the 12th century it had become the pre-eminent monastery in southwest France. The south portal created during this period is a masterpiece of Romanesque sculpture.

Abbey of St-Pierre
The church's exterior belongs to two periods: one part, in stone, is Romanesque, the other, in brick, is Gothic.

Christ in Majesty
The figure of Christ sits in judgment at the centre of the scene. He holds the Book of Life in His left hand and raises His right in benediction.

Tympanum
The lower register of the balanced, compact tympanum shows the expressive "24 Elders with crowns of gold" from St John's vision.

★ South Portal
The carved south portal (1100–1130) is a masterful translation into stone of St John's dramatic vision of the Apocalypse (Book of Revelation, Chapters 4 and 5). The Evangelists Matthew, Mark, Luke and John appear as "four beasts full of eyes". Moorish details on the door jambs reflect the contemporary cultural exchange between France and Spain.

Visitors' Checklist

Tarn-et-Garonne.
6 place Durand de Bredon (05 63 04 01 85). **Abbey open** 8am–6pm daily. **Closed** 1 Jan, 25 Dec. 6.30pm Mon–Fri, 7.30pm Sat, 10:30am Sun.

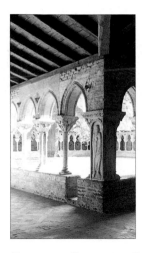

★ Cloister
The late 11th-century cloister is lined with alternate double and single columns in white, pink, green and grey marble. In all, there are 76 richly decorated arches.

Floorplan: Church and Cloister

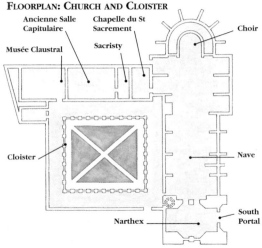

Ancienne Salle Capitulaire
Chapelle du St Sacrement
Choir
Musée Claustral
Sacristy
Cloister
Nave
South Portal
Narthex

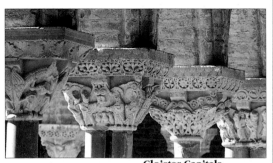

Cloister Capitals
Flowers, beasts and scenes from both the Old and New Testaments are featured in these superbly sculptured 11th century Romanesque capitals.

Star Features

- ★ South Portal
- ★ Cloister

Montauban ㉓

Tarn-et-Garonne. 54,000.
place Prax-Paris (05 63 63 60 60).
Sat.

Montauban deserves more attention than it usually gets, as Toulouse's little pink-brick sister and the capital of the 17th-century "Protestant Republic" of southern France. The painter Ingres was born in Montauban in 1780, and the town's great treasure is the **Musée Ingres**, an exceptional bequest of several paintings and 4,000 drawings. Part of the museum's collection includes works by sculptor Emile Bourdelle, an associate of Rodin, also from the town.

Above all, Montauban is a civilized shopping centre, with a double-arcaded main square (place Nationale) built in the 17th and 18th centuries. A few streets away lies the stark white **Cathédrale Notre-Dame**, built on the orders of Louis XIV in 1685, in the backlash against Protestant heresy.

Musée Ingres
Palais Episcopal. 05 63 22 12 91.
Open *Tue–Sun (Jul–Aug: daily).*
Closed *1 Jan, 14 Jul, 1 Nov, 11 Nov, 25 Dec.*

Gorges de l'Aveyron ㉔

Tarn-et-Garonne. *Toulouse.* *Montauban, Lexos.* *Montauban.* *Montauban (05 63 63 31 40).*

At the Gorges de l'Aveyron, the sweltering plains of Montauban change abruptly to cool, chestnut-wooded hills. Here the villages are of a different stamp from those of Périgord and Quercy, displaying an obsession with defence.

The château at Bruniquel, founded in the 6th century, is built over the lip of a precipice, reached by a steep walk through the village. Further along the D115, the village of Penne's position on the tip of a giant rock fang is even more extreme. The gorge narrows and darkens; from St-Antonin-Noble-Val, clamped to its rock face, the valley turns towards Cordes.

Cordes

Tarn. 🚶 970. 🚌 🚉 ℹ️ *place Bouteillerie (05 63 56 00 52).* 🚌 *Sat.*

Gloriously sited Cordes, lining a ridge above the river Cerou, is sometimes known as Cordes-sur-Ciel: a fitting description as the town seems suspended against the skyline. During the 13th-century Cathar wars the entire town was excommunicated. Devastating epidemics of plague later sent it into decline, and the town was in an advanced state of decay at the beginning of this century.

Restoration work under the care of the artist Yves Brayer began in the 1940s. The ramparts and many of the gates which the town's founder, Albigensian Count Raymond VII of Toulouse, built in 1222 have been well-preserved. Also intact are Gothic houses like the 14th-century **Maison du Grand Fauconnier**, with falcons carved on its façade, and the **Maison du Grand Veneur** (Great Huntsman's House) which line the unbelievably steep cobbled streets.

Today, lovely as it is from a distance, Cordes on its hilltop still exudes a sense of loss. The town of which Albert Camus once wrote, "Everything is beautiful there, even regret", is now completely dependent on tourism. "Medieval" crafts aimed at visitors abound, but nothing remains of the exuberant weaving, *pastel* (blue pigment) and leather industries which paid for so many of Cordes' ancient buildings.

Cathédrale de Ste-Cécile perched above the town of Albi

Albi

Tarn. 🚶 47,000. 🚌 🚉
ℹ️ *Palais de la Berbie, place Ste-Cécile (05 63 49 48 80).* 🚌 *Sat.*

Like many another large town in this part of the world, Albi is not only red, but also red hot, and definitely not for flying afternoon visits. You need to get up in the cool early morning to walk the streets around the market and the **Cathédrale de Ste-Cécile**.

Then make for the **Musée Henri de Toulouse-Lautrec** in the Palais de la Berbie ahead of the crowds. The museum contains the most complete permanent collection of the artist's work in existence, including paintings, drawings and his famous posters for the Moulin-Rouge. There are also canvases by Matisse, Dufy and Yves Brayer.

After a stroll around the beautiful terraced gardens of the Palais de la Berbie overlooking the river Tarn, head for the vast red-brick cathedral, built in the aftermath of the Albigensian crusade in 1265.

It was intended as a reminder to potential heretics that the Church meant business. From a distance, its semi-circular towers and narrow windows give it the appearance more of a fortress than a place of worship. Every feature, from the huge belltower to the apocalyptic fresco of the *Last Judgment*, is on a giant scale built deliberately to dwarf the average human being.

🏛 **Musée Henri de Toulouse-Lautrec**
Palais de la Berbie. 📞 *05 63 49 48 70.* **Open** *Apr–Sep: daily; Oct–Mar: Wed–Mon.* **Closed** *1 Jan, 1 May, 1 Nov, 25 Dec.* 📷 ♿

Castres

Tarn. 🚶 47,000. ✈️ 🚌 🚉
ℹ️ *3 rue Milhau-Ducommun (05 63 62 63 62).* 🚌 *Tue, Thu–Sat.*

Castres has been a centre for the cloth industry since the 14th century. Today it is also the headquarters of one of France's biggest pharmaceutical companies and a busy, relaxed, southern town. In the large collection of Spanish art in the **Musée Goya**, the artist himself is well represented by a large, misty council scene and by a series of powerful prints, *Los Caprichos*. Outside, the formal gardens between the town hall and the river Agout were designed in the 17th century by Le Nôtre *(see p169)*, the landscape architect of Vaux-le-Vicomte and Versailles.

🏛 **Musée Goya**
Hôtel de Ville. 📞 *05 63 71 59 30 or 05 63 71 59 27.* **Open** *Jul–Aug: daily; Sep–Jun: Tue–Sun.* **Closed** *1 Jan, 1 May, 1 Nov, 25 Dec.* 📷

Toulouse-Lautrec

Comte Henri de Toulouse-Lautrec was born in Albi in 1864. Crippled at 15 as a result of two falls, he moved to Paris in 1882, recording the life of the city's cabarets, brothels, racecourses and circuses. A dedicated craftsman, his bold, vivid posters did much to establish lithography as a major art form. Alcoholism and syphilis led to his early death at the age of 36.

Lautrec's *La Modiste* (1900)

Bastide Towns

BASTIDE TOWNS were hurriedly built in the 13th century by both the English and the French, to encourage settlement of empty areas before the Hundred Years' War. They are the medieval equivalent of "new towns", with their planned grid of streets and fortified perimeters. Over 300 bastide towns and villages still survive between Périgord and the Pyrenees.

A broad arcaded marketplace is the central feature of most bastides. Montauban's arcades still shelter a variety of shops.

The central square is surrounded by a grid of interconnecting streets and alleys. This differs markedly from the usual jumble of medieval houses and lanes.

Lauzerte, founded in 1241 by the Count of Toulouse, is a typical bastide town of grey stone houses. The town, long an English outpost, is perched for security on the brow of a hill.

The church could be used as a keep when the bastide's outer fortifications had been breached.

Stone houses protected the perimeter.

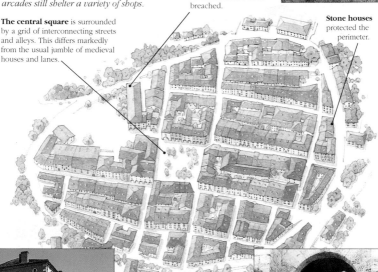

MONFLANQUIN

This military bastide town was built by the French in 1256 on a strategic north–south route. It changed hands several times during the Hundred Years' War.

Today, the bastides form a convenient network of market towns, known as the route des bastides. The best time to visit them is on market day, when the central squares are crammed with stalls.

Porte de la Jane in Cordes is a typical bastide feature. These narrow gateways were easily barred by portcullises.

Toulouse

TOULOUSE, THE MOST IMPORTANT TOWN in southwest France, is the country's fourth largest metropolis, and a major industrial and university city. The area is also famous for its aerospace industry (Concorde, Airbus, the Ariane space rocket all originated here), as shown by the new Cité de l'Espace just outside the city.

Best seen on foot, Toulouse has fine regional cuisine, two striking cathedrals, lively street life and a rose-brick Old Town which, as the French say, is "Pink at dawn, red at noon and mauve at dusk".

The river Garonne, crossed by the Pont Neuf, and bordered by tree-lined quays

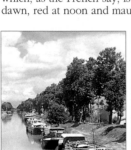

Houseboats at their moorings on the Canal du Midi

Exploring Toulouse

This warm southern city has steadily expanded, crescent-like, from its original Roman site on the Garonne. First it was a flourishing Visigoth city, then a Renaissance town of towered brick palaces built with the wealth generated by the *pastel* (blue pigment) and grain trades. The grandest of these palaces still survive in the Old Town, which has place du Capitole and the huge 18th-century **Hôtel de Ville** at its heart. Here, and in place St-Georges and rue Alsace Lorraine, is the main concentration of shops, bars and cafés.

The University of Toulouse, founded in 1229, has always supplied the city with an intellectual weight to match its wealth. Today the vocal student population keeps prices down in the city's many cafés, oyster bars and bookstores, and in the fleamarket, held on Sundays on place St-Sernin.

A ring of 18th- and 19th-century boulevards encircles the city, surrounded in turn by a tangle of autoroutes. Today, the ultra-modern driverless metro system connects the town centre with the suburbs.

✦ Les Jacobins

This church was begun in 1229 and completed over the next two centuries. It was the first Dominican convent, founded to combat dissent in the region. The Jacobins' convent became the founding institution of Toulouse University. Its church, a Gothic masterpiece, features a soaring, 22-branched palm tree vault in the apse. The belltower (1294) with no spire is much imitated in southwest France. The delicate Gothic Chapelle St-Antonin (1337) contains frescoes of the Apocalypse dating from 1341.

🏛 Musée des Augustins

21 rue de Metz. **[** 05 61 22 21 82. **Open** Wed–Mon. **Closed** public hols.

Toulouse became a centre of Romanesque art in Europe due to its position on the route to Santiago de Compostela (*see*

Palm vaulting in the apse of Les Jacobins

pp390–91). This museum has sculptures from the period, and incorporates cloisters from a 14th-century Augustinian priory, and 12th-century Romanesque capitals, many from the Basilique de Notre-Dame-de-la-Daurade. Also featured are 16th–19th-century French, Italian and Flemish paintings.

MONTAUBAN

Façade of Musée des Augustins

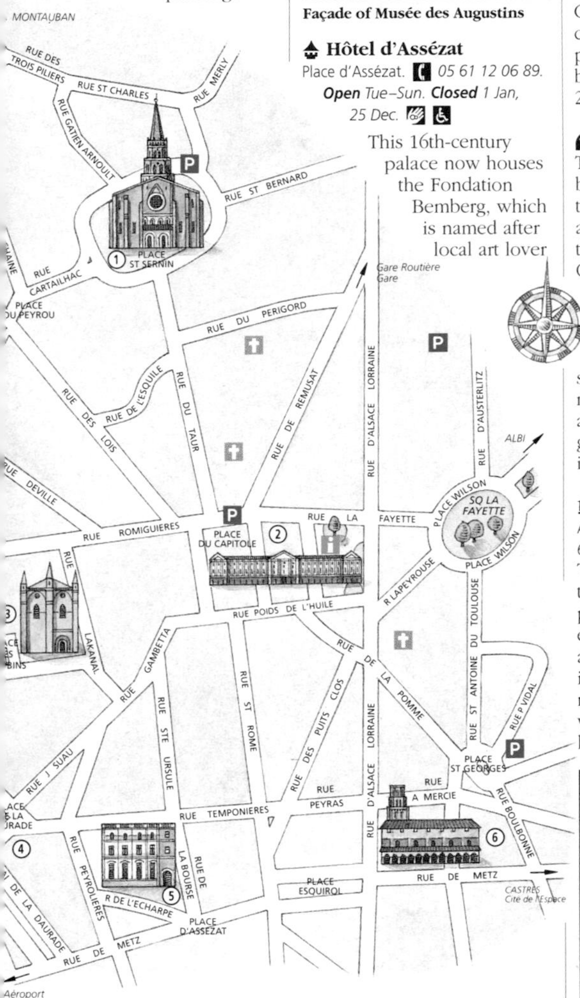

♠ Hôtel d'Assézat

Place d'Assézat. **【** 05 61 12 06 89. **Open** Tue–Sun. **Closed** 1 Jan, 25 Dec. 🎦 ᬀ

This 16th-century palace now houses the Fondation Bemberg, which is named after local art lover

Gare Routière
Gare

ALBI

Georges Bemberg. His fine collection covers Renaissance paintings, *objets d'art* and bronzes, as well as 19th- and 20th-century French paintings.

🔒 Basilique de St-Sernin

This is the largest Romanesque basilica in Europe, built in the 11th–12th centuries to accommodate pilgrims on their way to Santiago de Compostela. Highlights are the octagonal brick belfry, with rows of decorative brick arches topped by pepperpot turrets and a spire. Beautiful 11th-century marble bas-reliefs of Christ and the symbols of the Evangelists by Bernard Gilduin are in the ambulatory.

🏛 Cité de l'Espace

Avenue Jean Gonord. **【** 05 62 71 64 80. **Open** Tue–Sun. 🎦 ᬀ
To the southeast of Toulouse, this "space park" features a planetarium and interactive exhibits related to the exploration of space. One of these is a replica of the Ariane 5 rocket. In the control room, visitors can learn how to launch rockets and satellites.

CASTRES
Cité de l'Espace

Aéroport
FOIX

The tiered, 12th-century tower of Basilique de St-Sernin

KEY

🅿 Parking
🛈 Tourist information
🛉 Church

0 metres 250
0 yards 250

THE PYRENEES

PYRÉNÉES-ATLANTIQUES · HAUTES-PYRÉNÉES · ARIÈGE
HAUTE-GARONNE

THE MOUNTAINS *dominate life in the French Pyrenees. A region in many ways closer to Spain than France, over centuries its remote terrain and tenacious people have given heretics a hiding place and refugees an escape route. Today it is the last remaining wilderness in southern Europe and a habitat for rare animal species.*

Heading east from the Atlantic coast, the hills are wonderfully lush after the plains of Aquitaine. The deeper the Pyrenees are penetrated, the steeper the valley sides and the more gigantic the snow-clad peaks become. This is magnificent, empty, dangerous country, to be approached with caution and respect. In summer the region offers over 1,600 km (1,000 miles) of walking trails, as well as camping, fishing and climbing. In winter there is both cross-country and alpine skiing at the busy resorts along the border, much livelier than their Spanish counterparts.

Historically, the Pyrenees are known as the birthplace of Henri IV, who put an end to the Wars of Religion in 1593 and united France, though the region has been characterized more often by independent fiefdoms. The region's oldest inhabitants, the Basque people *(see p445)* have maintained their own language and culture, and their resorts of Bayonne, Biarritz and St-Jean-de-Luz reflect this, looking to the sea and to summer visitors for their livelihood.

Inland, Pau, Tarbes and Foix rely on tourism and medium-scale industry, while Lourdes receives four million pilgrims every year. For the rest, life has been regulated by agriculture, though economic restraints today are causing an exodus from the land.

Countryside around St-Lizier, in the heart of the Pyrenean countryside

◁ Barèges, a ski resort and spa town in the Hautes-Pyrénées

Exploring the Pyrenees

T HE TOWERING PYRENEES cut across southwest
France from the Mediterranean to the Atlantic
coast, encompassing the craggy citadel of
Montségur, the pilgrimage centre of Lourdes, Pau
in the hilly Béarn country, and the Basque port of
Bayonne. This formidable range, an unspoiled
paradise for walkers, fishermen and skiers, is as
lush on its French side as it is arid in Spain, and
contains the wild and beautiful Parc National des
Pyrénées. Throughout the region, visitors can
expect cool temperatures and grandiose scenery.
Lovers of art and architecture will be richly
rewarded by St-Bertrand-de-Comminges and St-
Jean-de-Luz, among the region's important sights.

Marzipan sweets, a speciality of
southwest France (see p387)

The galleried church in the Basque village of Espelette

GETTING AROUND

Access to the Basque coast in the
western Pyrenees is via the A63
from Bordeaux. The length of the
Pyrenees, including the mountain
valleys, is served by the A64 which
runs between Lannemesan, near
Tarbes, and Bayonne. Once you are
high up, expect narrow, twisting
roads and slow driving. The scenic
but demanding D918/118 corniche
road crosses 18 high passes
between the Atlantic and the
Mediterranean.

There are airports at Biarritz, Pau
and Lourdes. These three towns,
together with Orthez and Tarbes, are
on the rail route which loops south
between Bordeaux and Toulouse.

SIGHTS AT A GLANCE

Aïnhoa ④
Arreau ⑮
Bayonne ①
Biarritz ②
Foix ⑱
Forêt d'Iraty ⑧
Lourdes ⑫
Luz-St-Sauveur ⑭
Mirepoix ⑳
Montségur ⑲
Oloron-Ste-Marie ⑨
Orthez ⑤
Parc National des Pyrénées ⑬
Pau ⑩
St-Bertrand-de-Comminges ⑯
St-Jean-de-Luz ③
St-Jean-Pied-de-Port ⑦
St-Lizier ⑰
Sauveterre-de-Béarn ⑥
Tarbes ⑪

Wild pottock ponies on moorland in the Forêt d'Iraty

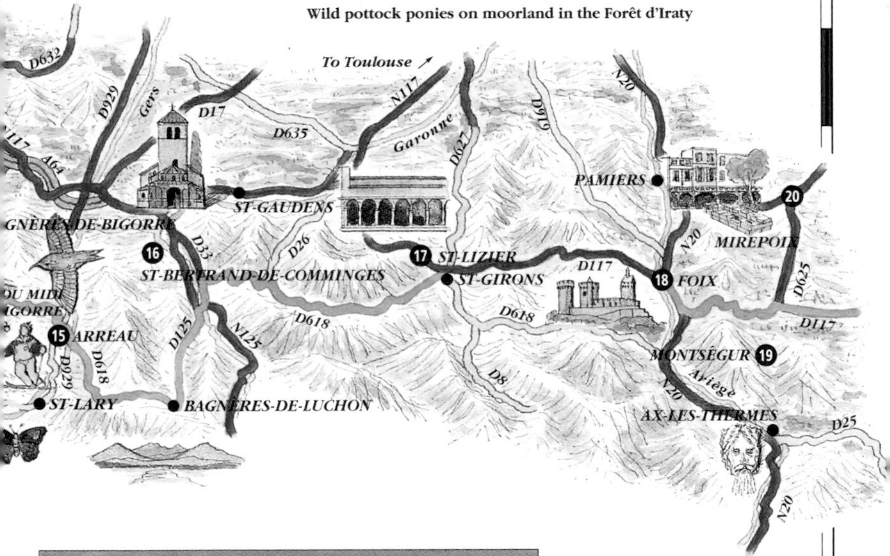

St-Jean-de-Luz seen from Ciboure, across the Nivelle estuary

KEY

▬ Motorway

▬ Major road

▬ Minor road

▬ Scenic route

〜 River

☆ Viewpoint

0 kilometres   25

0 miles   25

Bayonne ❶

Pyrénées-Atlantiques. 40,000.
place des Basques (05 59
46 01 46). daily.

BAYONNE, capital of the
French Basque country,
lies between two rivers – the
turbulent Nive which arrives
straight from the mountains,
and the wide, languid Adour.
An important town since
Roman times because of its
command of one of the few
easily passable roads to
Spain, Bayonne prospered as
a free port under English rule
from 1154 to 1451. Since then
it has successfully withstood
14 sieges, including a particularly bloody one directed by
Wellington in 1813.

Grand Bayonne, the district
around the cathedral, can be
easily explored on foot. The
13th-century **Cathédrale de
Sainte-Marie** was begun
under English rule and is
northern Gothic in style rather
than Pyrenean Romanesque.
Look for the handsome
cloister and the 15th-century
knocker on the north door –
if a fugitive could put a hand
to this, he was entitled to
sanctuary. The pedestrianized
streets around form a lively
shopping area, especially the
arcaded rue du Pont Neuf,
with cafés serving a Bayonne
speciality – hot chocolate –
and shops selling Bayonne
ham and the spicy local
Loukinkos sausage.
Petit Bayonne lies on the

**Grand Bayonne, clustered around
the twin-spired cathedral**

Lighthouse at Biarritz

opposite side of the quay-
lined river Nive. The **Musée
Basque** gives an excellent
introduction to the customs
and traditions of the Basque
nation, with reconstructed
house interiors and exhibits
on seafaring. Nearby, the
Musée Bonnat houses a
superb art gallery. The first
floor here is a must for art
lovers, with sketches by
Leonardo, Van Dyck,
Rembrandt and Rubens and
paintings by Goya, Constable,
Poussin and Ingres.

🏛 Musée Basque
1 rue Marengo. 05 59 59 08 98.
Closed indefinitely for refurbishment.
🏛 Musée Bonnat
5 rue Jacques Lafitte. 05 59 59 08
52. **Open** Wed–Mon.
Closed public hols.

Biarritz ❷

Pyrénées-Atlantiques. 29,000.
Javalquinto, square
d'Ixelles (05 59 22 37 10). daily.

BIARRITZ, WEST of Bayonne,
has a grandiose centre, but
has been developed along the
coast by residential suburbs.
The resort began as a whaling
port but was transformed into
a playground for the European
rich in the 19th century. Its
popularity was assured when
Empress Eugénie discovered
its mild winter climate during
the reign of her husband,
Napoleon III.

Nowadays about a quarter
of Biarritz's population are
retired people. The town has
three good beaches, with the
best surfing in Europe, two

casinos, and one of the last
great luxury hotels in Europe,
the Palais *(see p569)*, formerly the residence of Eugénie.

In the port des Pêcheurs, the
Musée de la Mer aquarium is
home to specimens of some
of the marine life found in
the Bay of Biscay. Next to it,
the Atalaye watch tower was
used until the 16th century
to send out smoke signals
whenever a school of whales
was seen approaching the
port. Below both, a narrow
causeway leads across to the
Rocher de la Vierge, offering
far-reaching views along the
whole of the Basque coast.

🏛 Musée de la Mer
Esplanade du Rocher-de-la-Vièrge,
14 plateau Atalaye. 05 59 24 02 59.
Open daily.

Altar in Eglise St-Jean-Baptiste

St-Jean-de-Luz ❸

Pyrénées-Atlantiques. 13,000.
place Maréchal Foch
(05 59 26 03 16). Tue & Fri.

ST-JEAN is a sleepy fishing
village out of season and
a scorching tourist town in
August, with shops to rival
the chic rue du Faubourg St-
Honoré in Paris. In the 11th
century whale carcasses were
towed into St-Jean to be
divided up by the whole
village. The natural harbour
protects the shoreline,
making it one of the few
beaches safe for swimming
along this stretch of coast.

One of the most important
historical events in St-Jean was
the wedding of Louis XIV
and the Infanta Maria Teresa

St-Jean-de-Luz, a fishing village that explodes into life in summer

of Spain in 1660, a union that had the effect of sealing the long-awaited alliance between France and Spain, only to embroil the two countries ultimately in the War of the Spanish Succession. This wedding took place at the **Eglise St-Jean-Baptiste**, still the biggest and best of the great Basque churches, a triple-galleried marvel with a glittering 17th-century altarpiece and an atmosphere of gaiety and fervour. The gate through which the Sun King led his bride was immediately walled up by masons: look for the plaque on the street marking the place.

Other sights which should not be missed in St-Jean include the **Maison Louis XIV** with its contemporary furnishings, where the king stayed in 1660. The port is busy in the summer, while the restaurants behind the covered markets serve sizzling bowls full of *chipirones* – squid cooked in their own ink – a local speciality.

🏛 Maison Louis XIV
Place Louis XIV. 📞 *05 59 26 01 56.*
Open *Jun–Sep: daily.* 🖼

Environs
On the other side of the river Nivelle, **Ciboure** was the birthplace of composer Maurice Ravel. It is characterised by 18th-century merchants' houses, steep narrow

streets and seafood restaurants. A two-hour coastal walk leads to the neighbouring village of **Socoa**, where the lighthouse on the clifftop offers a fine view of the coast all the way to Biarritz.

Basque men in traditional berets

Aïnhoa ❹

Pyrénées-Atlantiques. 🚶 *550.* 🚌

A TINY TOWNSHIP on the road to the Spanish border, Aïnhoa was founded in the 12th century as a waystation on the road to Santiago de Compostela *(see pp390–91).*

The main street of 17th-century whitewashed Basque houses and a galleried church from the same period survive.

Environs
There is a similar church in the village of **Espelette** nearby. Typically Basque in style, the galleries boosted the seating capacity and had the added effect of separating the men from the women and children in the main part of the church. Espelette is the trading centre for *pottocks*, an ancient local breed of pony, auctioned here at the end of January. It is also the shrine of the local crop, the red pimento pepper, especially in October when a pepper festival is held here.

In the opposite direction from Aïnhoa, at the foot of the St-Ignace pass, lies the pretty mountain village of **Sare**. From here you can reach the summit of la Rhune by cog railway. This provides the best vantage point in the entire Pays Basque.

Basque farmhouse near Espelette

Sauveterre-de-Béarn and the remains of the fortified bridge over the Gave d'Oloron

Orthez ❺

Pyrénées-Atlantiques. 🏘 *10,700.* 🚉
🚌 ℹ️ *Maison de Jeanne d'Albret,
rue du Bourg Vieux (05 59 69 02 75,
05 59 69 37 50).* 🛒 *Tue.*

ORTHEZ is an important Béarn market town, its 13th–14th-century fortified bridge a vital river crossing point over the Gave de Pau in the Middle Ages. It has a spectacular Tuesday morning market held from November to February, selling *foie gras*, smoked and air-cured Bayonne hams, and all kinds of poultry and fresh produce. Fine buildings line the rue du Bourg Vieux, especially the house of Jeanne d'Albret, mother of Henry IV, on the corner of rue Roarie. Jeanne's enthusiasm for the Protestant faith alienated both her own subjects and Charles X, and ultimately caused the Béarn region to be drawn into the Wars of Religion (1562–93).

Sauveterre-de-Béarn ❻

Pyrénées-Atlantiques. 🏘 *1,400.* 🚉
ℹ️ *La Mairie, Château de Nays
(05 59 38 50 17).* 🛒 *Wed & Sat.*

AN ATTRACTIVE market town, Sauveterre is well worth an overnight stay. It has breathtaking views southward over the Gave d'Oloron, the graceful single arch of the river's fortified bridge, and the 16th-century **Château de Nays**. Fishermen gather here for the annual world salmon-fishing championships, held in the fast-flowing Oloron between March and July.

Be sure, also, to visit the **Château de Laàs**, 9 km (5.5 miles) along the D27 from Sauveterre, which has an excellent collection of 18th-century decorative art and furniture – notably the bed Napoleon slept in (if he slept at all) on the night after his defeat at Waterloo.

⚜ **Château de Laàs**
📞 *05 59 38 91 53.* **Open** *Apr–Oct:
Wed–Mon.* 📷 ♿

The Château de Nays at Sauveterre in the Béarn region

St-Jean-Pied-de-Port ❼

Pyrénées-Atlantiques. 🏘 *1,500.* 🚉
🚌 ℹ️ *14 place Charles de Gaulle
(05 59 37 03 57).* 🛒 *Mon.*

ST-JEAN-PIED-DE-PORT is the old capital of Basse-Navarre and lies at the foot of the Roncesvalles Pass. Here the Basques crushed the rear-guard of Charlemagne's army in 778 and killed its commander, Roland, later glorified in the *Chanson de Roland*.

Throughout the Middle Ages this red sandstone fortress-town was famous as the last rallying point before entering Spain on the pilgrim road to Santiago de Compostela *(see pp390–91)*. As soon as a group of pilgrims was spotted, the townsfolk would ring the church bells to show them the way, and the pilgrims would sing in response.

Visitors and pilgrims in all seasons still provide St-Jean with its income. They enter the narrow streets of the upper town on foot from the Porte d'Espagne, and pass cafés, hotels and restaurants on the way up. The ramparts are worth the steep climb, as is the citadel with panoramic views.

On Mondays the town hosts a livestock market, Basque *pelote* matches and, in summer, running of the bulls.

Forêt d'Iraty 🔞

Pyrénées-Aquitaine. 🚌 🚉 *St-Jean-Pied-de-Port.* 🚋 *Larrau (05 59 28 51 29).*

A WILD PLATEAU of beech woods and moorland, the Forêt d'Iraty is famous for its cross-country skiing and walking. Here the ancient breed of Basque ponies, the *pottocks*, run half-wild. These creatures have not changed at all since the prehistoric inhabitants of the region traced their silhouettes on the walls of local caves.

The visitors' centre at Larrau publishes maps of local walks. The best begins at the Chalet Pedro car park, south of the lake on the Iraty plateau, and takes you along the GR10 to 3,000-year-old standing stones on the western side of the Sommet d'Occabé.

Oloron-Ste-Marie 🔞

Pyrénées-Atlantiques. 🚶 *11,000.* 🚌 🚉 🚋 *place de la Résistance (05 59 39 98 00).* 🛒 *Fri.*

OLORON, A SMALL TOWN at the junction of the Aspe and the Ossau valleys, has grown from a Celtiberian settlement. There are huge agricultural fairs here in May and September, and the town is famed for producing the famous classic French berets.

BASQUE CULTURE

Most of Basque country is in Spain, but around 10 per cent lies within France. The Basque people have their own complex language, isolated from other European tongues, and their music, games and folklore are equally distinct. French Basques are less fiercely separatist than their Spanish counterparts, but both are still deeply attached to their unique way of life.

Pelota, the traditional Basque game

Marble doorway of Eglise Ste-Marie

The town's great glory is the doorway of the Romanesque **Eglise Ste-Marie**, with its biblical and Pyrenean scenes. Spain lies just on the other side of the Somport pass at the head of the mountainous Aspe valley, and the influence of Spanish stonemasons is evident in Oloron's **Eglise Sainte-Croix** with its Moorish-style vaulting. These two churches are Oloron's only sights, leaving time to head up the Aspe valley to try one of the area's famous sheep's cheeses, or mixed cow and goat's cheeses.

A side road leads to Lescun, huddled around its church, beyond which is a spectacular range of saw-toothed peaks topped by the **Pic d'Anie** at 2,504 m (8,215 ft), one of the most beautiful spots in the Pyrenees. Sadly, at nearby Somport a controversial highway and tunnel project was permitted, despite it posing a threat to the traditional mountain agricultural economy, and the last habitat of the Pyrenean brown bear.

High moorland above the Forêt d'Iraty, long denuded of timber for use by the French and Spanish navies

Gobelin tapestry in the Château de Pau

Pau ⑩

Pyrénées-Atlantiques. 🏠 *87,000.* ✈
🚊 🚌 🛈 *place Royale (05 59 27 27 08).* 🛒 *Mon–Sat.*

A LIVELY university town, with elegant Belle Epoque architecture and shady parks, Pau is the capital of the Béarn region, and the most interesting big town in the central Pyrenees. The weather in autumn and winter is mild, so this has been a favourite resort of affluent foreigners, especially the English, since the early 19th century.

Pau is chiefly famous as the birthplace of King Henry IV. His mother, Jeanne d'Albret, travelled for 19 days by carriage from Picardy, in the eighth month of her pregnancy, just to have her baby here. She sang during her labour, convinced that if she did so, Henry would grow up as tough and resilient as she was. As soon as the infant was born, his lips were smeared with garlic and local Jurançon wine, in keeping with the traditional custom.

The town's principal sight is the **Château de Pau**, first remodelled in the 14th century for the ruler of Béarn, Gaston Phoebus *(see p453)*. It was heavily restored 400 years later. Marguerite d'Angoulême, sister of the King of France, resided here in the late 16th century, and transformed the town into a centre for the arts and free thinking.

The château's 16th-century Gobelin tapestries, made by Flemish weavers working in Paris, are fabulous, and the Musée Béarnais on the third floor is a veritable treasure house of information about the history, traditions and culture of the Béarn.

Outside, the boulevard des Pyrénées affords both glorious views of the gardens below and a glimpse of the highest Pyrenean peaks, which are often snow-capped all year round. Continue from here to the eclectic **Musée des Beaux Arts**, where there is a splendid Degas, the *Cotton Exchange, New Orleans;* Rubens' *Last Judgment;* and works by El Greco.

♣ Château de Pau
Rue du Château. 📞 *05 59 82 38 00.*
Open *daily.* **Closed** *1 Jan, 1 May, 25 Dec.* 📷 🚫 *Musée Béarnais open daily.* **Closed** *1 Jan, 1 May, 25 Dec.* 🚫

🏛 Musée des Beaux Arts
Rue Mathieu-Lalanne. 📞 *05 59 27 33 02.* **Open** *Wed–Mon.* **Closed** *public hols.* 🚫

Tarbes ⑪

Hautes-Pyrénées. 🏠 *48,000.* 🚊
🚌 🛈 *3 cours Gambetta (05 62 51 30 31).* 🛒 *Thu, Sat & Sun.*

T ARBES is the most prosperous town in the Bigorre region, a centre for chemical and engineering industries with good shops and a major agricultural market. The **Jardin Massey** in the middle of town was designed at the turn of the 19th century and is one of the loveliest parks in the southwest. It has many rare plants, including the North American sassafras. The cavalry museum in the **Musée Massey** is a must, with its dashing uniforms from 19th- and 20th-century regiments; nor are the thoroughbred stallions at the French National Stud.

🏛 Musée Massey
Jardin Massey. 📞 *05 62 36 31 49.*
Open *Jul–Aug: daily; Sep–Jun: Wed–Sun.* **Closed** *public hols.* 🚫

Lourdes ⑫

Hautes-Pyrénées. 🏠 *16,500.* 🚊 🚌
🚌 🛈 *place Peyramale (05 62 42 77 40).* 🛒 *alternate Thu.*

L OURDES, one of the great modern shrines of Europe, owes its celebrity to visions of the Virgin experienced by a 14-year-old girl, Bernadette Soubirous, in 1858.

Château de Pau, birthplace of Henry IV in 1553

Four million people annually visit the **Grotte Massabielle**, the cave where the visions occurred, and the one room on rue des Petits-Fossés where Bernadette's family lived, in search of a miracle cure for disability or disease.

If one is not led there by faith, Lourdes is best avoided, or left to those who really need it. Visit the **Grottes de Bétharram** for underground rides by boat and train through its vast caverns, or the **Musée Pyrénéen**, with fascinating exhibits on the first pioneering climbers who opened up these ranges.

⛏ Grottes de Bétharram
St-Pé-de-Bigorre. **📞** 05 62 41 80 04.
Open mid-Apr–mid-Oct: daily. 🖼

Spectacular limestone formations at the Grottes de Bétharram

Pilgrims participating in open-air mass at Lourdes

🏛 Musée Pyrénéen
Château Fort, rue du Fort. **📞** 05 62 42 37 37. **Open** Apr–mid-Oct: daily; mid-Oct–Mar: Wed–Mon. **Closed** public hols (winter only). 🖼

Parc National des Pyrénées ⓭

See pp450–51.

Luz-St-Sauveur ⓮

Hautes-Pyrénées. 🏘 1,200. 🚌 to Lourdes. 🚏 🏢 place du 8 mai (05 62 92 81 60). 🚌 Mon.

LUZ-ST-SAUVEUR is an attractive spa town, with an unusual church built in the 14th century by the Hospitaliers de Saint Jean de Jérusalem (later the Knights of Malta), an order established to protect pilgrims. The church is fortified with gun slits that look out over the town and valley, and provided protection for pilgrims on the way to Santiago de Compostela.

Environs
The elegant spa town of **Cauterets** makes a good base for climbing, skiing and walking in the rugged mountains of the Bigorre region.

Gavarnie is a former way-station on the Santiago de Compostela pilgrim route. A good track, accessible on foot or by donkey, leads from the village to the spectacular natural rock amphitheatre known as the **Cirque de Gavarnie**, one of the most popular tourist sights in the Pyrenean mountain range. Here the longest waterfall in Europe, at 240 m (787 ft), cascades off the mountain into space, encircled by eleven 3,000-m (9,800-ft) peaks.

The **Observatoire Pic du Midi de Bigorre** can be reached via Barèges, the Col de Tourmalet and then a 30-minute walk. The French are proud of the observatory, high in the Pyrenees. It has supplied the clearest images of Venus and other planets in the solar system so far obtained from the Earth's surface. The vast 2-m (6.5-ft) telescope mapped out the moon for NASA's Apollo missions.

🏛 Observatoire Pic du Midi de Bigorre
Le Sommet des Loisirs, Pic du Midi, Bagnères de Bigorre. **📞** 05 62 91 90 33. **Open** 25 Jun –Oct: daily (weather permitting). 🖼

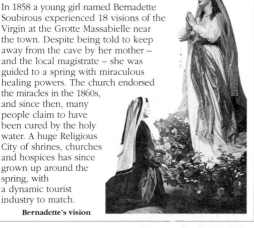

THE MIRACLE OF LOURDES

In 1858 a young girl named Bernadette Soubirous experienced 18 visions of the Virgin at the Grotte Massabielle near the town. Despite being told to keep away from the cave by her mother – and the local magistrate – she was guided to a spring with miraculous healing powers. The church endorsed the miracles in the 1860s, and since then, many people claim to have been cured by the holy water. A huge Religious City of shrines, churches and hospices has since grown up around the spring, with a dynamic tourist industry to match.

Bernadette's vision

Parc National des Pyrénées ⑬

Pyrenean ibex

THE PYRENEES national park, designated in 1967, extends 100 km (62 miles) along the French and Spanish frontier. It boasts some of the most spectacular scenery in Europe, ranging from meadows glimmering with butterflies to high peaks, snow-capped even in summer. Variations in altitude and climate make the park rich in flora and fauna. One of the most enjoyable ways to see it is on foot: within the park are 350 km (217 miles) of well-marked footpaths.

Vallée d'Aspe
Jagged peaks tower above the Vallée d'Aspe and the Cirque de Lescun. This area is now threatened by a new motorway (see p445).

Pic d'Anie
The limestone-flanked 2,504-m (8,215-ft) Pic d'Anie overlooks rich upland pastures watered by melting snow. In spring, the ground is ablaze with Pyrenean varieties of gentian and columbine, found nowhere else.

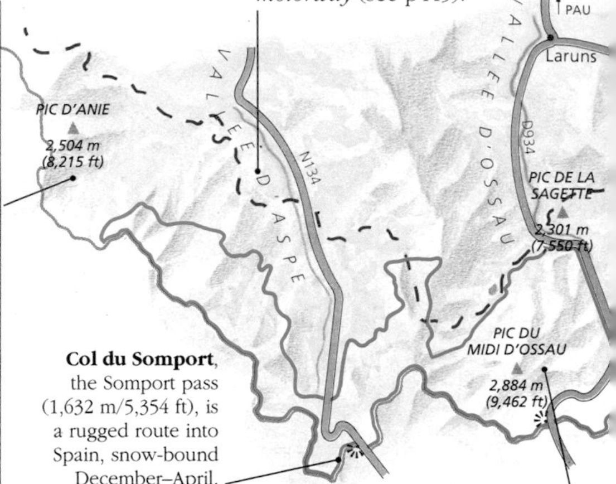

PIC D'ANIE
2,504 m (8,215 ft)

PIC DE LA SAGETTE
2,301 m (7,550 ft)

PIC DU MIDI D'OSSAU
2,884 m (9,462 ft)

↑ PAU

Laruns

Col du Somport, the Somport pass (1,632 m/5,354 ft), is a rugged route into Spain, snow-bound December–April.

Pic du Midi d'Ossau
A tough trail leads from the Bious-Artigues lake at the base of the Pic du Midi d'Ossau and encircles the formidable, tooth-shaped summit (2,884 m/9,462 ft).

PYRENEAN WILDLIFE

The Pyrenees are home to a rich variety of wild creatures, many of them unique to the range. The ibex, a member of the antelope family, is still numerous in the valleys of Ossau and Cauterets. Birds of prey include the Egyptian, griffon and bearded vultures. Ground predators range from the rare Pyrenean lynx, to civet, pine marten and stoat. The desman, a tiny aquatic mammal related to the mole, is found in many of the mountain streams.

Pyrenean fritillary *flowers through late spring and early summer in mountain pastures.*

The Turk's Cap Lily *flowers June–August on rocky slopes at up to 2,200 m (7,218 ft).*

rèche de Roland
*he famous breach in the sheer
rest of the Cirque de Gavarnie
orms a gateway between France
nd Spain.*

TIPS FOR WALKERS

The park is crossed by a network of numbered trails. Each is well-signposted and shows the length of time needed. En route are mountain huts offering a meal and a bed for the night. For maps and information visit the Park Office at Cauterets or the tourist office at Luz-St-Sauveur *(see p449)*, both open year-round.

Walking the trail in high summer

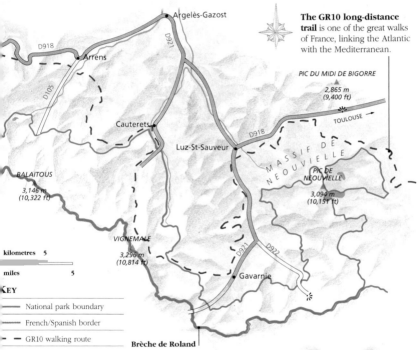

The GR10 long-distance trail is one of the great walks of France, linking the Atlantic with the Mediterranean.

Argelès-Gazost

D918

Arrens

D921

PIC DU MIDI DE BIGORRE
2,865 m
(9,400 ft)

TOULOUSE →

Cauterets

D918

Luz-St-Sauveur

M A S S I F   D E
N E O U V I E L L E

BALAITOUS
3,146 m
(10,322 ft)

*PIC DE
NEOUVIELLE*
3,094 m
(10,151 ft)

kilometres 5

miles 5

VIGNEMALE
3,296 m
(10,814 ft)

D921

D922

Gavarnie

KEY

— National park boundary

---- French/Spanish border

- - GR10 walking route

Brèche de Roland

*be Egyptian vulture is seen
ll over the Pyrenees, especially
n rocky cliff faces.*

Pyrenean bears *are close to
extinction but a few still live in
the Ossau and Aspe valleys.*

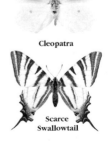

Cleopatra

**Scarce
Swallowtail**

These butterflies *are among
several colourful species found
at high altitudes.*

Arreau ⓯

Hautes-Pyrénées. 🏠 *860.* 🚌
🅘 *Château des Nestes (05 62 98 63 15).* 🛒 *Thu.*

A RREAU STANDS at the junction of the rivers Aure and Louron. A small, bustling half-timbered town with good shops and restaurants, this is the place to buy the basics (maps, walking boots, spiked walking sticks) for hiking or fishing in the mountains.

Environs

St-Lary Soulan is a ski resort up the valley, a base for exploring the entire Massif du Néouvielle in summer; the roads leading from the town will get you up to very high altitudes by car before you need to walk. Head for the village of Fabian and the smattering of lakes above it, where the GR10 *(see p451)* and other well-marked trails criss-cross the peaks. Here you may see golden eagles or an enormous lammergeier soaring over the snow fields.

St-Bertrand-de-Comminges ⓰

Haute-Garonne. 🏠 *220.* 🚉
Montregeau, then taxi. 🚌 🅘 *Les Olivetains, parvis de la Cathédrale (05 61 95 44 44).*

T HE PRETTY hilltop town of St-Bertrand is the most remarkable artistic and historic site in the Central Pyrenees and the venue for an acclaimed music festival in summer *(see p33).* Some of

Cloisters in the Cathédrale Ste-Marie, St-Bertrand-de-Comminges

the best sculpture in the region adorns the portal of the **Cathédrale Ste-Marie**. The adjoining Romanesque and Gothic cloisters contain sarcophagi, carved capitals and statues of the four Evangelists.

St-Bertrand's origins lie on the plain below, in the city founded by the great Roman statesman Pompey in 72 BC. At that time it consisted of two thermal baths, a theatre, a temple, a market and a Christian basilica. All were destroyed by Gontran, the grandson of Clovis *(see p202)* in 585, and six centuries were to pass before the Bishop of Comminges, Bertrand de l'Isle, saw the site as a potential location for a new cathedral and monastery. The town, which was relatively unimportant in political terms, became re-established as a major religious centre.

Inside the cathedral, look out for the 66 magnificent carved choirstalls and the 16th-century organ case. The tomb of Bertrand de l'Isle is situated at the far end of the choir, with

an altar beside it; the beautiful marble tomb in the Virgin's chapel just off the nave is that of Hugues de Châtillon, a wealthy local bishop who provided funds for the completion of the cathedral in the 14th century.

🔒 **Cathédrale Ste-Marie**
🕽 *05 61 89 04 91.* **Open** *daily* 🖼

Fresco in the Cathédrale St-Lizier

St-Lizier ⓱

Ariège. 🏠 *1,600.* 🅘 *place de l'Eglise (05 61 96 77 77).*

S T-LIZIER is located in the Ariège, a region famous for its steep-sided valleys and wild mountain scenery. The village dates back to Roman times, and by the Middle Ages was an important religious centre, only to be superseded in the 12th century by St-Girons nearby. St-Lizier has the distinction of possessing two cathedrals; the finest is the 12th–14th-century **Cathédrale St-Lizier** in the lower town. It boasts Romanesque frescoes and a cloister with carved columns,

The imposing 12th-century Cathédrale Ste-Marie above St-Bertrand

St-Lizier, with snow-capped mountains in the distance

but the **Cathédrale de la Sède** in the upper town, reached on foot through narrow streets, has the better view.

Foix ⑱

Ariège. 🏠 10,500. 🚉 🚌 🅸 45 cours Gabriel Fauré (05 61 65 12 12). 🖩 1st, 3rd & 5th Mon of each month.

Wᴵᵀᴴ ᴵᵀꜱ ʙᴀᴛᴛʟᴇᴍᴇɴᴛꜱ and towers, Foix stands foursquare above the junction of the rivers Arget and Ariège. In the Middle Ages, Foix's dynasty of counts ruled the whole of the Béarn area. Count Gaston Phoebus (1331–91) was the most flamboyant, a poet who surrounded himself with troubadours and wrote a famous treatise on hunting. He was a ruthless politician, who also had his own brother and his only son put to death.

Some of the pleasures of the medieval court are re-created in the local summer fair, the largest in France. At any time, the 15th-century keep of the **Château de Foix** is worth climbing just for the view. The small and much restored 14th-century **Eglise de St-Volusien**, on the banks of the river Ariège, is delightful in its simplicity and grace.

♠ Château de Foix
☎ 05 61 65 56 05. **Open** daily. **Closed** 1 Jan, 25 Dec. 🖩

The arcaded main square at Mirepoix

Montségur ⑲

Ariège. 🏠 100. 🅸 La Mairie (05 61 03 03 03 or 05 61 01 10 27). 🖩

Tʜᴇ ᴛᴏᴡɴ of Montségur is famous as the last stronghold of the Cathars (see p481). From the car park at the foot of the mount, a path leads up to the small fortress-town, occupied in the 13th-century by faydits (dispossessed aristocrats) and the Cathar garrison. The Cathars themselves lived outside the fortress, in houses clinging to the rock. Staunchly opposed to Catholic authority, the Cathar troops unwisely marched on Avignonnet in 1243 and massacred members of the Inquisitional tribunal. In retaliation, an army of 10,000 laid siege to Montségur for ten months. When captured, 225 Cathars burnt themselves to death rather than convert.

Mirepoix ⑳

Ariège. 🏠 3,000. 🚌 🅸 place du Maréchal Leclerc (05 61 68 83 76). 🖩 Mon & Thu.

Mᴵʀᴇᴘᴏᴵx ᴵꜱ ᴀ ꜱᴏʟᴵᴅ country bastide town (see p435) with a huge main square – one of the loveliest in the southwest – surrounded by beamed 13th–15th-century arcades and half-timbered houses.

The **cathedral**, begun in 1343 with the last additions made in 1867, boasts the widest Gothic nave (22m/72 ft) in France.

The best times to visit the town are on market days, when the square is covered with stalls selling a mass of local produce.

THE SOUTH OF FRANCE

Introducing the South of France

THE SOUTH is France's most popular holiday region, drawing millions of visitors each year to the Riviera resorts, and modern beach cities to the west. Agriculture is a mainstay of the economy, producing early fruits and an abundance of affordable wine. The new high-tech industries of Nice and Montpellier reflect the region's key role in the developing south coast sunbelt, while Corsica still preserves much of its natural beauty. The map shows the major sights of this sun-blessed region.

Pont du Gard, *a 2,000-year-old bridge (see p485), is a major feat of Roman engineering. It was a key link in the 17-km (10.5-mile) aqueduct, parts of which were underground, carrying fresh water from a spring at Uzès to Nîmes.*

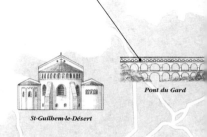

St-Guilhem-le-Désert

Pont du Gard

LANGUEDOC-ROUSSILLON
(See pp466–87)

Carcassonne

Peyrepertuse

St-Martin-de-Canigou

The Camargue *lies at the mouth of the Rhône delta, where marshland and inland seas support a rich selection of wildlife. Three visitors' centres give a good introduction to this fragile area and its population of pink flamingoes and white horses (see pp500–1).*

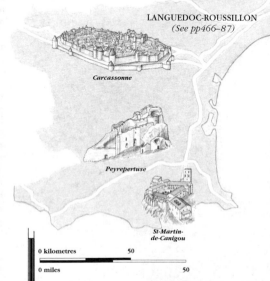

0 kilometres   50

0 miles   50

Avignon, *enclosed by massive ramparts, became papal territory when popes decamped from Rome (see p493) in the 14th century, taking up residence in the Palais des Papes which towers over the town. In the summer the town is the scene of the popular Avignon Festival.*

Palais des Papes, Avignon

Musée Matisse, Nice

PROVENCE AND THE COTE D'AZUR
(See pp488–521)

*Giacometti statue,
St-Paul-de-Vence*

Camargue

The Côte d'Azur *has attracted sunworshippers and celebrities since the 1920s (see pp464–5). The coast also offers some prize collections of 20th-century art (pp462–3) and yearly events such as the Cannes Film Festival and Antibes Jazz Festival.*

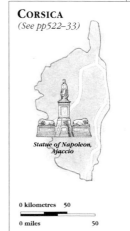

CORSICA
(See pp522–33)

*Statue of Napoleon,
Ajaccio*

| 0 kilometres | 50 |
| 0 miles | 50 |

Regional Food: the South

I<small>T'S A HEADY EXPERIENCE</small> just to stand, look and sniff in a Provençal market. Tables sag under piles of braided pink garlic, fresh and colourful peppers, tomatoes, aubergines, courgettes and asparagus. The Cavaillon melons are so ripe they've split, leaking sweet perfume. In the autumn and winter an earthy, fragrant scent fills the air; wild mushrooms, Swiss chards, cardoons, walnuts, quinces, pumpkins, fennel and wrinkled black olives all crowd the stalls. Coastal Provence is famous for fish soups, including *bouillabaisse* and *bourride*, a garlic fish stew. Lamb is the most common meat in Provence; the best comes from the Camargue and the Crau where lambs graze on herbs and salt-marsh grass. Languedoc-Roussillon

Rosemary supplies France with the first of the season's peaches, cherries and apricots. Its coastal waters provide a bountiful sea harvest of plump mussels, oysters and *tellines* (tiny clams). Further south the island of Corsica has a robust cuisine with a strong Italian influence, with chestnuts an important staple.

Salade Niçoise *comes in many versions but always includes lettuce, green beans, tomatoes, black olives, eggs and anchovies.*

Pistou soup *is a rich vegetable and bean soup flavoured with pistou, a sauce of basil, garlic and olive oil.*

Fish liquor

Croutons

Red snapper

Rouille (meaning "rust"), a mayonnaise of chillies and garlic

Conger eel

Monkfish

Red mullet

Bouillabaisse, *a fish soup originating in Marseille, is a luxury today. It consists of an assortment of local seafood including monkfish, mullet, snapper, scorpion fish and conger eel, flavoured with tomatoes, saffron and olive oil. Traditionally, the fish liquor is served first with croutons spread with rouille, a spicy mayonnaise. The fish is eaten afterwards.*

Ratatouille *is a stew of onions, aubergines, courgettes, tomatoes and peppers, cooked in olive oil and garlic.*

Pissaladière *is similar to pizza, garnished with onions, olives and anchovies. Every* boulangerie *in Provence sells it.*

Aïoli *is a sauce made of egg yolks, garlic and olive oil. It is served with salt cod, boiled eggs, snails or raw vegetables.*

Daube de boeuf *is a stew of beef, lamb or mutton with red wine, cooked in a pot-bellied casserole called a "daubière".*

Brandade de morue, *a speciality of Nîmes, is a purée of salt cod with cream, olive oil, garlic and potatoes.*

Tarte au citron *is a sweet-pastry pie filled with a creamy lemon mixture. Menton is well known for its supply of lemons.*

Fougasse *is a flattish, lattice-like bread variously studded with black olives, anchovies, onions and spices. The sweet version is flavoured with almonds.*

OLIVES AND OLIVE OIL

Most of the olive crop is crushed for oil. Ripe olives are black and the unripe ones are green; both can be preserved in brine or oil. At the end of the olive harvest it is customary to eat bread with *tapenade,* a paste of black olives, capers, anchovies and olive oil.

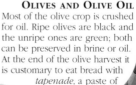

Tapenade

Black olives

Honey *comes in many flavours, depending on the diet of the bees, which can include a wide variety of flowers and herbs such as lavender, orange blossom, rosemary or thyme.*

Olive oil

Pitted olives

Lemon verbena   **Camomile**   **Lime flower**

TISANES

In the south of France, tisanes (flower and herb infusions or teas) are popular drinks, especially after meals. Lime flower *(tilleul)* is the most popular, considered good for the digestion and for sleep. Camomile tea stimulates the kidneys, and lemon verbena *(verveine)* soothes the liver.

France's Wine Regions: the South

A MASSIVE ARC stretching from Banyuls, in the extreme southwest corner of France, to Nice, close to the Italian border, encompasses the Mediterranean vineyards of Languedoc-Roussillon and Provence. This was for a century an area of mass-produced wine, and much is still of *vin de table* quality. Today, however, the more dynamic producers are applying new technology to traditional and classic grape varieties to revive southern France's nobler heritage of generous, warm, aromatic wines, redolent of sun-baked stone, the scent of wild herbs, and the shimmering waters of the Mediterranean.

Cellar sign, Banyuls

LOCATOR MAP

Languedoc-Roussillon & Provence

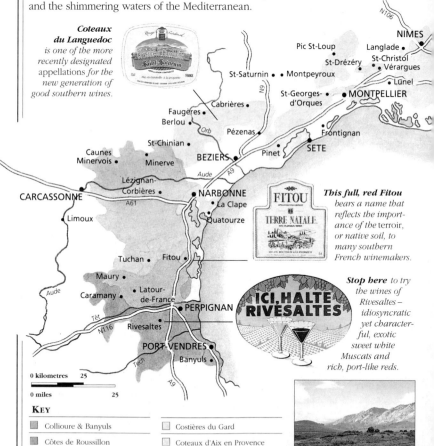

Coteaux du Languedoc *is one of the more recently designated appellations for the new generation of good southern wines.*

This full, red Fitou *bears a name that reflects the importance of the terroir, or native soil, to many southern French winemakers.*

Stop here *to try the wines of Rivesaltes – idiosyncratic yet characterful, exotic sweet white Muscats and rich, port-like reds.*

0 kilometres   25

0 miles   25

KEY

Collioure & Banyuls	Costières du Gard
Côtes de Roussillon	Coteaux d'Aix en Provence
Côtes de Roussillon Villages	Côtes de Provence
Fitou	Cassis
Corbières	Bandol & Côtes de Provence
Minervois	Coteaux Varois
Coteaux du Languedoc	Bellet

Rugged valley slopes in Corbières

Hand-picking grapes for Côtes de Provence red wine

WINE REGIONS

Both in the Provence wine region, east of Aix and Marseille, and in the larger Languedoc-Roussillon area to the west, new quality wine *appellations* are joining the more familiar names.

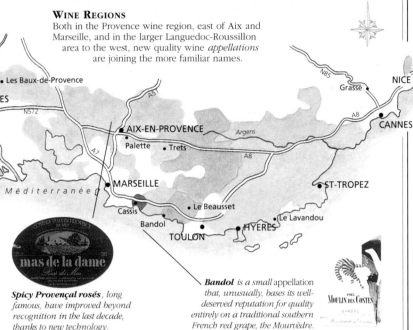

Spicy Provençal rosés, *long famous, have improved beyond recognition in the last decade, thanks to new technology.*

Bandol *is a small* appellation *that, unusually, bases its well-deserved reputation for quality entirely on a traditional southern French red grape, the Mourvèdre.*

KEY FACTS ABOUT WINES OF THE SOUTH

Location and Climate
A warm and sunny climate helps to create generously alcoholic wines. The flat coastal plains support acres of vines, but generally the best sites are on the schist and limestone hillsides.

Grape Varieties
Mass-production grapes such as **Carignan** and **Aramon** are giving way to quality varieties such as **Syrah**, **Mourvèdre** and **Grenache**. **Cabernet Sauvignon**, **Merlot** and **Syrah**, and the whites **Chardonnay**, **Sauvignon Blanc** and **Viognier**, are increasingly used for *vins de pays*. Rich, sweet whites are made from the aromatic, honeyed **Muscat** grape.

Good Producers
Corbières & Minervois: La Voulte Gasparets, Saint Auriol, Lastours, Villerambert-Julien, Daniel Domergue. *Faugères*: Château des Estanilles, Gilbert Alquier, Château de la Liquiere. *St Chinian*: Château Cazals-Viel, Domaine des Jougla, Cave de Roquebrun. *Coteaux du Languedoc and vins de pays*: Mas Jullien, Prieuré de St Jean de Bebian, Mas de Daumas Gassac, Pech-Celeyran. *Roussillon*: Domaine Gauby, Domaine de la Rectorie. *Provence:* Domaine Tempier, Domaine de Pibarnon, Domaine de Trevallon, Mas de la Dame, Mas de Gourgonnier, Domaine Richeaume, Domaine de la Bernarde, Commanderie de Peyrassol, La Courtade.

Artists and Writers in the South of France

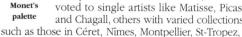

ARTISTS AND WRITERS have helped create our image of the South of France – the poet Stephen Liégeard even gave the Côte d'Azur its name in 1887. Many writers, French and foreign, found a haven in the warmth of the south. From Cézanne to Van Gogh, Monet to Picasso, artists have been inspired by the luminous light and brilliant colours of this seductive region. Today it is rich in art museums, some devoted to single artists like Matisse, Picasso and Chagall, others with varied collections such as those in Céret, Nîmes, Montpellier, St-Tropez, St-Paul-de-Vence and Nice *(see pp472–517).*

Monet's palette

Picasso and Françoise Gilot on the Golfe Juan, 1948

Paul Cézanne's studio in Aix-en-Provence *(see p501)*

FESTIVE LIGHT

THE IMPRESSIONISTS were fascinated by the effects of light, and Monet was entranced by "the glaring festive light" of the south which made colours so intense he said no-one would believe they were real if painted accurately. In 1883 Renoir came with him to the south, returning often to paint his voluptuous nudes in the filtered golden light. Bonnard too settled here, painting endless views of the red tiled roofs and palm trees.

Post-Impressionists Van Gogh and Gauguin arrived in 1888, attracted by the region's rich colours. Cézanne, who was born in Aix in 1839, analysed and painted the structure of nature, above all the landscape of Provence and his beloved Mont-Ste-Victoire. Pointillist Paul Signac came to St-Tropez to paint sea and sky in a rainbow palette of dots.

THE WILD BEASTS

THE FAUVES, DUBBED "Wild Beasts" for their unnaturally bright and wild colours, led one of the first 20th-century avant-garde movements, founded by Matisse in Collioure in 1905 *(see p25).* Other Fauves included Derain, Vlaminck, Marquet, Van Dongen and Dufy. Matisse visited Corsica in 1898, and then St-Tropez, and was inspired by the sensuality of Provence to paint the celebrated *Luxe, Calme et Volupté.* Eventually he settled in Nice, where he painted his great series of Odalisques. He wrote, "What made me stay are the great coloured reflections of January, the luminosity of daylight." The exquisite blue-and-white chapel he designed in Vence is one of the most moving of his later works *(see p513).*

Vincent Van Gogh's *Sunflowers* (1888)

PICASSO COUNTRY

THE SOUTH of France is, without question, Picasso country. His nymphs and sea urchins, his monumental women running on the beach, his shapes and colours, ceramics and sculpture are all derived from the hard shadows and bright colours of the south.

Pablo Picasso was born in Malaga in Spain in 1881, but he spent much of his life on the French Mediterranean, developing Cubism with Braque in Céret in 1911, and arriving in Juan-les-Pins in 1920. He was in Antibes when war broke out in 1939, where he painted *Night Fishing at Antibes*, a luminous nocturnal seascape. He returned in 1946 and was given the Grimaldi Palace to use as a studio. It is now a Picasso Museum *(see p511)*. He also worked in Vallauris, producing ceramics and sculptures *(see p512)*.

Deux Femmes Courant sur la Plage (1933) by Pablo Picasso

LOST CAVIAR DAYS

JUST AS F Scott Fitzgerald wrote the Jazz Age into existence, he created the glittering image of life on the Riviera with *Tender is the Night*. He and Zelda arrived in 1924 attracted, like many expatriate writers, by the warm climate and the cheap, easy living. "One could get away with more on

Scott and Zelda Fitzgerald with daughter Scottie

the summer Riviera, and whatever happened seemed to have something to do with art," he wrote. They passed their villa on to another American, Ernest Hemingway. Many other writers flocked there including Katherine Mansfield, DH Lawrence, Aldous Huxley, Friedrich Nietzsche, Lawrence Durrell and Graham Greene. Some, like Somerset Maugham, led a glamorous lifestyle surrounded by exotic guests. Colette was an early visitor to St-Tropez, and in 1954, Françoise Sagan captured the youthful hedonism of the time in her novel, *Bonjour Tristesse*.

NEW REALISM

IN THE 1950s Nice produced its own school of artists, the *Nouveaux Réalistes*, including Yves Klein, Arman, Martial Raysse, Tinguely, César, Niki de Saint Phalle and Daniel Spoerri *(see pp516–17)*. They explored the possibilities of everyday objects – Arman sliced violins, packaged and displayed trash; Tinguely exploded TV sets and cars. They had a light-hearted approach, "We live in a land of vacations, which gives us the spirit of nonsense," said Klein. He painted solid blue canvases of his personal colour, International Klein Blue, taking the inspiration of the Mediterranean to its limit.

PROVENÇAL WRITERS

The regions of Provence and Languedoc have always had a distinct literary identity, ever since the troubadours in the 12th–13th centuries composed their love poetry in the *langue d'oc* Provençal, a Latin-based language. In the last century, many regional writers have been inspired by the landscape and local traditions. They were influenced by the 19th-century Felibrige movement to revive the language, led by Nobel prize-winning poet Frédéric Mistral. Some, like Daudet and film-maker turned writer Marcel Pagnol, celebrate the Provençal character, others, such as Jean Giono, explore the connection between nature and humanity.

Frédéric Mistral in the *Petit Journal*

Beaches in the South of France

THE GLAMOROUS Mediterranean coast is France's foremost holiday playground. To the east lie the Riviera's big, traditional resorts such as Menton, Nice, Cannes and Monte-Carlo. To the west are smaller resorts in coves and bays like St-Tropez and Cassis. Further on is the long, sandy shore of Languedoc-Roussillon, where government investment since the 1960s has transformed mosquito-infested swamp into miles of clean, sandy beaches. Purpose-built resorts range from modernistic beach cities to replicas of fishing villages.

The beaches are sandy west of Antibes; eastwards, they are naturally shingly, so any sand is imported. Anti-pollution drives mean that most beaches are now clean, except in a few spots west of Marseille and around Nice. Beaches around towns often charge fees but are usually well-equipped.

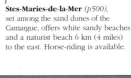

The Carlton Hotel logo

A rail poster by Domergue advertising the Côte d'Azur

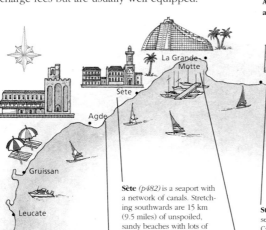

Sète •
Agde •
La Grande-Motte •
Stes-Maries-de-la-Mer •
Marseill
MEDITERRANEE

Gruissan
Leucate
Le Barcarès
Argelès Plage
Collioure

0 kilometres 25
0 miles 25

Sète *(p482)* is a seaport with a network of canals. Stretching southwards are 15 km (9.5 miles) of unspoiled, sandy beaches with lots of room, even in high season.

Stes-Maries-de-la-Mer *(p500),* set among the sand dunes of the Camargue, offers white sandy beaches and a naturist beach 6 km (4 miles) to the east. Horse-riding is available.

Cap d'Adge (p477) *is a vast modern resort with long, white sandy beaches and sports facilities of all kinds. It has Europe's largest naturist colony, accommodating 20,000 visitors.*

La Grande-Motte *(p485) is a huge purpose-built beach resort with excellent sports facilities, famous for its bizarre ziggurat architecture.*

In Victorian times *the Côte d'Azur, or Riviera, was the fashionable holiday venue of Europe's royalty and rich. They came to gamble and escape northern winters. Summer bathing did not come into vogue until the 1920s. Today the Riviera is busy all year round with the glamorous beaches and nightlife still a major attraction.*

Menton
Monaco
Nice — Cap Ferrat
Antibes
Cannes
Juan-les-Pins
St-Raphaël
St-Tropez
Cassis
La Ciotat
Toulon
Hyères

Menton *(p519)* has a warm climate in winter, giving beach weather all year. Its sheltered, shingly beaches are backed by beautiful villas.

Cannes *(p510)*, famous for its film festival, takes great pride in its golden beaches, keeping them scrupulously clean.

Cassis *(p503)* is a charming fishing village which has a popular casino, white cliffs and some lovely hidden creeks nearby.

Cap Ferrat (p518) *is a wooded peninsula which has a 10-km (6-mile) craggy cliff walk offering glimpses of grand villas and private beaches.*

St-Tropez (p506) *is flanked by golden beaches mostly occupied by stylish "clubs", offering amenities at a price.*

Nice (p516), *Côte d'Azur's capital, has 5 km (3 miles) of beaches along its seafront. Although pebbly, they are clean and the private ones are cheaper than in Cannes.*

LANGUEDOC-ROUSSILLON

AUDE · GARD · HÉRAULT · PYRÉNÉES-ORIENTALES

THE TWO DISTINCT PROVINCES of Languedoc and Roussillon stretch from the foothills of the Pyrenees on the Spanish border to the mouth of the Rhône. The flat beaches and lagoons of the coast form a purpose-built sunbelt accommodating millions of holiday-makers every year. In between is a dry, sunburned land producing half of France's table wine and the season's first peaches and cherries.

Beyond such sensuous pleasures are many layers of history, not least the unification of the two provinces. The formerly independent Languedoc once spoke Occitan, the tongue of the troubadours, and still cherishes its separate identity. Roussillon was a Spanish possession until the treaty of the Pyrenees in 1659. Its Catalan heritage is displayed everywhere from the road signs to the Sardana dance, and the flavour of Spain is evident in the popularity of bullfights, paella, and gaudily painted façades.

This stretch of coastline was the first place in Gaul to be settled by the Romans, their enduring legacy evident in the great amphitheatre at Nîmes and the magnificent engineering of the Pont du Gard. The abbeys of St-Martin-du-Canigou, St-Michel-de-Cuxa and St-Guilhem-le-Désert are superb examples of early Romanesque architecture, unaffected by Northern Gothic. The great craggy Cathar castles and the perfectly restored medieval Cité of Carcassonne bear witness to the bloody battles of the Middle Ages.

In parts, the region remains wild and untamed: from the high plateaux of the Cerdagne, to the wild hills of the Corbières or the remote uplands of Haut Languedoc. But it also has the most youthful and progressive cities in France: Montpellier, the ancient university city and capital of the region, and Nîmes with its exuberant *feria* and bullfights. The whole area is typified by an insouciant mixture of ancient and modern, from Roman temples and postmodern architecture in its cities to solar power and ancient abbeys in the mountains.

A sunny stretch of coastline at Cap d'Agde

◁ **The abbey of Saint-Martin-du-Canigou perched on Mount Canigou**

Exploring Languedoc-Roussillon

Languedoc-Roussillon combines miles of gentle coastline with a rugged hinterland. Its clean, sandy beaches are perfect for family holidays, with resorts ranging from traditional fishing villages to new purpose-built resorts. Inland is quieter, with acres of vineyards in the Corbières and Minervois and mountain walks in the Haut Languedoc and Cerdagne. A rich architectural heritage ranges from Roman to Romanesque, contrasting with the modern, vibrant atmosphere of the main cities.

Jousting on the canal, a regular summer event in Sète

Sights at a Glance

GETTING AROUND

Montpellier's international airport serves the region, with smaller airports at Perpignan and Nîmes. The TGV stops in Montpellier and a good rail network connects the main towns. The main motorways are the Autoroute des Deux Mers, giving access from the west, and the A9, following the coast. Smaller roads, even in the mountains, are well-maintained. Barges along the Canal du Midi are a leisurely alternative.

KEY

▬	Motorway
▬	Major road
▬	Minor road
▬	Scenic route
〰	River
☀	Viewpoint

0 kilometres	25
0 miles	25

The ruined Barbarossa tower at Gruissan on the Golfe du Lion

Cerdagne ●

Pyrénées-Orientales. ✈ Perpignan.
🚉 🚌 Mont Louis, Bourg Madame.
ℹ️ Mont Louis (04 68 04 21 97 or 04
68 04 21 18).

T HE REMOTE CERDAGNE, an
independent state in the
Middle Ages, is today divided
between Spain and France. Its
high plateaux offer skiing and
walking among clear mountain
lakes and pine and chestnut
forests. The Little Yellow Train
is an excellent way to sample
it in a day. Stops include
Mont Louis, a town fortified
by Vauban, Louis XIV's
military architect, which still
accommodates French troops;
the huge ski resort of **Font-
Romeu**; **Latour-de-Carol** and
the tiny village of **Yravals**
below it. Nearby **Odeillo** is the
site of a huge solar furnace,
45 m (150 ft) tall and 50
m (165 ft) wide.
Established in 1969, its
giant curved mirrors create a
remarkable sight in the valley.

Villefranche-de-Conflent ●

Pyrénées-Orientales. 🚶 260. 🚉 🚌
ℹ️ 1 place de l'Eglise (04 68 96 22 96).

I N MEDIEVAL TIMES Villefranche's
position at the narrowest
point of the Têt valley made
it an eminently defensible
fortress against Moorish
invasion. Today, fragments of
11th-century walls remain,
along with massive ramparts,
gates and Fort Liberia high
above the gorge, all built by

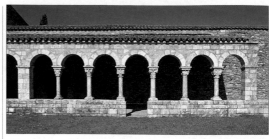
Abbey cloisters of St-Michel-de-Cuxa

Vauban in the 17th century.
The 12th-century **Eglise de St-
Jacques** has fine carved capitals from the workshops of St-
Michel-de-Cuxa, and Catalan
painted wooden statues, including a 14th-century *Virgin
and Child*. The 13th-century
oak door is embellished with
intricate local wrought ironwork, a craft which still
features on many of the shop
signs in town. From the streets

Statue in St-Jacques, Villefranche

of locally quarried pink marble
you can make the climb up to
the **Grottes des Canalettes**,
a superb underground setting
for concerts. Alternatively,
climb aboard the Little
Yellow Train up on to the
magnificent mountain plain of
the Cerdagne.

St-Michel-de-Cuxa ●

Prades, Pyrénées-Orientales. 📞 04 68
96 15 35. **Open** daily. **Closed** Sun am,
religious hols. 📷 ♿

P RADES, a small, pink marble
town in the Têt valley,
is typical of the local style.
The **Eglise St-Pierre** has a
southern Gothic wrought iron
belfry and a Baroque Catalan
interior. But the town is distinguished by the beautiful
pre-Romanesque abbey of
St-Michel-de-Cuxa which lies
3 km (2 miles) further up
the valley, and by the legacy
of the Spanish cellist Pablo
Casals. Casals spent many
years here in exile from
Franco's Spain; every August
the abbey provides the setting
for the Prades music festival
held in his memory.
An early example of mon-
astic architecture, St-Michel-
de-Cuxa abbey was founded
by Benedictine monks in 878
and rapidly became renowned
throughout France and Spain.
Distinctive keyhole arches
showing Moorish influence
pierce the massive walls of
the abbey church, which
was consecrated in 974. The
mottled pink marble cloisters,
with their superbly carved
capitals, were added later,
in the 12th century.
After the Revolution the
building was abandoned, and

THE LITTLE YELLOW TRAIN

Arrive early for the best seats in the carriages of *Le Petit
Train Jaune* which winds its way on narrow-gauge tracks
through gorges and across towering viaducts up into the
Cerdagne, stopping at small mountain stations along the
way. Built in 1910 to improve access to the mountains, it
now operates mainly for tourists, beginning at Villefranche-
de-Conflent and terminating at Latour-de-Carol.

The Little Yellow Train, with open carriages for summer visitors

its famous carvings looted. From 1913, George Grey Bernard, a visiting American artist, began to incorporate some of the capitals incorporated in local buildings. He sold the carvings to the Metropolitan Museum of Art in New York in 1925, where they formed the basis of the Cloisters Museum – a faithful re-creation of a Romanesque abbey in the unlikely setting of Manhattan.

St-Martin-du-Canigou ❹

Casteil. 📞 04 68 05 50 03. **Open** (guided tours only) mid-Jun–mid-Sep: daily (10am, noon, 2pm, 3pm, 4pm, 5pm); mid-Sep–mid-Jun: Wed–Mon (2:30pm, 3:30pm, 4:30pm). 🅿️

SAINT-MARTIN-DU-CANIGOU is situated in a spectacularly remote site a third of the way up Pic du Canigou, on a jagged spur of rock approached only by jeep or a 40-minute climb on foot from Casteil or by hiring a jeep from Vernet-les-Bains. The abbey was built between 1001 and 1026, and financed by Guifred, Count of Cerdagne, who abandoned his family and entered the monastery in 1035. He was buried there 14 years later in a tomb he carved from the rock himself, and which can still be seen. The church is early

Nun at St-Martin

Serrabone priory's chapel tribune, with columns of local marble

Romanesque, based on a simple basilican plan. Two churches are built, quite literally one on top of the other, making the lower church the crypt for the upper building.

The abbey complex is best viewed from above by continuing up the path. From there, its irregular design clinging to the rock is framed by the dramatic mountain setting – the ensemble a tribute to the ingenuity and vitality of its early builders.

Prieuré de Serrabone ❺

Serrabone. 📞 04 68 84 09 30. **Open** daily. **Closed** 1 Jan, 1 May, 1 Nov, 25 Dec. 🅿️

PERCHED HIGH UP on the northern flanks of Pic du Canigou, the sacred mountain of the Catalans, is the priory of Serrabone. A final lap of hairpin bends on the approach road (the D618) reveals the simple square tower and round apse of this remote Romanesque abbey, surrounded by a botanical garden of local herbs and woodland plants clinging to the mountain side.

Inside the cool, austere 12th-century building is a surprisingly elaborate chapel tribune, its columns and arches glowing from the local red-veined marble, carved by the anonymous Master of Cuxa, whose work appears throughout the region. Note the strange beasts and verdant flora featured in the capital carvings, especially the rose of Roussillon.

The 11th-century cloister of St-Martin-du-Canigou

Céret ⑥

Pyrénées-Orientales. 🏘 7,500. 🚌
ℹ av Clémenceau (04 68 87 00 53).
🛒 Sat.

CÉRET IS A CHERRY TOWN, surrounded by a glorious cloud of pink blossom in the early spring, and producing the very first fruits of the year. The tiled and painted façades and loggias of the buildings have a Spanish feel and the town was popular with Picasso, Braque and Matisse. Today, as a result, Céret is distinguished by the recently extended **Musée d'Art Moderne**, its sophisticated modern architecture housing a remarkable collection which includes Catalan artists Tapiès and Capdeville, a series of bowls by Picasso painted with bullfighting scenes, and works by Matisse, Chagall, Juan Gris and Salvador Dalí.

The town's Catalan heritage is evident in regular bullfights held in the arena, and in its Sardana dance festival at the end of August.

🏛 Musée d'Art Moderne

Bd Maréchal Joffre. 📞 04 68 87 27 76. **Open** May–Sep: daily; Oct–Apr: Wed–Mon. **Closed** 1 Jan, 1 May, 1 Nov, 25 Dec. 🐾 ⚿

Environs

From Céret the D115 follows the Tech valley to the spa

Statue by Aristide Maillol, Banyuls

town of **Amélie-les-Bains**, where fragments of Roman baths have been discovered. Beyond, in **Arles-sur-Tech**, the Eglise de Ste-Marie contains 12th-century frescoes, and a sarcophagus beside the church door which, according to local legend, produces drops of unaccountably pure water every year.

Catalan flag

Côte Vermeille ⑦

Pyrénées-Orientales. 🚉 Perpignan.
🚊 Collioure, Cerbère. 🚌 Collioure,
Banyuls-sur-Mer. 🚢 Port Vendres.
ℹ Collioure (04 68 82 15 47), Cerbère
(04 68 88 42 36).

HERE THE PYRENEES meet the Mediterranean, the coast road twisting and turning around secluded pebbly coves and rocky outcrops. The *vermeille* (vermilion-tinted) rock of the headlands gives this stretch of coast, the loveliest to be found in Languedoc-Roussillon, its name.

The Côte Vermeille extends all the way to the Costa Brava in northern Spain. With its Catalan character, it is as redolent of Spain as of France. **Argelès-Plage** has three sandy beaches and a palm-fringed promenade, and is the largest camping centre in Europe. The small resort of **Cerbère** is the last French town before the border, flying the red and gold Catalan flag to signal its true allegiance. All along the coast, terraced vineyards cling to the rocky hillsides, producing strong, sweet wines like Banyuls and Muscat. The difficult terrain makes harvesting a laborious process. Vines were first planted here by Greek settlers in the 7th century BC, and Banyuls itself has wine cellars dating back to the Middle Ages.

Banyuls is also famous as the birthplace of Aristide Maillol, the 19th-century sculptor, whose work can be seen all over the region. **Port Vendres**, with fortifications built by the indefatigable Vauban (architect to Louis XIV) is a fishing port, with anchovies its main catch.

The spectacular Côte Vermeille, seen from the coast road south of Banyuls

Collioure harbour, with one of its beaches and the Eglise Notre-Dame-des-Anges

Collioure ❽

Pyrénées-Orientales. 🏠 2,700. 🚉
🚌 🚹 place du 18 juin (04 68 82 15
47). 🛒 Wed & Sun.

THE COLOURS of Collioure
first attracted Matisse here
in 1905: brightly stuccoed
houses sheltered by cypresses
and gaily painted fishing boats,
all bathed in the famous luminous light, and washed by a
gentle sea. Other artists including André Derain worked here
under Matisse's influence and
were dubbed *fauves* (wild
beasts) for their wild experiments with colour. Art galleries
and souvenir shops now fill
the cobbled streets, but this
small fishing port has changed
surprisingly little since then,
with anchovies still its main
business. Three salting houses
are evidence of this tradition.

Three sheltered beaches,
both pebble and sand, nestle
round the harbour, dominated
by the bulk of the **Château
Royal**, which forms part of the
harbour wall. It was first built
by the Knights Templar in the
13th century, and Collioure
became the main port of
entry for Perpignan, remaining
under the rule of Spanish
Aragon until France took
over in 1659. The outer
fortifications were reinforced
ten years later by Vauban,
who demolished much of the
original town in the process.
Today the château can be

toured, or visited for its
exhibitions of modern art.

The **Eglise Notre-Dame-
des-Anges** on Collioure's
quayside was rebuilt in the
17th century to replace the
church which was destroyed
by Vauban. A former lighthouse was incorporated into
the fabric of the new church
as a belltower. Inside the
church are no fewer than
five Baroque altarpieces by
Joseph Sunyer and other
Catalan masters of the genre.

Be warned that Collioure
is extremely popular in July
and August, with visitors cram-
ming the tiny streets. Long
queues of traffic are possible,
too, though the building of
another route, the D86, has
helped to ease congestion.

⚓ Château Royal
📞 04 68 82 06 43. **Open** daily.
Closed 1 Jan, 1 May & 25 Dec. 🎫

Elne ❾

Pyrénées-Orientales. 🏠 6,500. 🚉
🚌 🚹 rue de Dr Bolte (04 68 22 05
07). 🛒 Mon, Wed & Fri.

THE ANCIENT TOWN of Elne
accommodated Hannibal
and his elephants in 218 BC
on his epic journey to Rome,
and was one of the most important towns in Roussillon until the 16th century. Today it
is famed for the 11th-century
**Cathédrale de Ste-Eulalie
et Ste-Julie**, with its superb
cloister. Milky blue-veined
marble has been carved into
exquisite capitals, embellished
with a riot of flowers, figures
and arabesques. The side nearest the cathedral dates from the
1100s, the remaining three are
13th–14th-century. From the
front of the cathedral are views
of the vines and orchards of
the surrounding plain.

Carved capital at Elne, showing "The Dream of the Magi"

A wide, sandy beach near Perpignan, almost purpose-built for family holidays

Perpignan ⑩

Pyrénées-Orientales. 🚉 108,000.
🚄 🚌 🏛 🈺 place Armand Lanoux
(04 68 66 30 30). 🔷 daily.

CATALAN PERPIGNAN has a distinctly southern feel, with palm trees lining the Têt river promenade, house and shop façades painted vibrant turquoise and pink, and the streets of the Arab quarter selling aromatic spices, couscous and paella.

Today Perpignan is the vibrant capital of Roussillon, and has an important position on the developing Mediterranean sunbelt. But it reached its zenith in the 13th and 14th centuries under the kings of Majorca and the kings of Aragon, who controlled great swathes of northern Spain and southern France. Their vast **Palais des Rois de Majorque** still straddles a substantial area in the south-ern part of the city.

Perpignan's strong Catalan identity is evident during the twice-weekly summer celebrations when the Sardana is danced in the place de la Loge. It is a key Catalan symbol, danced proudly by young and old. Arms raised, concentric circles of dancers keep step to the accompaniment of a Catalan woodwind band.

One of Perpignan's finest buildings, the **Loge de Mer**, lies at the head of the square. Built in 1397 to house the Maritime Exchange, only the eastern section retains the original Gothic design. The rest of the building was rebuilt in Renaissance style in 1540 with sumptuous carved wooden ceilings and sculpted window frames. While visitors are sometimes offended by the sight of a fast-food restaurant inside, the result is that the Loge de Mer has avoided becoming a hushed museum piece. Instead, it remains the centre of Perpignan life – elegant cafés cluster round it, producing a constant buzz of activity.

Devout Christ in St-Jean

Next door is the **Hôtel de Ville** with its pebble stone façade and wrought iron gates. Inside, parts of the arcaded courtyard date back to 1315; at the centre is Aristide Maillol's allegorical sculpture, *The Mediterranean* (1950).

To the east is the labyrinthine cathedral quarter of St-Jean, made up of small streets and squares containing some fine 14th- and 15th-century buildings.

🏛 Cathédrale St-Jean
Place de Gambetta.
Topped by a wrought iron belfry, this cathedral was begun in 1324 and was finally ready for use in 1509. It is constructed almost entirely from river pebbles layered with red brick, a style common throughout the region due to the scarcity of other building materials.

Inside the gloomy interior the nave is flanked by gilded altarpieces and painted wooden statues, with a massive pre-Romanesque marble font. A cloistered cemetery adjoins the church and the Chapel of

THE ANNUAL PROCESSION DE LA SANCH

There is a very Catalan atmosphere in Perpignan during the annual Good Friday procession of the Confraternity of La Sanch (Brotherhood of the Holy Blood). Originally dedicated to the comfort of condemned prisoners in the 15th century, members of the brotherhood still wear macabre red or black robes as they carry sacred relics and the crucifix from the Chapel of the Devout Christ to the cathedral.

the Devout Christ with its precious, poignantly realistic medieval wooden Crucifixion. The cathedral replaced the 11th-century church of St-Jean-le Vieux, whose superb Romanesque doorway can be glimpsed through the gates to the left of the main entrance.

⛨ Palais des Rois de Majorque
Rue des Archers. **☎** *04 68 34 48 29.*
Open *daily.* **Closed** *1 Jan, 1 May, 1 Nov, 25 Dec.* ⛨

Access to the vast 13th-century fortified palace of the Kings of Majorca is as circuitous today as it was intended to be for invading soldiers. Flights of steps zigzag within the sheer red-brick ramparts, begun in the 15th century and added to successively over the next two centuries. Eventually, the elegant gardens and substantial castle within are revealed, entered by way of the Tour de l'Hommage, from the top of which is a panoramic view of city, mountains and sea.

The palace itself is built around a central arcaded courtyard, flanked on one side by the Salle de Majorque, a great hall with a triple fireplace and giant Gothic arched windows. Adjacent, two royal chapels built one above the other shows southern Gothic style at its best: pointed arches, patterned frescoes and elaborate tilework demonstrating a distinct Moorish influence. The fine rose marble doorway of the upper King's Chapel is a typical example of the Roussillon Romanesque style,

Courtyard in the Hôtel de Ville

although the sculpted capitals are Gothic. Today the great courtyard is sometimes used for concerts.

🏛 Musée Catalan
Le Castillet. **☎** *04 68 35 42 05.* **Open** *Wed–Mon.* **Closed** *public hols.* ⛨
The red-brick tower and pink belfry of the Castillet, built as the town gate in 1368, was at one time a prison and is all that remains of the town walls. It now houses a collection of Catalan craft objects, including agricultural implements, kitchen furniture, looms, and glazed terracotta pots used for storing water and oil.

🏛 Musée Hyacinthe-Rigaud
16 rue de l'Ange. **☎** *04 68 35 43 40.*
Open *Wed–Mon.* **Closed** *public hols.*
This magnificent 17th-century mansion has an art collection dominated by Hyacinthe Rigaud (1659–1743), who was born in Perpignan and was court painter to both Louis XIV and Louis XV. Other

works range from the 13th century to the present day and include a large number of 14th- to 16th-century Catalan and Spanish paintings, among them the *Retable de la Trinité* (1489) by the Master of Canapost.

There are sculptures by Aristide Maillol, born in nearby Banyuls, and works by Raoul Dufy, Picasso, Jean-Baptiste Greuze, Jean-Auguste Ingres and Théodore Géricault. On the ground floor is a collection of Hispano-Moorish ceramics.

Fort tower and ramparts, Salses

Salses ⓫

Pyrénées-Orientales. 🚶 *2,500.* 🚉
🚌 🛈 *place de la République (04 68 38 66 13).* 🛒 *Wed.*

L OOKING LIKE a giant sand-castle against the ochre earth of the Corbières vineyards, the **Fort de Salses** stands at the old frontier of Spain and France. It guards the narrow defile between the mountains and the Mediterranean lagoons, and was built by King Ferdinand of Aragon between 1497 and 1506 to defend Spain's possession of Roussillon. Its massive walls and rounded towers are a classic example of Spanish military architecture, designed to deflect the new threat posed by gunpowder.

Inside were underground stabling for 300 horses and a subterranean passageway around the inner courtyard.

There is a wonderful view from the keep over the lagoons and surrounding coastline.

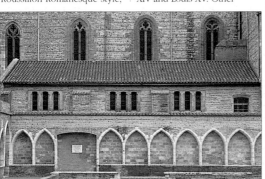
The pebble and red-brick Cathédrale de St-Jean in Perpignan

Vineyards covering the hilly terrain of the Corbières

Corbières 12

Aude. ✈ Perpignan. 🚉 Salses-le-
Château, Lézignan-Corbières.
🚌 Lézignan-Corbières, Salses-le-
Château, St Paul-de-Fenouillet. ℹ
Lézignan-Corbières (04 68 27 05 42).

STILL ONE of the wildest
parts of France with few
roads, let alone villages, the
Corbières is best known for
its wine and the great craggy
hulks of the Cathar castles *(see
p481)*. Much of the land is
untamed *garrigue* (scrubland)
fragrant with honeysuckle and
broom; promising south-facing
slopes have been cleared and
are planted with vines.

To the south are the spectacular medieval castles of
Peyrepertuse and **Quéribus**,
the latter one of the last Cathar
strongholds. **Villerouge-
Termenes** celebrates its
turbulent past with an annual
medieval banquet. To the
west is the barren, uninhabited
Razès area in the upper Aude
valley. Its best-kept secret is
the village of **Alet-les-Bains**,
with beautifully preserved
half-timbered houses and the
remains of a Benedictine
abbey, battle-scarred from the
Wars of Religion.

Narbonne 13

Aude. 🏛 46,000. 🚉 🚌 ℹ place
Roger Salengro (04 68 65 15 60).
🗓 Thu & Sun.

NARBONNE is a medium-
sized, cheerful town
profiting from the booming
wine region that surrounds it.
The town is bisected by the
tree-shaded Canal de la
Robine; to the north is the
restored medieval quarter with
many elegant shops and good
restaurants. Located here is
one of Narbonne's most
intriguing tourist attractions,
the **Horreum**. This underground warren of granaries
and grain chutes dates from
the 1st century BC, when
Narbonne was a major port
and capital of the largest
Roman province in Gaul.

The town prospered through
the Middle Ages until the 14th
century when the harbour
silted up and the course of
the river Aude altered, taking
Narbonne's fortunes with it.
By then, an important bishopric had been established and
an ambitious cathedral project,
modelled on the great Gothic
cathedrals of the North, was
underway. However, the full

grandiose design was abandoned and just the chancel,
begun in 1272, became the
**Cathédrale St-Just et St-
Pasteur** we see today.

It is still enormous, en-
hanced by 14th-century
sculptures, fine stained-glass
windows and an 18th-century
carved organ. Aubusson and
Gobelin tapestries adorn the
walls, and the Chapel of the
Anonciade houses a treasury
of manuscripts, jewelled
reliquaries and tapestries.

The unfinished transept
now forms a courtyard, and
between the cathedral and
the adjacent **Palais des
Archevêques** (Archbishops'
Palace), lie cloisters with four
magnificent galleries of 14th-
century vaulting.

This huge palace and cathedral complex dominates the
centre of Narbonne. Between
the Palais des Archevêques'
massive 14th-century towers
is the town hall, with a 19th-
century Neo-Gothic façade by
Viollet le Duc *(see p190)*, the
architect who so determinedly

The vaulted chancel of Cathédrale
St-Just et St-Pasteur in Narbonne

CANAL DU MIDI

From Sète to Toulouse the 240-km (149-mile)
Canal du Midi winds its way between plane
trees, vineyards and sleepy villages. The complex system of locks, aqueducts and bridges
is a remarkable feat of engineering, built by
the Béziers salt-tax baron Paul Riquet. Completed in 1681, it encouraged Languedoc trade
and established a vital link, via the Garonne
river, between the Atlantic and the Mediterranean. Today it is plied by holiday barges.

Tranquil waterway of the Canal du Midi

The Cistercian Abbaye de Fontfroide (1093), southwest of Narbonne

🏛 Musée Lapidaire
Eglise Notre-Dame de Lamourguier.
📞 04 68 65 53 58. **Open** Jul–Aug:
daily. **Closed** 14 Jul. 🅿 ♿

Environs
Thirteen kilometres (8 miles) southwest of Narbonne, the Cistercian **Abbaye de Font-froide** is worth visiting for its elegant cloister. The abbey is tucked away in a quiet valley, surrounded by cypress trees.

Golfe du Lion ⑭

Aude, Hérault. ✈ 🚉 🚌 Montpellier.
🚢 Sète. 🛈 Grande Motte (04 67 29 03 37).

UNTIL THE 1960s most of this coast was a mosquito-infested swamp, interspersed with tiny fishing villages. Vestiges of the past are found in small towns like **Gruissan** with its medieval Barbarossa tower, but government investment has transformed most of this 100-km (65-mile), sandy coastline into a series of holiday resorts. Modern architecture predominates, but the developments have been environmentally sensitive, and long coastal stretches have not been built up.

Port Leucate and **Port Bacarès** are both ideal for watersports. The huge beach development at **Cap d'Agde** accommodates thousands of people every year, and is the largest naturist resort in Europe. Inland, the old town of **Agde** is noted for its black basalt buildings, particularly the 12th-century, fortress-like **Cathédrale St-Etienne**.

restored medieval France. The palace itself is divided into the Palais Vieux (Old Palace) and the Palais Neuf (New Palace). Narbonne's most important museums are in the Palais Neuf, on the left as you enter through the low medieval arches of the passage de l'Ancre. The **Musée d'Archéologie et de Pré-histoire** collection includes fragments of Narbonne's Roman heritage, from milestones and parts of the original walls to an assemblage of domestic objects, coins, tools and glassware. The **Chapelle de la Madeleine** is decorated with a 14th-century wall painting and houses a collection of Greek vases, sarcophagi and mosaics.

In the archbishops' former apartments is the **Musée d'Art et d'Histoire**, which is as interesting for its luxurious furnishings and richly decorated ceilings as for its art collection. This includes some fine paintings by Canaletto, Brueghel, Boucher and Veronese as well as a large selection of local earthenware.

South of the Canal de la Robine are a number of fine mansions, including the Renaissance **Maison des Trois Nourrices** on the corner of rue des Trois-Nourrices and rue Edgard-Quinet. Nearby is the **Musée Lapidaire**, with architectural fragments from Gallo-Roman Narbonne, and the 13th-century Gothic **Basilique St-Paul-Serge**. The present building retains the crypt and some sarcophagi of an earlier church on this site.

🏛 Horreum
Rue Rouget-de-l'Isle. 📞 04 68 32 45 30. **Open** May–Sep: daily; Oct–Apr: Tue–Sun. **Closed** 1 Jan, 1 May, 14 Jul, 25 Dec. 🅿

🏛 Musée d'Archéologie et de Préhistoire/Musée d'Art et d'Histoire
Palais des Archevêques. 📞 04 68 90 30 54. **Open** May–Sep: daily; Oct–Apr: Tue–Sun. **Closed** 1 Jan, 1 May, 14 Jul, 25 Dec. 🅿

A wide, sandy beach on the Cap d'Agde

Carcassonne ⑮

THE CITADEL OF CARCASSONNE is a perfectly restored medieval town. It crowns a steep bank above the river Aude, a fairy-tale sight of turrets and ramparts overlooking the Basse Ville below. The strategic position of the citadel between the Atlantic and the Mediterranean and on the corridor between the Iberian peninsula and the rest of Europe led to its original settlement, consolidated by the Romans in the 2nd century BC. It became a key element in medieval military conflicts. At its zenith in the 12th century, it was ruled by the Trencavels who built the château and cathedral. Military advances and the Treaty of the Pyrenees in 1659, which relocated the French-Spanish border, left its superb fortifications obsolete and it fell into decline. The attentions of architectural historian Viollet-le-Duc *(see p190)* led to its restoration in the 19th century.

The Restored Citadel
Restoration of La Cité has always been controversial. Critics complain it looks too new, favouring a more romantic ruin.

★ **Château Comtal**
A fortress within a fortress, the château has a moat, five towers and defensive wooden galleries on the walls.

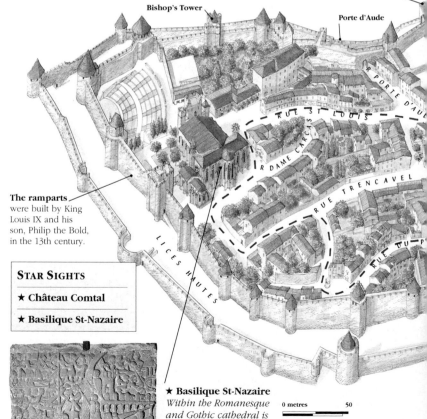

Bishop's Tower

Porte d'Aude

R PORTE D'AUL

RUE ST LOUIS

R DAME CARCAS

RUE TRENCAVEL

RUE TU P

L I C E S   H A U T E S

The ramparts
were built by King
Louis IX and his
son, Philip the Bold,
in the 13th century.

STAR SIGHTS

★ **Château Comtal**

★ **Basilique St-Nazaire**

★ **Basilique St-Nazaire**
*Within the Romanesque
and Gothic cathedral is
the famous Siege Stone,
said to depict the 1209
Siege of Carcassonne
by crusaders.*

| 0 metres | 50 |
| 0 yards | 50 |

KEY

- - - Suggested route

RELIGIOUS PERSECUTION

Carcassonne's strategic position meant it was often at the centre of religious conflict. The Cathars *(see p481)* were given sanctuary here in 1209 by Raymond-Roger Trencavel when besieged by Simon de Montfort in his crusade against heresy. In the 14th century the Inquisition continued to root out the Cathars. This painting depicts intended victims in the Inquisition Tower.

Les Emmurés de Carcassonne, JP Laurens

VISITORS' CHECKLIST

Aude. ⚑ 45,000. 🚉 Port du Canal du Midi (08 36 35 35 35). 🚌 bd de Varsovie. 🛈 Tour Narbonnaise, La Cité (04 68 25 07 04); 15 bd Camille-Pelleton (04 68 10 24 30). 🖳 Tue, Thu & Sat. 🎉 Festival de la Cité (all of Jul); l'Embrasement de la Cité (14 Jul); Les Médiévales (fortnight, around mid-Aug). **Château Comtal open** daily. **Closed** 1 Jan, 1 May, 14 Jul, 1 & 11 Nov, 25 Dec. 🖳

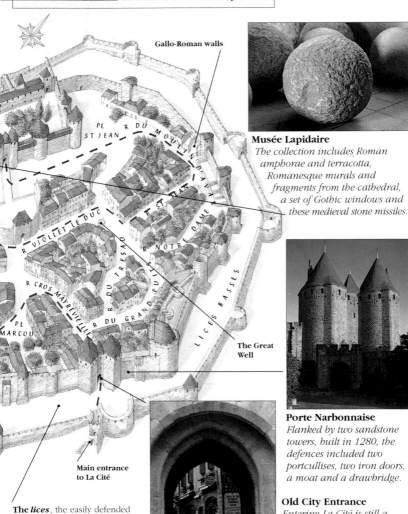

Gallo-Roman walls

Musée Lapidaire
The collection includes Roman amphorae and terracotta, Romanesque murals and fragments from the cathedral, a set of Gothic windows and these medieval stone missiles.

The Great Well

Porte Narbonnaise
Flanked by two sandstone towers, built in 1280, the defences included two portcullises, two iron doors, a moat and a drawbridge.

Main entrance to La Cité

Old City Entrance
Entering La Cité is still a step back in time, although it is one of France's top tourist destinations, filled with souvenir shops.

The *lices*, the easily defended spaces between the inner and outer ramparts, were also used for jousting, crossbow practice and for storage of timber and other materials.

Béziers with its medieval cathedral, seen from Pont Vieux in the southwest

Minerve ⑯

Hérault. 🚶 100. 🅹 La Mairie (04 68 91 81 43).

Iɴ ᴛʜᴇ ᴘᴀʀᴄʜᴇᴅ, arid hills of the Minervois, surrounded by vines and not much else, Minerve appears defiant on its rocky outcrop at the confluence of the rivers Cesse and Briant. It is defended by what the Minervois call the "Candela" (Candle), an octagonal tower which is all that remains of the medieval château. In 1210, the small town resisted the vengeful Simon de Montfort, scourge of the Cathars, in a siege lasting seven weeks. This culminated in the execution of 140 Cathars who were burned at the stake after refusing to renounce their faith.

Today visitors enter Minerve by a high bridge spanning the gorge. Turn right and follow the route of the Cathars past the Romanesque arch of the Porte des Templiers to the 12th-century **Eglise St-Etienne**. Outside the church is a crudely carved dove, symbol of the Cathars, and within is a 5th-century white marble altar table, one of the oldest artifacts in the region.

A rocky path follows the riverbed below the town, where the water has cut out caves and two bridges – the Grand Pont and the Petit Pont – from the soft limestone.

Béziers ⑰

Hérault. 🚶 76,000. ✈ 🚉 🚌 🅹 Palais des Congrès, 29 av Saint Saëns. (04 67 76 47 00). 🅵 Fri.

Fᴀᴍᴏᴜꜱ ꜰᴏʀ its bullfights and rugby, and the wine of the surrounding region, Béziers has several other points of interest. The town seems turned in on itself, its roads leading up to the massive 14th-century **Cathédrale St-Nazaire**, with its fine sculpture, stained glass and frescoes. In 1209, several thousand citizens were massacred in the crusade against the Cathars. The papal legate's troops were ordered not to discriminate between Catholics and Cathars, but to "Kill them all. God will recognize his own!"

Statue of the engineer Paul Riquet in the allées Paul Riquet, Béziers

The **Musée du Biterrois** holds exhibitions on local history, wine and the Canal du Midi, engineered in the late 17th century by Paul Riquet, Béziers' most famous son (see p476). His statue presides over the allées Paul Riquet, the broad esplanade at the foot of the hill. This is lined by two double rows of plane trees and large canopied restaurants, a civilized focus to this otherwise business-like town.

🏛 Musée du Biterrois
Caserne St-Jacques. 📞 04 67 36 71 01. **Open** Tue–Sun. **Closed** 1 Jan, Easter, 1 May, 25 Dec. 📷 ♿

Environs
Oppidum d'Ensérune is a superb Roman site, on a hill overlooking the Béziers plain and the mountains to the north. The original pre-Roman settlement is revealed in the substantial foundations of houses, some with huge terracotta storage jars buried in the floor. The **Musée de l'Oppidum d'Ensérune** has a good archaeological collection, from Celtic, Greek, and Roman vases to jewellery, funeral fragments and weapons.

🏛 Musée de l'Oppidum d'Ensérune
Nissan lez Ensérune. 📞 04 67 37 01 23. **Open** daily. **Closed** 1 Jan, 1 May, 1 & 11 Nov, 25 Dec. 📷 ♿ ground floor only.

The Cathars

THE CATHARS (from Greek *katharos*, meaning pure) were a 13th-century Christian sect critical of corruption in the established church. Cathar dissent flourished in independent Languedoc as an expression of separatism, but the rebellion was rapidly exploited for political purposes. Peter II of Aragon was keen to annex Languedoc, and Philippe II of France joined forces with the pope to crush the Cathar heretics in a crusade led by Simon de Montfort in 1209. This heralded the start of over a century of ruthless killing and torture.

CATHAR CASTLES
The Cathars took refuge in the defensive castles of the Corbières and Ariège. Peyrepertuse is one of the most remote, difficult to get to even today: a long, narrow stone citadel hacked from a high, craggy peak over 609 m (2,000 ft) high.

Cathars (also known as Albigensians) believed in the duality of good and evil. They considered the material world entirely evil. To be truly pure they had to renounce the world, and be non-violent, vegetarian and sexually abstinent.

The crusade against the Cathars was vicious. Heretics' land was promised to the crusaders by the pope, who assured forgiveness in advance of their crimes. In 1209, 20,000 citizens were massacred in Béziers and, the following year, 140 were burned to death in Minerve. In 1244, 225 Cathars died defending one of their last fortresses at Montségur.

CATHAR COUNTRY
Castles and towns with a Cathar association, some of them spectacular sites, are concentrated in Languedoc-Roussillon, the centre of Catharism in the Middle Ages.

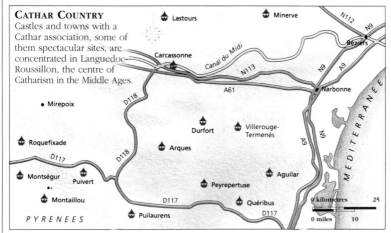

The impressive Grand Hotel *(see p571)* on quai de la Résistance, Sète

Sète 🄷

Hérault. 🄷 *42,000.* 🄷 🄷
🄷 *60 Grand' Rue Mario Roustan
(04 67 74 71 71).* 🄷 *Wed & Fri.*

Sète is a major fishing and
industrial port. It has a
gutsier, more raffish air than
much of the leisure-oriented
Mediterranean, with its shops
selling ships' lamps and

Cimetière Marin in Sète, burial
place of the poet Paul Valéry

propellers, and its quayside
restaurants full of hungry
sailors demolishing vast
platters of mussels, oysters
and sea snails straight off the
boat. Most of Sète's restaurants can be found in a stroll
along the Grand Canal, with
its Italianate houses painted
in pastel colours and with
wrought iron balconies overlooking Sète's network of
canals and bridges. Boisterous
water jousting tournaments,
which date back to 1666, form
part of the two-week festival
held in summer *(see p33)*.

Above the town is the
Cimetière Marin on Mont
St-Clair, where Sète's most
famous son, poet Paul Valéry
(1871-1945), is buried, and
where there is a small museum
dedicated to his memory.
From an observation platform,
there are breathtaking views
of the coast and the mountains
of the Cévennes. Beyond is
the Bassin de Thau, a major
oyster production centre,
and to the south are windswept, sandy beaches.

Pézenas 🄷

Hérault. 🄷 *8,000.* 🄷 🄷 *place
Gambetta (04 67 98 35 39).* 🄷 *Sat.*

Pézenas is a compact and
charming little town easily
appreciated in a gentle stroll
of its main sights, helpfully
indicated, and abounding in
revealing small details. Here
an exquisitely carved Renaissance window, there a fine old
doorway, in a niche a lovely
Madonna, all fragmentary
evidence of Pézenas' past
brilliance as the seat of local
government in the 16th–17th
centuries. Then the town also
played artistic host to many
glittering troupes of musicians
and actors, most notably the
dramatist Molière in the 1650s.

Best of all are the glimpses
of fine houses through courtyard doorways. Examples
include the **Hôtel des Barons
de Lacoste**, at 8 rue François-
Oustrin, with its beautiful
stone staircase, and the
Maison des Pauvres at 12
rue Alfred Sabatier, with its
three galleries and a staircase.

Look out for the medieval
shop window on rue Triperie-
Vieille, and just within the
14th-century **Porte Faugères**
(Faugères Gate) the narrow
streets of the Jewish ghetto,
which has a chilling feeling of
enclosure. Shops selling
antiques, secondhand goods
and books add to the pleasures of Pézenas. All around
the town, vines stretch as far
as the eye can see, covering
the prosperous plain.

The stone foyer of the Hôtel des
Barons de Lacoste in Pézenas

Parc Régional du Haut Languedoc ⑳

Hérault, Tarn. ✈ *Béziers*
🚋 *Bézier, Bédarieux.* 🚌 *St-Pons-de-Thomières, Mazamet, Lamalou-les-Bains.* 🛈 *St-Pons-de-Thomières (04 67 97 06 65).*

T HE HIGH LIMESTONE plateaux and wooded slopes of upper Languedoc are a world away from the coast. From the Montagne Noire, a mountainous region between Béziers and Castres, up into the Cévennes is a landscape of remote sheep farms, eroded rock formations and deep river gorges. Much of this area has been designated the Parc Régional du Haut Languedoc, the second largest of the French national parks after Ecrins.

St-Pons-de-Thomières is the entrance, with access to forest and mountain trails for walking and riding, plus a wildlife research centre, where one can glimpse the mouflons (wild mountain sheep), eagles and wild boar which were once a common sight in the region.

If you take the D908 from St-Pons through the park you pass the village of **Olargues** with its 12th-century bridge over the river Jaur. **Lamalou-les-Bains**, on the park's eastern edge, is a small spa town with a restored Belle Epoque spa building and theatre, and a soporifically slow pace.

Outside the park boundaries to the northeast there are spectacular natural phenomena. At the **Cirque de Navacelles**, the river Vis has joined up with itself cutting out an entire island. On it sits the peaceful village of Navacelles, visible from the road higher up. The **Grotte des Demoiselles** is one of the most magnificent in an area full of caves, where you walk through a calcified world. A funicular train takes visitors from the foot of the mountain to the top.

The **Grotte de Clamouse** is also an extraordinary experience, the reflections from underground rivers and pools flickering on the cavern roofs, with stalagmites resembling dripping candles and stalactites soaring Gothic columns.

🏛 **Grotte des Demoiselles**
St-Bauzille-de-Putois. 📞 04 67 73 70 02. **Open** daily. **Closed** 1 Jan, 25 Dec. 📷 ♿
🏛 **Grotte de Clamouse**
Rte de St-Guilhem-le-Désert, St-Jean-de-Fos. 📞 04 67 57 71 05. **Open** Mar–Oct: daily; Nov–Feb: Sun–Fri. 📷

Apse of St-Guilhem-le-Désert

St-Guilhem-le-Désert ㉑

Hérault. 🏠 200. 🚌 🛈 *Maison Communale (04 67 57 44 33).*

T UCKED AWAY in the Celette mountains, St-Guilhem-le-Désert is no longer as remote as when Guillaume of Aquitaine retired here as a hermit in the 9th century. After a lifetime as a soldier, Guillaume received a fragment of the True Cross from Emperor Charlemagne and established a monastery in this ravine above the river Hérault.

Vestiges of the first 10th-century church have been discovered but most of the building is a superb example of 11th–12th-century Romanesque architecture. Its lovely apsidal chapels dominate the heights of the village, behind which the carved doorway opens on to a central square.

Within the church is a sombre barrel-vaulted central aisle leading to the sunlit central apse. Only two galleries of the cloisters remain: the rest are in New York's Cloisters museum, along with carvings from St-Michel-de-Cuxa *(see p471).*

Extraordinary limestone formations at the Grotte de Clamouse

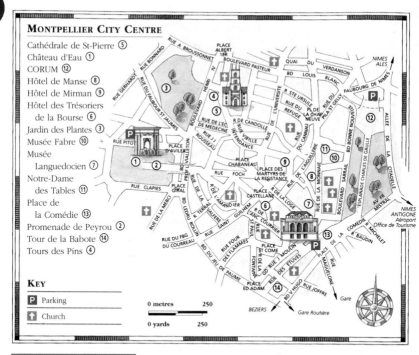

MONTPELLIER CITY CENTRE

Cathédrale de St-Pierre ⑤
Château d'Eau ①
CORUM ⑫
Hôtel de Manse ⑧
Hôtel de Mirman ⑨
Hôtel des Trésoriers
   de la Bourse ⑥
Jardin des Plantes ③
Musée Fabre ⑩
Musée
   Languedocien ⑦
Notre-Dame
   des Tables ⑪
Place de
   la Comédie ⑬
Promenade de Peyrou ②
Tour de la Babote ⑭
Tours des Pins ④

KEY

P Parking

✚ Church

0 metres   250

0 yards   250

**Open-air café in the place de la
Comédie, Montpellier**

Montpellier ㉒

Hérault. 🏛 *211,000.* ✈ 🚆 🚌
ℹ *allée de Tourisme, Le Triangle Bas
(04 67 58 67 58).* 🛍 *daily.*

MONTPELLIER is one of the
liveliest and most forward-
looking cities in the south, with
a quarter of its population
under 25. Sometimes on a
summer evening in university
term time it resembles more a
rock festival than the capital
of Languedoc-Roussillon.
Centre of the action is the
egg-shaped **place de la**

Comédie, known as "l'Oeuf"
("the egg"), with its 19th-cen-
tury opera house fronted by
the Fontaine des Trois Graces
and surrounded by buzzing
cafés. An esplanade of plane
trees and fountains leads to the
CORUM, an opera and conference centre typical of the
city's brave new architectural
projects. The best of these is
Ricardo Bofill's postmodern
housing complex known as
Antigone, which is modelled
on St Peter's in Rome.
   Montpellier was founded
relatively late for this region
of ancient Roman towns, developing in the 10th century
as a result of the spice trade
with the Middle East. The city's
medical school was founded
in 1220, partly as a result of
this cross-fertilization of
knowledge between the two
cultures, and remains one of
the most respected in France.
   Most of Montpellier was
ravaged by the Wars of Religion in the 16th century.
Only the **Tour de la Babote**
and the **Tours des Pins**
remain of the 12th-century
fortifications. There are few
fine churches, the exceptions
being the **Cathédrale de St-**

Pierre and the 18th-century
Notre-Dame des Tables.
   Reconstruction in the 17th
century saw the building of
mansions with elegant courtyards, stone staircases and
balconies. Examples open to
the public include **Hôtel de
Manse** on rue Embouque-
d'Or, **Hôtel de Mirman** near
place des Martyrs de la
Resistance and **Hôtel des
Trésoriers de la Bourse.**
The Hôtel des Lunaret houses
the **Musée Languedocien**
which exhibits Romanesque
and prehistoric artifacts.
   Another 17th-century building houses the **Musée Fabre**
with its collection of mainly
French paintings. Highlights
include Courbet's famous

PONT DU GARD ← To Uzès

Left bank

The bridge comprises
three tiers of
continuous arches.

Bonjour M. Courbet, Berthe Morisot's *L'Eté*, Robert Delaunay's *Nature Morte Portugaise*, and some evocative paintings of the region by Raoul Dufy and François Desnoyer.

A good place to view the city's position between mountains and sea is from the **Promenade de Peyrou**, a grand 18th-century square dominated by the **Château d'Eau** and the aqueduct which used to serve the city. Just to the north of here is the **Jardin des Plantes**. France's oldest botanical gardens, they were created in 1593.

🏛 **Musée Languedocien**
7 rue Jacques Coeur. 📞 *04 67 52 93 03*. **Open** *Mon–Sat*. **Closed** *public hols.* 🈺

🏛 **Musée Fabre**
39 bd Bonne Nouvelle. 📞 *04 67 14 83 00*. **Open** *Tue–Sun*. **Closed** *1 Jan, 1 May, 14 Jul, 1 & 11 Nov, 25 Dec.* 🈺 ♿

Château d'Eau, Montpellier

La Grande-Motte 🕗

Hérault. 🚶 *7,000*. 🚌 🛈 *place de la Mairie (04 67 56 42 00)*. 🅿 *Sun (& Thu: mid-Jun–mid-Sep)*.

THE BIZARRE white ziggurats of this modern beach resort exemplify the development of the Languedoc-Roussillon coast. One of a number of

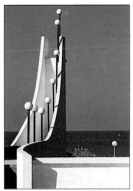

La Grande-Motte

beach cities on the lakes south of Montpellier, there are marinas and facilities for every kind of sport from tennis and golf to watersports, all flanked by golden beaches and pine forests. To the east are Le Grau-du-Roi, once a tiny fishing village, and Port-Camargue, with its big marina.

Aigues-Mortes 🕗

Gard. 🚶 *5,000*. 🚌 🛈 *Porte de la Gardette (04 66 53 73 00)*. 🅿 *Wed & Sun*.

THE BEST APPROACH to this perfectly preserved walled town is across the salt marshes of the Petite Camargue. Now marooned 5 km (3 miles) from the sea, the imposing defences of this once important port have become a tourist experience, worth visiting more for the effect of the ensemble than the tacky shops within. Aigues-Mortes ("Place of Dead Waters") was established by Louis XI in the 13th century to consolidate his power on the Mediterranean, and built according to

a strict grid pattern. By climbing up the **Tour de Constance** you can walk out onto the rectangular walls, which afford a superb view over the Camargue.

Environs
To the northeast is **St-Gilles-du-Gard**, also once an important medieval port. Today it is worth a detour to see the superbly sculpted 12th-century façade of its abbey church. This was originally established by the monks of Cluny abbey as a shrine to St Gilles, and a resting place on the famous pilgrimage route to Santiago de Compostela *(see pp390–91)*.

Pont du Gard 🕗

Gard. 🚌 *from Nîmes*.

NO AMOUNT OF FAME can diminish the first sight of the 2,000-year-old Pont du Gard. The Romans considered it the best testimony to the greatness of their Empire, and at 49 m (160 ft) it was the highest bridge they ever built. It is made from blocks of stone, hauled into place with an ingenious system of pulleys and a vast phalanx of slave labour. The huge build-up of calcium in the water channels suggests that the aqueduct was in continuous use for 400–500 years.

A dizzying view can be had by walking along the very top of the aqueduct, which originally carried water to Nîmes along a 50-km (31-mile) route from the springs at **Uzès**. This charming town has an arcaded marketplace and several fine medieval towers including the lovely 12th-century Tour Fenestrelle.

Water channel — To Nîmes →

Right bank

Roman inscriptions include a damaged phallus carving as a good luck symbol.

Some stones weighed up to six tonnes.

Nîmes

Arches of the Roman
amphitheatre

Listed number one on the tourist map of Nîmes is the bus stop designed by Philippe Starck, who is also credited with reworking the city's pedestrian zone. Such innovations are part of the city's current design renaissance. Architectural projects range from imaginative housing to a glittering new arts complex, under the guidance of a dynamic mayor. An important crossroads in the ancient world, Nîmes is equally well-known for its Roman antiquities such as the amphitheatre, the best preserved of its kind. The city is also famous for its festivals and bullfights. These are good times to see the rest of Nîmes with its museums, archaeological collections and Old Town of narrow streets and intimate squares.

Historic Nîmes

Nîmes has always had a turbulent history, and suffered particularly during the 16th-century Wars of Religion when the Romanesque **Cathédrale Notre-Dame et St-Castor** was badly damaged. During the 17th and 18th centuries the town prospered from textile manufacturing, one of the most enduring products being denim or "de Nîmes". Many of the fine houses of this period have been restored and elegant examples can be seen on rue de l'Aspic, rue des Marchands and rue de Chapitre in the Old Town. Just outside the town centre is the futuristic apartment building, **Nemausus I**.

The Roman gate, the **Porte Auguste**, built 20 years before the temple of **Maison Carrée**, was once part of one of the longest city walls in Gaul. Of the original arches still standing, two (large) were for carts and chariots and two (smaller) ones for pedestrians. The other major Roman remnant is the **Castellum**, where water used to arrive from the Pont du Gard (see p485). From the Castellum it was distributed around the city through thick pipes.

Jug from Musée Archéologique

♣ Jardin de la Fontaine

Quai de la Fontaine. **Open** daily. 🕭
When the Romans arrived in Nîmes, they found a town established by the Gauls, centred on source of a spring. They named the town Nemausus, after their river god. In the 18th century, formal gardens were constructed,

Jardin de la Fontaine, with a view over the city

and a network of limpid pools and cool stone terraces remains. High above the garden on Mont Cavalier is the octagonal Tour Magne, once a key part of the Roman walls.

Arms of the city in a sculpture by Martial Raysse

⋔ Les Arènes
Bd des Arènes. **[** 04 66 76 72 77. *Open* daily. *Closed* 1 Jan, 1 May, 25 Dec & on performance days. **⚕ &**
All roads lead to the amphitheatre, Les Arènes. Built at the end of the 1st century AD,

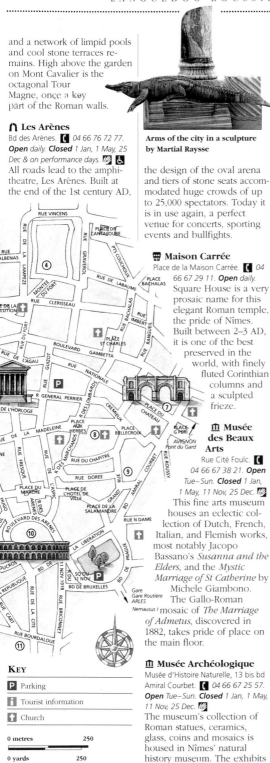

KEY
P	Parking
i	Tourist information
✝	Church

0 metres	250
0 yards	250

the design of the oval arena and tiers of stone seats accommodated huge crowds of up to 25,000 spectators. Today it is in use again, a perfect venue for concerts, sporting events and bullfights.

⊞ Maison Carrée
Place de la Maison Carrée. **[** 04 66 67 29 11. *Open* daily.
Square House is a very prosaic name for this elegant Roman temple, the pride of Nîmes. Built between 2–3 AD, it is one of the best preserved in the world, with finely fluted Corinthian columns and a sculpted frieze.

⋔ Musée des Beaux Arts
Rue Cité Foulc. **[** 04 66 67 38 21. *Open* Tue–Sun. *Closed* 1 Jan, 1 May, 11 Nov, 25 Dec. **⚕**
This fine arts museum houses an eclectic collection of Dutch, French, Italian, and Flemish works, most notably Jacopo Bassano's *Susanna and the Elders*, and the *Mystic Marriage of St Catherine* by Michele Giambono. The Gallo-Roman mosaic of *The Marriage of Admetus*, discovered in 1882, takes pride of place on the main floor.

⋔ Musée Archéologique
Musée d'Histoire Naturelle, 13 bis bd Amiral Courbet. **[** 04 66 67 25 57. *Open* Tue–Sun. *Closed* 1 Jan, 1 May, 11 Nov, 25 Dec. **⚕**
The museum's collection of Roman statues, ceramics, glass, coins and mosaics is housed in Nîmes' natural history museum. The exhibits

The Maison Carrée, now a museum

include important Iron Age menhir statues.

⋔ Carré d'Art
Place de la Maison Carrée. **[** 04 66 76 35 35. *Open* Tue–Sun. **⚕ &**
Nîmes' controversial arts complex, by the British architect Sir Norman Foster, opened in 1993. Five floors of this glass and steel temple, which was built in tribute to the Maison Carrée opposite, lie underground. The complex incorporates a library, a roof-terrace restaurant around a huge glass atrium, and the Musée d'Art Contemporain. The latter's French collection includes works by Raysse, Boltanski and Lavier.

Bullfight at Les Arènes in Nîmes

PROVENCE AND THE CÔTE D'AZUR

BOUCHES-DU-RHÔNE · VAUCLUSE · VAR
ALPES-DE-HAUTE-PROVENCE · ALPES-MARITIMES

ROM ITS HERB-SCENTED HILLS *to its yacht-filled harbours, no other region of France fires the imagination as strongly as Provence. The vivid landscape and luminous light have inspired artists and writers from Van Gogh to Picasso, Scott Fitzgerald to Pagnol.*

The borders of Provence are defined by nature: to the west, the Rhône; south, the Mediterranean; and north, where the olive trees end. To the east are the Alps and a border which has shifted over the centuries between France and Italy. Within is a contrasting terrain of plummeting gorges, Camargue saltflats, lavender fields and sun-drenched beaches.

Past visitors have left their mark. In Orange and Arles, the buildings of Roman *Provincia* are still in use. Fortified villages like Èze were built to withstand the Saracen pirates who plagued the coast in the 6th century.

In the 19th century, rich Europeans sought winter warmth on the Riviera; by the 1920s, high society was in residence all year, and their elegant villas remain.

The warm sunlight nurtures intense flavours and colours. Peppers, garlic and olives transform a netful of Mediterranean fish into that vibrant epitome of Provençal cuisine, *bouillabaisse.*

The image of Provence bathed in sunshine is marred only when the bitter Mistral wind scours the land. It has shaped a people as hardy as the olive tree, yet quick to embrace life to the full the moment the sun returns.

Cap Martin, seen from the village of Roquebrune

◁ **Lavender fields near the Gorges du Verdon**

Exploring Provence

THIS SUN-DRENCHED southeastern region is France's
most popular holiday destination. Sunworshippers
cram the beaches in the summer months, and entertainment includes jazz festivals, bull fights, car races,
casinos and *boules* games. Inland is a paradise
for walkers and nature
lovers, with remote
mountain pla-
teaux, perched
villages and
dramatic river
gorges.

Promenade des Anglais, Nice

SIGHTS AT A GLANCE

To Briançon

BARCELONNETTE

DIGNE-LES-BAINS

23

GETTING AROUND

The largest airport in the region, and second busiest in France, is Nice. Fly-drive packages are popular, although mainly recommended for touring inland. Traffic jams on coastal roads in high season can be avoided by using the autoroutes. Main coastal towns have good bus and rail links, and bikes can be hired at most rail stations. The Chemin de Fer de Provence railway line runs from Nice to Digne-les-Bains through spectacular mountain scenery. Mountain roads, though tortuous, are good.

MERCANTOUR

ALPES-MARITIMES **41**

MENTON **42**

GORGES DU LOUP

GORGES DU VERDON

VENCE **34** **33**
ST PAUL DE VENCE **35**
GRASSE **26**
BIOT **31**
VALLAURIS **30**
27

ÈZE **39** ROQUEBRUNE-CAP-MARTIN **40**
MONACO **43**
36 VILLEFRANCHE-SUR-MER **37**
NICE **38** CAP FERRAT
CAGNES-SUR-MER **32**
ANTIBES **29**
CAP D'ANTIBES **28**

DRAGUIGNAN

CANNES

FRÉJUS **24**
ST-RAPHAËL **25**

MASSIF DES MAURES

STE-MAXIME
ST-TROPEZ **22**
21

LE LAVANDOU

HYÈRES **19**

ÎLES D'HYÈRES **20**

KEY

	Motorway
	Major road
	Minor road
	Scenic route
	River
※	Viewpoint

0 kilometres 25

0 miles 25

Spectacular scenery near the quiet market town of Forcalquier

Mont Ventoux

Vaucluse. ⊠ *Avignon.* 🚌 *Orange.*
🚌 *Bédoin.* 🛈 *Bédoin (04 90 65 63 95).*

THE NAME means "Windy
Mountain" in Provençal,
and deservedly so. A variety
of flora and fauna may be
found on the lower slopes but
moss is the only plant life to
survive at the peak, where the
winter temperature can drop
to –27° C (–17° F). The bare
white scree at the summit
makes it look snowcapped
even during summer.

In 1336, the poet Petrarch
made the first recorded ascent
of the 1,909-m (6,261-ft) peak.
Today, a road leads to the
radio beacon pinnacle, but the
trip should not be attempted in
bad weather. At other times,
spectacular views from the top
make the effort worthwhile.

**Roman mosaic from the Villa du
Paon in Vaison-la-Romaine**

Vaison-la-Romaine

Vaucluse. 🏘 *5,500.* 🚌 🛈 *place du
Chanoine Sautel (04 90 36 02 11).*
🚊 *Tue.*

THIS SITE on the banks of the
Ouvèze has been settled
since the Bronze Age, but its
name stems from five centuries
as a prosperous Roman town.

Although the upper town,
dominated by the ruins of a
12th-century castle, has some
charming narrow streets, stone
houses and fountains, Vaison's
main attractions lie on the
opposite side of the river.

The **Roman City** is split into
two districts: Puymin and La
Villasse. At Puymin, an opulent
mansion, the Villa du Paon,
and a Roman theatre have
been uncovered. In 1992, the
river Ouvèze burst its banks,
taking many lives in Vaison

and the nearby area. Damage
to some ruins, such as the
Roman bridge, has since been
repaired. Also at Vaison is the
fine Romanesque **Cathédrale
Notre-Dame-de-Nazareth,**
with medieval cloisters.

🏛 **Roman City**
Fouilles de Puymin, place du Chanoine
Sautel. 📞 *04 90 36 02 11.*
Open *Wed– Mon.* **Closed** *1 Jan,
1 May, 25 Dec.* 🌐

Orange

Vaucluse. 🏘 *29,000.* 🚌 🚌 🛈 *cours
Aristide Briand (04 90 34 70 88).* 🚊 *Thu.*

ORANGE IS A thriving regional
centre. The fields and
orchards and, in particular, the
great vineyards of the Côtes du
Rhône make it an important
marketplace for produce such
as grapes, olives, honey and
truffles. In contrast, visitors
should explore the area around
the 17th-century Hôtel de Ville,
where attractive streets open
on to quiet, shady squares.
Orange has two of the greatest
Roman monuments in Europe.

🏛 **Roman Theatre**
Place du Théâtre. 📞 *04 90 51 17 60.*
Open *daily.* **Closed** *1 Jan, 25 Dec.*
🌐♿
Dating from the 1st-century
AD reign of Augustus, the
well-preserved theatre has
perfect acoustics. It is still in
use, a spectacular setting for
world-famous concerts. The
back wall ("the finest wall in
my kingdom", said Louis XIV)
rises to a height of 38 m (125
ft) and is 103 m (338 ft) wide.

🏛 **Triumphal Arch**
Avenue de l'Arc de Triomphe.
The triple-arched monument
was built about AD 20. It is

**Statue of Augustus Caesar in the
Roman Theatre at Orange**

elaborately decorated: battle
scenes and military trophies
are mingled with flowers and
fruits. Inscriptions to the glory
of Tiberius were added later.

🏛 **Musée de la Ville**
Place des Frères-Mounet. 📞 *04 90
51 18 24.* **Open** *daily.* **Closed** *1 Jan,
25 Dec.* 🌐
Relics here reflect the history
of Orange, including 400
marble fragments which
proved to be plans of the area
based on three surveys. The
earliest dates to the reign of
the Emperor Vespasian in the
1st century BC.

Châteauneuf-du-Pape

Vaucluse. 🏘 *2,100.* 🚌 *Sorgues,
then bus.* 🛈 *place du Portail
(04 90 83 71 08).* 🚊 *Fri.*

HERE, IN THE 14TH CENTURY,
the popes of Avignon
chose to build a new castle
(*château neuf*) and plant the
vineyards from which one of

View across the vineyards of Châteauneuf-du-Pape

the finest wines of the Côtes du Rhône is produced. Now almost every doorway in this attractive little town seems to open into a *vigneron*'s cellar.

After the Wars of Religion *(see pp50–51)*, all that remained of the papal fortress were a few fragments of walls and tower, but the ruins look spectacular and offer magnificent views across to Avignon and the Vaucluse uplands beyond.

Wine festivals punctuate the year, including the Fête de la Véraison in August *(see p34)*, when the grapes start to ripen, and the Ban des Vendages in September, when the grapes are ready to be harvested.

Avignon **⑤**

Vaucluse. **🏛** 87,000. **✕** **🚊** **🚌**
ℹ 41 cours Jean Jaurès (04 90 82 65 11). **🍴** Tue–Sun.

MASSIVE RAMPARTS enclose one of the most fascinating towns in southern France. The huge **Palais des Papes** *(see pp494–5)* is the dominant feature, but the town contains other riches. To the north of the Palais is the 13th-century **Petit Palais**, once the Archbishop of Avignon's residence. It has received such notorious guests as Cesare Borgia and Louis XIV. Now a museum, it displays Romanesque and Gothic sculpture and medieval paintings of the Avignon and Italian Schools, with works by Botticelli and Carpaccio.

The rue Joseph-Vernet and rue du Roi-René are lined with many splendid 17th- and 18th-century houses. There are also some notable churches, such as the **Cathédrale de Notre-Dame-des-Doms**, with its Romanesque cupola, and the 14th-century **Eglise St-Didier**. The **Musée Lapidaire** contains statues, mosaics and carvings from pre-Roman Provence. The **Musée Calvet** features a superb array of exhibits, such as wrought-iron works and Roman finds. It also gives an overview of French art during the past 500 years, with works by Rodin, Utrillo and Dufy.

The place de l'Horloge is the centre of Avignon's social life. Under the town hall's

Pont St-Bénézet and the Palais des Papes in Avignon

Gothic clock tower are pavement cafés and a merry-go-round from 1900. One of the prettiest streets is the rue des Teinturiers. Until the 19th century, brightly-patterned calico called *indiennes* was printed here, and it inspired today's Provençal patterns.

From mid-July until mid-August, Avignon's Festival takes place at the Palais des Papes *(see p33)*. France's

Open-air performance at the Avignon Festival

largest festival, it includes ballet, drama and classical concerts. The "Off" festival has street theatre and music from folk to jazz. Most commonly associated with Avignon is the song about dancing *Sur le Pont d'Avignon*. Built from 1171–1185, the **Pont St-Bénézet** had 22 arches, until most were destroyed by floods in 1668. One of the remaining arches bears the tiny Chapelle St-Nicolas. People danced on an island below the bridge but over the years, *sous* (under) has become *sur* (on).

🏛 Petit Palais
Place du Palais. **📞** 04 90 86 44 58.
Open Wed–Mon. **Closed** 1 Jan, 1 May, 14 Jul, 1 Nov, 25 Dec. **🎫**
🏛 Musée Lapidaire
27 rue de la République. **📞** 04 90 85 75 38. **Open** Wed–Mon. **Closed** some public hols. **🎫** **♿** **📷**
🏛 Musée Calvet
65 rue Joseph Vernet. **📞** 04 90 86 33 84. **Open** Wed–Mon. **Closed** some public hols. **♿** **🎫** **📷**

Palais des Papes

CONFRONTED WITH FACTIONAL STRIFE in Rome and encouraged by the scheming of Philippe IV of France, Pope Clement V moved the papal court to Avignon in 1309. Here it remained until 1376, during which time his successors transformed the modest episcopal building into the present magnificent palace. Its heavy fortification was vital to defend against rogue bands of mercenaries. Today it is empty of the luxurious trappings of 14th-century court life, as virtually all the furnishings and works of art were destroyed or looted in the course of the centuries.

Pope Clement VI (1342–52)

Benedict XII's cloister incorporates the guest and staff wings, and the Benedictine chapel.

Trouillas tower

Belltower

Military Architecture
The palace and its ten towers were designed as an impregnable fortress. It eventually covered an area of 15,000 sq m (148,000 sq ft).

La Gache tower

Corner tower

Champeaux gate

THE AVIGNON POPES

Seven "official" popes reigned in Avignon until 1376. They were followed by two "anti-popes", the last of whom, Benedict XIII, fled in 1403. Popes or anti-popes, few were known for their sanctity. Clement V died eating powdered emeralds, prescribed as an indigestion cure; Clement VI (1342–52) thought that the best way to honour God was through luxury. Petrarch was shocked by "the filth of the universe" at court. In 1367, Urban V tried to return the Curia (papal court) to Rome, a move that became permanent in 1376.

Benedict XII (1334–42)

Consistory Hall
Simone Martini's frescoes (1340) were taken from the cathedral to replace works destroyed by fire in the papal reception hall in 1413.

Papal Power
More like a war-lord's citadel than a papal palace, the building's heavy fortification reflects the insecure climate of 14th-century religious life.

★ Grand Tinel
A series of fine 17th- and 19th-century Gobelin tapestries now hang in the vast banqueting hall, where cardinals gathered to elect a new pope.

Angels' tower

★ Stag Room
Fourteenth-century hunting frescoes and ceramic tiles make Clement VI's study the palace's most lovely room.

Pope's chamber

Great courtyard

BUILDING THE PALACE

The palace comprises Pope Benedict XII's simple Palais Vieux (1334–42) and Clement VI's flamboyant Palais Neuf (1342–52). Ten towers, some of which are more than 50 m (164 ft) high, are set in the walls to protect its four wings.

The Great Chapel is 20 m (66 ft) high and covers an area of 780 sq m (8,400 sq ft).

KEY

☐	By Benedict XII (1334–42)
☐	By Clement VI (1342–52)

The Great Audience Hall is divided into two naves by five columns with bestiary sculpture on their capitals.

STAR FEATURES

★ Grand Tinel

★ Stag Room

Carpentras

Vaucluse. 25,500. 170 allée Jaurès (04 90 63 57 88). Fri.

IN 1320, CARPENTRAS became capital of the papal county of Venaissin, and remained so until 1791. Modern boulevards trace the former ramparts, with only one original gate, the Porte d'Orange, surviving.

In the Middle Ages the town was home to a large Jewish community, and it remains a Jewish centre. The 1367 **Synagogue** is the oldest in France. The Sanctuary has been restored but the baths and bakery are unchanged.

While not openly persecuted under papal rule, many Jews changed faith, entering **Cathédrale St-Siffrein** by the Porte Juive (Jews' Door).

The Law Courts were built in 1640 as the episcopal palace. Its Criminal Court has 17th-century carved tablets of the local towns. In the pharmacy of the Hôtel-Dieu, the 18th-century cupboards are painted with quaint figures of monkey "doctors". More regional art and history is on show at the **Musée Comtadin**.

Synagogue
Place de la Mairie. 04 90 63 39 97. **Open** Mon–Fri. **Closed** Jewish feast days.
Musée Comtadin
Bd Albin-Durand. 04 90 63 04 92. **Open** Wed–Mon. restricted.

Riverfront and watermill at Fontaine-de-Vaucluse

Fontaine-de-Vaucluse

Vaucluse. 500. chemin de la Fontaine (04 90 20 32 22).

THE MAIN ATTRACTION here is the source of the river Sorgue. It is the most powerful spring in France, gushing at up to 90,000 litres (19,800 gallons) per second from an underground river at the foot of a cliff. It powers a paper mill which still employs 15th-century techniques. There are also several museums. One is devoted to the poet Petrarch, who lived and wrote here, and another to the French Resistance of World War II. More bizarre is the macabre **Musée Historique de la Justice et de l'Injustice**, where the exhibits include a guillotine.

Gordes

Vaucluse. 2,000. Le Château (04 90 72 02 75). Tue.

PERCHED VILLAGES abound in Provence but Gordes is said to attract the most visitors, and it is easy to understand why. Dominated by a 16th-century château, the town forms such a harmonious whole that it might have been designed by an architect. The arcaded medieval lanes add to the attractive hilltop position.

Just south lies the **Village des Bories**, a bizarre, primitive habitat. Bories are tiny beehive-shaped huts built of overlapping dry stones. The construction techniques are thought to date back to Neolithic times. This group was inhabited from the 16th to the early 20th centuries.

The **Abbaye de Sénanque**, north of Gourdes, is one of the finest Romanesque Cistercian monastries in France.

Château de Gordes
04 90 72 02 75. **Open** Mon–Fri. **Closed** 1 Jan, 1 May, 25 Dec.
Village des Bories
Les Savourins, Route de Cavaillon. 04 90 72 03 48. **Open** daily.

Luberon

Vaucluse. Avignon. Cavaillon, Avignon. Apt. Apt (04 90 74 03 18).

A HUGE LIMESTONE range, the Montagne du Luberon is one of the most appealing areas of Provence. Rising to 1,125 m (3,690 ft), it combines

Perched village of Gordes

wild areas with picturesque villages. Almost the entire area is designated a regional nature park. Within it are more than 1,000 plant species and cedar and oak forests. The wildlife is varied, with eagles, vultures, snakes, beavers, wild boar and the largest European lizards. The park headquarters are in **Apt**, the capital of the Luberon.

Once notorious as the haunt of highwaymen, the Luberon hills now hide sumptuous holiday homes. The major village is **Bonnieux**, with its 12th-century church and 13th-century walls. Also popular are **Roussillon**, with red ochre buildings, **Lacoste**, the site of the ruins of the Marquis de Sade's castle, and **Ansouis**, with its 14th-century Eglise St-Martin and 17th-century castle. **Ménerbes**, drew to it the writer Peter Mayle, whose tales of life here brought this quiet region a worldwide audience.

Herb stall at St-Rémy-de-Provence

St-Rémy-de-Provence ⑩

Bouches-du-Rhône. 9,500. place Jean Jaurès (04 90 92 05 22). Wed & Sat.

FOR CENTURIES St-Rémy, with its tree-lined boulevards, fountains and narrow streets, had two claims to fame. One was that Vincent Van Gogh spent a year here, in 1889–90, at the St-Paul-de-Mausole hospital. *Wheat Field with Cypress* and *Ravine* are among the 150 works he produced here. St-Rémy-de-Provence was also the birthplace in 1503 of Nostradamus, known for his cryptic prophecies. But, in 1921, St-Rémy found new fame when archaeologists unearthed the fascinating Roman ruins at **Glanum**. Little remains of the ancient city, sacked in AD 480 by the Goths, but the site is very impressive. Around the ruins of an arch from the first century BC are the foundations of buildings, fragments of walls and a vast mausoleum, decorated with scenes such as the death of Adonis.

Glanum

04 90 92 23 79. ***Open*** *daily.* ***Closed*** *1 Jan, 1 May, 1 & 11 Nov, 25 Dec.*

Les Baux-de-Provence ⑪

Bouches-du-Rhône. 460. Arles. ilôt "Post Tenebras Lux" (04 90 54 34 39).

ONE OF THE STRANGEST places in Provence, the deserted citadel of Les Baux stands like a natural extension of a huge rocky plateau. The ruined castle and old houses overlook the Val d'Enfer (Infernal Valley), with its weird rocks, once the haunt of witches and goblins according to legend.

In the Middle Ages Les Baux was home to powerful feudal lords, who claimed descent from the Magus Balthazar. It was the most famous of the Provençal Cours d'Amour, at which troubadours sang the praises of high-born ladies. The ideal of everlasting but unrequited courtly love contrasts with the war-like nature of the citadel's lords.

The glory of Les Baux ended in 1632. It had become a Protestant stronghold and Louis XIII ordered its destruction.

Deserted medieval citadel of Les Baux-de-Provence

The living village below has a pleasant little square, the 12th-century **Eglise St-Vincent** and the **Musée Yves Brayer**. In 1821 bauxite was discovered (and named) here and the disused quarries now form the backdrop for spectacular audio-visual displays, known as the **Cathédrale d'Images**.

To the southwest are the ruins of the **Abbaye de Montmajour**. Its 12th-century Romanesque Eglise de Notre-Dame, is noted for its circular crypt.

Musée Yves Brayer

Hôtel des Porcelet. 04 90 54 36 99. ***Open*** *daily.* ***Closed*** *Jan–mid-Feb.*

Parading the Tarasque, 1850

Tarascon ⑫

Bouches-du-Rhône. 11,000. 59 rue des Halles (04 90 91 03 52). Tue.

ACCORDING TO LEGEND, the town takes its name from the Tarasque, a monster, half-animal and half-fish, which terrorized the countryside. It was tamed by Sainte Marthe, who is buried in the church here. An effigy of the Tarasque is still paraded through the streets each June *(see p33)*.

The 15th-century **Château** on the banks of the Rhône is Tarascon's most striking feature. One of the finest examples of Gothic military architecture in Provence, its sombre exterior gives no hint of the beauties within: the Flemish-Gothic courtyard; the spiral staircase; and painted ceilings of the banqueting hall.

On the opposite bank is Beaucaire, its own ruined castle surrounded by gardens.

Château

Bd du Roi René. 04 90 91 01 93. ***Open*** *daily.* ***Closed*** *1 Jan, 1 May, 1 & 11 Nov, 25 Dec.*

Arles ⑬

Emperor Constantine

FEW OTHER TOWNS IN PROVENCE combine all the region's charms so well as Arles. Its position on the Rhône makes it a natural, historic gateway to the Camargue (see pp500–1). Its Roman remains, such as the arena and Constantine's baths, are complemented by the ochre walls and Roman-tiled roofs of later buildings. A bastion of Provençal tradition and culture, its museums are among the best in the region. Van Gogh spent time here in 1888–9, but Arles is no longer the industrial town he painted. Visitors are now its main business, and entertainment ranges from the Arles Festival to bullfights.

Palais Constantine was once a grand imperial palace. Now only its vast Roman baths remain, dating from the 4th century AD. They are remarkably well-preserved and give an idea of the luxury that bathers enjoyed.

Musée Réattu

This museum, in the old Commandery of the Knights of Malta, houses witty Picasso sketches, paintings by the local artist Jacques Réattu (1760–1833) and sculptures by Ossip Zadkine, including La Grande Odalisque (1932), *above.*

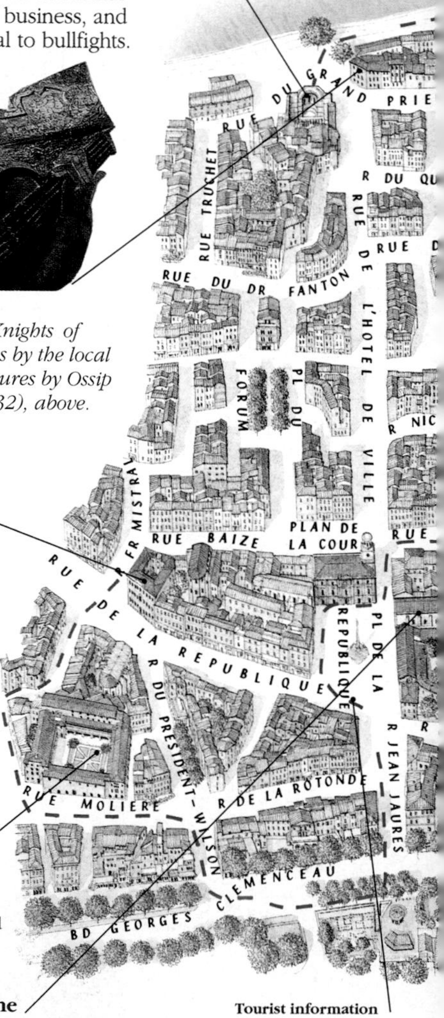

Museon Arlaten

In 1904 the poet Frédéric Mistral used his Nobel Prize money to establish this museum devoted to his beloved native Provence. Parts of the collection are arranged in room settings, and even the museum guides wear traditional Arles costume.

Espace Van Gogh, in a former hospital where the artist was treated in 1889, is a cultural centre devoted to his life and work.

★ Eglise St-Trophime

This church combines a noble 12th-century Romanesque exterior with superb Romanesque and Gothic cloisters. The ornate main portal is carved with saints and apostles.

Tourist information

| 0 metres | 100 |
| 0 yards | 100 |

LES ALYSCAMPS

A tree-lined avenue of broken medieval tombs is the focal point of these "Elysian Fields" to the southeast of Arles. It became Christian in the 4th century and was a prestigious burial ground until the 12th century. Some sarcophagi were sold and are in museums; others have been neglected. Mentioned in Dante's *Inferno*, painted by Van Gogh and Gauguin, it is a place for thought and inspiration.

Les Alyscamps **by Paul Gauguin**

VISITORS' CHECKLIST

Bouches-du-Rhône. 🏠 52,600. ✈ 25 km (13 miles) NW Arles. 🚉 av Paulin Talabot. 🅸 pl de la République (04 90 18 41 20). ⌂ Wed & Sat. 🎪 Arles Festival (Jul); Premices du Riz (Sep). **Museon Arlaten open** Jul–Sep: daily; Oct–Jun: Tue–Sun. **Closed** public hols. 🎫 **Musée Réattu open** daily. **Closed** public hols. 🎫

Notre-Dame-de-la-Major is the church in which the *gardiens* (cowboys) of the Camargue celebrate the feast day of their patron saint, St George. Although the building dates from the 14th to 17th centuries, a Roman temple existed on this spot hundreds of years earlier.

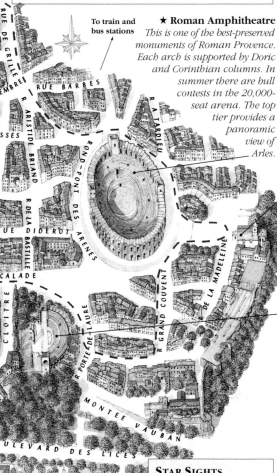

To train and bus stations

★ **Roman Amphitheatre**
This is one of the best-preserved monuments of Roman Provence. Each arch is supported by Doric and Corinthian columns. In summer there are bull contests in the 20,000-seat arena. The top tier provides a panoramic view of Arles.

★ **Roman Theatre**
Once a fortress, its stones were later used for other buildings. Today, the theatre stages the Arles Festival. Its remaining columns are called the "two widows".

STAR SIGHTS

★ **Roman Amphitheatre**

★ **Roman Theatre**

★ **Eglise St-Trophime**

KEY

– – – Suggested route

The Camargue ⑭

Sunset over the Camargue

THE RHONE DELTA was responsible for the formation of the 140,000 ha (346,000 acres) of wetlands, pastures, dunes and salt flats that make up the Camargue, but human efforts are needed to preserve it. The region now maintains a fragile eco-logical balance, in which a unique collection of flora flourishes, including tamarisk and narcissi, and fauna such as egrets and ibises. The pastures provide grazing for sheep, cattle and small white Arab-type horses, ridden by the *gardians* or cowboys, a hardy community who traditionally lived in thatched huts *(cabanes)* and still play their part in keeping Camargue traditions alive.

Camargue gardian

Black Bulls

In a Provençal bull contest (known as a course*), the animals are not killed. Instead, red rosettes are plucked from between their horns with a small hook.*

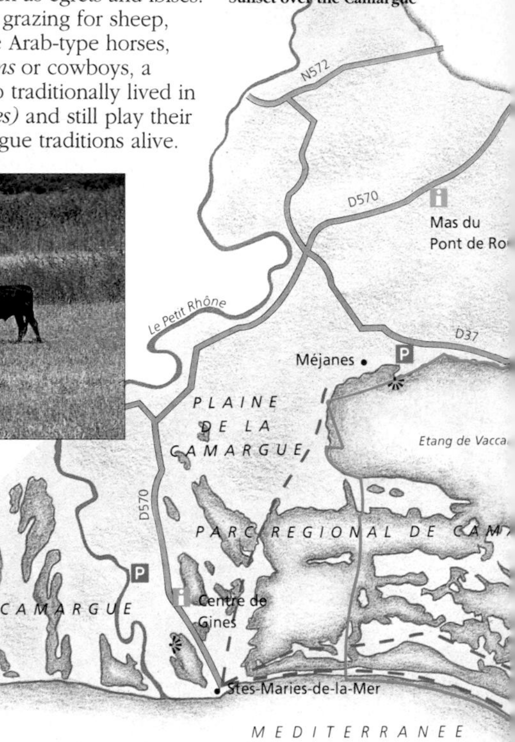

Mas du Pont de Ro

N572

D570

D37

Le Petit Rhône

Méjanes •

P L A I N E   D E   L A   C A M A R G U E

Etang de Vacca

P A R C   R E G I O N A L   D E   C A M

D570

P E T I T E   C A M A R G U E

Centre de Ginès

Stes-Maries-de-la-Mer

M E D I T E R R A N E E

0 kilometres   5
0 miles   5

Les Stes-Maries-de-la-Mer

The May gypsy pilgrimage to this fortified church marks the legendary arrival by boat in AD 18 of Mary Magdalene, St Martha and the sister of the Virgin Mary. Statues in the church depict the event.

Flamingoes

These striking birds are always associated with the Camargue, but the region supports many other breeds, including herons, kingfishers, owls and birds of prey. The area around Ginès is the best place to see them.

KEY

	Nature reserve boundary
— —	Walking routes
– –	Walking and cycling routes

VISITORS' CHECKLIST

Bouches-du-Rhône. ✈ *90 km (56 miles) east, Marignane-Marseille.* 🚂 *av Paulin Talabot, Arles.* 🚌 *av Paulin Talabot, Arles.* ℹ *5 av van Gogh, Les Stes-Maries-de-la-Mer; La Capelière, off D36B.* ☎ *04 90 97 82 55.* 🎪 *Les Pèlerinages (end May, end Oct).* **Musée Camarguais**, Mas du Pont de Rousty, Arles. ☎ *04 90 97 10 82.* **Open** *Apr–Sep: 9:15am–5:45pm daily; Oct–Mar: 10:15am–4:45pm Wed–Mon.* **Closed** *public hols.* 🅿 ♿

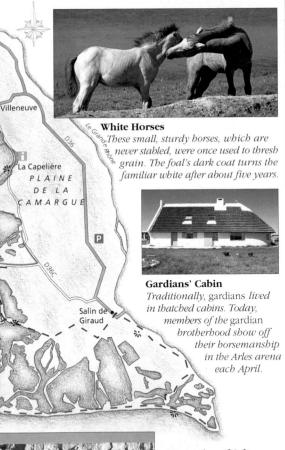

Villeneuve

Le Grande Rhône

D36

ℹ La Capelière

PLAINE DE LA CAMARGUE

🅿

D36C

Salin de Giraud

White Horses

These small, sturdy horses, which are never stabled, were once used to thresh grain. The foal's dark coat turns the familiar white after about five years.

Gardians' Cabin

Traditionally, gardians lived in thatched cabins. Today, members of the gardian brotherhood show off their horsemanship in the Arles arena each April.

Mountains of Salt

Sea salt is by far the largest "harvest" of the Camargue. Throughout the summer, vast brine pans evaporate and the crystals are heaped into shimmering camelles *up to 8 m (26 ft) high.*

Aix-en-Provence ⑮

Bouches du Rhône. 👥 *126,000.* 🚂 🚌 ℹ *2 place du Général de Gaulle (04 42 16 11 61).* 🚌 *daily.*

FOUNDED BY the Romans in 103 BC, Aix was frequently attacked, first by the Visigoths in AD 477, later by Lombards, Franks and Saracens. Despite this, the city prospered. By the end of the 12th century it was capital of Provence. A centre of art and learning, it reached its peak in the 15th century during the reign of "Good King" René. He is shown in Nicolas Froment's *Triptych of the Burning Bush* in the 13th-century Gothic **Cathédrale de St-Sauveur**, also noted for its 16th-century walnut doors, Merovingian baptistry and Romanesque cloisters. Aix's many museums include the **Musée Granet** of fine arts and archaeology, and the **Musée des Tapisseries** (tapestries), in the Palais de l'Archevêché.

Aix has been called "the city of a thousand fountains". Three of the best are situated on cours Mirabeau. On one side of this tree-lined avenue are 17th- and 18th-century buildings with wrought-iron balconies. On the other are the cafés which are so much a part of the city's social life.

The Old Town centres on place de l'Hôtel de Ville, with its colourful flower market.

In the northwest of town is the **Pavillon de Vendôme**, housing furniture and works of art by Van Loo.

Aix's most famous son is Paul Cézanne. His studio, the **Atelier Paul Cézanne**, is kept as it was when he died in 1906. Montagne Ste-Victoire, inspiration for many of his paintings, is 15 km (9 miles) east of Aix.

🏛 **Musée Granet**
place St-Jean de Malte. ☎ *04 42 38 14 70.* **Open** *Wed–Mon.* **Closed** *some public hols.* 🅿

🏛 **Musée des Tapisseries**
place de l'Ancien Archevêché. ☎ *04 42 23 09 91.* **Open** *Wed–Mon.* **Closed** *some public hols.* 🅿

🏛 **Atelier Paul Cézanne**
9 av Paul Cézanne. ☎ *04 42 21 06 53.* **Open** *daily.* **Closed** *some public hols.* 🅿

Old harbour of Marseille, looking towards the quai de Rive Neuve

Marseille ⑯

Bouches-du-Rhône. 🚉 800,000.
✈ 🚉 🚌 ⛴ 🚇 4 La Canebière
(04 91 13 89 00). 🛍 daily.

A GREEK SETTLEMENT, founded
in the 7th century BC,
then called Massilia, Marseille
was seized by the Romans in
49 BC. It became the "Gateway
to the West" for most Oriental
trade. France's largest port and
second-largest city has close
links with the Middle East
and North Africa. It is exotic,
cosmopolitan and lively, with
a reputation for corruption
and drug trafficking. The Vieux
Port was the setting for Marcel
Pagnol's comic trilogy, *Marius,
Fanny* and *César*, satirizing
the Marseillais character.

In Marseille, narrow stepped
streets, quiet squares and fine
18th-century façades contrast
with the bustle of boulevard
Canebière and the Cité
Radieuse, Le Corbusier's postwar radical housing complex.
A striking new landmark is
L'Hôtel du Département, the
local government headquarters,
a bright blue structure on
stilts, designed by the British
architect Will Alsop.

The old harbour now only
handles small boats, but its
daily fish market is renowned.
Gourmets agree that the

bouillabaisse (see p458) is
very authentic here.

Several museums in the
old harbour area include the
Musée des Docks Romains.
The wreck of a Roman ship
found in 1974 is on show at
the **Musée d'Histoire de
Marseille** and there are paintings of old Marseille at the
Musée de Vieux Marseille.

⛴ Château d'If
🎟 04 91 59 02 30. **Open** *daily.* 🖼
The Château d'If (Castle of
Yew) stands on a tiny island 2
km (1 mile) southwest of the
port. A formidable fortress, it
was built in 1524 to house
artillery, but never put to military use and later became a
prison. Alexandre Dumas'
fictional "Count of Monte
Cristo" was supposed to have
been imprisoned here, and
visitors can see a special cell,
complete with escape hole.

Most real-life inmates were
either common criminals or
political prisoners.

🏛 Notre-Dame-de-la-Garde
Built between 1853 and 1864,
this Neo-Byzantine basilica
dominates the city. Its belfry,
46 m (151 ft) high, is capped
by a huge gilded statue of the
Virgin. The lavishly decorated
interior has coloured marble
and mosaic facings.

🏛 Abbaye St-Victor
Similar to a fortress in
appearance, the abbey was
rebuilt in the 11th century
after destruction by the
Saracens. In the French
Revolution, the rebels used it
as a barracks and prison.

There is an intriguing crypt
in the abbey's church, with
an original catacomb chapel
and a number of pagan and
Christian sarcophagi.

On 2 February each year, St-
Victor becomes a place of
pilgrimage. Boat-shaped cakes
are sold to commemorate the
legendary arrival of St Mary
Magdalene, Lazarus and St
Martha nearly 2,000 years ago.

🏛 Cathédrale de la Major
Built in Neo-Byzantine style,
this is the largest 19th-century
church in France, 141 m (463
ft) long and 70 m (230 ft) high.
In the crypt are the tombs of
the bishops of Marseille. By it
is the small and beautiful Ancienne Cathédrale de la Major.

🏛 Vieille Charité
2 rue de la Charité.
🎟 04 91 14 58 80. **Open** *Tue–Sun.*
Closed *public hols.* 🖼 ♿
In 1640, the construction of a
shelter "for the poor and
beggars" of Marseille was
begun by royal decree. One
hundred years later, Pierre
Puget's hospital and domed

Le Corbusier's innovative Cité Radieuse in Marseille

Fish market at Marseille

church were finally opened.
Now, the restored building
houses the Musée d'Archéologie Egyptienne, with its fine
collection of Egyptian artifacts.

🏛 Musée des Beaux Arts

Palais Longchamp, place Henri Dunan.
📞 04 91 62 21 17. **Open** Tue–Sun.
Closed 1 Jan, 1 May, 25 Dec. 📷
This museum is housed in the
handsome 19th-century Palais
Longchamp. Works include
Michel Serre's graphic views
of Marseille's plague of 1721,
Pierre Puget's town plans for
the city and murals depicting
it in Greek and Roman times.

Cassis ⑰

Bouches-du-Rhône. 🏘 8,000. 🚊 🚌
🛈 place Baragnon (04 42 01 71 17).
🚢 Wed & Fri.

MANY OF THE VILLAGES along
this coast have been built
up, to the point where they
have all but lost their original
charm, but Cassis is still much
the same little fishing port that
attracted artists such as Dufy,
Signac and Derain. This is a
place in which to relax at a
waterside café, watching the
fishermen or street performers,
while enjoying a plate of seafood and a bottle of the local
dry white wine for which
Cassis is famous.

From Marseille to Cassis the
coastline forms narrow inlets,
the **Calanques**, their jagged
white cliffs (some as much as
400 m/1,312 ft high) reflected
in dazzling turquoise water.
Wildlife abounds here, with
countless seabirds, foxes, stone
martens, bats, large snakes and
lizards. The flora is no less
impressive, with more than
900 plant species, of which 50
are classified as rare. The En-
Vau and Sormiou Calanques
are especially lovely.

Toulon ⑱

Var. 🏘 170,000. ✈ 🚊 🚌 ⛴ 🛈
Place Raimu (04 94 18 53 00).
🚢 Tue–Sun.

THIS NAVAL BASE has a long
maritime history. In 1793 it
was captured by an Anglo-
Spanish fleet, but was boldly
retaken by the then-unknown
young commander Napoleon
Bonaparte. Nearly 150 years
later, Nazi troops took Toulon.
The French fleet, trapped in
the harbour, sank its own ships
to keep them from the enemy.

The **Musée de la Marine** is
a focus for this history, with
artifacts such as finely crafted
figureheads and model ships.

The tower of the former town
hall is virtually all that remains
of the pre-war quai Cronstadt.
Rebuilt and renamed quai
Stalingrad, its cafés and shops
make it a favourite meeting
place for Toulonnais. The war-
damaged Old Town has a few
original buildings, and the fish
market is worth a visit.

🏛 Musée de la Marine

Place Monsenergue. 📞 04 94 02 02
01. **Open** Jul–Aug: daily; Sep–Jun:
Wed–Mon. **Closed** public hols. 📷 ♿

Paul Signac's *Cap Canaille*, painted at Cassis in 1889

Tour of the Gorges du Verdon

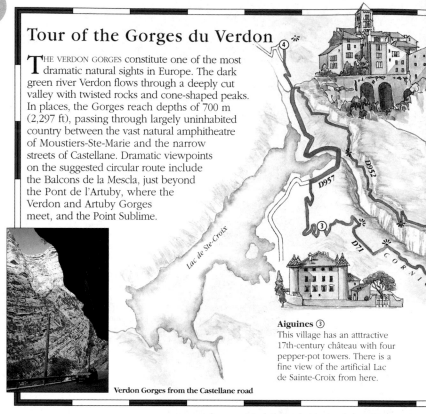

THE VERDON GORGES constitute one of the most dramatic natural sights in Europe. The dark green river Verdon flows through a deeply cut valley with twisted rocks and cone-shaped peaks. In places, the Gorges reach depths of 700 m (2,297 ft), passing through largely uninhabited country between the vast natural amphitheatre of Moustiers-Ste-Marie and the narrow streets of Castellane. Dramatic viewpoints on the suggested circular route include the Balcons de la Mescla, just beyond the Pont de l'Artuby, where the Verdon and Artuby Gorges meet, and the Point Sublime.

Verdon Gorges from the Castellane road

Aiguines ③
This village has an atttractive 17th-century château with four pepper-pot towers. There is a fine view of the artificial Lac de Sainte-Croix from here.

Hyères ⑲

Var. 👥 52,000. ✈ 🚉 🚌 ⛴
ℹ Rotonde Jean Salusse (04 94 65 18 55). 🛒 Tue, Sat & 3rd Thu of month.

TOWARDS THE END of the 18th century, Hyères became one of the first health resorts of the Côte d'Azur. Among its many distinguished visitors during the next century were Queen Victoria, Robert Louis Stevenson and Edith Wharton.

The main sights are found in the medieval streets of the Vieille Ville which lead past the spacious, flag-stoned place Massillon (scene of a colourful daily market) to a ruined castle and panoramic views over the coast.

Modern Hyères is imbued with a lingering Belle Epoque charm which has become popular with experimental film-makers. It continues to attract a health-conscious crowd and is a major centre for aquatic sports.

Fishing off Porquerolles, the largest of the Iles d'Hyères

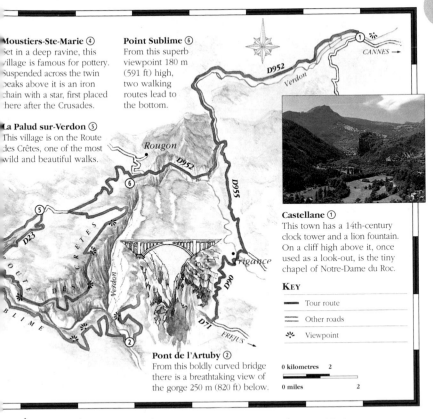

Moustiers-Ste-Marie ④
Set in a deep ravine, this village is famous for pottery. Suspended across the twin peaks above it is an iron chain with a star, first placed here after the Crusades.

Point Sublime ⑥
From this superb viewpoint 180 m (591 ft) high, two walking routes lead to the bottom.

La Palud sur-Verdon ⑤
This village is on the Route des Crêtes, one of the most wild and beautiful walks.

Castellane ①
This town has a 14th-century clock tower and a lion fountain. On a cliff high above it, once used as a look-out, is the tiny chapel of Notre-Dame du Roc.

KEY

━━━ Tour route

═══ Other roads

⚜ Viewpoint

Pont de l'Artuby ②
From this boldly curved bridge there is a breathtaking view of the gorge 250 m (820 ft) below.

0 kilometres   2

0 miles   2

Îles d'Hyères ⓴

Var. ✈ Toulon-Hyères. 🚌 🚗 ⛴
Hyères. 🛈 Hyères (04 94 65 18 55).

THIS GLAMOROUS TRIO of islands, sometimes referred to as the Iles d'Or, after the gold colour of their cliffs, can be easily reached by boat from mainland Hyères.

Porquerolles, the largest of the three, measures 7 km (4.5 miles) by 3 km (2 miles). It is covered in rich vegetation, much of which, for instance the Mexican bellombra tree, was introduced from a variety of exotic foreign climes.

The island's main town, also known as Porquerolles, looks more like a north African colonial settlement than any Provençal village. It was established in 1820 as a retirement town for Napoleon's most honoured troops.

All the island's beaches lie along the northern coastline. The best, the long, sandy Plage Notre-Dame, one of the finest beaches in Provence, sits in a sheltered bay about an hour's walk from Porquerolles.

A stroll around lush, hilly **Port-Cros**, covering just 2.5 sq km (1 sq mile), takes the best part of a day. It rises to 195 m (640 ft), the highest point on any of the islands.

Port-Cros has been a national park since 1963. A unique reserve of Mediterranean flora and fauna, its surrounding waters are also protected. There is even a 300 m (984 ft) scenic swimming route. You can buy a waterproof guide to the underwater wildlife, which includes rare rock fish.

The wild, virtually treeless **Île de Levant** is reached by boat from Port-Cros. Its main draw is the oldest naturist colony in France, Héliopolis, founded in 1931. The eastern half of the island, controlled by the French navy, is permanently closed to the public.

Massif des Maures ㉑

Var. ✈ Toulon-Hyères. 🚌 Hyères, Toulon or Fréjus. 🚗 Bormes-les-Mimosas. ⛴ Toulon. 🛈 Bormes-les-Mimosas (04 94 71 15 17).

THE DENSE WILDERNESS of pine, oak and sweet chestnut covering the Maures mountain range probably gave rise to its name, meaning dark or gloomy. It extends nearly 65 km (40 miles) between Hyères and Fréjus.

The D558 north of Cogolin offers a route to the heart of the Maures. Along the way is Garde-Freinet, well-known for its bottle cork industry.

Northwest of Cannet-des-Maures, in splendid isolation, lies the Romanesque Abbaye de Thoronet. With the abbeys at Sénanque, in Vaucluse, and Silvacane, in the Bouches-du-Rhône, it is known as one of the "Three Sisters" of Provence.

Harbourside at St-Tropez

St-Tropez ②

Var. 🏠 6,000. 🚌 🛈 quai Jean Jaurès (04 94 97 45 21). 🚢 Tue & Sat.

THE GEOGRAPHY of St-Tropez kept it untouched by the earliest development of the Côte d'Azur. Tucked away at the tip of a peninsula, it is the only north-facing town on the coast and so did not appeal to those seeking a warm and sheltered winter resort. In 1892 the painter Paul Signac was among the first outsiders to respond to its unspoiled charm, encouraging friends, such as the painters Van Dongen, Matisse and Bonnard, to join him. In the 1920s the chic Parisian writer Colette also made her home here. St-Tropez also began to attract star-spotters, hoping for a glimpse of celebrities such as the Prince of Wales.

During World War II the beaches around St-Tropez were the scene of Allied landings, and the town was heavily bombed. Then, in the 1950s, young Parisians began to arrive, and the Bardot-Vadim film helped to create the reputation of modern St-Tropez as a playground for gilded youth. The wild public behaviour and turbulent love affairs of Roger Vadim, Brigitte Bardot, Sacha Distel and others left fiction far behind. Mass tourism followed, with visitors once again more interested in spotting a celebrity than in visiting the **Musée de la Marine** in the 16th-century citadel above the town, or the **Musée de l'Annonciade** with its outstanding collection of

works by Signac, Derain, Rouault, Bonnard and others. Bardot had a villa at La Madrague, but tourists invaded her privacy, so she left.

Today, there are far more luxury yachts than fishing boats moored in St-Tropez harbour. Its cafés make ideal bases for people- and yacht-watching. Another centre of the action is place des Lices, both for the Harley-Davidson set and the morning market.

St-Tropez has its own small beaches but the best are to be found just outside the town, including the golden curve of Pampelonne, jammed with beach clubs and fashionable restaurants. This is the beach on which to see and be seen. St-Tropez has no train station, so driving and parking can be a nightmare in summer.

It is said that St-Tropez takes its name from a Roman soldier martyred as a Christian by the Emperor Nero. Each year in May a *bravade* in his honour takes place when an effigy of the saint is carried through the town to the accompaniment of musket fire.

Nearby are two small towns of differing character but equal charm. **Port-Grimaud** was only built in 1966 but the sensitive use of traditional architecture makes it seem older. Most of its "streets" are canals and many homes have their own mooring. Up in the hills, the winding streets of **Ramatuelle** have been restored to bijou perfection by the largely celebrity population.

🏛 **Musée de la Marine**
Montée de la Citadelle. 📞 04 94 97 49 53. **Open** mid-Dec–mid-Nov: Wed–Mon. **Closed** 1 Jan, 1 May, 25 Dec. 🖼

🏛 **Musée de l'Annonciade**
Place Grammont. 📞 04 94 97 04 01. **Open** Dec–Oct: Wed–Mon (Jul–Aug: daily). **Closed** 1 Jan, Ascension, 1 May, 25 Dec. 🖼

Stylish solution to the traffic problems in St-Tropez

BRIGITTE BARDOT

In 1956, Brigitte Bardot's film, *And God Created Woman*, was shot in St-Tropez by her new husband, Roger Vadim. By settling in St Tropez, "BB" the sex-goddess changed the fortunes of the sleepy little fishing village and ultimately the Côte d'Azur, making it the centre of her hedonistic lifestyle. In 1974, on her 40th birthday, she celebrated her retirement from films at Club 55 on Pampelonne Beach, and now devotes her time to her animal sanctuary.

Brigitte Bardot in 1956

Digne-les-Bains ㉓

Alpes-de-Haute-Provence. 🔊 *17,000.*
🚉 🚌 🛈 *Rond point du 11 Novembre*
(04 92 36 62 62). 🖢 *Wed, Sat.*

THIS CHARMING SPA town in
the foothills of the Alps
features in Victor Hugo's *Les
Misérables*: the hero stole a
bishop's candlesticks. A trip
on the *Train des Pignes* from
Nice offers superb views. Apart
from the spa, Digne also offers
a lavender festival *(see p34)*
and the **Fondation Alexandra
David-Néel**, a Tibetan centre.

**🏛 Fondation Alexandra
David-Néel**
27 av du Juin. 📞 *04 92 31 32 38.*
Open *daily.* 🚹

Fréjus ㉔

Var. 🔊 *45,000.* 🚉 🚌 🛈 *325 rue
Jean Jaurès (04 94 51 83 83).* 🖢
Wed & Sat (also Jul–Aug: Mon).

THE MODERN TOWN of Fréjus is
dwarfed in importance by
two impressive historic sites.
The remains of the Roman port
of **Amphithéâtre** (founded
by Julius Caesar in 49 BC) may
not be as complete as those at
Orange or Arles but they are
of exceptional variety. A great
amphitheatre, fragments of an
aqueduct, a theatre and part
of a rampart gateway remain.
The sea has receded over the
centuries and there are few
traces of the original harbour.
   The cathedral on place
Formigé marks the entrance
to the **Cité Episcopale**. The
fortified enclave includes the
5th-century baptistry, one of
the oldest in France, and the
cathedral cloister, its coffered
medieval roof decorated with
scenes from the Apocalypse.
   In 1959 Fréjus was hit by a
wall of water as the Malpasset
Barrage burst. To the north the
ruined dam can still be seen.

🏛 Amphithéâtre
Rue Henri Vadon. 📞 *04 94 51 83 83.*
Open *Wed–Mon.* **Closed** *1 Jan,
25 Dec.* 🚹
🏛 Cité Episcopale
58 rue de Fleury. 📞 *04 94 51 26 30.*
Open *Apr–Sep: daily; Oct–Mar:
Wed–Mon.* **Closed** *1 Jan, 1 & 11
Nov, 25 Dec.* 📷

THE CREATION OF A PERFUME

The best perfumes begin as a formula of essential
oils extracted from natural sources. The blend of
aromas is created by a perfumer called a "nose"
because of his or her exceptional sense of smell.
A perfume may use as many as 300 essences,
all painstakingly extracted from plants by
various methods: steam distillation, extraction
by volatile solvents and *enfleurage à froid*
(for costly or potent essences). With this process, pungent blossoms are placed onto layers of
Lavender fats for several days until the fats are saturated.
water The oils are then
"washed" out
with alcohol, and
when this evaporates,
it leaves the "pure"
perfume essence behind.   **Grasse flowers**

St-Raphaël ㉕

Var. 🔊 *28,000.* 🚉 🚌 🛈 *rue
Waldeck Rousseau (04 94 19 52 52).*
🖢 *daily.*

DELIGHTFULLY SITUATED, St-
Raphaël is a charming,
old-style Côte d'Azur resort
with Art Nouveau architecture
and a palm-fronded promenade. Aside from its beaches,
it offers a marina, a casino,
Roman ruins, a 12th-century
church and a museum with
treasures from a Roman wreck
found by Jacques Cousteau.
   It was here that Napoleon
Bonaparte landed in 1799 on
his return from Egypt.

Grasse ㉖

Alpes-Maritimes. 🔊 *43,000.* 🚌
🛈 *Palais des Congrès, cours Honoré
Cresp (04 93 36 66 66).* 🖢 *Tue–Sun.*

CRADLED BY HILLS, with
views out to sea,
Grasse is surrounded
by fields of flowers;
lavender, mimosa,
jasmine and roses.
Grasse has been the
centre of the world's
perfume industry
since the 16th cen-
tury, when Catherine
de' Médici set the
fashion for scented
leather gloves. At
that time, Grasse
was also known
as the centre
for leather
tanning. The

tanneries have gone, but the
perfume houses founded in
the 18th and 19th centuries are
still in business, although
today Grasse perfumes are
mostly made from imported
flowers or chemical essences.
Fragonard and Molinard have
their own museums, but the
best place to learn more is at
the **Musée Internationale
de la Parfumerie**, which has
a garden of fragrant plants.
   Grasse was the birthplace of
Jean-Honoré Fragonard, the
artist. The **Villa-Musée Fragonard** is decorated with murals
by his son. Fragonard's only
known religious work is in
the **Cathédrale de Nôtre-
Dame-du-Puy** in the Old
Town, with three paintings by
Rubens. The place aux Aires
and the place du Cours typify
the unspoiled charm of Grasse,
surrounded by narrow arcaded
streets with Renaissance staircases and balconies.

**🏛 Musée International
de la Parfumerie**
8 place du Cours. 📞 *04 93 36
80 20.* **Open** *Jun–Sep: daily;
Oct–May: Wed–Sun.*
Closed *public hols.*
📷 🚹
**🏛 Villa-Musée
Fragonard**
23 bd Fragonard. 📞 *04 93
36 01 61.* **Open** *Jun–Sep:
daily; Oct–May: Wed–Sun.*
Closed *public hols.* 📷 *(free
Wed & Sun).*

**Statue honouring
Jean-Honoré
Fragonard in Grasse**

Lavender fields near Puimoisson, Alpes-de-Haute-Provence ▷

High summer on the beach at Cannes, overlooked by the Carlton Hotel

Cannes ㉗

Alpes-Maritimes. 👥 70,000. ✈ ▤
🚢 🛈 *Palais des Festivals, 1 La Croisette (04 93 39 24 53).* ▤ *Tue–Sun.*

JUST AS GRASSE is synonymous with the perfume industry, the first thing that most people associate with Cannes is its many festivals, especially the International Film Festival held each May. There is, however, much more to the

city than these glittering events. It was Lord Brougham, the British Lord Chancellor, who put Cannes on the map, although Prosper Mérimée, Inspector of Historic Monuments, allegedly visited Cannes two months before him. Lord Brougham stopped here in 1834, unable to reach Nice due to a cholera outbreak there. Struck by the beauty and mild climate of what was then just a small fishing port,

he built a villa here. Other foreigners followed and Cannes became established as a top Mediterranean resort.

The Old Town which Lord Brougham knew is centred in the Le Suquet district, on the slopes of Mont Chevalier. Part of the old city wall can still be seen on place de la Castre, which is dominated by the **Notre-Dame de l'Espérance**, built in the 16th and 17th centuries in the Provençal Gothic style. An 11th-century watch tower is another attractive feature of the quarter, and the castle keep houses the **Musée de la Castre**, the eclectic finds of a 19th-century Dutch explorer, Baron Lycklama.

The famed **boulevard de la Croisette** is lined with gardens and palm trees. One side is occupied by luxury boutiques and hotels such as the Carlton, built in Belle Epoque style, whose twin cupolas were modelled on the breasts of La Belle Otero, a famous member of the 19th-century *demi-monde*. Opposite are some of the finest sandy beaches on this coast. Once one of the world's grandest thoroughfares, the glamour of the Croisette seems faded in the noise and fumes of summer.

🚢 Iles de Lérins
🚢 depart from: Gare Maritime, Vieux Port. 📞 *04 93 39 11 82. Summer: depart every 30 mins from 7:30am until 7pm; return noon, 3pm, 4pm, 5pm & 6pm. Winter: depart 10am, 11am, 12:15pm, 2pm, 3:15pm, 4.15pm; return noon, 3pm, 4pm & 5pm.*
Just off the coast from Cannes are the Iles de Lérins. The fort on **Ile Sainte-Marguerite** is

---

CANNES FILM FESTIVAL

The first Cannes Film Festival took place in 1946 and, for almost 20 years, it remained a small and exclusive affair, attended by the artists and celebrities who lived or were staying on the coast. The arrival of the "starlet", especially Brigitte Bardot, in the mid-1950s marked the change from artistic event to media circus, but Cannes remains the international marketplace for film-makers and distributors, with the *Palme d'Or* prize conferring high status on its winner. The annual film festival is held in the huge Palais des Festivals, opened in 1982. It has three auditoriums, two exhibition halls, conference rooms, a casino, night-club and restaurant.

Gérard Depardieu and family arriving at the festival

where the mysterious Man in the Iron Mask was imprisoned in the late 17th century. A favourite theory is that he was the illegitimate brother of Louis XIV. Visitors can see the tiny cell that held him for over ten years. **Ile Saint-Honorat** has an 11th-century tower in which the resident monks took refuge during raids by the Saracens. There are also five ancient chapels. Both islands offer peaceful woodland walks, fine views and quiet coves for swimming.

Beside the boulevard de la Croisette

Cap d'Antibes ❷

Alpes-Maritimes. 🚁 Nice. 🚌 🚍 Antibes. 🚢 Nice. 🛈 Antibes (04 92 90 53 00).

WITH ITS SUMPTUOUS villas in their lush grounds, this rocky, wooded peninsula, known as "the Cap" to its regular visitors, has been a symbol of luxury life on the Riviera since it was frequented by Scott Fitzgerald and the rich American set in the 1920s. One of the wealthiest of all, magnate Frank Jay Gould, invested in the resort of Juan-les-Pins and it became the focus of high life on the Cap. Today, memories of the Jazz Age live on at the Jazz Festival, when international stars perform under the pines *(see p33).*

At the highest point of the peninsula, the sailors' chapel of **La Garoupe** has a collection of votive offerings and a 14th-century Russian icon. Nearby is the **Jardin Thuret**, created in 1856 to acclimatize tropical plants. Much of the exotic flora of the region began its naturalization here.

🌿 Jardin Thuret
41 blvd du Cap. 📞 04 93 67 88 00. **Open** Mon–Fri. **Closed** public hols.

Antibes ❷

Alpes-Maritimes. 🏙 70,000. 🚌 🚍 🚢 🛈 11 place du Gal de Gaulle (04 92 90 53 00). 🛒 Tue–Sun.

THE LIVELY TOWN of Antibes was founded by the Greeks as Antipolis and settled by the Romans. In the 14th century, Savoy's possession of the town was contended by France until it fell to them in 1481, after which **Fort Carré** was built and the port, now a centre of Mediterranean yachting, was remodelled by Vauban.

The Château Grimaldi, formerly a residence of Monaco's ruling family, was built in the 12th century and retains its Romanesque tower. It now houses the **Musée Picasso**. In 1946 the artist used part of the castle as a studio and, in gratitude, donated all 150 works completed during his

The Goat (1946) by Pablo Picasso

stay, including *The Goat.* Most are inspired by his love of the sea, including *La Joie de Vivre.*

The pottery in the **Musée d'Archéologie** includes objects salvaged from shipwrecks from the Middle Ages to the 18th century.

🏛 Musée Picasso
Château Grimaldi. 📞 04 92 90 54 20. **Open** Tue–Sun. **Closed** public hols. 🌐 ♿

🏛 Musée d'Archéologie
1 av Meziere. 📞 04 92 90 54 35. **Open** Dec–Oct: Tue–Sun. **Closed** public hols. 🌐 ♿

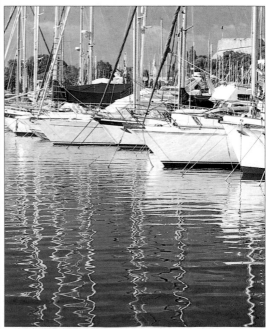

Sailing boats in the harbour at Antibes

Vallauris

Alpes-Maritimes. 24,000.
□ □ ▮ *square 8 mai 1945 (04 93 63 82 58).* ▲ *Tue–Sun.*

Vallauris owes its fame to the influence of Pablo Picasso, who rescued the town's dying pottery industry, and stimulated a revival of the craft. In 1951, the village commissioned Picasso to paint a mural in the deconsecrated chapel next to the castle, and his *War and Peace* (1952) is the chief exhibit of the **Musée Picasso**. In the main square is a bronze statue, *Man with a Sheep*, which Picasso donated to the town.

🏛 **Musée Picasso**
Place de la Libération. ▮ *04 93 64 16 05.* **Open** *Wed–Mon.* **Closed** *public hols.* 🞍 ♿ ground floor only.

Biot ㉛

Alpes-Maritimes. 8,000. □ □ ▮ *place de la Chapelle (04 93 65 05 85).* ▲ *Tue & Fri.*

A typical little hill village, Biot has retained its charm and has always attracted artists and artisans. The best known is Fernand Léger who made his first ceramics here in 1949. Examples of these, and other works by him are shown in the **Musée Fernand Léger** outside town. Its external wall boasts a huge mosaic by the artist.

The town is also famous for its bubble-flecked glassware. The craft of the glassblowers can be seen (and purchased) at the **Verrerie de Biot**.

🏛 **Musée Fernand Léger**
Chemin Val-de-Pôme. ▮ *04 92 91 50 30.* **Open** *Wed–Mon.* **Closed** *1 Jan, 1 May, 25 Dec.* 🞍 ♿
🏛 **La Verrerie de Biot**
Chemin des Combes. ▮ *04 93 65 03 00.* **Open** *daily.* **Closed** *25 Dec.* ♿

Renoir's studio at the Maison Les Collettes in Cagnes-sur-Mer

Cagnes-sur-Mer ㉜

Alpes-Maritimes. 43,000. □ □ ▮ *6 bd Maréchal Juin (04 93 20 61 64).* ▲ *Tue–Fri.*

Cagnes-sur-Mer is divided into three districts. The oldest and most interesting is Haut-de-Cagnes, with its steep streets, covered passageways and ancient buildings, including a number of Renaissance arcaded houses. The other districts are Cagnes-Ville, the modern town where hotels and shops are concentrated, and Cros-de-Cagnes, a sea-side fishing resort and yachting harbour. The **Château** in Haut-de-Cagnes was built in the 14th century and reworked in the 17th by Henri Grimaldi. Behind the fortress walls is a shady courtyard with a 200-year-old pepper tree. The surrounding marble columns conceal a museum devoted to the olive tree and a small collection of modern Mediterranean art. There is also a group of paintings bequeathed by *chanteuse* Suzy Solidor. The 40 works, all portraits of her, are by artists such as Marie Laurencin and Cocteau. On the ceiling of the banqueting hall is a vast illusionistic fresco of the *Fall of Phaeton* painted by Carlone in 1621–4.

The last 12 years of Pierre Auguste Renoir's life were spent in Cagnes, at the **Maison Les Collettes**, where the warm, dry climate eased his arthritis. The house has been kept almost exactly as it was

Exterior of the Musée Fernand Léger in Biot, with a mural by the artist

when he died in 1919 and contains ten of his paintings. It is set in a magnificent olive grove, in which can be seen his great bronze *Venus Victrix*.

♣ Château de Cagnes
📞 04 93 20 85 57. **Open** *Jul–Sep: daily; Oct–Jun: Wed–Mon.* **Closed** *mid-Nov–mid-Dec.* 🖼

⌂ Maison Les Collettes
📞 04 93 20 61 07. **Open** *Wed–Mon.* **Closed** *20 Oct–9 Nov & public hols.* 🖼

La Ferme des Collettes (1915) by Renoir, in Cagnes-sur-Mer

Gorges du Loup ㉝

Alpes-Maritimes. ✈ *Nice.*
🚊 *Cagnes-sur-Mer.* 🚌 *Grasse.*
🚏 *Nice.* ℹ *Grasse (04 93 36 66 66).*

THE RIVER LOUP rises in the Pre-Alps behind Grasse and cuts a deep path down to the Mediterranean. Along its route are dramatic cascades and spectacular views. The superb countryside is crowned by the perched villages for which the region is famous.

Gourdon owes much of its appeal to its ancient houses, grouped round a 13th-century **Château** built on the site of a Saracen stronghold and perched dizzyingly on the cliff-side. Its terraced gardens were laid out by Le Nôtre (*see p169*), who landscaped the gardens of Versailles. The museum houses a collection of naive art including a work by Henri Rousseau.

Tourrette-sur-Loup is a fortified village in which the ramparts are formed by the outer houses. It is surrounded by fields of violets, for which it is famous, grown for use in perfume and candied sweets.

♣ Château Gourdon
📞 04 93 09 68 02. **Open** *Jun–Sep: daily; Oct–May: Wed–Mon.* 🖼 ♿

Vence ㉞

Alpes-Maritimes. 🚶 *15,000.* 🚌
ℹ *place du Grand Jardin (04 93 58 06 38).* 🛒 *Tue, Thu & Fri.*

VENCE'S GENTLE CLIMATE has always been its main attraction; today it is surrounded by holiday villas. It was an important religious centre in the Middle Ages. The **Cathédrale**, built on the site of a temple of Mars, was restored by Vence's most famous bishop, Antoine Godeau. A 5th-century Roman sarcophagus serves as its altar and there are Carolingian wall carvings. Note, too, the 15th-century carved choir stalls and Godeau's tomb.

Just within the ramparts of the Old Town, which retains its 13th–14th-century town gates, is place du Peyra, once a Roman forum. Its urn-shaped fountain, built in 1822, still provides fresh water. On the edge of town, the **Chapelle du Rosaire** was built from 1946–51 and decorated by Henri Matisse,

Domed roof in Vence

in gratitude to the nuns who nursed him during an illness. On its white walls, biblical scenes are reduced to simple black lines tinted by splashes of light from the blue and yellow stained-glass windows.

♠ Chapelle du Rosaire
Av Henri Matisse. 📞 04 93 58 03 26. **Open** *Tue & Thu (Fri–Mon & Wed by appt only, 48 hrs notice reqd); school hols: Tue–Sat pm.* **Closed** *Nov.* 🖼 ♿

Market day in the Old Town of Vence

Street-by-Street: St-Paul-de-Vence ㉟

Restaurant sign,
St-Paul-de-Vence

ONE OF THE MOST famous and tourist-thronged hill villages of the Nice hinterland, St-Paul-de-Vence was once a French frontier post facing Savoy. Its 16th-century ramparts offer views over a landscape of cypress trees, and red-roofed villas with palm trees and swimming pools. The village has been heavily restored but its winding streets and medieval buildings are authentic. It has proved a magnet for artists, both established and aspiring, throughout the 20th century. Today galleries and studios dominate the village.

View of St-Paul-de-Vence
The local landscape is a favourite subject for artists. Neo-Impressionist Paul Signac (1863–1935) painted this view of St-Paul.

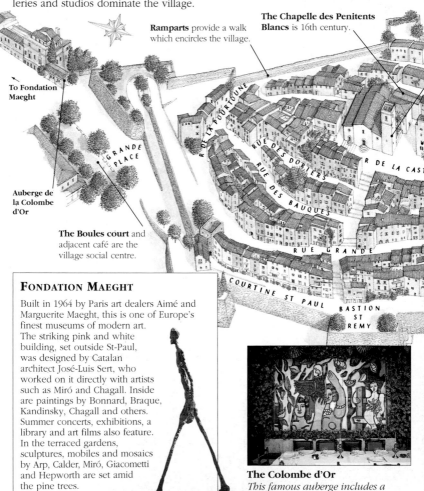

Ramparts provide a walk which encircles the village.

The Chapelle des Penitents Blancs is 16th century.

To Fondation Maeght

Auberge de la Colombe d'Or

The Boules court and adjacent café are the village social centre.

R DE LA FOURTOUNE
GRANDE PLACE
RUE DES DORIERS
RUE DES BAUQUES
R DE LA CAST
RUE GRANDE
COURTINE ST PAUL
BASTION ST REMY

FONDATION MAEGHT

Built in 1964 by Paris art dealers Aimé and Marguerite Maeght, this is one of Europe's finest museums of modern art. The striking pink and white building, set outside St-Paul, was designed by Catalan architect José-Luis Sert, who worked on it directly with artists such as Miró and Chagall. Inside are paintings by Bonnard, Braque, Kandinsky, Chagall and others. Summer concerts, exhibitions, a library and art films also feature. In the terraced gardens, sculptures, mobiles and mosaics by Arp, Calder, Miró, Giacometti and Hepworth are set amid the pine trees.

L'homme qui Marche
by Giacometti

The Colombe d'Or
This famous auberge includes a Léger mural (above) on the terrace; a Braque dove by the pool; a Picasso and a Matisse in the dining room.

Eglise Collégiale
Begun in the 12th century, the church's treasures include a painting of St Catherine, attributed to Tintoretto.

VISITORS' CHECKLIST

Alpes-Maritimes. 🚗 2,900.
🏛 12 place du Grand Jardin, Vence (04 93 58 37 60).
ℹ Maison de la Tour, 2 rue Grande (04 93 32 86 95).
Fondation Maeght open daily.

The Musée d'Histoire de Saint-Paul, contains tableaux of scenes from the town's past.

Le Donjon, a grim medieval building, was used as a prison until the 19th century.

Grand Fountain
This charming cobble-stoned place has a pretty urn-shaped fountain.

Rue Grande
The doors of the 16th- and 17th-century houses bear coats-of-arms.

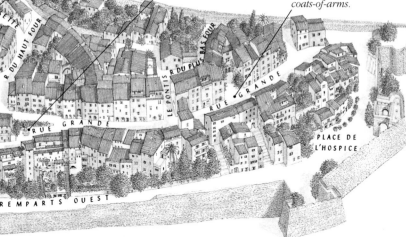

R DU HAUT FOUR
R DU PLUS BAS FOUR
LE PONTIS
RUE GRANDE
RUE GRANDE
PLACE DE L'HOSPICE
REMPARTS OUEST
SEITE

CELEBRITY VILLAGE

The Colombe d'Or (Golden Dove) auberge *(see p574)* was popular with many of the artists and writers who flocked to the Riviera in the 1920s. Early patrons included Picasso, Soutine, Modigliani, Signac, Colette and Cocteau. They often paid for their rooms and meals with paintings, resulting in the priceless collection that can be seen by diners today. The rich and famous have continued to come to St-Paul: Zelda and F Scott Fitzgerald had a dramatic fight over Isadora Duncan at dinner here one night, and Yves Montand married Simone Signoret on the terrace. A photo display of celebrity visitors in St-Paul museum features Sartre and de Beauvoir, Greta Garbo, Sophia Loren, Burt Lancaster and Catherine Deneuve.

Artist Marc Chagall (1887–1985), who moved to St-Paul-de-Vence in 1950

Nice ㊱

THE LARGEST RESORT on the Mediterranean coast and the fifth biggest city in France, with its second busiest airport, Nice was founded by the Greeks and colonized by the Romans. Its temperate winter climate and verdant subtropical vegetation have long attracted visitors. Until World War II it was favoured by aristocrats, including Tsar Nicholas I's widow who visited in 1856 and Queen Victoria who stayed in 1895. This glittering past has contributed to Nice becoming capital of the Côte d'Azur, and today it is also a centre for business conferences and package holidays. Nice has worthy museums, good beaches and an atmospheric street life. Best of all is Carnival: 18 days of celebrations finishing on Shrove Tuesday in a fireworks display and the Battle of the Flowers *(see p35).*

Nice's Old Quarter

Yachts at anchor in Nice harbour

Exploring Nice

The promenade des Anglais, running right along the seafront, was built in the 1830s with funds raised by the English colony. Today it is an 8-lane, 5-km (3-mile) highway, with galleries, shops and grand hotels like the **Negresco**, reflecting Nice's prosperity.

Nice also has a dark side, recorded in 1982 by English author, Graham Greene. He wrote a controversial attack on Jacques Médécin, the city's right-wing mayor, who fled to Paraguay to avoid standing trial in France.

Nice was Italian until 1860, and the pastel façades and balconies of the Old Town have a distinctly Italianate feel. It lies at the foot of a hill still known as the Château for the castle which once stood there. The district is fast being restored and its tall, narrow buildings now house artists and galleries, boutiques and restaurants. The daily flower and vegetable market in the

cours Saleya is a visual treat and a delight for shoppers.

The Cimiez district, on the hills overlooking the town, is the fashionable quarter of Nice. The old monastery of Notre-Dame-de-Cimiez is well worth a visit. Lower down on the hillside are the remains of an extensive Roman settlement with vestiges of the great baths and an amphitheatre. Artifacts from the excavations are on show at the archaeological museum, next door to the Musée Matisse.

🏛 Musée Matisse

164 av des Arènes de Cimiez.
[04 93 81 08 08. **Open** Wed–Mon.
Closed some public hols. 🎨 &

Inspired by the Mediterranean light, Matisse spent many years in Nice. The museum, housed in and below the 17th-century Arena Villa, displays drawings, paintings, bronzes, fabrics and artifacts. Highlights include *Still Life With Pomegranates* and his last completed work, *Flowers and Fruits.*

🏛 Palais Lascaris

15 rue Droite. [04 93 62 05 54.
Open Dec–Oct: Tue–Sun. **Closed** some public hols.

This stuccoed 17th-century palace is decorated with ornate woodwork, Flemish tapestries and illusionistic ceilings thought to be by Carlone. Its small but delightful collection includes a reconstruction of an 18th-century apothecary's shop.

🏛 Musée d'Art Contemporain

Promenade des Arts. [04 93 62 61 62. **Open** Wed–Mon. **Closed** 1 Jan, Easter, 1 May, 25 Dec. 🎨 &

The museum occupies a strikingly original complex of four marble-faced towers linked by glass passageways. The collection is particularly strong in Neo-Realism and Pop Art, with works by Andy Warhol, Jean Tinguely and Niki de Saint-Phalle. Also well-represented are such Ecole de Nice artists as César, Arman and Yves Klein.

***Blue Nude IV** (1952) by Henri Matisse*

An azure view – relaxing on the promenade des Anglais

🔒 Cathédrale Ste-Réparate

This 17th-century Baroque building is surmounted by a handsome tiled dome. Its interior is lavishly decorated with plasterwork, marble and original panelling.

🏛 Musée Chagall

Avenue du Docteur Ménard. **⚟** *04 93 53 87 20.* **Open** *Wed–Mon.* **Closed** *1 Jan, 1 May, 25 Dec.* 🖼 🕭
This is the largest collection of works by Marc Chagall, with paintings, drawings, sculpture, stained glass and mosaics. Best of all are the 17 canvases of the artist's *Biblical Message.*

🏛 Musée des Beaux Arts

33 avenue des Baumettes. **⚟** *04 92 15 28 28.* **Open** *Tue–Sun.* **Closed** *1 Jan, Easter, 1 May, 25 Dec.* 🕭
The 19th-century home of a Ukrainian princess displays works sent to Nice by Napoleon III after Italy ceded the city to France in 1860. Works by Dufy, Monet, Renoir and Sisley add to its appeal.

🏛 Palais Masséna

65 rue du France. **⚟** *04 93 88 11 34.* **Open** *Dec–Oct: Tue–Sun.* **Closed** *1 Jan, 25 Dec.* 🖼
This 19th-century palace is filled with paintings of the

VISITORS' CHECKLIST

Alpes-Maritimes. 👥 *345,000.* ✈ *7 km (4.5 miles) SW.* 🚌 *av Thiers (04 36 35 35 35).* 🚏 *prom des Arts (04 93 85 61 81).* ⛴ *quai du Commerce (04 93 66 13 66).* 🛈 *5 prom des Anglais (04 92 14 48 00).* 🏛 *Tue–Sun.* 🎭 *Carnival (Feb).*

Nice school, local folk art and ephemera such as Carnival posters, and a gold cloak once worn by Napoleon's beloved Josephine. It also contains works by the Impressionists and Provençal ceramics. The Italianate building belonged to the great-grandson of Napoleon's Nice-born Marshal.

🔒 Cathédrale Orthodoxe Russe St-Nicolas

Completed in 1912, the cathedral was built in memory of a young Tsarevitch who died of consumption here in 1865. The exterior is of pink brick and grey marble with elaborate mosaics. The interior is resplendent with icons and fine woodwork. The onion domes make this Nice's most exotic landmark.

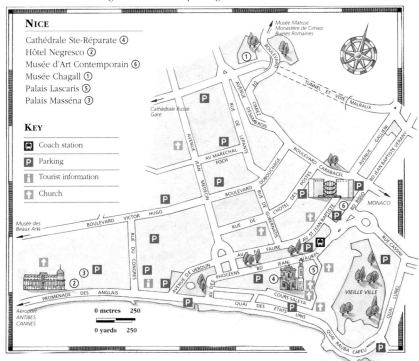

NICE

Cathédrale Ste-Réparate ④
Hôtel Negresco ②
Musée d'Art Contemporain ⑥
Musée Chagall ①
Palais Lascaris ⑤
Palais Masséna ③

KEY

🚌 Coach station

🅿 Parking

🛈 Tourist information

✝ Church

0 metres 250
0 yards 250

Chapelle St-Pierre, Villefranche

Villefranche-sur-Mer ㊲

Alpes-Maritimes. 🏘 8,000. 🚉 🚌
🛈 Jardin François Binon (04 93 01 73 68). 🛒 Tue, Sat, Sun & public hols.

O NE OF THE MOST perfectly
situated towns on the
coast, Villefranche lies at the
foot of hills forming a sheltered
amphitheatre. The town overlooks a beautiful natural harbour which is deep enough
to be a naval port of call.

The bright and animated
waterfront is lined by Italianate façades, with cafés and
bars from which to watch the
fishermen. Here, too, is the
medieval **Chapelle St-Pierre**,
which, after years of service
storing fishing nets, was restored in 1957 and decorated
by Jean Cocteau. His frescoes
depict non-religious images as
well as the life of St Peter.

Also worth a visit is the
16th-century **Citadelle St-
Elme**, incorporating the town
hall and two art galleries.

Behind the harbour, the
streets are narrow, winding,
and often stepped or enclosed
by overhanging buildings.
Walking through them, you get
the odd glimpse of the harbour. The vaulted 13th-century
rue Obscure has always provided shelter from bombardment, right up to World War II.

🔒 **Chapelle St-Pierre**
Port de Villefranche. 📞 04 93 76 90
70. **Open** mid-Dec–mid-Nov: Tue–Sun.
Closed 25 Dec. 🖼

Cap Ferrat ㊳

Alpes-Maritimes. ✈ Nice. 🚉 Nice.
🚌 Beaulieu-sur-Mer. 🚌 🛈 St-Jean-
Cap-Ferrat (04 93 76 08 90).

T HE PENINSULA of Cap Ferrat
boasts some of the most
sumptuous villas found on the
Riviera. From 1926 until the
author's death, the best-known
was Somerset Maugham's Villa
Mauresque, where he received
celebrities from Noël Coward
and Winston Churchill to the
Duke of Windsor.

Tall pines and high walls
guard most of the exclusive
villas, but possibly the finest
of all is open to the public.
The **Fondation Ephrussi de
Rothschild** is a terracotta
and marble mansion set in
themed gardens on the crest
of the cape. It belonged to
the Baroness Ephrussi de
Rothschild, who bequeathed
it to the Institut de France in
1934. It is furnished as she

left it, with her collections of
priceless porcelain, items that
belonged to Marie Antoinette,
tapestries and paintings, and
a unique collection of working
drawings by Fragonard.

The town of **Beaulieu** lies
where the cape joins the mainland, overlooking the Baie des
Fourmis. A pleasant marina
with an exceptionally mild
climate and very fine hotels,
it is the site of another unique
house, the extraordinary **Villa
Kerylos**. Built between 1902
and 1908 for archaeologist
Theodore Reinach in imitation
of an ancient Greek residence,
it contains lovingly reproduced
mosaics, frescoes and furniture.

🏛 **Fondation Ephrussi de
Rothschild**
Cap Ferrat. 📞 04 93 01 33 09. **Open**
daily. **Closed** 25 Dec. 🖼 ♿ 🎥
🏛 **Villa Kerylos**
Impasse Gustave Eiffel, Beaulieu.
📞 04 93 01 01 44. **Open** daily.
Closed 1 Jan, 25 Dec. 🖼 ♿ 🎥

Greek-style Villa Kerylos at Beaulieu on Cap Ferrat

Louis XV salon at the Fondation Ephrussi de Rothschild, Cap Ferrat

Eze ㊴

Alpes-Maritimes. 🏘 2,600. 🚉 🚌
🛈 place de Gaulle (04 93 41 26 00).

FOR MANY, EZE is the ultimate
perched village, balancing
on a rocky pinnacle high above
the Mediterranean. Every
summer, thousands of visitors
stream through the 14th-
century fortified gate and
throng the narrow streets. The
carefully restored, flower-
decked buildings are almost
all shops, galleries and craft
workshops. At the top of the
village, the ruined château is
surrounded by the lush tropical
plants of the **Jardin Exotique**.
The view from here is superb.

Further along the Upper
Corniche is the Roman
Alpine Trophy of **La Turbie**
(see pp42–3). Built in 6 BC,
the vast structure dominates
the surrounding village and
has magnificent views overlooking Monaco and Italy.

🌱 **Jardin Exotique**
Rue du Château. 📞 04 93 41 10 11.
Open daily. 🅰
🏛 **La Turbie**
Open daily. 🅰 📷

Roquebrune-Cap-Martin ㊵

Alpes-Maritimes. 🚉 Nice. 🚉 🚌
🛈 20 av Paul Doumer (04 93 35 62
87). 🚢 daily.

THE MEDIEVAL VILLAGE of
Roquebrune overlooks the
wooded cape where the villas
of the rich and famous still
abound. Visitors here have
included Coco Chanel and

Greta Garbo. The cape has
not always been kind to its
guests. Poet WB Yeats died
here in 1939 and the architect
Le Corbusier was drowned
off the coast in 1965.

In 1467 Roquebrune believed
that by performing scenes
from the Passion it escaped
the plague, and every August
it continues this tradition.

View from Roquebrune

Alpes-Maritimes ㊶

Alpes-Maritimes. 🚉 Nice. 🚉 Nice.
🚌 Peille. 🚢 Nice. 🛈 Peille (04 93
79 90 32).

IN THE HINTERLAND of the Côte
d'Azur, it is still possible to
find quiet, unspoiled villages
off the tourist track. The tiny
twin villages of **Peille** and
Peillon are typical. Both have
changed little since the Middle
Ages, perched on outcrops
over the Paillon river, their
streets a mass of steps and
arches. Peille, the more remote, even has its own dialect.
The Alpes-Maritimes countryside is also unspoiled, its

craggy gorges, tumbling rivers
and wind-swept plateaux just a
few hours from the coast. Of
note are the ancient rock carvings of the **Vallée des Merveilles** and rare wildlife in the
Parc National du Mercantour.

Menton ㊷

Alpes-Maritimes. 🏘 30,000. 🚉 🚌
🛈 Palais de l'Europe, avenue Boyer
(04 93 57 57 00). 🚢 daily.

MENTON'S BEACHES, with the
Alps and the golden
buildings and Belle Epoque
villas of the Old Town as a
backdrop, would be enough to
lure most visitors. In the 19th
century, Queen Victoria and
famous writers and poets often
holidayed here. Tropical gardens and citrus fruits thrive in
the town's perfect climate,
mild even in February for the
lemon festival (see p.35).

Among Menton's sights is the
Eglise St-Michel, a superb example of Baroque architecture
in yellow and pink stone. The
square before it is paved with
a mosaic of the Grimaldi coat
of arms. The **Hôtel de Ville**, in
the centre of town, was decorated in 1957 by Jean Cocteau.
Drawings, paintings, ceramics
and stage designs by the
renowned artist are displayed
in the **Musée Cocteau**,
housed in a 17th-century fort.

Inside the Palais Carnolès,
the **Musée des Beaux Arts**
features works from the Middle
Ages to the 20th century.

🏛 **Hôtel de Ville**
Place Ardoiono. 📞 04 92 10 50 00.
Open Mon–Fri. **Closed** public hols. 🅰
🏛 **Musée Cocteau**
Bastion du Port. 📞 04 93 57 72 30.
Open Wed–Mon. **Closed** public hols.
🏛 **Musée des Beaux Arts**
3 avenue de la Madone. 📞 04 93 35
49 71. **Open** Wed–Sun. **Closed**
public hols.

**Mosaic at the Musée Cocteau
in Menton**

Monaco ㊸

Travellers to monaco by car would do well to take
the Moyenne Corniche, one of the most beautiful
highways in the world, with incomparable views of the
Mediterranean coastline. Arriving among the skyscrapers
of Monaco today, it is hard to envisage the turbulence of
its history. At first a Greek settlement, later taken by the
Romans, it was bought from the Genoese in 1297 by
the Grimaldis who, in spite of bitter family feuds and at
least one political assassination, still rule as the world's
oldest monarchy. Monaco covers 1.9 sq km (0.74 sq
miles) and, although its size has increased by one-third
in the form of landfills, it still occupies an area smaller
than that of New York's Central Park.

Aerial view of Monaco

Grand Casino

Exploring Monaco

Monaco owes its renown
principally to its Grand
Casino. Source of countless
legends, it was instituted in
1856 by Charles III to save
himself from bankruptcy. The
first casino was opened in
1865 on a barren promontory
(later named Monte-Carlo in
his honour) across the harbour
from ancient Monaco-Ville. So
successful was Charles's
money-making venture that,
by 1870, he was able to abolish
taxation for his people. Today,
Monaco is a tax haven for
thousands, and its residents
have the highest per capita
income in the world.

Visitors come from all over
the world for the Grand Prix
de Monaco in May and the
Monte-Carlo Rally in January
(see p35). Many of the greatest
singers perform in the opera
season. There is a fireworks
festival (July–August), and an
international circus festival at
the end of January as well as
world-class ballet and concerts.
Facilities exist for every sort
of leisure activity, and there is
much else to enjoy without
breaking the bank, including
Fort Antoine and the neo-
Romanesque **Cathédrale**.

♛ Grand Casino
Place du Casino. **[** *00 377 92 16 21
21.* **Open** *daily.* **[**
Designed in 1878 by Charles
Garnier, architect of the Paris
Opéra *(see p93)*, and set in
formal gardens, the Casino
gives a splendid view over
Monaco. The lavish interior is
still decorated in Belle Epoque
style, recalling an era when
this was the rendezvous of
Russian Grand Dukes, English
lords and other adventurers.
Anyone can play the odds on
the one-armed bandits of the

Salle Blanche or the roulette
wheels of the Salle Europe.
Even the most exclusive of the
gaming rooms can be visited at
a price, but their tables are for
the big spenders only.

♟ Palais du Prince
Place du Palais. **[** *00 377 93 25 18
31.* **Open** *Jun–Oct: daily.* **[**
Monaco-Ville, the seat of
government, is the site of the
13th-century Palais du Prince.
The interior, with its priceless
furniture and carpets and its

Skyscrapers and apartment blocks of modern Monte-Carlo

MONACO'S ROYAL FAMILY

Since 1949, Monaco has been in the charge of its most effective ruler ever. Businesslike Prince Rainier III is descended from a Grimaldi who entered the Monaco fortress in 1297 disguised as a monk. Rainier's wife, former film star Grace Kelly, died tragically in 1982. Their son, Albert, is heir to the throne but his sisters, Caroline and Stephanie, are the main focus of media attention.

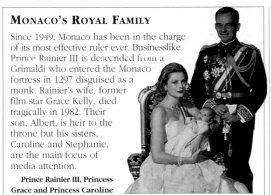

Prince Rainier III, Princess Grace and Princess Caroline

VISITORS' CHECKLIST

Monaco. 🏠 30,000. ✈ 7 km
(4.5 miles) SW Nice. 🚉 av Prince
Pierre (00 377 93 10 60 15). 🚌
2a bd des Moulins (00 377 92 16
61 16). 🚢 daily. 🎪 Festival du
Cirque (Jan–Feb); International
Fireworks Festival (Jul–Aug); Fête
Nationale Monégasque (Nov).

magnificent frescoes, is open to the public only during the prince's absence. The changing of the guard takes place daily at 11:55am.

🏛 Musée des Souvenirs Napoléoniens

Palais du Prince. 📞 00 377 93 25 18 31. **Open** Jun–mid-Nov: daily; mid-Dec–May: Tue–Sun. 🎫 ♿
A genealogical tree on the wall traces the family links between the Grimaldis and Bonapartes. Also on show are Napoleon's personal effects and

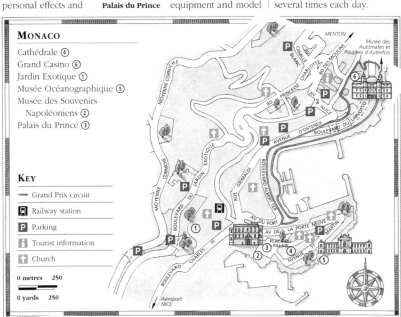

Guard outside the Palais du Prince

clothing, and portraits of Napoleon and Josephine.

✕ Musée Océanographique

Av Saint-Martin. 📞 00 377 93 15 36 00. **Open** daily. 🎫 ♿
This museum was founded in 1910 by Prince Albert I, using his casino profits. Its aquarium, fed with sea water, holds rare species of marine plants and animals. The museum houses an important scientific collection, diving equipment and model ships. Marine explorer Jacques Cousteau established his research centre here.

♣ Jardin Exotique

62 bd du Jardin Exotique. 📞 00 377 93 30 33 65. **Open** daily. **Closed** 19 Nov, 25 Dec. 🎫 ♿ to part of garden only.
These gardens are considered to be the finest in Europe, with a huge range of tropical and subtropical plants. In the park, a museum of anthropology offers evidence that bears, mammoths and hippopotami once lived on the coast here.

🏛 Musée des Automates et Poupées d'Autrefois

17 av Princesse Grace. 📞 00 377 93 30 91 26. **Open** daily. **Closed** 1 Jan, 1 May, 19 Nov, 25 Dec. 🎫
This museum houses over 400 dolls from the 18th century to the present. The delightful automata are set in motion several times each day.

MONACO

Cathédrale ④
Grand Casino ⑥
Jardin Exotique ①
Musée Océanographique ⑤
Musée des Souvenirs
   Napoléoniens ②
Palais du Prince ③

KEY

━━ Grand Prix circuit

🚉 Railway station

🅿 Parking

🚻 Tourist information

✝ Church

0 metres   250
0 yards   250

CORSICA

HAUTE-CORSE · CORSE-DU-SUD

CORSICA, *where the people speak their own Italian dialect, has all the attributes of a mini-continent. There are tropical palm trees, vineyards, olive and orange groves, forests of chestnut and indigenous pine, alpine lakes and cool mountain torrents filled with trout. Most distinctive of all is the parched maquis (scrub), heavy with the scent of myrtle, which Napoleon swore he could smell from the sea.*

The third largest island in the Mediterranean after Sicily and Sardinia, Corsica has been a problem and a bafflement to mainland France ever since 1769, when it was "sold" to Louis XV by the Genoese for 40 million francs. Before that, following years of struggle, the Corsican people had enjoyed 15 years of independence under the revered leadership of Pasquale Paoli. They understandably felt cheated by the deal with the French, and have resented them ever since. To holidaymakers visiting the island – in July and August tourists outnumber the inhabitants six to one – the Corsican-French relationship may be a matter of indifference. However, there is a strong (and sometimes quite violent) separatist movement, which does deter some tourists. As a result, Corsica's wild beauty has been preserved to an extent not seen in the rest of the Mediterranean.

For 200 years, from the 11th to the 13th century, Corsica was a colony of the old Tuscan republic of Pisa, whose builders founded beautifully proportioned Romanesque churches. These buildings are, along with the megalithic stone warriors in Filitosa, the noblest monuments to be seen here. For the rest, the birthplace of Napoleon is a place of wild seacoasts and mountain peaks, one of the last unspoiled corners of the Mediterranean: poor, depopulated, beautiful, old-fashioned and doggedly aloof.

The village of Oletta in the Nebbio region around St-Florent

◁ **A fisherman with feline friends in Bastia**

Exploring Corsica

CORSICA'S MAIN APPEAL is its scenery: a wildly beautiful landscape of mountains, forests, myrtle-scented maquis and countless miles of sandy beaches. Late spring (when the wild flowers are in bloom) and early autumn are the best times to visit – the temperature is moderate and there aren't too many visitors. The island is renowned for its superb hiking trails, some of which become cross-country skiing trails during the winter. Downhill skiing is also possible in February and March.

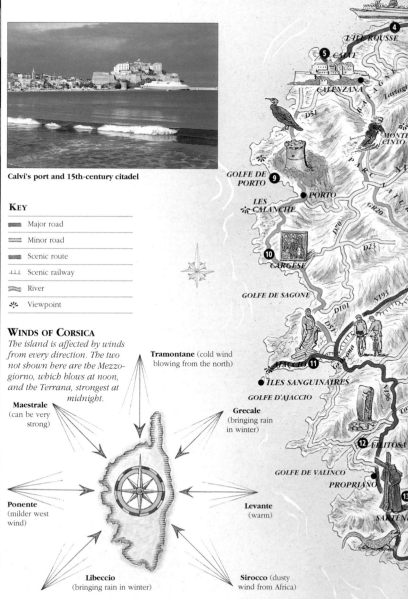

Calvi's port and 15th-century citadel

KEY

▬▬	Major road
═══	Minor road
▬▬	Scenic route
⊥⊥⊥	Scenic railway
≈≈	River
✻	Viewpoint

WINDS OF CORSICA

The island is affected by winds from every direction. The two not shown here are the Mezzogiorno, which blows at noon, and the Terrana, strongest at midnight.

Tramontane (cold wind blowing from the north)

Maestrale (can be very strong)

Grecale (bringing rain in winter)

Ponente (milder west wind)

Levante (warm)

Libeccio (bringing rain in winter)

Sirocco (dusty wind from Africa)

L'ÎLE ROUSSE

CALVI

CALENZANA

D51

MONTE CINTO

GOLFE DE PORTO

PORTO

LES CALANCHE

GR20

D70

D23

CARGESE

GOLFE DE SAGONE

D101

N193

AJACCIO

ÎLES SANGUINAIRES

GOLFE D'AJACCIO

N196

FILITOSA

GOLFE DE VALINCO

PROPRIANO

SARTENE

SIGHTS AT A GLANCE

The Calanche cliffs in the Golfe de Porto

GETTING AROUND

Car ferries (which should be booked well in advance) depart from Marseille, Nice and Toulon, arriving at Bastia, L'Île Rousse, Calvi, Ajaccio and Propriano. There are also ferries from Sardinia and the Italian ports of Genoa, Livorno and La Spezia. Small airports are based at Ajaccio, Bastia, Calvi and Figari (near Bonifacio). Corsica's roads are narrow, twisting and often tortuously slow, though breathtaking views reward the effort. A car is almost a must for exploring the island, as public transport is limited. Carry spare petrol – filling stations are few and far between.

| 0 kilometres | 20 |
| 0 miles | 10 |

Corte's Old Town, with its citadel high up on a rocky outcrop

Cap Corse ❶

Haute-Corse. ✈ *Bastia.* 🚊 *Bastia,*
Macinaggio, Rogliano. 🚌 *Bastia.*
🅹 *Bastia (04 95 31 00 89).*

CAP CORSE is the northern
tip of Corsica, 40 km (25
miles) in length but seldom
more than 12 km (7.5 miles)
wide, pointing like an accus-
atory finger towards Genoa.
There are two roads out of
Bastia to the cape: the D81
leading west across the mountains and joining up with the
D80 after the wine village of
Patrimonio; and the D80 travelling north along the eastern
shore to **Erbalunga** and
Macinaggio. Either way the
road is narrow and twisting, a
foretaste of what awaits you
nearly everywhere in Corsica.
From the coastal village of
Lavasina, the D54 leads left
off the D80 to Pozzo; from
here it is a 5-hour round trip on
foot to the 1,307-m (4,300-ft)
summit of **Monte Stello**, the
highest peak on the cape. The
360-degree view from the top
takes in St-Florent to the west,
the massif of central Corsica
to the south and the Italian
island of Elba to the east.
Further up the coast, the
restored **Tour de Losse** is one
of many 16th-century Genoese
towers along the coast – part
of an elaborate system which
enabled all Corsican towns to
be warned within two hours
of impending barbarian raids.
The charming 18th-century
fishing port of **Centuri**, near
the tip of the peninsula on the
west coast, is an ideal spot
for a delicious seafood feast.
Pino, a pretty little village

straggling down the green
mountainside further to the
south, has no hotel, only a
lovely little church dedicated
to the Virgin, full of model
ships placed there by mariners
grateful for her protection.
On the way south along the
vertiginous lower corniche,
be sure to turn left up the hill
to **Canari**. One of the larger
villages in this area, Canari has
a jewel of a 12th-century Pisan
church, Santa Maria Assunta,
a magnificent view across the
sea, and a thoroughly convivial
hotel-restaurant. All the by-
roads in this thickly wooded
area seem to lead somewhere
interesting. There are literally
dozens of picturesque hamlets
in the vicinity, and it should
be borne in mind that from
this point onwards the landscape becomes steadily less
attractive as the road winds
on past the old asbestos
workings and beaches of
black sand below **Nonza**.

The village of Erbalunga on the east coast of Cap Corse

Bastia ❷

Haute-Corse. 🏘 *39,000.* ✈ 🚊
🚌 🚢 🅹 *place St-Nicolas (04 95 31*
00 89). 🕭 *Tue–Sun.*

A THRIVING PORT and the
administrative capital of
Upper Corsica, Bastia is utterly
different in style from its sedate
west coast rival, Ajaccio. The
Genoese citadel and colourful
19th-century Italianate buildings around the old port are for
many people their first taste of
the authentic Mediterranean –
as it was half a century ago,
and as it stubbornly remains
in our imagination.
The centre of Bastiais life is
the **place St-Nicolas**, facing
the wharf where ferries from
the mainland and Italy arrive.
Heading south along the
waterfront you come to the
place de l'Hôtel de Ville,
site of a bustling outdoor
food market each morning.
Bordering the square are the
early 17th-century **Chapelle
de l'Immaculée Conception**,
with its ornate 18th-century
interior, and the mid-17th-
century **Eglise de St-Jean-
Baptiste**, whose façade
dominates the Vieux Port.
From here it is a short walk
up to the 16th-century **citadel**,
where there are two more
churches worth seeing: the
Baroque **Chapelle Sainte-
Croix**, with its striking *Black
Christ*, fished out of the sea by
Bastiais fishermen in 1428;
and the 15th-century **Sainte-
Marie**, which has a *Virgin*
made of a tonne of solid silver.

Bastia's Vieux Port seen from the Jetée du Dragon

St-Florent ❸

Haute-Corse. 🏛 *1,400*. 🔲 ℹ️
*Bâtiment Administratif (04 95 37
06 04)*. 🚹 *1st Wed of month*.

S T-FLORENT IS almost a
Corsican St-Tropez – chic,
affluent, and packed with
yachts from all over the
Mediterranean. Its citadel
(closed to visitors) dates from
1439, and is a fine example of
Genoese military architecture.
The town itself is pleasant to
wander around; its main
attraction, the 12th-century
Pisan **Cathédrale de Santa
Maria Assunta**, lies just inland
on the road to Poggio-d'Oletta.

Environs

A leisurely 4-hour circuit by car
of the **Nebbio** region, which
extends in an amphitheatre
around St-Florent, might take
in the following: **Santo Pietro
di Tenda**; **Murato**, famous for
its magnificent **Eglise de San
Michele de Murato**, a 12th-
century Pisan Romanesque
construction built of white and
green stone; the **San Stefano**
pass, with the sea on either
side; **Oletta**, which produces a
special blue cheese made from
ewes' milk; the **Teghime** pass;
and finally the wine village of
Patrimonio, where there is
a strange, big-eared menhir
dating from 900–800 BC.

Along the coast to the west
of St-Florent lies the barren, uninhabited **Désert des Agriates**.
If you can face the 10-km
(6-mile) haul to the sea – on
foot, by bike or by motorbike
– the Saleccia beach here is
by far the most beautiful and
solitary beach on the island.

San Michele de Murato

L'Île Rousse ❹

Haute-Corse. 🏛 *2,300*. 🔲 🔲 ⛴
ℹ️ *place Paoli (04 95 60 04 35)*.
🚹 *daily*.

F OUNDED IN 1758 by
Pasquale Paoli, leader of
independent Corsica, L'Île
Rousse is today a major
holiday resort and ferry
terminal. The centre of
town is the plane-shaded
place Paoli, dominated
by a marble statue of
Corsica's national hero.
On the north side of the
square is the covered
market, with the Old
Town just beyond.

In the summer months
L'Île Rousse becomes
hideously overcrowded,
its beaches a mass of
sun-starved bodies. It is
worth travelling 10 km
(6 miles) up the coast to
Lozari, which offers a magnificent, virtually unspoiled
stretch of sand.

Environs

One very pleasant way to
discover the **Balagne** region
is to take the tram from L'Île
Rousse to Calvi and back.
This odd little service runs
from June to September each
year, more or less keeping to
the coastline and stopping at
Algajola, Lumio and various
holiday villages along the way.

Calvi ❺

Haute-Corse. 🏛 *5,000*. 🔲 🔲 ⛴
ℹ️ *Port de Plaisance (04 95 65 16
67)*. 🚹 *daily*.

C ALVI, where Nelson lost his
eye in an "explosion of
stones" in 1794, is today half
military town, half cheap holiday resort. Its 15th-century
citadel is garrisoned by a
crack French regiment of the
foreign legion; while beyond
the ferry port is a seedy,
apparently endless camp-
site and trailer park.

The town makes a
half-hearted case for
being the birthplace of
Christopher Columbus,
but there is no real evi-
dence to support this.
A much better claim to
fame is the food, which is
very good and reasonably
priced by Corsican stan-
dards. There is also a very
respectable jazz festival
at Calvi in the third
week of June.

Outside town, the
19th-century **Chapelle
de Notre-Dame de la Serra**
is gloriously sited on a hilltop
commanding extensive views
in all directions.

**French foreign
legionnaire**

The Chapelle de Notre-Dame de la Serra, 6 km (3.5 miles) southwest of Calvi

Corte's 15th-century citadel seen at dawn

The Niolo ❻

Haute-Corse. 🚌 Bastia.
ℹ️ Calacuccia (04 95 48 05 22).

THE NIOLO, west of Corte, extends westward to the Vergio pass and the upper Golo basin, and to the east as far as the Scala di Santa Regina. It includes Corsica's highest mountain, the 2,700-m (8,859-ft) **Monte Cinto**, and its biggest river, the **Golo**, which meets the sea south of Bastia.

Alone of the various regions of Corsica, the Niolo persists in the cultivation of livestock as its economic mainstay.

The main town, **Calacuccia**, is suitable for excursions to Monte Cinto. The nearby ski resort of **Haut Asco** is best reached by the D147 from **Asco**, but enthusiasts can walk from Calacuccia (8–9 hours). To the south is the huge forest of **Valdu Niello**.

Corte ❼

Haute-Corse. 🏃 6,000. 🚌 🚂
ℹ️ 15 quartier Quatre Fontaines (04 95 46 26 70). 🚌 Fri.

IN THE geographical centre of Corsica, Corte was the chosen capital of the independence leader Pasquale Paoli from 1755–69, and today is the seat of the island's university. In the Old Town is the 15th-

century citadel, housing the **Musée de la Corse**. Its exhibits relate to traditional Corsican life and anthropology.

Corte is the best base for exploring nearby mountain areas, especially as it stands exactly halfway along the GR20, the legendary 220-km (137-mile) trail from Calenzana to Conca.

🏛 **Musée de la Corse**
La Citadelle. ☎ 04 95 45 25 45.
Open mid-Jun–mid-Sep: 10am–7:30pm daily; mid-Sep–mid-Jun: 10am–12:30pm, 2–5:45pm Tue–Sat.
Closed public hols. 🚫 ♿ 🖼

Environs
Don't miss the wildly beautiful **Gorges de la Restonica**, about 12 km (7.5 miles) out of town via the D623. Above these gorges adventurous walkers may wish to make the well-marked climb to the snow-fed **Lac de Melo** (allow 60–90 minutes); or the **Lac de Capitello**, 30 minutes further on, where the snow stays as late as early June. The path – in winter a cross-country ski trail – follows the river.

South of Corte, the **Forêt de Vizzavona** features beech and pine woodland crisscrossed by trout-filled streams and walking trails (notably the GR20). It is a perfect refuge from the summer heat and is also an excuse to take the small gauge train up from Ajaccio or Bastia, which stops at Vizzavona.

The Castagniccia ❽

Haute-Corse. ✈️ Bastia. 🚂 Corte, Ponte Leccia. 🚌 Piedicroce, La Porta, Valle-d'Alesani. ℹ️ Piedicroce (04 95 35 82 54).

EAST OF CORTE is the hilly, chestnut-covered region of Castagniccia (literally "small chestnut grove"), which most Corsicans agree is the very heart and kernel of the island. It was here that independence leader Pasquale Paoli was born in 1725, and that the revolts against Genoa and later France began in earnest in 1729. Alas, many of the villages in this beautiful, remote area are nearly empty, their inhabitants having joined the 800,000 or so Corsicans (almost three times the present population) who live and work in mainland France or Italy. It seems hard to believe that in the 17th century, when the great chestnut forests introduced here by the Genoese were at the height of their production, this was the most prosperous and populated region in Corsica.

The D71 from Ponte Leccia (north of Corte) to the east coast winds through the centre of the Castagniccia region, and to see it at a leisurely pace will take the best part of a day. Arm yourself with a picnic before you start, as there is little to be had in the way of supplies en route.

◁ Limestone cliffs of Bonifacio (see p533)

Golfe de Porto 9

Corse-du-Sud. ✈ 🚌 🚢 *Ajaccio.*
🚌 *Porto.* ℹ *Porto (04 95 26 10 55).*

Porto is sited at the head of the Golfe de Porto, one of the most beautiful bays in the Mediterranean, which for the sake of its fauna and flora has been included in UNESCO's list of the world's common cultural heritage sites. So far, the only effect of this on Porto town has been to send hotel and restaurant prices through the roof. The best things here are the sunset from the magnificent Genoese watchtower, and the boat heading out to the Calanche, Scandola and Girolata.

The **Calanche** begin 2 km (1.2 miles) out of Porto, on the road to Piana. These 300-m (1,000-ft) red granite cliffs plunge sheer to the sea, and are quite simply breathtaking. They are accessible only by boat or on foot: well-defined trails start from the Tête du Chien and the Pont de Mezanu, while boat tickets are available at Porto's Hôtel Le Cyrnée.

East of Porto are the Gorges de la Spelunca, accessed by a mule route punctuated by Genoese bridges.

The pretty village of **Piana**, just south of Porto, is a good starting point and a much nicer place to stay than Porto. Information about walking in this area can be obtained on the spot; one very worthwhile destination is the cove at **Ficajola** just below Piana – a truly delightful beach.

Porto's marina and Genoese watchtower

Environs

The road over the mountains from Porto to Calvi offers no more than a taste of this grandiose corner of Corsica – you have to take to the sea to view it properly (ferries from Porto and Galéria). **Girolata**, a tiny hamlet north of Porto, can be reached only by sea or via a mule track (4 hours round trip on foot) from a clearly marked point 23 km (14 miles) north of Porto on the D81.

At the mouth of the Golfe de Girolata, the **Réserve Naturelle de Scandola**, instituted in 1975, is the first land-and-sea reserve in France, covering over 1,000 hectares (2,500 acres) of sea, and a similar area of cliffs, caves and maquis. Marine life is abundant in these clear, protected waters; the birds include ospreys, puffins and falcons.

The town of Piana with the Calanche in the background

Cargèse's Greek rite church

Cargèse ⑩

Corse-du-Sud. 🏛 *900.* 🚌 ℹ *rue du Docteur Dragacci (04 95 26 41 31).*

CARGÈSE overlooks the sea from a promontory between the bays of Sagone and Pero. It is a small town with an odd history: many of the people who live here are the descendants of 17th-century Greek refugees from Turkish rule, given asylum in Corsica.

A few Cargèsiens still speak Greek, and their icon-filled Eastern (Greek) rite church still faces its Catholic counterpart in an attitude that must once have seemed deliberately confrontational. Nowadays the old rivalries have long since vanished, and the Orthodox priest and Catholic *curé* often stand in for one another.

There are many splendid beaches in the vicinity, notably at **Pero** and **Chiuni** just to the north, and at **Ménasina** and **Stagnoli** to the south.

Ajaccio ⑪

Corse-du-Sud. 🏛 *59,000.* ✈ 🚌 🚉 🚢 ℹ *place Foch (04 95 51 53 03).* 🗓 *Tue–Sun.*

AJACCIO, a noisy, busy town by Corsican standards, was the birthplace of Napoleon Bonaparte in 1769. Napoleon never returned to Corsica after crowning himself emperor of the French in 1804, but the town – modern capital of nationalist Corsica – celebrates his birthday every 15 August.

The **Cathédrale Notre-Dame de la Miséricorde**, where Napoleon was baptized on 21 July 1771, was built in the late 1500s. It houses Eugène Delacroix's famous painting *Vierge du Sacré-Coeur*.

A few streets away, the **Maison Bonaparte**, where Napoleon was born and spent his childhood, contains family portraits, period furniture and assorted memorabilia. The building was occupied for a brief spell by Hudson Lowe, Napoleon's future jailer on St-Helena, after the Bonaparte family was ejected by the citizens of Ajaccio in 1793.

Much more interesting is the superb collection of artworks assembled on the coat-tails of Napoleon by his unscrupulous uncle, Cardinal Fesch, who merrily looted churches, palaces and museums during the Italian campaign and brought the swag home to Ajaccio. Housed in the 19th-century Palais Fesch, the **Musée Fesch** contains the finest collection of Italian primitive art in France after the Louvre. Among its masterpieces are works by

Botticelli, Titian and Veronese. Next to the Palais Fesch stands the **Chapelle Impériale**, built in 1855 by Napoleon III to accommodate the tombs of the Bonaparte family.

From here, walk back along the quay to the Jetée de la Citadelle, which offers superb views of the town, the marina and the Golfe d'Ajaccio. The adjacent 16th-century **citadel** is occupied by the army.

🏛 Maison Bonaparte
Rue St-Charles. 📞 *04 95 21 43 89.* **Open** *Mon pm, Tue–Sat, Sun am.* 🖼
🏛 Musée Fesch
50 rue Fesch. 📞 *04 95 21 48 17.* **Open** *Jun–Sep: Tue–Sun; Oct–May: Sat–Tue.* **Closed** *public hols.* 🖼 ♿

Environs
From the quai de la Citadelle there are daily excursions to the **Îles Sanguinaires** at the mouth of the Golfe d'Ajaccio.

A statue-menhir at Filitosa

Filitosa ⑫

Centre Préhistorique de Filitosa, Corse-du-Sud. 📞 *04 95 74 00 91.* **Open** *daily.* 🖼 ♿ *museum only.*

THE 4,000-YEAR-OLD, life-size stone warriors of Filitosa are the most spectacular relics of megalithic man in Corsica. Discovered in 1946, these phallus-like granite menhirs represent an interesting progression from mere silhouettes to more detailed sculpture, etched with human features and even weapons.

The five most recent and most sophisticated figures (about 1500 BC) stand around a thousand-year-old olive

Statue of Napoleon by Laboureur in place Maréchal Foch, Ajaccio

The fortified Old Town of Bonifacio, with the harbour in the foreground

tree, in the field below a tumulus. Other finds, which include a heavily armed warrior with shield, helmet and sword, can be seen in the site's archaeological museum.

Sartène 🔞

Corse-du-Sud. 🚶 3,600. 🚌 🅸 rue Borgo (04 95 77 15 40). 🚌 winter: Tue & Sat; summer: Wed–Mon.

SARTENE is a medieval fortified town of narrow cobbled streets and grey granite houses rising above the Rizzanese valley. Founded by the Genoese in the early 16th century, it has survived attacks by Barbary pirates and centuries of bloody feuding among the town's leading families.

Despite all this, Sartène has a reputation for deep piety, reinforced each year by the oldest and most intense Christian ceremony in Corsica, the Good Friday Catenacciu (literally, the "chained one"). A red-hooded penitent, bare-foot and in chains, drags a wooden cross through the Old Town in a re-enactment of Christ's ascent to Golgotha.

Environs
Just outside town in Sartène's former prison, the **Musée de Préhistoire Corse** has a fascinating collection of artifacts from the Neolithic period, the Bronze Age and Iron Age.

🏛 Musée de Préhistoire Corse
Rue Croce. 🎧 04 95 77 01 09. **Open** mid-Jun–mid-Sep: Mon–Sat; mid-Sep–mid-Jun: Mon–Fri. **Closed** public hols. ♿

Bonifacio 🔞

Corse-du-Sud. 🚶 2,700. 🚌 🅱 🅸 place de l'Europe (04 95 73 11 88). 🚌 Wed.

BONIFACIO is the southern-most town in Corsica, dra-matically sited on a limestone cliff peninsula with some of the most stunning views in the Mediterranean *(see pp528–9).* Its handsome harbour at the foot of the cliffs is the focus of life: cafés, restaurants and bou-tiques abound and boats de-part regularly for neighbouring Sardinia and the uninhabited islands of Lavezzi and Cavallo.

From the harbour, steps lead up to Bonifacio's fortified Old Town. The citadel, which was built by the conquering Genoese at the end of the 12th century, has long been the town's main defensive post, and from 1963–83 was the headquarters of the French foreign legion. From here, wander down to the tip of the promontory to see the two old windmills and the ruins of a Franciscan monastery.

Côte Orientale 🔞

Haute-Corse & Corse-du-Sud. 🛧 Bastia 🚉 Porto-Vecchio, Aléria, Salenzara. 🚢 Bastia, Porto-Vecchio. 🅸 Aléria (04 95 57 01 50), Porto-Vecchio (04 95 70 09 58).

THE FLAT, rather dreary alluv-ial plain stretching from Bastia to Solenzara has been rich farmland since 1945, the year it was finally drained and rid of malaria. More recently, holiday resorts and even high-rise hotels have mushroomed along the coast, cashing in on its long, sandy beaches.

The best sight in **Mariana**, which is otherwise uncomfort-ably close to the Bastia-Poretta airport, is the early 12th-century cathedral of Mariana known as **La Canonica**. A short dis-tance away is the slightly older **Eglise de San Perteo**, surrounded by meadows.

About halfway down the coast, the port of **Aléria**, orig-inally a Greek colony and the base for Rome's conquest of Corsica in 259 BC, is interest-ing for its rich archaeological heritage. Just outside town, a museum housed in the 16th-century Fort de Matra chron-icles daily life in Roman Aléria.

Towards the southern tip of the island, the fortified town of **Porto-Vecchio**, built by Corsica's Genoese conquerors, is now an extremely popular seaside resort. The setting is perfect for the conventional seaside holiday, with umbrella pines, cork oak forests and glorious white sandy beaches within easy reach of the town, especially at **Palombaggia** and **Pinarello**.

The Golfe de Porto-Vecchio

TRAVELLERS' NEEDS

WHERE TO STAY

MANY OF FRANCE'S 22,000 registered hotels are charming, idiosyncratic and good value. On these four pages, the types of hotel on offer are summarized and tips provided on what to expect from French hotels. The hotel listings pages *(see pp540–75)* describe some of the best hotels around the country in every price category and style, from slick, modern chain hotels to small, classic, family-run establishments. Also included are *chambres d'hôte* (a sort of French bed and breakfast), which range from simple farms to grandiose châteaux, as well as the best hostels. France is one of the most popular countries in the world for self-catering holidays and information is given on renting a rural home or *gîte*, and how to get the most out of a camping holiday.

The Hôtel Euzkadi at Espelette in the Pyrenees *(see p569)*

THE CLASSIC FAMILY HOTEL

IF YOU'RE TOURING on a budget, the small, family-run, family-orientated hotel lurking in virtually every village and town is for you. It's likely to be the focal point of the village, with the bar and dining-room (if the food is up to standard) full of locals. The atmosphere is entirely informal, with children, cats and dogs happily at home. In the hotel's dozen or so bedrooms, old-fashioned charm will make up for a lack of sprightliness and, perhaps, the mere trickle of hot water from the shower.

The annual *Logis de France* guide details over 4,000 of these family-run, mainly one- and two-star hotel-restaurants. They tend to be located in small towns and rural locations; there are none in Paris. Most are no more than roadside inns, but off-the-beaten-track you will discover many converted farmhouses and inexpensive seaside hotels. While the *Logis* is a useful reference source, the quality of places listed can be uneven.

THE CHÂTEAU HOTEL

MANY OF FRANCE'S châteaux and mansions have been converted into luxury hotels. They include everything from Renaissance piles with sweeping lawns to medieval castles with battlements and keeps. Grand hotels can be found all over France, with rich pickings in the Loire, the Savoie, the Haute-Savoie and the Rhône delta. The properties included in the **Relais et Châteaux** brochure are recommended.

Typically, rooms are beautifully designed and the food is *haute cuisine*. Bedrooms range from grand suites to more simple abodes, often in converted farm-buildings, making it possible, if you're willing to forgo four-poster beds and antiques, to live in luxury without breaking the bank.

THE CITY HOTEL

EVERY BIG CITY has a clutch of hotels close to the train station or port. They range from cheap accommodation to a grand hotel or two. The most famous city hotels are the palace hotels in Paris and the Riviera resorts such as Nice and Cannes. Note that many city hotels do not have a restaurant or a salon and it is always worth checking the quality of the bedroom before you book it.

THE MODERN CHAIN HOTEL

OUTLETS OF MODERN hotel chains are useful for inexpensive pitstops if you're travelling through France. Many are situated on the outskirts of towns by motorways or main roads. The cheapest are the one-star, no-frills **Formula 1** motels, offering bedrooms with a double and single bed and no en suite facilities.

Two-star chains include **Ibis/ Arcade**, **Campanile**, **Climat de France** and **Inter Hôtel**. Three-star chains include **Novotel** and **Mercure/Altéa**; both offer en suite accommodation and allow one child to stay with no charge, provided the

Le Négresco in Nice on the Côte d'Azur *(see p573)*

The Meurice hotel in the Tuileries Quarter of Paris *(see p541)*

whole family sleeps in one room (Novotel has free accommodation for two under-16s).

THE RESTAURANT-WITH-ROOMS

THROUGHOUT FRANCE, many upmarket restaurants also offer accommodation. Usually, the bedrooms match the restaurant's smartness and are priced accordingly. Sometimes, though, gourmet restaurants have simple bedrooms hidden away upstairs – great finds for those who like to splash out on food while saving on lodging. Refer to the restaurant listings on pages 580–613.

MEALS AND FACILITIES

IN HIGH SEASON, many resort hotels insist on half board or *demi-pension* (a per person rate for the room, dinner and breakfast). There is also full board or *pension*, which covers lunch too. While it is cheaper to opt for inclusive rates, meals come from set or limited-choice menus, which often omit the more interesting dishes.

Many smaller family-run hotels do not provide meals on Sunday evenings and often stop serving dinner as early as 9pm on other days.

Rooms usually have double beds; twin or single beds must be requested when booking. All mid-range hotels have a choice of bathroom facilities. A short walk down the corridor to a separate bathroom can reduce the room rate considerably. A bathroom with a bath *(un bain)* is usually more expensive than one with a shower *(une douche); un cabinet de toilette* has a basin and bidet, without a bath, shower or a WC. If you do not have *pension* or *demi-pension* accommodation, breakfast is often charged as an extra. Go instead to the local café, as it tends to be cheaper and more filling.

Hôtel de l'Abbaye at Talloires in the French Alps *(see p564)*

GRADINGS

FRENCH HOTELS ARE GRADED from nought stars to four stars (plus "four star luxury"). Stars indicate precisely the hotel's facilities. Hotels with two or more stars must have a lift where appropriate, a phone in every bedroom and at least 40 per cent of their bedrooms en suite. Three-star hotels must offer breakfast in the bedroom and have 80 per cent en suite rooms. Only four-star hotels must have a restaurant and all of their rooms en suite.

PRICES

RATES, inclusive of tax and service, are quoted per room (apart from *pension* and *demi-pension* arrangements). There is usually a small supplement for a third person in a room for two, and little reduction for single travellers.

As a rule, the higher the star rating the more you pay. Rates for a double room start from about F130 per night for a one-star hotel and go up to F500 or more for a four-star hotel. Costs also vary geographically with remote rural areas like Brittany being the cheapest. For equivalent accommodation in fashionable areas like the Dordogne and Provence expect to pay 20 per cent more, and a further 20 per cent again for Paris and the Côte d'Azur. Prices vary seasonally too, with coastal and alpine areas putting up their tariffs by up to 50 per cent in peak periods.

BOOKING

ALWAYS BOOK well in advance for Paris, and for hotels in popular tourist areas in July and August.

In resort areas, most hotels shut down from October to March, so phone ahead when travelling out of season to make sure the place is open.

Reservations can normally be held with a credit card at all but the humblest hotels. If you want to make a booking while you are in France, there are tourist offices in all main cities which provide a hotel reservation service up to eight days in advance.

The dining room of the Grand Hôtel, Sète *(see p571)*

BED AND BREAKFAST

FRENCH bed and breakfasts, called *chambres d'hôte*, come in all shapes and sizes, from tiny cottages to elaborate châteaux full of family portraits and antiques, plus some *ferme-auberges (see p577).* In all cases you will stay in a private home, and should not expect hotel services or amenities. Many offer dinner – *table d'hôte* – on request, where you usually dine *en famille.* Over 5,000 rural *chambres d'hôte* are registered and inspected by **Gîtes de France.** Look out for the green *chambres d'hôte* signs at the side of the road.

Roadside signs also lead to many B&Bs that are not registered. Information on these is available from local tourist offices. There are also **Café-Couette** (literally coffee-quilt) B&Bs which include both urban and rural accommodation, with some 50 places in Paris alone. Reservations for all of Café-Couette's 500 B&Bs can be made through a central office after paying an annual membership fee.

SELF-CATERING

THE FABLED *gîte* is a rural holiday home often converted from a farmhouse or its out-buildings. A *gîte* holiday is a popular and cheap way to see France, particularly out of season, but you must book many months in advance for the best *gîtes.*

Gîtes de France registers some 40,000 *gîtes,* all inspected and graded to indicate the level of facilities. You can book from a selection of 2,500 in the company's main brochure (available from the London office), or direct. Each of its 95 regional offices produces a booklet with all the *gîtes* in its *département,* which comes with a booking form. These are also available through the head office in Paris, **Maison des Gîtes de France.**

France has plenty of other kinds of self-catering accommodation: expensive south-coast villas; ski resort chalets; city and coastal apartments. The *Allo Vacances* brochure, available through the **French Government Tourist Office,** gives the addresses of estate agents offering holiday lets.

The Gîtes de France logo

CAMPING

ELEVEN THOUSAND official sites are spread around France's diverse countryside. The **Fédération Française de Camping et de Caravaning** publishes a comprehensive list, updated every year. Gîtes de France's *Camping à la Ferme* guide covers some simpler sites on farm land.

Campsites are graded from one to four stars. Three- and four-star sites are usually impressively spacious with plenty of amenities and electricity connections for a percentage of tents and caravans. One- and two-star sites always have toilets, a public phone and running water (though in one-star sites sometimes only cold water). What they lack in facilities they often make up for in peacefulness and rural charm.

Note, some sites only accept visitors with a **camping carnet.** *Carnets* are available from the AA, RAC and the clubs listed on the facing page.

HOSTELS

HOSTELS are a money-saving option for single travellers, though cheap hotels are often no more expensive for those travelling with a partner.

The IYHF's Hostelling guide details the **FUAJ's** (Fédération Unie des Auberges de Jeunesse) 220 hostels around France, open to all ages and offering dormitory accommodation. If you are not a member of the **YHA** (Youth Hostel Association) in your home

A Bordeaux camp site in high season

country, you have to pay a small surcharge each time you stay in a French youth hostel.

UCRIF (Union des Centres de Rencontres Internationales de France) has 63 centres with a cultural bent scattered around France. All have single, shared and dormitory accommodation and a restaurant.

In summer, you can stay in university rooms. Contact **CROUS** (Centre Régional des Oeuvres Universitaires et Scolaires) for details.

Gîtes d'étapes are usually large farmhouses with dormitories close to walking, cycling and horse riding routes. Gîtes de France's *Gîtes d'Etapes* guide details 1,000 of these sites.

DISABLED TRAVELLERS

THE HOLIDAYS and Travel Abroad guide published by **RADAR** (Royal Association for Disability and Rehabilitation) provides details on wheelchair access to some privately owned hotels as well as the main hotel, youth hostel and self-catering chains.

The Carlton International Continental in Cannes *(see p572)*

The **CNRH** (Comité National pour la Réadaptation des Handicapés) holds information on accessible hotels. The **Association des Paralysés de France** also publishes a guide to accessible accommodation called *Où Ferons Nous Etape*.

Gîtes de France produces *Gîtes Accessibles aux Handicapés*, a guide to *gîtes* suitable for disabled people.

FURTHER INFORMATION

THE INVALUABLE *Traveller in France Reference Guide*, listing hotel chains, reservation agencies and companies for every type of package holiday, is published by the French Government Tourist Office. It also distributes *Logis de France* guides, and all the booklets for château-hotels, château-B&Bs and Café-Couette. However, it only distributes the *Relais et Châteaux* guide to personal callers.

The first port of call for all non-hotel accommodation in the French countryside should be Gîtes de France.

When in France, local tourist offices are the best source of information for B&Bs and self-catering accommodation.

Loisirs Acceuil are special booking agencies which deal with queries for hotels, campsites, *gîtes* and B&Bs in their area. There are 53 *Loisirs Acceuil*, found throughout France; the French Government Tourist Office provides contact numbers.

Choosing a Hotel

THE HOTELS in this guide have been selected across a wide price range for their excellent facilities and location. Many also have a highly recommended restaurant. The chart lists the hotels by region, starting with Paris; colour-coded thumb tabs indicate the regions covered on each page. For more details on restaurants, see pp580–613.

	Credit Cards	Children's Facilities	Parking Facilities	Swimming Pool	Garden
PARIS					
ILE ST-LOUIS: *Hôtel des Deux Iles.* Map 9 C4. ⓕⓕⓕ 59 rue St-Louis-en-l'Ile, 75004. 【 01 43 26 13 35. ᶠᵃˣ 01 43 29 60 25. *Rooms: 17.* It's a privilege to stay on the Ile St-Louis. The prices here are reasonable, although the bedrooms are quite small. 🖥 ▤ 📺	AE V	●	■		■
ILE ST-LOUIS: *Hôtel du Jeu de Paume.* Map 9 C4. ⓕⓕⓕ 54 rue St-Louis-en-l'Ile, 75004. 【 01 43 26 14 18. ᶠᵃˣ 01 40 46 02 76. *Rooms: 32* A welcoming, exemplary family hotel. Features include a glass-walled lift, wooden beams, old terracotta paving and a sauna. 🖥 📺	AE DC MC V	●			■
THE MARAIS: *Hôtel de la Place des Vosges.* Map 10 D4. ⓕⓕⓕ 12 rue de Birague, 75004. 【 01 42 72 60 46. ᶠᵃˣ 01 42 72 02 64. *Rooms: 16.* A charming old building close to one of the prettiest squares in Paris. The largest rooms, on the top floor, have good views. 🖥 📺	DC MC V				
THE MARAIS: *Hôtel de la Bretonnerie.* Map 9 C3. ⓕⓕⓕ 22 rue Ste-Croix de la Bretonnerie, 75004. 【 01 48 87 77 63. ᶠᵃˣ 01 42 77 26 78. *Rooms: 30.* Situated on a charming street, this is one of the most comfortable hotels in the Marais. Spacious bedrooms with antique furniture. 🖥 📺	MC V	●			
THE MARAIS: *St-Paul-le-Marais.* Map 10 D3. ⓕⓕⓕ 8 rue de Sévigné, 75004. 【 01 48 04 97 27. ᶠᵃˣ 01 48 87 37 04. *Rooms: 27* Old timber and stone create a rustic environment. If you want to be away from the traffic noise, ask for a room facing the courtyard. 🖥 📺	AE DC MC V	●			■
THE MARAIS: *Pavillion de la Reine.* Map 10 D3. ⓕⓕⓕⓕ 28 place des Vosges, 75003. 【 01 40 29 19 19. ᶠᵃˣ 01 40 29 19 20. *Rooms: 55.* This is the luxury hotel of the Marais. The bedrooms have been sumptuously renovated. The courtyard is a haven of peace. 🖥 ▤ 📺	AE DC MC V	●	■		
BEAUBOURG: *Hôtel Beaubourg.* Map 9 B2. ⓕⓕⓕ 11 rue Simon Lefranc, 75004. 【 01 42 74 34 24. ᶠᵃˣ 01 42 78 68 11. *Rooms: 28.* An extremely comfortable and well-equipped hotel, tastefully restored and decorated, with a pretty courtyard garden. 🖥 📺	AE DC MC V	●			■
BEAUBOURG: *Hôtel Britannique.* Map 9 A3. ⓕⓕⓕ 20 avenue Victoria, 75001. 【 01 42 33 74 59. ᶠᵃˣ 01 42 33 82 65. *Rooms: 40.* A reasonably priced, friendly, family-run hotel in a renovated 19th-century building. 🖥 📺	AE DC MC V	●			
LES HALLES: *Hôtel Agora.* Map 9 A2. ⓕⓕⓕ 7 rue de la Cossonerie, 75001. 【 01 42 33 46 02. ᶠᵃˣ 01 42 33 80 99. *Rooms: 29* A quirkily renovated hotel in a relatively quiet street. The cosy rooms are decorated with polished chests and old paintings. 🖥 📺	AE MC V	●			
LES HALLES: *Hôtel St-Merry.* Map 9 B3. ⓕⓕⓕ 78 rue de la Verrerie, 75004. 【 01 42 78 14 15. ᶠᵃˣ 01 40 29 06 82. *Rooms: 11* The building incorporates the austere St-Merry church and is decorated in 17th-century style with canopied beds and period rugs. 🖥	V				
TUILERIES QUARTER: *Hôtel Brighton.* Map 8 D1. ⓕⓕⓕ 218 rue de Rivoli, 75001. 【 01 47 03 61 61. ᶠᵃˣ 01 42 60 41 78. *Rooms: 70.* The bedrooms have high moulded ceilings and large windows looking either on to the courtyard or the Jardin des Tuileries. Courtyard rooms are quieter but less attractive. 🖥 📺	AE DC MC V	●			
TUILERIES QUARTER: *Hôtel de Crillon.* Map 7 C1. ⓕⓕⓕⓕⓕ 10 pl de la Concorde, 75008. 【 01 47 03 61 61. ᶠᵃˣ 01 44 71 15 02. *Rooms: 163.* Occupying an unrivalled position in the heart of the city, this hotel offers luxurious yet restrained elegance. Magnificent terrace. 🖥 ▤ 📺	AE DC MC V	●	■		■

Price categories for a standard double room (not per person) for one night, including tax and service charges, but not including breakfast.
(F) under F200
(F)(F) F200–400
(F)(F)(F) F400–600
(F)(F)(F)(F) F600–1,000
(F)(F)(F)(F)(F) over F1,000

CHILDREN'S FACILITIES
Cots and baby-sitting available. Some hotels provide children's portions and high chairs in the restaurant.

PARKING FACILITIES
Parking provided by the hotel in either a private car park or a private garage very close by.

SWIMMING POOL
Hotel pools are often quite small and are outdoors unless otherwise stated.

GARDEN
Hotel with garden, courtyard or terrace, often providing tables for eating outside.

Hotel	Credit Cards	Children's Facilities	Parking Facilities	Swimming Pool	Garden
TUILERIES QUARTER: *Hôtel du Louvre*. Map 8 E1. (F)(F)(F)(F) Place André Malraux, 75001. 01 44 58 38 38. FAX 01 44 58 38 01. **Rooms: 197.** If you stay in this hotel, book the Pissaro suite where the artist painted *Place du Théâtre Français*. Very good brasserie.	AE DC MC V	●			▪
TUILERIES QUARTER: *Intercontinental*. Map 8 D1. (F)(F)(F)(F) 3 rue de Castiglione, 75001. 01 44 77 11 11. FAX 01 44 77 14 60. **Rooms: 450.** This elegant late 19th-century hotel was designed by Charles Garnier, architect of the Paris Opéra, and is used for fashion shows.	AE DC MC V	●			▪
TUILERIES QUARTER: *Meurice*. Map 8 D1. (F)(F)(F)(F)(F) 228 rue de Rivoli, 75001. 01 44 58 10 10. FAX 01 44 58 10 15. **Rooms: 180.** A perfect example of successful restoration with excellent replicas of the original plasterwork and furnishings.	AE DC MC V	●			
TUILERIES QUARTER: *Ritz*. Map 4 D5. (F)(F)(F)(F)(F) 15 place Vendôme, 75001. 01 43 16 30 30. FAX 01 43 16 31 78. **Rooms: 187.** After a century, this hotel still lives up to its discreet, high reputation. Original Louis XVI furniture, fireplaces and chandeliers.	AE DC MC V	●	▪	●	▪
OPÉRA QUARTER: *Ambassador*. Map 4 E4. (F)(F)(F)(F) 16 bd Haussmann, 75009. 01 42 46 92 63. FAX 01 40 22 08 74. **Rooms: 289.** One of the best examples of Paris's Art Deco hotels, restored to its former glory with deep carpeting and antique furniture. The ground floor has crystal chandeliers and the food is outstanding.	AE DC MC V	●			
OPÉRA QUARTER: *Grand Hôtel*. Map 4 D5. (F)(F)(F)(F)(F) 2 rue Scribe, 75009. 01 40 07 32 32. FAX 01 42 66 12 51. **Rooms: 540.** Millions have been invested in this hotel – bedrooms are equipped with the utmost comfort and there is a health club.	AE DC MC V	●			
OPÉRA QUARTER: *Westminster*. Map 4 D5. (F)(F)(F)(F) 13 rue de la Paix, 75002. 01 42 61 57 46. FAX 01 42 60 30 66. **Rooms: 101.** The bedrooms are pleasantly furnished, some in period style with marble mantelpieces, chandeliers and 18th-century clocks.	AE DC MC V	●	▪		
INVALIDES QUARTER: *Pavillon*. Map 7 A2. (F)(F)(F) 54 rue Saint Dominique, 75007. 01 45 51 42 87. FAX 01 45 51 32 79. **Rooms: 20.** A small, family-run hotel that guarantees peace and quiet. Although the rooms are small, they are pleasantly decorated. Breakfast is served in the courtyard in summer.	AE DC MC V	●			▪
INVALIDES QUARTER: *Hôtel de Suède*. Map 7 B4. (F)(F)(F) 31 rue Vaneau, 75007. 01 47 05 00 08. FAX 01 47 05 69 27. **Rooms: 39.** This elegant, late 18th-century style hotel overlooks the park of the Hôtel Matignon, home of the prime minister.	AE MC V	●			▪
INVALIDES QUARTER: *Hôtel de Varenne*. Map 7 B2. (F)(F)(F)(F) 44 rue de Bourgogne, 75007. 01 45 51 45 55. FAX 01 45 51 86 63. **Rooms: 24.** A severe façade conceals a narrow courtyard where guests breakfast in the summer. Double glazing in the bedrooms minimizes street noise. Rooms overlooking the courtyard are quiet and cheerful.	AE MC V	●			▪
INVALIDES QUARTER: *Hôtel de Bourgogne & Montana*. Map 7 B2. (F)(F)(F)(F) 3 rue de Bourgogne, 75007. 01 45 51 20 22. FAX 01 45 56 11 98. **Rooms: 34.** Features include a mahogany bar, old lift and circular hall with pink marble columns. The bedrooms are more ordinary, except for those on the fourth floor, which have fantastic views.	AE DC MC V	●			
EIFFEL TOWER QUARTER: *Grand Hôtel Lévêque*. Map 6 F3. (F)(F) 29 rue Cler, 75007. 01 47 05 49 15. FAX 01 45 50 49 36. **Rooms: 50.** Very reasonable hotel with a superb location and friendly owners. Rooms vary in price and size but are all bright and airy.	AE MC V	●			

Price categories for a standard double room (not per person) for one night, including tax and service charges, but not including breakfast.

- Ⓕ under F200
- ⒻⒻ F200–400
- ⒻⒻⒻ F400–600
- ⒻⒻⒻⒻ F600–1,000
- ⒻⒻⒻⒻⒻ over F1,000

CHILDREN'S FACILITIES
Cots and baby-sitting available. Some hotels provide children's portions and high chairs in the restaurant.

PARKING FACILITIES
Parking provided by the hotel in either a private car park or a private garage very close by.

SWIMMING POOL
Hotel pools are often quite small and are outdoors unless otherwise stated.

GARDEN
Hotel with garden, courtyard or terrace, often providing tables for eating outside.

	Credit Cards	Children's Facilities	Parking Facilities	Swimming Pool	Garden
CHAILLOT QUARTER: *Alexander.* Map 1 B5. ⒻⒻⒻⒻⒻ 102 av Victor Hugo, 75116. ☏ 01 45 53 64 65. FAX 01 45 53 12 51. **Rooms:** 62. This comfortable, traditional hotel reflects the bourgeois self-confidence of avenue Victor Hugo. The small, quiet public rooms convey a sense of warmth and intimacy. 🖥 📺	AE DC MC V		■		■
CHAILLOT QUARTER: *Hôtel Paris Kléber Palace.* Map 5 C1. ⒻⒻⒻⒻⒻ 81 avenue Kléber, 75116. ☏ 01 44 05 75 75. FAX 01 44 05 74 74. **Rooms:** 83. Rooms in this hotel by Spanish architect Ricardo Bofill are elegant and luxurious. The lobby is planted with bamboo trees. 🖥 ▤ 📺	AE DC MC V		■	●	
CHAILLOT QUARTER: *Raphaël.* Map 2 D4. ⒻⒻⒻⒻⒻ 17 avenue Kléber, 75116. ☏ 01 44 28 00 28. FAX 01 45 01 21 50. **Rooms:** 90. Many films are shot in the Neo-Gothic bar of this timeless hotel where stars shelter from the paparazzi. A Turner hangs in the hall. 🖥 ▤ 📺	AE DC MC V	●	■		
CHAILLOT QUARTER: *Villa Maillot.* Map 1 C4. ⒻⒻⒻⒻⒻ 143 avenue de Malakoff, 75116. ☏ 01 53 64 52 52. FAX 01 45 00 60 61. **Rooms:** 42. A modern hotel with furnishings inspired by Art Deco. The rooms have large beds, jewellry safes and marble bathrooms. 🖥 ▤ 📺	AE DC MC V	●	■		■
CHAMPS-ELYSÉES: *Résidence Lord Byron.* Map 2 E4. ⒻⒻⒻⒻ 5 rue Chateaubriand, 75008. ☏ 01 43 59 89 98. FAX 01 42 89 46 04. **Rooms:** 31. This small, discreet hotel has a courtyard garden for summer breakfasts. The bedrooms are relatively quiet but not large. 🖥 📺	AE DC MC V	●			■
CHAMPS-ELYSÉES: *Atala.* Map 2 E4. ⒻⒻⒻⒻⒻ 10 rue Chateaubriand, 75008. ☏ 01 45 62 01 62. FAX 01 42 25 66 38. **Rooms:** 48. Situated in a quiet street close to the busy Champs-Elysées, the Atala's rooms overlook a tranquil garden with tall trees. The eighth-floor bedrooms have spectacular views of the Eiffel Tower. 🖥 ▤ 📺	AE DC MC V	●	■		■
CHAMPS-ELYSÉES: *Bristol.* Map 3 A4. ⒻⒻⒻⒻⒻ 112 rue du Faubourg St-Honoré, 75008. ☏ 01 53 43 43 00. FAX 01 53 43 43 01. **Rooms:** 194. One of the city's finest hotels. The large rooms are sumptuously decorated with antiques and have magnificent bathrooms. 🖥 ▤ 📺	AE DC MC V	●	■	●	■
CHAMPS-ELYSÉES: *Concorde La Fayette.* Map 1 C2. ⒻⒻⒻⒻⒻ 3 pl du Général Koenig, 75017. ☏ 01 40 68 50 68. FAX 01 40 68 50 43. **Rooms:** 970. A high-tech tower bristling with facilities including a fitness club, a shopping gallery and an amazing bar on the 33rd floor. 🖥 ▤ 📺	AE DC MC V	●			
CHAMPS-ELYSÉES: *George V.* Map 2 E5. ⒻⒻⒻⒻⒻ 31 avenue George V, 75008. ☏ 01 47 23 54 00. FAX 01 47 20 40 00. **Rooms:** 260 A legendary hotel dotted with secret salons, old furniture and paintings. It also has a wide range of facilities. 🖥 ▤ 📺	AE DC MC V	●	■		
CHAMPS-ELYSÉES: *Plaza Athénée.* Map 6 F1. ⒻⒻⒻⒻⒻ 25 avenue Montaigne, 75008. ☏ 01 53 67 66 65. FAX 01 53 67 66 66. **Rooms:** 211. A hotel for honeymooners and old aristocracy which conforms to the highest contemporary standards of luxury. 🖥 ▤ 📺	AE DC MC V	●	■		■
CHAMPS-ELYSÉES: *Royal Monceau.* Map 2 F3. ⒻⒻⒻⒻⒻ 37 avenue Hoche, 75008. ☏ 01 42 99 88 00. FAX 01 42 99 89 90. **Rooms:** 219. The elegant Royal Monceau takes in one of Paris's most luxurious health clubs and one of the city's best Italian restaurants. 🖥 ▤ 📺	AE DC MC V	●	■	●	
ST-GERMAIN-DES-PRÉS: *Hôtel Solférino.* Map 7 C2. ⒻⒻⒻ 91 rue de Lille, 75007. ☏ 01 47 05 85 54. FAX 01 45 55 51 16. **Rooms:** 33. A small bed and breakfast hotel close to the Musée d'Orsay with simply furnished rooms and a splendid rooftop view. Excellent value. 🖥 📺	AE MC V	●			

St-Germain-des-Prés: *Buci Latin.* **Map** 8 E4. ⒻⒻⒻⒻ AE
34 rue du Buci, 75006. **☎** *01 43 29 07 20.* **FAX** *01 43 29 67 44.* **Rooms:** *27.* DC
A trendy hotel with a minimalist decor which attracts a young crowd. MC
Several suites have balconies and big whirlpool baths. ▤ ▤ TV V

St-Germain-des-Prés: *Hôtel St-Germain-des-Prés.* **Map** 8 E4. ⒻⒻⒻⒻ AE
36 rue Bonaparte, 75006. **☎** *01 43 26 00 19.* **FAX** *01 40 46 83 63.* **Rooms:** *30.* MC
Although this charming and unusual Left Bank hotel is on a busy V
street the noise rarely intrudes. The bedrooms vary in size. ▤ ▤ TV

St-Germain-des-Prés: *Hôtel de l'Université.* **Map** 8 D3. ⒻⒻⒻⒻⒻ AE
22 rue de l'Université, 75007. **☎** *01 42 61 09 39.* **FAX** *01 42 60 40 84.* **Rooms:** *27.* MC
A converted 17th-century town house with antiques and tapestries V
in its public rooms. The basement is a 14th-century crypt. ▤ ▤ TV

Latin Quarter: *Esmeralda.* **Map** 9 A4. ⒻⒻ
4 rue St-Julien-le Pauvre, 75005. **☎** *01 43 54 19 20.* **FAX** *01 40 51 00 68.* **Rooms:** *19.*
The decor reflects contrasting ages and styles behind old stone walls
and under beamed ceilings. The best rooms overlook Notre-Dame. ▤

Latin Quarter: *Hôtel les Degrés de Notre-Dame.* **Map** 9 B4. ⒻⒻⒻ MC
10 rue des Grands-Degrés, 75005. **☎** *01 43 25 88 38.* **FAX** *01 40 46 95 34.* **Rooms:** *10.* V
Choose between a quiet bedroom or one with a wonderful view
of Notre-Dame from the window. Conveniently located. ▤ TV

Latin Quarter: *Hôtel des Grandes Ecoles.* **Map** 9 B5. ⒻⒻⒻ MC
75 rue Cardinal Lemoine, 75005. **☎** *01 43 26 79 23.* **FAX** *01 43 25 28 15.* **Rooms:** *50.* V
An astonishing cluster of three small houses with a garden. Two of
the buildings have retained their old-fashioned charm. ▤

Latin Quarter: *Hôtel des Grands Hommes.* **Map** 13 A1. ⒻⒻⒻⒻ AE
17 place du Panthéon, 75005. **☎** *01 46 34 19 60.* **FAX** *01 43 26 67 32.* **Rooms:** *32.* DC
Sorbonne teachers frequent this quiet family hotel close to the Jardin MC
du Luxembourg. The attic rooms have views of the Panthéon. ▤ ▤ TV V

Latin Quarter: *Hôtel de Notre-Dame.* **Map** 9 B5. ⒻⒻⒻⒻ AE
19 rue Maître Albert, 75005. **☎** *01 43 26 79 00.* **FAX** *01 46 33 50 11.* **Rooms:** *34.* MC
Situated in a quiet street with Notre-Dame just across the river, V
this small hotel makes an ideal base for exploring old Paris. ▤ TV

Latin Quarter: *Hôtel du Panthéon.* **Map** 13 A1. ⒻⒻⒻⒻ AE
19 place du Panthéon, 75005. **☎** *01 43 54 32 95.* **FAX** *01 43 26 64 65.* **Rooms:** *34.* DC
This hotel is managed by the same family as the Hôtel des Grands MC
Hommes and the welcome is equally warm. ▤ TV V

Luxembourg Quarter: *Perreyve.* **Map** 8 E5. ⒻⒻⒻ AE
63 rue Madame, 75006. **☎** *01 45 48 35 01.* **FAX** *01 42 84 03 30.* **Rooms:** *30.* DC
The bedrooms here are sober, simple and clean. The corner ones and MC
those in the attic on the sixth floor are the best. ▤ TV V

Luxembourg Quarter: *Récamier.* **Map** 8 E4. ⒻⒻⒻ MC
3 bis place St-Sulpice, 75006. **☎** *01 43 26 04 89.* **FAX** *01 46 33 27 73.* **Rooms:** *30.* V
A family hotel with no television sets or restaurant. Try to get a room
which looks on to both the courtyard and the square. ▤

Luxembourg Quarter: *Hôtel de l'Abbaye St-Germain.* ⒻⒻⒻⒻ AE
Map 8 D5. 10 rue Cassette, 75006. **☎** *01 45 44 38 11.* **FAX** *01 45 48 07 86.* **Rooms:** *46.* MC
Once an abbey, this elegant hotel still basks in a tranquil atmosphere. V
There is a pretty courtyard and a real fire in the salon. ▤ ▤ TV

Jardin des Plantes Quarter: *Le Jardin des Plantes.* **Map** 13 B1. ⒻⒻⒻ DC
5 rue Linné, 75005. **☎** *01 47 07 06 20.* **FAX** *01 47 07 62 74.* **Rooms:** *33.* MC
This cheerfully decorated hotel in a residential area near the gardens V
has a rooftop terrace and a sauna in the vaulted cellar. ▤ TV

Montparnasse: *Ferrandi.* **Map** 11 C1. ⒻⒻⒻ AE
92 rue du Cherche-Midi, 75006. **☎** *01 42 22 97 40.* **FAX** *01 45 44 89 97.* **Rooms:** *42.* DC
A quiet hotel with a fireplace in the lounge and comfortable MC
bedrooms, many with four-poster or canopied beds. ▤ ▤ TV V

Montparnasse: *L'Atelier Montparnasse.* **Map** 12 D1. ⒻⒻⒻ AE
49 rue Vavin, 75006. **☎** *01 46 33 60 00.* **FAX** *01 40 51 04 21.* **Rooms:** *17.* DC
Visitors receive a gracious family welcome at this original hotel. The MC
bathrooms have mosaic reproductions of famous paintings. ▤ ▤ TV V

Price categories for a standard double room (not per person) for one night, including tax and service charges, but not including breakfast.
- $\textcircled{F}$ under F200
- $\textcircled{F}\textcircled{F}$ F200–400
- $\textcircled{F}\textcircled{F}\textcircled{F}$ F400–600
- $\textcircled{F}\textcircled{F}\textcircled{F}\textcircled{F}$ F600–1,000
- $\textcircled{F}\textcircled{F}\textcircled{F}\textcircled{F}\textcircled{F}$ over F1,000

CHILDREN'S FACILITIES
Cots and baby-sitting available. Some hotels provide children's portions and high chairs in the restaurant.

PARKING FACILITIES
Parking provided by the hotel in either a private car park or a private garage very close by.

SWIMMING POOL
Hotel pools are often quite small and are outdoors unless otherwise stated.

GARDEN
Hotel with garden, courtyard or terrace, often providing tables for eating outside.

	Credit Cards	Children's Facilities	Parking Facilities	Swimming Pool	Garden
MONTPARNASSE: *Hôtel la Ste-Beuve.* Map 12 D1. $\textcircled{F}\textcircled{F}\textcircled{F}$ 9 rue Ste Beuve, 75006. ☎ 01 45 48 20 07. FAX 01 45 48 67 52. *Rooms:* 22. There is a warm and cosy atmosphere in this carefully restored hotel. Breakfast is served at bridge tables or at sofas in the salon. 🛏 ▤ 📺	AE MC V	●			
MONTPARNASSE: *Lenox Montparnasse.* Map 12 D2. $\textcircled{F}\textcircled{F}\textcircled{F}$ 15 rue Delambre, 75014. ☎ 01 43 35 34 50. FAX 01 43 20 46 64. *Rooms:* 52. The overall atmosphere is one of restrained elegance. Each of the six large suites on the upper floor has a fireplace. 🛏 📺	AE DC MC V	●			
MONTPARNASSE: *Villa des Artistes.* Map 12 D2. $\textcircled{F}\textcircled{F}\textcircled{F}$ 9 rue de la Grande Chaumière, 75006. ☎ 01 43 26 60 86. FAX 01 43 54 73 70. *Rooms:* 60. The main charm of this hotel, which aims to evoke the Belle Epoque, is the large patio garden where you can breakfast in peace. 🛏 ▤ 📺	AE DC MC V	●			▪
MONTMARTRE: *Timhôtel.* Map 4 E1. $\textcircled{F}\textcircled{F}\textcircled{F}$ 11 rue Ravignan, 75018. ☎ 01 42 55 74 79. FAX 01 42 55 71 01. *Rooms:* 60. This is one of Montmartre's most delightful hotels. It borders a quiet, charming square and there are good views from the top floors. 🛏 📺	AE DC MC V	●	▪		
MONTMARTRE: *Terrass.* Map 4 E1. $\textcircled{F}\textcircled{F}\textcircled{F}\textcircled{F}$ 12 rue Joseph-de-Maistre, 75018. ☎ 01 46 06 72 85. FAX 01 42 52 29 11. *Rooms:* 101. There are panoramic views over the rooftops of Paris from the upper floors. A few bedrooms retain original Art Deco woodwork. 🛏 📺	AE DC MC V	●	▪		▪

ILE DE FRANCE

	Credit Cards	Children's Facilities	Parking Facilities	Swimming Pool	Garden
BARBIZON: *Hostellerie la Dague* $\textcircled{F}\textcircled{F}$ 5 Grand rue, 77630. ☎ 01 60 66 40 49. FAX 01 60 69 24 59. *Rooms:* 25. This rustic yet chic ivy-hung hotel is popular with Parisians, so book well in advance. The traditional French restaurant is charming. 🛏 📺	DC MC V	●	▪		▪
FONTAINEBLEAU: *Hôtel de l'Aigle Noir* $\textcircled{F}\textcircled{F}\textcircled{F}\textcircled{F}$ 27 pl Napoléon, 77300. ☎ 01 60 74 60 00. FAX 01 60 74 00 01. *Rooms:* 57. This prestigious mansion overlooks Fontainebleau château and its vast park. Gourmet cuisine and impeccable service. 🛏 ▤ 📺	AE DC MC V	●	▪	●	▪
FONTENAY-TRÉSIGNY: *Le Manoir* $\textcircled{F}\textcircled{F}\textcircled{F}\textcircled{F}$ Départmentale 402, 77610. ☎ 01 64 25 91 17. FAX 01 64 25 95 49. *Rooms:* 20. This dreamy manor house set in vast grounds must be most visitors' idea of rural bliss. Distinguished guests arrive by helicopter. 🛏 📺	AE DC MC V	●	▪	●	▪
HERBEVILLE: *Le Mont au Vent* $\textcircled{F}\textcircled{F}\textcircled{F}$ 2 rue de Maule, 78580. ☎ 01 30 90 65 22. FAX 01 34 75 12 54. *Rooms:* 15. Set in appealing countryside, this small village hotel makes a good base for visiting Versailles. Price includes breakfast. Cash only.		●	▪	●	▪
ROISSY-CHARLES-DE-GAULLE: *Novotel Paris Roissy* $\textcircled{F}\textcircled{F}\textcircled{F}$ Charles de Gaulle Airport, 95705. ☎ 01 49 19 27 27. FAX 01 49 19 27 99. *Rooms:* 201. This standard chain hotel is one of the best emergency or en-route stop-overs. Convenience and efficiency are its hallmarks. 🛏 ▤ 📺	AE DC MC V	●	▪		
ST-GERMAIN-EN-LAYE: *La Forestière* $\textcircled{F}\textcircled{F}\textcircled{F}$ 1 av du Président Kennedy, 78100. ☎ 01 39 10 38 38. FAX 01 39 73 73 88. *Rooms:* 30. Exuding an air of rural sophistication, this secluded hotel is set in woodland. Enjoy the gastronomic delights in the restaurant. 🛏 📺	AE MC V	●	▪		▪
ST-GERMAIN-EN-LAYE: *Pavillon Henri IV* $\textcircled{F}\textcircled{F}\textcircled{F}\textcircled{F}$ 19–21 rue Thiers, 78100. ☎ 01 39 10 15 15. FAX 01 39 73 93 73. *Rooms:* 42. This sumptuous hotel-restaurant occupies an elegant lodge built by Henri IV where Louis XIV was born and Alexandre Dumas wrote *The Three Musketeers*. Panoramic views over the Seine Valley. 🛏 📺	AE DC MC V	●	▪		▪

VERSAILLES: *Hôtel de Clagny*   ⓕⓕ
6 impasse de Clagny, 78000. **[** *01 39 50 18 09.* FAX *01 39 50 85 17.* **Rooms:** *21.*
Conveniently close to the station and in a quiet location. The rooms are simply furnished and unremarkable but the welcome is genuine. 🔹 TV
Cards: DC MC V

VERSAILLES: *Trianon Palace*   ⓕⓕⓕⓕ
1 bd de la Reine, 78000. **[** *01 30 84 38 00.* FAX *01 39 49 00 77.* **Rooms:** *90*
Undoubtedly the most spendid hotel in the region, deserving the accolade "palace", blending in with the Classical lines of the Versailles park. The gourmet restaurant is the jewel in the crown. 🔹 ▤ TV
Cards: AE DC MC V

VILLEPREUX: *Château de Villepreux*   ⓕⓕⓕⓕ
Chemin de Grand-Maison, 78450. **[** *01 30 81 78 00.*
FAX *01 30 56 12 12.* **Rooms:** *10.*
This grand, privately owned chambres d'hôte has been in the Saint-Seine family for 200 years. Close to the St-Nom-la-Bretèche golf course. 🔹
Cards: MC V

LE NORD AND PICARDY

AMIENS: *Hôtel de Normandie*   ⓕⓕ
1 bis rue Lamartine, 80000. **[** *03 22 92 06 56.* FAX *03 22 82 22 89.* **Rooms:** *27.*
Five minutes' walk from the station and near the cathedral, this turn-of-the-century hotel represents quiet and simplicity in a busy city. 🔹 TV
Cards: MC V

AMIENS: *La Résidence*   ⓕⓕ
17 rue Porion, 80000. **[** *03 22 92 27 67.* FAX *03 22 92 46 16.* **Rooms:** *21.*
An exceptionally comfortable hotel with tastefully decorated rooms and antique furniture. Only a few steps from the cathedral. 🔹 TV
Cards: DC MC V

ARMBOUTS-CAPPEL: *Hôtel du Lac*   ⓕⓕⓕ
2 bordure du lac, 59380. **[** *03 28 60 70 60.* FAX *03 28 61 06 39.* **Rooms:** *66.*
South of Dunkerque, set beside a lake known for its abundant bird life, this is an exceptionally comfortable and modern hotel. 🔹 TV
Cards: AE DC MC V

BERCK-SUR-MER: *Hôtel Neptune*   ⓕⓕ
Esplanade Parmentier, 62600. **[** *03 21 09 21 21.* FAX *03 21 09 29 29.* **Rooms:** *63.*
An airy and elegant hotel on the seafront. Rooms are simple but stylish with white and blue decor. The restaurant has great sea views. 🔹 TV
Cards: AE MC V

BOULOGNE-SUR-MER: *Hôtel Métropole*   ⓕⓕⓕ
51 rue Thiers, 62200. **[** *03 21 31 54 30.* FAX *03 21 30 45 72.* **Rooms:** *25.*
Boulogne is notoriously short of hotels with character, but this one is exceptionally comfortable and convenient for shopping. 🔹 TV
Cards: AE DC MC V

CALAIS: *Le Climat de France*   ⓕⓕ
Digue G Berthe, 62100. **[** *03 21 34 64 64.* FAX *03 21 34 35 39.* **Rooms:** *45.*
Overlooking the beach is this comfortable and convenient hotel, a welcoming establishment with an inexpensive restaurant. 🔹 TV
Cards: AE DC MC V

CAMBRAI: *Le Mouton Blanc*   ⓕⓕ
33 rue Alsace Lorraine, 59400. **[** *03 27 81 30 16.* FAX *03 27 81 83 54.* **Rooms:** *32.*
Situated between the beautiful old church of St-Géry and the centre of the historic town, this hotel offers convenience and comfort. 🔹 TV
Cards: AE MC V

DUNKERQUE: *Welcome Hotel*   ⓕⓕ
37 rue du Prés Poincaré, 59140. **[** *03 28 59 20 70.* FAX *03 28 21 03 49.* **Rooms:** *39.*
This modern hotel is centrally situated and offers every convenience from mini-bar to cable TV. Restaurant and Mexican-style bar. 🔹 TV
Cards: AE MC V

FREVENT: *Le Vert Bocage*   ⓕⓕ
Monchel-sur-Canche, 62270. **[** *03 21 47 96 75.* FAX *03 21 03 24 17.* **Rooms:** *10.*
Set in its own large and well-laid out garden with a small lake, this modern, purpose-built hotel is a haven of calm and comfort. 🔹 TV
Cards: MC V

GOSNAY: *La Chartreuse de Val St-Esprit*   ⓕⓕⓕ
1 rue de Fouquières, 62199. **[** *03 21 62 80 00.* FAX *03 21 62 42 50.* **Rooms:** *56.*
A sumptuous, peaceful château with much of its original furniture. Its *restaurant gastronomique* specializes in fresh seafood, and the dining room is a setting in which to enjoy dining in style. 🔹 ▤ TV
Cards: AE DC MC V

GUISE: *Hôtel Champagne Picardie*   ⓕⓕ
41 rue A Godin, 02120. **[** *03 23 60 43 44.* **Rooms:** *12.*
A mansion in the historic town of Guise, the hotel backs on to its own substantial garden, which is overlooked by half the bedrooms. 🔹 TV
Cards: MC V

Price categories for a standard double room (not per person) for one night, including tax and service charges, but not including breakfast.
Ⓕ under F200
ⒻⒻ F200–400
ⒻⒻⒻ F400–600
ⒻⒻⒻⒻ F600–1,000
ⒻⒻⒻⒻⒻ over F1,000

CHILDREN'S FACILITIES
Cots and baby-sitting available. Some hotels provide children's portions and high chairs in the restaurant.

PARKING FACILITIES
Parking provided by the hotel in either a private car park or a private garage very close by.

SWIMMING POOL
Hotel pools are often quite small and are outdoors unless otherwise stated.

GARDEN
Hotel with garden, courtyard or terrace, often providing tables outside for eating outside.

	CREDIT CARDS	CHILDREN'S FACILITIES	PARKING FACILITIES	SWIMMING POOL	GARDEN
LAON: *Hôtel de la Bannière de France* ⒻⒻ 11 rue Franklin Roosevelt, 02000. ☎ 03 23 23 21 44. FAX 03 23 23 31 56. **Rooms:** 18. Charming coaching inn within the ancient walled town of Laon. Good views and a convenient stop to and from the Channel ports. 🍴 📺	AE DC MC V	●	▪		
LAON: *Hostellerie St-Vincent* ⒻⒻ 29 avenue Charles de Gaulle, 02000. ☎ 03 23 23 42 43. FAX 03 23 79 22 55. **Rooms:** 47. A comfortable and modern establishment, easy to find on the east side of this ancient town. Both hotel and restaurant are good value. 🍴 📺	AE MC V		▪		▪
LE TOUQUET: *Novotel-Thalamer* ⒻⒻⒻⒻ Front de Mer, 62520. ☎ 03 21 09 85 00. FAX 03 21 09 85 10. **Rooms:** 149. Large hotel on the seafront offering bright, functional rooms with superb views. Relax in the saltwater spa and sauna. 🍴 📺	AE MC V	●	▪	●	
LONGPONT: *Hôtel de l'Abbaye* ⒻⒻ 3 rue des Tourelles, 02600. ☎ 03 23 96 02 44. FAX 03 23 96 02 44. **Rooms:** 12. The name is taken from a 12th-century ruined abbey nearby and the hotel is almost as old. Good restaurant serving local cuisine. 🍴	MC V	●	▪		
MAUBEUGE: *Hôtel Shakespeare* ⒻⒻ 3 rue du Commerce, 59600. ☎ 03 27 65 14 14. FAX 03 27 64 04 66. **Rooms:** 35. Modern, functional and efficiently run hotel with a friendly atmosphere. There is a restaurant and a comfortable bar. 🍴 📺	AE DC MC V		▪		
MONTREUIL: *Le Darnetal* ⒻⒻ Place Darnetal, 62170. ☎ 03 21 06 04 87. FAX 03 21 86 64 67. **Rooms:** 4. Booking is essential at this hotel-restaurant in the old fortified town of Montreuil. Old-style rooms all with en-suite bathrooms. The dinner menu is excellent value, especially the oyster dishes. 🍴	AE DC MC V				
PÉRONNE: *Hostellerie des Remparts* ⒻⒻ 21 rue Beaubois, 80200. ☎ 03 22 84 01 22. FAX 03 22 84 31 96. **Rooms:** 16. Some rooms overlook the old fortifications of the town and their ornamental gardens. Substantial refurbishment has lessened its old-fashioned character. 🍴 📺	AE DC MC V	●	▪		▪
REUILLY-SAUVIGNY: *L'Auberge le Relais* ⒻⒻ 2 rue de Paris, 02850. ☎ 03 23 70 35 36. FAX 03 23 70 27 76. **Rooms:** 7. An old *ferme-auberge* with some modern additions in this tiny village. It has a glass conservatory overlooking a lovely garden. 🍴 ▤ 📺	AE DC MC V		▪		▪
ST-OMER: *Hôtel St-Louis* ⒻⒻ 25 rue d'Arras, 62500. ☎ 03 21 38 35 21. FAX 03 21 38 57 26. **Rooms:** 30. Situated right in the centre of a historic cathedral town is this 18th-century coaching inn. The bedrooms have been modernized, but the restaurant retains the flavour of the old days. 🍴 📺	MC V	●	▪		
ST-QUENTIN: *Grand Hôtel* ⒻⒻⒻ 6–8 rue Dachery, 02100. ☎ 03 23 62 69 77. FAX 03 23 62 53 52. **Rooms:** 24. Well-designed and tastefully decorated rooms. The restaurant, *Le Président*, is a must for dinner and breakfast as well. 🍴 📺	AE DC MC V	●	▪		
SARS-POTERIES: *Hôtel Fleuri* ⒻⒻ 65 rue du Général de Gaulle, 59216. ☎ 03 27 61 62 72. **Rooms:** 11. Simple but charming bed-and-breakfast accommodation with an excellent restaurant next door. 🍴	MC V		▪		▪
SEBOURG: *Hôtel et Restaurant Jardin Fleuri* ⒻⒻ 23 rue du Moulin, 59990. ☎ 03 27 26 53 31. FAX 03 27 26 50 08. **Rooms:** 10. Southeast of Valenciennes lies this quiet country hotel-restaurant in its own immense flower garden. There are tables outside and the restaurant, a short walk away, faces on to the village street. 🍴 📺	MC V		▪		▪

Vervins: *La Tour de Roy* ⓕⓕⓕ AE MC V
45 rue du Général Leclerc, 02140. 【 03 23 98 00 11. FAX *03 23 98 00 72*. **Rooms:** *18.*
An exceptionally comfortable and quiet hotel, with hand-painted bathrooms. There is a splendid garden and outdoor tables.

Wimereux: *Hôtel Paul et Virginie* ⓕⓕ MC V
19 rue Général de Gaulle, 62930. 【 03 21 32 42 12. FAX *03 21 87 65 85*. **Rooms:** *15.*
This attractive 19th-century building stands neatly between the beach and shops, in a delightful seaside town. Caters well for families.

CHAMPAGNE

Andelot: *Le Cantarel* ⓕⓕ MC V
Place Cantarel, 52700. 【 03 25 01 31 13. FAX *03 25 03 15 41*. **Rooms:** *8.*
Andelot lies northeast of Chaumont on the road to Neufchâteau. This hotel in the village square has a good, inexpensive restaurant.

Bourbonne-les-Bains: *Hôtel Jeanne d'Arc* ⓕⓕ AE MC V
Rue Amiral-Pierre, 52400. 【 03 25 90 46 00. FAX *03 25 90 46 00*. **Rooms:** *33.*
The town is a thermal spa and this well-equipped hotel is right beside the pump room. The surrounding countryside is magnificent.

Châlons-en-Champagne: *Hôtel du Pot d'Etain* ⓕⓕ V DC MC
18 place de la République, 51000. 【 03 26 68 09 09. FAX *03 26 68 58 18*. **Rooms:** *27*
This 15th-century private hotel in the centre of town is run by a family of bakers and there are fresh-baked croissants for breakfast.

Champillon: *Royal Champagne* ⓕⓕⓕⓕ AE DC MC V
Bellevue, 51160. 【 03 26 52 87 11. FAX *03 26 52 89 69*. **Rooms:** *29.*
Situated on the summit of the wooded Montagne de Reims, this 16th-century staging-post houses a welcoming hotel-restaurant.

Charleville-Mézières: *Le Clèves* ⓕⓕ AE DC MC V
43 rue de l'Arquebuse, 08000. 【 03 24 33 10 75. FAX *03 24 59 01 25*. **Rooms:** *47.*
This hotel is on a quiet street next door to the house where the poet Rimbaud was born. Smart and comfortable dining room.

Charleville-Mézières: *Le Relais du Square* ⓕⓕ AE DC MC V
3 place de la Gare, 08000. 【 03 24 33 38 76. FAX *03 24 33 56 66*. **Rooms:** *49.*
Despite the address, the hotel is out of earshot of the trains. There is a cosy bar and the hotel is connected to a decent restaurant.

Chaumont: *Le Grand Val* ⓕⓕ AE DC MC V
Route de Langres, 52000. 【 03 25 03 90 35. FAX *03 25 32 11 80*. **Rooms:** *52.*
On the road to Langres and Dijon stands this simple stone-built hotel with wood-panelling and fine views across the Marne Valley.

Epernay: *Hôtel de la Cloche* ⓕ AE MC V
3 place Mendès-France, 51200. 【 03 26 55 24 05. FAX *03 26 51 88 05*. **Rooms:** *19.*
This is the best hotel-restaurant in its category in Epernay, the capital of Champagne. *La Cloche* offers modest but sunny rooms and a good restaurant serving a choice of regional specialities.

Epernay: *Micheline & Jean-Marie Tarlant* ⓕⓕ MC V
Oeuilly, RN3, 51480. 【 03 26 58 30 60. FAX *03 26 58 37 31*. **Rooms:** *4.*
Grapepickers' cottages have been converted into guest rooms on this family-run wine estate. Breakfast is in a charming conservatory and can be followed by a visit to the champagne cellars below.

Etoges: *Château d'Etoges* ⓕⓕⓕ AE DC MC V
4 rue Richebourg, 51270. 【 03 26 59 30 08. FAX *03 26 59 35 57*. **Rooms:** *21.*
This impressive 17th-century château, with moat and decorative towers, is still inhabited and presented very much as a grand private home.

Haybes-sur-Meuse: *L'Ermitage Moulin Labotte* ⓕⓕ MC V
08170 Haybes-sur-Meuse. 【 03 24 41 13 44. FAX *03 24 40 46 72*. **Rooms:** *10.*
A remote 18th-century converted mill set in woodland. There is an atmospheric dining room with a slate floor and mill-wheel.

Langres: *Grand Hôtel de l'Europe* ⓕⓕ MC V
23–25 rue Diderot, 52200. 【 03 25 87 10 88. FAX *03 25 87 60 65*. **Rooms:** *28.*
The hotel is easy to find, in the main street of this market town. It is a listed 17th-century building, with a beautifully preserved dining room of the period, but with modernized bedrooms.

Price categories for a standard double room (not per person) for one night, including tax and service charges, but not including breakfast.
Ⓕ under F200
ⒻⒻ F200–400
ⒻⒻⒻ F400–600
ⒻⒻⒻⒻ F600–1,000
ⒻⒻⒻⒻⒻ over F1,000

CHILDREN'S FACILITIES
Cots and baby-sitting available. Some hotels provide children's portions and high chairs in the restaurant.

PARKING FACILITIES
Parking provided by the hotel in either a private car park or a private garage very close by.

SWIMMING POOL
Hotel pools are often quite small and are outdoors unless otherwise stated.

GARDEN
Hotel with garden, courtyard or terrace, often providing tables for eating outside.

Hotel	Price	Credit Cards	Children's Facilities	Parking Facilities	Swimming Pool	Garden
MAGNANT: *Le Val Moret* 10110 Magnant. ☎ 03 25 29 85 12. FAX 03 25 29 70 81. **Rooms:** 30. A single-storey modern motel on the autoroute from Calais to Dijon. Comfortable with a good and reasonably priced restaurant.	ⒻⒻ	AE MC V	●	▪		▪
MESNIL-ST-PÉRE: *L'Auberge du Lac* 10140 Mesnil-St-Pére. ☎ 03 25 41 27 16. FAX 03 25 41 57 59. **Rooms:** 15. This old-fashioned inn takes its name from the nearby lake in the Forêt d'Orient, where fishing, bathing and tennis are all available.	ⒻⒻ	MC V		▪		▪
MONTHERMÉ: *Le Franco-Belge* 2 rue Pasteur, 08800. ☎ 03 24 53 01 20. FAX 03 24 53 54 49. **Rooms:** 15. A family-run hotel overlooking the village square. The cuisine is home prepared using fresh garden produce.	ⒻⒻ	MC V	●			▪
REIMS: *Hôtel Crystal* 86 place Drouet d'Erlon, 51100. ☎ 03 26 88 44 44. FAX 03 26 47 49 28. **Rooms:** 31. This old-fashioned hotel borders the liveliest square in Reims yet is surprisingly quiet. In summer breakfast is served on the terrace.	ⒻⒻ	AE MC V				▪
REIMS: *Boyer les Crayères* 64 bd Henri Vasnier, 51100. ☎ 03 26 82 80 80. FAX 03 26 82 65 52. **Rooms:** 19. This is a renowned hotel on the gastronomic and champagne-tasting trail. Discreetly sumptuous, it occupies a Belle Epoque mansion, set in attractive grounds on the outskirts of Reims.	ⒻⒻⒻⒻⒻ	AE DC MC V	●	▪		▪
RETHEL: *Le Moderne* Place de la Gare, 08300. ☎ 03 24 38 44 54. FAX 03 24 38 37 84. **Rooms:** 22. A thoroughly modernized establishment that guarantees peace and comfort. Excellent local cuisine is served in the restaurant.	ⒻⒻ	AE DC MC V		▪		▪
ST-DIZIER: *Hôtel Gambetta* 62 rue Gambetta, 52100. ☎ 03 25 56 52 10. FAX 03 25 56 39 47. **Rooms:** 63. A modern establishment with conference facilities and an inexpensive restaurant. Many tourists come to St-Dizier to see the bird-life at the famous Lac du Der-Chantecoq nearby.	ⒻⒻ	AE DC MC V	●	▪		
SEDAN: *L'Auberge du Port* Bazeilles, 08140. ☎ 03 24 27 13 89. FAX 03 24 29 35 58. **Rooms:** 20. Exceptionally comfortable hotel on the banks of the river Meuse, ideal for visitors in search of peace and quiet. Meals on the terrace.	ⒻⒻ	AE DC MC V		▪		
SEPT-SAULX: *Le Cheval Blanc* Rue du Moulin, 51400. ☎ 03 26 03 90 27. FAX 03 26 03 97 09. **Rooms:** 25. Set among Champagne vineyards, this hotel-restaurant makes a convenient stop-over for visitors to Alsace and Burgundy. The gourmet restaurant is worth visiting in its own right.	ⒻⒻⒻ	AE DC MC V	●	▪		▪
TROYES: *Grand Hôtel* 4 av Maréchal-Joffre, 10000. ☎ 03 25 79 90 90. FAX 03 25 78 48 93. **Rooms:** 100. A large, modern establishment incorporating no less than eight restaurants, including a brasserie, pizzeria and *gastronomique*.	ⒻⒻ	AE MC V	●	▪	●	▪
TROYES: *Hôtel des Comtes de Champagne* 54–56 rue de la Monnaie, 10000. ☎ 03 25 73 11 70. FAX 03 25 73 06 02. **Rooms:** 27. This solid private mansion, located on a quiet street, was once the medieval bank of the Counts of Champagne. Individualistic rooms with period furniture. Perfect for exploring the city centre.	ⒻⒻ	MC V	●			▪
VIGNORY: *Le Relais Verdoyant* Quartier de la Gare, 52320. ☎ 03 25 02 44 49. FAX 03 25 01 96 89. **Rooms:** 7. An old converted country farm in a peaceful hamlet. Halfway between Chaumont and Joinville. Friendly and totally relaxing.	ⒻⒻ	MC V	●			▪

ALSACE AND LORRAINE

BAREMBACH: *Château de Barembach* ⓕⓕⓕ AE DC MC V
5 rue du Mal de Lattre, 67130. 【 *03 88 97 97 50.* FAX *03 88 47 17 19. Rooms: 15.*
An exquisite Renaissance château, now a family-run hotel. An ideal
holiday centre for outdoor activities with its own tennis court. 🚗 TV

COLMAR: *Hôtel Beauséjour* ⓕⓕ AE MC V
25 rue du Ladhof, 68000. 【 *03 89 41 37 16.* FAX *03 89 41 43 07. Rooms: 44.*
A family hotel – reasonably priced family rooms, some with kitchenette.
Facilities include children's play area, sauna and fitness room. 🚗 TV

COLMAR: *Hôtel le Maréchal* ⓕⓕⓕⓕ MC V
4–6 place des Six-Montagnes-Noires, 68000. 【 *03 89 41 60 32.*
FAX *03 89 24 59 40. Rooms: 30.*
A 16th-century timber-framed house, Colmar's premier city-centre hotel
is on the waterfront in the atmospheric Petite Venise quarter. 🚗 ▤ TV

EGUISHEIM: *Hostellerie du Pape* ⓕⓕ AE DC MC V
10 Grand rue, 68420. 【 *03 89 41 41 21.* FAX *03 89 41 41 31. Rooms: 33.*
An appealing hotel-restaurant set in the most perfectly preserved small
town, bordering the oldest quarter and well-placed for shops. 🚗 TV

EPINAL: *Hôtel de l'Europe* ⓕⓕ AE DC MC V
16 rue Blaudez, 88000. 【 *03 29 82 21 04.* FAX *03 29 64 23 47. Rooms: 36.*
Across the river from the Musée des Vosges, the hotel is an old building
carefully modernized, some rooms in Louis XV style. Sauna. 🚗 TV

GÉRARDMER: *M Paul Gegout* ⓕ
Le Phény, 123 Chemin des Rochottes, 88400. 【 *03 29 63 03 39. Rooms: 3.*
Farmhouse overlooking the Vosges mountains with simple, rustic
rooms and wonderful views. Excellent local cuisine.

METZ: *Grand Hôtel de Metz* ⓕⓕ AE DC MC V
3 rue des Clercs, 57000. 【 *03 87 36 16 33.* FAX *03 87 74 17 04. Rooms: 62.*
Close to the cathedral, market and restaurants, this established hotel
combines a Neo-Baroque lobby with countrified rooms. 🚗 TV

MOLSHEIM: *Hôtel Bugatti* ⓕⓕ AE MC V
Rue de la Commanderie, 67120. 【 *03 88 49 89 00.* FAX *03 88 38 36 00. Rooms: 45.*
Molsheim is where the great motor manufacturer Bugatti lived, and the
factory still stands across from the hotel. Guests can use the pool at the
Hôtel Diana and there are riding stables nearby. 🚗 TV

MULHOUSE: *Novotel Mulhouse–Sausheim* ⓕⓕⓕ AE DC MC V
Rue de L'Ile-Napoléon, 68390. 【 *03 89 61 84 84.* FAX *03 89 61 77 99. Rooms: 77.*
The Novotel chain offers great family bargains and caters well for
children – there is a toddlers' play area. 🚗 ▤ TV

NANCY: *Hôtel Albert Ier et Astoria* ⓕⓕ AE DC MC V
3 rue Armée-Patton, 54000. 【 *03 33 40 31 24.* FAX *03 33 28 47 78. Rooms: 85.*
This welcoming hotel is just a few minutes' walk from place Stanislas. The
decor is modern and the rooms well-equipped, comfortable and quiet. 🚗 TV

NANCY: *Grand Hôtel de la Reine* ⓕⓕⓕⓕ AE DC MC V
2 place Stanislas, 54000. 【 *03 83 35 03 01.* FAX *03 83 32 86 04. Rooms: 48.*
As well as the elegant luxury of this 18th-century palace in the town's main
square, the Stanislas restaurant is excellent. 🚗 TV

OBERNAI: *Hôtel des Vosges* ⓕⓕ MC V
5 place de la Gare, 67210. 【 *03 88 95 53 78.* FAX *03 88 49 92 65. Rooms: 20.*
There is nothing pretentious about this functional, modern hotel.
Standards are high and the restaurant is excellent value. 🚗 TV

REMIREMONT: *Hôtel du Cheval de Bronze* ⓕⓕ AE MC V
59 rue Charles de Gaulle, 88200. 【 *03 29 62 52 24.* FAX *03 29 62 34 90. Rooms: 35.*
An old-fashioned hotel that is a useful stop-over for travellers crossing
Alsace or Lorraine and a good base for exploring the Vosges. There is
no restaurant but the owner is happy to recommend. 🚗 TV

RIBEAUVILLE: *Hôtel de Mouton* ⓕⓕ MC V
5 place de la Sinne, 68150. 【 *03 89 73 60 11.* FAX *03 89 73 74 62. Rooms: 14*
A delightful 14th-century wine-grower's house in the old quarter.
Spacious, charming rooms and inexpensive restaurant. 🚗 TV

For key to symbols see back flap

Price categories for a standard double room (not per person) for one night, including tax and service charges, but not including breakfast.
- F under F200
- FF F200–400
- FFF F400–600
- $FFFF$ F600–1,000
- $FFFFF$ over F1,000

CHILDREN'S FACILITIES
Cots and baby-sitting available. Some hotels provide children's portions and high chairs in the restaurant.

PARKING FACILITIES
Parking provided by the hotel in either a private car park or a private garage very close by.

SWIMMING POOL
Hotel pools are often quite small and are outdoors unless otherwise stated.

GARDEN
Hotel with garden, courtyard or terrace, often providing tables for eating outside.

	Price	CREDIT CARDS	CHILDREN'S FACILITIES	PARKING FACILITIES	SWIMMING POOL	GARDEN
SAVERNE: *Chez Jean* 3 rue de la Gare, 67700. ☎ 03 88 91 10 19. FAX 03 88 91 27 45. **Rooms:** 25. A four-storeyed traditional Alsatian house with views of the hills behind the town. There is a delightful wine bar downstairs. 🖨 TV	FFF	AE DC MC V		■		■
SÉLESTAT: *Auberge des Alliés* 39 rue des Chevaliers, 67600. ☎ 03 88 92 09 34. FAX 03 88 92 12 88. **Rooms:** 17. The decor of this charming *logis de France* is one of exposed beams, polished wood and decorative knick-knacks. 🖨 TV	FF	MC V				
STRASBOURG: *Au Cerf d'Or* 6 place de l'Hôpital, 67000. ☎ 03 88 36 20 05. FAX 03 88 36 68 67. **Rooms:** 37. The main hotel has more charming rooms, but the annexe offers a small pool and sauna. Nearby are several waterfront restaurants. 🖨 TV	FF	MC V	●		●	
STRASBOURG: *Relais Mercure* 3 rue Maire Kuss, 67000. ☎ 03 88 32 80 80. FAX 03 88 23 05 39. **Rooms:** 52. An old-fashioned red-brick hotel with very helpful management. 🖨 ▤ TV	FF	AE MC V				■
STRASBOURG: *Régent Petite France* 5 rue des Moulins, 67000. ☎ 03 88 76 43 43. FAX 03 88 76 43 76. **Rooms:** 72. The city's most prestigious and ideally located deluxe hotel. Set in a converted watermill, it overlooks the Petite France district. 🖨 ▤ TV	$FFFFF$	AE DC MC V	●	■		
VERDUN: *Hostellerie du Coq Hardie* 8 avenue de la Victoire, 55100. ☎ 03 29 86 36 36. FAX 03 29 86 09 21. **Rooms:** 35. This handsome Lorraine hotel offers traditional comfort and a friendly reception. Delicious traditional cooking, but rather expensive. 🖨 TV	FFF	AE DC MC V		■		
WANTZENAU: *Le Moulin de la Wantzenau* 3 impasse de Moulin, 67610. ☎ 03 88 59 22 22. FAX 03 88 59 22 00. **Rooms:** 20. An imposing converted mill that makes a pleasant place to stop en route to Lorraine and Germany. Peaceful atmosphere. 🖨 TV	FFF	AE MC V	●	■		■

NORMANDY

	Price	CREDIT CARDS	CHILDREN'S FACILITIES	PARKING FACILITIES	SWIMMING POOL	GARDEN
L'AIGLE: *Hôtel du Dauphin* Place de la Halle, 61300. ☎ 02 33 84 18 00. FAX 02 33 34 09 28. **Rooms:** 30. A fine stone-built inn close to the biggest market in Normandy. High-class, traditional hospitality and business facilities. 🖨 TV	FF	AE DC MC V	●	■		
ALENÇON: *Hôtel le Chapeau Rouge* 3 boulevard Duchamp, 61000. ☎ 02 33 26 20 23. FAX 02 33 26 54 05. **Rooms:** 14. A modern, serviceable hotel ten minutes' walk from the town centre. The restaurant (of the same name) next door is English-run. 🖨 TV	FF	AE MC V	●	■		
BAGNOLES DE L'ORNE: *Hôtel de Normandie* 2 av de la Ferté-Macé, 61140. ☎ 02 33 30 80 16. FAX 02 33 37 06 19. **Rooms:** 20. A handsome old stone-built inn with a highly recommended restaurant. In addition to its own attractive garden there is a fine view from the front across wooded countryside and park. Reasonably priced. 🖨 TV	FF	AE DC MC V	●	■		■
BALISNE: *Hôtel Moulin de Balisne* Le Moulin de Balisne, 27130. ☎ 02 32 32 03 48. FAX 02 32 60 11 22. **Rooms:** 12. Set in its own vast park, this delightful country hotel is good value. The conversion of the ancient mill has been tastefully done. 🖨 TV	FF	AE DC MC V	●	■		■
BÉNOUVILLE: *Le Manoir d'Hastings* 18 avenue de la Côte-de-Nacre, 14970. ☎ 02 31 44 62 43 FAX 02 31 44 76 18. **Rooms:** 15. A modern hotel built on to a 17th-century building which is now the restaurant. Each bedroom has its own sitting-room. Helpful staff. 🖨 TV	FFF	AE DC MC V	●	■		■

BRIONNE: *Auberge du Vieux Donjon* ⒻⒻ
Pl Frémont-des-Essarts, 27800. **[** *02 32 44 80 62.* **FAX** *02 32 45 83 23.* **Rooms:** *8.*
A perfect old-fashioned country inn on the edge of the market square.
For centuries farmers have come here to enjoy a hearty meal. 🖼 📺
MC V

CABOURG: *Grand Hôtel* ⒻⒻⒻⒻ
Promenade Marcel-Proust, 14390. **[** *02 31 91 01 79.* **FAX** *02 31 24 03 20.* **Rooms:** *70.*
A huge, white Belle Epoque hotel standing on the seafront with vast
rooms and balconies. Marcel Proust often stayed here. 🖼 📺
AE DC MC V

CAEN: *Le Relais des Gourmets* ⒻⒻⒻ
15 rue de Geôle, 14000. **[** *02 31 86 06 01.* **FAX** *02 31 39 06 00.* **Rooms:** *28.*
A modern hotel built and decorated in traditional style, with an elegant
dining room. Impressive views of Caen château. 🖼 📺
AE DC MC V

CAEN: *Hôtel Mercure* ⒻⒻⒻ
1 rue Courtonne, 14000. **[** *02 31 47 24 24.* **FAX** *02 31 47 43 88.* **Rooms:** *114.*
Despite its central location, an atmosphere of quiet elegance pervades,
with every attention paid to the comfort of the guests. 🖼 ▤ 📺
AE DC MC V

CEAUX: *Le Relais du Mont* ⒻⒻ
Labuvette, 50220. (Route N175.) **[** *02 33 70 92 55.* **FAX** *02 33 70 94 57.* **Rooms:** *28.*
Facing west with splendid sunsets over Mont-St-Michel, this modern
hotel has family rooms available and an excellent restaurant. 🖼 📺
AE MC V

DEAUVILLE: *Hôtel Normandy* ⒻⒻⒻⒻ
38 rue J-Mermoz, 14800. **[** *02 31 98 66 22.* **FAX** *02 31 98 66 23.* **Rooms:** *300.*
Despite its modernization, this friendly hotel has retained its original
charm. Meals are served in the courtyard under the apple trees. 🖼 📺
AE DC MC V

EVREUX: *Le Paris* Ⓕ
32 rue de la Harpe, 27000. **[** *02 32 39 12 97.* **Rooms:** *6.*
Quietly situated in a pedestrianized street, close to the cathedral and the town
centre. Clean, simple rooms are sensibly priced, and the welcome is warm.
AE DC MC V

FALAISE: *Hôtel de la Poste* ⒻⒻ
38 rue Georges-Clemenceau,14700. **[** *02 31 90 13 14.* **FAX** *02 31 90 01 81.* **Rooms:** *20.*
The hotel accommodation is comfortable and the restaurant is very
good value. The busy street quietens down at night. 🖼 📺
AE DC MC V

FÉCAMP: *Hôtel de l'Univers* Ⓕ
5 place St-Etienne, 76400. **[** *02 35 28 05 88.* **FAX** *02 35 27 82 58.* **Rooms:** *16.*
An inexpensive and family-run hotel in the centre of this attractive,
busy fishing port. Facilities remain simple but staff are attentive. 🖼 📺
MC V

FONTENAI-SUR-ORNE: *Le Faisan Doré* ⒻⒻ
Route de Paris, 61200. **[** *02 33 67 18 11.* **FAX** *02 33 35 82 15.* **Rooms:** *14.*
A large, moderately priced and impressively professional hotel. There
is a beautiful garden with a terrace for dining out in summer. 🖼 📺
AE MC V

GACÉ: *Castel le Morphée* ⒻⒻ
2 route de Lisieux, 61230. **[** *02 33 35 51 01.* **FAX** *02 33 35 51 62.* **Rooms:** *11.*
Large, turreted house set back from the road. Rooms in the main
building are elegant, those in the annexe more cottage-like. 🖼 📺
AE DC MC V

GRANDCAMP-MAISY: *Hôtel Duguésclin* ⒻⒻ
4 quai Crampon, 14450. **[** *02 31 22 64 22.* **FAX** *02 31 22 34 79.* **Rooms:** *30.*
Friendly and efficiently run modern hotel on the seafront in this small
fishing port. Boasts an excellent restaurant. 🖼 📺
AE MC V

GRANVILLE: *Hôtel Normandy Chaumière* ⒻⒻ
20 rue Dr Paul Poirier, 50400. **[** *02 33 50 01 71.* **FAX** *02 33 50 15 34.* **Rooms:** *6.*
The hotel is close to shops, restaurants and casino in this charming
town. Highly recommended restaurant serving excellent seafood. 🖼 📺
MC V

HONFLEUR: *La Ferme St-Siméon* ⒻⒻⒻⒻ
Rue A-Marais, 14600. **[** *02 31 89 23 61.* **FAX** *02 31 89 48 48.* **Rooms:** *34.*
Ancient farmhouse on the Seine estuary, beautifully converted in to guest
rooms. Renoir, Cézanne and other Impressionists used to meet here. 🖼 📺
AE MC V

ISIGNY-SUR-MER: *Hôtel de France* ⒻⒻ
17 rue Emile-Demagny, 14230. **[** *02 31 22 00 33.* **FAX** *02 31 22 79 19.* **Rooms:** *19.*
A friendly and comfortable small hotel in this picturesque fishing port.
Local ingredients are favoured in the excellent restaurant. 🖼 📺
MC V

Price categories for a standard double room (not per person) for one night, including tax and service charges, but not including breakfast.
- Ⓕ under F200
- ⒻⒻ F200–400
- ⒻⒻⒻ F400–600
- ⒻⒻⒻⒻ F600–1,000
- ⒻⒻⒻⒻⒻ over F1,000

CHILDREN'S FACILITIES
Cots and baby-sitting available. Some hotels provide children's portions and high chairs in the restaurant.

PARKING FACILITIES
Parking provided by the hotel in either a private car park or a private garage very close by.

SWIMMING POOL
Hotel pools are often quite small and are outdoors unless otherwise stated.

GARDEN
Hotel with garden, courtyard or terrace, often providing tables for eating outside.

	Credit Cards	Children's Facilities	Parking Facilities	Swimming Pool	Garden
LISIEUX: *Grand Hôtel de l'Espérance* ⒻⒻ 16 boulevard Ste-Anne, 14100. ☎ 02 31 62 17 53. FAX 02 31 62 34 00. **Rooms:** 100. This traditional half-timbered Norman building is on a busy street but double-glazing ensures peace and quiet. 🛏 📺	AE DC MC V		■		
MESNIL-VAL: *Hostellerie de la Vieille Ferme* ⒻⒻⒻ 23 rue de la Mer, 76910. ☎ 02 35 86 72 18. FAX 02 35 86 12 67. **Rooms:** 33. Set in its own park, this 18th-century farmhouse has several attractively converted outbuildings that make up the hotel complex. 🛏 📺	AE DC MC V	●	■		■
MORTAGNE-AU-PERCHE: *Hostellerie Genty-Home* ⒻⒻ 4 rue Notre-Dame, 61400. ☎ 02 33 25 11 53. FAX 02 33 25 41 38. **Rooms:** 8. A traditional stone-built inn in the centre of this unspoiled market town. Inside the decor varies from functional in the hotel to ornate in the reproduction Louis XV gastronomic restaurant. 🛏 📺	AE MC V	●	■		■
MORTAIN: *Hôtel de la Poste* ⒻⒻ Place des Arcades, 50140. ☎ 02 33 59 00 05. FAX 02 33 69 53 89. **Rooms:** 28. Situated on the spectacular Cherbourg peninsula, Mortain has a lovely river overlooked by this family-run hotel. 🛏 📺	MC V		■		■
PONT-AUDEMER: *Belle-Isle-sur-Risle* ⒻⒻⒻⒻ 112 Route de Rouen, 27500. ☎ 02 32 56 96 22. FAX 02 32 42 88 96. **Rooms:** 19. Set on an island in its own large garden of ancient trees and roses, the hotel boasts exceptionally comfortable bedrooms and superb cuisine in the arched basement. 🛏 📺	AE DC MC V	●	■	●	■
PONT DE L'ARCHE: *Hôtel de la Tour* ⒻⒻ 41 quai Foch, 27340. ☎ 02 35 23 00 99. FAX 02 35 23 46 22. **Rooms:** 16. A pretty 18th-century Norman house with comfortably renovated rooms, overlooking either the patio garden, the ramparts or the river. 🛏 📺			■		■
ROUEN: *Hôtel de Bordeaux* ⒻⒻ 9 place de la République, 76000. ☎ 02 35 71 93 58. FAX 02 35 71 92 15. **Rooms:** 48. A functional, friendly and well-run hotel overlooking the Seine on one side and the cathedral towers on the other. English spoken. 🛏 📺	AE DC MC V	●			
ROUEN: *Hôtel de Lisieux* ⒻⒻ 4 rue de la Savonnerie, 76000. ☎ 02 35 71 87 73. FAX 02 35 89 31 52. **Rooms:** 30. The staff are friendly and helpful, the rooms are spacious, some of them with views of the river and cathedral. This establishment offers excellent value and the owner is very welcoming. 🛏 📺	AE DC MC V				
SAINT-LÔ: *Hôtel des Voyageurs* ⒻⒻ 5–7 avenue de Briovère, 50000. ☎ 02 33 05 08 63. FAX 02 33 05 14 34. **Rooms:** 31. A professional establishment where the rooms are comfortable and quiet. The restaurant specializes in seafood. 🛏 📺	AE DC MC V	●	■		■
ST-PATERNE: *Château de St-Paterne* ⒻⒻⒻ 72610 St-Paterne. ☎ 02 33 27 54 71. FAX 02 33 29 16 71. **Rooms:** 8. This is not so much a hotel as a family château, where a fixed-menu is served *en famille*. The De Valbrays still live in this beautiful château, set in its own park just on the outskirts of Alençon. 🛏 📺	AE MC V	●	■		■
SÉES: *Hôtel du Cheval Blanc* ⒻⒻ 1 place St-Pierre, 61500. ☎ 02 33 27 80 48. FAX 02 33 28 58 05. **Rooms:** 9. A discreet and comfortable hotel on the route south from the Channel ports. It represents the best of French provincial hospitality. 🛏 📺	MC V				
VERNON: *Hôtel d'Evreux* ⒻⒻ 11 place d'Evreux, 27200. ☎ 02 32 21 16 12. FAX 02 32 21 32 73. **Rooms:** 18. An 18th-century coaching inn with a romantic courtyard where, on warm summer evenings, guests can enjoy fine cuisine outside. 🛏 📺	AE DC MC V	●	■		■

BRITTANY

AUDIERNE: *Le Goyen* ⓕⓕⓕ AE MC V
Place Jean-Simon, 29770. **☎** *02 98 70 08 88.* **FAX** *02 98 70 18 77.* **Rooms:** *27.*
Most of the bedrooms in this restored old building overlook the fishing port which supplies the hotel's superb restaurant. 🛏 TV

BREST: *Hôtel de la Corniche* ⓕⓕ AE MC V
1 rue Amiral-Nicol, 29200. **☎** *02 98 45 12 42.* **FAX** *02 98 49 01 53.* **Rooms:** *16.*
This modern hotel, built of local stone in the Breton style, is on the west side of the city near the naval base. It is convenient as a base for walks along the scenic coastline. Facilities include a tennis court. 🛏 TV

CANCALE: *Hôtel Richeux* ⓕⓕⓕⓕ AE DC MC V
Le Point du Jour, 35260. **☎** *02 99 89 64 76.* **FAX** *02 99 89 88 47.* **Rooms:** *13.*
A charming Art-Deco villa with views of the bay of Mont-St-Michel.
The rooms are furnished with antiques. 🛏 TV

CARNAC: *Lann Roz* ⓕⓕⓕ AE MC V
36 avenue de la Poste, 56340. **☎** *02 97 52 24 36.* **FAX** *02 97 52 29 93.* **Rooms:** *13.*
A friendly hotel with a pretty garden ten minutes' walk from the beach.
The restaurant has a fine wine list. 🛏 ▤ TV

CESSON-SÉVIGNÉ: *Hôtel Germinal* ⓕⓕ AE MC V
9 cours de la Vilaine, 35510. **☎** *02 99 83 11 01.* **FAX** *02 99 83 45 16.* **Rooms:** *20.*
A river runs on both sides of this converted mill. The decor is rustic with traditional wooden furniture. 🛏 TV

DINARD: *Le Prieuré* ⓕⓕ MC V
1 place Général de Gaulle, 35800. **☎** *02 99 46 13 74.* **FAX** *02 99 46 81 90.* **Rooms:** *4.*
A reservation is essential at this hotel facing the western edge of Prieuré beach. Its restaurant is exceptionally good value. 🛏 TV

FOUGÈRES: *Balzac Hôtel* ⓕⓕ AE DC MC V
15 rue Nationale, 35300. **☎** *02 99 99 42 46.* **FAX** *02 99 99 65 43.* **Rooms:** *20.*
In one of the prettiest towns in western France, this quiet hotel furnished in 18th-century style offers a warm welcome. 🛏 TV

GROIX (ÎLE DE): *Hôtel de la Marine* ⓕⓕ MC V
7 rue Général-de-Gaulle, 56590. **☎** *02 97 86 80 05.* **FAX** *02 97 86 56 37.* **Rooms:** *22.*
An old stone house filled with traditional furniture standing in the middle of the island of Groix. A relaxing hideaway. 🛏

LA FORÊT-FOUESNANT: *Le Manoir du Stang* ⓕⓕⓕⓕ
29940 La Forêt-Fouesnant. **☎** & **FAX** *02 98 56 97 37.* **Rooms:** *24.*
A fabulous Renaissance manor house set in a large park with woodland and a lake. The interior features ancient panelling and antique furniture which has been in the family for generations. 🛏

LAMBALLE: *Hôtel de l'Angleterre* ⓕⓕ AE DC MC V
29 boulevard Jobert, 22400. **☎** *02 96 31 00 16.* **FAX** *02 96 31 91 54.* **Rooms:** *20.*
A comfortable hotel opposite the railway station, suitable for an inexpensive overnight stop. Reasonable fixed-price menu. 🛏 TV

MORLAIX: *Hôtel de l'Europe* ⓕⓕ AE DC MC V
1 rue d'Aiguillon, 29600. **☎** *02 98 62 11 99.* **FAX** *02 98 88 83 38.* **Rooms:** *60.*
This Second Empire hotel is filled with furniture from earlier periods.
The brasserie and grill are excellent value. Centrally located. 🛏 TV

PÉNESTIN: *Hôtel Loscolo* ⓕⓕⓕ MC V
La Pointe de Loscolo, 56760. **☎** *02 99 90 31 90.* **FAX** *02 99 90 32 14.* **Rooms:** *16.*
A modern building on a cape with magnificent sea views to both sides and good walking nearby. The restaurant serves rich cuisine. 🛏 TV

PLÉVEN: *Le Manoir de Vaumadeuc* ⓕⓕⓕⓕ AE DC MC V
22130 Pléven. **☎** *02 96 84 46 17.* **FAX** *02 96 84 40 16.* **Rooms:** *14.*
This old manor house, with its graceful bay windows and fine staircase, dates back to the 15th century. The park around it includes a beautiful rose garden. 🛏

PLOUGASTEL-DAOULAS: *Hôtel Kastel Roc'h* ⓕⓕ AE MC V
Roc'h Kérézen, 29470. **☎** *02 98 40 32 00.* **FAX** *02 98 04 25 40.* **Rooms:** *45.*
Near Océanopolis and the marina, this hotel has some family rooms which makes it a good base for a holiday with children. 🛏 TV

For key to symbols see back flap

Price categories for a standard double room (not per person) for one night, including tax and service charges, but not including breakfast.
- Ⓕ under F200
- ⒻⒻ F200–400
- ⒻⒻⒻ F400–600
- ⒻⒻⒻⒻ F600–1,000
- ⒻⒻⒻⒻⒻ over F1,000

CHILDREN'S FACILITIES
Cots and baby-sitting available. Some hotels provide children's portions and high chairs in the restaurant.

PARKING FACILITIES
Parking provided by the hotel in either a private car park or a private garage very close by.

SWIMMING POOL
Hotel pools are often quite small and are outdoors unless otherwise stated.

GARDEN
Hotel with garden, courtyard or terrace, often providing tables for eating outside.

	CREDIT CARDS	CHILDREN'S FACILITIES	PARKING FACILITIES	SWIMMING POOL	GARDEN
PLUMAUDAN: *Le Plessis* ⒻⒻ 22350 Plumaudan. 📞 02 96 86 00 44. **Rooms:** 3. A comfortable 18th-century farmhouse in the Breton countryside near Dinan. Friendly relaxed atmosphere. Serves only vegetarian meals.			■		■
QUIBERON: *Hôtel Bellevue* ⒻⒻⒻ Rue Tiviec, 56170. 📞 02 97 50 16 28. **FAX** 02 97 30 44 34. **Rooms:** 40. Forming an L-shape around its swimming pool, the Bellevue is near the seafront and casino. It has a comfortable lounge and bar. 🖥 📺	AE MC V	●	■	●	■
QUIMPER: *La Tour d'Auvergne* ⒻⒻⒻ 13 rue des Réguaires, 29000. 📞 02 98 95 08 70. **FAX** 02 98 95 17 31. **Rooms:** 42. A recently refurbished hotel with a pretty courtyard and a friendly family atmosphere. The bedrooms are spacious and comfortable. 🖥 📺	AE MC V	●	■		
ROSCOFF: *Hôtel Bellevue* ⒻⒻ Rue Jeanne-d'Arc, 29680. 📞 02 98 61 23 38. **FAX** 02 98 61 11 80. **Rooms:** 18. An old Breton house enjoying fine views of the sea and the old port. To the rear is a pleasant garden with deckchairs where drinks are served. The restaurant specializes in fish and Loire white wines. 🖥 📺	MC V	●	■		■
ST-MALO: *Hôtel Elisabeth* ⒻⒻⒻ 2 rue des Cordiers, 35400. 📞 02 99 56 24 98. **FAX** 02 99 56 39 24. **Rooms:** 17. Situated within the ramparts of the old town, the building has a 17th-century façade. English satellite TV is available. 🖥 📺	AE DC MC V	●	■		
VANNES: *La Marébaudière* ⒻⒻ 4 rue Aristide-Briand, 56000. 📞 02 97 47 34 29. **FAX** 02 97 54 14 11. **Rooms:** 41. A peaceful hotel decorated with flair. Some of the beds are antique. The beautifully preserved old walled town is a short walk away. 🖥 📺	AE MC V	●	■		■

THE LOIRE VALLEY

	CREDIT CARDS	CHILDREN'S FACILITIES	PARKING FACILITIES	SWIMMING POOL	GARDEN
AMBOISE: *Le Choiseul* ⒻⒻⒻⒻ 36 quai Charles-Guinot, 37400. 📞 02 47 30 45 45. **FAX** 02 47 30 46 10. **Rooms:** 32. An ivy-covered manor set in elegant grounds. The famous cellars can be visited. A sophisticated restaurant serves fish cooked in wine. 🖥 📺	AE MC V	●	■	●	■
AZAY-LE-RIDEAU: *Le Clos Philippa* ⒻⒻ 10 rue Pineau, 37190. 📞 02 47 45 26 49. **Rooms:** 4. Guests at this 18th-century house have the use of the owner's drawing room, sitting room, library and grounds. There is no restaurant. 🖥	MC V		■		
AZAY-LE-RIDEAU: *Manoir de la Rémonière* ⒻⒻⒻ La Chapelle St-Blaise, 37190. 📞 02 47 45 24 88. **FAX** 02 47 45 45 69. **Rooms:** 6. A manor house standing in romantic grounds which are perfect for children to play in. Meals include homegrown vegetables. 🖥			■	●	■
BEAUGENCY: *Hotel de la Sologne* ⒻⒻ 6 place St-Firmin, 45190. 📞 02 38 44 50 27. **FAX** 02 38 44 90 19. **Rooms:** 16. This old-fashioned hotel is on the main square, overlooking the ruined castle keep. Breakfast is served in an attractive winter garden. 🖥 📺	MC V	●	■		
BEAUGENCY: *Hotel de l'Abbaye* ⒻⒻⒻ 2 quai de l'Abbaye, 45190. 📞 02 38 44 67 35. **FAX** 02 38 44 87 92. **Rooms:** 18. Ask for a room in one of the former monastic cells of this restored abbey beside the river. The restaurant is good but overpriced. 🖥 📺	AE DC MC V		■		■
LA BOHALLE: *L'Hermitage* ⒻⒻ 5 route de Brain, 49800. 📞 02 41 54 96 05. **Rooms:** 2. Run by a Scottish-French couple, this *chambres d'hôtes* in a charming fishing village on the north bank of the Loire is a simple but welcoming place to stay. The owners are happy to advise on local sights.		●	■		■

BOURGUEIL: *Châteaux des Réaux* ⓕⓕⓕ AE MC V
Le Port-Boulet, 37140. 【 02 47 95 14 40. FAX 02 47 95 18 34. *Rooms: 17.*
A lovingly restored brick and stone Renaissance château in a
wine-growing area. The owners enjoy showing it to visitors. 🔗

BRÉHÉMONT: *Les Brunets* ⓕⓕ
37130 Bréhémont. 【 02 47 96 55 81. *Rooms: 3.*
This charming country house in an unspoiled village on the Loire is
owned by a welcoming English couple. 🔗 TV

BRÉHÉMONT: *Le Castel de Bray et Monts* ⓕⓕⓕ MC V
Le Bourg, 37130. 【 02 47 96 70 47. FAX 02 47 96 57 36. *Rooms: 9.*
An attractive 18th-century mansion which sits next to a stream in ample
grounds. The rooms are charming and breakfast is excellent. 🔗 TV

CHAMBORD: *Hôtel Saint-Michel* ⓕⓕ MC V
41250 Chambord. 【 02 54 20 31 31. FAX 02 54 20 36 40. *Rooms: 38.*
Book ahead at this old-fashioned hotel and ask for a room with a view
of the château. The restaurant is stuffy but the cuisine good. 🔗 TV

CHAMPIGNÉ: *Château des Briottières* ⓕⓕⓕⓕ AE DC MC V
49330 Champigné. 【 02 41 42 00 02. FAX 02 41 42 01 55. *Rooms: 8.*
Classical, family-run white château once used as a film set. Romantic
dinners are on offer as well as food and wine-tasting trips. 🔗

CHARTRES: *Grand Monarque* ⓕⓕⓕⓕ AE DC MC V
22 place des Epars, 28005. 【 02 37 21 00 72. FAX 02 37 36 34 18. *Rooms: 54.*
An efficiently managed modern hotel on the edge of the old quarter.
It has a recommended gourmet restaurant. 🔗 TV

CHENONCEAUX: *Hostel du Roy* ⓕⓕ AE MC V
9 rue de Dr Bretonneau, 37150. 【 02 47 23 90 17. FAX 02 47 23 89 81. *Rooms: 37.*
A sprawling hotel-restaurant with simple but appealing bedrooms and
a dining room hung with hunting trophies. Local wines served. 🔗 TV

CHINON: *Hôtel Diderot* ⓕⓕ AE DC MC V
4 rue Buffon, 37500. 【 02 47 93 18 87. FAX 02 47 93 37 10. *Rooms: 27.*
An elegant, creeper-clad 18th-century house on a quiet street. The
bedrooms are simple but some have good views. 🔗

CHINON: *Hôtel de France* ⓕⓕ AE DC MC V
47 place de Gen-de-Gaulle, 37500. 【 02 47 93 33 91. FAX 02 47 98 37 03. *Rooms: 30.*
This underrated hotel, comfortable and friendly but without frills, is
situated in the Old Quarter a short way from the scenic main street. 🔗 TV

CHINON: *Hostellerie Gargantua* ⓕⓕ AE MC V
73 rue Voltaire, 37500. 【 02 47 93 04 71. *Rooms: 7.*
With its pointed roof and turret, this old building overlooking the river
is a local landmark. Its cuisine blends the traditional and modern. 🔗

FONDETTES: *Manoir du Grand Martigny* ⓕⓕⓕⓕ
37230 Fondettes. 【 02 47 42 29 87. FAX 02 47 42 24 44. *Rooms: 7.*
Wild and wooded grounds surround this quirky manor house which
is less formal than other Loire château hotels. There is no restaurant. 🔗

FONTEVRAUD-L'ABBAYE: *Hôtellerie Prieuré St-Lazare* ⓕⓕⓕ AE MC V
49590 Fontevraud-L'Abbaye. 【 02 41 51 73 16. FAX 02 41 51 75 50. *Rooms: 52.*
This atmospheric hotel is housed in the former St-Lazare priory, within
the famous abbey complex. 🔗 TV

GENNES: *Le Prieuré* ⓕⓕⓕⓕ AE DC MC V
Chênehutte-les-Tuffeaux, 49350. 【 02 41 67 90 14. FAX 02 41 67 92 24. *Rooms: 35.*
Most of the rooms in this luxurious Renaissance manor look out on
to the Loire. A gourmet restaurant adds to the appeal. 🔗 TV

GIEN: *Hôtel du Rivage* ⓕⓕⓕ AE DC MC V
1 quai de Nice, 45500. 【 02 38 37 79 00. FAX 02 38 38 10 21. *Rooms: 19.*
This riverside hotel is renowned for its exquisite cuisine which is
supervised by the owner, Christian Gaillard. 🔗 ▤ TV

LA CHARTRE-SUR-LE-LOIR: *Hôtel de France* ⓕⓕ MC V
20 place de la République, 72340. 【 02 43 44 40 16. FAX 02 43 79 62 20. *Rooms: 28.*
This hotel in the town centre has a garden beside the river. Its
restaurant serves generous portions and has won awards. 🔗 TV

Price categories for a standard double room (not per person) for one night, including tax and service charges, but not including breakfast.
- Ⓕ under F200
- ⒻⒻ F200–400
- ⒻⒻⒻ F400–600
- ⒻⒻⒻⒻ F600–1,000
- ⒻⒻⒻⒻⒻ over F1,000

CHILDREN'S FACILITIES
Cots and baby-sitting available. Some hotels provide children's portions and high chairs in the restaurant.

PARKING FACILITIES
Parking provided by the hotel in either a private car park or a private garage very close by.

SWIMMING POOL
Hotel pools are often quite small and are outdoors unless otherwise stated.

GARDEN
Hotel with garden, courtyard or terrace, often providing tables for eating outside.

	CREDIT CARDS	CHILDREN'S FACILITIES	PARKING FACILITIES	SWIMMING POOL	GARDEN
LE MANS: *Ibis Centre* ⒻⒻ Quai Ledru-Rolin, 72000. ▮ 02 43 23 18 23. ᴼ 02 43 24 00 72. *Rooms: 85.* Overlooking the river and the Old Quarter, this is the best hotel in Le Mans for budget travellers. It serves a good buffet breakfast. ▤ 📺	AE DC MC V		■		■
LOCHES: *Hôtel de France* ⒻⒻ 6 rue Picois, 37600. ▮ 02 47 59 00 32. ᴼ 02 47 59 28 66. *Rooms: 19.* This elegant hotel is situated near the medieval gate. Guests are expected to take half-board. The restaurant is excellent. ▤ 📺	DC MC V		■		■
LUYNES: *Domaine de Beauvois* ⒻⒻⒻ Route de Cleré, 37230. ▮ 02 47 55 50 11. ᴼ 02 47 55 59 62. *Rooms: 40.* Built around a 15th-century tower and overlooking its own lake, the Domaine has large rooms and a celebrated restaurant. ▤ 📺	AE DC MC V	●	■	●	■
MARÇAY: *Château de Marçay* ⒻⒻⒻⒻ 37500 Marçay. ▮ 02 47 93 03 47. ᴼ 02 47 93 45 33. *Rooms: 38.* Service and cuisine in this elegant château-hotel are impeccable. There are good views over the surrounding parkland and vineyards. ▤ 📺	AE DC MC V	●	■	●	■
MONTBAZON: *Château d'Artigny* ⒻⒻⒻⒻ Route de Monts, 37250. ▮ 02 47 34 30 30. ᴼ 02 47 34 30 39. *Rooms: 55.* The grandiose classical exterior is matched by a formal Empire-style interior. A gourmet restaurant serves regional specialities. ▤ 📺	AE DC MC V	●	■	●	■
MONTLOUIS-SUR-LOIRE: *Château de la Bourdaisière* ⒻⒻⒻⒻ 25 rue de la Bourdaisière, 37270. ▮ 02 47 45 16 31. ᴼ 02 47 45 09 11. *Rooms: 17.* A magnificent château which has been refurbished as luxury accommodations. Gabrielle d'Estrées, Henri IV's mistress, was born here in 1565. Facilities include tennis courts and horseback riding. ▤ 📺	MC V		■	●	■
MONTREUIL-BELLAY: *Demeure des Petits Augustins* ⒻⒻ 49260 Montreuil-Bellay. ▮ 02 41 52 33 88. *Rooms: 3.* Guests are made welcome in this 17th-century town mansion. The spacious, individually styled bedrooms look over a charming courtyard. The "white" suite is especially recommended. ▤	MC V	●	■		■
MONTREUIL-BELLAY: *Splendid Hôtel* ⒻⒻ 139 rue Docteur-Gaudrez, 49260. ▮ 02 41 53 10 00. ᴼ 02 41 52 45 17. *Rooms: 60.* An old-fashioned hotel in the centre of town with an excellent regional restaurant. The annexe has quieter, more stylish rooms. ▤ 📺	MC V	●	■	●	■
MUIDES-SUR-LOIRE: *Château de Colliers* ⒻⒻⒻⒻ 41500 Muides-sur-Loire. ▮ 02 54 87 50 75. ᴼ 02 54 87 03 64. *Rooms: 5.* This château, set among woods a short drive east of Blois, combines grandeur with rusticity. In the 18th century it belonged to an aristocratic governor of Louisiana. ▤	MC V	●	■		■
NANTES: *Jules Verne* ⒻⒻ 3 rue du Couëdic, 44000. ▮ 02 40 35 74 50. ᴼ 02 40 20 09 35. *Rooms: 65.* A modern hotel on a pedestrian square, offering friendly service and comfortable rooms. Parking in the nearby place du Commerce. ▤ ▤ 📺	AE DC MC V	●	■		
NANTES: *Hôtel la Perouse* ⒻⒻⒻ 3 allée Duquesne, 44000. ▮ 02 40 89 75 00. ᴼ 02 40 89 76 00. *Rooms: 46* This chic hotel which opened in 1993 offers crisp, contemporary design and efficient service. It is reasonably quiet for a city hotel. ▤ ▤ 📺	AE DC MC V	●	■		
NOIZAY: *Château de Noizay* ⒻⒻⒻⒻ 37210 Noizay. ▮ 02 47 52 11 01. ᴼ 02 47 52 04 64. *Rooms: 14.* A compact Renaissance château set in Classical gardens on the right bank of the Loire. The rooms are discreetly and elegantly furnished. In good weather breakfast is served on the terrace. ▤ 📺	AE MC V	●	■	●	■

ONZAIN: *Domaine des Hauts de Loire* ⒻⒻⒻⒻ — AE DC MC V
Route d'Herbault, 41150. 🄴 02 54 20 72 57. FAX 02 54 20 77 32. **Rooms:** 15.
A count's former hunting lodge with large grounds and a lake, this is
an unashamedly expensive place to relax and enjoy good food. 🄴 TV

ROCHECORBON: *Les Hautes Roches* ⒻⒻⒻⒻ — AE MC V
86 quai de la Loire, 37210. 🄴 02 47 52 88 88. FAX 02 47 52 81 30. **Rooms:** 15.
The underground rooms hewn into the chalk in this "troglodyte" hotel
are less spacious but more atmospheric than the rest. 🄴 TV

ROMORANTIN-LANTHENAY: *Grand Hôtel Lion d'Or* ⒻⒻⒻⒻ — AE DC MC V
69 rue Clémenceau, 41200. 🄴 02 54 94 15 15. FAX 02 54 88 24 87. **Rooms:** 16.
This former 17th-century staging post is now a gastronomic halt in a
historic but untouristy town in the watery Sologne landscape. 🄴 ▤ TV

ST-JULIEN-LE-PAUVRE: *Château de la Renaudière* ⒻⒻⒻ
72240 St-Julien-le-Pauvre. 🄴 02 43 20 71 09. **Rooms:** 3.
A gracious château, owned by the Marquis de Mascureau, set among
rolling meadows between Le Mans and Laval. The family enjoys
introducing visitors to the lesser-known châteaux of the region. 🄴

ST-LAMBERT-DES-LEVÉES: *La Croix de la Voulte* ⒻⒻ
Route de Boumois, 49400. 🄴 02 41 38 46 66. FAX 02 41 38 46 66. **Rooms:** 4.
The rooms in this old manor outside Saumur are all different and the
furnishings stylish. Ask for directions when you book. 🄴

SAUMUR: *Hôtel Anne d'Anjou* ⒻⒻⒻ — AE DC MC V
32–34 quai Mayaud, 49400. 🄴 02 41 67 30 30. FAX 02 41 67 51 00. **Rooms:** 50.
The decor in this elegant mansion beside the river Loire is sophisticated
and romantic. The courtyard and grand staircase are impressive. 🄴 TV

TOURS: *Hôtel Balzac* ⒻⒻ — AE DC MC V
47 rue de la Scellerie, 37000. 🄴 02 47 05 40 87. FAX 02 47 05 67 93. **Rooms:** 18.
Cosy and welcoming, this old-fashioned hotel is situated between the
theatre and the cathedral. Drinks are served in the courtyard. 🄴 TV

TOURS: *Hôtel Moderne* ⒻⒻ — AE MC V
1–3, rue Victor Laloux, 37000. 🄴 02 47 05 32 81. FAX 02 47 05 71 50. **Rooms:** 23.
A convenient location, a warm welcome and a good restaurant easily
make up for rooms which are comfortable but a little shabby. 🄴 TV

TOURS: *Hôtel de l'Univers* ⒻⒻⒻⒻ — AE MC V
5 boulevard Heurteloup, 37000. 🄴 02 47 05 37 12. FAX 02 47 61 51 80. **Rooms:** 85.
Statesmen, including Winston Churchill, and royals have stayed at this
luxurious Belle Epoque hotel. The rooms have antique furniture. 🄴 TV

VARADES: *Le Grand Patis* ⒻⒻ
44370 Varades. 🄴 02 40 83 42 28. **Rooms:** 5.
Rooms in this restored château are simple, clean and spacious. Two
have stone balconies overlooking the peaceful, leafy grounds. 🄴

VOUVRAY: *Château de Jallanges* ⒻⒻⒻⒻ — AE MC V
Vallée de Vaugoudy, 37210. 🄴 02 47 52 11 18. FAX 02 47 52 11 18. **Rooms:** 6.
An imposing Renaissance brick mansion, now a family home, with
stylish and comfortable rooms. Guests are taken on a guided tour
from chapel to turrets. A good base for exploring Touraine. 🄴

BURGUNDY AND FRANCHE-COMTÉ

ARBOIS: *Jean-Paul Jeunet* ⒻⒻⒻ — DC MC V
9 rue de l'Hôtel de Ville, 39600. 🄴 03 84 66 05 67. FAX 03 84 66 24 20. **Rooms:** 18.
In the centre of this picturesque town, Jeunet offers modern amenities
and comfort. Good selection of Jura wines in the restaurant. 🄴 TV

ARNAY-LE-DUC: *Chez Camille* ⒻⒻⒻ — AE DC MC V
1 place Edouard-Herriot, 21230. 🄴 03 80 90 01 38. FAX 03 80 90 04 64. **Rooms:** 11.
An attractive and tastefully decorated hotel with spacious bedrooms
and antique furniture. The hotel offers warmth and peace with its huge
open fire in the salon and double-glazing. Traditional cuisine. 🄴 TV

AUTUN: *Les Granges* ⒻⒻ
Monthélon, 71400. 🄴 03 85 52 22 99. **Rooms:** 3.
This working farm is a good base to explore the Burgundian country-
side and Autun. Friendly owners but no restaurant and cash only. 🄴

Price categories for a standard double room (not per person) for one night, including tax and service charges, but not including breakfast.
Ⓕ under F200
ⒻⒻ F200–400
ⒻⒻⒻ F400–600
ⒻⒻⒻⒻ F600–1,000
ⒻⒻⒻⒻⒻ over F1,000

CHILDREN'S FACILITIES
Cots and baby-sitting available. Some hotels provide children's portions and high chairs in the restaurant.

PARKING FACILITIES
Parking provided by the hotel in either a private car park or a private garage very close by.

SWIMMING POOL
Hotel pools are often quite small and are outdoors unless otherwise stated.

GARDEN
Hotel with garden, courtyard or terrace, often providing tables for eating outside.

Hotel	Price	Credit Cards	Children's Facilities	Parking Facilities	Swimming Pool	Garden
AUTUN: *Hôtel St-Louis* — 6 rue de l'Arbalète, 71400. ☎ 03 85 52 21 03. FAX 03 85 86 32 54. **Rooms:** 44. This quiet hotel was once a staging post. Rooms vary in price, the most expensive being Napoleon's former bedchamber. 🚗 TV	ⒻⒻ	AE MC V	●	■		■
BEAUNE: *Hôtel du Parc* — Route Verdun, Levernois, 21200. ☎ 03 80 24 63 00. FAX 03 80 24 21 19. **Rooms:** 25. A quiet, quaint country hotel on the outskirts of Beaune, set in a beautiful park. A good base for visiting the nearby vineyards. 🚗 TV	ⒻⒻ	MC V	●	■		■
BEAUNE: *Le Home* — 138 route Dijon, 21200. ☎ 03 80 22 16 43. FAX 03 80 24 90 74. **Rooms:** 20. Set back from the main road in a charming courtyard is this simple, homely hotel just outside the town. Clean and comfortable. 🚗	ⒻⒻ	MC V	●	■		
BEAUNE: *Hôtel du Cep* — 27 rue Maufoux, 21200. ☎ 03 80 22 35 48. FAX 03 80 22 76 80. **Rooms:** 49. In the heart of the Old Town is this subdued and elegant hotel, tastefully renovated in a Renaissance style. Each bedroom is named after a wine of the Côte d'Or vineyards. Restaurant and bar. 🚗 TV	ⒻⒻⒻⒻ	AE DC MC V	●	■		■
BESANÇON: *Hôtel Mercure Parc Micaud* — 3 avenue E Droz, 25000. ☎ 03 81 80 14 44. FAX 03 81 53 29 83. **Rooms:** 91. A luxury modern hotel on the waterfront offering comfort, good breakfasts and an excellent restaurant called *Le Vesontio*. 🚗 TV	ⒻⒻⒻ	AE DC MC V	●	■		
BOUILLAND: *Le Vieux Moulin* — 21420 Bouilland. ☎ 03 80 21 51 16. FAX 03 80 21 59 90. **Rooms:** 26. A recently renovated mill located in one of the most spectacular villages in Burgundy. The chef is renowned for his creativity. 🚗 TV	ⒻⒻⒻⒻ	MC V	●	■	●	■
CHABLIS: *Hostellerie de Clos* — Rue Jules-Rathier, 89800. ☎ 03 86 42 10 63. FAX 03 86 42 17 11. **Rooms:** 26. The owner has renovated a medieval convent in the middle of this famed village. The rooms are modern and comfortable, the garden is delightful and the restaurant is one of the best in the region. 🚗 TV	ⒻⒻⒻ	AE MC V	●	■		■
CHAILLY-SUR-ARMANÇON: *Château de Chailly* — 21320 Chailly-sur-Armançon. ☎ 03 80 90 30 30. FAX 03 80 90 30 00. **Rooms:** 45. A Japanese industrialist has restored this magnificent château, installing every detail of luxury including a golf course. 🚗 TV	ⒻⒻⒻⒻⒻ	AE DC MC V	●	■		■
CHÂTEAU CHINON: *Hôtel du Vieux Morvan* — 8 place Gudin, 58120. ☎ 03 86 85 05 01. FAX 03 86 85 02 78. **Rooms:** 24. François Mitterrand learned he had become President here – for years he visited this hotel and always stayed in room 15. The manageress has since retired but the hotel retains its rustic, old-world style. 🚗 TV	ⒻⒻ	MC V		■		
CLUNY: *Hostellerie de Bourgogne* — Place de l'Abbaye, 71250. ☎ 03 85 59 00 58. FAX 03 85 59 03 73. **Rooms:** 12. This old-fashioned auberge is located next door to the magnificent Cluny abbey. Excellent restaurant serving refined cuisine. 🚗 TV	ⒻⒻⒻ	AE DC MC V	●	■		■
DIJON: *Hostellerie le Sauvage* — 64 rue Monge, 21000. ☎ 03 80 41 31 21. FAX 03 80 42 06 07. **Rooms:** 21. This city hotel is conveniently located for the main sights and the historic centre. The restaurant specializes in steaks and grills. 🚗 TV	ⒻⒻ	MC V		■		■
FLAVIGNY-SUR-OZERAIN: *Mme Marc Brigand* — 21150 Flavigny-sur-Ozerain. ☎ 03 80 96 20 91. **Rooms:** 3. Simple accommodation in an old-fashioned house brought to life by its breezy owners. Meals available and cash only.	Ⓕ					■

FONTETTE: *Hôtel Crispol* ⓕⓕⓕ
St-Père-sous-Vezelay, 89450. 【 03 86 33 26 25. FAX 03 86 33 33 10. **Rooms:** 12.
Well-planned and chic decor in this very luxurious and modern
hotel. Generous and imaginative local cooking. 🔧 TV
Cards: AE MC V

GEVREY-CHAMBERTIN: *Hôtel des Grands Crus* ⓕⓕ
Route des Grands Crus, 21220. 【 03 80 34 34 15. FAX 03 80 51 89 07. **Rooms:** 24.
A light and airy, old-style hotel with wonderful views over the vine-
yards. No restaurant but several good restaurants in the village. 🔧
Cards: MC V

GEVREY-CHAMBERTIN: *Mme Geneviève Sylvain* ⓕⓕ
14 rue de l'Eglise, 21220. 【 03 80 51 86 39. **Rooms:** 3.
Welcoming owners run this spacious *chambres d'hôte*. Ideal location
for exploring the village restaurants and local wine-tastings. 🔧

JOIGNY: *La Côte St-Jacques* ⓕⓕⓕⓕ
14 Faubourg Paris, 89300. 【 03 86 62 09 70. FAX 03 86 91 49 70. **Rooms:** 29.
Known as a mini Versailles, this glamorous and glossy hotel
sits beside the river Yonne. The restaurant is outstanding. 🔧 ▤ TV
Cards: AE DC MC V

LEVERNOIS: *Le Parc* ⓕⓕⓕⓕ
21200 Levernois. 【 03 80 22 22 51. FAX 03 80 24 21 19. **Rooms:** 25.
Set in the heart of beautiful park land, this hotel offers a relaxing retreat.
Hot-air ballooning is possible in the area. 🔧 TV
Cards: AE DC V

LIGNY-LE-CHATEL: *Relais Saint-Vincent* ⓕⓕ
14 Grande-Rue, 89144. 【 03 86 47 53 38. FAX 03 86 47 54 16. **Rooms:** 15.
An ancient half-timbered house, well equipped with modern comforts.
The restaurant serves regional specialities. 🔧 TV
Cards: MC V

OYE-ET-PALLET: *Hôtel Parnet* ⓕⓕ
11 rue de la Fauconnière, 25160. 【 03 81 89 42 03. FAX 03 81 89 41 47. **Rooms:** 17.
In the Jura mountains, this is a great place to take a cross-country
skiing vacation. Clean, comfortable and calm. Good food. 🔧 TV
Cards: MC V

POLIGNY: *Hostellerie des Monts de Vaux* ⓕⓕⓕ
39800 Poligny. 【 03 84 37 12 50. FAX 03 84 37 09 07. **Rooms:** 10
An elegant old coaching inn on the outskirts of Poligny. Friendly
owners, good Jura cuisine and wine, and tennis courts. 🔧 TV
Cards: AE DC MC V

PULIGNY-MONTRACHET: *Le Montrachet* ⓕⓕⓕ
Place des Marroniers, 21190. 【 03 80 21 30 06. FAX 03 80 21 39 06. **Rooms:** 32.
A quiet resting spot in the heart of Burgundy wine country. The
restaurant serves good food and has an excellent wine list. 🔧 TV
Cards: AE DC MC V

ST-GERVAIS-EN-VALLIÈRE: *Moulin d'Hauterive* ⓕⓕⓕ
Chaublanc, 71350. 【 03 85 91 55 56. FAX 03 85 91 89 65. **Rooms:** 21.
A converted watermill in a secluded setting with a tennis court and
sauna. The owner serves inventive home-cooking. 🔧 TV
Cards: AE MC V

ST-PÈRE-SOUS-VÉZELAY: *Mme Demeule* ⓕⓕ
Le Petit Cléret, Fontette, 89450. 【 03 86 33 25 87. **Rooms:** 2.
This charming period house is run as a *chambres d'hôte* by two
animal lovers. Choose the upstairs room under the eaves.

SAULIEU: *La Côte d'Or* ⓕⓕⓕⓕ
2 rue Argentine, 21210. 【 03 80 90 53 53. FAX 03 80 64 08 92. **Rooms:** 27.
Regarded as one of the best and most innovative restaurants in France.
Some of the older rooms are relatively inexpensive. 🔧 TV
Cards: AE DC MC V

TONNERRE: *L'Abbaye St-Michel* ⓕⓕⓕⓕ
Montée de St-Michel, 89700. 【 03 86 55 05 99. FAX 03 86 55 00 10. **Rooms:** 15.
A renovated abbey which now houses a celebrated Burgundy
restaurant. The hotel blends old and modern styles. 🔧 TV
Cards: AE DC MC V

TOURNUS: *Château de Beaufer* ⓕⓕⓕⓕ
71700 Tournus. 【 03 85 51 18 24. FAX 03 85 51 25 04. **Rooms:** 6.
Choose between a room in the ivy-clad 16th-century château or one in the
annexe. Restaurants are a short drive away.
Cards: MC V

VÉZELAY: *Cabalus* ⓕⓕ
Rue St Pierre, 89450. 【 03 86 33 20 66. FAX 03 86 33 38 03. **Rooms:** 7.
This 12th-century building, the abbey's former hostelry, is in the middle
of the Old Town. There are good views from some of the rooms. 🔧
Cards: MC V

		Price categories info	CREDIT CARDS	CHILDREN'S FACILITIES	PARKING FACILITIES	SWIMMING POOL	GARDEN

Price categories for a standard double room (not per person) for one night, including tax and service charges, but not including breakfast.
Ⓕ under F200
ⒻⒻ F200–400
ⒻⒻⒻ F400–600
ⒻⒻⒻⒻ F600–1,000
ⒻⒻⒻⒻⒻ over F1,000

CHILDREN'S FACILITIES
Cots and baby-sitting available. Some hotels provide children's portions and high chairs in the restaurant.

PARKING FACILITIES
Parking provided by the hotel in either a private car park or a private garage very close by.

SWIMMING POOL
Hotel pools are often quite small and are outdoors unless otherwise stated.

GARDEN
Hotel with garden, courtyard or terrace, often providing tables for eating outside.

	Credit Cards	Children's	Parking	Pool	Garden
VÉZELAY: *L'Espérance* ⒻⒻⒻⒻ St-Père-sous-Vézelay, 89450. 📞 03 86 33 20 45. FAX 03 86 33 26 15. **Rooms:** 21. Some of the rooms overlook the garden; others are in a renovated mill. Above all, guests come for the famous restaurant. 🚗 TV	AE DC V	●	■	●	■
VONNAS: *Georges Blanc* ⒻⒻⒻⒻⒻ 01540 Vonnas. 📞 04 70 50 90 90. FAX 04 74 50 08 80. **Rooms:** 32. A sumptuous hotel-restaurant with luxurious rooms built and furnished in a modern country style using stone, tiles and tapestries. 🚗 ▤ TV	AE DC MC V	●	■	●	■

THE MASSIF CENTRAL

	Credit Cards	Children's	Parking	Pool	Garden
AUBUSSON-D'AUVERGNE: *Au Bon Coin* Ⓕ 63120 Aubusson-d'Auvergne. 📞 04 73 53 55 78. FAX 04 73 53 56 29. **Rooms:** 6. The friendly owner of this rustic inn is also the mayor of the town and the tasty cuisine reflects his pride in local culinary traditions.	MC V	●			■
BEAULIEU-SUR-DORDOGNE: *Château d'Arnac* ⒻⒻⒻ Nonards, 19120. 📞 05 55 91 54 13. FAX 05 55 91 52 62. **Rooms:** 3. The hospitable English owners have restored this château, keeping some original details. The grounds include a small lake. Dinner available. 🚗			■		■
BELCASTEL: *Le Vieux Pont* ⒻⒻⒻ 12390 Belcastel. 📞 05 65 64 52 29. FAX 05 65 64 44 32. **Rooms:** 7. An annexe to the Fagegaltier sisters' imaginative but affordable restaurant which overlooks the medieval village and its castle. 🚗 TV	MC V		■		
CALVINET: *Hôtel Beauséjour* ⒻⒻ Route de Maurs, 15340. 📞 04 71 49 91 68. FAX 04 71 49 98 63. **Rooms:** 12. A recently renovated hotel filled with light which has a highly distinctive cuisine. The town is renowned for its schist roofs. 🚗 TV	MC V	●	■		
CHAMALIÈRES: *Hôtel Radio* ⒻⒻⒻ 43 avenue Pierre-Curie, 63400. 📞 04 73 30 87 83. FAX 04 73 36 42 44. **Rooms:** 26. Quiet Art Deco building perched on a hill overlooking Clermont-Ferrand and dotted with early radio sets. First-class cuisine. 🚗 TV	AE DC MC V	●	■		■
FLORAC: *Grand Hôtel du Parc* ⒻⒻ 47 avenue Jean-Monestier, 48400. 📞 04 66 45 03 05. FAX 04 66 45 11 81. **Rooms:** 60. There is an old-fashioned atmosphere to this cavernous hotel set in attractive grounds. The prices are not those of a grand hotel. 🚗 TV	AE DC MC V	●	■	●	■
LAGUIOLE: *Michel Bras* ⒻⒻⒻⒻ Route de l'Aubrac, 12210. 📞 05 65 44 32 24. FAX 05 65 48 47 02. **Rooms:** 15. The Auvergne's most prestigious chef, whose cuisine is renowned for its use of wild plants, offers superb, ultra-modern rooms overlooking the Aubrac plateau. The atmosphere is surprisingly unstuffy. 🚗 TV	AE MC V	●	■		■
LAQUEUILLE: *Les Clarines* ⒻⒻ Laqueuille-Gare, 63820. 📞 04 73 22 00 43. FAX 04 73 22 06 10. **Rooms:** 12. Simple rooms and dependable food are available at this converted farmhouse high up in the midst of rolling countryside. 🚗 TV	AE DC MC V		■		■
MILLAU: *Château de Creissels* ⒻⒻ Route de Ste-Afrique, 12100. 📞 05 65 60 16 59. FAX 05 65 61 24 63. **Rooms:** 31. A converted 13th-century *bastide* with a vaulted dining room and modern bedrooms. Straightforward regional food is on the menu. There are stunning views over the Tarn valley. 🚗	AE DC MC V	●	■	●	■
MOULINS: *Hôtel de Paris-Jacquemart* ⒻⒻⒻⒻ 21 rue de Paris, 03000. 📞 04 70 44 00 58. FAX 04 70 34 05 39. **Rooms:** 28. A stylish stopover, near the cathedral at the gateway to the Massif Central. The restaurant has a garden. 🚗 TV	AE DC MC V	●	■		■

MUR-DE-BARREZ: *Auberge de Barrez* Ⓕ Ⓕ — AE MC V
Avenue du Carladez, 12600. **⌂** *05 65 66 00 76.* **FAX** *05 65 66 07 98.* **Rooms:** *18.*
A welcoming and comfortable modern hotel in the heart of hiking country. Christian Gaudel's excellent cooking is a bonus. 🚗 TV

NAJAC: *Ousial del Barry* Ⓕ Ⓕ — AE MC V
Place du Bourg, 12270. **⌂** *05 65 29 74 32.* **FAX** *05 65 29 75 32.* **Rooms:** *20.*
This rustic inn overlooks the square of one of France's most picturesque villages. The cuisine is highly distinctive. 🚗 TV

NEUVÉGLISE: *Auberge du Pont Lanau* Ⓕ Ⓕ — MC V
15260 Neuvéglise. **⌂** *04 71 23 57 76.* **FAX** *04 71 23 53 84.* **Rooms:** *8.*
This inn in the Gorges de la Truyère has small but well-proportioned rooms and serves good food with a regional accent. 🚗 TV

PLAISANCE: *Les Magnolias* Ⓕ Ⓕ — AE MC V
Rue des Magnolias, 12550. **⌂** *05 65 99 77 34.* **FAX** *05 65 99 70 57.* **Rooms:** *6.*
Giant magnolias several hundred years old surround this unspoilt 14th-century country mansion furnished with antiques. 🚗 TV

PONTAUMUR: *Hôtel de la Poste* Ⓕ Ⓕ — MC V
Avenue du Marronnier, 63380. **⌂** *04 73 79 90 15.* **FAX** *04 73 79 73 17.* **Rooms:** *15.*
A pleasantly decorated modern hotel in a small country town. The owner-chef believes in promoting the finest local ingredients. 🚗 TV

PONTEMPEYRAT: *Hôtel Mistou* Ⓕ Ⓕ Ⓕ — AE MC V
Craponne-sur-Arzon, 43500. **⌂** *04 71 50 62 46.* **FAX** *04 77 50 66 70.* **Rooms:** *24.*
A delightfully quiet and secluded hotel in a converted old mill. Fun-loving Bernard Roux offers consistently inventive cooking. 🚗

ROANNE: *Troisgros* Ⓕ Ⓕ Ⓕ Ⓕ — DC MC V
Place Jean-Troisgros, 42300. **⌂** *04 77 71 66 97.* **FAX** *04 77 70 39 77.* **Rooms:** *19.*
What was once a humble station hotel has become a luxurious place to stay and a world-famous culinary attraction. 🚗 ▤ TV

ST-BONNET-LE-FROID: *Auberge des Cimes* Ⓕ Ⓕ Ⓕ — AE MC V
43290 St-Bonnet-le-Froid. **⌂** *04 71 59 93 72.* **FAX** *04 71 59 93 40.* **Rooms:** *19.*
Gourmet pilgrims compete for rooms at this exceptional village inn run by an inspired chef whose reputation is growing. 🚗 ▤ TV

ST-FLOUR: *Le Bout du Monde* Ⓕ Ⓕ — MC V
St-Georges, 15100. **⌂** *04 71 60 15 84.* **FAX** *04 71 73 05 10.* **Rooms:** *14.*
You'll get an old-fashioned welcome at this hotel in a quiet river valley. The restaurant serves local dishes at unbeatable prices. 🚗 TV

ST-HILAIRE-LE-CHÂTEAU: *Hôtel du Thaurion* Ⓕ Ⓕ — AE DC MC V
23250 St-Hilaire-le-Château. **⌂** *05 55 64 50 12.* **FAX** *05 55 64 90 92.* **Rooms:** *19.*
This renovated staging post has been in the owner's family for 200 years. His cuisine is based on old local recipes. 🚗 TV

ST-JEAN-DU-BRUEL: *Hôtel du Midi Papillon* Ⓕ — MC V
12230 St-Jean-du-Bruel. **⌂** *05 65 62 26 04.* **FAX** *05 65 62 12 97.* **Rooms:** *19.*
A quiet, friendly hotel overlooking a flower garden and a river. The food is good and breakfast especially recommended. 🚗

ST-PRIVAT-D'ALLIER: *La Vieille Auberge* Ⓕ Ⓕ — V
Route de Saugues, 43580. **⌂** *04 71 57 20 56.* **Rooms:** *17.*
A recently renovated, pleasantly rustic village inn. The roooms and the food (hearty and straightforward) are excellent value. 🚗

SALERS: *Hostellerie de la Maronne* Ⓕ Ⓕ Ⓕ — AE MC V
Le Theil, St Martin Valmeroux 15140. **⌂** *04 71 69 20 33.* **FAX** *04 71 69 28 22.* **Rooms:** *21.*
Built as a 19th-century mansion, this stylish hotel is a haven of peace. Its restaurant is a treat for gourmets. 🚗 TV

VICHY: *Le Pavillon d'Enghien* Ⓕ Ⓕ Ⓕ — AE DC MC V
32 rue Callou, 03200. **⌂** *04 70 98 33 30.* **FAX** *04 70 31 67 82.* **Rooms:** *22.*
There's something of Vichy's pre-war spa atmosphere to this small, reasonably priced hotel opposite the Callou Baths. 🚗 TV

VILLEFORT: *Hôtel Balme* Ⓕ Ⓕ — AE DC MC V
Place du Portalet, 48800. **⌂** *04 66 46 80 14.* **FAX** *04 66 46 85 26.* **Rooms:** *18.*
An unusual hotel which has a mini-museum devoted to the chestnut. The cuisine is influenced by the chef's travels in the Orient. 🚗

For key to symbols see back flap

Price categories for a standard double room (not per person) for one night, including tax and service charges, but not including breakfast.
Ⓕ under F200
ⒻⒻ F200–400
ⒻⒻⒻ F400–600
ⒻⒻⒻⒻ F600–1,000
ⒻⒻⒻⒻⒻ over F1,000

CHILDREN'S FACILITIES
Cots and baby-sitting available. Some hotels provide children's portions and high chairs in the restaurant.

PARKING FACILITIES
Parking provided by the hotel in either a private car park or a private garage very close by.

SWIMMING POOL
Hotel pools are often quite small and are outdoors unless otherwise stated.

GARDEN
Hotel with garden, courtyard or terrace, often providing tables for eating outside.

	Credit Cards	Children's Facilities	Parking Facilities	Swimming Pool	Garden
VITRAC: *Auberge de la Tomette* ⒻⒻ 15220 Vitrac. 📞 04 71 64 70 94. FAX 04 71 64 77 11. **Rooms:** 19. The main hotel stands in a flowery park. Its handsome dining room has attractive panelling. 🛏 📺	AE MC V	●		●	●
YDES: *Château de Trancis* ⒻⒻⒻⒻ 15210 Ydes. 📞 04 71 40 60 40. FAX 04 71 40 62 13. **Rooms:** 7. On the fringes of the Auvergne regional park, this stylish château offers well-equipped rooms and an ornate Louis XIV salon. 🛏 📺	AE MC V	■		●	■

THE RHÔNE VALLEY AND FRENCH ALPS

	Credit Cards	Children's Facilities	Parking Facilities	Swimming Pool	Garden
AIX-LES-BAINS: *Hôtel Le Manoir* ⒻⒻ 37 rue Georges-1er, 73105. 📞 04 79 61 44 00. FAX 04 79 35 67 67. **Rooms:** 73. A charming old hotel in the Parc du Splendide-Royal, within walking distance of the thermal baths. 🛏 📺	AE DC MC V	●	■	●	■
ALBERTVILLE: *Hôtel Million* ⒻⒻ 8 place de la Liberté, 73200. 📞 04 79 32 25 15. FAX 04 79 32 25 36. **Rooms:** 28. Established in 1770 by an ancestor of the present owner, this hotel is known for its restaurant which serves superb *savoyard* cuisine. 🛏 📺	AE DC MC V	●	■		■
ANNECY: *Hôtel de l'Abbaye* ⒻⒻ 15 chemin de l'Abbaye, 74940. 📞 04 50 23 61 08. FAX 04 50 27 77 65. **Rooms:** 18. A charming hotel-restaurant occupying a former 15th-century Dominican convent surrounded by gardens. 🛏 📺	AE DC MC V	●	■		■
BAGNOLS: *Château de Bagnols* ⒻⒻⒻⒻⒻ 69620 Bagnols. 📞 04 74 71 40 00. FAX 04 74 71 40 49. **Rooms:** 20. This exquisite 13th-century château north of Lyon is set on a hilltop surrounded by Beaujolais vineyards. 🛏 🍽 📺	AE DC MC V	●	■		■
BOURG-EN-BRESSE: *Hôtel du Prieuré* ⒻⒻⒻ 49–51 boulevard de Brou, 01000. 📞 04 74 22 44 60. FAX 04 74 22 71 07. **Rooms:** 14. A charming hotel surrounded by gardens and 16th-century stone walls, only a minute's walk from the famous Eglise de Brou. The large bedrooms are furnished in French country style. 🛏 📺	AE DC MC V	●	■		■
CHAMBÉRY: *Hôtel des Princes* ⒻⒻ 4 rue de Boigne, 73000. 📞 04 79 33 45 36. FAX 04 79 70 31 47. **Rooms:** 45. Set in the grandest section of the Old Town, this pleasantly old-fashioned hotel offers comfortable rooms and a good restaurant. 🛏 📺	AE DC MC V	●	■		
CHAMONIX-MONT-BLANC: *Le Hameau Albert 1er* ⒻⒻⒻⒻⒻ 119 impasse du Montenvers, 74402. 📞 04 50 53 05 09. FAX 04 50 55 95 48. **Rooms:** 30. This large but welcoming chalet-style hotel offers elegantly furnished rooms with stupendous views of Mont Blanc. Its restaurant has a reputation for serving the best food in town. 🛏 📺	AE DC MC V	●	■	●	■
COMBLOUX: *Aux Ducs de Savoie* ⒻⒻⒻ 253 route du Bouchet, 74920. 📞 04 50 58 61 43. FAX 04 50 58 67 43. **Rooms:** 50. The rooms in this modern hotel are well-equipped and some of them face Mont Blanc. A five-course meal is served every night. 🛏 📺	AE DC MC V	●	■		■
CORDON: *Le Cordonant* ⒻⒻ 74700 Cordon. 📞 04 50 58 34 56. FAX 04 50 47 95 57. **Rooms:** 16. A friendly family-run hotel west of Chamonix offering comfortable rooms with views of Mont Blanc and an excellent *table d'hôte* menu. 🛏 📺	MC V		■		■
COURCHEVEL: *La Sivolière* ⒻⒻⒻⒻⒻ 1850 Route des Chenus, 73120. 📞 04 79 08 08 33. FAX 04 79 08 15 73. **Rooms:** 30. Attracting such distinguished guests as the Spanish royal family, this tastefully decorated hotel lies at the foot of the pistes. 🛏 📺	MC V	●	■		

EVIAN-LES-BAINS: *Hôtel Royal* ⒡⒡⒡⒡
Rive Sud du Lac-de-Génève, 74500. **(** 04 50 26 85 00. **FAX** 04 55 37 28 92. **Rooms:** 156.
This imposing turn-of-the-century hotel houses six restaurants and offers everything from jogging trails to a children's club. 🛏 📺
Cards: AE DC MC V ● ▪ ● ▪

EVIAN-LES-BAINS: *Hôtel de la Verniaz et ses Chalets* ⒡⒡⒡
Avenue d' Abondance, 74500. **(** 04 50 75 04 90. **FAX** 04 50 70 78 92. **Rooms:** 35.
Set on a hill above Evian, this glamorous establishment consists of a central villa and five chalets, each with its own garden. 🛏 ▤ 📺
Cards: AE DC MC V ● ▪ ● ▪

GRENOBLE: *Parc Hôtel* ⒡⒡⒡
10 place Paul-Mistral, 38027. **(** 04 76 85 81 231. **FAX** 04 76 46 49 88. **Rooms:** 52.
Grenoble's leading modern hotel offers comfortably furnished rooms with many amenities. Staff are friendly and helpful. 🛏 ▤ 📺
Cards: AE DC MC V ●

LA CHAPELLE-EN-VERCORS: *Hôtel Bellier* ⒡⒡
26420 La Chapelle-en-Vercors. **(** 04 75 48 20 03. **FAX** 04 75 48 25 31. **Rooms:** 12.
Set in the Vercors massif southwest of Grenoble, this family-run chalet-style hotel is friendly and unassuming. 🛏 📺
Cards: AE DC MC V

LAMASTRE: *Château d'Urbillac* ⒡⒡⒡⒡
Route de Vernoux, 07270. **(** 04 75 06 42 11. **FAX** 04 75 06 52 75. **Rooms:** 13.
A 16th-century château restored with rooms in 19th-century style and set in a vast area of parkland in the beautiful Ardèche region. 🛏
Cards: AE DC MC V ▪ ● ▪

LE POËT LAVAL: *Les Hospitaliers* ⒡⒡⒡⒡
26160 Le Poët Laval. **(** 04 75 46 22 32. **FAX** 04 75 46 49 99. **Rooms:** 22.
A beautifully restored hotel in the centre of a tiny medieval hilltop village east of Montélimar. First-class service and cuisine. 🛏
Cards: AE DC MC V ▪ ●

LES ROCHES-DE-CONDRIEU: *Hôtel Bellevue* ⒡⒡
Quai du Rhône, 38370. **(** 04 74 56 41 42. **FAX** 04 74 56 47 56. **Rooms:** 18.
This friendly modern hotel southwest of Vienne has comfortable rooms with balconies and a pleasant restaurant overlooking the river Rhône.
Cards: AE MC V ▪

LYON: *Hôtel des Artistes* ⒡⒡⒡
8 rue Gaspard-André, 69002. **(** 04 78 42 04 88. **FAX** 04 78 42 93 76. **Rooms:** 45.
Close to place Bellecour and next door to the Théâtre des Célestins, this delightful hotel is a favourite haunt of actors and revue artists. 🛏 📺
Cards: AE DC MC V ●

LYON: *Hôtel Carlton* ⒡⒡⒡
4 rue Jussieu, 69002. **(** 04 78 42 56 51. **FAX** 04 78 42 10 71. **Rooms:** 83.
In the heart of the Presqu'île near the Rhône, this recently renovated hotel still retains traces of its elegant Belle Epoque days. 🛏 ▤ 📺
Cards: AE DC MC V ● ▪

LYON: *Cour des Loges* ⒡⒡⒡⒡⒡
6 rue du Boeuf, 69005. **(** 04 78 42 75 75. **FAX** 04 72 40 93 61. **Rooms:** 63.
A luxury hotel occupying four renovated Renaissance mansions in the heart of Vieux Lyon. Bedrooms are modern in style. 🛏 ▤ 📺
Cards: AE DC MC V ● ● ▪

MALATAVERNE: *Domaine du Colombier* ⒡⒡⒡
Route de Donzère, 26780. **(** 04 75 90 86 86. **FAX** 04 75 90 79 40. **Rooms:** 25.
Occupying a 14th-century abbey south of Montélimar, this welcoming hotel has stylish rooms and a big garden with swimming pool. 🛏 📺
Cards: AE DC MC V ● ● ▪

MANIGOD: *Hôtel de la Croix-Fry* ⒡⒡⒡
Route du Col de la Croix-Fry, 74230. **(** 04 50 44 90 16. **FAX** 04 50 44 94 87. **Rooms:** 12.
High on a mountain pass east of Annecy, this delightful chalet-style hotel combines Alpine rustic with comfort and facilities. 🛏 📺
Cards: AE MC V ▪ ● ▪

MEGÈVE: *Le Fer à Cheval* ⒡⒡⒡⒡⒡
36 route du Crêt-d'Arbois, 74120. **(** 04 50 21 30 39. **FAX** 04 50 93 07 60. **Rooms:** 41.
A charming hotel with an authentic Savoy atmosphere. Guests are served dinner around a stone fireplace in winter. 🛏 📺
Cards: AE MC V ● ● ▪

MORZINE: *Hôtel Champs-Fleuris* ⒡⒡⒡⒡
La Cuisat, 74110. **(** 04 50 79 14 44. **FAX** 04 50 79 27 75. **Rooms:** 45.
Surrounded by forested mountains in the high Savoy, this hotel is popular year-round. T-lifts and gondolas a few paces away. 🛏 📺
Cards: MC V ▪ ● ▪

PÉROUGES: *Hostellerie du Vieux Pérouges* ⒡⒡⒡⒡
Place du Tilleul, 01800. **(** 04 74 61 00 88. **FAX** 04 74 34 77 90. **Rooms:** 28.
This historic Bresson inn is a filmmaker's dream, converted from 13th-century buildings and set in a medieval hilltop village. 🛏 📺
Cards: MC V ● ▪ ▪

For key to symbols see back flap

Price categories for a standard double room (not per person) for one night, including tax and service charges, but not including breakfast. Ⓕ under F200 ⒻⒻ F200–400 ⒻⒻⒻ F400–600 ⒻⒻⒻⒻ F600–1,000 ⒻⒻⒻⒻⒻ over F1,000	**CHILDREN'S FACILITIES** Cots and baby-sitting available. Some hotels provide children's portions and high chairs in the restaurant. **PARKING FACILITIES** Parking provided by the hotel in either a private car park or a private garage very close by. **SWIMMING POOL** Hotel pools are often quite small and are outdoors unless otherwise stated. **GARDEN** Hotel with garden, courtyard or terrace, often providing tables for eating outside.

	CREDIT CARDS	CHILDREN'S FACILITIES	PARKING FACILITIES	SWIMMING POOL	GARDEN

SAINT-LATTIER: *Le Lièvre Amoureux*   ⒻⒻ
Quartier de la Gare, 38840. **☎** 04 76 64 50 67. **FAX** 04 76 64 31 21. **Rooms:** 12.
Facing the foothills of the Vercors, just east of Valence, is this small, welcoming hotel with a charming old-fashioned atmosphere. ⌂
AE DC MC V — ● ■ ● ■

TALLOIRES: *Hôtel de l'Abbaye*   ⒻⒻⒻⒻ
Route du Port, 74290. **☎** 04 50 60 77 33. **FAX** 04 50 60 78 81. **Rooms:** 31.
An elegant hotel occupying a former 17th-century Benedictine abbey, beautifully situated on the shores of Lac d'Annecy. ⌂
AE DC MC V — ● ■ ■

TALLOIRES: *Hôtel Beau-Site*   ⒻⒻⒻ
74290 Talloires. **☎** 04 50 60 71 04. **FAX** 04 50 60 79 22. **Rooms:** 29.
This elegant hotel is especially noted for its warm and friendly atmosphere. Boating and watersports on the nearby lake. ⌂ TV
AE DC MC V — ● ■ ● ■

POITOU AND AQUITAINE

ARCACHON: *Arc-Hôtel-sur-Mer*   ⒻⒻⒻⒻ
89 boulevard de la Plage, 33120. **☎** 05 56 83 06 85. **FAX** 05 56 83 53 72. **Rooms:** 30.
An outdoor pool, sandy beach nearby, sea views and pleasant location enhance the appeal of this comfortable resort hotel. ⌂ ▤ TV
AE DC MC V — ● ■ ● ■

BEQUEY-CADILLAC: *Hôtel du Château de la Tour*   ⒻⒻ
Route départementale 10, 33410. **☎** 05 56 76 92 00. **FAX** 05 56 62 11 59. **Rooms:** 32.
An appealing hotel with good facilities in a historic village. A good base to explore surrounding wine country. ⌂ TV
AE DC MC V — ● ■

BORDEAUX: *Grand Hôtel Français*   ⒻⒻⒻ
12 rue du Temple, 33000. **☎** 05 56 48 10 35. **FAX** 05 56 81 76 18. **Rooms:** 35.
A good value hotel in the centre of town with attractively decorated, comfortable and quiet rooms. No restaurant. ⌂ ▤ TV
AE DC MC V — ●

CIERZAC: *Moulin de Cierzac*   ⒻⒻ
17520 Cierzac. **☎** 05 45 83 01 32. **FAX** 05 45 83 03 59. **Rooms:** 10.
South of Cognac is this small hotel-restaurant in a 17th-century country house with a vast collection of Cognac, "the water of life". ⌂ TV
AE MC V — ● ■

COGNAC: *Les Pigeons Blancs*   ⒻⒻⒻ
110 rue Jules Brisson, 16100. **☎** 05 45 82 16 36. **FAX** 05 45 82 29 29. **Rooms:** 7.
A small, excellent value hotel-restaurant which has been in the same family since the 18th-century. ⌂ TV
AE DC MC V — ● ■

CONFOLENS: *Hôtel de Vienne*   ⒻⒻ
4 rue de la Ferrandie, 16500. **☎** 05 45 84 09 24. **FAX** 05 45 84 11 60. **Rooms:** 15.
A basic but good value hotel with a perfect setting beside the river Vienne, with a lovely flowered terrace used for meals. Traditional decor and food. Ask for a room with a view. ⌂
MC V — ■

COULON: *Hôtel du Marais*   ⒻⒻ
46-48 quai Louis Tardy, 79510. **☎** 05 49 35 90 43. **FAX** 05 49 35 81 98. **Rooms:** 18.
Situated in the mysterious fens of the Marais Poitevin is this lovely little hotel. Boat hire is available in the town. ⌂ TV
MC V

EUGÉNIE-LES-BAINS: *Les Prés d'Eugénie*   ⒻⒻⒻⒻⒻ
40320 Eugénie-les-Bains. **☎** 05 58 05 06 07. **FAX** 05 58 51 10 10. **Rooms:** 43.
The illustrious chef Michel Guérard draws worshippers to his delightful hotel, cuisine and thermal spa. Less costly accommodation is available in the same grounds. Truly a treat to stay here. ⌂ TV
AE DC MC V — ● ■ ● ■

GRADIGNAN: *Le Chalet Lyrique*   ⒻⒻ
169 cours du Général-de-Gaulle, 33170. **☎** 05 56 89 11 59. **FAX** 05 56 89 53 37. **Rooms:** 44.
Not too far away from the Bordeaux-Mérignac airport, this is a pleasant stop-over with a magnificent patio. ⌂ ▤ TV
AE DC MC V — ■ ■

GRENADE-SUR-L'ADOUR: *Pain Adour et Fantaisie* ⒻⒻⒻ — AE DC MC V
14–16 place de Tilleuls, 40270. **☎** 05 58 45 18 80. **FAX** 05 58 45 16 57. **Rooms:** 11.
Timber and stone adorn this graceful 18th-century hotel set beside the
river Adour. A memorable setting and acclaimed cuisine. 🚪 ▤ TV

HIERSAC: *Hostellerie de Maine Brun* ⒻⒻⒻ — AE DC MC V
La Vigerie, 16290. **☎** 05 45 90 83 00. **FAX** 05 45 96 91 14. **Rooms:** 20.
A mill on the pretty banks of the Nouère has become a supremely
relaxing hotel with much to enjoy – cuisine, wines and Cognac. 🚪 TV

HOSSEGOR: *Hôtel de la Plage* ⒻⒻ — MC V
Place des Landais, 40150. **☎** 05 58 41 76 41. **FAX** 05 58 41 76 54. **Rooms:** 7.
Situated in a very popular summer resort is this good value, attractive
hotel on the beach. Ask for a room with a sea view. 🚪 TV

LA ROCHELLE: *Les Brises* ⒻⒻⒻ — AE MC V
Ch. de la Digue de Richelieu, 17000. **☎** 05 46 43 89 37. **FAX** 05 46 43 27 97. **Rooms:** 50.
A comfortable and well-liked hotel to the west of this handsome and
bustling city. Wonderful views out to sea and the offshore islands. 🚪 TV

MAGESCQ: *Relais de la Poste* ⒻⒻⒻ — AE DC MC V
40140 Magescq. **☎** 05 58 47 70 25. **FAX** 05 58 47 76 17. **Rooms:** 12.
A small hotel with gardens and pools perfectly combining comfort,
celebrated cuisine, fine wines and family tradition. 🚪 TV

MARGAUX: *Relais de Margaux* ⒻⒻⒻⒻ — AE DC MC V
Chemin de l'Ile Vincent, 33460. **☎** 05 57 88 38 30. **FAX** 05 57 88 31 73. **Rooms:** 31.
The high price at this luxurious hotel is money well spent. Peaceful
setting, handsome grounds, pool, tennis and exquisite food. 🚪 TV

MIMIZAN: *Au Bon Coin du Lac* ⒻⒻⒻ — AE V
34 avenue du lac, 40200. **☎** 05 58 09 01 55. **FAX** 05 58 09 40 84. **Rooms:** 8.
The cuisine at this small hotel is a prime draw, not to mention its very
agreeable setting among pine trees and beside a lake. 🚪 TV

NIEUIL: *Château de Nieuil* ⒻⒻⒻⒻ — AE DC MC V
16270 Nieuil. **☎** 05 45 71 36 38. **FAX** 05 45 71 46 45. **Rooms:** 14.
King François I hunted in the extensive park embracing this spectacular
Renaissance château, transformed in the 1930s into a hotel. 🚪 TV

POITIERS: *Château Clos de la Ribaudière* ⒻⒻⒻ — AE DC MC V
Chasseneuil-du-Poitou, 86360. **☎** 05 49 52 86 66. **FAX** 05 49 52 86 32. **Rooms:** 43.
A restored 19th-century house in a riverside park near Poitiers – a
haven of peace and comfort away from the busy city. 🚪 TV

RETJONS: *L'Hostellerie Landaise* Ⓕ — MC V
40120 Retjons. **☎** 05 58 93 36 33. **Rooms:** 6.
Architecturally a true *auberge landaise*, set in its own park with duck-
dimpled lake. A delightful overnight stop and a very talented chef. 🚪

ROYAN: *Family Golf Hôtel* ⒻⒻⒻ — MC V
28 boulevard Garnier, 17200. **☎** 05 46 05 14 66. **FAX** 05 46 06 52 56. **Rooms:** 30.
An unpretentious hotel on the seafront in a large and lively resort just
north of the Gironde. Central but no restaurant. 🚪 TV

SABRES: *Auberge des Pins* ⒻⒻ — AE MC V
Route de la Piscine, 40630. **☎** 05 58 07 50 47. **FAX** 05 58 07 56 74. **Rooms:** 24.
Deep in the forests of the Landes Regional Park, this comfortable
auberge has been called the very model of a family hotel. 🚪 TV

ST-CLAUD: *Le Bragier* ⒻⒻ
16450 Saint-Claud. **☎** 05 45 71 47 49. **Rooms:** 3.
On the edge of open meadows and woods in a rural hamlet is this
vegetarian chambres d'hôte where guests are encouraged to feel at home. 🚪

ST-EMILION: *Château Meylet* ⒻⒻ
"La Gomerie", 33330. **☎** 05 57 24 68 85. **Rooms:** 4.
A renovated, homely farmhouse surrounded by its own vineyards –
perfect for exploring the area. Price includes a lovely breakfast. 🚪

ST-EMILION: *Hostellerie Plaisance* ⒻⒻⒻⒻ — AE DC MC V
5 place du Clocher, 33330. **☎** 05 57 24 72 32. **FAX** 05 57 74 41 11. **Rooms:** 12.
An excellent small hotel in a striking building in the upper part of this
town, famous for its wine. Delicious food is served. 🚪 ▤

For key to symbols see back flap

Price categories for a standard double room (not per person) for one night, including tax and service charges, but not including breakfast.

- Ⓕ under F200
- ⒻⒻ F200–400
- ⒻⒻⒻ F400–600
- ⒻⒻⒻⒻ F600–1,000
- ⒻⒻⒻⒻⒻ over F1,000

CHILDREN'S FACILITIES
Cots and baby-sitting available. Some hotels provide children's portions and high chairs in the restaurant.

PARKING FACILITIES
Parking provided by the hotel in either a private car park or a private garage very close by.

SWIMMING POOL
Hotel pools are often quite small and are outdoors unless otherwise stated.

GARDEN
Hotel with garden, courtyard or terrace, often providing tables for eating outside.

	CREDIT CARDS	CHILDREN'S FACILITIES	PARKING FACILITIES	SWIMMING POOL	GARDEN
VELLUIRE: *Auberge de la Rivière* ⒻⒻ Rue Fouarne, 85770. ☎ 05 51 52 32 15. FAX 05 51 52 37 42. *Rooms: 11.* A secluded, ivy-covered inn on the banks of the river Vendée. Rooms are comfortable with river views. Worth staying for the superb food. 🍴 📺	MC V		▓		
VILLENEUVE-DE-MARSAN: *Francis Darroze* ⒻⒻⒻ 57 Grand rue, 40190. ☎ 05 58 45 20 07. FAX 05 58 45 82 67. *Rooms: 15.* A country house hotel set in pine-shaded grounds. Darroze is a distinguished family name with a long tradition of fine cuisine. 🍴 📺	AE DC MC V	●	▓	●	▓

PÉRIGORD, QUERCY AND GASCONY

	CREDIT CARDS	CHILDREN'S FACILITIES	PARKING FACILITIES	SWIMMING POOL	GARDEN
ALBI: *Hostellerie du Vigan* ⒻⒻ 16 place du Vigan, 81000. ☎ 05 63 54 01 23. FAX 05 63 47 05 42. *Rooms: 40.* A very good value hotel in the centre of town which is unpretentious, comfortable and inexpensive. Excellent restaurant. 🍴 📺	AE DC MC V	●	▓		▓
ALBI: *Hôtel St-Clair* ⒻⒻ 8 rue St-Clair, 81000. ☎ 05 63 54 25 66. *Rooms: 11.* An 18th-century hotel that has been in the same family for generations. Nicely converted and furnished with antiques. Centrally located. 🍴 📺	MC V		▓		
AUVILLAR: *d'Astros* ⒻⒻ Le Pin, 82340. ☎ 05 63 95 95 20. FAX 05 63 95 93 55. *Rooms: 4.* A small, friendly guest house set well off the tourist track in a large, secluded garden. Also caters for vegetarians and special diets. 🍴		●	▓		
BEYNAC: *Hôtel Bonnet* ⒻⒻ 24220 Beynac. ☎ 05 53 29 50 01. FAX 05 53 29 83 74. *Rooms: 21.* This small village hotel is named after the family who have owned it for years. Simple, airy and traditional in style. 🍴	MC V	●			
BRANTÔME: *Le Chatenet* ⒻⒻⒻ 24310 Brantôme. ☎ 05 53 05 81 08. FAX 05 53 05 85 52. *Rooms: 8.* Off the busy riverside road lies this beautifully restored 17th-century manor house. Facilities include tennis courts and a clubhouse. 🍴 📺	MC V	●	▓	●	
BRANTÔME: *Le Moulin de l'Abbaye* ⒻⒻⒻⒻ 1 route de Bourdeilles, 24310. ☎ 05 53 05 80 22. FAX 05 53 05 75 27. *Rooms: 20.* A handsome, old creeper-covered mill standing next to the river Dronne. The dining room extends to a terrace over the river. 🍴 📺	AE DC MC V	●	▓		
CAHORS: *Terminus* ⒻⒻⒻ 5 avenue Charles-de-Freycinet, 46000. ☎ 05 65 35 24 50. FAX 05 65 22 06 40. *Rooms: 22.* A good find in the heart of truffle country, only two minutes from the station. Elegant 1920s-style decor and stained-glass windows. 🍴 📺	AE MC V	●	▓		
CARSAC-AILLAC: *Le Relais du Touron* ⒻⒻ 24200 Carsac-Aillac. ☎ 05 53 28 16 70. FAX 05 53 28 52 51. *Rooms: 12.* Set in wooded countryside just east of Sarlat is this serene, 19th-century small mansion. Simple but exquisitely cooked food. 🍴	MC V	●	▓		
CHAMPAGNAC-DE-BELAIR: *Hôtel Moulin du Roc* ⒻⒻⒻ 24530 Champagnac-de-Belair. ☎ 05 53 02 86 00. FAX 05 53 54 21 31. *Rooms: 14.* In a beautiful setting by a quiet stream just outside Brantôme is this converted walnut mill. Indoor pool and wonderful food. 🍴 📺	AE DC MC V	●	▓	●	
COLY: *Manoir d'Hautegente* ⒻⒻⒻⒻ 24120 Coly. ☎ 05 53 51 68 03. FAX 05 53 50 38 52. *Rooms: 12.* Just north of Sarlat is this picturesque mansion, once the mill and forge of an abbey. Family-run, friendly hotel with log fires, private fishing, swimming pool and library. 🍴 📺	AE MC V	●	▓	●	

CONDOM: *Hôtel des Trois Lys* ⓕⓕⓕ AE MC V
38 rue Gambetta, 32100. 05 62 28 33 33. FAX 05 62 28 41 85. **Rooms:** 10.
In the heart of Armagnac country is this well-run 17th-century hotel.
Breakfast is served on the patio.

DOMME: *Hôtel de l'Esplanade* ⓕⓕ AE MC V
24250 Domme. 05 53 28 31 41. FAX 05 53 28 49 92. **Rooms:** 25.
Perched on the cliff-top is this hotel with a panoramic dining terrace.
Rooms are tastefully decorated, some with fantastic views.

DURAS: *Hostellerie des Ducs* ⓕⓕ MC V
47120 Duras. 05 53 83 74 58. FAX 05 53 83 75 03. **Rooms:** 15.
Situated between the Dordogne and Garonne rivers is this simple,
family-run hostelry overlooking a 14th-century fortress.

FLORIMONT-GAUMIERS: *La Daille* ⓕⓕ
24250 Dordogne. 05 53 28 40 71. **Rooms:** 4.
A short drive from Gaumier's, this stone-built farmhouse
has marvellous views. Good food.

GARABIT: *Hôtel-restaurant Beau Site* ⓕⓕ DC MC V
Garabit, Loubaresse, 15320. 05 71 23 41 46. FAX 05 71 23 46 34. **Rooms:** 17.
Well named for its spectacular views of the lake and Eiffel's viaduct, this hotel
also offers large, comfortable rooms, good food and a heated pool.

LACAVE: *Le Pont de l'Ouysse* ⓕⓕⓕ AE DC MC V
46200 Lacave. 05 65 37 87 04. FAX 05 65 32 77 41. **Rooms:** 14.
A chic restaurant-with-rooms not far from Rocamadour. Inventive
variations on local dishes are on offer.

LA COQUILLE: *Hôtel des Voyageurs* ⓕⓕ MC V
Rue de la République, 24450. 05 53 60 18 29. FAX 05 53 60 18 29. **Rooms:** 10.
This small village hotel is friendly and comfortable.
Enjoy delicious regional food in the tartan dining room.

LES EYZIES-DE-TAYAC: *Le Moulin de la Beune* ⓕⓕ AE MC V
24620 Les Eyzies-de-Tayac. 05 53 06 94 33. FAX 05 53 06 98 06. **Rooms:** 20
Huge, comfortable rooms in this converted mill. Reasonably priced
and efficiently run. The restaurant has a very good reputation.

LES EYZIES-DE-TAYAC: *Le Centenaire* ⓕⓕⓕ AE DC MC V
24620 Les Eyzies-de-Tayac. 05 53 06 68 68. FAX 05 53 06 92 41. **Rooms:** 20.
A luxurious, modern hotel just outside the town. Spacious bedrooms
with balconies overlooking the lawn and swimming pool.

MARQUAY: *Hôtel des Bories* ⓕⓕ MC V
24620 Marquay. 05 53 29 67 02. FAX 05 53 29 64 15. **Rooms:** 30.
An unassuming hotel offering outstanding value. Family-run with basic
rooms and beamed ceilings. Lake with watersports nearby.

MERCUÈS: *Château de Mercuès* ⓕⓕⓕⓕ AE DC MC V
46090 Mercuès. 05 65 20 00 01. FAX 05 65 20 05 72. **Rooms:** 31.
Situated beside the Lot river is this 12th-century turreted château which
has been tastefully modernized. Generous breakfasts.

MEYRONNE: *La Terrasse* ⓕⓕ MC V
46200 Meyronne. 05 65 32 21 60. FAX 05 65 32 26 93. **Rooms:** 18.
This converted monastery has some of its bedrooms in the adjacent
9th-century château. Meals are eaten in the large dining room.

NONTRON: *Le Grand Hôtel* ⓕⓕ MC V
3 place A-Agard, 24300. 05 53 56 11 22. FAX 05 53 56 59 94. **Rooms:** 28.
Very reasonably priced and well-run hotel in the centre of this market
town. Swimming pool, pretty garden and good, honest food.

PÉRIGUEUX: *Hôtel Perigord* ⓕⓕ MC V
74 rue Victor Hugo, 24000. 05 53 53 33 63. FAX 05 53 08 19 74. **Rooms:** 20.
Close to the old centre of this delightful town is this fabulous
little find. The restaurant offers good value, traditional cuisine.

RIBÉRAC: *Pauliac* ⓕⓕ MC V
Celles, 24600. 05 53 91 97 45. FAX 05 53 90 43 46. **Rooms:** 5.
A basic, well-restored farmhouse set in a tiny hamlet. There is a
terraced garden and tables outside. Good, wholesome food.

Price categories for a standard double room (not per person) for one night, including tax and service charges, but not including breakfast.

- **F** under F200
- **F F** F200 – 400
- **F F F** F400 – 600
- **F F F F** F600 – 1,000
- **F F F F F** over F1,000

CHILDREN'S FACILITIES
Cots and baby-sitting available. Some hotels provide children's portions and high chairs in the restaurant.

PARKING FACILITIES
Parking provided by the hotel in either a private car park or a private garage very close by.

SWIMMING POOL
Hotel pools are often quite small and are outdoors unless otherwise stated.

GARDEN
Hotel with garden, courtyard or terrace, often providing tables for eating outside.

Hotel	Credit Cards	Children's Facilities	Parking Facilities	Swimming Pool	Garden
ROCAMADOUR: *Domaine de la Rhue* **F F F** 46500 Rocamadour. ☎ 05 65 33 71 50. FAX 05 65 33 72 48. **Rooms:** 12. Only a few minutes' drive from Rocamadour is this peaceful hotel – a 19th-century stone building, imaginatively converted. Spacious rooms. 🚗	MC V	●	■	●	
ST-CIRQ-LAPOPIE: *Hôtel de la Pélissaria* **F F F** 46330 St-Cirq-Lapopie. ☎ 05 65 31 25 14. FAX 05 65 30 25 52. **Rooms:** 10. A tiny hotel in a cliff-top village above the Lot river. The rooms have tiled floors, white walls, exposed beams and pine doors. 🚗 TV	MC V			●	
SARLAT-LA-CANÉDA: *Hostellerie de Meysset* **F F F** Route des Eyzies, 24200. ☎ 05 53 59 08 29. FAX 05 53 28 47 61. **Rooms:** 26. Built in local style and set in its own park is this pleasant rural hotel. French windows open on to the lawn. Excellent food. 🚗	AE DC MC V	●	■		
TAMNIÈS: *Hôtel Laborderie* **F F** 24620 Tamniès. ☎ 05 53 29 68 59. FAX 05 53 29 65 31. **Rooms:** 32. Between Sarlat and Les Eyzies lies this family-run, modern hotel. Log fires in winter and swimming and outdoor meals in summer. 🚗 TV	MC V		■		
TOULOUSE: *Hôtel Albert 1er* **F F** 8 rue Rivals, 31000. ☎ 05 61 21 17 91. FAX 05 61 21 09 64. **Rooms:** 50. A good value hotel, centrally situated with cheerful rooms and modern bathrooms. Small lounge and breakfast room but no restaurant. 🚗 ▤ TV	AE DC MC V	●			
TOULOUSE: *Hôtel Jean-Mermoz* **F F F** 50 rue Matabiau, 31000. ☎ 05 61 63 04 04. FAX 05 61 63 15 64. **Rooms:** 53. Modern hotel in the centre of town which is comfortable, friendly and surprisingly quiet. Pleasant garden and restaurant. 🚗 ▤ TV	AE DC MC V	●	■		■
VIEUX MAREUIL: *Château de Vieux-Mareuil* **F F F** Rte Angoulême-Périgueux, 24340. ☎ 05 53 60 77 15. FAX 05 53 56 49 33. **Rooms:** 14. Spacious bedrooms and delicious cuisine can be found at this 15th-century fortified hotel. Acres of parkland to explore. 🚗 TV	AE DC MC V	●	■		■

THE PYRENEES

Hotel	Credit Cards	Children's Facilities	Parking Facilities	Swimming Pool	Garden
AÏNHOA: *Hôtel-Restaurant Ithurria* **F F F** 64250 Aïnhoa. ☎ 05 59 29 92 11. FAX 05 59 29 81 28. **Rooms:** 27. With its cosy rooms, beamed dining room and gourmet cooking, this old coaching inn in one of the prettiest Basque villages is a satisfying place to stay. 🚗 TV	AE MC DC V	●	■	●	
ANGLET: *Château de Brindos* **F F F F** Allée du Château, 64600. ☎ 05 59 23 17 68. FAX 05 59 23 48 47. **Rooms:** 14. Life is calm and gracious here beside the peaceful lake. The beach is only a short drive away and there is also a golf course nearby. 🚗 TV	AE DC V	●	■	●	■
ARGELÈS-GAZOST: *Hôtel le Miramont* **F F** 44 avenue des Pyrénées, 65400. ☎ 05 62 97 01 26. FAX 05 62 97 56 67. **Rooms:** 28. A stylish, comfortable hotel with a garden in a small spa town. The attractive restaurant serves delicious food. 🚗 TV	MC V		■		
ARREAU: *Hôtel d'Angleterre* **F F** Route de Luchon, 65240. ☎ 05 62 98 63 30. FAX 05 62 98 69 66. **Rooms:** 24. Four rivers flow through little Arreau, past slate-roofed houses. This 17th-century inn serving savoury mountain food is good value. It makes a suitable base for exploring the stunning countryside. 🚗 TV	MC V	●	■		■
BARBAZAN: *Hostellerie de L'Aristou* **F F** Route Sauveterre, 31510. ☎ 05 61 88 30 67. FAX 05 61 95 55 66. **Rooms:** 7. This pleasant country house has a fine restaurant and is ideal for exploring the nearby Roman ruins. 🚗 TV	AE DC MC V	●	■		

BIARRITZ: *Château du Claire de Lune* ⓕⓕⓕ
48 avenue Alan-Seeger, 64200. **℡** *05 59 41 53 20*. **FAX** *05 59 41 53 29*. **Rooms:** *16.*
This Belle-Époque mansion converted into a relaxing hotel is
set back from the crowded coast amid scented gardens. 🛏 TV
AE DC MC V

BIARRITZ: *Hôtel Windsor* ⓕⓕⓕ
Avenue Edouard-VII, 64200. **℡** *05 59 24 08 52*. **FAX** *05 59 24 98 90*. **Rooms:** *49.*
Standing above the famous Grande Plage, and with recently decorated
family rooms, this is a great spot for a lively holiday. 🛏 TV
AE DC MC V

BIARRITZ: *Hôtel du Palais* ⓕⓕⓕⓕⓕ
1 avenue de l'Impératrice, 64200. **℡** *05 59 41 64 00*. **FAX** *05 59 41 67 99*. **Rooms:** *156.*
A magnificent hotel of enduring grandeur and elegance. The service
and food are impeccable; the mood refreshingly unstuffy. 🛏 TV ▤
AE DC MC V

ESPELETTE: *Hôtel Euzkadi* ⓕⓕ
64250 Espelette. **℡** *05 59 93 91 88*. **FAX** *05 59 93 90 19*. **Rooms:** *32.*
The generous, savoury Basque cooking has made this characterful
hotel enormously popular. 🛏
V

FOIX: *Hôtel Audoye-Lons* ⓕⓕ
6 place G-Duthil, 09000. **℡** *05 61 65 52 44*. **FAX** *05 61 02 68 18*. **Rooms:** *39.*
The big, period bedrooms and glass-enclosed dining room of this half-
timbered house in the Old Town are right above the river. 🛏 TV
AE DC MC V

GAVARNIE: *Hôtel Vignemale* ⓕⓕⓕ
65120 Gavarnie. **℡** *05 62 92 40 00*. **FAX** *05 62 92 40 08*. **Rooms:** *24.*
This recently modernized hotel makes a comfortable base to walk the
mountain trails or merely to enjoy the Cirque de Gavarnie. 🛏 TV
AE MC V

NUZENAC: *L'Oustal* ⓕⓕ
Unac, 09250. **℡** *05 61 64 48 44*. **Rooms:** *5.*
High in the wild Arriège, not far from Ax-les-Thermes, is this appealing
rural hostelry with marvellous views and excellent cuisine. 🛏
MC V

OLORON-STE-MARIE: *L'Alysson* ⓕⓕ
Boulevard des Pyrénées, 64400. **℡** *05 59 39 70 70*. **FAX** *05 59 39 24 47*. **Rooms:** *34.*
The most comfortable hotel in a picturesque riverside town, with
good food served in a modern dining room. 🛏 TV
MC V

PAU: *Grand Hôtel du Commerce* ⓕⓕ
9 rue Maréchal-Joffre, 64000. **℡** *05 59 27 24 40*. **FAX** *05 59 83 81 74*. **Rooms:** *51.*
Conveniently located near the royal château, this popular, traditional
hotel has comfortable rooms and a reasonable restaurant. 🛏 TV
AE DC MC V

ST-ETIENNE-DE-BAÏGORRY: *Hôtel Arcé* ⓕⓕⓕ
64430 St-Etienne-de-Baïgorry. **℡** *05 59 37 40 14*. **FAX** *05 59 37 40 27*. **Rooms:** *22.*
Deep in the Basque Country is this welcoming family hotel in a
wonderful setting beside the fast-flowing Nive des Aldudes. 🛏 TV
MC V

ST-GIRONS: *Hôtel Eychenne* ⓕⓕⓕ
8 avenue Paul-Laffont, 09200. **℡** *05 61 04 04 50*. **FAX** *05 61 96 07 20*. **Rooms:** *60.*
The antique furnishings, garden, swimming pool and excellent
restaurant combine to give this hotel true distinction. 🛏 TV
MC V

ST-JEAN-DE-LUZ: *La Devinière* ⓕⓕⓕ
5 rue Loquin, 64500. **℡** *05 59 26 05 51*. **FAX** *05 59 51 26 38*. **Rooms:** *9.*
Quiet and tiny, with snug rooms elegantly furnished and an intimate
garden, this gem of a hotel is in the heart of the old city. 🛏
MC V

ST-JEAN-DE-LUZ: *Le Parc Victoria* ⓕⓕⓕⓕ
5 rue Cépé, 64500. **℡** *05 59 26 78 78*. **FAX** *05 59 26 78 08*. **Rooms:** *12.*
A glorious garden and swimming pool set off this Victorian mansion,
furnished in the style of the 1930s, near the beach. 🛏 TV
AE DC MC V

ST-JEAN-PIED-DE-PORT: *Hôtel les Pyrénées* ⓕⓕⓕ
19 pl du Gén-de-Gaulle, 64220. **℡** *05 59 37 01 01*. **FAX** *05 59 37 18 97*. **Rooms:** *20.*
Relaxing, if pricy, this hotel with its renowned Basque-based cuisine
provides a refuge from the summer crowds. 🛏 TV ▤
AE MC V

ST-JEAN-PIED-DE-PORT: *Hôtel Larramendy Andreinia* ⓕ
Esterençuby, 64220. **℡** *05 59 37 09 70*. **FAX** *05 59 37 36 05*. **Rooms:** *26.*
Set in a tiny village on the rippling river Nive, this Basque
hotel is an ideal base for ramblers. 🛏 TV
MC V

Price categories for a standard double room (not per person) for one night, including tax and service charges, but not including breakfast.
Ⓕ under F200
ⒻⒻ F200–400
ⒻⒻⒻ F400–600
ⒻⒻⒻⒻ F600–1,000
ⒻⒻⒻⒻⒻ over F1,000

CHILDREN'S FACILITIES
Cots and baby-sitting available. Some hotels provide children's portions and high chairs in the restaurant.

PARKING FACILITIES
Parking provided by the hotel in either a private car park or a private garage very close by.

SWIMMING POOL
Hotel pools are often quite small and are outdoors unless otherwise stated.

GARDEN
Hotel with garden, courtyard or terrace, often providing tables for eating outside.

Hotel	Price	Credit Cards	Children's Facilities	Parking Facilities	Swimming Pool	Garden
SARE: *Hôtel Arraya* — Place du village, 64310. ☎ 05 59 54 20 46. FAX 05 59 54 27 04. **Rooms:** 20. This centrally located, modern hotel guarantees peace and comfort. Every bedroom has an en-suite bathroom. 🛏 📺	ⒻⒻⒻ	AE MC V		■		■
TARBES: *Hôtel de l'Avenue* — 778–80 av Bertrand-Barère, 65000. ☎ 05 62 93 06 36. **Rooms:** 28. A small family-run hotel only a two-minute walk from the station. The quietest rooms overlook an interior courtyard. 🛏 📺	ⒻⒻ	MC V	●	■		

LANGUEDOC-ROUSSILLON

Hotel	Price	Credit Cards	Children's Facilities	Parking Facilities	Swimming Pool	Garden
AIGUES-MORTES: *Hôtel des Croisades* — 2 rue du Port, 30220. ☎ 04 66 53 67 85. FAX 04 66 53 72 95. **Rooms:** 14. With friendly staff and a delightful garden, this hotel is excellent value for money. 🛏 ▤ 📺	ⒻⒻ	MC V		■		■
AIGUES-MORTES: *Hôtel Saint-Louis* — 10 rue de l'Amiral-Courbet, 30220. ☎ 04 66 53 72 68. FAX 04 66 53 75 92. **Rooms:** 22. This charming hotel is tucked within the stout stone walls of a lively city built by the saint-king Louis IX. The Camargue is nearby. 🛏 📺	ⒻⒻⒻ	AE DC MC V	●	■		■
BARJAC: *Hôtel le Mas du Termes* — Route de Bagnol-sur-Cèze, 30430. ☎ 04 66 24 56 31. FAX 04 66 24 58 54. **Rooms:** 32. Situated in beautiful country near the Ardèche gorges is this distinctive old hotel. The restaurant serves home-produced wine. 🛏 📺	ⒻⒻⒻ	MC V	●	■	●	
BÉZIERS: *Grand Hôtel du Nord* — 15 place Jean-Jaurès, 34500. ☎ 04 67 28 34 09. FAX 04 67 49 00 37. **Rooms:** 40. A sturdy town house off the central avenue, handy for the sights. The back rooms are quieter, with views across to the Orb river. 🛏 📺	ⒻⒻ	AE DC MC V		■		
BOUZIGUES: *La Côte Bleue* — Avenue Louis-Tudesq, 34140. ☎ 04 67 78 31 42. FAX 04 67 78 35 49. **Rooms:** 32. With its comfortable rooms, swimming pool and famous terraced restaurant on the seashore, this hotel is justifiably popular. 🛏 📺	ⒻⒻ	MC V		■	●	■
CARCASSONNE: *Hôtel du Donjon* — 2 rue du Comte-Roger, 11000. ☎ 04 68 71 08 80. FAX 04 68 25 06 60. **Rooms:** 37. Right in the heart of the medieval city, this superb 14th-century building is full of modern comforts. 🛏 ▤ 📺	ⒻⒻⒻ	AE DC MC V		■		
CARCASSONE: *Hôtel Mercure la Vicomté* — 18 rue C Saint-Saens, 11000. ☎ 04 68 71 45 45. FAX 04 68 71 11 45. **Rooms:** 61. At the eastern entry to the medieval city, this is a comfortable place for a stopover away from the summer crowds. 🛏 ▤ 📺	ⒻⒻⒻ	AE DC MC V	●	■		
CASTILLON-DU-GARD: *Le Vieux Castillon* — Rue Citernasse, 30210. ☎ 04 66 37 61 61. FAX 04 66 37 28 17. **Rooms:** 35. Restored buildings in a medieval village near the Pont du Gard have been made into a stylish and discreet hotel. Even the pool is artfully set beside a ruined wall. 🛏 📺	ⒻⒻⒻⒻ	AE MC V	●	■	●	■
CÉRET: *La Terrasse au Soleil* — Route de Fontfrède, 66400. ☎ 04 68 87 01 94. FAX 04 68 87 39 24. **Rooms:** 27. A peaceful and comfortable hotel set between the mountains and the sea giving splendid views. There is a good restaurant. 🛏 ▤ 📺	ⒻⒻⒻⒻ	DC MC V	●	■	●	■
COLLIOURE: *Relais de Trois Mas* — Route de Port-Vendres, 66190. ☎ 04 68 82 05 07. FAX 04 68 82 38 08. **Rooms:** 23. The hotel consists of several tastefully restored buildings amid pine-shaded gardens. Every room has a sea or harbour view and some have terraces. The restaurant, La Balette, is renowned. 🛏 ▤ 📺	ⒻⒻⒻ	MC V	●	■	●	■

FUILLA: *Rozinante* ⓕⓕ
7 Cami Ribere Enclose, 66820. 【 04 68 96 34 50. FAX 04 68 96 34 50. **Rooms:** 3.
Nestling under Mount Canigou, this delightful guesthouse
boasts its own pool and luxurious lawns.

MINERVE: *Relais Chantovent* ⓕⓕ MC V
34210 Minerve. 【 04 68 91 14 18. FAX 04 68 91 81 99. **Rooms:** 10.
The hotel buildings are spread out in the narrow streets. The rooms
in the annexe, a converted village house, have great character. 🖼

MONTPELLIER: *Hôtel Guilhem* ⓕⓕⓕ AE DC MC V
18 rue JJ-Rousseau, 34000. 【 04 67 52 90 90. FAX 04 67 60 67 67. **Rooms:** 33.
An appealing bed-and-breakfast hotel, run by friendly owners, which
provides peace and seclusion in a busy city. 🖼 📺

NARBONNE: *Grand Hôtel du Languedoc* ⓕⓕ AE DC V
22 boulevard Gambetta, 11100. 【 04 68 65 14 74. FAX 04 68 65 81 48. **Rooms:** 40.
A cheerful city hotel only a short walk from the cathedral, shops
and museums. Its Belle Epoque-style restaurant is popular. 🖼 📺

NÎMES: *Hôtel Plazza* ⓕⓕ AE DC MC V
10 rue Roussy, 30000. 【 04 66 76 16 20. FAX 04 66 67 65 99. **Rooms:** 28.
A peaceful location and well-equipped bathrooms and bedrooms
make this modernized hotel good value. 🖼 ▤ 📺

NÎMES: *Imperator Concorde* ⓕⓕⓕⓕ AE DC V
Quai de la Fontaine, 30000. 【 04 66 21 90 30. FAX 04 66 67 70 25. **Rooms:** 61.
Nîmes' grandest hotel stands close to 17th-century gardens and
fountains, and some remarkable Roman architecture. 🖼 ▤ 📺

PERPIGNAN: *Hôtel de la Loge* ⓕⓕ AE DC MC V
1 rue des Fabriques-Nabot, 66000. 【 04 68 34 41 02. FAX 04 68 34 25 13. **Rooms:** 22.
In the heart of the city, close to the sights, is this calm, 16th-century
Catalan mansion with a mosaic forecourt and fountain. 🖼 ▤ 📺

PEYRIAC-MINERVOIS: *Château de Violet* ⓕⓕⓕⓕ AE DC MC V
Route de Pépieux, 11160. 【 04 68 78 10 42. FAX 04 68 78 30 01. **Rooms:** 12.
Timbered ceilings and huge fireplaces add atmosphere to this château
which presides over its own domain of parks and vineyards. 🖼 📺

PONT DE MONTVERT: *Hôtel des Cévennes* ⓕⓕ
48220 Pont de Montvert. 【 04 66 45 80 01. **Rooms:** 10.
This traditional granite auberge overlooks the rushing Tarn. Choose rooms
1, 2 or 3 for a river view. The dining room offers a panorama of the village. 🖼

PRADES: *Grand Hôtel Thermal* ⓕⓕⓕ AE MC V
Molitg-les-Bains, 66500. 【 04 68 05 00 50. FAX 04 68 05 02 91. **Rooms:** 70.
A spa hotel in the mountains, surrounded by palm trees and
adjacent to a lake. Spacious, peaceful and very good value. 🖼 📺

QUILLAN: *Hôtel Cartier* ⓕⓕ AE MC V
31 bd Charles de Gaulle, 11500. 【 04 68 20 05 14. FAX 04 68 20 02 57. **Rooms:** 30.
A comfortable, modest hotel-restaurant in the centre of town. 🖼 📺

ST-CYPRIEN-PLAGE: *Le Mas d'Huston* ⓕⓕⓕⓕ AE DC MC V
66750 St-Cyprien-le-Plage. 【 04 68 37 63 63. FAX 04 68 37 64 64. **Rooms:** 50.
A relaxing hotel by the beach with all the pleasures of a bustling
resort to hand. The restaurant overlooks a golf course. 🖼 ▤ 📺

SÈTE: *Grand Hôtel* ⓕⓕⓕ AE DC MC V
17 quai du Mar de Lattre de Tassigny, 34200. 【 04 67 74 71 77.
FAX 04 67 74 29 27. **Rooms:** 45.
Built in Belle Epoque style, this hotel overlooking Sète's Grand Canal
has a splendid palm-filled atrium and rooms with balconies. 🖼 ▤ 📺

SOMMIÈRES: *Auberge du Pont-Romain* ⓕⓕ AE DC MC V
2 rue Emile-Jamais, 30250. 【 04 66 80 00 58. FAX 04 66 80 31 52. **Rooms:** 18.
Behind a forbidding façade is a wonderful garden leading down to a
riverbank. The bedrooms are large, some with garden views. 🖼

UZÈS: *Le Mas d'Oléandre* ⓕⓕ
Saint-Médiers, 30700. 【 04 66 22 63 43. **Rooms:** 6.
A carefully restored farmhouse set in a secluded village surrounded by
vineyards. A good base for exploring and close to local restaurants. 🖼

Price categories for a standard double room (not per person) for one night, including tax and service charges, but not including breakfast.
- ⓕ under F200
- ⓕⓕ F200–400
- ⓕⓕⓕ F400–600
- ⓕⓕⓕⓕ F600–1,000
- ⓕⓕⓕⓕⓕ over F1,000

CHILDREN'S FACILITIES
Cots and baby-sitting available. Some hotels provide children's portions and high chairs in the restaurant.

PARKING FACILITIES
Parking provided by the hotel in either a private car park or a private garage very close by.

SWIMMING POOL
Hotel pools are often quite small and are outdoors unless otherwise stated.

GARDEN
Hotel with garden, courtyard or terrace, often providing tables for eating outside.

	CREDIT CARDS	CHILDREN'S FACILITIES	PARKING FACILITIES	SWIMMING POOL	GARDEN
UZÈS: *Château d'Arpaillargues* ⓕⓕⓕⓕ 30700 Uzès. ☎ 04 66 22 14 48. FAX 04 66 22 56 10. **Rooms:** 29. An 18th-century château with tastefully decorated bedrooms, varying in size. Enjoy the exquisite cuisine by the pool or on the terrace. 🛏 📋 📺	AE DC MC V	●	■	●	●
VILLENEUVE-LES-BÉZIERS: *Maison Viner* ⓕⓕ 7 rue de la Fontaine, 34420. ☎ 04 67 39 87 15. FAX 04 67 39 87 15. **Rooms:** 4. Beautifully restored period bed-and-breakfast just 5 km (3 miles) from the Mediterranean. Evening meals and picnic lunches available. 🛏		●			■

PROVENCE AND THE CÔTE D'AZUR

	CREDIT CARDS	CHILDREN'S FACILITIES	PARKING FACILITIES	SWIMMING POOL	GARDEN
AIX-EN-PROVENCE: *Hôtel des Augustins* ⓕⓕⓕⓕ 3 rue de la Masse, 13100. ☎ 04 42 27 28 59. FAX 04 42 26 74 87. **Rooms:** 29. A converted 12th-century convent with large and commodious rooms in traditional Provençale style. A haven of peace in the heart of Aix. 🛏 📋 📺	AE DC MC V		■		
AIX-EN-PROVENCE: *Mas d'Entremont* ⓕⓕⓕⓕ Montée d'Avignon, Célony, 13090. ☎ 04 42 17 42 42. FAX 04 42 21 15 83. **Rooms:** 18. This old Provençal farmhouse is now a luxurious hotel set in terraced tennis grounds just outside Aix. Spacious and tastefully decorated. 🛏 📋 📺	MC V	●	■	●	●
ANTIBES: *Mas Djoliba* ⓕⓕⓕ 29 av de Provence, 06600. ☎ 04 93 34 02 48. FAX 04 93 34 05 81. **Rooms:** 13. A traditional Provençale hotel just a short walk from the centre and beach. Set in a pretty garden it offers comfortable rooms in a rustic style. 🛏	AE DC MC V		■	●	●
ARLES: *Hôtel d'Arlatan* ⓕⓕⓕ 26 rue du Sauvage, 13631. ☎ 04 90 93 56 66. FAX 04 90 49 68 45. **Rooms:** 41. Situated in the heart of Arles, this hotel dates from the 16th-century. Stone walls and a cavernous fireplace decorate the salon. 🛏 📋 📺	AE DC MC V	●	■		●
AVIGNON: *Hôtel de la Mirande* ⓕⓕⓕⓕⓕ 4 place de la Mirande, 84000. ☎ 04 90 85 93 93. FAX 04 90 86 26 85. **Rooms:** 20. An exquisite establishment with richly decorated rooms in Provençal style and fine antiques. There is a relaxing inner courtyard. 🛏 📋 📺	AE DC MC V	●	■		■
AVIGNON: *L'Europe* ⓕⓕⓕⓕ 12 place Crillon, 84000. ☎ 04 90 14 76 76. FAX 04 90 85 43 66. **Rooms:** 47. This has been Avignon's most refined hotel since Napoleon's day. Bedrooms are vast and elegant; the salon is splendidly bedecked with tapestries above marble floors. Superb restaurant. 🛏 📋 📺	AE DC MC V		■		
BEAULIEU-SUR-MER: *Le Métropole* ⓕⓕⓕⓕⓕ 15 bd du Marechal Leclerc, 06310. ☎ 04 93 01 00 08. FAX 04 93 01 18 51. **Rooms:** 46. An Italianate palace complete with Mediterranean terrace, offering luxurious rooms and views across to St-Jean-Cap-Ferrat. 🛏 📋 📺	AE MC V		■	●	■
BEAURECUEIL: *Relais Sainte-Victoire* ⓕⓕⓕ 13100 Beaurecueil. ☎ 04 42 66 94 98. FAX 04 42 66 85 96. **Rooms:** 10. A small hotel set in a beautiful pastoral scene next to open fields under Mont-Ste-Victoire. Good value and a highly regarded restaurant. 🛏 📋 📺	AE DC MC V	●	■	●	●
BORMES-LES-MIMOSAS: *Le Bellevue* ⓕ 14 place Gambetta, 83230. ☎ 04 94 71 15 15. **Rooms:** 12. Small, simple family-run hotel with spacious bedrooms and balconies, overlooking a nest of terracotta roofs to the sea. 🛏	MC V				
CANNES: *Carlton International* ⓕⓕⓕⓕⓕ 58 bd de la Croisette, 06400. ☎ 04 93 06 40 06. FAX 04 93 06 40 25. **Rooms:** 354. Home to stars during the film festival and business people the rest of the year, the Carlton rivals Le Négresco as the Riviera's glittering jewel. A private beach allows you to book in direct from your yacht. 🛏 📋 📺	AE DC MC V	●	■		

DIGNE-LES-BAINS: *Hôtel du Grand-Paris* Ⓕ Ⓕ Ⓕ
19 bd Thiers, 04000. 【 *04 92 31 11 15.* FAX *04 92 32 32 82.* **Rooms:** *29.*
Once a convent, this atmospheric hotel offers comfortable rooms and
medieval surroundings in the heart of the town. 🚗 TV
AE DC MC V

FONTVIEILLE: *La Régalido* Ⓕ Ⓕ Ⓕ Ⓕ
Rue Mistral, 13990. 【 *04 90 54 60 22.* FAX *04 90 54 64 29.* **Rooms:** *15.*
This peaceful converted olive mill is one of the most welcoming and
luxurious hotels in the area – covered in ivy, with a flowery garden.
Rooms are tastefully decorated, some with terraces. 🚗 ▤ TV
AE DC MC V

FOX AMPHOUX: *L'Auberge du Vieux Fox* Ⓕ Ⓕ Ⓕ
Place de l'Eglise, 83670. 【 *04 94 80 71 69.* FAX *04 94 80 78 38.* **Rooms:** *8.*
Parts of this hotel date back to the 11th century, when it was a staging
post. Rooms are small but the sweeping views are splendid. 🚗 TV
AE MC V

JUAN-LES-PINS: *La Jabotte* Ⓕ Ⓕ
13 av M-Mauray, Cap d'Antibes, 06160. 【 *04 93 61 45 89.* FAX *04 93 61 07 04.* **Rooms:** *13.*
Five minutes' walk from the centres of Juan-les-Pins and Antibes,
this friendly hotel has a lot to offer for its price. It is also possible
to stay in one of the bungalows on the terrace. 🚗 TV
AE MC V

LA CADIÈRE D'AZUR: *Hostellerie Bérand* Ⓕ Ⓕ Ⓕ Ⓕ
Rue Gabriel Peri, 83740. 【 *04 94 90 11 43.* FAX *04 94 90 01 94.* **Rooms:** *40.*
A friendly hotel and restaurant on the high street of this village. Four
converted buildings with individually styled bedrooms. 🚗 ▤ TV
AE MC V

LES ARCS-SUR-ARGENS: *Logis du Guetteur* Ⓕ Ⓕ Ⓕ
Place du Château, 83460. 【 *04 94 73 30 82.* FAX *04 94 73 39 95.* **Rooms:** *10.*
This 11th-century château sits on top of a hill overlooking the village.
Atmospheric vaulted dining room and spacious bedrooms. 🚗 TV
AE DC MC V

LES BAUX-DE-PROVENCE: *Le Mas d'Aigret* Ⓕ Ⓕ Ⓕ Ⓕ
13520 Les Baux-de-Provence. 【 *04 90 54 33 54.* FAX *04 90 54 41 37.* **Rooms:** *15.*
A smart, personal hotel only a short walk from the medieval citadel.
The dining room and some of the bedrooms of this intriguing old
farmhouse have been cut out of rock. 🚗 TV
AE DC MC V

NICE: *Hôtel Windsor* Ⓕ Ⓕ Ⓕ
11 rue Dalpozzo, 06000. 【 *04 93 88 59 35.* FAX *04 93 88 94 57.* **Rooms:** *60.*
A friendly, family-run hotel with a palmed garden. Simple bedrooms
with modern murals, French windows and balconies. 🚗 ▤ TV
AE DC MC V

NICE: *Le Négresco* Ⓕ Ⓕ Ⓕ Ⓕ Ⓕ
37 prom des Anglais, 06000. 【 *04 93 16 64 00.* FAX *04 93 88 35 68.* **Rooms:** *143.*
The most famous hotel on the Riviera, recently renovated to even
more lofty heights of Belle Epoque grandeur. 🚗 ▤ TV
AE DC MC V

PEILLON: *Auberge de la Madone* Ⓕ Ⓕ Ⓕ
06440 Peillon. 【 *04 93 79 91 17.* FAX *04 93 79 99 36.* **Rooms:** *20.*
A family-run modern inn in the remarkable perched village of Peillon.
Imaginative regional menus and comfortable bedrooms. 🚗
MC V

REILLANNE: *Auberge de Reillanne* Ⓕ Ⓕ
Le Pigeonnier, 04110. 【 *04 92 76 45 95.* **Rooms:** *7.*
A beautiful old country house in the east Lubéron, secluded and off
the tourist track. The hotel is simple yet alluring – books line the
ancient shelves and the 20th century seems to have barely begun. 🚗
MC V

ROUSSILLON: *Le Mas de Garrigon* Ⓕ Ⓕ Ⓕ
Route de St-Saturnin d'Apt, 84220. 【 *04 90 05 63 22.* FAX *04 90 05 70 01.* **Rooms:** *9.*
Set in pines in a secluded corner of Haute Provence, this traditional
country house is a perfect retreat. Classical music plays in the comfort-
able salons and each room has a private terrace. 🚗 TV
AE DC MC V

SAIGNON: *Auberge du Presbytère* Ⓕ Ⓕ
Place de la Fontaine, 84400. 【 *04 90 74 11 50.* FAX *04 90 04 68 51.* **Rooms:** *10.*
A small auberge in the square of this unspoiled hilltop village. Simple,
atmospheric bedrooms, local cuisine and the village bar. 🚗
AE MC V

ST-JEAN-CAP-FERRAT: *Clair Logis* Ⓕ Ⓕ Ⓕ
12 av Centrale, 06230. 【 *04 93 76 04 57.* FAX *04 93 76 11 85.* **Rooms:** *18.*
This seductively old-fashioned villa with its large, mature garden is
very good value. The larger rooms are in the main building. 🚗
AE DC MC V

	CREDIT CARDS	CHILDREN'S FACILITIES	PARKING FACILITIES	SWIMMING POOL	GARDEN
Price categories for a standard double room (not per person) for one night, including tax and service charges, but not including breakfast. Ⓕ under F200 ⒻⒻ F200–400 ⒻⒻⒻ F400–600 ⒻⒻⒻⒻ F600–1,000 ⒻⒻⒻⒻⒻ over F1,000 **CHILDREN'S FACILITIES** Cots and baby-sitting available. Some hotels provide children's portions and high chairs in the restaurant. **PARKING FACILITIES** Parking provided by the hotel in either a private car park or a private garage very close by. **SWIMMING POOL** Hotel pools are often quite small and are outdoors unless otherwise stated. **GARDEN** Hotel with garden, courtyard or terrace, often providing tables for eating outside.					
LES SAINTES-MARIES-DE-LA-MER: *Hostellerie de Cacharel* ⒻⒻⒻ Route de Cacharel, 13460. **[** 04 90 97 95 44. **FAX** 04 90 97 87 97. **Rooms:** 15. *Gardiens* or Provençal cowboys used to inhabit this ancient ranch in the heart of the marshes. The hotel is surprisingly comfortable with large rooms and relaxing salons. Horse riding is available on site.	AE DC MC V	●	▪	●	●
ST-PAUL-DE-VENCE: *La Colombe d'Or* ⒻⒻⒻⒻⒻ Place De-Gaulle, 06570. **[** 04 93 32 80 02. **FAX** 04 93 32 77 78. **Rooms:** 25. An old farmhouse once populated by Impressionist painters is now home to film stars and models. The rooms are luxurious but the real stars are originals by Picasso and Matisse *(see p514).*	AE DC MC V	●	▪	●	●
ST-RÉMY-DE-PROVENCE: *Le Château de Roussan* ⒻⒻⒻ Route de Tarascon, 13210. **[** 04 90 92 11 63. **FAX** 04 90 92 50 59. **Rooms:** 21. One of the most beautiful hotels in Provence – a converted 18th-century château set in extensive formal grounds.	AE MC V		▪		▪
ST-RÉMY-DE-PROVENCE: *Le Mas de Carassins* ⒻⒻⒻ 1 chemin Gaulois, 13210. **[** 04 90 92 15 48. **Rooms:** 10. A 19th-century farmhouse on the outskirts of town, decorated in a country-style. Expect a friendly atmosphere and helpful staff.	MC V		▪		▪
ST-TROPEZ: *Lou Cagnard* ⒻⒻ Avenue P Roussel, 83990. **[** 04 94 97 04 24. **FAX** 04 94 97 09 44. **Rooms:** 19. A very popular, good value hotel in the newest part of town, a short walk to the port. Cheerful bedrooms and pleasant courtyard.	MC V		▪		▪
SALON-DE-PROVENCE: *L'Abbaye de Sainte-Croix* ⒻⒻⒻⒻ Route du Val-de-Cuech, 13300. **[** 04 90 56 24 55. **FAX** 04 90 56 31 12. **Rooms:** 24. This converted 12th-century abbey retains its medieval charm. The bedrooms, originally the monks' cells, vary in size.	AE DC MC V	●	▪	●	▪
SEILLANS: *Hôtel les Deux Rocs* ⒻⒻ Place Font d'Amont, 83440. **[** 04 94 76 87 32. **FAX** 04 94 76 88 68. **Rooms:** 14. A captivating 18th-century mansion hotel in the peaceful village square. Strong family atmosphere and excellent traditional food.	MC V		▪		▪
TOURTOUR: *La Petite Auberge* ⒻⒻⒻ 83690 Tourtour. **[** 04 94 70 57 16. **FAX** 04 94 70 54 52. **Rooms:** 11. For peace and quiet, beautiful views and a rustic setting, head to Tourtour and this small auberge.	MC V	●	▪	●	▪
TRIGANCE: *Château de Trigance* ⒻⒻⒻⒻ 83840 Trigance. **[** 04 94 76 91 18. **FAX** 04 94 85 68 99. **Rooms:** 10. A unique and romantic hideaway in the mountain valleys. Four-poster beds, tapestries and vaulted ceilings adorn this 11th-century château, carefully restored by the owner. Access by private road.	AE DC MC V		▪		▪
VAISON-LA-ROMAINE: *Le Beffroi* ⒻⒻⒻ Rue de L'Evêché, Haute Ville, 84110. **[** 04 90 36 04 71. **FAX** 04 90 36 24 78. **Rooms:** 22. This 16th-century hotel seduces its guests with antiques, fireplaces, tiled floors and paintings. Each room is individually furnished.	AE DC MC V	●	▪	●	▪
VENCE: *Auberge les Seigneurs* ⒻⒻ Place du Frêne, 06140. **[** 04 93 58 04 24. **FAX** 04 93 24 08 01. **Rooms:** 6. This restaurant-with-rooms is a medieval time capsule. Bedrooms are spartan but cheap. Good choice of Provençal specialities.	AE DC MC V	●		●	
VILLEFRANCHE-SUR-MER: *Hôtel Welcome* ⒻⒻⒻ 1 quai Courbet, 06230. **[** 04 93 76 76 93. **FAX** 04 93 01 88 81. **Rooms:** 32. This tall, narrow building stands over a fish restaurant near the old port. Most of the small but comfortable bedrooms have seaside balconies. The same family has run this hotel for half a century.	AE DC MC V	●	▪		

CORSICA

AJACCIO: *Hôtel Dolce Vita* ⓕⓕⓕⓕ — AE DC MC V
Route des Sanguinaires, 20000. **℡** 04 95 52 00 93. **FAX** 04 95 52 07 15. *Rooms: 32.*
Functional, modern hotel overlooking the sea with direct access to the
beach. Flashy decor and a floodlit swimming pool. 🅿 ▤ 📺

BARCAGGIO: *La Giraglia* ⓕⓕⓕ
Ersa, 20275. **℡** 04 95 35 60 54. **FAX** 04 95 35 65 92. *Rooms: 13.*
Off the tourist track, this modest seaside hotel with rustic rooms is ideal
for a peaceful stay. There are good seafood restaurants next door. 🅿

BASTIA: *Hôtel de la Corniche* ⓕⓕⓕ — AE DC MC V
San-Martino-di-Lota, 20200. **℡** 04 95 31 40 98. **FAX** 04 95 32 37 69. *Rooms: 19.*
A simple but good value hotel on a winding road 10 minutes' drive
from Bastia. Breathtaking views from the terrace. 🅿 📺

BONIFACIO: *Résidence du Centre Nautique* ⓕⓕⓕⓕ — AE DC MC V
Quai Nord, 20169. **℡** 04 95 73 02 11. **FAX** 04 95 73 17 47. *Rooms: 10.*
A perfect stop by the harbour for sailing enthusiasts. The rooms have
been converted into small duplexes. 🅿 ▤ 📺

BONIFACIO: *Hôtel Genovese* ⓕⓕⓕⓕ — AE DC MC V
Quartier de la Citadelle, 20169. **℡** 04 95 73 12 34. **FAX** 04 95 73 09 03. *Rooms: 14.*
A luxury hotel in the Old Town that was once the legionnaires' barracks.
Refined, modern decor with grand rooms and suites. 🅿 ▤ 📺

CALVI: *Auberge de la Signoria* ⓕⓕⓕⓕ — AE MC V
Rte de la Forêt de Bonifato, 20260. **℡** 04 95 65 93 00. **FAX** 04 95 65 38 77. *Rooms: 10.*
The owners have renovated their large house, retaining its
original character. A haven of seclusion and peace – candlelit dinners
served on the terrace under the palm trees. 🅿 ▤ 📺

CALVI: *Hôtel Balanéa* ⓕⓕⓕ — AE DC MC V
6 rue Clémenceau, 20260. **℡** 04 95 65 94 94. **FAX** 04 95 65 29 71. *Rooms: 37.*
Recently renovated hotel in the centre of town beside the harbour.
Spacious and well-decorated rooms with large bathrooms. 🅿 ▤ 📺

FELICETO: *Hôtel Mare e Monti* ⓕⓕ — AE DC MC V
20225 Feliceto. **℡** 04 95 63 02 00. **FAX** 04 95 63 02 01. *Rooms: 18.*
Set at the foot of rocky cliffs overlooking the sea, the house has been
in the same family since 1870. Expect a warm welcome and delicious,
traditional food, including fresh fruit from the garden. 🅿

L'ILE ROUSSE: *A Pastorella* ⓕⓕ — AE DC MC V
Monticello, 20220. **℡** 04 95 60 05 65. **FAX** 04 95 60 21 78. *Rooms: 12.*
Just inland, this traditional hotel sits in the village square. Originally a
bar and restaurant, rooms of various sizes have been added. 🅿

L'ILE ROUSSE: *Santa Maria* ⓕⓕⓕ — AE DC MC V
Route du Port, 20220. **℡** 04 95 60 13 49. **FAX** 04 95 60 32 48. *Rooms: 56.*
A modern hotel situated between two beaches with small but light and
comfortable rooms with balconies. Meals are served on request. 🅿 ▤ 📺

PIANA: *Les Roches Rouges* ⓕⓕⓕ — AE DC MC V
20115 Piana. **℡** 04 95 27 81 81. **FAX** 04 95 27 81 76. *Rooms: 30.*
An old Corsican house that has been refurbished – the rooms are plain
but there is a lovely restaurant with terrace and superb views. 🅿 📺

PORTICCIO: *Le Maquis* ⓕⓕⓕⓕ — AE DC MC V
20166 Porticcio. **℡** 04 95 25 05 55. **FAX** 04 95 25 11 70. *Rooms: 27.*
A stylish hotel consisting of white-shuttered buildings centred on a
terrace and freshwater pool. Excellent cuisine. 🅿 ▤ 📺

SARTÈNE: *Villa Piana* ⓕⓕ — AE DC MC V
Route de Propriano, 20100. **℡** 04 95 77 07 04. **FAX** 04 95 73 45 65. *Rooms: 32.*
A large, friendly Provençal-style villa with a splendid view across the
town to the mountains. The rooms are bright and airy, decorated in a
rustic style. Floodlit tennis courts. 🅿

SPELONCATO: *A Spelunca* ⓕⓕ — MC V
20226 Speloncato. **℡** 04 95 61 50 38. **FAX** 04 95 61 53 14. *Rooms: 18*
A magnificent hotel in the former palace of a local cardinal. Huge grand
rooms and excellent value. No restaurant. 🅿 📺

WHERE TO EAT

THE FRENCH consider eating well an essential part of their national birthright. There are few other places where people are as passionately knowledge-able about their cuisine and their wine. Restaurant reviews, as well as cooking and food shows on television, are avidly followed and the general quality of both fresh food and restaurant offerings is vastly better in France than it is in most other European countries.

This introduction to the restaurant listings, which are arranged by region and town *(see pp580– 613)*, looks at the different types of restaurant in France and gives practical tips on eating out, reading menus, ordering and service – everything you need to know to enjoy your meal. At the front of the book is a guide to a typical menu and an introduction to French wine *(see pp20–23)*. The main food and wine features are at the beginning of each of the five regional sections.

FRENCH EATING HABITS

THE TRADITIONAL large meal at noon survives mainly in rural regions. Nowadays, lunch is increasingly likely to consist of a sandwich, salad or a steak in a café, while dinner is the main meal of the day. Usually, lunch is from noon to 2pm and dinner is from 8 to 10pm, with last orders taken 30 minutes before closing time.

Some family-owned places are closed at weekends, so it may be difficult to find a meal anywhere outside your hotel on Sundays, except in large cities. Off the beaten track and in resort towns, restaurants and hotels are often closed out of season, so it is advisable to ring ahead.

Over the past few decades, French eating habits have changed dramatically. The growing popularity of the cuisine of former French colonies means that North African and Vietnamese places are now easy to find, as are Chinese restaurants. Burger and Tex-Mex joints are also popular with young people. As city-dwellers and suburbanites in France have become almost as health-conscious as other Europeans, there has been an explosion of "light" foods; and the rise of the *hypermarchés* (hypermarkets) has resulted in less fresh produce on the menu as more frozen and prepared food is eaten.

REGIONAL COOKING

ONE OF the great pleasures of travelling in France is sampling the country's regional

Taverne Magenageuse in Mougins, Provence *(see p612)*

cuisine. In every *département* of France, menus will nearly always include local special-ities, which reflect predominant local products and agriculture. A good way to divide France gastronomically is the butter/olive oil divide. In the north, butter is generally used in cooking; in the south, olive oil; and in the southwest, goose and duck fat predominate.

Each region takes great pride in its own cuisine. Nationally, the best known dishes come from four regions: Alsace, a province with close German ties; the southwest, where *cassoulet*, a rich stew of white beans, tomatoes, sausage and duck is a well-loved dish; the Alps, which gave *fondue* to the nation; and Provence, famed for *bouillabaisse*, a rich fish soup from Marseille.

The gastronomic capital of France is, however, considered to be Lyon, which boasts a significant proportion of France's best restaurants and many superb no-nonsense bistros known as *buchons*.

La Cigale, a Belle Epoque brasserie in Nantes *(see p595)*

RESTAURANTS

ENCOMPASSING the whole alphabet of French cuisine, restaurants in France range from tiny white washed places with rush-bottomed chairs to stately, wood-panelled château dining rooms and the top kitchens of famous chefs. Many hotels have fine restaurants open to non-residents, a selection of which can be found in the hotel listings *(see pp540–75).*

Prices for restaurants of the same rating are more-or-less consistent throughout France except in large cities, where they can be more expensive. The quality of the food and service, though, is the most significant price factor and you can easily spend up to F1,000 per head to eat at one of the top establishments.

There is a number of different kinds of French cuisine that you may come across. *Haute cuisine* is the traditional cooking method, where the flavour of the food is enhanced with rich sauces. *Nouvelle cuisine* challenged this method, especially for the diet-conscious, in using light rather than creamy sauces which bring out the texture and colour of the ingredients. *Cuisine bourgeoise* is French home cooking. *Cuisine des Provinces* uses high quality ingredients to prepare traditional rural dishes. Many top chefs favour *cuisine moderne,* which releases the natural flavour of the food. There has also been a revival of traditional methods.

BISTROS

WHEN THE FRENCH go out to eat, they are most likely to visit the broadest class of restaurant, the bistro. Bistros vary enormously – some urban bistros are formally decorated, while those in smaller cities and in the country tend to be more casual. Generally they offer a good, moderately

The restaurant L'Excelsior at Nancy in Lorraine *(see p589)*

priced meal from a traditional menu of an *entrée* or *hors d'oeuvre* (starter), *plats mijotés* (simmered dishes) and *grillades* (grilled fish and meats), followed by cheese and dessert.

BRASSERIES

BRASSERIES have their origin in Alsace and were originally attached to breweries; the name brasserie actually means brewery. Usually found in larger cities, they are big, bustling places, many with fresh shellfish stands outside. They serve beer on tap as well as a *vin de la maison* (house wine) and a variety of regional wines. Menus include simple fish and grilled meat dishes along with Alsatian specialities like *choucroute garnie* (sauerkraut with sausage and pork). Prices are very much on a par with those you would pay at bistros. Like cafés, brasseries are usually open from morning until night and serve food all day long.

(Camembert cheese label reads: CAMEMBERT FABRIQUÉ EN NORMANDIE — LE FIN NORMAND — AFFINÉ — VÉRITABLE — LAITERIE DE)

Camembert

FERME-AUBERGES

IN THE COUNTRY you may eat at a simple "farm inn", where good, inexpensive meals, often made with fresh farm produce, are taken with your host's family as part of your room and board. For more details on *ferme-auberges,* see under Bed and Breakfast on page 538.

CAFÉS

CAFÉS REPRESENT the soul of France. Every place but the tiniest hamlet can be counted on to have a café, open as a rule from early in the morning until 10pm or so. They serve drinks, coffee, tea, simple meals and snacks such as salads, omelettes and sandwiches throughout the day, and usually provide a cheaper breakfast than most hotels.

As well as serving refreshments, cafés are a good source of information and provide the traveller with endless opportunities to observe the French at their most relaxed.

In villages, almost the entire population might drift in and out of the single café during the course of a day, while large cities have cafés that cater for a specific clientele, such as workers or students. In Paris's most famous cafés, celebrated intellectuals and artists have gathered to discuss their ideas *(see p142).*

Auberge du XII Siècle at Saché in the Loire Valley *(see p595)*

Tables outside a café in the Old Town of Nice on the Côte d'Azur

BISTRO ANNEXES

WITHIN THE PAST few years, baby-bistros or bistro annexes have appeared in larger cities, especially Paris and Lyon, as a new category of restaurant. They are lower-priced sister eateries of the famous – and much more expensive – restaurants run by well-known chefs. Many of them offer *prix-fixe* (fixed-price) menus and the chance to sample the cooking of a celebrated kitchen in relaxed surroundings.

FAST FOOD

IF YOU WANT to avoid the American fast food chains, wine bars and *salons du thé* are also good value for light meals. Cafeterias, found in some shopping centres, serve tasty food at reasonable prices.

RESERVATIONS

IN CITIES and larger towns it is always best to make a reservation, especially from May to September. This rarely applies to cafés or in the country, where you can walk into most places without a reservation. However, if you are travelling in remote rural and resort areas off season, it is worth checking first that the restaurant is open all year.

If you have a reservation and your plans change, then you should call and cancel. Smaller restaurants, in particular, must fill all their tables to make a profit, and "no-shows" threaten their livelihood.

READING THE MENU AND ORDERING

WHEN THE MENU is presented, you'll usually be asked if you'd like an aperitif. Since many French people do not drink spirits before a meal, this could be Kir (white wine mixed with a dash of blackcurrant liqueur), vermouth, light port (drunk in France as a cocktail) or a soft drink.

Opening the menu, *les entrées* or *hors d'oeuvre* are starters. *Les plats* are the main courses, and most restaurants will offer a *plat du jour*, or daily special; these are often seasonal or local dishes of particular interest. A selection of dishes from a classic French menu is given on pages 20–21.

Cheese is served as a separate course between the main course and dessert. Coffee is served black, unless you specify *"crème"*. Alternatively, you can ask for a *tisane*, or herbal tea.

WINE

AS RESTAURANTS put a large mark-up on wine, it is better to further your connoisseurship with bottles purchased in shops, rather than when dining out. Local wine, however, is often served in carafes. Ordering a *demi* (50 cl) or *quart* (25cl) carafe is a cheap way to try out a region's wines.

French law divides the country's wines into four classes, in ascending order of quality: Vin de Table, Vin de Pays, Vin Délimité de Qualité Supérieure (VDQS) and Appellation d'Origine Contrôlée (AOC).

The blended Vin de Table wines are rarely found in restaurants, but in choosing a regional wine (Vins de Pays upwards), refer to the wine features in the regional sections of this book. For an introduction to French wine, see pages 22–3.

When in doubt, order the house wine. Few restaurants will risk their reputation on an inferior house wine, and they often provide value for money.

WATER

TAP WATER is supplied on request free of charge, and is perfectly safe to drink. The French also pride themselves on their wide range of mineral waters. Favourite mealtime brands include Evian and the slightly fizzy Badoit.

Le Moulin de Mougins *(see p612)*

HOW TO PAY

VISA/Carte Bleue (V) is the most widely accepted credit card in France. Mastercard/Access (MC), American Express (AE) and Diners Club (DC) are also in common use. The abbreviations shown in brackets are used in the restaurant listings to indicate which restaurants take which card.

La Tour d'Argent in the Latin Quarter of Paris *(see p583)*

Always carry plenty of cash, especially when touring the countryside, as many smaller restaurants still do not take any credit cards. If in doubt, ask when you make a reservation.

SERVICE AND TIPPING

THE PACE of a French meal is generally leisurely. People think nothing of spending four hours at the table, so if you are pressed for time, go to a café or brasserie. A service charge of 12.5 to 15 per cent is almost always included in the price of your meal, but most French people leave a few additional francs behind in a café, and an additional 5 per cent or so of the total bill in other restaurants. In the grander restaurants, which pride themselves on their service, an additional tip of 5 to 10 per cent is correct.

Two francs is sufficient for toilet attendants, and F5 an item is appropriate for the cloakroom attendant.

DRESS CODE

EVEN WHEN DRESSED casually, the French are generally well-turned out; visitors should aim for the same level of presentable comfort. Running shoes, shorts, beach clothes or active sportswear are unacceptable everywhere except cafés or beachside places.

The restaurant listings indicate which restaurants require men to wear a jacket and tie (see pp580-613).

CHILDREN

FRENCH CHILDREN are introduced early to restaurants and as a rule are well-behaved. Consequently, children are well-received almost everywhere in France. However, few restaurants provide special facilities like high-chairs or baby seats, as children are expected to behave sensibly, and there is often not much room for push-chairs.

PETS

DOGS are usually accepted at all but the most elegant restaurants. As the French are

The Eychenne hotel-restaurant at St-Girons in the Pyrenees (see p607)

great dog lovers, do not be surprised to see your neighbour's dog sitting on the next door *banquette*.

SMOKING

IN SPITE OF recent strict legislation requiring restaurants to provide their clientele with smoking and non-smoking sections, a laissez-faire attitude prevails in most places. The patron of one Paris bistro now carries a portable no-smoking sign which he hangs on the wall over the table of anyone who requests a non-smoking table. If you are sensitive to smoke, ask for a window table.

The Hôtel Royal at Evian-les-Bains in the French Alps (see p563)

WHEELCHAIR ACCESS

THOUGH THE RESTAURANTS of newer hotels usually provide wheelchair access, it is often restricted elsewhere. A word when you are booking your table should ensure that you are given a conveniently located table and assistance, if needed, when you arrive.

The listings show restaurants with special facilities.

Refer also to page 539 of this book, which gives the names and addresses of some organizations which provide advice to disabled travellers in France.

VEGETARIAN FOOD

FRANCE REMAINS difficult for vegetarians, although some progress has been made in recent years. In most non-vegetarian restaurants the main courses are firmly orientated towards meat and fish. However, you can often fare well by ordering from the *entrées* and should never be timid about asking for a dish to be served without its meat content. Provided you make your request in advance, most smart restaurants will prepare a special vegetarian dish.

Only larger cities and university towns are likely to have fully fledged vegetarian restaurants. Otherwise cafés, pizzerias, crêperies and oriental restaurants are good places to find vegetarian meals.

PICNICS

PICNICKING is the best way to enjoy the wonderful fresh produce, local bread and cheeses from the markets and enticing shops to be found all over France. For more details about the shops and markets of France, see pages 62–3.

Picnics are also a good way to eat cheaply and enjoy the French countryside. Picnicking areas along major roads are well marked and furnished with tables and chairs.

Choosing a Restaurant

THE RESTAURANTS in this guide have been selected across a wide range of price categories for their good value, exceptional food and interesting location. This chart lists the restaurants by region, starting with Paris. Use the colour-coded thumb tabs, which indicate the regions covered on each page, to guide you to the relevant section of the chart. *Bon Appétit!*

		Credit Cards	Children's Facilities	Fixed-Price Menu	Good Wine List	Outdoor Tables
PARIS						
Ile de la Cité: *Le Caveau du Palais.* **Map 8 F3.** 17–19 place Dauphine, 75001. **(** *01 43 26 04 28.* Enjoy a selection of superb fish and meat dishes smoke-grilled over wood in this ancient stone-walled cellar. Closed Saturdays and Sundays.	ⓕⓕ	AE MC V		■	●	■
Ile de la Cité: *Le Vieux Bistrot.* **Map 9 B4.** 14 rue du Cloître-Notre-Dame, 75004. **(** *01 43 54 18 95.* An authentic, honest bistro, frequented by many Parisian restaurateurs and entertainment stars. The food here is unpretentious and very good.	ⓕⓕⓕ	V			●	■
Ile St-Louis: *Au Franc Pinot.* **Map 9 C4.** 1 quai de Bourbon, 75004. **(** *01 46 33 60 64.* The wine bar is on the ground floor and the restaurant is in the cellar. Excellent food and atmosphere.	ⓕ	MC V		■		
Ile St-Louis: *Le Monde des Chimères.* **Map 9 C4.** 69 rue St-Louis-en-l'Île, 75004. **(** *01 43 54 45 27.* A bistro in a 300-year-old house serving traditional family cooking made only with fresh produce.	ⓕⓕⓕ	MC V		■		
The Marais: *Baracane.* **Map 10 E4.** 38 rue des Tournelles, 75004. **(** *01 42 71 43 33.* In spite of its touristy location this tiny restaurant serving southwestern cuisine has very good quality food at reasonable prices.	ⓕⓕ	MC V		■		
The Marais: *Le Bar à Huîtres.* **Map 10 E3.** 33 bd Beaumarchais, 75003. **(** *01 48 87 98 92.* Oysters and other shellfish predominate here. You can compose your own appetizer platter, then follow with a choice of fish or meat dishes.	ⓕⓕⓕ	AE MC V	●	■		■
The Marais: *Miravile.* **Map 9 B3.** 72 quai de l'Hôtel Ville, 75004. **(** *01 42 74 72 22.* The menu here is inventive and exciting, featuring such dishes as rabbit with olives, and lobster with potatoes. Vegetarian dishes available.	ⓕⓕⓕ	AE MC V		■	●	
The Marais: *L'Ambroisie.* **Map 10 D3.** 9 pl des Vosges, 75004. **(** *01 42 78 51 45.* This discreet, romantic spot is one of only five Michelin three-star restaurants in Paris. Reservations are accepted one month ahead. **&**	ⓕⓕⓕⓕ	AE MC V			●	
Beaubourg: *Benoît.* **Map 9 B2.** 20 rue St Martin, 75004. **(** *01 42 72 25 76.* This is the Rolls-Royce of Paris bistros. The excellent traditional cuisine includes assorted cold salads, house *foie gras* and *boeuf à la mode.*	ⓕⓕⓕⓕ			■	●	
Les Halles: *Chez Elle.* **Map 9 A2.** 7 rue des Prouvaires, 75001. **(** *01 45 08 04 10.* The menu is classic bistro, changing with the seasons and always based on fresh, local produce. Desserts are traditional and delicious, including the crème caramel.	ⓕⓕ	AE MC V		■		■
Les Halles: *Le Grizzli.* **Map 9 B3.** 7 rue St-Martin, 75004. **(** *01 48 87 77 56.* The owner orders much of the produce from his native southwest, including cured ham, cheese, and wines made by his family.	ⓕⓕ	AE MC V		■		■
Les Halles: *Au Pied de Cochon.* **Map 8 F1.** 6 rue Coquillière, 75001. **(** *01 40 13 77 00.* This famous institution in the heart of Les Halles is open every day, all day and all night, serving copious amounts of grilled pigs' trotters and shellfish. Hearty cuisine and atmosphere but be prepared to queue after 10pm.	ⓕⓕ	AE DC MC V		■		■

Average prices for a three-course meal for one, including a half-bottle of house wine, tax and service:
(F) under F150
(F)(F) F150–F250
(F)(F)(F) F250–F350
(F)(F)(F)(F) F350–F500
(F)(F)(F)(F)(F) over F500

CHILDREN'S FACILITIES
Some restaurants have high chairs and offer smaller portions for children.
FIXED-PRICE MENU
A good-value fixed-price menu on offer at lunch, dinner or both, often with three or more courses.
GOOD WINE LIST
Denotes a wide range of good wines, or otherwise a more specialised selection of local wines.
OUTDOOR TABLES
Facilities for eating outdoors, on a terrace, or in a garden or courtyard, often with a good view.

Restaurant	Price	CREDIT CARDS	CHILDREN'S FACILITIES	FIXED-PRICE MENU	GOOD WINE LIST	OUTDOOR TABLES
TUILERIES QUARTER: *Le Grand Louvre.* **Map 8 F2.** Le Louvre, 75001. (01 40 20 53 41. It is rare to find such a good restaurant in a museum. André Daguin, a gastronomic star from the southwest, developed the menu.	(F)(F)	AE DC MC V		■		
TUILERIES QUARTER: *Armand au Palais Royal.* **Map 8 F1.** 6 rue de Beaujolais, 75001. (01 42 60 05 11. Situated behind the Palais Royal, this charming restaurant was once a stable, but this is no reflection on the food, which is very Parisian.	(F)(F)	AE MC V		■		■
TUILERIES QUARTER: *L'Espadon.* **Map 4 D5.** 15 pl Vendôme, 75001. (01 43 16 30 80. Part of the Ritz, this is one of the Parisian restaurants most highly rated by Michelin. Modern classic cuisine from chef Guy Legay. 🚹 🍴	(F)(F)(F)(F)(F)	AE DC MC V	●	■	●	●
TUILERIES QUARTER: *Le Grand Véfour.* **Map 8 F1.** 17 rue de Beaujolais, 75001. (01 42 96 56 27. An 18th-century two-star Michelin restaurant, considered by many to be the most attractive in the city. This is the place for special occasions. 🚹 🍴	(F)(F)(F)(F)(F)	AE MC V		■	●	
OPÉRA QUARTER: *A G Le Poète.* 27 rue Pasquier, 75008. (01 47 42 00 64. Soft lighting and red velvet decor provide a romantic setting for inspired cooking, with dishes such as red mullet and baby scallops on creamed wild nettles.	(F)(F)	AE MC V		■		
OPÉRA QUARTER: *Chartier.* **Map 4 F4.** 7 rue du Faubourg Montmartre, 75009. (01 47 70 86 29. This cavernous restaurant packs in the crowds with its quick service and basic French food at budget prices. Popular with students, travellers and local *habitués*, the place bustles with an infectious bonhomie.	(F)	AE MC V		■		
OPÉRA QUARTER: *Café Runtz.* **Map 4 F5.** 16 rue Favart, 75002. (01 42 96 69 86. This pleasant brasserie is one of the few genuine Alsatian places in Paris where you can get regional specialities in copious amounts.	(F)(F)	AE DC MC V		■		
OPÉRA QUARTER: *Le Vaudeville.* **Map 4 F5.** 29 rue Vivienne, 75002. (01 40 20 04 62. The attractive Art Deco interior provides an appealing backdrop to the food: good shellfish, the chef's famous smoked salmon, and classic standbys like pigs' trotters and *andouillette* (tripe sausage).	(F)(F)	AE DC MC V	●	■		■
OPÉRA QUARTER: *Lucas Carton.* **Map 3 C5.** 9 pl de la Madeleine, 75008. (01 42 65 22 90. Awarded three Michelin stars, the cuisine here is imaginative and exotic. The decor is stunning, the service crisp and the crowd very dressy. 🍴	(F)(F)(F)(F)(F)	MC V		■	●	
INVALIDES QUARTER: *Thoumieux.* **Map 7 A2.** 79 rue St-Dominique, 75007. (01 47 05 49 75. This well-run restaurant is excellent. Ingredients are fresh, and virtually everything is made on the premises, including *foie gras* and *rillettes* (similar to pâté). The *cassoulet* (stew of white beans and meat) is a speciality here.	(F)(F)	AE V	●	■		
INVALIDES QUARTER: *L'Arpège.* **Map 7 B3.** 84 rue de Varenne, 75007. (01 45 51 47 33. Chef owner Alain Passard's restaurant is near the Musée Rodin. His lobster and turnip vinaigrette, and the duck Louise Passard are classics.	(F)(F)(F)(F)(F)	AE DC MC V		■	●	
EIFFEL TOWER QUARTER: *La Serre.* **Map 7 A2.** 29 rue de l'Exposition, 75007. (01 45 55 20 96. A small, cosy neighbourhood restaurant of a type that is becoming increasingly rare. Rustic specialities include *pot au feu* and *cassoulet*.	(F)(F)	MC V	●	■		

For key to symbols see back flap

Average prices for a three-course meal for one, including a half-bottle of house wine, tax and service:
Ⓕ under F150
Ⓕⓕ F150–F250
Ⓕⓕⓕ F250–F350
Ⓕⓕⓕⓕ F350–F500
Ⓕⓕⓕⓕⓕ over F500

CHILDREN'S FACILITIES
Some restaurants have high chairs and offer smaller portions for children.

FIXED-PRICE MENU
A good-value fixed-price menu on offer at lunch, dinner or both, usually with three courses.

GOOD WINE LIST
Denotes a wide range of good wines, or a more specialized selection of local wines.

OUTDOOR TABLES
Facilities for eating outdoors, on a terrace, or in a garden or courtyard, often with a good view.

Restaurant	Price	Credit Cards	Children's Facilities	Fixed-Price Menu	Good Wine List	Outdoor Tables
CHAILLOT QUARTER: *La Butte Chaillot.* **Map 2 D5.** 110 bis, av Kleber, 75116. 01 47 27 88 88. This is one of chef Guy Savoy's most recent restaurants. The sophisticated cuisine and the modern decor attract a very stylish crowd.	Ⓕⓕⓕ	AE MC V	●	■		■
CHAILLOT QUARTER: *Le Relais du Parc.* **Map 5 C1.** 55–57 av Raymond Poincaré, 75116. 01 44 05 66 10. Master chef, Joël Robuchon, of the Michelin three-star Jamin restaurant, set the menu for this chic bistro. It features simple but delicious dishes.	Ⓕⓕⓕ	AE DC MC V		■	●	
CHAILLOT QUARTER: *Le Port-Alma.* **Map 6 E1.** 10 av de New-York, 75116. 01 47 23 75 11. The dishes here are influenced by the chef's native southwest France. Try the *bourride* (fish soup with garlic) or the sea bass in salt crust.	Ⓕⓕⓕⓕ	AE DC MC V		■		
CHAILLOT QUARTER: *Alain Ducasse.* **Map 9 C1.** 59 av Raymond Poincaré, 75116. 01 47 27 12 27. In a dining room decorated with *trompe l'oeil* and sculptures, Alain Ducasse creates the great classic dishes from meticulously chosen ingredients.	Ⓕⓕⓕⓕⓕ	AE DC MC V	●	■	●	
CHAMPS-ELYSÉES: *Berry's.* **Map 3 B3.** 44–46 rue de Naples, 75008. 01 40 75 01 56. The bistro annexe of the excellent Grenadin restaurant features the cuisine of Le Berry, a region in the heart of France. Berry does a delicious leek and goat's cheese tart and the pork dishes are also very tasty.	Ⓕⓕ	MC V		■		■
CHAMPS-ELYSÉES: *Le Cercle Ledoyen.* 1 av Duti, 75001. 01 53 05 10 00. Walls and ceiling of the handsome dining room are decorated with Parisian scenes. Food is simple yet refined: grilled brill with wild mushrooms, pheasant with quince and a wonderful range of chocalate desserts.	Ⓕⓕⓕ	AE DC MC V		■		
CHAMPS-ELYSÉES: *La Fermette Marbeuf 1900.* **Map 2 F5.** 5 rue Marbeuf, 75008. 01 53 23 08 00. Come here to dine amid the stunning Belle Epoque decor. La Fermette serves good brasserie-style food, including a commendable set menu with many wines of *appellation contrôlée* status.	Ⓕⓕⓕ	AE DC MC V		■	●	■
CHAMPS-ELYSÉES: *Lasserre.* 17 av Franklin D Roosevelt, 75008. 01 43 59 53 43. For over 50 years, charismatic owner René Lasserre has laboured to maintain one of the finest menus in Paris. Main courses are classics, desserts sublime.	Ⓕⓕⓕⓕⓕ	AE MC V		■	●	
CHAMPS-ELYSÉES: *Au Petit Colombier.* **Map 2 D3.** 42 rue des Acacias, 75017. 01 43 80 28 54. The slightly rustic ambience of this comfortable restaurant complements the traditional provincial cuisine. An excellent place for a relaxing evening.	Ⓕⓕⓕⓕ	AE MC V		■	●	
CHAMPS-ELYSÉES: *Taillevent.* **Map 2 F4.** 15 rue Lamennais, 75008. 01 45 61 12 90. Taillevent is the most elegant of Paris's three-star restaurants. The service, wine list and cuisine of Phillippe Legendre make it memorable.	Ⓕⓕⓕⓕⓕ	AE DC MC V			●	
ST-GERMAIN-DES-PRÉS: *Le Petit St-Benoît.* **Map 8 E3.** 4 rue St-Benoît, 75006. 01 42 60 27 92. This is the place for anyone who's on a budget or who wants to mix with the locals. The food is simple and tasty, and good value.	Ⓕ					■
ST-GERMAIN-DES-PRÉS: *Marie et Fils.* **Map 8 F4.** 34 rue Mazarine, 75006. 01 43 26 69 49. Situated in the heart of St-Germain, this trendy restaurant provides delicious food – rabbit *terrine*, tuna steaks and excellent desserts.	Ⓕⓕ	AE MC V		■	●	■

St-Germain-des-Prés: *Restaurant Jacques Cagna.* **Map** 8 F4. Ⓕ Ⓕ | AE MC V
14 rue des Grands Augustins, 75006. ▐ *01 43 26 49 39.*
This elegant 17th century town house is a showcase for the excellent
classic-cum-contemporary cuisine of the chef/owner Jacques Cagna. ▐

St-Germain-des-Prés: *La Vigneraie* Ⓕ Ⓕ | MC V
16 rue du Dragon, 75006. ▐ *01 45 48 57 04.*
This bustling Art Deco brasserie attracts a glittering clientele including
politicians and actors. Traditional dishes are its forte.

Latin Quarter: *Le Michalain.* **Map** 9 B5. Ⓕ | AE MC V
18 rue du Cardinal Lemoine, 75005. ▐ *01 44 07 29 50.*
A cosy bistro, about 10 minutes' walk from the Odéon, offering friendly
service and very good food at budget prices.

Latin Quarter: *Le Bistrot d'A Côté.* **Map** 9 B5. Ⓕ Ⓕ | AE MC V
16 bd Saint-Germain, 75005. ▐ *01 43 54 59 10.*
The latest of star chef Michel Rostang's bistros, the menu offers a superb
selection of seafood and meat dishes cooked in classic Lyonnais style.

Latin Quarter: *Loubnane.* **Map** 9 A4. Ⓕ Ⓕ | AE DC MC V
29 rue Galande, 75005. ▐ *01 43 26 70 60.*
This Lebanese restaurant serves generous mezzes under the watchful eye of a
patron whose main aim in life is the happiness of his customers.

Latin Quarter: *La Tour d'Argent.* **Map** 9 B5. Ⓕ Ⓕ Ⓕ Ⓕ Ⓕ | AE DC MC V
15–17 quai de la Tournelle, 75005. ▐ *01 43 54 23 31.*
Established in 1582, La Tour d'Argent consistently maintains top-class
status. The wine cellar must be one of the best in the world. ▐

Luxembourg Quarter: *Perraudin.* **Map** 12 F1. Ⓕ
157 rue St-Jacques, 75005. ▐ *01 46 33 15 75.*
Generations of students have come here to tuck into the home-spun meals
at this authentic turn-of-the-century bistro. The set menu is a bargain.

Luxembourg Quarter: *Polidor.* **Map** 8 F5. Ⓕ
41 rue Monsieur-le-Prince, 75006. ▐ *01 43 26 95 34.*
Artists, poets and writers have been attracted to this homely bistro
for decades. James Joyce was once a regular customer.

Luxembourg Quarter: *Au Petit Marquéry.* **Map** 13 B3. Ⓕ Ⓕ | AE DC MC V
9 bd de Port-Royal, 75013. ▐ *01 43 31 58 59.*
Cold lobster *consommé* with caviar, mushroom salad with *foie gras* and
cod with spices are some of the unusual dishes served here.

Luxembourg Quarter: *La Petite Cour.* **Map** 8 E4. Ⓕ Ⓕ | AE MC V
8 rue Mabillon, 75006. ▐ *01 43 26 52 26.*
An old restaurant with a Napoleon III interior and a courtyard.
The menu includes skate with cabbage and beef stew with carrots.

Luxembourg Quarter: *L'Ecaille de PCB.* **Map** 8 E4. Ⓕ Ⓕ Ⓕ | AE MC V
5 rue Mabillon, 75006. ▐ *01 43 26 73 70.*
A calm restaurant with steamship-style decor. Exclusively for fish and
seafood lovers, the menu draws especially on big, deep sea catches.

Montparnasse: *La Coupole.* **Map** 12 D2. Ⓕ Ⓕ | AE DC MC V
102 bd du Montparnasse, 75014. ▐ *01 43 20 14 20.*
This is a lively and boisterous place all through the day and night. It has
been popular with artists and thinkers since 1927. Serves vegetarian dishes.

Montparnasse: *L'Ostréade.* **Map** 11 B2. Ⓕ Ⓕ | AE MC V
11 bd Vaugirard, 75015. ▐ *01 43 21 87 41.*
Next to the Gare Montparnasse, this is an attractive seafood restaurant.
The roast lobster, roast sea bass and Brittany oysters are delicious.

Montparnasse: *La Regalade.* **Map** 12 D5. Ⓕ Ⓕ | MC V
49 av Jean Moulin, 75014. ▐ *01 45 45 68 58.*
The food here is outstanding at a remarkable price. Chef Yves
Camdeborde reinvents bistro cooking in his own inimitable style. ▐

Montparnasse: *La Cagouille.* **Map** 11 C3. Ⓕ Ⓕ | AE MC V
10–12 pl Constantin Brancusi, 75014. ▐ *01 43 22 09 01.*
This is considered one of the best fish restaurants in Paris. The shellfish
platter is recommended. Also look out for the seasonal items on the menu

For key to symbols see back flap

				Average prices for a three-course meal for one, including a half-bottle of house wine, tax and service: Ⓕ under F150 ⒻⒻ F150–F250 ⒻⒻⒻ F250–F350 ⒻⒻⒻⒻ F350–F500 ⒻⒻⒻⒻⒻ over F500	**CHILDREN'S FACILITIES** Some restaurants have high chairs and offer smaller portions for children. **FIXED-PRICE MENU** A good-value fixed-price menu on offer at lunch, dinner or both, usually with three courses. **GOOD WINE LIST** Denotes a wide range of good wines, or a more specialized selection of local wines. **OUTDOOR TABLES** Facilities for eating outdoors, on a terrace, or in a garden or courtyard, often with a good view.	CREDIT CARDS	CHILDREN'S FACILITIES	FIXED-PRICE MENU	GOOD WINE LIST	OUTDOOR TABLES

Restaurant	Price	Credit Cards	Children's Facilities	Fixed-Price Menu	Good Wine List	Outdoor Tables
MONTPARNASSE: *L'Assiette.* **Map 11 C4.** 181 rue du Château, 75014. **[** 01 43 22 64 86. Formerly a simple *charcuterie* now turned restaurant, L'Assiette is a popular address with politicians and stars. The food is still very good.	ⒻⒻⒻⒻ	AE MC V			●	
MONTMARTRE: *Au Grain de Folie.* **Map 4 F1.** 24 rue La-Vieuville, 75018. **[** 01 42 58 15 57. This is a good-value vegetarian restaurant, portions are generous and organic wine is available. The speciality is the mixed vegetarian platter.	Ⓕ			■		
MONTMARTRE: *Le Maquis* 69 rue Caulaincourt, 75018. **[** 01 42 59 76 07. A pleasant bistro where you can enjoy a simple but delicious meal on the tree-shaded terrace. Very good value.	ⒻⒻ	MC V		■		■
MONTMARTRE: *La Pomponette.* **Map 4 E1.** 42 rue Lepic, 75018. **[** 01 46 06 08 36. This is a restaurant to remember Montmartre by – the yellowing walls are covered with engravings, etchings, paintings and old photos of Montmartre as it was. Even the food has its own bohemian flavour.	ⒻⒻ	MC V		■	●	
MONTMARTRE: *Charlot Roi des Coquillages.* **Map 4 E2.** 12 place de Clichy, 75009. **[** 01 53 20 48 00. Specialities here include *bouillabaisse* and a copious shellfish platter. The decor has retained its original 1930s style.	ⒻⒻⒻ	AE DC MC V	●	■		
MONTMARTRE: *Beauvilliers* 52 rue Lamarck, 75018. **[** 01 42 54 54 42. Stepping into this restaurant, you are imbued with a sense of *joie de vivre*. Chef Edouard Carlier's cuisine is always exciting. 🅣	ⒻⒻⒻⒻ	AE DC MC V		■		■

ILE DE FRANCE

Restaurant	Price	Credit Cards	Children's Facilities	Fixed-Price Menu	Good Wine List	Outdoor Tables
BARBIZON: *La Clé d'Or* 73 rue Grande. **[** 01 60 66 40 96. This recently restored inn retains its old-world charm. Its specialities are shellfish, seafood and game in season.	ⒻⒻ	AE DC MC V	●	■	●	■
BARBIZON: *Hostellerie les Pléiades* 21 rue Grande. **[** 01 60 66 40 25. Once the artist Daubigny's studio, this restaurant offers traditional cuisine such as kidneys and sweetbreads with wild mushrooms.	ⒻⒻⒻ	AE MC DC V	●	■	●	■
DAMPIERRE: *Auberge Saint-Pierre* 1 rue de Chevreuse. **[** 01 30 52 53 53. This half-timbered inn faces the grand Château de Dampierre. The menu offers classics such as *magret de canard* and *tête de veau* (calf's head).	ⒻⒻⒻ	MC V	●	■	●	■
DAMPIERRE: *Les Ecuries du Château* Château de Dampierre. **[** 01 30 52 52 99. Situated within the château, Les Ecuries offers a classic menu of seafood and meat dishes in a sophisticated setting.	ⒻⒻⒻ	AE DC MC V		■	●	
FONTAINEBLEAU: *Le Caveau des Ducs* 24 rue de Ferrare. **[** 01 64 22 05 05. Offers standard classic French cuisine in intimate rustic surroundings near to the fabulous Château de Fontainebleau.	ⒻⒻⒻ	AE MC V	●	■	●	■
MAISONS-LAFFITTE: *Le Tastevin* 9 avenue Eglé. **[** 01 39 62 11 67. Outstanding cooking and carefully selected wines served in delightful surroundings make Michel Blanchet's restaurant one of the best in the Paris suburbs. Specialities include fish, seafood and poultry.	ⒻⒻⒻⒻ	AE DC MC V		■	●	■

RAMBOUILLET: *Auberge Villa Marinette* Ⓕ Ⓕ | MC V
20 av Général de Gaulle, D 906, Gazeran. 🕻 *01 34 83 19 01.*
Diners come here to enjoy the blend of Alsatian and Ile de France
specialities which include home-made *terrines* and fish dishes.

RUEIL-MALMAISON: *Relais de St-Cucufa* Ⓕ Ⓕ | AE V
114 rue Général-de-Miribel. 🕻 *01 47 49 79 05.*
Whether lunching on the terrace or dining by the fire, guests can enjoy
specialities such as the crayfish ravioli or steamed salmon.

VERSAILLES: *Restaurant Chez Lazare* Ⓕ | AE MC V
18 rue de Satory. 🕻 *01 39 50 41 45.*
This fun South-American restaurant makes a change from French
classic cuisine. Seated below tiers of copper pots, diners tuck into
grilled fish and steaks. The fixed-price menu is for lunch only.

VERSAILLES: *Brasserie La Fontaine (Trianon Palace)* Ⓕ Ⓕ | AE DC MC V
1 bd de la Reine. 🕻 *01 30 84 38 47.*
The annexe to Les Trois Marches is no gourmet paradise
but allows visitors to enjoy a meal at acceptable prices in a beautiful
place. Serves seafood, grilled meats and rich chocolate desserts.

VERSAILLES: *Les Trois Marches (Trianon Palace)* Ⓕ Ⓕ Ⓕ Ⓕ Ⓕ | AE DC MC V
1 bd de la Reine. 🕻 *01 39 50 13 21.*
The restaurant is part of the sumptuous palace overlooking the formal
gardens. The *haute cuisine* matches the splendour of the place.

LE NORD AND PICARDY

ABBEVILLE: *Au Châteaubriant* Ⓕ Ⓕ | AE MC V
1 place de l'Hôtel de Ville. 🕻 *03 22 24 08 23.*
The *Quiche Picarde* (flan with sweet onions, ham and sour cream) and
steak in mushroom and Calvados sauce are recommended.

AMIENS: *La Couronne* Ⓕ Ⓕ | MC V
64 rue Saint-Leu. 🕻 *03 22 91 88 57.*
To start, try a portion of home-made spicy duck pâté, followed by salt marsh
lamb from the Somme Abbey nearby, accompanied by a Chinon wine.

ARRAS: *La Rapière* Ⓕ | AE MC V
44 Grand'Place. 🕻 *03 21 55 09 92.*
There are several menus, but the *menu régional* offers good value and
a varied selection of dishes. The chicken cooked in beer is delicious. 🕭

ARRAS: *La Faisanderie* Ⓕ Ⓕ Ⓕ Ⓕ | AE DC MC V
45 Grand'Place. 🕻 *03 21 48 20 76.*
La Faisanderie is a classified historic building with a splendid brick-
vaulted dining room. The menu changes according to season.

AVESNES-SUR-HELPE: *La Crémaillière* Ⓕ Ⓕ | AE DC MC V
26 place Général Leclerc. 🕻 *03 27 61 02 30.*
A great place, with a menu featuring stuffed quails
and other local dishes.

CALAIS: *La Diligence* Ⓕ Ⓕ Ⓕ | AE DC MC V
5–7 rue Edmond Roche. 🕻 *03 21 96 92 89.*
This is a very refined restaurant, even by high French standards. Snails
with mushrooms, and *fricassée* of sole and crayfish are irresistible.

CAMBRAI: *L'Escargot* Ⓕ Ⓕ | AE DC MC V
10 rue Général de Gaulle. 🕻 *03 27 81 24 54.*
Mme Maton, the owner, has a regular clientele for her *plat du jour,*
which changes regularly. She also makes her own *terrines* and *foie gras.*

COUDEKERQUE-BRANCHE: *Le Soubise* Ⓕ Ⓕ | AE DC MC V
49 2 bis route de Bergues. 🕻 *03 28 64 66 00.*
The chef changes his menu according to what he finds in the morning
market. The fresh vegetables are cooked in a variety of unusual ways
and the delicious fruit tarts are all home-made.

DOUAI: *La Terrasse* Ⓕ Ⓕ Ⓕ | MC V
36 terrasse St-Pierre. 🕻 *03 27 88 70 04.*
Breast of duck with fresh figs, and fillet of *sandre* (perch) on a bed
of sweet onions give some idea of the splendid cuisine available here.

Average prices for a three-course meal for one, including a half-bottle of house wine, tax and service:
F under F150
FF F150–F250
FFF F250–F350
FFFF F350–F500
FFFFF over F500

CHILDREN'S FACILITIES
Some restaurants have high chairs and offer smaller portions for children.

FIXED-PRICE MENU
A good-value fixed-price menu on offer at lunch, dinner or both, usually with three courses.

GOOD WINE LIST
Denotes a wide range of good wines, or a more specialized selection of local wines.

OUTDOOR TABLES
Facilities for eating outdoors, on a terrace, or in a garden or courtyard, often with a good view.

	Price	Credit Cards	Children's Facilities	Fixed-Price Menu	Good Wine List	Outdoor Tables
DURY-LES-AMIENS: *L'Aubergade* 78 Route Nationale, Saleux. ☎ 03 22 89 51 41. Try the chef's prize-winning *Charlotte de pommes de terre au pain d'épice et foie gras* (potato and spiced bread baked with *foie gras*).	FFF	AE MC V	●	■	●	■
HALLINES: *L'Hostellerie St-Hubert* 1 rue du Moulin. ☎ 03 21 39 77 77. The restaurant is situated in its own park at the edge of the river Aa. Offers a classic French menu with an impressive selection of cheeses.	FFF	DC MC V	●	■	●	
LILLE: *La Pâte Brisée* 65 rue de la Monnaie. ☎ 03 20 74 29 00. Set in the Old Town, this rustic bistro specializes in bountiful servings of quiches, tarts, gratins and mixed salads. It's always packed at lunchtime, so arrive early.	F	MC V	●	■		
LILLE: *Restaurant aux Moules* 34 rue de Béthune. ☎ 03 20 57 12 46. As its name suggests, mussels are the order of the day here, with a wide selection of styles. Local dishes such as *carbonnade flamande* are also good. Wash down your choice with local beer and enjoy the bustling, 1930s brasserie atmosphere.	FF	AE DC MC V	●	■		
LONGUEAU: *La Potinière* 2 av Henri Barbusse. ☎ 03 22 46 22 83. Popular with the locals, this cosy restaurant offers a daily menu based on freshly bought produce. Dishes are richer in winter.	FF	MC V	●	■		
MONTREUIL-SUR-MER: *Auberge de la Grenouillère* Rue de la Grenouillère, La Madeleine-sous-Montreuil. ☎ 03 21 06 07 22. This is an excellent restaurant, only 3 km (2 miles) west of Montreuil, for sampling French provincial cooking: braised quails with langoustines and frogs' legs are just two of the specialities.	FFF	AE DC MC V	●	■		■
POIX-DE-PICARDIE: *L'Auberge de la Forge* Route Nationale 29, Caulières. ☎ 03 22 38 00 91. A traditional Picardy inn that serves good, old-fashioned, hearty fare: try the salt-marsh lamb or trout with *foie gras*.	FFF	V	●	■	●	
ROYE: *La Flamiche* 20 place de l'Hôtel de Ville. ☎ 03 22 87 00 56. Braised eel and local wild duck with forest mushrooms are two particular favourites with diners here. Start with a *flamiche* (covered tart) of leeks or baked langoustines with grapefruit.	FFFF	AE DC MC V	●	■		
ST-QUENTIN: *Le Pot d'Etain* Route Nationale 29, Holnon. ☎ 03 23 09 34 35. This is a newly opened, purpose-built hotel-restaurant with the emphasis on practicality and good service. The food is unpretentiously wholesome. ♿	FF	AE DC MC V	●	■	●	■
SANGATTE: *Les Dunes* Route Nationale 48, Blériot-Plage. ☎ 03 21 34 54 30. By the beach, a short drive from the Channel Tunnel, this restaurant serves great seafood, including a cassoulet of mussels and cockles flambéed in whisky. ♿	FF	AE DC MC V	●	■		■
SARS-POTERIES: *L'Auberge Fleurie* 67 rue Général de Gaulle. ☎ 03 27 61 62 48. Situated in pretty countryside, L'Auberge is an ancient, rather grand converted farmhouse. Game, venison, wild boar and partridge are in abundance in winter. A variety of shellfish also appears on the menu.	FFF	AE DC MC V		■		■
WIMEREUX: *La Liégeoise* La digue. ☎ 03 21 31 61 15. At this fish restaurant, a salad of red mullet with balsamic vinegar makes a good start to the meal, followed by braised turbot with scallops. ♿	FF	AE DC MC V	●	■	●	

CHAMPAGNE

Restaurant	Price	Cards
AIX-EN-OTHE: *Auberge de la Scierie* La Vove. **[** *03 25 46 71 26.* This creeper-clad inn stands in a lovely garden by the river. The superb menu includes veal kidneys with cranberries, and snails in puff pastry.	⑤⑤⑤	AE DC MC V
AMBONNAY: *Auberge Saint-Vincent* 1 rue St Vincent. **[** *03 26 57 01 98.* This elegant restaurant with Louis XIII ceilings is a pleasure to dine in. The menu changes according to the season.	⑤⑤⑤	AE DC MC V
AUBRIVES: *Debette* 2 place Louis Debette. **[** *03 24 41 64 72.* Ardennes specialities here include smoked ham, trout, and game *terrines*. Splendid desserts are made with fruit from the owner's garden. **&**	⑤	AE MC V
BIÈVRES: *Relais de St-Walfroy* Bièvres. **[** *03 24 22 61 62.* An unusual dish on the menu is the braised guinea-fowl with tiny mirabelle plums. There is also the perennial classic, *canard à l'orange*.	⑤	MC V
CHALONS-EN-CHAMPAGNE: *Les Ardennes* 34 place de la République. **[** *03 26 68 21 42.* The patron, M Bouffonais, worked at the Savoy in London in the 1950s. His restaurant is a fine 17th-century house in this picturesque town. The menu is exceptionally wide with an extravagant selection of desserts.	⑤⑤	AE MC V
CHAUMONT: *Bleu Comme Orange* 11 rue Saint-Louis. **[** *03 25 01 26 87.* Situated in the Old Quarter of Chaumont, this lively restaurant is always packed with locals at midday. It is essentially a *crêperie*, providing imaginative combinations of fillings.	⑤	MC V
EPERNAY: *L'Auberge Champenoise* Moussy. **[** *03 26 54 03 48.* After visiting some of the vast champagne cellars in Epernay, this friendly inn is an excellent place to stop for an inexpensive meal.	⑤	MC V
L'EPINE: *Aux Armes de Champagne* 31 avenue du Luxembourg. **[** *03 26 69 30 30.* This gourmet restaurant situated in a pretty village just north of Châlons-en-Champagne serves delicious regional specialities.	⑤⑤⑤	AE DC MC V
FLORENT-EN-ARGONNE: *Auberge de la Menyère* Rue Basse. **[** *03 26 60 93 70.* The restaurant is a well-preserved, 400-year-old house set in a magnificent forest. Come in the hunting season to sample game with wild mushrooms.	⑤⑤	MC V
JOINVILLE: *Le Soleil d'Or* 9 rue des Capucins. **[** *03 25 94 15 66.* Its monastic interior belies the restaurant's elegant service and eclectic menu. Try the tart of scallops with sweet basil. **&**	⑤⑤	AE DC MC V
LANGRES: *Le Lion d'Or* Rue des Angesl. **[** *03 25 87 03 30.* This charming restaurant not only offers good regional food but also a panoramic view of Lake Liez.	⑤⑤	MC V
LE MESNIL-SUR-OGER: *Le Mesnil* 2 rue Pasteur. **[** *03 26 57 95 57.* Just south of Epernay, between Cramant and Verbis, this gourmet restaurant is situated in one of the prettiest villages in Champagne, amid vineyards. The *patron* is happy to show diners around his cellars.	⑤⑤⑤	MC V
NOGENT-SUR-SEINE: *Au Beau Rivage* 20 rue Villiers-aux-Choux. **[** *03 25 39 84 22.* Situated at the water's edge, this restaurant has a terrace overlooking the river. The menu is particularly strong on fish cooked with fresh herbs.	⑤⑤	MC V
REIMS: *La Coupole* 73 place Drouet d'Erlon. **[** *03 26 47 86 28.* La Coupole caters to all tastes, including vegetarian. The menu includes a wide range of *hors d'oeuvres*, imaginative salads and good fruit sorbets.	⑤⑤	AE DC MC V

<table>
<tr><td rowspan="2">

Average prices for a three-course meal for one, including a half-bottle of house wine, tax and service:
Ⓕ under F150
ⒻⒻ F150–F250
ⒻⒻⒻ F250–F350
ⒻⒻⒻⒻ F350–F500
ⒻⒻⒻⒻⒻ over F500

</td><td>

CHILDREN'S FACILITIES
Some restaurants have high chairs and offer smaller portions for children.
FIXED-PRICE MENU
A good-value fixed-price menu on offer at lunch, dinner or both, usually with three courses.
GOOD WINE LIST
Denotes a wide range of good wines, or a more specialized selection of local wines.
OUTDOOR TABLES
Facilities for eating outdoors, on a terrace, or in a garden or courtyard, often with a good view.

</td></tr>
</table>

	Price	CREDIT CARDS	CHILDREN'S FACILITIES	FIXED-PRICE MENU	GOOD WINE LIST	OUTDOOR TABLES
REIMS: *Le Vigneron* Place Paul Jamot. **【** *03 26 47 00 71.* This popular restaurant is particularly recommended for those who wish to sample dishes with a strong local flavour. A reservation is essential.	ⒻⒻⒻ	MC V		▨		▨
REIMS: *Les Crayères* 64 boulevard Vasnier. **【** *03 26 82 80 80.* Set in ample grounds, this celebrated restaurant runs tours of its wine cellar. Specialities include smoked salmon and cream of caviar.	ⒻⒻⒻⒻⒻ	AE DC MC V			●	▨
ST-DIZIER: *La Gentilhommière* 29 rue Jean Jaurès. **【** *03 25 56 32 97.* Caul-wrapped chopped fillet of lamb with tarragon, and pikeperch with a rich sauce made of the local forest mushrooms, are two favourites here. **&**	ⒻⒻ	MC V				
ST-DIZIER: *Hôtellerie du Moulin* Eclaron (9 km from St-Dizier). **【** *03 25 04 17 76.* Estimable food cooked with a light touch across a wide range of dishes in this wood-frame logis. **&**	ⒻⒻ	MC V	●	▨	●	
ST-IMOGES: *La Maison du Vigneron* Route Nationale 51. **【** *03 26 52 88 00.* Both a champagne house and a chic restaurant. Regional dishes are served and diners can accompany their meals with the owner's champagne. **&**	ⒻⒻ	AE DC MC V	●	▨	●	▨
TROYES: *Le Jardin Gourmand* 31 rue Paillot de Montabert. **【** *03 25 73 08 30.* Set in the heart of the historic quarter, the restaurant occupies a romantic courtyard. This is the place to try the town's speciality – *andouillettes*.	ⒻⒻ	MC V		▨		▨
TROYES: *Le Bourgogne* 40 rue Général de Gaulle. **【** *03 25 73 02 67.* Le Bourgogne is considered Troyes' finest restaurant (unfortunately closed in August). Try the *mousseline* of pike or the hearty lamb stew.	ⒻⒻⒻ	MC V		▨	●	
ALSACE AND LORRAINE						
BORNY: *Le Jardin de Bellevue* 58 rue Claude Bernard. **【** *03 87 37 10 27.* The chef has written a popular book about traditional Lorraine cuisine updated, and uses his own garden produce when available. **&**	ⒻⒻ	MC V	●	▨	●	▨
COLMAR: *Le Caveau Saint-Pierre* 24 rue de la Herse. **【** *03 89 41 99 33.* Reached by a boardwalk running alongside a canal in Colmar's pretty "Little Venice." At weekends in winter, the speciality to choose is the classic *baeckoff* (stew).	ⒻⒻ	V	●	▨		
COLMAR: *La Maison des Têtes* 19 rue des Têtes. **【** *03 89 24 43 43.* The façade of this unique 17th-century brasserie is a classified historic monument. Serves traditional Alsace fare such as *choucroute*. **&**	ⒻⒻⒻ	AE DC MC V	●	▨	●	▨
DOLE: *Les Templiers* 35 Grande rue. **【** *03 84 82 78 78.* Adventurous dishes served in a truly sumptuous Gothic setting, and all at reasonable prices.	ⒻⒻ	AE DC MC V		▨		
HAGUENAU: *Restaurant Barberousse* 8 place Barberousse. **【** *03 88 73 31 09.* Astonishingly good value, the lunchtime menu particularly. The dishes are unpretentious local fare: home-made *foie gras* and *terrines, choucroute* with meat or fish and good hot desserts. **&**	ⒻⒻ	MC V	●	▨		▨

MARLENHEIM: *Le Cerf* ⓕⓕⓕⓕ
30 rue du Général de Gaulle. 03 88 87 73 73.
This fine restaurant likes customers to arrive hungry. Alsatian cuisine here
is at its richest, and the portions are immense. Vegetarians are welcomed.
AE DC MC V

METZ: *Restaurant des Roches* ⓕⓕ
29 rue des Roches. 03 87 74 06 51.
Predominantly a fish restaurant – fillet of turbot with basil is very good,
but there are plenty of meat dishes. The *soufflé glacé* is recommended.
AE DC MC V

MULHOUSE: *Restaurant de la Poste* ⓕⓕⓕ
7 rue Général de Gaulle, Riedisheim. 03 89 44 07 71.
Six generations of chefs have worked here to establish the reputation
of this excellent restaurant. The menu is imaginative and varied.
AE MC V

NANCY: *L'Excelsior* ⓕⓕ
50 rue Henri Poincaré. 03 83 35 24 57.
Take a step back in time and enjoy a delightful meal in this magnificent
listed historic monument. The cuisine is classic French.
AE DC MC V

RIQUEWIHR: *Au Péché Mignon* ⓕ
5 rue de Dinzheim. 03 89 49 04 17.
This rustic restaurant offers robust Alsatian specialities, the food is
described as *cuisine grand-mère* – homely, copious and old-fashioned.
MC V

SAVERNE: *Taverne Katz* ⓕⓕ
80 Grand-Rue. 03 88 71 16 56.
The cosy, polished-wood interior provides a perfect setting for traditional
food such as *spaetzle* (Alsatian noodles) and *jambonneau braisé* (ham).
MC V

SÉLESTAT: *Restaurant Jean-Fredéric Edel* ⓕⓕ
7 rue des Serruriers. 03 88 92 86 55.
Home-made *foie gras*, and tender fillets of chicken with an exceptionally
fine *choucroute* are two of the specialities in this renowned restaurant.
AE DC MC V

STRASBOURG: *Zum Strissel* ⓕ
5 place de la Grande Boucherie. 03 88 32 14 73.
An old-fashioned wine cellar in a 14th-century building near the cathedral.
It serves mixed-meat stew, onion tart and pitchers of Alsatian wines.
MC V

STRASBOURG: *Restaurant au Crocodile* ⓕⓕⓕⓕⓕ
10 rue de l'Outre. 03 88 32 13 02.
This is probably Strasbourg's most exclusive restaurant. Visitors dine in
opulent surroundings and their every whim is attended to. One of the
recommended dishes is baked perch with smoked eel and carp roe.
AE DC MC V

TURCKHEIM: *Auberge du Brand* ⓕⓕ
8 Grand rue. 03 89 27 06 10.
The cuisine has a regional flavour but it is not as resolutely Alsatian as
in the neighbouring *winstubs* (winebars). The service is prompt and
discreet, and individual requests for vegetarian dishes are catered for.
MC V

VERDUN: *Le Coq Hardi* ⓕⓕⓕ
8 avenue de la Victoire. 03 29 86 36 36.
This gourmet restaurant is the best in Verdun, a city with few
good quality, moderately priced restaurants.
AE DC MC V

NORMANDY

ACHERIE: *Le Manoir de l'Acherie* ⓕⓕ
50800 St Cécil. 02 33 51 13 87.
Calvados (apple brandy) is the flavour here – ham and even whiting
are cooked in it and, of course, the apple tart is flambéed with it.
AE MC V

ARGENTAN: *Auberge de l'Ancienne Abbaye* ⓕⓕ
25 rue St-Martin. 02 33 39 37 42.
The Auberge is located in Argentan's oldest church, now a listed site
of historical interest. It is a treat to dine in its magnificent interior, where
carved stone blends in with massive oak beams. Serves vegetarian dishes.
AE DC MC V

AUDRIEU: *Château d'Audrieu* ⓕⓕⓕⓕ
Audrieu. 02 31 80 21 52.
This 18th century château was transformed into a luxurious hotel and
restaurant in 1976. This is the place for an elegant dinner.
MC V

Average prices for a three-course meal for one, including a half-bottle of house wine, tax and service:
Ⓕ under F150
ⒻⒻ F150–F250
ⒻⒻⒻ F250–F350
ⒻⒻⒻⒻ F350–F500
ⒻⒻⒻⒻⒻ over F500

CHILDREN'S FACILITIES
Some restaurants have high chairs and offer smaller portions for children.

FIXED-PRICE MENU
A good-value fixed-price menu on offer at lunch, dinner or both, usually with three courses.

GOOD WINE LIST
Denotes a wide range of good wines, or a more specialized selection of local wines.

OUTDOOR TABLES
Facilities for eating outdoors, on a terrace, or in a garden or courtyard, often with a good view.

Restaurant	Price	Credit Cards	Children's Facilities	Fixed-Price Menu	Good Wine List	Outdoor Tables
BAYEUX: *Le Lion d'Or*	ⒻⒻⒻ	AE DC MC V	●	■	●	
LE BEC-HELLOUIN: *Restaurant de la Tour*	ⒻⒻ	AE DC MC V	●	■		■
CHAMPEAUX: *Au Marquis de Tombelaine*	ⒻⒻ	MC V	●	■	●	■
CHERBOURG: *La Cendrée*	Ⓕ	MC V	●	■		■
COSQUEVILLE: *Au Bouquet de Cosqueville*	ⒻⒻⒻ	MC V	●	■	●	■
CRESSERONS: *La Valise Gourmande*	ⒻⒻ	MC V		■	●	■
DEAUVILLE: *Le Dauphin*	ⒻⒻⒻ	AE MC V		■	●	
DEAUVILLE: *Le Spinnaker*	ⒻⒻⒻ	AE MC V	●	■	●	
DIEPPE: *La Marmite Dieppoise*	ⒻⒻ	MC V	●	■		
DOZULÉ: *Le Pavé d'Auge*	ⒻⒻ	MC V	●	■		
GISORS: *Hostellerie des Trois Poissons*	ⒻⒻ	V		■		■
HONFLEUR: *Le Champlain*	ⒻⒻ	AE MC V	●	■		

BAYEUX: *Le Lion d'Or*
71 rue St-Jean. ☎ 02 31 92 06 90.
This 17th-century inn has been run by the same family since 1929, and serves delicious food. Try the unusual *foie gras* of duck with honey, hot *andouille* (tripe sausage) or the mouth-watering forest mushroom tart.

LE BEC-HELLOUIN: *Restaurant de la Tour*
Place Guillaume-le-Conquérant. ☎ 02 32 44 86 15.
It's best to reserve in advance to sample the traditional Norman cuisine here. After your meal you can buy Calvados and cider to take home with you.

CHAMPEAUX: *Au Marquis de Tombelaine*
Sartilly. ☎ 02 33 61 85 94.
The dishes to go for here are homemade *foie gras*, oysters and lobster Thermidor, accompanied by a bottle of Burgundy and ending with cheese.

CHERBOURG: *La Cendrée*
18–20 passage Digard. ☎ 02 33 93 67 04.
This simple but friendly restaurant offers probably the best value in town. It is popular with the locals and reservation is advisable.

COSQUEVILLE: *Au Bouquet de Cosqueville*
Hameau Remond. ☎ 02 33 54 32 81.
The specialities include lobster cooked in whisky, and turbot baked with leeks and truffles. For dessert try a fresh *crêpe* or *crème brûlée*. ⅗

CRESSERONS: *La Valise Gourmande*
7 route de Lion-sur-Mer. ☎ 02 31 37 39 10.
Traditional Normandy food is served here against a setting of old beams and oak furniture. Try the mussels in butter, and *tergoule* (rice pudding).

DEAUVILLE: *Le Dauphin*
Le Breuil-en-Auge, Pont l'Evêque. ☎ 02 31 65 08 11.
A reservation is essential for this much sought-after restaurant in a small hamlet. The owners M and Mme Lecomte spare no effort in making your visit a memorable one, and they take great pride in their cooking.

DEAUVILLE: *Le Spinnaker*
52 rue Mirabeau. ☎ 02 31 88 24 40.
A one-star Michelin fish restaurant, this is one of Normandy's finest. The baked lobster in cider vinegar or turbot with shallots must be sampled. ⅗

DIEPPE: *La Marmite Dieppoise*
8 rue St Jean. ☎ 02 35 84 24 26.
Dieppe is one of the best places in France for seafood. The chef's *Marmite Dieppoise* is a tasty combination of fish and shellfish in a cream sauce.

DOZULÉ: *Le Pavé d'Auge*
Beuvron-en-Auge. ☎ 02 31 79 26 71.
The highly talented chef at Le Pavé d'Auge likes to serve food made from local ingredients. The menu is strong on fish, with a assortment of meat and poultry dishes. The cheese platter has a good selection.

GISORS: *Hostellerie des Trois Poissons*
13 rue Cappeville. ☎ 02 32 55 01 09.
This half-timbered house, with an attractive terrace for summer dining, offers rabbit cooked in cider as its speciality.

HONFLEUR: *Le Champlain*
6 place Hamelin. ☎ 02 31 89 14 91.
This family-run business uses only fresh farm produce. Favourites are scallops in puff pastry with orange butter, and sautéed veal kidneys.

HONFLEUR: *La Ferme St-Siméon* ⓕⓕⓕⓕⓕ
Rue A-Marais. 02 31 89 23 61.
It is a delight to enjoy a light lunch here on the terrace. The food is exquisitely prepared, featuring local seafood, poultry, fruits and cheese.
AE MC V

LA FERTÉ MACÉ: *Auberge le Clouet* ⓕⓕ
Chemin le Clouet. 02 33 37 18 22.
An hour or two spent exploring the delightful, historic market town should end with a meal of local specialities on this floral terrrace.
MC V

LOUVIERS: *Le Clos Normand* ⓕⓕ
16 rue de la Gare. 02 32 40 03 56.
Mme Deniau, the owner, loves to prepare food for appreciative guests in this attractive 1890s town house. Vegetarian dishes served on request.
AE MC V

LYONS-LA-FORÊT: *La Licorne* ⓕⓕⓕ
Place Benserade. 02 32 49 62 02.
The high quality belies the price in this 17th-century inn, where diners eat in front of a massive fireplace. Vegetarians are catered for.
AE DC MC V

MONT-ST-MICHEL: *Hôtel Saint-Pierre* ⓕ
Grand-Rue. 02 33 60 14 03.
Lamb grazed on the salt marshes, known as *agneau pré-salé*, features on the menu. Crab and sole are other favourites in this 15th-century building.
AE MC V

MONT-ST-MICHEL: *La Mère Poulard* ⓕⓕⓕⓕ
Grande-Rue. 02 33 60 14 01.
Visitors from all over Europe come here to sample the famous *omelette Mère Poulard* cooked in a long-handled pan over a wood fire.
AE DC MC V

NONANT-LE-PIN: *Hôtel Saint-Pierre* ⓕ
Nonant-le Pin. 02 33 39 94 04.
Set in the middle of France's horse-breeding country, the restaurant is on the road to the Dordogne and Spain. The menu is simple but imaginative.
MC V

PUTANGES-PONT-ECREPIN: *Hôtel du Lion Verd* ⓕ
Place de l'Hôtel-de-Ville. 02 33 35 01 86.
The owner is especially proud of her veal cooked in local cider. The lunchtime menu is very good value. Vegetarian dishes are available.
MC V

ROUEN: *La Marmite* ⓕⓕ
3 rue Florence 02 35 71 75 55.
This attractive restaurant is housed in an 18th-century building. It stays open late for guests to enjoy the romantic candle-lit atmosphere.
AE MC V

ROUEN: *Restaurant Gill* ⓕⓕⓕⓕ
9 quai de la Bourse. 02 35 71 16 14.
The *panaché de poissons* is a colourful dish of succulent fish and seafood. Another speciality is pigs' trotters with lentils.
AE DC MC V

ST-GERMAIN DE TALLEVENDE: *Auberge Saint-Germain* ⓕⓕ
Place de l'Eglise. 02 31 68 24 13.
This is an ideal restaurant for families, with a menu of good home-cooking that caters to all tastes, including vegetarian.
MC V

THIBERVILLE: *La Levrette* ⓕ
10 rue de Lieurey. 02 32 46 80 22.
Plain home cooking at competitive prices is the attractive feature of this friendly place. Try the local free-range poultry.
V

TROUVILLE-SUR-MER: *Brasserie les Vapeurs* ⓕⓕ
160 boulevard Fernard-Moureaux. 02 31 88 15 24.
Situated opposite the fish market, the seafood served here is truly fresh and flavoursome. You will be tempted to come back for more.
AE MC V

VEULES-LES-ROSES: *Les Galets* ⓕⓕⓕ
3 rue Victor Hugo. 02 35 97 61 33.
If you wish to have a meal by the sea, Les Galets is just the place. A reservation is necessary as it is very popular with the locals.
AE DC MC V

VILLERS-BOCAGE: *Les Trois Rois* ⓕⓕ
2 place Jeanne d'Arc. 02 31 77 00 32.
The special menu here, known as *mon marché*, consists of dishes created by the owner from the catch of the day, fresh every morning.
AE DC MC V

For key to symbols see back flap

Average prices for a three-course meal for one, including a half-bottle of house wine, tax and service: ⓕ under F150 ⓕⓕ F150–F250 ⓕⓕⓕ F250–F350 ⓕⓕⓕⓕ F350–F500 ⓕⓕⓕⓕⓕ over F500	**CHILDREN'S FACILITIES** Some restaurants have high chairs and offer smaller portions for children. **FIXED-PRICE MENU** A good-value fixed-price menu on offer at lunch, dinner or both, usually with three courses. **GOOD WINE LIST** Denotes a wide range of good wines, or a more specialized selection of local wines. **OUTDOOR TABLES** Facilities for eating outdoors, on a terrace, or in a garden or courtyard, often with a good view.			

	Prices	Credit Cards	Children's Facilities	Fixed-Price Menu	Good Wine List	Outdoor Tables
BRITTANY						
AURAY: *La Closerie de Kerdrain* 20 rue Louis Billet. **[** 02 97 56 61 27. A manor house with an imposing stone staircase and First Empire tapestries in the dining room. Specialities include sea bass and clams.	ⓕⓕⓕ	AE DC MC V	●	■		■
BELLE-ISLE-EN-TERRE: *Le Relais de l'Argoat* 9 rue de Guic. **[** 02 96 43 00 34. This old coaching inn on the edge of a pretty village has two dining rooms with a very friendly atmosphere. An excellent cheeseboard.	ⓕⓕ	MC V	●	■		
CHEVAIGNÉ: *La Marinière* Route du Mont-St-Michel. **[** 02 99 55 74 64. An old-fashioned country restaurant set in parklands. Mainly a fish restaurant, with good Normandy cheeses and Loire wines.	ⓕⓕ	AE DC MC V		■	●	
CONCARNEAU: *Le Galion* 15 rue St-Guénolé. **[** 02 98 97 30 16. Situated on the tip of a peninsula, the restaurant is almost surrounded by water. It serves a wide range of fish in a romantic setting.	ⓕⓕⓕ	AE DC MC V	●	■	●	
DINAN: *Chez la Mère Pourcel* 3 place des Merciers. **[** 02 96 39 03 80. This restaurant is in a stunning old Gothic building. The menu changes seasonally and the standard is consistent, with excellent Loire wines.	ⓕⓕⓕ	AE MC V	●	■	●	■
FOUGÈRES: *Restaurant des Voyageurs* 10 place Gambetta. **[** 02 99 99 14 17. In the town centre, the dining room has a high ceiling and massive chandeliers. The cuisine is local, with hearty game dishes in winter.	ⓕⓕ	AE MC V	●	■		
HÉDÉ: *L'Hostellerie du Vieux Moulin* Ancienne route de St-Malo. **[** 02 99 45 45 70. The old mill was part of a complex built in the 19th century to supply water power, and it has views of the ruins of Hédé Castle. There are particularly good lunches of scallops, grilled langoustines and duck.	ⓕⓕⓕ	AE DC MC V	●	■		■
LE CONQUET: *Les Boucaniers* 3 rue Poncelin. **[** 02 98 89 06 25. A *crêperie* in a granite building done up as a fisherman's cottage. Try the crêpes with goat's cheese, or orange and chocolate.	ⓕ	MC V	●			■
LORIENT: *Le Neptune* 15 ave de la Perrière. **[** 02 97 37 04 56. Try for a table in the rear dining room with conservatory. A wide range of fish is served, but go for lobster flambé or fricassée of monkfish.	ⓕⓕ	AE DC MC V	●	■		
MORLAIX: *La Marée Bleue* 3 rampe St-Melaine. **[** 02 98 63 24 21. Standing in the shadow of the viaduct, this old town house has become a first-class restaurant. Customers return often for the flawless fish dishes.	ⓕⓕ	MC V	●	■	●	
PAIMPOL: *La Vieille Tour* 13 rue de l'Eglise. **[** 02 96 20 83 18. This is a friendly, old-fashioned restaurant with the dining room on the first floor. Some rare delicacies are served, including ravioli stuffed with crayfish tails or cherry-filled chocolate mousse in raspberry sauce.	ⓕⓕ	MC V	●	■		
PLÉLAN-LE-GRAND: *L'Auberge du Presbytère* Treffendel. **[** 02 99 61 00 76. In an old priest's house that has altered little over the centuries, the chef serves poultry and pigeon in a number of traditional dishes.	ⓕⓕ	MC V	●	■		■

PLOMEUR: *Le Relais Bigouden* — Ⓕ Ⓕ — MC V
Rue Pen Allée. **【** *02 98 82 04 79.*
A cheerful and friendly restaurant full of fresh flowers, where the specialities include duck cooked in fresh lime and lobster in a ragoût.

PLOUNÉRIN: *Restaurant Patrick Jeffroy* — Ⓕ Ⓕ Ⓕ Ⓕ — MC V
Le Bourg. **【** *02 96 38 61 80.*
The restaurant has 45 seats in two dining rooms. The crayfish with artichokes are a must, complemented by cider from the local château.

PONT L'ABBÉ: *Le Relais de Ty-Boutic* — Ⓕ Ⓕ — MC V
Route de Plomeur. **【** *02 98 87 03 90.*
A serious "foodie", the chef has won several prizes. His best dishes are monkfish with cider, and langoustines with leeks.

QUIBERON: *Le Relax* — Ⓕ Ⓕ — AE DC MC V
27 boulevard Castéro. **【** *02 97 50 12 84.*
With lovely views over the sea and a pretty garden, you will find a wide selection of superbly cooked fish here, changing seasonally.

QUIMPER: *L'Ambroisie* — Ⓕ Ⓕ — AE DC MC V
49 rue Elie Fréron. **【** *02 98 95 00 02.*
A short walk from the cathedral, this newly decorated restaurant has Francis Bacon prints on the walls. The fish and desserts are excellent.

RENNES: *Le Corsaire* — Ⓕ Ⓕ — AE DC MC V
52 rue d'Antrain. **【** *02 99 36 33 69.*
In a grand town house, Le Corsaire is renowned locally. The braised oxtail and the *abalones* are specialities. Good Muscadet wines.

RENNES: *Le Palais* — Ⓕ Ⓕ Ⓕ — AE DC MC V
7 place du Parlement de Bretagne. **【** *02 99 79 45 01.*
In the Old Quarter of Rennes, this is an elegant setting in which to sample some of the best cooking in the region. Impeccable service combines with first-class local produce, and the desserts are amazing.

ST-BRIEUC: *Amadeus* — Ⓕ Ⓕ Ⓕ — V
22 rue de Gouët. **【** *02 96 33 92 44.*
One of the oldest buildings in this historic town, the oak beams and stone walls remain. Fish predominates – fillet of sole dished up with duck liver is exceptional – and there is a wide range of desserts.

ST-MALO: *Le Franklin* — Ⓕ — AE DC MC V
4 chaussée du Sillon. **【** *02 99 40 50 93.*
A restaurant overlooking the sea. Specialities include fish cooked with spices and *pré-salé* lamb which is raised on the salt-marshes.

VITRÉ: *La Taverne de l'Ecu* — Ⓕ Ⓕ — AE MC V
12 rue Baudrairie. **【** *02 99 75 11 09.*
A half-timbered Renaissance house with a courtyard and a 16th-century dining room. The fish is delicate and tasty.

THE LOIRE VALLEY

AMBOISE: *Le Manoir St Thomas* — Ⓕ Ⓕ Ⓕ — AE DC MC V
Place Richelieu. **【** *02 47 57 22 52.*
The elaborate, Renaissance-style decor, and the ability of the chef, combined with a sensational wine cellar, make this place irresistible.

ANGERS: *Restaurant La Ferme* — Ⓕ — AE MC V
2 place Freppel. **【** *02 41 87 09 90.*
A hectic restaurant which spills outdoors in summer. Rustic dishes like *coq au vin* and snails are favoured, as is the white Anjou wine.

ANGERS: *La Terrasse* — Ⓕ Ⓕ — MC V
La Pointe de Bouchemaine, Bouchemaine. **【** *02 41 77 11 96.*
Located in a hamlet on the confluence of the rivers Loire and Maine, this panoramic restaurant cooks freshly caught eels, pike, salmon and other freshwater fish over an open fire.

ANGERS: *La Salamandre* — Ⓕ Ⓕ Ⓕ — AE DC MC V
1 boulevard du Maréchal-Foch. **【** *02 41 88 99 55.*
The slightly kitsch interior belies the strength of the food. Sample ravioli stuffed with lobster, steaks, fish soups and rich cheeses.

Average prices for a three-course meal for one, including a half-bottle of house wine, tax and service:
Ⓕ under F150
ⒻⒻ F150–F250
ⒻⒻⒻ F250–F350
ⒻⒻⒻⒻ F350–F500
ⒻⒻⒻⒻⒻ over F500

CHILDREN'S FACILITIES
Some restaurants have high chairs and offer smaller portions for children.
FIXED-PRICE MENU
A good-value fixed-price menu on offer at lunch, dinner or both, usually with three courses.
GOOD WINE LIST
Denotes a wide range of good wines, or a more specialized selection of local wines.
OUTDOOR TABLES
Facilities for eating outdoors, on a terrace, or in a garden or courtyard, often with a good view.

Restaurant	Price	Credit Cards	Children's Facilities	Fixed-Price Menu	Good Wine List	Outdoor Tables
BEAUGENCY: *Le P'tit Bateau* 54 rue du Pont. **[** *02 38 44 56 38.* Near the château, Le P'tit Bateau is the most appealing restaurant in town. It is popular with the locals and offers fresh fish, game and wild mushrooms, all washed down with regional wines.	ⒻⒻ	AE DC MC V		▪		▪
BLOIS: *La Mesa* 11 rue Vauvert. **[** *02 54 78 70 70.* Eat outside in the pretty square in the summer, and sample unusual salads from the Loire region, fish, veal and a range of tasty *crudités*.	Ⓕ	AE MC V		▪		
BLOIS: *Le Duc de Guise* 15 place Louis XII. **[** *02 54 78 22 39.* A boisterous family-orientated Italian restaurant by the château. Pizzas are cooked in traditional fashion, in wood-fired ovens. 🅱	ⒻⒻ	AE MC V	●	▪		▪
BLOIS: *La Péniche* Promenade du Mail. **[** *02 54 74 37 23.* Located on a beautifully restored barge on the river. Fresh fish is served amid tables adorned with linen and flowers.	ⒻⒻ	AE DC MC V		▪	●	
BOURGES: *La Courcillière* Rue de Babylone. **[** *02 48 24 41 91.* Bordering the marshes with a view over the river Yèrre, it is worth the 20-minute walk from town to enjoy the freshwater fish and duck.	ⒻⒻ	AE MC V	●	▪		▪
BOURGES: *Le Jardin Gourmand* 15 bis, boulevard Ernest-Renan. **[** *02 48 21 35 91.* A gourmet restaurant in an old town house decorated with elegance and style. Specialities include seafood, curried lamb and poultry.	ⒻⒻ	AE MC V		▪	●	▪
BOURGUEIL: *L'Auberge la Lande* Borgueuil. **[** *02 47 97 92 41.* This auberge, set in an old town house, uses only local produce for its simple but delicious dishes. There is a good choice of local Borgueil wines.	ⒻⒻ	MC V		▪	●	
CHARTRES: *Le Buisson Ardent* 10 rue au Lait. **[** *02 37 34 04 66.* With a splendid view of the cathedral, this restaurant is in the oldest part of Chartres. The new chef's baked salmon in vinaigrette and cod in coriander are very tasty.	ⒻⒻ	MC V	●	▪		●
CHARTRES: *Le Grand Monarque* 22 place des Epars. **[** *02 37 21 00 72.* Established in a large farmhouse dating from the 17th century, the interior was refurbished in 1987. The food is variable but can be excellent, and there is a first-rate wine cellar.	ⒻⒻⒻ	AE DC MC V	●	▪	●	▪
CHEVERNY: *Le Pousse-Rapière* Rue Nationale. **[** *02 54 79 94 23.* Facing the château, the restaurant serves dishes from the Loire and Gascony; the Gascon influence shows in the *foie gras* and *cassoulet*.	ⒻⒻ	AE MC V	●	▪	●	
CHINON: *Les Années 30* 78 rue Voltaire. **[** *02 47 93 37 18.* An elegant little eatery on the way up to the château. Pike, pork *rillons* (cooked in fat and served cold) and *coq au vin* are served in an airy dining room, or out on the terrace.	ⒻⒻ	MC V	●	▪	●	▪
FONTEVRAUD-L'ABBAYE: *La Licorne* Allée Sainte-Cathérine. **[** *02 41 51 72 49.* The elegant setting and pretty courtyard, plus the oysters and asparagus, make this a popular place to dine. Reserve tables in summer.	ⒻⒻⒻ	AE DC MC V		▪		▪

GIEN: *Le Rivage*
1 quai de Nice. ☎ *02 38 37 79 00.*
Eat on the flower-lined terrace overlooking the Loire. Sample rich
meat dishes, an interesting cheese board and unusual local wines.
Ⓕ Ⓕ | AE DC MC V

LA BOHALLE: *Auberge de la Gare*
3 impasse de la Gare. ☎ *02 41 80 41 20.*
After a dinner of snails, seafood, steak and good local cheeses
take a stroll down to the riverbank behind this welcoming inn.
Ⓕ | MC V

LAMOTTE-BEUVRON: *Hôtel Tatin*
5 avenue de Vierzon. ☎ *02 54 88 00 03.*
The menu of game, trout and local red wine is overshadowed by this
restaurant's famous dessert, *tarte Tatin* (upside-down apple pie).
Ⓕ Ⓕ | AE DC MC V

LE MANS: *La Cité d'Aleth*
7 & 9 rue de la Vieille Porte. ☎ *02 43 28 73 81.*
A family-run crêperie in Le Vieux Mans, which offers crêpes of all
descriptions, complemented by salads and fruity desserts. ⓑ
Ⓕ | MC V

LE MANS: *Le Grenier à Sel*
26 place de L'Eperon. ☎ *02 43 23 26 30.*
Well-situated for exploring the Old Town, this restaurant specializes
in fish served with light sauces. ⓑ
Ⓕ Ⓕ | AE MC V

LE MANS: *La Vie en Rose*
55 Grand Rue. ☎ *02 43 23 27 37.*
Stone walls and rose-coloured decor create a soft mood. The cuisine
is essentially *nouvelle.* Portions of seafood are beautifully presented.
Ⓕ | AE DC MC V

MONTBAZON: *La Chancelière*
1 place des Marronniers. ☎ *02 47 26 00 67.*
A firm favourite with the locals, the dining room is newly decorated
and offers well-cooked pigs' trotters, sweetbreads and regional fare.
Ⓕ Ⓕ Ⓕ Ⓕ | MC V

NANTES: *La Taverne de Maitre Kanter*
1 place Royale. ☎ *02 40 48 55 28.*
Part of a reliable chain, this Alsatian tavern excels with its offerings
of *choucroute* (sauerkraut) and cold meats. Try the beers, too.
Ⓕ | AE DC MC V

NANTES: *La Cigale*
4 place Graslin. ☎ *02 51 84 94 94.*
The interior of this Belle Epoque brasserie is decorated with tiles
and gilding; the quality and choice of cuisine are also exceptional.
Ⓕ Ⓕ | MC V

NANTES: *Torigai*
Ile de Versailles. ☎ *02 40 37 06 37.*
On an island in the river Erdre, in a conservatory full of exotic plants,
sample the incomparable blending of Oriental and French cooking. ⓑ
Ⓕ Ⓕ Ⓕ Ⓕ | AE MC V

ORLÉANS: *Auberge de la Croix Blanche*
Marcilly-en-Villette. ☎ *02 38 76 10 14.*
Twenty km (12 miles) south of Orléans, discover an auberge offering
delicate fish, satisfying cheeses, dessert trolley and good Sauvignon wine.
Ⓕ Ⓕ | MC V

ORLÉANS: *La Chancellerie*
27 place du Martroi. ☎ *02 38 53 57 54.*
This brasserie is on the town's main square and draws people in
with its liveliness. Staple brasserie fare is enlivened by the wines.
Ⓕ Ⓕ | AE MC V

ORLÉANS: *La Tête de l'Art*
Cloître St-Pierre-Empont. ☎ *02 38 54 14 39.*
An enthusiastic young clientele makes the atmosphere animated here.
The *tête de veau, coq au vin* and vast salads are very good value. ⓑ
Ⓕ | MC V

SACHÉ: *Auberge du XII Siécle*
Rue Principal. ☎ *02 47 26 88 77.*
In an old, listed building in the centre of town, regional specialities such
as *sandre* (a local fish) and *escargots* are on the menu.
Ⓕ Ⓕ Ⓕ | AE MC V

SAUMUR: *Auberge St-Pierre*
6 place St-Pierre. ☎ *02 41 51 26 25.*
This auberge is hidden in an old-fashioned square near the château.
Their regional specialities include pike in butter and *coq au vin.* ⓑ
Ⓕ | AE MC V

Average prices for a three-course meal for one, including a half-bottle of house wine, tax and service: Ⓕ under F150 ⒻⒻ F150–F250 ⒻⒻⒻ F250–F350 ⒻⒻⒻⒻ F350–F500 ⒻⒻⒻⒻⒻ over F500	**CHILDREN'S FACILITIES** Some restaurants have high chairs and offer smaller portions for children. **FIXED-PRICE MENU** A good-value fixed-price menu on offer at lunch, dinner or both, usually with three courses. **GOOD WINE LIST** Denotes a wide range of good wines, or a more specialized selection of local wines. **OUTDOOR TABLES** Facilities for eating outdoors, on a terrace, or in a garden or courtyard, often with a good view.	**CREDIT CARDS**	**CHILDREN'S FACILITIES**	**FIXED-PRICE MENU**	**GOOD WINE LIST**	**OUTDOOR TABLES**
SAUMUR: *Les Caves de Marson* Ⓕ Rou-Marson. 〔 *02 41 50 50 05.* Booking is essential at this troglodyte restaurant, with a fixed-price menu including pancakes with beans and goat's cheese.		MC V	●	▪		
TOURS: *La Renaissance* ⒻⒻ 64 rue Colbert. 〔 *02 47 66 63 25.* Exposed beams and low lighting create the ambience here. The cuisine is classic French with a sprinkling of regional favourites.		MC V	●	▪	●	
TOURS: *Les Naiades* ⒻⒻ 63 rue Blaise Pascal. 〔 *02 47 05 27 92.* The dining room has recently been renovated in Louis XV style. The pan-roasted prawns and pigeon in couscous should not be missed.		MC V	●	▪	●	
TOURS: *La Roche Le Roy* ⒻⒻⒻⒻ 55 rue de St-Avertin. 〔 *02 47 27 22 00.* Another Michelin-starred establishment, rather formal in a romantic manor house. The emphasis is on seasonal fish and game. 〔		AE MC V	●	▪	●	▪
TOURS: *Jean Bardet* ⒻⒻⒻⒻⒻ 57 rue Groisson. 〔 *02 47 41 41 11.* The gastronomic temple of the Loire. With two Michelin stars and a dazzling wine list, diners revel in oysters, lobster, scallops and truffles of all kinds. Prices are better not taken into consideration!		AE DC MC V	●	▪	●	
TOURS: *Barrier* ⒻⒻⒻⒻ 101 avenue de la Tranchée. 〔 *02 47 54 20 39.* Having been excellent, this restaurant is now slipping, but worth a visit for the pot-roasted langoustines.		AE MC V	●	▪		
VENDOME: *Le Vieux Moulin* Ⓕ 21–23 rue du Change. 〔 *02 54 72 29 10.* Set in a well-converted mill, the brasserie is better known for its ambience than the strength of its pleasant, but unexceptional, food.		MC V	●	▪		▪
VILLANDRY: *Domaine de la Giraudière* Ⓕ Route de Druye. 〔 *02 47 50 08 60.* A roadside working farm ideal for a countrified lunch. The food is all home-grown or made: pâtés, stuffed tomatoes, quiches and omelettes.				▪		▪
VOUVRAY: *La Cave Martin* Ⓕ 66 vallée Coquette. 〔 *02 47 52 62 18.* Carved into the rocks around wine caves, this restaurant has a typical rustic menu of *andouillettes* (tripe sausages), duck and salads.		AE MC V	●	▪		▪
BURGUNDY AND FRANCHE-COMTÉ						
BEAUNE: *La Bouzerotte* ⒻⒻ Bouze les Beaune. 〔 *03 80 26 01 37.* In winter, a roaring fire makes this the cosiest place in Burgundy. In summer, enjoy the warm evenings and the cuisine on the terrace. The hearty regional dishes are all cooked to order.		MC V	●	▪		▪
BEAUNE: *La Ciboullette* ⒻⒻ 69 rue Lorraine. 〔 *03 80 24 70 72.* The basic decor is in contrast with the standard of bistro cooking, which is the best value in Beaune. Solid, simple dishes include steak and pork.		MC V	●	▪		
BEAUNE: *Le Gourmandin* ⒻⒻ 8 place Carnot. 〔 *03 80 24 07 88.* A stainless steel modern interior is warmed by the buzzing crowds. The chef provides good, satisfying bistro cooking like *boeuf bourguignon*.		MC V		▪		▪

BEAUNE: *Les Coquines* ⓕⓕ AE DC MC V
Ladoix Serrigny. 🄲 *03 80 26 43 58.*
Feast on solid Burgundy cooking, with the emphasis on quantity. The
restaurant is located in a vineyard and the wines are exceptional.

BEAUNE: *Jean Crotet* ⓕⓕⓕ AE DC MC V
Route de Combertault, Levernois. 🄲 *03 80 24 73 58.*
"Serious" cuisine is served up in a beautiful old mansion. The Bresse
chicken and braised spiced sweetbreads are carefully cooked. 🄰

CHAGNY: *Château de Bellecroix* ⓕⓕⓕ AE DC MC V
Route Nationale 6. 🄲 *03 85 87 13 86.*
This charming mansion was once the property of the Order of the
Knights of Malta and boasts a Neo-Gothic dining room. Local
dishes are a speciality and the desserts are mouth-watering. 🄰

CHAGNY: *Lameloise* ⓕⓕⓕⓕ AE MC V
36 place d'Armes. 🄲 *03 85 87 08 85.*
The cheapest Michelin three-star restaurant in France, this family-
run restaurant is not in the slightest pretentious. It exudes warmth
and offers classic Burgundy cooking, done to perfection.

CHATEAUNEUF: *La Fontaine* ⓕⓕ AE MC V
Chateauneuf. 🄲 *03 85 26 26 87.*
An extravagant pink and pistachio mosaic interior sets the scene for
inventive and flavoursome interpretations of traditional dishes.

CHATEAUNEUF: *Hostellerie du Château* ⓕⓕⓕ AE MC V
Chateauneuf. 🄲 *03 80 49 22 00.*
Set in a picturesque medieval village, this modestly priced inn is simple
and welcoming. The straightforward food is good value for money.

DIJON: *Le Bistrot des Halles* ⓕⓕ MC V
10 rue Bannelier. 🄲 *03 80 49 94 15.*
At lunchtime, this bistro is roaring. Next to the market, it attracts all
sorts of food merchants and local business people, who come here
to enjoy fish pâté, steak tartare and grilled lamb chops.

DIJON: *Le Chabrot* ⓕⓕ V
36 rue Monge. 🄲 *03 80 30 69 61.*
The cosy interior and chatty owner make this restaurant as popular as
the good fixed-price menu. Burgundy wine is served by the glass.

DIJON: *Breuil La Chouette* ⓕⓕ AE DC MC V
1 rue de la Chouette. 🄲 *03 80 30 18 10.*
An exponent of "old school" cuisine, the chef has injected new life
into classics such as frogs' legs and salmon. Huge cellar
of Burgundy wines. 🄰

DIJON: *Jean-Pierre Billoux* ⓕⓕⓕ AE MC V
13 place de la Libération. 🄲 *03 80 38 05 05.*
Run by the most renowned chef in Dijon, its cooking effectively
combines rustic traditional ingredients with novel flavours. 🄰

FONTANGY: *Ferme Auberge de la Morvandelle* ⓕ
Précy-sous-Thil. 🄲 *03 80 84 33 32.*
This is a working farm, open to guests only at the weekend. Book in
advance to experience rabbit, guinea fowl and home-made tarts. 🄰

GEVREY-CHAMBERTIN: *Le Bon Bistrot* ⓕⓕ V
Rue de Chambertin. 🄲 *03 80 34 33 20.*
Mouthwatering Burgundian delicacies are served at very reasonable
prices for this region. On fine days you can dine on the terrace.

GEVREY-CHAMBERTIN: *La Sommellerie* ⓕⓕⓕ MC V
7 rue Souvert. 🄲 *03 80 34 31 48.*
Stylish service and regional cuisine meet in a wine-coloured dining
room. Salmon ravioli with caviar and the Côtes de Nuit wine are a must.

GEVREY-CHAMBERTIN: *Les Millésimes* ⓕⓕⓕⓕ DC MC V
25 rue de l'Eglise. 🄲 *03 80 51 84 24.*
This family concern, in a wine-making cellar, provides friendly service,
exotic cuisine and wonderful wines. Veal, sweetbreads, truffles and
a superb cheese board make it a firm favourite with all who visit.

For key to symbols see back flap

Average prices for a three-course meal for one, including a half-bottle of house wine, tax and service:
- Ⓕ under F150
- ⒻⒻ F150–F250
- ⒻⒻⒻ F250–F350
- ⒻⒻⒻⒻ F350–F500
- ⒻⒻⒻⒻⒻ over F500

CHILDREN'S FACILITIES
Some restaurants have high chairs and offer smaller portions for children.

FIXED-PRICE MENU
A good-value fixed-price menu on offer at lunch, dinner or both, usually with three courses.

GOOD WINE LIST
Denotes a wide range of good wines, or a more specialized selection of local wines.

OUTDOOR TABLES
Facilities for eating outdoors, on a terrace, or in a garden or courtyard, often with a good view.

	CREDIT CARDS	CHILDREN'S FACILITIES	FIXED-PRICE MENU	GOOD WINE LIST	OUTDOOR TABLES
LA CROIX-BLANCHE: *Le Relais Mâconnais* ⒻⒻ Berze la Ville. ☏ 03 85 36 60 72. Burgundy beef cooked with red Mâcon wine, and slices of duck liver in strawberry vinegar are on the menu of this acclaimed restaurant. ♿	AE DC MC V	●	■		■
MARCIGNY SOUS THIL: *L'Auberge Pénélopé* Ⓕ Marcigny. ☏ 03 80 64 52 34. A country inn on a quiet backroad. The unprepossessing exterior hides culinary invention at very reasonable prices. Worth a detour. ♿	MC V		■		
MEURSAULT: *Relais de la Diligence* Ⓕ 23 rue de la Gare. ☏ 03 80 21 21 32. In a drab location by an old station, the Relais bulges with locals on Sunday lunchtimes. The quantity and quality of dishes such as *coq au vin* and *boeuf bourguignon* is superb. ♿	AE DC MC V	●	■		
NITRY: *La Beursaudière* ⒻⒻ Chemin de Ronde. ☏ 03 86 33 62 51. The staff wear peasant costume. A full four-course meal – plainly presented but very appetizing – is served at a reasonable price. ♿	AE DC MC V	●	■		■
QUARRÉ-LES-TOMBES: *Auberge de l'Atre* ⒻⒻⒻⒻ Les Lavaults. ☏ 03 86 32 20 79. The decorative interior of this restaurant in the Morvan region contrasts with the rustic simplicity of the building. It is known locally to offer the best value in its price range. ♿	AE DC MC V	●	■		
RABOLIOT: *Le Raboliot* Ⓕ Place Marché. ☏ 02 38 97 44 52. In a village just off the A6, the style here is an eclectic mixture of Corsican and French cooking, with hefty portions of game in season.	MC V	●	■		
SAINTE-MAGNANCE: *La Chenevotte* ⒻⒻ Route Nationale 6. ☏ 03 86 33 14 79. A simple country inn with no pretensions. The decor is wooden and rustic, and the food is heartwarming. Go for Burgundy specialities like *coq au vin*.	MC V	●	■		
ST-LAURENT-SUR-SAÔNE: *Le St-Laurent* ⒻⒻ 1 quai Bouchacourt. ☏ 03 85 39 29 19. 1900s kitsch fills George Blanc's city bistro, which serves adventurous versions of local specialities. The white Mâcon wine is good value. ♿	AE MC V	●	■		■
ST-PÈRE-SOUS-VÉZELAY: *Le Pré des Marguerites* ⒻⒻ St-Père-sous-Vézelay. ☏ 03 86 33 20 45. Somewhat antiseptic inside, this annexe to *L'Espérance* offers up a rustic menu of traditional Burgundian dishes in a cold environment. ♿	AE MC V	●	■		■
ST-PÈRE-SOUS-VÉZELAY: *L'Espérance* ⒻⒻⒻⒻⒻ St-Père-sous-Vézelay. ☏ 03 86 33 39 10. Arguably the greatest eating experience in Burgundy. An airy dining room leads on to a terrace with expansive views. Marc Meneau, one of France's finest chefs, turns traditional dishes into modern classics. ♿	AE DC MC V	●	■	●	
SAULIEU: *La Poste* ⒻⒻ 1 rue Grillot. ☏ 03 80 64 05 67. This is a former coaching inn with well-preserved charm. Try sole and turbot *terrine* or pigeon in truffle juice, along with good local wines. ♿	AE DC MC V	●	■	●	
SAULIEU: *La Côte d'Or* ⒻⒻⒻⒻⒻ 2 rue d'Argentine. ☏ 03 80 64 07 66. Old-fashioned decor misleads here. The chef serves up an imaginative *cuisine moderne*, including rabbit livers, snail and nettle soup and perch in wine. Very sumptuous with an extensive wine list.	AE DC MC V	●	■	●	

SINCEY-LES-ROUVRAY: *Ferme Auberge de la Mothe* Ⓕ
Sincey-les-Rouvray. **[** *03 80 64 71 13.*
A 15th-century château run as a family *ferme auberge*. Open only at
weekends, it offers fresh, home-produced country food. **&**

TOURNUS: *Restaurant Greuze* ⒻⒻⒻⒻ *AE MC V*
1 rue A Thibaudet. **[** *03 85 51 09 11.*
Here's the place to enjoy some of the best classic cooking in France.
The restaurant is a monument to a bygone age, serving cognac-infused
quenelles, buttery frogs' legs and creamy choux pastry starters. **&**

VILLARS-FONTAINE: *Auberge du Coteau* Ⓕ *V*
Villars-Fontaine, D35 W of Nuits St-Georges. **[** *03 80 61 10 50.*
Set among the vineyards of the Haute-Côtes de Nuits, this cosy inn
serves hearty Burgundy fare at great prices.

VILLENEUVE-SUR-YONNE: *Auberge la Lucarne aux Chouettes* ⒻⒻ *AE MC V*
Quai Bretoche. **[** *03 86 87 18 26.*
Renovated by actress Leslie Caron, this restaurant has a lovely setting
by the river Yonne. The staff try very hard to please. **&**

VONNAS: *L'Ancienne Auberge* ⒻⒻⒻ *AE MC V*
Place de Marché. **[** *04 74 50 90 50.*
The clientele is often wealthy Parisians rather than locals. Fancier and
more expensive than most bistros, it is still well worth a visit. **&**

VONNAS: *Georges Blanc* ⒻⒻⒻⒻⒻ *AE DC MC V*
Vonnas. **[** *04 70 50 90 90.*
A popular shrine of cooking, with smooth service in a dining
room crammed with antiques. The inventive menu includes
fish and game. **&**

THE MASSIF CENTRAL

AUMONT-AUBRAC: *Prouhèze* ⒻⒻⒻ *V*
2 route du Languedoc. **[** *04 66 42 80 07.*
The award-winning chef uses only the freshest ingredients to create
elegant and unusual flavours. The presentation is often a little basic. **&**

AURILLAC: *A la Reine Margot* ⒻⒻ *MC V*
19 rue Guy-de-Veyre. **[** *04 71 48 26 46.*
The place to sample the rustic dishes of the Auvergne. The high-
quality hams, pork and beef are the pride of the region.

BESSE-EN-CHANDESSE: *Les Mouflons* ⒻⒻ *AE MC V*
Route de Super-Besse. **[** *04 73 79 56 93.*
The fish is locally caught and delicious; taste the salmon trout or the
turbot with *cèpes*, washed down with lively local Chanturgue red wine.

BOURGES: *Jacques-Coeur* ⒻⒻ *AE DC MC V*
3 place Jacques-Coeur. **[** *02 48 70 12 72.*
Diners enjoy local specialities against a medieval backdrop. The cooking
can be bland; the best bet is the scallops, kidneys or Loire salmon. **&**

BOUSSAC: *Le Relais Creusois* ⒻⒻⒻ *MC V*
Route de la Châtre. **[** *05 55 65 02 20.*
Expect the luxury here to come from the high standard of cuisine, not
the surroundings. The desserts are exquisite, as are the Bordeaux wines.

CLERMONT-FERRAND: *Le Chardonnay* Ⓕ *V*
1 place Philippe-Marcombes. **[** *04 73 90 18 28.*
As well as enjoying hearty Auvergne cuisine, wine-lovers can consult
the *patron-sommelier* for his selection from the wide range of superb
wines, many of which can be sampled by the glass.

CLERMONT-FERRAND: *Le Charade* ⒻⒻ *AE DC MC V*
51 rue Bonnabaud. **[** *04 73 93 59 69.*
The new chef is gaining confidence and making tasty salads, duck and
a range of delicious desserts. The fixed-price menu includes wine. **&**

ESPALION: *Le Méjane* ⒻⒻⒻ *AE DC MC V*
8 rue Méjane. **[** *05 65 48 22 37.*
Exceptionally good value for a menu that includes dishes such as
confit of rabbit with *foie gras* and snails with garlic cream. **&**

Average prices for a three-course meal for one, including a half-bottle of house wine, tax and service:
Ⓕ under F150
ⒻⒻ F150–F250
ⒻⒻⒻ F250–F350
ⒻⒻⒻⒻ F350–F500
ⒻⒻⒻⒻⒻ over F500

CHILDREN'S FACILITIES
Some restaurants have high chairs and offer smaller portions for children.

FIXED-PRICE MENU
A good-value fixed-price menu on offer at lunch, dinner or both, usually with three courses.

GOOD WINE LIST
Denotes a wide range of good wines, or a more specialized selection of local wines.

OUTDOOR TABLES
Facilities for eating outdoors, on a terrace, or in a garden or courtyard, often with a good view.

	CREDIT CARDS	CHILDREN'S FACILITIES	FIXED-PRICE MENU	GOOD WINE LIST	OUTDOOR TABLES
LAGUIOLE: *Michel Bras* ⒻⒻⒻⒻ Route de l'Aubrac. ☏ 05 65 44 32 24. A wall of glass gives views over the Aubrac countryside from Michel Bras' hilltop restaurant. The goat's and sheep's cheeses are recommended.	AE DC V	●	■		
LIMOGES: *Philippe Redon* ⒻⒻ 3 rue d'Aguesseau. ☏ 05 55 34 66 22. Philippe Redon offers first-class local ingredients, particularly fish. The dishes are conventional but well-cooked and the wines are good value.	AE DC MC V	●	■	●	
MONTSALVY: *Auberge Fleurie* Ⓕ Place du Barry. ☏ 04 71 49 20 02. A friendly village inn with a cheery atmosphere and a motherly chef who prepares wonderful mushroom omelettes and green salads. ♿	MC V	●	■	●	■
MURAT: *Le Jarrousset* ⒻⒻⒻ Route Nationale 122. ☏ 04 71 20 10 69. This is a discreet, unfussy restaurant. The chef uses local ingredients like green lentils and "free-range" veal, cooked to perfection. ♿	MC V	●	■	●	■
RODEZ: *Le St-Amans* ⒻⒻ 12 rue de la Madeleine. ☏ 05 65 68 03 18. Ttraditional cooking with sophistication – the *cassoulet des fruits de mer* is flavoured with aniseed, the pigeon with a touch of cocoa. ♿	MC V		■		
ROYAT: *La Belle Meunière* ⒻⒻ 25 avenue de la Vallée. ☏ 04 73 35 80 17. The chef, Jean-Claude Bon, won a Gault Millau award for his repertoire of regional dishes. The menu is regularly updated, but the classics include cabbage stuffed with pigs' trotters and *crêpes* with Bleu d'Auvergne cheese. ♿	AE DC MC V	●	■		■
ST-ETIENNE: *Nouvelle* ⒻⒻ 30 rue St-Jean. ☏ 04 77 32 32 60. Elegant setting and attentive staff as well as the culinary treats make this a very popular restaurant. Advance booking is advised to ensure a chance to sample the inventive cuisine.	AE MC V		■		
ST-JEANNE-EN-VAL: *La Bergerie* ⒻⒻ Sarpoil. ☏ 04 73 71 02 54. This restaurant has become a local favourite, so booking is essential in the evening. Choose from an ever-changing, inventive menu. ♿	AE DC MC V	●	■		
ST-JULIEN-CHAPTEUIL: *Vidal* ⒻⒻⒻ Place du Marché. ☏ 04 71 08 70 50. Top quality local produce is served here, and the menus change according to the season. ♿	AE MC V	●	■		
VICHY: *La Veranda* ⒻⒻ 3 place Joseph-Aletti. ☏ 04 70 31 78 77. Part of the Aletti Palace Hotel, La Veranda serves rock lobster, beef and regional cheeses in modern surroundings.	AE DC MC V	●	■		

THE RHÔNE VALLEY AND FRENCH ALPS

	CREDIT CARDS	CHILDREN'S FACILITIES	FIXED-PRICE MENU	GOOD WINE LIST	OUTDOOR TABLES
AIX-LES-BAINS: *Lille* ⒻⒻ Grand-Port. ☏ 04 79 63 40 00. One of the best restaurants in Aix, especially for the elaborate fish dishes. It is close to the landing stages for the lake steamers. ♿	AE DC MC V	●	■		■
BOURG-EN-BRESSE: *Jacques Guy* ⒻⒻⒻ 19 place Bernard. ☏ 04 74 45 29 11. The local speciality, *Bresse* chicken, is perfection, as are the *terrines* and *hors d'oeuvres*. Desserts and wines are also superb. ♿	AE DC MC V	●	■	●	■

CHAMBÉRY: *La Chaumière*   (F)
14 rue Denfert-Rochereau. **[** *04 79 33 16 26.*
A cosy dining room that serves good quality traditional dishes. The
fish, duck and *foie gras* are particular bargains.   *AE MC V*

CHAMBÉRY: *La Vanoise*   (F)(F)
44 av Pierre-Lanfrey. **[** *04 79 69 02 78.*
Fish straight from the region's lakes are accompanied by the delicate
sauces of chef Philippe Lenain. Menus change every 15 days.   *AE MC V*

CHAMONIX: *Albert 1er*   (F)(F)(F)
119 impasse Montenvers. **[** *04 50 53 05 09.*
The superb cooking of chef Pierre Carrier at this one-Michelin-star
restaurant is matched by the wonderful views over Mont Blanc.
The *foie gras* is especially recommended.   *AE DC V*

CHAMONIX: *L'Impossible*   (F)(F)
Route des Pélerins. **[** *04 50 53 20 36.*
Originally a farmhouse, the rustic dining room is warmed by a huge fire.
There is an emphasis on cheese dishes such as traditional *raclette* and
fondue. Entrecôte and tournedos steaks can be ordered too.   *MC V*

COLLONGES-AU-MONT-D'OR: *Paul Bocuse*   (F)(F)(F)(F)
50 quai de la Plage. **[** *04 72 42 90 90.*
Try specialities like black truffle soup with pastry and fillet of sole with
coriander and vanilla butter. The wines are also of a high standard.   *AE DC MC V*

COURCHEVEL: *La Bergerie*   (F)(F)(F)
Route de Nogentil. **[** *04 79 08 24 70.*
Popular with the rich and famous, this is a two-tiered restaurant with
dancing on the ground floor. Lunches and drinks are served upstairs.   *AE MC V*

COURCHEVEL: *Le Chabichou*   (F)(F)(F)
Quartier des Chenus. **[** *04 79 08 00 55.*
Reserve seats by the huge windows to enjoy views of the mountains.
The cuisine is creative and exotic at one of the most popular (but
expensive) restaurants in this extensive resort.   *AE DC MC V*

EVIAN-LES-BAINS: *Savoy*   (F)(F)
17 quai Charles Besson. **[** *04 50 83 15 00.*
The restaurant offers views of the lake and across into Switzerland. The
Savoyard specialities include *fondue* and *gratin dauphinois*.   *AE DC MC V*

GRENOBLE: *Amerindia*   (F)
4 place des Gordes. **[** *04 76 51 58 39.*
A bright and cheerful restaurant on a South American theme, with an
enjoyable choice of vegetarian options on the menu.   *MC V*

GRENOBLE: *Le Berlioz*   (F)(F)(F)
4 rue de Strasbourg. **[** *04 76 56 22 39.*
Housed in an 18th-century mansion, this restaurant features a different
seasonal menu with regional specialities each month.   *AE DC MC V*

LYON: *Le Bouchon aux Vins*   (F)(F)
62 rue Mercière. **[** *04 78 42 88 90.*
A very popular restaurant serving regional cuisine. Try the
charcuterie, rabbit and *pot-au-feu*, with praline tarts for dessert.   *AE MC V*

LYON: *Le Mercière*   (F)(F)
56 rue Mercière. **[** *04 78 37 67 35.*
A busy, top-value restaurant where booking is essential. The fixed-
price menu provides very substantial dishes, and the *à la carte* is a
rare treat. Its offerings include snails, monkfish and mussels.   *AE DC MC V*

LYON: *Léon de Lyon*   (F)(F)(F)(F)
1 rue Pléney. **[** *04 78 28 11 33.*
The expert chef and owner serves local food with a modern twist
in a two-storey building set on the Presqu'Île in the heart of the city.
The menu changes ten times a year.   *AE MC V*

LYON: *La Tour Rose*   (F)(F)(F)(F)(F)
22 rue du Boeuf. **[** *04 78 37 25 90.*
In a Renaissance convent, the chef concentrates on flavoursome fish
and vegetables, also providing a huge cheeseboard and good wines.   *AE DC MC V*

	Credit Cards	Children's Facilities	Fixed-Price Menu	Good Wine List	Outdoor Tables

Average prices for a three-course meal for one, including a half-bottle of house wine, tax and service:
Ⓕ under F150
ⒻⒻ F150–F250
ⒻⒻⒻ F250–F350
ⒻⒻⒻⒻ F350–F500
ⒻⒻⒻⒻⒻ over F500

Children's Facilities
Some restaurants have high chairs and offer smaller portions for children.
Fixed-Price Menu
A good-value fixed-price menu on offer at lunch, dinner or both, usually with three courses.
Good Wine List
Denotes a wide range of good wines, or a more specialized selection of local wines.
Outdoor Tables
Facilities for eating outdoors, on a terrace, or in a garden or courtyard, often with a good view.

Restaurant	Price	Credit Cards	Children's Facilities	Fixed-Price Menu	Good Wine List	Outdoor Tables
MEGÈVE: *Le Chamoix* Place de l'Eglise. ▐ 04 50 21 25 01. A popular restaurant in the centre of town, serving such regional specialities as smoked ham.	Ⓕ	MC V		■		
MEGÈVE: *Les Enfants Terribles* Place de l'Eglise. ▐ 04 50 58 76 69. A refined menu on which expensive ingredients like truffles and *foie gras* are used to brighten up locally inspired dishes. ▐	ⒻⒻ	AE MC V	●	■		■
MORZINE: *La Chamade* Morzine. ▐ 04 50 79 13 91. The extravagant draped design of the dining room is complemented by beautifully presented main courses and delicate, exotic desserts. ▐	ⒻⒻ	AE DC MC V	●			■
PÉROUGES: *Hostellerie du Vieux Pérouges* Place du Tilleul. ▐ 04 74 61 00 88. In a 13th-century timbered building, this restaurant is exceptionally good. Try *Ypocras*, a liqueur made to a recipe from medieval times.	ⒻⒻⒻ	MC V	●	■		
ROANNE: *Chez Troisgros* Place de la Gare. ▐ 04 77 71 66 97. One of the most prestigious restaurants in France, with elegant contemporary decor. Dishes include salmon with sorrel. ▐	ⒻⒻⒻⒻⒻ	AE DC MC V	●	■	●	
TALLOIRES: *Villa des Fleurs* Route du Port. ▐ 04 50 60 71 14. The lake in the grounds here is picturesque, and it also provides the restaurant's main attraction – a rare, succulent fish called *féra*.	ⒻⒻⒻ	MC V	●	■		■
TALLOIRES: *Le Père Bise* Route du Port. ▐ 04 50 60 72 01. A mixture of locals and wealthy tourists gather to worship at one of France's gastronomic shrines. The faultless food and panoramic views of the garden and lake somewhat offset the horror of the prices! ▐	ⒻⒻⒻⒻⒻ	AE DC MC V	●	■		■
THONON-LES-BAINS: *Le Belvédère* 3 rue des Ursules. ▐ 04 50 71 75 64. Close to the shores of Lac Léman, Le Belvédère mainly serves *feuilletés*, light, flaky pastries filled with meat and vegetables in various styles.	Ⓕ	MC V	●	■		
VALANCE: *Restaurant Pic* 285 avenue Victor-Hugo. ▐ 04 75 44 15 32. Fillet of sea bass in caviar, *charolais* beef and intricate desserts have helped the reputation of this establishment to grow. ▐	ⒻⒻⒻⒻⒻ	AE DC MC V		■	●	
VIENNE: *Magnard* 45 cours Brillier. ▐ 04 74 85 10 43. Traditional cuisine includes fillet of turbot with mussels, tournedos in a morel-flavoured sauce and chicken with shrimp. ▐	ⒻⒻ	MC V	●	■		■

POITOU AND AQUITAINE

Restaurant	Price	Credit Cards	Children's Facilities	Fixed-Price Menu	Good Wine List	Outdoor Tables
ANGOULÊME: *Auberge du Pont de la Meure* Nersac. ▐ 05 45 90 60 48. A combined café-restaurant beside the Charente river. Salads of chicken livers, stewed eel and goat in garlic are worth a special trip.	ⒻⒻ	AE DC MC V		■	●	
BORDEAUX: *La Mamounia* 51 rue Lafourie-Monbadon. ▐ 05 56 81 21 84. A draped ceiling lends a tent-like atmosphere to this smart Moroccan restaurant, which is a haven for vegetarians. Couscous is the main item on the menu. Sweet mint tea is served with your meal. ▐	Ⓕ	AE DC MC V				

BORDEAUX: *La Tupina* ⓕⓕ — AE DC MC V
6 rue Porte de la Monnaie. **☎** 05 56 91 56 37.
Dishes are cooked over an open fire in a friendly atmosphere. Bistro
food predominates, such as charcoal-grilled poultry and *pétoucles* (scallops).

BORDEAUX: *Chez Philippe* ⓕⓕⓕ — AE DC MC V
1 place du Parlement. **☎** 05 56 81 83 15.
A casual, lively spot specializing in fresh fish and shellfish, with the
deserved reputation of being the best fish restaurant in Bordeaux.

BORDEAUX: *Le Clavel St-Jean* ⓕⓕ — MC V
44 rue Charles-Domercq. **☎** 05 56 92 63 07.
This modern bistro is one of the few places where Bordeaux wine can
be sampled by the glass. The menus are good and varied. ♿

BORDEAUX: *Le Chapon Fin* ⓕⓕⓕⓕ — AE DC MC V
5 rue de Montesquieu. **☎** 05 56 79 10 10.
Thick, meaty soup with chunks of pigeon and chestnuts, rich eel and
red wine stew and local oysters are some of the treats in store here. ♿

BOULIAC: *Le Bistroy* ⓕⓕ — AE DC MC V
3 place Camille-Hostein. **☎** 04 57 97 06 06.
This buzzing place gets its food from the neighbouring top restaurant
St-James, meaning the same sensational cuisine at lower price. ♿

COGNAC: *Les Pigeons Blancs* ⓕⓕ — AE DC MC V
110 rue Jules Brisson. **☎** 05 45 82 16 36.
Owned by the same family since the 18th century, this old post house
is an attractive place to eat. The service, wine and food are excellent. ♿

CROUTELLE: *La Chenaie* ⓕⓕ — AE MC V
Ligugé. **☎** 05 49 57 11 52.
Deep in the Poitevin hills, this cheery farmhouse offers tasty *salade
de langouste*, rabbit with artichokes and rich local goat's cheese. ♿

ILE DE RÉ: *Café du Phare* ⓕ — MC V
St-Clément-des-Baleines. **☎** 05 46 29 46 66.
A café beneath the lighthouse serves the local speciality, *poutargue*
(cod's roe, shallots and sour cream), in Art Deco surroundings. ♿

JARNAC: *Restaurant du Château* ⓕⓕ — AE MC V
15 place du Château. **☎** 05 45 81 07 17.
A traditional establishment, immensely popular with the locals, which
produces prawn salads, sea bass and cabbage stuffed with rabbit.

LANGON: *Claude Darroze* ⓕⓕⓕⓕ — AE DC MC V
95 cours du Général Leclerc. **☎** 05 56 63 00 48.
Gaudy *trompe l'oeil* decor should not detract from the generosity and
quality of the food, best washed down with a premium local claret. ♿

LA ROCHELLE: *Yachtman* ⓕⓕⓕ — AE DC MC V
23 quai Valin. **☎** 05 46 50 63 14.
Diners enjoy fresh seafood in comfortable portside surroundings. The
cellar has a small but choice range of local wines.

LA ROCHELLE: *Richard Coutanceau* ⓕⓕⓕⓕ — AE DC MC V
Plage de la Concurrence. **☎** 05 46 41 48 19.
Overlooking the beach, this is a big, bright restaurant run by a rising
young chef. Simple, authentic dishes combine with exotic desserts. ♿

MARGAUX: *Le Savoie* ⓕⓕ — V
Rue de la Poste. **☎** 05 57 88 31 76.
This little town house, next to a *maison du vin*, offers good-value
menus made up of simple yet original dishes, with fish as a speciality. ♿

MIMIZAN: *Au Bon Coin du Lac* ⓕⓕⓕⓕ — AE MC V
34 avenue du Lac. **☎** 05 58 09 01 55.
Plushness and luxury abound at this lakeside eatery. There are views
of the lake from both the dining room and pretty terrace. ♿

NIORT: *Les Mangeux du Lumas* ⓕⓕ — MC V
La Garette. **☎** 05 49 35 93 42.
Sample a favourite local treat, *lumas* – tiny snails – bathed in butter,
cream or a regional aperitif known as *pineau des Charentes*. ♿

Average prices for a three-course meal for one, including a half-bottle of house wine, tax and service:
- Ⓕ under F150
- ⒻⒻ F150–F250
- ⒻⒻⒻ F250–F350
- ⒻⒻⒻⒻ F350–F500
- ⒻⒻⒻⒻⒻ over F500

CHILDREN'S FACILITIES
Some restaurants have high chairs and offer smaller portions for children.

FIXED-PRICE MENU
A good-value fixed-price menu on offer at lunch, dinner or both, usually with three courses.

GOOD WINE LIST
Denotes a wide range of good wines, or a more specialized selection of local wines.

OUTDOOR TABLES
Facilities for eating outdoors, on a terrace, or in a garden or courtyard, often with a good view.

	CREDIT CARDS	CHILDREN'S FACILITIES	FIXED-PRICE MENU	GOOD WINE LIST	OUTDOOR TABLES
PAUILLAC: *Château Cordeillan-Bages* ⒻⒻⒻⒻ Route des Châteaux. ☎ 05 56 59 24 24. The award-winning wine waiter at this establishment, right in the heart of Bordeaux country, will guide you through the extensive wine list to find the perfect accompaniment to a splendid meal. ♿	AE DC MC V	●	■	●	■
POITIERS: *Maxime* ⒻⒻ 4 rue St-Nicholas. ☎ 05 49 41 09 55. A chic restaurant for sophisticated palates. Dishes include tender duck in delicious Hungarian Tokay wine, monkfish and ravioli of hot oysters.	AE MC V		■		
ROYAN: *La Jabotière* ⒻⒻⒻ Pontaillac. ☎ 05 46 39 91 29. Modern cuisine is offered in a renovated beachfront restaurant. Choose the ravioli of rabbit in pistachio oil, fresh sole and apple gratin. ♿	AE MC V	●	■		■
ST-EMILION: *Hostellerie de Plaisance* ⒻⒻ Place du Clocher. ☎ 05 57 24 72 32. Enjoy the view over the roofs of the medieval town and sample good regional cuisine along with superb wines from across the country. ♿	AE DC MC V	●	■	●	
SAINTES: *Brasserie Louis* ⒻⒻ 116 avenue Gambetta. ☎ 05 46 74 16 85. A local favourite, this is a crowded brasserie serving wonderful seafood – the *fruits de mer* are a must. Very good value.	V	●	■		■

PÉRIGORD, QUERCY AND GASCONY

	CREDIT CARDS	CHILDREN'S FACILITIES	FIXED-PRICE MENU	GOOD WINE LIST	OUTDOOR TABLES
ALBI: *Hostellerie du Vigan* ⒻⒻ 16 place Vigan. ☎ 05 63 54 01 23. An unpretentious and inexpensive, rather business-like place to eat, which produces good local dishes at remarkable value. ♿	AE DC MC V	●	■		
ALBI: *Le Moulin de la Mothe* ⒻⒻ Rue de la Mothe. ☎ 05 63 60 38 15. The restaurant is close to the cathedral in pretty grounds. Its typical Tarn dishes include perch fillets and roast pigeon. ♿	AE MC V	●	■	●	■
AUCH: *L'Auberge de Lartigue* Ⓕ Saramon. ☎ 05 62 65 41 22. Don't be put off by appearances – this is wonderful, off-the-beaten-track Gascony. The *foie gras* comes in a variety of forms, all superb. ♿		●	■		■
AUCH: *Restaurant Roland Garreau* ⒻⒻⒻⒻⒻ 2 place de la Libération. ☎ 05 62 61 71 71. Avoid the experimental nature of some of the dishes and stay with the classics – *assiette des trois foie gras*, fresh goose and sweet wines.	AE DC MC V	●	■	●	
BARBOTAN-LES-THERMES: *La Bastide Gasconne* ⒻⒻ Barbotan-les-Thermes. ☎ 05 62 08 31 00. The reputation of this restaurant is going up with the locals, always a good sign. Flawless dishes such as "pizza" of asparagus tips and mushrooms, sweetbreads and tuna marinated with green olives are served impeccably.	AE MC V	●	■		■
BERGERAC: *Le Cyrano* ⒻⒻ 2 boulevard Montaigne. ☎ 05 53 57 02 76. Copious and enticing regional food at a premium – a fixed-price menu of astonishing value. Wash it all down with local Bergerac wines.	AE DC MC V	●	■	●	
BRANTÔME: *Les Frères Charbonnel* ⒻⒻⒻ 57 rue Gambetta. ☎ 05 53 05 70 15. Bargain-priced wines, hearty salad, red mullet in lobster sauce and *foie gras* can be enjoyed while watching the ducks on the Dronne. ♿	AE DC MC V	●	■	●	■

BRANTÔME: *Moulin de L'Abbaye*   ⓕⓕⓕⓕ   AE DC V
1 route de Bourdeilles. 【 05 53 05 80 22.
Dine in luxury on traditional Perigord cooking complemented
by dishes such as *terrine* of brill. 🔊 🍽

BRANTÔME: *Le Moulin du Roc*   ⓕⓕⓕⓕ   AE DC MC V
Champagnac-de-Belair. 【 05 53 02 86 00.
A converted oil mill in a romantic spot overlooking the river Dronne.
The cooking is inconsistent but the fish is recommended. 🔊

CAHORS: *Le Troquet des Halles*   ⓕ   MC V
55 rue St-Maurice. 【 05 65 22 15 81.
This is a locals' restaurant right beside the market. The food is robust
and good – with a very cheap fixed-price menu. 🔊

CAHORS: *Claude Marco*   ⓕⓕ   AE V
Lamagdelaine. 【 05 65 35 30 64.
A rustic restaurant with a cosy oak-beamed dining room and a delightful
terrace. An abundance of regional specialities are on offer, such as *foie gras*.

CAHORS: *Le Balandre*   ⓕⓕⓕ   AE MC V
5 avenue Charles-de-Freycinet. 【 05 65 30 01 97.
An immaculate dining room where you can enjoy generous helpings
of typical southwestern fare and a good selection of Cahors wines. 🔊

DOMME: *L'Esplanade*   ⓕⓕⓕⓕ   AE MC V
Place de la Barre. 【 05 53 28 31 41.
Avoid high prices here by sticking to trout, salmon or rack of lamb.
There are panoramic views from the huge yellow-and-blue restaurant. 🔊

LES-EYZIES-DE-TAYAC: *Cro-Magnon*   ⓕⓕⓕ   AE DC MC V
Les Eyzies-de-Tayac. 【 05 53 06 97 06.
An old-fashioned, vine-covered restaurant with beams and a giant fire-
place. *Foie gras*, pigeon and goose feature on a good regional menu. 🔊

MARMANDE: *Restaurant Trianon*   ⓕⓕ   MC V
Route d'Agen. 【 05 53 20 80 94.
Fresh produce such as monkfish, pigeon and the house speciality of
lamprey eel from the river Garonne are on offer here. 🔊

MONTAUBAN: *Le Ventadour*   ⓕⓕ   MC V
23 quai Villebourbon. 【 05 63 63 34 58.
A popular place with the local townspeople, who appreciate the plain
cooking and reasonable prices at this central restaurant.

MONTFORT-CAUDON: *La Ferme*   ⓕⓕ   MC V
Caudon-de-Vitrac. 【 05 53 28 33 35.
It is worth a detour to sample the rustic charm of this restored farmhouse.
Rye bread soup, thick ham and lamb chops come in huge portions.

MONTRÉAL-DU-GERS: *Chez Simone*   ⓕⓕⓕ   AE DC MC V
Montréal-du-Gers. 【 05 62 29 44 40.
Another restaurant very much admired by people in the know, due to
the generous helpings of excellent locally produced *foie gras*.

PERIGUEUX: *Au Petit Chef*   ⓕ   DC MC V
5 place du Coderc. 【 05 53 53 16 03.
Choose the lowest price menu, comprising soup, a buffet of hors d'oeuvres,
main course, and pâtisserie – all home-made. Shut on Saturday evenings.

PÉRIGUEUX: *Hôtel-Restaurant Périgord*   ⓕⓕ   V
74 rue Victor-Hugo. 【 05 53 53 33 63.
A delightful hotel, set in a leafy garden, serving highly regarded cuisine,
in its charmingly old-fashioned dining room. 🔊

POUDENAS: *A La Belle Gasconne*   ⓕⓕⓕ   AE DC MC V
Poudenas. 【 05 53 65 71 58.
Set in a 13th-century mill, the dining room is built over the river. The
food is similarly spectacular; try the pike, *foie gras*, pork and pigeon.

PUYMIROL: *Les Loges de l'Aubergade*   ⓕⓕⓕⓕ   AE DC MC V
52 rue Royale. 【 05 53 95 31 46.
One of the great restaurants of the southwest, this is not to be missed.
The beautiful medieval building on a hilltop adds to the wonder. 🔊

Average prices for a three-course meal for one, including a half-bottle of house wine, tax and service:
Ⓕ under F150
ⒻⒻ F150–F250
ⒻⒻⒻ F250–F350
ⒻⒻⒻⒻ F350–F500
ⒻⒻⒻⒻⒻ over F500

CHILDREN'S FACILITIES
Some restaurants have high chairs and offer smaller portions for children.
FIXED-PRICE MENU
A good-value fixed-price menu on offer at lunch, dinner or both, usually with three courses.
GOOD WINE LIST
Denotes a wide range of good wines, or a more specialized selection of local wines.
OUTDOOR TABLES
Facilities for eating outdoors, on a terrace, or in a garden or courtyard, often with a good view.

	CREDIT CARDS	CHILDREN'S FACILITIES	FIXED-PRICE MENU	GOOD WINE LIST	OUTDOOR TABLES
ROCAMADOUR: *Jehan de Valon* ⒻⒻⒻ Cité Médiévale. 【 05 65 33 63 08. There are great views from this restaurant in the pedestrianized medieval town centre. Lamb and duck liver are specialities.	AE DC MC V	●	■		■
TOULOUSE: *A la Truffe de Quercy* Ⓕ 17 rue Croix-Baragnon. 【 05 61 53 34 24. Traditional recipes have been handed down from father to son for 70 years in this rustic family restaurant. Try the *cassoulet.* 🖢	MC V		■		
TOULOUSE: *La Côte de Bœuf* ⒻⒻ 12 rue des Gestes. 【 05 61 21 19 61. Small, efficient and supremely friendly restaurant offering huge steaks and known for its generous portions. The best value in town. 🖢	MC V		■		■
TOULOUSE: *Brasserie des Beaux-Arts* ⒻⒻⒻ 1 quai de la Daurade. 【 05 61 21 12 12. An authentic brasserie serving local dishes. There is always a queue. Try the oysters with house Riesling wine. 🖢	AE DC MC V	●	■	●	■
TOULOUSE: *Les Jardins de l'Opéra (D. Toulousy)* ⒻⒻⒻⒻ 1 place du Capitole. 【 05 61 23 07 76. Without question one of the best places to eat in Toulouse. Found in a pretty courtyard in the middle of town, it produces great local cuisine.	AE DC MC V		■	●	■
VILLEFRANCHE-DE-LAURAGAIS: *Hôtel de France* Ⓕ 106 rue de la République. 【 05 61 81 62 17. You are in *cassoulet* country here, and this 19th-century auberge prides itself on its reputation for making one of the best and most authentic in the region.	AE DC MC V	●	■		

THE PYRENEES

AINHOA: *Ithurria* ⒻⒻⒻ Ainhoa. 【 05 59 29 92 11. In the prettiest village of the Basque region, this eatery serves delicious local fare such as lamb and purée of salt cod, with rosé Rioja wines.	AE DC MC V	●	■		
ARCANGUES: *Moulin d'Alotz* ⒻⒻⒻ Arcangues. 【 05 59 43 04 54. A well-converted mill where the chef offers light country cooking such as pan-fried langoustine and turbot roasted with ceps. 🖢	MC V	●	■		■
ARGELÈS-GAZOST: *Hostellerie le Relais* ⒻⒻ 25 rue du Maréchal-Foch. 【 05 62 97 01 27. The excellent value of the fixed-price menu makes this worth a detour; wide views of the mountains and reasonable wines add to the charm.	MC V	●	■		■
AUDRESSEIN: *l'Auberge d'Audressein* ⒻⒻ Route de Luchon. 【 05 61 96 11 80. This family-run logis is housed in a converted 19th-century forge and serves some of the best local cuisine around, with game and *foie gras* strongly featured.	AE DC MC V	●	■	●	■
BAYONNE: *Euzkalduna* Ⓕ 61 rue Pannecau. 【 05 59 59 28 02. This is the place to try the aromatic, spicy, often peppery dishes that characterize Basque cuisine. The fish soup is excellent as are the fried squid and mussels in vinaigrette. It is open for lunch only.				●	
BIARRITZ: *Les Platanes* ⒻⒻ 32 avenue Beausoleil. 【 05 59 23 13 68. Top-flight cooking, using only fresh products, in a friendly setting. The dining room will only seat 20 and it is advisable to book ahead. 🖢	AE MC V	●	■		

BIARRITZ: *Ramona*
5 rue Centre. **[** *05 59 24 34 66.*
Enjoy the very good value, wide-ranging fixed-price menus in a Belle
Epoque brasserie. The local wines are of a high calibre. **&**

CIBOURE: *Arrantzaleak*
Avenue Jean-Poulou. **[** *05 59 47 10 75.*
An unassuming seafront building hides a dream. Wonderfully fresh fish
is grilled on the open fire dominating the no-frills dining room. **&**

ESPELETTE: *Euzkadi*
Espelette. **[** *05 59 93 91 88.*
The locals gather here on Sundays for their favourite seasonal game,
salmon, peppers, omelette, blood sausage and substantial Rioja wines.

EUGÉNIE-LES-BAINS: *Les Prés d'Eugénie-Michel Guérard*
Eugénie-les-Bains. **[** *05 58 05 06 07.*
The creator of *cuisine minceur* is chef here. Choose from a low-calorie
menu or a truly gourmet, richer one. All desserts are made to order. **&**

GUÉTHARY-BIDART: *Les Frères Ibarboure*
Chemin de Talienia. **[** *05 59 54 81 64.*
In an 18th-century manor amid woods, this is a rare treat – the regional
fare is full-flavoured and faultless. The bill is surprisingly light. **&**

JURANÇON: *Ruffet*
3 avenue Chateau-Touzet. **[** *05 59 06 25 13.*
Good, traditional cuisine, a warm welcome and amiable service entice
diners to return. The duck comes in a number of guises, all delicious. **&**

PAU: *La Gousse d'Ail*
12 rue du Hédas. **[** *05 59 27 31 55.*
A pleasant, brick and stucco restaurant with beams and a big fireplace.
Its excellent value makes it stand out in an area full of bistros. **&**

PAU: *Chez Pierre*
16 rue Louis-Barthou. **[** *05 59 27 76 86.*
A fine chef, an elegant setting in a 19th-century town house and a series
of creative dishes have ensured the reputation of this restaurant. **&**

ST-GIRONS: *Eychenne*
8 avenue Paul Laffont. **[** *05 61 66 34 19.*
A pretty restaurant in an old seminary, with period furniture. It has two
gardens where diners can enjoy pigeon, duck and fish specialities.

ST-JEAN-DE-LUZ: *Auberge Kaïku*
17 rue de la République. **[** *05 59 26 13 20.*
Regional Basque dishes such as cuttlefish and pasta, shrimps or beef
with truffles are served in the oldest house in town. **&**

ST-JEAN-DE-LUZ: *Petit Grill Basque*
2 rue St Jacques. **[** *05 59 26 80 76.*
Simple, good Basque home-cooking (fish soup, squid, chicken
croquettes) served by jolly waitresses. Very good value. **&**

ST-JEAN-PIED-DE-PORT: *Chalet Pedro*
Forêt d'Iraty. **[** *05 59 37 02 52.*
A chalet in the mountains which caters for skiers and locals alike. Slow
service does not spoil fresh trout or mushroom and garlic omelette. **&**

ST-JEAN-PIED-DE-PORT: *Pyrénées*
19 place Charles de Gaulle. **[** *05 59 37 01 01.*
A renowned restaurant serving the best local produce: Pyrenean
suckling lamb, salmon and, in season, wild morel mushrooms. **&**

ST-SAVIN: *Le Viscos*
St-Savin. **[** *05 62 97 02 28.*
In summer, eat outside on the flower-filled terrace overlooking the
river Lavedan. Specialities are monkfish and *foie gras.* **&**

URT: *Auberge de la Galupe*
Place du Port. **[** *05 59 56 21 84.*
A fishermans' inn making use of fine local produce – Montauzer ham,
salmon and eels from the Adour river, and sweet Jurançon wine. **&**

For key to symbols see back flap

		CREDIT CARDS	CHILDREN'S FACILITIES	FIXED-PRICE MENU	GOOD WINE LIST	OUTDOOR TABLES

Average prices for a three-course meal for one, including a half-bottle of house wine, tax and service:
Ⓕ under F150
ⒻⒻ F150–F250
ⒻⒻⒻ F250–F350
ⒻⒻⒻⒻ F350–F500
ⒻⒻⒻⒻⒻ over F500

CHILDREN'S FACILITIES
Some restaurants have high chairs and offer smaller portions for children.
FIXED-PRICE MENU
A good-value fixed-price menu on offer at lunch, dinner or both, usually with three courses.
GOOD WINE LIST
Denotes a wide range of good wines, or a more specialized selection of local wines.
OUTDOOR TABLES
Facilities for eating outdoors, on a terrace, or in a garden or courtyard, often with a good view.

LANGUEDOC-ROUSSILLON

Restaurant	Price	Credit Cards	Children's Facilities	Fixed-Price Menu	Good Wine List	Outdoor Tables
AIGUES-MORTES: *La Camargue* 19 rue de la République. ☎ 04 66 53 86 88. Dine to gypsy and flamenco music in this popular venue. Try the seafood paella or *rabo di taureau* (bull's tail stew). Fun and good value. ♿	Ⓕ	MC V	●	▪		▪
AIGUES-MORTES: *Restaurant les Enganettes* 12 rue Morceau. ☎ 04 66 53 69 11. Excellent regional specialities are served in a rustic setting. Portions are very generous and all the food is freshly prepared.	Ⓕ	MC V		▪		
ANDUZE: *Auberge des Trois Barbus* Générargues. ☎ 04 66 61 72 12. Imaginative cooking with *foie gras* and truffles is presented in a rustic auberge. Lunch by the pool and soak up the views across the valley.	ⒻⒻⒻ	AE MC V	●	▪		▪
ARLES-SUR-TECH: *Hôtel les Glycines* Rue du Jeu-de-Paume. ☎ 04 68 39 10 09. Tasty food based on local produce, and many regional wines. There is a pretty garden which is ideal for summer dining. ♿	ⒻⒻ	AE MC V	●	▪	●	▪
BÉZIERS: *Le Framboisier* 12 rue Boeildieu. ☎ 04 67 49 90 00. A gastronome's delight, this is an elegant establishment with a classic menu and long list of fine Languedoc-Roussillon wines. ♿	ⒻⒻⒻ	AE DC MC V	●	▪		
BOUZIGUES: *La Côte Bleue* Avenue Louis Tudesq. ☎ 04 67 78 30 87. Overlooking the saltwater lagoon of the Bassin de Thau, this is a large and airy restaurant which offers fresher-than-fresh seafood and fish. ♿	ⒻⒻ	AE MC V	●	▪		▪
CARCASSONNE: *Le Languedoc* 32 allée d'Iéna. ☎ 04 68 25 22 17. This pleasant restaurant is below the walled city in the less crowded town. *Cassoulet*, the filling bean stew that is the regional speciality, is a must, and there is a range of salads, savoury dishes and desserts.	ⒻⒻ	AE DC MC V	●	▪		
CARCASSONNE: *Brasserie Le Donjon* 4 rue Porte d'Aude. ☎ 04 68 25 95 72. An elegant, refreshingly modern brasserie in an otherwise completely medieval town. Regional specialities of *foie gras* and cassoulet. ♿	ⒻⒻ	AE DC MC V	●	▪		▪
CASTELNAUDARY: *Grand Hôtel Fourcade* 14 rue des Carmes. ☎ 04 68 23 02 08. In an Old Town bordering the Canal du Midi, this is an old-fashioned place to eat, with *cassoulet* the highlight of an interesting menu.	ⒻⒻ	AE DC MC V	●	▪		▪
CASTELNOU: *L'Hostal* Carrer de la Patore. ☎ 04 68 53 45 42. In an artists' village, this restaurant fills up at the weekend, when locals flock in for *cargolade*, the Catalan feast of grilled meat and snails.	ⒻⒻ	AE DC MC V	●	▪		▪
CÉRET: *Les Feuillants* 1 boulevard Lafayette. ☎ 04 68 87 37 88. A top-class restaurant in the foothills of the Pyrenees, with a remarkablewine list. Especially good are the lamb, cuttlefish and red mullet.	ⒻⒻⒻⒻ	AE MC V	●	▪	●	▪
COLLIOURE: *La Frégate* Quai de l'Amirauté. ☎ 04 68 82 06 05. Wonderful fish soups, local anchovies and *bouillinades* (fish platters) are among the favourites in this jolly, quayside restaurant.	ⒻⒻ	MC V	●	▪		▪

COLLIOURE: *La Balette* ⓕⓕⓕ MC V
Route de Port-Vendres. 【 04 68 82 05 07.
Beautifully set above the bay, this is a very popular place in summer –
a reservation is essential. Seafood stars in a wide range of Catalan dishes.

CUCUGNAN: *Auberge du Vigneron* ⓕⓕ MC V
2 rue Achille-Mir. 【 04 68 45 03 00.
Atmospheric restaurant in the former wine cellar of a charming inn,
serving dishes featuring duck and fruit in tasty combinations. 🕭

FLORENSAC: *Léonce* ⓕⓕⓕ AE DC MC V
8 place de la République. 【 04 67 77 03 05.
It is well worth seeking out this restaurant, where the cooking is
inspired by local dishes. The fish dishes and desserts are heavenly.

LE VIGAN: *Le Mas Quayrol* ⓕⓕ MC V
Aulas. 【 04 67 81 12 38.
A warm welcome and quality food are to be found here. The menu is
inventive, tasty and versatile, with fresh fish to the fore. 🕭

MINERVE: *Relais Chantovent* ⓕⓕ MC V
Minerve. 【 04 68 91 14 18.
The pretty medieval town, with its deep ravine, should not be missed,
neither should the regional cooking and good wines at the Relais. 🕭

MONTPELLIER: *Chandelier* ⓕⓕⓕⓕ AE MC V
267 rue Léon Blum. 【 04 67 15 34 38.
Inventive seafood and fish dishes such as crayfish fritters and sea bass
with crushed olives are the stock-in-trade here.

MONTPELLIER: *La Réserve Rimbaud* ⓕⓕⓕ AE DC MC V
820 avenue de St-Maur. 【 04 67 72 52 53.
Sophisticated food at affordable prices in a relaxed riverside setting.
Grilled clams, and monkfish in cream and wine, are savoury treats. 🕭

NARBONNE: *L'Auberge des Vignes* ⓕⓕ AE MC V
Domaine de l'Hospitalet, route de Narbonne Plage. 【 04 68 45 28 50.
In the middle of a vineyard this restaurant serves Mediterranean cuisine,
such as fish of the day served with *tapenade* and saffron juice. 🕭

NARBONNE: *La Table St-Créscent* ⓕⓕ AE DC MC V
Domaine St-Crésent le Viel. 【 04 68 41 37 37.
In an 8th-century oratory, this delightful restaurant serves elegant food
including a superb aubergine canelloni. Well chosen selection of local wines.

NÎMES: *Nicolas* ⓕ MC V
1 rue Poise. 【 04 66 67 50 47.
Regional fare at good-value prices in a packed but friendly and
unpretentious atmosphere.

PERPIGNAN: *Casa Sansa* ⓕ AE MC V
3 rue Fabriques-Couvertes. 【 04 68 34 21 84.
A 14th-century wine cellar decorated with Catalan artifacts provides
the setting for true Catalan food: spicy meatballs, prawns and anchovies.

PERPIGNAN: *Le Chapon Fin* ⓕⓕⓕ AE DC MC V
18 boulevard Jean-Bourrat. 【 04 68 35 14 14.
The restaurant serves fine Catalan food such as partridge stew with
peppers and oranges, as well as seafood and truffles. 🕭

PERPIGNAN: *Le Mas Vermeil* ⓕⓕⓕ DC V
Traverse de Cabestany. 【 04 68 66 95 96.
The menu is unpretentious and simple, leaning towards the rich Catalan
style. Dine in the garden restaurant, complete with fountains. 🕭

PORT-VENDRES: *La Côte Vermeille* ⓕⓕ AE MC V
Quai du Fanal. 【 04 68 82 05 71.
At this quayside restaurant, the culinary arts are concentrated
on delicate seafood and fish, but other dishes can be ordered. 🕭

SAILLAGOUSE: *L'Atalaya* ⓕⓕⓕ MC V
L10, Saillagouse. 【 04 68 04 70 04.
A pretty auberge perched above the village. The original cuisine offers
pigeon in cranberry sauce, salmon mousse with dill and *foie gras*. A find!

For key to symbols see back flap

Average prices for a three-course meal for one, including a half-bottle of house wine, tax and service:
- Ⓕ under F150
- ⒻⒻ F150–F250
- ⒻⒻⒻ F250–F350
- ⒻⒻⒻⒻ F350–F500
- ⒻⒻⒻⒻⒻ over F500

CHILDREN'S FACILITIES
Some restaurants have high chairs and offer smaller portions for children.

FIXED-PRICE MENU
A good-value fixed-price menu on offer at lunch, dinner or both, usually with three courses.

GOOD WINE LIST
Denotes a wide range of good wines, or a more specialized selection of local wines.

OUTDOOR TABLES
Facilities for eating outdoors, on a terrace, or in a garden or courtyard, often with a good view.

Restaurant	Price	Credit Cards	Children's Facilities	Fixed-Price Menu	Good Wine List	Outdoor Tables
ST-MARTIN-DE-LONDRES: *Les Muscardins* 19 route des Cévennes. 📞 04 67 55 75 90. A bright, cheerful restaurant with a notable list of local wines. Gourmets often return to savour the adventurous cooking of the Rousset family, who base their menu on regional produce – fish, lamb and pigeon. ♿	ⒻⒻⒻ	AE DC MC V		■	●	
ST-PONS-DE-THOMIÈRES: *Auberge de Cabarétou* St-Pons-de-Thomières. 📞 04 67 97 02 31. Set amid a forest with views across Haut Languedoc, this auberge is memorable for its combination of classic and modern local cuisine.	ⒻⒻ	AE DC MC V	●	■		
SÈTE: *Palangrotte* 1 rampe Paul-Valéry. 📞 04 67 74 80 35. A good place to go to sample a plate of oysters, for which this area is justifiably famous.	ⒻⒻ	AE DC MC V		■		■
TAURINYA: *Auberge des Deux Abbayes* 2 place de l'Oratoire. 📞 04 68 96 49 53. This restaurant in a mountain setting serves regional dishes including Banyuls-style goose pâté and Collioure anchovies. ♿	ⒻⒻ	MC V	●	■		
VILLEFRANCHE-DE-CONFLENT: *Auberge St-Paul* Place de l'Eglise. 📞 04 68 96 30 95. Originally a 13th-century chapel, this inn offers a good variety of local produce, cooked with a personal touch and Catalan influence. ♿	ⒻⒻⒻ	MC V		■		

PROVENCE AND THE CÔTE D'AZUR

Restaurant	Price	Credit Cards	Children's Facilities	Fixed-Price Menu	Good Wine List	Outdoor Tables
AIX-EN-PROVENCE: *Mas d'Entremont* 315 Route Nationale 7. 📞 04 42 17 42 42. Glass walls open on to the surrounding park, and the menu is wonderful, but with few local dishes. A good Provençal wine list. ♿	ⒻⒻⒻ	MC V	●	■	●	■
AIX-EN-PROVENCE: *Le Bistro Latin* 18 rue de la Couronne. 📞 04 42 38 22 88. An intimate restaurant on two floors, serving excellent meals at good prices, and imaginative local specialities like sole with lobster sauce.	ⒻⒻ	AE MC V		■	●	
AIX-EN-PROVENCE: *L'Aix Quis.* 22 rue Leydet. 📞 04 42 27 76 16. Stylish fish and meat dishes in a restaurant that is fast becoming the culinary headquarters of Aix. Try the delicious six-course menu. ♿	ⒻⒻⒻ	AE MC V		■		
ARLES: *L'Escaladou* 23 rue de la Porte de Laure. 📞 04 90 96 70 43. This pretty Provençal restaurant is close to the bull ring in the centre of town. Choose the good local fish with piles of fresh vegetables. ♿	ⒻⒻ		●	■		
ARLES: *Le Vaccarès* Place du Forum. 📞 04 90 96 06 17. Provençale food in elegant surroundings. The chef here particularly enjoys putting a spin on classic dishes. The seafood and soups are especially recommended.	ⒻⒻⒻ	AE MC V		■		■
AVIGNON: *La Fourchette* 17 rue Racine. 📞 04 90 85 20 93. A relaxed alternative to Avignon's smarter restaurants. Prices are reasonable and there is a range of 12 mouthwatering desserts. ♿	ⒻⒻ	MC V		■		
AVIGNON: *Hiély-Lucullus* 5 rue de la République. 📞 04 90 86 17 07. Avignon gastronomes have been flocking here for 60 years. Quality is as good as ever; try specialities like *foie gras* and *meringue glacée*.	ⒻⒻⒻ	MC V	●	■	●	

Biot: *Auberge du Jarrier* ⒻⒻⒻ — AE, MC, V
30 passage de la Bourgade. 📞 04 93 65 11 68.
An unpretentious restaurant with an array of seafood, delicate fish and intriguing cheeses. Reserve a week in advance in season. ♿

Cagnes-sur-Mer: *Le Cagnard* ⒻⒻⒻ — AE, DC, MC, V
Rue du Sous-barri. 📞 04 93 20 73 21.
Housed in a medieval inn in the ramparts of the village, this superb restaurant offers a classic menu with delicacies such as roast pigeon.

Cannes: *Royal Gray* ⒻⒻⒻ — AE, DC, MC, V
38 rue des Serbes. 📞 04 92 99 79 60.
It is difficult to eat more lavishly than at the Royal Gray, long the doyen of Cannes' restaurants. ♿

Cavaillon: *Restaurant Prévot* ⒻⒻⒻ — AE, MC, V
353 avenue de Verdun. 📞 04 90 71 32 43.
A gastronomic treat in the heart of a pretty market town. The food is elegant and delicious; try the aubergines and langoustines. ♿

Châteauneuf-du-Pape: *La Mère Germaine* ⒻⒻⒻ — MC, V
Place de la Fontaine. 📞 04 90 83 54 37.
A once outstanding restaurant that is now recovering its reputation. It has superb views of the vineyards and pleasant, unobtrusive service. ♿

Châteaux-Arnoux: *La Bonne Etape* ⒻⒻⒻⒻⒻ — AE, DC, MC, V
Chemin du Lac. 📞 04 92 64 00 09.
Set among lavender fields and olive groves, the flavour is Provençal, with expertly crafted dishes such as *courgettes farcies* and lamb.

Col d'Eze: *La Bergerie* ⒻⒻ — AE, MC, V
Grande Corniche. 📞 04 93 41 03 67.
Winter by the fire, summer on the terrace – the hearty, warming food includes lamb in herbs, washed down with copious local wine. ♿

Cuers: *Le Lingoustou* ⒻⒻⒻ — AE, DC, MC, V
Route de Pierrefeu. 📞 04 94 28 69 10.
Traditional Provençal specialities served in refined style, winning a Michelin star. The setting is suitably rustic, amid rolling vineyards.

Gigondas: *Les Florets* ⒻⒻ — AE, DC, MC, V
Route des Dentelles. 📞 04 90 65 85 01.
Locals pack the dining room, sampling the good regional food. In summer, eat on the terrace overlooking the Dentelles de Montmirail. ♿

La Garde Freinet: *Auberge Sarrasin* Ⓕ — MC, V
Route Nationale 98. 📞 04 94 43 67 16.
A rural dining room where a fire roars in winter and flowers adorn the tables in summer. Try *cassoulet Provençal* washed down with rosé. ♿

Les Baux-de-Provence: *L'Oustau de Baumanière* ⒻⒻⒻⒻⒻ — AE, DC, MC, V
Val d'Enfer. 📞 04 90 54 33 07.
Two Michelin stars, views over the medieval village and a memorable menu – a blend of ancient local dishes and *nouvelle cuisine*.

Lourmarin: *Le Moulin de Lourmarin* ⒻⒻⒻ — AE, DC, MC, V
Rue Temple. 📞 04 90 68 06 69.
The millstones are still intact in this luxurious converted olive mill, and the food is delicious – especially the fish and Lubéron game.

Marseille: *Dar Djerba* ⒻⒻ — MC, V
15 cours Julien. 📞 04 91 48 55 36.
A North African restaurant serving delicious couscous dishes in an intimate atmosphere. ♿

Marseille: *Miramar* ⒻⒻⒻⒻ — AE, DC, MC, V
12 quai du Port. 📞 04 91 91 10 40.
The *bouillabaisse* is one of the most authentic in Marseille – but at a price. There is also a huge selection of seafood. ♿

Monaco: *Le Périgourdin* Ⓕ — AE, MC, DC, V
5 rue des Oliviers. 📞 00377 93 30 06 02.
Two minutes walk from the casino, this friendly restaurant offers all the riches of Périgord cuisine – such as *foie gras* – at bargain prices.

Average prices for a three-course meal for one, including a half-bottle of house wine, tax and service:
(F) under F150
(F)(F) F150–F250
(F)(F)(F) F250–F350
(F)(F)(F)(F) F350–F500
(F)(F)(F)(F)(F) over F500

CHILDREN'S FACILITIES
Some restaurants have high chairs and offer smaller portions for children.
FIXED-PRICE MENU
A good-value fixed-price menu on offer at lunch, dinner or both, usually with three courses.
GOOD WINE LIST
Denotes a wide range of good wines, or a more specialized selection of local wines.
OUTDOOR TABLES
Facilities for eating outdoors, on a terrace, or in a garden or courtyard, often with a good view.

Restaurant	Credit Cards	Children's Facilities	Fixed-Price Menu	Good Wine List	Outdoor Tables
MONTE-CARLO: *Café de Paris* (F)(F)(F) Place du Casino. 04 92 16 20 20. A re-creation of a Belle Epoque brasserie. Among the specialities are *pavé de saumon* and Charolais beef with morels.	AE DC MC V				■
MOUGINS: *Le Moulin de Mougins* (F)(F)(F)(F)(F) Notre Dame-de-Vie. 04 93 75 78 24. Now only with two Michelin stars, but still managing to stay ahead of competition. *The* restaurant for stars during the Cannes Film Festival.	AE DC MC V		■	●	
NICE: *Nissa Socca* (F) 5 rue Sainte-Réparate. 04 93 16 18 35. Features vast plates of *socca* (chick-pea bread) with pasta and carafes of red wine. Crowded, usually taking over the street in summer.		●			■
NICE: *Le Chantecler (Negresco)* (F)(F)(F)(F) 37 promenade des Anglais. 04 93 88 39 51. Long the bastion of gastronomy in Nice, the restaurant retains immaculate standards established when Russian princes came to dine in the last century. Seafood and fish feature strongly.	AE DC MC V	●	■	●	
ORANGE: *La Roselière* (F) 4 rue du Renoyer. 04 90 34 50 42. Chalkboards propped against stone walls display the daily-changing menu, with every dish lovingly prepared from local produce.			■		■
ST-AGNES: *Le Logis Sarrasin* (F)(F) 40 rue de Sarrasin. 04 93 35 86 89. A simple, family-run restaurant in the Alpine foothills behind Menton, offering six huge courses of local game and Italian specialities.			■		
ST-JEAN-CAP-FERRAT: *Le St-Jean* (F) Place Clemenceau. 04 93 76 04 75. In the busy town square, this restaurant serves up simple but excellent food, such as pizzas cooked over wood, pastas and fish. The first floor terrace is perfect for balmy summer evenings.	AE MC V	●			■
ST-JEAN-CAP-FERRAT: *Le Sloop* (F)(F) Nouveau port de St-Jean. 04 93 01 48 63. Amid the smart yachts of St-Jean's picturesque and buzzing port, Le Sloop specializes in light and delicious seafood.	AE MC V	●	■	●	■
ST-RÉMY-DE-PROVENCE: *Le Jardin de Fréderic* (F)(F) 8 bd Gambetta. 04 90 92 27 76. This small, family-run restaurant housed in a villa serves local dishes such as onion tart, and poached turbot with sorrel.	MC V		■		
ST-VALLIER-DE-THIERY: *Le Relais Impérial* (F) Route Napoléon, Route Nationale 85. 04 93 42 60 07. In an agreeable atmosphere, and with friendly service, this is one of the few places to offer an authentic *pissaladière* – onions, olives and anchovies cooked in dough – with superb Provençal white wines.	AE DC MC V	●	■	●	
SÉGURET: *La Table du Comtat* (F)(F)(F) Séguret. 04 90 46 91 49. Truffles, pigeon and wild boar grace the menu of local produce. A memorable view forms the backdrop and the cellar stuffed with Côtes du Rhône provides a fitting accompaniment.	AE DC MC V	●	■		
TOUET-SUR-VAR: *Auberge des Chasseurs* (F)(F) Touët. 04 93 05 71 11. Local game makes for appetizing and filling dishes at this country auberge, where the wild boar and blue trout are excellent.	AE DC MC V	●	■		■

VENCE: *Auberge des Seigneurs* ⓕⓕ
Place du Frêne. **[** *04 93 58 04 24.*
Come with an appetite to this medieval auberge, complete with
roaring fire and five succulent courses, including the local blue trout
and tender lamb, cooked in front of you on a spit.
AE DC MC V

VENCE: *Le Vieux Couvent* ⓕⓕ
68 av Générale Leclerc. **[** *04 93 58 78 58.*
Housed in a former 17th-century convent, this restaurant is popular
for Provençale fare with an inventive touch.
MC V

VILLEFRANCHE-SUR-MER: *Mère Germaine* ⓕⓕⓕⓕ
Quai Courbet. **[** *04 93 01 71 39.*
Bouillabaisse and *sole tante marie* (sole with mushrooms) are served
in this friendly restaurant overlooking the beach. **&**
AE MC V

CORSICA

BASTELICACCIA: *Auberge Seta* ⓕⓕ
Bastelicaccia Suaralta. **[** *04 95 20 00 16.*
Not far from Ajaccio is this restaurant with a verandah and splendid
views over the sea. Fish dominates the menu.
MC V

BONIFACIO: *Stella d'Oro* ⓕⓕ
7 rue Doria. **[** *04 95 73 03 63.*
A family institution, with steep prices and a hearty local atmosphere.
Fish and fowl feature heavily on the menu.
AE DC MC V

CALVI: *L'Ile de Beauté* ⓕⓕⓕⓕ
Quai Landry. **[** *04 95 65 00 46.*
This restaurant is on the quayside and concentrates on perfect fish
creations such as oysters with lime and lobster. The dining room on
the first floor specializes in meat dishes. Neither is cheap! **&**
AE DC MC V

CAURO: *U Barracone* ⓕⓕ
Barracone. **[** *04 95 28 40 55.*
A quiet place to eat in the countryside near Cauro. The menu includes
tournedos with morel mushrooms and *crêpes* with orange coulis. **&**
AE DC MC V

CORTE: *Auberge de la Restonica* ⓕⓕ
Vallée de la Restonica. **[** *04 95 46 09 58.*
Run by an ex-international footballer, this is a rural hillside inn with
a dining room opening on to views of the forest. Simple, good food. **&**
MC V

L'ILE ROUSSE: *La Bergerie* ⓕⓕ
Route de Monticello. **[** *04 95 60 01 28.*
Dine in the shady garden of this pretty converted farmhouse. Try a
sea-urchin omelette accompanied by a bottle of Corsican wine. **&**
MC V

PORTO: *Le Soleil Couchant* ⓕ
Porto Marine. **[** *04 95 26 10 12.*
On the terrace, there are wonderful views over the marina. The local
fare is very good value; the *charcuterie* and sheeps' cheeses excel.
MC V

PORTO-VECCHIO: *Auberge du Maquis* ⓕⓕ
Ferruccio. **[** *04 95 70 20 39.*
Order kid or wild boar and it will be roasted in front of you in this
peaceful country retreat, a short drive from Porto-Vecchio.

PORTO-VECCHIO: *Le Regina* ⓕⓕ
Route de Bastia. **[** *04 95 70 14 94.*
A rather regal restaurant with a complicated cuisine prepared from
the finest local produce. Seafood, sweetbreads and pastas are served
in elaborate forms. The wine list is the best on the island.
AE DC MC V

ST-FLORENT: *La Gaffe* ⓕⓕ
Port de St-Florent. **[** *04 95 37 00 12.*
Savour fresh, appetizing mussels and lobster in lemon and mint,
while sitting on the shady terrace watching the boats sail by. **&**
AE DC MC V

SARTÈNE: *La Chaumière* ⓕⓕ
39 rue du Capitaine-Benedetti. **[** *04 95 77 07 13.*
Carved out of the granite hillside, this Corsican inn serves traditional
island cooking: *charcuterie*, tripe and wild boar, with local wines.
AE DC MC V

For key to symbols see back flap

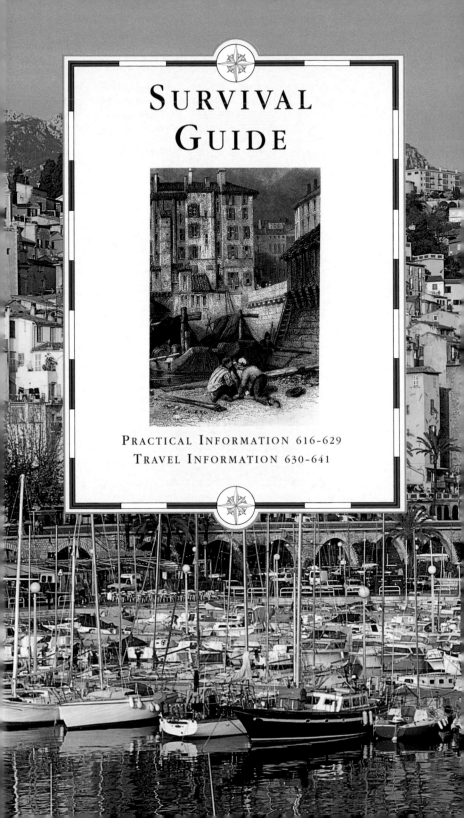

SURVIVAL
GUIDE

PRACTICAL INFORMATION

FRANCE is justifiably proud of its many attractions, for which it has excellent tourist information facilities. Both in France and abroad, French Government Tourist Offices are an invaluable source of reference for practical aspects of your stay. Most towns and villages in France have a tourist information office; the relevant

Tourist information logo

address and telephone number is provided for each town and area listed in this guide. Domestic tourism in France creates holiday migrations, especially between 14 July and 31 August. Consequently, the hotel and restaurant trades are seasonal. A little forward planning will allow you to avoid the pitfalls of seasonal closure.

MANNERS

THE FRENCH have rituals of politeness which are easy to pick up. In shops be ready to say *Bonjour* before asking for what you want, then *merci* when you receive your change, and *merci, au revoir* when you get your purchases and leave.

Shake hands when introduced to someone, or at any time when you see a hand proffered. In small communities, many people may greet you with a *Bonjour* in the street even if they have never seen you before.

For other useful expressions, refer to the phrase book on pages 671–2.

VISAS

CURRENTLY THERE are no visa requirements for EU nationals or visitors from the United States, Canada or New Zealand who plan to stay in France for under three months. Visitors from most other countries, including Australia, require a tourist visa.

Visas should be obtained prior to departure from your local French consulate. Anyone planning to study or work in France should apply to their local French consulate several months in advance about visa requirements.

TAX-FREE GOODS AND CUSTOMS INFORMATION

VISITORS RESIDENT outside the European Union can reclaim the sales tax TVA, or VAT, on French goods if they spend more than F2,000 in one shop, get a *détaxe* receipt and take the goods out of the

country within six months. The form should be handed in at customs when leaving the country. The reimbursement will be sent on to you.

Exceptions for *détaxe* rebate are food and drink, medicines, tobacco, cars and motorbikes, though tax can be reimbursed for bicycles. More information and advice is available from the **Centre des Renseignements des Douanes**, but this is usually in French.

Sign for tourist office in smaller towns and villages

TOURIST INFORMATION

ALL MAJOR CITIES and large towns have *offices de tourisme*. Small towns and even villages have *syndicats d'initiative*. Both will give you town plans, advice on accommodation, and information on regional recreational and cultural activities.

You can also get information before you leave for France from **French Government Tourist Offices**, or by phoning or writing to local tourist offices (see headings for each town

in this guide) or the appropriate CRT *(Comité Régional de Tourisme)* – ask the FGTO for the address.

ADMISSION CHARGES

MOST MUSEUMS and monuments in France charge an entrance fee, usually from F15 to F40. This may be reduced or waived on Sundays. Those under seven and over 60 are admitted free at all times. Discounts are often available to people under the age of 26, carrying a *Carte Jeune Internationale* (International Youth Card), and students *(see facing page)*.

OPENING HOURS

THIS GUIDE lists which days of the week sights are open. Generally, hours are from 10am–5:40pm with one late evening per week. Most sights close on public holidays. National museums and sights are normally closed on Tuesdays, with a few exceptions which close on Mondays. Municipal museums normally close on Mondays. Churches open every day but shut at lunchtime. Always check the opening hours for private museums as they may not comply with standard opening times.

See page 622 for details on opening hours for shops; page 620 for banks; and pages 576–7 for restaurants.

Colonne de la Grande Armée

Sign to monument of cultural importance

Visitors taking the weight off weary feet

FACILITIES FOR THE DISABLED

DETAILED LISTINGS by town are provided in *Guide Rousseau H comme Handicapés*, available from **Les Editions La Route Robert** and French bookshops. *Touristes Quand Même* details services in the main towns in French, with translations in English and German of the most common phrases. It is issued free by **CNRH** (Comité National Français de Liaison pour la Réadaptation des Handicapés), and is also available from **Paris Convention and Visitors Bureau Headquarters**. The **CIDJ** (Centre d'Information et de Documentation Jeunesse) offers information for young disabled travellers. The UK-based organization **RADAR** provides information on wheelchair access, as does the **Association des Paralysés de France** *(see p539)*.

FRENCH TIME

FRANCE IS ONE HOUR ahead of Greenwich Mean Time (GMT). The French use the 24-hour clock, so 7pm = 19:00, for example.

Queuing for the Eiffel Tower

STUDENT INFORMATION

STUDENTS WITH valid ID cards (an International Student Identity Card or the French *carte jeunes*) benefit from many discounts. **CIDJ** offices provide a comprehensive service for students.

ELECTRICAL ADAPTORS

THE VOLTAGE in France is 220 volts. Plugs have two round pins, or three round pins for applications which need to be earthed. Some hotels offer built-in adaptors for shavers only.

Standard French two-pin plug for electrical appliances

CONVERSION CHART

Imperial to metric
1 inch = 2.54 centimetres
1 foot = 30 centimetres
1 mile = 1.6 kilometres
1 ounce = 28 grams
1 pound = 454 grams
1 pint = 0.6 litre
1 gallon = 4.6 litres

Metric to imperial
1 millimetre = 0.04 inch
1 centimetre = 0.4 inch
1 metre = 3 feet 3 inches
1 kilometre = 0.6 mile
1 gram = 0.04 ounce
1 kilogram = 2.2 pounds
1 litre = 1.8 pints

EMBASSIES

Australia
4 rue Jean Rey, 75015 Paris.
Map 6 D3. ☎ *01 40 59 33 00*.

United Kingdom
35 rue du Faubourg St-Honoré
Paris 75008. **Map** 3 C5. **Consulate**:
16 rue d'Anjou, 75008 Paris. **Map**
3 C5. ☎ *01 44 51 31 00*.
Consular offices: Bordeaux,
Lille, Lyon, Marseille.

FRENCH GOVERNMENT TOURIST OFFICES

Australia
French Tourist Bureau
BNP Building, 12th floor
12 Castlereagh Street, Sydney
NSW 2000. ☎ *(2) 9231 52 44.*
FAX *(2) 9221 86 82.*

Paris
Maison de la France, 8 av de l'Opéra,
75001 Paris. **Map** 8 E1. ☎ *01 42
96 10 23.* **FAX** *01 42 86 08 94.*

UK
French Government Tourist
Office, 178 Piccadilly, London
W1V 0AL. ☎ *0891 244 123.*
FAX *(0171) 493 6594.*

USEFUL ADDRESSES

Centre des Renseignements des Douanes
23rue de l'Université, 75007
Paris. **Map** 14 F3.
☎ *01 40 24 65 10.* **FAX** *01 40 24
65 30.* **Open** *9am–5pm Mon–Fri.*

CIDJ
101 quai Branly, 75015 Paris.
Map 6 E2. ☎ *01 44 49 12 00.*
Open *9:30am–6pm Mon–Fri,
9:30am–1pm Sat.*

CNRH
236 bis, rue de Tolbiac,
75013 Paris. ☎ *01 53 80 66 66.*

Paris Convention and Visitors Bureau Headquarters
127 av des Champs-Elysées, 75008
Paris. **Map** 2 E4. ☎ *01 49 52 53 54.*
☎ *01 49 52 53 56 (in English).*
Open *9am–8pm Mon–Sat,
11am–6pm Sun.* **Closed** *25
Dec, 1 Jan.*

Personal Security and Health

O N THE WHOLE, France is a safe place for visitors: take normal precautions, such as sensible care of your possessions at all times, and avoid isolated and unlit urban areas at night. If you fall ill during your stay, pharmacies generally offer good advice. Consulates and consular departments at your embassy are a good source of help and advice in an emergency *(see p617)*. For serious medical problems, this section gives the numbers of the emergency services.

French pharmacy sign

PERSONAL SECURITY

V IOLENT CRIME is rare in France, though there can be random incidents. If you are involved in an argument or a car accident avoid confrontation. In potentially difficult situations you should stay calm and speak French if you can, as your efforts may defuse the situation.

LEGAL ASSISTANCE

I F YOU HAVE a comprehensive insurance policy which covers legal advice in France, from organizations like Europ Assistance or Mondial Assistance, this will help with the legal aspects of insurance claims, for instance after an accident. If you do not have this cover, telephone your nearest consulate *(see p617)*, or, as a last resort, telephone the local *Ordre des Avocats* (lawyers' association) for the name of a good local lawyer.

Gendarme   Fireman

INTERPRETERS

T RANSLATION and interpretation is offered by professional translators. Contact the **Société Française des Traducteurs Professionels** through Minitel *(see p624)*.

PERSONAL PROPERTY

M AKE SURE you insure your possessions before arrival. Beware of pickpockets, especially on the Paris metro during the rush hour. Keep all valuables securely concealed and if carrying a handbag or case, never let it out of your sight. Also, only take as much cash as you think you will need. Traveller's cheques are the safest method of carrying large sums of money.

Telephone or visit the police to report crimes which take place in towns, missing persons or stolen property, robbery or assault. The *commissariat de police* is the headquarters. In small towns and villages, go to the *mairie* (town hall), which will only be open during office hours. If your passport is lost or stolen, call your consulate *(see p617)*.

The white-gloved motorcyclists who patrol the motorways are the *CRS (Compagnie Républicaine de Sécurité)*. If you are involved in a traffic accident outside a town you may be asked to accompany the other driver to the nearest *gendarmerie*. The *gendarmerie nationale* is a military organization which deals with all crimes outside urban areas. Making a statement (a *PV* or *procés-verbal*) can be a lengthy process. Take your identity papers (and your vehicle papers, if relevant) with you when you go to make a statement.

MEDICAL TREATMENT

A LL EUROPEAN UNION nationals are entitled to French social security coverage. However, treatment must be paid for and hospital rates vary widely. Reimbursements may be obtained if you have acquired your E111 form before you travel (available from post offices in the UK), but the process is long and complicated.

All travellers should consider purchasing travel insurance. Non-EU nationals are obliged to carry medical insurance, taken out before they arrive.

In the case of a medical emergency call **SAMU** *(Service d'Aide Médicale Urgence)*. However, it is often faster to call **Sapeurs Pompiers** (the fire service), who offer a first aid and ambulance service. This is particularly true in rural areas where the local fire-station is likely to be much

---

DIRECTORY

EMERGENCY NUMBERS

Ambulance (SAMU)
 15 or 18 *(Sapeurs Pompiers)*.

Fire (Sapeurs Pompiers)
 18.

Police and Gendarmerie
 17.

INTERPRETERS

Société Française des Traducteurs Professionels
 Minitel 3616 SFTRAD.

closer than the ambulance service based in town. The paramedics are called *secouristes*.

Casualty departments *(service des urgences)* in public hospitals can deal with most medical problems. Your consulate should be able to recommend an English-speaking doctor in the area.

Police car

PHARMACIES

I N FRANCE, pharmacists can diagnose health problems and suggest appropriate treatments. They are also trained to identify mushrooms: take any you are unsure about to them to eliminate the danger of poisoning.

Pharmacies have a green cross outside. A card in the window will give details of the nearest *pharmacie de garde* for night openings.

Fire engine

Ambulance

Fire hazard poster

IN THE OPEN AIR

F OREST FIRES are a major risk in many parts of France. High winds can mean fires spread rapidly in winter as well as summer. Keep well away from an area where there is a fire, as its direction can change quickly. Make sure you do not start a fire with campfires or a cigarette butt.

When walking in the mountains or sailing, notify your route to the relevant authority and observe local regulations posted in the area.

During the hunting season (Sep–Feb and especially Sundays) dress in visible colours when out walking. Avoid areas where hunters are staked out in hides or beating through the undergrowth *(see p629)*.

PUBLIC TOILETS IN FRANCE

Modern pay toilets are now found in many towns. Do not let children under ten use the toilets on their own as the automatic cleaning function can be dangerous. The best policy is to use toilets in cafés or restaurants where you are a customer, or go to a department store. Traditional *pissoirs* and keyhole toilets, still found in some towns, are often not very clean. Toilet facilities are provided on the *autoroute* at drive-in rest areas every 20 km (12 miles), as well as at the major service areas.

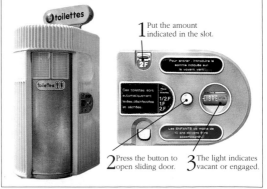

1 Put the amount indicated in the slot.

2 Press the button to open sliding door.

3 The light indicates vacant or engaged.

Banking and Local Currency

Y OU MAY BRING any amount of currency into France, but if you intend to re-export more than F50,000, you should declare it on arrival. Traveller's cheques are the safest way to carry money abroad, but credit cards, which can be used to withdraw local currency from an automatic teller machine, are by far the most convenient. Bureaux de change are located at airports, large railway stations, and in some hotels and shops, but banks usually offer the best rates of exchange.

Credit card cash dispenser

USING BANKS

M OST FRENCH BANKS have a bureau de change, but rates can vary. Many banks now have ATMs (automatic teller machines) outside, which you can normally use with cards in the **Visa/Carte Bleue** or **Mastercard** (Access) groups. Instructions are often given in French, English and German. Bear in mind that ATMs may run out of notes before the end of the weekend.

If there is no ATM, you can withdraw up to F2,000 per day on Visa at the foreign counter of a bank showing the Visa sign. The Bank will need to obtain telephone authorization for such withdrawals first.

BANKING HOURS

A S A GENERAL RULE, banks in northern France are open Mon–Fri approximately 9am– 4:30 or 5:15pm. However, some are open only till noon, and many will close at noon on the working day before a holiday.

In southern France, banks are normally open Tue–Sat, approxi- mately 8am–12 noon and from 1:30–4:30pm. Around a public hol- iday, they are usually closed from Friday noon to Tuesday morning.

OTHER SOURCES

G IRO BANK ACCOUNT holders can use the postcheque system to obtain cash from post offices, often open longer hours than banks.

Outside Paris, independent bureaux de change are rare

except in major railway stations and areas with a high density of tourists.

Privately owned bureaux de change can have variable rates: check commission and minimum charges first.

CARDS AND CHEQUES

T RAVELLER'S CHEQUES can be obtained from **American Express**, **Thomas Cook** or your bank. If you know that you will spend most of them, it is best to have them issued in French francs. American Express cheques are widely accepted in France. If cheques are exchanged at an Amex office no commission is charged. In the case of theft, cheques are replaced at once.

Because of the high com- missions charged, many French businesses do not accept the American Express credit card. The most com- monly used credit card is Carte Bleue/Visa. Eurocard/ Mastercard (Access in UK) is also widely accepted.

Credit cards issued in France are now "smart cards", which means they have a *puce* (a microchip capable of storing data). Many retailers have machines designed to read both smart cards and magnetic strips. If your conven- tional card cannot be read in the smart card slot you will be told you have a *puce morte*. Persuade the cashier to try swiping the card through the magnetic reader *(bande magnétique)*. You may also be asked to tap in your PIN code *(code confi-*

Machine to read credit cards

dentiel) and press the green key *(validez)* on a small keypad by the cash desk.

EUROCHEQUES

W ITH EUROCHEQUES you can write cheques in francs for the exact amount of a purchase up to a limit of F1,400; several cheques can be written to cover a larger sum. Cheques are guaranteed by a Eurocheque card. Euro- cheques can also be used to obtain cash from a bank.

DIRECTORY

FOREIGN BANKS

American Express
11 rue Scribe, 75009 Paris.
Map 4 D5. **[** *01 47 77 70 00.*

Thomas Cook
25 boulevard des Capucines, 75002 Paris.
[*01 42 96 26 78.*

Barclays
21 rue Lafitte, 75009 Paris.
Map 4 F4. **[** *01 44 79 79 79.*

Midland
20 bis av Rapp, 75007 Paris.
Map 1 C4. **[** *01 44 42 70 00.*

LOST CARDS AND TRAVELLER'S CHEQUES

American Express
[*01 47 77 72 00 (cards)*
[*0800 90 86 00 (cheques)*
or reverse charge call to UK:
[*0171-222 9633.*

Visa/Mastercard/Carte Bleue
[*01 42 77 11 90 in Paris*
or reverse charge call to UK:
[*0604 230 230.*

Currency

THE FRENCH UNIT OF CURRENCY is the franc, which is indicated by the letter "F" before or, more usually, after the amount. It is distinguished from the Swiss or Belgian franc by the use of the letters "FF". There are 100 centimes to the franc, but their value is now so small that 1 centime coins are no longer in circulation.

Bank Notes
French bank notes come in the denominations F20, F50, F100, F200 and F500. They increase in size progressively according to their value.

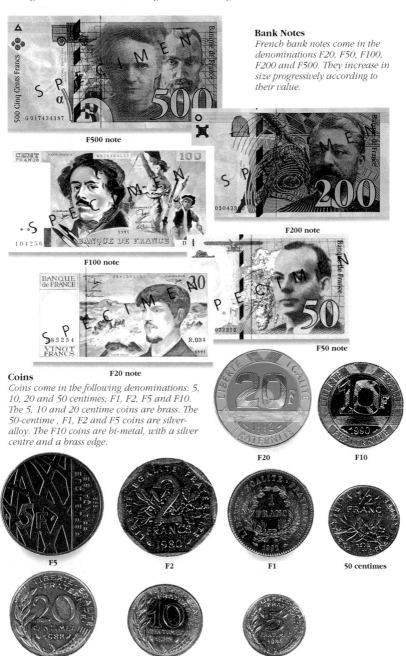

F500 note

F200 note

F100 note

F50 note

F20 note

Coins
Coins come in the following denominations: 5, 10, 20 and 50 centimes; F1, F2, F5 and F10. The 5, 10 and 20 centime coins are brass. The 50-centime, F1, F2 and F5 coins are silver-alloy. The F10 coins are bi-metal, with a silver centre and a brass edge.

F20

F10

F5

F2

F1

50 centimes

20 centimes

10 centimes

5 centimes

Shopping

SHOPPING IN FRANCE is a delight. Whether you go to the hypermarkets and department stores, or seek out the small specialist stores and markets, you will be tempted by stylish French presentation and the quality of goods on offer. Renowned for its food and wine, France also offers world-famous fashion, pottery, porcelain and crystal.

This section gives guidelines on opening hours, and the range of goods stocked by the different types of stores and markets. There are also tips on how to buy wine straight from the vineyards and wine co-operatives, and a size conversion chart to make clothes shopping easier.

Olive Oil from Baux

Fresh nectarines and melons on sale at a market stall

OPENING HOURS

FOOD SHOPS open at about 7am and close around noon for lunch. After lunch most are open until 7pm or later. Bakeries often stay open until 1pm or later, serving snacks at lunchtime.

Shops which do not close at lunchtime include some supermarkets, department stores and most hypermarkets.

General opening hours for non-food shops are around 9am–6pm Mon–Sat, often with a break for lunch. Many of these shops are closed on Monday mornings.

Food shops (and news-agents) are open on Sunday mornings. Virtually every shop in France is closed on Sunday afternoon, except for the last weeks before Christmas when hypermarkets remain open all day. Smaller shops may be closed one day of the week, usually Monday. However, those in tourist regions are often open every day in the high season.

LARGER SHOPS

HYPERMARKETS (*hypermarchés* or *grandes surfaces*) can be found on the outskirts of every sizeable town: look for signs indicating *centre commercial*. Among the biggest are Carrefour, Casino, Auchan and Continent. Discount petrol is often sold, but you may have to pay for it in cash. Check before you fill up.

Department stores (*grands magasins*), such as the cheap and cheerful Monoprix and Prisunic, are often found in town centres. Others, like the more upmarket Printemps and Galeries Lafayette, can be found both in town and out-of-town centres.

A local bakery, which will often sell pâtisseries as well as bread

SPECIALIST SHOPS

ONE OF THE PLEASURES of shopping in France is that specialist shops for food still flourish despite the new large supermarkets. The *boulangerie*, for bread, is frequently combined with a *pâtisserie* selling cakes and pastries. The *traiteur* sells prepared foods. Cheese shops (*fromagerie*) and other shops specializing in dairy products (*laiterie*) may also be combined, while the *boucherie* (butcher's) and *charcuterie* (delicatessen) are often separate shops. For general groceries go to an *épicerie fine*.

Cleaning and household products are available from a *droguerie*, but hardware is bought from a *quincaillerie*. The term *Papeterie* (stationer's) covers both the expensive, specialist retailers and the colourful, seductive sections in hypermarkets.

MARKETS

THIS GUIDE LISTS the market days for every town featured. To find out where the market is, ask a passerby for *le marché*. Markets usually finish promptly at noon and don't re-open in the afternoon.

Look for local producers, including those with only one or two special items to sell, as their goods are often cheaper and of better quality.

By law, price tags include the origin of all produce: *pays* means local. Chickens from Bresse are marketed wearing a red, white and blue badge giving the name of the producer as proof of authenticity. If you are visiting markets over several weeks, look for items just coming into season, such as fresh walnuts, the first wild asparagus, early artichokes or tiny *fraises des bois* (wild strawberries).

At the market, you can also buy spices, shoes and clothes, and some offbeat peculiarities such as decorative cabbages.

There is a full calendar of important seasonal regional markets in France, specializing in such things as truffles, hams, garlic, *foie gras* and livestock. *Foires artisanales* may be held at the same time as the seasonal fairs, selling local produce and crafts.

REGIONAL PRODUCE

FRENCH REGIONAL specialities can be bought outside their area of origin. It is, however, interesting to buy them locally as their creation and flavour reflect the traditions, tastes and climate of the region.

Provence, in the south, prides itself on the quality of its olive oil, the best of which is made from the first cold pressing and lovingly decanted every day for a week. In the temperate north, Camembert is the product of fresh Norman milk that has been cured for at least three weeks. Popular drinks are also associated with particular regions. Pastis, made from aniseed, is popular in the south, while calvados, made from apples, is from the north *(see p245)*.

Location also determines quality. Lyon's culinary importance stems from the distinctive cheeses that come from the surrounding dairy region, and the proximity of Bresse for chickens, Charolais for beef and the Alsace region for sausages.

Sausages and cheeses, regional specialities on offer in a Lyon market

WINE

IN WINE-producing areas, follow the *dégustation* (tasting) signs to vineyards *(domaines)* where you can taste the wine. You will be expected to buy at least one bottle. Wine co-operatives sell the wine of small producers. Here you can buy wine in five- and ten-litre containers *(en vrac)*, as well as in bottles. The wine is often rated AOC, *appellation d'origine controlée*, selling at

Pastis 51, drunk in the south

less than F10 a litre. As wine sold *en vrac* is "duty-free", customers receive a *laissez-passer* (permit) indicating their destination. Bottled wine sold by co-ops is duty-paid.

HOUSEHOLD AND KITCHEN GOODS

WHEN BUYING goods for the home, the best department stores are Alinéa, Cèdre Rouge and Habitat, whose stock in France is geared to the Gallic market. Despalles is good for garden furniture, and Le Roy Merlin is the hypermarket of the DIY world.

It is surprisingly rare to see the whole range of kitchen goods available in a specialist shop. Try instead the kitchen

section of department stores. General hardware shops stock cast-iron cookware and cooking equipment. White china is found in specialist stores.

A good variety of pottery is available anywhere in France at reasonable prices, but particularly near the centres where it is made, such as at Aubagne near Marseille, and Vallauris near Grasse *(see p512)*.

Other fine examples of French craftsmanship come from Limoges, a world-famous centre for porcelain since the 18th century *(see p168)*, and Baccarat, renowned for fine crystal since 1764.

CLOTHING

ELEGANT AND CASUAL clothes can be found even in quite small towns. Paris, however, remains the centre for fashion; refer to pages 136–7 for details on men and women's fashion.

Provençal dried herbs for culinary use and making teas

SIZE CHART

For Australian sizes follow the British and American conversions.

Women's dresses, coats and skirts

French	34	36	38	40	42	44	46
British	8	10	12	14	16	18	20
American	6	8	10	12	14	16	18

Women's shoes

French	36	37	38	39	40	41
British	3	4	5	6	7	8
American	5	6	7	8	9	10

Men's suits

French	44	46	48	50	52	54	56	58
British	34	36	38	40	42	44	46	48
American	34	36	38	40	42	44	46	48

Men's shirts

French	36	38	39	41	42	43	44	45
British	14	15	15½	16	16½	17	17½	18
American	14	15	15½	16	16½	17	17½	18

Men's shoes

French	39	40	41	42	43	44	45	46
British	6	7	7½	8	9	10	11	12
American	7	7½	8	8½	9½	10½	11	11½

Communications

FRENCH TELECOMMUNICATIONS are today sophisticated and efficient. They are run by France Télécom; the postal service is La Poste. Public telephones are located in most public places, including on the streets. If you are phoning abroad from France, the best way is to use a telephone card *(télécarte)*.

Bureaux des postes (post offices) are identified by the blue-on-yellow La Poste sign. La Poste used to be called the PTT, so road signs often still indicate PTT.

Foreign language newspapers are available in most large towns. Some TV channels and radio stations broadcast foreign-language programmes.

Sign for public telephone

TELEPHONING IN FRANCE

PAYPHONES TAKE coins (F1, F2, F5 and F10) or plastic telephone cards *(télécartes)*. Cards are cheaper and more convenient to use than coins. They are sold in either 50 or 120 units and can be bought at post offices and *tabacs* (tobacconists) and some newsagents. For local calls, a unit lasts up to six minutes. Many phones now also accept credit cards (with a PIN number).

In cafés, payphones are coin-operated and are reserved for the use of patrons. Post offices have telephone booths *(cabines)* where you can telephone first and pay after the call. This is cheaper than making long-distance calls from hotels, which often add hefty surcharges.

The Minitel electronic directory can also be used free in post offices.

Home Direct calling service, or *pays directe*, lets you book the call through an operator in your country, and pay by credit card or by reversing the charges. Sometimes you can also call a third country.

In October 1996, all telephone numbers in France changed from eight to ten digits, and the old "16" code was dispensed with. For calls to and within Paris and the Ile de France, the prefix 01 is now added to the original eight-digit number; a 02 prefix is added for northwestern regions; 03 for the northeast; 04 for the southeast (including Corsica); and 05 for the southwest. When phoning from abroad, omit the initial 0 from the new area code, ie dial 33 followed by nine digits.

USING A PHONECARD TELEPHONE

1 Lift receiver and wait for a dialling tone.

2 Insert the *télécarte*, arrow side up, in the direction that the arrow is pointing.

3 The display will show how many units are stored on the card and then tell you to dial.

4 Key in the number and wait to be connected.

5 If you want to make another call, do not replace the receiver; simply press the green follow-on call button.

6 When you have finished the call, replace the receiver. The card will emerge from the slot. Remove it.

7 If card runs out in mid-call, it will re-emerge; remove it and insert another.

French phonecard

HOW TO KEY INTO MINITEL

Minitel provides a variety of services through a screen and keyboard connected to the telephone line. To use Minitel, press the telephone symbol and enter the Minitel number and code. For directory information, press the telephone symbol and key in 3611. When beeping starts, press Connexion/Fin. Specify the service or name of supplier required. Enter town or area. Press Envoi to search. To disconnect, press Veille or Connexion/Fin. Charges vary and are displayed on the screen.

TV AND RADIO

THE ARTE CHANNEL broadcasts foreign films, documentaries and concerts every evening, dubbed in French, or with French subtitles. M6 is mainly music, pop and jazz, as well as dubbed US sitcoms and detective series. Canal+ specializes in sport and films. Foreign films are first screened with subtitles and then a dubbed version is shown later in the month. Listings indicate whether the screening will be *v.o. (version originale)* or *v.f. (version française)*. Films on channels FR2 and FR3 are dubbed, except late on Friday and late on Sunday.

Radio France Internationale (738 MW) broadcasts news in English from 4–5pm daily. The French radio news station, France Inter, broadcasts news and weather and traffic reports. The BBC monthly magazine "Worldwide" gives the wavelengths and programme guides for BBC World service broadcasts.

Foreign newspapers sold in France

USING A COIN-OPERATED TELEPHONE

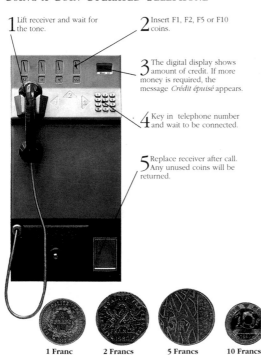

1 Lift receiver and wait for the tone.

2 Insert F1, F2, F5 or F10 coins.

3 The digital display shows amount of credit. If more money is required, the message *Crédit épuisé* appears.

4 Key in telephone number and wait to be connected.

5 Replace receiver after call. Any unused coins will be returned.

| 1 Franc | 2 Francs | 5 Francs | 10 Francs |

NEWSPAPERS AND MAGAZINES

ENGLISH LANGUAGE newspapers printed in Europe and widely available on the day of publication are the *Financial Times*, the *Guardian International*, and the *International Herald Tribune*. The *European*, published every Friday, and English language magazines like the *Economist*, *USA Today*, and *Newsweek* are easy to find, especially at *maisons de la presse* (newsagents) and railway kiosks in large towns and cities. Many other English newspapers and the major Swiss, Italian, German and Spanish titles are sold the day after publication.

The most influential French newspapers are, from right wing to left: *Le Figaro*, *France Soir*, *Le Monde*, *Libération* and *L'Humanité*.

Special interest magazines listing events all over France are: *Diapason*, for music; *Beaux Arts*, for art; and *Art Presse* for all the arts. See page 140 for listings magazines in Paris.

USEFUL FRENCH DIALLING CODES

- All domestic calls require a two-digit area prefix followed by eight digits. The area codes are:
  Paris and Ile de France 01; northwest 02; northeast 03; southeast 04; southwest 05.
- For operator service, dial 13.
- For international information, dial:
  12 for Germany;
  13 for other European countries;
  14 for the rest of the world.
- To make direct international calls, dial 00, wait for the tone, then dial the country code, area code and the number.
- The front pages of the A–H telephone directory gives the cost of calls per minute for each country and lists their country code.
- The country codes for the following are:
  Australia: 61; **Canada and USA**: 1; **Eire**: 353; **France**: 33; **New Zealand**: 64; **UK**: 44.
  Always omit the initial 0 of the area code.

LA POSTE

Road sign giving directions to the post office

USING LA POSTE

LA POSTE (the Post Office) used to be called the P.T.T. *(postes, télégraphes, téléphones)* and although the signs have been changed on post office buildings, some road signs still give directions to the P.T.T.

The postal service in France is fast and reliable. However, it is not cheap, especially when sending a parcel abroad, as all sea-mail services have been discontinued.

At La Poste, postage stamps *(timbres)* are sold singly or in *carnets* of seven or ten. Common postage stamps are also sold at *tabacs*. You can also consult telephone directories *(annuaires)*, buy phonecards, cash postcheques, send or receive money orders *(mandats)*, and call abroad.

Post offices also provide, for a small collection fee, a mail holding service *(poste restante)* so you can receive mail, care of post offices in France. As an address, the sender should write the recipient's surname in block capitals before the Christian name, followed by "Poste Restante", then the postcode and name of the town it is to be sent to. Unless specified otherwise, mail will go to that town's main post office *(recette principale)*.

Post offices usually open from 9am–5pm Mon–Fri, often with a break for lunch, and 9am–noon on Saturdays.

A distinctive yellow French mail box

SENDING A LETTER

LETTERS ARE POSTED in yellow mail boxes which often have separate slots for the town you are in, the *département* and other destinations *(autres destinations)*.

There are eight different price zones for international mail. EU countries are the cheapest, Australasia the most expensive. You can also buy aerograms, which cost the same for all countries.

A postman *(un facteur)*

POSTCODES

ALL FRENCH ADDRESSES have five-digit postcodes. The first two digits represent the *département (see opposite)*. If they are followed by 000, this indicates the main town in that *département*, so, for example, Bordeaux is 33000. France's largest cities, Paris, Lyon and Marseille, are divided into *arrondissements*, which are shown in the last two digits of the postcode.

A variety of standard issue French stamps

Carnet of ten stamps

The town hall in Compiègne

LOCAL GOVERNMENT IN FRANCE

A COMPLEX JIGSAW, France's local government operates in a three-tier system – *région*, *département* and *commune*. The country used to comprise separate semi-autonomous provinces or duchies, like Provence and the smaller Anjou. During the Revolution, these were replaced by a standard-sized network of 96 *départements*. These are administrative units mostly named after rivers, for example Haute-Loire, each ruled by a "prefect" appointed in Paris.

The system had its strengths, but was too state-controlled for a modern democracy. Now some of the prefect's power has gone to the *département*'s elected council. For some functions the *départements* have been grouped into 22 *régions*, each with an elected assembly. Several, like Brittany and Alsace, roughly correspond to the old provinces; others are hybrids, like Centre and Rhône-Alpes.

At a lower level, France remains split up into around 35,000 *communes* (parishes or boroughs), ranging from big cities like Paris or Lyon to tiny villages. Each *commune* has its elected mayor, a figure of great local influence, ruling from the *mairie* (town hall). This system is cumbersome, yet village communes refuse to merge, so great is the pull of local pride.

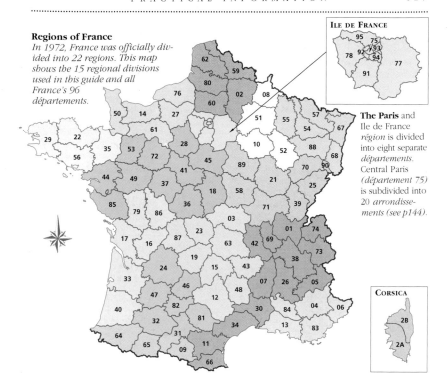

Regions of France

In 1972, France was officially divided into 22 regions. This map shows the 15 regional divisions used in this guide and all France's 96 départements.

ILE DE FRANCE

The Paris and Ile de France *région* is divided into eight separate *départements*. Central Paris *(département 75)* is subdivided into 20 *arrondissements (see p144)*.

CORSICA

THE DÉPARTEMENTS OF FRANCE

PARIS AND ILE DE FRANCE

75 Paris
77 Seine-et-Marne
78 Yvelines
91 Essonne
92 Hauts-de-Seine
93 Seine-St-Denis
94 Val-de-Marne
95 Val-d'Oise

NORTHEAST FRANCE

Le Nord and Picardy

02 Aisne
59 Nord
60 Oise
62 Pas-de-Calais
80 Somme

Champagne

08 Ardennes
10 Aube
51 Marne
52 Haute-Marne

Alsace and Lorraine

54 Meurthe-et-Moselle
55 Meuse
57 Moselle
67 Bas-Rhin
68 Haut-Rhin
88 Vosges

WESTERN FRANCE

Normandy

14 Calvados
27 Eure
50 Manche
61 Orne
76 Seine-Maritime

Brittany

22 Côtes-du-Nord
29 Finistère

35 Ille-et-Vilaine
56 Morbihan

The Loire Valley

18 Cher
28 Eure-et-Loir
36 Indre
37 Indre-et-Loire
41 Loir-et-Cher
44 Loire-Atlantique
45 Loiret
49 Maine-et-Loire
53 Mayenne
72 Sarthe
85 Vendee

CENTRAL FRANCE

Burgundy and Franche-Comté

21 Côte d'Or
25 Doubs
39 Jura
58 Nièvre
70 Haute-Saône
71 Saône-et-Loire
89 Yonne
90 Territoire de Belfort

The Massif Central

03 Allier
12 Aveyron
15 Cantal
19 Corrèze
23 Creuse
43 Haute-Loire
48 Lozère
63 Puy-de-Dôme
87 Haute-Vienne

Rhône Valley and French Alps

01 Ain
05 Hautes Alpes
07 Ardèche
26 Drôme
38 Isère
42 Loire

69 Rhône
73 Savoie
74 Haute-Savoie

SOUTHWEST FRANCE

Poitou and Aquitaine

16 Charente
17 Charente-Maritime
33 Gironde
40 Landes
79 Deux-Sèvres
86 Vienne

Périgord, Quercy and Gascony

24 Dordogne
32 Gers
46 Lot
47 Lot-et-Garonne
81 Tarn
82 Tarn-et-Garonne

The Pyrenees

09 Ariège
31 Haute-Garonne
64 Pyrénées-Atlantiques
65 Hautes-Pyrénées

THE SOUTH OF FRANCE

Languedoc-Roussillon

11 Aude
30 Gard
34 Hérault
66 Pyrénées-Orientales

Provence and the Côte d'Azur

04 Alpes-de-Haut-Provence
06 Alpes-Maritimes
13 Bouches-du-Rhône
83 Var
84 Vaucluse

Corsica

2A Corse-du-Sud
2B Haute-Corse

Specialist Holidays and Outdoor Activities

A COUNTRY AS RICHLY DIVERSE in culture and geography as France offers an amazing variety of sport and leisure activities. For the best in entertainment and spectator sports, festivals and annual events, see *France through the Year* on pages 32–5. Information on current leisure and sporting activities in a particular region is available from the tourist offices listed for each town in this guide. The suggestions below cover some of the most popular as well as some more unusual pursuits.

Hiking along the Gorges du Verdon in Provence *(see pp504–5)*

SPECIALIST HOLIDAYS

F RENCH GOVERNMENT TOURIST Offices *(see p617)* have an extensive range of information on travel companies offering special interest holidays. Send off for *The Traveller in France Reference Guide*.

Educational courses include language learning, very often combined with other activities. Request *Cours de francais pour étudiants étrangers* from the cultural counsellor's office of your **French Embassy**, or send for *Le Petit Guide* from **Ulysses International**.

Young people can enjoy a French-speaking holiday by working part time on the restoration of historic sites with **R.E.M.P.ART** *(Association pour la Réhabilitation et Entretien des Monuments et du Patrimoine Artistique)*.

There is a wide range of gastronomic courses available, teaching classical cuisine or regional cookery. Wine appreciation courses for various levels of expertise are also available. Craft activities include courses for tapestry, sculpture and painting.

Nature lovers can enjoy the *parcs nationaux*, and can join organized bird watching and botanical trips in many areas, including the Camargue, the Cévennes and Corsica.

The Guide des Jardins de France from **Editions Hachette** is a useful reference guide when visiting France's many beautiful gardens.

GOLF AND TENNIS

T HERE ARE golf courses all over France, especially along the north and south coasts and in Aquitaine. French players have to reach a minimum standard and obtain a licence in order to play, so take your handicap certificate with you. Most top courses offer weekend or longer tutored breaks geared to any level of player. *Le Guide des Golfs de France* from **Editions Sand et Menges** will give details.

Tennis is very popular in France and courts for hourly hire can be found in almost every town. Take your own equipment with you as hire facilities may not be available.

Mountain bikes, wonderful for exploring

Escaping into the forest at Fontainebleau *(see pp170–71)*

WALKING, CYCLING AND HORSERIDING

M ORE THAN 30,000 km (19,000 miles) of *Grandes Randonnées* (long-distance tracks) and the shorter *Petites Randonnées* are clearly waymarked. The routes vary in difficulty and include long pilgrim routes, alpine crossings and tracks through national parks. *Topo Guides*, published by **Fédération Française de la Randonnée Pédestre**, describe the *GR* tracks in French with details of transport connections, overnight stops and food shopping. They also have a more general guide to walking, *Guide du Randonneur*.

Some *Grandes and Petites Randonnées* are open to mountain bikes and horses. For detailed advice on cycling in France, contact the **CTC** (Cyclists' Touring Club) or the **Fédération Française de Cyclotourisme**. Local tourist offices in France provide details about riding facilities in their area. *Gîtes d'étapes (see p539)* offer dormitory accommodation close to well-known tracks.

MOUNTAIN SPORTS

A PART FROM down-hill skiing and *ski de fond* (cross-country skiing), catered for by numerous travel operators, the mountains, especially the Alps and Pyrenees, are enjoyed in the

Canoes at St-Chély, near the Gorges du Tarn *(see pp360–61)*

summer by rock-climbers and mountaineers. Contact the **Féderation Française de la Montagne et de l'Escalade** for more information.

AERONAUTICAL SPORTS

Learning to fly in France can be much cheaper than in the UK. Information on schools can be obtained from the **Fédération Nationale Aéronautique**. There are also plenty of opportunities to learn the exhilarating skills of gliding, paragliding and hang gliding. For more information, contact the **Fédération Française de Vol Libre**.

Paragliding or *parapente* off the cliffs of Chamonix *(see pp312–13)*

WATER SPORTS

White-water rafting, kayaking and canoeing take place on many French rivers, especially in the Massif Central. More information can be obtained from The **Fédération Française de Canoë-Kayak**. The Atlantic coast around Biarritz offers some of the best surfing and windsurfing in Europe. Sailing and water-skiing are also popular all over France. Training schools and equipment hire are found both at the coast and on lakes.

Swimming facilities are generally good, although beaches in the South of France can be very crowded *(see pp464–5)*.

FIELD SPORTS

Although hunting is a popular sport in France, a *permis de chasser* is essential. This involves passing an exam in French, which makes it difficult for visitors to take part. There are regional variations of season depending on the activity. Details are displayed in local town halls.

All kinds of fishing, for both fresh and seawater fish, are available, depending on the area. Local fishing shops sell the *carte de pêche*, which gives details of regulations.

NATURISM

There are nearly 50 centres in France for naturism, mostly in the south, southwest and Corsica. Information is available in English from French Government Tourist Offices or **Fédération Française de Naturisme**.

PUBLIC EVENTS

To join the French enjoying their spare time, look out for football and rugby matches, or cycling races. Special seasonal markets and local *fêtes* often combine antiques fairs and *boules* tournaments with rock and pop concerts.

TRAVEL INFORMATION

RANCE has highly advanced transport systems, with Paris at the hub of its air, rail and road networks. Paris's two main airports have direct flights to North America, Africa, Japan and the rest of Europe. The city's six major railway stations connect it to some 6,000 destinations in France and provide links to the whole of Europe. France is also well connected by sea, with frequent ferry crossings in the English Channel and the Mediterranean.

ARRIVING BY AIR

RANCE IS SERVED by nearly all international airlines. Some airports near the border, such as Geneva, Basle and Luxembourg, can also be used for destinations in France.

The main British airlines with regular flights to France are **British Airways** and **British Midland**, and the main French airline is **Air France**. From the United States there are regular flights through American Airlines and Delta. Air Canada runs flights from Canada, and **Qantas** provides connecting flights from Australia and New Zealand.

AIR FARES

IRLINE FARES are at their highest during the peak summer season in France, usually from July to September. Different airlines, however, may have slightly different high summer season periods, so check with the airlines or an

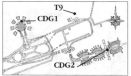

Charles de Gaulle Airport
Terminals CDG1, CDG2 and T9 are linked by shuttle buses and mini-metro trains. Departures are on the lower level and arrivals on the upper.

CDG1 is used for international flights, except those of Air France.

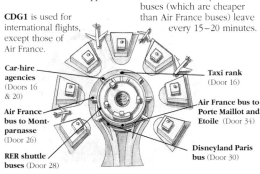

Car-hire agencies
(Doors 16 & 20)

Air France bus to Montparnasse (Door 26)

RER shuttle buses (Door 28)

Taxi rank (Door 16)

Air France bus to Porte Maillot and Etoile (Door 34)

Disneyland Paris bus (Door 30)

PARIS CHARLES DE GAULLE/ROISSY (CDG)

HERE ARE TWO main terminals: CDG1 and CDG2. T9 is for charter flights. Taxis to central Paris cost F200–300.

Air France buses go to Porte Maillot and Charles de Gaulle-Etoile. The journey takes about 40 minutes. Air France buses also go to Montparnasse TGV train station every hour. RATP buses (which are cheaper than Air France buses) leave every 15–20 minutes.

No. 350 goes to Gare du Nord and Gare de l'Est, and No. 351 goes to Place de la Nation. Journeys take about an hour, but times may vary, depending on traffic conditions.

All the major car hire companies can be found at the airport. A limousine service is also available, but this must be reserved in advance, and costs F700–F900 to Paris.

A fast, reliable and cheap way to the centre is by train. Metro Express RER reaches Gare du Nord and Châtelet in 35 minutes. Trains leave every 15 minutes.

CDG2 also has its own TGV station, with direct lines to Lille (1hr) and Lyon (2hrs), and connections to other branches of the TGV network.

Major expansion is underway at CDG2, due for completion in 2003, so layouts may alter.

Airport Information
[i] *01 48 62 22 80.*

CDG2 is used for all Air France flights and for short-hop international flights by other carriers.

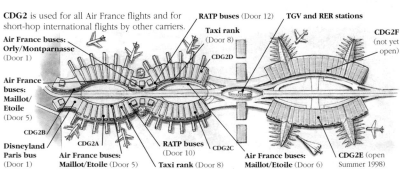

RATP buses (Door 12)   **TGV and RER stations**

Taxi rank (Door 8)

CDG2F (not yet open)

Air France buses: Orly/Montparnasse (Door 1)

CDG2D

Air France buses: Maillot/ Etoile (Door 5)

CDG2B

Disneyland Paris bus (Door 1)   **Air France buses: Maillot/Etoile** (Door 5)

CDG2A

RATP buses (Door 10)   **Taxi rank** (Door 8)

CDG2C

Air France buses: Maillot/Etoile (Door 6)

CDG2E (open Summer 1998)

agent to find out which fares will apply when you travel.

APEX fares are booked in advance. They cannot be changed or cancelled without penalty and there are also minimum and maximum stay requirements. Note that children often travel more cheaply than adults.

Fierce competition between airlines means there are some very attractive discounts on offer. Look around for the best deals; reputable discount agents provide some very good ones. The addresses of a selection of recommended discount travel agents are listed on page 633. These agents offer both charter and regular scheduled flights at competitive prices. Many of them have representatives in other countries.

Getting to or from France on the national carrier, Air France

FLIGHT TIMES

FLIGHT TIMES to Paris from various cities are: London: 1 hour; Dublin: 90 minutes; Montreal: 7½ hours; New York: 8 hours; Los Angeles: 12 hours; Sydney: 23 hours.

INTERNATIONAL AIRPORTS

MAIN AIRPORTS in France serving international and domestic flights are listed overleaf, along with transport details. Below are details of Paris's two main airports.

Orly Airport
The two terminals, Orly Sud and Orly Ouest, are linked by shuttle bus, but they are within walking distance of one another.

Orly Ouest is used almost exclusively for domestic flights.

ORLY AIRPORT (ORY)

THERE ARE two terminals: Orly Sud and Orly Ouest. Taxis take 25–45 minutes to the city centre, depending on the traffic, and cost F100–180.

Air France buses leave the airport every 12 minutes and take around 30 minutes to reach the centre of Paris, stopping at Les Invalides and Montparnasse.

The RATP Orlybus leaves every 13 minutes and takes about 50 minutes to reach the Denfert-Rochereau metro.

The Jet Bus, which connects Orly to Villejuif-Louis Aragon metro, departs from the airport every 12 minutes.

Shuttle buses link the airport with RER Orlyrail services at nearby Rungis. Trains for Gare d'Austerlitz leave every 15 minutes, and take 45 minutes.

A train service, Orlyval, links up with the Roissy Rail RER line B at Antony station nearby, with trains leaving every 4–7 minutes for Châtelet. The journey takes 30 minutes.

Car rental companies at the airport include Avis, Budget, Century, Citer, EuroDollar, Europcar, Eurorent and Hertz. A chauffeur-driven limousine to Paris costs F650–800.

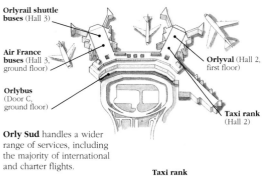

Orlyrail shuttle buses (Hall 3)

Air France buses (Hall 3, ground floor)

Orlybus (Door C, ground floor)

Orlyval (Hall 2, first floor)

Taxi rank (Hall 2)

Orly Sud handles a wider range of services, including the majority of international and charter flights.

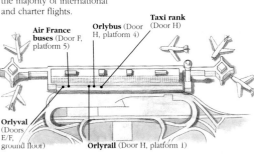

Air France buses (Door F, platform 5)

Orlybus (Door H, platform 4)

Taxi rank (Door H)

Orlyval (Doors E/F, ground floor)

Orlyrail (Door H, platform 1)

Airport Information
🛈 01 49 75 15 15.

FRANCE BY AIR

THE MAIN domestic airline is **Air Inter Europe**. **TAT** (Touraine Air Transport) and **Air Littoral** also have a number of routes, as does Air France, and there are many small airlines that operate within just one region.

Unless you are eligible for discounts, you may find it cheaper and faster to travel on the high-speed railways *(see p635)*, given the time taken to reach out of town airports.

Air Inter Europe offers many discounted fares, based on the red, white and blue calendar system: peak flights are red *(rouge)*; off-peak flights are designated *bleu* (blue) or *blanc* (white). Discounts are based on various combinations of age and frequency of travel.

Domestic flights can be booked from abroad with travel agents or Air France.

AIRPORT	INFORMATION	DISTANCE FROM CITY
Bâle-Mulhouse	03 89 90 31 11	25 km (16 miles)
Bastia (Poretta)	04 95 54 54 54	20 km (13 miles)
Bordeaux (Mérignac)	05 56 34 50 50	12 km (8 miles)
Lille (Lesquin)	03 20 49 68 68	8 km (5 miles)
Lyon (Satolas)	04 72 22 72 21.	25 km (16 miles)
Marseille (Marignane)	04 42 14 14 14.	25 km (16 miles)
Montpellier Fréjorgues	04 67 20 85 00	7 km (4 miles)
Nantes Atlantique	02 40 84 80 00	12 km (8 miles)
Nice (Côte d'Azur)	04 93 21 30 30	6 km (4 miles)
Strasbourg	03 88 64 67 67	12 km (8 miles)
Toulouse (Blagnac)	05 61 42 44 00	7 km (4 miles)

CROSSING THE CHANNEL

THERE ARE SEVERAL crossings between UK and Continental ports. The Channel Tunnel provides a direct link between London and Paris.

Stena Sealink has 90-minute crossings from Dover to Calais and four-hour crossings from Newhaven to Dieppe. **P&O European Ferries** has a 75-minute crossing from Dover to Calais and a six-hour crossing from Portsmouth to Le Havre. It also operates a six-hour service from Portsmouth to Cherbourg. **Sally Viking Line** operates a 2½-hour service from Ramsgate to Dunkirk and a four-hour service to Oostende. **Brittany Ferries** runs

a nine-hour service from Portsmouth to St-Malo. They also have a service to Santander in Spain and to Biarritz, near the French border, and sail from Cork in Eire to Roscoff.

North Sea Ferries sail from Hull to Zeebrugge in Belgium, with good road links to northeast France; P&O sail from Felixstowe to Zeebrugge.

Hoverspeed operates 35-minute hovercraft services between Dover and Calais. The high-speed catamaran is run by **Seacat** between Folkestone and Boulogne, and takes 55 minutes.

THE CHANNEL TUNNEL

THE CHANNEL Tunnel was inaugurated by the Queen and President Mitterrand in 1994. A car-carrying shuttle service, which is operated by **Eurotunnel**, runs between Folkestone and Calais. The passenger service, **Eurostar**, links London and Ashford with Paris *(see p634)*.

Eurotunnel logo

OTHER CROSSINGS

CAR FERRIES sail to Corsica from Marseille and Nice all year round, or from Toulon between April and October. The ferries are run by **SNCM Ferryterranée**. In the high season, SNCM also sail weekly to Sardinia from Marseille and Toulon. SNCM also go to Tunis and Algiers from Marseille.

From April to September **Corsica Marittima** (CMT) operates a three-hour car ferry service between Bastia in Corsica and Livorno in Italy, and an overnight crossing from Porto Vecchio in Corsica to Livorno. **Compagnie Marocaine de Navigation** offers a luxury two-night car ferry service between Sète and Tangier.

Plying the Mediterranean with SNCM Ferryterranée

Taxi Fare to the City	Bus Details	Car Rental
F240–260	City centre 30 mins	Avis, Budget, Citer-EuroDollar, Europcar, Hertz
F180–250	City centre 25 mins	Avis, Budget, Citer-EuroDollar, Europcar, Hertz-Filipi Auto
F160–200	Gare St-Jean 30–45 mins	ADA, Avis, Budget, Citer-EuroDollar, Europcar, Eurorent, Hertz
F100–130	Lille SNCF 20 mins	Avis, Budget, Citer-EuroDollar, Europcar, Hertz
F200–250	Perrache SNCF 40 mins. Also to Chambery, Geneva Apt Valence, St-Etienne and ski resorts	Avis, Budget, Century, Citer-EuroDollar, Eurorent, Hertz
F200–250	St-Charles SNCF 25 mins	Avis, Budget, Citer-EuroDollar, Europcar, Eurorent, Hertz
F80–100	City centre 20 mins	ADA, Avis, Budget, Citer-EuroDollar, Europcar, Eurorent, Hertz
F100–130	City centre 20 mins	ADA, Avis, Budget, Citer-EuroDollar, Europcar, Eurorent, Hertz
F100–120	Gare Routière 20 mins	Avis, Budget, Citer-EuroDollar, Europcar, Eurorent, Hertz, Mattei
F150–200	City centre 30 mins	ADA, Avis, Budget, Citer-EuroDollar, Europcar, Eurorent, Hertz
F100–130	Gare Routière Marengo 20 mins	ADA, Avis, Budget, Citer, Europcar, Eurorent, Hertz, Spanghero

DIRECTORY

AIRLINES

Air France
📞 0802 802 802.
📞 0181–742 6600 in UK.

Air Inter Europe
📞 0802 802 802.

Air Littoral
📞 0803 834 834.

British Airways
📞 0820 802 902.
📞 0990 444 000 in UK.

British Midland
📞 01 48 62 55 65.
📞 0181–745 7321 in UK.

Qantas
📞 01 44 55 52 05.
📞 0181–846 0466 in UK.

TAT
📞 0803 805 805.

TRAVEL AGENCIES

Bordeaux
Usit Voyages, 284 rue St-Cathérine, 33000 Bordeaux.
📞 05 56 33 89 90.

Lyon
Council Travel, 36 quai ... illeton, 69002 ... 7 09 56.

Nice
Council Travel,
37 bis rue d'Angleterre,
06000 Nice.
📞 04 93 82 23 33.

Usit Voyages,
10 rue de Belgique, 06000 Nice.
📞 04 93 87 34 96.

Paris
Council Travel,
1 place de l'Odéon,
75006 Paris.
📞 01 44 41 89 89.

Nouvelle Frontières,
66 bd St-Michel, 75006
Paris. 📞 01 46 34 55 30.

O. T. U.
119 rue St-Martin, 75004
Paris. 📞 01 40 29 12 12.

Usit Voyages,
12 rue Vivienne, 75002
Paris. 📞 01 42 44 14 00.

Usit Voyages,
6 rue de Vaugirard,
75006 Paris.
📞 01 42 34 56 90.

Toulouse
Usit Voyages,
5 rue des Lois, 31000
Toulouse.
📞 05 61 11 52 42.

London
Council Travel,
28A Poland Street,
London W1V 3DB.
📞 0171–437 7767.

Nouvelle Frontières,
11 Blenheim Street,
London W1Y 0QP.
📞 0171–629 7772.

Trailfinders,
215 Kensington High St
London W8 6BD.
📞 0171–937 5400.

Travel Cuts,
295 Regent Street,
London W1R 7YA.
📞 0171–255 1944.
FAX 0171–528 7532.

FERRY SERVICES

Brittany Ferries
📞 02 33 88 44 88.
📞 01202 44 11 36 in UK.

Compagnie Marocaine de Navigation
📞 01 45 22 27 52.

Corsica Marittima (CMT)
📞 04 95 54 66 95.

Hoverspeed
📞 03 21 46 14 14.
📞 01304 240 241 in UK.

North Sea Ferries
📞 01482 77177 in UK.

P&O European Ferries
📞 03 21 46 10 10.
📞 0990 980 980 in UK.

Seacat
📞 03 21 46 14 14.
📞 01304 240 241 in UK.

Stena Sealink
📞 03 21 46 78 30.
📞 01233 647 047 in UK.

SNCM Ferryterranée
📞 0836 57 95 00 (24-hrs for all ports).

Marseille
Embark at Joliette ferry terminal.

Nice
Embark at quai du Commerce.

Toulon
Embark at Gare Maritime.

CHANNEL TUNNEL

Eurostar
📞 01233 617 575.

Eurotunnel
📞 0990 353 535.

Travelling by Train

SNCF

SNCF logo

THE FRENCH state railway, Société Nationale des Chemins de Fer (**SNCF**), provides an excellent rail network which covers nearly all of France. Even where lines have been closed for economic reasons, SNCF runs bus services, which are free to people with rail passes. The best trains are, however, confined to the *Grandes Lignes* which radiate out of Paris. Travelling off these major lines can be slow so it is sometimes quicker to make your way cross-country via Paris.

fee. Not all trains have restaurant cars or bars, even on long journeys. TGV trains have bars with light meals, but reservations must be made in advance for the at-seat meal service available in first class.

Note that for Lille, Mâcon and Vendome the TGV stop is in a different location from the main station.

ARRIVING IN FRANCE

TRAINS FROM the UK through Dieppe and ports in Normandy arrive in Paris at Gare St-Lazare, or at the Gare du Nord from Boulogne and Calais. Most trains from Scandinavia, Holland and Belgium also arrive at the Gare du Nord.

The terminus for trains from Brittany ports is the Gare Montparnasse on the Left Bank. Trains from southern France, the Alps, Italy, Switzerland and Greece arrive at Gare de Lyon in eastern Paris, the city's main station. The Gare d'Austerlitz on the Left Bank serves southwest France, Spain and Portugal. The Gare de l'Est serves eastern France, Switzerland, Austria and Germany.

Eurostar's passenger service through the Channel Tunnel runs between Waterloo International and the Gare du Nord. **Hoverspeed City Link** provides connecting train travel between London and Paris, with fast Channel crossings via Folkestone.

Travelling by train and car through France with Motorail

TRAVELLING AROUND FRANCE BY TRAIN

FRANCE HAS ALWAYS been known for the punctuality of its trains, and now also for a positive attitude to investment in the rail system. Apart from the four types of TGV, *Trains à Grande Vitesse*, there are many other frequent train services such as the Corail express, the Motorail service *(Trains Autos Couchette* or *TAC*, sometimes called *TAA)*.

Rail traveller with luggage trolley

There are also very good local and suburban train services in the largest cities, and the excellent RER (*Reseau Express Régionale)* train network in the Paris area.

Services such as Train + Auto and Train + Vélo, are also available – you reserve a rental car or bike when you buy your train ticket and collect it from the station of arrival. Train + Hotel provides pre-booked accommodation at your destination. Train de Nuit/Hôtel de Jour gives sleeping car passengers use of a hotel room and its services the following day for half-price. Information on all these services is available from the **Rail Europe** office in London. In France, leaflets are available at most stations. Overnight services are popular in France. Most long distance trains have couchettes, which you must reserve for a

RER

Symbol for Paris suburban trains

FARES

TICKETS BOOKED in France are normally subject to supplements, as indicated by the *calendrier voyageurs*, a red, white and blue calendar. Red is for peak-time travel, and blue for the cheapest fares. Many of the discounts offered (up to 60 per cent) for rail travel are only available on blue days. Fares are also dependent on the distance of the journey, whether you travel first/second class, a reservation fee and the station surcharge. Reservations are compulsory for all TGV trains.

SNCF issues cards which entitle holders to discount fares: *carte vermeil* for the over 60s; *carte à deux* for couples sharing an address; and *carte Kiwi* for up to four people travelling with a child. There are also 12–25 fares for those under 26; *découvertes* fares for advance booking; and *séjours* return fares for trips over 1,000 km (600 miles). Rail passes bought outside the country for use in France include Eurodomino tickets, which allow three, five or ten days' travel in a month. Eurotrain fares are for travellers under 26, and are valid for two months.

Air France Rail offers a combined air and rail package which includes flights from a choice of five British airports to Charles de Gaulle and then unlimited train travel in France with a Eurodomino pass for either a 3, 5 or 10 day period, including transfers in Paris.

Specialist agencies **Travel Cuts** and issue the

allows anyone under 26 one month's unlimited travel in France and 25 other European countries. The slightly more expensive InterRail Plus 26 Card is for travellers over 26. A 10-day pass is also available. Note, you must be a resident to buy an InterRail in France. InterRail passengers must still pay reservation fees and surcharges where applicable.

PRIVATE RAILWAYS

PRIVATELY RUN RAILWAYS are numerous but mostly serve as tourist attractions rather than transport options. However, **Chemins de Fer de Provence** runs the Train des Pignes over the 150-km (90-mile) spectacular route from Nice to Digne. In Corsica, **Chemins de Fer de la Corse** operates two routes, Bastia-Calvi and Calvi-Ajaccio.

A high-speed TGV link

TGV RAIL SERVICE

Trains à Grande Vitesse, or high-speed trains, travel at speeds up to 300 km/h (185 mph). There are three routes. TGV Nord from Paris Gare du Nord, TGV Atlantique from Paris Gare Montparnasse and TGV Sud-Est from Paris Gare de Lyon.

KEY

- ▬ Nord
- ▬ Atlantique
- ▬ Sud-Est

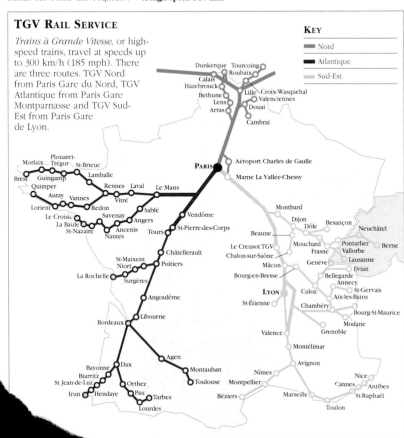

To Book in France

AUTOMATIC TICKET and reservation machines *(billetterie automatique)* are found at main stations. They take credit cards or coins. You can also check train times and fares and make reservations by phoning **SNCF** or by using the Minitel system *(see p624)*. Tickets may be purchased by credit card, then collected at the station.

Reservations are compulsory for travel by TGV, on public holidays, and for a *couchette* or *siège inclinable* (reclinable seat) and must be made at least five minutes before departure. Both reservations and tickets must be validated in a *composteur* machine before boarding the train *(see below)*.

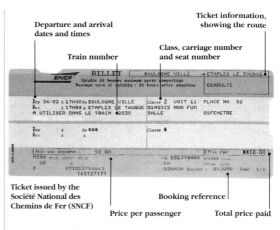

Departure and arrival dates and times

Train number

Ticket information, showing the route

Class, carriage number and seat number

Ticket issued by the Société National des Chemins de Fer (SNCF)

Price per passenger

Booking reference

Total price paid

An automatic ticket machine

To Book in the UK

BOOKING SERVICES by post, telephone and fax for all tickets to and within France can be made through **Rail Europe** who also give information on prices and departure times. There is a £5 per person booking fee, up to a maximum of £15 per booking. Tickets are sent out by registered post the same day if paid by credit card and after five days if paid for by check.

If you intend to travel by Motorail, it is a good idea to get the booklet *French Railways, the Expressway into Europe* first, as there are many

choices of route, fare, and sleeping accommodation.

The Rail Europe office in London offers the full range of discount tickets *(see p634)*, including InterRail. Bookings can be made up to two months in advance and, if you call in person, not less than two days before departure.

Reservations made in the UK may prove difficult to change in France. You may have to buy another reservation, or in the case of Motorail, another ticket and claim a refund later after your return. If you want to change your booking, it is better to do so before leaving for France, where possible, as Rail Europe only charge a small amendment fee.

Tickets for **Eurostar** can be booked direct from this company or via Rail Europe.

Timetables

FRENCH RAILWAY timetables change twice a year in May and September. French Railways sell the *Ville à Ville* timetable, which lists major routes from Paris. They also sell the regional timetables for the Atlantic coast, the southeast and the northeast.

Free leaflets give information on travelling with children, reduced fares, train travel for the disabled and the TGV network *(see pp634–5)*. Some regions, such as Provence-Alpes-Côte d'Azur, now have a regional TER *(Transports Express Régionaux)* timetable which includes coach travel.

Bear in mind that trains in France are punctual. Your train will almost certainly leave on time!

Composteur Machine
Orange composteur machines are located in station halls and at the head of each platform. Insert tickets and reservations separately, printed side up, in the machine. The composteur will punch your ticket and print the time and date on the back. A penalty may be imposed by the inspector on the train if...

ARRIVING BY COACH

COACH TRAVEL is the cheapest way to get to France. The modern coaches operated by **Eurolines** travel to 270 destinations in Europe, including many in France.

There are three departures daily to Paris from Victoria Coach Station in London, dropping off at Bagnolet and in Versailles. The trip takes about nine hours and tickets may be purchased from the **National Express** office at Victoria. Eurolines offer one-way tickets, returns and round trips throughout Europe.

Hoverspeed City Sprint uses the faster hovercraft crossing and takes about 6 hours from Victoria Coach Station to Paris, with a drop-off point 15 minutes by metro from the Gard du Nord.

TRAVELLING AROUND FRANCE BY COACH

LONG-DISTANCE coaches generally only operate where trains don't offer a good service (for example, Geneva to Nice). SNCF (the state railway) operates some coaches and issues regional TER *(Transports Express Régionaux)* combined timetables and tickets.

Eurolines offer a wider range of destinations than most. They also offer excursions and arrange accommodation.

There are many local buses, which run from the town's *Gare Routière* (which is often at the Gare SNCF). Timetables are geared to carry students and people going to work, so the morning departure time from a village may be very early.

TAXIS

IN THE PROVINCES prices vary from one region to another. All taxis must carry meters *(compteurs)*. The pick-up charge should be about F12 plus F3.60 or more per km. You may be able to agree a price for a long journey. Look for a *station de taxi* outside airports or railway stations or in the centre of town. As hailing a taxi is only common practice in France's large cities, you have to book a taxi by telephone in rural areas.

CYCLE TRAVEL

ALTHOUGH CYCLING is popular in France, there are not many trains on which you can take your bicycle. The ones upon which you may are indicated on the timetable by a bicycle symbol. In most instances, however, a bicycle has to be sent as a separate package. The drawback is that you may have to wait up to four days for delivery.

Alternatively, you can hire a bicycle. Through the SNCF, you can reserve a rental bike at a number of stations when you buy your ticket *(see Train + Vélo p634)*. Cycle shops in many towns have touring cycles or mountain bikes for hire, and may also hire mopeds and light motorcycles.

Rural France is ideal for cycling due to its large network of uncrowded roads. There are, however, few cycle lanes in towns. For more details on waymarked cycle routes, see page 628.

HITCH-HIKING

IT IS NOT EASY to get around France by hitch-hiking. You must look clean and "normal" to have any chance of a lift, especially since it is car, rather than lorry, drivers who will be your best bet. The safest and easiest way to hitch-hike long-distance is through **Allo-stop**. This organization has branches in many major towns and will set you up with lifts for a very reasonable rate.

On the Road

The classic Citroën 2 CV

FRANCE HAS one of the densest road networks in Europe, with modern motorways which allow quick and easy access to all parts of the country. However, you can save money on tolls and explore France in a more leisurely way by using some of the other high-quality roads which dissect the country. This section outlines both alternatives and gives instructions on how to use the motorway toll booths and French parking meters (*horodateurs*), as well as some of the rules governing driving in France. There are also tips on where to buy petrol, how to get weather and traffic forecasts, where to hire a car and how to get the best road maps.

Motorway and D-road signs

GETTING TO FRANCE BY CAR

THERE IS A GOOD choice of car-ferry operators from the UK (*see p632*). You can profit from discount fares for short breaks, a flat rate for a car with up to five passengers, or by buying tickets for the crossing in conjunction with Motorail (*see pp634 and 637*).

You can also take the car on the Eurotunnel shuttle (*p632*) through the Channel Tunnel.

WHAT TO TAKE

MANY MOTOR INSURERS now offer a green card, which gives full cover abroad, as a free extension with fully comprehensive policies. The AA, RAC and Europ Assistance have special policies providing a rescue and recovery service.

It is compulsory to take the original registration document for the car, a current insurance certificate and a valid driving licence. You should also carry a passport or National ID card. A sticker showing the country of registration should be dis-

played near the rear number plate. The headlights of right-hand drive cars must be adjusted for left-hand driving or have deflector kits fitted (available at most ports). You must also carry a red warning triangle, spare head-light bulbs, a first-aid kit and a fire extinguisher. If you are caught without these you are liable to be fined. When driving in ski resorts in winter, snow chains (*chaînes*) are essential.

BUYING PETROL IN FRANCE

PETROL (*essence*) is expensive in France, especially on the *autoroutes*. Large supermarkets and hypermarkets sell petrol at a discount. A map (*la carte de l'essence moins chère*), available from French Government Tourist Offices (*see p617*), shows the location of stores which are close to motorway exits. Petrol coupons are not accepted in France. Filling up the tank is known as *faire le plein*.

Diesel fuel (*gazole* or *gasoil*) is comparatively cheap and is sold everywhere, as is unleaded petrol (*sans plomb*).

Some of the most widely available car hire firms in France

RULES OF THE ROAD

UNLESS ROAD signs indicate otherwise, *priorité à droite* means that you must give way to any vehicle joining the road from the right. Most major roads outside built-up areas have the right of way indicated by *passage protegé* signs. Cars already on a roundabout have right of way.

Contrary to convention in the UK, flashing headlights in France means the driver is claiming the right of way.

Other French motoring rules, including parking regulations, are summarized in the **RAC** publication *The European Motoring Guide*. Rules include the compulsory wearing of seat belts, and no overtaking where there is an unbroken white centre-line.

40 km/h (25 mph) speed limit

SPEED LIMITS AND FINES

SPEED LIMITS in France are as follows:
• On autoroutes: 130 km/h (80 mph); 110 km/h (70 mph) when it rains.
• On dual carriageways: 110 km/h (70 mph); 90–100 km/h (55–60 mph) when it rains.
• On other roads: 90 km/h (55 mph), 80 km/h (50 mph) when it rains.
• In towns: 50 km/h (30 mph). This applies anywhere in a village, hamlet or city, unless marked otherwise. In some places it may be lower. Normal limits may not be shown.

On-the-spot fines may be demanded, especially from visitors, for speeding offences and for drink-driving offences. Fines are also imposed for not carrying the proper documentation and for breaking the rules of the road.

Sign indicating one-way system

No entry for any vehicles

***Passage protegé* ends, *priorité à droite* starts**

MOTORWAYS

MOST MOTORWAYS in France have a toll system *(autoroutes à péage)*, which can be expensive. There are short sections which are free, usually close to major centres. Tolls can be paid with either credit cards or cash. Where only small sums are involved, you throw coins into a large receptacle and the change is given automatically.

Much of the *autoroute* network has been built in the last 20 years. It includes good and frequent rest areas and picnic spots 10–20 km (6–12 miles) apart, petrol stations at every 40 km (25 miles), and emergency telephones every 2 km (1¼ miles). Service areas include shops, takeaway food and restaurants, fax and telephone facilities.

OTHER ROADS

IN FRANCE the RN *(route nationale)* and D *(départementale)* roads are a good alternative to motorways. *Bis/Bison futée* signs are posted for alternative routes which avoid heavy traffic.

Sunday is usually a good day to travel as there are very few trucks on the road. Try to avoid travelling at the French holiday rush periods known as *grands départs*. The worst times are weekends in mid-July, and at the beginning and end of August when holidays begin and end.

If you are by-passing rather than driving into Paris, it is more advisable to take the motorways on either side of the city, avoiding the busy *boulevard péripherique* which encircles Paris.

ROAD CONDITIONS AND WEATHER FORECASTS

LOCAL RADIO stations report on road conditions – look out for motorway signs listing their frequencies. **CRICR** (Centre Régional d'Information et de Coordination Routière) lines give general information on regional road conditions. The **CNIR** (Centre National d'Information Routière) line covers the whole of France.

The **RAC** sell a tailor-made route-planning information service, giving scenic options and road conditions.

To get weather forecasts in English for the English Channel ring **Marinecall**, and for selected cities in France, call the **Holiday Weatherline**.

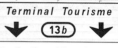

Sign for Channel Tunnel terminal

USING THE AUTOROUTE TOLL

When you join an autoroute, collect a ticket from the machine. This identifies your starting point on the autoroute. You do not pay until you reach an exit toll. You are charged according to the distance travelled and the type of vehicle used.

Motorway Sign
These signs indicate the name and distance to the next toll booth. They are usually blue and white; some show the tariff rates for cars, motorbikes, trucks and caravans.

Toll Booth with Attendant
When you hand in your ticket at a manned toll booth, the attendant will tell you the cost of your journey on the autoroute and the price will be displayed. You can pay with coins, notes, credit cards or with a Eurocheque in French francs. A receipt is issued on request.

Automatic Machine
On reaching the exit toll, insert your ticket into the machine and the price of your journey is displayed in French francs. You can pay either with coins or by credit card. The machine will give change and can issue a receipt.

USING AN HORODATEUR MACHINE

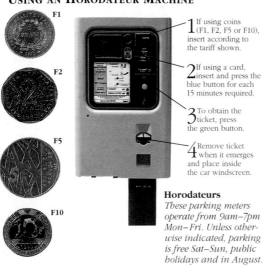

F1

F2

F5

F10

1 If using coins (F1, F2, F5 or F10), insert according to the tariff shown.

2 If using a card, insert and press the blue button for each 15 minutes required.

3 To obtain the ticket, press the green button.

4 Remove ticket when it emerges and place inside the car windscreen.

Horodateurs
These parking meters operate from 9am–7pm Mon–Fri. Unless otherwise indicated, parking is free Sat–Sun, public holidays and in August.

PARKING

Parking regulations vary from town to town. Most operate pay-and-display systems *(horodateurs)*. Some machines accept a parking payment card, which can be bought at tobacconists. Provincial towns often offer free parking from noon to 1:30pm. Parking is normally limited to two hours. In small towns, parking is confined to one side of the street only, alternating at different times of the month. Signs indicate where parking is allowed.

In larger cities, especially Paris, finding a parking space can be a problem. Due to the competition for spaces, cars are frequently "bumped" to create more room.

If you are in an area where parking discs are in use, the local tourist office will supply you with one.

CAR HIRE

All the main international car-hire companies operate in France. It is worth ringing around before you leave for France as there are many special offers for rentals booked and prepaid in the UK or USA. Two smaller companies offer very competitive rates. **Century**

Self Drive operate outside airport terminal buildings, usually from a hotel lobby in the immediate vicinity. They will collect you when you arrive. The other option is **Hire for Lower**, brokers who use cars owned by other car hire companies, like **Budget** and **Citer**. Hiring from either of these companies may work out at half the price of the standard rental.

For car hire booked in combination with flights, your travel agent can usually organize a good deal. SNCF (the French state railway) offers combined train and car-hire fares called Train + Auto

(see p634) with collection points at 200 stations in France. Phone **Rail Europe** for information.

For non-EU residents planning to drive in France for a minimum of three weeks, the best option is the short-term tax-free purchase-and-buy-back service (sometimes called TT leasing) offered by **Citroën**, **Peugeot** and **Renault**.

Information on chauffeur-driven car hire can be obtained from the **Automobile Club de l'Ile de France**.

MAPS

In this guide, each chapter begins with a map of the region showing all the sights and giving useful tips on getting around. If you plan to use autoroutes extensively, *Enjoy your trip on the French Motorways* is a good foldout map of the autoroute network with useful information on the back. The more general *France Tourist Map* marks historic sites and also has useful information on the back. You can get both maps at French Government Tourist Offices *(see p617)*.

For driving shorter distances and for cycling, it is very pleasant to use the smaller D *(département)* roads marked in yellow or white on **Michelin** maps, and often quite empty of traffic. The red Michelin maps of France (scale 1:1,000,000) are useful for planning a trip. The excellent Michelin atlas of France has generously overlapping maps

Mountain cyclists in the Alps

at a scale of 1:200,000. At the same scale, a series of regional maps with yellow covers is sold in different sheet sizes. Maps showing the whole country are also available (red covers). Larger scale maps (green covers) are currently only available for the south of France and the area surrounding Paris. A new series of *Cartes Zoom*, also at 1:100,000 scale, focus on the areas round Toulouse, Bordeaux, Clermont-Ferrand and Nantes.

IGN (Institut Géographique National) is the equivalent of the British Ordnance Survey. The whole of France is available in sheets at 1:250,000, 1:100,000, 1:50,000 and 1:25,000. Their atlas is published in conjunction with the **AA** as *The Big Road Atlas to*

France. **Espace IGN**, just off the Champs-Elysées in Paris, is a haven for map lovers. For super clarity and detail use the *Daily Telegraph* (*Recta Foldex* in France) series from **Roger Lascelles**. Refer to page 628 for walking and cycling maps.

In France, all newsagents and petrol stations stock the more commonly used maps. In the UK, **Stanfords** is famous for its range. Waterstone's bookshops also have a good selection. For more specialized requests try **Roger Lascelles**, **France House**, or World Leisure Marketing *(see p629)*.

The town maps included in this guide locate all the important sights. You can

A selection of French road maps

usually get town plans free from tourist offices, although for large towns you might need the more detailed maps published by Michelin.

DIRECTORY

CAR HIRE

ADA
℡ 01 49 58 44 44 (Paris).

Avis
℡ 01344-70 70 70 (UK).
℡ 01 47 55 61 00 (Paris).

Budget
℡ 0800 181181 (UK).
℡ 01 40 35 33 33 (Paris).

Century Self Drive Ltd
℡ 0442 216512 (UK).
℡ 01 34 29 00 08 (Paris).

Citer-EuroDollar
℡ 01 44 38 60 00 (Paris).

Europcar
℡ 0345 222 525 (UK).
℡ 01 45 00 08 06 (Paris).

Eurorent
℡ 01 44 38 55 55 (Paris).

Hertz
℡ 0990 996 699 (UK).
℡ 01 39 38 38 38 (Paris).

Hire for Lower
℡ 0171-491 1111 (UK).

TRAIN + AUTO

Rail Europe
℡ 0171-203 7000 (UK).

TT LEASING

Citroën
19 bis rue Friant
75014 Paris.
Map 11 C5 (off "N 306").
℡ 01 45 40 30 30.
FAX 01 45 39 10 07.

Peugeot Sodexa
℡ 0800 44 24 44 (Paris).

Renault Eurodrive
Renault Ventes Spéciales
Exportation,
186 av Jean-Jaurès,
75019 Paris.
℡ 0800 05 15 15 (Paris).
FAX 01 42 41 83 47 (Paris).

Australia: International Market Development
℡ (2) 229 33 44.
FAX (2) 290 39 63.

CAR HIRE WITH CHAUFFEUR

Automobile Club de l'Ile de France
14 av de la Grande Armée,
75017 Paris.
Map 2 D4.
℡ 01 40 55 43 00.

WEATHER FORECASTS

Holiday Weatherline
℡ 0839 444070 forecasts for France.

Marinecall
℡ 0839 444071 forecasts for the Channel.

NATIONAL ROAD CONDITIONS

RAC
RAC House, Bartlett Street, South Croydon, Surrey CR2 6XW.
℡ 0345 333 222.
℡ 0800 550 055 for guides.

REGIONAL ROAD CONDITIONS

CRICR Bordeaux
℡ 05 56 96 33 33.

Lille
℡ 03 20 47 33 33.

Lyon
℡ 04 78 54 33 33.

Marseille
℡ 04 91 78 78 78.

Metz
℡ 03 87 63 33 33.

Paris Region
℡ 01 48 99 33 33.

Rennes
℡ 02 99 32 33 33.

MAPS

AA
30–31 Haymarket
London SW1X 4EU.
℡ 0990 989 989.

Espace IGN
107 rue la Boétie
75008 Paris. **Map** 2 F5.
℡ 01 43 98 80 00.
FAX 01 43 98 51 08.

France House
Digbeth Street, Stow-on-the-Wold, Gloucestershire GL54 1BN.
℡ 0451 870 871.
FAX 0451 830 869.

Michelin
℡ 01 45 66 12 34 (Paris).
℡ 0923 415 000 (UK).

Roger Lascelles
47 York Road, Brentford, Mddx TW8 0QP.
℡ 0181-847 0935.
FAX 0181-568 3886.

Stanfords
12–14 Long Acre
London WC2E 9LP.
℡ 0171-836 1321.
FAX 0171-836 0189.

General Index

Acknowledgments

DORLING KINDERSLEY would like to thank the following people whose contributions and assistance have made the preparation of this book possible.

MAIN CONTRIBUTORS

John Ardagh, Rosemary Bailey, Judith Fayard, Lisa Gerard-Sharp, Alister Kershaw, Alec Lobrano, Anthony Roberts, Alan Tillier, Nigel Tisdall.

CONTRIBUTORS AND CONSULTANTS

JOHN ARDAGH is a writer and broadcaster, and author of many books on France, among them *France Today* and *Writers' France*.

ROSEMARY BAILEY has written and edited several guides to regional France, including *Burgundy*, the *Loire Valley* and the *Côte d'Azur*.

ALEXANDRA BOYLE is a writer and editor who has worked in publishing in England and France for 20 years.

ELSIE BURCH DONALD, editor and writer, is the author of *The French Farmhouse*.

DAVID BURNIE B.Sc. has written over 30 books on natural sciences, including *How Nature Works*.

JUDITH FAYARD, an American based in Paris, was Paris bureau chief for *Life* magazine for 10 years, and is now European editor of *Town & Country*. She contributes to various publications, including the *Wall Street Journal*.

LISA GERARD-SHARP is a writer and broadcaster and author of several regional guides to France and Italy.

COLIN JONES is Professor of History at Exeter University. His books include *The Longman Companion to the French Revolution* and *The Cambridge Illustrated History of France*.

ALISTER KERSHAW is an Australian writer and broadcaster who has lived in the Loire Valley for 30 years.

ALEC LOBRANO is an American writer, based in Paris. He is the European editor of *Departures* magazine and contributes to *International Herald Tribune*, *Los Angeles Times* and *The Independent*.

ANTHONY ROBERTS is a writer and translator who has lived in Gascony for 15 years, contributing to various publications including *The Times*, *World of Interiors* and *Architectural Digest*.

ANTHONY ROSE is the wine correspondent of *The Independent* and co-author of *The Grapevine*.

JANE SIGAL is the author of two books on French food, *Normandy Gastronomique* and *Backroom Bistros, Farmhouse Fare*.

ALAN TILLIER is the main contributor to the *Eyewitness Guide to Paris*. He has lived in Paris for more than 20 years as correspondent for various journals, including the *International Herald Tribune*, *Newsweek* and *The Times*.

NIGEL TISDALL is a travel writer and author of guides to Brittany and Normandy.

PATRICIA WELLS is food critic of the *International Herald Tribune* and author of the *Food Lovers' Guide to Paris* and the *Food Lovers' Guide to France*.

ADDITIONAL CONTRIBUTORS

Caroline Bugler, Ann Cremin, Bill Echikson, Adrian Gilbert, Peter Graham, Marion Kaplan, Jim Keeble, Alexandra Kennedy, Fred Mawer, Clive Unger-Hamilton.

ADDITIONAL PHOTOGRAPHY

Jo Craig, Michael Crockett, Mike Dunning, Philip Enticknap, Steve Gorton, Alison Harris, John Heseltine, Roger Hilton, Eric Meacher, Neil Mersh, Roger Moss, Robert O'Dea, Alan Williams, Peter Wilson.

ADDITIONAL ILLUSTRATIONS

Dinwiddie Maclaren, John Fox, Nick Gibbard, Paul Guest, Stephen Gyapay, Kevin Jones Associates, Chris Orr, Robbie Polley, Sue Sharples.

ADDITIONAL CARTOGRAPHY

Colourmap Scanning Limited; Contour Publishing; Cosmographics; European Map Graphics; Meteo-France. Street Finder maps: ERA Maptec Ltd (Dublin), adapted with permission from original survey and mapping by Shobunsha (Japan).

CARTOGRAPHIC RESEARCH

Jennifer Skelley, Rachel Hawtin (Lovell Johns); James Mills-Hicks, Peter Winfield, Claudine Zante (Dorling Kindersley Cartography).

DESIGN AND EDITORIAL ASSISTANCE

Louise Abbott, Peter Adams, Laetitia Benloulou, Steve Bere, Jane Branneky, Arwen Burnett, Margaret Chang, Maggie Crowley, Fay Franklin, Tom Fraser, Emily Green, Elaine Harries, Sasha Heseltine, Elaine Hewson, Paul Hines, Nicholas Inman, Nancy Jones, Siri Lowe, Francesca Machiavelli, Lesley McCave, Ella Milroy, Malcolm Parchment, Shirin Patel, Alice Peebles, Marianne Petrou, Salim Qurashi, Caroline Radula-Scott, Marisa Renzullo, Rupert Small, Andrew Szudek, Dawn Terrey, Fiona Wild.

SPECIAL ASSISTANCE

Mme Jassinger, French Embassy Press Department; Peter Mills and Christine Lagardère, French Railways Ltd.

PHOTOGRAPHIC REFERENCE

Altitude, Paris; Sea and See, Paris; Editions Combier, Maçon; Thomas d'Hoste, Paris.

PHOTOGRAPHY PERMISSIONS

DORLING KINDERSLEY would like to thank the following for their assistance and kind permission to photograph at their establishments: The Caisse Nationale des Monuments Historiques et des Sites; M. A. Leonetti, the Abbey of Mont St-Michel; Chartres Cathedral; M. Voisin, Château de Chenonceau; M. P Mistral, Cité de Carcassonne, M. D. Vingtain, Palais des Papes, Avignon; Château de Fontainebleau; Amiens Cathedral; Conques Abbey; Fontenay Abbey; Moissac Abbey; Vézelay Abbey, Reims Cathedral and all the other churches, museums, hotels, restaurants, shops, galleries and sights too numerous to thank individually.

PICTURE CREDITS

t = top; tl = top left; tc = top centre;
tr = top right; cla = centre left above;
ca = centre above; cra = centre right above;
cl = centre left; c = centre; cr = centre right;
clb = centre left below; cb = centre below;
crb = centre right below; bl = bottom left;
b = bottom; bc = bottom centre;
br = bottom right; (d) = detail.

Works of art have been reproduced with the permission of the following copyright holders; ©ADAGP, Paris and DACS, London 1994: 25tl, 59tl, 61tl (detail), 88c, 89ca, 95t, 109b, 514bl; ©DACS, London 1994: 24c, 24cb, 25c, 25cb, 26bl, 60–61, 84cl, 86t, 86b, 89t, 203t, 341t, 371br, 412t, 463t, 472t, 498ca, 503b, 511t, 512b, 514tr, 514br, 519b; © J Fabris: 25c; © Succession H. Matisse/DACS 1994; 25b, 88b, 516b.

Photos achieved with the assistance of the EPPV and the CSI: 132–3; Photo of Euro Disneyland ® Park and the Euro Disneyland Paris ® 168cr; The characters, architectural works and trademarks are the property of The Walt Disney Company. All rights reserved; Courtesy of the Maison Victor Hugo, Ville de Paris:'87t; Musée National des Châteaux de Malmaison et Bois-Preau: 163b; Musée de Montmartre, Paris: 129t; Musée National de la Legion d'Honneur: 56t; © Sundancer: 138bl.

The publisher would like to thank the following individuals, companies and picture libraries for permission to reproduce their photographs: AIR FRANCE/D TOULORGE: 631t; ALPINE GARDEN SOCIETY/CHRISTOPHER GREY-WILSON: 450bl, 450br; AGENCE PHOTO AQUITAINE: D. Lelann 411tl; ANCIENT ART AND ARCHITECTURE COLLECTION: 43 crb, 46c, 46cb, 48br, 53bl, 242–3b, 325bl, 372t, 424t, 428b; PHOTO AKG, BERLIN: 41cra, 42bl, 50bc, 51crb, 392t,

393b; ARCHIVES PHOTOGRAPHIQUES, PARIS/DACS: 412t; ATELIER DU REGARD/A ALLEMAND: 432cl, 432cr, 432b.

BIBLIOTHEQUE NATIONALE, DIJON: 45cb; F. BLACKBURN: 451bl; GERARD BOULLAY/PHOTOLA: 83bl, 83cra; BRIDGEMAN ART LIBRARY: Albright Knox Art Gallery, Buffalo, New York 265br; Anthony Crane Collection 201br; Bibliothèque Nationale, Paris 46cr–47cl, 48t, 49cr, 65bl; British Library, London 48bl, 64br, 282c, 283br, 283tl; Bonhams, London 55tc, 58tl; Château de Versailles, France 65tr; Christies, London 25c, 503b; Giraudon 24tr, 24tl, 52cr–53cl, 53tl, 55tl, 65bc, 171b, 324c, 333c, 355t; Guildhall Library, Corporation of London 407b; Hermitage, St Petersburg 25bl; Index 462b; Kress Collection, Washington DC 283bl; Lauros-Giraudon 42t, 65br; Musée des Beaux Arts, Quimper 233c; Musée Condé, Chantilly 46tl, 53tr, 64bl, 65tc, 65tcl, 65cb, 194t, 283c; Musée d'Orsay, Paris 24cb; Paul Bremen Collection 245t; Sotheby's New York 51tl; V&A Museum, London 328b; Walters Art Gallery, Baltimore, Maryland 346t; JOHN BRUNTON: 504b; MICHAEL BUSSELLE: 172–3.

CAMPAGNE, CAMPAGNE: 340t; C. Guy 315t; Lara 181cr; B. Lichtstein 207b, 314cl; Pyszel 180bl; CNMHS, PARIS/DACS: Longchamps Delehaye 203tl; CASTELET/GROTTE DE CLAMOUSE: 483b; COLLECTION CDT GARD: 315bl; CDT LOT: 429b; CEPHAS: Stuart Boreham 250–1; Hervé Champollion 312tr, 324t, 340b; Mick Rock 34c, 388tl, 388cl, 461t, 508–9; JEAN LOUP CHARMET: 43b, 46br, 48clb, 54t, 58cl, 58clb, 59tl, 59tc, 60bl, 60br, 61crb, 204b, 233b, 255br, 259b, 264t, 271b, 290br, 333br, 348b, 349t, 351c, 391cr, 391br, 411b, 465t, 497t; CITÉ DES SCIENCES ET L'INDUSTRIE: Michel Lamoureux 133c; Pascal Prieur 132tr, 132ca; Michel Viard 132cb; BRUCE COLEMAN: Udo Hirsch 361br; Flip de Nooyer 377br; Hans Reinhard 313tl, 313tr; PHOTOS EDITIONS COMBIER, MACON: 193t; JOE CORNISH: 112, 224–5, 360br, 438.

DANSMUSEET, STOCKHOLM/PETER STENWALL: 60cr–61cl; DOHERTY: 235tc; E. DONARD; 31tr, 31c, 31cl, 31bc; EDITIONS D'ART DANIEL DERVEAUX: 390cr–391cl; PHOTO DASPET, AVIGNON: 494bl.

ET ARCHIVE: 290bl; Cathedral Treasury, Aachen 4t; 44cl; Musée Carnavalet, Paris 57tl; Museum of Fine Arts, Lausanne 51br; Musée d'Orsay, Paris 57cra; Musée de Versailles 52b; 289bl; National Gallery, Scotland 54br; Victoria and Albert Museum, London 49tl; 333bl; MARY EVANS PICTURE LIBRARY: 9c, 42br, 46bl, 47c, 49b, 50tl, 52cla, 54c, 58b, 59cr, 59br, 61br, 108c, 109cl, 167b, 173c, 181t, 187b, 225c, 269t, 281b, 283tr, 291bl, 305c, 356b, 383c, 445t, 455c, 463b, 498tl, 535c, 615c; Explorer 27b, 50clb.

PHOTO FLANDRE, AMIENS: 193b; FRANCE TÉLÉCOM: 624cr; M Reynard 624b; FRENCH RAILWAYS/SNCF: 634bl, 635t.

GIRAUDON, PARIS: 8–9, 15t, 25cra, 25br, 42ca, 44tl, 44clb, 45tl, 46cl, 48cr–49cl, 52tl, 52clb, 54cl, 56cl, 56cr–57cl, 323br, 337br, 359b, 481cb MS Nero EII pt.2 fol. 20V0; Lauros-Giraudon 40tl, 40bc, 41t, 41crb, 41cb, 41br, 43tc, 45tr, 47crb, 51cr, 56clb, 56br, 341b, 481cl; Musée d'Art Moderne, Paris 25tl; Musée de Beaux Arts, Quimper 24cl; Telarci 45cr; RONALD GRANT ARCHIVE: 17b, 62clb.

SONIA HALLIDAY PHOTOGRAPHS: Laura Lushington 299tr; ROBERT HARDING PICTURE LIBRARY: 26bl, 33tr, 35tr, 35cl, 39b, 108tr, 131bl, 230tl, 233tr, 312bl, 312br, 313br, 339t, 390cla, 427cr, 451tr, 479b, C. Bowman 442t; Explorer, Paris 35cr, 63br, 97br, 169b, 352t, 361tr, 450cb, 451tl, 474b, 487br, 617b, 628b, 640b; R.Francis 82clb, 626c; D.Hughes 382–3; W.Rawlings 45br, 63tl, 227tl, 246b; A.Wolfitt 22tr, 160, 538b; JOHN HESELTINE: 135c; HONFLEUR, MUSÉE BOUDIN: 252b; DAVID HUGHES: 2–3, 357t, 357b; THE HULTON DEUTSCH COLLECTION: 181br, 291br, 463c, 506b; FJ Mortimer 180tl.

THE IMAGE BANK: Peter Miller 362; IMAGES: 313c, 450cl, 450tr.

JACANA: F Gohier 450tl; JM Labat 451bc; TREVOR JONES: 194b.

MAGNUM PHOTOS LTD: Bruno Barbey 16b, 27tr, 32bl; R Capa 462tr; P Halsman 515b; P Zachman 15b; THE MANSELL COLLECTION: 27tl, 272t, 285b, 449b, 494tl; JOHN MILLER: 214b, 326tr, 397b; MUSÉE DE L'ANNONCIADE, ST-TROPEZ: 514tr; MUSÉE DES BEAUX ARTS, CARCASSONNE: 479tl; MUSÉE DES BEAUX ARTS, DIJON: 333tl; MUSÉE DES BEAUX ARTS DE LYON: 371tr, 371bl, 371br; MUSÉE DE LA CIVILISATION GALLO-ROMAINE, LYON: 43cr, 368cl; MUSÉE DEPARTMENTAL BRETON, QUIMPER: 264bl; MUSÉE FLAUBERT, ROUEN: 255bl; MUSEUM NATIONAL D'HISTOIRE NATURELLE, PARIS: 134c; COURTESY OF THE MUSÉE MATISSE, NICE: 516b; MUSÉE NATIONAL D'ART MODERNE, PARIS: 88clb, 89t, 89cr, 89cb, 325br; Succession Henri Matisse 88bl; MUSÉE RÉATTU, ARLES: M Lacanaud 498ca; CLICHÉ MUSÉE DE SENS/J.P. ELIE: 320tl; MUSÉE TOULOUSE-LAUTREC, ALBI: 434b.

SERVICE NATIONAL DES TIMBRES POSTE ET DE LA PHILATÉLIE: designed by Eve Luquet 626bl;

NETWORK PHOTOGRAPHERS: Barry Lewis 328t; Rapho/Mark Buscail 628tl; Rapho/De Sazo 628tr; Rapho/Michael Serraillier 629b.

PICTURES COLOUR LIBRARY: 325t, 392b, 416, 534, 614–5; MICHEL LE POER TRENCH: 26br; CENTRE GEORGES POMPIDOU: Bernard Prerost 89b; POPPERFOTO: 241c; PYRENEES MAGAZINE/DR: 390bl.

REDFERNS: William Gottlieb: 60clb; RETROGRAPH ARCHIVE: M. Breese 464tl, 464tr; RÉUNION DES MUSÉES NATIONAUX: Musée des Antiquités Nationales 393c; Musée Guimet 107t; Musée du Louvre 53ca, 97bl, 98t, 98bl, 98br, 99tl, 99c, 99b; Musée Picasso 84cl, 86b, 463t; Musée de Versailles 169t; RF Reynolds 235bc; REX FEATURES: Sipa 18t; ROCAMADOUR: 427t; ROGER-VIOLLET: 109tc; FOUNDATION ROYAUMONT: J Johnson 162t.

SIPA PRESS: 128bl; PHOTO SNCM/SOUTHERN FERRIES: 632b; SPECTRUM COLOUR LIBRARY: P Thompson 239b; FRANK SPOONER PICTURES: Bolcina 33b; Uzan 62br; Simon 63ca; Gamma Press 35b, 63crb; JEAN MARIE STEINLEN: 394; TONY STONE IMAGES: 312c, 316; SYGMA: 521t; C de Bare 32t; Walter Carone 140t; P Forestier 304–5; Frederic de la Fosse 510b; D Goldberg 17c; L'Illustration 104tl; Keystone 131crb; T Prat 426c; L de Raemy 63bl; Sunset Boulevard 131br.

EDITIONS TALLANDIER: 38, 40cb, 43tl, 44br, 44br–45bl, 47t, 47b, 48cl, 49tr, 50br, 54clb, 54bl, 54cr–55cl, 55crb, 55bl, 57tr, 57crb, 57br, 59bl, 59bc, 60cla, 60crb, 61tc, 61tr; © TMR/A.D.A.G.P, PARIS AND DACS, LONDON 1994 – COLLECTION L. TREILLARD: 61tl detail.

JEAN VERTUT: 40br–41bl; VISUAL ARTS LIBRARY: 24b.

WORLD PICTURES: 313bl.

ZEFA: 168c, 341t; O. ZIMMERMAN/MUSÉE D'UNTERLINDEN 6800 COLMAR: 217t.

Front Endpaper: All special photography except JOE CORNISH lbl; THE IMAGE BANK rcb; PICTURES COLOUR LIBRARY lcr; JEAN MARIE STEINLEIN lcl; TONY STONE IMAGES rca.

Jacket: All special photography except CEPHAS/MICK ROCK front t; MICHAEL BUSSELLE front cbr; ROBERT HARDING PICTURE LIBRARY spine t.

Phrase Book

IN EMERGENCY

Help!	Au secours!	oh se**koor**
Stop!	Arrêtez!	aret-**ay**
Call a doctor!	Appelez un médecin!	apuh-lay uñ medsañ
Call an ambulance!	Appelez une ambulance!	apuh-**lay** oon oñboo-**loñs**
Call the police!	Appelez la police!	apuh-**lay** lah poh-**lees**
Call the fire department!	Appelez les pompiers!	apuh-lay leh poñ-**peeyay**
Where is the nearest telephone?	Où est le téléphone le plus proche?	oo ay luh tehleh**fon** luh ploo prosh
Where is the nearest hospital?	Où est l'hôpital le plus proche?	oo ay l'**opee**tal luh ploo prosh

COMMUNICATION ESSENTIALS

Yes	Oui	wee
No	Non	noñ
Please	S'il vous plaît	seel voo **play**
Thank you	Merci	mer-**see**
Excuse me	Excusez-moi	exkoo-**zay** mwah
Hello	Bonjour	boñz**hoor**
Goodbye	Au revoir	oh ruh-**vwar**
Good night	Bonsoir	boñ-**swar**
Morning	Le matin	matañ
Afternoon	L'après-midi	l'apreh-**meedee**
Evening	Le soir	swar
Yesterday	Hier	eeyehr
Today	Aujourd'hui	oh-zhoor-**dwee**
Tomorrow	Demain	duhmañ
Here	Ici	ee-**see**
There	Là	lah
What?	Quel, quelle?	kel, kel
When?	Quand?	koñ
Why?	Pourquoi?	poor-**kwah**
Where?	Où?	oo

USEFUL PHRASES

How are you?	Comment allez-vous?	kom-moñ tal**ay** voo
Very well, thank you.	Très bien, merci.	treh byañ, mer-**see**
Pleased to meet you.	Enchanté de faire votre connaissance.	oñshoñ-**tay** duh fehr votr kon-ay-**sans**
See you soon.	À bientôt.	byañ-**toh**
That's fine	Voilà qui est parfait	vwalah kee ay par**fay**
Where is/are...?	Où est/sont...?	oo ay/soñ
How far is it to...?	Combien de kilomètres d'ici à...?	kom-**byañ** duh keelo-metr d'ee-**see** ah
Which way to...?	Quelle est la direction pour...?	kel ay lah deer-ek-**syoñ** poor
Do you speak English?	Parlez-vous anglais?	par-**lay** voo oñg-**lay**
I don't understand.	Je ne comprends pas.	zhuh nuh kom-**proñ** pah
Could you speak slowly please?	Pouvez-vous parler moins vite s'il vous plaît?	poo-**vay** voo par-**lay** mwañ veet seel voo play
I'm sorry.	Excusez-moi.	exkoo-**zay** mwah

USEFUL WORDS

big	grand	groñ
small	petit	puh-**tee**
hot	chaud	show
cold	froid	frwah
good	bon	boñ
bad	mauvais	moh-**veh**
enough	assez	as**say**
well	bien	byañ
open	ouvert	oo-**ver**
closed	fermé	fer-**meh**
left	gauche	gohsh
right	droit	drwah
straight ahead	tout droit	too drwah
near	près	preh
far	loin	lwañ
up	en haut	oñ oh
down	en bas	oñ bah
early	de bonne heure	duh bon **urr**
late	en retard	oñ ruh-**tar**
entrance	l'entrée	l'on-**tray**
exit	la sortie	sor-**tee**
toilet	les toilettes, les WC	twah-let, vay-**see**
free, unoccupied	libre	leebr
free, no charge	gratuit	grah-**twee**

MAKING A TELEPHONE CALL

I'd like to place a long-distance call.	Je voudrais faire un interurbain.	zhuh voo-dreh fehr uñ añter-oorbañ
I'd like to make a collect call.	Je voudrais faire une communication PCV.	oon komoonikah-**syoñ** peh-seh-veh
I'll try again later.	Je rappelerai plus tard.	zhuh rapel-**eray** ploo tar
Can I leave a message?	Est-ce que je peux laisser un message?	es-**keh** zhuh puh leh-**say** uñ mehsazh
Hold on.	Ne quittez pas, s'il vous plaît.	nuh kee-**tay** pah seel voo play
Could you speak up a little please?	Pouvez-vous parler un peu plus fort?	poo-**vay** voo par-**lay** uñ puh ploo for
local call	la communication locale	komoonikah-**syoñ** low-**kal**

SHOPPING

How much does this cost?	C'est combien s'il vous plaît?	say kom-**byañ** seel voo play
I would like ...	je voudrais...	zhuh voo**dray**
Do you have?	Est-ce que vous avez?	es-**kuh** voo zavay
I'm just looking.	Je regarde seulement.	zhuh ruh**gar** suhl**moñ**
Do you take credit cards?	Est-ce que vous acceptez les cartes de crédit?	es-**kuh** voo zaksept-**ay** leh kart duh kreh-**dee**
Do you take traveler's checks?	Est-ce que vous acceptez les chèques de voyage?	es-**kuh** voo zaksept-**ay** leh shek duh vwa**yazh**
What time do you open?	A quelle heure vous êtes ouvert?	ah kel urr voo zet oo-**ver**
What time do you close?	A quelle heure vous êtes fermé?	ah kel urr voo zet fer-**may**
This one.	Celui-ci.	suhl-wee-**see**
That one.	Celui-là.	suhl-wee-**lah**
expensive	cher	shehr
cheap	pas cher, bon marché	pah shehr, boñ mar-**shay**
size, clothes	la taille	tye
size, shoes	la pointure	pwañ-**tur**
white	blanc	bloñ
black	noir	nwahr
red	rouge	roozh
yellow	jaune	zhohwn
green	vert	vehr
blue	bleu	bluh

TYPES OF SHOPS

antiques shop	le magasin d'antiquités	maga-**zañ** d'oñteekee-**tay**
bakery	la boulangerie	booloñ-**zhuree**
bank	la banque	boñk
book store	la librairie	lee-**brehree**
butcher	la boucherie	boo-**shehree**
cake shop	la pâtisserie	patee-**sree**
cheese shop	la fromagerie	fromazh-**ree**
dairy	la crémerie	krem-**ree**
department store	le grand magasin	groñ maga-**zañ**
delicatessen	la charcuterie	sharkoot-**ree**
drugstore	la pharmacie	farmah-**see**
fish seller	la poissonnerie	pwasson-**ree**
gift shop	le magasin de cadeaux	maga-**zañ** duh kadoh
greengrocer	le marchand de légumes	mar-**shoñ** duh lay-**goom**
grocery	l'alimentation	alee-moñta-**syoñ**
hairdresser	le coiffeur	kwa**fuhr**
market	le marché	marsh-**ay**
newsstand	le magasin de journaux	maga-**zañ** duh zhoor-**no**
post office	la poste, le bureau de poste, le PTT	pohst, boo**roh** duh pohst, peh-teh-teh
shoe store	le magasin de chaussures	maga-**zañ** duh show-**soor**
supermarket	le supermarché	soo pehr-**marshay**
tobacconist	le tabac	tabah
travel agent	l'agence de voyages	l'azhoñs duh vwayazh

SIGHTSEEING

abbey	l'abbaye	l'abay-**ee**
art gallery	le galerie d'art	galer-**ree** dart
bus station	la gare routière	gahr roo-tee-**yehr**

cathedral	la cathédrale	katay-**dral**
church	l'église	l'ayg**leez**
garden	le jardin	zhar-**dañ**
library	la bibliothèque	beeblee**co**-tek
museum	le musée	moo-**zay**
tourist information office	les renseignements touristiques, le syndicat d'initiative	roñsayn-**moñ** too-rees-**teek**, sandee-ka d'eenee-syat**eev**
town hall	l'hôtel de ville	l'ohtel duh veel
train station	la gare (SNCF)	gahr (es-en-say-ef)
private mansion	l'hôtel particulier	l'ohtel partikoo-**lyay**
closed for public holiday	fermeture jour férié	fehrmeh-**tur** zhoor fehree-**ay**

STAYING IN A HOTEL

Do you have a vacant room?	Est-ce que vous avez une chambre?	es-kuh voo-**zavay** oon shambr
double room, with double bed	la chambre à deux personnes, avec un grand lit	shambr ah duh pehr-**son**, avek un groñn lee
twin room	la chambre à deux lits	shambr ah duh lee
single room	la chambre à une personne	shambr ah oon pehr-**son**
room with a bath, shower	la chambre avec salle de bains, une douche	shambr avek sal duh bañ, oon doosh
porter	le garçon	gar-**son**
key	la clef	klay
I have a reservation.	J'ai fait une réservation.	zhay fay oon rayzehrva-**syoñ**

EATING OUT

Have you got a table?	Avez-vous une table libre?	avay-**voo** oon tahbl leebr
I want to reserve a table.	Je voudrais réserver une table.	zhuh voo-**dray** rayzehr-**vay** oon tahbl
The check please.	L'addition s'il vous plaît.	l'adee-**syoñ** seel voo **play**
I am a vegetarian.	Je suis végétarien.	zhuh swee vezhay-**tehryañ**
Waitress/waiter	Madame, Mademoiselle/Monsieur	mah-**dam**, mah-demwah**zel**/muh-**syuh**
menu	le menu, la carte	men-**oo**, kart
fixed-price menu	le menu à prix fixe	men-**oo** ah pree feeks
cover charge	le couvert	koo-**vehr**
wine list	la carte des vins	kart-deh vañ
glass	le verre	vehr
bottle	la bouteille	boo-**tay**
knife	le couteau	koo-**toh**
fork	la fourchette	for-**shet**
spoon	la cuillère	kwee-**yehr**
breakfast	le petit déjeuner	puh-**tee** deh-**zhuh-nay**
lunch	le déjeuner	deh-**zhuh-nay**
dinner	le dîner	dee-**nay**
main course	le plat principal	plah prañsee-**pal**
appetizer, first course	l'entrée, le hors d'oeuvre	l'oñ-**tray**, or-duhvr
dish of the day	le plat du jour	plah doo zhoor
wine bar	le bar à vin	bar ah vañ
café	le café	ka-**fay**
rare	saignant	**say**-noñ
medium	à point	ah **pwañ**
well-done	bien cuit	byañ **kwee**

MENU DECODER

l'agneau	l'anyoh	lamb
l'ail	l'eye	garlic
la banane	ba**nan**	banana
le beurre	burr	butter
la bière, bière à la pression	bee-**yehr**, bee-**yehr** ah lah pres-**syoñ**	beer, draft beer
le bifteck, le steack	beef-**tek**, stek	steak
le boeuf	buhf	beef
bouilli	boo-**yee**	boiled
le café	kah-**fay**	coffee
le canard	kanar	duck
le chocolat	shoko-lah	chocolate
le citron	see-**troñ**	lemon
le citron pressé	see-**troñ** press-**eh**	fresh lemon juice
les crevettes	kruh-**vet**	prawns
les crustacés	kroos-ta-**say**	shellfish
cuit au four	kweet oh foor	baked
le dessert	deh-**ser**	dessert

l'eau minérale	l'oh **meeney**-ral	mineral water
les escargots	leh zes-kar-**goh**	snails
les frites	freet	chips
le fromage	from-**azh**	cheese
le fruit frais	frwee freh	fresh fruit
les fruits de mer	frwee duh mer	seafood
le gâteau	gah-**toh**	cake
la glace	glas	ice, ice cream
grillé	gree-**yay**	grilled
le homard	omahr	lobster
l'huile	l'weel	oil
le jambon	zhoñ-**boñ**	ham
le lait	leh	milk
les légumes	lay-**goom**	vegetables
la moutarde	moo-**tard**	mustard
l'oeuf	l'uf	egg
les oignons	leh zon**yoñ**	onions
les olives	leh zo**leev**	olives
l'orange	l'oroñzh	orange
l'orange pressée	l'oroñzh press-**eh**	fresh orange juice
le pain	pan	bread
le petit pain	puh-**tee** pañ	roll
poché	posh-**ay**	poached
le poisson	pwah-**ssoñ**	fish
le poivre	pwavr	pepper
la pomme	pom	apple
les pommes de terre	pom-duh **tehr**	potatoes
le porc	por	pork
le potage	poh-**tazh**	soup
le poulet	poo-**lay**	chicken
le riz	ree	rice
rôti	row-**tee**	roast
la sauce	sohs	sauce
la saucisse	soh**sees**	sausage, fresh
sec	sek	dry
le sel	sel	salt
la soupe	soop	soup
le sucre	sookr	sugar
le thé	tay	tea
le toast	toast	toast
la viande	vee-**yand**	meat
le vin blanc	vañ bloñ	white wine
le vin rouge	vañ roozh	red wine
le vinaigre	vee**naygr**	vinegar

NUMBERS

0	zéro	zeh-**roh**
1	un, une	uñ, oon
2	deux	duh
3	trois	trwah
4	quatre	katr
5	cinq	sañk
6	six	sees
7	sept	set
8	huit	weet
9	neuf	nerf
10	dix	dees
11	onze	oñz
12	douze	dooz
13	treize	trehz
14	quatorze	ka**torz**
15	quinze	kañz
16	seize	sehz
17	dix-sept	dees-**set**
18	dix-huit	dees-**weet**
19	dix-neuf	dees-**nerf**
20	vingt	vañ
30	trente	tront
40	quarante	karoñt
50	cinquante	sañkoñt
60	soixante	swasoñt
70	soixante-dix	swasoñt-**dees**
80	quatre-vingts	katr-vañ
90	quatre-vingts-dix	katr-vañ-**dees**
100	cent	soñ
1,000	mille	meel

TIME

one minute	une minute	oon mee-**noot**
one hour	une heure	oon urr
half an hour	une demi-heure	oon **duh-mee** urr
Monday	lundi	luñ-**dee**
Tuesday	mardi	mar-**dee**
Wednesday	mercredi	mehrkruh-**dee**
Thursday	jeudi	zhuh-**dee**
Friday	vendredi	voñdruh-**dee**
Saturday	samedi	sam-**dee**
Sunday	dimanche	dee-**moñsh**

TITLES PUBLISHED TO DATE

THE GUIDES THAT SHOW YOU WHAT OTHERS ONLY TELL YOU

COUNTRY GUIDES

AUSTRALIA • FRANCE • GREAT BRITAIN • GREECE:
ATHENS & THE MAINLAND • THE GREEK ISLANDS
IRELAND • ITALY • PORTUGAL
SPAIN • THAILAND

REGIONAL GUIDES

CALIFORNIA • FLORENCE & TUSCANY
FLORIDA • HAWAII • LOIRE VALLEY
NAPLES WITH POMPEII & THE AMALFI COAST
PROVENCE & THE COTE D'AZUR • SARDINIA
SEVILLE & ANDALUSIA • VENICE & THE VENETO

CITY GUIDES

AMSTERDAM • ISTANBUL • LISBON • LONDON
MOSCOW • NEW YORK • PARIS • PRAGUE
ROME • SAN FRANCISCO • ST PETERSBURG
SYDNEY • VIENNA • WARSAW

TO BE PUBLISHED IN SPRING 1999
MADRID • BUDAPEST • DUBLIN